APPLIED
ECONOMICS

Eighth
Edition

Edited by
ALAN GRIFFITHS
& STUART WALL

APPLIED ECONOMICS

An Introductory Course

Longman
London and New York

Pearson Education Limited,
Edinburgh Gate,
Harlow,
Essex CM20 2JE,
England
and Associated Companies throughout the world.

*Published in the United States of America
by Pearson Education Inc., New York*

*Visit us on the world wide web at:
http://www.awl-he.com*

© Addison Wesley Longman Limited 1984
This edition © Pearson Education Limited 1999

First published 1984
Second edition 1986
Third edition 1989
Fourth edition 1991
Fifth edition 1993
Sixth edition 1995
Seventh edition 1997
Eighth edition 1999

ISBN 0 582 41454 7

British Library Cataloguing-in-Publication Data
A catalogue record for this book is available from the British Library

Library of Congress Cataloging-in-Publication Data
Applied economics : an introductory course / Alan Griffiths & Stuart
  Wall (editors). – 8th ed.
     p.   cm.
  Includes bibliographical references and index.
  ISBN 0-582-41454-7
  1. Economics. 2. Great Britain—Economic conditions—1945-1993.
  I. Griffiths, Alan, 1944- . II. Wall, Stuart, 1946- .
  HB171.5.A65   1999
  330—dc21   98-51498
                                                                              CIP

*The publisher has made every attempt to obtain permission to reproduce material in this book from the appropriate
source. If there are any errors or omissions please contact thepublisher who will make suitable acknowledgement
in the reprint.*

Set in 10/12pt Erhardt
Typeset by 32
Produced by Addison Wesley Longman Singapore Pte. Ltd.
Printed in Singapore

Contents

Contents

As any teacher or student of economics well knows, the vitality of the subject depends largely upon a continual synthesis of theory with observation, and observation with theory. Unfortunately this exercise is costly in terms of the time and the effort involved in finding sources, in assembling and interpreting data, and in searching journals and periodicals for informed comment on contemporary events. That the exercise is, however, ultimately worth while, is eloquently expressed by the late Professor James Meade in the following quotation taken, with his permission, from a letter to the authors:

> The great tradition of Political Economy in this country is the application of basic economic analysis to the central economic problems of the time. For this purpose students must have a knowledge of institutions and quantitative relationships over a very wide range of sectors of the economy; and this instruction about the facts must be accompanied with guidance about methods of applying economic theory to the problems which arise over a very wide range of topics. Guidebooks to the UK economy which combine information and analysis in this way are all too rare; and the authors are to be highly commended for undertaking a comprehensive survey of this kind.

Our hope is that *Applied Economics* will take the reader some distance along this route, by combining information with analysis over thirty separate topic areas. The book also examines in detail the major economic issues arising within each topic area. Although the focus of *Applied Economics* is the UK, extensive reference is made throughout to the experience of the other advanced industrialized countries, helping the reader place any observations on the UK in a broader international context.

Each chapter concentrates on a particular topic area and begins with a synopsis, setting out the issues to be investigated, and ends with a conclusion, reviewing the major findings. The largely self-contained nature of each chapter gives the book a useful degree of flexibility. For instance chapters can be read selectively, in any order appropriate to the reader's interest or to the stage reached in a programme of study. This may be helpful to the reader as courses rarely follow the same sequence of topics. On the other hand the topics have been arranged with an element of progression, so that the reader may begin at Chapter 1 and read the following chapters, arranged in four separate 'parts', consecutively. The book then takes the form of a 'course' in applied economics.

Applied Economics is designed for undergraduate students in the first and second years of degree courses in economics, the social sciences and business studies, and for those taking professional and postgraduate courses with an economic content. The material will also be useful to many involved in Higher and National Diplomas and Certificates, and to the serious A level student. Much of the content begins at an introductory level and is suitable for those with little or no previous exposure to economics, although the diverse nature of the various topic areas inevitably means some variation in the level of analysis, and indeed in the balance between information and analysis. Overall, the book is best read in conjunction with a good introductory text on economic theory.

We are indebted to many individuals for help during the course of this project. The major debt is, however, clearly owed to those who contributed the various chapters, and this is acknowledged more fully at the end of the book. Finally, for patience and forbearance during many months of absence from normal family activities, our thanks go to Sylvia and Eleanor. Of course any errors and omissions are entirely our responsibility.

We were delighted that the first seven editions of *Applied Economics* were so well received by teachers and students across a wide range of courses. Our intention is to keep the book at the forefront of economic debate and events. Accordingly, in this eighth edition we have thoroughly updated all the data and empirical material and added new economic analysis where appropriate, including a new chapter on the economics of social problems and additional material on trading blocs and EU-related issues. We have also included a supplement from the *Financial Times* on page 744 which gives students an insight into how to read the financial pages. Written by a highly regarded journalist, this piece will help the reader to understand better the relationship between the world of the 'city' and the 'real' economy.

If you have any comments about this text we would be delighted to hear from you. Please either complete the tear out section at the back of the book, or E-mail us on b&e.feedback@awl.co.uk.

Alan Griffiths, Stuart Wall. Cambridge 1999

Acknowledgements

We are grateful to the following for permission to reproduce copyright material:

Table 3.3 a and b from FAME (Financial Analysis Made Easy) CD-ROM, 122a Oct. 1998, Bureau van Dijk, London; Figure 4.1 from *Quarterly Report on Small Business Statistics*, Business Finance Division, Sept. 1998, Bank of England; Table 7.4 from FT 500, *Financial Times*, 25 Jan. 1998; Table 9.1 and Figure 9.3 from *Competition in the Supply of Petrol*, OFT 229, Office of Fair Trading, 1998; Figure 9.4 from *The Supply of Beer*, House of Commons Papers, Command 651, Figure 9.6 from *Black and Decker*, House of Commons Papers, Command 805, Crown copyright is reproduced with the permission of the Controller of Her Majesty's Stationery Office; Table 12.1 and Table 12.5 from *Transport Statistics Great Britain*, Department of Transport and the Regions (DETR), Crown copyright is reproduced with the permission of the Controller of Her Majesty's Stationery Office, 1998; Table 12.6 from The Capital at Risk: Transport in London Task Force Report, Confederation of British Industry, 1989; Table 12.7 from Local Transport Today, 23 May 1996, Landor Publishing, London; Figure 17.2 from *Competitiveness of UK Manufacturing Industry*, Second Report, Trade and Industry Committee, House of Commons, 1994, Crown copyright is reproduced with the permission of the Controller of Her Majesty's Stationery Office; Figure 21.4 from The Bank of England's Operations in Sterling Money Markets, *Bank of England Quarterly Bulletin Report*, May 1997, Bank of England; Table 21.4 from Financial Statistics, Oct. 1998, Crown copyright is reproduced with the permission of the Controller of Her Majesty's Stationery Office; Table 21.7 from CSO, Crown copyright is reproduced with the permission of the Controller of Her Majesty's Stationery Office; Figure 22.1 from The inflation target of five years on, *Bank of England Quarterly Bulletin*, 37, (King, 1997), Bank of England; Figure 22.2 and Figure 22.3 from *Bank of England Inflation Report*, Aug. 1998, Bank of England; Figure 23.7 and Table 23.7 from OECD *Economic Outlook* No. 63, June 1998, copyright OECD, 1998.

Whilst every effort has been made to trace the owners of copyright material, in a few cases this has proved impossible and we take this opportunity to offer our apologies to any copyright holders whose rights we may have unwittingly infringed.

Chapter 1

Changes in the UK economic structure

In this chapter we review the changing economic structure of the UK, particularly the declining significance of industrial output and employment as compared with the service sector. Some comparisons are made with international experience. Alternative explanations of industrial decline are examined, such as economic 'maturity', low-wage competition, the advent of North Sea oil, 'crowding out' by the non-market public sector and low UK productivity *vis-à-vis* its competitors. We consider whether the changes observed in the UK are a cause for concern, or merely a reflection of changes experienced in other advanced industrialized countries.

The popular view of the UK as an industrial economy, a manufacturing nation, is now inaccurate. Over the past thirty years the structure of the economy has been transformed. Manufacturing now contributes only around 18% of total output and employs almost 5 million fewer people than in 1964. One of the most prominent of today's industries, North Sea oil and gas, did not even exist twenty-five years ago, and service activities now dominate the economy both in terms of output and employment. There are even suggestions that the UK is becoming a 'post-industrial' economy, i.e. one in which information-handling activities are predominant. We shall consider the causes and consequences of these changes, and in so doing point out that structural change has implications for other important economic issues.

Structure defined

An economy may be analysed in terms of its component parts, often called 'sectors'. Sectors may be widely drawn to include groups of industries (e.g. the engineering industries) or narrowly drawn to identify parts of industries (e.g. fuel-injection equipment), depending on our purpose. Structural change is often discussed in terms of the even more widely drawn 'primary', 'secondary' and 'tertiary' (service) sectors. It will be useful at the outset to define these, and other conventional sector headings: (a) *the primary sector* – includes activities directly related to natural resources, e.g. farming, mining and oil extraction; (b) *the secondary sector* – covers all the other goods production in the economy, including the processing of materials produced by the primary sector. Manufacturing is the main element in this sector which also includes construction and the public utility industries of gas, water and electricity; (c) *the tertiary sector* – includes all the private sector services, e.g. distribution, insurance, banking and finance, and all the public sector services, such as health and defence; (d) *the goods sector* – the primary and secondary sectors combined; and (e) *the production industries* – includes the entire secondary sector except construction, together with the coal and coke industries and the extraction of mineral oil and natural gas. There is an index of industrial production on this basis, and the term 'industry' usually refers to this sector heading.

Structural change means change in the relative size of the sectors, however defined. We may judge size by output (contribution to Gross Domestic Product (GDP)),[1] or by inputs used, either capital or labour. Usually more attention is paid to labour because of the interest in employment and also because it is more easily measured than capital.

Through time we should *expect* the structure of an economy to change. The pattern of demand for a country's products will change with variations in income or taste, affecting in turn both output and employment. If economic growth occurs and real incomes rise, then the demand for goods and services with high and positive income elasticities will tend to increase relative to those with low or even negative income elasticities[2]. For example, between 1983 and 1997 total real consumer expenditure at 1990 prices rose by 35.2%, but expenditure on goods and services classified as 'recreation, entertainment and education' increased by 57%, whilst expenditure on 'food' increased by only 11.6%. Within the 'recreation, entertainment and education' category, consumer tastes favoured 'radio, TV and other durable goods', where real spending increased by 186%; by contrast spending on 'newspapers and magazines' rose by only 3.1% in real terms. These changes have clear implications for the pattern of output and employment.

The pattern of demand is also responsive to changes in the age structure of the population. The UK, like other developed countries, is experiencing important demographic changes which mean that by 1998 there were 1.68 million fewer people in the 16–24 year old age group than in 1981. So, for example, the 'recreation, entertainment and education' sector may find this a constraint on its growth, unless it can adapt to the changing characteristics of the market. This smaller age cohort will form fewer new households than previous cohorts, so reducing demand for housing, furniture and consumer durables below what it would otherwise have been. In the longer term, a further demographic factor will be the continuing rise in the numbers of people aged over 75, who will place increasingly heavy demands on the medical and care services.

It is not only the demand side which initiates structural change. The reduced supply of young people in the labour market in the early 1990s increased their earnings relative to other workers, which encouraged firms such as supermarkets to recruit older workers. Employers may also respond by substituting capital for labour and so changing employment patterns, or by raising product prices which would reduce the growth of output and in turn influence employment.

Also on the supply side, technical progress makes possible entirely new goods and services, as well as new processes for producing existing goods and services. In Chapter 23 we note that microelectronics not only gives us new products, such as word processors and video games, but also reduces costs of production, whether through the introduction of robotics in manufacturing, or computerized accounting methods in banking services. Where such 'process innovation' raises total factor productivity, unit costs fall. The supply side is therefore itself initiating new patterns of demand, output and employment, by creating new products or by reducing the prices of existing products and raising quality.

Changes in resource availability may also initiate structural change, as happened so dramatically with oil in 1973 and again in 1979. When the oil-producing and exporting countries (OPEC) restricted world output, oil-based products rose sharply in price, with *direct* consequences for substitutes (e.g. coal and gas) and complements (e.g. cars). In response to higher oil prices not only did the demand for substitutes rise, and for complements fall, but decisions had also to be taken throughout the economy, by both producers and consumers, to use less energy. As a result there was a decline in output and employment in energy-intensive industries, a prime example being steel.

Oil has had further *indirect* effects on the structure of the UK economy by means of the exchange rate. The development of North Sea oil production enabled the UK to be self-sufficient in oil by 1980, but also bestowed 'petro-currency' status on the pound. This meant that the sterling exchange rate was now responsive to changes in oil prices, which between 1979 and 1983 tended to keep the pound higher than would otherwise have been the case. The result was to make UK exports dearer and imports cheaper in the early 1980s, with adverse consequences for output and employment in sectors facing international competition, both abroad and at home. During 1986 this was partially reversed. The oil price halved and sterling fell 9.2% (on average), providing a stimulus to industrial output during 1987. Although by 1990 the UK was not much more than self-sufficient in oil, the pound still behaved as a petro-currency during the Gulf crisis. Following the invasion of Kuwait by Iraq, and the consequent rise in the oil price, the pound appreciated by just over 6% during July and August 1990. The trade surplus in oil peaked at £8.1 bn in 1985 and fell to a low of £1.2 bn by 1991. Since then it has been rising with the rapid growth in oil production and reached £4.6 bn in 1997.

International competition is a potent force for change in the economic structure of the UK. Changing consumer tastes, the creation of new products and changing comparative costs result in the redistribution of economic activity around the world. The demise of the UK motorcycle industry in the face of Japanese competition, for example, was the result of UK manufacturers failing to meet consumer demand for lighter, more reliable, motorcycles which Japan could produce more cheaply. As we see in Chapter 26, for most products the major impact on UK output and employment has come not from Japanese producers, but from those EU countries which, unlike Japan, have unrestricted access to the UK market. Membership of the EU inevitably meant accepting some restructuring of the UK economy, in accordance with European comparative advantages. This is certainly true for industrial production, with the EU a protected free trade area, though less true for agriculture (see Chapter 28).

Decisions on the location of industrial production are increasingly taken by *multinational enterprises*. In the UK motor industry, decisions taken by Ford and General Motors during the 1970s and early 1980s to supply more of the European market from other EU plants, contributed to the fall in UK car output from 1.3 million in 1977 to 1.1 million in 1987, despite real consumer spending on cars and vehicles more than doubling in that period. By 1997 inward investment by Nissan, Toyota, Honda, BMW and Peugeot-Citroen had contributed to an increase in car production to over 1.5 million.

Structural change in the UK

The data we shall use to trace changes in the UK economic structure are contained in Tables 1.1, 1.2 and 1.4. The choice of the years in these tables is not arbitrary; 1964, 1969, 1973, 1979, 1990 and 1997 are the peaks of successive business cycles. By using these years we shall be comparing like with like. Some activities, e.g. construction, show much more fluctuation in output and employment during the course of a trade cycle than do others, e.g. the public sector services. We must therefore compare years which have similar economic conditions if we are to avoid reaching wrong conclusions. It is, however, interesting to observe the way the recession of the early 1980s affected the different sectors, so data are provided for 1981.

Changes in output   Table 1.1 presents index numbers of output at constant factor cost,[3] recording changes in the volume of output for the various sectors. Data for GDP at factor cost is also given so that comparisons can be made between the individual sectors and the economy as a whole.

In the **primary sector**, *agriculture, hunting, forestry and fishing* grew slightly slower than GDP between 1964 and 1979. After 1979 this sector's output was more influenced by the agricultural policy of the European Union than by the UK business cycle. So agricultural output grew strongly through the recession of the early 1980s and, just as perversely, fell during the upswing of 1994 and 1995. Within *mining and quarrying* there are two very contrasting industries; coal, which

Table 1.1   Index numbers of output at constant factor cost (1990 = 100).

	1964	1969	1973	1979	1981	1990	1997
Primary							
Agriculture, hunting, forestry and fishing	55.0	59.0	69.5	71.3	81.2	100	93.3
Mining and quarrying	187.0	136.1	104.3	109.2	115.7	100	77.7
Coal and nuclear fuel	295.0	213.2	166.1	144.4	143.8	100	45.4
Oil and gas extraction	–	–	–	88.8	99.2	100	179.7
Secondary							
Manufacturing	72.6	85.4	94.6	90.6	77.7	100	104.3
Construction	65.9	74.4	77.4	69.4	60.5	100	93.3
Electricity, gas and water supply	45.3	55.1	69.6	80.4	81.9	100	126.8
Tertiary							
Distribution, hotels and catering, repairs	61.0	65.5	76.0	76.6	69.9	100	113.0
Transport and storage	60.2	66.7	79.3	81.5	77.9	100	121.4
Post and telecommunication	30.6	40.2	50.2	59.7	62.7	100	152.4
Financial, intermediation, real estate, renting and business activities	27.6	34.5	42.3	49.6	54.3	100	118.7
Ownership of dwellings	63.3	73.3	79.8	90.8	92.6	100	110.1
Public administration, national defence and social security	85.1	89.1	98.0	98.0	102.2	100	90.6
Education, health and social work	57.9	67.2	76.5	92.4	94.2	100	109.5
Other services	51.8	54.7	59.0	68.3	70.5	100	135.6
GDP	58.7	66.4	74.9	80.0	76.5	100	112.9
Production industries	62.6	73.3	81.4	87.6	78.9	100	109.4

Sources: ONS (1998) *Economic Trends*, July; ONS (1998) *Monthly Digest of Statistics*, July, and previous issues.

is the only industry where output has fallen throughout the period, and the oil and gas extraction industry which grew very rapidly in the late 1970s and early 1980s. *Coal* output fell by just over half between 1964 and 1979. High real energy prices after the 1973 and 1979 oil price 'shocks' improved the prospects of the coal industry, but at the same time made feasible the rapid exploitation of high cost North Sea oil, which was increasingly to act as a substitute for coal. Coal output fell by around 30% between 1979 and 1990 and then by a further 55% between 1990 and 1997 as the privatized electricity generating companies made their 'dash for gas'. *Oil and gas extraction* had peaked at an index number of 137 in 1987 before falling to the 100 in 1990 shown in the table (the halving of the oil price in 1986 may have been a factor in this decline). Since 1990 the offshore oil and gas extraction industry has enjoyed a remarkable revival in which output increased by nearly 80% over the seven years to 1997 to register an all-time high. Earlier forecasts of declining output proved to be wrong as new techniques enabled more oil and gas to be profitably produced both from existing fields and also from new smaller fields which might previously have been uneconomic.

In the **secondary sector**, 1973 is again a significant date. Output from both manufacturing and construction rose steadily between 1964 and 1973 (at annual rates of 2.9 and 1.8% respectively), but between 1973 and 1979 output from both these sub-sectors actually fell, and fell still more sharply in the recession between 1979 and 1981. *Manufacturing* output fell by as much as 12.9 points or 14.2% in this recession. The recovery after 1981 took manufacturing output to a new peak by 1990 which was just 5.4 points above the previous peak seventeen years earlier in 1973. All of that gain in output was then lost in the recessionary years of 1991 and 1992, before the upturn from 1993 which left manufacturing output in 1997 only 4.3% above that of 1990 and just 9.7 points (or 10.2%) above the level of 1973. Over a period of 24 years this rate of growth represents virtual stagnation.

Output in the *construction* industry follows a similar path to that in manufacturing up to 1981. The industry was then a leading sector in the boom of the eighties, far outstripping manufacturing, with growth of almost 40 points or 66% between 1981 and 1990 (i.e. 5.7% per annum). Output of the industry then fell by 6.7% between 1990 and 1997. *Electricity, gas and water supply* shows none of the volatility of construction. The long run growth of output in this sector tends to exceed that of GDP and does not become negative during recessions.

The index of output for the *production industries* (see earlier definition), is presented in the last row of Table 1.1. We see that industrial production grew between 1964 and 1973 by 18.8 points, an annual rate of 2.9%, but then grew more slowly between 1973 and 1979, and fell sharply between 1979 and 1981. This definition includes the contribution of North Sea oil and gas, which helped to compensate for the sharp decline of output in manufacturing since 1973. Exploitation of a non-renewable natural resource is, however, more akin to the consumption of capital than it is to the production of goods and services. The North Sea is providing the UK with a once-and-for-all 'windfall' gain in output over other less fortunate countries. To some extent this masked the full extent of the decline in *non-oil industrial output* which fell by 14.6% between 1973 and 1981, resulting in *non-oil GDP* being 2.5% lower in 1981 than in 1973.

After 1981, growth of UK industrial output resumed, led by the recovery of manufacturing output, and averaged 2.9% per year through to 1988. Industrial output in the 1980s was again growing at the rates of the 1960s, and changing oil output did not significantly affect the index. Industrial production then fell back under the impact of recession, falling 4.1 points between 1990 and 1992 before recovering after 1993.

International comparisons highlight the failure of British industry during the 1960s and 1970s. Industrial production in the industrial market economies (OECD) grew at a weighted average of 6.2% per annum between 1960 and 1970, slowing to what in the UK would still have been regarded as a healthy 2.3% per annum between 1970 and 1983. So British industrial output in the 1960s grew at less than half the average rate of the industrial market economies as a whole, and during the late 1970s contracted as industrial production in these countries continued to grow. However during the 1980s the growth of UK industry relative to the rest of the OECD clearly improved. The OECD index of industrial production shows growth in the UK of 35% for the period 1980–97, against an average growth for the whole OECD of 36%. We can conclude that although the UK's rate of relative decline as an industrial producer has been greatly reduced since the 1970s, it has not yet been halted.

In the **tertiary or service sector**, Table 1.1 shows that output grew in every sub-sector throughout the whole 1964–79 time period. Even during the recession of 1979–81 output fell in only two of the eight sub-sectors. The pace-setters have been the communications, and financial services sectors. The thrust of Government policy since 1979 has ensured that public sector services have grown more slowly than the rest of the sector. Indeed, since 1990, public administration along with defence and social security as a group has seen a fall in measured output.

The contrast in growth experience between the service sector and the industrial sector has changed the share of total output attributable to each (see Table 1.2). However, even in the service sector, growth of output in the UK at 2.9% per annum between 1964 and 1981 lagged behind the average for the industrial market economies which was 3.9%. Between 1981 and 1997 UK service sector growth was, at 2.8% per annum, a relative improvement as the average for the industrial market economies had fallen to a similar figure. The poor UK industrial performance outlined above may also have contributed to this relatively poor service sector performance, since many services are marketed to industry or to people whose incomes are earned in industry. A growing industrial sector generates an induced demand for the output of the service sector.

The GDP can be obtained by aggregating the various sectors outlined above. It grew from 58.7 in 1964 to 80.0 in 1979, i.e. by around 36%. This represents an average annual growth rate of about 2.2% between 1964 and 1979, slowing to 1.1% between 1973 and 1979. The GDP actually declined between 1979 and 1981 by 4.4% whilst the OECD average GDP continued to rise slowly. By international standards the UK growth performance was poor between 1964 and 1981. For instance the weighted average annual growth rate for industrial market economies, our key trading partners, was 5.1% between 1960 and 1970 and 3.2% between 1970 and 1979. In the eight years following the recession of 1981, UK real GDP grew at an average of 3.3% per annum, well above the UK rates of the 1960s, and above the OECD average of 3.1%. During the 1980s, therefore, the UK's relative economic decline was halted, but even at these higher rates its reversal was likely to be a slow process. Events since 1988 have confirmed this view, with UK real GDP growing at 2.1% per annum between 1988 and 1997 compared to the OECD average of 2.4%.

Changes in shares of output

Table 1.2 uses percentage shares of total output (GDP at factor cost), to show changes in the relative importance of the sectors presented in Table 1.1.

The **primary sector** was in relative decline between 1964 and 1973 because of the contraction of output in coal-mining. From a low point of 4.2% of GDP in 1973, the primary sector sharply increased its share to 6.7% in 1979 and 9.5% in 1984 (not shown), an unusual trend in a developed economy and almost entirely attributable to the growth of North Sea oil and gas production. By 1990 the primary sector's share had slumped to 3.9%. This dramatic change was caused, in part, by the collapse of oil prices during 1986. Self-sufficiency in oil has meant that the UK's national interest in energy prices is no longer necessarily the same as that of the other (non-oil-producing) industrial nations.

The **secondary sector's** share of output fell from a peak of 42.0% in 1969 to only 31.5% in 1990; the recession then further reduced this to 26.8% in 1997. This long term decline in the secondary sector is inevitable as the share of manufacturing in GDP falls. By 1990 manufacturing produced only 22.5% of UK output, which fell further to 19.8% by 1997.

The **tertiary sector's** share of output has grown throughout the period since 1969, necessarily so as the shares of the primary and secondary sectors have fallen. The financial sector trebled its share of output between 1964 and 1997 to become the largest sector in output share (unfortunately the data has been aggregated with the imputed rent from ownership of dwellings since 1990).

With the exception of the growth of the North Sea sector, these changes in economic structure have occurred throughout the advanced industrial countries (see Table 1.3). The fall in the share of manufacturing in GDP in the UK is typical

Table 1.2   Percentage shares of GDP at factor cost*.

	1964	1969	1973	1979	1990	1997
Primary	5.8	4.3	4.2	6.7	3.9	3.8
Agriculture, forestry and fishing	1.9	1.8	2.9	2.2	1.8	1.4
Mining and quarrying including oil and gas extraction	3.9	2.5	1.1	4.5	2.1	2.4
Secondary	40.8	42.0	40.9	36.7	31.5	26.8
Mineral oil processing	0.5	0.5	0.4	0.6	} 22.5	} 19.8
Manufacturing	29.5	30.7	30.0	27.3		
Construction	8.4	8.4	7.3	6.2	6.9	4.9
Electricity, gas and water supply	2.4	2.4	2.8	2.6	2.1	2.1
Tertiary	53.8	53.0	54.9	56.5	64.4	69.4
Distribution, hotels, catering, repairs	14.0	13.3	13.1	12.7	13.5	14.3
Transport and storage	4.4	4.4	4.7	4.8	} 7.6	} 8.9
Post and telecommunication	1.6	1.9	2.3	2.5		
Financial intermediation, real estate, renting and business activities	8.3	8.6	10.7	11.0	} 22.6	} 25.1
Ownership of dwellings	5.4	5.5	5.1	5.8		
Public administration, national defence and social security	7.6	7.0	6.1	6.1	6.3	5.2
Education, health and social work	6.9	7.1	7.7	8.1	8.9	11.4
Other services	5.6	5.2	5.1	5.7	5.5	4.5

Calculated from GDP at factor cost, at current prices and unadjusted for financial services and residual error.
*Totals may not sum to 100 due to rounding.
Source: ONS (1998) *United Kingdom National Accounts*, and previous issues.

Table 1.3 Industrial
market economies
distribution of GDP:
percentages.

	1960	1980	1985	1996
Agriculture	6.0	3.1	2.6	1.9
Industry	41.0	36.5	34.2	29.4
(manufacturing)	(30.4)	(24.7)	(23.2)	(21.3)
Services	53.0	60.4	63.2	68.6

Sources: OECD (1998) *OECD in Figures* and previous issues; OECD (1997) *Country Surveys* (various).

of the other industrial market economies, and the growth in the share of the service sector has been similar to the average for such economies. This has led some to interpret the changes in UK economic structure as inevitable, giving more recently industrialized countries a glimpse of the future. However, to be complacent because the *relative* position of the sectors in the UK has changed in line with that in other advanced industrialized countries, is to ignore the UK's dramatic and unrivalled fall in the *volume* of non-oil industrial production between 1973 and 1981, outlined above in the section on changes in output (p. 5). Of especial concern has been the negligible growth rate of manufacturing output in the UK between 1973 and 1997; indeed the volume figure for UK manufacturing in 1997 is only 10.2% above that for 1973 (see Table 1.1 above).

Changes in employment

Employment has obviously been influenced by the changes in output already described. It has also been influenced by changes in technology, which have affected the labour required per unit of output. Table 1.4 gives numbers employed in each sector, together with percentage shares of total employment. The table shows that in the **goods sector** (primary and secondary) there were fewer jobs in 1979 than in 1964, with a still more rapid decline in jobs between 1979 and 1997.

In the **primary sector**, employment was reduced by 60% between 1964 and 1990. The contraction in coal output inevitably sent employment in *mining and quarrying* into severe decline. After 1990 this accelerated as the coal industry lost some of its electricity generation market to gas and was itself made ready for privatization. By 1997 coal industry employment stood at only 13,900, having been over 300,000 in the early 1970s. Such was the growth of output per worker in *agriculture* that employment was reduced by 1997 to half its 1964 level, despite an increase in output of almost 80%. The rise of the North Sea sector had directly created only 24,000 jobs in *oil and natural gas* by 1981. Renewed interest in gas helped raise this to 36,000 by 1990 but although output soared after 1990, employment again fell. The outcome was that between 1964 and 1997 the primary sector's share of total employment fell from 5.1% to 1.4%.

In the **secondary sector**, employment fell by 2.07 million between 1964 and 1979, and again by almost 4 million between 1979 and 1997. Manufacturing, as the largest part of this sector, suffered most of these job losses, with manufacturing employment falling by almost 5 million in the period 1964–97. The *share* of manufacturing in total employment fell from 38.1% in 1964 to as little as 18% in 1997.

As employment fell in the goods sector between 1964 and 1979, employment in the **tertiary sector** expanded by 2,378,000, enabling total employment to be held at around 23 million. This expansion was concentrated in the financial sector, and in various professional and scientific services.

Table 1.4 Employees in employment, UK at mid June.

	1964 ('000s)	1964 (% of total employment)	1973 ('000s)	1973 (% of total employment)	1979 ('000s)	1979 (% of total employment)	1981 ('000s)	1981 (% of total employment)	1990 ('000s)	1990 (% of total employment)	1997 ('000s)	1997 (% of total employment)
Agriculture, forestry and fishing	540	2.3	432	1.9	368	1.6	363	1.6	314	1.4	244	1.1
Mining and quarrying			336	1.5	304	1.3	285	1.3	126	0.5	41	0.2
Extraction of mineral oil and natural gas			5	–	20	0.1	24	0.1	36	0.2	31	0.1
Total primary	1,201	5.1	773	3.4	692	3.0	672	3.0	476	2.1	316	1.4
Manufacturing	8,909	38.1	7,861	34.7	7,259	31.3	6,221	28.4	4,709	20.5	4,002	18.0
Construction	1,659	7.1	1,320	5.8	1,253	5.4	1,130	5.2	1,143	5.0	817	3.7
Other energy and water supply			364	1.6	366	1.6	366	1.7	241	1.1	141	0.7
Total secondary	10,978	46.9	9,573	42.4	8,911	38.5	7,748	35.4	6,093	26.6	4,960	22.4
Distribution, hotels and catering, repairs	1,665	7.1	3,950	17.4	4,252	18.4	4,172	19.1	4,912	21.4	5,027	22.8
Transport			1,062	4.7	1,051	4.5	987	4.5	921	4.0	963	4.4
Communication			445	2.0	422	1.8	438	2.0	471	2.0	440	2.0
Banking, finance, insurance, business services and leasing	9,513	40.7	1,442	6.4	1,663	7.2	1,738	7.9	3,480	15.2	3,800	17.2
Public administration, defence and social security			1,664	7.3	1,721	7.4	1,623	7.4	1,442	6.3	1,322	6.0
Education and health			2,781	12.3	2,876	12.4	2,908	13.3	5,125	22.4	5,248	23.8
Other services			976	4.3	1,571	6.8	1,600	7.3				
Total tertiary	11,178	47.8	12,320	54.4	13,556	58.5	13,465	61.4	16,351	71.3	16,800	76.3
Total employment	23,357		22,664		23,158		21,891		22,920		22,076	

Source: ONS (1998) *UK National Accounts* and previous issues; *Labour Market Trends* (1998), May.

Table 1.5 Industrial market economies distribution of the labour force: percentages.

	1960	1980	1985	1996
Agriculture	17.3	6.5	5.5	3.8
Industry	36.7	34.5	31.7	28.3
(manufacturing)	(27.2)	(25.0)	(22.7)	(20.6)
Services	46.0	59.0	62.8	67.9

Source: OECD (1998) *OECD in Figures*, and previous issues; OECD (1997) *Country Surveys* (various).

The rough balance between employment losses in the goods sector and gains in the service sector broke down after 1979. Between 1979 and 1981 service sector employment actually fell slightly. Not until 1984 did the growth of service sector employment again compensate for the loss of goods sector employment. Over the whole period 1979–97 service sector employment grew by 3.2 million whilst employment in the goods sector fell by 4.3 million. As a result total employment fell by 1.08 million, at a time when the number of people in the labour force was steadily increasing (see Chapter 23).

Similar changes in the pattern of employment have, however, taken place throughout the industrial world (see Table 1.5). By comparison with other advanced economies the UK now has relatively small agricultural and industrial sectors, leaving services with a larger than average share of total employment.

Causes of structural change

Stage of maturity   As the world's oldest industrial nation the UK might reasonably lay claim to being its most developed or 'mature' economy. Several variants of the maturity argument provide explanations of industrial decline which appear rather reassuring.

A first variant suggests that the changing pattern of UK employment since 1964 may be seen as analogous to the transfer of workers from agriculture to industry during the nineteenth century; a transfer necessary to create the new industrial workforce. In a similar way, the argument here is that those previously employed in industrial activities were required for the expansion of the service sector in the 1960s and 1970s. However, this line of argument looks rather weak from the mid- to late 1970s onwards, with rising unemployment surely providing the opportunity for service sector expansion without any marked decline in industrial sector employment.

The hypothesis that economic maturity is associated with falling industrial employment may be crudely tested by reference to Table 1.6. In the period 1964–79 the experience of the UK, Austria, Belgium, West Germany, the Netherlands, Sweden and Switzerland lends support to the hypothesis, whilst the experience of Canada, the USA, France and Norway contradicts it. Italy and Japan also experienced rising industrial employment, but it might be contentious to call these economies 'mature' in this period. Between 1964 and 1979, the evidence does therefore suggest that decline in industrial employment in the UK was by no means an inevitable result of economic development. The data between 1979 and 1983 are more difficult to interpret as they cover a period of recession, but only Japan and Austria experienced a rise in industrial employment in these years. However, data

Table 1.6 Changes in industrial employment (%)*.

	1964–79	1979–83	1983–96
UK	−14.8	−18.9	−7.9
Canada	+35.7	−8.7	+9.7
US	+27.2	−6.4	+6.9
Japan	+28.3	+4.1	+8.2
Austria	−3.2	+8.3	+0.2
Belgium	−18.6	−15.2	−8.2
France	+2.3	−7.4	−20.1
Germany	−10.3	−8.5	+24.0
Italy	+2.2	−3.8	−12.5
The Netherlands	−14.0	−12.4	+12.3
Norway	+9.1	−2.7	−8.4
Sweden	−10.9	−7.1	−18.1
Switzerland	−21.1	−3.3	−9.4

*Calculated from data in OECD (1997) *Labour Force Statistics 1976–96*, and previous issues; OECD *Country Surveys* (various).

for the years 1983 to 1996 do seem to refute any simple hypothesis that economic maturity must inevitably bring with it a fall in industrial employment. Canada, the USA, Japan, Austria, Germany, and the Netherlands, all experienced increases in industrial employment. In the UK the decline in industrial employment accelerated during the early 1990s, resulting in an overall fall of nearly 8% for the 1983–96 period as a whole.

A second variant of the 'maturity' argument is that our changing economic structure simply reflects the changing pattern of demand that follows from economic development. It has been argued that consumer demand in a mature economy shifts away from goods and towards services (higher income elasticities) and that this, together with increased government provision of public sector services, adds impetus to the growth of the tertiary sector. This may be a sound explanation for some of the UK's structural change, but not all. The pattern of UK demand simply does not fit such a stylized picture; for instance, UK trade data clearly show UK demand for manufactured imports growing faster than UK manufactured exports (see Chapter 26). This growth in manufactured imports is hardly consistent with a major switch of UK demand away from industries producing goods.

In a third variant of the 'maturity' argument, Rowthorn and Wells (1987) have pointed out that the demand for manufactured goods is at least as income elastic as the demand for services, when valued at constant prices, that is, in terms of volume. A successful industrial sector would therefore achieve increases in the volume of output at least matching the growth of GDP. Faster growth of productivity in the industrial sector could then cause prices to fall relative to those in the service sector, thereby reducing the industrial sector's *share* of both output at current prices and employment. The 'maturity' argument should, in the view of Rowthorn and Wells, be based on *productivity* changes and not on demand changes. In the case of the UK, the relatively slow growth in the *volume* of industrial output hardly supports this variant of the 'maturity' argument.

A fourth variant of the argument is that the UK has always been a reluctant manufacturing nation, and that we are now specializing in services, a sector in which we enjoy a comparative advantage and a protected domestic market. However since the mid-1970s, any need to exploit comparative advantages in services could again have been met from unused resources rather than by reducing industrial output and employment.

Low-wage competition   Foreigners, especially from the Third World, make a convenient scapegoat for UK problems and are particularly blamed for providing 'unfair', low-wage competition. Wages in the Third World are extremely low but are often accompanied by low productivity, a lack of key categories of skilled labour, and a shortage of supporting industrial services and infrastructure. The UK is not unique in facing this competition and is itself a low-wage economy by developed country standards. In some sectors (e.g. textiles and cheap electrical goods) Third World competition has been important but, as yet, the scale of Third World involvement in the export of world manufactures is too small (around 14% of OECD manufactured imports in 1997) to be regarded as a major cause of UK structural change. As we see in Chapter 26, the main competition comes from other industrial market economies, and not from low-wage developing countries. We should also remember that countries like the previously high growth Asian 'Tiger' economies provide important export markets for manufactured goods, and so have contributed to world economic growth, with the recent slump in these economies creating problems for the export sectors of many industrialized economies, such as the UK.

The North Sea   Free market economists often argue that the contribution of North Sea oil to the UK balance of payments has meant inevitable decline for some sectors of the economy. The mechanism of decline is usually attributed to the exchange rate, with the improvement in the UK visible balance (via removal of the oil deficit) bringing upward pressure on sterling. In terms of the foreign exchange market, higher exports of oil increase the demand for sterling, and lower imports of oil decrease the supply of sterling. The net effect has been a higher sterling exchange rate than would otherwise have been the case, particularly in the late 1970s and early 1980s. The status of sterling as a petro-currency may also attract an increased capital inflow, further raising the demand for sterling, and with it the sterling exchange rate. The higher price of sterling then makes UK exports more expensive abroad, and imports cheaper in the UK. United Kingdom producers of industrial exports, and import substitutes, are the most seriously disadvantaged by a high pound, since the major part of UK trade is in industrial products (around two-thirds of both exports and imports). In this way a higher pound produces a decline in industrial output and employment.

The argument that North Sea oil, through its effect on the exchange rate, inevitably resulted in the decline in UK manufacturing output and employment observed in the late 1970s and early 1980s, is rather simplistic. The government could have directed surplus foreign exchange created by oil revenues towards imported capital equipment. This increase in imports of capital equipment would have eased the upward pressure on the pound,[4] whilst providing a basis for increased future competitiveness and economic recovery. Equally, the upward pressure on sterling could have been alleviated by macroeconomic policies aimed at raising aggregate demand, and with it spending on imports, or by lower interest rates aimed at reducing capital inflow.

North Sea oil cannot be wholly to blame for the observed decline in UK industrial output and employment. These structural changes began in the mid-1960s, yet North Sea oil only became a significant factor in the UK balance of payments in 1978. The periods of high exchange rate between 1978 and 1981, whilst certainly contributing to industrial decline, were by no means an inevitable consequence of North Sea oil. Different macroeconomic policies could, as we have seen, have produced a lower exchange rate, as happened after withdrawal from the Exchange Rate Mechanism in September 1992.

'Crowding out'   Bacon and Eltis (1976) argued that the decline of British industry was due to its being displaced ('crowded out') by the growth of the non-market public sector. Some of the (then) public sector, such as steel, is itself industrial and markets its output in the same way as any private sector company. However, some of the public sector, such as health and education, provides services which are not marketed, being free at the point of use. This non-market public sector uses resources and generates income, but does not supply any output to the market. It requires investment goods for input, and consumes goods and services, all of which must be provided by the market sector.

We might usefully illustrate the 'crowding out' argument by first taking a closed economy with no government sector. Here the income generated in the market would equal the value of output. The income-receivers could enjoy all the goods and services they produced. However they could no longer do so if a non-market (government) sector is now added, since the non-market sector will also require a proportion of the goods and services produced by the market sector. The market sector must therefore forgo some of its claims on its own output. It is one of the functions of taxes to channel resources from the market sector to support non-market (government) activity. The rapid growth of the public sector after 1945, it is argued, led to too rapid an increase in the tax burden (see Chapter 19), which adversely affected investment and attitudes to work, to the detriment of economic growth. Also, in the face of rising tax demands, workers in both market and non-market sectors sought to maintain or improve their real disposable income, thereby creating inflationary pressures.

If the market sector does not accommodate the demands of a growing non-market sector by forgoing claims on its own output, then in an open economy adjustment must be made externally. The higher overall demand *of both sectors combined* can then only be met either by reducing the exports of the market sector, or by increasing imports. A rising non-market public sector in this way contributes to balance of payments problems.

Bacon and Eltis saw the rapid growth of the non-market public sector as the cause of higher taxes, higher interest rates (to finance public spending), low investment, inflationary pressures and balance of payments problems. The growth of the non-market public sector has in these ways allegedly 'crowded out' the market sector, creating an economic environment which has been conducive to UK decline.

These ideas provided intellectual backing to the Conservative Party's approach to public spending and tax policies after 1979. The irony is that attempts to cut public spending and taxation after 1979 simply accelerated industrial decline, eroded the tax base and prevented the desired reduction of the tax burden (see Chapter 19). Bacon and Eltis's ideas provide a coherent theory of industrial decline helping us to appreciate some of the complex linkages in the process. However, experience since 1979 calls into question the basic propositions. High unemployment during the 1980s made it impossible to argue that industry was denied labour, although it did lack capital investment. It may be that low investment had more to do with low expected returns than with the high interest rates said to be necessary to finance the growth of public expenditure. There are, of course, several other determinants of UK interest rates in addition to public expenditure. The 'crowding out' argument also neglects the importance of public sector services as *inputs* to the private sector. Of the non-marketed services, education is especially important in increasing the skills of the work force.

Productivity

The total output of any economy is determined partly by the quantity of factor input (labour, capital, etc.), and partly by the use to which factors are put. Different economies may achieve different volumes of total output using similar quantities of factor input, because of variations in productivity. Productivity is the concept relating output to a given input, or inputs.

Productivity is usually expressed in terms of labour as input, i.e. labour productivity, or capital as input, i.e. capital productivity. However, a productivity measure which relates output to *both* labour and capital inputs is called *total factor productivity* (TFP). We now seek to investigate the UK's productivity performance relative to other countries with the aid of these measures.

The most widely used measure of a country's economic efficiency is *labour productivity* and this is often defined as output (or value added) per person employed. However, since there may be changes in the structure of jobs between full- and part-time or in the length of the working week or number of holidays, then a more useful measure of labour productivity is arguably output (value added) *per person hour*.

A much debated issue is whether or not the UK has been catching up with other major competitors in terms of productivity. An important recent study of the UK's relative productivity performance (O'Mahony 1998) is the basis for Tables 1.7 and 1.8.

Table 1.7 shows the growth rates of labour productivity defined as value added per hour worked in the UK and a number of its main competitors between 1950 and 1996. These growth rates are an average for labour productivity across *all* sectors of the respective economies, including agricultural, industrial and service sectors. We see that the UK performance has averaged about 2.5% per annum over the 1950–96 period, about 1% per annum better than in the US over this period, but has lagged well behind the annual growth rates of labour productivity achieved by France, Germany and Japan.

What matters, of course, is not only the *growth* in labour productivity but the *base level* from which that growth takes place. To compare *absolute levels* of labour productivity between the UK and her main competitors, we need to refer to Table 1.8 (column L).

Table 1.7 Growth rates of labour productivity* (% per annum) 1950–96.

	UK	US	France	Germany	Japan
1950–96	2.48	1.57	3.71	3.87	4.48
1950–73	2.72	2.37	4.62	5.18	6.11
1973–96	2.23	0.78	2.79	2.56	3.06

* Value added per hour worked.
Source: Adapted from O'Mahony (1998) Table 1.2.

Table 1.8 Labour and total factor productivities (UK = 100).

	US		France		Germany		Japan	
	L	T	L	T	L	T	L	T
Whole economy								
1950	182	128	75	71	68	68	39	48
1979	154	133	130	123	131	117	79	82
1996	120	112	132	121	129	112	90	80
Manufacturing								
1973	302	171	97	119	79	114	43	87
1979	193	170	162	150	151	139	114	109
1996	160	137	144	125	120	106	122	103
Distributive trades								
1973	178	134	119	112	74	88	15	62
1979	161	143	150	131	119	108	72	75
1996	171	146	136	120	108	104	96	95
Financial and business services								
1973	194	159	90	173	55	137	30	81
1979	151	151	138	165	137	135	51	76
1996	115	113	114	121	169	131	56	59

Notes: L = labour productivity, T = total factor productivity (TFP).
Source: Adapted from O'Mahony (1998) Tables 1.2 and 1.5.

From Table 1.8 (which uses index numbers based on UK = 100) we can see that UK labour productivity for the *whole economy* has improved over time in relation to the US. For example, in 1950 the US was 82% more productive than the UK, but by 1996 was only 20% more productive than the UK. However, France and Germany have come from behind the UK in 1950 to pass the UK's level of labour productivity by the 1970s. Japan's performance, starting from very low levels of labour productivity after the dislocation of World War II, has also been impressive, though labour productivity remains below the level of the UK. The table certainly suggests that there has been some narrowing of the labour productivity gap with the US and Germany since 1979, but there has been a marginal deterioration in labour productivity with France and Japan since 1979. Overall, the UK's labour productivity level for the whole economy still remained significantly below that of the US, France and Germany in 1996, with deficits of 20%, 32% and 29% respectively.

In terms of levels of TFP, Table 1.8 (column T) provides some useful comparisons. From the table we can see that for the *whole economy* the UK remains at a disadvantage *vis-á-vis* its major competitors, namely the US (12%), France (21%) and Germany (12%), though the UK has an advantage of 20% over Japan. In the period since 1979 there is evidence of the UK having begun to narrow the TFP gap with its major competitors, though there is clearly scope for further improvements in this respect.

Table 1.8 also provides information on the levels of labour productivity (L) and TFP (T) in some of the most important *sectors* of the respective economies between 1973 and 1996. The three sectors shown in the table account for some 60% of GDP in these countries and provide an insight into the comparative productivity performance of these countries in both manufacturing and services. Comparing the UK with the US, we see that the UK's relative productivity performance for both labour and TFP improved in manufacturing and in the financial/business services, but not in the distributive trades. Comparing the UK with France and Germany, we see that the UK's relative productivity performance for both labour and TFP deteriorated in manufacturing and the distributive trades between 1973 and 1979 and then improved from 1979 onwards. For the financial/business services sector the UK's productivity performance relative to France and Germany follows a less obvious pattern.

What is clear is that in 1996 the UK still faced a substantial disadvantage in levels of labour productivity and TFP in all three sectors as compared to France and Germany.

- First, taking *labour productivity*, the recorded disadvantages in 1996 with France for the manufacturing, distributive trades and financial/business services sectors were 44%, 36% and 14% respectively, and with Germany 20%, 8% and an astonishing 69% respectively.
- Secondly, taking *total factor productivity*, the recorded disadvantages in 1996 with France for the manufacturing, distributive trades and financial/business services sectors were 25%, 20% and 21% respectively, and with Germany 6%, 4% and 31% respectively.

Although calculating productivity data is notoriously complex and prone to error, such a systematic underperformance by the UK in sectors which even include financial services, is clearly some cause for concern. This analysis would suggest that the UK cannot necessarily depend on higher productivity in services to compensate for any productivity deficit recorded in manufacturing. At this point it will be useful to consider productivity in manufacturing in rather more detail.

Manufacturing productivity

The UK's productivity in manufacturing has always been in the forefront of discussion because the sector is so open to global competitive forces. Table 1.9 gives a brief summary of trends in labour productivity for the whole economy and for manufacturing, together with trends in manufacturing output in the UK between 1964 and 1998. We see that output per person employed in manufacturing has risen

Table 1.9 United Kingdom productivity and manufacturing output (1990 = 100).

Year	UK output per person employed		Manufacturing output
	Whole economy	Manufacturing	
1964	58.1	45.3	72.6
1969	67.0	53.8	85.4
1973	76.2	63.4	94.6
1979	81.7	65.8	90.6
1990	100.0	100.0	100.0
1998*	114.8	120.4	101.6

*First quarter.
Source: ONS (1998) *Economic Trends*, October, and previous issues.

by 75.1 points on 1964, much more than the 56.7 points recorded for the whole economy. This is certainly supportive of the view that manufacturing is a vital 'engine for growth'. However, we can also see that manufacturing *output* has only increased by 29 points since 1964. Indeed, since 1990 UK manufacturing output has been essentially static, growing by only 1.6 points. Hardly surprising then that we noted significant job losses in the manufacturing sector in Table 1.4 (p. 9), since a relatively rapid labour productivity growth and a static output are invariably associated with a reduction in employment.

Although much discussion of the UK's performance in terms of productivity has centred on the manufacturing sector, it should be noted that this sector is not a cohesive entity; rather it is made up of many sub-sectors with divergent records over time. A recent major study of UK manufacturing productivity (Cameron and Proudman 1998) showed that although the overall growth of manufacturing output may have been stagnant, there were significant differences between sub-sectors of manufacturing. The study investigated output growth and labour productivity in 19 sub-sectors of manufacturing over the period 1970–92. Their results suggest that there has been an important shift in the contribution of the various sub-sectors to manufacturing output, with nine sectors experiencing positive rates of output growth (led by computing, pharmaceuticals, aerospace, electronics and precision instruments), whilst the other ten sectors experienced negative rates of growth of output (led by iron and steel, basic metals, minerals and machinery). Interestingly, the sectors experiencing positive rates of growth of output also tended to be those which experienced higher rates of growth of labour productivity.

Two further conclusions of the study might also be noted. First, the authors investigated whether changes in overall manufacturing productivity were due to the re-location of resources *between* sectors (i.e. from low to high productivity sectors) or due to productivity growth *within* the sectors over time. They concluded that over 90% of the increase in labour productivity was due to *within*-sector productivity growth. This suggests that explanations of changes in productivity should concentrate on factors which affect productivity *within* industries and even plants. Second, the study looked at whether productivities across the various sectors of manufacturing have tended to converge. They concluded that whilst productivity in a number of sectors appeared to settle at levels just below the manufacturing mean, the productivities of a few sectors (such as computing, pharmaceuticals and aerospace) remained consistently above the mean and tended to move further above the mean over time. This evidence of divergence between sectors of UK manufacturing raises the question of whether the progressively higher productivity levels achieved in particular manufacturing sectors is the result of differences in the nature of the *technologies* used in these sectors, or is the result of other factors involving capital intensity, labour skills or openness to trade. We will return to some of these questions later in the chapter.

Productivity and capital investment

The contribution of *capital investment* to variations in the rate of output growth between nations has been an important topic of research for many years, the argument being that the greater the investment in plant and equipment, the greater the capacity of the economy to grow (see Ch. 17). Recent research has looked at the role of investment in tangible assets (plant, machinery and equipment) and in human capital (training, etc.) in influencing the growth of nations (Dougherty and Jorgenson

1997). They found that for the period 1960–89, the two main factors explaining the recorded differences in levels of output per head between countries were identified as the *level* of capital input and the *quality* of labour input. They concluded that one of the most serious deficiencies in the UK *vis-á-vis* other countries was the low recorded level of capital per head. The earlier study by O'Mahony (1998) provides further evidence on this issue of capital intensity, i.e. different levels of capital per unit of labour across nations and sectors.

Table 1.10 uses capital per hour worked with the UK as the base (100) for the index in each year. It shows that over the period 1950–95, the level of capital per hour worked for the *whole economy* was substantially higher in other countries than in the UK. Although the UK has narrowed this capital intensity gap with the US over the 1950–95 period from 310 down to 131, the gap has actually widened for the UK *vis-á-vis* France, Germany and Japan. By 1995 the US had a capital intensity advantage of 31%, France 36%, Germany 55% and Japan 40% in terms of capital per hour worked.

When we look at the three individual sectors of manufacturing, distributive trades and financial/business services, we can see some important patterns.

- In the *manufacturing* sector, all the competitors to the UK have a capital intensity advantage over the UK. By 1995 the US had 51% more capital per hour worked in manufacturing than the UK, with corresponding figures of 50% for France, 40% for Germany and 60% for Japan. Although the UK has narrowed this capital intensity gap in manufacturing relative to the US over the whole period, the gap has actually widened since 1979 relative to France, Germany and Japan.
- In the *distributive trades* sector the UK was clearly at a disadvantage in 1995 in terms of capital per hour worked against all the countries in Table 1.10, with the gap widening in all countries except France since 1979.

Table 1.10 Relative levels of capital per hour worked (UK = 100).

	US	France	Germany	Japan
Whole economy				
1950	310	120	98	51
1979	166	123	153	86
1995	131	136	155	140
Manufacturing				
1950	178	143	146	113
1979	167	141	139	116
1995	151	150	140	160
Distributive trades				
1950	175	164	174	72
1979	150	163	121	79
1995	158	160	139	120
Financial/ business services				
1950	146	91	96	47
1979	100	59	103	35
1995	107	93	138	88

Source: Adapted from O'Mahony (1988) Tables 1.7 and 1.8.

- In the *financial/business services* sector the trend in capital intensity since 1979 has been adverse for the UK in comparison with all four countries, though the UK still has an advantage against France (7%) and Japan (12%), but a disadvantage against the US (7%) and Germany (38%).

In contrast to the more recent trends in labour productivity noted earlier, there has been no great improvement since 1979 in Britain's capital intensity levels relative to the other four countries. A relatively low level of capital intensity for the UK is of some concern in the context of studies such as Oulton (1997). In a more general survey of growth in 53 countries over the period 1965–90, Oulton found that the most important way of raising growth rates was by increasing the growth rate of capital stock, i.e. raising capital per worker. Of course, the relatively low levels of investment in the UK may be a rational response to low returns, so that whilst low investment may contribute to low productivity, low productivity may in turn discourage investment. For example, Oulton noted that the pre-tax rate of return for investment in UK companies (excluding North Sea oil) averaged only 8.7% per annum between 1988 and 1997, with the private rate of return on human capital around the same figure. Since the cost of capital averaged around 5–7% per annum over the same period, the payoff for investing in either physical or human capital in the UK was hardly attractive!

Productivity and labour skills

The above account points to the importance of capital intensity in enhancing productivity. Of course the productivity of a nation also depends on the skills of its management and workforce in making the best use of whatever resources are available. Management is responsible for selecting projects, organizing the flow of work and the utilization of resources, so that effective management is a 'necessary' condition for good productivity performance. It is not, however, 'sufficient' since a labour force which possesses inappropriate skills, or which refuses to adapt its work practices and manning levels to new technology will prevent advances in productivity, whatever the merits of management. A major issue in many industries is workers' lack of flexibility between tasks, resulting in overmanning and also acting as a disincentive to innovation. Lack of flexibility can result from union restrictive practices, but is also caused by badly trained workers and managers who are unable to cope with change. There is evidence of low standards in UK education which mean that many school leavers are ill-equipped for the growing complexity of work.

Throughout British industry there is less emphasis on training than in other countries. Only around 50% of 18 year olds in the UK were in full time or part time education or training in 1998, much less than the 80% figure for Germany, France Netherlands and Belgium, suggesting that young people as a group in the UK are among the least educated and trained in Europe. When considering the whole labour force, that is the stock of human capital rather than the flow, the situation is probably even worse. Davies and Caves (1987) had pointed out that British managers were only marginally better qualified than the population at large: for example very few production managers were graduate engineers. Amongst production workers only a quarter in Britain had completed an apprenticeship compared with about half in Germany. Very few British foremen had formal qualifications for their job but in Germany foremen were trained as craftsmen and then took the further qualification of *Meister*. In fact only 14% of UK technicians and 3% of UK foremen possessed higher intermediate qualifications, compared to 36% of German technicians and 64% of German foremen (Steedman *et al.* 1991). The study by O'Mahony (1998) also confirms the UK's skills deficit against Germany at the intermediate level. Higher levels of skill have arguably enabled German firms to make better use of their capital equipment and to adapt to change of all kinds, so investment in human capital raises productivity of both physical capital and labour, whilst also achieving consistently higher quality of output.

Overall some progress has been made in narrowing the productivity gaps previously identified for the UK *vis-à-vis* its major competitors. However, the UK is still at a considerable productivity disadvantage in terms of many of its competitors. A similar picture emerges from our review of capital intensity and the quality of the work force.

Nevertheless it is important to remember that the whole question of productivity differences is much more complex than might at first appear. For example, a NIESR research project investigated the reasons for observed differences in productivity between the US and Europe in two quite different sectors, namely the biscuit sector and the precision industry sector (Mason and Finegold 1997). The survey did find that some of the reasons for the higher US productivity could be related to higher physical capital investment per worker in these sectors in the US as compared to Europe. However, the most important factor underlying the productivity gap was found to be the greater economies of scale available in the US sectors compared to the European sectors, a factor which is often overlooked in studies comparing productivity performances. That the reasons for productivity differences are complex is apparent from comparisons in 1998 between Nissan's Sunderland plant, which produces 98 cars per employee per year, and the Rover Group plant at Longbridge, which produces 33 cars per employee per year. Investigations revealed that as compared to Nissan's Sunderland plant, the Longbridge plant was older, had a more complex layout, and suffered from a lower demand for its product range, suggesting that simplistic conclusions from productivity comparisons must be treated with some caution. Certainly the existence of relatively inefficient car plants is by no means a British phenomenon. For example, the Renault plant at Sandouville, France, produces only 36 cars per employee per year and the Volkswagen plant at Emden, Germany, produces only 28 cars per employee per year.

A more detailed comparison of labour productivity and capital utilization in six manufacturing and service industries across the five leading industrialized countries has been undertaken by the McKinsey Global Institute (McKinsey Report 1998). These comparisons covered car assembly, food processing, food retailing, hotels, telecommunications and software production. Figure 1.1 provides a snapshot of some of the results, with the data presented as averages across the six industries from the countries concerned over the period 1994–96, UK = 100. This McKinsey study reinforces some of our earlier data, revealing a clear productivity gap between the UK and its major competitors in both labour productivity and TFP, though not in capital productivity as compared with France and Germany.

Labour productivity across these six sectors is 37% higher in the US than in the UK, and 26% higher in both Germany and France than in the UK. Similar, if less substantial, productivity gaps are revealed using the TFP measure, but UK capital productivity is only behind the US (by 10%), being ahead of France (by 8%) and Germany (by 7%). However, capital investment per hour worked is some way behind all our competitors.

Fig. 1.1.   UK comparative productivity and capital intensity, 1994–96.
Source: Adapted from McKinsey Global Institute, in Kaletsky (1998).

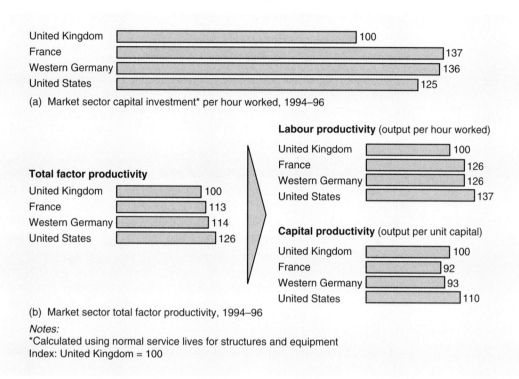

(a) Market sector capital investment* per hour worked, 1994–96

(b) Market sector total factor productivity, 1994–96

Notes:
*Calculated using normal service lives for structures and equipment
Index: United Kingdom = 100

In seeking to probe behind these productivity differences, the McKinsey Report concludes that 'UK management often fails to adopt global best practices even when in some cases these are readily understandable and achievable'.

Relative unit labour costs (RULC)

It would still be possible to remain price-competitive with overseas producers even with low labour productivity, if real wages were also low. Labour costs per unit of output (unit labour costs) are determined by the wages of the workers as well as the output per worker. International competitiveness, in terms of unit labour costs, is also influenced by exchange rates. Depreciation of the currency can even compensate for poor productivity and high money wages, though it also has the effect of raising import prices.

Figure 1.2 reveals the sources of the changes in UK cost competitiveness in manufacturing since 1976, relative to its major competitors. The UK's *relative productivity* is shown by Schedule 'C', which indicates the changes in UK manufacturing productivity *relative* to its major competitors since 1976. We see that in 1998 UK manufacturing productivity had risen by around 10% on its 1976 level relative to those competitors. The *relative cost of UK labour* had, however, risen by as much as 80% over this period (Schedule 'B'). The impact of these changes on UK competitiveness was, however, moderated by a fall in the *effective exchange rate* to around 88% of its 1976 level (Schedule 'D'). As a result, *relative unit labour costs* (RULC) were around 44% above their 1976 level (Schedule 'A'). Whilst significant, a

44% increase in RULC is certainly much less than the 80% increase in relative labour costs over this period.

The calculation of RULC is as follows:

$$\frac{\text{Relative labour costs}}{\text{Relative productivity}} \times \frac{\text{sterling effective}}{\text{exchange rate}} = \text{RULC} \qquad \left(\frac{1.80}{1.10} \times 0.88 = 1.44\right)$$

We should not of course conclude from this that the 1976 position was 'just right'. Nevertheless we have already shown that manufacturing output and employment had fallen dramatically between 1976 and 1998. A restoration of UK competitiveness, even to 1976 levels would in all probability generate more output and more employment than currently experienced.

The above formula emphasizes that lower *relative unit labour costs* could be achieved either by reducing relative labour costs, or by raising relative productivity, or by lowering the effective exchange rate, or indeed by a combination of all three. If the *exchange rate alone* were to be used, a *depreciation* of 30% would have been required in 1998 in order to restore RULC in the UK to its 1976 level.

Figure 1.2 draws attention to the fact that the sterling effective exchange rate *appreciated* between 1978 and 1981 (see also Chapter 25). This happened at the very time that relative labour costs were rising rapidly and relative productivity was falling. Hardly surprising, therefore, that the UK's competitive position deteriorated by about 50% during this period, as indicated by the sharp rise in RULC. This was a major factor in the marked decline in manufacturing output and employment in the UK between 1979 and 1981.

After 1980/81 the competitive position improved (RULC is on a downward trend) as the decline of the sterling effective exchange rate more than compensated for the resumed rise in relative labour costs. Notice that improvements in relative productivity contributed little to the falling RULC after 1983. By 1990 there was again concern about the competitive position of the UK as the pound rose to around

Fig. 1.2. Cost contributions: sources of changes in UK cost competitiveness in manufacturing.
Sources: National Economic Development Office (1987); *Economic Trends* (various); *European Economy* (various).

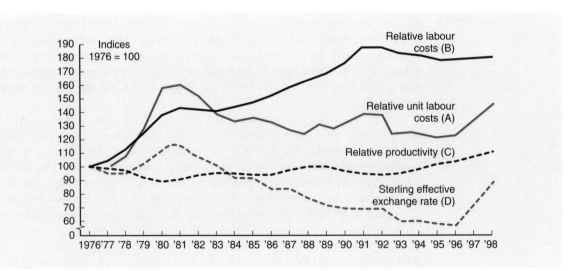

3.0 DM. This concern was re-inforced by UK entry into the Exchange Rate Mechanism (ERM) at the (high) central parity of £1 = 2.95 DM in October 1990. However the enforced withdrawal of the UK from the ERM on 16 September 1992 (see Chapter 28) led to the pound depreciating by more than 14% in the following months. This went some way to meeting the 27% depreciation estimated as being required in 1991 to restore RULC to its 1976 level in Fig. 1.2. It has certainly brought about a sharp fall in RULC from September 1992 onwards which has contributed to the recovery of output and improved the balance of trade. However, of recent concern has been the strong appreciation in the sterling effective exchange rate over the 1996–98 time period. It has risen by more than 20% over this two-year period, in turn raising RULC by around 17%, despite a modest fall in the ratio of relative labour costs to relative productivity. Clearly upward movements in the sterling effective exchange rate can more than offset any labour cost/labour productivity improvements.

The major study by O'Mahony (1998) reinforces many of these points. For example, Table 1.11 presents *levels* of relative unit labour costs (RULC) for the four countries identified between 1973 and 1995 (UK = 100), providing a further insight into the competitive position of the UK. In terms of the *whole economy*, in 1995 the UK had a small (5%) competitive disadvantage relative to the US in terms of RULC, but was actually more cost efficient on this measure than France (by 18%), Germany (by 30%) and Japan (by 90%). Although not shown in this table, in terms of particular *sectors*, the US had RULC advantages over the UK in manufacturing (80), distributive trades (91) and financial/business services (65), but France, Germany and Japan all had significantly higher RULC than the UK in all these sectors. For example, the RULCs of these countries in manufacturing were much higher than in the UK, e.g. France (111), Germany (164) and Japan (129). It is only when we look at *all* elements, namely relative labour costs, relative labour productivity and relative exchange rates, as in Table 1.11, that we can get a reasonably accurate picture of international competitiveness.

The UK would therefore appear to be more cost competitive than its disappointing comparative productivity data might have indicated. Nevertheless it is important that the productivity gaps already identified be narrowed or removed. It is certainly doubtful as to whether the apparent alternative option of a low-wage, low-productivity industrial economy is viable, given the role of technology. Technical change is frequently embodied in the latest capital equipment, and has the effect of changing not just the volume of output per worker, but also the quality of products. For instance, robot welders and paint-sprayers on car production lines offer a dependable quality which previously more labour-intensive methods did not. If, as a consequence of lower real wages, older and more labour-intensive methods are retained in the face of competition from new technology, markets will often still be

Table 1.11 Relative unit labour costs (UK = 100).

	US	France	Germany	Japan
Whole economy				
1973	123	128	147	131
1979	92	124	131	133
1989	94	96	104	144
1995	95	118	130	190

Source: Modified from O'Mahony (1998) Table 1.15.

lost on the basis of quality, *even if* prices can be held at apparently low levels. In these circumstances, the UK would be producing goods under similar conditions to many newly industrializing Third World countries.

Low productivity, not fully compensated by low wages or by a lower exchange rate, leaves UK companies in a weak market position. They are faced with the choice of raising prices and risking lost orders, or continuing to sell on lower profit margins. Markets differ in their sensitivity to rising prices, but in all markets rising prices tend to reduce sales *volume*, which usually means less employment. Multinational companies located in the UK may, to avoid raising price, supply an increasing proportion of their market from overseas plants, again reducing UK output and employment (see Chapter 7).

Firms which absorb rising unit costs by taking lower profit margins may be able to maintain their levels of output and employment, at least in the short run. But in the long run profits are vital to industrial investment, both in providing investment finance and in influencing expectations of future rates of return, and hence investment plans. Investment is also required in many industries to raise productivity, and thereby profits, and so we come full circle. Profits depend on productivity, which is affected by investment, which depends on profits! The process is self-reinforcing; low productivity gives low profits, low investment and therefore little productivity improvement. In contrast, once productivity is raised, profits and investment increase, which further raises productivity. This cumulative upward spiral is still further reinforced in that market share and factor incomes rise, so that demand is created for still higher output. New technology is also more easily accepted in situations of rising output, perhaps leading to still higher profits, stimulating further investment, and so driving the process on. The UK's problem is to further improve on its productivity performance, given the substantial gaps which still persist relative to its main competitors across a number of industrial and service sectors.

The consequences of low productivity and poor competitiveness have been felt mainly in the manufacturing sector of the economy, largely because its exposure to international competition is greater than that of the service sector. Structural change, in the form of a *reduced share* of output and employment for the manufacturing sector, is then almost inevitable. In the UK this has also become a decline in the *absolute level* of employment in manufacturing and, since 1973, virtual stagnation of the absolute level of output of the manufacturing sector.

Consequences of structural change

Deindustrialization   There is little agreement as to what 'deindustrialization' actually means. For some time politicians on the left have used the term to mean loss of industrial employment. Others extend the term to include situations of declining industrial output, and still others to include declining *shares* of employment or output.

We have shown that the UK has undergone deindustrialization on each and every one of these criteria. Declining industrial employment is not unusual in other advanced economies (see Table 1.6), and neither is a decline in the industrial sector's share of employment (Table 1.5) or of GDP (Table 1.3). Where the UK is unusual is in the insignificant growth of non-oil industrial production in the 26 years since 1973.

Declining industrial employment need not be a problem; there is every indication that many British people would not freely choose industrial employment. There will, however, be the problem of rising unemployment if declining industrial employment is not compensated by increasing non-industrial employment. Until 1979 this problem did not arise; as we saw in Table 1.4, employment levels were broadly maintained until 1979, but since then the growth of service sector employment has *not* compensated for falling industrial employment. The costs of deindustrialization have been particularly felt in those regions where declining industries were concentrated. The Midlands, the North, Yorkshire and Humberside, the North West, Wales and Scotland all experienced a prolonged period with unemployment rates well above 10% during the 1980s, as the industrial base contracted. However, there has been a considerable narrowing of the unemployment differential between regions as the recession of the early 1990s bit deep into the previously expanding service sector activities throughout the UK (see Chapter 23).

Some writers view these changes as part of a move towards a post-industrial society, where the main activities involve the creation and handling of information. However, a decline in the *share* of industrial activity within the economy would be less worrying if *absolute* industrial output had grown since 1973 at the same rate as in other advanced economies.

A decline in manufacturing activity may cause a still more serious employment impact than that given by the official statistics. This is because manufacturing is characterized by many more *backward-linkages* than is the service sector (Greenhalgh, 1994). For example, in order to make cars the vehicle manufacturer will buy in some engine components, metal products and textiles from other manufacturers and will also purchase the services of vehicle transporters, accountants, bankers, designers etc. Manufacturing and services display very different patterns of inter-industry purchases, which can be examined using statistical input-output tables. In particular, the rate of purchase of service output by manufacturing firms is a much larger proportion per unit of gross output than is the purchase of manufactured goods for use as inputs by services. Whereas Greenhalgh found that each £1 spent on manufacturing gross output created £1.61 of employment income in *all* sectors, that same £1 spent on service gross output created only £0.56 of employment income in *all* sectors. Clearly manufacturing sustains a far higher proportion of jobs (*directly and indirectly*) than it might appear to us from data on sectoral shares, such as Table 1.4 above.

Deindustrialization may not only put these backward-linkages at risk but also a variety of *forward-linkages*. The suggestion here is that innovations, whether measured by patents or survey records, are heavily concentrated in the manufacturing sector. Again Greenhalgh (1994) found that 87% of innovations were developed in the manufacturing (and primary) sector, and 80% of all first commercial adoptions of innovations took place in this sector. Deindustrialization clearly puts at risk the 'seed-corn' of domestic technology, which in turn has balance of payments implications (see below) as UK trade becomes progressively geared to high-technology products.

Growth prospects   As we saw in Table 1.9, it is manufacturing which has led the way in productivity growth. Manufacturing lends itself to rapid growth of labour productivity because of the scope for capital investment and technical progress. Growth of manufacturing output, of GDP and of productivity, are closely related, and manufacturing has in the past been the engine for growth. As workers found new jobs in manufacturing during the nineteenth century they left agriculture and other relatively low-productivity sectors. Those in the new jobs raised their productivity, and the average productivity of those remaining in agriculture was raised by the removal of marginal workers. At the same time rising incomes in manufacturing generated new demand for goods and services, the multiplier process encouraging still further growth of output, and with it productivity. Indeed Greenhalgh (1994) points out that in the eight-year period 1985–93, manufacturing contributed about 70% of the average rise in output per worker in the whole economy.

In parts of the service sector there is little scope for improved productivity; even the concept itself is often inappropriate. First, because there is often no clear output – how do you measure the output of doctors, or nurses? Second, even where a crude output measure is devised, it often fails to take into account the quality of service – are larger class sizes an increase or decrease in educational productivity? The national accounts often resort to measuring output by input (e.g. the wages of health workers), so that productivity is by definition equal to 1. There are, however, some services where productivity can be meaningfully measured and in these there is scope for productivity growth, especially where the new information technologies can be applied. But many workers who lose manufacturing jobs move into service sector jobs, where their productivity may be lower, into unemployment or out of the labour market altogether. There is no mechanism for growth in this process, quite the reverse.

Balance of payments   An alternative definition of deindustrialization is offered by Singh, based on the traditional role of manufacturing in UK trade flows. Historically the UK was a net exporter of manufactures, so that surplus foreign exchange was earned which enabled the country to run a deficit on its trade in food and raw materials. Singh (1977) defines an 'efficient' manufacturing sector as one which 'not only satisfies the demands of consumers at home but is also able to sell enough of its products abroad to pay for the nation's import requirements'. Singh also states that this is subject to the restriction that 'an efficient manufacturing sector must be able to achieve these objectives at socially acceptable levels of output, employment and exchange rate'. A country such as the UK would then be 'deindustrialized' if its manufacturing sector did not meet these criteria, leaving an economic structure inappropriate to the needs of the country. It can be argued that this is indeed the position in the UK. The current account can only be kept in balance by surpluses in the oil and service sectors and by earnings from overseas assets. Any reflation of aggregate demand stimulates an even faster growth in imports of manufactured goods which pushes the current account towards deficit. By the end of the 1980s boom the UK again had a worryingly large current account deficit (see Chapter 26). The decline of UK manufacturing has recreated the balance of payments constraint on macroeconomic policy which many had hoped North Sea oil would remove. This, allied to the fact that UK output and employment are hardly at *socially acceptable* levels, suggests that the UK could be regarded as 'deindustrialized' on Singh's definition.

It might be argued that the service sector can take over the traditional role of manufacturing in the balance of payments accounts. A difficulty here is that unlike manufactures many services cannot, by their nature, be traded internationally (e.g. public sector services), with the result that trade in manufactures is on a vastly bigger scale than trade in services (see Chapter 26). The House of Commons Trade and Industry Committee (1994) pointed out that a 2.5% rise in service exports is required merely to offset a 1% fall in manufacturing exports. In some services which can be traded, the UK is already highly successful (e.g. financial services), and if even bigger surpluses are to be earned then the UK would have to move towards a monopoly position in those services. In fact, international competition is increasing in traded services and the UK may find it difficult to hold its current share of the market.

Other economists have pointed out that Singh's definition would leave most of the non-oil-producing industrial countries categorized as 'deindustrialized' because, despite growing industrial output, their macroeconomic policies were constrained by their balance of payments positions after the 1973 and 1979 oil price rises. This observation does not invalidate the conclusion that deindustrialization in the UK has had serious balance of payments consequences.

Inflation If deindustrialization in the UK is so advanced that the economy is not capable of producing goods to match the pattern of market demand, then there may be implications not only for imports but also for prices. Any increase in overall demand will meet a shortage of domestic suppliers in many industrial sectors. This will both encourage import substitution and provide opportunities for domestic suppliers to raise prices. As a result, despite continuing high unemployment, there may be little effective spare capacity in the UK in sectors where deindustrialization has been excessive. Supply side constraints created by structural change may then have increased the likelihood of the UK experiencing demand-led inflation in the event of a sustained increase in aggregate demand, such as that of the late 1980s. In response to such constraints government policy has moved towards strengthening the supply side, as with the Conservative government's labour market reforms and Labour government measures such as the New Deal.

Conclusion

There have been profound structural changes in the UK economy since 1964, resulting in relative stagnation of industrial output and declining industrial employment, and these have transformed the sectoral balance of the economy. The causes of these changes are not agreed. We reviewed various suggestions, such as economic 'maturity', low-wage competition, the advent of North Sea oil, 'crowding out', and low productivity. Our view has been that low productivity, resulting in a substantial loss of competitiveness, has been central to the structural changes observed. Certainly no other major industrial country has experienced the fall in volume of non-oil industrial output recorded in the UK after 1973. The consequences of industrial decline are widespread, contributing to unemployment and balance of payments problems, increasing inflationary pressures and hampering growth. Judged by the growth of output and productivity there was an improvement in the performance of the UK economy during the 1980s. The UK has reduced the productivity gap with other OECD countries and has increased industrial output at a rate close to the OECD average. Nevertheless, UK manufacturing output in 1998 was only 7.3% more in volume terms than it had been in 1973.

Theory of the firm

Chapter 2

Company accounts as a source of financial information

Companies in the UK are required by Act of Parliament to publish accounts on an annual basis.

This chapter examines the content and presentation of conventional accounts, and identifies a number of useful accounting ratios which can be calculated. The 1998 accounts of Tesco p.l.c. have been used for illustration. Tesco is one of Britain's leading food retailers, with 586 stores throughout the United Kingdom. It also operates stores in the Republic of Ireland, France and Central Europe. The chapter concludes with a detailed analysis of the Financial Times Share Information Service, and the indices and ratios it contains.

Company accounts and the assessment of company performance

The separation of control and ownership in the majority of public companies[1] creates an atmosphere in which management might wish to present to shareholders as favourable a picture as possible of the company's activities. Fear of the effects of competition and of adverse investor reaction may also mean that companies seek to give away as little as possible – usually by disclosing the legal minimum of information. Most p.l.c.'s, however, regard the presentation of their annual accounts as a matter of corporate pride, and pay great attention to the quality and relevance of the documents.

Published financial statements should provide sufficient information to enable shareholders and potential shareholders to make economic decisions about whether to buy, hold or sell shares in a company.

An examination of the typical elements that make up a company report reveals a mixture of statutory items, requirements of the accounting profession, additional Stock Exchange requirements and voluntary disclosures. The most important items within annual reports are the following:

(a) Chairman's review;
(b) Directors' report;
(c) Balance sheet;
(d) Profit and loss account;
(e) Statement of total recognised gains and losses;

(f) Note of historical cost profits and losses;
(g) Notes to the accounts (including statement of accounting policies);
(h) Cash flow statement;
(i) Auditors' report;
(j) Historical summary.

It is worth while investigating each of these elements to identify those features which may be helpful in assessing a company's overall performance.

Chairman's review

There is no statutory requirement for a chairman to report separately from his or her directors, so any statement usually contains voluntary information. The chairman's review of operations often seeks to explain why the company has performed as it has over the past year, indicating strategy for the immediate future. Plans for expansion, diversification, overseas growth and the development of new products would usually be included.

However, the chairman's position as the figurehead of the company demands that he or she maintains confidence in the company's activities, so the chairman is likely to concentrate on the encouraging aspects of performance and play down the weak points. Thus John Gardiner, chairman of Tesco, stated:

> The company continues to move ahead in an increasingly competitive UK marketplace. We are also investing in new areas of growth for the long term, such as the Central European retail market and the provision of financial services. There will be start-up costs associated with these developments. Looking ahead, we will work the business harder both to improve the shopping trip for customers and to increase profits for the Group.

Directors' report

This includes a statement of the principal activities of the company and of any significant changes that have taken place in the holding of fixed assets (e.g. property sales or the acquisition of subsidiaries). Details of the directors and their shareholdings in the company are also mentioned as any significant change in their holdings may reflect their view of the company's future prospects.

Balance sheet

This shows the position of the company at its financial year end, usually 31 December, but for a retailer like Tesco, the relatively 'quiet' date of the last Saturday in February 1998 (28th) was used. It details the assets of the business and balances them against its liabilities; in other words, what the company *owns* (assets) is exactly matched by what it *owes* (liabilities) in terms of funds required to finance those assets.

The balance sheet is essentially a 'snapshot' of the state of the company on one day, though the actual position could of course appear very different a few days before or after. A number of criticisms can be made of the way balance sheets are normally presented. They do not show how the final position was arrived at; for instance, the company may attempt to 'clean up' its balance sheet by repaying loans just before the year end only to incur the debt again early in the new financial year. This is known as 'window dressing'. They also ignore those items which cannot be measured objectively in monetary terms, such as expertise or harmonious labour relations.

Accounting ratios   Despite these difficulties, the construction of several simple ratios from the information contained within the balance sheet can give a clear assessment of the company's performance by making the following comparisons:

- with its *own* performance in previous time periods.
- with that of *other companies* in the same sector, and/or
- with *accepted standards* of performance, i.e. with particular values ('norms') for each ratio.

Figure 2.1 shows the 1998 balance sheet for Tesco p.l.c. Several accounting ratios have been calculated by extracting the 1998 figures from the table and *comparing them* with the corresponding (net of VAT) annual sales turnover (£16,452m for Group sales to outside customers – see the profit and loss account of Fig. 2.2). For comparative purposes the same ratios have been calculated for Kingfisher p.l.c., also in the retailing sector (Woolworths, Superdrug, Comet, etc.), and, as a contrast, for Blue Circle Industries p.l.c. in the manufacturing (building materials) sector.

Fig. 2.1.   Balance sheet. *Source:* Adapted from Tesco p.l.c., 1998.

Consolidated Balance Sheet
28 February 1998

	1998 £m	1997 £m
Fixed assets		
Tangible assets	6,311	5,826
Investments	185	23
	6,496	5,849
Current assets		
Stocks	584	550
Debtors	133	78
Investments	196	80
Cash at bank and in hand	29	65
	942	773
Creditors: falling due within one year	2,712	2,101
Net current liabilities	(1,770)	(1,328)
Total assets less current liabilities	4,726	4,521
Creditors: falling due after more than one year	812	611
Provisions for liabilities and charges	38	20
	3,876	3,890
Capital and reserves		
Called up share capital	110	109
Share premium account	1,528	1,431
Other reserves	40	40
Profit and loss account	2,198	2,310
Equity shareholders' funds	3,867	3,890

Gearing ratio   This reflects the financial risk to which the company is subject, by measuring the capital structure of the company and the degree to which it relies on external borrowings. Gearing can be calculated in various ways, including:

$$\text{Gearing ratio} = \frac{\text{external borrowing}}{\text{total capital employed}}$$

$$= \frac{\text{loan capital} + \text{bank overdraft}}{\text{loan capital} + \text{bank overdraft} + \text{ordinary shares and reserves}}$$

The total capital employed is made up of external borrowings (debentures,[2] other loans and bank borrowing) and internally generated funds (ordinary shares and reserves). The *cost* of external borrowing is loan interest payments, whilst that for internal funds is the dividend that must be paid to shareholders.

The gearing ratio shows the proportion of total capital that is provided externally and gives an indication of the burden of interest payments to which the company is committed irrespective of its profitability. A gearing ratio around 33.3% is usually regarded as acceptable for a company, suggesting that it is not over-reliant on external borrowing. A figure in excess of this indicates a relatively highly geared company. High gearing ratios are most suitable to those companies with steady and reliable profits, whose earnings are sufficient to cover interest payments and where total dividends are low. Wide fluctuations in profitability make the highly geared company extremely vulnerable to a downturn in market conditions – profits may be so low that interest payments cannot be covered, leading to receivership. The 1998 accounts reveal a gearing ratio of 26.5% for Tesco, (607 + 792)/ (607 + 792 + 3,876), a value lower than the 34% of Blue Circle but greater than Kingfisher's 22%. Tesco had £225m investments and cash at bank and in hand at the balance sheet date, which when offset against loans and overdrafts, effectively reduces its gearing level to only 22%.

A drawback of the ratio is that it is concerned only with borrowings on which interest charges are incurred. It ignores completely liabilities which constitute interest-free loans. One such major item is that of 'trade creditors' – money which is owed by the company to its suppliers. The ratio tends to understate the dependence of companies on external borrowings, so it is useful to extend the 'loan' item to 'all liabilities'. The numerator would then become: 'short and long-term liabilities' and produce a ratio which is a more realistic basis for comparison when linked with 'shareholders' funds'. The ratios for the three companies are: Tesco 92%; Blue Circle 112%; Kingfisher 111%.

Operating ratios   These can be used to gauge the efficiency with which various aspects of the company's trading are managed.

Stock turnover ratio.   The holding of stock, in the form of unsold finished, and partly finished, goods, is an expensive activity for companies, so that considerable attention is paid to the stock turnover ratio:

$$\text{Stock turnover ratio} = \frac{\text{average stocks}}{\text{sales turnover}}$$

Fig. 2.2. Profit and loss
account.
Source: Adapted from
Tesco p.l.c., 1998.

Group Profit and Loss Account
53 weeks ended 28 February 1998

	Total 1998 £m	Total 1997 £m
Sales at net selling prices	17,779	14,984
Value added tax	1,327	1,097
Turnover excluding value added tax	16,452	13,887
Operating expenses		
Normal operating expenses	15,505	13,081
Employee profit sharing	35	32
Integration costs	95	–
Operating profit	817	774
Loss on disposal of discontinued operations	(8)	–
Net loss on disposal of fixed assets	(1)	–
Loss from interests in associated undertakings	(15)	–
Profit/(loss) on ordinary activities before interest	793	774
Net interest payable	(65)	(24)
Profit on ordinary activities before taxation	728	750
Profit before integration costs, loss on disposal of discontinued operations and net loss on disposal of fixed assets	832	750
Integration costs	(95)	–
Loss on disposal of discontinued operations	(8)	–
Net loss on disposal of fixed assets	(1)	–
Tax on profit on ordinary activities	223	230
Profit for the financial year	505	520
Dividends	255	225
Retained profit for the financial year	250	295

	pence	pence
Earnings per share	23.1	24.1
Adjustment for integration costs after taxation	3.7	–
Adjusted for net loss on disposal of fixed assets and loss on disposal of discontinued operations after taxation	0.4	–
Adjusted earnings per share	27.2	24.1
Fully diluted earnings per share	22.6	23.5
Adjusted for integration costs after taxation	3.6	–
Adjusted for net loss on disposal of fixed assets and loss on disposal of discontinued operations after taxation	0.4	–
Adjusted fully diluted earnings per share	26.6	23.5
Dividends per share	11.60	10.35

This ratio reflects the level of stockholding used to support sales (see Fig. 2.2). We would expect companies to carry the minimum level of stock (inventories) consistent with the efficient running of the business. The appropriate figure will vary widely according to the industrial sector involved. Tesco's ratio is only 3.8% ((584 + 550)/2)/14,887, a figure which reflects the extremely fast throughput of their stock, on average being sold every 14 days. Kingfisher's ratio was 13.1% (48 days) whilst Blue Circle had a ratio of 13.6% (50 days).

Debtors' turnover ratio.   This ratio can be used to monitor a company's credit control procedures, by comparing the amount it is owed by consumers, to whom credit facilities have been extended, with its total sales.

$$\text{Debtors' turnover ratio} = \frac{\text{debtors}}{\text{sales turnover}}$$

$$= \frac{\text{average amount owed to the group by customers}}{\text{sales turnover}}$$

Businesses like retail supermarkets are run almost exclusively on a cash-and-carry basis so have almost zero debtors. However, the tendency for retail supermarkets to introduce their own charge card for credit trading (e.g. Marks and Spencer, 1985, Tesco, 1996) increases the debtors' figure. Even so, it may generate sufficient additional sales actually to reduce the debtors' turnover ratio. For other businesses an average credit period might be nine weeks, equivalent to a debtors' turnover figure of around 17%. Retailers Tesco and Kingfisher showed figures of 0.7%* (2.5 days' sales) and 8.5% (31 days' sales) respectively.

Creditors' turnover ratio.   This ratio indicates the size and period of credit a company receives from its suppliers, by comparing the total amount the company owes to its creditors with its sales.

$$\text{Creditors' turnover ratio} = \frac{\text{creditors}}{\text{sales turnover}}$$

$$= \frac{\text{average amount owed by the group to its suppliers}}{\text{sales turnover}}$$

It may (after evaluating the possibility of pre-payment discounts) be very much in the company's interests to exploit its suppliers by extending the credit period. However, Tesco shows a figure of 6% (899[†]/14,887), reflecting its close links with its suppliers. Kingfisher (5.1%) and Blue Circle (6.7%) show similar figures.

It is important to avoid confusion between the term 'creditors' when meaning 'trade creditors' (i.e. money owed to suppliers) as against meaning 'total creditors' (i.e. liabilities of all varieties). All further references in this chapter will equate 'creditors' with 'trade creditors'.

*((133 + 78)/2)/14,887
[†](972 + 826)/2

Liquidity ratios   These give an indication of the company's short-term financial position. In other words, the availability of cash or marketable assets with which to meet current liabilities.

Current ratio.   The current ratio measures the extent to which currently available assets cover current liabilities, i.e. those requiring repayment within one year.

$$\text{Current ratio} = \frac{\text{current assets}}{\text{current liabilities}}$$

$$= \frac{\text{stocks} + \text{debtors} + \text{cash}}{\text{overdraft} + \text{creditors} + \text{taxation} + \text{dividends}}$$

A figure of 2.0 may be taken as prudent, showing that current liabilities are more than covered by current assets. A ratio value of more than 2.0 is not necessarily a sign of strength, since it may mean excessive stocks or debtors, or an uneconomic use of liquid funds.

Food retailers are unusual in that their rapid turnovers, together with the cash-and-carry nature of their business, will give relatively low 'stock' and 'debtor' items respectively. In this way 'current assets' will be small, and so a very low current ratio is to be expected. Tesco's 1998 figure of 0.35 (942/2,712) must be viewed in this context. By comparison, Blue Circle's 1.6 reflects the high level of stocks which manufacturers carry. Kingfisher's ratio of 1.2 is typical of a predominantly 'non-food' retailer.

Quick assets ratio (acid test).   This ratio provides a better indication of short-term liquidity by ignoring stockholdings and concentrating on those assets which are more easily convertible into cash.

$$\text{Quick assets ratio} = \frac{\text{current assets} - \text{stocks}}{\text{current liabilities}}$$

A yardstick of 1.0 is usually sought, indicating that sufficient liquid assets are available to cover current liabilities. Blue Circle is just above the manufacturing sector average with a ratio of 1.2.

Traders with a rapid turnover of cash sales will have a lower level of current assets, and often a very low ratio. This is the case with Tesco's quick assets ratio of only 0.13 ((942 − 584)/2,712) for 1998. Kingfisher's ratio is 0.63.

The current and quick assets ratios are probably the best-known and most widely used financial ratios, so it is no surprise that some companies might resort to 'window-dressing' of the accounts in order to create an impression that these ratios are a little better than they actually are.

The calculation of the above six ratios from balance sheet information, i.e. (a) *gearing* ratio; (b) *operating* ratios: stock turnover; debtors' turnover; creditors' turnover; and (c) *liquidity* ratios: current; quick assets. These ratios permit an assessment of a company's performance with regard to accepted standards across a given sector. This assessment is further improved by considering the information provided by the profit and loss account.

Profit and loss account

This is a summary of transactions for a stated period, usually a year, and sets revenues against costs in order to show the company's profit or loss. The statement discloses summarized figures for the expenses of the business (e.g. the cost of goods sold), but makes no evaluation of the risks incurred in order to earn the given profit levels. Neither is there any indication of the degree to which the given profit level conforms with the company's objectives.

Figure 2.2. shows the profit and loss account of Tesco for 1998 and indicates the various deductions that take place from sales revenue to derive profit or loss. Part of the profit is distributed to shareholders in the form of dividends, with the balance being retained by the company to boost reserves. Dividends may still be paid to shareholders even when losses have been incurred, if profits from previous years are available.

The profit figure remains the single most important figure in the company accounts and various profitability measures can be employed to assess relative performance.

Profit margin

$$\text{Profit margin} = \frac{\text{profit before interest and tax}}{\text{sales turnover}}$$

The profit margin is a ratio of profit, after the deduction of trading expenses but before the payment of interest on borrowings (financing charges) and corporation tax, to sales turnover. A normal figure of 8–10% would be typical for manufacturing industry. Activities such as food retailing, with high volumes and competitive prices, might expect a ratio around 3%, which might still yield high absolute levels of profit. In fact, Tesco exhibits an encouraging result with a ratio of 4.8% (793/16,452) for its profit margin. Kingfisher earned 8.3%, whilst Blue Circle produced 13.3%.

Return on assets

$$\text{Return on assets} = \frac{\text{profit before interest and tax}}{\text{total assets}}$$

Measurement of the rate of return on total assets offers a popular alternative assessment of profitability, despite the fact that it compares a 'dynamic' item (profits) with a 'static' item (total assets). On this basis the Tesco figure is 10.7% (793)/ (6,496 + 942), whereas Blue Circle yields 9.9%, and Kingfisher 14.3%.

Calculations of the return on assets will clearly vary, sometimes substantially, with the basis used for measurement. This is a strong argument for using a standard approach and accountants are expected, under their *Statement of Standard Accounting Practice (SSAP) No. 12*, to reassess the value of assets at regular intervals to avoid outdated valuations being used.

A consideration of these profitability ratios, together with earlier information on leverage, operating and liquidity ratios, can give an overall impression of Tesco's financial position in 1998. The company has maintained a relatively high profit margin and return on assets, whilst having a low gearing ratio. Its working capital situation would cause alarm in a different type of business, but the very fast throughput of stock ensures that the cash flow is more than adequate to meet liabilities as they fall due.

Statement of total
recognised gains and
losses

This is a primary financial statement (i.e. of equal standing to the profit and loss account, balance sheet and cash flow statement), which was introduced by *Financial Reporting Standard (FRS) 3* in 1992. It enables users of accounts to consider *all* gains and losses (not just 'trading' profits) in assessing the company's overall performance. Fig. 2.3 shows Tesco p.l.c.'s statement, which, for 1997/98, showed that the company, whilst making an after-tax profit of £505m (as shown in the profit and loss account) lost £14m on foreign exchange adjustments, bringing the total 'recognised' gains down to £491m. The statement was introduced to prevent companies from misleading shareholders by 'hiding' non-trading losses (e.g. on revaluation of properties and foreign currency transactions) in notes to the accounts, rather than giving them the prominence they warranted. The classification of the statement of total recognised gains and losses as a *primary* statement ensured that such vital information can no longer be concealed.

Fig. 2.3.   Statement of
total recognised gains
and losses.
Source: Adapted from
Tesco p.l.c., 1998.

Statement of Total Recognised Gains and Losses
52 weeks ended 28 February 1998

	Group	
	1998 £m	1997 £m
Profit for the financial year	505	520
Loss on foreign currency net investments	(14)	(12)
Total recognised gains and losses relating to the **financial year**	491	508

Note of historical cost
profits and losses

This is a memorandum statement, also introduced by FRS 3 designed to present the profits or losses of companies which have *revalued* their assets on a more comparable basis with those that have not. Tesco did not revalue its assets, but Fig. 2.4 is the statement of Blue Circle Industries p.l.c. showing that the effect of revaluing assets was to reduce profits by £2.2m in the year.

Fig. 2.4.   Note of
historical cost profits and
losses.
Source: Adapted from
Blue Circle Industries
p.l.c., 1997.

Note of Historical Cost Profits and Losses
52 weeks ended 31 December 1997

	1997 £m	1996 £m
Profit on ordinary activities before tax	246.3	297.6
Difference between historical cost depreciation charge and the actual depreciation charge calculated on the revalued amount	2.2	2.3
Historical cost profit on ordinary activities before tax	248.5	299.9
Historical cost profit for the year retained after tax, minority interests and dividends	19.7	77.2

Notes to the accounts (including statement of accounting policies)

There is far more information contained in notes to the accounts than is within the balance sheet and profit and loss account. The regulatory framework of accounting has broadened since the early 1970s to include not only the Companies Acts but also *Statements of Standard Accounting Practice and Financial Reporting Standards*, which are issued by the accountancy profession to standardize procedures and suggest 'best practice'.

The notes always commence with a statement of the accounting policies adopted by the company (an extract is shown in Fig. 2.5), and there will follow many pages of detailed information needed either to comply with the Acts or the relevant accounting standards required by the profession. It is unusual for companies to give more than the minimum requirements, but the auditors' report (see Fig. 2.7) will confirm whether or not such requirements have been met.

Cash flow statement

Until 1991, nearly all companies had to prepare a *Statement of Source and Application of Funds* (SSAF) as part of their audited annual accounts. This statement placed the emphasis on where the company raised funds (e.g. profits and asset sales), and what it did with the funds generated (e.g. increasing working capital). A new Accounting Standards Board which had been formed in 1990 issued its first Financial Reporting Standard (FRS 1) in 1991 entitled *Cash Flow Statements* to replace the previous standard requiring the SSAF. It is a recognition that the generation of *cash* is of far greater importance than the disclosure of an inflow of *funds*, particularly as an indicator of impending insolvency. Because the SSAF was based on working capital movements, liquidity problems could be disguised, and a significant decrease in cash could be concealed by increases in stock and debtors.

One much quoted example was that of Polly Peck p.l.c., the crashed fruit to electronics conglomerate, which showed a £172m *funds inflow* in its 1989 accounts, yet would have recorded a £130m *cash outflow* had FRS 1 been applied. David Tweedie, chairman of the ASB, said (1991) on the introduction of FRS 1 that 'It is right that cash flow should be the subject of the board's first standard. Recent experience had demonstrated all too clearly that adequate information on cash is an essential element of a company's financial statements. Cash is the lifeblood of a business, if it dwindles the business will die. But it is also a very difficult figure to fiddle.'

Figure 2.6 shows the cash flow statement of Tesco p.l.c., and it can be seen that despite it being a 'profitable' year, there was a *decrease* in cash of £128m. Trading activities generated over £1bn of cash, but taxation (£238m), purchase of fixed assets (£805m) and the purchase of subsidiaries (£649m) combined to contribute to the overall cash outflow in the year.

Auditors' report

The auditors are required to report to shareholders ('the members') on whether the company accounts have been properly prepared, in accordance with the Companies Act, and whether they give a true and fair view of the activities of the company. Figure 2.7 provides a typical example. The auditors may qualify their approval of the accounts if they feel that the records have not been well kept or if all the information they require is not available. Such qualifications usually fall into two categories: (1) those relating to accounting policy, and (2) those relating to unsatisfactory levels of information.

Fig. 2.5.   (Extract from)
accounting policies.
Source: Adapted from
Tesco p.l.c., 1998.

Accounting Policies

Basis of financial statements

The financial statements have been prepared in accordance with applicable accounting standards, under the historical cost convention, and are in accordance with the Companies Act 1985.

Basis of consolidation

The Group profit and loss account and balance sheet consist of the financial statements of the parent company and its subsidiary undertakings, all of which are prepared to or around 28 February 1998 apart from Global T.H., Tesco Polska Sp. z o.o., Tesco Stores ČR a.s. and Tesco Stores SR a.s. which had 31 December 1997 year ends.The results of Catteau S.A. have been included to 24 February 1998, its date of disposal. In the opinion of the directors it is necessary for the Continental European companies to prepare financial statements to an accounting date earlier than the rest of the Group to enable the timely publication of the Group financial statements.

Any excess or deficiency of purchase consideration in relation to the fair value of attributable net assets of subsidiary undertakings at the date of acquisition is adjusted in reserves.

The Group's share of associated undertakings' profits or losses is included in the Group profit and loss account and added to the cost of investments in the balance sheet. The accounting policies of associated undertakings are adjusted on consolidation to achieve consistent Group accounting policies.

Stocks

Stocks comprise goods held for resale and development properties and are valued at the lower of cost and net realisable value. Stocks in stores are calculated at retail prices and reduced by appropriate margins to the lower of cost and net realisable value.

Money market investments

Money market investments are stated at cost. All income from these investments is included in the profit and loss account as interest receivable and similar income.

Fixed assets and depreciation

Fixed assets include amounts in respect of interest paid, net of taxation, on funds specifically related to the financing of assets in the course of construction.

Depreciation is provided on an equal annual instalment basis over the anticipated useful working lives of the assets, after they have been brought into use, at the following rates:

Land premiums paid in excess of the alternative use value on acquisition – at 4% of cost.
Freehold and leasehold buildings with greater than 40 years unexpired – at 2.5% of cost.
Leasehold properties with less than 40 years unexpired are amortised by equal annual instalments over the unexpired period of the lease.
Plant, equipment, fixtures and fittings and motor vehicles – at rates varying from 10% to 33%.

Fig. 2.6.   Cash flow
statement.
Source: Adapted from
Tesco p.l.c., 1998.

Group Cash Flow Statement
53 weeks ended 28 February 1998

	1998 £m	1997 £m
Net cash inflow from operating activities	1,156	1,219
Returns on investments and servicing of finance		
Interest received	28	44
Interest paid	(116)	(84)
Interest element of finance lease rental payments	(6)	(7)
Net cash outflow from returns on investments and servicing of finance	(94)	(47)
Taxation		
Corporation tax paid (including advance corporation tax)	(238)	(228)
Capital expenditure and financial investment		
Payments to acquire tangible fixed assets	(805)	(703)
Receipts from sale of tangible fixed assets	82	91
Increase in fixed asset investments	–	12
Net cash outflow for capital expenditure and financial investment	(723)	(600)
Acquisitions and disposals		
Purchase of subsidiary undertakings	(649)	(112)
Net cash acquired with subsidiary	65	3
Sale of subsidiary undertakings	259	–
Net cash disposed of as part of sale of subsidiary undertakings	(2)	–
Purchase of interests in associated undertakings	(32)	(17)
Net cash outflow from acquisitions and disposals	(359)	(126)
Equity dividends paid	(214)	(194)
Cash (outflow)/inflow before use of liquid resources and financing	(472)	24
Management of liquid resources		
Increase in short term deposits	(116)	(29)
Financing		
Ordinary shares issued for cash	38	31
Redemption of E.C.S.C. loans 1996	–	(74)
Increase in other loans	443	60
Capital element of finance leases repaid	(21)	(18)
Net cash inflow/(outflow) from financing	460	(1)
Decrease in cash in the period	(128)	(6)
Reconciliation of net cash flow to movements in net debt		
Decrease in cash in period	(128)	(6)
Cash (inflow)/outflow from (increase)/decrease in debt and lease financing	(422)	32
Loans and finance leases acquired with subsidiary	(20)	–
Loans and finance leases disposed of as part of sale of business	10	–
Cash used to increase liquid resources	116	29
Amortisation of 4% unsecured deep discount loan stock	(3)	(3)
Foreign exchange differences	5	12
(Increase)/decrease in net debt	(442)	64
Net debt at 22 February 1997	(749)	(813)
Net debt at 28 February 1998	(1,191)	(749)

Fig. 2.7. Auditors'
Report.
Source: Adapted from
Tesco p.l.c., 1998.

Auditors' Report
To the Shareholders of Tesco p.l.c.

We have audited the financial statements on pages 16 to 39 which have been prepared under the historical cost convention, the accounting policies set out on pages 20 and 21 and the directors' emoluments and share details included on pages 10 to 14.

Respective responsibilities of directors and auditors

As described above, the company's directors are responsible for the preparation of financial statements. It is our resonsibility to form an independent opinion, based on our audit, on those statements and to report our opinion to you.

Basis of opinion

We conducted our audit in accordance with Auditing Standards issued by the Auditing Practices Board. An audit includes examination, on a test basis, of evidence relevant to the amounts and disclosures in the financial statements. It also includes an assessment of the significant estimates and judgements made by the directors in the preparation of the financial statements, and of whether the accounting policies are appropriate to the company's circumstances, consistently applied and adequately disclosed.

We planned and performed our audit so as to obtain all the information and explanations which we considered necessary in order to provide us with sufficient evidence to give reasonable assurance that the financial statements are free from material misstatement, whether caused by fraud or other irregularity or error. In forming our opinion we also evaluated the overall adequacy of the presentation of information in the financial statements.

Opinion

In our opinion the financial statements give a true and fair view of the state of affairs of the company and of the Group as at 28 February 1998 and of the profit and cash flows of the Group for the year then ended and have been properly prepared in accordance with the Companies Act 1985.

Price Waterhouse

Chartered Accountants
and Registered Auditors
London
20 April 1998

Historical summary Over 90% of the companies subject to the requirements of the Stock Exchange Listing Agreement provide some sort of historical summary, usually over a five- or ten-year period, but with no uniform approach to content (Fig. 2.8). It gives a simple overall picture of the company's progress, along with difficulties encountered, such as problems of coping with inflation over the period or with changing accountancy practice.

Fig. 2.8.   Five year
record.
Source: Adapted from
Tesco p.l.c., 1998.

Five Year Record

Year ended February

	1994 £m	1995 £m	1996 £m	1997 £m	1998 £m
Turnover excluding VAT					
UK	8,347	9,655	11,560	13,118	14,640
Northern Ireland and Republic of Ireland	–	–	–	–	1,028
Rest of Europe	253	446	534	769	784
	8,600	10,101	12,094	13,887	16,452
Operating profit – pre-integration costs					
UK	513	600	713	760	866
Northern Ireland and Republic of Ireland	–	–	–	–	49
Rest of Europe	8	17	11	14	(3)
	521	617	724	774	912
Operating margin					
UK	6.1%	6.2%	6.2%	5.8%	5.9%
Northern Ireland and Republic of Ireland	–	–	–	–	4.8%
Rest of Europe	3.2%	3.8%	2.1%	1.8%	–
Total group	6.1%	6.1%	6.0%	5.6%	5.5%
Share of loss from associated undertakings	–	–	–	–	(15)
Net interest (payable)/receivable	7	(22)	(43)	(24)	(65)
Underlying profit	528	595	681	750	832
Wm Low/Ireland integration costs	–	(39)	–	–	(95)
Loss on disposal of discontinued activities	–	–	–	–	(8)
Net loss on disposal of fixed assets	(93)	(5)	(6)	–	(1)
Profit before taxation	435	551	675	750	728
Taxation	(136)	(170)	(209)	(230)	(223)
Profit after taxation	299	381	466	520	505
Underlying fully diluted earnings per share	18.8p	20.1p	21.9p	23.5p	26.6p
Earnings per share	15.2p	18.9p	22.2p	24.1p	23.1p
Dividend per share	7.75p	8.60p	9.60p	10.35p	11.60p
Net worth – £m	2,749	3,104	3,588	3,890	3,876
Return on shareholders' funds	19.4%	20.3%	20.4%	20.1%	21.4%
Return on capital employed	15.7%	16.2%	16.9%	17.1%	18.4%
Net assets per share	140p	151p	167p	179p	176p
UK food retail productivity £					
Turnover per employee	138,658	140,842	143,355	146,326	146,404
Profit per employee	8,522	8,752	8,841	8,478	8,660
Wages per employee	13,922	13,941	13,948	14,222	14,500
Weekly sales per sq. ft.	16.37	17.00	18.31	19.74	21.12
UK food retail statistics					
Market share in food and drink shops	10.7%	12.0%	13.6%	14.6%	15.2%
Number of stores	430	519	545	568	586
Total sales area – '000 sq. ft.	11,006	12,641	13,397	14,036	14,585
Sales area opened in year – '000 sq. ft.	790	830	685	603	680
Average store size (sales area) – '000 sq. ft.	25,700	24,900	25,600	26,300	26,600
Average sales area of stores opened in year – '000 sq. ft.	33,100	28,200	30,700	25,800	26,700
Full-time equivalent employees	60,199	68,552	80,650	89,649	99,997
Share price – pence					
Highest	260	255	338	370	539
Lowest	179	202	245	263	339
Year end	223.5	252	271	349	517

International Accounting Standards

In addition to the accounting standards produced by the UK profession, many other countries have their own 'national' standards. In 1973, an organization called the International Accounting Standards Committee (IASC), was established with the object of harmonising standards on a world wide basis. It has representatives from over seventy countries, and the members seek to encourage compliance between their own national standards and those agreed by the IASC. In most cases, compliance with a UK Financial Reporting Standard will ensure automatic compliance with the relevant International Accounting Standard.

One major problem that members face is that there is no internationally agreed conceptual framework within which the objectives of financial reporting can be agreed, due largely to the differing economic systems operating within the member countries.

External sources of financial information

Of the various elements in the company accounts, the chairman's review is probably the most widely read. None of the other elements, despite the importance of the information contained, receives more than the passing attention of the average reader. Users of financial information still often prefer to use secondary sources of information, including those provided by the Central Statistical Office, the financial press and other external agencies. Details of the comprehensive information provided by the *Financial Times* is given on pp. 744–6. Two specific features are here considered in detail: The FTSE All-Share Index, and data on individual share price movements.

FTSE All-Share Index: sector share movements   The All-Share Index[3] integrates the movements of some 850 constituent shares, covering 8 sector groups, and 35 individual sectors, based on April 1962 = 100. Figure 2.9 shows the nature of the information provided. Various indices (see below) and trends are published separately for each sector group, as well as for selected sectors within those groups. Data for the Sevices sector only is shown in Figure 2.9.

A comparison of *sector* index numbers with that for the All-Share Index allows the buoyant and depressed sectors to be quickly and clearly identified. For instance, 'Pharmaceuticals' (9,830.11) and 'Life Assurance' (7,260.04) represent the high-fliers when compared to the All-Share figure of 2,576.02, whilst 'Diversified Industrials' (1104.93) and 'Construction' (1,236.66) are the laggards.

FT data on individual share movements   The *individual company* Share Information Service – of which Fig. 2.10 is an abstract – can usefully be viewed in conjunction with the All-Share Index. The performance of an individual company can then be assessed in the context of the performance of the industrial sector in which it operates.

Share (equity) price movements are published daily, with shares ordered alphabetically within particular industrial sectors. The price quoted is the middle

Fig. 2.9. (Extract from)
FTSE actuaries share
indices.
Source: Adapted from
Financial Times 27/8/98.

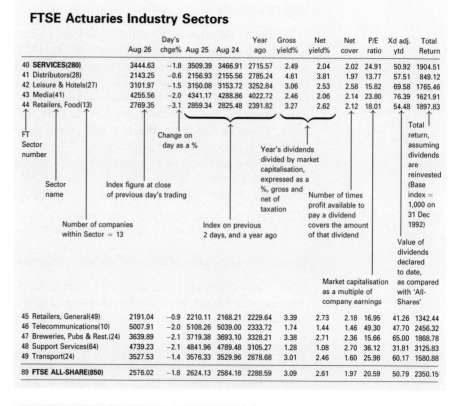

FTSE Actuaries Industry Sectors

	Aug 26	Day's chge%	Aug 25	Aug 24	Year ago	Gross yield%	Net yield%	Net cover	P/E ratio	Xd adj. ytd	Total Return
40 **SERVICES(280)**	3444.63	−1.8	3509.39	3466.91	2715.57	2.49	2.04	2.02	24.91	50.92	1904.51
41 Distributors(28)	2143.25	−0.6	2156.93	2155.56	2785.24	4.61	3.81	1.97	13.77	57.51	849.12
42 Leisure & Hotels(27)	3101.97	−1.5	3150.08	3153.72	3252.84	3.06	2.53	2.58	15.82	69.58	1765.46
43 Media(41)	4255.56	−2.0	4341.17	4288.86	4022.72	2.46	2.06	2.14	23.80	76.39	1621.91
44 Retailers, Food(13)	2769.35	−3.1	2859.34	2825.48	2391.82	3.27	2.62	2.12	18.01	54.48	1897.83
45 Retailers, General(49)	2191.04	−0.9	2210.11	2168.21	2229.64	3.39	2.73	2.18	16.95	41.26	1342.44
46 Telecommunications(10)	5007.91	−2.0	5108.26	5039.00	2333.72	1.74	1.44	1.46	49.30	47.70	2456.32
47 Breweries, Pubs & Rest.(24)	3639.89	−2.1	3719.38	3693.10	3328.21	3.38	2.71	2.36	15.66	65.00	1868.78
48 Support Services(64)	4739.23	−2.1	4841.96	4789.48	3105.27	1.28	1.08	2.70	36.12	31.81	3125.83
49 Transport(24)	3527.53	−1.4	3576.33	3529.96	2878.68	3.01	2.46	1.60	25.98	60.17	1580.88
89 **FTSE ALL-SHARE(850)**	2576.02	−1.8	2624.13	2584.18	2288.59	3.09	2.61	1.97	20.59	50.79	2350.15

FT
Sector
number

Sector
name

Number of companies
within Sector = 13

Index figure at close
of previous day's trading

Change on
day as a %

Index on previous
2 days, and a year ago

Year's dividends
divided by market
capitalisation,
expressed as a
%, gross and
net of
taxation

Number of times
profit available to
pay a dividend
covers the amount
of that dividend

Market capitalisation
as a multiple of
company earnings

Total
return,
assuming
dividends
are
reinvested
(Base
index =
1,000 on
31 Dec
1992)

Value of
dividends
declared
to date,
as compared
with 'All-
Shares'

Fig. 2.10. FT Share
Information Service.
Source: Adapted from
Financial Times 27/8/98.

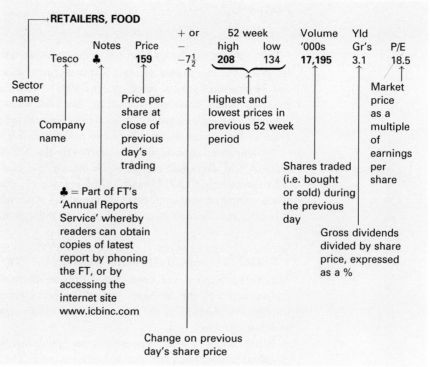

→ **RETAILERS, FOOD**

	Notes	Price	+ or −	52 week high	low	Volume '000s	Yld Gr's	P/E
Tesco	♣	**159**	−7½	**208**	134	**17,195**	3.1	18.5

Sector
name

Company
name

Price per
share at
close of
previous
day's
trading

♣ = Part of FT's
'Annual Reports
Service' whereby
readers can obtain
copies of latest
report by phoning
the FT, or by
accessing the
internet site
www.icbinc.com

Change on previous
day's share price

Highest and
lowest prices in
previous 52 week
period

Shares traded
(i.e. bought
or sold) during
the previous
day

Gross dividends
divided by share
price, expressed
as a %

Market
price
as a
multiple
of
earnings
per
share

price, i.e. midway between the buy and sell prices on the stock market. Figure 2.10 shows the specific information provided for Tesco p.l.c. in the food retailers sector.

The FT of Thursday 27 August 1998 (see Fig. 2.10) revealed that at the close of the day's trading the Tesco share price stood at 159 p, down $7\frac{1}{2}$ p from the previous day's closing price. We can make a more thorough assessment of Tesco's current position if we examine some of the technical headings of Figures 2.9 and 2.10, in conjunction with Tesco's own annual report. Figure 2.11 shows the derivation of Tesco's key data.

Price/earnings ratio: Tesco 18.5, Sector 18.01, All-Share 20.59   The price/earnings (P/E) ratio is the most important single measure of how the market views the company, and is the most common means of comparing the market values of different shares. The P/E ratio tells us the number of years' earnings that will be necessary to accumulate the current share price. Usually the more highly regarded the company, the higher its P/E ratio, with the market anticipating a sustained earnings performance over a lengthy period. The P/E ratio will depend in part upon the company's past record, but also upon that of the industrial sector of which it is a part, and upon the overall level of the stock market. A P/E ratio of 17–22 was regarded as typical in August 1998.

$$\text{P/E ratio} = \frac{\text{share price}}{\text{earnings per share}}$$

where earnings per share is profit after tax divided by the number of ordinary shares.

The sector figure of 18.01 for food retailers (see Fig. 2.9) is itself lower than average (20.59), whilst Tesco's own P/E ratio of 18.5 probably indicates market sentiment regarding Tesco's dominant place within the sector whilst recognising the intense competition from other retailers such as J. Sainsbury and Asda. Changes in future expectations will affect both share price and the P/E ratio, of which the share price is the numerator.

Net cover: Tesco 1.98, Sector 2.12, All-Share 1.97   This indicates the level of safety regarding the payment of dividends compared with profit levels. The average number of times that the profit *available* for dividend 'covers' the dividend itself is 2.12 in the food retailers sector; i.e. for every £ paid in dividends, there was £2.12 of profits available. This is slightly safer than the overall 'All Share' average of 1.97.

Gross dividend yield: Tesco 3.0%, Sector 3.27%, All-Share 3.09%   This shows the return on the investment before the deduction of income tax at the basic rate, as a percentage of the share price.

$$\text{Gross dividend yield} = \frac{\text{gross dividend per share}}{\text{share price}} \times 100$$

These technical figures, particularly the P/E ratio and the gross dividend yield, provide an excellent indication of current company performance and prospects. If this FT information is used alongside balance sheet information, company reports, particularly that of the auditors, and press statements about recent company activities, then the shareholder will be better able to assess the management of his or her investment.

Fig. 2.11. FT ratios:
Tesco p.l.c. (1998).

Conclusion

Clive Jenkins, a former trade union leader, is reputed to have complained that 'published accounts are utterly and absolutely useless' (Holmes and Sugden 1997). Clearly there remain opportunities to revise the content and improve the presentation of company accounts so that they provide the shareholder with a better service. Nevertheless our earlier analysis makes it difficult to agree with Mr Jenkins. Various accounting ratios, properly understood, give useful insights into specific aspects of company performance. Taken together they can also provide a more general guide to overall company prospects. The content of the published accounts, together with external sources, notably the FT Share Information Service, provide an excellent basis for the assessment of company performance and the evaluation of investments. Some further information on the various FT indices can be found at the end of the book.

Key points

- All limited companies in the UK have to publish financial information.
- All p.l.c.s have to appoint an independent auditor to report to the shareholders on the truth and fairness of the financial statements.
- The majority of the financial information contained within the annual report is required by either legislation (the Companies Acts) or Stock Exchange regulations.
- There are four primary financial statements: the balance sheet, the profit and loss account, the cash flow statement and the statement of total recognised gains and losses.
- Accounting ratios can be grouped into gearing, operating (e.g. stock turnover), liquidity (e.g. acid test) and profitability (e.g. margin).
- The cash flow statement was introduced by FRS 1. It shows whether the company had a net cash inflow or outflow during the year. Even though a company may be profitable, it may go out of business through its inability to pay its creditors or repay a loan (or loan interest) which falls due.
- The FTSE All-Share Index shows key information for nearly 40 sectors. Individual share information is found each day (except Sunday) in the Share Information Service pages of the *Financial Times*.

Notes

1. Evidence suggests that in the majority of public companies, the controlling management has little or no stake in the ownership of the company. The directors of Tesco p.l.c., for example, had beneficial ownership of only 0.09% of the company's issued equity capital (1.9m shares out of a total issued share capital of over 2 billion).
2. Fixed interest stocks issued by companies, usually redeemable at a set date, and backed by an agreement similar to a mortgage.
3. The All-Share Index is an arithmetic average of price relatives weighted to reflect the market valuation of the shares included.

$$\text{All-Share Index} = \frac{w_1(P_1/S_1) + w_2(P_2/S_2) + \ldots + w_{850}(P_{850}/S_{850})}{w_1 + w_2 + \ldots + w_{850}}$$

where w_{1-850} = market valuations (i.e. current share price × number of ordinary shares) for each share included;

P_{1-850} = current share price of each share;

S_{1-850} = base year share prices for April 1962.

4. A bonus issue is a transfer of a company's reserves to its shareholders by means of a free pro rata distribution of shares to existing owners of equity capital.

<table>
<tr><td>

References and
further reading

</td><td>

Financial Reporting Standard 1 (1991) Accounting Standards Board.
Financial Reporting Standard 3 (1992) Accounting Standards Board.
Holmes, G. and **Sugden, A.** (1997) *Interpreting Company Reports and Accounts.* Prentice-Hall.
Statement of Standard Accounting Practice 12 (1977) Accounting Standards Board.
Tweedie, D. (1991) *Accountancy Age*, 26 September.

</td></tr>
</table>

The following web sites are relevant to this chapter:

http://www.ftse.com
http://www.tesco.co.uk
http://www.ft.com
http://www.icbinc.com

Chapter 3

Firm objectives and firm behaviour

Economists have put forward various theories as to how firms behave in order to predict their reaction to events. At the heart of such theories is an assumption about firm objectives, the most usual being that the firm seeks to maximize profits. The first part of the chapter examines a number of alternative objectives open to the firm. It begins with those of a maximizing type, namely profit, sales revenue, and growth maximization, predicting firm price and output in each case. A number of non-maximizing or behavioural objectives are then considered. The second part of the chapter reviews recent research into actual firm performance, and attempts to establish which objectives are most consistent with how firms actually operate. We see that although profit is important, careful consideration must be given to a number of other objectives if we are accurately to predict firm performance. The need for a perspective broader than profit is reinforced when we consider current management practice in devising the corporate plan.

Firm objectives

The objectives of a firm can be grouped under two main headings: maximizing goals and non-maximizing goals. We shall see that marginal analysis is particularly important for maximizing goals. This is often confusing to the student who, rightly, assumes that few firms can have any detailed knowledge of marginal revenue or marginal cost. However, it should be remembered that marginal analysis does not pretend to describe *how* firms maximize profits or revenue. It simply tells us *what* the output and price must be if they do succeed in maximizing these items, whether by luck or by judgement.

Maximizing goals   Profit maximization   The profit-maximizing assumption is based on two premises: first, that owners are in control of the day-to-day management of the firm; second, that the main desire of owners is for higher profit. The case for profit maximization as 'self-evident' is, as we shall see, undermined if either of these premises fails to hold.

Profit is maximized where marginal revenue (MR) equals marginal cost (MC), i.e. where the revenue raised from selling an extra unit is equal to the cost of producing that extra unit. In Fig. 3.1 total profit (TP) is a maximum at output Q_p, where the vertical distance between total revenue (TR) and total cost (TC) is the greatest ($TP = TR - TC$). Had the marginal revenue and marginal cost curves been presented in Fig. 3.1, they would have intersected at output Q_p.

To assume that it is the owners who control the firm neglects the fact that the dominant form of industrial organization is the public limited company (plc), which is usually run by managers rather than by owners. This may lead to conflict between the owners (shareholders) and the managers whenever the managers pursue goals which differ from those of the owners. This conflict is referred to as a type of *principal–agent* problem and emerges when the shareholders (principals) contract a second party, the managers (agents), to perform some tasks on their behalf. In return, the principals offer their agents some compensation (wage payments). However, because the principals are divorced from the day-to-day running of the business, the agents may be able to act as they themselves see fit. This independence of action may be due to their superior knowledge of the company as well as their ability to disguise their actions from the principals. Agents, therefore, may not always act in the manner desired by the principals. Indeed, it may be the agents' goals which predominate. This has led to a number of managerial theories of firm behaviour, such as sales revenue maximization and growth maximization.

Fig. 3.1. Variation of output with firm objective.

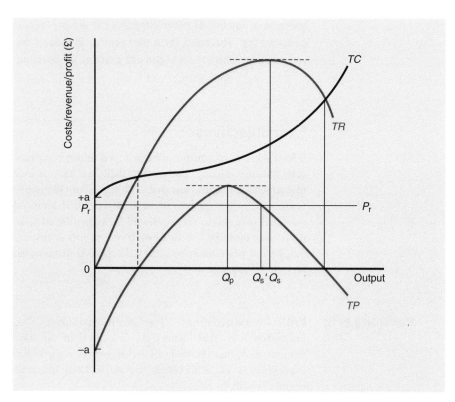

Sales revenue maximization   Baumol (1959) has suggested that the manager-controlled firm is likely to have sales revenue maximization as its main goal rather than the profit maximization favoured by shareholders. His argument is that the salaries of top managers, and other perks, are more closely correlated with sales revenue than with profits.

Williamson's (1963) managerial theory of the firm is similar to Baumol's in stressing the growth of sales revenue as a major firm objective. However, it is broader based, with the manager seeking to increase satisfaction through the greater expenditure on both staff levels and projects made possible by higher sales revenue. Funds for greater expenditure can come from profits, external finance and *sales revenue*. In Williamson's view, however, increased sales revenue is the easiest means of providing additional funds, since higher profits have in part to be distributed to shareholders, and new finance requires greater accountability. Baumol and Williamson are describing the same phenomenon, though in rather different terms.

If management seeks to maximize sales revenue without any thought to profit at all (pure sales revenue maximization) then this would lead to output Q_s in Fig. 3.1. This last (Q_s^{th}) unit is neither raising nor lowering total revenue, i.e. its marginal revenue is zero.

Constrained sales revenue maximization   Both Baumol and Williamson recognize that some constraint on managers can be exercised by shareholders. Maximum sales revenue is usually considered to occur well above the level of output which generates maximum profits. The shareholders may demand at least a certain level of distributed profit, so that sales revenue can only be maximized subject to this constraint.

The difference a profit constraint makes to firm output is shown in Fig. 3.1. If P_r is the minimum profit required by shareholders, then Q_s' is the output which permits the highest total revenue whilst still meeting the profit constraint. Any output beyond Q_s' up to Q_s, would raise total revenue *TR* – the major objective – but reduce total profit *TP* below the minimum required (P_r). Therefore Q_s' represents the constrained sales revenue maximizing output.

So far we have assumed that the goals of owners (profits) have been in conflict with the goals of management (sales revenue). Marris (1964), however, believes that owners and managers have a *common* goal, namely maximum growth of the firm.

Growth maximization   Marris (1964) argues that the overriding goal which *both* managers and owners have in common is growth. Managers seek a growth in demand for the firm's products or services, to raise power or status. Owners seek a growth in the capital value of the firm to increase personal wealth.

It is important to note, therefore, that it is through the *growth* of the firm that the goals of both managers and owners can be achieved. Also central to the analysis of Marris is the ratio of retained to distributed profits, i.e. the 'retention ratio'. If managers distribute most of the profits (low retention ratio), shareholders will be content and the share price will be sufficiently high to deter takeover. However, if managers distribute less profit (high retention ratio), then the retained profit can be used for investment, stimulating the growth of the firm. In this case shareholders may be less content, and the share price lower, thereby increasing the risk of a takeover bid.

The major objective of the firm, with which both managers and shareholders are in accord, is then seen by Marris as maximizing the rate of growth of the firm's demand *and* the firm's capital ('balanced growth'), subject to an acceptable retention ratio. Figure 3.2 shows the trade-off between higher balanced growth and the average profit rate.[1]

For 'balanced growth' to increase, more and more investment in capital projects must be undertaken. Since the most profitable projects are undertaken first, any extra investment must be reducing the average profit rate. Point Z is where the balanced growth rate is at a maximum (G_1), with an implied retention ratio so high that all profitable investment projects have been pursued, giving an average profit rate P_{r1}. Risk avoidance by managers may, however, enforce a lower retention ratio with more profits distributed. Point Y is such a constrained growth-maximizing position (G_2), with a lower retention ratio, lower investment and higher average profit (P_{r2}) than at point Z. How close the firm gets to its major objective, Z, will depend on how constrained management feels by the risk of disgruntled shareholders, or a takeover bid, should the retention ratio be kept at the high rates consistent with points near to Z.

Non-maximizing goals   The traditional (owner control) and managerial (non-owner control) theories of the firm assume that a single goal will be pursued. The firm then attempts to achieve the highest value for that goal, whether profits, sales revenue or growth. The *behaviouralist* viewpoint is rather different, and sees the firm as an organization with various groups, workers, managers, shareholders, customers, etc., each of which has its own goal, or set of goals. The group which achieves prominence at any point of time may be able to guide the firm into promoting its goal-set over time. This dominant group may then be replaced by another giving greater emphasis to a totally different goal-set. The traditional and managerial theories which propose the maximization of a single goal, are seen by behaviouralists as being remote from the organizational complexity of modern firms.

Fig. 3.2.   Trade-off between average profit and balanced growth.

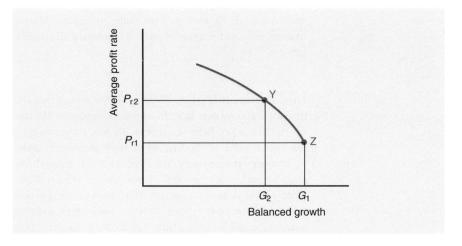

Satisficing   One of the earliest behavioural theories was that of Simon (1959) who suggested that in practice managers are unable to ascertain when a marginal point has been reached, such as maximum profit with marginal cost equal to marginal revenue. Consequently, managers set themselves *minimum* acceptable levels of achievement. Firms which are satisfied in achieving such limited objectives are said to 'satisfice' rather than 'maximize'. This is not to say that satisficing leads to some long-term performance which is less than would otherwise be achieved. The achievement of objectives has long been recognized as an incentive to improving performance and is the basis of the management technique known as management by objectives (MBO). Figure 3.3 illustrates how the attainment of initially limited objectives might lead to an improved long-term performance.

At the starting point 1, the manager sets the objective and attempts to achieve it. If, after evaluation, it is found that the objective has been achieved, then this will lead to an increase in aspirational level (3B). A new and higher objective (4B) will then emerge. Thus, by setting achievable objectives, what might be an initial minimum target turns out to be a prelude to a series of higher targets, perhaps culminating in the achievement of some maximum target, or objective. If, on the other hand, the initial objective is not achieved, then aspirational levels are lowered (3A) until achievable objectives are set. Simon's theory is one in which no single objective can be presumed to be the inevitable outcome of this organizational process. In fact, the final objective may, as we have seen, be far removed from the initial one.

Coalitions and goal formation   If a firm is 'satisficing', then who is being satisfied – and how? Cyert and March (1963) were rather more specific than Simon in identifying various groups or coalitions within an organization. A *coalition* is any group which, at a given moment, shares a consensus on the goals to be pursued.

Workers may form one coalition wanting good wages and work conditions and some job security; managers want power and prestige as well as high salaries; shareholders want high profits. These differing goals may well result in group conflict, e.g. higher wages for workers may mean lower profits for shareholders. The behavioural theory of Cyert and March, along with Simon, does not then view the

Fig. 3.3. Development of aspiration levels through goal achievement.

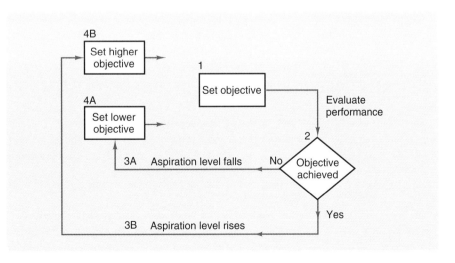

firm as having one outstanding objective (e.g. profit maximization), but rather many, often conflicting, objectives.

It is not just internal groups which need to be satisfied. There is an increasing focus by leading organizations on *stakeholders*, i.e. the range of both internal and external groups which relate to that organization. Freeman (1984) defined stakeholders as 'Any group or individual who can affect or is affected by the achievement of the organization's objectives'. Cyert and March suggest that the aim of top management is to set goals which resolve conflict between opposing groups. This approach has been reinforced by the 'Tomorrow's Company Inquiry Report' (RSA 1994) which noted that sustainability of the *company* can only occur where it meets the expectations of its stakeholders.

Contingency theory   The contingency theory of company behaviour suggests that the optimal solutions to organizational problems are derived from matching the internal structure and processes of the firm with its external environment. However the external environment is constantly changing as industrial markets become more complex, so that the optimum strategy for a firm will change as the prevailing environmental influences change. The result of this is that firms may not have a single goal such as the maximization of profits or sales, but will have to vary their goals and strategies as the environment changes around them. Contingency theory helps us to understand why firms will not always be able to follow a single optimizing course through time.

To summarize, the various behavioural theories look at the *process* of decision-making. They recognize that the 'organization' is not synonymous with the owner – nor with any other single influence, but rather that the firm has many objectives which relate to the many different groups acting within the organization. These objectives may be in conflict and so management will use a number of techniques in order to reduce that conflict. The behavioural approach has been criticized for its inability to yield precise predictions of firm activity in particular settings. However, where management processes are recognized, such as in strategic planning (see p. 63), then specific short-term predictions can be made.

Does firm objective matter?   The economist is continually seeking to predict the output and price behaviour of the firm. Figure 3.1 indicates that firm *output* does indeed depend upon firm objective, with the profit-maximizing firm having a lower output than the sales-maximizing firm (pure and constrained). If we remember that price is average revenue (i.e. total revenue/total output) we can see from Fig. 3.4 that firm *price* will also vary with firm objective.

Price in the *pure sales-maximizing* firm $= \tan \theta_s = R_1/Q_s$
Price in the *profit-maximizing* firm $\quad = \tan \theta_p = R_2/Q_p$
$$\tan \theta_s < \tan \theta_p$$

i.e. the price of the pure sales-maximizing firm is below that of the profit-maximizing firm.

It is clear that it really *does* matter what objective we assume for the firm, since both output and price depend on that objective. We turn now to firm performance to assess which of the objectives, if any, can be supported by how firms actually behave.

Fig. 3.4. Variation of price with firm objective.

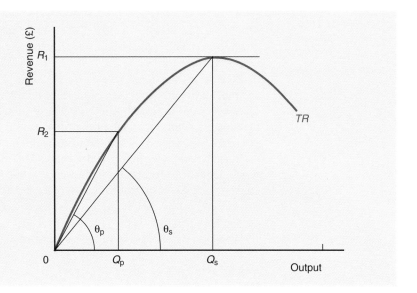

Firm behaviour

Ownership and control in practice

Profit maximization is usually based on the assumption that firms are owner-controlled, whereas sales and growth maximization usually assume that there is a separation between ownership and control. The acceptance of these alternative theories was helped by early research into the ownership of firms. Studies in the US by Berle and Means in the 1930s, and by Larner in the 1960s, suggested that a substantial proportion of large firms (44% by Berle and Means and 85% by Larner) were manager-controlled rather than owner-controlled. Later research has, however, challenged the definition of 'owner-control' used in these early studies. Whereas Berle and Means assumed that owner-control is only present with a shareholding of more than 20% in a public limited company, Nyman and Silberston (1978) used a much lower figure of 5% after research had indicated that effective control could be exercised by owners with this level of shareholding. This would suggest that owner-control is far more extensive than previously thought. Leech and Leahy (1991) found that 91% of British public limited companies are owner-controlled using the 5% threshold figure, but only 34% are owner-controlled using a 20% threshold figure. Clearly the degree of ownership control is somewhat subjective, depending crucially on the threshold figure assigned to shareholding by owners in order to exercise effective control.

A further aspect of owner-control involves the role of financial institutions and pension funds. Between them they now own over 76% of the shares of public companies in the UK, compared to only 36% in 1963, while individual share ownership has declined from 54% to around 20% over the same period. Financial institutions are more likely than individuals to bring influence to bear on chief executives, being experienced in the channels of communication and sensitive to indices of firm performance. The effect of this influence is seen by many as moving the firm towards the profit-maximizing (owner-controlled) type of objective.

Profit   **Profit maximization**   In a major study, Shipley (1981) concluded that only 15.9% of his sample of 728 UK firms could be regarded as 'true' profit-maximizers. This conclusion was reached by cross-tabulating replies to two questions shown in Table 3.1.

Because answers to questionnaires can often be given loosely, Shipley considered as 'true' maximizers only those who claimed both to maximize profit (answered (a) to Question 1) and to regard profit as being of overriding importance (answered (d) to Question 2). Only 15.9% of all the firms replied with both 1(a) and 2(d), and were considered by Shipley as true profit-maximizers.

A similar study by Jobber and Hooley (1987) found that 40% of their sample of nearly 1,800 firms had profit maximization as their prime objective. In a more recent study of 77 Scottish companies by Hornby (1994), 25% responded as 'profit maximizers' to the 'Shipley test'. The percentage of satisficers was very similar in both studies (Shipley 52.3%, Hornby 51.9%).

Given the significance of the profit-maximizing assumption in economic analysis, these results may seem surprising. However, some consideration of the decision-making process may serve to explain these low figures for profit maximization. Firms in practice often rely on pre-set 'hurdle' rates of return for projects, with managers given some minimum rate of return as a criterion for project appraisal. As a result they may not consciously see themselves as profit-maximizers, since this phrase suggests marginal analysis. Yet in setting the hurdle rates, top management will be keenly aware of the marginal cost of funding, so that this approach may in some cases relate closely to profit maximization. In other words, the response of management to questionnaires may understate the true significance of the pursuit of profit.

Profit as part of a 'goal set'   Although few firms appear to set out specifically to maximize profit, profit is still seen (even in response to questionnaires) as an important factor in decision-making. In the Shipley study the firms were asked to list their principal goal in setting price and target profit was easily the most frequently cited, with 73% of all firms regarding it as their principal goal. Even more firms (88%) included profit as at least part of their 'goal set'.

Table 3.1   Sample of 728 firms.

	All respondents (%)
(1) Does your firm try to achieve:	
(a) Maximum profits,	47.7
(b) 'Satisfactory' profits?	52.3
(2) Compared to your firm's other leading objectives, is the achievement of a target profit . . . regarded as being:	
(a) Of little importance	2.1
(b) Fairly important	12.9
(c) Very important	58.9
(d) Of overriding importance?	26.1
Those responding with both 1(a) and 2(d)	15.9

Source: Adapted from Shipley (1981).

Profit – long term vs short term   Long-term profit may be even more important than short-term profit in firm objectives. Senior managers are well aware that poor profitability in the long term may lead to their dismissal or the takeover of their firm, quite apart from an increased risk of insolvency. Indeed Shipley found that 59.7% of his sample gave priority to long-term profits, compared to only 20.6% giving priority to short-term profits. Shipley found long-term profit to be a significant influence in all sizes of company, though particularly in those of medium/large size. More recently, a survey by the *Financial Times* (1998) of 77 Finance Directors of FTSE 100 companies found that 98% considered the priority of investors to be long-term performance of the company rather than its performance in the short term.

Studies of the behaviour of firms in technology based markets has provided further support for the emphasis on longer term profit perspectives (Arthur, 1996). Arthur suggests that when a technology reaches a certain critical mass of usage, then the market is 'locked in' and the only rational choice for new users is then to adopt the established technology. He cites Microsoft Windows as being a typical example of this, with the continued increase in use of Windows providing an example of a market system operating positive feedback. Arthur suggests that average (and marginal) revenues might even rise in technology based markets as volume exceeds the 'critical mass' for that established technology, rather than decline as in standard theory. This phenomenon has often led to a strategy of giving away products reflecting new technologies at their introduction stage in order to create lock-in. The objective of this strategy for technology based markets might arguably still be profit maximization, but only in the longer term.

Profit and reward structures   There has been a great deal of concern throughout the 1990s that managers in large firms have paid too little regard to the interests of shareholders, especially as regards profit performance of the company. Indeed a number of celebrated cases in the press have focused on the apparent lack of any link between substantial rises in the pay and bonuses of chief executives (e.g. in the privatized utilities) and any improvements in company performance.

The majority of empirical studies have indeed found little relationship between the remuneration of top managers and the profit performance of their companies. In the UK, Storey *et al.* (1995) found no evidence of a link between the pay of top managers and the ratio of average pre-tax profits to total assets, with similar results for studies by Jensen and Murphy (1990) and Barkema and Gomez-Meija (1998) in the US. Table 3.2 confirms this picture with only three of the 20 firms appearing in the ten highest sales revenue and ten highest profit rankings being in the list of the ten highest paid CEOs (namely the CEOs of the computer chip manufacturer Intel, of the finance company Morgan Stanley DW and of the business services company Cendant).

However, the absence of any proven link between the profitability of a firm and the reward structures it offers to its CEO and other top managers does not necessarily mean that profit-related goals are unimportant. Firms increasingly offer top managers a remuneration 'package', with pay but one element of a total remuneration 'package' involving bonus payments and share options as well as salary. In this case higher firm profitability, and therefore dividend earnings per share, may help raise the share price and with it the value of the total remuneration package. Indeed Ezzamel and Watson (1998) have suggested that the total remuneration package offered to CEOs is directly related to the 'going rate' for corporate profitability. It may therefore be that top

Table 3.2 Ten highest ranked US corporations by sales revenue, profit and CEO remuneration.

Rank	Sales revenue maximizers*	Profit maximizers[†]	Highest paid CEOs[‡]
1	Republic Industries	Microsoft	Travelers Group
2	US Office Products	Intel	Conseco
3	Duke Energy	Coca-Cola	HealthSouth
4	Morgan Stanley DW	Schering-Plough	Occidental Petroleum
5	CHS Electronics	Merck	AlliedSignal
6	Bell Atlantic	Bank of New York	Intel
7	Cendant	Bristol-Myers Squibb	HBO & Co
8	Foundation Health Systems	CoreStates Financial	Monsanto
9	Washington Mutual	EMC	Morgan Stanley DW
10	UtilitCorp United	Berkshire Hathaway	Cendant

*using % change in revenues from 1996 to 1997.
[†]using 1997 profits as % of 1996 revenues.
[‡]using 1997 remuneration data.
Sources: Sales Revenue and Profit Maximization (*Fortune* 1998); CEO Pay (*Forbes* 1998).

management have more incentives for seeking profit-related goals than might at first be apparent.

To summarize, therefore, although there may be no open admission to profit maximization, the strong influence of owners on managed firms, the use of pre-set hurdle rates and the presence of profit-related reward structures, may in the end lead to an objective, or set of objectives, closely akin to profit maximization.

Sales revenue

Sales revenue maximization Baumol's suggestion that management-controlled firms will wish to maximize sales revenue was based on the belief that the earnings of executives are more closely related to firm revenue than to firm profit. A number of studies have sought to test this belief. For example, in a study of 177 firms between 1985 and 1990, Conyon and Gregg (1994) found that the pay of top executives in large companies in the UK was most strongly related to *relative sales growth* (i.e. relative to competitors). They also found that it was only weakly related to a long-term performance measure (total shareholder returns) and not at all to current accounting profit. Furthermore, growth in sales resulting from take-overs was more highly rewarded than internal growth, despite the fact that such take-overs produced on average a lower return for shareholders and an increased liquidity risk. These findings are in line with other recent UK research (Gregg, Machin and Szymanski 1993 and Conyon and Leech 1994) and with a study of small UK companies by Conyon and Nicolitsas (1998) which also found sales growth to be closely correlated with the pay of top executives.

As well as a linkage between the growth of sales revenue and executive income there is also general support for the contention that *firm size* is directly related to executive income. Studies by Gregg *et al.* (1993) and Rosen (1990) concur with much earlier studies, such as Meeks and Whittington (1975), who found that the larger the asset value of the company, the larger the executive salary.

What does seem clear from these various findings is that top management appears to be able to revise the rules for their own remuneration according to circumstance. Principals (shareholders) would appear to have little effective control over agents (management) remuneration in major public corporations where ownership and control are separated.

Sales revenue as part of a 'goal set'   The results of Shipley's analysis tell us little about sales revenue *maximization*. Nevertheless, Shipley found that target sales revenue was the fourth-ranked principal pricing objective, and that nearly half the firms included sales revenue as at least part of their set of objectives. Larger companies cited sales revenue as an objective most frequently; one-seventh of companies with over 3,000 employees gave sales revenue as a principal goal compared to only one-fourteenth of all the firms. Since larger companies have greater separation between ownership and management control this does lend some support to Baumol's assertion. The importance of sales revenue as part of a set of policy objectives was reinforced by the study of 193 UK industrial distributors by Shipley and Bourdon (1990), which found that 88% of these companies included sales revenue as one of a number of objectives. However, we see below that the nature of planning in large organizations must also be considered and that this may temper our support for sales revenue being itself the major objective, at least in the long term.

Strategic planning and sales revenue   Current thinking on strategic planning would support the idea of short-term sales maximization, but only as a means to other ends (e.g. profitability or growth). Research in the mid-1970s by the US Strategic Planning Institute linked market share – seen here as a proxy for sales revenue – to profitability. These studies found that high market share had a significant and beneficial effect on both return on investment and cash flow, at least in the long term. However, in the short term the high investment and marketing expenditure needed to attain high market share, reduces profitability and drains cash flow. Profit has to be sacrificed in the short term if high market share, and hence future high profits, are to be achieved in the long term.

Constrained sales revenue maximization   The fact that 88% of all companies in Shipley's original study included profit in their goal set indicates the relevance of the profit constraint to other objectives, including sales revenue. The later study by Shipley and Bourdon (1990) reached a similar conclusion, finding that 93% of the UK industrial distributors surveyed included profit in their goal set.

Growth   There are a number of reasons why firms should wish to grow, although in the 1990s the term 'growth' would appear to apply to asset value and market share rather than workforce. Marris (1964) suggests that managers seek to increase their status by increasing the 'empire' in which they work. Others would argue that although growth is an important company objective it is a means to an end, e.g. higher profit, rather than an end in itself as Marris would suggest.

When we examine the facts, however, there is little to indicate that faster growth really does mean higher profits. If, for the purposes of illustration, we equate profitability with % profit margin, we can see from Table 3.3(a) that none of the top ten UK firms with the highest % profit margin are in the top ten growth firms, with only Cable and Wireless, John Swire and Sons and Diageo close to the top ten fastest growing firms. Moreover Glaxo Wellcome, the UK firm with the highest profitability ranking, is 80th in the growth ranking. From Table 3.3(b) we can see that none of the top ten UK firms with the fastest growth (% change in total assets over past two

Table 3.3 (a) The ten most profitable UK companies in 1997 (% profit margin) and their position in the growth ranking of the top 100 UK companies.

(a) Ranking in profitability	Firm	Rank in growth
1	Glaxo Wellcome	80
2	Cable and Wireless	11
3	John Swire & Sons Ltd	14
4	Esso Exploration and Production	40
5	Rio Tinto	66
6	Cadbury Schweppes	72
7	BG plc	92
8	Smithkline Beecham	76
9	Zeneca	73
10	Diageo	19
(b) Rank in growth	Firm	Rank in profitability
1	Granada Group plc	18
2	British Steel	55
3	BAT Industries	46
4	BT	11
5	Rover	96
6	General Motors	84
7	Scottish Power	14
8	British Airways	45
9	Shell International	79
10	BP International	73

(b) The ten fastest growing UK companies in 1997 (% change in total assets over the last two financial years) and their position in the profitability ranking of the top 100 UK companies.

Source: Financial Analysis Made Easy (FAME) (CD-ROM), 112a October 1998.

years) are in the top ten most profitable firms, with only BT, Scottish Power and Granada close to such a ranking. The other top ten growth firms are low down in the profitability rankings, such as British Steel which is 2nd in growth but only 55th in profitability. Table 3.3 is in line with the results of a study by Whittington (1980) who found that profit levels did *not* increase as the firm grew in size. This lends some support to those, like Marris, who see growth as a separate objective to profit.

In fast-moving markets, such as high-technology electronics and pharmaceuticals, companies need flexibility to move rapidly to fill market niches. To achieve this, some firms are moving in quite the opposite direction to growth, i.e. they are de-merging. 'De-merging' occurs when the firm splits into smaller units, each separately quoted on the Stock Exchange. For example, since 1996 Hanson plc, the US–UK conglomorate, has de-merged its coal, power, tobacco and chemical interests to concentrate on building materials, rather similar to the situation of ICI which, in 1992, had de-merged its pharmaceutical interests, giving 'birth' to the new company Zeneca. Such de-merging is a clear sign that professional investors do not merely equate larger size to greater profit.

In a similar vein, Tom Peters, co-author of *In Search Of Excellence*, says that 'quality and flexibility will be the hallmarks of the successful economy for the foreseeable future'. This premise leads to a view that size, with its inherent inflexibility and distance from the end-customer, is a *disadvantage*. Indeed, analysis by the Strategic Planning Institute (Buzzel and Gale 1987) shows an *inverse* relationship between market size and the rate of return on investment in the US. In market segments of less than $100m (£62m), the return on investment averaged 27% in their study; however, where firms operated in market segments of over $1bn (£620m), the return averaged only 11%. They found that organizations sought to reduce the disadvantages of size by restructuring, either by de-merging or by the creation of smaller, more dynamic

Strategic Business Units (SBUs), which are able to meet the demands of the market more rapidly. This is well illustrated by the decision of DuPont, in its 1994 restructuring programme, to split its six Chemicals and Specialities sectors into twenty-three SBUs, for precisely this reason.

Non-maximizing behaviour

We have seen that the non-maximizing or behavioural theories concentrate on how firms actually operate within the constraints imposed by organizational structure and firm environment. Recent evidence on management practice broadly supports the behavioural contention, namely that it is unhelpful to seek a single firm objective as a guide to actual firm behaviour. This support, however, comes from a rather different type of analysis, that of portfolio planning.

Work in the US by the Boston Consulting Group on the relationship between market share and industry growth gave rise to an approach to corporate planning known as 'portfolio planning'. Firms, especially the larger ones, can be viewed as having a collection or 'portfolio' of different products at different stages in the product life cycle. If a product is at an early stage in its life cycle, it will require a large investment in marketing and product development in order to achieve future levels of high profitability. At the same time another product may have 'matured' and, already possessing a good share of the market, be providing high profits and substantial cash flow.

The usual strategy in portfolio planning is to attempt to balance the portfolio so that existing profitable products are providing the funds necessary to raise new products to maturity. This approach has become a classic part of strategic decision making.

If a firm is using the portfolio approach in its planning then it may be impossible to predict the firm's behaviour for individual products or market sections on the basis of a single firm objective. This is because the goals of the firm will change for a given product or market sector *depending on the relative position of that product or market sector within the overall portfolio*. Portfolio planning, along with other behavioural theories, suggests that no single objective is likely to be useful in explaining actual firm behaviour, at least in specific cases.

Conclusion

The traditional theory of the firm assumes that its sole objective is to maximize profit. The managerial theories assume that where ownership and control of the organization are separated, the objective which guides the firm will be that which the management sets. This is usually thought to be maximization either of sales revenue or growth. It is important to know which, if any, of the maximizing objectives are being pursued, since firm output and price will be different for each objective. Behavioural theory tends to oppose the idea of the firm seeking to maximize any objective. For instance, top management may seek to hold the various stakeholder groups in balance by adopting a set of minimum targets. Even where a single group with a clear objective does become dominant within the firm, others with alternative objectives may soon replace it.

In practice, profit maximization *in the long term* still appears to be important. Sales revenue seems quite important as a short-term goal, though even here a profit target may still be part of the goal set. The prominence of the profit target may be an indication that ownership is not as divorced from the control of large firms as may once have been thought. One reason why sales revenue may be pursued in the short term is found in an analysis of current strategic planning techniques, which link short-term sales revenue to long-term profit. Sales revenue may therefore be useful for explaining short-term firm behaviour, but with profit crucial for long-term behaviour. Those who, like Marris, argue that growth is a separate objective from profit, find some support in the lack of any clear relationship between growth and profitability. Growth may also be a means of securing greater stability for the firm. It may reduce internal conflict, by being an objective around which both owner-shareholders and managers can agree, and possibly reduces the risk of takeover. Also large firms experience, if not higher profits, then less variable profits (see Whittington 1980 and Schmalensee 1989). A widely used technique in the management of larger firms, portfolio planning, would seem to support the behaviouralist view, that no single objective will usefully help predict firm behaviour in a given market.

Key points	

- Separation between ownership by shareholders (principals) and control by managers (agents) makes profit maximization less likely.
- Maximization of sales revenue or asset growth (as well as profit) must be considered in manager-led firms.
- The objectives pursued by the firm will influence the firm's price and output decisions.
- Different groupings (coalitions) may be dominant within a firm at different points of time. Firm objectives may therefore change as the coalitions in effective control change.
- Organizational structure may result in non-maximizing behaviour; e.g. the presence of diverse stakeholders may induce the firm to set minimum targets for a range of variables as a means of reducing conflict.
- Shipley's seminal work (supported by later studies) found less than 16% of the firms studied to be 'true' profit maximizers.
- However Shipley found that 88% of firms included profit as part of their 'goal set'.
- Separation between ownership and control receives empirical support, though small 'threshold' levels of shareholdings may still secure effective control in modern plcs.
- Profit remains a useful predictor of long-term firm behaviour though sales revenue may be better in predicting short-term firm behaviour.
- Profit maximization may not be acknowledged as a goal by many firms, yet in setting 'hurdle rates' senior managers may implicitly be following such an objective.
- Profitability and executive pay appear to be largely unrelated, suggesting other mangerial objectives might be given priority (sales revenue, growth, etc.). However, total renumeration 'packages' for top executives may be linked to profitability, helping to align the interests of managers more closely to the interests of shareholders.
- Portfolio planning points to a variety of ever-changing objectives guiding firm activity rather than any single objective.

Notes

1. Average profit rate is total profit divided by total capital employed.

References and further reading

Arthur, W. B. (1996), Increasing returns and the new world of business, *Harvard Business Review*, July–August, pp. 100–9.

Barkema, H. G. and Gomez-Meija, L. R. (1998) Managerial compensation and firm performance, *Academy of Management Journal*, **41**, 2.

Baumol, W. J. (1959) *Business Behaviour, Value and Growth*, Macmillan.

Berle, A. A. and Means, G. C. (1934) *The Modern Corporation and Private Property*, Macmillan, New York.

Buzzel, R. and Gale, B. (1987) *The PIMS Principles*, Strategic Planning Institute.

Conyon, M. and Gregg, P. (1994) Pay at the top: a study of the sensitivity of top director remuneration to company specific shocks, *National Institute Economic Review*, August.

Conyon, M. and Leech, D. (1994) Executive compensation, corporate performance and ownership structure, *Oxford Bulletin of Economics and Statistics*, **56**, pp. 229–47.

Conyon, M. J. and Nicolitsas, D. (1998) Does the market for top executives work? CEO pay and turnover in small UK companies, *Small Business Economics*, **11**, 2.

Cyert, R. M. and March, J. G. (1963) *A Behavioural Theory of the Firm*, Prentice-Hall, New York.

Ezzamel, M. and Watson, R. (1998) Market compensation earnings and the bidding-up of executive cash compensation: evidence from the United Kingdom, *Academy of Management Journal*, **41**, 2.

Financial Times (1998) Shares in the action, 27 April.

Forbes (1998) Executive compensation: who gets paid what?, 18 May.

Fortune (1998) Global 500, 3 August.

Freeman, R. E. (1984) *Strategic Management: a stakeholder approach*, Pitman, Boston.

Gregg, P., Machin, S. and Szymanski, S. (1993) The disappearing relationship between directors' pay and corporate performance, *British Journal of Industrial Relations*, **31**, pp. 1–9.

Henderson, B. (1970) Intuitive strategy, *Perspectives*, **96**, The Boston Consulting Group, Boston.

Hornby, W. (1994) *The Theory of the Firm Revisited: a Scottish perspective*, Aberdeen Business School.

Jensen, M. C. and Murphy, K. J. (1990) Performance pay and top management incentives, *Journal of Political Economy*, 98.

Jobber, D. and Hooley, G. (1987) Pricing behaviour in UK manufacturing and service industries, *Managerial and Decision Economics*, **8**, pp. 167–77.

Leech, D. and Leahy, J. (1991) Ownership structure, control type classifications and the performance of large British companies, *Economic Journal*, **101**.

Main, B. G. M. (1991) Top executive pay and performance, *Management and Decision Economics*, **12**, pp. 219–29.

Marris, R. (1964) *The Economic Theory of Managerial Italism*, Macmillan.

Meeks, G. and Whittington, G. (1975) Directors' pay, growth and profitability, *Journal of Industrial Economics*, **24**, 1, Sept.

Nyman, S. and Silberston, A. (1978) The ownership and control of industry, *Oxford Economic Papers*, **30**, 1, March.

Rosen, S. (1990) Contracts and the market for executives, *NBFR Working Paper*, 3542.

RSA (1994) *Tomorrow: Company Inquiry.*

Schmalensee, R. (1989) Intra-industry profitability in the US, *Journal of Industrial Economics,* **36,** 4.

Shipley, D. D. (1981) Primary objectives in British manufacturing industry, *Journal of Industrial Economics,* **29,** 4, June.

Shipley, D. and **Bourdon, E.** (1990) Distributor pricing in very competitive markets, *Industrial Marketing Management,* **19.**

Simon, H. A. (1959) Theories of decision making in economics, *American Economic Review,* **69,** 3, June.

Storey, D., Watson, R. and **Wynarczyk, P.** (1995) The remuneration of non-owner managers in UK unquoted and unlisted securities market enterprises, *Small Business Economics,* **7.**

Whittington, G. (1980) The profitability and size of United Kingdom companies, *Journal of Industrial Economics,* **28,** 4.

Williamson, O. E. (1963) Managerial discretion and business behaviour, *American Economic Review,* **53,** Dec.

Chapter 4

The small firm

The small firm is the subject matter of this chapter. It begins by outlining the difficulties of finding an adequate definition, along with problems of measurement. Fragmentary statistical evidence is reviewed, to see whether the small firm really is becoming more important in UK employment and net output, and to compare the small firm in the UK with its position in other countries. We consider the historical reasons for the neglect of the small firm, and why, in more recent times, there has been a resurgence of interest in them. Measures to help the small firm are outlined, from both government and private sources. The chapter concludes with a cautionary note against placing too heavy a reliance on the small firm for economic regeneration.

Definition of the small firm

The difficulties of deriving a single, simple definition of a small firm were amply illustrated in the Bolton Committee Report of 1971. The committee's terms of reference had defined small firms as broadly those with not more than 200 employees, but in practice it found this definition to be totally inadequate. Instead, it suggested that a definition was needed which emphasized those characteristics of small firms which might be expected to make their performance and their problems significantly different from those of large firms. They concluded that three main characteristics had to be taken into account:

1. A small firm is one that has a relatively small share of its market.
2. It is managed by its owners or part-owners in a personalized way, and not through the medium of a formalized management structure.
3. It is independent, in the sense that it does not form part of a large enterprise, so that its owner-managers are free from outside control when taking their principal decisions.

These characteristics formed the 'economic' definition of the small firm. However, to make this operational, the committee needed a statistical definition, although it recognized that no single quantifiable definition could be entirely satisfactory. In attempting to reflect the three characteristics above, the committee found that for statistical purposes the criteria of a small firm would have to vary from sector to sector. For manufacturing it retained the usual '200 employees or less' definition, though in construction and mining the upper limit for small firms was reduced to '25 employees or less'. In the motor trades, retailing and miscellaneous services, the statistical definition was based not on the number of employees, but on a specified upper limit for annual turnover, e.g. £200,000 for the motor trades, and £50,000 for retailing and miscellaneous services. For road transport the definition adopted was based on the number of vehicles operated (less than five), whereas in catering all enterprises were to be included except multiples and brewery-managed public houses.

Problems of defining the small firm are not confined to the UK. It has been pointed out that the definition often used for small firms varies widely, from less than 50 employees in the Netherlands, to less than 1,000 employees in the USA! Whether within a single country, or between countries, there will inevitably be a strong element of arbitrariness in the statistical definition used for the small firm.

Importance of the small firm

The problem of finding an appropriate statistical definition for small firms makes it difficult to assess their contribution to economic activity, and the dearth of government statistics in the small business field compounds the difficulty. For instance, in a survey of the Paisley area in 1982, Dr Alan Leyston found that 70% of the small firms contacted had never filled in any government census or leaflet relating to their business. Indeed, establishments employing fewer than twenty persons are not required to complete returns for the Census of Production. It is hardly surprising, therefore, that even when the statistical definition of the small firm has been agreed, the lack of data may still cause estimates of the number of small firms to vary widely.

Table 4.1 shows the size distribution of private sector firms in UK manufacturing. The contribution of small firms (with less than 200 employees) fell between 1958 and 1968 in terms of both employment and net output, but rose between 1968 and 1995. Since 1968 the sharpest rise has been for firms with less than 100 employees; from 13.5% of total employment in 1968 to 37.2% in 1995, and from 11.5% of total net output in 1968 to 27.3% in 1995.

The data in Table 4.1 provide information about the presence of small firms in manufacturing but do not provide an adequate picture of the economy as a whole. Since 1995, information on the size distribution of *all* UK firms has been improved with the introduction of the new Inter-Departmental Business Register (IDBR). This register

Table 4.1 Analysis of private sector enterprises by size of employment (all manufacturing).

Size of firm	1958 Total employment (%)	1958 Total net output (%)	1968 Total employment (%)	1968 Total net output (%)	1995 Total employment (%)	1995 Total net output (%)
1–24	5.8	5.2	5.9	5.2 ⎫		
25–99	9.9	8.4	7.6	6.3 ⎬	37.2	27.3
100–199	8.0	6.9	5.6	4.7 ⎭	12.1	10.4

Sources: Adapted from Office for National Statistics (1998) *Production and Construction Inquiries, (PA1002) Summary Volume, 1998*, Table 5.

keeps statistics of all businesses registered for VAT and also those businesses which operate a PAYE scheme. This means that the IDBR includes small businesses below the VAT threshold but with a PAYE system, together with those businesses trading in goods exempt from VAT but operating a PAYE system, e.g. small firms in finance, insurance and education. Of course, the IDBR does not collect information on unregistered businesses, i.e. those which do not register for VAT or operate PAYE systems. Thus, figures for activities such as sole proprietors and partnerships have to be estimated from the Labour Force Survey (LFS) and added to the IDBR figures.

Table 4.2 shows that there were some 3,708,000 businesses in the UK in 1997. The new category 'class size zero' includes enterprises which consist of one or more self-employed people with *no employees*. This category reflects the growth of self-employment in the UK, but while it accounts for 68.1% of the total number of businesses it only accounts for some 13.6% of total employment and 4.8% of total turnover. Small businesses of fewer than 50 employees can be seen from the table to account for nearly half of total employment and over a third of total turnover. If we include small and medium-sized enterprises (SMEs), i.e. businesses employing less than 250 employees, then such businesses account for around 60% of employment and turnover. The total number of businesses in the UK rose from 2.4m in 1979 to 3.7m in 1997 and since most of the *new* businesses are small, this reflects a significant growth in the small firm sector.

As we see later in the chapter, the 1980s saw a renewed interest in the role of the small firm in the UK, with a variety of policy measures directed towards its support. As a result the relative size of the small firms sector in the UK is now much closer to that in other countries than it was at the beginning of the 1980s. As Table 4.3 indicates, in 1997 the small (micro) firm in the UK employing less than 10 persons made up 95% of all enterprises and provided some 30.3% of all employment and 23.1% of total turnover.

While the figures for the contribution for micro enterprises were similar in the UK and the EU, it is interesting to note that small and medium-sized enterprises tended to contribute rather less to employment and turnover in the UK than in the EU. The mirror image of this can be seen in the greater contribution that large firms make to employment and turnover in the UK as compared to the EU.

Table 4.2 Number of businesses, employment and turnover share by size band (1997).

Employment size band	Number of businesses (thousands)	Share of total (per cent)		
		Businesses	Employment	Turnover
0	2,524	68.1	13.6	4.8
1–4	803	21.7	10.0	12.0
5–9	192	5.2	6.6	6.3
10–19	107	2.9	7.2	7.9
20–49	50	1.3	7.3	8.5
50–99	15	0.4	5.1	5.8
100–199	8	0.2	5.3	6.3
200–249	2	–	1.7	2.1
250–499	3	0.1	5.3	7.9
500+	4	0.1	37.9	38.3
Total	3,708	100.0	100.0	100.0

Note: figures rounded.
Source: Adapted from Department of Trade and Industry (1998) Table 1.

Table 4.3 **Shares of
enterprises, employment
and turnover: UK and EU
(1997).**

%	Micro (0–9)	Small (10–49)	Medium (50–249)	Large (250+)
Enterprises:				
UK	95.0	4.2	0.6	0.2
EU	93.0	5.9	0.9	0.2
Employment:				
UK	30.3	14.5	12.2	43.2
EU	33.0	19.0	14.0	34.0
Turnover:				
UK	23.1	16.4	14.4	46.3
EU	25.4	20.4	19.2	35.0

Source: Eurostat (1997) p. 27 and Table 4.2; Bank of England (1998).

The neglect of small firms

Early economic theory was broadly favourable to the small firm. The theory of perfect competition had shown that in markets where many small firms produced identical products, the eventual equilibrium would be at the 'technical optimum', i.e. the level of output with lowest average cost. Monopoly, on the other hand, was regarded with suspicion, the exploitation of market power giving the opportunity for restricting output and raising prices (see Ch. 9, Fig. 9.1).

The rise of limited liability and the development of the capital market had, by the end of the nineteenth century, made it easier for firms to raise finance for growth. There was also a greater awareness that increased size could secure substantial economies of scale. These developments shifted the focus of attention away from small firms and towards large firms. During the inter-war period, economic theory gave further grounds for viewing large-scale production in a more favourable light. The theory of imperfect competition developed during the 1930s showed that many small firms producing differentiated products could, as with monopoly, produce output below the technical optimum, with prices above the competitive level.

Bannock (1981) argues that after the Second World War attitudes towards large firms became still more positive, with attention being focused on the innovatory role of large firms. Particularly influential was the American economist Schumpeter, who wrote in 1943 that 'the large-scale establishment . . . has come to be the most powerful engine in [economic] progress and in particular of the long-run expansion of total output' (Bannock 1981). Price competition in traditional competitive theory was, to Schumpeter, less important than the 'gales of creative destruction' which replaced old products, processes and organizations, with new ones. Technical progress to bring about these innovative changes would, in Schumpeter's view, require substantial monopoly profits to fund research and development (R & D). The large sums needed to research and develop products in the aerospace, nuclear and computer industries lent weight to this argument. The fact that in the two decades after the Second World War, increasing industrial concentration coincided with the most rapid and sustained period of economic growth in the twentieth century was seen by many as supporting Schumpeter's view.

British government policy reflected this growing preoccupation with larger size as a means of reaping economies of scale and reducing unit costs of production, so that UK products would become more competitive on world markets. For example, in 1966 the government announced the formation of the Industrial Reorganization Corporation (IRC). The White Paper inaugurating the IRC had emphasized the need for increased concentration in British industry, so that firms could benefit from economies of scale in production and increase expenditure on R & D. The IRC was set up to encourage the reorganization of UK industry, which in practice led to it promoting mergers through financial and other assistance. Although the IRC was wound up in 1971, the Industry Acts of 1972 and 1975 continued financial help to industry on a selective basis in order to encourage modernization, efficiency and expansion, in particular through the activities of the National Enterprise Board (NEB). However, emphasis on increasing size as a means of achieving greater efficiency began to wane by the early 1970s, with a reawakening of interest in small firms.

The renewed interest in small firms

Empirical and other evidence began to accumulate in the late 1960s which challenged the views of Schumpeter that large firms must be the engine of economic progress.

First, it began to be felt that large firms might not always be the most innovative. Instead of large firms growing still larger by capturing new markets as a result of product and process innovation, they often grew by taking over existing firms with established products and processes. A study by Hannah and Kay (1977) had shown that virtually all the increase in concentration that occurred in the UK between 1957 and 1973 resulted from mergers between existing companies and not from internal growth.

Second, evidence began to be published which indicated that small firms were themselves beginning to play an important role in innovation. The Bolton Committee had found in its survey of important innovations between 1945 and 1970, that small firms only accounted for some 10% of these innovations, but that this was twice as high as their share of total R & D. It has been argued, therefore, that small firms use skilled manpower and research equipment more efficiently than larger firms. Similarly in a nationwide study of 800 firms, covering 1,200 innovations, Oakey, Thwaites and Nash (1980) had found that 23% of these innovations came from single-site independent companies. In the fast-growing instrument engineering and electronic sectors, the small firms' share of innovations was even higher. The fact that small firms had been prominent in the most dynamic, high-technology sectors, suggested that they still had an important role to play as innovators.

Third, Prais (1976) produced evidence that the growth in size of firms (business units) was not, in the main, due to the growth in size of plants (production units). According to his calculations the share of the 100 largest manufacturing plants remained at about 11% between 1930 and 1968, whilst the share of the 100 largest *firms* rose from about 22% to 41% in the same period. Concentration had increased because firms had built or acquired more plants, not because they had built larger ones. Put another way, Prais showed that increasing concentration was not explained by increased technical economies of scale at plant level. The small firm may therefore be able to compete with the large firm even though it produced in relatively small plants.

Fourth, evidence began to accumulate that acquisitions do not always have particularly beneficial effects on financial performance. A number of studies (Singh

1971; Meeks 1977) showed that the profitability of the combined enterprise usually fell after merger. In fact Newbold (1970) found that only 18% of all the mergers investigated could be linked in any way to technical or financial economies of scale. Again, such evidence gave grounds for optimism that the small firm may be at less of a disadvantage in terms of profitability than had earlier been thought.

Fifth, there was evidence that small firms had contributed a major part of the recorded gains in employment whilst larger firms had been shedding labour. Birch (1979) in his study of changes in employment in the USA, concluded that small firms (those with twenty or fewer employees) generated 66% of all new jobs in the USA in the period 1969-76. In the UK, Gudgin (Gudgin, Brunskill and Fothergill 1979) showed that the main source of employment growth in the regions has been through the setting-up of new, small, indigenous firms, rather than through the inward migration of large firms. Gudgin's studies indicated that small firms originate in a localized fashion, with people working in small firms more likely to set up in business themselves than the employees of large firms. The existence of a greater number of small firms might therefore increase prospects for gains in employment through new 'start-ups'. Also, in the UK, the 'shake-out' of jobs in recession had appeared to come mainly from large firms (see Ch. 7) which again added to government interest in small firms.

Sixth, the role of small firms in foreign trade had been shown to be more significant than had previously been thought. Hannah and Kay (1977) quoted unpublished figures from a survey undertaken in 1973 by the Department of Trade. These showed that firms with a turnover of less than £10m exported 14.5% of turnover, whilst firms with a turnover of over £250m exported only 10%.

For all these reasons there has been a renewed interest in the small firm, which has been reflected in recent government policy.

Measures to help small firms

Small firms and government   Since the early 1980s the then Conservative government and the current Labour government have sought to stimulate the supply side of the economy, with special attention being paid to the small-firms sector. Specifically, action has been taken in three directions.

Equity and loan capital   The flow of equity and loan capital has been augmented to enable an individual who wishes to exploit an idea or to expand his business to do so. The following schemes have been introduced.

The Enterprise Investment Scheme   The Enterprise Investment Scheme (EIS) was introduced in January 1994 and is the successor to the former Business Expansion Scheme (BES) which had been operating since 1983. The BES had become expensive to run and only a fraction of the funds had actually found their way to small manufacturing companies. Much of the equity investment had been placed in private rented properties which gave 'safe' returns, rather than being invested in the more dynamic but risky manufacturing sector.

The EIS was introduced to encourage equity investment in small (and therefore 'high risk') unquoted companies. It also sought to encourage 'business angels' (outside investors with some business background who might contribute both capital and management expertise) to invest in such companies. The scheme was modified in 1998 and offers income tax relief at 20% on annual investments of up to £150,000 a year in the ordinary shares (equity) of companies which qualify. A person who was previously unconnected with the company can also become a paid director and qualify for tax relief.

Gains made on the sale of equities held for the full five years are exempt from capital gains tax. Also, any losses experienced when selling the shares after this period can be set off against income tax. To qualify for the EIS, companies must have carried on an approved trade wholly or mainly in the UK for a period of three years after the date of issue of shares, but they need not be resident or incorporated in the UK.

Loan Guarantee Scheme.   This was introduced in June 1981 as a pilot scheme for three years. It was intended to cover situations where potential borrowers were unable to provide sufficient collateral, or where the banks considered the risk went beyond their normal criteria for lending. The government now encourages 'authorised' financial institutions to lend to small firms by guaranteeing 70% of each loan to those companies which have been trading for less than two years and 85% of each loan for those companies trading for more than two years. Loans of up to £100,000 (£250,000 for established businesses) can be guaranteed for between two to ten years. In return for the guarantee, the borrower pays the Department a premium of *extra* interest of 1.5% a year on the outstanding loan, for variable interest loans. The premium is only 0.5% a year for fixed interest loans. Over the period 1981–98, some 60,000 loans valued at around £2.1bn have been guaranteed.

Venture Capital Trusts.   The Venture Capital Trust (VCT) was introduced by the Finance Act 1995 to encourage individuals to invest in smaller, unlisted trading companies. The first twelve VCTs launched under the scheme had raised over £105m by April 1996. Basically the VCT invests in a range of trading companies whose assets must not exceed £10m, i.e. it invests in relatively small companies. VCTs are exempt from Corporation tax on any capital gains arising on the disposal of their investments. Individuals who invest, i.e. buy shares, in a VCT are exempt from income tax on their dividends from ordinary shares and are also exempt from Capital Gains Tax when they dispose of their shares.

Alternative Investment Market (AIM).   The Unlisted Securities Market (USM) was introduced in November 1981 to enable small and medium sized firms to acquire venture capital on the London Stock Exchange. Its attractiveness declined in the early 1990s partly because the Stock Exchange rules regarding a full listing had been relaxed in response to changes in European Union directives. This meant that the advantages to companies of being on the USM rather than on the Official Stock Exchange List had been eroded. The USM ceased trading in December 1996.

The demand for a replacement market to the USM was evident in the early 1990s with the growth of trading under Rule 4.2 of the London Stock Exchange. This rule permitted member firms to deal in specific securities which were neither listed nor quoted on the USM. It had been formulated to provide an occasional dealing facility in unquoted companies for members of the Stock Exchange. The main benefits of trading under Rule 4.2 was that trading rules were less stringent than under the Full Listing or the USM.

In June 1995 the *Alternative Investment Market* was opened to meet the demand for a low cost and accessible investment market for small and growing companies. Its trading rules are less demanding than those for the Full Listing and the old USM but are on a more formal basis than trading under Rule 4.2. For example, the cost of a full listing is often high because companies need to appoint mandatory 'sponsors' who check whether the Listing Rules have been followed. In the new market, the responsibility for the accuracy of the documents rests on the company directors alone. The new market would, in addition, be accessible to companies raising small amounts of capital and those with few shareholders. Investors in AIM companies benefit from the same tax breaks as apply to unquoted companies, including Inheritance Tax relief, Capital Gains Tax relief and relief under the Enterprise Investments Scheme and Venture Capital Trusts. Further, there would be no minimum or maximum limits set on the size of the company joining the market nor on the size of the issue. In brief, the Alternative Investment Market operates under rules which depend more on companies themselves disclosing the basic information rather than on their having to fulfil the strict suitability criteria for a full listing. The hope is that the market will be attractive to small companies, providing the finance and flexibility they need.

By June 1998, there were 307 companies trading on the AIM with a market capitalisation of £7bn. Companies on the AIM include Peel Hotels, Majestic Wine and Ask Central (restaurants). By the late 1990s some observers began to point out that the cost of an AIM float could be as high as £250,000, not too far short of the cost of a full listing. The result has been that many very small firms are beginning to use the Ofex market, leaving AIM for those companies looking to raise £2m or more.

Tax allowances and grants   In order to help small businesses, tax allowances have been modified, and grants offered.

Corporation tax.   This has been made more generous for small firms – small companies in 1999 pay a reduced rate of 20% on their profits (up to a profit limit of £300,000) compared to a standard rate of 30%. The allowances which can be used by small firms to set against corporation tax had also been increased. Small firms can now set 40% of the cost of investment in machinery and plant against corporation tax during the first year, after which this tax-free allowance falls to 25% in each subsequent year. As a result small firms are expected to pay some £149m less in corporation tax in 1999–2000. To qualify for such allowances a company must satisfy at least two of the following three conditions. A turnover of less than £11.2m, assets of less than £5.6m and employment of less than 250 workers.

The Enterprise Initiative.   As part of this initiative, grants have been provided for companies employing fewer than 25 people in the Development Areas under the

Regional Enterprise Grant Scheme. This operated from 1991–97. For *investment* projects the Department of the Environment paid 15% of the expenditure on fixed assets up to a maximum grant of £15,000 and for *innovation projects* the DOE paid 50% of eligible costs up to £25,000 to firms in Development Areas employing fewer than 50 employees (see Ch. 11).

Support for Products Under Research (SPUR). This scheme operated from 1991–97 and provided grants to small firms to help develop new products and processes which represent a significant technological advance. To qualify, companies had to have less than 250 employees and sales of less than Ecu20m (£3.9m). SPUR grants have usually been for up to £50,000 or 30% of the project cost. Between 1991 and 1997 SPUR helped over 700 projects and offered £100m of support.

The Small Firms Merit Award for Research and Technology (SMART). This is a scheme formed in 1986 offering financial support to promote technical or commercial feasibility studies into innovative technology. A new SMART scheme was introduced in April 1997 which combined the previous SMART and SPUR schemes with the innovation element of the Regional Enterprise Grant. Individuals and independent small companies with fewer than 50 employees can submit proposals for funding 75% of the total cost (up to £45,000) of feasibility studies into innovative technology. Larger independent businesses with fewer than 250 employees can apply for funding up to 30% of the total development cost of new products and processes. The scheme is more flexible than its predecessors and decisions are made within strict time targets. In 1997/98, the first year of the new scheme, some 1,250 applications were successful.

The Small Firms Training Loans (SFTL). These were introduced in 1996 for firms with up to 50 employees, which seek to establish a system of lifelong learning for employees. This initiative is part of the government's 'Investment in People Standard', with SFTL loans of between £500 and £125,000 available from high street banks to help with training costs. Repayment of the loans are deferred for between 6 and 12 months and are interest-free during the deferred period.

Other sources of advice and training for small firms By 1998 there were a number of providers of advice, information and training for small firms.

Training and Enterprise Councils (TECs). The network of 82 TECs in England and Wales were charged with the responsibility of taking forward the government's strategy for training in the 1990s. These independent companies are run by boards of directors led by private sector business leaders and are contracted by the government both to provide the whole country with a skilled workforce and to support and co-ordinate local economic development. The TECs provide advice, counselling, training and consultancy facilities for small firms.

Chambers of Commerce. These also provide information and support services for small firms while the *Local Enterprise Agencies* (LEAs) offer advice and counselling to new and expanding businesses and often work under contract to the local TEC. There are now over 400 LEAs throughout the UK.

Business Links. These were established in 1993 and form the final major source for the provision of core services which local small businesses may need. These are partnerships between the TECs, Chambers of Commerce, LEAs and local authorities, and bring together the most important business development services in a single, accessible location. At the heart of each Business Link are the Personal Business Advisers (PBAs) who foster growth by helping to provide information and advice. The Business Links are designed for smaller companies with 20–200 employees and also specialize in services in the areas of export, consultancy, innovation, design and business skills. In recent times the emphasis has been on each of the 89 Business Links acting as 'one stop shops', providing almost all the advice/services needed by SMEs. The Business Link Network Company (BLNC) has been established to provide executive support for all the Links in order to improve their effectiveness. In 1998 Business Links advised around 72,000 businesses.

All these training initiatives are absolutely essential since surveys in the early 1990s showed that between 80% and 90% of small companies had no business training and received no formal preparation for company board responsibility. The continued need for such support was highlighted in the influencial Small Business Research Centre Report (1992), which cited a lack of marketing, sales and management skills as significant barriers to growth. This same report was useful in revealing the small firm's own perspective of government policy. Smaller firms were seen to regard the interest rate as highly significant, with almost one-third regarding it as the most important policy hindering firm performance. Overall economic policy was seen as hindering small firm prospects, though taxation policy was seen as broadly neutral. The most helpful policies were seen as being the provision of investment incentives and measures to make the labour market more flexible. The research covered over 2,000 firms in both manufacturing and service sectors employing up to 500 persons, though over half of the firms employed between 10 and 99 persons.

Another useful survey of the problems facing UK SMEs involved a sample of around 1,000 small firms compiled by NatWest/SBRT in their 'Quarterly Survey of Small Business' (1998). Figure 4.1 shows that the three most important problems faced by UK SMEs over the last 14 years have involved low turnover, government regulations and cash-flow/payments. Low turnover was identified by almost 50% of firms as the most important problem in the immediate aftermath of the economic slowdown of the early 1990s and is still cited as such by around 30% of SMEs. Cashflow payments problems are seen as the main source of concern by around 15% of UK SMEs. Sometimes the source of this problem may be high interest rates on loans or the lack of demand in times of recession. However, a persistent element would seem to involve late payments. For example, a recent survey by Grant Thornton (Bank of England 1998) found that the UK was as low as ninth in the EU league as regards average payment periods. It had an average payment delay of 49 days, longer than countries such as Denmark (32 days), Norway (33 days) and Germany (34 days), but shorter than France (63 days) and Italy (81 days). Excessive government regulations are seen by less than 10% of UK SMEs as the main problem. It is interesting to note that the NatWest/SBRT survey found a lack of skilled employees to be in fourth place as regards the most important problem faced by UK SMEs.

Fig. 4.1. Problems facing small firms.
Source: Bank of England (1998).

Note: The cashflow/payments option was not
included in the questionnaire until 1990.

——— Low turnover
– – – Cashflow/payments
········· Govt regulations

Small firms and the banks

Sources of finance for UK industry vary with the size of company. Smaller firms rely on personal savings at the start-up stage but then obtain some 60% of external finance from banks, although very small firms also use hire purchase and leasing arrangements. The relationship between smaller firms and banks is therefore of vital importance for this sector of UK industry. As has been noted in many surveys, the central problem of financial support for small firms is not necessarily the *availability* of finance but its *cost*. The rate of interest for the smallest firms employing less than 30 employees is between 3% and 5% above base rates and this is often doubled if the overdraft is exceeded, even if only briefly.

Another problem for UK small firms is the *debt structure*. As can be seen in Table 4.4 the debt structure of the UK smaller firms differs significantly from elsewhere in the European Union. The most obvious difference is in the high proportion of UK overdraft finance with some 70% of all external funding coming from this source, compared to an EU average of 53%. The major disadvantage of overdrafts is that they are payable on demand and therefore restrict the ability of smaller firms to take a long-term view. However, past criticisms of the UK banks for 'short-termism', i.e. lending for only short periods of time compared to other advanced industrialized countries, would now appear somewhat misplaced! We can see from Table 4.4 that

Table 4.4 Sources of external funding (%) and lengths of loans.

Country	Sources of external funding (%)			Length of loans (%)		
	Overdraft	Lease & hire-purchase	Loans	Up to 3 years	3–5 years	Over 5 years
UK	70	41	43	9	11	20
Germany	48	41	73	17	16	34
France	46	38	59	8	23	22
Spain	14	40	59	19	14	10
EU average	53	33	51	14	13	17

Source: Adapted from Bank of England (1998).

only 9% of UK loans are for less than 3 years compared to an EU average of 14%, whereas 20% of UK loans are for more than 5 years compared to an EU average of only 17%.

Another major issue regarding the relationship between UK banks and small firms concerns the *basis on which loans were provided*. A detailed study in 1992 of financing arrangements in the Netherlands, Germany and the UK found that UK bank officials who were assessing company risk were more dependent on a narrow range of financial information while in the other countries more importance was placed on managerial information and on the potential of the entrepreneur (Deakins and Philpott 1993). Again, the Bank of England has noted some 'improvement' in the UK in that the commercial banks now appear to be taking lending decisions based less on security and more on cash flow and business plans.

A final problem is that UK banks have been criticised for not providing small firms with sufficient *liquidity* to avert bankruptcy, unlike the German banking system which is more flexible in such situations. This seems to indicate that there may be failures of understanding among UK banks of how to help small businesses in both growth and recession periods. In contrast with Germany and Japan, the UK has no regional banks which are likely to have greater knowledge of local industry and can develop mutual trust between bank and small firms. Also the big UK commercial banks often lack a strong local or regional career structure, so that managers are often shifted across country and find it difficult to get to know their locality before they are moved on. However, the National Westminster Bank has recently begun a scheme whereby managers are moved only within each of their 19 regions.

As a result of sustained criticism of bank treatment of small firms, the Institute of Directors conducted a survey of 323 firms employing fewer than 100 persons in July 1992 (Institute of Directors 1992). Around half of the firms surveyed paid only 1–2% above base rate and 90% of all firms surveyed paid less than 4% above base rate. Only 16% of firms had had their overdraft facility reduced in the past 12 months. This report tended to view criticisms of bank treatment of small businesses as being somewhat exaggerated although it did not undermine the validity of the more serious problems noted above.

European Union Policy for small firms

Within the European Commission, Directorate General XXIII has the responsibility for policies for small and medium-sized enterprises (SMEs). Help for small and medium-sized firms in the EU is provided by many agencies and it might be useful to take a few examples from the current programme for SMEs which runs from 1997 until 2000. Within this programme some £85m will be spent on projects which improve the business and financial environment for SMEs in Europe in order to enhance their competitiveness. Such projects include establishing a network of business schools (BENE) across Europe to develop training modules for SME managers plus seed-capital funds to help SMEs in their start-up phase.

Other forms of EU help for SMEs involve the *European Investment Bank* (EIB) which provides loans through some 130 financial intermediaries to support SME investments. Some £700m was allocated in 1997 to help set up new SMEs in the technology sector. The EIB also created a 'European Technology Facility' in 1998 with over £100m available to support projects by growth-orientated, high-technology

SMEs. The *European Investment Fund* (EIF) also provides guarantees for the loans of financial institutions which help SMEs to invest in the medium or long term. The EIF is also able to participate in the equity of enterprises which specialize in the financing of SMEs. Other funds for SMEs are available through the *European Regional Development Fund* (ERDF), which now spends 10% of its budget on SMEs. The *European Social Fund* (ESF) spends 14% of its funds on promoting a systematic approach to training by SMEs in the poorer regions of the EU.

Finally, Directorate General XXIII has supported the development of European stock markets specifically designed to help SMEs. For example, the Nouveau Marche in Paris and the EASDAQ in Brussels specialize in helping young, relatively small companies gain access to equity funds more easily and cheaply.

Conclusion

Renewed interest in small firms derives from changes in economic thought and has been given impetus by the particular policies pursued by the government, partly for ideological reasons, partly as a means of producing new jobs, and partly as a corollary of 'supply side' monetarist policies. However, there is a danger in placing too heavy an emphasis on the role of small firms in rebuilding the UK's industrial base. Figures from the DTI in the late 1990s showed that 45% of VAT registered businesses failed to survive the first three years. Storey (1982) had already shown that most small firms stay static or die. In his study of all the new manufacturing firms started in Cleveland, County Durham, and Tyne and Wear from 1965 to 1978, he found that only 774 survived out of 1,200. Of the survivors, more than half still had less than ten employees in 1982, and nearly three-quarters had less than twenty-five. In fact, the probability of a new business employing more than 100 people after a decade was less than three-quarters of 1%. For every new job created by a small firm in these three counties over the thirteen-year period, four jobs were lost from large companies employing over 1,000 persons. Storey *et al.* (1987) found that in their survey of single-plant independent manufacturing companies in northern England, one-third of the new jobs were found in less than 4% of the new starters. More recent research (Storey 1994) has also shown that it is incorrect to assume that countries which have experienced the most rapid increase in new firm formation (measured in terms of increase in self employment) are those which have experienced the fastest growth of employment creation. The same survey has also pointed out that investment in government training schemes for small company entrepreneurs at the start-up or at later stages is not necessarily related to the future success of small companies. The evidence shows that success is more closely related to the original educational attainment of the business owner. In other words, it may be more important to improve the level of the UK's general education as a whole, if small firms are to thrive.

For all these reasons, the net advantages of small firms may be less than is commonly supposed. Nevertheless small firms are able to find market niches, especially where economies of scale are not easily obtained, as in providing specialized items for small markets, and in developing products used as components by large firms. Also the movement towards a higher proportion of employment being in the service sector where traditionally smaller firms have been dominant, suggests an increasingly important role for smaller firms in the UK economy. Indeed a UK survey of more than 2,000 firms by the Small Business Research Centre (1992) found that, even in recession, 64% of small firms planned modest growth over the next 3 years and 23% planned substantial growth. The authors suggest that the small firms sector does indeed have considerable potential for raising output and employment, whatever the phase of the business cycle. However, one should not forget that even during periods of economic recovery important problems still remain for the small firm sector. Around 30% of managers of SMEs cite that low turnover remains a major problem, with cashflow payments (12%) and government regulations (7%) also featuring as sources of concern (Bank of England 1998). Therefore, the health of the small firm sector is still firmly dependent (via turnover) on the performance of the macro-economy, both national and international.

Key points

- Definitions of the small firm vary within and between countries.
- UK manufacturing firms with less than 100 employees now account for around 37.2% of total employment, compared to only 13.5% in 1968.
- Across all industrial sectors, firms with less than five employees account for around 90% of the total number of firms. However such firms only account for around 24% of total employment and 17% of total turnover.
- The small firm is increasingly seen by governments as a focus of new growth and employment opportunities.
- Small firm support has focused on three main areas. Easier access to equity and loan capital, increased tax allowances and grants, and less government interference.
- Banks provide the main source (60%) of external finance for small firms in the UK, increasingly in the form of medium to longer term loans, though high exposure to overdraft finance remains a problem in the UK.
- Small firms in the UK see interest rate policy, general macroeconomic policy and taxation policy as the governmental policies with most impact on themselves.
- Low turnover is by far the most important single problem identified by small firms in the UK.
- European policy towards SMEs is becoming increasingly influential with large-scale funds available to support a broad range of initiatives.

References and further reading

Bank of England (1998) Quarterly Report on Small Business Statistics, Business Finance Division, Sept.
Bannock, G. (1981) *The Economics of Small Firms*. Blackwell, Oxford.
Bannock, G. and **Daly, M.** (eds) (1994) *Small Business Statistics*. Paul Chapman.
Birch, D.L. (1979) *The Job Generation Process*. Massachusetts Institute of Technology (mimeo).
Deakins, D. and **Philpott, T.** (1993) *Comparative European Practices in the Finance of Small Firms: UK, Germany and Holland*. Small Business Research Group, University of Central England Business School.

Department of Trade and Industry (1996) Small Firms in Britain Report 1996.

Department of Trade and Industry (1998) *Small and Medium-sized Enterprises (SME) Statistics for the United Kingdom 1997.* Small Firms Statistical Unit, July.

Hannah, L. and Kay, J.A. (1977) *Concentration in Modern Industry.* Macmillan.

Eurostat (1997) Enterprises in Europe, 4th Report.

Institute of Directors (1992) *Survey of Banks and Interest Rates – Perceptions of Small Businesses* (mimeo).

Meeks, G. (1977) *Disappointing Marriage: a study of the gains from merger.* University of Cambridge, Department of Applied Economics, Occasional Paper 51, CUP, Cambridge.

Newbold, A. (1970) *Management and Merger Activity.* Guthstead, Liverpool.

Prais, S.J. (1976) *The Evolution of Giant Firms in Britain.* CUP, Cambridge.

Singh, A. (1971) *Takeovers.* CUP, Cambridge.

Small Business Research Centre Report (1992) *The State of British Enterprise,* University of Cambridge.

Storey, D. (1982) *Entrepreneurship and the New Firm.* Croom Helm.

Storey, D. (1994) *Understanding the Small Business Sector.* Routledge, London.

Storey, D., Keasey, K., Watson, R. and **Wynarczyk, P.** (1987) *The Performance of Small Firms.* Croom Helm.

Chapter 5

Mergers and acquisitions in the growth of the firm

A well-established maxim suggests that a company must grow if it is to survive. Mergers and acquisitions have become two of the more widely used methods of achieving growth in recent years, accounting for about 50% of the increase in assets and 60% of the increase in industrial concentration. The years 1984–89 and 1994–96 provided a sustained merger boom greater than that experienced in either 1968 or 1972, in that the *expenditure* on mergers was extremely high compared to the number of mergers involved. This chapter examines the types of merger activity, such as horizontal, vertical, conglomerate and lateral mergers, and the motives for such activity. These include financial motives which may be related to valuations placed on a firm's assets, the desire to increase 'market power' or to secure economies of scale and managerial motives related more to firm growth than profitability. Trends in merger activity and legislation affecting merger activity are considered both in the UK and the EU. The UK approach to mergers is then contrasted with that of the USA. The chapter concludes with a brief review of recent tendencies to de-merge.

Definitions

One of the most significant changes in the UK's industrial structure during this century has been the growth of the large-scale firm. For example, the share of the 100 largest private enterprises in manufacturing net output has risen from 22% in 1949 to a maximum of 42% in 1975, before falling back to around 30% by the late 1990s. Most of the growth in size was achieved by acquisition or merger rather than by internal growth.

A *merger* takes place with the mutual agreement of the management of both companies, usually through an exchange of shares of the merging firms with shares of the new legal entity. Additional funds are not usually required for the act of merging, and the new venture often reflects the name of both the companies concerned.

A *takeover* (or acquisition) occurs when the management of Firm A makes a direct offer to the shareholders of Firm B and acquires a controlling interest. Usually the price offered to Firm B shareholders is substantially higher than the current share price on the stock market. In other words, a takeover involves a direct transaction between the management of the acquiring firm and the stockholders of the acquired firm. Takeovers usually require additional funds to be raised by the acquiring firm (Firm A) for the acquisition of the other firm (Firm B), and the identity of the acquired company is often subsumed within that of the purchaser.

Sometimes the distinction between merger and takeover is clear, as when an acquired company has put up a fight to prevent acquisition. However, in the majority of cases the distinction between merger and takeover is difficult to make. Occasionally the situation is complicated by the use of the words 'takeover' and 'merger'. For example, in 1989 the press announced that SmithKline Beckman, the US pharmaceutical company, had 'taken over' the UK company Beecham for £4,509m. However, technically speaking it was a 'merger' because a new company SmithKline Beecham was created which acquired the shares of the two constituent companies to form a new entity.

Types of merger

Four major forms of merger activity can be identified: horizontal integration, vertical integration, the formation of conglomerate mergers, and lateral integration.

Horizontal integration   This occurs when firms combine at the same stage of production, involving similar products or services. During the 1960s over 80% of the total number of UK mergers were of the horizontal type, and despite a subsequent fall in this percentage, some 80% of mergers in the late 1990s were still of this type. The British Airways takeover of British Caledonian in 1988, the merger of Royal Insurance and Sun Alliance to form Royal Sun Alliance in 1996, and the Hong Kong and Shanghai Banking Corporation's acquisition of Midland Bank in 1992, were examples of horizontal mergers. Horizontal integration may provide a number of economies at the level both of the plant (productive unit) and the firm (business unit). *Plant economies* may follow from the rationalization made possible by horizontal integration. For instance, production may be concentrated at a smaller number of enlarged plants, permitting the familiar technical economies of greater specialization, the dovetailing of separate processes at higher output,[1] and the application of the 'engineers' rule' whereby material costs increase as the square but capacity as the cube. All these lead to a reduction in cost per unit as the size of plant output increases. *Firm economies* result from the growth in size of the whole enterprise, permitting economies via bulk purchase, the spread of similar administrative costs over greater output, and the cheaper cost of finance, etc.

Vertical integration   This occurs when the firms combine at different stages of production of a common good or service. Only about 5% of UK mergers are of this type. Firms might benefit by being able to exert closer control over quality and delivery of supplies if the vertical integration is 'backward', i.e. towards the source of supply. Factor inputs might also be cheaper, obtained at cost instead of cost + profit. The takeover of Texas Eastern, an oil exploration company, by Enterprise Oil in 1989, serves as an example of backward vertical integration. Of course, vertical integration could be 'forward' – towards the retail outlet. This may give the firm merging 'forward' more control of wholesale or retail pricing policy, and more direct customer contact. The purchase of the regional electricity company, MANWEB, by Scottish Power in 1995 was an example of vertical forward integration between a producer and a distributor of electricity.

Vertical integration can often lead to increased control of the market, infringing monopoly legislation. This is undoubtedly one reason why they are so infrequent. Another is the fact that, as Marks and Spencer have shown, it is not necessary to have a controlling interest in suppliers in order to exert effective control over them. Textile suppliers of Marks and Spencer send over 75% of their total output to Marks and Spencer. Marks and Spencer have been able to use this reliance to their own advantage. In return for placing long production runs with these suppliers, Marks and Spencer have been able to restrict supplier profit margins whilst maintaining their viability. Apart from low costs of purchase, Marks and Spencer are also able to insist on frequent batch delivery, cutting stockholding costs to a minimum.

Conglomerate merger This refers to the adding of different products to each firm's operations. Diversification into products and areas with which the acquiring firm was not directly involved before, accounted for only 13% of all mergers in the UK in the 1960s. However, by the late 1980s the figure had risen to 34%. The major benefit is the spreading of risk for the firms and shareholders involved. Giant conglomerates like Unilever (with interests in food, detergents, toilet preparations, chemicals, paper, plastics, packaging, animal feeds, transport and tropical plantations – in seventy-five separate countries), are largely cushioned against any damaging movements which are restricted to particular product groups or particular countries. The various *firm economies* outlined above may also result from a conglomerate merger. The ability to buy companies relatively cheaply on the stock exchange and to sell parts of them off at a profit later, became an important reason for conglomerate mergers in the 1980s. The takeovers by Hanson p.l.c. of the Imperial Group, Consolidated Goldfields and the Eastern Group in 1986, 1989 and 1995 respectively, provide good examples of the growth of a large conglomerate organization.

Despite these benefits of diversification, the recession of the early 1990s led many firms to revert back to more familiar 'core' businesses. As a result, only some 10% of new UK mergers in the 1990s could be classified as conglomerate mergers. For example, the de-merger of Hanson plc in 1996 produced four businesses with recognizable 'core' activities, namely tobacco, chemicals, building and energy.

Lateral integration This is sometimes given separate treatment, though in practice it is difficult to distinguish from a conglomerate merger. The term 'lateral integration' is often used when the firms which combine are involved in different products, but in products which have *some element of commonality*. This might be in terms of factor input, such as requiring similar labour skills, capital equipment or raw materials; or it might be in terms of product outlet. For example, the takeover of Clerical Medical, the life assurance company, by Halifax Building Society for £800m in 1996, involved the linking of companies with different products but within the same financial sector. The increase in savings by an ageing population together with a reduction in mortgage business, meant that the Halifax had surplus funds which it could now direct into insurance policies using Clerical and Medical's strong presence among independent financial advisers. These advisors could also act as distribution channels for other Halifax products as well as for those of its Clerical Medical subsidiary.

Economic theory and merger activity

A number of theories have been put forward to explain the underlying motives behind merger activity. However, when these various theories are tested empirically the results have often been inconsistent and contradictory. An interesting survey article on merger activity in 1989 noted that as many as *fourteen* separate motives were frequently cited in support of merger activity (Mueller 1989). Despite these obvious complications, it may be useful at this stage to explain some of the main factors which seem to motivate mergers, if only to understand the complexity of the process.

The value discrepancy hypothesis

This theory is based on a belief that two of the most common characteristics of the industrial world are imperfect information and uncertainty. Together, these help explain why different investors have different expectations of the prospects for a given firm.

The value discrepancy hypothesis suggests that one firm will only bid for another if it places a greater value on the firm than that placed on the firm by its current owners. If Firm B is valued at V_A by Firm A and V_B by Firm B then a takeover of Firm B will only take place if $V_A > V_B$ + costs of acquisition. The difference in valuation arises through Firm A's higher expectations of future profitability, often because A takes account of the improved efficiency with which it believes the future operations of B can be run.

It has been argued that it is in periods when technology, market conditions and share prices are changing most rapidly that past information and experience are of least assistance in estimating future earnings. As a result differences in valuation are likely to occur more often, leading to increased merger activity. The value discrepancy hypothesis would therefore predict high merger activity when technological change is most rapid, and when market and share price conditions are most volatile.

Evidence   Gort's (1969) test of the value discrepancy hypothesis in the USA gives some support, finding a statistically significant relationship between merger rate and the parameters noted above. In the UK the merger booms of the late nineteenth century, of the 1920s, the 1960s and the mid-1980s, seem also to have occurred during periods of accelerating technological change and volatile share prices. However, although this theory points to the general economic conditions surrounding merger activity, it rarely provides an insight into the particular reasons behind merger activity.

The valuation ratio

One factor which may affect the likelihood of takeover is the valuation ratio, as defined below:

$$\text{Valuation ratio} = \frac{\text{market value}}{\text{asset value}} = \frac{\text{no. of shares} \times \text{share price}}{\text{book value of assets}}$$

If a company is 'undervalued' because its share price is low compared to the value of its assets, then it becomes a prime target for the 'asset stripper'. If a company attempts to grow rapidly it will tend to retain a high proportion of profits for reinvestment, with less profit therefore available for distribution to shareholders. The consequence may be a low share price, reducing the market value of the firm in relation to the book value of its assets, i.e. reducing the valuation ratio. It has been argued that a high valuation ratio will deter takeovers, whilst a low valuation ratio will increase the vulnerability of the firm to takeover. In the early 1980s, for example, the property company British Land purchased Dorothy Perkins, the womenswear chain, because its market value was seen as being low in relation to the value of its assets (prime high street sites). After stripping out all the freehold properties for resale, the remainder of the chain was sold to the Burton Group.

In recent years the asset value of some companies has been seriously underestimated for other reasons. For example, many companies have taken years to build up brand names which are therefore worth a great amount of money; but it is often the case that these are *not* given a money value and are thus not included in the asset value of the company. As a result, if the market value of a company is already low in relation to the book value of its assets, then the acquirer gets a double bonus. One reason why Nestlé was prepared to bid £2.5bn (regarded as a 'high' bid, in relation to its book value) for Rowntree Mackintosh in 1988 was to acquire the 'value' of its consumer brands cheaply, because they were not shown on the balance sheet. Finally, it is interesting to note that when the valuation ratio is low and a company would appear to be a 'bargain', a takeover may originate from *within* the company; in this case it is referred to as a management buy out (MBO).

Evidence   Kuehn (1975) in his study of over 3,500 companies in the UK (88% of companies quoted on the Stock Exchange) between 1957 and 1969, found that those firms which maintained a high valuation ratio were much less susceptible to takeover. Figure 5.1 indicates this inverse relation between valuation ratio and the probability of acquisition. The suggestion is that potential raiders are deterred by the high price to be paid, reflecting a more realistic market valuation of the potential victims' assets. However, the valuation ratio may not be as important as Kuehn's study implies. For example Singh (1971), in a study of takeovers in five UK industries (which included

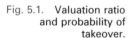

Fig. 5.1. Valuation ratio and probability of takeover.

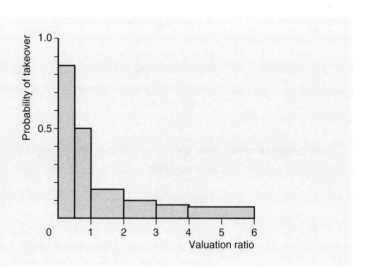

food, drink and electrical engineering industries) between 1955 and 1960, found that a relatively high valuation ratio may not always guarantee protection against takeover. An even stronger conclusion against the valuation ratio hypothesis was drawn by Newbold (1970), when he compared the valuation ratios of 'victim' firms with those of the 'bidding' firms during the merger period of 1967 and 1968. His conclusion was that the valuation ratio of actual 'victim' firms exceeded the average for the industry in thirty-eight cases but was below the average in only twenty-six cases. In other words, a high valuation ratio did not seem to deter takeover activity. Levine and Aaronovitch (1981) came to a similar conclusion in their study of 109 mergers in manufacturing and services, noting that as many as 14% of the successful 'bidding' firms had a valuation ratio below 1, which one might have expected to result in their becoming 'victim' firms.

Some confirmation of the view that a high valuation ratio may not deter takeover activity has come from a survey of merger activity in the US manufacturing and mining sectors, between 1940 and 1985. This survey related merger activity to a measure called the Tobin q. This measure is similar to the valuation ratio explained above, except that the market value of a company is measured against the 'replacement value' of the company's assets. The study found a *positive* relationship between mergers and the Tobin q, i.e. a high Tobin q or valuation ratio was associated with a high level of merger activity – the reverse of the more usually accepted hypothesis (Golbe and White 1988).

The market power theory

The main motive behind merger activity may often be to increase monopoly control of the environment in which the firm operates. Increased market power may help the firm to withstand adverse economic conditions, and increase long-term profitability.

Three situations are particularly likely to induce merger activity aimed at increasing market power:

1. Where a fall in demand results in excess capacity and the danger of price-cutting competition. In this situation firms may merge in order to secure a better vantage point from which to rationalize the industry.
2. Where international competition threatens increased penetration of the domestic market by foreign firms. Mergers in electronics, computers and engineering, have in the past produced combines large enough to fight off such foreign competition.
3. Where a tightening of legislation makes many types of linkages between companies illegal. Firms have in the past adopted many practices which involved collusion in order to control markets. Since restrictive practices legislation has made many of these practices illegal between companies, merger, by 'internalizing' the practices, has allowed them to continue.

For these reasons merger activity may take place to increase a firm's market power. However, the very act of merging usually increases company size, both in absolute terms and in relation to other firms. It is clear, therefore, that increased size will be both a by-product of the quest for increased market power, and itself a cause of increased market power.

Evidence   Newbold (1970) in his study of thirty-eight mergers between 1967 and 1968 found that the most frequent reason cited by managers for merger activity was risk reduction (48% of all mergers), as firms sought to control markets along the lines of market power theory. These conclusions were substantiated in a study by Cowling, Cubbin and Hall (1980) of nine major UK mergers, which concluded that the mergers did generate elements of market power, often to the detriment of consumers.

There is also fragmentary evidence that the termination of restrictive agreements encouraged some firms to combine formally. Elliot and Gribbin (1977) found that the five-firm concentration ratio increased faster in industries in which restrictive practices had been terminated than in those in which no such practices existed.

Empirical work does suggest that an increase in the size of a firm raises its market power. For example, Whittington (1980) found that large firms often experience less variability in their profits than small firms, indicating that large firms may be less susceptible to changing economic circumstances as a result of their greater market power. Studies by Aaronovitch and Sawyer (1975) also show that large firms are less likely to be taken over than small or medium-sized ones, and that a given percentage increase in size for an already large firm reduces the probability of takeover much more than the same percentage increase for a small to medium-size firm. It would appear that size, stability and market power are closely interrelated.

It may also be that profitability and market power are closely related. This would seem to be the implication of the results of a survey into 146 out of the top 500 UK firms. A questionnaire was sent to these companies asking for the responses of their respective Chief Executive Officers to a number of questions relating to merger activity (Ingham *et al.* 1992). From the responses to questions relating to the motives for mergers, the survey found that the single most important reason for mergers and acquisitions was the expectation of increased profitability. This was closely followed by the second most important reason – the pursuit of market power. It is therefore possible that the desire for market power and the profit motive are highly interrelated, or at least are thought to be so by significant 'players' in the market.

Nevertheless the *actual results* of merger activity provide little evidence that any increase in market power is effective in raising firm profitability. For example, Ravenscraft and Scherer (1987) conducted a detailed analysis of 6,000 acquisitions in the US between 1950 and 1976 and revealed that post-merger profitability was generally disappointing, with the profitability of around two-thirds of the merged companies *below* the average achieved prior to merger.

Economies of scale It is often argued that the achievement of lower average costs (and thereby higher profits) through an increase in the scale of operation is the main motive for merger activity. As we noted in the earlier part of this chapter such economies can be at two levels. First, at the level of the plant, the production unit, including the familiar technical economies of specialization, dovetailing of processes, engineers' rule, etc. Second, at the level of the firm, the business unit, including research, marketing, administrative, managerial and financial economies. To these plant- and firm-level economies we might add the 'synergy' effect of merger, the so-called '2 + 2 > 4' effect, whereby merger increases the efficiency of the combined firm by more than the sum of its parts. Synergy could result from combining complementary activities as, for example, when one firm has a strong R & D team whilst another firm has more effective production control personnel.

Evidence Economies of scale seem less important in merger activity than is traditionally supposed. Prais (1976) points out that technical economies, through increased plant size, have played only a small part in the growth of large firms. For instance, the growth of the 100 largest plants (production units) in net output has been much slower than the growth of the 100 largest firms (business units) in net output. Firms seem to grow not so much by expanding plant size to reap technical economies, but by acquiring more plants. Of course, evidence that firms seek to grow as an enterprise or business unit, through adding extra plants, could still be linked to securing 'firm level' economies of scale.

Newbold (1970), however, found that only 18% of firms surveyed admitted to any motive that could be linked to plant- or firm-level economies of scale. Cowling, Cubbin and Hall (1980) concluded in similar vein that the 'efficiency gains' (economies of scale) from mergers were difficult to identify in the firms examined. Finally, Whittington (1980) found profitability to be independent of firm size, and we have already noted that the study by Ravenscraft and Scherer (1987) noted a decline in the profitability of two-thirds of the now larger combined firms in the period following the mergers. This might also seem to argue against any significant economies of scale, otherwise larger firms, with much lower costs, might be expected to secure higher profits.

Although we cannot test the synergy effect directly, there is case evidence that it plays a part in encouraging merger activity. Nevertheless, the hopes of substantial benefits through this effect are not always realized. Unsuccessful attempts at pursuing synergy are widespread, notably by companies who mistakenly believe that they have the management and marketing expertise to turn around loss-making companies into efficient, profitable ventures. Indeed the survey by Ingham, Kran and Lovestam, mentioned earlier, placed the 'pursuit of marketing economies of scale' as the third most important reason for mergers. However, this reason was given rather infrequently, i.e. it was ranked well behind 'profitability' and 'market power'. Again, although recent EU annual reports on competition policy seem to indicate that the synergies to be derived from 'combining complimentary activities' are an important motive for merger activity, this reason was also ranked well behind 'strengthening of market share' and 'expansion'.

Managerial theories In all the theories considered so far, the underlying principle in merger activity is, in one way or another, the pursuit of profit. For example, market power theory suggests that through control of the firm's environment, the prospects of profit, at least in the long run, are improved. Economies of scale theory concentrates on raising profit through the reduction of cost. Managerial theories on the other hand (see also Ch. 3) lay greater stress on non-profit motives.

With the rise of the public limited company there has been a progressive divorce between ownership by shareholders, and control by management. This has given managers greater discretion in control of the company, and therefore in merger policy. The suggestion by Marris, Williamson, and others, is that a prime objective of managers is growth of the firm, rather than absolute size. In these theories the growth of the firm raises managerial utility by bringing higher salaries, power, status, and job security to managers. Managers may therefore be more interested in the rate of growth of the firm than in its profit performance.

Managerial theories would suggest that fast-growing firms, having already adopted a growth-maximization approach, are the ones most likely to be involved in merger activity. These theories would also suggest that fast-growing firms will give higher remuneration to managers, and will raise job security by being less prone to takeover.

Evidence   It does appear that it is the fast-growing firms that are mainly involved in merger activity. For example, Singh (1971, 1975) noted that the acquiring firms had a significantly higher growth rate than the acquired firms, and possessed many of the other attributes of a growth maximizer, such as a higher retention ratio (see Ch. 3), higher gearing and less liquidity (Ch. 2). Similarly Aaronovitch and Sawyer (1975) reported that in the period before an acquisition, the acquiring firm generally grew much faster than the acquired firm. Ravenscraft and Scherer (1987) in their major study of 6,000 US acquisitions concluded that the pursuit of growth rather than profit was a key factor in explaining merger activity.

As regards higher managerial remuneration through growth, Firth (1980) found a significant increase in the salaries of directors of the acquiring company after merger. The chairman's salary increased by an average of 33% in the two years following merger, compared to only 20% for the control group of companies not engaged in merger activity. More recent research carried out between 1985 and 1990 on a sample of 170 UK firms (Conyon and Gregg 1994) showed that the remuneration of the top director was closely related to sales growth. The research also showed that company sales growth through acquisition raised the top directors' remuneration significantly above that which could have been achieved by internal or organic growth.

Managerial theories place less stress on profit performance, and more on growth of the firm. The fact that, at least in the short run, the profit level often deteriorates for the acquiring firms is taken by some as further evidence in support of the managerial approach. A number of studies have showed that firms involved in mergers tended to have lower profitability levels than non-merging firms; in studies by Meeks (1977), Kumar (1985), Cosh et al. (1985) and Ravenscraft and Scherer (1987), mergers were found to have negative effects on profitability.

We have already noted that large firms, whilst not necessarily the most profitable (Meeks and Whittington 1975), were less likely to be taken over than small to medium-sized firms. In fact, any given percentage increase in size was much more significant in reducing the probability of takeover for the large firm, than it was for the small to medium-sized firm (Aaronovitch and Sawyer 1975; Singh 1975). The small to medium-sized firm has therefore an incentive to become large, and the large firm still larger, if takeovers are to be resisted. Further evidence in support of the suggestion that small to medium-sized firms are active in acquisitions came from a survey of some 2,000 firms in UK manufacturing industry between 1960 and 1976 (Kumar 1985). The study concluded that there was indeed a tendency for firm growth through acquisitions to be *negatively* related to firm size. Once firms become large they appear to be more 'stable' and less prone to takeover. Such evidence is consistent with managerial theories which stress the importance of growth as a means of enhancing job security for managers. However it should be noted that the merger boom of the late 1980s showed that even large firms were no longer safe from takeovers; this was in part due to firms now having easier access to the finance required for takeover activity.

The evidence clearly points away from traditional economies of scale, whether at the level of 'plant' or 'firm', as the motive for merger. Survival of the firm, and control of its environment, seems to be at the heart of most merger activity. This often implies the sacrifice of profit, at least in the short run. Such an observation is consistent with market power and managerial theories, both of which concentrate on objectives other than short-run profit (see also Ch. 3).

Mergers and the public interest

Although there is clearly much debate about the motivation behind merger activity, there is a broad consensus that the resulting growth in firm size will have implications for the 'public interest'. Before a more detailed investigation into the legislation and institutions involved in regulating merger activity in the UK, EU and US, it may be helpful to consider the potential impacts of a merger on economic efficiency and economic welfare, which are two key elements in any definition of the 'public interest'.

Economic efficiency   The idea of economic efficiency may usefully be broken down into two separate elements.

- *Productive efficiency.* This involves using the most efficient combination of resources to produce a *given level* of output. Only when the firm is producing a given level of output with the *least-cost* methods of production available do we regard it as having achieved 'productive efficiency'.
- *Allocative efficiency.* This is often taken to mean setting a price which corresponds to the marginal cost of production. The idea here is that consumers pay firms exactly what it costs them to produce the last (marginal) unit of output; such a pricing strategy can be shown to be a key condition in achieving a so-called 'Pareto optimum' resource allocation, where it is no longer possible to make someone better off without making someone else worse off. Any deviation of price *away from* marginal cost is then seen as resulting in 'allocative inefficiency'.

What may pose problems for policy makers is that the impacts of proposed mergers may move these two aspects of economic efficiency in *opposite directions*. For example, economies of scale may result from the merger having increased firm size, with a lower cost of producing any given output thereby improving productive efficiency. However, the greater market power associated with increased size may give the enlarged firm new opportunities to raise price above (or still further above) its costs of production, including marginal costs, thereby reducing allocative efficiency.

We may need to balance the gain in productive efficiency against the loss in allocative efficiency to get a better idea of the overall impact of the merger on the 'public interest'.

Economic welfare   Economic welfare is a branch of economics which often involves ideas of consumer surplus and producer surplus.

- *Consumer surplus.* This is the benefit to consumers of being willing to pay *more* for a product than they actually have to pay in terms of the going market price. It is usually measured by the area underneath the demand (willingness to pay) curve and above the ruling market price. So in Fig. 5.2, if the ruling market price is $0P$ and quantity sold $0Q$, then area *afd* corresponds to the 'consumer surplus', in the sense that consumers are willing to pay $0afQ$ for $0Q$ units, but only have to pay $0dfQ$ (price × quantity), giving a consumer surplus of *afd*.

- *Producer surplus.* This is the benefit to producers of receiving a price *higher* than the price they actually needed to get them to supply the product. In Fig. 5.2 we shall assume for simplicity that the MC curve is the firm's supply curve (you should know that this actually *is* the case in a perfectly competitive industry!). So in Fig. 5.2, if the ruling market price is $0P$ and the quantity sold $0Q$, then area *dfig* corresponds to the 'producer surplus', in the sense that producers are willing to supply $0Q$ units at a price of $0g$ but actually receive a price of $0P$, giving them a producer surplus of *dg* per unit, and a total producer's surplus of *dfig* on all $0Q$ units solds.

Figure 5.2 is useful in illustrating the fact that a proposed merger might move productive and allocative efficiencies in opposite directions. For simplicity we assume the curves displayed to be linear, and the firm to be at an initial price/quantity equilibrium of P/Q with marginal cost MC (for a profit-maximizing firm MR would have intersected MC at point *i*). Now suppose that the merger/take-over results in the (enlarged) firm using its market power to raise price from P to P_1, cutting output from Q to Q_1, *but* that at the same time the newly available scale economies cut costs so that MC shifts downwards to MC_1.

Clearly we have to balance a loss of allocative efficiency against a gain in productive efficiency in order to assess the overall impact on the 'public interest'. To do this we can usefully return to the idea of economic welfare, and the associated consumer and producer surpluses.

If we regard the total welfare resulting from a resource allocation as being the sum of the consumer surplus and the producer surplus, we have:

- Pre-merger   *afd* + *dfig*
- Post-merger   *abc* + *bckj*

Fig. 5.2. Mergers, economic efficiency and economic welfare. Welfare gain (*ghkj*) and welfare loss (*cflk*) from merger.

In terms of total welfare (consumer surplus + producer surplus) we can note the following impacts of the merger.

- Gain of welfare   *ghkj*
- Loss of welfare   *cflk*

The 'gain of welfare' (*ghkj*) represents the improvement in productive efficiency from the merger, as the Q_1 units still produced require less resources than before, now that the scale economies have reduced costs (shifting MC down to MC_1).

The 'loss of welfare' (*cflk*) represents the deterioration in allocative efficiency from the merger; price has risen (P to P_1) and marginal costs have fallen (MC to MC_1), further increasing the gap between price and marginal cost. As a result of the price rise from P to P_1, output has fallen from Q to Q_1. This loss of output has reduced economic welfare since society's willingness to pay for these lost $Q - Q_1$ units (area under the demand curve from $Q - Q_1$, i.e. *cfQQ₁*) exceeds the cost of producing them (sum of all the marginal costs from $Q - Q_1$, i.e. *klQ Q₁*) by *cflk*.

Clearly the overall welfare effect ('public interest') could be positive or negative, depending on whether the welfare gains exceed the welfare losses, or vice versa (in Fig. 5.2 the losses outweigh the gains). No pre-judgement can therefore be made that a merger will, or will not be, in the public interest. As Stewart (1996) notes, everything depends on the extent of any price rise and on the demand and cost curve configurations for any proposed merger. It is in this context that a Monopolies and Mergers Commission investigation and other methods of enquiry into *particular* proposals might be regarded as important in deciding whether any merger should proceed or be abandoned.

Merger booms

Figure 5.3 shows the trends in number and value (at constant 1997 prices) of merger activity in the UK between 1967 and 1997. Four clear merger cycles can be identified, namely 1967–69, 1971–74, 1983–90 and 1992–97. There has been a tendency for the number and value of mergers to move in the same direction, although the most recent merger cycle has seen the value of mergers rise whilst the number of mergers has tended to fall, indicating a small number of larger mergers taking place in recent times.

The most notable features which have tended to galvanize such merger and takeover activity were the following.

- First, the growth of national and international markets has created circumstances favourable to economies of scale, while at the same time world tariff barriers have been reduced under the guidance of GATT (now the WTO). The result has been fierce competition between nations which has often led to a rationalization of production since larger firms have been seen as having important cost advantages.
- Second, improved communication methods, often involving information/ telecommunication technologies, have made it easier for large companies to grow, while the adoption by many companies of a multi-divisional structure has encouraged horizontal mergers.
- Third, there has been a rapid growth in the number and type of financial intermediaries, such as insurance companies and investment trusts. They have

Fig. 5.3. Mergers and acquisitions in the UK 1967–97.
Source: Adapted from Datastream.

begun investing heavily in company equity, thereby providing a ready source of finance for companies who want to issue more shares and then to use the money received to support a takeover bid. At the same time, there has been a dilution of managerial control (see Ch. 3). This 'divorce of ownership from control' has made takeover activity easier because directors now have a less-close relationship with the company, and are therefore less committed to its continuing in an unchanged form.

- Fourth, many of the periods of intense merger activity have seen an increase in the 'gearing ratio' of companies, i.e. an increase in the ratio of debt (debenture and bank borrowing) to shares (equity). Loan finance has proven attractive because the interest paid on debentures and loans has been deducted from company profits *before* it is taxed. Therefore companies have had a tax incentive to issue loan stock, the money from which they have then been able to use to mount a takeover bid.

The motives for such intense takeover activity have been varied. For example, many of the 1985–87 mergers were of the *horizontal* type suggesting that one important motive for such activity was production economies arising from rationalization. This motive may have been strengthened by the desire to integrate technology and to improve marketing expertise in order to increase market power. There is also some evidence that *target* companies in this period tended to be less dependent on debt finance, which suggests that some acquisitions may have been due to the desire of the *acquirer* to increase cash flow and to reduce its dependency on debt finance. A study of 38 UK takeovers between 1985 and 1987 (Manson, Stark and Thomas 1994) seemed to provide some evidence of such motives. They found that the takeovers studied did produce operating gains in terms of both cash flow and market values.

During this period, mergers were largely financed by share issues. The value of the more dynamic bidder's share would often tend to be higher than the value of the target company's share, giving the bidder the opportunity to exchange the minimum number of its shares for every one of the target company's. This meant that the takeover deal was relatively 'cheap' for the bidder so that its earnings per share (EPS – total earnings/total no. of shares) would not fall too much to worry its existing shareholders and the stock market in general. After the stock market crash in late 1987, however, the decrease in share prices and the rise in interest rates meant that takeovers increasingly involved cash deals rather than share issues.

Mergers and acquisition activity in the 1992–97 period has been triggered by many factors, including merger opportunities in utilities such as electricity and water, and attempts to secure greater market share in the pharmaceutical, telecommunications and finance industries in order to gain scale economies and provide a base for global expansion.

Control of mergers and acquisitions

We have seen that mergers may be a means of extending market power. We now consider how the UK, the EU and the USA, have sought to exercise control over merger activity in order to prevent the abuse of such power.

The UK experience   United Kingdom legislation has been tentative in its approach to merger activity, recognizing the desirable qualities of some monopoly situations created through merger; it therefore seeks to examine each case on its individual merits. The first UK legislation, the Monopolies and Restrictive Practices (Inquiry and Control) Act, dates from 1948 and set up the Monopolies Commission. This Act empowered the Board of Trade (now the Department of Trade and Industry) to instruct the commission to report on situations in which any one firm (unitary monopoly), or group of firms acting together, could restrict competition through the control of at least one-third of the market. Although the commission was successful in revealing the extent of monopoly power in the UK, its position as an advisory body left it powerless to effect change. The commission took on average more than two years to complete a report, and the majority of its recommendations were virtually ignored.

Monopolies and mergers legislation   The 1965 Monopolies and Mergers Act provided for the investigation of mergers or acquisitions which might produce or strengthen a monopoly, if they involved the takeover of assets in excess of £5m. The Board of Trade could prohibit those cases found by the commission to be 'contrary to the public interest', and could set conditions under which certain mergers might be allowed to proceed. The effect of the 1965 Act was to slow down the trend towards greater industrial concentration rather than seriously to inhibit the growth of larger firms. Indeed, the Labour government of the late 1960s actively promoted mergers in engineering and computers, with the assistance of the Industrial Reorganization Corporation (IRC), in order to make better use of scarce entrepreneurial talent and to provide units of sufficient size to compete effectively on an international basis. The political climate has remained a major factor in the implementation of mergers policy, so that the vast majority of mergers and acquisitions proceed unopposed. Since 1965, less than 3% of mergers eligible for consideration by the Monopolies Commission have, in fact, been referred to it, with fewer than 1% ruled against the public interest. The 1973 Fair Trading Act together with the 1980 Competition Act represent the current state of monopoly and merger legislation, and have introduced a number of changes.

1. The unitary monopoly definition is extended to situations where 25% or more (rather than 33%) of the market is controlled by a single buyer or seller. This market share test may be applied to sales at local, as well as at national level. In addition, monopoly situations stemming from nationalization can now be investigated.
2. Under the Acts, two interconnected companies (e.g. a parent + subsidiary) which control 25% or more of the market share can now be investigated, as can two quite distinct companies operating in such a way as to restrict competition without any formal agreement, e.g. the case of price leadership or tacit collusion (see Ch. 6).
3. As regards mergers, investigation can take place when the merging firms together control 25% or more of the market, or when the merger involves gross assets of over £70m.
4. The 1973 Fair Trading Act created the Office of Fair Trading (OFT) and new post of Director-General of Fair Trading (DGFT). The Director-General can refer cases of monopoly situations to the renamed Monopolies and Mergers Commission (MMC), and chairs a mergers panel which can collect information on mergers which fall within current legislation. He may then advise the Secretary of State on whether the mergers investigated (by the panel) should be referred to the commission for a decision on whether or not they are against the 'public interest'.

After the preparation of the commission's report (a delay of around three months), the Director-General recommends action to the Secretary of State based on the commission's conclusions. However, as is apparent from the flow chart (Fig. 5.4), various alternative outcomes are possible. We might usefully follow through Fig. 5.4, using recent data and cases for illustration.

About 28% of takeover bids are contested by the boards of 'raided' companies or by third parties (a), and in over 40% of cases the boards are able to defend themselves successfully, so that the proposals are abandoned (b). Of the cases that remain (voluntary mergers and unsuccessful defences by boards), only a small proportion, less than 3%, are recommended for referral by the Director-General of Fair Trading to the MMC (c). For example, only 171 proposed mergers were actually referred to the MMC between 1950 and 1995.

The Director-General may refer mergers to the MMC if he feels that they will infringe the public interest through adverse effects on competition. Where such considerations are unclear, as with conglomerate mergers, strong additional circumstances are usually necessary to bring about referral. However, the Director-General has no power to implement his decisions, as shown by five instances in 1982, 1990, 1991, 1993 and 1998 when his recommendations were overruled:

1. His advice to refer the takeover by Woolworth of the Dodge City do-it-yourself chain in 1982 was rejected by the Secretary of State (d), who allowed the deal to go through without investigation on the grounds that jobs would otherwise be lost in areas of high unemployment.
2. In February 1990 the Secretary of State, Mr Nicolas Ridley, overruled the recommendation of the DGFT. He decided to refer the bid by Ransomes (the maker of grass cutting machinery) for Westwood (a garden tractor maker) to the

Fig. 5.4. The referral procedure.

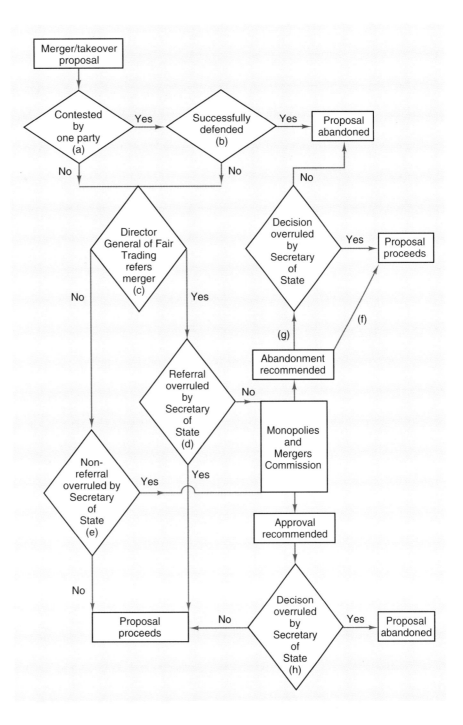

MMC despite the fact that the DGFT did not feel that a referral was needed (e). He felt that the merged company would have an unacceptably high UK market share in 'ride-on' domestic lawnmowers. The MMC's report recommended that the takeover was not against the public interest and it was allowed to continue.

This was only the third time in a decade that the Secretary of State had overruled the DGFT in this way.

3. Another 'overrule' soon followed in 1991 when the DGFT decided to refer the proposed takeover by BPB Industries (Europe's biggest plasterboard manufacturer) of the plasterboard interests of Poilet, the diversified French building materials group. Again this was overruled by the then Secretary of State, Peter Lilley (d). The Director-General felt that BPB was too dominant in the UK market and that the only competition it was experiencing at the time was from imports. Thus, the takeover by BPB of a French competitor would have strengthened BPB's market power even further. However, the Secretary of State felt that the merger would *not* alter significantly the degree of competition in the industry. Subsidiaries of German manufacturers had recently begun to produce plasterboards in the UK. In addition, UK competitors in plasterboard manufacture had entered joint ventures with foreign firms (e.g. Redland with a French firm). As a result, BPB's share of the UK plasterboard market had fallen from 95% to 65%, convincing the Secretary of State that there was no need for referral.

4. In February 1993 the DGFT advised the then Secretary of State for Trade and Industry, Mr Michael Heseltine, to refer two takeover situations to the MMC, namely the GEC acquisition of Philips' infra-red components business and the hostile bid by Airtours for Owners Abroad. The Secretary of State rejected the DGFT's advice (d) on the grounds that the mergers might help to rationalise the industries concerned and create strong competitive companies. In the Owners Abroad case, it was felt that barriers to entry into the market were low and that the merger of these two companies would provide strong competition for the market leader, Thompson Holidays. The proposals were allowed to proceed.

5. In August 1998, Margaret Beckett, the Secretary of State for Trade and Industry, overruled a decision by the MMC in a case relating to the Scottish bus industry (f). First Group, the transport company, had made a £96m acquisition of the Glasgow-based SB Holdings in 1997. The acquisition was referred by the DGFT to the MMC, which decided that such a merger might act against the public interest and recommended that First Group should sell a division of its Scottish operations in order to decrease the company's market power before the merger could proceed. However, the Secretary of State reversed the ruling in August 1998, arguing that soon after First Group had bought the bus company, a rival, Stagecoach had entered the Glasgow bus market, thus increasing competition. Allowing the proposed merger to proceed without First Group having to sell a division of its Scottish operations was contrary to the view of the MMC which felt that such dis-investment was necessary in the interests of competition.

The MMC was strengthened by the 1973 Fair Trading Act, being given a free hand to define the 'public interest', so that it could more easily maintain and promote competitive trading conditions. However, the decision-making process involved in the referral of mergers has remained somewhat arbitrary and unsatisfactory to the companies concerned. The very action of referral has itself led to the immediate abandonment of about one-third of proposed mergers – as with the referral of Argyll Foods' bid for Linfood. Argyll had borrowed £20m to build up a 30% stake in Linfood but decided not to incur the estimated £1.75m in interest charges necessitated by the usual six months wait for the conclusion of the commission investigation.

When the MMC has reported, it is by no means certain that its recommendations will be implemented. For instance, if the MMC rules a proposal against the public interest, *but by less than a two-thirds majority*, the Secretary of State has no powers to implement the MMC recommendation (f) preventing the merger taking place. Therefore the proposal must proceed despite the MMC recommendation. The acquisition of Herbert Morris, the engineering firm, by Babcock and Wilcox was one bid which went ahead in such circumstances. Even if the ruling is achieved with a two-thirds majority the Secretary of State *need not* implement the recommendation of the MMC even though he now has the power to do so (g). This happened for the first time in December 1982 with the decision to allow Charter Consolidated, the South African mining company, to bid for Anderson Strathclyde, the Glasgow-based mining engineers, despite the greater than two-thirds majority by the MMC against the bid. If, on the other hand, the MMC recommends approval of the merger, it is still not clear that it can proceed as the Secretary of State may overrule the decision and propose the abandonment of the merger (h). As well as the problems noted above, both referrals by the Director-General and approvals of the Secretary of State often give the impression of extensive behind-the-scenes political activity, rather than a detailed assessment of economic arguments.

The UK approach to mergers is based on the principle that they can be forbidden if they operate, or can be expected to operate, against the public interest. A Labour government Green Paper in 1978 argued that it was wrong to place the onus on the MMC to find that a merger was against the public interest because it tended to encourage the MMC to look for problems. As a result, it recommended that the MMC should not only recognize the possibility that a loss of competition might result from mergers but also that benefits might accrue. However, when the Conservative government came to power in 1979, its new Competition Act of 1980 cast a more sceptical attitude towards the supposed benefits from mergers, especially conglomerate ones. In a practical sense, most of the references to the MMC since July 1984 have followed the guidelines proposed by the then Secretary of State, Norman Tebbitt. These guidelines suggest that, apart from the statutory 'market share' criterion, references should be made to the MMC on the more practical grounds of possible loss of competition as a result of the merger. For example in 1990, the MMC rejected the Kingfisher/Dixons merger in the UK retail market for electrical appliances, because it would 'clearly remove competition between the two market leaders; in our view it would also significantly weaken competition in the retailing of electrical appliances'. The paramount importance of 'competition factors' as the main criterion for decisions as to whether proposed mergers should be referred to the MMC was also reiterated in 1992, during the takeover battle for the Midland Bank between Lloyds Bank and the Hong Kong and Shanghai Banking Corporation. The proposed Lloyds Bank–Midland merger was referred to the MMC on 'competition grounds', given the dominant position the merged bank would have had in high-street banking. However the proposed merger between HKSB Corporation and Midland was cleared of competition implications, and was therefore *not* referred to the MMC. In the event Lloyds withdrew its rival bid, making any referral unnecessary.

However, since 1992, the UK approach to mergers and competition seems to have shifted ground. Under Michael Heseltine, the DTI appeared to have become a stronger advocate of an industrial policy based on the creation of national champions capable of competing in global markets – as reflected in the DTI's competitiveness White Paper of May 1994.

The situation became yet more confused in April 1996 when Ian Laing, the Secretary for Trade and Industry, announced that 'fostering competition' rather than the 'creation of national champions' should be the main criterion for assessing merger policy. This case involved the refusal by the minister to allow either National Power's £2.8bn bid for Southern Electric or PowerGen's £1.9bn bid for Midland Electricity to proceed. An added complication being that the Minister also overruled an earlier MMC decision which had recommended that the acquisition be allowed.

Despite the problems of policy noted above, the Companies Act of 1989 did attempt to modify and improve merger operations in three main ways.

First, the Act provides for a formal pre-notification procedure to help reduce the uncertainties involved in merger policy. Under this procedure, the companies involved must submit a merger notice to the OFT, together with a completed questionnaire containing basic details of the proposed merger, and a fee to cover the cost of merger reference. In uncomplicated cases the details given in the questionnaire will be the basis of the DGFT's recommendation to the Secretary of State. Generally, companies will have automatic clearance if no merger reference is made to the MMC within twenty days of the receipt of the notice.

Second, even if the DGFT has recommended that the Secretary of State should make a reference to the MMC, the Secretary of State need not in fact make the reference. Instead he might ask the companies involved in the proposed merger to sell off some of their assets in order to decrease any excess power they may acquire as a result of the merger. If they agree to this, the Secretary of State may still allow the merger without reference to the MMC.

Third, parties to a merger which has been referred to the commission are prohibited from acquiring each other's shares during the period of the reference, except with the consent of the Secretary of State.

Basically, these new aspects are merely modifications to the main aspects of merger legislation, which otherwise remain intact.

Self-regulatory controls   As well as the legal controls noted above, there are also self-regulatory controls on UK merger activity which are imposed by the Stock Exchange and the Panel on Takeovers and Mergers, both of which are responsible to the *Council for the Securities Industry*. The London Stock Exchange imposes self-regulatory controls on all companies which are listed on the Stock Exchange or on the Alternative Investment Market (AIM). These rules were mainly developed in order to keep all shareholders adequately informed of certain important changes in share ownership. For example, the quotations department of the Stock Exchange must be given certain information about listed companies which acquire more than 5% of the assets of another company or which divest more than 5% of their own assets. If the figure is between 5% and 15%, only the Stock Exchange and the press need be notified; but if the figure rises to 15% or more, the Department of Trade and Industry, the shareholders, and the press should be notified. The *Council for the Securities Industry* also issues a 'City Code on Takeovers and Mergers'. This is administered by the Panel on Takeovers and Mergers and relates to both listed and unlisted companies but not to private companies. One function of the Code is to make sure that each shareholder is treated equally during takeover bids. For example, an offer given to some shareholders early in a bid, and which they have accepted, must also be left open to all other shareholders. Another function of the Code is to set out 'rules' for the conduct of companies during a takeover, covering items such as 'insider dealing' and other complicated aspects of such bids. If companies fail to follow these rules, the Council can refuse them the facilities of the securities market.

Insider dealing   On a wider issue, the whole question of 'insider dealing' came to the fore during this period. This type of dealing occurs when company shares are bought by those who have special privileged information about the future of the company, e.g. the possibility of an imminent takeover. By buying shares *before* a takeover announcement, for example, they can make huge gains as share prices rise when the excitement of the takeover begins. Basically, the UK has one of the most advanced insider-dealing regulations in the world.

The latest UK legislation regulating insider dealing came into force in 1994 and extended the scope of the main Companies Securities (Insider Dealing) Act of 1985. The new provisions were contained in the 1993 Criminal Justice Act and followed a requirement to implement an EU Directive on the subject. Under the new law it is a criminal offence for an individual who has inside information to deal in price affected securities (such as shares, debt securities, gilts and derivatives whose price movements could be sensitive to certain information), or to encourage another person to deal. It is also a criminal offence for such an individual to disclose the information to another person, other than as part of his/her professional work. The dealing in question must either be on a regulated market (basically all EU primary and secondary markets) or it may be off-market but involve professional intermediaries who deal in securities.

The new legislation expands the scope of the 1985 Act by widening the definition of who can be considered an 'insider' and by extending, for the first time, the definition of the securities covered to derivative products. The definition of dealing has been widened to include subscribing for shares (as well as the buying and selling of shares), thus making the legislation applicable to underwriting transactions. Also the territorial scope of the legislation was extended to most EU markets rather than only UK markets and the burden of proof was shifted from the prosecution to the defence. Whether the legislation achieves its main aim of making convictions for insider dealing easier, remains to be seen, especially since insider dealing is a criminal offence, so that the amount of proof needed for conviction is substantial, leading to few being convicted. For example, in 1995 the Stock Exchange investigated 1,500 unusual share trading operations but only 43 were referred to the prosecuting authority. A city 'think tank' report in 1996 recommended that to increase the number of convictions, insider dealing should be made a *civil* offence. This would mean that a lower burden of proof would then be required for conviction and those harmed by insider dealing would now be able to recover damages.

MMC and UK competition: an assessment of policy   The MMC has been involved in most areas of competition policy, although its focus has broadened over time. For example, between 1950 and 1995, the MMC has investigated 377 cases, of which 171 were merger cases and 138 monopoly cases, with merger cases becoming increasingly more important (e.g. 91 merger cases between 1987 and 1995). Most of the MMC reports over the 1950–96 period (54.3%) involved manufacturing, followed by Transport and Communication (14.7%) and Banking and Finance (10.1%) (OECD 1996).

Criticisms of the MMC and of UK competition policy in general have become more voluble during the second half of the 1990s.

- Firstly, the MMC has been criticized as lacking in both resources and professionalism. It has one full-time chairman, three part-time deputy chairmen, 31 part-time commissioners and only 100 staff. Many argue that with such restricted resources, the MMC is often 'out-gunned' by lawyers representing the firms under investigation. Further, the fact that detailed analysis of complex markets depends on the judgements of a few individuals for whom MMC membership is only a part-time occupation, is seen by some as unprofessional.
- Secondly, there is often an element of ideological inconsistency between government policy and subsequent MMC decisions. For example, in 1995, Ian Laing, the minister in charge of competition policy, allowed through the Scottish Power bid for MANWEB without referring it to the MMC. Yet in 1996, the minister overruled the positive recommendations of the MMC and prevented similar 'vertical' takeovers of Southern Electricity and Midland Electricity (the two regional electricity companies) by National Power and PowerGen respectively.
- Thirdly, there is arguably some strategic confusion in the implementation of competition policy. For example, blocking the National Power and PowerGen takeovers of regional electricity companies increases potential bids from *overseas* companies for both generating companies.

Proposals for amending UK competition policy came to a head with the introduction of a new Competition Bill in 1998, which would come into force in late 1999. This Bill sought to strengthen UK competition law by introducing prohibitions on various types of restrictive agreements along the lines of Articles 85 and 86 of the EU code (see below). Fines are to be imposed on firms which engage in cartels or in other serious anti-competitive arrangements, and on firms which abuse their market power. Competitors and customers damaged by anti-competitive behaviour deemed to be in breach of the law will now be entitled to seek damages, and any alleged anti-competitive action can now be halted pending detailed investigations. As far as the abuse of a dominant market position is concerned, the Bill aims to strengthen the 1973 Fair Trading Act, with the DGFT now having stronger investigatory powers, including the capacity to fine abusers. Consumers or firms adversely affected by anti-competitive practices may now challenge any decisions made by the DGFT by being given the right of appeal to a new Competition Commission. This Competition Commission has been empowered to take over the functions of the MMC when the Competition Bill comes into force in late 1999. Overall, these changes bring UK competition policy more into line with that of the EU, increasing elements of legal prohibition for various restrictive arrangements and bringing new opportunities for legal redress by those adversely affected by such arrangements.

The EU experience   Many European countries have long histories of state intervention in markets so it is hardly surprising that the European Commission accepts the case for intervention by member governments. Apart from agriculture, competition is the only area in which the EU has been able to implement effectively a common policy across member countries. The Commission can intervene to control the behaviour of monopolists, and to increase the degree of competition, through authority derived directly from the Treaty of Rome:

1. Article 85 prohibits agreements between enterprises which result in the restriction of competition (notably relating to price-fixing, market-sharing, production limitations and other restrictive practices). This article refers to any agreement affecting trade between member states and therefore applies to a large number of British industries.
2. Article 86 prohibits a dominant firm, or group of firms, from using their market power to exploit consumers.
3. Articles 92–94 prohibit government subsidies to industries or individual firms which will distort, or threaten to distort, competition.

Mergers and EU industry

Statistics on mergers and major acquisitions involving Community (EU) firms are shown in Table 5.1. The table classifies mergers into four categories. 'National' deals are defined as mergers which involve firms from the same country whilst 'Community' deals involve firms from at least two different member states. The 'EU-International' category covers deals where EU companies acquire firms of non-EU origin and 'International-EU' describes the situation where the bidder is a firm from outside the Community which acquires one or more EU firms.

Table 5.1 shows that the total number of all types of merger reached a peak around 1989–90, before subsequently falling as the European recession of the early 1990s took hold. It can be seen that around 56% of all EU mergers still occur between firms from the same Member State, with around 17% of all EU mergers involving cross-border deals between EU firms. Mergers by EU companies with other companies outside the EU (i.e. international) seem to have fluctuated over the period, though Europe remains consistently attractive for non-European (international) investors. Although not shown in this table, some 55% of EU mergers involve companies in the industrial sector and 45% involve companies in the service sector. The most active industrial sectors for merger activity have been the electrical, chemical and machinery sectors, while the most active service sectors for merger activity have been business services and wholesale distribution.

An interesting strategic view of the merger process has been indicated by surveys of top executives across six of Europe's most actively acquisitive countries (Angwin and Savill 1997). The results showed that the top four reasons for expanding into other countries through acquisitions were, in order:

Table 5.1 Mergers and acquisitions involving EU firms 1987–97. Numbers and percentages (in brackets).

	National	Community	EU-Intern.	Intern.-EU
1987	1,928 (71.2)	262 (9.7)	401 (14.8)	116 (4.2)
1988	2,604 (65.0)	548 (13.7)	675 (16.8)	181 (4.5)
1989	4,344 (63.0)	1,330 (19.3)	698 (10.1)	523 (7.6)
1990	4,225 (60.8)	1,479 (21.4)	691 (9.9)	552 (7.9)
1991	4,292 (65.3)	1,160 (18.0)	501 (7.3)	498 (9.8)
1992	3,792 (65.3)	968 (16.7)	476 (8.2)	573 (9.8)
1993	3,543 (63.7)	875 (15.7)	538 (9.7)	608 (10.9)
1994	3,764 (62.8)	913 (15.2)	588 (9.8)	729 (12.2)
1995	3,492 (59.4)	989 (16.8)	706 (12.0)	693 (11.8)
1996	3,072 (56.0)	973 (17.7)	745 (13.5)	705 (12.8)

Sources: AMDATA; EU Commission.

- the growing similarity between both national and EU markets;
- the ability to find a good strategic fit;
- establishing a market presence overseas ahead of others; and
- obtaining greater growth potential at a lower cost abroad than at home.

The most appropriate *target company* for acquisition was quoted as being a company which has a good strategic fit with the acquirer, is financially healthy, and has a relatively strong market (or market niche) position. Over the last decade corporate mergers have tended to involve the core activities of the merging companies, resulting in more horizontal-type mergers. For example the purchase by Volkswagen of Rolls Royce for £430m in 1998 was aimed at strengthening its core activities, with higher volumes permitting the scale economies which might allow more effective competition in world markets, while at the same time improving the strategic fit, since Volkswagen wanted to compete more actively in the luxury car market in which Rolls Royce had a greater presence.

A number of advantages were cited by the top executives surveyed for using acquisitions rather than joint ventures or other methods of entry into other EU markets, with an important one being that acquisitions were seen as a faster and less risky method of building up a critical mass in another country.

European competition policy has been criticized for its lack of comprehensiveness but in December 1989, the Council of Ministers agreed for the first time on specific cross-border merger regulations. The criteria for judging whether a merger should be referred to the European Commission covered three aspects. First, the companies concerned must have a combined world turnover of more than 5bn ECU (though for insurance companies the figure was based on total assets rather than turnover). Second, at least two of the companies concerned in the merger must have a Community-wide turnover of at least 250m ECU each. Third, if both parties to the merger have two-thirds of their business in one and the same member state, the merger was to be subject to national and not Community controls.

The Commission must be notified of merger proposals which meet the criteria noted above within one week of the announcement of the bid and it will vet each proposed merger against a concept of 'a dominant position'. Any creation or strengthening of a dominant position will be seen as incompatible with the aims of the Community if it significantly impedes 'effective competition'. The Commission has one month after notification to decide whether to start proceedings and then four months to make a final decision. If a case is being investigated by the Commission it will not also be investigated by national bodies such as the British Monopolies and Mergers Commission for example. Member states may prevent a merger which has already been permitted by the Community only if it involves public security, involves some aspects of the media or if competition in the local markets is threatened.

Review of EU merger regulation

A number of reservations were expressed about the 1990 legislation. First, a main aim of the legislation was to introduce the 'one stop shop' which meant that merging companies would either be liable to European *or* national merger control and not both. However, as can be seen above, there were situations where national merger control could override EU control in certain instances so that there may be a 'two stop shop'! Second, it was not clear how the rules would apply to non EU companies. For example, it was quite possible that two US or Japanese companies each with the required amount of *sales* in the Community, but with no actual Community *presence*, could merge. While such a case would certainly fall within the EU merger rules, it was not clear how seriously the Commission would pursue its powers in such cases. Third, guidelines were also needed on joint ventures. The new regulations make a distinction between 'concentrative' joint ventures and 'cooperative' joint ventures which needed further clarification. The new Commission rules applied to the first type which was seen to concentrate power, but not to the second (which was merely seen as a method to coordinate competitive behaviour). The second type was to be covered by articles 85 and 86 of the Treaty of Rome as before. As can be seen, there were still problems to be resolved, but the first major breakthrough had been achieved.

In March 1998 a number of amendments were made to the scope of EU cross-border merger regulations in effect increasing the number of mergers which can be referred to the EU Commission. The threshold (turnover) figures noted earlier had been criticized for being set at too high a level, so that only large mergers could be referred *exclusively* to the Commission, thereby meeting the 'one stop shop' principle. Of course such an approach suited many individual member countries of the EU which did not want to cede to the Commission their own national authority to investigate mergers. However, by 1996 the EU Commission had suggested a 'middle road' whereby the old higher thresholds could remain but in which other thresholds would be introduced to allow more mergers to be dealt with exclusively by the Commission.

The result of these amendments means that the three original criteria for exclusive reference to the Commission (p. 106) still remain, but other criteria have been added to cover some mergers which would not be large enough to qualify under the ECU 5bn and ECU 250m rules described earlier. For example, the Commission can now assume exclusive jurisdiction for any merger if the following three new, and rather complicated, conditions *all* hold true. First, if the combined aggregate world-wide turnover of the undertakings concerned exceeds ECU 2.5bn *and* second, if in each of at least three Member States, the combined aggregate turnover of the undertakings concerned is more than ECU 100m *and* third, if in each of the same three Member States, the aggregate turnover of each of at least two of the undertakings concerned exceeds ECU 25m.

The new amendments will be reviewed in the year 2000. The Commission believes that the new thresholds may result in more companies having the choice of making only one filing to the Commission instead of multiple national filings (i.e. there will now be more 'one stop shop' opportunities). Of course the difficulty of calculating more turnover figures than before will add to the complexity of the whole process. To date the Commission has handled around 80 merger cases per year since 1991, and the new legislation will perhaps increase this by another eight mergers per year.

The US experience   American legislation reflects a much more vigilant attitude towards mergers, dating from the Sherman Anti-Trust Act of 1890. Monopolies were considered illegal from the outset, resulting in a much less flexible approach to the control of monopoly power. Present merger legislation in the US is covered under the Clayton Act (1914), the Celler/Kaufman Act (1950) and the Hart–Scott–Rodino Act (1976), with the laws being enforced by the Federal Department of Justice and the Federal Trade Commission.

Since 1968 US merger guidelines have directed attention to the market power exerted by the four largest companies in any market. The rigidity of using merely the four largest companies (see the discussion on Fig. 5.5 below) for evaluating merger proposals has been extensively criticized, and in June 1982 the US Justice Department issued new proposals. These included establishing a new 'screening' index to alert the Justice Department as to which merger proposals were worthy of closer scrutiny and which should be immediately prohibited or 'nodded through'. That index was to reflect the whole market and not just the four largest firms.

The so-called 'Herfindahl–Hirschman Index' of market concentration was devised for this screening purpose, together with a number of guidelines for policy action. This index is constructed simply as:

$$\sum_{i=1}^{n} (\% \text{ market share})^2$$

for all n companies in the market. Using a squaring procedure places greater emphasis on the large firms in the market. We can illustrate this by first considering an index which adopts an additive procedure. If a simple additive procedure had been used over all n companies:

Market A: Index $= 1(70) + 30(1) = 100$
Market B: Index $= 4(20) + 20(1) = 100$

Here the markets would be evaluated as equally competitive, yet a strong case could be made for Market B being the more competitive. Using the Herfindahl–Hirschman Index we have:

Market A: Index $= 1(70)^2 + 30(1)^2 = 4{,}930$
Market B: Index $= 4(20)^2 + 20(1)^2 = 1{,}620$

Fig. 5.5. Hypothetical markets in the construction of market concentration indices.

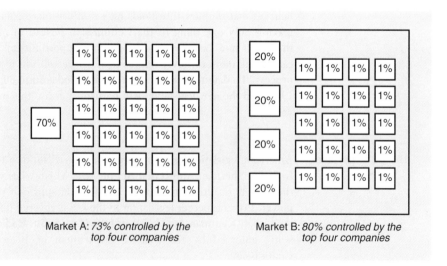

Market A: *73% controlled by the top four companies*

Market B: *80% controlled by the top four companies*

The lower the index, the more competitive the market, so that Market B is deemed more competitive. The index could, in fact, vary in value from 10,000 (i.e. 100^2) for a pure monopoly, to almost zero for a perfectly competitive industry. For example, an industry consisting of 1,000 companies each with a tiny 0.1% share of the market would produce an index value of only 10 (i.e. $1,000 (0.1)^2$).

Once constructed, the interpretation of the index is still, however, subjective. Figure 5.6 illustrates the range of the index and the three zones of index value identified by the US Justice Department for policy purposes. The chosen dividing lines appear somewhat arbitrary, though it is clear from the guidelines that the two extreme zones are viewed in radically different lights. The central zone (1,000–1,800) represents a policy 'grey' area, requiring more detailed scrutiny of the proposed merger. In practice, mergers in this zone will only receive approval if there is evidence of easy entry into the market, freely available substitutes and no collusive arrangements between existing members. The intention in this central zone is to prevent further acquisitions in the market by a market leader, whilst allowing smaller companies to combine more freely. The 'highly concentrated' zone (> 1,800) of the index would, for instance, include any market in which two companies have shares of over 30%, so that their potential for growth of market share by further acquisition is slim – even the addition to one of these firms of a further 2% of acquisition would trigger the 100-point condition. Yet in the same market, two smaller companies with market shares of less than 5% each could combine without infringing anti-trust

Fig. 5.6. The Herfindahl Index as an instrument of merger policy.

policies. The purchase of just one of the competing companies in hypothetical Market A of Fig. 5.5 by the dominant firm would increase the index to 5,070 (i.e. $1(71)^2 + 29(1)^2$), triggering the 100-point condition in the process and attracting the attentions of the Justice Department.

To see how such guidelines would operate within the UK context, it might be interesting to take the Monopolies and Mergers Commission report on the UK insulation market, published in May 1991. The merger which was investigated was between Morgan Crucible Plc, an international group based in the UK, and Manville Corporation, a US company. Both companies produced RCF (Refactory Ceramic Fibre) which is used in the steel, petrochemical and aluminium industries as a high temperature heat insulator. The market for RCF in the UK was supplied by the following companies; Carborundum (50%), Morgan Crucible (27%), Kerlane (12%), Manville (9%) and others (2%).

Under the Herfindahl–Hirschman index the industry would already have been regarded as concentrated, with a value of 3,458 (i.e. $1(50)^2 + 1(27)^2 + 1(12)^2 + 1(9)^2 + 1(2)^2$). However, the merger would have increased the market share of the combined group to 36%, so that the index would have risen to 3,944 (i.e. $1(50)^2 + 1(36)^2 + 1(12)^2 + 1(2)^2$). The increase of 486 would have been much higher than the 100 point criterion for attracting the attention of the US Justice Department. Interestingly, this merger was allowed to go ahead in the UK on the basis that Carborundum, the BP owned company, was continuing to grow, and that the French company, Kerlane, was also increasing its share of the market. In other words, all companies would retain some power in the UK market and competition could still continue. Although US merger policy is not *solely* dictated by the value of the index, the adverse initial movement of the index would certainly have created a context in which subsequent investigation in the US was less likely to decide in favour of the merger than in the UK.

Despite the attractive simplicity of this index, a number of criticisms have been directed towards it. First, the index cannot cope adequately with vertical or conglomerate mergers since they cannot be viewed merely in terms of increasing market concentration. As a result, even with this index, non-horizontal mergers between companies in different industries or market sectors remain an area of uncertainty in terms of Justice Department reaction. Second, there is often no clear way to determine in exactly which market the market share should be measured. For example, in the investigation into the proposed British Airways/American Airlines alliance in 1998, the carriers themselves asserted that the relevant market was travel between the US and Europe (where their combined market share is modest), while EU officials focused on travel between the US and the UK (where their combined market share is substantial). Third, even where the definition of the market is clear, the relation between changes in the index and changes in market power may be rather obscure. For example, although two firms, Coca Cola and Pepsi Cola, control 75% of sales of the US soft drinks industry, such market concentration has in no way diminished the aggressive price competition between these rivals.

Officials have increasingly resorted to a range of indicators in addition to the Herfindahl–Hirschmann index in order to evaluate proposed mergers. For example, a key issue may be whether mergers are likely to drive prices higher. In 1997, the proposed merger of Staples and Office Depot, the two superstore office chains, seemed to provide no problem in terms of market concentration as thousands of other US retailers also sell office supplies. However, when the Federal Trade Commission (FTC) used electronic scanners to scrutinize data on sales price and quantities for every item sold, they found a distinctive pattern. Staple's prices were found to be lower in cities where Office Depot had a store compared to cities where Office Depot had none. This was seen by the FTC as evidence that the proposed merger would in all probability allow Staples to raise prices after the merger. The merger was therefore blocked. It is often technological developments, such as the availability of powerful computer resources and electronic retail price scanners in this example, which have permitted such data to be collected and analysed, providing additional indicators to be used alongside the Herfindahl–Hirschmann index as an aid to decision making.

Corporate restructuring

Two of the most important developments during the 1980s and 1990s have been the acceleration in the trend towards corporate restructuring, and the financing of takeovers by 'leveraged debt'.

While larger mergers have been continuing, other forms of restructuring seem to have gone against this trend. Restructuring has taken two directions; the taking apart of diversified conglomerates, and the putting together of focused global companies. There are obvious advantages in creating diversified conglomerates, such as less risk of financial distress and a decreased threat of being taken over. However, in recent years many larger conglomerates have found that they need to concentrate on operating a more limited range of companies or divisions, especially those which can generate cash. For example, Pearson plc, which owns the *Financial Times* and a large number of publishing companies (e.g. Penguin, Pitman, Addison-Wesley Longman, Prentice-Hall) has sold many of its non-media related companies during 1997/98, such as those involved with leisure interests (e.g. Madame Tussaud's, Warwick Castle) and financial services, in order to focus on its core, media-related activities. In similar vein, the former conglomerate BTR sold its aerospace business in 1998 as part of the process of turning itself into a more focused engineering group.

The restructuring of companies into a relatively more focused area of operation during the 1980s and 1990s has been made more possible by the emergence in the UK and abroad of the 'leveraged buyout'. This means that companies obtain a high percentage of the finance they need in order to take over another company by issuing high interest unsecured bonds (Junk Bonds) or by borrowing through high interest unsecured loans (mezzanine finance). The former was a method favoured in the US while the latter form of borrowing is the favoured UK method. This development has had two important repercussions for corporate strategy. First, it has meant that even managers of very large companies can be subject to a takeover bid from a smaller company which has managed to borrow large amounts of debt finance. Being large *per se* is, therefore, no guarantee of safety from being taken over. Second, it has become easier, through leveraged buyouts, to take over a large diversified conglomerate, to sell off parts of it, and then to re-focus the company on its 'core' activity. There has been a tendency in recent years for such 'deconglomeration' to be used in order to increase the cash flow of an acquiring company, thereby helping to service the larger debt created by the takeover, while also increasing the competitiveness of the company in its core activities, to the benefit of shareholders.

Conclusion

Corporate restructuring through mergers and acquisitions became increasingly important in the late 1980s and again in the mid to late 1990s, as had previously been the case during certain periods of the 1950s and 1970s. The 1980s saw the build-up of conglomerate types of mergers, while the 1990s has seen a shift towards mergers between companies within the same sector, as companies move closer to their 'core' activities. Economic theory and statistical analysis do little to suggest that there are substantial benefits from merger activity, although such activity does appear consistent with managerial motives, such as higher status and remuneration.

UK legislation on mergers and takeovers has required some modification in order to tighten controls on anti-competitive arrangements and to bring UK and EU policy into closer alignment. On a more global scale, the chapter has looked at merger regulation in the US and in the EU.

Key points

- Types of merger activity include horizontal, vertical, conglomerate and lateral.
- Suggested reasons for merger include at least one company believing it can add value beyond the costs of merger (value discrepancy hypothesis), a low valuation of share price relative to assets (valuation ratio) and the desire for greater market power.
- Other reasons include the securing of substantial economies of scale at plant and/or enterprise level. The former would be mainly technical economies by rationalization of production into larger plants.
- There is little evidence to suggest that merger activity increases shareholder value but considerable evidence to suggest that merger activity may diminish profitability and shareholder value.
- Mergers which result in over 25% of the industry output being in the hands of a single company or group of related companies may be referred to the Monopolies and Mergers Commission (MMC). So too may mergers involving gross assets over £70m.
- Few mergers are actually referred to the MMC – only 171 between 1950 and 1995. Less than 3% have been disallowed.
- 'Competition factors' seem to be the most important reason for referral to the MMC.
- UK regulations of mergers and various restrictive arrangements are moving closer to the EU model, with prohibition and legal redress (e.g. fines) more available as remedies to injured parties.

Note

1. This refers to the fact that a higher level of output may be required before the separate processes involved in producing the good 'dovetail' so that there is no idle capacity. Suppose two processes are required to produce good X. Process A needs a specialized machine which can produce twenty units per hour and Process B needs a machine able to produce thirty units per hour. Only when output has risen to sixty units per hour will there be no idle capacity. For smaller output than sixty at least one machine cannot be fully used.

References and further reading

Aaronovitch, S. and Sawyer, M. (1975) Mergers, growth and concentration, *Oxford Economic Papers*, **27**, 1, March.

Angwin, D. and Savill, B. (1997) Strategic perspectives on European cross-border acquisitions: a view from top European executives, *European Management Journal*, **15**, 4, August.

Conyon, M.J. and Gregg, P. (1994) Pay at the top: a study of the sensitivity of top director remuneration to company specific shocks, *National Institute Economic Review*, **149**, August.

Cosh, A.D., Hughes, A. and Singh, M.S. (1980) The causes and effects of takeovers in the UK: an empirical investigation for the late 1940s at the microeconomic level, in Mueller, D.C. (ed.), *The Determinants and Effects of Mergers*. Gelschlager, Gunn and Hain.

Cosh, A.D., Hughes, A. and Singh, M.S. (1985) Institutional investment, company performance and mergers: empirical evidence for the UK: *A report to the Office of Fair Trading*, mimeo, Cambridge.

Cowling, K., Cubbin, J. and Hall, S. (1980) *Mergers and Economic Performance*. CUP, Cambridge, Ch. 5.

Elliot, D. and Gribbin, J.D. (1977) The abolition of cartels and structural change in the United Kingdom, in Jacquemin, A. P. and de Jong, H. W. (eds) *Welfare Aspects of Industrial Markets*. Leidin Nijhoff, The Hague.

Firth, M. (1979) The profitability of takeovers and mergers, *Economic Journal*, **89**.

Firth, M. (1980) Takeovers, shareholders' return and the theory of the firm, *Economic Journal*, **82**.

Golbe, D.L. and White, L. (1988) A time-saving analysis of mergers and acquisitions in the US economy, in Auerbach, A. J. (ed.) *Corporate Takeovers: Causes and Consequences*. University of Chicago Press.

Gort, M. (1969) An economic disturbance theory of mergers, *Quarterly Journal of Economics*, **82**.

Griffiths, A. (1992) Competition policy and EC industry, in Griffiths, A. (ed.) *European Community Survey*. Longman.

Ingham, H., Kran, I. and Lovestam, A. (1992) Mergers and profitability, *Journal of Management Studies*, **2**, March.

Kuehn, D.A. (1975) *Takeovers and the Theory of the Firm*. Macmillan.

Kumar, M.S. (1985) Growth, acquisition and firm size: evidence from the United Kingdom, *The Journal of Industrial Economics*, **33**, March.

Levine, P. and Aaronovitch, S. (1981) The financial characteristics of firms and theories of merger activity, *Journal of Industrial Economics*, **30**.

Manson, S., Stark, A. and Thomas, H. (1994) A cash flow analysis of the operational gains from takeovers, *The Chartered Association of Certified Accountants*, Research Report No. 35.

Meeks, G. (1977) *Disappointing Marriage: a study of the gains from merger*. University of Cambridge, Department of Applied Economics, Occasional Paper 51, CUP, Cambridge.

Meeks, G. and Whittington, G. (1975) Director's pay, growth and profitability, *Journal of Industrial Economics*, **24**, 1, Sept.

Mueller, D.C. (1989) Mergers, *International Journal of Industrial Organization*, **7**.

Newbold, A. (1970) *Management and Merger Activity*. Guthstead, Liverpool.

OECD (1996) *Economic Surveys: UK*, Tables 20, 21.

Office of Fair Trading (1992) Annual Report of the Director of Fair Trading, 1991, HMSO, June.

Prais, S.J. (1976) *The Evolution of Giant Firms in Britain*. CUP, Cambridge.

Ravenscraft, D.J. and **Scherer, F.M.** (1987) *Mergers, Sell-offs and Economic Efficiency*, Brookings Institution, Washington, D.C.

Singh, A. (1971) *Takeovers*. CUP, Cambridge.

Singh, A. (1975) Takeovers, economic natural selection and the theory of the firm: evidence from the post-war United Kingdom experience, *Economic Journal*, **85**, Sept.

Stewart, G. (1996) Takeovers, *Economic Review*, **14**, 1 and 2.

Whittington, G. (1980) The profitability and size of UK companies, *The Journal of Industrial Economics*, **28**, 4, June.

Chapter 6

Oligopoly

In this chapter we first record the growth of market domination by the few, using the most recent statistics on the size distribution of firms, on concentration ratios, and on advertising expenditures. We then consider attempts to explain and predict behaviour in oligopoly markets, closely relating theory to actual practice. Attempts to explain firm behaviour when there is no collusion have involved various reaction curve models (including kinked demand), and more recently game theory. However, collusion can and does take place, sometimes formally, as in cartels, or more often tacitly, under various types of price leadership.

Definition and measurement of oligopoly

Oligopoly may be defined as an industry in which there are few firms and many buyers. However, this definition begs two important questions. First, how many is 'few'? Broadly speaking, the number of firms should be sufficiently small for there to be 'conscious interdependence', with each firm aware that its future prospects depend not only on its own policies, but also on those of its rivals. Second, what is an industry? In theory, an industry is defined as a group of firms whose products are close substitutes for one another (i.e. the products have high and positive cross-elasticities of demand).[1] In practice, precise calculations of cross-elasticities of demand are impossible to make, and an industry is defined either by approximate similarity of output (such as the confectionery industry) or by similarity of the major input (such as the rubber industry, which makes a wide variety of goods from shoe soles to tyres).

Bearing in mind these problems of precise definition, the rise of oligopoly can be charted in a variety of ways.

Concentration ratios   Perhaps the most usual method of measuring the degree of oligopoly is through concentration ratios. These show the proportion of output or employment in a given industry, or product grouping, accounted for by, say, the three, four or five largest firms. Table 6.1 presents five-firm concentration ratios for both net output and employment in terms of various *industrial groups* and clearly shows that some are more dominated by large firms than others. In the tobacco industry the five

	Net output (%)	Employment (%)
Tobacco	99	98
Motor vehicles and their engines	84	80
Cement, lime and plaster	80	82
Aerospace equipment manufacture and repair	73	68
Ice cream, cocoa, chocolate and sugar confectionery	73	61
Domestic type electrical appliances	57	56
Insulated wire and cable	51	56
Pharmaceutical products	51	32
Glass and glassware	49	45
Footwear	48	44
Brewing and malting	38	45
Textile finishing	29	27
Printing and publishing	16	13
Leather goods	15	12

Source: Adapted from Business Monitor (1995).

largest firms account for 99% of net output and 98% of employment, whereas in the leather goods industry the five largest firms account for a mere 15% of net output and 12% of employment.

Although three- and five-firm concentration ratios are the most useful in assessing changes in concentration for particular products and industries within manufacturing, the 100-firm concentration ratio is useful for the manufacturing sector as a whole (Table 6.2). This ratio can be traced back as far as 1909, and gives an indication of the progressive concentration of economic power within that sector of the economy, at least until the mid/late 1970s. Since then, the domination of the largest 100 firms has begun to recede. (Unfortunately, changes in the method of data collection for the UK Annual Census of Production mean that Table 6.1 and 6.2 represent the latest data available.)

Overall, the previous tables reveal a clear tendency for UK markets to be dominated by a few large firms, though with a resurgence of smaller-firm activity in recent years (see Ch. 3). The concentration ratios for *product groups* are also useful in revealing a further characteristic of oligopoly, namely the increased differentiation and branding of products. Large firms often compete with each other in *specific product groups*, so that the concentration ratios in product groups can be very high. Unfortunately there is only fragmentary data for concentration by product group. Nevertheless the most recent estimate for the five-firm concentration ratio in the *product* beer at 61% is higher than that in the *industry* brewing and malting (Table 6.1). Similarly, the five largest firms selling refrigerators and washing machines in the UK account for over 95% of the market in both product groups, but the five-firm concentration ratio for the industrial group 'Domestic electrical appliances' is much lower (Table 6.1). This is because makers such as Hotpoint, AEG and Zanussi in refrigerators, and Hotpoint, Hoover and Creda in washing machines, *each produce* a variety of models themselves. To the consumer, therefore, the rise of oligopoly may

Year	1909	1935	1958	1968	1975	1985	1992
(%)	16.0	24.0	32.0	41.0	41.7	38.8	33.4

Sources: Sawyer (1981); *Business Monitor (1995)* and others.

Table 6.3 Five-firm concentration ratios (C5EU) at the EU level by industry and type.

Ten most concentrated	%	Ten least concentrated	%
Optical instruments (AR)	73.1	Metal structures (C)	5.7
Computers/office equipment (R)	71.2	Meat products (C)	5.7
Electric lamps/lighting (R)	64.7	Plastics (C)	5.6
Motor vehicles (AR)	62.9	Wooden structures (C)	5.5
Domestic/office chemicals (R)	62.9	Silk (C)	5.3
Man-made fibres (R)	62.6	Clothing (C)	4.3
Aerospace (R)	57.0	Wooden containers (C)	4.1
Tobacco (A)	56.1	Metal treatment (C)	3.8
Rubber (A)	48.7	Other wood products (C)	3.2
Domestic electrical appliances (AR)	46.4	Wooden furniture (C)	3.1

Notes: The % figures represent the combined production of the five largest EU firms as a percentage of total EU production, for each industry.

The industry 'types' are in brackets, where:

A = advertising intensive

AR = advertising and research intensive

R = research intensive

C = conventional

Source: Adapted from Davies and Lyons (1996).

not be immediately apparent. There may often *seem* to be extensive competition between a wide variety of brands of product. In fact, these are often produced by only a few major competing firms. The market for soap powders is one example, with most of the leading brands produced by Proctor and Gamble and Lever Brothers. By using product groups, we can move behind the veil of branding to see the true extent of market domination by the few.

Evidence of market domination by the few is also present in manufacturing at the European level. Table 6.3 shows the ten *most concentrated* industries and the ten *least concentrated* industries in the EU, using the five-firm concentration ratios for the respective industries. It can be seen that the most concentrated EU industries are either in the advertising intensive industries (A), the research intensive industries (R), or industries which are *both* advertising and research intensive (AR). On the other hand, the least concentrated EU industries are all in the so-called conventional industries (C) producing fairly homogenous products for which competition is mainly based on price.

The advertising and/or research intensive industries, are characterized by product differentiation rather than product homogeneity, by non-price competition rather than price competition. High advertising and/or research and development expenditure in relation to turnover can create competitive advantages which allow a small number of large enterprises to dominate these industrial sectors. These competitive advantages may relate to successful branding created and reinforced by advertising and/or technological innovations resulting from substantial R&D investment. Non-technical scale economies tend to be more important for these industries than the plant-based technical scale economies, with the opposite the case for the 'conventional' industries.

Advertising expenditure

Data on advertising are a useful, if indirect method, for gauging both the rise of oligopoly markets, and the tendency towards product differentiation. Advertising is essentially aimed at binding consumers to particular brands for reasons other than

Rank	Company	Advertising (£m)
1	BT	83.97
2	Ford Motor Co.	72.11
3	Vauxhall Motors	67.22
4	Kellogg (UK)	65.58
5	Proctor and Gamble	64.05
6	CSO	58.42
7	Elida Fabergé	55.62
8	Rover Cars	48.28
9	Renault (UK)	45.34
10	Lever Bros.	45.34

Source: Adapted from *Media Week*, 29 August 1997.

price. Estimates in the USA of branded, processed foods, put their prices almost 9% higher than 'private label' equivalents – similar products packaged under the retailer's own name – due solely to more extensive media advertising.[2]

One way of understanding the impact of advertising on oligopolistic markets is to study the total advertising expenditure of the top ten *companies*, as listed in Table 6.4. For example, two companies which compete aggressively with each other in the *household stores and toiletries* sectors are Proctor and Gamble and Lever Brothers, and in 1997 they were fifth and tenth in the advertising league. If we take the clothes washing market, Proctor and Gamble's products (such as Ariel Future and Daz Automatic) are in competition with Lever Brothers' products (such as Persil Automatic and Persil New Generation). In the *automobile industry*, companies such as Ford, Vauxhall, Rover and Renault are all included in the top ten advertisers. Finally, it is also worth noting the presence of three very large *confectionery* groups in the top advertisers. Although not shown in this table, Mars Confectionery was the seventeenth largest advertiser in 1997 with Nestlé Rowntree (24) and Cadbury Confectionery (71) also intensive advertisers. Thus the UK confectionery market is in the hands of a few firms who sell extensive ranges of branded goods and compete vigorously with each other.

The companies noted above all advertise their branded products intensively in order to 'bind' the consumer to the product for reasons other than price. Where successful, such advertising may help *shift* the demand curve outwards, raising market share, while simultaneously causing the demand curve to pivot and become steeper. Demand then becomes less price elastic, creating new opportunities for raising both price and revenue. Table 6.5 shows the advertising expenditure on the

Rank	Brand	Company	Advertising (£m)
1	Coca Cola	Coca Cola	31.41
2	Ariel	Proctor and Gamble	21.91
3	Persil	Lever Bros.	20.59
4	Always	Proctor and Gamble	15.60
5	Kellogg's Corn Flakes	Kellogg	12.53
6	Fairy Dish Care	Proctor and Gamble	12.06
7	Pampers Nappies	Proctor and Gamble	11.68
8	Pepsi	Pepsico	10.91
9	Pedigree Chum	Pedigree Petfoods	10.87
10	Nescafé Gold Blend	Nestlé	10.64

Source: Adapted from *Marketing*, 6 August 1998.

top ten branded products in the grocery, drink and personal care sectors. This table reflects the competition between brands, as in the drinks industry (Coca-Cola , Pepsi) and the detergent industry (Ariel, Persil). Branding activity is, of course, also rife in other industrial sectors such as automobiles where the top five companies (Opel/GM, Ford, Renault, VW and Fiat) account for 54% of the market and brands such as Peugeot 106 and 306, Fiat Uno, Renault Clio, Rover 400 and Honda Civic are all extensively advertised.

Oligopoly in theory and practice

The central task of market theory is to predict how firms will set prices and output. In perfect competition and pure monopoly we can make definite predictions. In perfect competition it can be shown that in the long run price will be equal to the lowest possible average costs of the firm – what Adam Smith called 'the natural price'. In pure monopoly the firm seeking to maximize profits will restrict output and raise prices until marginal revenue exactly equals marginal cost.

In oligopoly, where there are few firms in the market, and where there is product differentiation, there can be no such precision. Where the number of firms is sufficiently small for each firm to be aware of the pricing policy of its rivals, it will have to try to anticipate its rivals' reactions to its own pricing decision. Further, where products are differentiated, the firm will have to estimate the degree of brand loyalty customers have for its products – the greater that loyalty, the smaller the effect of price changes on consumer demand. This constant need to anticipate the reaction both of rivals and consumers, creates a high degree of uncertainty in oligopoly markets.

Despite this uncertainty, the importance of the oligopoly-type of market structure in modern economies has encouraged the quest for theories to explain and predict firm behaviour. Although little progress seems to have been made in devising a general theory of oligopoly behaviour, some progress has been made in understanding the behaviour of *particular* firms in *particular* oligopoly situations. We might usefully review a number of such theories, keeping a close eye on firm practice.

Non-collusive oligopoly

First, we consider situations in which each firm decides upon its strategy without any formal or even tacit collusion between rivals. There are essentially three approaches the firm can adopt to handle interdependence when oligopoly is non-collusive:

1. The firm could assume that whatever it decides to do, its rivals *will not* react, i.e. they will ignore its strategies. This assumption may reasonably be valid for day-to-day, routine decisions, but is hardly realistic for major initiatives. The Cournot duopoly model is, however, of this type. Each firm simply observes what the other does, and then adopts a strategy that maximizes its own profits. It makes no attempt to evaluate potential reactions by the rival firm to its own profit-maximizing strategy.
2. The firm could assume that rivals *will* react to its own strategies, and use past experience to assess the form that reaction might take. This 'learning' process underlies the reaction-curve model of Stackleberg. It also underlies the kinked-demand model (see below), with firms learning that rivals do not match price increases, but certainly do match any price reductions.

3. Instead of using past experience to assess future reactions by rivals, the firm itself could try to identify the *best possible* move the opposition could make to each of its own strategies. The firm could then plan counter measures if the rival reacts in this (for the rival) optimal way. As we see below, this is the essence of game theory.

Approaches (2) and (3) might lead us to expect a considerable amount of price movement, as rivals incessantly formulate strategy and counter-strategy. In practice, however, the oligopolistic industries experience *short bursts* of price-changing activity (often linked to price warfare), together with longer periods of relatively stable or rigid prices. We briefly review these two types of situation, noting the relevance of kinked-demand theory to stable prices, and conclude our discussion of non-collusive behaviour with an outline of game theory.

Price warfare   Price-cutting is a well-attested strategy for oligopoly firms, both for raising and defending market share. This can, of course, lead to a competitive downward spiral in firm prices, resembling a 'price war'. Examples of this abound. We will see, in Chapter 9, how price warfare developed amongst petrol retailers. In 1996, for example, stagnant demand for petrol due to increasing taxes and more fuel-efficient cars coupled with competition from supermarkets, led the UK's largest petrol retailer, Esso, to announce aggressive price cuts to maintain its dominant position. Shell, BP and Conoco (Jet) responded by matching or undercutting Esso price cuts. The catalyst for the new strategy was that Esso's share of the petrol market had fallen to around 17% as compared to the supermarkets' share of 25%.

Intense company rivalry and price warfare is also a recognized practice in the oligopolistic US computer market. In March 1996, leading US personal computer manufacturers cut prices of their desk-top and network server models by more than 20% in an attempt to capture increased market share. Digital Equipment's 26% price reduction was met by a 21% reduction from Hewlett-Packard followed in turn by 20% price reductions by Compaq and IBM.

Price warfare continued to be a feature of competition during the 1990s as various factors converged to force the oligopolistic food retailing groups to react to new market conditions. For example, the accelerated expansion in the number of superstores between 1985 and 1998 had increased capacity too rapidly. The major food retailers were now finding it increasingly difficult to achieve enough sales in such new superstores to earn an adequate return on their investment. Also, they were under continued pressure from low priced stores such as Aldi, Netto and Kwik Save; Aldi and Netto being non-UK food retailers selling both familiar brands and their own brands at a discount, by keeping staffing, advertising and design costs to a minimum. The result was a series of price skirmishes which have involved aggressive price cuts by Gateway, Asda, Tesco and Sainsbury.

In 1996, the cross-channel business saw a fierce outbreak of price warfare. Of the 35m passengers using the cross-channel route, 35% went by Eurotunnel, 32% by P&O European Ferries and 20% by Stena Line. Between 1993 and 1996, peak season cross-channel fares fell by 60% as the ferries tried to resist the challenge of the Channel Tunnel. For example, the standard brochure fares for a crossing in the summer of 1996 involving a car and four passengers were heavily discounted on the shorter Dover/Calais (ferries) and the Folkestone/Calais (Le Shuttle) routes. Actual ferry prices were cut to around 40% of the standard return price while Le Shuttle prices were cut to 80% of their normal fares. Most of the operators were charging around £100 for a return fare involving a car and four passengers. In order to use its ships to capacity, P&O's policy was to match any rival company's discount.

Clearly in oligopolistic markets, where only a few firms dominate, a price-cutting strategy by one is likely to be followed by others. After short bursts of price warfare, the market may settle down into prolonged periods of price stability, although the fact that firms no longer compete in price may not mean an absence of competition. In periods of price stability, non-price competition often becomes more intense, with advertising, packaging and other promotional activities now used to raise or defend market share. For example, in the food retailing business, advertising is a well known form of non-price competition. In 1997, Sainsbury spent £30m on advertising, Tesco £16m and Asda £14m. Coupled with this overall advertising strategy, there have been other efforts at product differentiation, such as the 'green grocer' campaigns to promote environmentally friendly products. Similarly, the loyalty cards introduced by Tesco (Clubcard), Safeway (Added Bonus Card) and Sainsbury (Reward card) have been designed to reinforce brand loyalty and make customers less price sensitive. In economic terms, this was designed to make demand curves less elastic, giving the supermarkets more opportunity to raise prices at a later date if necessary.

Non-price competition may take forms other than advertising and quality considerations. In the mid 1990s when price competition was intense in the travel industry, there were still signs that companies were using other non-price methods to increase market share. For example, Thompson's industrial strategy of *vertical integration* towards the market (owning Lunn Poly and Britannia Airways) was strengthened further in 1994 by its purchase of the Country Holidays Group which gave it a major interest in the UK holiday lettings industry. Vertical integration was also involved in the acquisition by Thomas Cook in 1998 of the US Carlson group (owner of Caledonian Airways and the tour operator 'Inspirations'). *Take-over* strategies are also an important 'non price' method by which firms in oligopolistic industries compete with one another.

Price stability   That price in oligopoly will tend to have periods of stability is, in fact, predicted by economic theory.

Kinked demand. In 1939 Hall and Hitch in the UK and Sweezy in the USA proposed a theory to explain why prices often remain stable in oligopoly markets, even when costs rise. A central feature of that theory was the existence of a kinked-demand curve.

To illustrate this we take an oligopolistic market which sells similar, but not identical products, i.e. there is some measure of product differentiation. If one firm raises its price, it will then lose some, though not all, of its custom to rivals. Similarly, if the firm reduces its price it will attract some, though not all, of its rivals' custom. How much custom is lost or gained will depend partly on whether the rivals follow the initial price change.

Extensive interviews with managers of firms in oligopoly markets led Hall and Hitch to conclude that most firms have learned a common lesson from past experience of how rivals react. Namely, that if the firm were to raise its price above the current level (*P* in

Fig. 6.1), its rivals *would not* follow, content to let the firm lose sales to them. The firm will then expect its demand curve to be relatively elastic (*dK*) for price rises. However, if the firm were to reduce its price, rivals *would* follow to protect their market share, so that the firm gains few extra sales. The firm will then expect its demand curve to be relatively inelastic (*KD′*) for price reductions. Overall the firm will believe that its demand curve is kinked at the current price *P*, as in Fig. 6.1.

One can intuitively see why this belief will lead to price stickiness, since the firm will rapidly lose market share if it raises price, and gain little from reducing price. A kinked-demand (average revenue) curve of the form *dKD′*, will have a discontinuity (L−M) in its associated marginal revenue curve below the kink point K.[3] The marginal cost curve could then vary between MC_1 and MC_2 without causing the firm to alter its profit-maximizing price *P* (or its output *Q*).

A number of industries have exhibited price stability, despite rising costs. The UK confectionery industry, presently dominated by Mars, Nestlé Rowntree (absorbed Rowntree Mackintosh in 1988) and Cadbury Schweppes, is a good example of this tendency. During some periods in the 1980s, price wars were often avoided, though competition between these companies still continued in other forms. For example, in the mid 1980s non-price competition took the form of product weight. In one such period, Mars raised the weight of Mars bars by 10%; Cadburys raised the weight of its Fruit and Nut by 14% and Rowntree Mackintosh raised the weight of Cabana by 15% and increased the chocolate content of KitKat by 5%. In all of these cases the firms accepted rises in their costs, i.e. more ingredients per bar, *without changing price*.

Similarly in 1990, competition in the UK snacks market increased as the three major companies, KP Foods, Smiths and Walkers (owned by the US company, PepsiCo), and Golden Wonder (the Dalgety subsidiary), looked for new ways of competing. KP foods introduced its new crisp-like snack called 'Frisp' and spent £4.4m on marketing it in the first three months alone. To prevent being squeezed out by its two big rivals, Golden Wonder planned to launch a few new products in the middle of 1990 and in the meantime increased the packet size of all its crisps and snacks from 28 gm to 30 gm *without raising prices*. In terms of our kinked oligopoly

Fig. 6.1. Kinked demand curve and price stability.

Notes: *d–d′* = Demand curve when rivals *do not* follow price changes
D–D′ = Demand curve when rivals *do* follow price changes
dKD′ = Kinked demand curve
dLMN = Associated marginal revenue curve

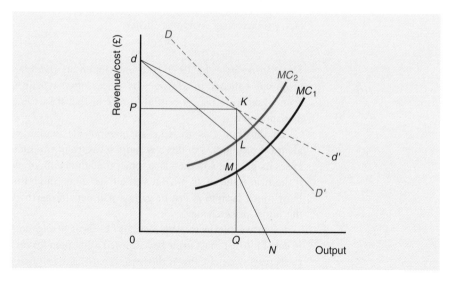

model, the companies noted above preferred to accept the higher costs of non-price competition (which can be illustrated by the upward shift in the MC curve), rather than engage in price warfare, in order to gain market share. The reason for this is that companies sometimes believe they have a better idea of the costs and benefits involved in *non-price competition* as compared to the unknown risks of getting involved in price-competition. When a company becomes involved in price-competition, gains and losses are more difficult to assess because they depend on the *reactions* of competitors to the initial company's pricing strategy.

Despite the usefulness of the kinked oligopoly model as a descriptive tool in the understanding of oligopoly behaviour, it still faces a number of problems:

1. The theory does not explain how oligopolists actually *set* an initial price; merely why a price, once set, might be stable. Kinked demand is *not* a theory of price determination.
2. The observed stickiness of prices may have little to do with the rival-firm reaction patterns of kinked-demand theory. It is, for instance, administratively expensive to change prices too often.
3. The assertion, implicit in kinked-demand theory, that prices are more 'sticky' under oligopoly than under other market forms, has not received strong support from empirical studies (Wagner 1981). For instance, Stigler, in a sample of 100 firms across 21 industries in the USA, had concluded as early as the 1940s that oligopoly prices hardly merited the description 'sticky'. Domberger, in a survey of twenty-one UK industries, found that the *more* oligopolistic the market, the more variable was price (Domberger 1980).
4. The precise nature of any kink in the demand curve may depend on the economic conditions prevailing at the time. For example, a study of 73 small owner-managed firms in Scotland found that price increases were more likely to be followed during booms, whilst falls were more likely to be followed during times of recession (Bhaskar, Machin and Reid 1991).

Game theory   One of the more recent attempts to assess non-collusive behaviour by oligopolists has involved game theory. The intention is to go beyond the rather general reaction patterns of earlier theory, to more explicit assessments of strategy and counter-strategy. We might usefully illustrate the principles involved by a simple two-firm (duopoly) game, involving market share. By its very nature, a market share game must be 'zero sum', in that any gain by one 'player' must be offset exactly by the loss of the other(s).

Suppose Firm A is considering two possible strategies to raise its market share, a 20% price cut or a 10% increase in advertising expenditure. Whatever initial strategy A adopts, it anticipates that its rival, Firm B, will react by using either a price cut or extra advertising to defend its market share. Firm A now evaluates the market share it can expect for each initial strategy and each possible counter-strategy by B. The outcomes expected by A are summarized in the pay-off matrix of Table 6.6.

If A cuts price, and B responds with a price cut, A receives 60% of the market. However, if B responds with extra advertising, A receives 70% of the market. The 'worst' outcome for A (60% of the market) will occur if B responds with a price cut. If A adopts the strategy of extra advertising, then the 'worst' outcome for A (50% of the market) will again occur if B responds with a price cut. If A expects B to play the

Table 6.6 Firm A's pay-off matrix.

		Firm B's strategies	
		Price cut	Extra advertising
Firm A's strategies	Price cut	60*[†]	70[†]
	Extra advertising	50*	55

* 'Worst' outcome for A of each A strategy.
[†] 'Worst' outcome for B of each B strategy.

game astutely, i.e. choose the counter-strategy best for itself (worst for A), then A will choose the price-cut strategy as this gives it 60% of the market rather than 50%. If A plays the game in this way, selecting the best of the 'worst possible' outcomes for each initial strategy, it is said to be adopting a 'maxi–min approach' to the game.

If B adopts the same maxi–min approach as A, *and* has made the same evaluation of outcomes as A, it also will adopt a price-cut strategy. For instance, if B adopts a price-cut strategy, its 'worst' outcome would occur if A responds with a price cut – B then gets 40% of the market (100% minus 60%), rather than 50% if A responds with extra advertising. If B adopts extra advertising, its 'worst' outcome would again occur if A responds with a price cut – B then receives 30% . The best of the 'worst possible' outcomes for B occurs if B adopts a price cut, which gives it 40% of the market rather than 30%.

In this particular game we have a stable equilibrium, without any resort to collusion. Both firms initially cut price, then accept the respective market shares which fulfil their maxi–min targets – 60% to A, 40% to B. There could then follow the price stability which we have seen to be a feature of some oligopoly situations. In some games the optimal strategy for each firm may not even have been an initial price cut, but rather non-price competition (such as advertising). Game theory can predict both price stability and extensive non-price competition.

The problem with game theory is that it can equally predict unstable solutions, with extensive price as well as non-price competition. An unstable solution might follow if each firm, faced with the pay-off matrix of Table 6.6, adopts entirely different strategies. Firm B might not use the maxi–min approach of A, but take more risk.[4] Instead of the price cut it might adopt the 'extra advertising' strategy, hoping to induce an advertising response from Firm A and gain 45% of the market, but risk getting only 30% if A responds with a price cut. Suppose this is what happens. Firm A now receives 70% of the market, but B only receives 30%, which is below its initial expectation of 45%. This may provoke B into alternative strategy formulation, setting off a further chain reaction. The game may then fail to settle down quickly, if at all, to a stable solution, i.e. one in which each firm receives a market share which meets its overall expectation. An unstable solution might also follow if each firm evaluates the pay-off matrix differently from the other. Even if they then adopt the same approach to the game, one firm at least will be 'disappointed', possibly provoking action and counteraction.

If we could tell *before the event* which oligopoly situations would be stable, and which unstable, then the many possible outcomes of game theory would be considerably narrowed. At present this is beyond the state of the art. However, game theory has been useful in making more explicit the *interdependence* of oligopoly situations. Here we have used game theory in a situation in which the firms did not collude. Game theory can also show (in games which are *not* zero sum) that collusion between firms may sometimes improve the position of all. It is to such collusive behaviour that we now turn.

Collusive oligopoly   When oligopoly is non-collusive, the firm uses guesswork and calculation to handle the uncertainty of its rivals' reactions. Another way of handling that uncertainty in markets which are interdependent is by some form of central co-ordination; in other words, collusion. At least two features of collusive oligopoly are worth emphasizing. First, the objectives that are sought through collusion. Second, the methods that are used to promote collusion – these may be formal, as in a cartel, or informal, via tacit agreement.

Objectives of collusion   *Joint profit maximization.*   The firms may seek to co-ordinate their price, output and other policies to achieve maximum profits for the industry as a whole. In the extreme case the firms may act together as a monopoly, aggregating their marginal costs and equating these with marginal revenue for the whole market. If achieved, the result would be to maximize joint profits, with a unique industry price and output (P_1Q_1), as in Fig. 6.2.

A major problem is, of course, how to achieve the close co-ordination required. We consider this further below, but we might note from Fig. 6.2 that co-ordination is required both to *establish* the profit-maximizing solution for the industry P_1Q_1, and to *enforce* it once established. For instance, some agreement must be reached on sharing the output Q_1 between the colluding firms. One solution is to equate marginal revenue for whole output with marginal cost in each separate market,[5] with Firm A producing Q_A and Firm B, Q_B. Whatever the agreement, it must remain in force – since if any firm produces above its quota, this will raise industry output, depress price and move the industry away from the joint profit-maximizing solution.

Deterrence of new entrants – limit-pricing.   Firms may seek to co-ordinate policies, not so much to maximize short-run profit but rather some longer-run notion of profit (see Ch. 3). A major threat to long-run profit is the potential entrance of new firms into the industry. Economists such as Andrews and Bain have therefore suggested that oligopolistic firms may collude with the objectives of setting price below that which maximizes joint profits, in order to deter new entrants. The 'limit price' can be defined as the highest price which the established firms believe they can charge without inducing entry. Its precise value will depend upon the nature and extent of

Fig. 6.2. **Joint profit maximization in duopoly.**

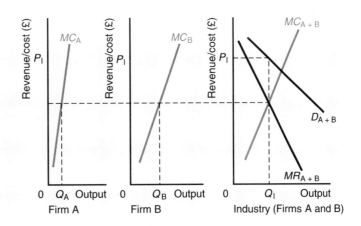

the 'barriers to entry' for any particular industry. The greater the barriers to entry, the higher the 'limit price' will be.

Substantial economies of scale are a 'barrier to entry', in that a new firm will usually be smaller than established firms, and will therefore be at a cost disadvantage. Product differentiation itself, reinforced by extensive advertising, is also a barrier – since product loyalty, once captured, is difficult and expensive for new entrants to dislodge. Other barriers might include legally enforced patents to new technologies in the hands of established firms, and even inelastic market demands. This latter is a barrier in that the less elastic the market demand for the product, the greater will be the price fall from any extra supply contributed by new entrants.

The principle of 'limit-pricing' can be illustrated from Fig. 6.3.

Let us make the analysis easier by supposing that each established firm has an identical average cost (AC) curve, and sells an identical output, Q_F, at the joint profit-maximizing price P_I set for the industry. Suppose a new firm, with an identical cost profile, is considering entering the industry, and is capable of selling E units in the first instance. Despite the initial cost disadvantage the new firm believes it can survive. One way of preventing the survival of the new firm, perhaps even deterring its entry, would be for the colluding established firms to reduce the industry price to P_L. Although this would reduce their own excess profits in the short run (by VW per unit) the new entrant would make a loss selling E at price P_L, since price would be less than average cost at that output. It would have needed to produce as much as output S *immediately* at the price P_L, even to have just covered its average costs.

The greater the barriers to the entry of new firms, the higher the 'limit price', P_L, can be, i.e. the closer P_L can be to P_I. The most favourable situation for established firms would be if barriers were so great that P_L were at, or above, P_I. In other words, established firms could set the joint profit-maximizing price without inducing entry.

An example of the occurrence of high barriers to entry and relatively high limit prices could be seen in the French market for natural spring water during the early 1990s. In 1992 the French market for such bottled water was dominated by three companies, Nestlé, Perrier and BSN, and the barriers to entry into the industry were high. For example, the transport costs of bringing non-French water to the market

Fig. 6.3. Limit pricing as a barrier to entry.

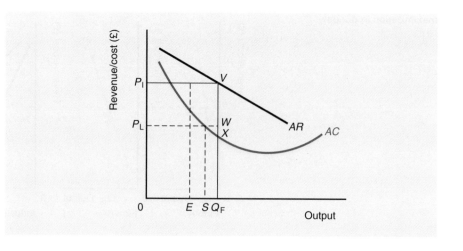

were substantial and persuading French retailers to stock new brands was difficult. Advertising costs were also heavy, helping create strong brand loyalties in France for the products of the three companies. Finally, the fact that the companies held 82% of the market share by volume constituted an additional problem for prospective new entrants. (European Commission 1994.) As a result, these companies were able to increase their prices substantially during the period, thus keeping their limit prices high and maximising their joint profits.

Occasionally a limit-pricing policy is explicitly adopted, as in the early 1960s when the three major petrol wholesalers, Shell/BP, Esso and Regent were threatened with new entrants. In 1963 Shell announced a price reduction 'to make the UK market less attractive to newcomers and potential newcomers'. Again, in 1973 the Monopolies and Mergers Commission (MMC) found evidence of limit-pricing by Kellogg concluding that 'when fixing its prices, therefore, Kellogg has as an objective the preservation of its share of the market against potential competitors'.

An obvious constraint to limit-pricing is that prices cannot be set below X in Fig. 6.3, the level at which the established firms begin to make excess profits (normal profit included in average cost), at least not for any length of time. The established firms may therefore resort to non-price competition to reinforce barriers against new entrants. For instance, the petrol companies sought extensive 'solus' agreements, giving discounts to retailers dealing exclusively with them, and sought to buy up retail outlets directly. In the detergent industry, Lever Brothers, by introducing new brands, have increased product differentiation and raised barriers to entry. As much as 58% of their turnover comes from new brands introduced in the past thirteen years. Extensive advertising (as shown by Tables 6.4 and 6.5) is yet another way of increasing barriers to entry into a market or industry. Advertising can be used to increase brand loyalty, thus making it difficult for new firms with a new product to enter a market. Increased advertising can be used by firms already in the industry not only to keep other firms out, but also to drive out existing firms which have newly entered the industry.

To investigate this latter proposition, a study was undertaken into the behaviour of forty-two companies operating in various consumer goods markets, such as electric shavers, deodorants, washing up liquids and kettles, over the period 1975 to 1981. The study investigated the advertising strategy of companies *already in* these oligopolistic markets after new firms with new products had managed to enter those markets (Cubbin and Domberger 1988). The results of the study showed that increased advertising was used as a weapon in an attempt to drive out new entrants in 38% of markets studied, and that the response of the firms already in the market to the new entrants depended on the *structure of the oligopoly* and the *nature of the market*. For example, in a tightly competitive oligopoly situation, where a dominant firm controlled more than 30% of the market, it was more likely that the new entrant would be exposed to increased advertising competition than in a looser oligopoly where there was no clear dominance by one firm. Similarly, increased advertising competition was more likely to face new entrants in static markets, i.e. those in which demand is not growing. This is partly because growing markets tend to be dominated by new consumers with less attachment to the products of existing firms. Advertising in this situation is therefore a less-certain weapon for driving out a new entrant, as compared to a market in which demand is static.

We now turn briefly to the methods which firms have actually used to promote collusion in oligopolistic markets.

Methods of collusion   *Formal collusion – cartels.*   Formal collusion often takes the form of a cartel - in other words, the establishment of some central body with responsibility for setting the industry price and output which most nearly meets some agreed objective. Usually it also has the responsibility for sharing that total output between the members. Cartels are against the law in most countries, including the UK. However, in the UK the Cement Makers' Federation was an exception. Up to 1987 it still held monthly meetings in which deliveries, prices and market shares were discussed. The three main companies sharing the market were Blue Circle (60%), Rio Tinto Zinc (22%) and Rugby Portland (18%), with their common price calculated on a formula which averaged the costs of different producers. The Restrictive Practices Court permitted the cartel to continue on the basis that a common price agreement enables cement capacity to be controlled in an orderly way. Nevertheless, increased concentration of the cement industry in the last few years raised the possibility of intervention by the MMC and this, together with international competition from cheap European imports (especially from Greece), caused the cartel to be abandoned in 1987.

Various cartels operate internationally. The most famous is OPEC, in which many, but not all (the UK is not a member) oil-exporting countries meet regularly to agree on prices and set production quotas. Whilst OPEC worked successfully in the mid-1970s in raising oil prices, in the worldwide economic slump of the early 1980s co-ordination has proved increasingly difficult. As demand for oil has fallen, exporters have been faced with the necessity of cutting production quotas to maintain prices; and some, such as Iran and Nigeria with major internal economic problems, have been unwilling to do this, preferring to cut prices and seek higher market share. Of course the Iraqi pressure on OPEC countries to curtail production and raise prices, and the subsequent Kuwait invasion, contributed to higher oil prices in the early 1990s. However by 1992/93, the continued fall in demand for oil under worldwide recessionary conditions, allied to some additional oil supplies (e.g. from the Gulf States), revived the disagreements between those cartel members in favour of price cuts and those in favour of tighter quotas. The International Air Transport Association (IATA) is the cartel of international airlines, and has sought to set prices for each route. During the 1970s it was seriously weakened by price-cutting competition from non-member airlines, such as Laker Airways. It has been further weakened by worldwide recession in the late 1980s and early 1990s, with lower incomes causing demand for air travel, with its high-income elasticity, to fall dramatically. To fill seats, the member airlines began to compete amongst themselves in terms of price, often via a complex system of discounts. The experiences of OPEC and IATA suggest that cartels are vulnerable both to price-cutting amongst members when demand for the product declines, and to competition from non-members.

Another example of an international cartel was brought to light by investigations during 1990 into the activity of the International Telegraph and Telephone Consultative Committee (CCITT), a Geneva based 'club' consisting of the main international telephone companies of the major industrial countries (*Financial Times* 1990). Major international telephone companies such as AT&T (USA), British Telecom (UK), Deutsche Bundespost (Germany), France Telecom (France), Telecom Canada (Canada) and KDD (Japan) belong to the group. The CCITT had a book of 'recommendations' for its member companies which included two important features. First, it suggested a complicated method of sharing the revenues received from international telephone calls. When international phone calls are made from the UK to Japan, for example, BT receives the money for the call but it has to pay KDD in Japan for delivering the call to its final destination in that country. The particular method used to calculate the distribution of the revenue received for the call between the various international telephone companies tended to penalize any company that attempted to cut its telephone prices. This in turn made it difficult for both existing or new companies to decrease prices because their profits would also fall. Second, it suggested that members of the group should not lease too much of their international telephone circuits to other private companies, since this could increase potential competition.

The effect of the first 'rule' was to provide high profit margins for telephone companies because prices were kept artificially high by the peculiar revenue sharing scheme. Meanwhile, new technological advances had decreased the *real* costs per minute of using a transatlantic cable from $2.53 per minute in 1956 to $0.04 in 1988. While costs had fallen drastically, the price charged for a peak call from the US to the UK and Italy remained at $2 and $4 per minute respectively! As a result profit margins on international calls (i.e. profits divided by revenue) of some of the top earners were as follows: Japan (75%), Canada (68%), US (63%), Britain (58%), W Germany (48%) and France (43%). British Telecom earned a profit of between £600m and £800m on its international business during the 1988/9 financial year, depending on the accounting definitions used. The second 'rule' made it difficult for new companies to enter this market because most of the international cables were built by members of the CCITT and new operators had to get permission from these companies in order to lease cable space from them. If they were not allowed more space on international cables, then new companies had to use satellite links which were more expensive and of lower quality than cable links.

Tacit collusion – price leadership.   Although cartels are illegal in most countries, various forms of tacit collusion undoubtedly occur. In 1776, Adam Smith wrote in his *Wealth of Nations* that entrepreneurs rarely meet together without conspiring to raise prices at the expense of the consumer. Today the most usual method of tacit collusion is price leadership, where one firm sets a price which the others follow.

1 **Dominant-firm leadership.** Frequently the price leader is the dominant firm. In the late 1960s Brooke Bond controlled 43% of the market for tea, well ahead of the second largest firm Typhoo with only 18% of the market. Brooke Bond's price rises were soon matched by those of other firms, bringing the industry to the attention of the Prices and Incomes Board in 1970. Sealink, with 34% of the cross-Channel market, seems to have been the price leader in ferry travel to the Continent in the 1980s. In the car industry, Ford has frequently acted as the dominant market leader by being first with its price increases. In 1990, companies who bought fleet cars from Ford, Rover, Vauxhall and Peugeot Talbot, accused the big car manufacturers of operating a price cartel led by Ford. By initiating two separate price rises (amounting to a total of 8.5% by the middle of 1990), Ford was seen as the dominant leader of a 'cartel' by the fleet car buyers.

2. **Barometric-firm leadership.** In some cases the price leader is a small firm, recognized by others to have a close knowledge of prevailing market conditions. The firm acts as a 'barometer' to others of changing market conditions, and its prices are closely followed. In the mid-1970s Williams and Glyn's, a relatively small commercial bank, took the lead in reducing bank charges in response to

rising interest rates. Maunder also found this sort of price leadership in the glass bottle and sanitary ware markets of the 1960s and early 1970s (Maunder 1972). Since the mid-1970s there have been signs that the 'minor' petrol wholesalers have had an increasing influence on petrol prices (see Ch. 9). Again a recent study suggests that the barometric form of price leadership can be seen in the North American newsprint industry where some thirty firms produce most of the newsprint. The authors of the study found a tendency for a leader to emerge which then acts as an 'anchor' for the calculations of other firms in the industry and as a 'trigger' for any price adjustment within the group when cost or demand conditions change (Booth *et al.* 1991).

3. **Collusive-price leadership**. This is a more complicated form of price leadership; essentially it is an informal cartel in which prices change almost simultaneously. The parallel pricing which occurred in the wholesale petrol market (noted in Ch. 9) until the mid-1970s, suggested this sort of tacit group collusion. In practice it is often difficult to distinguish collusive-price leadership from types in which firms follow price leaders very quickly. The French market for spring water, referred to earlier in the chapter, is one where both the setting of parallel prices and price leadership were present. Between 1987 and 1992 the prices of bottled water sold by Nestlé, Perrier and BSN rose in almost a simultaneous or parallel way, with Perrier being the price leader. Although the three companies did not have a collusive price arrangement, their behaviour was reminiscent of a close 'tacit' form of oligopolistic interdependence.

Sometimes it is difficult to prove that this sort of collusion is present when all the firms in an industry are influenced by a third factor outside their control but which they all have to respond to quite rapidly, thus *appearing* to show collusion. For example, the Office of Fair Trading investigated parallel pricing and excess profits in the petrol wholesaling business in 1989/90. Although the sector comprised 69 petrol wholesalers, it was still dominated by Esso, Shell, BP, Texaco and Mobil who accounted for 65% of the market. The report found that there was no evidence of price collusion by the wholesalers because they seemed to adjust their prices fairly simultaneously to the common world oil price reflected by the Rotterdam spot market. Also the allegations that the oil companies implemented price rises more quickly than price falls were rejected by the report. They found that when Rotterdam prices rose, UK wholesalers delayed price rises to avoid losing market share, and when Rotterdam prices fell, the wholesalers' price fell after a short delay, but in smaller steps. Over time it is sometimes difficult to distinguish between periods of actual collusive price leadership from periods of 'apparent' collusive price leadership.

Conclusion

That oligopoly has become a progressively more important form of market structure in the UK is clear from the data, particularly from concentration ratios. Interdependence is a key feature of such markets, which makes the outcome of any strategy by a firm uncertain, depending to a large extent on how the rivals react. Price competition may be a particularly hazardous strategy, perhaps leading to a 'price war'. In any case, to the extent that kinked-demand theory is valid, the profit-maximizing price may not change even for wide variations in cost. For both these reasons there may be extensive periods of price stability. Even so, there may still be close competition between firms for market share, though this will be mainly of the non-price variety – advertising, packaging, new brands, etc. Non-price competition, by increasing product differentiation, real or imagined, may benefit firms not only by raising market share, but by providing greater future control over price – extra brand loyalty making demand curves less price-elastic.

The uncertainty of rival reactions, whether price or non-price, can be mitigated by guesswork, based on past experience (reaction curves), or by trying to evaluate the rivals' optimal counter-strategy (game theory). Collusion between firms may be a still more secure way of reducing uncertainty, and avoiding mutual damage. This could be arranged formally, as in cartels, or informally by some form of tacit collusion (information agreements, price leadership, etc.). Although we may be no nearer a general model of oligopoly behaviour, we have made some progress in predicting how firms react under particular circumstances at particular times.

Key points

- Concentration ratios for both product and industry groups have risen over time, implying a more oligopolistic market structure.
- 'Recognized interdependence between the few' is a key feature of oligopoly markets.
- Where firms develop their own strategies independently we speak of 'non-collusive behaviour'.
- Even in this case firms will seek to anticipate how their rivals might react to any strategy they might adopt.
- Past experience might be a guide to rival reactions, as in the 'kinked demand' model. Firms learn that rivals match price cuts but not price rises. The model predicts price stability.
- Even where there is little price competition, there may be extensive non-price competition.
- 'Game' simulations may be used to predict the outcomes of different combinations of action/reaction. Games may or may not have stable equilibria depending on the strategies each firm adopts.
- To avoid uncertainty, collusion may occur, whether formal (cartels) or informal (tacit).
- Informal collusion may include various types of price leadership models as well as agreements of various kinds.
- To be successful firms must abide by the rules of collusive agreements, e.g. producing no more than their allocated quotas.

Notes

1. Cross-elasticity of demand is defined as the percentage change in quantity demanded of X, divided by the percentage change in price of Y. If X and Y are close substitutes, then a small fall in price of Y will lead to a substantial decrease in demand for X. This gives a high positive value for the quotient.
2. See, for instance, Jump (1982), which suggested that brand loyalty permitted prices to be 9% higher for branded processed foods in the USA than for supermarket own-brand equivalents.

3. This is because each demand curve, dd' and DD' respectively, will have its own separate marginal revenue curve, bisecting the horizontal between the vertical axis and demand curve in question.
4. The maxi–min approach is a rather conservative strategy in that it assumes that the rival reacts to your strategy in the worst possible way for you.
5. A distribution of the joint profit-maximizing output such that aggregate $MR = MC$ in each separate market, is often called the 'ideal' distribution. From Fig. 6.2 we can see that there is no other distribution which will raise total profits for the industry. For instance, one extra unit produced by Firm B will add more to cost than is saved by one less unit produced by Firm A (i.e. $MC_B > MC_A$). Whether the firms will acquiesce in such a share-out is quite another matter.

References and further reading

Bhaskar, V., Machin, S. and Reid, G. (1991) Testing a Model of the Kinked Demand Curve, *The Journal of Industrial Economics*, **39**, 3, March.

Booth, D.I., Kanetkar, V., Vertinsky, I. and Whistler, D. (1991) An Empirical Model of Capacity Expansion and Pricing in an Oligopoly with Barometric Price Leadership: A Case Study of the Newsprint Industry of North America, *The Journal of Industrial Economics*, **39**, 3, March.

Business Monitor (1995) PA 1002 Report on the Census of Production 1993.

Cubbin, J. and Domberger, S. (1988) Advertising and Post-entry Oligopoly Behaviour, *The Journal of Industrial Economics*, **37**, Dec.

Davies, S. and Lyons, D. (1996) *Industrial Organisation in the EU*, Clarendon Press, Oxford.

Domberger, S. (1980) Mergers, Market Structure and the Rate of Price Adjustment, in Cowling, K. *et al.*, *Mergers and Economic Performance*, CUP, Cambridge, Ch. 13.

European Commission (1994) European Economy, No. 57, Part C.

Financial Times (1990) Reconnecting Charges with Costs, 3 April.

Jump, N. (1982) Corporate Strategy in Mature Markets, *Barclays Bank Review*, **57**, 4, Nov.

Marketing Week (1994) Prices War Continues on Wider Front, 5 August, p. 11.

Marketing Week (1996) The UK's Top 100 Advertisers, 10 May.

Maunder, P. (1972) Price Leadership: An Appraisal of its Character in some British Industries, *The Business Economist*, **4**.

Sawyer, M.C. (1981) *The Economics of Industries and Firms*, Croom Helm.

Wagner, L. (ed.) (1981) *Readings in Applied Micro-economics*, 2nd edn, OUP, Oxford.

Chapter 7

The multinational corporation

This chapter focuses on the 'globalization' of business and the growing importance of the multinational corporation. Aided by a host of 'enabling technologies', notably inexpensive air travel and microchip-based communications systems, the world's largest companies have become truly global in scope. From Beijing to London to Tierra del Fuego, today's teenagers universally drink Coca-Cola, eat McDonalds' hamburgers, wear Levi jeans and listen to Madonna on MTV. Their parents drive cars produced by a handful of global auto makers, filling them up with petrol refined by an even smaller number of world-wide oil companies. This chapter reviews the changing pattern of production by multinational corporations, going on to consider the reasons for the increasing globalization of business. It then considers the implications of this phenomenon for the UK economy.

What is a multinational corporation?

The terms 'multinational', 'transnational' and 'international' corporation (or enterprise) are often used interchangeably. A multinational may be defined as a company which owns or controls production or service facilities in more than one country. In other words, a multinational is *not* simply a company which trades internationally by exporting its products (or by licensing overseas producers), it actually *owns* (via a wholly or partly-owned subsidiary) or *controls* (via a branch plant, joint venture or minority shareholding) productive facilities in countries outside its home country. Such overseas productive facilities may be acquired by taking over existing locally-owned capacity (e.g. Nestlé's famous acquisition of Rowntree in 1988 or BMW's takeover of Rover in 1994) or by investing directly in new (or 'greenfield site') plant and equipment (e.g. Nissan's plant in Washington or Toyota's car factory in Derby).

From a statistical point of view there are two main methods of ranking the world's top multinationals. First, ranking them according to the amount of foreign assets they control and second ranking them in terms of a 'transnationality index'. Table 7.1 ranks the top ten multinationals according to the value of foreign assets they control and we can see that six of the top ten are from the US, two from Japan, one from

Table 7.1 World's top
ten multinationals ranked
by foreign assets, 1996.

Ranking					
Foreign assets	Trans. index	Company	Country	Industry	Trans. index (%)
1	83	General Electric	US	Electronics	30.7
2	32	Shell, Royal Dutch	UK/Neth.	Petroleum	66.6
3	75	Ford Motor Co.	US	Automotive	37.7
4	22	Exxon Corp.	US	Petroleum	72.7
5	85	General Motors	US	Automotive	30.3
6	52	IBM	US	Computers	54.3
7	79	Toyota	Japan	Automotive	35.0
8	49	Volkswagen Group	Germany	Automotive	55.3
9	71	Mitsubishi Corp.	Japan	Diversified	41.4
10	38	Mobil Corp.	US	Petroleum	62.3

Note: Trans. index = transnationality index.
Source: UNCTAD (1998), p. 48.

Germany and one from UK/Netherlands. They are primarily based in the petroleum, automotive and electronics/computing sectors. However, Table 7.1 also provides each company's transnationality index and its transnationality ranking. The *transnationality index* takes a more comprehensive view of a company's global activity and is calculated as the average of the following ratios: foreign assets/total assets; foreign sales/total sales; and foreign employment/total employment. For example, we can see that the largest multinational company is General Electric in terms of the foreign assets it owns. However, its transnationality index of 30.7% means that it is only ranked 83rd in terms of this criteria. The reason for this is that even though it has large investments overseas in absolute value, in *percentage* terms, most of its assets, sales and employment are still located in the US. This is in contrast with Exxon Corporation where over 70% of its overall activity is based abroad.

If we wanted to find the companies which operate mostly outside their home country, then we would have to look at the ten top multinationals in terms of the *transnationality index*. These are shown in Table 7.2 and here we see the dominance of EU companies in sectors such as food/beverages, pharmaceuticals/chemicals and electrics/electronics. The companies with the highest transnationality index are often

Table 7.2 World's top
ten multinationals ranked
by the transnationality
index, 1996.

Ranking					
Trans. index	Foreign assets	Company	Country	Industry	Trans. index (%)
1	34	Seagram Co.	Canada	Beverages	97.3
2	12	Asea Brown Boveri	Swtz./Sweden	Electrical	96.1
3	11	Nestle SA	Switzerland	Food	95.3
4	50	Thomson Corp.	Canada	Printing/Publ.	94.9
5	83	Solvay SA	Belgium	Chem./Pharm.	92.2
6	56	Holderbank Financiere	Switzerland	Construction	89.8
7	62	Electrolux AB	Sweden	Electrical	88.7
8	18	Unilever	Neth./UK	Food	87.1
9	21	Roche Holdings	Switzerland	Pharmaceuticals	87.0
10	52	Michelin	France	Rubber/plastics	84.4

Note: Trans. index = transnationality index.
Source: UNCTAD (1998), p. 45.

from the smaller countries as a more restricted domestic market induces them to operate abroad if they are to maximize their growth in terms of revenue or profits.

Technical definitions of multinationals, however, fail to convey the true scope and diversity of global business, which covers everything from the thousands of medium-sized firms which have overseas operations to the truly gigantic multinationals like IBM, General Motors and Ford. Some multinationals are vertically integrated, with different stages of the same productive process taking place in different countries (e.g. British Petroleum). Others are horizontally integrated, performing the same basic production operations in each of the countries in which they operate (e.g. Marks and Spencer). Many multinationals are household names, marketing global brands (e.g. Rothmans International, IBM, British Airways). Others are holding companies for a portfolio of international companies (e.g. Diageo) or specialize in capital goods that have little name-recognition in the high street (e.g. BTR, Hawker Siddley, GKN).

How important are the multinationals?

In 1998 the United Nations Division on Transnational Corporations and Investment estimated that there are presently 53,607 multinationals, collectively controlling a total of 448,917 foreign affiliates. Table 7.3 provides an overview of multinational activity. It shows that the sales of multinationals' foreign affiliates exceed global exports and amount to 31% of world Gross Domestic Product (GDP). It also shows that foreign direct investment has grown at approximately twice the rate of growth of exports for much of the period. Although not shown in Table 7.3, the gross output of the foreign affiliates of multinationals was $2 trillion (i.e. $2,000bn) in 1997, accounting for nearly 7% of world GDP. The same affiliates also accounted for 32.5% of world exports. Ranked by either turnover or GDP, half of the world's largest economic 'units' are multinationals, rather than countries. Only fourteen nation states have a GDP which exceeds the turnover of Exxon, Ford or General Motors.

Historically, the bulk of multinational activity was concentrated in the *developed* world. Indeed, as recently as the mid-1980s, half of all multinational production took place in only five countries – the United States, Canada, the UK, Germany and the Netherlands. This pattern is now changing rapidly. The rapid industrialization and economic growth in the newly-industrializing nations of the world has led to a sharp increase in multinational investment in Asia and (to a lesser extent) Latin America. Some of these countries, notably the 'four tigers' (Taiwan, South Korea, Hong Kong and Singapore), now have per capita GDP levels which

Table 7.3 Multinational activity in a global context.

	1997 ($bn)	Average annual growth rates (%)				
		1981–85	1986–90	1991–95	1996	1997
FDI outflows	424	0.8	27.1	15.1	−0.5	27.1
FDI outward stock	3,541	5.4	21.0	10.3	11.5	13.7
Sales of foreign affiliates of MNCs	9,500	1.3	16.6	13.4	6.0	7.3
World gross domestic product	30,551	2.1	12.1	5.5	0.8	6.0
World gross fixed capital formation	5,393	0.7	12.5	2.6	−0.1	5.0
Total exports of goods and services	6,432	−0.1	14.6	8.9	2.9	3.0

Source: UNCTAD (1998), p. 2.

exceed those of most European nations and their indigenous companies are now beginning to establish production facilities in the 'old world', although the 1997 'Asian crisis' may temporarily slow or even reverse this process. Figure 7.1 shows that the old bi-polar world (dominated by North America and Europe) is now giving way to a tri-polar economy, comprising the 'Triad' of North America, the European Union and East and South-East Asia. These three regions account for approximately 75% of the world's exports and 60% of manufacturing output and almost all multinational activity.

It is estimated that between 1997 and the year 2010, world GDP will nearly double from its present level of $30,000bn to $55,000bn, with the share of the developing world rising from one-third to one-half over the same period. Figure 7.2 shows the changing pattern of *foreign direct investment* (fdi) by which domestic companies acquire control over productive facilities overseas. While there is a strong cyclical pattern evident, with foreign direct investment in the rich industrial countries higher during the world boom than in the recessionary years of the early 1990s, investment in the developing countries shows a strong secular increase over the period 1989–97.

Figure 7.2 also reflects the reintegration of the former centrally planned economies of central and eastern Europe into the world economy. These former centrally planned economies are included in the category 'developing countries'. Although the total volume of inward foreign investment is still relatively low (central and eastern Europe attracted only 3.8% of total global inflows in the period 1994–97), inflows have increased strongly since the transition process began in 1989. In this region, 60% of the inflows are associated with the privatization of former state-owned enterprises (compared with 8% in the other developing countries). Unsurprisingly, countries that have pushed ahead with market reform,

Fig. 7.1. **The changing global map of production and trade.** *Source:* Adapted from Dicken (1998).

A multi-polar global economy – the 'triad' of economic power

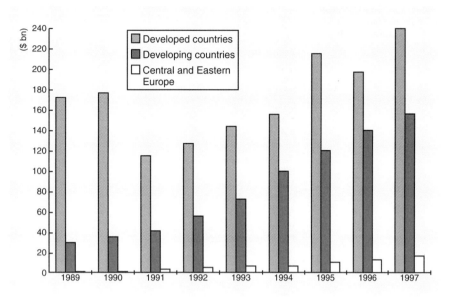

Fig. 7.2. Inflows of foreign direct investment. *Source:* UNCTAD (1998), pp. 361–5.

and privatization in particular, have attracted the bulk of the foreign investment, both by creating international confidence in their future economic and political stability and by providing the opportunities for foreign companies to buy local production and distribution facilities. Poland and the Czech Republic, for example, have been highly successful in attracting multinationals like Ford, Volkswagen and Philip Morris. Countries which have resisted or delayed market reform, notably many of the states of the former Soviet Union have, in contrast, found foreign companies unwilling to risk large-scale inward investment.

Multinationals and the UK economy

Multinationals play a central role in the UK economy. Table 7.4 gives one indication of their importance. It lists the top 20 UK-based companies, ranked by annual turnover. Of this number, 18 are truly multinational (only Sainsbury and Tesco do not have extensive overseas interests, although Marks and Spencer have shown that foreign subsidiaries can be profitably operated in the retail sector). BP and Shell, for example, boast production and distribution facilities in over 100 countries; ICI and Unilever have a similarly extensive presence in the world's chemicals markets. BT and British Gas have both dramatically internationalized their operations since privatization in the 1980s and now profess their ambition to become global corporations.

The UK still ranks as a major home to multinationals, reflecting its colonial past and the vast assets accumulated pre-1914. Although Table 7.5 suggests that the *number* of home-based multinationals is smaller than in the other countries represented, the *value* of their contribution to multinational activity is substantially greater, as can be seen in Table 7.6. Outward foreign investment from Britain has remained high in the post-war years, with UK home-based multinationals responsible for over 16% of all fdi outflows from the developed economies in 1997, whilst only

Table 7.4 The UK's top twenty companies by turnover, 1997.

Company	Turnover (£bn)	Sector
Shell Transport and Trading*	74.2	Petroleum
British Petroleum	43.4	Petroleum
Unilever	33.5	Food
Tesco	17.7	Retail grocery
British Telecom	15.6	Telecommunications
Diageo	13.7	Leisure
Sainsbury	12.9	Retail grocery
ICI	11.0	Industrial chemicals
British Airways	8.6	Airlines
British Aerospace	8.5	Aircraft manufacture
BTR	8.1	Engineering/electrics
Marks and Spencer	7.8	Retail
Smithkline Beecham	7.0	Pharmaceuticals
Asda	6.9	Retail
Inchcape	5.9	Engineering
P&O Steam Navigation	5.7	Shipping
British Gas	5.3	Utilities
Bass	5.3	Leisure
Boots	5.2	Retail
Zeneca	5.2	Pharmaceuticals

*This is the UK side of Royal Dutch Shell – figures are for the whole group.
Source: Financial Times (1998a).

Table 7.5 Home and host to multinationals.

	Parent corporations based in country: home	Foreign affiliates based in country: host
France	2,078	9,351
Germany	7,569	11,445
United Kingdom	1,059	2,609
Japan	4,231	3,014
United States	3,379	18,901
Total (5 countries)	18,316	45,320
Developed countries	43,442	96,620

Source: UNCTAD (1998), p. 3.

Table 7.6 FDI outflows from five main home economies ($bn) for multinationals.

	1986–91	1992	1993	1994	1995	1996	1997
France	18	31	21	24	16	30	25
Germany	16	20	15	17	39	30	34
United Kingdom	26	19	27	34	44	34	58
Japan	33	17	14	18	23	23	26
United States	26	39	75	73	92	75	115
Total (5 countries)	119	126	152	166	214	192	258
Developed countries	169	180	206	241	306	283	360

*Annual average.
Source: UNCTAD (1998), p. 367.

representing around 2% of all home-based multinationals (see Table 7.6). Moreover, despite the UK's increasingly close economic and political ties with other member states of the European Union (EU), the bulk of *outward* foreign direct investment still goes to the United States where UK multinationals retain a pre-eminent position in terms of the value of US assets controlled.

As a host country, the UK is also an important destination for *inward* direct investment by foreign multinationals (see Table 7.5). Of the Financial Times top 500 companies operating in the UK, 313 are foreign-owned, with Germany (87), France (77), Switzerland (28) and the Netherlands (17) being the most important European nations. Just as UK multinationals dominate foreign direct investment in the United States, however, so US multinationals account for the lion's share of foreign direct investment in the UK; and led by Nissan, Sony, Toyota and Honda, Japanese and Korean multinationals are also increasing their stake in the UK economy. In the last few years, 120 major Japanese companies have set up in the UK. Over 30% of all Japanese foreign direct investment in the EU to date has been in the UK and the Confederation of British Industry (CBI) estimates that, by the year 2010, subsidiaries of Japanese multinationals could produce as much as 20% of the UK's industrial output.

The UK economy is thus particularly affected by the globalization of business, being simultaneously home of, *and* host to, a large number of multinationals producing a rapidly growing proportion of its output. Multinational companies (both UK companies and foreign companies in the UK) account for an estimated 30% of GDP in the UK and almost half manufacturing employment. Most activity is concentrated in capital-intensive, high technology sectors – computers, automobiles, electronics, pharmaceuticals and chemicals. One-third of UK exports and imports by value are estimated to be *intra-firm* (within firm) transactions, as multinationals import and export the intermediate products which tie together production processes which are vertically integrated across national frontiers.

Why do companies become multinational?

Multinationals are very heterogeneous in nature. Most large companies are multinational, but there are many medium-sized companies which also have overseas operations. This heterogeneity makes it difficult to generalize about the reasons why firms become multinational. Nevertheless, there is broad agreement amongst economists that the primary motivation for multinational activity is to seek higher or more secure profits in the long term – for example, by strengthening the company's market position.

Ultimately, any such consideration of the motives for establishing overseas operations must focus on one or other side of the profit and loss account; that is, becoming multinational is either driven by a desire to cut costs or, alternatively, by the prospect of greater revenues. One way of categorizing these two motives is to distinguish between multinationals which are *cost-oriented* and those which are *market-oriented*.

Cost-oriented multinationals are those which internationalize their operations by *vertical integration*; e.g. integrating backwards in search of cheaper or more secure inputs into the productive process. The oil companies like Exxon, Shell and BP were early examples of this approach. In order to secure control of strategic raw materials in oil fields around the world, they established overseas extraction operations in the early years of the twentieth century with the aim of shipping crude oil back to their home markets for refining and sale. More recently, many US and European companies have integrated forwards by establishing assembly facilities in SE Asia in order to take account of the relative abundance of cheap, high quality labour (see

Fig. 7.3.
Manufacturing labour
costs ($ per hour, 1995).
Source: Adapted from
Economist (1996).

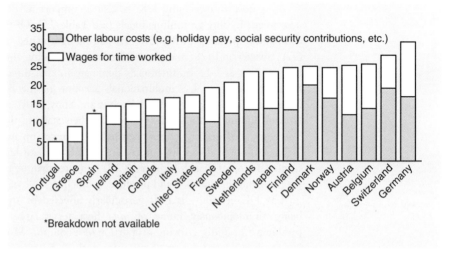

*Breakdown not available

Figure 7.3). Companies like America's ITT ship semi-manufactured components to the region, where they are assembled by local labour into finished products which are then re-exported back to the home market. Such home countries are sometimes termed 'production platforms', which underscores their role as providers of a low-cost input into a global, vertically integrated production process.

Market-oriented multinationals   are those whose internationalization is motivated by the promise of new markets and greater sales; i.e. the internationalization process takes the form of *horizontal* (rather than vertical) *integration* into new geographic markets, with companies gradually switching from exporting (or licensing) to establishing first a sales outlet and finally full production facilities overseas (see Figure 7.4).

Figure 7.5 shows the spectacular divergence in economic performance between the world's major economies which is expected over the next quarter of a century. It shows that currently, in terms of market size, the global economy is dominated by rich industrial countries like the United States, Japan, Germany, France, Italy and the UK. However, by the year 2020, China will be the world's largest market, with India, Indonesia, South Korea, Thailand and Taiwan all moving into the 'top ten'. Therefore it is increasingly likely that market orientated companies will be drawn to these areas.

Extending the product life cycle   A more subtle variation on this theme is that firms may internationalize in order to extend the 'product life cycle' of their products. The underlying thesis is that products have a finite economic life, going through four stages or phases (see Figure 7.6). In the *introduction phase*, the product is slow to win over consumers, who are unfamiliar with the new innovation; many products fail at this stage. But for those which are successful, sales gradually build up in the following *growth phase*, as the product becomes established. At some point, the product reaches *maturity* – there are few new users to win over and most sales are on a replacement basis; the product becomes standardized and competition becomes

Fig. 7.4. Evolution of a
market-orientated
multinational.

Fig. 7.5.   Growth of the global economy, 1992–2020.
Source: World Bank.

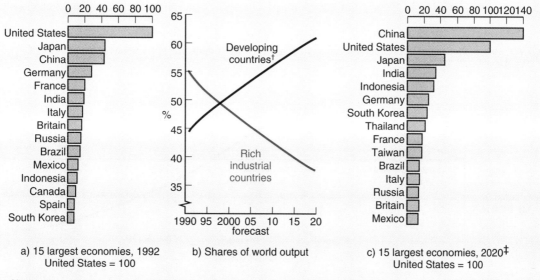

a) 15 largest economies, 1992   b) Shares of world output   c) 15 largest economies, 2020‡
    United States = 100   United States = 100

Notes:
†Including Eastern Europe and former Soviet Union
‡Forecasts assume countries grow at regional rates projected in the World Bank's 'Global Economic Prospect'

Fig. 7.6. Product life cycle.

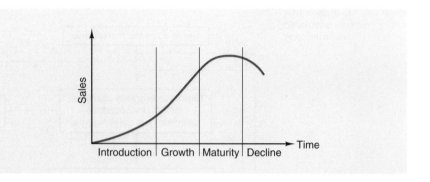

cut-throat. Finally, either because a new substitute challenges the product or because consumer tastes simply move on, the product moves into a period of *decline*, with sales steadily falling. The Sony Walkman provides a useful illustration of this cycle. It was first introduced to a sceptical Japanese market, where it was initially derided as a 'portable cassette player with no speakers and no facility to record tapes'. Gradually, it became established, stimulating a raft of 'me-too' copies by other companies until the market became saturated. Currently, the market is under attack from new formats, including portable CD players and the minidisc system which allows material to be recorded on to small CD-like diskettes.

The link between the product life cycle and internationalization stems from the fact that a product may be at *different stages of its life cycle* in *different geographic markets*, giving rise to changing configurations of supply and demand which variously favour local production, and/or exporting, and/or importing from cheaper overseas suppliers.

Consider Fig. 7.7, which illustrates one possible scenario for a US manufacturer. In *Phase I* (introduction), production is concentrated in the United States, with the

Fig. 7.7. Stages/phases in the product life cycle and the switch from domestic to overseas production.

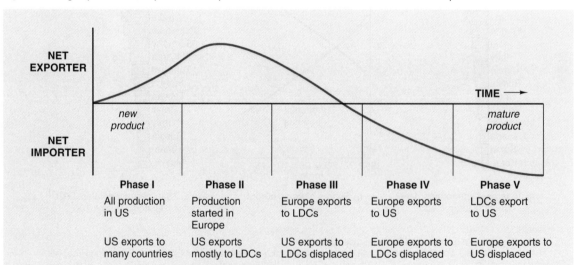

innovating companies exporting to other countries. As the US market matures and production techniques become standardized, production starts up in the expanding, lower cost European market; these new lower-cost producers are able to initially displace imports into Europe from the United States (in *Phase II*) and then increasingly challenge US competitors for a share of developing country markets (in *Phase III*) and finally the US market itself (in *Phase IV*). In due course, however, the technology spreads to the developing world, whose producers are gradually able to take on and out-compete the now higher-cost European companies, first in their own markets (*Phase IV*) and ultimately in the US market as well (*Phase V*). In this way, the product life cycle drives production *out* of the innovating country to lower cost producers overseas.

Advances in enabling technologies   While cost-orientation and market orientation clearly provide important *motives* for investing and producing overseas, the acceleration in the pace of globalization is also intimately tied up with advances in *enabling technologies* which have reduced the costs of doing business across national frontiers. These include:

1. *improved communications*, including cheap air travel, satellite telephone and fax facilities, computers and IT-based communications systems like internet.
2. *the globalization of consumer markets*, through television, video and popular music. These media make it cheaper for established producers to penetrate new markets in developing countries; and
3. *new organizational technologies*, e.g. the rise of the divisional corporate structure based on product or geographic divisions or matrices. This makes managing complex global companies more feasible.

Benefits of producing overseas compared to exporting   One way of exploring the decision by a domestic company to internationalize its production is to consider the advantages of producing at home *vis-à-vis* overseas.

Consider a **market-oriented** company first. By exporting, the company can concentrate production in a single plant at home, reaping the advantages of lower production costs which flow from economies of scale and avoiding the costs of managing an overseas facility. By producing overseas, however, the company can avoid the costs of transporting its products and incurring tariffs. All other things equal, the greater the scope for economies of scale and the higher the costs of managing offshore facilities, the more likely a firm will be to forego internationalization in favour of a large domestic plant; conversely, the smaller the scope for economies of scale and the higher the transports costs and tariffs faced when exporting, the greater the incentive to invest directly in overseas capacity.

Figure 7.8a illustrates these basic principles graphically. It shows the demand (average revenue) and marginal revenue schedules it faces in its *overseas* market. For simplicity, the *marginal cost of production* (whether at home or abroad) is assumed to be constant at C_1 (n.b., with a given fixed cost, this implies that average total costs decline as production increases). The *marginal cost of supplying the overseas market* from a domestic production platform is C_2, where $C_2 - C_1$ is equal to the unit costs of *transport* and *tariffs*. The firm faces *fixed* production costs of F_1

Fig. 7.8.

(a) Demand and marginal revenue in an *overseas* market.
Market-oriented company

(b) Demand and marginal revenue in a *home* market.
Cost-oriented company

if it produces at home and F_2 if it produces abroad (where F_2 is assumed to be greater than F_1, given the higher costs of managing an overseas production facility). Consider its options.

- If the firm *exports to the overseas market*, it will set C_2 equal to marginal revenue, charging a price P_2 and earning profit equal to $P_2ACC_2 - F_1$.
- If the firm *establishes an overseas production facility*, then it will set C_1 equal to marginal revenue, charging a price P_1 and earning profit equal to $P_1BDC_1 - F_2$.

Clearly, the firm's decision rule is:

1. if $P_2ACC_2 - F_1 > P_1BDC_1 - F_2$, then produce at home and export to overseas market;
2. if $P_1BDC_1 - F_2 > P_2ACC_2 - F_1$, then produce overseas.

All other things equal, the *higher the transport costs and / or tariffs levied on exports* to the overseas market (i.e. C_2 compared to C_1), the greater the relative attractiveness of overseas production *vis-à-vis* exporting; similarly, all other things equal, the *lower the relative fixed costs of producing overseas* (i.e. F_2 compared to F_1), the more attractive overseas production. The gap $F_2 - F_1$ will be reduced by advances in enabling technologies which, as we have noted, cut the costs of doing business across national frontiers.

Hence, the decision for a market oriented firm to locate overseas rather than export hinges critically on the transport and tariff costs of serving overseas markets and the relative fixed costs of production. The greater the former, and the smaller any gap as regards the latter ($F_2 > F_1$), the more favourable the situation is to multinational activity.

The same diagram can also be reinterpreted to illustrate the decision facing a **cost-oriented** multinational. In this case (Fig. 7.8b), the demand and marginal revenue schedules are drawn for the *home market*. C_2 is now the company's marginal cost of producing at home for its domestic market, while C_1 represents the marginal cost of supplying the home market from an overseas production platform and shipping back to the home market. Despite the costs of transport and tariffs, it is assumed here that overseas production is subject to lower supply costs, for example because of lower labour costs.

- If the firm *produces at home*, it sets marginal production cost C_2 equal to marginal revenue, charging a price P_2 and earning profit $P_2ACC_2 - F_1$.
- If the firm *produces abroad*, it sets marginal supply cost C_1 equal to marginal revenue, charging a price P_1 and earning profit $P_1BDC_1 - F_2$.

Its decision rules are now:

1. if $P_2ACC_2 - F_1 > P_1BDC_1 - F_2$, then produce at home;
2. if $P_1BDC_1 - F_2 > P_2ACC_2 - F_1$, then produce overseas and export to home market.

All other things equal, the *lower the relative marginal costs of supplying from overseas* (i.e. C_1 compared to C_2), the greater the relative attractiveness of overseas production *vis-à-vis* domestic production; similarly, all other things equal, the *lower the relative fixed costs of producing overseas* (i.e. F_2 compared to F_1) the more attractive overseas production.

Hence, the decision for a cost-oriented firm to serve its home market from an offshore production facility rather than producing at home hinges on the relative variable costs of overseas production and relative fixed costs. The greater the (variable) cost discrepancy in favour of overseas supply, and the smaller any gap as regards overseas fixed costs compared to domestic fixed costs (i.e. F_2 compared to F_1), the more favourable the situation is to multinational activity.

It should be remembered that labour cost (an important variable cost) can be an important determinant of production location even within major industrialized countries. For example in 1998, the US Department of Labour calculated that the hourly compensation costs of production workers in the UK were $14.19 in the UK as compared to US ($17.74), France ($19.34), Japan ($21.04), Sweden ($24.56) and Germany ($31.87) . The 1,500 German subsidiaries operating in the UK see the relatively low labour costs in the UK as giving them an attractive production advantage which they can exploit by exporting their UK-produced goods back to Germany and to other European countries. (*Financial Times* 1998b).

Location and internalization

The above explanations of internationalization are, however, only partial. They fail to explain why cost-oriented companies do not simply import the inputs they need from independent producers in low-cost countries rather than integrating backwards; similarly, they do not explain why market-oriented companies should operate their own production facilities in foreign markets rather than licensing local manufacturers to produce their products. A full explanation needs to account for both 'location' (i.e. why a good is produced in *two or more* countries rather than simply one) and 'internalization' (i.e. why production in different locations is done by the *same* firm rather than different firms).

Dunning (1993) attempted to synthesize different theoretical perspectives on multinationals with the evidence provided by case studies. He concluded that companies will only become involved in overseas investment and production when the following conditions are all satisfied:

1. companies possess an 'ownership-specific' advantage over firms in the host country (e.g. assets which are internal to the firm, including organization structure, human capital, financial resources, size and market power);
2. these advantages are best exploited by the firm itself, rather than selling them to foreign firms. In other words, due to market imperfections (e.g. uncertainty), multinationals choose to bypass the market and 'internalize' the use of ownership-specific advantages via vertical and horizontal integration (such internalization reduces transactions costs in the presence of market imperfections); and
3. it must be more profitable for the multinational to exploit its ownership-specific advantages in an overseas market than in its domestic market – i.e. there must additionally exist 'location specific' factors which favour overseas production (e.g., special economic or political factors, attractive markets in terms of size, growth or structure, low 'psychic' or 'cultural' distance, etc.).

The decisions of multinationals to produce abroad are, therefore, determined by a mixture of motives – ownership specific, locational , and internationalization factors – as noted above. These are also summarized in a more effective way in Table 7.7.

Honda case study However, to understand the complexity of motives which underlie multinational activity it may be helpful to consider an actual example, namely Honda Europe. Figure 7.9 shows the Honda motorcycle network in Europe together with its outside supply links. Honda is very much a multinational company with a *transnationality index* of over 50%. It began by exporting motorcycles to Europe, but this was quickly followed by its first European overseas affiliate in 1962. This affiliate, Honda Benelux NV (Belgium) was set up in order to establish strong bonds with European customers as well as to provide a 'learning' opportunity before Honda brought its automobile production to Europe. Figure 7.9 shows that, by the late 1990s, Honda's operations have widened significantly, with its affiliates in Germany acting as its main European regional headquarters. Honda Deutschland Gmbh coordinates the production and marketing side, while Honda R&D Europe is engaged in research, engineering and designing for all the affiliates in Europe.

Honda's key *assembly* affiliates are Honda Industriale SpA (Italy) which is wholly owned, and Montessa Honda SA (Spain) which is majority owned (88%). These companies were originally designed to concentrate on the assembly of specific types of motorcycle model appropriate to the different European locations in order to benefit from various economies of scale. At the same time, each assembler exported its own model to the other Honda locations in Europe in order to gain economies in joint production and marketing; in other words any given model is produced in one location, but a full range of models is offered for sale in all locations. Finally, in the international context , Honda's European models are also exported to its subsidiaries in the US, Brazil and Japan, while its European network imports large and medium-sized motorcycles from its US and Brazil affiliates.

As far as motorcycle parts are concerned, engines and key parts were initially

Table 7.7. Types of international production: some determining factors.

Types of international production	(O) Ownership advantages (the 'why' of MNE activity)	(L) Location advantages (the 'where' of production)	(I) Internationalization (the 'how' of involvement)	Strategic goals of MNEs	Illustration of types of activity that favour MNEs
Natural resource seeking	Capital, technology, access to markets; complementary assets; size and negotiating strengths	Possession of natural resources and related transport and communications infrastructure; tax and other incentives	To ensure stability of supplies at right price; control markets	To gain privileged access to resources *vis-à-vis* competitors	(a) Oil, copper, bauxite, bananas, pineapples, cocoa, hotels (b) Export processing, labour intensive products or processes
Market seeking	Capital, technology, information, management and organizational skills; surplus R&D and other capacity; economies of scale; ability to generate brand loyalty	Material and labour costs; market size and characteristics; government policy (e.g. with respect to regulations and to import controls, investment incentives, etc.)	Wish to reduce transaction or information costs, buyer ignorance, or uncertainty, etc; to protect property rights	To protect existing markets, counteract behaviour of competitors; to preclude rivals or potential rivals from gaining new markets	Computers, pharmaceuticals, motor vehicles, cigarettes, processed foods, airline services
Efficiency seeking (a) of products (b) of processes	As above, but also access to markets; economies of scope, geographical diversification, and international sourcing of inputs	(a) Economies of product specialization and concentration (b) Low labour costs; incentives to local production by host governments	(a) As for second category plus gains from economies of common common governance (b) The economies of vertical integration	As part of regional or global product rationalization and/or to gain advantages of process specialization	(a) Motor vehicles, electrical appliances, business services, some R&D (b) Consumer electronics, textiles and clothing, cameras, pharmaceuticals
Strategic asset seeking	Any of first three that offer opportunities for synergy with existing assets	Any of first three that offer technology, markets and other assets in which firm is deficient	Economies of common governance; improved competitive or strategic advantage; to reduce or spread risks	To strengthen global innovatory or production competitiveness; to gain new product lines or markets	Industries that record a high ratio of fixed to overhead costs and which offer substantial economies of scale or synergy
Textile and distribution (import and export)	Market access; products to distribute	Source of inputs and local markets; need to be near customers; after-sales servicing, etc.	Need to protect quality of inputs; need to ensure sales outlets and to avoid under-performance or misrepresentation by foreign agents	Either as entry to new markets or as part of regional or global marketing strategy	A variety of goods, particularly those requiring contact with subcontractors and final consumers
Support services	Experience of clients in home countries	Availability of markets, particularly those of 'lead' clients	Various (see above categories)	As part of regional or global product or geographical diversification	(a) Accounting, advertising, banking, producer goods (b) Where spatial linkages are essential (e.g. airlines and shipping)

Source: Adapted from Dunning (1993).

supplied from Japan. However in 1985 Honda acquired a 25% stake in Peugeot Motorcycles SA and began producing small engines in France for scooters and mopeds. These engines were then supplied to its Italian and Spanish assemblers of scooters and mopeds. Following this, medium-sized engines began to be produced in Honda Italia Industriale, both for its own models and for Montessa Honda, while the latter began producing frames and other parts locally. Large-sized engines were still, however, supplied from Japan.

This study of Honda illustrates the complex set of motives underlying multinational activity which were discussed earlier. The traditional technical economies of scale were exploited to reduce average costs as were the more market-based advantages from producing within the EU with its 370 million consumers. In addition, the improved communications within the EU and the rise of more sophisticated corporate structures enabled Honda to integrate operations both

Fig. 7.9. Honda: EU motorcycle networks and supply links.
Source: UNCTAD (1996), p. 102.

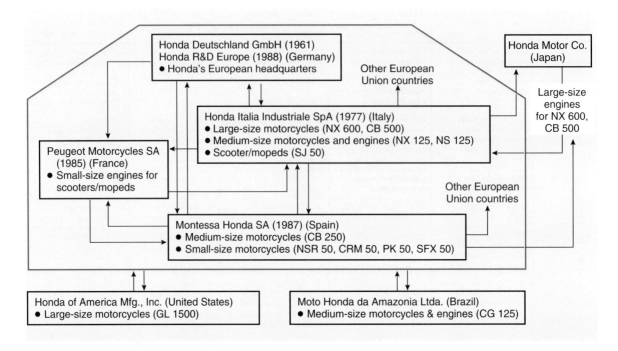

horizontally, through affiliate specialization in particular models, and vertically, through specialization of affiliates in the production of parts. Honda was able to capitalize on its well-known ownership-specific advantages of excellent quality engineering and sound business skills, and to combine this with an intelligent strategy for locating production within the largest consumer market in the world. The Honda experience also helps to illustrate the nature of multinational *inter-firm* activity within a sophisticated market dominated by product differentiation.

The impact of multinationals on the UK economy

The UK is unusually exposed to the influence of multinationals. As noted above, the UK is an important *home* country of multinationals, with the majority of its top companies operating overseas subsidiaries. By the end of the 1990s, official records show that the UK was the home for 1,059 parent corporations which operated internationally. Since the register does not give a complete picture of the involvement of smaller companies, we can take this to be an underestimate of the total number although it provides a useful guideline as to the number of medium to large UK multinational companies. However, we can supplement this data by using the flows of foreign direct investment from the UK as a measure of UK's multinational involvement in the world's economy. Here we find that during the second half of the 1990s the UK accounted for 28% of total EU outflows of FDI, ahead of Germany and France.

The UK is also a major *host* country for foreign multinationals. For example, in 1997, although foreign-owned businesses in agriculture, manufacturing and distribution accounted for only 0.6% of total UK enterprises, they accounted for as much as 11% of total UK employment and 23% of total UK turnover. Three countries, namely the US, Germany and Japan, had a particularly strong presence in the UK, accounting for over 60% of all foreign multinational employment and turnover in the UK. The US had, by far, the most dominating presence in the UK, accounting for some 42% of all foreign multinational employment in the UK and 37% of all foreign multinational turnover in the UK. In manufacturing, the presence of foreign multinationals is even more dominant, accounting for 19% of UK manufacturing employment and 26% of manufacturing net output (Duffus and Gooding 1997).

What are the implications for the UK economy of such openness to multinationals? Advocates of multinationals argue that the economy benefits from their activities, with outward and inward foreign direct investment accelerating industrial restructuring and ensuring the most efficient allocation of resources. On the other hand, critics argue that outward foreign direct investment by UK-owned multinationals denies the economy sorely-needed investment and jobs, while the influx of foreign multinationals undermines the nation's economic sovereignty.

An economic cost-benefit appraisal of multinational activity

It is clear that there are strongly contrasting views of multinationals. However, such divergent views are often coloured by implicit assumptions about the nature of the multinationals involved and, as noted in the introduction, international companies are so heterogeneous in their nature that generalizations are both difficult and potentially dangerous. For example, the precise balance of economic costs and benefits that a foreign multinational imposes on the UK economy depends upon:

1. how the multinational establishes itself in the UK (e.g. via a greenfield site investment or the takeover of locally-owned productive assets, etc.);
2. whether funds used for the investment are raised locally or 'imported';
3. the function of the multinational (e.g. whether it is cost- or market-oriented); and
4. characteristics of host and parent economies (e.g. the extent to which there is 'culture dissonance').

Fig. 7.10.

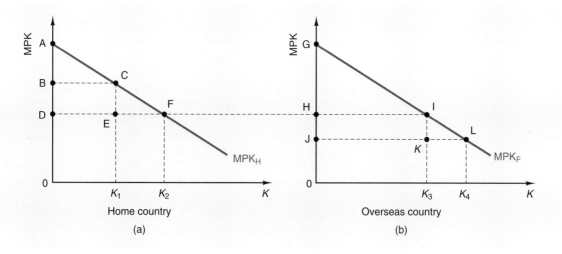

Home country
(a)

Overseas country
(b)

These costs and benefits can be explored in more detail under six main headings. Consider each in turn.

Foreign direct investment and economic welfare

Direct investment by a foreign multinational is widely regarded as an unambiguous improvement in economic welfare. Figures 7.10a and 7.10b illustrate the potential economic gains from cross-border investment by multinationals in search of the highest marginal rate of return on capital. These figures show the marginal product of capital in both the home country (MPK_H) and overseas (MPK_F) respectively. Initially, in the absence of multinational activity, capital is relatively less abundant in the home country and with a capital stock, K_1, the marginal product of capital is B. GDP is given by the area under the curve, $0ACK_1$, of which $0BCK_1$ is the reward to capital and BAC is the reward to labour. Similarly, in the overseas sector, the capital stock is K_4, giving rise to a marginal product of capital equal to J and a GDP of $0GLK_4$, of which $0JLK_4$ is the reward to capital and JGL the reward to labour.

Given this disparity between the marginal productivity of capital in different countries, profit-maximizing multinationals will reallocate capital from overseas to the home country, increasing the capital stock from K_1 to K_2, while reducing it overseas from K_4 to K_3. GDP in the home country will rise to $0AFK_2$, an increase of K_1CFK_2. GDP overseas will fall to $0GIK_3$, a reduction of K_3ILK_4. However, remember that a proportion of GDP is a reward to capital and, in the case of multinational investment in the home country, this profit will be repatriated overseas. Hence, for the home country, the net gain from the inward investment is only EFC (the reward to labour), with K_1EFK_2 being repatriated by the foreign multinationals. Conversely, overseas, the loss of GDP (K_3ILK_4) is offset by the repatriated profit K_1EFK_2. Since K_1K_2 (the increase in the capital stock in the home country) is equal to K_3K_4 (the decrease in the capital stock overseas), and D (new marginal product of capital at home) is equal to H (new marginal product of capital overseas), then area K_1EFK_2 must exceed area K_3ILK_4. Thus, the home country benefits as a result of the multinational activity (by the amount of the value-added by its domestic labour force) and overseas producers gain (because the reward from the extra production generated by the use of their capital exceeds its opportunity cost in the overseas market).

This conventional analysis of the impact of multinational investment implicitly assumes, however, that the investment constitutes a reallocation of productive capital from overseas to the host country. In practice, this assumption may be violated in *two* ways.

First, multinationals frequently finance overseas investment either from the retained profits earned by their existing productive or sales operations in the target country or by raising the capital on the local capital market. In both cases, the multinational's investment may simply displace domestic investment that would otherwise have taken place. Figure 7.11 illustrates this dilemma.

An investment financed by a capital inflow from the parent multinational overseas bypasses the domestic market for loanable funds, leaving the balance of domestic savings and investment unchanged at I_2, with rate of interest r_0. However, raising funds locally to finance the investment increases the demand for loanable funds (from D to D′), leading to a rise in interest rates (from r_0 to r_1) and the crowding out of domestic investment (which falls from I_2 to I_1).

Secondly, multinational investment more frequently involves the takeover of existing assets, rather than greenfield site investment in new plant and equipment. Table 7.8 gives details of the largest foreign acquisitions that have taken place in the

Fig. 7.11. Investment financed from overseas versus investment financed locally.

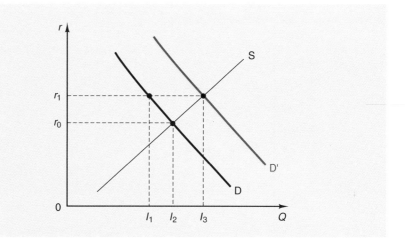

last three years. In this case, the total capital stock of the host country is unaffected by the foreign direct investment, with the ownership of existing assets simply being transferred from local investors to the foreign multinational. Figure 7.12 gives an impression of the scale of such takeover activity, in both the UK and overseas markets. Note here that UK *domestic* refers to acquisitions by UK companies in the UK; UK *outward* refers to UK companies acquiring overseas companies; UK *inward* refers to overseas companies acquiring UK companies.

Technology transfer It is widely held that multinational activity by more efficient foreign multinationals promotes technology transfer to the benefit of domestic companies. For example, when Nissan established a car plant in the north-east of England, it demanded much higher standards of UK component suppliers than the incumbent national producers like Ford and Rover. Nissan's engineers assisted these supplying companies to upgrade their production processes in order to meet their requirements. The result was the creation of a strong positive externality: the international competitiveness of the UK car supply industry was strengthened and, as a direct consequence, the quality of the inputs to domestic auto makers improved.

This so-called 'technology transfer' is clearly maximized by such 'direct linkages' with domestic suppliers, which occurs when incoming multinationals like Sony, Nissan, Honda and Toyota work closely with domestic suppliers to raise the standard of

Table 7.8 Largest foreign takeovers announced in 1997 of UK companies valued at over $1bn (£610m).

Target company	Sector	Acquiring company	Sector	Acquirer's nationality
BAT Industries – Financial	Insurance	Zurich Versicherungs	Insurance	Switzerland
Mercury Asset/Management	Investment	Merrill Lynch	Investment	US
Redland plc	Rubber/misc.	La farge SA	Stone/clay	France
Makro Holdings – European	Retail	Metro Group	Real estate	Germany
Perkins Engines Group	Machinery	Caterpillar Inc	Machinery	US
ICI – white pigment	Chemical	E. I. du Pont de Nemours	Chemical	US
Vendome Luxury Group	Misc. manuf.	Richemont (Rembrant grp)	Tobacco	Switzerland

Source: UNCTAD (1998), pp. 315–16.

Fig. 7.12.   Acquisition activity.
Sources: Amdata; *Business Briefing* (various).

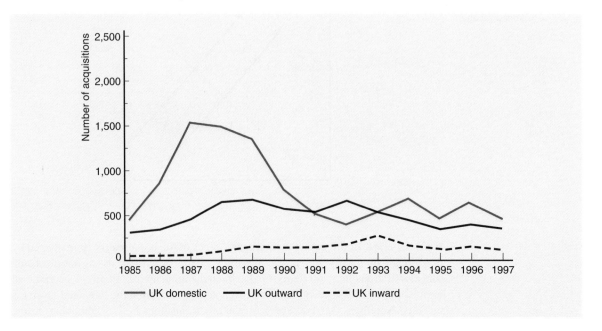

UK-produced inputs. There are, however, also positive indirect 'demonstration effects' which may promote technology transfer. At its simplest, these relate to attempts by less efficient local producers to imitate the superior processes and organization advantages of the foreign interlopers.

There are, however, clear limitations to technology transfer. Most obviously, one of the most powerful drivers for foreign investment is the advantage to a multinational of internalizing an ownership-specific advantage. Such considerations militate against the notion that a foreign multinational will willingly share the technologically-based sources of its competitive advantage over local rivals. Moreover, in the case of Japanese multinationals, their historical advantage was built upon close relationships with Japanese suppliers. For example, the big four Japanese motorcycle companies (Honda, Yamaha, Suzuki and Kawasaki) rely heavily on a very limited number of domestic suppliers (e.g. Bridgestone for tyres, Nippon Denso for electronic components, etc.). Early dissatisfaction with UK suppliers with regard to quality and reliability of deliveries has led to a number of these Japanese suppliers following their major customers into the European market, thereby reducing the potential scope for technology transfer via linkages with local suppliers.

A final problem relates to the issue of cultural dissonance. The psychic distance between US and UK companies is relatively small. Both share a broadly common culture, a common language and they have a reasonably high level of mutual understanding. The success of multinationals from, say, Japan or other parts of East and South-East Asia is built on a very different set of social and cultural values, which are not easily transferable to the UK setting. Companies like Sony, Nissan and Honda have all reported difficulties in establishing Japanese-style work practices, which many economists regard as an integral part of that country's corporate success. The operation of 'just-in-time' (or 'kanban') production processes and 'quality circles' rely on employee loyalty to his/her company, which in Japan is reinforced by lifetime employment and a shared set of values which emphasizes collectivism. Such techniques are much less easily transposed to western cultures with their stress on individualism and self-determination.

Balance of payments As noted above, the positive balance of payments impact of multinational activity depends, in the first instance at least, on whether the funds are imported (a capital inflow) or raised locally. Even if the capital is imported, however, the ultimate balance of payments effect may still be negative. At its simplest, multinationals invest in productive facilities overseas because they believe that the net present value of the profits they will be able to repatriate exceeds the capital investment they will make. It follows that, if a multinational invests rationally, the initial capital inflow must be at least matched by the net present value of future outflows on current account (i.e. net payments of interest, profit and dividend abroad). In crude money terms, the total value of the repatriated returns to capital will dwarf the original investment made.

Moreover, the speed with which an initial capital inflow is reversed by outflows on the current account depends critically on the function of the multinational. In the case of a market-oriented company intent on 'jumping tariffs', the multinational may attempt to import part-finished products, using cheap local labour to assemble the final product. Volkswagen was accused of this technique during the 1970s in Brazil, when it established a manufacturing plant in which workers assembled 'complete knock-down kits' into finished cars which were sold, tariff-free, in the Brazilian market. The impact on the current account was strongly negative, with visible imports being inflated by the cost of the kits and invisible imports being increased by the repatriated profits. Most countries (including Brazil) now have extensive 'rules of origin' to prevent such 'screwdriving operations' being used by multinationals as a device for evading tariffs.

In Britain's case, however, inward foreign direct investment has historically been generally outweighed by higher outward capital flows. Table 7.9 shows that both inward and outward investment fell during the 1990–92 recession. During the subsequent recovery, inward investment has picked up much more strongly than outward investment, so that the traditional relationship between the two has been reversed. Insofar as the resumption of economic growth in Britain came earlier than in continental Europe, making inward investment attractive to foreign companies strapped for investment opportunities in their home markets, inward investment may fall back as national business cycles come more into line with each other. Table 7.9 also highlights the strongly positive contribution that net earnings on overseas assets have made to Britain's current account over the last two decades (N.B. net interest, profits and dividends also includes interest received on portfolio investments), but shows the sharp decline resulting from the surge in inward investment after 1992.

Employment Faced with persistently high levels of unemployment in many European countries, it is perhaps understandable that so many states should court foreign multinationals in the belief that their investments will create local employment. Recent investments by major Japanese and US multinationals have, for example, been accompanied by strong competition on the part of national and regional governments in the EU to attract the investment in the hope of generating work. The relationship between

Table 7.9 The impact of multinationals on the UK's balance of payments.

	Direct inward investment	Direct outward investment	Net interest, profit and dividends
1976	1,853	2,419	1,580
1977	2,546	2,399	265
1978	1,962	3,520	808
1979	3,030	5,809	1,201
1980	4,355	4,867	−182
1981	2,932	6,005	1,251
1982	3,027	4,091	1,460
1983	3,386	5,147	2,830
1984	−181	6,042	4,344
1985	4,504	8,430	2,298
1986	5,837	11,849	4,622
1987	9,449	19,147	3,757
1988	12,006	20,883	4,424
1989	18,567	21,503	3,388
1990	18,520	10,544	1,630
1991	9,032	8,841	320
1992	8,513	10,845	5,059
1993	46,818	17,135	13,512
1994	31,836	16,412	−3,561
1995	14,400	26,900	1,680
1996	21,075	28,213	2,198
1997	22,200	36,200	1,205

Source: ONS, *Economic Trends* (various).

government regional assistance and the presence of foreign multinational activity is dealt with more specifically in Chapter 11 on Regional and Urban Policy. The ultimate employment effect of multinational activity is, however, rather more complex. The net employment effect is a function of three factors:

1. direct job creation, which depends on the size of the foreign–owned subsidiary and the labour (or capital) intensity of its production processes;
2. indirect job creation, which depends on linkages with local suppliers and the value-added by domestic factors of production; and
3. the 'Trojan horse' effect, namely the displacement of domestic incumbents by the more efficient multinational company, which depends upon the latter's market power.

In practice, it is difficult to gauge the net employment effect of multinational activity in the UK. There is no question that direct job creation has been significant, as witnessed by the eagerness of local authorities in areas of high unemployment to woo potential investors to their region. The UK government estimates that nearly 500,000 jobs have been created by overseas businesses in the country between 1979 and 1998. However, indirect job creation (like technology transfer) is clearly limited by the extent to which foreign multinationals rely on imported intermediate products (e.g. inputs shipped from the parent company for local assembly). Under pressure from the EU, Japanese multinationals in the UK, for example, are attempting to raise the percentage of 'local' (i.e. EU) content in finished products to 80%, but at present the average is only 67%. Finally, to the extent that (by definition) foreign multinationals enjoy ownership-specific advantages over domestic rivals, their success is likely to be at the expense of the declining market share enjoyed by the existing incumbents – direct (and indirect) jobs gains may thus be offset by induced job losses in the adversely affected companies. The difficulty of estimating this Trojan horse effect in the UK is that the foreign multinational's output may compete with (and displace) exports from other countries, rather than with domestic production; by the same token, part or all of the multinational's output may be exported (e.g. to other states in the EU). Hence, the UK may enjoy the direct job gains, while the Trojan horse losses (which could well be larger) may fall on third countries, inside or outside the EU. In recent years, certain EU governments, notably France, have expressed precisely this fear, suspecting that the Japanese-led renaissance of the UK's consumer electronics and car industries will be at the expense of French, German and Italian workers.

In the UK , the Trojan horse effect is seen when foreign multinationals, often with UK government subsidies, create employment in the UK but at a high cost per worker and by displacing indigenous companies. For example, it has been calculated in the late 1990s that the subsidy given to the Korean Lucky Goldstar (LG) electronics company to locate production in South Wales amounted to £40,000 per job created – while indigenous investment could generate more high quality jobs for a much lower subsidy of between £2,000 and £3,000 per job (*Financial Times* 1998b).

Industrial structure The ownership-specific advantage often enjoyed by foreign multinationals is their market size and power. One consequence of this is, inevitably, the displacement of less efficient domestic producers. Under certain circumstances, it is sometimes argued that foreign direct investment may result in the truncation of the host economy (i.e. the gradual loss of those economic sectors critical to self-sustained growth) and its subsequent dependence on overseas multinationals for continued growth and employment. *In extremis*, it is sometimes claimed that the widespread presence of foreign multinationals may lead to a loss of economic sovereignty on the part of the host country's government. The counter argument is that, at least in the case of the UK, foreign direct investment has positively benefited the UK's economic structure, channelling funds into those sectors (e.g. high technology manufacturing, car production, etc.) in which the economy enjoys a comparative advantage and thereby accelerating economic restructuring.

Taxation Multinationals are widely accused by governments of arranging intra-company transactions in order to minimize their tax liabilities, effectively forcing countries to compete to provide the lowest tax regime. Consider a simplified example in which a multinational's production is vertically integrated, with operations in two countries. Basic manufacture takes place in country A and final assembly and sale in country B (see Table 7.10). In country A, the corporate tax rate is 25%, while in country B it is 50%. Suppose the company's costs (inputs, labour, etc.) in country A are $40m and it produces intermediate products with a market value of $50m; if it were to sell these intermediate products in the *open market*, it would declare a profit of $10m in country A, incurring a tax liability of $2.5m in that country.

However, suppose the products are actually intended for the parent company's subsidiary in country B. In Scenario 1, the 'transfer price' (i.e. the internal price used by the company to calculate profits in different countries) is set at the market price of $50m in country A for the intermediate products which are now to be 'shipped' to country B for incorporation into the final product. The operation in country B incurs additional costs of $40m, after which the final product is sold in country B for $100m; thus the

Table 7.10 Multinational tax avoidance.

$m	Scenario 1		Scenario 2	
	Country A	Country B	Country A	Country B
Costs	40	90	40	100
Sales	50	100	60	100
Profit	10	10	20	0
Tax liability	2.5	5	5	0
Total tax	7.5		5	

subsidiary will declare a profit of $10m and incur a tax liability of $5m. The company as a whole will face a total tax liability of $7.5m in countries A and B taken together.

Consider an alternative scenario (Scenario 2), in which the company sets a transfer price *above* the market price for the intermediate products manufactured in the low-tax country, A. With a transfer price of $60m rather than $50m and the same costs of $40m, the subsidiary in country A incurs a higher tax liability (25% of $20m), but this is more than offset by the lower (in fact, zero) tax liability incurred by the subsidiary in country B. Because the latter is now recording its total costs (including the cost of the intermediate products 'bought' from the subsidiary in country A) as being $100m rather than $90m, its profits and tax liability fall to zero. As a result, the total tax liability faced by the company on its international operations is only $5m, rather than $7.5m.

The basic issue is that the multinational has earned a total profit of $20m on its vertically integrated operation; i.e. $100m actual sales revenue in B minus $80m costs in A + B. However, by setting transfer prices on intra-company sales and purchases of intermediate products appropriately, the company can 'move' this profit to the lowest tax country, thereby denying the higher tax country (in this case, country B) the tax revenue to which it is entitled. Such transfer pricing can, of course, only succeed when there is no active market for the intermediate products being traded. If the tax authorities in country B can refer to an open market price for the intermediate product, the inflated transfer price being paid can be identified. However, to the extent that many multinationals internalize cross-border operations because they have ownership-specific advantages (e.g. control of a specific raw material or technology), it may be that comparable intermediate products are not available on the open market. For this reason, high-tax countries may find they lose tax revenues to lower-tax centres as business becomes increasingly globalized. This creates, in turn, an incentive for countries to 'compete' for multinational tax revenues by offering low tax rates; the result of such competition is a transfer of income from national governments to the shareholders of multinational companies.

Conclusion

Multinationals play a more influential role in the UK economy than in any other major, developed country in the world. Most of the household-name companies in Britain – BP, ICI, Ford, Kellogg, Heinz, Cadbury – are multinationals. In the past, companies became multinational to secure resources and markets or to overcome the transport costs associated with exporting. Increasingly, multinationals are becoming genuinely global, performing different stages of an integrated productive process in different countries to exploit natural and government-induced differences in factor costs as we saw in the case of Honda. There is a fierce debate about the benefits and costs of multinational activity for individual economies like the UK. What is clear, however, is that the growth of multinationals will continue into the next century and that an increasing proportion of UK companies will do the majority of their business overseas, while an ever-higher share of UK production will be controlled by foreign companies.

Indeed, it is already becoming increasingly meaningless to think of companies as 'British' or 'foreign'. Is Ford, an 'American' company which designs and builds cars in the UK, 'foreign'? Is Attock Oil, a 'British' oil exploration and production company which operates only in North America and SE Asia, 'British'? As companies become increasingly global in nature, the convention of labelling a company's nationality by reference to the nationality of its controlling shareholders will become redundant. Imagine the Ford Motor Company of the 21st Century, owned by Japanese shareholders, run by an American chief executive, producing components across the EU and assembling them in Turkey for sale in Russia. In what sense is such a multinational 'American', 'Japanese' or even 'European'? The multinational of the future is likely to be genuinely 'stateless'. Already the trend towards statelessness is well underway and the implications of this phenomenon are liable to be profound.

Key points

- A 'multinational' is a company which owns or controls production or service facilities in more than one country.
- There are some 54,000 multinational companies, the sales revenue of which amounts to around 31% of world GDP. Only 14 nation states have a GDP greater than the annual turnover of Exxon, Ford or General Motors.
- Multinationals account for around 30% of GDP in the UK and almost half of manufacturing employment.
- Foreign multinationals account for 11% of UK employment and 23% of UK turnover. The US dominates the scene, accounting for 42% of all foreign multinational employment in the UK and 37% of all foreign multinational turnover.
- Successful multinational activity from the home base usually depends on the possession of 'ownership-specific' advantages over firms in the host country, together with 'location-specific' advantages which favour overseas production.
- Cost-oriented multinationals mainly focus on reducing costs of production via overseas production (often via vertical integration); market-oriented multinationals mainly focus on easier sales access to overseas markets via overseas production (often via horizontal integration).
- Being both a 'home' country to (UK) multinationals as well as a 'host' to foreign multinationals, results in substantial flows of outward and inward foreign direct investment (fdi).
- The costs and benefits of multinational activity for the UK (or indeed any country) can usefully be assessed under six main headings:
  - (i) fdi and economic welfare
  - (ii) technology transfer
  - (iii) balance of payments
  - (iv) employment
  - (v) industrial structure
  - (vi) taxation

References and further reading

Buckley, P. J. (1992) *New dimensions in international business*, Edward Elgar.

Cleeve, E. (1994) Transnational corporations and internationalisation: a critical review, *British Review of Economic Issues*, Vol 16, No 40.

Crum, R. and Davies, S. (1991) *Multinationals*, Heinemann Educational.

Dicken, P. (1998) *Global shift: transforming the world economy*, 3rd edn, Paul Chapman.

Duffus, G. and Gooding, P. (1997) Globalisation: scope, issues and statistics, *Economic Trends*, No 528, November.

Dunning, J. (1996) Globalisation, foreign direct investment and economic development, *Economics and Business Education*, Vol IV, No 3.

Dunning, J. H. (1993) *Multinational enterprises and the global economy*, Addison-Wesley.

Economist (1996) *Economic Indicators*, 27 April.

Financial Times (1998a) *FT 500*.

Financial Times (1998b) West-Midlands popular as manufacturing base, *Reporting Britain*, 16 July.

Financial Times (1998b) Regions take an inward look at a growing problem, 21 May.

Greenaway, D. (1993) Trade and foreign direct investment, *European Economy*, No 52.

Kene, P. B. (1994) *The international economy*, Cambridge University Press.

Kobrun, S. J. (1991) An empirical analysis of the determinants of global integration, *Strategic Management Journal*, Vol 12.

Norman, G. (1995) Japanese foreign direct investment: the impact on the European Union, in N. Healey (ed.), *The economics of the new Europe: from Community to Union*, Routledge.

Thomsen, S. (1992) Integration through globalisation, *National Westminster Bank Quarterly Review*, August.

UNCTAD (1996) *World Investment Report: investment, trade and international policy arrangements*, Geneva.

UNCTAD (1998) *World Investment Report 1998 – trends and determinants*, Geneva.

Winters, L. (1991) GATT: the Uruguay Round, *The Economic Review*, Vol 9, No 2, November.

Young, S., Hood, N. and Hamill, J. (1988) *Foreign multinationals and the British economy*, Croom Helm.

Chapter 8

Privatization and deregulation

Public ownership of industries is now in retreat throughout the world as governments privatize. Since the early eighties the UK has provided a model of privatization which has been influential in policy making, both in other industrial countries and in developing countries. The collapse of the Soviet Union and the Eastern European Communist regimes has led to privatization programmes which totally dwarf those of the UK. This chapter summarizes the original case for nationalization and considers the arguments for and against privatization. There is also a discussion of the case for regulating the activities of the privatized companies as well as the contrary view in favour of less regulation (i.e. deregulation).

Nature and importance

Public (or state) ownership of industry in the UK has mainly been through *public corporations*, which are trading bodies whose chairpersons and board members are appointed by the Secretary of State concerned. These *nationalized industries*, as they are often called, are quite separate from government itself. They run their businesses without close supervision but within the constraints imposed by government policy. These constraints include limits to the amounts they can borrow and therefore invest and may also include limits to the wages and salaries they can offer. Not all public corporations are, however, nationalized industries. There are some public corporations, such as the BBC, which are *not* classed as nationalized industries.

Public ownership can also take the form of direct share ownership in private sector companies. So, for example, after the collapse of the DAF motor vehicle group in 1993, the Netherlands government provided 50 per cent of the equity and loan capital for DAF Trucks N.V. which took over some of the failed group's activities. In a similar way the UK government held a majority holding in British Petroleum for many years prior to its complete privatization in 1987.

Privatization in the UK has reduced the number of nationalized industries to a mere handful of enterprises accounting for less than 2% of UK GDP, around 3% of investment and under 1.5% of employment. By contrast, in 1979 the then nationalized industries were a very significant part of the economy, producing 9% of GDP, being responsible for 11.5% of investment and employing 7.3% of all UK employees. The scale of the transfer of public sector businesses since 1979 to private ownership is further indicated in Table 8.1 (p. 164), which lists the businesses privatized by sector.

Reasons for nationalization

Looking back from the perspective of the late 1990s, the reader may well ask why the state ever became so heavily involved in the production of goods and services. Yet between the 1940s and the 1980s this was one of the most contentious issues in British politics, both between the major parties and within the Labour Party. The first post-war Labour government (1945–51) achieved a major programme of nationalization which was opposed by the Conservative Party at the time but broadly left in place by subsequent Conservative governments. The apparent consensus on the scale of the nationalized industries was, however, broken after 1979 as Conservative governments under Mrs Thatcher developed the policy of privatization. We now consider a range of arguments used in favour of nationalization.

Political   The political case for nationalization centred on the suggestion that private ownership of productive assets creates a concentration of power over resources which is intolerable in a democracy. Until 1995 the Labour Party appeared to embrace this idea in Clause 4 of its constitution which promised public ownership of the means of production, distribution and exchange. The founders of the Labour Party saw public ownership as a necessary step towards full scale socialism and one which would aid economic planning. This developed into a policy of nationalizing the 'commanding heights' of the economy which the 1945 Labour government identified as the transport industries, the power industries and the iron and steel industries; the Post Office had always been state owned and at that time also included telephones. There were always many in the Labour Party who were opposed to a literal interpretation of Clause 4 and saw that there were other means of regulating economic activity besides outright public ownership. By the 1990s, after the collapse of the Eastern European socialist economies, there were few remaining advocates of economic planning and the Labour Party abandoned the old Clause 4 by a large majority at a special conference in 1995.

Post-war reconstruction   After the Second World War some industries, e.g. the railways, were extremely run-down, requiring large-scale investment and repair. For these, the provision of state finance through nationalization seemed a sensible solution. In other industries, e.g. steel, nationalization was a means of achieving reorganization so that economies of scale could be fully exploited. In still other industries, e.g. gas and electricity, reorganization was required to change the industry base from the local to the national.[1] A different government might, of course, have used policy measures other than nationalization, such as grants and tax reliefs, to achieve these objectives.

The public interest   There are many situations where commercial criteria, with their focus on profitability, are at odds with a broader view of the public interest, and in such cases nationalization is one solution. For instance, the Post Office aims to make a profit overall, but in doing so makes losses on rural services which are subsidized by profits made elsewhere – a 'cross-subsidy' from one group of consumers to another. Some object to cross-subsidization, arguing that it interferes with the price mechanism in its role of resource allocation when some consumers pay less than the true cost of the services they buy, whilst others pay more than the true cost. However, in the case of the Post Office cross-subsidization seems reasonable, if only because we may all want to send letters to outlying areas from time to time, and all derive benefit from the existence of a full national postal service. A private sector profit-orientated firm might not be prepared to undertake the loss-making Post Office services.

State ownership may also be a means of promoting the public interest when entire businesses are about to collapse. The state has sometimes intervened to prevent liquidation, as in 1970 when the Conservative government decided to rescue Rolls-Royce rather than see the company liquidated. Prestige, strategic considerations, effects on employment and on the balance of payments all played a part in the argument, as the judgement of the market was rejected in favour of a broader view of the public interest. In the long run the markets were proved wrong and the decision to intervene commercially correct, as the company is now a world leader in aero-engine technology and has been successfully returned to the private sector.

State monopoly   The 'natural monopoly' argument is often advanced in favour of nationalization of certain industries. Economies of scale in railways, water, electricity and gas industries are perhaps so great that the tendency towards monopoly can be termed 'natural'. Competing provision of these services, with duplication of investment, would clearly be wasteful of resources. The theory of the firm suggests that monopolies may enjoy supernormal profits, charging higher prices and producing lower output than would a competitive industry with the same cost conditions. However, where there are sufficient economies of scale, the monopoly price could be lower and output higher than under competition (see Ch. 9, Fig. 9.1). Monopoly might then be the preferred market form, especially if it can be regulated. Nationalization is one means of achieving such regulation.

Presence of externalities   Externalities occur when economic decisions create costs or benefits for people other than the decision-taker; these are called social costs or social benefits. For example, a firm producing textiles may emit industrial effluent, polluting nearby rivers and causing loss of amenity. In other words, society is forced to bear part of the cost of private industrial activity. Sometimes those who impose external or social costs in this way can be controlled by legislation (pollution controls, Clean Air Acts), or penalized through taxation. The parties affected might be compensated, using the revenue raised from taxing those firms creating social costs. On the other hand, firms creating external or social benefits may be rewarded by the receipt of subsidies. In other cases nationalization is a possible solution. If the industry is run in the public interest, it might be expected that full account will be taken of any externalities. For instance, it can be argued that railways reduce road usage, creating social benefits by relieving urban congestion, pollution and traffic accidents. This was one aspect of the case for subsidizing British Rail through the passenger service obligation grant which, in the mid-1990s, amounted to around £1bn. The grant enabled British Rail to continue operating some loss making services. Nationalization is therefore one means of exercising public control over the use of subsidies when these are thought to be in the public interest.

Improved industrial climate

There was hope after 1945 that the removal of private capital would improve labour relations in the industries concerned, promoting the feeling of co-ownership. The coal industry in particular had a bitter legacy of industrial relations. From nationalization until the strike of 1973, industrial relations in the coal industry, judged by days lost in disputes, seemed to have dramatically improved over pre-war days. Nevertheless, for the nationalized industries as a whole, it is fair to say that the hopes of the 1940s were not fulfilled, perhaps because the form of nationalization adopted in the UK did little to involve workers in the running of their industries. Participation in management, worker directors, genuine consultation and even an adequate flow of information to workers are no more common in the UK public sector than they are in the private sector.

Redistribution of wealth

Nationalization of private sector assets without compensation is a well-tried revolutionary means of changing the distribution of wealth in an inegalitarian society. Nationalization in the UK has not, unlike the Soviet Union in 1917, been used in this way; in the UK there has almost always been 'fair' compensation. Indeed, the compensation paid between 1945 and 1951 was criticized as over-generous, enabling shareholders to get their wealth out of industries which, in the main, had poor prospects (e.g. railways, coal) in order to buy new shareholdings in growth industries (e.g. chemicals, consumer durables). Once 'fair' compensation is accepted in principle in state acquisitions of private capital, then nationalization ceases to be a mechanism for redistribution of wealth.

An alternative to 'fair' compensation is confiscation. However, it would have serious consequences for UK capital markets. Ownership of assets in the UK would, in future, carry the additional risk of total loss by state confiscation, which could influence decisions to invest in new UK-based plant and equipment, and to buy UK shares. The ability of UK companies to invest and to raise finance might therefore be undermined. The transfer of assets might also prove inequitable, since shares are held by pension funds and insurance companies on behalf of millions of small savers who would then be penalized by confiscation.

Privatization

Privatization means the transfer of assets or economic activity from the public sector to the private sector. It is more than just a synonym for denationalization and has many facets. Sometimes the government has kept a substantial shareholding in privatized public corporations (initially 49.8% in BT). In other cases a public corporation has been sold in its entirety (e.g. National Freight Corporation). Government-owned shares in companies which were not public corporations have also been sold (e.g. British Petroleum, Amersham International). Where public sector corporations and companies are not attractive propositions for *complete* privatization then profitable assets have been sold (e.g. Jaguar Cars from the then British Leyland and also British Rail Hotels). The divide between public and private sectors may be broken down by joint ventures such as the formation of

Allied Steel and Wire by British Steel and GKN. In the local authority sector in the period 1979–1997, a total of 1.4 million dwellings were sold to tenants, whilst over the same period local authority house building became insignificant. Throughout the public sector many activities were opened up to market forces by inviting tenders. The cleaning of public buildings and local authority refuse collection are examples of former 'in-house' services which are now put out to tender. Private sector finance and operation of facilities and services is also now established in the prison service.

Early privatizations, for example BT in 1984, were usually simple transfers of existing businesses to the private sector. Increasingly privatizations have become much more complex, often being used to restructure industries by breaking up monopolies and establishing market-based relationships between the new companies. For example, in 1990/91 the privatization of the Central Electricity Generating Board created three companies – National Power and Power Gen in the private sector and Nuclear Electric which remained state owned, at least initially. Nuclear Electric has since been partially privatized under that name, whilst leaving Magnox Electric in state ownership. These generating companies sell electricity to the regional supply companies through the National Grid, which is also open to any other generator or importer of electricity. Similar ingenuity was applied to the privatization of British Rail by separating ownership of the track (Railtrack) from the train operating companies and also the train leasing companies. The train operating companies are in this case franchisees who have successfully tendered for contracts to operate trains for a specified period. The UK government was insistent that British participation in the Channel Tunnel project would be entirely via tenders from the private sector. Nevertheless the project received crucial support from the French government. The private sector is also involved in raising funds for a wide range of public sector projects under the Private Finance Initiative (PFI). This channels funds into what would previously have been public sector projects and so creates new sources of finance in a partnership between the public and private sectors (Myers 1998).

Market forces have also been introduced into the unlikely areas of social services, the health services and education – especially higher education. In health and social services this has involved the purchaser/provider model in which, for example, doctors have used their limited budgets to buy hospital services needed by their patients. Funds, and hence the use of resources, are then controlled by *purchasers* rather than by the *providers*. As a result, doctors have an incentive to use hospitals offering, in their judgement, the 'best' service as described by some combination of quality and value for money. (However, as we note in Ch. 13, the incoming Labour government has sought to modify some of these market arrangements.) In higher education, the funding of universities has been closely linked to the numbers of students enrolling. It follows that any failure to enrol students, perhaps through offering unpopular courses, would drive a university into deficit and possible bankruptcy. Resources in this sector were previously allocated by administrators, now a market test is applied.

Table 8.1 shows the extent of privatization in the UK to 1998/99, both in terms of the number of businesses and their spread across major sectors of the economy. The total value of privatization receipts to the Treasury has been estimated at over £70bn. Clearly the scope for further privatization among the remaining nationalized industries is now limited as there are so few left, but there are many possibilities in the activities currently run by the Civil Service and Local Authorities. Of the

Table 8.1 **Major privatizations: a sectoral breakdown.**

Mining, Oil, Agriculture and Forestry
British Coal, British Petroleum, Britoil, Enterprise Oil
Land Settlement, Forestry Commission, Plant Breeding Institute

Electricity, Gas and Water
British Gas
National Power, PowerGen
Nuclear Electric
Northern Ireland Electric, Northern Ireland Generation (4 companies)
Scottish Hydro-Electric, Scottish Power
National Grid
Regional Electricity Distribution (12 Companies)
Regional Water Holding Companies (10 Companies)

Manufacturing, Science and Engineering
AEA Technology
British Aerospace, Short Bros., Rolls-Royce
British Shipbuilders, Harland and Wolff
British Rail Engineering
British Steel
British Sugar Corporation
Royal Ordnance
Jaguar, Rover Group
Amersham International
British Technology Group Holdings (ICL, Fairey, Ferranti, Inmos)

Distribution, Hotels, Catering
British Rail Hotels

Transport and Communication
British Railways
National Freight, National and Local Bus Companies
Motorway Service Area Leases
Associated British Ports, Trust Ports, Sealink
British Airways, British Airports Authority (and other airports)
British Telecommunications, Cable and Wireless

Banking, Finance, etc.
Girobank

remaining nationalized industries, the Post Office is the prime candidate for privatization. The previous Conservative government made clear its preference for privatization in a 1994 White Paper. However, there is still a strong consumer attachment to the idea of the Royal Mail and a tradition of public service which stretches back into the nineteenth century.

The case for privatization

A commitment to privatize wherever possible became established in the Conservative Party during Mrs Thatcher's first term. By 1982 the late Mr Nicholas Ridley, then Financial Secretary to the Treasury, expressed this commitment as follows:

> It must be right to press ahead with the transfer of ownership from state to private ownership of as many public sector businesses as possible.... The introduction of competition must be linked to a transfer of ownership to private citizens and away from the State. Real public ownership – that is ownership by people – must be and is our ultimate goal.

Mr Ridley made a case for privatization which focused on the traditional Conservative antipathy to the state. On this view the transfer of economic activity from the public to the private sector is, in itself, a desirable objective. By the early 1980s privatization was also supported by adherents of 'supply side' economics with its emphasis on free markets. Privatization would expose industries to market forces which would benefit consumers by giving them choice, and also lower prices as a result of efficiency gains within the privatized companies.

Supply side benefits   The breaking of a state monopoly (e.g. Mercury competing with BT) would, in this view, enable consumers to choose whichever company produced the service they preferred. That company would then generate more profit and expand in response to consumer demand, whilst competitive pressure would be put on the company losing business to improve its service or go into liquidation. BT's progressive reductions in 'phone charges have clearly been at least partly in response to competition. The pressure to meet requirements should also improve internal efficiency (X efficiency) as changes can be justified to workers and managers by the need to respond to the market. The old public corporations had increasingly been seen as producer led, serving the interests of management and workers rather than those of consumers and shareholders (in this case tax-payers). Privatization introduces market pressures which help to stimulate a change of organizational culture.

Trade unions can be expected to discover that previous customs and work practices agreed when in the public sector are now challenged by privatization, as the stance taken by management changes from when it was a nationalized industry, and thereby raises corporate efficiency. Similarly competition in the product market will force moderation in wage demands and increased attention to manning levels, again raising efficiency. Privatization contributes in these various ways to the creation of 'flexibility' in labour markets, higher productivity and reduced unit labour costs.

The stock market provides a further market test for privatized companies. Poor performance in meeting consumer preferences or in utilizing assets should result in a share price which underperforms the rest of the market and undervalues the company's assets, ultimately leaving it vulnerable to takeover by a company able to make better use of the assets. Supporters of privatization place more faith in these market forces than in the monitoring activities of Departments of State and Parliamentary Committees.

Wider share ownership   The Conservative Party also emphasized wider share ownership. By 1998, share ownership in the UK had spread to 22% of the adult population, having been only 7% as recently as 1981. The total number of UK shareholders is about the same as the number of trade-unionists. This increase in shareholding is largely due to privatization. A new group of shareholders has been attracted and become participants in the 'enterprise culture'. Additionally 90% of the employees in the privatized companies have become shareholders in the companies they work for, at least initially. Worker share ownership is advocated as a means of involving workers more closely with their companies and achieving improved industrial relations. This has been taken further by selling companies to their managers (e.g. Leyland Bus 1987) or to consortiums of managers and workers (e.g. National Freight 1982). The latter is regarded as a highly successful example, profits having grown more than tenfold since privatization.

Reductions in PSBR   Privatization has also been seen as a way in which the PSBR can be cut, at a stroke! The finance of external borrowing by the nationalized industries is regarded in accounting terms as being part of public expenditure, which then ceases when these industries become privately owned. Sale of assets or shares also increases government revenue, again reducing the PSBR in the year of the sale. Over the period 1979–99 the Treasury gained £70bn from asset sales. Privatization made a very significant contribution to the budget surpluses of the late 1980s and to curbing the size of the budget deficits of the 1990s. Privatization proceeds have reduced the PSBR as a proportion of GDP by more than 1.5% during the late 1980s, and by a still significant, if smaller, percentage in other years.

Managerial freedom   The activities of state-owned organizations are constrained by their relationship with the government. They lack financial freedom to raise investment capital externally because the government is concerned about restraining the growth of public expenditure (see Ch.18). Privatization is then seen as increasing the prospects for raising investment capital, thereby increasing efficiency and lowering prices.

Control by Whitehall extends to granting approval for specific capital projects of more than £20 million. Supporters of privatization argue that civil servants are not the best people to participate in essentially commercial decisions and that the process is unwieldy and time-consuming for top managers.

Removal of the financial controls on nationalized industries is *not* seen as a satisfactory alternative to privatization, largely because the nationalized industries would then gain an unfair advantage against private sector competitors in that losses would ultimately be underwritten by the tax-payer. The Green Paper 'The Future of the Postal Services' in 1994 claimed that the removal of financial controls would create 'risk free' businesses which would compete unfairly against private sector companies for funds in the capital market. Furthermore the nationalized industries would also compete with other public sector services, such as health and education, for a share of public expenditure. On these grounds the Green Paper favoured, instead of financial liberalization, selling 51% of Royal Mail and Parcelforce to effectively remove them from the public sector, whilst retaining a close link between government and the Royal Mail consistent with the 'important role the Royal Mail plays in our life'.

A further limitation on nationalized industries is the political near-impossibility of diversification. In many cases this would be the sensible corporate response to poor market prospects but it is not an option likely to be open to a nationalized concern. Since privatization, however, companies *have* been able to freely exploit market opportunities. So, for example, most of the regional electricity companies have become suppliers of gas as well as electricity.

The 'globalization' of economic activity also, in this view, leaves nationalized industries at a distinct disadvantage. For example, no private oil company would follow the nationalized British Coal in confining its activities to one country where it happened to have reserves. This international perspective is an important reason why the Post Office management have seen privatization as 'the only (option) which offers us the freedom to fight off foreign competition'. In the postal services, increased competition is expected from the Dutch Post Office, which has been privatized, and from further liberalization of other national postal services expected within the European single market. The difficulties of an international strategy for nationalized industries are shown by the failure of the attempted Renault–Volvo merger in 1993. The then nationalized status of Renault contributed substantially to Swedish (Volvo) shareholder opposition to the merger.

Privatization, then, is seen by its supporters as a means of greatly improving economic performance.

The case against privatization   Privatization may be opposed for all the reasons that nationalization was originally undertaken (see above). Additionally both the rationale of the policy and its implementation may be criticized.

Absence of competition   An essential aspect to the case *for* privatization is the creation of competitive market conditions. However, some state-owned industries have always faced stiff competition in their markets (for example, British Airways and the former Austin-Rover), so that privatization of these industries might be considered irrelevant on the basis of this 'competitive market conditions' argument.

The government also faces a dilemma as regards creating competitive market conditions when privatizing public utilities which are monopolies; namely that it has another, and potentially conflicting, objective which is to raise money for the Treasury. Breaking up state monopolies in order to increase competition reduces the market value of the share offer; monopolies are likely to be worth more as share offers because they reduce uncertainty for investors. Critics would say that the government has allowed the creation of competition to be secondary to creating attractive share issues which sell easily. The result has been the transfer of public utility monopolies intact to the private sector, creating instead private sector monopolies.

Nevertheless, competitive pressures are being applied to some of the previously public utility monopolies in their newly privatized form. For example, at the time of privatization, British Gas appeared to be a classic natural monopoly. Since then consistent pressure from the regulatory authorities has created competitive market conditions in the supply of gas to industry, to such an extent that by the end of 1998 the British Gas share of the market was below 30% and competitive supply had been extended to the domestic market for gas across the whole country. As regards BT, from the very beginning its monopoly position was challenged by Mercury. However opportunities for new entrants created by rapid technical change have been even more significant in eroding the market dominance of BT. Cable TV companies can now provide highly competitive phone services using their fibre optic cable systems; additionally many large organizations have created their own phone networks and the Internet and digital TV are creating still further opportunities for communication.

The technical and regulatory changes in the telecommunication and gas industries have benefited consumers but should not be confused with the issue of the desirability of privatization. Consumers might well feel that these desirable outcomes could have been achieved under public ownership. If so, critics might then argue that consumers could have experienced still greater benefit from technical innovation because, under privatization, lax regulatory regimes have allowed excessive levels of profit, to the benefit of shareholders and executives rather than consumers.

Presence of externalities   The rationale for privatization is at its weakest when externalities exist. Indeed the former nationalized industries contained many examples of such externalities, which was one of the reasons for their original public ownership. The now privatized rail companies are *not* able to charge road users for any benefits (e.g. less congestion) created by the lower levels of road traffic which rail services create. In the water industry there is a vested interest in encouraging consumption to increase turnover, even if this means the need to build new reservoirs with a consequent loss of land, disruption to everyday life and dramatically changed landscapes. In the case of the electricity industry, the competitive market among the generators has had nearly terminal implications for the coal industry. New contracts for coal supplies to the electricity generating companies have only been secured by British Coal at world prices, well below the prices previously agreed. As employment in mining has plummeted, the cost has been borne by society. Miners' families and local communities have become much poorer, whilst public expenditure on unemployment and social security benefits has risen and tax revenues have been reduced by the rising unemployment. At a time of high unemployment, organizations which lower their *private* costs by making more workers redundant invariably create *social* costs (externalities). There is also the issue of the long term *strategic* role of the coal industry. The German government has long recognised these wider aspects of industrial policy and has arranged a levy on electricity users to compensate the electricity generators for offering coal prices which are over three times the world price. German electricity prices in the late 1990s were some 30–40% higher than those in the rest of Europe. The UK government has taken a contrary view and decided that the nuclear industry rather than the coal industry should be subsidised. In doing so it has, of course, departed from its free market philosophy and further endangered the coal industry by subsidising a competitor.

Undervaluation of State assets   The extension of share ownership does not in itself attract much criticism. The issues which have provoked criticism include the pricing and the marketing of the shares. It is argued that valuable national assets have been sold at give-away prices. This criticism is made of both privately negotiated deals and the public share offers. An example of the former is the offer for Austin Rover made by British Aerospace in March 1988 which valued a company which has received a total of £2.9bn of public funds at only £150m and this on condition that the government wrote off £1.1bn of accumulated losses and injected a further £800m. The deal could be presented as giving away £650m and a company with net assets of more than £1.1bn. The generosity of the government's approach was confirmed when the European Commission ruled that the £800 million government injection of capital must be reduced to £572 million, in the interests of fair competition in the EU motor market. The Commission also insisted that British Aerospace repay £44.4 million which it received from the government as 'sweeteners' during the deal. The government's prime objective was to return Rover to the private sector as quickly as possible in the belief that the benefits would soon outweigh any losses on the deal. There were also the provisos that the company remain under British ownership (see below) and that employment be maintained. These provisos severely restricted the number of potential buyers.

In most cases public share offers have been heavily over-subscribed and large percentage profits have been made by successful applicants. Rolls-Royce shares, for example, were issued part paid at 85p on 20 May 1987 and moved to 147p by the close of business that day, a profit of 73% before dealing costs. British Telecom shares reached a premium of 86% on the first day. The electricity privatization has, to date, raised some £6.5 billion, but the assets involved have a value of £28 billion. Hardly surprisingly, the Regional Electricity Company shares had a first day premium of almost 60%, and the Electricity Generating Companies a premium of almost 40%.

Underpriced issues have cost the Treasury substantial revenues and have also conditioned a new class of small shareholders to expect quick, risk-free capital gains. These expectations were encouraged by barrages of skilful advertising. Not surprisingly many of the new shareholders cashed in their windfall gains by selling their shares. As a result share ownership in the new companies quickly became more concentrated. For example the 1.1 million BA shareholders at the flotation in February 1987 had reduced to 0.4 million by early October. Despite this there is no doubt that there has been a considerable extension of share ownership, although the majority of shareholders have shares in only one company. In fact 54% of investors hold shares in only one company and only 17% have shares in more than four companies. Parker (1991) concludes that privatization has *widened* share ownership but not *deepened* it. Indeed, the institutional investors raised their proportion of shareholdings during the 1980s at the expense of the private investor, whose proportion of total shareholdings fell from 30% to 20% during this period.

Short-termism   The discipline of the capital markets may prove a very mixed blessing for some of the privatized companies if they become subject to the City's alleged 'short termism'. The large investment fund managers are often criticized for taking a short-term view of prospects. This would be particularly inappropriate for the public utilities where both the gestation period for investment and the pay-back period tend to be lengthy. The freedom with which ownership of assets changes hands on the stock market is not always in the public interest. The acquisition of B Cal in 1987 by the newly privatized BA, for example, was investigated by the Monopolies and Mergers Commission (MMC) and approved on condition that BA gave up some of the routes acquired. There was also concern at the 22% holding in BP which the Kuwait Investment Office acquired very cheaply in the aftermath of the 1987 stock market crash. The MMC ruled that the Kuwait holding be reduced to 11%. The limitations of privatization and excessive reliance on the markets was illustrated in 1994 by BMW's takeover of the Rover Group from British Aerospace. The government had originally set a period of five years in which Rover could not be sold to a foreign buyer but, within a few months of the expiry of the limitation, the last British controlled volume car producer was sold to the German company. Of course it is by no means clear that retaining national control of companies is a desirable objective. The takeover could arguably be welcomed as a benefit of

European integration which will strengthen the European car industry. However if national control *is* desired, as it was when British Aerospace bought Rover, then this is an example of the weakness of privatization as a substitute for industrial policy. The French government's plans to retain a controlling majority interest in Renault after privatization illustrates an alternative approach, although the UK government would tend not to view such a compromise as a 'privatization'.

Opportunity costs   The flow of funds into privatization offers has been diverted from other uses. It is reasonable to suppose that applicants for shares are using their savings rather than reducing their consumption. Large sums of money leave the building societies during privatizations, and other financial institutions are also deprived of funds. This raises the possibility that what is merely a restructuring and change of ownership of state industry may be reducing the availability of funds for other organizations which would use them for real capital investment. The effects of privatization issues on the financial markets are much the same as the effects of government borrowing, raising the same possibilities of 'crowding out'.

The contribution of privatization to reducing the PSBR has been widely criticized as 'selling the family silver'. The sales involve profitable assets and, after privatization, the Exchequer loses the flow of returns from them. Schwartz and Lopes (1993) have pointed out that the sale price of assets should equal the net present value of expected future returns on them. If this were the case, then the 'family silver' argument would lose some of its power and rest on the use to which the proceeds were put – that is consumption or investment. However most privatization issues in the UK *have* been underpriced in the view of the markets (see above).

McWilliams and Pragnell (1996) have pointed out that the PSBR is a relatively recent concern in that targets for the PSBR were only introduced in 1976, and they stress that there are other ways of defining public borrowing. Much of the current interest in levels of public borrowing relates to the convergence criteria for European Monetary Union agreed in the Maastricht Treaty. The definition being used for the Maastricht criteria does not in fact include the borrowing of nationalized industries as part of public borrowing. It also excludes privatization receipts from government revenue and expenditure, whereas the UK practice counts these receipts as negative public expenditure, thereby lowering the public sector borrowing requirement. McWilliams and Pragnell comment that a simple change in accounting definitions could have a profound disincentive effect on the government's desire to privatize and could even reinstate the public corporation as a sensible way of providing public and indeed commercial services without increasing public borrowing under the Maastricht definition. In essence they see the current constraints on public corporations as arising out of a prejudice against public sector activity and the setting of unnecessarily tight borrowing limits.

Burden on taxpayers   A final criticism of privatization is a moral one, that the public are being sold shares which, as taxpayers, they already collectively own. The purchasers of the shares benefit from the dividends paid by the new profit seeking enterprises, at the expense of taxpayers as a group. Those taxpayers who do not buy the shares, perhaps because they have no spare cash, are effectively dispossessed.

Regulation of privatized companies

The privatization of public utility companies with 'natural' monopolies creates the possibility that the companies might abuse their monopoly power. In these cases UK privatizations have offered reassurance to the public in the form of regulatory offices for each privatized utility, for example OFTEL for telecommunications and OFWAT for the water industry. Where privatized companies like Rover and British Airways are returned to competitive markets, arguably there is no need for specific regulation beyond the normal activities of the Office of Fair Trading (OFT) and the Monopolies and Mergers Commission (MMC). If a privatized company finds its regulator's stipulations unacceptable, then it may appeal to the MMC.

Objectives of regulators   Regulators have two fundamental objectives. Firstly, they attempt to create the constraints and stimuli which companies would experience in a competitive market environment. For example, companies in competitive markets must bear in mind what their competitors are doing when setting their prices and are under competitive pressure to improve their service to consumers in order to gain market share. Regulation can *simulate* the effects of a competitive market by setting price caps and performance standards. Secondly, regulators have the longer term objective of encouraging *actual* competition by easing the entry of new producers and by preventing privatized monopoly power maintaining barriers to entry. An ideal is the creation of markets sufficiently competitive to make regulation unnecessary. The market for gas has moved substantially in this direction. British Gas, when first privatized, had an apparent classic natural monopoly in the supply of gas to industry, but by the end of 1998 the British Gas market share was below 30% for industrial users and since 1998 the company has faced nation-wide competition in the supply of gas to domestic consumers. Similarly, the Regulator insisted on the introduction of competition into the supply of electricity to domestic consumers by 1998.

Problems facing regulators   Regulators have an unenviable role as they try to create the constraints and stimuli of a competitive market. Essentially they are arbitrating between the interests of consumers and producers. *Other things being equal*, attempts by regulators to achieve improvements in service levels will cause increases in costs and so lower profits, whilst price caps on services with price inelastic demand will also reduce profits by *preventing* the regulated industries raising prices and therefore revenue. Lower profits, and the expectation of lower profits, have immediate implications for dividend distributions to shareholders and so for share prices. At this point other things are unlikely to remain equal. The privatized company subject to a price cap may well look for ways of lowering costs to allow profits to be at least maintained, or perhaps raised. In most organizations there are economies to be gained by reducing staffing levels and the utility companies have dramatically reduced their numbers of employees. Investment in new technology may also enable unit costs to be lowered so that profits are greater than they otherwise would have been.

The wave of takeovers among the electricity companies in 1995 and 1996 raised further issues for regulation and indeed for wider competition policy. At privatization care had been taken to separate electricity generation from distribution in England and Wales in order to protect consumers from the market power of vertically integrated electricity companies. It was no surprise, therefore, that when Scottish Power (a generating company) launched a takeover of MANWEB (a distribution company) the regulator recommended an investigation by the MMC. The Minister, however, did not make a referral and the bid went ahead. The Minister later contradicted this approach by referring similar bids by National Power for Southern Electric and Powergen for Midlands Electricity to the MMC. Indeed he even rejected the subsequent MMC recommendation that the deals be allowed to go ahead. The Minister now saw vertical integration as causing 'significant detriments to competition', in a clear reversal of his earlier stance on the MANWEB case.

The monopoly power of the water companies has also been widely criticized. Takeovers by water companies in Northwest England and Wales have now led to even more powerful companies which are *joint* water/electricity utility companies for their areas. There is obvious scope for economies if one company deals with the same consumers for both water and electricity. Nevertheless consumers who were unhappy about dealing with a privately owned water monopoly are likely to be even more concerned about the development of 'multi-utility companies'. Again a weakness is exposed in UK competition policy in that takeovers are monitored on a case by case basis. As critics have pointed out a careful review is now needed of what is essentially a restructuring of the public utilities.

Establishing a price cap   In deciding on a price cap the regulator has in mind some 'satisfactory' rate of profit on the value of assets employed. A key issue is then the valuation of the assets. If the basis of valuation is *historical*, using the market value at privatization plus an estimate of investment since that date, then the company will face a stricter price cap than if *current* market valuations are used for assets. This is because historic valuations will usually be much smaller than the current valuations and so will justify much smaller total profits and therefore lower prices to achieve that profit. During 1996 the OFGAS regulator and British Gas were in dispute about gas transportation charges, which nicely illustrated this point. Ms Clare Spottiswoode, the regulator, at first proposed a cut in transportation charges which would have reduced prices to the average domestic gas consumer by £30 per year from March 1997. After protests from British Gas, the regulator *raised* the valuation of the gas transportation company TransCo's assets from an estimated £9–£11bn to £11.7bn. This change of asset valuation gave the regulator the opportunity of accepting higher gas profits and prices, allowing the gas price reduction to be eased to £28 per year. Further cuts of 2.5% per annum follow until 2001. The regulator is expecting productivity growth of 4% per year to accommodate the price cuts, whereas British Gas has warned of widespread job losses.

Price caps are often associated with job losses. In an economy with less than full employment it may then be argued that such cost savings in the privatized companies are only achieved at the expense of extra public expenditure on welfare benefit. However, a counter-argument is that lower public utility prices benefit all consumers, with lower costs of production across the economy stimulating output and creating employment.

It may be over-simplistic to assume that privatized companies will invariably respond to a price cap by cutting costs as much as possible in order to maximize profits over the medium term period of the price cap. The planning period in public utilities is likely to be much longer than the four or five years of a regulator's price review period. If a company meets its price cap and service requirements by making excessively large efficiency savings so that its profits and share price grow quicker than the average for large companies, then there will be great public pressure on the regulator to be much tougher next time. The goals of regulated companies probably include avoiding the long term regulatory regime becoming too 'tight'. At the same time the regulator may depend on the company for a great deal of the information needed for the task of regulation. So there is the possibility of the regulator's independence being compromised, which has been called 'capture' of the regulator. Clearly the relationship between regulator and regulated company is complex, so that simple predictions of action and reaction are difficult to make.

Costs of regulation Whilst regulation should produce clear benefits for the consumers of each privatized company, there are inevitable costs involved in running regulatory offices and also costs for the regulated company which has to supply information and present its case to the regulator. It is likely that companies will go further than this and try to *anticipate* the regulator's activities, so incurring further costs. It is not at all clear that having separate regulatory offices for each industry is a cost-effective arrangement. Concentration of *all* regulation in one agency might be more efficient and lead to more consistency in the treatment of different industries. It would also enable a consideration of the implications of decisions in one industry on competitive conditions in other industries. OFTEL, for example, has sought to increase competition in the rapidly changing telecommunications market by forcing BT to allow cable TV companies favourable access to its transmission networks. Yet these cable companies themselves have monopoly power in their own markets!

Differences in the regulatory regimes have certainly contributed to the astonishing difference between the weak share performance of the gas and telecommunications industries and the strong share performance of the water and electricity industries which have outperformed the FTSE 100 index by 60% and 101% respectively. High returns in the stock market are usually associated with risk. However neither the water industry nor electricity can be viewed as risky; indeed they would normally be seen as unspectacular but steady income generators rather than as growth stocks.

Regulation and deregulation

Regulation Regulation may be defined as the various *rules* set by governments or their agencies which seek to control the operations of firms. We have already discussed the role of the regulators for the privatized industries who themselves are part of this broad regulatory process.

Regulation is one of the mechanisms available to governments when dealing with the problem of 'market failure'. Of course market failure can take many forms although, as Stewart (1997) points out, four broad categories can usefully be identified.

- *Asymmetric information*. Here the providers may have information not available to the purchasers. For example in recent cases involving the mis-selling of pensions the companies involved were found to have withheld information from purchasers. Stricter regulation of the sector has been the government's response to this situation.

- *Externalities.* In the case of negative externalities, regulations may be used to bring private costs more closely into line with social costs (as with environmental taxes) or to restrict social costs to a given level (as with environmental standards).
- *Public goods.* Regulation may be required if such goods are to be provided at all. The idea of a public 'good' (which may, of course, be a service) is that it has the characteristics of being non-excludable and non-exhaustible, at least in the 'pure' case. Non-excludable refers to the difficulty of excluding those who do not wish to pay for the 'good' (e.g. police or defence); non-exhaustible refers to the fact that the marginal cost of providing an extra unit of the 'good' is effectively zero (e.g. an extra person covered by the police or defence forces). The non-excludable condition prevents a private market developing, since it is difficult to make 'free riders' actually pay for the public good. The non-exhaustible condition implies that any price that is charged should, for allocative efficiency (see Ch. 5, p. 93), equal marginal cost and therefore be zero. Private markets guided by the profit motive are hardly in the business of charging zero prices! Both conditions imply that the 'good' is best supplied by the public sector at zero price, using general tax revenue to fund provision (in the 'pure' public good case).
- *Monopoly.* Regulation may be required to prevent the abuse of monopoly power. In Ch. 5 we considered a variety of regulations implemented by the Office of Fair Trading. Figure 5.1 (p. 88) was used to show that regulations involving the Monopolies and Mergers Commission may be used to prevent or modify certain proposed mergers which are arguably against the public interest (e.g. where gains in 'productive efficiency' are more than offset by losses in 'allocative efficiency').

The *forms* of regulation are too innumerable to capture in a few headings. The various rules can involve the application of maximum or minimum prices, the imposition of various types of standards, taxes, quotas, procedures, directives, etc., whether issued by national bodies (e.g. UK government or its agencies) or international bodies (e.g. EU Commission, World Trade Organization, etc.).

Although a strict classification of the numerous types of regulation would seem improbable, McKenzie (1998) makes a useful distinction.

- Regulations aimed at *protecting* the consumer from the consequences of market failure.
- Regulations aimed at *preventing* the market failure from happening in the first place.

In terms of the Financial Sector, the Deposit Guarantee Directive of the EU is of the former type. This *protects* customers of accredited EU banks by restoring at least 90% of any losses up to £12,000 which might result from the failure of a particular bank. In part this is a response to asymmetric information, since customers do not have the information to evaluate the credit-worthiness of a particular bank, and might not be able to interpret that information even if it *was* available.

The Capital Adequacy Directive of the EU is of the latter type. This seeks to *prevent* market failure (such as a bank collapse) by directly relating the value of the capital a bank must hold to the riskiness of its business. The idea here is that the greater the value of capital available to a bank, the larger the buffer stock which it can use to absorb any losses. Various elements of the Capital Adequacy Directive force the banks to increase their capital base if the riskiness of their portfolio (indicated by various statistical measures) is deemed to have increased. In part this is in response to the potential for negative externalities in this sector. One bank failure can invariably lead to a 'domino effect' and risk system collapse with incalculable consequences for the sector as a whole.

In these ways the regulatory system for EU financial markets is seeking to provide a framework within which greater competition between banks can occur, while at the same time addressing the fact that greater competition can increase the risks of bank failure. It is seeking both to protect consumers should any mishap occur and at the same time to prevent such a mishap actually occurring.

Overall we can say that those who support any or all of these forms of regulation, in whatever sector of the economy, usually do so in the belief that they improve the allocation of resources in situations characterized by one or more types of market failure.

Deregulation

Deregulation may be defined as efforts to *remove* the various rules set by governments or their agencies which seek to control the operation of firms.

One of the major arguments in favour of deregulation involves 'public interest theory'. The suggestion here is that regulations should be removed whenever it can be shown that this will remove or reduce the 'deadweight loss' typically shown to result from various types of market interference.

Figure 8.1 can be used to show how a particular market regulation, here a quota scheme, can result in a 'deadweight loss'. In this analysis *economic welfare* is defined as consumer surplus plus producer surplus. The *consumer surplus* being the amount consumers are willing to pay over and above the amount they need to pay; the *producer surplus* being the amount producers receive over and above the amount they need for them to supply the product.

In Fig. 8.1 we start with an initial demand curve DD and supply curve SS giving market equilibrium price P_1 and quantity Q_1. However, the *regulation* here is that should the market price fall below a particular level P_2, then the government is directed to intervene. It is required to use a *quota* arrangement to prevent market price from falling below P_2; in other words P_2 is a minimum price which is set by regulation at a level which is above the free market price P_1. In terms of Fig. 8.1, if

Fig. 8.1. Welfare loss with a quota scheme $0Q_2$ raising price (P_2) above the market clearing level P_1

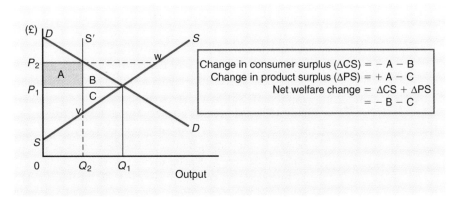

the quota is set at Q_2, then the effective supply curve becomes SvS', since no more than Q_2 can be supplied whatever the price. The result is to raise the 'equilibrium' price to P_2 and reduce the 'equilibrium' quantity to Q_2. However, the quota regulation has resulted in a *loss of economic welfare* equivalent to the area B plus area C. The reduction in output from Q_1 to Q_2 means a loss of area B in consumer surplus and loss of area C in producer surplus which exactly offsets the loss of area A in consumer surplus. However, the higher price results in a gain of area A in producer surplus. This means that the *net* welfare change is negative, i.e. there is a 'deadweight loss' of area B + area C.

'Public interest theory' is therefore suggesting that deregulation should occur whenever the net welfare change of *removing regulations* is deemed to be positive. In terms of Fig. 8.1 it might be argued that removing the regulation whereby the government (or its agent) seeks to keep price artificially high at P_2 will give a *net* welfare change which is positive, namely a net gain of area B + area C. In other words, allowing the free market equilibrium price P_1 and quantity Q_1 to prevail restores the previous deadweight loss via regulation. Put another way, public interest theory is suggesting that deregulation should occur whenever the outcome is a net welfare gain, so that those who gain can, at least potentially, more than compensate those who lose.

Of course a similar analysis can be carried out in terms of other types of regulation incurring a deadweight loss *vis-à-vis* the free market equilibrium. In Ch. 28 we show how the operation of price support schemes using *central purchasing* arrangements by the Common Agricultural Policy of the EU can incur deadweight loss, when intervention prices are set above the world market price for certain agricultural products.

The empirical difficulties of placing a money value on changes in consumer surplus and producer surplus should not, of course, be underestimated. In terms of Fig. 8.1 it involves accurate estimates of both the demand and supply (or cost) curves facing the firm or industry. Issues of 'weighting' must also be considered, for example whether a £1 gain of producer surplus is the same in welfare terms as a £1 loss of consumer surplus. Certainly such a 'one for one' weighting was used in Fig. 8.1, with +A gain of producer surplus under the quota regarded as exactly offsetting the −A loss of consumer surplus previously earned under the initial free market situation. Some might argue that a given monetary value to consumers should be given a greater 'weight' in terms of economic welfare than a similar monetary value received by producers!

Whether deregulation will yield a net welfare gain or loss (i.e. be in, or against, the public interest) clearly involves both theoretical and empirical aspects, and may need to be considered on a case-by-case basis. Certainly deregulation *is* gathering momentum in the major industrialized economies. For example it has been estimated that in 1977 some 17% of US GNP was derived from the output of fully regulated industries, whereas that figure had declined to around 5% of GNP in current times. Winston (1993), in a wide-ranging study of the impacts of deregulation across the US industrial and service sectors, found substantial net gains to have resulted from deregulatory activity. For instance, in the US airlines sector he estimated the net benefit of the elimination of all regulations on air fares in 1983 to have been in the range of $4.3bn. to $6.5bn over a ten-year period.

Interestingly, empirical estimates of the impact of deregulation have had the greatest difficulty in placing monetary values on predicted or actual changes in the *quality* of goods or services. For example, predictions as to the likely impact of deregulation on the mean and variance of travel times for passengers and freight in the transport sector have been noticeable by their absence from empirical studies or their inaccuracy when compared with eventual outcomes.

Our earlier discussion in Ch. 5 (pp. 93–5) reinforced this point about the difficulty of evaluating the net welfare change from deregulation. It showed how 'public interest theory' may often have to weigh the gains in terms of 'productive efficiency' against the losses in terms of 'allocative efficiency' when trying to evaluate whether a regulation (e.g. restricting a proposed merger) is, or is not, operating in the overall public interest.

Conclusion

Despite the advance of privatization, there remains a strong case for some form of government intervention in selected industries, for example to protect the public interest, prevent abuse of monopoly power and compensate for externalities. It does not, however, follow that nationalization is the best form of government intervention. The extent of privatization since 1979 has radically changed the role of the state in the UK economy and makes it very unlikely that there will ever again be the range of state industries which existed at that date. Indeed, there is now a world-wide shift of policy in favour of privatizing state-owned assets. The performance of both state owned and privatized industry is difficult to evaluate. It has not been convincingly demonstrated that the form of ownership of an organization is the most important influence on its performance. Of much greater importance would seem to be the degree of competition and the effectiveness of regulatory bodies. Certainly greater powers are being given to many of the regulators of the previously nationalized industries in an attempt to prevent the abuse of monopoly power by the now privatized utilities. Regulators may impose price-caps and use other devices to prevent consumers being 'exploited' in monopoly-type situations. They may also seek to open markets to additional competition by encouraging new entrants. Nevertheless there is also a counter-movement which seeks to *remove* regulations where these are thought to operate against the public interest. Such attempts at deregulation are widespread, though it should not be forgotten that the reason many regulations exist is to protect consumers from the adverse consequences of various types of 'market failure'.

Key points	

- In 1979 the nationalized industries produced some 9% of GDP, 12% of investment and 7% of total employment. However, by 1998 their contribution was much smaller, only around 2% of GDP, 3% of investment and 2% of total employment.
- Privatization is the transfer of assets or economic activity from the public sector to the private sector.
- The term 'privatization' is often used to cover many situations: the outright sale of state-owned assets, part-sale, joint public/private ventures, market testing, contracting out of central/local government services, etc.
- The case *for* privatization includes allegedly greater productive efficiency (lower costs) via the introduction of market pressures. These are seen as creating more flexibility in labour markets, higher productivity and reduced unit labour costs. More widespread share ownership, a lower PSBR, easier access to investment capital, greater scope for diversification, and the absence of civil service oversight, are often quoted as 'advantages' of privatization.
- The case *against* privatization includes suggestions that state monopolies have often merely been replaced by private monopolies, with little benefit to consumers, especially in the case of the public utilities. The loss of scale economies (e.g. 'natural monopolies'), the inability to deal effectively with externalities, undervaluation of state assets, the subsequent concentration of share ownership, 'short-termism' of the city, are often quoted as disadvantages of privatization.
- Regulators have been appointed for a number of public utilities in an attempt to *simulate* the effects of competition (e.g. limits to price increases and to profits), when there is little competition in reality.
- Other regulations are widely used in all economic sectors in order to protect consumers from 'market failure' and to prevent such failures actually occurring.
- There is considerable momentum behind removing regulations (i.e. deregulation) where this can be shown to be in the 'public interest'. However, evaluating the welfare change from deregulation is a complex exercise.

Notes	

1. For example, the transition from private to public ownership meant the takeover of some 550 separate local concerns in the electricity industry and over 1,000 local concerns in the gas industry.

References and further reading	

Bishop, M., Kay, J. and **Mayer, C.** (1994) *Privatization and Economic Performance*, Oxford University Press.
Helm, D. (1994) British Utility Regulation Theory, Practice and Reform, *Oxford Review of Economic Policy*, **10**, 3.
McKenzie, G. (1998) Financial Regulation and the European Union, *The Economic Review*, April.
McWilliams, D. and **Pragnell, M.** (1996) Who will Miss the PSBR? *Financial Times*, 30 September.

Myers, D. (1998) The Private Finance Initiative – a Progress Report, *The Economic Review*, April.

Oxford Review of Economic Policy (1997) *Competition in Regulated Industries*, **13**, 1, Spring.

Parker, D. (1991) Privatization Ten Years On: a critical analysis of its rationale and results, *Economics*, Winter.

Schwartz, G. and **Lopes, P.S.** (1993) Privatization: Expectations, Trade-offs and Results, *Finance and Development*, June.

Stewart, G. (1997) Why Regulate?, *The Economic Review*, September.

Wilson, J. (1994) Competitive Tendering and UK Public Services, *The Economic Review*, April.

Winston, C. (1993) Economic Deregulation, *Journal of Economic Literature*, **XXXI**, September.

Chapter 9

Pricing in practice

The first part of this chapter briefly illustrates how economic *theory* can predict a variety of prices for a product, depending on the structure of the market and the objectives of the firm. The second and major part looks at pricing in *practice*, using recent research findings to illustrate how firms actually price their products. Costs clearly play a role in price-setting, although a variety of other factors must also be considered, including market-share strategies, the phase of the product life cycle, the degree of product differentiation, product line and prestige pricing strategies, and the role of distributors. Chapter 3, 'Firm objectives and firm behaviour', could usefully be read before beginning this chapter.

Pricing in theory

Price and market structure   For simplicity we shall initially assume that the firm's objective is to maximize profits. Given this objective the price charged may still vary depending on the type of market structure within which the firm operates. This is well illustrated by a comparison between the extreme market forms of perfect competition and pure monopoly.

Perfect competition vs pure monopoly   Under perfect competition, price is determined for the industry (and for the firm) by the intersection of demand and supply, at P_C in Fig. 9.1. As the reader familiar with the theory of the firm will know, the supply curve, S, of the perfectly competitive industry is also the marginal cost (MC) curve of the industry. Suppose now that the industry is taken over by a single firm ('pure monopoly'), and that costs are initially unchanged. It follows that the marginal cost curve remains in the same position; also that the demand curve for the perfectly competitive industry becomes the demand (and average revenue (AR)) curve for the monopolist. The marginal revenue (MR) curve must then lie inside the negatively sloped AR curve. The profit-maximizing price for the monopolist is P_M, corresponding to output Q_M where $MC = MR$. Price is higher under monopoly than under perfect competition (and quantity, Q_M, is lower). This is the so-called 'classical' case against monopoly.

Fig. 9.1.   Price under perfect competition and monopoly.

Our intention here is merely to point out that price will tend to *differ* for firms depending on the type of market within which they operate. In our comparison of extreme market forms, the final outcome for price may or may not be higher under monopoly than under competition. It is in part an empirical question. If economies of scale were sufficient to lower the *MC* curve below *MC'* in Fig. 9.1, then the monopoly price would be below that of perfect competition. Price will however, except by coincidence, *be different* under these two market forms, as it would under other market forms, such as monopolistic competition or oligopoly.

Price and firm objective

So far we have assumed that the firm has a single objective, i.e. profit maximization. If there are other objectives then there will tend to be a still wider range of possibilities for price. We saw in Fig. 3.4 that a sales-maximizing objective would usually lead to a lower price than would a profit-maximizing objective. The situation becomes even more complicated when we examine behavioural or non-maximizing objectives, as these yield not a unique price, but a range of price outcomes for any given market structure. Clearly firm price depends also on firm objective.

Price, market structure and firm objective

Price thus depends on both market structure and firm objective. Since there are many possible combinations of these, any given product or service can experience a wide array of possible prices.

From Fig. 9.2 we see that the four market structures can lead to at least four different price outcomes (P_1–P_4) for objective 1. A further four prices (P_5–P_8) might result from objective 2, and so on, giving at least sixteen prices[1] for the four market structures and the four firm objectives. To derive guidelines for price-setting from theory, which will have general validity, is clearly a daunting if not impossible task.

Fig. 9.2. Market
structure, firm objective
and price.

Pricing in practice

We now turn to practice to see whether observation will give us more help than theory in determining price.

Cost-plus pricing   We first examine the influence of cost on price. The suggestion here is that it is not so much the demand side of the market that affects price, but rather the supply side, via costs of production.

Cost-plus pricing is a description given to a number of practices whereby price is closely related to costs of production. Most cost-plus pricing strategies add a certain percentage profit mark-up to the firm's costs, in order to arrive at a final price. The precise outcome for price will vary from firm to firm for three main reasons:

1. There is the problem of selecting which costs to include in the pricing decision. Some firms may include only variable costs in the base for the mark-up. Interestingly this is called 'marginal costing' by accountants even when the base is average variable cost. Other firms may include both variable and fixed costs in the base (full-cost pricing). When the firm is producing more than one product, full-cost pricing faces the problem of apportioning total fixed costs between the various products. For instance, if a factory was already producing Product A, and a new Product B was introduced using the same machinery, what part, if any, of the unchanged capital costs should be allocated to B? Product B may be asked to 'absorb' some proportion of the fixed costs already included in the price of A. Different firms will make different decisions on how to absorb fixed costs across their various products.

2. Whatever the costs to be included in the base, there is the problem of estimating the 'normal' level of output at which the firm will operate. This estimate is important since *average cost* (both the variable and fixed elements) and therefore the size of the cost base, will vary with output, i.e. with capacity utilization.

3. Whatever the costs included, and the estimate of capacity utilization, there is the problem of calculating the percentage mark-up to be added to costs. Some firms may set a relatively constant percentage mark-up, whilst others may vary the percentage according to firm objective and market circumstance.

An array of price outcomes is therefore possible for a firm, depending on the practices it adopts in dealing with each of the three problems outlined above. Although cost-plus pricing cannot therefore yield precise predictions for firm price, it does put price-setting in a particular perspective. The emphasis is upon *costs* influencing price, and then producers selling what they can at that price. Demand has little influence on price-setting in cost-plus theory, except perhaps in affecting the size of the mark-up to be added to costs. Any extra demand is met from stocks, or by lengthening the order book, rather than by the immediate price rise predicted by market theory.

Empirical evidence   The empirical evidence for cost-plus pricing, in one firm or another, is rather impressive. Hall and Hitch (1939), in their survey of entrepreneurs in the 1930s, found that most adopted a full-cost pricing approach. Hague (1948) came to a similar conclusion in his study of twenty firms in the Midlands, finding that price was set by adding a largely conventional profit margin to average total cost. An intensive study by Coutts, Godley and Nordhaus (1978) of seven UK industries, also lent support to cost-plus pricing. Their study set out to test the relative importance of costs, demand, taxes, government intervention, and international trade, on the price of manufactured goods in the UK over the period 1957–73. The results suggested that firms had very limited and specific rules about the process of price determination and that costs of production were the most important single influence on price. More recently, Shipley and Bourdon (1990) found that in their sample of 193 industrial distributors almost 52% used a cost-plus pricing approach, whilst Blinder (1992) found cost-plus pricing to be ranked third highest in his study of 72 US companies. Hall *et al.* (1996), in a major survey of the pricing policy of 654 UK companies, found that cost-based pricing was recognized as 'important' by over 47% of these companies. It was ranked overall as the second most important pricing strategy which those companies actually pursue.

In practice, there are a number of reasons for the popularity of cost-based pricing methods. One reason is that many firms do not change their prices very often, in part because of the substantial costs involved in searching for the information necessary to *identify* the profit-maximizing price. Moreover, even having identified some 'optimal' price firms also face the cost of *implementing* the adjustments to current pricing and policy strategies. Given such costs Blinder found that firms in his US study usually changed their prices only annually. Similarly Dahlby (1992) showed that the average length of the pricing period for Canadian insurance premiums was as high as 15 months, whilst the Small Business Research Trust (1995) found that 42% of a sample of 350 small UK firms changed their prices at most only once a year and often even less frequently. Hall *et al.* (1996) also found that the firms studied tended to let at least six months elapse before changing prices. Of course, the frequency of price change tends to vary from sector to sector, with retailers much more likely to change their prices more frequently than construction or manufacturing firms. Nevertheless, the general sense is that prices appear to be 'sticky', i.e. relatively unresponsive to the frequent changes affecting the general demand conditions, and more closely associated with cost than demand.

Reinforcing this view is the evidence that firms often tend to rely upon changes in material costs as a reason for changing prices. For instance Hall *et al.* (1996) found that firms were approximately four times more likely to *raise* their price due to increases in costs as opposed to increases in demand. Similarly, they found that firms were much more likely to *reduce* their prices due to decreases in costs as opposed to decreases in demand.

Nevertheless, although it is clear that the prices of both domestic and internationally traded products are related to cost, market factors can still play a part. For example, when demand is relatively price inelastic, Eichner (1987) found that the mark-up on costs is likely to be higher. He found a higher mark-up to be particularly likely in market situations where there are fewer substitutes available, when new entrants face substantial barriers and when there was little chance of government retaliatory action (e.g. anti-trust referrals to the Monopoly and Mergers Commission, etc.). These are obviously situations in which higher profits can more easily be made. Some therefore see cost-plus pricing as being less divorced from market factors than might at first appear. Shipley and Bourdon support this view, finding that 27% of the industrial distribution firms they studied raised the mark-up when demand increased and 41% reduced the mark-up when demand decreased.

Much of this analysis, whilst finding empirical support for cost-plus pricing strategies, suggests that firms do respond to major shifts in market situations by varying the percentage mark-up according to the ease or difficulty of making profit. This has led some commentators to argue that cost-plus pricing is actually a rule of thumb for setting the profit-maximizing price in situations when firms rarely have detailed knowledge of marginal revenue and cost, and even if they had would find it administratively too difficult and expensive to change the profit-maximizing price (MC = MR) with every market fluctuation.

We now turn to price-setting practices that are more broadly based than cost.

Market-share strategies

Although prices appear to be 'sticky', when prices are changed this is often for reasons of strategy rather than in response to variations in cost. For instance, prices may be reduced to raise market share, or to defend existing market share in the face of greater competition. Jobber and Hooley (1987) found that market-share pricing objectives were practised more by larger firms. Grant's study of the oligopolistic *wholesale* petrol market (Grant 1982; see also OFT 1998) seemed to present a clear case of market-share strategies exerting a dominant influence on price-setting. As we see from Table 9.1, five

Table 9.1 Share of UK refined output, 1988 and 1996.

	Market share (%)	
	1988	1996
Esso	18.0	17.9
BP	9.2	}17.1
Mobil	10.3	
Shell	15.4	13.2
Texaco	12.9	10.7
Total majors	65.8	58.9
Others	34.2	41.1
Total	100.0	100.0

Source: OFT (1998).

firms accounted for over 65% of the volume of petrol sold in the UK in 1988 and four firms for some 59% by 1996.

There is evidence to suggest that these 'major' oil companies have often followed a pattern of parallel pricing since the early 1970s, charging roughly the same wholesale price within a geographic region. They have also offered similar discounts for 'solus' agreements, where the retailer takes all his petrol from the one company. As a result the *relative* market share of the individual 'majors' has remained rather static during much of the past 30 years. The *absolute* market share of the 'majors' in petrol refining has, however, fallen substantially over this period from over 78% in 1970 to the 59% recorded in 1996. In recent times the majors have also lost market share in petrol retailing, namely to the superstores (Tesco, Safeway, etc.) which have increased their share of petrol retailing from 5% in 1990 to 23% in 1996 (OFT 1998).

Aggressive pricing policies by the majors have sometimes broken out in an attempt to defend their market share against both other majors and the non-majors. For example, Esso launched its 'PriceWatch' campaign in January 1996. This saw prices cut to the extent that its margin on the price per litre fell to 1p (OFT 1998). Since petrol is a relatively homogenous product with little attendant brand loyalty, the other oil majors and the supermarkets also had to cut their prices to support their *relative* market share. When prices are dictated in this way by market-share strategies they may bear little relationship to the costs of production, at least in the short-run. This can be seen in Fig. 9.3, where the falling net profit margins for the four majors reflected their commitment to defending their relative market share via aggressive pricing strategies.

From this analysis we can see that short-term pricing policy can be dictated by market-share strategies. Parallel pricing has been used by the majors to avoid mutually damaging encroachment on their respective market shares. However when times get difficult, price wars can still break out. When prices *are* dictated by market-share strategies they may bear little relationship to costs of production, at least in the short run. This view was confirmed by Hall *et al.* (1996) in a survey of 654 UK companies. Over 65% of companies stated that their most important pricing strategy was 'market-led pricing', with prices set either at the highest level the market could bear or at a level which has taken full account of their competitors' pricing strategies.

Fig. 9.3. Change in % in net margins of oil majors in UK refining, wholesaling and retailing operations, 1992–96. *Source:* OFT (1998).

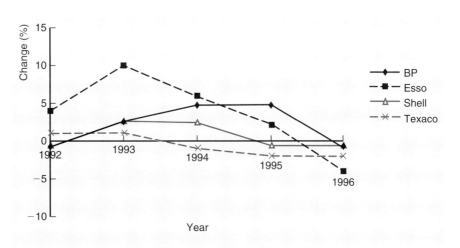

Life-cycle strategies   The pricing strategy of the firm will not only be affected by considerations of market share. The position of the product in its life cycle will also influence price. It has long been recognized that products frequently have a finite market life, and that within that life they change their strategic role (see also Chapter 3 on portfolio planning). The three broad phases of the life cycle which products go through after their successful introduction (most products fail!) are often described as the growth phase, the maturity phase and the decline phase.

Growth phase   In the growth phase the product's market share, and possibly the total market size, is increasing. It is normal for those first into a market to support growth by high marketing expenditure. Market leaders may be forced in this phase to make a choice between two types of strategy. They can adopt a 'skimming' strategy, charging a *high* price which creams off a small but lucrative part of the market. Producers of fashion products, which have a short life and high innovative value as long as only a few people own them, often adopt a skimming strategy.

Alternatively market leaders can adopt a 'penetration' strategy, charging a *low* price and raising marketing expenditure in order to establish a much larger market presence. The penetration strategy is more likely to deter early competition and may ultimately prove more profitable if the firm can afford to wait for a return on its initial outlay. The firm can then delay raising the price of its product until *after* it has secured a substantial market presence. Redmond (1989) concluded that penetration pricing by pioneer firms in a range of industries had a measurable influence in raising the eventual concentration of those industries in maturity.

How much of a role cost plays in the determination of price during the growth phase will depend on the individual firm. It is not unknown for companies who market aggressively to set prices *below* average cost in order to gain high market share, in the expectation that costs will fall as output and experience increase. This is particularly so in high-technology industries. In similar vein strategy of giving away products based on the ownership of high technology processes and products has been adopted by firms offering global products. The rationale is to lock the market into that technology, thereby making any change to alternative technologies and their associated products too expensive. The current battle between Netscape (Navigator™) and Microsoft (Explorer™) for the *de facto* standard world-wide web browser is a good example of this approach.

Maturity phase   As time passes the product reaches maturity. Both the firm and the market are then in a situation which can be expected to continue for some time. The strategic pricing decisions will in this phase depend largely on the market share that has already been established and on the quality of the product compared to that of its competitors.

For a company with a high market share and a high-quality product, the policy is often to charge relatively high prices, supported by high marketing and product development expenditure in order to maintain the position of leadership. Prices may, however, still be well in excess of average total cost, since technical costs in the maturity phase are often low as a result of scale economies. Again, prices may diverge from cost during the maturity phase of the product life cycle.

Take, for example, the disposable nappy. This is a relatively mature product, yet producers are constantly seeking ways of updating the design of disposable nappies, with higher prices often associated with the updated version of this (mature) product. The point here is that the 'update' gives some latitude for price variation (increase). Vishwanath and Mark (1997) have shown that Proctor and Gamble, the makers of Pampers Baby-Dry and Pampers Premium disposable nappies, have continuously invested in strategic products such as these in order to maintain the 'mature phase' for as long as possible; i.e. to use updating-investment as a means of delaying the onset of the 'decline phase'.

Decline phase   Over time many products fall into 'decline', perhaps through changing social habits or because of technological innovation. Even so manufacturers will usually try to maintain their high price in the decline phase by relying upon the brand loyalty of those customers who remain. When products become 'obsolete', such as video games like 'Doom' and 'Quake', manufacturers may attempt to re-package such products as 'classics'. Where successful this strategy will allow them to continue to profit from earlier investment in such products, even during the decline phase.

Pricing policy may in these various ways be shaped by factors other than cost; here the phase of the product life cycle has played an important role.

Market segmentation strategies   There is a trend in advanced economies towards wider variety in consumer choice and greater specialization in industrial products. In other words the markets are far less homogeneous than had been thought; being constructed of *segments* which can be distinguished from each other. For example, cosmetics were once considered one market, but new product development, branding and packaging have segmented this in many ways. The Body Shop has targeted higher income consumers interested in using cosmetics that have not been tested on animals and which pose no threat to the environment, permitting a price premium for many of its cosmetic products. Similarly for the snack foods market, the Phileas Fogg brand had virtually created a niche market of 'adult nibbles' by the mid-1990s, with the prices about 20% higher than the common snacks. Their target market being identified as adult buyers who are entertaining guests. These forms of *life-style segmentation* are now used by many firms in preference to the social class distinctions of the previous three decades.

The price of goods and services may increasingly be related to the demand characteristics of the market segment, rather than to the actual costs of production. For example, the changing lifestyles of consumers are giving rise to changes in demand elasticity and buying habits. A number of studies have confirmed the idea that, by assembling goods in one place, a shop saves its customers 'search' costs. The *one stop shop* customers are prepared to *pay more* for the convenience of being able to buy all the household groceries in one shopping visit.

The beer market provides a further example of how market segmentation can form the basis of pricing strategies, rather than the costs of producing the various products. In the Monopolies and Mergers Commission Report (MMC 1989b) on the 'Supply

Fig. 9.4. The price of
beer (pounds per bbl).
Source: MMC (1989b).

of Beer' it was concluded that lager was more highly priced than beer but that 'the high price of lager was not justified by the cost of producing it'. Figure 9.4 shows the costs of producing four different types of draft beer. The cost of producing draft lager is less than packaged beer, for instance, yet its contribution to profits is considerably higher – the highest in fact of all the beers. Lager is attractive to younger drinkers, whose demand is apparently less sensitive to price. The demand for lager therefore displays a lower price elasticity, and in consequence a higher percentage mark-up on costs can be charged.

Price discrimination strategies

Price discrimination may also result in prices bearing little or no relation to cost. Conventional economic theory tells us that there are two conditions necessary for price discrimination, i.e. the charging of *different prices for the same product in different markets*. First, for price discrimination to be *possible*, there must be barriers (e.g. distance, time, etc.) preventing consumers switching from the dearer to the cheaper market. Second, for price discrimination to be *profitable*, there must be differences in price elasticity of demand between the markets. The profit-maximizing condition would then be that marginal cost for whole output be equal to marginal revenue *in each separate market*. In this way economic theory would predict higher prices in markets for which demand was less elastic, irrespective of cost conditions.

The market for motor vehicles has provided a clear example of price discrimination. Cars produced in a given location have been sold at substantially higher prices in the UK than in the rest of Europe. United Kingdom import legislation and the fact that European models were left-hand drive made it difficult to transfer cars across markets, so that the price differential persisted for many years. Another example is the price of telephone calls. The increase in demand for lines during business hours means that a premium can be charged over this period. Price sensitive users will wait for 'cheap rate' periods before making calls. This illustrates how demand affects the *price* of a service which *costs* virtually the same to provide, whatever time of day it is used.

Product differentiation strategies

Product differentiation refers to attempts by the firm to make its product different from other products. This may be achieved by changing the characteristics of the product, through R & D expenditure, or by changing consumer perceptions of the product, through additional marketing expenditure. Product differentiation enables the firm to lessen the prospect of facing direct competition and to move towards a more monopolistic position, with greater control over price.

In some cases product differentiation is becoming more difficult. Petrol companies, for instance, found product differentiation virtually impossible after the star/octane ratings were made public. Similarly, packaged food manufacturers with well-known brands such as Birds Eye and Heinz are being put under increasing pressure from retailers' own brands, some of which are now perceived as being of higher quality. Despite these difficulties many manufacturers are successful in differentiating their products and in gaining premium prices because of it.

An example of this was the introduction of 'Pepsi Max' by PepsiCo Inc. As a result of market research, PepsiCo established that the majority of consumers of Diet Pepsi were in fact female. Further research concluded that the reason for this was that men objected to purchasing goods that were labelled 'diet'. In order to allow full exploitation of the low calorie cola market, PepsiCo launched Pepsi Max, a sugar free cola drink, with no connotations with diet whatsoever. So, through the use of extensive market research, PepsiCo were able to identify an under-exploited niche in the cola market and create a unique product to exploit this (Sellars 1994).

It is in the firm's interest to establish the *extent* to which product differentiation gives it control over price, i.e. what the customer is prepared to pay. Kraushar (1982) describes how market research helps solve the problem of discovering exactly what the market will bear. Two techniques are frequently used: buy–response questions and multi-brand choice.

Buy–response and multi-brand choice   The buy–response test is where a large sample of respondents are shown the product and asked 'If you saw this product in your local store, would you pay £x, £y, £z ... etc. for it?' The list will typically contain ten prices. A large number of responses makes it possible to construct a buy–response curve, giving the percentage of buyers at different price levels. In the example shown in Fig. 9.5, 90% of those willing to buy would pay up to 40p for the product, and 35% would pay up to 56p. The flatter the buy–response curve the more control the firm has over price.

The multi-brand choice test is where respondents are asked to rate the products in question against similar products. The question may take the form 'If we add this feature to our product, making it different from our competitors', would you pay an extra £x, £y, £z ... etc. for it?' The aim is to establish a *relative* price for the product.

Kraushar cites a number of examples where these two approaches to price determination have been used successfully. Using buy–response curves, a manufacturer's undercoat paint was found to be more price-sensitive than his gloss paint. The manufacturer decided therefore to keep the price of his undercoat paint at the same level as that of cheaper competitors' 'own brands'. However, with gloss paint being less sensitive to price, the manufacturer was able to raise the price of this product relative to his competitors'.

Fig. 9.5. A typical buy–
response curve.

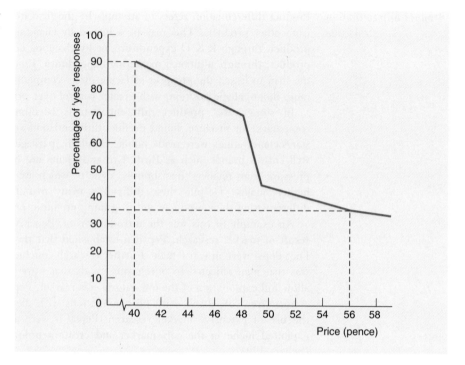

Product line price The point here is that where a firm produces a set of related products in a *product line*, then the pricing of one item may be influenced by factors other than the cost of producing that item. Suppose, for example, that a firm manufactures a product line consisting mainly of *complementary products*, as with a particular type of camera and its various accessories. The manufacturer may seek to maximize return on the *whole product line*, setting a price for the 'core' or central product (car or camera) low enough to attract customers to the components or accessories which can then be priced with a higher mark-up on cost.

On the other hand, the product line may consist mainly of *substitute products*, e.g. the manufacture of standard and de-luxe models of car or camera. Where two or more products in the line are substitutes, the price of the bottom-of-the-line product may be set artificially below that which a conventional mark-up on cost might suggest. If consumers are satisfied with the inexpensive first-time purchase, then the next time they make a repeat purchase they may buy a product in the higher quality range which earns the manufacturer a larger mark-up. The sale of automobiles tends to follow such considerations.

We can therefore see that the determination of prices in a *product line* is dependent on many factors other than costs. For example Sony, which produces the Walkman personal stereo, has a range of prices from £16.99 for the basic EX17 personal stereo, to £155 for a top-of-the-range FX665 personal stereo, with each successive model in the range offering additional features. The price of the various different models in the product range are determined not only by cost differences, but also by competitors' prices, consumers' perceptions of the additional features offered, and by the producers' objective to (in many cases) maximize the return to the *whole* product line rather than any single item contained within it. Psychology also plays a part in product line pricing since if the increments in price between two successive models in a range are too small, consumers, in the main, will opt for the more advanced model.

Prestige pricing strategies This type of pricing practice occurs when manufacturers price their products at a deliberately high level in the belief that consumers equate high prices with high quality. In this way an *increase in price* may even lead to an *increase in demand*, as in the case of Grand Metropolitan's 'Haagen Dazs' ice-cream. Indeed, through the introduction in 1993 of a new super premium product, 'Haagen Dazs Extraas', the company was able to convince consumers that this was a true prestige product. Despite a higher price this resulted in its US market share rising by 20% over an eight month period. *Prestige pricing strategies* can also occur in markets where consumers may have no other means of judging the product's exact quality so that they take the price as the best indicator of quality. For example, people often feel that branded drugs are more effective than the chemically equivalent generic drugs because they have been priced at a higher level.

If manufacturers *can* create an association in the consumers' mind that premium prices mean higher quality and exclusiveness, then they can engage in prestige pricing. For example, *designer* jeans and sports apparel sold in stores are often four times the price of mass market jeans and shirts; but the quality is rarely four times as high!

Influence of retailers on price Whatever lengths manufacturers go to in establishing the retail price for a product, they have to take account of the profit margins of the intermediaries – the distributors, both wholesalers and retailers. The power to control prices would in some markets appear to be moving out of the hands of producers and into the hands of distributors.

Brewers distribute their beers to a number of different types of trade channels. A Monopolies and Mergers Commission report in 1989 stated that the price, and the amount of contribution to profits, varied according to the channel used. In *Managed Houses* where they have most control, the wholesale price of draft lager averaged £128.23 per bbl (a beer barrel (bbl) is 36 gallons or 288 pints). In *Free Houses* the price averaged £116.49 per bbl. However, in Free Houses where a low interest loan had been provided by the Brewery (giving the Brewery more control), the price was £126. 11 per bbl. These differences are illustrated in Fig. 9.6. Prices of beer are influenced by demand (as we saw earlier) and, as we can see here, by the extent of control of the brewer over the retailer.

Brewing is another example of the producer successfully exerting control on price. However, as *retailers* become more powerful, they may be able to wrest control of prices from the producer. Bulk buying and a large share of the premium price grocery market makes such retailers as Tesco, Sainsbury, Safeway and Marks and Spencer formidable buyers who can significantly influence price. Furthermore such companies as these develop *strategic alliances* with suppliers. The powerful buyers provide technical and marketing expertise to the supplier and are willing to make long term commitments to the supplier in return for price and quality performance targets. As early as 1981, the major multiples were found to be enjoying lower costs and charging customers lower prices. Since then they have further increased market

Fig. 9.6. The price of
lager by type of trade
channel.
Source: MMC (1989b).

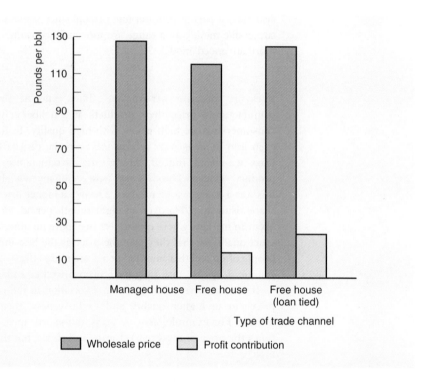

share, enlarged the ranges of 'own brand' (see Chapter 6, Table 6.5) goods and increased the dependence of suppliers upon them through computerised stock systems. One particular way in which retailers demonstrate their power is through the use of loss leaders.

Loss Leaders. A loss leader is a low priced item used to attract customers. For example, a well known branded product, which the customer uses for a reference price, might be subject to *deep discounting* by the retailer; here the retail price may be at, or even below, the invoiced cost. Such pricing can create, in the mind of the customer, what the John Lewis Partnership has described as a 'convincing aura of good value'. For suppliers of well known brands, however, this action by retailers can be damaging. It can reduce the perceived value of the product and discourage other retailers from selling it. When B&Q (DIY superstores) reduced the selling prices of Black and Decker power tools in 1989, Black and Decker retaliated by withholding supplies. This was illegal under the Resale Prices Act 1976 unless there was reasonable cause to believe that the retailer had been using them as loss leaders. Black and Decker normally gave a 15% margin to the retailer and decided that any retailer charging a price which reduced that to 12.5% or below was cutting the price by too much. The Monopolies and Mergers Commission disagreed, saying that a general rule of this type was too sweeping and that individual cases need to be looked at (MMC 1989a). They therefore disallowed Black and Decker's bid to withhold supplies, saying that it was 'anti-competitive'. Again we have an example where the retailer (here supported by statute) influenced the price despite the wishes of the producer, causing the final price to deviate from cost.

Discounts and price reductions   There are various methods by which the large retailers obtain reductions in the price of goods purchased from manufacturers and wholesalers. Manufacturers and wholesalers often have published price lists but these only give an indication of what is actually being charged. Prices, especially prices for large retailers, are a matter for negotiation, and reductions from stated prices come in a number of ways. The MMC report (1981: Chapter 4) describes some of the more common ones, which include:

Discounts for bulk delivery. Depending on quantity delivered in a 'drop'.
Special discounts. Negotiated discounts which take account of the overall relationship with the retail customer.

Retrospective discounts or rebates. Discounts made on the basis of quantities actually sold, sometimes called 'over-riders'. These are negotiated at the beginning of a contract, and if the quantity sold reaches an appropriate level, then the discount becomes operative and is given at the end of the contract period.

Favourable credit terms. Allowing some retail customers longer to pay, thereby reducing their costs.

Special promotions. In this case wholesalers and manufacturers pay for the price reduction passed on to the final customer, so that the retailer's short-term profit does not suffer.

In addition to these price benefits, other non-price incentives may be given to retailers. These include payments to cover the costs of shelf-filling, point-of-sale advertising, staff training, etc.

When retailers have substantial buying power, the producers are far less able to set prices purely on a cost-plus basis. Although producers may not formally *change* their percentage mark-up on cost, they often do so in practice by varying the discounts permitted to retailers in the light of market conditions.

Conclusion

Pricing decisions depend both on the structure of the market in which the firm operates and the objectives it pursues. There are, in fact, a variety of market structures and a variety of firm objectives, so that theory predicts a wide range of price outcomes. Can observation of firm practice lead us to more definite conclusions? Costs certainly determine the price floor, since in the long term price cannot fall below average total cost if the firm is to stay in business. However, those who support cost-plus theories would argue that everyday prices are closely related to cost. There is a considerable body of empirical support for cost-plus price-setting, though there is also evidence that the percentage mark-up on cost varies with both market circumstance and with firm strategy. The phase of the product life cycle may also influence price, as may the firm's degree of 'success' in setting prices which discriminate between markets, or in establishing product differentiation. Finally, the nature of the retail outlets used by the firm will affect the price, with the producer having less freedom to dictate price where retail outlets themselves have a large customer base.

Key points	

- Estimates of the level of output and decisions as to the costs to be included are vital elements in cost-plus pricing.
- The percentage mark-up on cost seems to rise as market conditions improve, suggesting that demand factors as well as costs play a part here.
- In a major survey of 654 UK companies, over 47% regarded cost-based pricing as 'important' (Hall *et al.* 1996).
- Other influences on price include firm objective, market structure, stage reached in the product life cycle, pursuit of market segmentation or price discrimination strategies, etc.
- Product differention, product-line pricing and prestige pricing strategies may also influence price.
- The major survey of 654 UK companies reported above also found 'market led' pricing to be the most important pricing strategy for over 65% of companies (Hall *et al.* 1996).
- Although often neglected by economists, the market power of distributors may influence price at least as much as producers.

Notes	

1. For instance, it is assumed in Fig. 9.2 that the four firm objectives are of the maximizing type, with only a single price outcome for each objective. Equally, Fig. 9.2 assumes that for each objective and market structure there is a single price outcome covering both short- and long-run time periods. If either of these assumptions is relaxed, there might be more than sixteen different price outcomes from our figure. See also Eichner (1987).

References	

Blinder, A. (1992) Why are prices sticky? *American Economic Review*, May.

Coutts, K., Godley, G. and **Nordhaus, W.** (1978) *Industrial Pricing in the UK*, CUP.

Dahlby, B. (1992) Price adjustment in an automobile insurance market, *Canadian Journal of Economics*, **25**.

Eichner, A. S. (1987) Prices and pricing, *Journal of Economic Issues*, December.

Grant, R. M. (1982) Pricing behaviour in the UK wholesale market for petrol 1970–80: a 'structure-conduct analysis', *Journal of Industrial Economics*, **30**, 3, March.

Hague, D. C. (1948) Economic theory and business behaviour, *Review of Economic Studies*, **16**.

Hall, R. L. and **Hitch, C. J.** (1939) Price theory and business behaviour, *Oxford Economic Papers*, 2, May.

Hall, S., Walsh, M. and **Yates, T.** (1996) How do UK companies set prices?, *Bank of England Quarterly Bulletin*, May.

Jobber, D. and **Hooley, G.** (1987) Pricing behaviour in UK manufacturing and service industries, *Managerial and Decision Economics*, **8**, pp. 167–77.

Kraushar, P. (1982) How to research prices, *Management Today*, January.

MMC (1981) *Discounts to Retailers*, House of Commons Papers, 311, HMSO.

MMC (1989a) *Black and Decker*, House of Commons Papers, Command 805.

MMC (1989b) *The Supply of Beer*, House of Commons Papers, Command 651.

Office of Fair Trading (1998) *Competition in the Supply of Petrol*, OFT229.

Redmond, W. H. (1989) Effects of new product pricing on the evolution of market structure, *Journal of Product Innovation Management,* **6,** 2, June.

Sellars, P. (1994) Pepsi opens a second front, *Fortune,* **8,** August.

Shipley, D. and **Bourdon, E.** (1990) Distributor pricing in very competitive markets, *Industrial Marketing Management,* **19.**

Small Business Research Trust (1995) *Pricing Policies,* **3,** 4.

Vishwanath, V. and **Mark, J.** (1997) Your brand's best strategy, *Harvard Business Review,* May–June.

Chapter 10

Economics of the environment

In recent years there has been considerable interest in the impact of economic decisions on the environment. In this chapter we start by reviewing the position of the environment in models of national income determination. We then look at a number of important contemporary issues involving the environment, such as the debates on sustainable growth and global environmental change. The application of cost–benefit principles to environmental issues is also considered together with problems of valuation. The use of market-based incentives in dealing with environmental problems, such as taxation and tradeable permits, is reviewed, as is the use of 'command and control' type regulations. We conclude by examining a number of case studies which show how environmental considerations can be brought into practical policy making.

Role of the environment

The familiar circular flow analysis represents the flow of income (and output) between domestic firms and households. Withdrawals (leakages) from the circular flow are identified as savings, imports, and taxes, and injections into the circular flow as investment, exports, and government expenditure. When withdrawals exactly match injections, then the circular flow is regarded as being in 'equilibrium', with no further tendency to rise or fall in value.

All this should be familiar from any introductory course in macroeconomics. This circular flow analysis is often considered to be 'open' since it incorporates external flows of income (and output) between domestic and overseas residents via exports and imports. However, many economists would still regard this system as 'closed' in one vital respect, namely that it takes no account of the constraints imposed upon the economic system by environmental factors. Such a 'traditional' circular flow model assumes that natural resources are abundant and limitless, and generally ignores any waste disposal implications for the economic system.

Fig. 10.1 provides a simplified model in which linkages between the conventional economy (circular flow system) and the environment *are* now introduced. The natural environment is seen as being involved with the economy in at least three specific ways.

Fig. 10.1. Economy/
environment linkages.

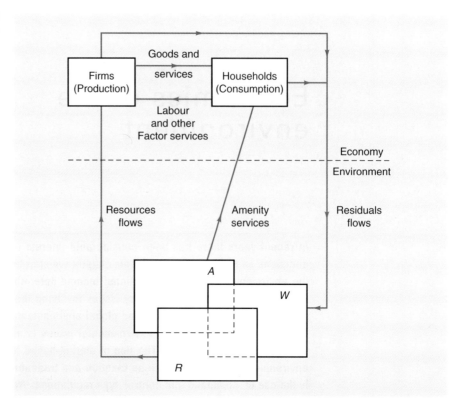

1. *Amenity Services (A)*   The natural environment provides consumer services to domestic households in the form of living and recreational space, natural beauty, and so on. We call these 'Amenity Services'.
2. *Natural Resources (R)*   The natural environment is also the source of various inputs into the production process such as mineral deposits, forests, water resources, animal populations and so on. These natural resources are in turn the basis of both the renewable and non-renewable energy supplies used in production.
3. *Waste Products (W)*   Both production and consumption are activities which generate waste products or residuals. For example, many productive activities generate harmful by-products which are discharged into the atmosphere or watercourses. Similarly, sewage, litter and other waste products result from many consumption activities. The key point here is that the natural environment is the ultimate dumping place or 'sink' for all these waste products or residuals.

We have now identified three *economic* functions of the environment: namely, it functions as a direct source of consumer utility (A), as a resource supplier (R) and as a waste receptor and assimilator (W). Moreover, these functions interact with other parts of the economic system and also with each other. This latter point is the reason for showing the three boxes A, R and W as overlapping each other in Fig. 10.1. For example, a waterway may provide amenity services (A) to anglers and sailors, as well as aesthetic beauty to onlookers. At the same time it may also provide water resources

(R) to firms situated alongside which can be used for power, for cleaning, as a coolant or as a direct input into production. Both consumers and producers may then discharge effluent and other waste products (W) into the waterway as a consequence of using this natural resource. All three functions may readily co-exist at certain levels of interaction. However, excessive levels of effluent and waste discharge could over-extend the ability of the waterway to assimilate waste, thereby destroying the Amenity and Resource functions of the waterway. In other words the three economic functions of the natural environment constantly interact with each other, as well as with the economic (circular flow) system as a whole. Later in the chapter we shall look at ways of providing economic incentives or regulations which might bring about *optimum* levels of interaction between each function and within the economic system as a whole.

By bringing the environment into our modelling of the economy we are essentially challenging the traditional view that the environment and the economy can be treated as separate entities. Everything that happens in the economy has a potential environmental impact. For example, excessive price support for agricultural products under the Common Agricultural Policy (CAP – see Ch. 28) will encourage over-production of agricultural produce. Land which might otherwise be left in its natural state may then be brought into agricultural use, and increased yields may be sought by additional applications of fertilizers and pesticides. Hedgerows may be cut back to provide larger and more economical units of cultivation, and so on. In other words, most types of economic policy intervention will impact the environment directly or indirectly. Equally, policies which seek to influence the environment will themselves impact the economic system. As we shall see, attempts to reduce CO_2 (carbon dioxide) emissions may influence the relative attractiveness of different types of energy, causing consumers to switch between coal, gas, electricity, nuclear power and other energy forms. There will be direct effects on output, employment and prices in these substitute industries and, via the multiplier, elsewhere in the economy. We must treat the traditional economic system and the environment as being dynamically interrelated.

Sustainable growth

Economic activity can be viewed as being primarily concerned with the conversion of natural resources into products. Products can therefore be regarded as embodied energy and materials. However, when products decay they become waste and it is the environment which must ultimately handle that waste. An increased output of products, via economic growth, will inevitably produce still more waste. This in turn brings into focus the 'first law of thermodynamics'.

First Law of Thermodynamics   This states that we cannot create or destroy energy and matter. We cannot therefore add to the finite stock of energy, and other environmental resources. Equally, whatever energy or natural resources we use up in consumption or production activities must end up somewhere else in the environmental system. Resources cannot be destroyed; they can only be converted or assimilated in one way or another.

In this view, the earth is a closed system in which a finite set of resources is available for current and future growth. In other words the capacity of the economy to produce still more products is constrained or limited by the availability of natural resources. Even if resources are sufficient to permit growth, the extra production will simply 'drag through' more materials and energy embodied in products, which the environment must ultimately assimilate, since matter and energy cannot be destroyed. Wherever possible, materials must therefore be recycled, renewable energy sources must be used in preference to non-renewable sources, and waste emissions must be limited to the extent that the earth can safely absorb these 'residuals'. This approach has led many economists to propose limiting our demand for goods and services in order to attain a level of economic growth that can be 'sustained' over future generations.

The question then follows as to whether it is possible to separate or 'decouple' the economy from those constraints imposed by environmental considerations. Put another way, is it possible to change the current *ratio* between economic growth and any adverse environmental impacts? There are at least two ways in which this might be done.

Decoupling the economy from the environment

1. **Technological change**   As we note in Chapter 23 and elsewhere in this book, new technology can raise output per unit of factor input (i.e. factor productivity). This can be as true for 'environmental input' as for capital or labour input. For example, the increased use of 'clean' technologies in the high income countries has reduced the environmental damage inflicted per unit of raw material consumed. As we can see from Fig. 10.2 the growth path of damaging pollutants has to some extent been successfully decoupled from the growth path of Gross Domestic Product (GDP) in the high income OECD countries. For instance, since 1970 the GDP of the OECD countries has risen by over 80%, yet sulphur oxide emissions have *fallen* by 38%, particulate emissions by 60% and lead emissions by over 85%. Whilst more can still be done, technological change is certainly one way in which

Fig. 10.2. Breaking the link between growth in GDP and pollution. *Source:* Adapted from World Bank (1992).

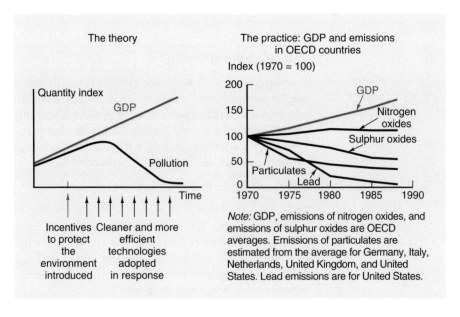

Note: GDP, emissions of nitrogen oxides, and emissions of sulphur oxides are OECD averages. Emissions of particulates are estimated from the average for Germany, Italy, Netherlands, United Kingdom, and United States. Lead emissions are for United States.

we can change the ratio between economic growth and adverse environmental impacts.

Of course the invention and application of clean technologies is not without cost. Improvements such as those shown in Fig. 10.2 have been achieved as the result of annual expenditures on anti-pollution policies equivalent to 0.8–1.5 per cent of GDP since the 1970s. About half of these expenditures were incurred by the public sector and half by the private sector.

Technology can also help 'decoupling' by developing new production processes which reduce the energy input required per £ of GNP. This has, in fact, happened in the UK. In 1998 our real GNP was some 50% higher than in 1970, yet our energy consumption was broadly the same. In other words we were producing each £1 of GNP with only two-thirds of the energy input required in 1970.

2. Conservation and recycling   Conservation is a second means by which we can reduce the impact of economic growth on the environment. Since matter and energy cannot be created, the idea here is to use only the minimum necessary amount of existing materials and energy to achieve any given output target. Recycling can also help in this respect. For instance, if we recycle a tonne of crushed glass we can make a saving of around 25% in terms of the oil and raw material originally used to make that glass. Again, all metal production uses a lot of energy, particularly aluminium production. However, if we recycle aluminium, then we save 95% of the energy that would otherwise be used to make the same amount of new aluminium. It is estimated that some 77% by weight of the materials used in new car manufacture are now recycled in the UK. Steps have been taken to *design* items in a way that facilitates recycling; for example, BMW has designed cars for 90% recyclability by weight (Royal Commission 1994).

National income valuations   We have seen how growth of GDP may bring with it environmental costs. First, there may be costs of pollution to the health of a country's citizens, which might be given a monetary value (e.g. by estimating the additional number of working days lost). Second, there are resource costs involved in running down the stock of natural resources and therefore the country's capacity for future production. Attempts are being made to express such environmental factors in terms of the National Accounts. A recent Mexican study (World Bank 1992) gives some idea of the adjustments which might be involved. Mexico's net national product fell by almost seven per cent when an adjustment was made to take into account the depletion of oil, forests and groundwater associated with recent levels of recorded economic growth. Table 10.1 gives some further indication of the estimated impact on national income of environmental damage in selected countries.

Sustainable economic welfare

Rather more sophisticated attempts to capture environmental costs within a national accounting framework have been made by economists such as Jackson and Marks (1994 and, with Ralls and Stymne, 1997). An Index of Sustainable Economic Welfare (ISEW) has been calculated for the USA and UK. Essentially, any increase in the

Table 10.1 Summary of
national environmental
damage estimates.

Country	Form of environmental damage	Year	Percentage GNP
Burkina Faso	Crop, livestock and fuelwood losses due to land degradation	1988	8.8
Ethiopia	Effects of deforestation on fuelwood supply and crop output	1983	6.0–9.0
Madagascar	Land burning and erosion	1988	5.0–15.0
Malawi	Soil erosion	1990	0.5–3.1
Mali	On site soil erosion losses	1988	0.4
Nigeria	Soil degradation, deforestation, water pollution, other erosion	1989	17.4
Indonesia	Soil erosion and deforestation	1984	4.0
Hungary	Pollution damage	late 80s	5.0
Poland	Pollution damage	1987	2.1–4.4
Czechoslovakia	Pollution damage	1988	5.0
Germany*	Pollution damage	1988	2.1–4.4
Netherlands	Some pollution damage	1986	0.5–0.8
USA[†]	Air pollution control	1981	0.8–2.1
	Water pollution control	1985	0.4

*Pre-unification.
[†]Benefits of environmental policy, i.e., avoided damages rather than actual damages.
Source: Adapted from Pearce (1991b).

GNP figure is *adjusted* to reflect the following impacts which are often associated with rising GNP:

1. monies spent correcting environmental damage (i.e. 'defensive' expenditures);
2. decline in the stock of natural resources (i.e. environmental depreciation);
3. pollution damage (i.e. monetary value of any environmental damage not corrected).

By failing to take these environmental impacts into account, the conventional GNP figure arguably does *not* give an accurate indication of *sustainable economic welfare*, i.e., the flow of goods and services that an economy can generate without reducing its future production capacity. Suppose we consider the expenditure method of calculating GNP. It could be argued that some of the growth in GNP is due to expenditures undertaken to mitigate (offset) the impact of environmental damage. For example, some double-glazing may be undertaken to reduce noise levels from increased traffic flow, and does not therefore reflect an increase in economic well being, merely an attempt to retain the status quo. Such 'defensive expenditures' should be subtracted from the GNP figure (item 1. above). So too should be expenditures associated with a decline in the stock of natural resources. For example, the monetary value of minerals extracted from rock is included in GNP but nothing is subtracted to reflect the loss of unique mineral deposits. 'Environmental depreciation' of this kind should arguably be subtracted from the conventional GNP figure (item 2. above). Finally, some expenditures are incurred to overcome pollution damage which has not been corrected; e.g., extra cost of bottled water when purchased because tap water is of poor quality. Additional expenditures of this kind should also be subtracted from the GNP figure, as should the monetary valuation of any environmental damage which has *not* been corrected (item 3. above).

We are then left with an Index of Sustainable Economic Welfare (ISEW) which subtracts rather more from GNP than the usual depreciation of physical capital.

ISEW = GNP *minus* depreciation of physical capital

                  minus defensive expenditures

                  minus depreciation of environmental capital

                  minus monetary value of residual pollution

As we can see from Fig. 10.3 the effect of such adjustments is quite startling. The UK GNP per capita (unadjusted) was 2.5 times greater in real terms in 1996 than it was in 1950 (Jackson *et al.* 1997). This corresponds to a 2.0% average annual growth in real GNP, 1950–1996. However the adjustment outlined above for each year over the period gives an ISEW per head for the UK which is just 1.25 times higher in real terms than it was in 1950. This corresponds to a mere 0.5% average annual growth in real ISEW, 1950–1996. Such 'environmental accounting' is suggesting an entirely different perspective on recorded changes in national economic welfare.

Global environmental changes

The issue of reducing the environmental costs of economic growth has become all the more pressing, given an increasing awareness of the global environmental changes currently underway.

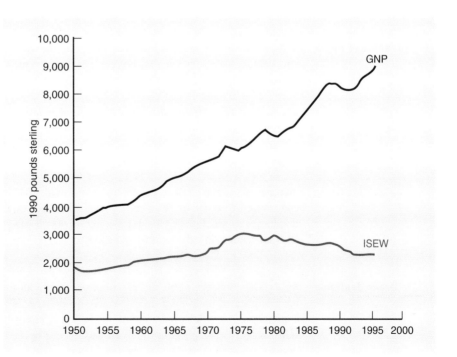

Fig. 10.3. Real GNP and ISEW per capita, UK 1950–1996.
Note: ISEW = Index of Sustainable Economic Welfare.
Source: Adapted from Jackson *et al.* (1997).

Fig. 10.4.   The population explosion.

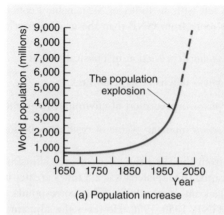

(a) Population increase

(b) A comparison of population increase in developing and developed countries

Country	1982 Population (millions)	Estimated 2050 Population (millions)	% Increase 1982–2050
Bangladesh	93	357	284
Brazil	127	279	120
China	1008	1450	44
India	717	1513	111
Indonesia	153	332	117
Mexico	73	182	149
Nigeria	91	471	418
Pakistan	87	302	247
USA	226	288	27
USSR	265	358	35

Population and resource use

Over the next 40 years the World Bank expects the world's population, now at 5.3bn, to grow by more than two-thirds to over 9bn (Fig. 10.4).

In most parts of the world this growth will involve a rapid increase in urban dwellers. Only in Africa will more than half the population still be living off the land. As a result food demand is expected to double over the next 40 years, while global industrial output and energy consumption is expected to more than treble. Indeed, over the last generation, gross global product (GGP) has been growing at more than 3% a year. If growth continues at this rate, then 250 years from now the GGP would be 1,600 times larger than its present size.

Various environmental problems are seen as inevitable side-effects of this growth in industrial output and in energy consumption.

Greenhouse effect

This refers to the trapping of heat between the earth's surface and gases in the atmosphere, especially carbon dioxide. Currently some six billion tonnes of carbon dioxide (CO_2) are released into the atmosphere each year, largely as a result of burning fossil fuels. In fact carbon dioxide constitutes some 56% of these 'greenhouse gases', with chlorofluorocarbons (CFCs) used mainly in refrigerators, aerosols and air-conditioning systems, accounting for a further 23% of such gases, the rest being methane (14%) and nitrous oxide (7%). By trapping the sun's heat these gases are in turn raising global temperature (global warming). On present estimates, temperatures are expected to increase by a further 1.3°C by 2020 and 3°C by the year 2070. An increase of merely half a degree in world temperature this century has already contributed to a rise of 10cm in sea levels. Higher sea levels (via melting ice caps), flooding, various climatic changes causing increased desertification and drought, have all been widely linked to global warming.

Ozone depletion

As well as contributing to the greenhouse effect, chlorofluorocarbons (CFCs) have been implicated in eroding the protective ozone layer in the upper atmosphere. As a consequence ultraviolet radiation has increased in intensity, producing higher rates of skin cancer, cataract related illnesses and even crop failures as ultraviolet radiation destroys proteins and nucleic acids in plants.

The linkage between environment and economy can be usefully illustrated here. Ozone depletion and the associated increases in ultraviolet radiation are expected to cut by one-fifth the yields of vegetable crops such as peas, barley and oil-seed rape by the end of the century. These and other species of plants are highly sensitive to ultraviolet radiation and show a 1% fall in yield for every 1% reduction in the protective ozone layer. Plants exposed to higher levels of UV-B radiation are often smaller, less fertile in terms of reproduction, and have a lower oil and protein content (e.g. soya bean). Cereal crops such as wheat are also affected. With a 10% reduction in the ozone layer already experienced over Europe in the past ten years, the impact of reduced crop yields is expected to be seen in progressively higher food prices than would otherwise have been the case.

Deforestation In an attempt to meet the demand for wood as a resource and to clear forests for farming and ranching, the tropical rainforests are being depleted at a rate of around 1% a year. This is likely to further increase the greenhouse effect as the rainforests, in net terms, take in carbon dioxide and give out oxygen, thereby providing a 'carbon absorption service'.

If countries individually, and jointly, are to improve environmental management then targeted policies are needed to ensure that environmental values are properly reflected in economic activity by both the private and public sectors. One way of seeking to evaluate the full economic and environmental impacts of projects and policies is the use of a cost-benefit approach.

Cost-benefit analysis and the environment

Cost-benefit analysis (CBA) is an attempt to provide a monetary valuation of the perceived costs and benefits of any particular investment project (see Chapter 12). We can use this technique to evaluate the impact of projects seeking to improve environmental quality.

Fig 10.5 presents a simplified model in which the marginal pollution costs (MPC) attributable to production are seen as rising with output beyond a certain output level, Q_A. Up to Q_A the amount of pollution generated within the economy is assumed to be assimilated by the environment with zero pollution costs. In this model we assume that pollution is a 'negative externality', in that firms which pollute are imposing costs on society that are not paid for by those firms.

At the same time the marginal *net* private benefit (MNPB) of each unit of output is assumed to decline as the level of economic activity rises. MNPB is the addition to private benefit received by firms from selling the last unit of output minus the addition to private costs incurred by producing that last unit of output.

If the pollution externality was *not* taken into account, then firms would produce up to output Q_B at which MNPB = 0. Only here would total net private benefit (i.e. total profit) be a maximum. However, the *socially optimum* level of output is Q_S, where MNPB = MPC. Each unit of output *beyond* Q_S adds more in pollution costs to society than it does to net private benefit, and is therefore socially inefficient to produce. Equally it would be socially inefficient to forsake producing any units *up to* Q_S, since each of these units adds more to net private benefit than to pollution costs for society.

Fig. 10.5. Finding an
optimum level of
pollution.

Fig. 10.5. Finding an optimum level of pollution.

Note:
MNPB = Marginal Net Private Benefit
MPC = Marginal Pollution Cost

Note that in this analysis the social optimum does *not* imply zero pollution. Rather it suggests that the benefits to society are greatest at output Q_S, with pollution costs being positive at Q_SX. We return to this idea of seeking 'acceptable' levels of pollution below.

The valuation issue   A key element in finding any socially efficient solution to the negative environmental effects of increased production clearly involves placing a *monetary value* on the marginal private and social costs (or benefits) of production. In terms of Figure 10.6 we need some monetary valuation which will permit us to estimate both the MNPB and the MPC curves.

The idea of 'willingness to pay' underlies many of the methods used by economists in an attempt to place a monetary value on benefits and costs, especially where no market prices exist. Individuals are asked, using *surveys* or *questionnaires*, how much they would be willing to pay for some specified environmental good, such as improved water quality or the preservation of a threatened local amenity. For example, in Ukunda, Kenya, residents had three sources of water – door-to-door vendors, kiosks and wells – each requiring residents to pay different costs in money and time. Water from door-to-door vendors cost the most but required the least collection time. A study found that the villagers were willing to pay a substantial share of their incomes – about eight per cent – in exchange for this greater convenience and for time saved. Such valuations can be helpful in seeking to make the case for extending reliable public water supply even to poorer communities.

Questionnaires and surveys of willingness-to-pay have been widely used in the UK to evaluate the recreational benefits of environmental amenities (Willis 1991). Other valuation methods may also be used. For example, where no price is charged for entry to recreational sites, economists have searched for private market goods whose consumption is *complementary* to the consumption of the recreational good in question. One such private complementary good is the travel costs incurred by individuals to gain access to recreational sites. The 'price' paid to visit any site is uniquely determined for each visitor by calculating the travel costs from his/her location of origin. By observing people's willingness to pay for the private complementary good it is then possible to infer a price for the non-price environmental amenity.

In Fig. 10.6, the demand curve D_{VISITS} shows the overall trend relationship between travel costs and visit rates for all the visitors interviewed. Using this information we can estimate the average visitor's (V_1) total recreational value $(V_1 \times P_1)$ for the site. Multiplying this by the total number of visitors per annum allows us to estimate the total annual recreational value of the site.

A further technique often used in deriving valuations where no prices exist, is the so-called 'hedonic price' method. This estimates the extent to which people are, for example, willing to pay a house price premium for the benefit of living within easy access of an environmental amenity.

Using all such methods, the value of non-priced recreation on the Forestry Commission sites in the UK was estimated to be £53 million per annum in 1988, almost as large as the total income from the sale of timber from those sites.

Total economic value

In recent years there has been considerable discussion as to how to find the 'total economic value' (TEV) of an environmental asset. The following identity has been suggested:

Total Economic Value $\equiv$ Use Value + Option Value + Existence Value

The idea here is that 'use value' reflects the practical uses to which an environmental asset is currently being put. For example, the tropical rainforests are used to provide arable land for crop cultivation or to rear cattle in various ranching activities. The forests are also a source of various products, such as timber, rubber, medicines, nuts, etc. In addition, the forests act as the 'lungs' of the world, absorbing stores of carbon dioxide and releasing oxygen, as well as helping to prevent soil erosion and playing an important part in flood control.

Fig. 10.6. The relationship between the number of visits to a site and the price of the visit.

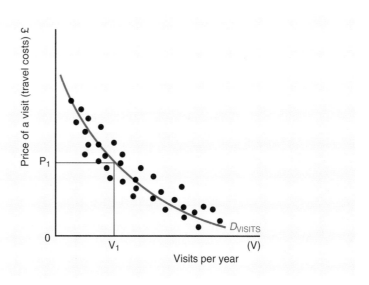

There are clear difficulties in placing reliable monetary estimates on all these aspects of the 'use value' of the rainforest. However, it is even more difficult to estimate 'option value', which refers to the value we place on the asset *now* as regards functions which might be exploited some time in the *future*. For example, how much are we willing to pay to preserve the rain forest in case it becomes a still more important source of herbal and other medicines? This is a type of insurance value, seeking to measure the willingness to pay for an environmental asset now, given some probability function of the individual (or group) wishing to use that asset in various ways in the future.

Finally, 'existence value' refers to the value we place on an environmental asset as it is today, independently of any current or future use we might make of that asset. This is an attempt to measure our willingness to pay for an environmental asset simply because we wish it to continue to exist in its present form. Many people subscribe to charities to preserve the rainforests, other natural habitats or wildlife even though they may never themselves see those habitats or species. Existence value may involve inter-generational motives, such as wishing to give one's children or grandchildren the opportunity to observe certain species or ecosystems.

Although much remains to be done in estimating TEV, a number of empirical studies have been undertaken. For instance, the Flood Hazard Research Centre in the UK estimated that in 1987/88 people were willing to pay £14 to £18 per annum in taxes in order that recreational beaches (use value) be protected from erosion (Turner 1991). The researchers also surveyed a sample of people who did *not* use beaches for recreational use. They estimated that these people were willing to pay £21 to £25 per annum in taxes in order to preserve these same beaches (existence value).

Overall, many estimates are finding that the 'option' and 'existence' values of environmental assets often far exceed their 'use' value. For example, existence values for the Grand Canyon were found to outweigh use values by the startling ratio of 60 to 1 (Pearce 1991a). In similar vein, *non-users* of Prince William Sound, Alaska, devastated by the Exxon Valdez oil spill in 1989 placed an extremely high value on its existence value (O'Doherty 1994). The amounts non-users were estimated (via interviews) as willing to pay to *avoid* the damage actually incurred came to $2.8 billion, i.e. $31 per US household. This approach whereby interviewees are asked about the value of a resource 'contingent' on its not being damaged, is often termed 'contingent valuation.'

We now turn to the important policy issue of how we can provide market incentives or regulations which will result in a socially optimum level of environmental damage (output Q_S in Fig. 10.5), rather than the higher levels of environmental damage which would result from an unfettered free market in which externalities were ignored (output Q_B in Fig. 10.5).

Market-based and non-market-based incentives

In free-market or mixed economies the market is often seen as an efficient means of allocating scarce resources. Here we look at ways in which the *market* could be used to provide incentives to either firms or consumers in order to bring about a more socially optimum use of environmental assets.

Market-based incentives

a) Environmental taxes   An environmental tax is a tax on a product or service which is detrimental to the environment, or a tax on a factor input used to produce that product or service. An environmental tax will increase the *private* costs of producing goods or services which impose negative 'externalities' on society. In terms of Fig. 10.5 earlier, an appropriate tax could convert the marginal *pollution* cost curve (MPC) into the firm's own marginal cost curve (MC). This is because the firm itself now has to pay a 'price' (the tax) for the pollution it imposes on society. The firm itself would then have a profit based incentive to produce the socially optimum level of output Q_S, since its own profits would now be maximized at MNPB = MPC, instead of producing the socially inefficient output Q_B. Using environmental taxes in this way is often said to be a policy of 'internalising' the externality. In other words the firm itself now has the incentive to take the externality into account in its own decision making.

Of course, in practice, there are many problems in devising a tax rate which will exactly equate marginal pollution cost (MPC) with marginal cost (MC) for the firm. Such a (Pigouvian) tax would need to impose private costs which vary with output in a way which exactly mirrors the amount of marginal pollution cost related to each additional unit of output.

A move towards environmental taxes is in line with the 'polluter-pays' principle adopted by the OECD in 1972. This principle states that 'the polluter should bear the cost of measures to reduce pollution decided upon by public authorities to ensure that the environment is in an 'acceptable state'. The idea behind adopting this principle across member states was to avoid the distortions in comparative advantages and trade flows which could arise if countries tackled environmental problems in widely different ways. Slightly less than 2% of UK total tax revenue is currently yielded by explicitly environmental taxes, although if general taxes on energy are also included in a looser definition of 'environmentally related' taxes, then this figure rises to some 8.5% of UK total tax revenue.

b) Tradeable permits   Another market-based solution to environmental problems could involve tradeable permits. Here the polluter receives a permit to emit a specified amount of waste, whether carbon dioxide, sulphur dioxide or whatever. The *total* amount of permits issued for any pollutant must, of course, be within currently accepted guidelines of 'safe' levels of emission for that pollutant. Within the overall limit of the permits issued, individual polluters can then buy and sell the permits between each other. The distribution of pollution is then market directed even though the overall total is regulated. The expectation being that those firms which are already able to meet 'clean' standards will benefit by selling permits to those firms which currently find it too difficult or expensive to meet those standards.

Under the United States Clean Air Act legislation it is possible to trade permits. The Tennessee Valley Authority, for example, has agreed to buy allowances to emit 10,000 tons of sulphur dioxide, a key cause of acid rain, from privately owned Wisconsin Power and Light. Similarly, Duquesne Light of Pittsburgh has bought allowances from the same Wisconsin company to emit between 15,000 and 25,000 tons of sulphur dioxide. Under the Clean Air Act, utilities have been required to cut emissions of sulphur dioxide in half by the year 2000, i.e. from a national total of 19 million tons to 9 millions tons.

There are, arguably, at least two main benefits from this market in tradeable permits. First, costs of production will be lower than they otherwise would be in producing power consistent with the new overall environmental targets. This is because there will be a cost saving for those companies with permits which would otherwise either have to purchase expensive technology (e.g. 'scrubbers') to meet lower sulphur emissions or to change capital equipment to deal with harder, lower sulphur coal. This cost saving is, arguably, achieved at no overall rise in projected levels of sulphur pollution since the 'cleaner' companies now have an incentive to *more than meet* the lower targets of sulphur emission, exchanging 'unneeded' permits for cash on the market.

Secondly, the market in tradeable permits will help to avoid other sources of environmental damage which would otherwise occur. For instance, the market will help avoid the hazards involved in transporting large amounts of hard, low-sulphur coal from the western states of the US to the eastern states in which most of the soft, high sulphur coal is produced and in which most of the 'offending' power utilities reside. It will now be possible for the power utilities in the east to purchase permits from power utilities elsewhere, thereby avoiding the disruption of adapting capital equipment and working practices, as well as avoiding any environmental costs associated with bulk transport of cargo over long distances.

The Kyoto agreement in December 1997, has for the first time, accepted the principle of carbon trading between nations. Countries are to be allocated quotas for maximum annual emissions of carbon dioxide. Should any country produce *less than* its quota, it will be able to sell its 'right to pollute' to other countries.

c) Bargains   The idea here is that if we assign 'property rights' to the polluters giving them the 'right to pollute', or to the sufferers giving them the 'right not to be polluted', then bargains may be struck whereby pollution is curbed. For instance, if we assign these property rights to the polluters, then those who suffer may find it advantageous to compensate the polluter for agreeing *not* to pollute. The suggestion being that compensation will be offered by the sufferers as long as this is less than the value of the damage which would otherwise be inflicted upon them. Alternatively, if the property rights are assigned to the sufferers, who then have the 'right' not to be polluted, then the polluters may find it advantageous to offer the sufferers sums of money which would allow the polluters to continue polluting. The suggestion being that the polluters will offer compensation to the sufferers as long as this is less than the private benefits obtained by expanding output and thereby increasing pollution. Under either situation, economists such as R. Coase have shown that clearly assigned property rights can lead to 'bargains' which bring about output solutions closer to the social optimum than would otherwise occur.

From Fig. 10.7 we can see that, with no regulation, the polluter will seek to maximize *total* net private benefits (profits) producing at Q_B, whereas Q_S is the social optimum.

The introduction of property rights can, however, change this situation. If the *polluter* is given the property rights, then the sufferer will (provided polluter and sufferer have the same information!) find it advantageous to *compensate/bribe* the polluter to cease output at Q_S. For any *extra* output beyond Q_S the losses to the sufferer exceed the benefits to the polluter (eg $X + Y > X$ at output Q_B). There is clearly scope for a negotiated solution at output level Q_S.

Fig. 10.7.   Negotiation
under property rights.

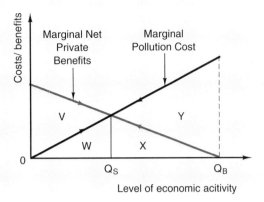

A similar negotiated outcome can be expected under the Coase theorem if the *sufferer* is given the property rights. This time the polluter will (given symmetry of information) find it advantageous to *choose* the socially optimum output Q_S and offer compensation equivalent to W to sufferers. For any *extra* output beyond Q_S the gains to the polluter are more than offset by the (actionable) losses to the sufferers (e.g. X < X + Y at output Q_B). There is, again, clearly scope for a negotiated solution at output level Q_S.

The principle of 'sufferer pays' is already in evidence. For example, Sweden assists Poland with reducing acid rain because the acid rain from Poland damages Swedish lakes and forests. Similarly, the Montreal Protocol of 1987 sought to protect the ozone layer by including provisions by which China, India and other developing countries were to be compensated by richer countries for agreeing to limit their use of chlorofluorocarbons (CFCs). On this basis, Brazil has argued that it is up to the developed countries to compensate it for desisting from exploiting its tropical rainforests, given that it is primarily other countries which will suffer if deforestation continues apace.

Non-market-based incentives: regulations

Many current environmental policies make use of regulations. Standards are set for air or water quality and the polluter is then left free to decide on how best to achieve these minimum standards. The regulator then monitors the environmental situation and takes action against any producers found to be in violation of the standards set.

In the UK, the Environmental Protection Act (1989) laid down minimum environmental standards for emissions from over 3,500 factories involved in chemical processes, waste incineration and oil refining. The factories have to meet these standards for all emissions, whether into air, water or onto land. Factory performance is monitored by a strengthened HM Inspectorate of Pollution, the costs of which are paid for by the factory owners themselves. The Act also provided for public access to information on the pollution created by firms. Regulations were also established on restricting the release of genetically engineered bacteria and viruses and a ban was imposed on most forms of straw and stubble burning from 1992 onwards. Stricter regulations were also imposed on waste disposal operations, with local authorities given a duty to keep public land clean. On-the-spot fines of up to £1,000 were instituted for persons dropping litter.

Regulations have also played an important part in the five 'Environmental Action Programmes' of the EU, which first began in 1973. For example, specific standards have been set for minimum acceptable levels of water quality for drinking and for bathing. As regards the latter, regular monitoring of coastal waters must take place, with as many as 19 separate tests undertaken throughout the tourist season.

Of course regulations may be part of an integrated environmental policy which also involves market-based incentives. We have already seen how the tradeable permits system in the US is working in tandem with the standards imposed by the US Clean Air Act.

We now review a number of key environmental issues to examine the relative merits of market-based and non-market-based incentives for dealing with environmental problems.

Applications of environmental policies

Global warming The whole debate on curbing emissions of CO_2 usefully highlights a number of issues:

- a non-zero level of pollution as socially efficient;
- the respective advantages and disadvantages of market and non-market-based incentives in achieving socially efficient solutions.

We have already addressed some of the environmental implications of global warming. There are clearly significant social damage costs associated with emissions of CO_2, which rise at an increasing rate with the total level of emissions. This situation is represented by the *Total Damage Costs* curve in Fig. 10.8a.

However, seeking to reduce CO_2 emissions will also impose costs on society. For instance we may need to install expensive flue-desulphurization plants in coal burning power stations, or to use (less efficient) sources of renewable energy (e.g. wind, wave, solar power). These various costs are represented by the *Total Abatement Costs* curve in Fig. 10.8a. We might expect these Total Abatement Costs to rise at an increasing rate as we progressively *reduce* the level of CO_2 emissions, since the easier and less costly means of cutting back on CO_2 emissions are likely to have been adopted first.

In Fig. 10.8a, we can see that the consequence of taking *no action* to reduce CO_2 emissions would leave us at Q_P, with zero abatement costs but high total damage costs.

What must be stressed here is the importance of seeking to identify *both* types of cost. On occasions environmentalists focus exclusively on the damages caused by global warming, whereas producers concern themselves solely with the higher (abatement) costs of adopting less CO_2 intensive methods of production.

The analysis is simplified (Fig. 10.8b) by using *marginal* changes in the damage costs or abatement costs related to each extra tonne of CO_2 emitted or abated. The socially optimum level of CO_2 emissions is where marginal damage costs exactly equal marginal abatement costs, i.e. output Q_S in Fig. 10.8b. To emit more CO_2 than Q_S would imply marginal damage costs to society *greater than* the marginal cost to society of abating that damage. Society is clearly disadvantaged by any emissions in excess of Q_S. Equally, to emit less CO_2 than Q_S, would imply marginal damage costs to society *less than* the marginal cost to society of abating that damage. In this case society is disadvantaged by seeking to cut CO_2 emissions below Q_S.

Fig. 10.8. Using abatement and damage cost curves in finding a socially optimum level of pollution.

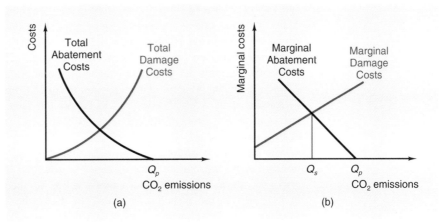

(a)   (b)

Setting the targets   If we are to apply our analysis in practical ways we must seek to *value* both the marginal damage and the marginal abatement cost curves. Again we are faced with the conceptual problem of placing a valuation on variables to which monetary values are at present only rarely attached, if at all. In addition, in a full cost–benefit analysis we must select a rate of discount (see Ch. 12) to enable a comparison to be made between effects in the distant future and the costs of policies introduced today.

Uncertainty will therefore clearly be involved in any attempt to evaluate the costs and benefits of policy action or inaction. The target for *reducing* CO_2 emissions ($Q_P - Q_S$ in Fig. 10.8b) to the socially optimum level will clearly be affected by such uncertainty. Analysts often use 'scenarios' of high, medium and low estimates for marginal damage and marginal abatement cost curves. For instance, Nordhaus (1989, 1991) estimated each of these marginal cost curves for both CO_2 emissions and for the broader category of Greenhouse Gases, based on US data. His *high* estimate of marginal damage costs was calculated at $66.00 per tonne of CO_2, his *low* estimate at only $1.83 per tonne of CO_2. We can use Fig. 10.8b, above, to illustrate this analysis. In the high estimate case, the marginal damage cost curve shifts vertically upwards, Q_S falls, and the 'target' reduction in CO_2 emissions (i.e. $Q_S - Q_P$) increases. On this basis Nordhaus advocates reducing CO_2 emissions by 20%. It is hardly surprising (in view of the valuation discrepancy noted above) that in his low estimate case, the marginal damage cost curve shifts vertically downwards in Fig. 10.8b, Q_S rises, and the target reduction in CO_2 emissions (i.e. $Q_S - Q_P$) falls. On this basis Nordhaus only advocates reducing CO_2 emissions by about 3%.

Government policy   The UK government's policy is to stabilize CO_2 emissions at their 1990 level by the year 2005. In practice this will mean a reduction in CO_2 emissions in 2005 by between 20% and 50%, compared to their estimated uncontrolled levels by that date. This would be rather higher than the restrictions advocated by Nordhaus, even in his 'high' cost scenario.

Achieving the targets   Whatever the targets set for reduced emissions, which policy instruments will be most effective in achieving those targets? The discussion by Ingham and Ulph (1991) is helpful in comparing market and non-market policy instruments. Many different methods are available for bringing about any given total reduction in CO_2 emissions. Users of fossil fuels might be induced to switch towards fuels that emit less CO_2 within a given total energy requirement. For instance oil and gas emit, respectively, about 80% and 60% as much CO_2 per unit of energy as coal. Alternatively, the total amount of energy used might be reduced in an attempt to cut CO_2 emissions.

Another issue is whether we seek to impose our target rate of reduction for CO_2 emissions on *all* sectors of the UK economy. Table 10.2 gives the sectoral breakdown of CO_2 emissions.

Should we then ask for a *uniform* reduction of say, 25% across all sectors? This is unlikely to be appropriate since *marginal abatement* cost curves are likely to differ across sectors and, indeed, across countries. For instance, it has been estimated that to abate 14% of the air pollution emitted by the textiles sector in the USA will cost $136m per annum. However to abate 14% of the air pollution emitted by each of the machinery, electrical equipment and fabricated metals sectors respectively, will cost $572m, $729m and $896m (World Bank 1992). As well as differing between industrial sectors *within* a country, abatement costs will also differ between countries. For example, it has been estimated that a 10% reduction in CO_2 emissions by 2010 (as compared to 1988 emission levels) will cost 400 ECU per tonne of CO_2 abated in Italy, but only 200 ECU per tonne abated in Denmark, and less than 20 ECU per tonne abated in the UK, France, Germany and Belgium (European Economy 1992).

This point can be illustrated by taking just two sectors in the UK – say electricity generation and transport – and by assuming that they initially emit the same amount of CO_2. Following Ingham and Ulph (1991) suppose that the overall target for reducing CO_2 emissions is the distance O'O in Fig. 10.9.

We must now decide how to allocate this total reduction in emissions between the two sectors. In Fig. 10.9 we measure reductions in CO_2 emissions in electricity generation from left to right, and reductions in CO_2 emissions in transport from right to left. Point A, for example, would divide the total reduction in emissions into OA in electricity generation and O'A in transport. A *marginal abatement cost* (MAC) curve is now calculated for each sector. In Fig. 10.9 we draw the MAC curve for electricity generation as being lower and flatter than that for transport. This reflects the greater fuel-switching possibilities in electricity generation as compared to transport, both within fossil fuels and between fossil and non-fossil (solar, wave, wind) fuels. In other words, any marginal reduction in CO_2 emissions in electricity generation is likely to raise overall costs by *less* in electricity generation than in transport. In transport there are far fewer fuel-substitution possibilities; the major means of curbing CO_2 emissions in transport being improved techniques for energy efficiency or a switch from private to public transport.

Given these *different* marginal abatement cost curves for each sector in Fig. 10.9, how then should we allocate our reduction between the two sectors? Clearly we

Table 10.2 UK sectoral breakdown of CO_2 emissions.

Sector	CO_2 emissions (%)
Electricity generation	39
Industry	24
Transport	17
Domestic	14

Source: Adapted from Ingham and Ulph (1991).

Fig. 10.9. Finding the 'efficient' or 'least-cost' solution for reducing CO₂ emissions in a two-sector model.

should seek a solution by which the given total reduction in emissions is achieved at the least total cost to society: we shall call this the *efficient* or *least-cost* solution. In Fig. 10.9, this will be where marginal abatement costs are the same in both sectors, i.e. at point B in the diagram. We can explain this by supposing we were initially *not* at B, but at A in Fig. 10.9, with equal reductions in the two sectors. At point A, marginal abatement costs in transport are AC but marginal abatement costs in electricity generation are only AF. So by abating CO₂ by *one more* tonne in electricity generation and *one less* tonne in transport, we would have the same total reduction in CO₂ emissions, but would have saved CF in costs. By moving from point A to the 'efficient' point B, we would save the area CFE in abatement costs.

It follows, therefore, that for any given target for total reduction in CO₂ emissions, 'efficiency' will only occur if the marginal cost of abatement is the same across all sectors of the economy (and indeed across all methods of abatement). Pollution control policies which seek to treat all sectors equally, even where marginal abatement costs differ widely between sectors, may clearly fail to reach an 'efficient' solution.

Policy implications We have previously seen that environmental policy instruments can be broadly classified into two types: market-based and non-market-based. *Market-based* policy instruments would include setting a tax on emissions of CO₂ or issuing a limited number of permits to emit CO₂ and then allowing a market to be set up in which those permits are traded. *Non-market-based* policy instruments would include regulations and directives. For example, in the UK, the Non-Fossil Fuel Obligation currently imposed on privatized electricity companies requires them to purchase a specified amount of electricity from non-fossil fuel sources.

We can use Fig. 10.9 to examine the case for using a tax instrument (market-based) as compared to regulation (non-market-based). A tax of BE on CO_2 emissions would lead to the 'efficient' solution B. This is because polluters have a choice of paying the tax on their emissions of CO_2 or of taking steps to abate their emissions. They will have an incentive to abate as long as the marginal cost of abatement is lower than the tax. So electricity generating companies will have incentives to abate to OB, and transport companies to O'B, in Fig. 10.9 above. Since every polluter faces the same tax, then they will end up with the same marginal abatement cost. Here 'prices', amended by tax, are conveying signals to producers in a way which helps co-ordinate their (profit maximizing) decisions in order to bring about an 'efficient' (least cost) solution.

The alternative policy of government regulations and directives (non-market-based instrument) in achieving the 'efficient' solution at B in Fig. 10.9, would be much more complicated. The government would have to estimate the marginal abatement cost curve for *each sector*, given that such curves differ between sectors. It would then have to estimate the different percentage reductions required in each sector in order to equalize marginal abatement costs (the 'efficient' solution). It is hardly reasonable to suppose that the government could achieve such fine tuning in order to reach 'efficient' solutions.

The market-based solution of tax has no administrative overhead. Producers are simply assumed to react to the signals of market prices (amended by taxes) in a way which maximizes their own profits. Regulations, on the other hand, imply monitoring, supervision and other 'bureaucratic' procedures. Ingham and Ulph (1991) found that using a tax policy as compared with seeking an *equal proportionate reduction* in CO_2 emissions by regulations, resulted in total abatement costs being 20% lower than they would have been under the alternative regulatory policy.

In a recent simulation by Cambridge Econometrics (Cowe 1998), a 'package' of seven green taxes, including a carbon tax based on industrial and commercial energy use, was estimated as cutting CO_2 emissions by 13% on 1990 levels by the year 2010. Rather encouragingly, this package of green taxes was estimated as raising a further £27bn in tax revenues by 2010, which could be used to cut employers' national insurance by 3%, leading to almost 400,000 extra jobs. Only a small (−0.2%) deterioration was predicted for the balance of payments and for inflation (prices rising by 0.5%) by 2010 and GDP was even predicted to have received a small boost (+0.2%) by this package of green taxes. Such simulation studies are useful in that they 'model' impacts of tax measures throughout the economy, although one must carefully check the assumptions which underlie the equations used in computer models.

Transport and the environment

Many of the detailed issues involving transport are considered in Chapter 12. Here we focus on the environmental implications of various scenarios envisaged for the growth of transport, and the various policy instruments which might be applied to influence transport outcomes.

That transport has moved to centre-stage as regards environmental concern is amply illustrated by the plethora of major reports on transport and the environment (e.g. Royal Commission 1994 and 1997, House of Commons 1994). This is hardly surprising given facts such as the following and our earlier discussions on global warming and climatic change:

Table 10.3 Transport and environmental costs (£bn per annum in 1994 prices).

	Eighteenth Report	Newbery	Maddison *et al.*
Air pollution	2.0–5.2	2.8–7.4	19.7
Climate change	1.5–3.1	0.4	0.1
Noise and vibration	1.0–4.6	0.6	2.6–3.1
Total environmental costs	4.6–12.9	3.8–8.4	22.4–22.9
Road accidents	5.4	4.5–7.5	2.9–9.4
Quantified social and environmental costs other than congestion costs	10.0–18.3	8.3–15.9	25.3–32.3

Note:
'Eighteenth Report' refers to the Royal Commission on Environmental Pollution (1994). Details of the studies by Newbery (1995) and Maddison *et al.* (1996) can be found at the end of the chapter.
Source: Adapted from Royal Commission on Environmental Pollution (1997).

- Total UK carbon dioxide emissions fell by 10% between 1970 and 1990, but emissions from transport increased by 65%.
- Transport accounts for the whole of the net increase projected in UK carbon dioxide emissions between 1970 and 2020 (an increase of 39 million tonnes of carbon a year).
- Two-thirds of that projected increase in carbon dioxide emissions is accounted for by private cars.

Nor is there any longer much doubt as to the serious impact of the negative externalities associated with road transport, as Table 10.3 usefully indicates. This table excludes congestion costs (see Chapter 12) and a number of other environmental costs, yet still calculates the environmental costs of road transport at between £8.3bn and £32.3bn per annum depending on which of the three studies is used and on whether the lower or upper estimates are selected in any given study. This is equivalent to between 1% and 4% of UK GDP per annum. Even allowing for the uncertainty indicated by the differing estimates of each study and by the lower and upper ranges of the calculations, negative externalities of such magnitude have forced transport to the forefront of environmental debate.

The Royal Commission on Environmental Pollution (1994) set a range of *targets* for transport-related pollutants at specific future dates. For example, to limit emissions of carbon dioxide from surface transport in the year 2000 to the 1990 level, and in the year 2020 to no more than 80% of the 1990 level. To achieve such targets it proposed a range of *policy instruments* which included a blend of market-based and non-market-based instruments.

Market-based instruments   There is a clear preference to use such instruments wherever feasible, yet a recognition that other approaches may sometimes be needed.

> Although economic instruments utilising the price mechanism are not a complete alternative to direct regulation, they tend to be more efficient. (Royal Commission 1994: 106)

The commission reviews a number of possible road charges which relate the amount paid to the environmental costs imposed by journeys or movements. These included charges related to distance travelled, to use of road space (road pricing), to pollutants emitted, to parking space, and to fuel used. The 'pollutant emitted' charge was attractive to the commission as it would correspond to the Pigouvian environmental tax previously discussed (p. 211). A German proposal is for data on the use of the vehicle during the year to be stored in an electronic management system, displayed during an annual test on emissions and passed on to the tax authorities. The technology and necessary EU legislation for such a tax is not immediately available, and this was considered of interest for the medium term. For the present, the focus of attention became the charge on fuel used.

Fuel duty was regarded as having a number of advantages as an economic instrument for influencing decisions about additional journeys:

- *The amount of tax paid varies with the environmental costs:* The amount of fuel used and duty paid is in the main proportional to the amount of carbon dioxide emitted, and (for any given vehicle) is closely reflected in the quantities of other substances emitted. Fuel consumption is substantially higher in congested urban traffic, and is therefore correlated to some degree with situations in which a vehicle is contributing to higher concentrations of pollutants, and where there is a higher exposure to the noise and vibration it is producing.
- *It is simple to administer:* It costs little to collect, is difficult to avoid or evade, and can easily be modified.
- *Road users have discretion about how to respond:* Road users may respond either by reducing the number or length of their journeys or by reducing their use of fuel in other ways, such as switching to a smaller or more fuel-efficient vehicle or driving in a more fuel-efficient way.
- *It is possible to vary the rate of fuel duty to provide an incentive to use environmentally less damaging forms of fuel:* As in the case of the existing small differentials in favour of diesel and unleaded petrol.
- *A fuel duty already exists.*

Fig. 10.10. Relationship between fuel price and fuel use by road vehicles. *Source:* Adapted from Royal Commission (1994).

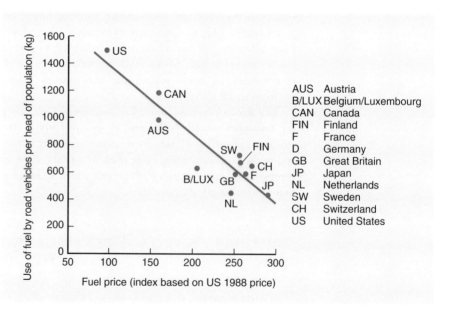

AUS	Austria
B/LUX	Belgium/Luxembourg
CAN	Canada
FIN	Finland
F	France
D	Germany
GB	Great Britain
JP	Japan
NL	Netherlands
SW	Sweden
CH	Switzerland
US	United States

Table 10.4 Combined
effect of recommended
measures on carbon
dioxide emissions from
surface transport, million
tonnes carbon/year.

	1990	Cars 19.7	Road 30.5	Total 32.3	% of 1990 100
Baseline	2000	22.4	34.7	36.4	113
Doubling of fuel prices by 2005		20.2	31.3	33.2	103
Enforcement of 60 mph and 70 mph speed limits		19.1	30.1	32.0	99
40% improvement in fuel efficiency of new cars by 2005		18.4	29.1	31.1	97
Halving of growth of car traffic in urban areas		18.2	28.9	30.9	96
Baseline	2020	26.9	42.9	44.7	138
Doubling of fuel prices by 2005		18.2	29.5	32.0	99
Enforcement of 60 mph and 70 mph speed limits		17.1	28.4	30.9	96
40% improvement in fuel efficiency of new cars by 2005		13.1	23.8	26.3	82
Halving of growth of car traffic in urban areas		12.6	23.2	25.7	80

Source: Adapted from Royal Commission (1994) Appendix D.

Empirical studies have indicated that variations in fuel duty do indeed have an *effect* on road transport use. The Department of Transport has estimated that a 10% increase in the price of fuel in real terms would lead to a fall in fuel use of up to 3%, of which half would be the result of reduced vehicle use. The Royal Commission concluded that in order to meet the target of limiting carbon dioxide emissions from road transport to 1990 levels by this means alone, the price of fuel would need to double, relative to the price of other goods, by the year 2005. This would require an increase in fuel duty of some 9% a year (in real terms) for ten years (a further 4% above the government's already stated intention of 5% a year).

Certainly there is international evidence to indicate the effectiveness of higher fuel prices deterring fuel use by road vehicles, as can be seen in Fig. 10.10.

Non-market based instruments The Royal Commission's recommended measures for achieving its CO_2 targets for the years 2000 and 2020 are set out in Table 10.4. These clearly involve a mix of market and non-market based instruments. For example, emissions of various pollutants (including CO_2) increase fairly rapidly at vehicle speeds over 55 m.p.h., as do car accidents. There is therefore a recommendation for stricter enforcement by the regulatory authorities of the speed limits on various roads. Note that *all* the measures in Table 10.4 are needed to meet the target of carbon dioxide at 80% of 1990 levels by the year 2020.

Many other subsidiary *regulations* also underly these recommendations. For example 'that more stringent standards be applied in the emissions element of the annual MOT test, and that this element become obligatory for all cars a year after registration' (instead of 3 years as at present). This recognises the fact that there is a tendency for pollution emissions to increase with age of vehicle, for any given distance travelled.

As the Royal Commission concludes:

> Government must use an appropriate combination of direct regulation and economic instruments to force the pace of technological development and foster markets for new products. In the case of noise levels and the emission of pollutants, direct regulation in the form of EU legislation should continue to be the primary method used to reduce the environmental impact of vehicles. Direct regulation should extend beyond compliance with limits for new vehicles to include much more effective enforcement of environmental standards applying to the existing fleet. (Royal Commission 1994: 144).

Implementation of policy types

The World Bank (1992) has concluded that 'regulatory policies, which are used extensively in both industrial and developing countries, are best suited to situations that involve a few public enterprises and non-competitive private firms.' It also concludes that economic incentives, such as charges, will often be less costly than regulatory alternatives (see Table 10.5). For instance, to achieve the *least-cost* or *efficient* solution of point B in Fig. 10.9 above, is estimated as costing some 22 times more in the US if particulate matter is abated by regulations, rather than by using market-based instruments. Similarly, achieving this least-cost solution by regulating sulphur dioxide emissions in the UK is estimated as costing between 1.4 and 2.5 times as much as compared to using market-based instruments.

However, regulatory policies are particularly appropriate when it is important not to exceed certain thresholds, e.g. emissions of radioactive and toxic wastes. In these cases it is clearly of greater concern that substantial environmental damage be avoided than that pollution control be implemented by policies which might prove to be more expensive than expected. However, where the social costs of environmental damage do *not* increase dramatically if standards are breached by small margins, then it is worthwhile seeking the least-cost policy via market incentives rather than to spend excessive amounts on regulation to avoid any breach at all.

With market-based policies, all resource users or polluters face the same price and must respond accordingly. Each *user* decides on the basis of their own utility/profit preferences whether to use fewer environmental resources or to pay extra for using more. On the other hand, with regulations it is the regulators who take such decisions on the behalf of the users, e.g. *all* users might be given the same limited access to a scarce

Table 10.5 Simulation studies of alternative policies for controlling air pollution.

Pollutant	Geographic area	Ratio of costs of regulatory policies to those of least-cost policy (percent)
Sulphates	Los Angeles, Calif.	110
Nitrogen dioxide	Baltimore, Md.	600
Particulate matter	Baltimore, Md.	420
Sulphur dioxide	Lower Delaware Valley	180
Particulate matter	United States	2,200
Hydrocarbons	All US Dupont plants	420
Sulphur dioxide	Five regions of the United States	190
Sulphur dioxide	United Kingdom	140–250

Source: Adapted from World Bank (1992).

environmental resource. Regulators are, of course, unlikely to be well informed about the relative costs and benefits faced by users or the valuations placed on these by such users.

Market-based policies have another advantage, namely that they price environmental damage in a way which affects all *polluters*, providing uniform 'prices' to which all polluters can respond (see Fig. 10.9), thereby yielding 'efficient' or 'least cost' solutions. By contrast, regulations usually only affect those who fail to comply and who therefore face penalties. Further, regulations which set minimizing standards give polluters no incentives to do better than that minimum.

Conclusion

Our review of environmental concerns and possible remedial policies has, of necessity, been selective. We have considered the competing claims of market- and non-market-based incentives towards achieving socially efficient solutions. Market-based incentives often help avoid the necessity of external bodies seeking to evaluate marginal abatement cost and marginal damage cost curves. This is certainly an advantage in an area where such valuations are notoriously difficult. Nevertheless there are situations where regulations or a judicious mix of markets and regulations, may be the most appropriate way forward. In any case all the interdependences of any proposed solution must be fully taken into account before any final decisions are made. What is beyond dispute is that the environment and the economic system are highly interrelated, and neither can be considered in isolation from the other.

Key points

- The environment interacts with the circular flow, providing amenity services, natural resources and the assimilation of waste products.
- The 'First Law of Thermodynamics' states that we cannot create or destroy energy and matter. We must therefore pay close attention to the conservation of natural resources and the disposal of waste products.
- The above 'law' may also lead to the idea of 'environmental limits to growth'.
- An 'Index of Sustainable Economic Welfare' (ISEW) adjusts the conventional GNP figure for environmental impacts. On this basis the growth of ISEW per head for the UK in the period 1950–96 is a mere 0.5% per annum, much less than the growth in real GNP per head of 2.0% per annum over the same period.
- The optimum level of pollution for society is unlikely to be zero. Rather it will occur at the (positive) level at which marginal damage costs exactly equal marginal abatement costs.
- Assessing such an optimum involves finding solutions to problems of *valuation* of environmental impacts, especially where no market prices exist.
- Policy instruments which might be used to achieve a social optimum include both market-based incentives (taxes, tradable permits and negotiation) and non-market-based incentives (various standards and regulations).
- There is evidence to suggest that in most cases a given objective can be achieved at least-cost by a combination of market-based policy instruments.

References and further reading

Cowe, R. (1998) Green taxes come up against pain barrier, *Guardian*, 2 Feb.

European Economy (1992) The Climate Challenge, Economic Aspects of the Community's Strategy for Limiting CO_2 Emissions, **51**, May.

European Environment Agency (1996) Environmental Taxes, Copenhagen.

House of Commons (1994) *Transport-Related Air Pollution in London*, Vol 1, Report, Minutes of Proceedings and Appendices.

Ingham, A. and **Ulph, A.** (1991) Economics of Global Warming, *The Economic Review*, **9**, 2.

Jackson, T. and **Marks, N.** (1994) Measuring Sustainable Economic Welfare – A Pilot Index: 1950–1990, *Stockholm Environment Institute*.

Jackson, T., Marks, N., Ralls, J. and **Stymne, S.** (1997) Sustainable Economic Welfare in the UK 1950–1996, *New Economics Foundation*, London.

Kerry Turner, R., Pearce, D. and **Bateman, I.** (1994) *Environmental Economics*, Harvester Wheatsheaf, Hemel Hempstead.

Maddison, D., Pearce, D. *et al.* (1996) *Blueprint 5: The True Costs of Road Transport*, Earthscan Publications Ltd.

Newbery, D. M. (1995) Economic Effects of (18th Report) Recommendations, *Economic Journal*, **105**, Sept.

Nordhaus, W. (1991) To Slow or not to Slow: the Economics of the Greenhouse Effect, *Economic Journal*, **101**.

O'Doherty, R. (1994) Pricing Environmental Disasters, *Economic Review*, **12**, 1.

Oxford Review of Economic Policy (1990) Economic Policy Towards the Environment, **6**, 1.

Pearce, D. (1991a) Towards the Sustainable Economy: Environment and Economics, *Royal Bank of Scotland Review*, **172**, Dec.

Pearce, D. (1991b) Economics and the Environment, *Economics, Journal of the Economics Association*, **XXVII**, Pt 1, 113.

Royal Commission on Environmental Pollution (1994) Transport and the Environment, Eighteenth Report.

Royal Commission on Environmental Pollution (1997) Transport and the Environment – Developments since 1994, Twentieth Report.

Tietenberg, T. (1994) *Environmental Economics and Policy*, Harper Collins.

Turner, K. (1991) Environmental Economics, *Developments in Economics: an Annual Review*, **7**.

UK Environmental Accounts (1998) HMSO.

Willis, K. (1991) The Priceless Countryside: the Recreational Benefits of Environmental Goods, *Royal Bank of Scotland Review*, **172**, Dec.

World Bank (1992 and 1994) World Development Reports.

Chapter 11

Regional and urban policy

This chapter surveys the regional and urban problems experienced by the UK over the last twenty to thirty years. The difficulties of defining a region are examined, together with 'convergent' and 'divergent' theories of regional development. The policies used by successive governments to alleviate the 'regional problem' are noted, and their effectiveness assessed. The urban dimension to the regional problem is then discussed and government policy outlined. The chapter ends with a brief assessment of the effectiveness of urban policy.

The regions and their characteristics

Simply defined, a region is a portion of the earth's surface that possesses certain characteristics (physical, economic, political, etc.) which give it a measure of unity and differentiate it from surrounding areas, enabling us to draw boundaries around it. The commonly perceived regions of the UK, mainly counties, were formalized into 'economic planning regions' in 1964. Although certain economic criteria were used in the groupings of counties, the regions were largely established on the basis of administrative convenience.

There is nothing absolute about these planning regions. The Local Government Act of 1972 dramatically altered the county boundaries, and this led to the redrawing of the economic planning regions. These were then called Standard Planning Regions but in 1994 the system changed once more with the establishment of the Government Offices for the Regions (GORs).

The GORs act as regional arms for three government departments, namely the Department of the Environment, Transport and the Regions, the Department for Education and Employment, and the Department of Trade and Industry. Their role is to work in partnership with local communities, including local government, in order to promote economic prosperity in the region as a whole. With the introduction of the GORs in April 1994, the boundaries of the UK regions were redrawn, and as from 1998, statistics for the regions have been based on the GOR boundaries.

In a further change, local government reorganization between 1995 and 1998 has introduced Unitary Authorities (UA) to replace the County and Local District Authorities in some areas of England and Wales, whilst Unitary Councils were established in Scotland and Unitary Boards/Districts in Northern Ireland. The new GOR regions and their sub-regions are shown in Figs. 11.1 and 11.2.

Fig. 11.1. The
Government Office
Region boundaries
(GORs).

The regional problem

Traditionally a 'regional problem' is said to exist when a region departs from the 'national average' in a number of important respects:

1. High and persistent unemployment.
2. Low level and growth of GDP per head.

Fig. 11.2. The UK: regional, sub-regional and urban organization. *Sources:* ONS (1998) *Adapted from Regional Trends.*

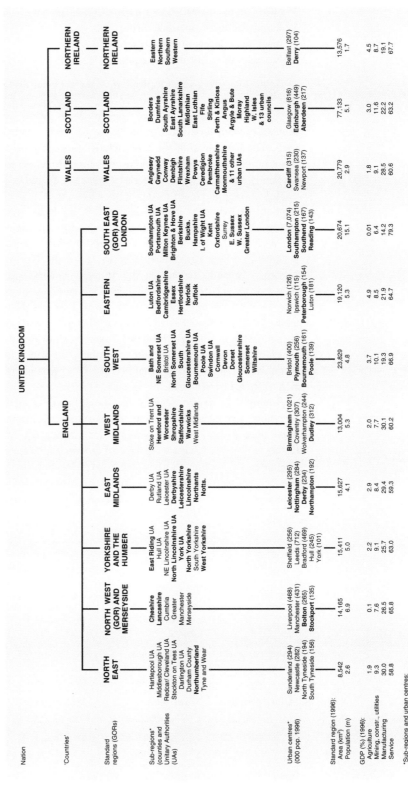

3. Heavy dependence upon a narrow industrial base.
4. Rapid decline in manufacturing.
5. Inadequate levels of infrastructure.
6. Net migration out of the region.

Table 11.1 gives some indication of the regional disparities with reference to the first two criteria.

A number of attempts have been made to group regions in terms of common economic characteristics. For instance, the terms 'core' and 'periphery' are often used. The 'core area' of the UK includes those regions which have experienced the most rapid economic advance in the past three decades. The South East, East Midlands and the Eastern region are usually placed in this category. In 1997, for example, unemployment in the South East was 70% of the national average, but the standard of living, as indicated by GDP per head, was 14.5% above the national average. The 'periphery' can be subdivided into an 'inner periphery', which contains the West Midlands, the South West, and Yorkshire and the Humber, and an 'outer periphery', which contains the North West, the North East, Wales, Scotland and Northern Ireland. Regions in the 'outer periphery' are characterized by relatively slow growth, stagnation or decline, and contain most of the old industrial areas of the UK. In 1997, unemployment in the North East was 32% above the national average whilst GDP per head was 15.7% below that average. Regions in the 'inner periphery' are somewhat in between these two extremes, showing rather more signs of 'economic health' than regions in the 'outer periphery'. In 1997, for example, West Midlands was only 2% below the national average as regards unemployment, and 6.5% below as regards GDP per head.

Attempts to group regions on these broad economic grounds are, however, becoming less meaningful. The rise of microelectronic technology, the growing importance of multinational activity (see Chapter 7), and the effects of the Single European Act (see Chapter 28) have all contributed to a more 'footloose', and therefore geographically mobile, pattern of industrial location. In today's complex and rapidly changing industrial environment, any spatial grouping of 'standard' regions into 'core' or 'periphery' may be less appropriate than hitherto. Indeed there is evidence to suggest

Table 11.1 Index of regional variation in GDP per head and unemployment (UK = 100).

		GDP per head			Unemployment		
		1971	1981	1996	1971	1981	1997
Core	South East	113.8	114.5	114.5	59	71	70
	East Midlands	96.5	100.0	94.2	85	90	80
	Eastern	93.8	97.3	108.8	91	81	84
Inner periphery	West Midlands	102.7	90.6	93.5	85	120	98
	South West	94.7	95.9	94.7	95	87	78
	Yorks/Humber	93.2	93.0	89.5	112	104	108
Outer periphery	North West	96.1	94.3	90.8	113	122	106
	North East	87.1	94.3	84.3	163	130	132
	Wales	88.4	86.8	83.1	128	128	111
	Scotland	93.0	98.7	99.1	170	120	117
	Northern Ireland	74.3	72.2	81.2	221	159	123

Sources: ONS (1998) *Economic Trends*, October, and previous issues.

the emergence in the l990s of 'areas of prosperity' centred on urban regions, which are likely to grow much faster than other parts of their GOR region.

However, the three core areas defined in Table 11.1 still contribute 46.6% of total UK GDP and have an important weight in the economy. A similar concern still remains about the continuing influence of the North/South 'divide', which involves a broader definition of Britain's regions than that given in Table 11.1 The recession of the early l990s tended to hit the UK's service orientated industries more than manufacturing, so that the North appeared to have been relatively less affected by the recession than the South. However, in 1998 the South (defined as East Midlands, Eastern, South East and South West) still contributed 54.4% of UK GDP as compared to 52.6% in 1979. As a result, the core and periphery and similar concepts may still remain useful tools of reference during the late 1990s.

Free market or government intervention?

From Table 11.1 it is clear that regional disparities do exist in the UK in terms of both unemployment and income per head. Whether or not these disparities constitute a 'problem', requiring government intervention, depends on one's view of the economic system. Certainly changes in demand and supply in any economy will have different effects on individual regions, since each has its own particular industrial structure. A change in the pattern of demand can cause some regions to increase production, employment and income, when they contain the industries which produce the goods and services now demanded. Similarly, regions which produce commodities for which demand has decreased, will find themselves with declining production, employment and income. As a result, growing regions will diverge positively from the national norm, while declining regions will diverge negatively.

It has been argued that in a dynamic economy regional disparities will be short run, as in time market forces will tend to equalize the situation across regions (convergence). This could occur through a movement into the high-unemployment/ low-income regions of firms attracted by lower wage costs. At the same time there will be an outward migration of labour from these 'disadvantaged' regions to the relatively prosperous regions where demand, employment and wages are higher. It follows that if labour and capital are perfectly mobile, with no impediment to firms moving into and out of regions, regional differences should disappear. For example, in the disadvantaged regions unemployment would fall and wages would rise as firms relocate themselves in these areas. Similarly, in the more prosperous regions unemployment would rise and wages fall as firms move out to low-wage/low-cost areas. Given sufficient time, and no imperfections, this view suggests that there would be no need for government intervention to solve the 'regional problem', since market forces will eventually cause regions to 'converge'.

The case for intervention   In practice, imperfections exist and even those who believe in the market mechanism may still advocate some form of regional policy. First, neither labour nor capital is perfectly mobile. There may be a lack of knowledge on the part of employees or employers of opportunities in other regions; or there may be high 'costs' of movement as with the need for rehousing, the breaking of social ties and the expensive relocation of plant and machinery. Second, there may be restrictions on the price of labour or capital, such as maximum or minimum wages, or limits on the dividends which firms issue. These imperfections may reduce the incentives for both labour and capital to flow out of 'disadvantaged' and into 'advantaged' regions and vice versa. Under these circumstances even the free-market adherent might admit the need for government intervention to offset these market imperfections. This may take the form of policies to promote labour mobility or to coax firms to move into more disadvantaged regions. Government intervention is then seen as necessary to *enhance* the workings of the market mechanism.

Another view of the regional problem sees a still more urgent need for government intervention. Market forces are regarded as acting in a way which will aggravate rather than ameliorate regional disparities. Intervention is no longer a *supplement* to market forces but must be strong enough to *offset* them. Any fall in output and employment in a region will reduce the size of the regional market and erode economies of scale. Also labour migration from declining regions may consist of the younger, better educated, more adaptable component of the regional labour force, leaving behind a less productive labour force. New firms may no longer wish to locate production in such regions even if wages are lower. As regional output declines and unemployment rises, local authority rates may become inadequate to sustain basic infrastructure and services, further disadvantaging a region already in decline. In this view, government policy has to be strong enough to prevent regions constantly 'diverging', with poor regions getting poorer and rich regions getting richer. Such a policy might seek to inhibit the movement of labour out of disadvantaged regions by giving firms incentives to locate in these regions.

To sum up, if, as in the first view, the regions are seen as 'converging' over time, then government intervention need only strengthen the 'natural' market forces making for equality. However if, as in the second view, the regions are seen as 'diverging' over time, then a greater degree of government intervention may be needed. Otherwise market forces will cause regions to become 'polarized' into areas of very low output, employment and income on the one hand, and very high output, employment and income on the other.

Regional policy in the UK

In the UK the need for government intervention in the regions was accepted as far back as 1934, with the passing of the first of three Special Areas Acts. These aimed to help the depressed areas by setting up government trading estates, subsidizing rents and providing low-interest loans. Since then legislation affecting the regions has been embodied in a variety of Industry and Finance Acts.

The Assisted Areas (AAs)

The basic principle guiding UK regional policy has been to identify specific geographical areas requiring assistance – mainly on the basis of above-average unemployment rates.

As Fig. 11.3 shows, there are currently three main types of area designated for regional assistance:

1. Development Areas (DAs) – first broadly identified in 1934, and since then redefined on a number of occasions. They remained more or less unchanged from the Industrial Development Act of 1966 until 1979, when the incoming

Fig. 11.3. The Assisted
Areas from August 1993.

Conservative government began a review of regional aid. The review resulted in
the Industrial Development Act of 1982 (revised 1984 and 1993) which severely
curtailed the amount of assistance for Development Areas and reduced the
number and size of areas eligible for aid. The most recent modification to the
Assisted Areas map of Great Britain was in August 1993, when it was calculated
that the DAs would cover about 16% of the total working population.

2. Intermediate Areas (IAs) – originated with the Hunt Report of 1969. It was
recognized that some areas would, without assistance, become the Development
Areas of the future. These were substantially reduced in spatial extent after the
1982 Act, but increased again in 1984 (in part, so that the areas concerned could
qualify for European Regional Development Fund (ERDF) aid – see below).

3. Northern Ireland – receives special regional assistance due to the particular
problems of that area.

Between 1967 and 1984 certain parts of the Development Areas were designated as *Special Development Areas*. These were initially areas which had suffered severe unemployment because of colliery closures and were therefore made eligible for higher levels of assistance. This differentiation *within* the Development Areas was terminated by the Conservative government in 1984.

By 1993, when the latest changes to the Assisted Area map occurred, the government's approach involved using a range of indices as the basis for drawing the new map. They included such indices as current unemployment, structural unemployment, long-term unemployment, activity rates, etc. The government's strategy was to concentrate more on the difficulties experienced by local economies in order to identify certain localities more disadvantaged than others, even within a small geographical area. This formed the basis of the 'split' areas which are a *mixture* of Development and Intermediate Areas, as seen in Fig. 11.3. In 1993, for the first time, areas such as London, the South Coast and parts of the East Anglian coast were given Assisted Area status, reflecting the localized problems within such areas. The present Assisted Areas map covers 34% of the total population, as compared to the 35% coverage of the previous 1984 map.

Once areas have been designated, UK policy has been of two types: first, to offer financial incentives to firms located in, or moving to, these areas; and second, to control expansion by firms outside these areas. Although the Industrial Development Certificate (IDC) is no longer used as a policy tool by the government, it is included here as an example of an expansion control measure. As we shall see, the extent of financial inducement or control has varied with the type of area and with shifts in government policy emphasis.

The situation shown in Fig. 11.3 is, however, about to change. New European Commission guidelines on regional aid adopted in December 1997 are designed to lower the proportion of the European Union's population covered by regional aid. This means that the proportion of the UK designated as a type of Assisted Area will be reduced by a quarter by the year 2000 as part of the Commission's drive to lower the total value of overall aid to industry. The Assisted Areas map for the UK will be much less extensive after that date, perhaps covering some 25% of the total population rather than the current 34%.

The policy instruments

Financial incentives In 1988, the then Conservative government recommended an overhaul of the Department of Trade and Industry (DTI) in order to improve Britain's competitiveness, innovativeness and the skills of individuals, especially in AAs and inner cities. Regional financial assistance was seen by the government as a subsidy that was damaging industry's efficiency and therefore its ability to compete, especially in view of the 'open market' of the EU after 1992. These revisions to regional policy were undertaken in the belief that payment of continuous subsidies to industries in AAs was an inappropriate way for central government to encourage an attitude of self-help and a spirit of enterprise and competitiveness. Hence, it was argued that if the regions were ever to experience *convergence*, much of the impetus would have to come from within the regions themselves, and government could only really facilitate this process – it could not legislate it, nor could it make certain areas or industries forever dependent upon the public purse.

A major consequence of the DTI's reorganization was to shift the focus of regional aid away from support for traditional industries and more towards encouragement of new company formation. This meant changing the balance of regional financial assistance – Regional Development Grants (RDGs), long the mainstay of regional policy aid, were terminated in 1988, and the emphasis shifted to Regional Selective Assistance and to a new scheme of other grants and incentives for smaller firms in both AAs and under various government Urban initiatives.

Regional Selective Assistance (RSA)   This is the main instrument of UK regional industrial policy. It is a discretionary grant towards projects of any size in both the manufacturing and service sectors and is open to both domestic and international investors. It has three overlapping objectives: first, to create and safeguard jobs; second, to attract and retain internationally mobile investment; and third, to contribute to improving the competitiveness of disadvantaged regions. The RSA is usually administered either as a capital-related or job-related grant. Capital-related project grants are normally used to help cover the costs of land purchase and site preparation or the acquisition of plant and machinery; job-related project grants are normally used to help cover the costs of hiring and training staff. Around two-thirds of the RSA budget is spent on grants of less than a £1m and some 60% of such grants go to UK-owned companies. Each £1m of RSA is, on average, matched by around £10m of company investment and each £1m of RSA has been estimated to create or safeguard some 237 jobs. For example, the RSA grant has helped to attract new investments such as the production of the X400 Jaguar at Halewood in 1997/98, thereby safeguarding 2,400 jobs. The amount spent on RSA grants has averaged £130m per year between 1997 and 1999.

Regional Enterprise Grants (REG) and other assistance   One of the main aspects of the government changes to regional incentives in 1988 was its emphasis on schemes designed to support the wealth-creating process among small and medium-sized firms. As a result companies in Assisted Areas employing fewer than twenty-five people were able to apply for two Regional Enterprise Grants. The first was an *investment* grant of 15% towards the costs of fixed assets, subject to a maximum grant of £15,000. The second was an *innovation* grant of 50% designed to support product and process development in small companies with a maximum grant limit of £25,000. However, both REGs were discontinued in 1996/97 after evaluations of the schemes concluded that they were less effective than alternatives available through the RSA. In addition to the REG, the government has been developing its Business Links network which, by July 1998, comprised eighty-nine Business Link companies. Each company is a partnership between local Chambers of Commerce, TECs, Enterprise Agencies and Local Authorities, and is designed to offer business in its area a single point of access to high quality advice, information and support services. Such services range from consultancy and financial services to design and management training.

European Regional Development Fund   Since 1973 the UK has had access to a further potential source of regional assistance, the EU. It was only in 1975, however, with the establishment of the European Regional Development Fund (ERDF), that EU funds became available for regional support on a systematic basis. The ERDF is financed out of the general budget of the EU and allocates most of its funds to member countries on a quota basis rather than for specific regional projects. The funds are given directly to member governments, and are intended to be *additional to* regional aid already given by those governments. Between 1975 and 1999 the UK had received over £10bn from the fund. Unfortunately there have been criticisms that these funds were used to replace rather than supplement regional expenditure by member governments. In an attempt to counter this, 5% of all ERDF funds have been allocated on a non-quota basis, linked to specific projects proposed by member governments. Some 80% of the cost of the regional/social fund is now allocated to the four poorest members of the EU and the fund is encouraging designated Assisted Areas in all EU countries to construct *coherent* development programmes rather than submit large numbers of individual projects.

The ERDF is part of the wider *European Structural Funds* initiative which designated six objectives for European areas suffering from structural decline. Of those six, three objectives have been identified for regional enterprise initiatives. Objective 1 covers the most problematic regions lagging behind the rest of the EU, i.e. where GDP per capita is 75% or less of the EU average. By 1996, Northern Ireland, the Highlands and Islands, and Merseyside had qualified for assistance under this priority objective. Objective 2 covers regions in industrial decline, such as the North East, North West, Yorks and Humberside, West Midlands and South Wales. Finally, Objective 5(b) covers the development of certain rural areas of the South West, Wales, the North of England and Scotland. Some 2.8% of the UK's population is covered under Objective 1, 35% under Objective 2 and 5% under Objective 5(b), thus covering some 43% of the UK population in total. ERDF grants normally pay up to 50% of the eligible cost of a project although it can be more in Objective 1 areas. The rest, i.e. 'matching funds', must be found by the prospective ERDF recipient from its own funds or from funds it can raise from other grant awarding bodies. In 1999, for example, some £1bn was allocated to the UK from the structural funds with 60% going to the English regions, 16% to Scotland, 17% to Northern Ireland and 7% to Wales.

The European Commission has, however, suggested reforming the use of the European Structural Funds under its 'Agenda 2000' proposals. It is expected that the possible enlargement of the EU to include countries from Central and Eastern Europe will result in the funds available under the ERDF being restricted to present EU members (such as the UK) after the year 2000.

Expansion control   Industrial Development Certificate   The principal method used by successive British governments between 1947 and 1981 to try to control the regional distribution of manufacturing industry was the Industrial Development Certificate (IDC). This was first introduced in the Town and Country Planning Act of 1947. Under the Act, any proposed new industrial development in excess of 5,000 square feet (465 square metres) had to obtain an Industrial Development Certificate (IDC) from the Board of Trade before planning permission for development could be granted. The certificate could be withheld at the discretion of the Board of Trade if the development would create industrial congestion or if it was not consistent with the 'proper' distribution of industry.

The effectiveness of regional policy

It is difficult to assess the effectiveness of regional policy, for a number of reasons. First, detailed statistics have only been readily available on the regions since the mid-1970s. Second, the areas qualifying for assistance have themselves been frequently redefined. For example, since 1979 the Development Areas have been 'reduced' in size to such an extent that they now only include 16% of the employed population in Britain, in contrast to 40% in previous years. Third, any assessment of the impact of regional policy involves a comparison of the actual situation with an *estimate* of what would have happened had there been no such regional policy.

Despite these problems attempts have been made to assess the effects of regional policy over the last thirty to forty years. These attempts fall into two broad categories: first, those which measure the total impact of policy on employment creation and factory/office building in AAs; second, those which assess the effectiveness of particular instruments of regional policy, such as grants, tax incentives and IDCs.

I. Effects of policy on employment and firms

The 1960–1979 period   A detailed study of the impact of regional policy on job gains and firm relocations in Assisted Areas (AAs) by Moore, Rhodes and Tyler (1986) came to the conclusion that over two decades of 'active' regional policy covering 1960–81, about 945,000 jobs were created or safeguarded in AAs as a result of government programmes. Some 90% of these jobs were still in place in 1981. As far as firm relocations are concerned, policy induced movements of factories from more prosperous areas to AAs yielded a net gain of 2,085 firms between 1945 and 1978, with 58% of the moves occurring during the more active policy period of 1966–78. However, in general, some 8,000 firms moved from one county to another between 1945 and 1980, of which only about 12% appear to have been 'persuaded' to move by government policy.

As well as trying to determine the total impact of regional policy on the economies of AAs by aggregating gross and net gains in numbers of jobs and of factory moves, regional economists have also sought to demonstrate relationships between the *actual numbers involved*, and *variations in the intensity of government intervention policy* over given time periods. Figure 21.5 shows the relationship between the growth of manufacturing employment in selected regions and changes in regional policy.

In Fig. 11.4 an attempt is made to define periods when regional policy was 'active' or strong, and periods when regional policy was 'passive' or weak. Periods of 'active' as distinct from 'passive' regional policy were defined as those periods in which the amount spent on regional incentives increased significantly and in which IDCs were issued far more sparingly in the non-assisted areas.

The amount of employment in any region will depend in part on the balance of industries in that region (i.e. industrial structure), and in part on the growth of output from such industries. Given the industrial structure of an Assisted Area, the

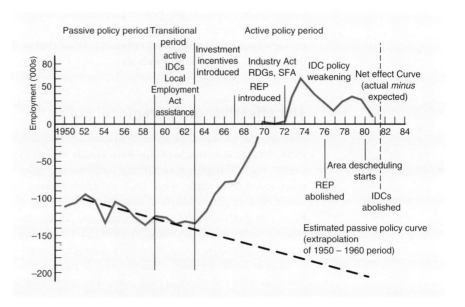

maximum employment which that region could be 'expected' to create would occur if each of its industries grew at the national average rate. This 'expected' level of employment was calculated for the four named Assisted Areas as a whole, for each year since 1950, and compared with the actual level of employment in those areas in each year. If actual employment in the Assisted Areas had reached the 'expected' level, then the 'net effect' curve (actual *minus* expected) would have recorded zero on the vertical axis. The fact that in the first few years 'actual' employment was around 100,000 below that 'expected', suggests that the Assisted Areas really do have more serious employment problems than elsewhere.

During the 'passive' period from 1950 to 1959, with little or no regional assistance, actual unemployment fell progressively further behind the 'expected' level. This provides some support for the 'divergent' view of the regional problem (see earlier), i.e. that without intervention the position of the assisted regions will progressively deteriorate. The dashed line in Fig. 11.4 projects this trend during the 'passive' period through to 1981. In other words, it provides an indication of what might have happened if regional policy had not become more 'active'. However, from 1963 a variety of incentives were introduced (see above) in the Assisted Areas, together with a more stringent application of IDCs preventing expansion in the advantaged regions. We can see from Fig. 11.4 that actual employment gets closer and closer to the 'expected' level up to 1970, and after 1970 even exceeds it. 'Active' policy began to slacken in the mid-1970s, with a number of incentives abolished (e.g. Regional Employment Premium (REP) in 1976 – see below), and a less stringent application of IDCs. As a result actual employment had begun to fall towards the 'expected' level in the late 1970s, early 1980s.

The 1980–1998 period   As noted previously, the importance attached to regional policy initiatives decreased after the return of the Conservative government in 1979. Regional assistance became less general and more selective in scope, as government philosophy shifted away from a wider view of the regional problem towards the promotion of new enterprises and the growth of self employment. Unfortunately, this policy shift does not seem to have narrowed the basic differences between the Assisted Areas and the more prosperous regions of Britain. For example, during the period 1979 to 1990, employment growth fell by 100,000 in the Assisted Areas, while employment growth rose by 1.3m in the South. Within these figures, the number of self employed rose by only 200,000 in the Assisted Areas while in the South the increase was 1.3m (Martin and Tyler 1992).

A similar picture emerges as regards the growth of new businesses. Here it is useful to look at both the rate of *new* business registrations and also the *net change* in the number of businesses in the 'South' as compared to the 'North' of Britain. The former measure will provide an idea of the dynamic changes in new business *formation*, while the latter (since it takes into consideration both the births and deaths of firms) gives a picture of the overall *net effect* on the total stock of businesses. Between 1981 and 1989, new business registrations per 1,000 employees were 94.5 in the South, but only 66.5 per 1,000 employees in the North. Net changes in the number of businesses per 1,000 employees were 17.5 in the South, but only 11.4 in the North. Clearly, the North continues to suffer more problems than the South in terms of both lower rates of new firm creation and the retention of existing firms.

However, in the mid 1990s it was argued that the tide had now turned. It was pointed out that in the recession of 1990–92 the South East had experienced a greater than average fall in net business formation (−3.1%) as compared to the traditional problem areas such as the North (−2.4%), North West (−2.4%) and Wales (−2.5%). At the same time the South East had seen the highest growth in unemployment. Partly in response to this phenomenon, the UK Assisted Areas map had been redrawn in 1993 to include more regions in the South East.

Perhaps, one of the ways in which regional grants are still relevant to regional development is that they may make the regions somewhat more attractive to foreign

Table 11.2 GDP, regional assistance, and the location of foreign manufacturing output.

	GDP[1]	Manufacturing[2]		RSA assistance[3]	
		UK	Foreign	UK	Foreign
Scotland	99	65	35	411	365
Wales	83	70	30	342	356
North East	84	70	30	181	184
West Midlands	94	74	26	133	134
North West	91	78	22	127	63
Yorks/Humber	90	83	17	126	37
Merseyside	–	73	27	63	32
South West	95	84	16	40	40
East Midlands	94	84	16	26	5
South East	115	70	30	17	6
London	123	74	26	10	3
Eastern	109	72	28	7	3
UK	**100**	**75**	**25**	**1,482**	**1,416**

Notes:
[1]GDP (1996) based on UK = 100.
[2]Percentage of gross value added in each region, 1995.
[3]Number of companies receiving RSA, 1987–97.
Sources: Financial Times (1998) *Reporting Britain*, 11 June, and Table 11.1.

multinationals. Table 11.2 provides some information which may be relevant to this debate. It includes figures for each region in terms of GDP, shares of manufacturing output contributed by UK and by foreign firms, and the number of UK and foreign firms in receipt of government assistance via the RSA. We can see from Table 11.2 that the share of foreign firms in regional manufacturing output is greater in Scotland, Wales and the North East. These three regions also account for 77% of the total number of foreign firms receiving government assistance under the RSA. The government estimates that some 500,000 jobs have been created in the UK by such overseas business since 1979. However, the situation is not without its critics. For example, it has been argued that regions of the UK such as Wales still have below average GDP even though they have high ratios of foreign inward investment. It has also been argued that the concentration of foreign manufacturing production in Wales has given that regional economy a bias towards middle to low-quality jobs in export-orientated manufacturing companies which are highly vulnerable to changes in world market conditions; further, the relatively small contribution of the service sector in Wales, which tends to include activities of a higher value-added nature than manufacturing, has arguably only compounded the situation. Such critics argue that the role of government assistance as a means of promoting inward investment and jobs cannot be divorced from the need to create a balanced view of development in each region.

However, improved job prospects and the growth of new companies depend not only on the prospects of government grants but also on how macroeconomic forces (such as relatively lower wages in the UK) and microeconomic policies (such as urban policies) affect the *regions*. Nevertheless whichever way we look at the problem, a regional perspective is still critical if we wish to enjoy a healthy and prosperous national economy.

II. Effectiveness of policy instruments

Criticism of regional policy instruments has become part of a 'performance evaluation' procedure since the mid-1970s, particularly when it has been able to identify their 'cost-effectiveness' on a job creation basis. Research into the gross Exchequer *cost per job* in British DAs during the period 1960–81 demonstrated that the most cost effective instrument was IDC policy with its minor administrative cost. The next least expensive instrument was RSA, with a cost per job (at 1981 prices) of £17,000, followed by investment incentives at £25,000 per job and by REP, the most expensive instrument, at £73,000 per job (Moore, Rhodes and Tyler 1986). Not surprisingly, with governments determined to reduce spending from the late-1970s onwards, RSA emerged as the favoured policy instrument.

Investment incentives have formed a central part of regional policy since its inception in 1934. Investment grants and tax incentives were designed to encourage firms to set up in the disadvantaged regions. Surveys in the 1960s and 1970s seemed to show that capital grants may have had a significant effect on the movement of industry to Assisted Areas. However, financial incentives have been criticized for being capital-biased, thus encouraging the movement of capital- rather than labour-intensive firms into the Assisted Areas. Another criticism was that these incentives, whether grants or tax allowances, were often 'automatic', being given to *all* firms in the Assisted Areas irrespective of whether they were creating new employment or not. It was this persistent criticism and the suspicion that grants were going mostly to companies who would have invested in the Assisted Areas even *without* government assistance which led to the termination of RDG schemes in 1988 and the creation of the discretionary RSA assistance, which was much more selective in the projects chosen for help.

The *Regional Employment Premium* (REP) was used as a policy weapon in the UK from 1967 to 1976 and was, in effect, a direct-labour subsidy paid to all employers in the Assisted Areas to encourage the retention of existing employment and the creation of new employment. However, the benefits of a flat-rate subsidy such as the REP were eroded by inflation during the early 1970s, reducing its attractiveness to employers. Also, as with financial incentives, the REP was criticized for being available to all manufacturing establishments in the Development Areas 'whether new or old, expanding or contracting, progressive or asleep' (Moore and Rhodes 1976: 218). Another criticism was that the REP may well have encouraged firms to retain a higher labour/capital ratio than might have been dictated by economic efficiency alone. The REP was abolished in early 1976.

Industrial Development Certificates (IDCs) were simple to operate and were of only minor administrative cost to the Exchequer. However, there was no guarantee that a firm refused an IDC in, say, the South East, would actually build the factory in an Assisted Area. Projects for expansion could be shelved or moved abroad, particularly if the company refused permission to develop was a multinational. Industrial Development Certificate-type controls were more effective in redistributing employment when the economy was relatively buoyant than they were in recession when every region became desperate for jobs. In such circumstances all regions, including the relatively prosperous ones, were reluctant to accept restrictions on the expansion of firms through IDC control. It was partly as a result of this inadequacy that the use of IDCs was suspended in December 1981.

The urban problem

Urban–rural shift One of the most striking features of the post-war period has been the shift in employment and population from London and the large conurbations towards towns and cities in more rural areas. This shift is clearly shown in Table 11.3 where the statistics show a significant decrease in manufacturing employment in the mainly urban areas between 1960 and 1991. If we take changes in total employment (which includes services etc. as well as manufacturing), then the figures continue to show a relative shift in total employment from large urban areas towards rural areas over the shorter 1971–91 period.

Table 11.3 Employment change by urban–rural category '000s (%).

	Manufacturing employment 1960–91		Total employment 1971–91	
London	−979	(−73.2)	−716	(−18.0)
Conurbations	−1,392	(−61.0)	−795	(−17.5)
Free-standing cities	−631	(−47.0)	−114	(−3.7)
Large towns	−388	(−42.0)	+156	(+6.7)
Small towns	−284	(−17.4)	+425	(+8.2)
Rural areas	+238	(+45.4)	+759	(+14.3)
Great Britain	−3,443	(−42.8)	−283	(+1.2)

Source: Gudgin (1996) (modified).

Such shifts in employment and population away from the large urban areas have been due to a number of reasons. First, it became increasingly obvious that urban areas could not provide adequate factory floorspace for industries to expand. Automation and the adoption of new techniques led to a demand for greater floorspace per employee, causing firms to seek suitable sites outside major conurbations. Second, the cost of acquiring land in urban areas to establish new factories or to extend old ones was high compared to that in other regions. Third, some surveys have shown that over 60% of UK manufacturing industry is now 'footloose', being less affected by specific locational factors. This means that factors such as proximity to the large markets of the main conurbations are now less important. Fourth, it has been noted that manufacturing plants in urban areas tend to be larger than in non-urban areas. For example, Fothergill and Gudgin (1982) found that 68% of workers in Teesside were employed in large plants (500+ employees), with similar figures for Merseyside (64%) and Clydeside (56%). Such plants are often a part of large firms, such as multinationals, so that any company reorganization, rationalization or relocation may have a significant effect on employment in these urban areas.

Finally, the urban–rural shift has been explained in terms of an 'enterprise theory' (Keeble and Tyler 1995). The suggestion here is that rural settlements (as distinct from urban locations) are more able to attract a relatively high proportion of actual or potential entrepreneurs because of the more desirable residential environment. This in turn creates a pool of specialized and complex skills which results in the growth of niche markets, producing new and innovatory products. The improved accessibility of many rural settlements to modern telecommunications, transport, and financial services, make the rural locations increasingly more attractive vis-à-vis their urban counterparts.

All these factors have encouraged the movement of employment and population away from large urban areas, presenting a major problem for the inner core of many large cities.

The inner-city problem

During the post-war period employment and population have declined in the major conurbations, with the most serious decline occurring in the inner-city areas of such conurbations. For instance, between the early 1950s and the mid-1970s employment declined by 20% in the conurbations as a whole, but by 33% in the inner-city areas. However, in the suburban areas employment remained steady, whilst in small towns and rural areas employment rose.

Further evidence of inner-city problems includes the fact that the share of unskilled and semi-skilled workers in the labour force is significantly higher in such areas than in outer-city areas or in the nation as a whole. Inner cities also appear to have a higher proportion of low-income racial minorities. These low-skilled, low-income groups find it difficult to move from their low-cost, council accommodation in the inner city, to high-cost, owner-occupied accommodation in suburban or rural areas. For example, the London Planning Advisory Committee in 1987 reported that there was a growing east/west divide within the city with the residents of inner and east London far more likely to be unskilled or semi-skilled and working in declining economic activities than the residents of outer and west London. The committee also reported that parts of inner London had unemployment rates of over 20%. Such divisions continued into the 1990s with unemployment in inner London in 1995

Table 11.4
Unemployment rates in
the inner areas of the six
major conurbations of the
UK 1951–95 (%).

Inner area of	1951	1961	1971	1995
London	2.5	3.1	5.9	16.6
West Midland	1.2	1.4	4.8	15.1
Manchester	2.0	3.8	8.2	18.0
Merseyside	4.5	5.8	9.8	17.4
Tyneside	4.0	4.6	9.4	17.2
Clydeside	4.5	6.0	9.0	15.3
United Kingdom	2.1	2.8	5.2	8.2

Sources: Gudgin, Moore and Rhodes (1982); Travers and Minors (1995).

being 16.6%, or nearly double the outer London rate of 9.2%. Similarly, the percentage of the population on income support was 22.5% in inner London as compared to only 12.9% in the more affluent outer London area (Travers and Minors 1995).

The severity of the urban and inner-city problem is reflected in the fact that most of the metropolitan areas or major cities shown in Fig. 11.3 have been designated as 'inner-urban areas' for policy purposes (see below). The problems of inner-urban areas within the major conurbations are reflected in Table 11.4. Since 1951, only in the West Midland conurbation has inner-urban unemployment been significantly below the national average, though after 1981 even this conurbation had unemployment rates above the national average.

The movement of manufacturing employment away from the inner-urban areas was encouraged by the government's *New Towns* policies in the 1950s and 1960s. This was later followed by increased availability of grants and incentives for firms locating in the Assisted Areas. Inner-urban areas also suffered from the more active use of IDC policy, which made it more difficult for firms to locate within inner-urban areas. The general improvement in communications and rising real incomes were further factors in encouraging more people to live outside inner-urban areas, in suburbs, smaller towns and rural communities. A more recent survey has also shown that small firms in *rural* areas are likely to take on more labour than similar firms in urban areas, especially when the rural firms expansion was due to higher wage and other costs in the urban areas (North and Smallbone 1993).

Urban policy in the UK

Since the Second World War government policy towards the plight of urban and inner-city areas can be divided into four phases: 1945–65, 1965–77, 1977–88 and 1988–98.

1945–65 During this phase the government's policy was to limit the growth of major conurbations in an attempt to solve some of the pressing problems of urban congestion. *Green Belts* were established around major conurbations to prevent their expansion, and *New Towns* were built outside the major conurbations to take up any urban overspill. After 1947 the use of IDCs further restricted the growth of industries in the urban areas, whilst the Location of Offices Bureau sought to redistribute office work away from the conurbations, especially London.

1965–77   From the middle of the 1960s the government's attitude towards the inner-city problem began to change. Attention began to be drawn to the fact that the UK non-white population had grown to some half a million and was largely concentrated in cities. Fears were expressed that race riots similar to those of the US in 1967–68 might occur in the UK and this helped focus government attention on the urban problem. This emphasis was strengthened by the findings of the Plowden Report on children's education in 1967. This report identified deprived areas in inner cities which needed special help and led to the setting-up of *Educational Priority Areas* (EPAs) in 1969. In 1968 an *Urban Programme* was also established which, under the Local Government Grants (Social Needs) Act of 1969, was provided with a fund of £20–25m over four years. The aim of the Urban Programme was to provide resources for capital projects and educational schemes, such as pre-school playgroups, in order to raise the level of social services in areas of acute social need. In 1969 the *Community Development Project* was established to research into new ways of solving social deprivation in large urban communities.

1977–88   During this period the focus of attention began to shift to the economic problems of inner cities. The seeds of change began with the Labour government's White Paper *Policy for the Inner Cities* in 1977. This sought to strengthen the economies of inner-city areas, to improve the physical fabric of such areas to alleviate social problems, and to secure a new balance between inner-city areas and the rest of the region in terms of population and jobs. The White Paper also proposed the extension of local authority power to assist industry, and this was introduced through the Inner Urban Areas Act of 1978 which empowered local authorities to declare industrial and commercial improvement areas and to give financial assistance to companies which located in such areas.

With the election of the Conservative government in 1979 new initiatives were introduced to add to, and modify, existing legislation. Under the Local Government Planning and Land Act of 1980, Enterprise Zones and Urban Development Corporations (UDCs) were set up. In 1984 the first Free Zones (originally called Freeports) were designated, and in 1988 Simplified Planning Zones (SPZs) were created, having fewer financial advantages than Enterprise Zones but retaining the benefits of fewer planning regulations.

Enterprise Zones reflected the government's desire to release the private sector from restrictive financial and administrative controls, encouraging firms to set up in the more derelict parts of inner-city areas. Initially, eleven zones were designated in 1981, with the number rising to a maximum of twenty-seven by the end of 1989. These Enterprise Zones enjoy a number of privileges for ten years from their date of inception; the most important being exemption from the Business Rate, and 100% tax allowances for capital expenditure on commercial or industrial buildings. Companies setting up in Enterprise Zones are also exempt from development land tax, and face fewer local authority planning regulations and controls than they would in other areas. However, in 1988 the then Conservative government announced that no more zones would be created in England as it was becoming particularly worried about the consequences of the cost of the zones to the Exchequer.

Urban Development Corporations (UDCs).   The role of the local authorities in allocating resources has been eroded by such legislation as Enterprise Zones. Their powers were further reduced under the 1980 Act by the creation of new agencies for urban renewal with special powers and resources, the Urban Development Corporations (UDCs). The UDCs were designed to undertake substantial programmes of land acquisition and reclamation in an attempt to secure the greatest possible involvement of the private sector companies in their areas. Similarly, the UDCs are involved in environmental improvement and infrastructure provision in these areas. The first generation of Urban Development Corporations were formed in the London Docklands and in Merseyside in 1980 and were given special powers to promote urban renewal in those areas. The second generation, formed in 1987, included Trafford Park, the Black Country, Teesside and Tyne and Wear. By the late 1980s these had been joined by a third generation covering Central Manchester, Leeds, Sheffield and Bristol. The fourth, and most recent, generation of UDCs included the Birmingham Heartlands and Plymouth, designated in 1992/93. These corporations are financed mainly by Exchequer grants and employ around 500 permanent staff in total. The UDCs are limited-life bodies and are now preparing their completion and succession strategies. Leeds and Bristol UDCs were wound up in 1995 and all the UDCs had been wound up by March 1998.

Free Zones.   Six areas were designated for Free Zone status in 1984, including Birmingham, Belfast, Cardiff, Liverpool, Prestwick and Southampton. However, by 1994, Belfast and Cardiff had left the list but Hull, Tilbury and Humberside had been added. Within the Freeports, goods are to be exempt from customs duties and (possibly) VAT, unless the goods are subsequently transported from the Freeport to the rest of the UK. The intention of the Freeports is to attract business and investment into the areas, particularly since goods *not destined for import into the UK* can be handled *without* tariff charges. This should help the UK gain a greater share of the rapidly growing intermediate processing and servicing activities via global specialization (see Chapter 7).

In addition to the measures noted above, this period saw the growth of a 'package' of measures to combat inner city problems. These included the Urban Programme, the Urban Development Grant and the Derelict Land Programme.

Urban Programme.   Up to the early 1990s the Urban Programme was the major mechanism for allocating funds to the inner cities. The programme has continued to operate, despite changes in emphasis, up to the present time although spending on the whole scheme has fallen dramatically (see Table 11.5) as other schemes have been introduced. The Urban Programme is designed to provide support for a wide range of projects submitted by fifty-seven local authorities, called Urban Programme areas (UPs). In particular it provides funding to enable local authorities to make assistance available in their locality for *specific projects* which involve the private sector organizations and which encourage enterprise and the development of new businesses. Broadly speaking the main aims of the Urban Programme are:

1. To promote the regeneration of local economies. This involves supporting projects which build new, or convert old, factory units and which create training opportunities and jobs for the labour force in those areas.

2. To improve the physical environment of local economies. This involves modernizing shops and other buildings while also improving parks, waterways and footpaths etc.
3. To meet social and housing needs directly. Social needs include the provision of community centres, sports facilities and health projects while housing needs encompass improvements in refuge accommodation and helping to improve conditions on housing estates which have environmental problems.

Up to 1988, the key instrument for funding parts of the Urban Programme was the *Urban Development Grant* (UDG) but this was abolished in May 1988 and was replaced by the *City Grant* explained below. However, since 1994/95 the funding of the Urban Programmes has come directly from the Single Regeneration Budget (see below) and most of the remaining Urban Programme projects were completed in 1997.

Another component of the urban package, although not strictly defined as being within the Urban Programme, is the *Derelict Land Programme*. Under the Derelict Land Act of 1982, the Secretary of State for the Environment is empowered to pay grants to public bodies, voluntary organizations, private firms and individuals to enable derelict land to be reclaimed, improved or brought into use again. The grant varies between 50% and 100%, depending on the location of the site and the institutions or persons applying.

1988–98   As noted earlier in the chapter, in March 1988 the Conservative government launched a series of new initiatives to help promote enterprise investment and employment in the inner-city areas and also published a new government booklet entitled *Action for Cities*. The booklet defined a range of inner city initiatives which were to be the foundation of government urban policy during the 1990s. Some of the initiatives included in the booklet, such as the Urban Programme and the Urban Development Corporations, were not in fact new, but were now collected together under the Action for Cities 'umbrella'. However, other initiatives were new, including the following elements.

First, a new, simplified *City Grant* noted above was introduced to replace the Urban Development Grant (UDG), the Urban Regeneration Grant (URG) and the private sector part of the Derelict Land Grant (DLG). It was designed to support capital investments undertaken by the private sector in property and business development especially in the priority areas. The total project value must be above £200,000 and the private sector must convince the Department of the Environment that the project will provide jobs, private housing or other benefits. Also, to receive the grant the Department must be satisfied that the project is unable to proceed because the costs incurred in the development (including allowance for a reasonable profit) exceed the market value of the project. If the application is successful then the grant would cover this deficit and would therefore allow projects which benefit the community to continue despite the apparent problems of covering all essential costs. The *City Grant* applications are made directly to the local offices of the DOE (instead of through the local authorities as with the UDG) and appraisals of the projects are to be made within ten weeks. These procedures simplified and streamlined the grant system.

Second, measures were introduced to make more unused and under-utilized land in urban areas available for development by requiring publication of information about land held in public ownership.

Third, the government factory builder, the English Industrial Estates, provided grants for the conversion of suitable buildings for use as managed workshops.

Fourth, the Manpower Services Commission (the forerunner of the Training Agency) was allowed to increase its staff in inner-city areas in order to advise unemployed people and also to give financial support to inner-city areas (Compacts). Here groups of employers work with schools to guarantee a job with training for all young people aged sixteen to eighteen leaving school and who have met an agreed standard while at school. Many of these initiatives have now been taken over in modified form by the 104 *Training and Enterprise Councils* (TECs) who are responsible for delivering a range of training programmes on behalf of the Department for Education and Employment.

To add to the plethora of different measures which were introduced, it is worth noting two additional schemes and one major reorganization.

First, the creation by the Department of Trade and Industry from 1985 onwards of eight City Action Teams (CATs). These teams consist of senior officials and other representatives who attempt to coordinate the work of their different government departments within inner-city areas. They also encourage partnerships between business, local and central government and the voluntary sector in inner-city areas and act as the primary focal point with local authorities for the City Challenge (see below). The work of these teams was subsumed within the Government Offices for the Regions in 1994. In 1986, under the same initiative, sixteen Inner-City Task Forces composed of smaller teams of civil servants and people on secondment from the private sector, were formed to work directly with local businesses or local councils in an attempt to stimulate economic development, employment and training in inner-city areas. In 1997/98 the Task Forces assisted around 2,000 businesses and provided up to 6,000 jobs and 19,000 training places, before being wound up in 1998.

Second, in order to improve the targeting of government resources as part of the Action for Cities programme, the *City Challenge* was introduced in 1991. Under this scheme local authorities, in conjunction with the private sector, compete for government resources (i.e. funds diverted from various existing inner-city schemes) by submitting *action plans* for scrutiny. These plans must be environmentally imaginative whilst also helping to sustain economic activity in key inner-city localities. By 1998 a total of 31 City Challenge action plans were each receiving £7.5m a year, ongoing for five years. All these action plans will have been completed by 1999.

Single regeneration budget

By the late 1990s a plethora of schemes had been created to deal with various aspects of the Urban problem, as can be seen in Table 11.5.

In April 1994 a total of twenty targeted government programmes from the DOE, DTI, Employment and Home Office Departments were brought together into a new Single Regeneration Budget (SRB). The aim of the SRB was to fill the gaps in main programmes where these were not sufficiently flexible to tackle particular regeneration needs. The Secretary of State for the Environment, Transport and the Regions is accountable to Parliament for the SRB and is guided by a Ministerial Committee on Regeneration on the use of the Budget.

The SRB is currently administered by the Government Offices for the Regions (GOR), although certain parts of the Budget such as the Challenge Fund and English Partnerships are destined to be taken over by the new Regional Development Agencies (RDAs) by the year 2000.

Table 11.5 Regeneration expenditure (DOE only), £m.

Single regeneration budget	1990–91 outturn	1992–93 outturn	1994–95 outturn	1998–99 plans
UDCs	553.2	430.6	258.0	0.5
Docklands Light Railway	54.0	84.4	29.1	52.0
English Partnerships (URA)	118.9	153.3	191.7	298.4
Housing Action Trusts	–	26.5	92.0	87.5
Challenge Fund	–	–	–	567.3
Estate Action	180.0	348.0	372.6	99.0
City Challenge	–	72.6	233.6	6.8
Urban Programme	225.8	236.2	67.8	
Business Start-up Scheme	113.1	62.1	63.8	
Local Initiative Fund	9.9	49.7	34.5	
Task Forces	20.9	23.6	15.7	4.1
Compacts	5.8	5.4	5.2	
City Action teams	7.7	4.6	0.2	
Others	81.2	87.7	94.1	
Sub total	1,370.5	1,584.7	1,458.3	1,115.6
New Towns	−333.2	−168.9	−135.3	−103.1
European Structural Funds	2.1	26.9	158.4	220.5
Others	6.9	13.6	34.9	20.8
Total Regeneration	1,046.3	1,456.3	1,516.3	1,253.8

Source: Adapted from Department of the Environment, Transport and the Regions (1998) Annual Report, and previous issues.

As can be seen in Table 11.5, the main element of the SRB is the *Challenge Fund*, based on a national competitive bidding process, through which funds are allocated for new regeneration initiatives in urban areas. For example, funds are used to support employment, training, housing and crime prevention initiatives, as well as stimulating projects directed towards the ethnic minority communities in urban areas. The first three rounds of bidding under the Challenge Fund covered the period 1995–97 and created or safeguarded some 666,000 jobs, as well as helping stimulate some £7.2bn private sector spending in those areas.

Another important element of the SRB Fund is the *English Partnerships*, whose objectives are to promote job creation, inward investment and environmental improvement in urban areas by reclaiming and developing vacant or derelict land. The English Partnerships involve both the private sector and the Local Authorities in a variety of urban projects. For example, English Partnerships was involved in the long-term regeneration of the Greenwich Peninsula in London, and in the ten-year project to bring 56,000 jobs to some of the old coal-field regions of the UK.

Finally, the SRB also covers the six *Housing Action Trusts* (HATs) which, with the agreement of their tenants, took over some of the most deprived local authority estates in order to improve the quality of housing and communal conditions. In 1997/98 for example, the HATs built 814 new homes, renovated a further 370 homes and created nearly 500 jobs in poor urban areas of London and Liverpool.

The effectiveness of urban policy

Although greater emphasis has been placed on urban policy over the last few years, it has not been without its critics.

First, it has been argued that resources directed to urban policies have been insufficient, accounting for only 4% of the Department of the Environment, Transport and the Regions planned spending in 1998/99. In the same period, for example, the total amount to be spent on the English Partnerships (£298m); and the Challenge Fund (£567m) combined was less than central government spending on arts and libraries.

Second, it is claimed that urban policies have failed to ensure that new jobs created in the inner cities were filled by unemployed inner-city residents. Evidence suggests that higher-skilled commuters from outside the inner-city areas often 'crowd out' inner-city residents in the competition for employment. To redress the balance it has been suggested that marginal subsidies be provided for firms which recruit unemployed inner-city residents. Such schemes could also be designed to favour employers making the greatest contribution to improving the skill and job experience of inner-city residents.

Third, the UDG was criticized for being more helpful in attracting renewal schemes to areas which *already* have a reasonable degree of economic activity. In a study of 41 UDG sponsored projects in operation during the mid-1980s it was found that many of the schemes would have gone ahead even without UDG grants. In fact 64% of the total employment generated by the UDG sponsored projects would have been created even without the government subsidy. In other words, companies were likely to have come to those areas even if they had not been offered subsidies (Martin 1989). In parts of the North-East and South Wales it may take more than 'pump priming' to persuade private capital to invest in areas of serious urban decay. There is, as yet, little evidence that national financial institutions such as pension funds and insurance companies are 'risking' capital by investing in projects which were eligible for UDGs.

A report by Price Waterhouse on the impact of the City Grant and its predecessors (the UDG and the Urban Regeneration Grant) covering thirty-six projects was completed in 1993. It indicated that the grants had been important in creating confidence in the local economies but that the actual job creation had been 19% below the figure initially predicted for the schemes. Further, some 46% of the jobs created were jobs displaced from other premises in the area. Hence, the *net* additional jobs were only half the numbers initially predicted. Hotels were the most efficient at generating net additional jobs and they also employed the highest proportion of employees from within the inner-city areas. However, they were also the most 'expensive' in that they absorbed £1 of government grants for every £2.8 of private investment (i.e. 35%) as compared to retail (14%), offices (15%) and industrial (25%). In general, the cost per job at £14,280 for the City Grants compared relatively favourably with other public sector job creation initiatives.

Fourth, there is a danger that programmes such as the Urban Development Corporations may not solve the unemployment problem because many of the jobs created in these areas often go to people who live outside the area. For example, a report by the House of Commons Employment Committee in 1988 found that although the overall increase in employment in the London Dockland Corporation area had risen from 27,213 in 1981 to 36,000 in 1987, the majority of this increase represented a relocation of jobs from outside Docklands. It also pointed out that the skills demanded by the new companies entering the London Dockland Development Corporation scheme did not match the skills of the local population. Finally, the committee found that most of the new jobs created in this area tended to be in office or service work and that manufacturing employment had actually declined. As a result the unemployment level in this area was higher in 1988 than at the launch of the scheme in 1981.

The problems of unemployment and deprivation continue in the urban areas despite the myriad of schemes shown in Table 11.5. A Policy Studies Institute report in 1992 demonstrated that the urban areas with the highest deprivation experienced the worst unemployment and that their relative position *deteriorated* during the 1980s. Also there was a higher level of unemployment *after* completion of training schemes among people from urban programme areas, as compared with those from other areas. Some of the problem may lie in what some see as the official view that the key criterion for effective policy is the cost per job created. For others, the key criterion should be the creation of the maximum number of jobs in the deprived areas. It is interesting to note that an evaluation of local economic policy in Britain found that although the various initiatives had produced overall value for money for the public exchequer, the problems for disadvantaged groups in obtaining employment persisted (Foley 1992).

Fifth, there is a danger that urban policies could be detrimental to industrial growth as a whole. By limiting their aid to firms which locate in highly urbanized areas, governments may discourage production taking place in more suitable locations, leading to a less efficient allocation of resources. There is also the difficulty that inner cities may gain firms and employment at the expense of the suburbs, or other areas, so that there is no net gain to the economy as a whole.

A survey assessing the impact of urban policy on the Urban Programme Areas (UPAs) found that the *unemployment* gaps between UPA and non-UPA areas had narrowed over the last part of the 1980s but that there was no discernible narrowing of the difference between the two types of areas in terms of *job creation* or *new firm foundation*. In fact, the benefit accruing to the deprived inner city areas were less than those accruing to the areas on the periphery of these deprived inner city areas (Department of the Environment 1994).

A report on thirteen Enterprise Zones which had completed their ten year life cycle in 1993/94 serves to illustrate some of these problems (Department of the Environment 1995). Out of 51,100 permanent jobs created in the thirteen zones over the ten year period, 33,424 would have been there even without the zone designation and some 26,269 of the jobs had merely been diverted to the zones from nearby areas. Taking other multiplier effects into consideration, the net additional permanent jobs created by the Zones was estimated as 23,150, at a total cost of between £1,450–£1,850 per job, per year.

Finally, the effectiveness of urban policy depends on a rational and clear strategic view of how to tackle urban problems. The City Challenge initiative could be usefully assessed in this light. Unfortunately, the City Challenge promoted centralization rather than a free market, in that the government (through the competitive bidding process) was given more control over how Urban Programme authorities spend their resources. Also, co-operation between authorities was hindered by the fact that authorities were made to bid against each other for funds. On top of this, the City Challenge did not provide a net addition to the general Urban Programme fund, since the resources were taken from other urban initiatives. Finally, local authorities who were successful in obtaining City Challenge funds often had to bring more of their own funds into the scheme, sometimes at the cost of reducing spending on other deprived areas within the local authority (Atkinson and Moon 1994).

The Regional Development Agencies (RDAs)

The incoming Labour government of 1997, as well as devolving power to Scotland and Wales, has established nine English Regional Development Agencies (RDAs), resembling those already in existence in Wales and Scotland, i.e. the Welsh Development Agency (WDA) and the Scottish Development Agency (SDA) respectively. The boundaries of the RDAs will be the same as those already existing under the Government Offices of the Regions (GORs) and will retain the same regional names (e.g. Eastern Development Agency for the Eastern GOR, etc.). Each RDA is, in effect, a non-departmental public body, with the Secretary of State appointing each RDA Board member (between eight and fifteen). Those appointed to Board membership in each region are to reflect a mix of interests, such as business, education, voluntary sector, etc.

The functions of each RDA are defined to include taking a leadership role in developing and implementing regional economic strategies to improve the economic competitiveness of the region. The RDAs will also be involved with regional regeneration as they will administer the SRB Challenge Fund as well as exercising the functions of the Rural Development Commission and English Partnerships. They will also provide advice to the DTI on allocating RSA grants for their region and will help assemble a range of support facilities such as recruitment, training, site location, etc. for any inward investment projects into their region.

This change in emphasis of regional policy in England towards the RDA model is not without its critics. Some argue that the RDAs will inevitably be involved in wasteful competition, with regions seeking to outbid each other in an attempt to secure inward investment. Others argue that the plans for the RDAs concentrate too much on economic development, with the result that environmental or sustainable development objectives are hardly mentioned in their remit (Mawson 1998).

Conclusion

Despite the problems of definition, it has long been recognized that some areas of the UK suffer a greater degree of economic difficulty than do others. Government policies have attempted to alleviate such problems and have experienced some measure of success, creating up to 800,000 extra jobs in the Assisted Areas since the 1960s. However, critics have commented that the 'costs' have been high, at £40,000 per job created, with much of the benefit going to companies such as ICI, Shell and BP, which often would have located plants in the Assisted Areas without financial help.

In the 1970s the regional problem was aggravated by economic and social difficulties experienced in the large conurbations, especially within the inner cities. Policies to counteract these problems were slow to develop, though in the 1980s and 1990s government policy has been much more active with the development of Enterprise Zones, UDCs and inner-city initiatives such as *Action for Cities*, and with the new organizational changes brought about by the Single Regeneration Budget in 1994. However, an integrated policy may be required, incorporating both government and industry views, and taking account of both the regional and urban dimension, if the UK is successfully to combat the difficulties noted above. To promote such integration, from April 1999 the new Regional Development Agencies have been given the task of co-ordinating the various policy initiatives at the regional level. The long-run 'costs' of *not* developing an effective, integrated, policy may far outweigh any short-term monetary 'benefits' from reduced government spending.

Key points

- A *regional problem* exists where a region departs from the 'national average' in terms of various characteristics: e.g. levels of unemployment, GDP per head, outward migration, etc.
- 'Core' regions are those which have experienced the most rapid economic advance in the past three decades or so: e.g. South East, East Midlands, East Anglia.
- 'Periphery' regions have experienced less favourable conditions: 'inner' and 'outer' peripheries are often identified.
- Intervention in terms of regional policy is usually advocated by those who feel that market forces alone will not eliminate regional disparities.
- Various types of *Assisted Area* (AA) are now identified in the UK. *Development Areas* (DAs) receive most help and *Intermediate Areas* (IAs) rather less. *Split* areas are now used for those on the margin of these categories.
- Most policy instruments now involve a range of financial incentives rather than direct controls.
- The *Urban Problem* involves aspects such as the urban–rural shift of population and economic activity, often reflected in particular inner-cities problems.
- Policies have included Enterprise Zones, Urban Development Corporations and Grants and various inner-city initiatives.
- The Regional Development Agencies (RDAs) are to play an increasingly important role in regional and urban policy in England.

References and further reading

Atkinson, R. and **Moon, G.** (1994) The city challenge initiative: an overview and preliminary assessment, *Regional Studies*, **28**, 1.

Blake, N. (1995) The regional implications of macroeconomic policy, *Oxford Review of Economic Policy*, **11**, 2, Summer.

Department of the Environment (1994) Assessing the Impact of Urban Policy, Inner City Research Programme.

Department of the Environment (1995) Final Evaluation of Enterprise Zones, PA Cambridge Economic Consultants.

Financial Times (1998) Regions take an inward look at the growing problem, May, p. 11.

Foley, P. (1992) Local economic policy and job creation: a review of evaluation studies, *Urban Studies*, **29**.

Fothergill, S. and **Gudgin, G.** (1982) *Unequal Growth: urban and regional employment change in the UK*, Heinemann.

Gudgin, G. (1996) Regional problems and policy in the UK, *Oxford Review of Economic Policy*, **11**, 2.

Gudgin, G., Moore, B. and **Rhodes, J.** (1982) Employment problems in the cities and regions of the UK: prospects for the 1980s, *Cambridge Economic Policy Review*, **8**, 2, University of Cambridge, Department of Economics, Gower.

Keeble, D. and **Tyler, P.** (1995) Enterprising behaviour and the urban–rural shift, *Urban Studies*, **32**, 6.

Martin, R. (1998) Regional incentive spending for European regions, *Regional Studies*, **32**, 6.

Martin R. and **Tyler, P.** (1992) The regional legacy, in J. Michie (ed.) *The Economic Legacy 1979–1992*, Academic Press.

Martin, S. (1989) New jobs in the inner city: the employment impacts of projects assisted under urban development Grant Programme, *Urban Studies*, **26**, 6, December.

Mawson, J. (1998) Regional development agencies and sustainable development, *Regional Studies*, **32**, 4, Review section.

Moore, B. C. and **Rhodes, J.** (1976) A quantitative analysis of the effects of the regional employment premium and other regional policy instruments, in Whiting, A. (ed.) *The Economics of Industrial Subsidies*, HMSO.

Moore, B. C. and **Rhodes, J.** (1977) *Methods of Evaluating the Effects of Regional Policy*, OECD, Paris.

Moore, B., Rhodes, J. and **Tyler, P.** (1986) *The Effect of Government Regional Economic Policy*, DTI, HMSO.

North, D. and **Smallbone, D.** (1993) Employment generation and small business growth in different geographical environments, Small Firms Conference, Nottingham.

Robson, B. (1997) Urban renewal and regional development, *Developments in Economics*, **13**, Causeway Press.

Travers, T. and **Minors, M.** (1995) *London 1995*, London Research Centre.

Tyler, J., Moore, B. and **Rhodes, J.** (1979) Regional policy and growth in development areas, paper presented to the Social Science Research Council Urban and Regional Economic Seminar Group, Newcastle.

Chapter 12

Transport

Transport is an important sector of the UK economy and has been the subject of increasing debate in recent years. This chapter will deal with certain aspects of that debate, notably the problems of road transport congestion and the move to a more deregulated transport sector. The last 40 years have seen a dramatic change in the patterns of demand for transport. For example, in 1952 only 27% of passenger kilometres travelled were by car, van and taxi, while public transport (both road and rail) accounted for 60%. Today, however, the share has changed, with 86% of passenger kilometres now being by car, van and taxi with public transport accounting for only 12%. Such a substantial change has significant implications for road congestion and the environment. In this chapter we therefore concentrate mainly on the *road transport sector*, and on the car in particular.

Characteristics of transport

Firstly, transport is a service which is seldom demanded for its own sake and can be viewed as a 'derived demand'. In other words, the demand for the private car, public transport and freight haulage, is 'derived' from the need to transfer passengers and goods from one destination to another. Each journey undertaken can be seen as 'unique' in terms of both time and space, and cannot therefore be stored or transferred.

Secondly, the transport sector (both passenger and freight operators) is affected by the peak and off-peak nature of demand. There will be periods of maximum or peak demand, e.g. on a *daily* basis when commuters travel into a major conurbation to work, or on a *seasonal* basis when holidaymakers use road, rail or airline transport during summer periods. Peak periods are present in the transport sector because of the derived nature of demand and because transport is consumed immediately and is therefore non-storable. Spare capacity at one time of the day or season *cannot* be used at another time of the day or season. Also the indivisibility of supply means that public transport may be running at full capacity into the urban area in the peak period, but operating empty on the return journey. As a result there are often problems of over supply during off-peak periods.

Thirdly, the transport sector has, over the years, been subject to varying degrees of state intervention. When the Conservative government was elected in 1979, the transport sector was characterized by public ownership and substantial government intervention, particularly in the provision of public transport. The 1980s saw a period of rapid change, with a substantial scaling down of state intervention in the sector. For example, the *1980 Transport Act* deregulated the long distance express coach market allowing increased competition. The National Freight Corporation was privatized in 1982 and subsequent years saw the deregulation of local bus provision as a result of the *1985 Transport Act*. Other transport companies were privatized, such as British Airways in 1987 and NBC in 1988. In addition there was the franchising of rail services from 1995 onwards.

Fourthly, 'externality' effects are a characteristic of transport. These include effects such as pollution through emissions from car exhausts, noise from aircraft and motorways, and traffic congestion. At present 71% of carbon monoxide and 48% of nitrogen oxide emissions are associated with road transport in the UK. These impose costs on the community and are generally *not* taken into account by the transport provider (company or individual) who is usually only concerned with the *private costs* (such as fuel, wear and tear, etc.) of the journey undertaken. Intervention by the state has therefore been required to deal with these external effects, especially where companies or individuals have failed to take full account of the *social* implications of their actions. This has led, for example, to the introduction of emission tests for carbon monoxide as part of the MoT test for cars and light vehicles and an increase in roadside enforcement programmes in order to remove the worst offenders from the road.

Fifthly, other characteristics of transport may be gauged from the changing nature of travel over the last decade. Table 12.1 gives a summary of passenger travel in Great

Table 12.1   Passenger transport by mode: 1987–97.

	Billion passenger kilometres/percentage													
	Road													
	Buses and coaches		Cars and vans[1]		Motor cycles		Pedal cycles		All road		Rail[2]		Air		All modes[3]
	Per cent		Per cent		Per cent		Per cent		Per cent		Per cent		Per cent		Per cent
1987	47	8	500	83	7	1	6	1	560	93	40	7	4	1	604	100
1988	46	7	536	84	6	1	5	1	593	93	41	6	5	1	639	100
1989	47	7	581	85	6	1	5	1	639	93	40	6	5	1	684	100
1990	46	7	588	85	6	1	5	1	645	93	40	6	5	1	690	100
1991	44	6	584	86	6	1	5	1	639	94	38	6	5	1	682	100
1992	43	6	587	86	5	1	5	1	640	94	38	6	5	1	682	100
1993	43	6	585	86	4	1	5	1	637	94	37	5	5	1	679	100
1994	43	6	596	87	4	1	5	1	648	94	35	5	5	1	689	100
1995	44	6	596	86	4	1	4	1	648	94	36	5	5.9	0.9	690	100
1996	44	6	609	86	4	1	4	1	661	94	38	5	6.3	0.9	706	100
1997	43	6	619	86	4	1	4	1	670	93	41	6	6.8	0.9	717	100

Notes:
[1]Includes taxis.
[2]Former British Rail companies plus Urban Rail Systems.
[3]Excluding travel by water within the UK (including Channel Islands), estimated at 0.6 billion passenger kilometres in 1997.
Source: DETR (1998c).

Britain over the period 1987-97. It shows that there was an increase in passenger transport by 19% over the period, with travel by cars and vans increasing by 24%. *Cars* dominate passenger transport and have expanded their share of this sector from 83% to 86% over the period in question. Over the same period there has been a decline in *bus* and *coach* passenger kilometres, both in absolute and relative terms. In fact in terms of passenger kilometres, bus and coach travel has fallen by 8.5% between 1987 and 1997, and their share of overall passenger kilometres travelled in Great Britain has steadily declined throughout the period. Domestic air travel, although it has grown by 70% between 1987 and 1997, still only accounts for 0.9% of overall travel.

Table 12.2 compares Great Britain with a number of other countries in terms of passenger kilometres travelled between 1985 and 1995. In all of these countries the major mode of transport is the private road vehicle. This is the case in Japan even though travel by rail is an important mode. In fact it is interesting to note that in Japan, 37% of all passenger kilometres travelled are by rail.

Finally, another characteristic of transport is the changing nature of the *freight* market. In terms of freight transport, Table 12.3 gives figures in billion tonne kilometres and percentage, by mode, over the period 1987–97. It shows that there has been a 20% increase in freight transported over the ten year period and, as with passenger transport, roads can be seen as the major form of transport, with 67% of the share in 1997.

Table 12.2 Passenger transport by national vehicles on national territory: 1985 and 1995.

	Billion passenger kilometres							
	Cars and taxis		Buses and coaches		Rail excluding metro systems		Total of these modes	
	1985	1995	1985	1995	1985	1995	1985	1995
Great Britain	441.0[1]	606.0[1]	49.0[1]	44.0[1]	29.7[2]	29.3	519.7	679.3
Belgium	67.4	91.2	9.0	12.5	6.6	6.8	83.0	110.5
Denmark	43.2	61.5	8.8	9.9	4.9	5.0	56.9	76.4
France	494.4	664.3	37.0	40.5	62.1	55.6	593.5	760.4
Germany	564.2	741.5	94.0[1]	68.6[1]	66.0	63.6	724.2	873.7
Greece	66.6	95.0	5.8	5.6	1.7	1.6	74.1	102.2
Irish Republic	30.4	42.4	2.6	3.0	1.0	1.3	34.0	46.7
Italy	373.7	615.3	68.1	79.0	40.3	52.4	482.1	746.7
Netherlands	118.0[1]	146.8[1]	13.0[1]	14.3[1]	9.0	14.0	140.0	175.1
Spain	119.8[1]	211.4[1]	31.8[1]	40.2[1]	17.2	16.6	168.8	268.2
Sweden	71.6	91.7	9.0	9.2	6.8	6.4	87.4	107.3
Norway	33.1	41.8[3]	3.7	4.7[3]	2.2	2.7[3]	39.0	49.2
Switzerland	62.2[1]	75.1[3]	4.1[1]	5.7[3]	9.0	12.1[3]	75.3	92.9
Japan	384.0	591.0	105.0	100.0	330.1	400.0	819.1	1091.0
USA	3,449.0	4,561.0	151.0	178.0[4]	18.2	22.0	3,618.2	4,761.0

Notes:
[1]National and foreign vehicles.
[2]Figures for 1985 are based on calender years whereas 1995 are based on financial year 1995/96.
[3]1994 data.
[4]Intercity transport and school buses only.
Source: Adapted from DETR (1998c).

Table 12.3 Freight
transport by mode (in
billion tonne kilometres
and percentages):
1987–97.

	Billion tonne kilometres (percentages)					
	1987	1989	1991	1993	1995	1997
All traffic						
Road[1]	113.3	137.8	130.0	134.5	149.6	157.1
Rail	17.3	17.3	15.3	13.8	13.3	16.9
Water	54.1	57.9	57.7	51.2	52.6	48.2
Pipeline	10.5	9.8	11.1	11.6	11.1	11.2
All modes	195.2	222.8	214.1	211.1	226.6	233.4
Percentage of all traffic						
Road[1]	58	62	61	64	66	67
Rail	9	8	7	7	6	7
Water	28	26	27	24	23	21
Pipeline	5	4	5	5	5	5
All modes	100	100	100	100	100	100

Note:
[1]All goods vehicles, including those up to 3.5 tonnes gross vehicle weight.
Source: Adapted from DETR (1998c).

The demand for transport

The quantity of a good or service demanded is dependent upon a number of factors, such as its own price, the price of other goods or services (particularly close substitutes and complements), and income. For example, private car ownership is not only a function of the price of motor vehicles, but also of fuel prices, the price of alternative forms of transport, and income levels. Income is an important factor in determining both the demand for transport in general, and the *particular mode* of transport a passenger uses.

Table 12.4 gives figures for motoring expenditure, fares and other travel costs for households with different levels of income in the UK over the 1996–97 period. As one would expect, it clearly shows that travel expenditure increases with income with those households in the lowest 10% income group having an average weekly expenditure on *motoring* of £4.88 whilst the highest 10% spend £98.49. For *all* households the average is £41.20. For *bus and coach* fares the figures reveal that expenditure declines at higher income levels. As illustrated in Table 12.4, the fifth income decile group spent £1.54 on average per week whilst the top decile group spent £1.16 per week, leading one to suggest that bus and coach travel can be viewed in economic terms as an *inferior good*.

For *rail transport, Family Spending 1996–97* (Office for National Statistics 1997) reveals a different trend with higher income groups spending more on that mode of travel. As illustrated in Table 12.4 the highest 10% of income earners spent on average £4.39 per week on rail and tube fares compared to an average for *all households* of £1.29.

Predicting the demand for transport in the future is a difficult process since it depends on how the variables affecting demand change over time. For example, forecasts in terms of car ownership and in particular, cars per person are predicted to increase by 31% between 1997 and 2031. In terms of vehicle kilometres then the

Table 12.4   Detailed household expenditure by gross income decile group, 1996–97.

Commodity or service	Lowest ten per cent	Second decile group	Third decile group	Fourth decile group	Fifth decile group	Sixth decile group	Seventh decile group	Eighth decile group	Ninth decile group	Highest ten per cent	All households
	Average weekly household expenditure (£)										
Motoring	4.88	8.38	15.11	24.26	33.19	44.80	48.15	60.44	74.38	98.49	41.20
Percentage standard error	*12.7*	*15.0*	*7.4*	*5.9*	*5.3*	*4.6*	*4.1*	*3.8*	*4.3*	*4.3*	*1.9*
Cars, vans and motorcycles purchase	1.21	2.24	3.82	6.13	12.46	17.44	15.74	23.74	30.67	45.56	15.90
Spares and accessories	–	0.70	0.62	1.50	1.32	1.95	2.51	3.17	4.05	3.97	1.99
Car and van repairs and servicing	0.72	0.82	1.80	2.92	2.71	4.42	5.01	5.54	5.71	8.61	3.83
Motor vehicle insurance and taxation	1.06	1.60	2.84	4.13	5.23	6.55	7.77	8.66	10.27	11.98	6.01
Petrol, diesel and other motor oils	1.46	2.66	5.26	7.96	10.15	13.02	15.09	16.94	20.51	24.75	11.78
Other motoring costs	0.33	0.37	0.75	1.61	1.33	1.42	2.03	2.38	3.17	3.63	1.70
Fares and other travel costs	1.98	2.43	3.56	4.64	7.36	6.36	9.21	9.22	11.37	18.41	7.45
Percentage standard error	*10.1*	*11.5*	*8.1*	*11.1*	*25.6*	*11.5*	*16.1*	*11.0*	*10.6*	*15.9*	*5.7*
Rail and tube fares	0.22	0.18	0.30	0.34	0.87	0.85	1.25	1.51	2.96	4.39	1.29
Bus and coach fares	0.97	0.93	1.45	1.32	1.54	1.35	1.57	1.75	1.76	1.16	1.38
Air and other travel and transport	0.66	1.05	1.69	2.21	2.54	3.14	5.87	4.68	5.91	7.33	3.51
Bicycles, boats, purchase and repair	–	–	–	0.76	–	1.02	0.52	1.29	0.74	–	1.28

Source: Adapted from Office for National Statistics (1997).

forecast for cars and taxis is an increase of 50% over the same period whereas goods vehicles are forecast to increase by 69%. In 1997 there were approximately 21.7m private cars licenced in Great Britain. As Table 12.5 reveals, however, we have not as yet reached saturation level in terms of car ownership, for there are still 30% of households who do *not* own a car.

With regards to forecasting car ownership, the Department of Transport used the *National Road Traffic Forecasts* 1988 (Goodwin 1990) to make the following observation:

'Many factors are likely to influence the growth of car ownership and use. They include income, the cost of buying and running cars, journey requirements (work and non-work), quality of public transport services and the way people's expectations and preferences about car ownership change over time. ... It seems likely that car ownership will eventually reach a limit – or "saturation level" – as a larger proportion of the population acquires cars. Since no country appears to have reached this limit yet, the level of saturation must be assumed. For these forecasts, saturation has been assumed to occur when 90% of the driving age group of 17–74-year-olds owns a car; (100% car ownership is unlikely because some people will be prevented or deterred by disabilities or other factors). On this basis, saturation would correspond to 650 cars per thousand people. The forecasts of growth in national car ownership are essentially about the rate and path with which the saturation level is approached.'

Forecasts of future traffic, particularly the private car, are essential for a central government which has to decide on the allocation of funds for future road development. For, as stated by the Department of Transport in 1989:

Traffic forecasts are important in assessing whether the benefits from a road improvement, over its life-time, justify the initial cost and in determining the standard of provision. They enable a balance to be struck between providing extra capacity before it is needed and the cost of adding to capacity at a later stage. Traffic forecasts also play a part in predicting the environmental impacts of traffic, such as noise and air pollution.

Such forecasts are difficult to determine owing to the high degree of uncertainty about the future and for this reason the basis of the forecasts involves two differing assumptions, namely that of low economic growth and that of high economic growth. The forecasts therefore provide a range of values ('scenarios') to cover the

Table 12.5 **Households with regular use of cars, 1986–96.**

	Percentage/households				
	No car	One car	Two cars	Three or more cars	Great Britain (millions)
1986	38	45	15	3	21.3
1987	36	45	16	3	21.5
1988	35	44	17	3	21.7
1989	34	44	18	4	21.9
1990	33	44	19	4	22.1
1991	32	45	19	4	22.4
1992	32	45	20	4	22.6
1993	31	45	20	4	22.9
1994	32	45	20	4	23.1
1995	30	45	21	4	23.3
1996	30	45	21	4	23.5

Source: DETR (1998c).

uncertainties involved. It is possible, however, for the outcome to fall outside the forecast range, with the Department of Transport being unable to forecast traffic levels accurately. A good example of this was seen with the M25, for which forecasts were undertaken in the 1970s when oil prices were high and economic growth low. This led the Department of Transport to *underestimate* the likely demand for transport along the route. For example, between 1982 and 1987 they forecast an increase in road traffic of between 9% and 16%, but the *actual* increase was 22%. The main reason for this was that the forecast assumed a growth of GDP of between 8% and 15% over the 5-year period, but GDP actually grew by 18%. Also the price of fuel was forecast to rise in real terms, whereas it actually fell.

In the absence of unexpected changes in behaviour the latest official forecast for all motor vehicle traffic will from 1996 increase by 3–15% by 2001, 17–39% by 2011 and 36–84% by 2031.

Road transport congestion

Congestion costs arise because the addition of more vehicles onto a road network reduces the speed of other vehicles and so increases the average time it takes to complete any particular journey.

It is possible to gain some understanding of congestion by studying the relationship between speed and flow along a particular route. Figure 12.1 shows a *speed-flow curve* for the movement of vehicles along a particular road. It shows how motorists interact and impose delays and costs on each other. In a free flow situation (around point A) there is little or no interaction between vehicles and therefore speeds (subject to the legal speed limit) are relatively high. However, as extra vehicles join the road, average speed is reduced; nevertheless an increased flow will still occur until point B is reached. The flow of vehicles depends upon the number of vehicles joining the road and the speed of the traffic. For the *individual user*, maximum efficiency is where the speed is at its highest, i.e. point A. In terms of the *system as a whole*, however, the maximum

Fig. 12.1.   Speed–flow curve.

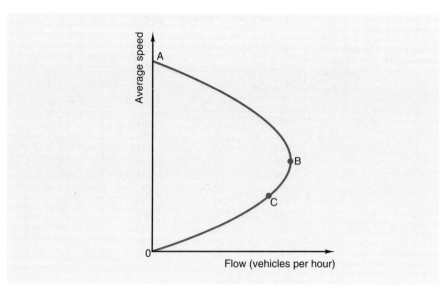

efficiency is at point B, before the speed-flow curve turns back on itself (i.e. where the maximum flow of vehicles is achieved). Once at point B, the road is said to have reached its capacity at the maximum flow level. Motorists may continue to enter the road after B because they may lack perfect information, thus slowing down the whole flow. Point C may therefore be used to represent the speed-flow situation during a peak period. At this point the traffic is in a stop-start situation, perhaps where the traffic flow is subject to a bottleneck. This gives rise to high *external* costs which the motorist is not taking into account. These costs will tend to increase the closer the road is to full capacity.

The costs of congestion

It is clear that a major strategy is needed to tackle the congestion problem, not only in urban areas but also on inter-urban routes. Congestion undermines competitiveness and hinders certain conurbations, particularly London, from attracting people and business. It also imposes a financial cost on the business community in terms of increased commuter times and delays in the delivery of goods. One estimate calculated that congestion costs are over £3bn per year in London and the six major English conurbations alone, and suggested that the total national congestion bill could be in the region of £10bn per year (The British Road Federation 1988).

The Confederation of British Industry estimates that delays on the M25 cost £1bn per year, and that London's inadequate transport system costs the nation around £15bn per annum, almost two thirds of which relates to London and the South East. In the CBI report 'The Capital at Risk', published in 1989, the following figures were given for the average additional costs incurred in London and the South East. This information was compiled from data provided by those national companies which could compare their distribution costs in London and the South East with other areas. The results are shown in Table 12.6 and reveal that the £15bn per annum consists of, amongst other things, increased staff and vehicle requirements and additional fuel costs. This figure should however be treated with extreme caution.

Specific businesses such as British Telecom and the Royal Mail put the cost of congestion to themselves at £7.25m and £10.4m per annum, respectively. These costs were measured in terms of fleet inefficiency, lost driver's time, and extra vehicle costs. According to the CBI, every British household has to spend at least £5 per week *more than it needs to* on goods and services in order to meet the costs to business of road and rail congestion. This is equal to 2p on the basic rate of income tax. The CBI estimate that if traffic delays could be reduced, thereby raising average speeds by 1.5 mph, then London's economy would be better off by £1m per day. A more recent

Table 12.6 Congestion costs in London and the South East.

Average additional costs due to congestion incurred in London/South East	
Productivity lost due to lateness of staff	1%
Delivery time and cost penalties within M25	30%
Additional staff/drivers needed to beat congestion	20%
Additional vehicles needed	20%
Additional vehicle service/repair costs	20%
Additional fuel costs	10%
Estimated total additional transportation costs in the London area	20%

Statistics were compiled from information provided by national organizations that could compare distribution costs in London and the South East with other areas.
Source: Confederation of British Industry (1989).

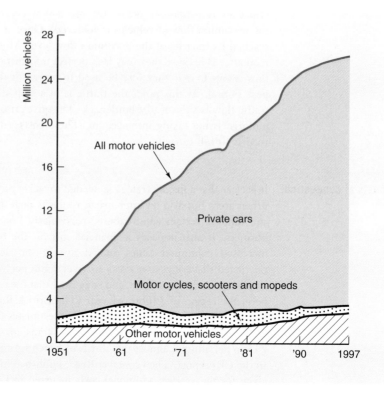

Fig. 12.2.   Motor vehicles
licensed, 1950–97.
Source: Adapted from
Transport Statistics,
Great Britain (1998), ONS.

report undertaken by the National Economic Research Associates (NERA) in 1997 estimates the total cost of road congestion to road users to be £7bn. This can be split into the cost to business (£2.5bn) and the cost to private motorists, private van drivers and bus passengers (£4.5bn).

In terms of traffic speeds, the situation has worsened over the last 20 years. In Central London, the morning and evening peak period travel speeds were 12.7 and 11.8 mph respectively in 1968–70, whereas by 1996 they had fallen to 10.0 and 10.2 mph respectively. Figure 12.2 gives some indication of the causes of congestion. There has been a dramatic rise in the number of licensed vehicles over the period 1951 to 1997, made up almost entirely of private cars.

The theory of urban road transport congestion   An economic model can be used to simplify the various issues involved in transport congestion, as shown in Figure 12.3. The horizontal axis measures the flow of vehicles per hour along a particular route. The vertical axis measures the cost per trip, including time costs. Two demand curves are shown, both of which have a negative slope because it is assumed that motorists will reduce their driving if the cost of driving increases. The demand curve D_1 refers to the *off-peak* demand for the route. It is the aggregate demand of all motorists who wish to use the route. If the cost per trip is C_0, and demand is D_1, then this will produce a flow of F_0 along the route. When making a journey, a motorist is not likely to take account of the congestion cost of that journey and may in fact only consider his or her own *marginal private cost* (MPC).

Fig. 12.3.   Equilibrium
traffic flow.

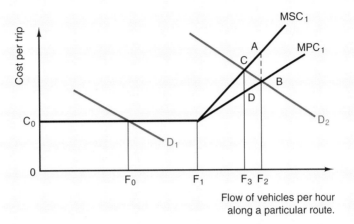

MPC includes costs such as the price of petrol used and the opportunity cost of the time the motorist spends travelling. There can, however, be costs incurred on *other* road users which the individual motorist will not take into account. These are 'external costs' and include such things as the pollution and noise borne by society as a whole and the congestion borne by other road users. These are shown by the *marginal social cost* curve (MSC) in Figure 12.3. For simplicity Figure 12.3 assumes that congestion is the *only* externality; hence MPC is shown as equal to MSC for some range of traffic flow up to F_1 because there is no congestion until that flow is reached. (Of course if we allowed for the pollution which occurs from exhaust gases at low mileage, then MSC would be above MPC at all levels of traffic flow.) If motorists *did* take into account the social costs of a journey, then they might decide that the journey was not worth making, at least not at that time of day or by that particular route.

In the Figure it can be seen that the flow of traffic can increase up to F_1 without congestion, because it is possible for the additional cars to enter the road without slowing down any other driver. It can be seen, therefore, that there is no divergence between marginal private cost and marginal social cost. However at flows above F_1, congestion is apparent because additional drivers slow down the overall traffic flow and the individual motorist's MPC per trip increases. Each motorist is now beginning to interfere with other road users, affecting their costs but ignoring those costs when deciding whether or not to make a particular trip. As the flow of traffic increases beyond F_1 there is also a *divergence* between the MPC and the MSC, as shown in the figure by lines MPC_1 and MSC_1 (MSC is equal to MPC plus the social cost of congestion). This is mainly brought about through increased travel times, as each additional driver entering the road imposes an extra delay (perhaps only small) on every other driver. If the demand for the route at the peak period is of the normal shape D_2, then the traffic flow will be F_2. Here F_2B will be the (private) cost per trip *to the motorist*, and the external costs which the motorist has *not* taken into account will be equal to AB. At a flow of F_2 there is therefore *allocative inefficiency*, as the 'real' or social cost of congestion has not been accounted for by the private motorist.

Policy options for urban road congestion – demand policies

There are various policies which have been designed to improve the use of existing road capacity. These include policies which can be introduced to influence the *demand* for road space; there are also policies designed to expand road capacity, which can be viewed as *supply* side policies. These various policies will be covered in this section. However at this stage it is also worth mentioning that there is a 'laissez faire' approach which is an alternative solution for permitting an equilibrium level of road transport congestion to emerge. For instance, if congestion gets 'too bad' in a particular region, then it may persuade companies and individuals to move to less prosperous regions which do not have the same level of congestion. The problem with this 'laissez faire' approach is that the transport network may be operating at, or near, full capacity at certain times, and therefore even small fluctuations in demand can cause long delays and create problems for safety. For example, in London, ambulances which reached accidents at an average speed of 25 mph in 1975, now reach accidents at an average of 11 mph.

Road pricing   When undertaking a journey, each driver is comparing the private benefit of each trip with the private cost of each trip. Drivers will add their vehicles to the flow whenever their marginal private benefit exceeds their marginal private cost. New roads could be built to meet the demand during the peak period, or demand could be restrained, or a mixture of the two policies could be undertaken. In Figure 12.3 above, the flow of F_3 could be achieved by placing a tax (a road price) of CD on the road user, so raising marginal private costs from MPC_1 to equal those of MSC_1; this would thereby reduce the traffic flow from F_2 to F_3. This road pricing option would bring about a 'more efficient allocation' of a scarce resource, because the marginal private benefit (as measured by the demand curve) is now equal to the marginal social cost curve. Road pricing is an option which is gaining in popularity. As yet, however, there are very few examples of schemes in operation worldwide. One scheme which had trials in 1993 was Congestion Metering in Cambridge (Ison 1996). Although it received a great deal of attention there are no plans to proceed with the scheme. D. Newbery has commented that 'As road space is a valuable and scarce resource, it is natural that economists should argue that it should be rationed by price – road-users should pay the marginal social cost of using the road network if they are to make the right decisions about whether (and by which means) to take a particular journey, and, more generally, to ensure that they make the correct allocative decisions between transport and other activities' (Newbery 1990).

Urban road pricing which involves charging for road use, was suggested as a possible solution to the urban congestion problem as long ago as 1964, when the Ministry of Transport produced the Smeed Report. Road pricing could be introduced by using meters attached to cars in the form of an electronic numberplate. As a car entered a congested area or stretch of road, the meter would be activated by sensors in the road. A charge would then be registered and a bill for the congestion caused sent to the motorist periodically. This was the method used in the Hong Kong Electronic Road Pricing experiment, 1983–85 (Hau 1990). Current technology would involve the use of the smartcard as with Cambridge congestion metering (Ison 1996). As well as dissuading the marginal car user from using the road, it would also provide the authorities with revenue which could be used to construct more roads or to improve the public transport system. In November 1991 then Department of Transport initiated research into the case for and against, and the practical feasibility of, implementing Congestion Charging within the M25. The findings of 'The London Congestion Charging Research Programme' were published in 1995. A range of charges and structures were tested. For example, it was estimated that an £8 charge to enter an inbound Central London cordon, charged throughout the working day, would reduce total vehicle kilometres within the charged area by 22% while journey speeds would increase by 32%. As regards the implementation costs then, according to the London Congestion Charging Research Programme, in terms of an automatic charge collection the lowest cost for installation was estimated to be an inbound Central London cordon based on using read–write tags. If two million vehicles were equipped, the cost of implementation would be £85m with an operating cost of £55m per annum, at 1991 prices. More sophisticated technology would be more costly to implement. It is estimated that considerable revenue would be raised from Congestion Charging. At a charge of £8 to enter an inbound Central London cordon it would raise £465m per annum in revenue with an increase in public transport revenue of £40m and a reduction in the revenue from parking of £80m, giving an overall net revenue of £420m (the London Congestion Charging Research Programme 1995).

One of the criticisms levelled at road pricing is its effect on increasing the inflation rate. However, if it succeeded in reducing the total costs of commercial activities, then this is a false worry. Road pricing should not be viewed as a revenue maximizing tax, but as an efficiency maximizing tax. It could then be the key to medium-term relief from congestion and could provide the funds for the long-term upgrading of roads and public transport.

In addition, there are a number of problems to be addressed when considering the implementation of a road pricing policy. First, there need to be accurate estimates of elasticities of demand and of marginal external costs. Second, the issue of equity and the problem of practically implementing the scheme, both need to be considered. For example, what charge should be made for congestion and how would it vary depending on the level of traffic and the time of day? Third, road pricing could be seen as an invasion of privacy, which was one of the reasons for it not being continued in Hong Kong after the initial experiment. However some writers view the lack of understanding of the new charges by car owners as a possible reason for its lack of success, for there was a failure to realize in Hong Kong that the charges of $2–$3 per day would replace the annual licensing fee (Newbery 1990).

Road pricing is certainly an option and it is currently receiving serious consideration.

Supplementary licences   An alternative form of pricing in congested urban areas could be a system of *supplementary licences*. Such a system was introduced in Singapore in 1975 under which a vehicle owner purchased and displayed a licence when the vehicle travelled into a designated area. In Singapore, motorists had to buy a licence to enter the business district between 7.30 am and 10.15 am. In June 1989 the scheme was extended to the evening peak period between 5.00 pm and 7.00 pm. It was found that traffic fell by as much as 76% during this period, which suggests that road users are sensitive to such a fiscal penalty. It is also interesting to note that the introduction of the supplementary licence did *not* lead to a large increase in the use of public transport in Singapore. This may have been due to the growth of car sharing, which could be viewed as a benefit of the scheme. A system such as supplementary licences can be perceived as being inflexible and labour intensive. Therefore an electronic road pricing (ERP) automatic alternative has been phased in from April 1998. In-vehicle-units have been fitted to the windscreens of vehicles and smart cards made available to motorists from banks, post offices and petrol stations. The smart card can be charged up with monetary units (cash card) at automatic teller machines. The smart card is inserted in the in-vehicle-unit and detectors at overhead gantries at ERP control points deduct monetary units from the smart card at a predetermined rate. If there is a violation or error through such things as there being no in-vehicle-unit, no smart card or lack of monetary balance on the card, then cameras photograph the rear number plate of the vehicle so that it can be issued with a notice of traffic offence. In terms of Figure 12.3 above, the aim of both the supplementary licence or ERP scheme is to shift the demand curve D_2 to the left to reduce the traffic flow towards F_1.

Finally, it is worth noting that road pricing (including supplementary licences) involves rationing the congested infrastructure at peak times, here by using the price mechanism, and is an example of 'the polluter pays' principle. Obviously important in such a scheme is the destination of the revenue collected. If it went into the general exchequer fund, then it might be presented as just another tax. However it could be directed towards the provision of new road capacity or towards improving the public transport network.

Subsidizing public transport   Another approach designed to shift the demand to the left in Figure 12.3 is *subsidizing public transport*. This method was used in the 1970s by a number of UK metropolitan councils. For example in Sheffield, bus fares were reduced by 55% in real terms over the period 1975–81. In addition to financial implications, the problem faced by this method is in persuading car users to *transfer* from private to public transport, since they often perceive themselves as being the *victims* of congestion rather than the *cause* of it. To be successful this policy requires a long-term improvement in public transport and a cross elasticity of demand between public and private transport substantially greater than zero. An added problem is that increased income levels lead to increased car ownership, thus lowering the demand for public transport. The Public Transport sector therefore becomes more reliant on certain groups of travellers, namely the young, the elderly and those on low incomes, i.e. on a market which is getting smaller (Goodwin 1990). The Department of Transport comments that 'The level of traffic on roads in London is a reflection largely of individual choice, not the non-availability of other modes of travel'. However, it could be the case that individuals are not paying the true cost of motoring, i.e. there are 'hidden subsidies' which have the effect of making single car occupancy an attractive proposition, particularly in the peak period. This results in an inefficient use of road capacity.

Parking restrictions   One policy which has been extensively used in urban areas since the 1960s is *parking restraints*. The aim has been, through parking meters and restrictions on on-street parking, to limit the supply of parking spaces, so reducing the demand for urban routes. This policy, too, has limitations in that removing parking facilities from a road essentially increases the size of the road and may therefore encourage extra traffic flows. At the same time, parking restraints encourage illegal parking which may add to congestion. This is one of the main reasons for the introduction of wheel clamps in Central London in 1986 and policies such as the tow-away scheme introduced in Cambridge in 1991, subsequently abandoned in 1996 given its unprofitability.

City Councils have sought to use pricing policies at their car parks to encourage shopping and other short stay motorists, while at the same time discouraging long stay commuters. However, the success of this policy has been hindered to some extent by their lack of control over privately operated car parks and by high volumes of through traffic in most congested areas. Parking charges are also unable to discriminate between length of journey or route taken. Pricing policies could be used to encourage motorists to park at peripheral, out of town, car parks, which could be part of a park-and-ride scheme. Such schemes operate in Oxford, Cambridge and York.

Limiting car ownership and use   There are three further ways of influencing the demand for road space. The first is to *limit car ownership*. This could be achieved by imposing either import restrictions, a registration tax, or a system of rationing on cars. As yet, this is not something which has been advocated in the UK but it does occur in certain parts of the world, not only to deal with traffic congestion but also to save energy. For example, in Singapore a quota system is in operation where vehicle owners tender for a 'certificate of entitlement' without which they cannot own a vehicle. The second method is to introduce a system of *car sharing* which, if successful, would also shift demand to the left in Figure 12.3. The third method is to *increase the road fuel duty*. This was introduced by the Chancellor of the Exchequer in the March 1993 Budget. The road fuel duty was increased by 10% and it was announced that in future Budgets the duty would be increased, in real terms, by at least 3%. Although the stated reason for this policy was environmental, directed towards reducing carbon dioxide emissions, it would also act as a disincentive to car ownership and use. This policy, whilst being welcomed by the Royal Commission on Environmental Pollution (1994) is perceived to be insufficient to achieve its environmental objectives. The Commission recommends that the duty on fuel should be doubled in price, relative to the prices of other goods, by the year 2005, if emissions targets are to be achieved.

Policy options for urban road congestion – supply policies   As well as demand policies to deal with the urban road congestion problem, *supply side policies* (such as new road building) can be implemented. An urban road building strategy can be examined by the use of Figure 12.4.

Increasing the number of lanes, or building new roads, will shift the marginal private cost and marginal social cost curves from MPC_1 and MSC_1 respectively, to MPC_2 and MSC_2. The diagram implies that before the road capacity was expanded, congestion occurred beyond a traffic flow of F_1, but now occurs at a point beyond F_4. The reason for this is that road construction increases road capacity, so that an increased flow is now possible before the costs of congestion appear. If demand is taken to be D_2, then a flow of F_5 will now use the road and although there will be some congestion (note that MSC_2 is greater than MPC_2 at F_5 by the distance GH) this will be somewhat less than the congestion *before* the new road expansion, which was AB in Figure 12.4.

Fig. 12.4. Equilibrium
traffic flow: supply side
policies.

There is, however, a limitation with this strategy. If the road network is expanded and improved, then individuals who previously used public transport may now begin to use their own car. New traffic will therefore be *generated*, as those who did not make a particular trip previously are now encouraged to do so, and motorists who travelled via a different route may now be persuaded to use the route(s) in question. Also peak and off-peak travel can, to some extent, be viewed as substitutes, so that off-peak travel may fall. It could therefore be argued that increasing a road's capacity will result in more vehicles using the route, i.e. a case of supply generating its own demand. This means that the level of demand may well be underestimated. In fact demand could become almost perfectly elastic, as with demand curve D_3 in Figure 12.4. If this were to be the case, then the flow of traffic along the particular route would be F_6 and not F_5, and the social cost which had not been taken into account would be EF and not GH. The final situation may not, then, be significantly different from the initial external cost of AB in Figure 12.4. In other words, a similar congestion problem would still persist.

Government transport policy

In July 1998 the government published a White Paper on the Future of Transport entitled 'A New Deal for Transport: Better for Everyone' in which it was recognized that there was a need to improve public transport and reduce car dependency. As such, a commitment was made to create an improved integrated transport system more able to tackle congestion and its associated pollution. The main aim of the White Paper is perceived as to 'increase personal choice by improving the alternatives and to secure mobility that is sustainable in the long term'. There is a recognition that road building ('predict and provide') is not the answer to the growth in traffic. Integration is central to the government's thinking as stated in the White Paper (DETR 1998b).

By an *integrated* transport policy they mean:

- integration *within and between different types of transport* – so that each contributes its full potential and people can move easily between them;
- integration *with the environment* – so that our transport choices support a better environment;
- integration *with land use planning* – at national, regional and local level, so that transport and planning work together to support more sustainable travel choices and reduce the need to travel;
- integration *with our policies for education, health and wealth creation* – so that transport helps to make a fairer, more inclusive society.

Over the years, the state has attempted to influence transport in a number of ways:

Quality   This has mainly been concerned with safety. In 1930 the Road Traffic Act was introduced, which required both bus operators and freight hauliers to licence their vehicles with regional Traffic Commissioners. This policy was viewed, essentially, as one of protecting the public interest. This follows from the fact that, for both the road haulier and the bus operator, the capital costs of vehicle purchase are relatively low, so that there is a low barrier to entry into the industry. As a result profits can be driven down, which in turn could lead to operators trying to reduce their costs, with possibly adverse effects on safety standards. In recent years there have been a number of transport disasters and this has clearly made the whole area of transport safety a major political issue. An important question is whether increased competition will lead to reduced safety standards!

Quantity   The licensing system has also been used as a form of regulatory control. Successive governments have been of the opinion that quantitative controls on transport were necessary in order to make sure that existing capacity was fully utilized. Such controls have applied to the road haulage and bus industries. One of the implications of licensing has been the cross-subsidization of bus services. Until 1986, the provision of unprofitable services was closely linked to the granting of licences for route monopolies by the traffic commissioners. Although certain services, such as late evenings, weekends and certain rural routes, were unprofitable, they were viewed as being 'socially' worthwhile. The financial losses on such routes were supported from the profits which the operators earned on the more profitable routes, so that cross-subsidization clearly took place. However cross-subsidization was only possible as long as operators did have monopolies; with a deregulated bus sector this was less likely.

Ownership   Railways and parts of the road haulage and bus passenger transport sector have been under public ownership. The main reasons put forward for such ownership include the suggestion that if the subsidization of such services was needed, then it would be easier for the government rather than private companies to control that particular operation. Government control would also allow for an improved co-ordination of services. The government's stance on state ownership has changed, however, in the last 15 years, as with the sale of the National Freight Corporation to its employees in 1982, and of the National Bus Company following the deregulation of the bus industry in 1986 and the franchising of rail services.

Resource allocation   A major area of direct government involvement in the transport sector concerns the large amounts of public expenditure invested in the road network. Expenditure by Central Government through the Highways Agency on National Roads (namely maintaining, renewing, improving and extending) is planned to be £1,349m in 1998–99.

Government intervention in the transport sector, characterized by state monopolies, public ownership and investment based on state priorities, can be contrasted with a 'laissez-faire' approach. The latter involves leaving the sector to the workings of the free market, with quality, quantity and resource allocation being determined by consumer preferences. In a 'pure' laissez faire situation, transport services are provided by privately owned firms and the finance of those services is based on customer fares. In this free market there would be no statutory control on entry into the sector and no financial support for those operators facing difficulties. However the transport sector has not been left to the free market, for many of the reasons mentioned above, although there has been a move in recent years to allow certain parts of the transport sector to operate in a 'freer' market. This has been the case with the private financing and construction of the Channel Tunnel, the deregulation of the bus industry and the private financing of road construction. In terms of more government involvement, there is a mounting case for government to consider seriously a road pricing policy to counteract the problems of road congestion which are hindering the efficient working of the market mechanism and resulting in a misallocation of resources. There is now a general consensus that road supply cannot realistically be expanded sufficiently to meet demand. The need for demand management policies has therefore become more widely accepted and these will become an increasingly important part of any government's transport policy in the foreseeable future.

Private road construction   In May 1989 the government published a Green Consultation Paper entitled 'New Roads by New Means' which set out proposals for the private funding of roads. Private sector companies would now be invited to bid for contracts to design, build, finance and operate (DBFO) privately financed road schemes. As well as building new motorways, the improvement to existing roads was also envisaged.

There have only been a limited number of private sector projects, for example the Channel Tunnel, the Severn bridge and the Dartford river crossing, but despite this, the government did not perceive road building as purely a public sector monopoly.

The rationale for private sector roads is based on the premise that it allows (in theory at least) more roads to be built than would be the case if government funded road schemes were the only ones undertaken. Also, because private road builders would be using their own finance plus that of their shareholders, they would have to bear the risk of financial failure. This being so, greater care would be taken to ensure that projects were completed on time and within the financial constraints laid down.

Essentially, it would mean that the risk would be transferred from the public sector to the private sector.

Roads would, of course, only be built if the construction company believed that demand was sufficient to generate an adequate return on the capital investment. The private road builders would charge for the use of such roads, which would ensure that the users paid directly for the resources they consumed. In return for being charged for the use of the road, the user would receive a higher quality road service. However there are a number of issues which need to be considered as regards private sector road projects. If a system of tolls were used they could create problems in being collected which could in itself create congestion. They may also create problems of road design, because the number of toll exits has to be limited. However the problem of toll collection could, to some extent, be dealt with by having vehicles fitted with an electronic identity plate. This would allow cars to pass through a toll point with a pre-paid bank account being directly debited. Tolls would be based on what motorists were prepared to pay, although in monopoly situations (such as river crossings) the government would have to fix a maximum charge in line with the 'public interest'. It is likely, however, that private sector finance would only be attracted to those parts of the country which were experiencing relatively higher levels of economic growth, and that the public sector would have to provide for the less economically attractive regions.

Another question which needs to be addressed is whether any increased involvement by the private sector in road construction will lead to a net addition to the total road programme, or simply to a displacement of public sector expenditure on roads.

In saying this, a number of roads are being planned or are in fact under construction, such as the A1(M) improvement near Peterborough which is based on the DBFO contractural arrangements. The contract involves the private sector in providing or improving a particular road and with its management over a thirty year period. The private sector raises the funds and is remunerated by the government based on the useage of the road. Essentially a 'shadow toll' system is used. A 'shadow toll' is one where the private construction company makes an agreement to build or improve a road and is then reimbursed by the government, depending on the number of vehicles which use the road. One benefit of using such a 'shadow toll' is that it avoids the disruption of the traffic flow caused by the collection of actual tolls. Construction work will start in 1999 on the Birmingham Northern Relief Road as a new private finance project.

Deregulation of the bus industry

Prior to 1930, the local urban and rural bus industry operated in a competitive market structure with no government regulation. There was fierce competition between rival bus companies (using surplus war vehicles) and this period was associated with a high number of accidents, unscheduled and irregular intervention by 'pirate' operators at peak times, and other types of wasteful duplication.

It was for these reasons that, in 1930, the *Road Traffic Act* was introduced, which was to form the basis of bus industry regulation for 50 years. Under the Act, Traffic Commissioners were responsible for the issue of road service licences (a licence being required for each route operated), the quality of vehicles and the level of fares.

The period 1930 to 1980 was therefore a restrictive one for the local bus service industry. A comprehensive public transport network was provided under a protectionist system, with a licence acting as a barrier to entry, since a licence gave the operator a monopoly on a particular route for the duration of the licence. In 1930 the industry was dominated by private bus operators but, as it developed, the state took a progressively larger role, as with the formation in 1968 of the National Bus Company (NBC) and the Scottish Bus Group (SBG). This meant that by 1986 the industry consisted of state owned operators, the local authority sector and independent companies which mainly operated in the contract hire sector (including school bus provision).

Changes were regarded as necessary by the mid 1980s. There had been a steady decline in patronage, with bus and coach passenger travel falling from 42% of total travel in 1953, to 8% in 1983. The growth in the use of the private car, fare increases in excess of the inflation rate, increased operating costs and the decline in the service provided, were seen as the chief reasons for the decline in bus/coach travel.

The Conservative government started on the changes with the *1980 Transport Act*, which abolished road service licences for long distance express coach travel, and with the decision to establish the 'trial areas' of Devon, Hereford and Worcester, and Norfolk, for local bus service deregulation. For long distance coach travel, the Act allowed companies which met certain safety standards to enter the market and to offer whatever service they chose. By 1989, passenger prices on the main trunk roads were 15% lower in real terms, and coach frequency 70% higher, as compared to the position prior to deregulation (Thompson and Whitfield 1990).

The 1984 White Paper on Buses stated:

> The total travel market is expanding. New measures are needed urgently to break out of the cycle of rising costs, rising fares, reducing services, so that public transport can win a bigger share of this market. We must get away from the idea that the only future for bus services is to contract painfully at large cost to taxpayers and ratepayers as well as travellers. Competition provides the opportunity for lower fares, new services, more passengers. For these great gains, half measures will not be enough. Within the essential framework of safety regulation and provision for social needs, the obstacles to enterprise, initiative and efficiency must be removed.

The White Paper led to the *1985 Transport Act*, through which (by October 1986) road service licensing requirements were abolished outside London. Provision was also made in the Act for the privatization of the National Bus Company. The Passenger Transport Executives operating in metropolitan areas were to be converted into independent companies, still owned by the local authorities but which now had the option to privatize them. Local bus operators had to register their routes and times and to give sufficient notice of withdrawal of services. There was also the introduction of competitive tendering for the unprofitable bus routes.

So the main objective of the 1985 Act was to introduce competition into the bus sector, providing the opportunity for independent bus operators which did not offer licensed services before 1986, now to do so. It was envisaged that there would be a number of benefits from deregulation.

- Firstly, increased competition should allow greater choice for the consumer and provide a service which is more responsive to the preferences of the consumer.
- Secondly, there should now be a closer relationship between bus operating costs and the fares charged, the reason for this being the ending of cross-subsidization, whereby certain routes were overcharged in order to subsidize non-profitable

routes. This was helped, of course, by the freedom of entry for new operators after 1986, which in principle should compete away any 'monopoly profits' from charging excessive fares on routes, unrelated to costs.

• Thirdly, providing a greater potential for innovation in bus travel under deregulation, which was less likely in the absence of competition. One such innovation following deregulation has been the introduction of mini-bus services.

• Fourthly, a reduction in the subsidies obtained by bus operators to undertake unprofitable services. The revenue support from government had increased from £10m in 1972 to £529m in 1982. It could be argued that such subsidies created a protective wall behind which bus operators could operate inefficient services.

There were, however, reservations as to the likely success of bus deregulation, most notably the view that it could lead to a wasteful duplication of services on the profitable routes, especially at peak periods, with a resulting increase in the level of congestion in a number of urban areas. Further, it was feared that the intended reduction in the level of subsidy to the bus sector after deregulation might lead to a rise in the level of fares, thereby diminishing bus use.

Bus services since deregulation   In terms of local bus services in England (outside London), there has in fact been an increase in annual bus kilometres travelled. In 1985–86, the year before deregulation, 1,423m bus kilometres were undertaken, whereas by 1996–97 around 1,863m bus kilometres were recorded, an increase of 31%. Care must, however, be taken when interpreting these figures. In evidence to the House of Commons Transport Committee (1993) on the government's proposals for the deregulation of buses in London, two reasons were suggested as to why the recorded increase in bus kilometres might be misleading:

> first, there has been a growth in the proportion of small buses, which may in some cases increase the probability of passengers not being able to get on the first bus to come; second, some proportion of the mileage run by competing bus companies is attributable to one bus closely shadowing another, and in this case a rise in total vehicle mileage does not bring proportionate benefits to passengers.

Nevertheless it is likely that there has indeed been some increase in the provision of local bus services.

Although there has been an *increase in bus kilometres travelled* since deregulation, there has also been a *decrease in passenger journeys* in England from 4,808m in 1985/ 86 to 3,758m in 1996/97, a decline of 22.3%. There is little doubt that deregulation has been a contributing factor to the decline in bus use by passengers. One reason, at least immediately after deregulation, being the confusion which passengers experienced due to the changes in service times, routes and operators resulting from deregulation. Higher fares may also have played a part in the reduction in passenger journeys. In Great Britain in 1996/97, local bus fares increased by 5%, which represented a real fare increase of 3%. Over the last decade, fares in Great Britain have increased by 26% in real terms (DETR 1997). A factor in these price increases has been the reduction in Local Authority subsidies for bus services, which fell by over £520m in real terms between 1985–86 and 1996–97. Another factor in the recorded price increases was the ending of the 'cheap fares policies' by the Public Transport Executives (PTEs) in Metropolitan areas over the period 1985–87. Of course the reduction in passenger use of buses has been a trend over a long period of time, closely related to the increase in car ownership and use.

Deregulation of buses can also be assessed in terms of its impact on operating costs. Over the period 1985–86 to 1996–97 bus operating costs fell from 153 p per vehicle kilometre (excluding depreciation at 1996/97 prices) to 81 p in 1996/97.

According to the government's White Paper on the Future of Transport 1998 bus deregulations outside London caused substantial upheaval because of 'bus wars' and confusion over changing service patterns. There have been some good examples of innovation but frequent changes to bus services, poor connections and the reluctance of some bus operators to participate in information schemes or through-ticketing has undermined bus services. In this climate, it was not easy for buses to match the levels of comfort, reliability and access offered by the private car.

In response to this the proposal is for 'Quality Partnerships' to be developed. These already exist in a number of towns and cities but the view is that they need to be more widespread. These partnerships are between local authorities and the bus operators, with local authorities providing traffic management schemes such as bus priority at traffic lights, bus lanes and park-and-ride sites, and operators providing an improved quality of service.

BR privatization

In July 1992 the government published a White Paper entitled New Opportunities for the Railways (Cm 2012) in which it put forward plans for the privatization of BR, the objective being to 'improve the quality of railway services by creating many new opportunities for private sector involvement'. The ensuing Railways Act 1993 provided for the privatization of British Rail and incorporated a number of major changes.

A new track authority has been established, namely *Railtrack*, which owns and manages the railway infrastructure, in particular, the track, signalling and stations. Railtrack is also responsible for coordinating the timetable of services, for making sure that safety standards are adhered to (although ultimately the safety of the network is the responsibility of the Health and Safety Executive) and for investing in new, and modernizing existing, infrastructure. The majority of Railtrack's revenue comes from charging the users of the track and from income obtained through the leasing of stations. Stations, given their prime site location in many towns and cities and thus their potential for new office and shopping development, are in fact likely to prove important sources of revenue.

The *rail regulator* has responsibility for:

  (i) issuing licences to operators who meet safety criteria;
 (ii) ensuring that the competition is fair;
(iii) making sure that passenger interests are protected;
 (iv) ensuring that Railtrack acts as a responsible and efficient steward of the national rail network;
  (v) promoting the development of rail freight.

In terms of freight, the rail regulator is keen to see an increase in rail usage. As a result significant freight grants have been paid. In 1997/98 £30m was spent to 'tip the balance in favour of rail haulage where the environmental benefits justify that'. Over 4 million lorry trips will have been saved as a result of grants awarded since

Table 12.7   The first seven franchise awards.

Franchise	TOC	Franchise length (years)	Subsidy year one	Subsidy final year	Average rate of subsidy cut p.a.
South West Trains	Stagecoach	7	£54.7m	£40.3m	£2m
Great Western	Management	10	£53.2m	£38.2m	£2.1m
InterCity East Coast	Sea Containers	7	£64.6m	0	£9.2m
Gatwick Express	National Express Group	15	−£4.6m	−£22.6m	n/a
Network South Central	CGEA	7	£85.3m	£34.6m	£7.2m
Midland Main Line	National Express Group	10	£16.5m	−£10m	n/a
London, Tilbury and Southend	Prism	15	£29.5m	£11.2m	£1.2m

Source: Local Transport Today, 23 May 1996.

the scheme began (DETR 1998b). Passenger trains have been restructured into 25 *train operating companies*, franchised for a period of between 5 and 20 years. The normal period is for 7 years and Table 12.7 illustrates the first seven franchises awarded to the 25 now in force.

The *Office of Passenger Rail Franchising* (OPRAF) is responsible for negotiating franchises with the private sector companies who want to operate a passenger train service. The Director of OPRAF has been responsible for specifying the length and cost of the franchise as well as the *passenger service requirements*. These requirements have covered areas such as the frequency of trains, the first and last trains, stations served, weekend provision, limits with regard to overcrowding and maximum journey times. Now that the franchising process is complete his main statutory functions include deciding whether to veto any proposed closures of passenger services, encouraging railway investment and identifying new franchise opportunities.

The implications. The privatization of British Rail has offered a number of opportunities, although difficulties have been experienced. In terms of the opportunities, the Department of Transport, in a paper entitled 'Britain's Railways: A New Era', March 1994, stated that privatization would:

(i) allow competition to be introduced into the provision of rail services, improving efficiency and the quality of service;
(ii) mean that additional investment could be provided by the private sector; and
(iii) allow subsidies to continue, but their allocation would be such that it would be clearer to see where they were being spent.

It is certainly the case that a privatized sector has allowed companies such as bus operators to run rail services. This has created a number of attractive opportunities in that they have similar skills, bus companies being experienced public transport operators with considerable market knowledge in terms of service design, passenger requirements, publicity and marketing.

A view has been expressed that British Rail has been over bureaucratic in the past which meant it was slow to change and take advantage of new ideas. It has also been stated that British Rail had a management structure which was engineering dominated and weaker in terms of customer relations. Proponents of privatization argue, therefore, that it allowed managers the opportunity to become more customer oriented.

There have, however, been a number of difficulties associated with rail privatization. Potential franchisees have been deterred from entering the rail sector by the fear that they would have insufficient control over their operation. For example, although the operating company has been able to propose the timetable, the ultimate responsibility has rested with Railtrack. The provision of a train service is the total sum of many factors. The franchisee, however, has only a limited influence over certain aspects of its operation. This has certainly been the case in terms of the track, the signalling, and the quality and availability of the rolling stock.

It has been argued that rather than reducing the level of bureaucracy there has been an increase, with hundreds of contracts and a fragmentation of responsibility. Since the franchising of services began there appears to have been a deterioration in the punctuality and reliability of rail services. In the first quarter of 1998, for example, passenger complaints almost doubled compared with the same period in 1997.

In response to this the government White Paper on the Future of Transport (DETR 1998b) outlines plans for the introduction of a Strategic Rail Authority (SRA) providing a focus for strategic planning of the passenger and freight railways, with appropriate powers to influence the behaviour of key industry players.

The specific aims of the SRA will be to:

- bring together passenger and freight interests;
- promote better integration and interchange;
- provide strategic vision; and
- get better value for public subsidy in terms of fares and network benefits.

Conclusion

This chapter has attempted to identify, and analyse, a number of the current issues facing the transport sector, notably road congestion and the role of the state in transport provision. Transport, as a derived demand, is an important sector of the UK economy, accounting for some 15% of household expenditure. The period 1987–97 has seen a 19% increase in the demand for passenger transport and this is expected to continue into the next century, with the car dominating. Income has been viewed as a major factor in determining that demand and its future growth. Forecasting the future patterns of demand is seen as essential for governments when deciding on the allocation of funds to possible new road developments. The increased reliance on the car has created a major problem of congestion, particularly in urban areas, and in recent years this has become more of a political issue. A number of possible solutions have been examined, originating from both the supply and demand sides. On the supply side, it is clear that it is not possible to provide sufficient road capacity to meet the likely growth in demand. Demand needs therefore to be 'managed', and demand side policies have been extensively used. However, road pricing has not, as yet, been implemented in the UK, although it is viewed by many to be the best method of dealing with the congestion problem, all be it part of a package of measures.

The public sector plays an important role in the transport sector, both as regards its expenditure on such aspects as the national roads system and its ownership of parts of the sector. The last 20 years have, however, seen a move towards a transport sector operating in a 'freer' market. Major parts of the sector have been privatized, the bus industry has been deregulated and there has been increased private sector involvement in the provision of the transport infrastructure. This chapter has sought to examine the possible reasons for this move towards a free market sector, together with the likely advantages and disadvantages.

Key points

- In the 1950s only 25% of passenger journeys were by car; today the figure has risen to over 80%. Future estimates suggest that motor vehicle traffic will increase by between 36% and 84% by the year 2031 on unchanged policies.
- Transport is a service which is a *derived* demand, with important peak and off-peak characteristics.
- Transport, particularly road transport, is a major source of pollution and of other externalities, e.g. congestion.
- A *speed-flow curve* is a useful means of analysing congestion.
- The CBI estimates that every British household must spend at least an *extra* £5 per week in order to meet the costs to business of road and rail congestion.
- Policy options to deal with congestion are various. Those involving *demand* include road pricing, supplementary licences, subsidies to public transport, parking restrictions and limits to car ownership. Those involving *supply* include more extensive and better integrated transport networks.

References and further reading

Confederation of British Industry (1989) The Capital at Risk: Transport in London Task Force Report.

Department of the Environment, Transport and the Regions (DETR) (1997) Transport Statistics Report. Bus and Coach Statistics, Great Britain 1996/97, October, London, The Stationery Office.

Department of the Environment, Transport and the Regions (DETR) (1998a) The Government's Expenditure Plans 1998–99, Annual Report.

Department of the Environment, Transport and the Regions (DETR) (1998b) *A New Deal for Transport: Better for Everyone*, Government's White Paper on the Future of Transport (Cm. 3950).

Department of the Environment, Transport and the Regions (DETR) (1998c) *Transport Statistics Great Britain 1998*, London, The Stationery Office.

Department of Transport (1984) *Buses*, HMSO (Cmnd 9300).

Department of Transport (1989) *New Roads by New Means – Bringing in Private Finance*, HMSO (Cmnd 698).

Department of Transport (1992) *New Opportunities for the Railways*, HMSO (Cmnd 2012).

Goodwin, P. B. (1990) Demographic Impacts, Social Consequences, and the Transport Debate, *Oxford Review of Economic Policy*, **6**, 2, Summer.

Government Office for London (1995) *The London Congestion Charging Research Programme*, HMSO.

Hau, T. (1990) Electronic Road Pricing: Developments in Hong Kong 1983–1989, *Journal of Transport Economics and Policy*.

House of Commons Transport Committee (1993) Fourth Report, The Government's Proposals for the Deregulation of Buses in London, HMSO.

Ison, S. (1996) Pricing Road Space: Back to the Future? The Cambridge Experience. *Transport Reviews*, **16**, 2, pp. 109–26.

National Economic Research Associates (NERA) (1997) The Costs of Road Congestion in Great Britain, NERA Briefing Paper.

Newbery, D. M. (1990) Pricing and Congestion: Economic Principles Relevant to Pricing Roads, *Oxford Review of Economic Policy*, **6**, 2, Summer.

Office for National Statistics (ONS) (1997) Family Spending, a Report on the 1996–97 Family Expenditure Survey, London, The Stationery Office.

Royal Commission on Environmental Pollution (1994) Eighteenth Report, Transport and the Environment, HMSO (Cmnd 2674).

Thompson, D. J. and **Whitfield, A.** (1990) Express Coaching: Privatization, Incumbent Advantage and the Competitive Process, Centre for Business Strategy Working Paper, London Business School.

Chapter 13

Social policy

This chapter will focus on the various methods by which resources might be allocated within the social policy area. In this sense it might be more accurately titled 'The Economics of Social Problems' or even 'Welfare State Economics'. After briefly reviewing the nature of the welfare state, we look at a number of market and quasi-market means of resource allocation. The context for our analysis will be three key areas of welfare provision; namely health care, education and housing. Of course relevant materials can also be found in other chapters, especially those involving the Distribution of Income and Wealth (Chapter 14), Public Expenditure (Chapter 18), Taxation (Chapter 19), and Unemployment (Chapter 23).

The Welfare State

The term 'welfare state' is broadly applied to those social welfare services in an economy which are organized and provided by the government. Indeed some two thirds of public spending is represented by welfare services such as health, education, housing and social security (see Chapter 18).

It may be useful at the outset to identify what the welfare state seeks to achieve. The popular view is that it seeks to relieve poverty – but far broader aims have been advanced in favour of the welfare state. Following Hills (1994, 1995), at least four key (if overlapping) aims can be identified in support of the public provision or finance of welfare services.

1. Relief of poverty and redistribution of income towards the long-term poor.
2. Smoothing out the level of income over the life cycle: i.e., acting as a kind of 'savings bank' between periods of high and low earning and during periods of non-employment, e.g. while undertaking education or in retirement.
3. Insurance for everyone against life's risks: e.g. long-term illness, unemployment, early retirement, family breakdown and so on.
4. Redistribution towards particular groups with greater needs: e.g. the sick, the disabled, the unemployed or those with pressing family circumstances (e.g. single parents).

Given these broad aims of welfare policy it would be unrealistic to expect only the poor to receive welfare services. Nevertheless there is much debate as to whether the 'wrong' people are benefiting from welfare spending, such as middle-class households receiving child benefit or high income households receiving state pensions. The period of economic recession in the early 1990s helped to heighten such concern since all welfare services are either direct transfer payments from tax revenue or involve government provision at (subsidized) prices considerably below cost, and sometimes at even zero prices. This latter point obviously brings into play the whole issue of the Public Sector Borrowing Requirement (PSBR). This has changed for the UK from being *negative* (i.e. tax revenue exceeding government spending) at around 3% of GDP (£15bn) in 1988, to being *positive* (i.e. government spending exceeding tax revenue) at around 1% of GDP (£5bn) in 1997/98. Concern that unchanged welfare policies might in due course lead to a sharp rise in the PSBR has made this area of vital policy concern to governments.

Before considering some of the future problems facing the welfare state, it might be helpful to review briefly the extent to which it is 'succeeding' in meeting the four aims outlined above.

Relief of poverty   The first involves the relief of poverty and redistribution towards the long term poor. This is considered in some detail in Chapter 14 but Fig. 13.1 provides a useful overview. We can see that the *net* effect of receiving all kinds of benefits, whether in cash (e.g. state pension, income support) or kind (e.g. state education, NHS), as compared to paying all kinds of taxes, is strongly redistributive. The bottom five deciles of income groups are net 'gainers', while the top five deciles of income groups are net 'losers', which of course is in line with the first aim outlined above.

Fig. 13.1. Net gains and losses from benefits and taxes, 1991. *Sources:* Hills (1994); *Economic Trends* (various).

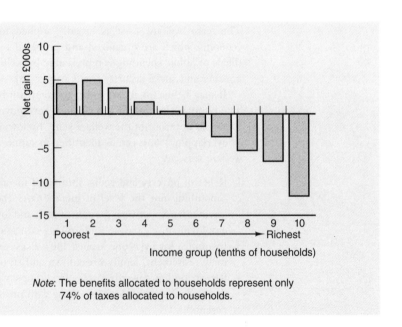

Note: The benefits allocated to households represent only 74% of taxes allocated to households.

Life-cycle redistribution   The second and third aims of the welfare state involve an element of *life-cycle redistribution* between good times and bad times, which to some extent is relevant to everyone, rich or poor alike.

Figure 13.2 shows how equivalent income[1] varies with age for an individual progressing through the present tax/benefit system. It is based on a computer simulation as an actual life history would involve an individual progressing through many *different* welfare systems.

- *Original income* makes no allowance for taxes and benefits in cash or kind and is clearly very unequal through time. It rises steeply in the late teenage/early 20s, then flattens out to peak in late middle age before falling sharply in retirement.
- *Net income* allows for taxes and cash benefits. Together they reduce the original income available to spend during the working years, but increase it during retirement.
- *Final income* allows for benefits in kind, such as free or subsidised education and health services. These clearly add to net income for all age groups, but especially for those in retirement.

As we can see from Fig. 13.2 the tax/benefit system succeeds in 'smoothing out' final income over the life cycle. People 'pay into' the welfare system in net terms when original incomes are relatively high, but 'draw out' from it when original incomes are relatively low.

Taking this lifetime perspective into account, the tax/benefit system is also effective in redistributing income from the *lifetime rich* to the *lifetime poor*. The bottom five decile groups by lifetime income receive more lifetime benefits (in cash and kind) than they pay in lifetime taxes, so that the *net lifetime gain* (benefits minus taxes) is positive for the bottom five decile groups. Only for the sixth from bottom decile group do we find neutrality with neither gain nor loss via the welfare system.

Interestingly in terms of *gross lifetime benefits* from social security, national health and education subsidies etc., *all* deciles of lifetime income groups receive a broadly similar amount, with only slightly more received by the poorest three deciles. Of course these bottom deciles pay much less in lifetime tax and social security contributions to finance these lifetime benefits, so that the richer deciles largely 'self-finance' these gross lifetime benefits. As an average (in 1991 prices) some £133,000 can be expected to be received as gross benefit across the lifetime of an individual almost irrespective of lifetime income group membership. Of this gross benefit, around £98,000 is, on average, self-financed

Fig. 13.2.   Impact of Welfare State on lifetime income. *Source:* Hills (1994) and *LSE Lifemod Simulation Model.*

(i.e. some 74%). In other words nearly three-quarters of what the welfare state does is akin to operating as a 'lifetime savings bank', with people paying in during the 'good' times, to support themselves during the 'bad' times. Only one quarter of what the welfare state does is redistributive in a lifetime context.

Redistribution towards particular groups   Turning to the fourth aim of the welfare state, namely redistribution towards particular groups, clearly the sick, the disabled, the unemployed, etc. are likely to be represented in the lower deciles of lifetime income and in that sense will be net beneficiaries of the welfare system. A more detailed analysis of the prospects for those groups is presented in Chapters 14 (Distribution of Income and Wealth), 19 (Taxation) and 23 (Unemployment).

The Welfare State and the long-run

Prospective changes in the welfare state may disrupt some of the patterns we have identified. For example, the current system relies on those generations *in work* paying more into the system than they receive in benefits to cover the needs of those generations currently in retirement. In other words the system works on a 'pay as you go' principle, rather than banking the contributions of each generation for the future use of that generation once it has retired. Those who are currently aged 59 years have, on average, paid £40,000 more into the system than they have as yet received; the implied inter-generational contract being that they will receive most, if not all, of this back over the rest of their lives during retirement. However if the share of GDP allocated to the welfare state is reduced, with greater emphasis on private insurance to cover future welfare needs, then this inter-generational contract will be breached. Those in work will then have to pay much more over their working lives (to cover both their own future needs and those currently retired or about to retire) than they can expect to receive back over their entire life-cycle. In some sense they will be 'paying twice' – once for previous generations who, now being too old, lack the opportunity of private insurance provisions – and once for themselves.

Demographic pressures are also putting the welfare state under great strain. By 2030 the proportion of the population over 65 years is expected to be 18.4%, almost 4% higher than in 1998. Such an ageing population is expected to increase the UK *dependency ratio* – the non-working population divided by the working population – from 0.52 in 1998 to 0.62 by 2030; implying that those in work will need to support a greater number of retired persons. This is, of course, a key reason why some policy-makers regard it as inevitable that the implied inter-generational contract will be breached, as already discussed. If the present system were to continue, each worker would be required to contribute some 18% *more* in real income to sustain the current level of welfare provision into the year 2030. To improve the quality of welfare provision in the future would require still greater real income contributions from those in work.

Of course a period of sustained economic growth might make such scenarios for the funding of future welfare provision appear far too pessimistic. For example, if economic growth were to halve unemployment then, by the end of this century (despite an ageing population), the real contribution of each worker needed to sustain the current level of welfare provision would fall, and continue to fall over the period to 2030.

Quasi-markets in welfare provision

The provision of many welfare services is increasingly being undertaken by what might be called *quasi markets* or *internal markets* instead of being directly controlled by a government department, as previously. In many cases the state ceases to provide the services in question, relying instead on independent institutions to compete against each other to win contracts to supply such services. As well as competition on the supply side there is usually a purchasing aspect on the demand side of the quasi market, often state funded. Since outcomes (in terms of allocation of resources) are determined by the interaction of supply and demand, typical of any market, we can reasonably use the term 'market' to describe these emerging mechanisms of welfare provision. However, there are a number of aspects on both the supply and demand sides which are untypical of any market – hence the term 'quasi'.

Many types of service provider   On the supply side there is a wider variety of types of service provider than is usual in a market – for example, private 'for profit' organizations, private 'not for profit' organizations (e.g. voluntary bodies and charities), and various public organizations, etc. There is therefore a greater than usual diversity of ownership structures and organizational objectives than is typical of more conventional markets.

Use of vouchers or budgets rather than cash   On the demand side, consumer purchasing power is often expressed in terms of *vouchers*, or *budgets* allocated for specific purposes, rather than in terms of cash changing hands.

Use of agents or intermediaries in purchasing   On the demand side, instead of market preferences being expressed by the consumer directly, as in normal markets, the consumer's preferences are often expressed indirectly by an agent or intermediary (e.g. a GP, health authority, care manager, etc.).

Many advocates of these emerging quasi markets argue that they promote greater efficiency in supply, respond more rapidly to consumer preferences and are more accountable to those who fund their operation. Critics argue that the market conditions necessary for such favourable outcomes do not exist in most welfare sectors. As a consequence, movements towards quasi market provision will increase administrative and other transaction costs and lead to greater inequalities amongst recipients of such services. Before considering the operation of these quasi markets in the particular sectors of health care, education and housing, it may be useful to consider the contribution of conventional economic theory to an understanding of their operation. Indeed, economic theory suggests a number of conditions which must be met if the more favourable outcomes claimed for quasi markets are to occur (Le Grand 1992).

1. *The market structure must be competitive in both supply and demand, with many providers and many purchasers.* If markets are to operate 'efficiently', in terms of price, output and quality, dissatisfied purchasers must be able to seek alternative

sources of supply (i.e. there must be an absence of monopoly in supply). Similarly suppliers must not be dependent on a few, powerful purchasers, otherwise price can be kept artificially low and many potentially efficient suppliers can be driven out of business (i.e. there must be an absence of monopsony in demand).

2. *Accurate, easily accessible information as to the cost and quality of provision must be available to both suppliers and purchasers.* Otherwise suppliers will be unable to cost and price their activities appropriately, and purchasers will be unable to monitor the price and quality of the services they receive. 'Market failure' in respect of this condition could, for example, lead to suppliers reducing costs by lowering the quality of services without purchasers being aware of the fact.

3. *Profit must be a significant factor in motivating suppliers.* Price is a key 'signal' in markets and if suppliers do not respond to the signal of higher prices and profits by increasing supply, because profit is not a motivating factor, then resource allocation will be impaired. It follows that an over-representation of voluntary and charitable bodies in provision, pursuing various 'praiseworthy' aims, may lead to unpredictable and arguably 'inefficient' responses by suppliers to market signals.

4. *There must be few opportunities in the market for 'adverse selection' or its opposite, 'cream skimming'.* Both are the consequence of a lack of symmetry in the information available to sellers and buyers and may inhibit the existence of a market. In the case of 'adverse selection', purchasers who know themselves to be 'bad risks' but who are not known to be so by providers, may be over-represented in the market. This will reduce profitability for providers and may even cause the welfare provision to cease as suppliers make excessive losses. On the other hand 'cream skimming' can impair market efficiency by permitting providers to use information available only to themselves to select purchasers who are 'good risks', thereby raising profits. In this case welfare services may fail to reach those who most require them.

We shall refer back to some of the aspects of quasi-markets considered in this section as we look in more detail at the provision of particular welfare services.

Health care

Since the National Health Service (NHS) was instituted in 1948 following the earlier Beveridge Report (1942), the majority of health care services have been provided via a relatively centralized administrative structure. A single organization funded by the state, namely the Department of Health, both purchased and provided health care services along two main routes:

1. via the Family Practitioner Committees (FPCs) to the general practitioners (GPs), dentists and pharmacists, who had contracts with the NHS to provide 'front-line' medical care;
2. via the Regional Health Authorities (RHAs) and the District Health Authorities (DHAs), which operated the hospitals and the community units, e.g. midwives and district nurses.

Those in the front line services would either treat patients themselves or refer them to the hospital sector. Costs would be incurred at the point of treatment and would be covered by a budgetary allocation at each point in the system.

Fig. 13.3. Demand and supply of health care.

The mandate of the NHS is to provide health care services according to need, free at the point of delivery. It was, and continues to be, financed from central government tax revenues via the Consolidated Fund. Some 80% of funding is via these tax revenues with another 14% via a proportion of the National Insurance contributions of employers and employees, with only around 4% of NHS receipts currently funded via charges for prescriptions, dental services etc. The consequence for resource allocation of providing health care services essentially free at the point of delivery can be discussed using Fig. 13.3.

We assume demand for health care services to be downward sloping with respect to price: i.e. people demand fewer treatments per time period if price rises. If a market were established with demand D_1 and a short-run supply S_1 (here perfectly inelastic supply), then a price P_1 would be established with an equilibrium number of treatments demanded and supplied per year of Q_1. If demand now increases to D_2, then *price adjusts* in the market, rising to P_2 to allocate the unchanged Q_1.

However as we have seen, the NHS does not operate by price adjustment but by *quantity adjustment*, (since service is free at the point of treatment); with the initial demand D_1, at zero price $0Q_2$ treatments are demanded. This requires the supply curve of treatments to shift rightwards to S_2 if the NHS is to satisfy this demand. If demand now rises to D_2, supply must further increase to S_3, since no price adjustment is permitted. Otherwise $Q_3 - Q_2$ patients would be untreated; i.e. a rise in waiting lists. It is clear that by relying mainly on quantity adjustment, the NHS must either allocate more resources to health care in the face of increased demand or accept a rise in waiting lists.

Factors behind the demand for health care services

A commonly observed trend in the UK, as in other advanced industrialized countries, has been that of a substantial and persistent increase in demand for health care services.

A number of well-attested factors underlie this increase:

1. *A high income elasticity of demand for health care services.* The rise in NHS spending has grown more than in proportion to any rise in National Income (here GNP at constant prices).
2. *An ageing population.* We have already noted the rapid increase in the proportion of elderly people in the UK population. By the year 2011 it is estimated that 17% of the population will be aged over 65 years compared to only 11% in 1951, with 4.5% over 80 years compared to only 1.4% in 1951, those over 75 years are (together with new born infants), the main source of increased expenditure on health care services.
3. *Increased deprivation/economic recession.* Evidence has begun to accumulate that health care needs are related to aspects of deprivation, such as unemployment, low income, etc. We note in Chapter 23 that each successive business cycle has tended to exhibit a higher level of unemployment at any given stage than have previous business cycles. Evidence has been collected which indicates that those Regional Health Authorities with the highest unemployment rates are those which issue the most prescriptions per year, suggesting that rising unemployment is associated with increasing ill health.
4. *Advances in medical technology.* New methods and procedures are available today to treat conditions which previously would have been left untreated.
5. *Higher expectations.* With greater awareness by patients of rights and opportunities (e.g. Patients' Charter), there is a progressively higher expectation of treatment than in earlier times.

Of course the list could readily be extended; what has become abundantly clear is that demand has outstripped supply in many health care specialities, with waiting lists frequently growing as a means of rationing by quantity adjustment rather than price adjustment.

Supply and cost factors

In addition to the problem of ever increasing demand, the NHS faced substantial *cost increases* in real terms. For example, over the 1979–92 time period:

- cost per GP consultation rose by 86% in real terms;
- cost of drugs rose by 55% in real terms;
- cost of dental services rose by 30% in real terms.

The only source of cost reduction was in hospital treatment; down 30% in real terms over the period as in-patient stay fell from an average of 10 days to 6.5 days.

With the NHS costing over £32bn per year (second only to Social Security among the spending departments) employing over one million persons, dispensing 435 m drug prescriptions per year, treating 8 m in-patients and 20 m out-patients per year, the scope for governmental concern by the early 1990s at rising costs and expenditures was obvious.

Creating an internal (quasi) market

In April 1991 the then Conservative government introduced major changes into the UK health care market. The responsibility for *purchasing* health care was now separated from the responsibility for *providing* it.

According to the White Paper preceding the 1991 reforms, the health service reforms were intended to achieve two objectives, namely:

To give patients, wherever they live in the UK, better health care and greater choice of the services available (and to produce) greater satisfaction and rewards for those working in the NHS who successfully respond to local needs and preferences.

These objectives were to be accomplished by the implementation of a number of key measures.

- First, increased delegation of responsibilities from central to local levels, for example, the delegation of functions from Regions to Districts, and from Districts to individual hospitals.
- Second, certain of the larger hospitals were invited to apply to become NHS Hospital Trusts. Trust status would permit the hospital increased freedom of action in terms of local pay settlements, easier access to borrowing, more choice in deciding upon output mix (e.g. types of speciality) and new opportunities to retain profit. There would then be hospitals managed directly by the District Health Authority (DHA) and hospitals with NHS Trust status.
- Third, all hospitals in the future were to be free to offer their services, at agreed prices, to any DHA in the UK, and to the private sector. Previously hospitals within a given area normally treated only patients originating from within that area.
- Fourth, a facility was to be provided for the larger general practices to hold and operate their own budgets, for the purchase of services directly from hospitals and to cover drug prescribing costs. This meant the creation of a new category of General Practitioner Fund Holders (GPFH). For smaller practices the GPs could *combine* to form various types of commissioning groups, purchasing on behalf of individual GPs within such groups.

The new NHS structure introduced in 1991 was to be as shown in Fig. 13.4(a). The Department of Health (through the NHS Executive) allocates funds to Regional Health Authorities (RHAs) according to demographic 'needs'. These are in turn allocated to District Health Authorities (DHAs), NHS Trusts and GP Fundholders. Notice the beginnings of extensive contractual relationships between the various 'players' (dashed lines).

Note that the internal market established in 1991 was *not* a private market in the normal sense. It was not the patients who were to make the purchasing decisions, as they do in the case of US health care for example; rather it was the DHAs and the GPs who were to have the spending power, allocated to them from the RHA or, as in the case of the GP Commisioning Groups, allocated to them from the DHA. On the basis of this budget allocation, the purchaser can then effect a health treatment on behalf of the patient in any one of three ways. Treatment may be purchased: first, from a (managed) hospital administered by a DHA; second, from a hospital with Trust status; third, from a private sector hospital, i.e. one totally outside the NHS.

Note that in Table 13.1 we have included the private sector. The 'purchasers' will include private patients paying directly for treatment or, more usually, through health insurance schemes (e.g. BUPA). The 'providers' include private hospitals which may offer services to NHS patients. Equivalently, NHS hospitals may offer services to private patients. Some exchange between the public and private sector has occurred previously but its extent was expected to increase under the new reforms.

The Conservative government argued in 1991 that the introduction of competition on the supply side would encourage efficiency. Providers competing for contracts with purchasers would have to be efficient or face a possible loss of business.

Fig. 13.4.   Structure of the National Health Service after the 1991 and 1998 reforms.

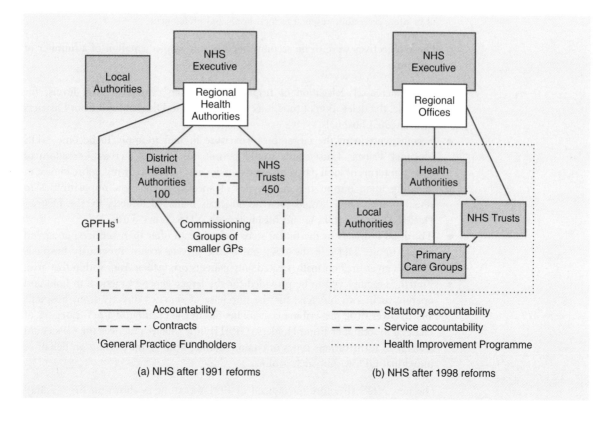

(a) NHS after 1991 reforms   (b) NHS after 1998 reforms

Purchasers, because they had finite budgets, would have incentives to seek out efficient providers. The government also argued that this system would increase patient choice.

However the efficiency benefits claimed for this internal (quasi) market in health care depend upon the 'signals' or incentives given to both providers and purchasers and the nature of their likely response to such signals (Propper 1993). We now consider this in more detail: first, the incentives to purchasers; second, the incentives to providers.

Incentives to purchasers   **District Health Authority (DHA)**   As purchasers, districts were to be responsible for assessing the health care needs of their populations, prioritizing needs, developing contracting arrangements for the services they wish to purchase, and monitoring

Table 13.1 Purchasers and providers.

Purchasers	Providers
District Health Authority (DHA) GP Fund Holders (GPFH) GP Commisioning Groups Private patients	NHS Trust hospitals District managed hospitals Private hospitals

provider performance. They received a budget, which was a function of the number and age of the persons for whom they were responsible.

The incentives for increased efficiency facing DHAs were, however, rather limited. There were no direct sanctions for failing to meet the needs of their consumers. Managers were not rewarded on the basis of health care outcomes and so were not directly rewarded for doing what the new system intended them to do. It was relatively costly for districts to gather information about the *outcomes* of care from different providers since they had no direct contact with patients. This high cost of acquiring information meant that at the margin, districts probably under-collected such information.

General Practice Fund Holders (GPFH)   Alongside districts, the 1991 reforms gave larger general practices (providers of primary care) the opportunity to become fundholders and to assume a purchasing role. The financing for this role came from top-slicing part of the budget of the DHA in which the fundholding practice was located. Fundholders were free to place contracts with whichever hospitals they wished, and in some cases to substitute their own services for existing ones, e.g. they could now offer minor surgical procedures directly.

GP fundholders had more discretion than non-fundholding GPs about how and when their patients were treated. They had better access than the DHAs to information about the outcomes of care from different providers since they saw patients *before* and *after* treatment. The costs of gathering information were therefore lower and, in this respect, fundholders were likely to be more efficient than DHAs in acting as consumers' agents.

Competition on the purchasing side between agents rather than individuals – may arguably have given purchasers the incentive to be more responsive to patient needs. However it may also have increased the risk of 'cream skimming'. This is because each purchasing agent – DHA, GPFH or Commissioning Group of smaller GPs – receives a sum of money per person for whom they were responsible, adjusted for age. General Practitioner Fund Holders were, as we have noted, in a good position to identify directly any 'bad risks', i.e. patients who were likely to require recurrent health care. They could then reject these 'bad risks' from their list of patients, thereby reducing costs. In contrast the DHAs had to treat *all* patients, so that the pool of patients available to them may have become over-represented by those deemed 'bad risks' (i.e. adverse selection). Many saw the risks of a two-tier system developing in which healthier patients would receive priority treatment from GP fundholders.

Incentives to providers   The *providers* were to be the NHS managed hospitals, NHS trust hospitals and private hospitals. The difference between the first two, the directly managed hospitals under DHA control and the trust hospitals responsible to the Department of Health, was mainly in terms of the greater contractual freedom of the latter. Trust hospitals could set their own pay scales, decide themselves on the quantity and mix of factor inputs and types of specialism they offered (output mix).

Neither managed nor trust hospitals could make profit on their services. Prices had to be based on *average cost*, with no cross-subsidies or price discrimination. However, this average cost pricing policy could itself lead to inefficiencies. In

Fig. 13.5. Problems with
average cost pricing.

Fig. 13.5. Problems with average cost pricing.

Fig. 13.5 we assume, for simplicity, that two hospitals, A and B, have *identical* average and marginal cost curves. We can see that although each hospital treats a different number of patients, they each have the same average cost $\overline{C}$ in a situation where Q_A treatments take place in hospital A and Q_B treatments take place in hospital B, and therefore both hospitals charge the same price via the earlier directive on average cost pricing. However an efficient allocation of resources (patients) would be one which allowed hospital A to charge a *lower price* than B, since scale economies are still potentially available to A which would reduce average costs with extra treatments (unlike hospital B where average costs would increase with extra treatments). This lower price would then attract patients to hospital A which can provide treatment at a lower (average) cost than hospital B. Therefore the regulation insisting on average cost pricing did not permit the (quasi) market for health care to send appropriate signals to patients. Resource allocation would then be inefficient where patients (or their agents) chose the identically priced hospital B rather than A. (Note that a marginal cost pricing principle would be more appropriate here – since MC_A at $Q_A <$ MC_B at Q_B.)

Put another way, the internal market was not structured in such a way as to allow profit signals on particular activities to guide resource allocation. Even if such profit signals had existed, the fact that all three types of provider (including even the private hospitals) may not have followed a clear profit maximizing objective might have deflected them from reacting 'appropriately' to the profit signals. It is sometimes argued that the publicly owned managed and trust hospitals are dominated by senior managers or medical staff who seek 'break even' targets, rather than maximum profits. Such non-profit maximizing objectives may even extend to private hospitals, some of which have charitable status. It can hardly be surprising if non-profit maximizing hospitals fail to respond to profit related signals in ways predicted by economic theory, even when such profit signals *are* transmitted in the market!

Another criticism of the operation of the internal market was that funds did not always follow the patient immediately. The result being that the efficient providers have sometimes been unable to treat more patients even when the demand has been there, since they have run out of funds. As a result treatments have had to cease in some 'efficient' hospitals once their initial targets have been met.

Characteristics of an internal market and health care provision

It may be that certain aspects of the 1991 reforms establishing an internal market were unlikely to succeed because of *intrinsic characteristics* of the market for health care provision. For example, competition is only likely to yield efficiency gains where excess capacity exists in a market. This is hardly the case in health care provision where almost all indicators point to under-supply (i.e. excess demand). In a case of under-supply in a pure market, *price* will allocate the restricted supply amongst the competing consumers (see Fig. 13.3 above). In a quasi market, where regulations of various kinds are imposed which prevent a 'pure' price adjustment, an element of *rationing* may be inevitable. Arguably it may then be better to use certain 'objective' means of rationing rather than consumer purchasing power or the arbitrary judgements of the service providers.

A number of other problems were seen, by critics, as likely to prevent the internal market from making a significant contribution to the improvement of health care.

Asymmetry of information   When the provider and purchaser were one and the same, as with the DHAs before 1991, the quality of health care provision could be monitored through internal channels. However they became separated after the creation of the internal market in 1991, the problem then being that while the providers may be aware of any diminution in quality of service, the purchasers may not. This *asymmetry of information* between seller and buyer is a classic instance of 'market failure' which may lead to an inefficient allocation of resources, with purchasers paying more than the competitive price for any given quality of service.

High transaction costs   The main means by which purchasers seek to gain assurances as to the price and quality of provision is by the issuing of contracts, which may of necessity be rather detailed. Drawing up such contracts takes time and money, as does the whole tendering process between rival providers and the eventual requirements for issuing and processing invoices and other documents between contracting parties. These *transactions costs* may absorb some or all of any efficiency gains via the internal market. Before the creation of the internal market some 5% of total health care spending in the UK involved administrative costs; there were fears that the internal market might raise this figure nearer to the 20% of total health care spending involving the various transaction costs commonly experienced in the US.

Non-contestable markets   To avoid excessive transaction costs, there may be the incentive for individual providers and purchasers to develop *long-term relationships* in response to the creation of an internal market. The billing and invoicing system of the respective parties might then be simplified and made compatible, as might other aspects of provision. Familiarity and convenience may then serve to make it difficult for *potential new entrants* to secure existing contracts when these are due for renewal. This lack of opportunity for new entrants may permit existing providers in the internal market to be less efficient than is technically feasible, as a result of the long-term relationships established between providers and purchasers. In other words these long-term relationships may make the internal health care market less contestable (by new entrants) than hitherto.

Monopoly provision   Some districts and regions within the internal market may be too small, in themselves, to support more than one (or perhaps even one) 'efficient' service provider. This may be the case where significant economies of scale are available in respect of various types of treatment, giving large hospitals a cost advantage. Significant travel costs (transport, time and convenience) may then deter patients (or their agents) from undermining the higher cost provision in these local monopoly cases by seeking treatment in other regions and districts.

Table 13.2 would suggest that in the case of processing blood samples, for example, very significant economies of scale do exist. A tenfold increase in throughput spreads the fixed equipment costs over much larger output, thereby reducing average fixed costs and contributing to a significant reduction in average total costs.

The move since 1991 to an internal or quasi market in health care clearly created some opportunities for efficiency gains but it also created other conditions which may in principle offset any such gains. The incoming Labour government in 1997 felt that, on balance, the disadvantages of the internal market outweighed the advantages. It therefore introduced a White Paper in 1998 which sought to reform the NHS.

The 1998 NHS reforms   The NHS White Paper (1998) set out to replace the internal market by a system of integrated care, outlined in Fig. 13.4(b) (p. 286). The focus of the reforms can be seen as providing a greater emphasis on *national planning* of health provision, with delivery a matter of *local responsibility* and involving *partnership* between the various providers.

The White Paper sets out a 10-year programme for reform. The Health Authorities (HAs) have been reconstituted and given stronger powers to improve the health of residents in their region and district. Over time they are to lose their responsibility for direct commissioning. Instead their main objective will be to work with local authorities, NHS trusts and Primary Care Groups (PCGs) to draw up three-year Health Improvement Programmes within which all local NHS bodies will operate.

HAs will allocate funds to PCGs which will then take the responsibility for commissioning services, working closely with local authority social services. The

Table 13.2 Average total costs for blood samples at different scales of operation.

| Item | Cost per test in pence Throughput: 000s samples | | | | |
	50	100	200	400	500
Labour	2.5	2.5	2.5	2.5	2.5
Consumables	2.5	2.5	2.5	2.5	2.5
Equipment	10	5	2.5	1.25	1
Overheads and phlebotomy costs	25	25	25	25	25
Average total cost	40	35	32.5	31.25	31

Source: Adapted from Bowers (1994).

Fig. 13.7. The decision
to invest in education.

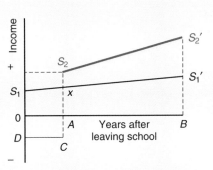

which develops from within'. Research by Robert Barro, for example, suggests that a 10% increase in educational attainment increases growth by 0.2% per year.

To what extent is the market capable of providing an appropriate level of education or training? What role might there be for an internal or quasi market in this area? Before seeking to address these issues it may be useful to review the circumstances under which the purchaser or provider, respectively, might be induced to invest in a given amount of education or training.

In Fig. 13.7, suppose the individual can leave school without training at 16 years and progress along the income pathway $S_1 S_1'$. Alternatively the individual can 'invest' in $0A$ years of training, paying directly the sum $0ACD$ as costs for this training. On completion, the higher marginal revenue product of the employee raises his or her earning potential to $S_2 S_2'$. In addition the (full time) training period has meant an opportunity cost of $0AXS_1$ income foregone during the training period. Only if lifetime benefits exceed the lifetime costs of training is it likely that the 'investment' in training will be regarded as worthwhile. In other words the extra benefits $XS_1' S_2' S_2$ must be greater than the extra costs $0ACD + 0AXS_1$. All sums must, since they occur at different times, be discounted to a present value equivalent.

Research by London Economics (Chote 1994) for the Committee of Vice Chancellors and Principals shows how attractive an investment in higher education can be. For example, a woman *graduate* of equivalent profile to a non-graduate in other respects, would by the age of 49 years be taking home some 70% more pay than her non-graduate counterpart. In similar vein, Schmitt (1995) reports that a male *graduate* in the UK can expect to receive a weekly wage some 90% in excess of that for a non-graduate of otherwise similar profile. Perhaps the most comprehensive survey of this issue (IFS 1998) has involved the life profiles of 2,500 individuals born in a particular week in March 1958. The study concludes that male graduates in their early 30s earned 15 to 20% more than similar aged men who completed A levels but did not undertake hgher education. For women the average gain due to a degree was even higher, around 35%.

Problems for a pure market   It is unlikely that a pure market will lead to an 'efficient' level of provision for education or training. This can be illustrated in Fig. 13.8. Suppose untrained labour has a Marginal Revenue Product of MRP_0 to the firm, and is paid the wage ($=MRP_0$) of W_0. Suppose also that the firm which provides the training does so at a cost of ($V - W_0$) per week. The total cost to the

Fig. 13.8. The firm's decision to train labour.

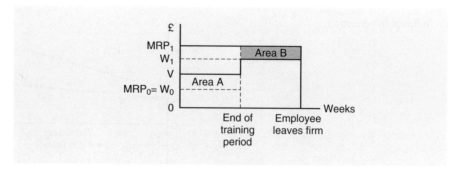

firm of providing training during the training period is therefore given by area A. However at the end of the training period, suppose the Marginal Revenue Product of trained labour rises to MRP_1 ($>MRP_0$). To recoup the training costs the firm will now need to pay a wage *below* MRP_1 (say W_1). The minimum condition necessary to make it worthwhile for the firm to support training is that:

$$\underbrace{\left(\begin{array}{c}\text{Cost of training}\\\text{during training period}\end{array}\right)}_{\text{Area A}} = \underbrace{\left(\begin{array}{c}\text{Excess of MRP after}\\\text{training over wage paid}\end{array}\right)}_{\text{Area B}}$$

Again, of course, this equation must be expressed in present value terms, with all future sums involved discounted to their present value equivalents.

A problem for a *pure market* to be established in training would be the risks of 'poaching'. For example, a rival firm could offer to pay the trained worker at the end of the training period between W_1 and MRP_1 and still find this transaction profitable since it has not itself incurred the training costs A. If the worker leaves the company which has funded the training *before* sufficient time has elapsed for area B (in present value terms) to at least equal area A, then the company has lost at the expense of its rival. Such 'poaching', if extensive, would negate any incentives for individual firms themselves to offer an appropriate level of training opportunities.

Quasi markets in education and training

Many of the reforms proposed for enhancing access to education and training involve aspects of the quasi markets discussed earlier.

On the *provider* side a centralized state agency (Department for Employment and Education or Department of Trade and Industry) is being progressively replaced by market-type mechanisms for resource allocation. In the schools, inducements have been provided for schools to 'opt-out' of local authority control and to receive direct grants from central government. Budgets are increasingly allocated to schools according to their individual characteristics (formula funding) – if more pupils are attracted, more income is received. Schools have also been given greater opportunities for managing their own budgets (Local Management of Schools – LMS), becoming in effect semi-independent providers.

On the *purchaser side*, under open enrolment parents have greater choice, within limits, as to the school to which they send their child. Training and Enterprise Councils (TECs) can act as agents for consumers, selecting the educational institutions or training bodies they will fund to provide particular vocational or training courses, or even providing such courses themselves. Greater awareness of the results of different educational institutions (e.g. National League Tables) are aimed at giving 'purchasers' better information as to the quality of service provision. In total, many of these reforms have similarities with a *voucher system*, whereby parents, students or TECs choose a particular provider, and a budget allocation directly follows that choice. Indeed, pilot projects have been run whereby education and training vouchers have been allocated to students directly to a given value which can then be spent on courses of their choice.

As in the case of health care, the view of the then Conservative government was that increased competition among providers for the vouchers/expenditure of purchasers would raise both the efficiency of supply and the choice of consumers. We now consider a number of broad issues raised by the development of such quasi markets in education and training.

Problems for quasi market provision

Cream skimming and adverse selection   As with health care, the extent of efficiency gains from quasi markets depends upon providers being unable to 'cream skim' by taking only those most likely to succeed. If certain schools *are* able to do this, other (non opted-out) schools will have a progressively adverse pool from which to draw their pupils, and disparities between schools will widen rather than narrow. There is evidence to suggest that a quasi market in which only a minority of schools opt out is indeed likely to result in elements of selection. For example detailed studies such as Mortimore *et al.* (1988) found that only about 5% of what actually takes place in schools affects 'outcomes' (e.g. exam results). Over 64% of the variance in pupil achievements could be explained by initial attainment and social background. With such a large part of the likely outcomes for pupils outside the direct influence of the schools, Glennerster (1993) concluded that 'any school entrepreneur acting rationally would seek to exclude pupils who would drag down the overall performance of the school, its major selling point to parents'.

Poor information and externalities.   Following on from the previous point, a selective system might (say critics) create rather misleading information and a variety of negative externalities as compared to an initially non-selective system. This is in line with the earlier point that in quasi markets there needs to be *symmetry of information between providers and purchasers*. In a competitive and selective system, educational providers may have incentives *not to reveal* relevant factors, and parents (purchasers) may be unable to extract that information. Of course such 'secrecy' may also be the case in non-selective schools as a defence mechanism for teachers. In any case Parents' Charters and National League Tables may help remedy information deficiencies by ensuring that schools reveal specific aspects of information about themselves. 'Value added' league tables may give still more relevant information to parents (prospective purchasers).

Selectivity may also lead to certain *negative externalities*. For example, the loss of local community ties fostered by non-selective local schools; the loss of the improved educational outcomes attributed to average and below average children mixing together in non-selective schooling. Opponents of this view would cite the *positive externalities* selection might give to brighter children able to progress more rapidly in a cohort of children with similar ability.

Sunk costs   A quasi market will lead to 'winners' and 'losers', with some schools expanding and others contracting. The corollary of this is that there will be more frequent entry to, and exit from, individual schools by children. *Sunk costs* are costs which cannot be recovered on exit from a market, and arguably these will be high in an educational context where schools have become part of a community. Any closure of the less successful schools will then incur substantial sunk costs. Similarly the disruption costs to children from frequent upheaval will be considerable. Critics of this view would argue that the decline and even closure of inadequate schools is a 'price worth paying' for higher standards.

As in the case of health care, there can be no presumption that quasi markets in education and training must of necessity create greater efficiency and choice. The issues are complex and require thorough analysis and empirical investigation. Certainly the momentum is towards extending such quasi markets with reports such as Social Justice (1994) recommending the creation of individual learning accounts (i.e. transferable vouchers) for both pupils and employees. However the Social Justice Report recognized that pure market solutions will not work in the case of training, so it also proposes that *minimum standards* be set for all employers. For instance all employers, whether providing training or not, might be required to set aside up to 2% of payroll, reclaimable in part or full depending on the amount of training they themselves actually provide. Employers unable or unwilling to provide that level of training themselves would be required to put the *difference* into their employees' individual learning accounts or to pay the TECs to reimburse companies who do provide such training. Again the aim is to use quasi markets rather than 'pure' markets to redress a situation in which nearly two-thirds of UK employers invest less than 2% of payroll costs in training, whereas three-quarters of French employers invest more than 2% and in Germany an average of 3.5% of payroll is given towards training related programmes (Social Justice 1994).

Housing

As in the case of health care and education, resources in the *housing sector* are increasingly allocated via quasi markets. The housing associations have largely replaced the local authorities as the main providers of social housing in the UK. Government policy has largely switched from subsidizing bricks and mortar to subsidizing individual 'purchasers', via means tested housing benefit. These 'purchasers' can then exercise some choice, subject to certain restrictions, as to the sector (whether local authority, housing association or private landlord) and type of property which will receive their 'voucher-type' payment.

Before examining some of the quasi market issues involving housing, it may be useful to review briefly some of the main developments in so vital a sector.

Housing market developments

Growth of owner occupation   Owner occupied housing is both an *asset* (wealth) and a *consumption good* (providing housing services which must otherwise be paid for). A rise in house prices is therefore significant in terms of a wealth effect (leading to extra consumer spending) and in changing in favour of owner occupation in preference to the now more expensive renting of property. The fact that wealth in housing was seen (during much of the 1970s and 1980s) to be more easily *transformed* into purchasing power than wealth in other assets such as insurance policies or pensions, further increased the attractiveness of owner occupation. As we can see from Table 13.3, owner occupation has risen dramatically over this century, from 10% in 1914 to 67% in 1996, with particularly rapid growth in the 1981–91 period, partly due to attractive terms for the purchase of council houses by tenants (an average of 40% discount for existing tenants wishing to purchase).

Decline in rented sector   In parallel with the growth of owner occupation there has been a significant decline in the rented sector, from 90% in 1914 to below 30% in 1996. The switch towards owner-occupation has come mainly from the local authority (public rented) sector which declined from 31.4% of the housing stock in 1979 to only 21.8% in 1991.

Increase in availability and real price of housing   Other interesting trends shown in Table 13.3 include the data on the rise in the stock of dwellings from some 8m units in 1901 to over 24m units in 1996. This increase in the stock of dwellings has occurred at almost twice the rate at which the population has increased, so that the *number of persons per dwelling* has roughly halved from 4.78 to 2.48 over the period. We can also see that since shortly before the Second World War the index of *real house prices* almost quadrupled, though falling with the advent of the recessionary period in 1988/89 (having reached 210 in 1988).

Increase in housing contribution to net wealth   The rises in the stock of dwellings, in the rate of owner occupation and in real house prices (up to 1988) have all contributed to a significant increase in *housing net wealth* held by the personal sector. Whereas housing was only 20% of the total net wealth of the personal sector in 1968, by 1996 that figure had doubled to around 40%. This is hardly surprising

Table 13.3 Trends in housing data in the UK.

	Owner occupation %	Stock of dwellings (millions)	UK population: stock of dwellings	Index of real house prices (1971 = 100)
1901	10.0	8.01	4.78	–
1911	–	8.94	4.71	–
1921	–	7.98	5.52	–
1931	–	9.40	4.90	–
1939	33.0	11.50	4.20	51
1945	–	11.10	4.32	61
1951	34.5	12.39	4.05	87
1961	44.4	16.42	3.21	71
1971	52.1	18.20	3.05	100
1981	58.6	21.18	2.64	140
1991	68.0	23.00	2.52	182
1994	67.8	23.70	2.49	174
1996	67.0	24.60	2.48	197

Source: Annual Abstract of Statistics (various); *Social Trends* (1998); Miles (1992).

since between 1939 and 1988 the total number of houses roughly doubled and the real price roughly trebled, giving a sixfold increase in the value of the real stock of housing. Clearly a strong housing market has played a key part in consumer confidence via a positive wealth effect, especially during the 'boom' years of the 1980s. Indeed there is ample evidence to support the view that the housing market led to significant 'equity withdrawal', supporting consumer spending during those years. *Equity withdrawal* is where net new lending on housing *exceeds* the amounts recorded as having actually been spent on housing! For example, in the peak year of 1988, equity withdrawal has been calculated at some £200bn for that year.

Increase in negative equity   The corollary of the above is that the onset of recession has caused the housing market to play a key part in eroding consumer wealth and confidence. In particular there has been a significant rise in *negative equity*. This is the situation whereby the value of the mortgage debt outstanding on the house *exceeds* the current market value of the house. The decline in house prices since 1988 had led to a situation where over one million houses were estimated as having negative equity in 1995. The effect of this decline in house prices on consumer confidence is particularly important in the UK which has a higher ratio of net equity in housing to GDP (at 1.68) than has any other industrialized country except Japan.

Increasing government subsidy   One of the concerns for government has been the increasing cost of housing subsidy, both to the owner-occupied and rented sectors.

As regards the *owner-occupied sector*, the main source of subsidy is via mortgage interest tax relief (MIRAS). This dates back to 1805, when allowances were permitted on various forms of loan interest. The Treasury has had to meet an increasing bill, totalling some £7bn in 1998. Today the (tax paying) borrower pays interest less 65% on the first £30,000 of their mortgage, and the lender claims the tax relief from the Inland Revenue. The system is known as MIRAS (Mortgage Interest Relief At Source). At present rates of interest in the housing market of around 7.0%, this amounts to an annual subsidy of £504 per £30,000 of mortgage (i.e. £30,000 × 7.0% = £2,100; at 23% standard rate of tax = £483). Clearly such mortgage interest relief has been a further factor encouraging owner-occupation, and partly reflects a government philosophy in favour of a home-owning democracy.

As regards the *rented sector*, housing benefit has become increasingly important as a means of subsidising the entire rented sector, whether local authority or private rented property. In 1998, over 3 million households received means-tested Housing Benefit to cover part or all of their rent and, for those on Income Support, interest payments on mortgages up to £125,000. Despite the tightening of qualification rules, Housing Benefit rose dramatically from £5.1bn in 1988 to over £10bn in 1998. Despite the laudable intentions of such benefit, we see in Chapter 19 how it contributes to the more general problem of poverty and unemployment 'traps'. For example, Housing Benefit is reduced by 65 pence for every extra pound earned after tax, discouraging many people from moving out of dependency and into various types of (low paid) employment.

Housing market and bequests The housing market is a key factor in the transmission of wealth from one generation to another. Hamnett *et al.* (1991) found that in a random sample, 60% of all persons inheriting over £1000 did so via the houses of their parents. The substantial rise in owner-occupation noted above and the continued rise in life expectancy will make bequests of housing wealth still more important in the future. It is expected that the number of housing bequests will exceed 200,000 per year by 2000, and will double in the following 25 years.

Quasi markets in housing Although an extremely diverse sector, many of the current developments and proposed reforms involving housing incorporate aspects of *quasi markets* (p. 281). In particular moves in the rented sector towards subsidizing people (rather than bricks and mortar) with portable housing benefits, are, in effect, voucher-type purchasing power characteristic of quasi markets on the demand side. On the supply side quasi market characteristics are also developing in the housing sector. For example Housing Associations with an approximately 55:45 public–private mix, are increasingly replacing local authorities as providers of new social housing. The Social Justice Report (1994) similarly called for Local Housing Companies, with a mix of private and public capital, to play a leading role in providing new social housing. Although beyond our brief to investigate the relative merits of these various quasi market solutions, we can clearly state a number of principles as to why *some form* of 'quasi', as opposed to 'pure' market solution will be needed in a housing context.

1 Externalities The widespread presence of *externalities*, both positive and negative, in the housing market makes it unlikely that 'pure' market solutions will be efficient. For example, if one person renovates his house, he and his neighbours may benefit from a rise in house value. Yet only if the marginal *private* benefit exceeds the marginal private cost to the renovator will he go ahead with the housing investment. Such calculations will usually be made without taking into account any marginal *social* benefits, here the rise in house values of neighbours. In this case underprovision of housing investment would occur in a 'pure' market because of 'market failure' in the context of unaccounted positive externalities.

2 Complementary markets A related argument for intervention involves cases where a market only operates efficiently for a *combination of products* rather than a single product in isolation. There are many situations in the housing sector where an appropriate 'price' can only be assigned if *all* the aspects of housing redevelopment are brought together in a single package. Hence the need for public or quasi public bodies to be involved in major housing schemes, such as the London Dockland Development Corporation.

3 Institutional conventions Certain *conventions* by the lending institutions may preclude a market being established, even where benefits exceed costs. For example building societies have sometimes 'redlined' *entire geographical areas as high risk* and precluded all mortgage applications from such areas, independently of their individual

merits. Similarly 'statistical screening' practices by lenders may disadvantage entire groups of potential borrowers (e.g. the self-employed are ascribed a 'high risk' score). For these and other reasons there may need to be public provision or at least a public guarantee of loan finance advanced by private sector lenders.

4 Imperfect information   Efficient markets depend on full knowledge of the prices and qualities of the products traded in the market. Clearly building societies, banks and estate agents go some way to resolving this informational problem in the housing market, especially where they have branches throughout the country and can therefore advise on regional price variations. However, the fact that long and complex selling chains are still frequent (often breaking down and preventing purchase), and that building surveys are often the source of dispute or have to be repeated, suggests that the market is some way from entirely resolving this problem of imperfect information. Arguably the state has a role to play in at least guaranteeing minimum standards of professional competence for those involved in the market, though others would advocate that it should play a much more extensive informational role.

5 Absence of market makers   An alleged 'flaw' in the market for housing is the absence of a market maker. The function of a market maker is to both buy and sell the commodity in question, thereby establishing a market for it. Unlike, say, dealers in second-hand cars, none of the professional agencies in the housing sectors appear willing to act as market makers. The mortgage providers (building societies, banks etc.) see their role as merely funding a contract for property; the estate agents see their role as merely introducing prospective sellers to prospective buyers. No one (except the occasional housing developer) sees their role as being that of taking the prospective buyer's *existing* property onto their books at an agreed price, thereby enabling the buyer to complete the purchase. Of course such market making would be expensive for those acting as 'principal agent' in this way, and wide margins would be required between the purchase and sale price. Nevertheless this may be a 'price' traders would be willing to pay to reduce the delay, uncertainty and frequent breakdown of selling chains. The state may again have a role to play in facilitating the operation of such 'market makers' in one way or another.

In all these ways, 'quasi' as opposed to 'pure' markets are arguably more appropriate for the housing sector. Whether in any particular situation a quasi market is more efficient than a centralised administrative system of resource allocation, must be decided on a case-by-case basis.

Conclusion

The chapter has reviewed some of the four key aims, outcomes and prospects for social policy in the context of the welfare state. Three particular areas of policy have been examined: health care, education and training, and housing. It has been noted that many of the emerging means of provision in these areas involved 'quasi' rather than 'pure' market provision, as an alternative to the previously centralized and administrative means of resource allocation. Some of the conditions under which quasi markets are likely, or unlikely, to yield 'efficient' allocative solutions have been noted, in general, and in each particular area or sector.

Key points

- Welfare services such as health, education, housing and social security make up around two-thirds of all public spending.
- The Welfare State has several objectives, including relief of poverty, life-cycle redistribution and help for particular disadvantaged groups, such as the sick, disabled and unemployed.
- The provision of welfare services is making increasing use of *quasi* or *internal* markets.
- Quasi markets have particular characteristics: many types of service provider, use of vouchers rather than cash, use of intermediaries (agents) in purchasing.
- An excess demand at zero price in the market for health care can only be closed by increased supply or some form of 'rationing'.
- Such 'rationing' might be made more explicit and objective by the use of indicators such as QALYs (Quality Adjusted Life Years) and estimates of the cost per QALY gained.
- The UK internal market in health care has sought to separate *purchasers* from *providers* and to introduce more accountability and competition. In 1998 various reforms have started to move the NHS away from an internal market.
- Problems such as *cream skimming*, *adverse selection*, *asymmetry of information*, presence of *negative externalities*, etc. are present in most types of welfare provision, whether health, education and training, or housing.

Note

1. 'Equivalent income' is where gross income for a household is adjusted depending on the 'needs' of the household; e.g. the number of children or dependents.

References and further reading

Barr, N. (1993) *The Economics of the Welfare State*, 2nd edn, Weidenfeld and Nicolson.

Barr, N. and **Whynes, D.** (1993) *Current Issues in the Economics of Welfare*, Macmillan.

Bowers, P. (1994) *Managerial Economics for the Service Industries*, Chapman and Hall.

Chote, R. (1994) Time the Campus went to Market, *Independent on Sunday*, 14 August.

Glennerster, H. (1993) The Economics of Education, in Barr, N. and Whynes, D., *The Economics of the Welfare State*, Weidenfeld and Nicolson.

Hamnett, C. *et al.* (1991) *Safe as Houses*, Paul Chapman Publishing.

Hills, J. (1994) Who Gains from the Welfare State? *The Economic Review*, April.

Hills, J. (1995) Funding the Welfare State, *Oxford Review of Economic Policy*, **11**, 3.

IFS (1998) *Higher Education, Employment and Earnings in Britain*, Institute of Fiscal Studies.

Le Grand, J. (1992) Quasi Markets in Welfare, *The Economic Review*, November.

Le Grand, J., Propper, C. and **Robinson, R.** (1992) *The Economics of Social Problems,* 3rd edn, Macmillan.

Machin, S. (1996) Wage Inequality in the UK, *Oxford Review of Economic Policy,* **12, 1.**

Maclennan, D. and **Gibb, K.** (1993) Political Economy, Applied Welfare Economics and Housing in the UK, in Barr, N. and Whynes, D., *The Economics of the Welfare State,* Weidenfeld and Nicolson.

Miles, D. (1992) Housing and the Wider Economy in the Short and Long Run, *National Institute Economic Review,* February.

Mooney, G. (1994) *Key Issues in Health Economics,* Harvester Wheatsheaf.

Mortimore, P. *et al.* (1988) The Junior School Project: Understanding School Effectiveness, ILEA Statistics Section.

Propper, C. (1993) Incentives in the New UK Health Care Market, *The Economic Review,* February.

Schmitt, J. (1995) *The Changing Structure of Male Earnings in Britain, 1974–88,* in Machin, S. *op. cit.*

Social Justice (1994) Stategies for National Renewal.

Social Trends (1998) ONS.

Chapter 14

Distribution of income and wealth

In this chapter we review the changes that have taken place in the distribution of income and wealth in the UK. We see that there has been a significant increase in inequality of incomes in the UK since the late 1970s, though not at every income level. We assess the usefulness of the Gini coefficient as an index of inequality, and use it to compare the income distribution of the UK with that of other countries. Income from employment is examined in some detail as this provides over 63% of all income received. Factors resulting in income inequality are considered together with policies which might correct the inequalities observed. Although wealth is difficult to measure, we note a progressive tendency towards a more equal distribution in the 1970s, but little change since then. In fact there is some evidence of greater inequality in recent years at the top and bottom ends of the income distribution. This chapter concludes with a brief review of poverty in the UK.

Distribution and justice

Throughout the history of economics, the distribution of income and wealth has been a major concern. There has not only been a desire to explain the observed pattern of distribution, but also a belief that basic issues of justice and morality were involved. Positive and normative economics are therefore difficult to separate in this area.

Commutative justice There are two main views of justice in distribution. The first may be called 'commutative justice', where it is held that each person should receive income in proportion to the value of labour and capital they have contributed to the productive process. This view underlies the ideology of the free market economy, with some economists seeking to show that commutative justice will automatically be achieved under free competition, since each factor will receive the value of its marginal product. Disparities in the distribution of income and wealth are then seen as being quite consistent with 'commutative justice'.

Distributive justice   The second view may be called 'distributive justice', where it is believed that people should receive income according to need. Given that people's needs are much the same, 'distributive justice' implies approximate equality in income distribution. This view underlies the ideology of socialism. The socialist sees the free market as a kind of power struggle, through which certain groups are exploited; hence their advocacy of various forms of social control of the economy to achieve 'distributive justice'.

Issues in distribution

In the debate about distribution, there are five specific areas of concern:

1. The distribution of income between persons, irrespective of the source of that income. Included here is income from labour (wages and salaries), and from the ownership of capital (dividend and interest) and land (rent).
2. The distribution of income between factors of production, in particular between labour and capital. Advocates of the free market believe that income accrues to labour and capital according to their relative productivity, whilst critics explain their relative shares as the outcome of a continuous conflict in which capital seeks to exploit labour, and labour to resist.
3. The distribution of earnings between different types of labour. Again, believers in the free market see differences in earnings between occupational groups as being caused by differences in relative productivity. Critics explain such differentials through the relative bargaining power of the labour groups in question.
4. The distribution of wealth. In the nineteenth century virtually all wealth was held by a small elite, who lived off the profits from it, whilst the majority lived by the 'sweat of their brows'. The injustice of this was a major spur to socialism. More recently, defenders of capitalism have argued that wealth has become progressively more evenly distributed, so that the majority benefit from profits – 'We are all capitalists now'!
5. Poverty. Free market ideologists have always acknowledged that a small minority will be unable to compete in the labour market, and will therefore be poor; so from Adam Smith onwards most economists accepted the need for some protection of the poor. Critics, however, have argued that poverty was, and remains, widespread.

In this chapter, we shall attempt to assess the facts in each of these five areas of concern, and to look more closely at the conflicting explanations. We shall start by looking at the overall distribution of income between people.

Income distribution between people

The overall picture   The most vivid illustration of income distribution is Pen's 'Parade of Dwarfs' (Pen 1971). In the course of *an hour* the entire population passes by, each person's height in relation to average height signifying their income in relation to average income. In the first minute we see only matchstick people such as women doing casual work. After ten to fifteen minutes dustmen and ticket collectors pass by, though only three feet high. After thirty minutes, when half the population has passed, skilled manual workers and senior office clerks appear, though these are still well under five feet tall. In fact we only reach the average height twelve minutes before the hour ends, when teachers, executive class civil servants, social workers and sales representatives pass by. After this, height increases rapidly. Six minutes before the end come farmers, headmasters and departmental heads of offices, standing about six feet six inches. Then come the giants: the fairly ordinary lawyer at eight feet tall, the family doctor at twenty-one feet, the chairman of a typical public company over sixty feet, and various film stars and tycoons resembling tower blocks.

This illustration demonstrates two little-understood features of the personal income distribution. First, that the mean or average income is way above median income; the median-income receiver being the person who arrives after thirty minutes, with half the population poorer and half richer. Roughly three-quarters of the population have less than the mean or average income. Put another way, the median income is only about 85% of average income. Broadly speaking, this is because at the top end there are considerable numbers of very rich people who pull the average up. Second, that amongst the top quarter of income receivers are people in fairly ordinary professions, such as teachers and sales representatives, who would perhaps be surprised to learn that the great majority of the population were significantly less well-off than themselves.

Definition of income

When we come to collect precise data about income we find various problems of definition. Should we deduct taxes and add transfer payments? Should we count capital gains as income? This latter question raises the problem of distinguishing between income which is a flow, and wealth which is a stock. Income is defined in theory, *as the amount a person could have spent whilst maintaining the value of his wealth intact*. By this definition capital gains should count as income, but for simplicity of data collection they are excluded from official tables. A further question is whether an imputed rent should be credited as income to those who own their dwelling. Again, strictly it should, as a dwelling is a potential source of income which could be spent without diminishing wealth, but for simplicity it is usually excluded. Finally, what should count as the income receiver, the individual or the household? In practice we normally use the 'tax unit' – the individual or family which is defined as one unit for tax purposes.

The Lorenz curve and the Gini coefficient

The conventional means of illustrating income distribution is the Lorenz curve, shown in Fig. 14.1. The horizontal axis shows the cumulative percentage of population; the vertical axis the cumulative percentage of total income they receive. The diagonal is the 'line of perfect equality' where, say, 20% of all people receive 20% of all income.

Table 14.1 presents figures for the distribution of income in the UK at selected dates since 1961. The data for 1991 are plotted in Fig. 14.1 as a continuous line, and are known as the Lorenz curve. The degree of inequality can be judged by the extent to which the Lorenz curve deviates from the diagonal. For instance, the bottom 20% only received 7.6% of total income in 1991, so that the vertical difference between Lorenz curve and diagonal represents inequality. To assess inequality over the whole range of the income distribution, the Gini coefficient is calculated. It is the ratio of

Fig. 14.1. Lorenz curve and Gini coefficient.

Table 14.1 Percentage shares of income after tax in the UK (before housing costs).

Income receivers	1961	1971	1979	1981	1985	1991
Bottom 10%	4.2	4.4	4.7	3.5	3.6	3.0
Bottom 20%	9.4	9.9	11.0	9.0	8.9	7.6
Bottom 30%	15.3	15.6	17.5	15.4	15.5	13.9
Bottom 40%	22.3	22.4	24.2	22.3	22.4	20.3
Bottom 50%	30.5	30.1	32.2	29.8	30.1	27.5
Bottom 60%	40.1	39.0	41.2	38.3	38.8	36.2
Bottom 70%	51.0	49.6	51.8	48.5	49.6	46.7
Bottom 80%	63.1	62.0	64.3	61.1	62.2	59.2
Bottom 90%	78.0	76.7	79.6	76.3	77.4	75.0
Bottom 100%	100.0	100.0	100.0	100.0	100.0	100.0
Gini coefficient	0.260	0.262	0.248	0.259	0.279	0.337

Source: Adapted from Goodman and Webb (1994).

enclosed area between Lorenz curve and diagonal, to total area underneath the diagonal. If there was no inequality (i.e. perfect equality), the Lorenz curve would coincide with the diagonal, and the above ratio would be zero. If there was perfect inequality (all the income going to the last person) then the Lorenz curve would coincide with the horizontal axis until that last person, and the above ratio would be 1. The Gini coefficient therefore ranges from zero to 1 with a rise in the Gini coefficient suggesting less equality. The value of the Gini coefficient is, in fact, calculated for each year in Table 14.1.

The figures from Table 14.1, as well as confirming the conclusions we drew from Pen's 'Parade of Dwarfs', show that during the 1960s the Gini coefficient remained relatively constant, suggesting no significant change in the distribution of income. The period from 1971 to 1979 saw a sustained fall in the coefficient, suggesting that the income distribution became progressively more equal. However the trend has been broken in the 1980s and early 1990s, with the Gini coefficient rising, i.e. less equality (Jenkins 1994).

The Gini coefficient can, however, only give an overall impression. More detailed inspection shows that the bottom 20% of income receivers were worse-off in 1991 with only 7.6% of income, compared to 11% in 1979. What has happened is that the relative position of the lower-income groups has worsened, and that of some of the higher-income groups improved. The top 10% received 25% of income in 1991 but only 20.4% in 1979. When one Lorenz curve lies below another *at every point* we can confidently say that a rise in the Gini coefficient must mean less equality. This appears to be the case for *all* deciles of income in 1991 as compared to 1979. If the Lorenz curves intersect we have to balance less equality at one part of the income distribution with greater equality at another part.

If we had compared the 1961 and 1985 Lorenz curves, we would have found just such an intersection. For instance, there was *less equality* for the bottom 50% of income earners in 1985 (30.1% of income) as compared with 1961 (30.5% of income). However there was *greater equality* for the bottom 30% of income earners in 1985 (15.5% of income) as compared with 1961 (15.3% of income). So the rise in the overall Gini coefficient, from 0.260 in 1961 to 0.279 in 1985, must be treated with some care as it does *not*, in this case, mean less equality throughout the income distribution.

International comparisons

International comparisons of income distributions and their associated Gini coefficients have been difficult to undertake because various countries have different definitions of income and different methods of collecting data. However, recent work by A. B. Atkinson has provided an important insight into income distribution in both Europe and the US (Atkinson 1996). Table 14.2 presents the income distribution for various countries in the late 1980s, using cumulative decile shares. This table contains the same information as Table 14.1. For example, the income distribution for Finland shows that the bottom 10% of income earners (S_{10}) earn 4.5% of all income, whereas the bottom 20% of income earners (S_{20}) earn 10.8% of all income, and so on. The Gini coefficient for the entire distribution is given in the last column on the right (G_0).

If these figures were drawn for each country then we would have a series of Lorenz curves of the kind shown in Fig. 14.1 with each Lorenz curve representing a

Table 14.2 Income distribution in European countries and the US in the 1980s: cumulative decile shares of total income (%).

	S_{10}	S_{20}	S_{30}	S_{40}	S_{50}	S_{60}	S_{70}	S_{80}	S_{90}	G_0
Finland	4.5	10.8	18.1	26.4	35.6	45.6	56.6	68.6	82.2	0.207
Luxemburg	4.3	10.2	17.1	24.8	33.5	43.1	53.9	66.0	80.4	0.238
Belgium	4.2	10.2	17.1	25.0	33.8	43.5	54.3	66.4	80.3	0.235
Netherlands	4.1	10.1	16.9	24.5	33.0	42.5	53.2	65.3	79.4	0.268
Germany	4.0	9.8	16.6	24.2	32.9	42.5	53.2	65.3	79.4	0.250
Norway	3.9	9.8	16.9	24.9	33.9	43.7	54.6	66.7	80.6	0.234
Portugal	3.4	8.0	13.9	20.9	28.9	38.1	48.5	60.8	75.8	0.310
Sweden	3.3	9.5	16.9	25.3	34.6	44.8	55.9	68.2	81.9	0.220
Italy	3.1	8.0	13.9	20.7	28.7	38.0	48.7	61.2	76.2	0.310
France	3.0	8.3	14.6	21.8	29.9	39.1	49.5	61.6	76.3	0.296
Switzerland	2.8	8.0	14.1	21.0	29.0	37.8	47.7	58.9	72.5	0.323
Spain	2.8	7.4	13.2	20.1	28.2	37.5	47.9	60.2	75.5	0.320
UK	2.5	7.5	13.5	20.5	28.7	38.2	49.1	61.8	77.1	0.304
Ireland	2.5	7.1	12.6	19.3	27.1	36.3	47.0	59.6	75.1	0.330
US	1.9	5.7	11.2	18.0	26.2	35.7	46.9	60.2	76.3	0.341

Note: The results are for the distribution among persons of household disposable income adjusted by an equivalence scale equal to (household size)$^{0.5}$.
Sources: Modified from Atkinson (1996).

country's income distribution. The countries in Table 14.1 are ranked from low to high inequality, using the share of the *bottom decile* income group as the initial indicator; i.e. the greater the share of income accounted for by the bottom 10% of income earners, the less inequality we initially assume to occur in that country's distribution of income. Of course we know that the Lorenz curves can intersect each other, making generalizations about the bottom decile less useful.

The Gini coefficients based on the *whole distribution* are given on the right of Table 14.2 and yield a similar ranking (from low to high) of inequality to that implied by the bottom decile of income earners, although the ordering is not exactly the same. Despite these problems, useful conclusions can be drawn from such tables. For example if all the Lorenz curves were mapped, there would be a clear group of mainland Northern European countries at the top (Finland, Belgium, Luxembourg, Norway and Sweden), i.e. with the lowest income inequalities. In the middle would be countries such as France, Italy and Portugal, and at the bottom, i.e. with highest income inequalities, would be a grouping containing Switzerland, Spain, the UK and Ireland, together with the US. The Gini coefficient for the US suggests the least equal distribution of income of all the countries considered. The weighted average Gini coefficient for Europe was 0.288 as compared to that for the US of 0.341, indicating that inequality of income in Europe as a whole is still less than such income inequality in the US. Interestingly, this 5% (0.053) *difference* in Gini coefficient between Europe and the US is less than the difference between some European countries. For example, when comparing Finland with Switzerland or Sweden with Ireland, we find the differences in Gini coefficients are closer to 10%. The UK has more inequality in terms of the overall Gini coefficient (0.304%) than has Europe as a whole (0.288), though some six countries (see Table 14.2) have still greater inequality than the UK. However in terms of the bottom 10% of income earners, the UK's ranking is lower still, with only Ireland equivalent to it and the US below it, suggesting that this group of income earners is particularly vulnerable in the UK.

These trends have been substantiated by another major cross-country comparison of income inequality (Gottshalk and Smeeding 1997). They calculate an inequality measure which they call the '90/10 ratio'. The 90 refers to the ratio of the income of a person at the 90th percentile to the median income for the whole country whereas the 10 refers to the ratio of the income of a person at the 10th percentile to the median income. By *dividing* these two ratios we derive the 90/10 ratio for the UK in the mid-1990s as 206/44 or 4.67, suggesting that a person at the 90th percentile enjoys nearly five times the income of a person at the 10th percentile. Only the ratio for the US at 5.78 was found to be higher than the UK's, while the ratio for most European countries varied within the range from Finland (2.74) to Ireland (4.30).

The next question which might be asked in the international context is what has happened to the distribution of income *over time*? Has it become more or less unequal? Atkinson (1996) presents data of *changes* in the Gini coefficient of different countries over time. A rise in the index suggests that overall inequality has risen, and a fall in the index suggests that overall inequality has fallen. Income inequality appears to have remained relatively steady or actually fallen in the US, Germany, France, Italy and Finland, whilst in the UK there has been a significant increase in inequality, indicated by a rise of over 40% (0.40) in the Gini coefficient between 1977 and 1991. This trend is substantiated by the rise of 36% (0.36) in the Gini coefficient between 1979 and 1991 shown in Table 14.1 earlier. No other country has experienced this rate of increase – Sweden since 1988 being the only other major country experiencing a clear increase in inequality. This trend has been further confirmed by Gottshalk and Smeeding (1997), who concluded from their data that the UK Gini coefficient had risen at twice the rate of the US between 1978 and 1991.

Income distribution between factors of production

Definition of factors

In analysing the share of income between labour, capital and land there are initial problems of definition. First, under labour do we include workers and managers, thereby combining wages and salaries, since both are paid in return for work? Some argue that salaries for managers include a profit element, since they exert direct control over capital and they carry entrepreneurial risks. In practice it is impossible to separate any profit element in salaries, and payments to workers and managers are counted together. More difficult is the income of the self-employed, since this undoubtedly includes payment for both labour and capital services; a separate category is, in fact, usually made for the self-employed.

Measurement of factor shares

Table 14.3 shows pre-tax income to various factors as a percentage of total income. The share for labour has tended to increase, at least until recently. It has been estimated that at the beginning of the century labour's share was only 50% . This increase has not, however, been at the expense of profits but of rent, which has declined from about 25% to a negligible proportion (part of 'other income' in Table 14.3). This follows mainly from the decline in the relative importance of agriculture, and the rise in owner-occupation of dwellings. It is, however, of note that relatively high levels of unemployment since 1981, and a sustained upturn in the economy, contributed to a significant shift of income away from employment and towards corporate profit, at least up to 1989. However, there was a shift away from profits under the impact of economic recession up to 1992 (when the share of company profits fell to 11.9%) before recovering once more after 1993 (see Table 14.3). The privatization programme has also reduced the share of public corporations and general government enterprises, within 'Gross Trading Profits'.

One may question the importance of factor shares in overall income distribution. Whether the changes in factor shares shown in Table 14.3 reflect greater inequality in household incomes depends on how unequally distributed these earnings from different factor sources are across the various income groups. For example, the table

Table 14.3 Factor shares as a percentage of total income.

	1973	1977	1981	1989	1997
Income from employment	66.9	67.2	69.1	64.5	63.2
Income from self-employment	10.2	8.4	8.4	10.9	10.7
Gross trading profits					
Companies	12.5	13.0	10.9	15.2	14.9
Public corporations and					
Central government enterprises	3.1	3.8	3.3	1.5	0.6
Other income*	7.3	7.6	8.3	7.8	10.6
	100.0	100.0	100.0	100.0	100.0

*Rent income, and an imputed charge for consumption of non-trading capital.
Source: ONS (1998) *Economic Trends*, April, and previous issues.

suggests that the distribution of factor shares has shifted away from employment and towards self-employment and profits over the last 16 years. If we knew that income from these two sources is more unevenly distributed across income groups than income from employment, then this shift in factor shares towards self-employment and profits could result in an increase in the overall inequality of income between different groups of people.

Studies have, in fact, shown that income from self-employment and from investments (rent, dividends and interest) are more important sources of income for the lowest and highest income groups than for the middle income groups. For example in 1992/93, income from self-employment accounted for 18% of total income for the *bottom 10% income group* while investment income accounted for 13%. For the *top 10% income group* the figures were 17% and 10% respectively (Ryan 1996). On the other hand, for the middle income groups, the respective shares of self-employment and investment income were much less. In other words, the growth in the importance of self-employment and profits (income from investments) in the 1980s as seen in Table 14.3 has contributed to an increase in income inequality. Indeed a recent study (Jenkins 1996) outlines the growth of income inequality among the self-employed sector during the 1980s. However, as Table 14.3 indicates, the most important factor share is income from employment (62.5%) so that we must pay particular attention to this income source when seeking to identify causes of income inequality.

There are two main types of theoretical explanation of factor shares. The first emphasizes the role of market forces and starts with a microeconomic analysis of factor markets. If there is perfect competition in goods and factor markets, each factor will receive precisely its marginal revenue product; in other words, it will receive income in proportion to its productive value. The rising share to the factor labour would be viewed from this standpoint as reward for a greater contribution to production.

An alternative approach has been to explain factor shares in terms of power. Marx saw capitalists as exploiting labour, receiving 'surplus value' from the fact that the efforts of workers yield returns over and above their wages. Marx believed that this exploitation would increase as production became more capital-intensive and labour was displaced, creating a pool of unemployment which would depress wages, and therefore the share of labour in National Income. Eventually, the decline in people's ability to purchase the output of the capitalist factories, combined with the workers' resentment at their poverty, would cause crisis and revolution.

Neither theory is wholly adequate. Assumptions, such as perfect competition in labour markets, required by orthodox theory are clearly unrealistic (see Chapter 15). Similarly, Marx's prediction of a declining wage and factor share for labour has not been fulfilled.

The earnings distribution

Since over 62% of total income accrues to the factor labour (Table 14.3), it follows that differing returns to the various factors (labour, capital or land) are unlikely to be the main explanation of income inequality. Rather, we must turn our attention to variations in income between different groups *within* the factor labour, i.e. the earnings distribution.

Earnings by occupation   Table 14.4 shows the relative earnings of the main occupational groups according to the Standard Occupational Classification (SOC) introduced for the first time in 1991. Each figure represents the average earnings of the members of that group as a percentage of overall average male earnings. We can see that the first three categories of non-manual workers earn significantly more than the average. These categories include managers in industry and in local/central government; professionals, such as engineers, teachers, scientists and solicitors; and associate professional and technical employees such as technicians, surveyors and computer programmers. However, it is also true that non-manual workers in occupations such as clerical and secretarial earn, on average, less than manual occupations such as craft workers and machine operators. Indeed a more detailed analysis also reveals that certain manual occupations, such as plant drivers and scaffolders, earn as much as teachers and certain classes of management. Although the overall picture is complicated, it can be seen that inequalities of earnings are clearly present in UK society.

A hidden source of inequality between occupations is the difference in value of fringe benefits and pension entitlement. As early as 1979 the Diamond Commission found that this typically adds 36% to the pre-tax salary of a senior manager, and 18% to that of a foreman, whilst unskilled workers enjoy little or no such benefits.

Table 14.4 Earnings of occupational groups. Average (gross weekly) earnings of full-time male employees in selected occupations, as a percentage of average (gross weekly) earnings of all full-time male employees (April 1998).

Non-manual	
Managers and administrators	146
Professional occupations	133
Associate professional and technical	121
Sales	80
Personal and protection services	80
Clerical and secretarial	68
Manual	
Craft and related occupations	84
Plant and machine operators	78
Other occupations	66

Source: Adapted from ONS (1998) *New Earnings Survey, Part A.*

Earnings by sex   Table 14.5 shows female earnings in relation to male earnings. The position of women improved significantly during the 1970s – a period which saw the introduction of equal pay legislation – though women continued to earn substantially less than men. The momentum towards equal pay seems to have slowed down during the 1980s and early 1990s, with the earnings of both manual and non-manual females making little further progress as compared to males.

Table 14.5 Average gross weekly female earnings as a percentage of average male earnings.

	1970	1976	1998
Manual	50	62	64
Non-manual	51	61	65

Source: ONS (1998) *New Earnings Survey, Part A,* and previous issues.

Earnings trends   Figure 14.2 shows that there have been significant changes *over time* in the real earnings gap between high and low wage earners. The figure traces the growth in real

Fig. 14.2. Real hourly
male earnings by
percentile
(Index 1966 = 100).
Sources:
Financial Times (1994);
New Earnings Survey
(1998).

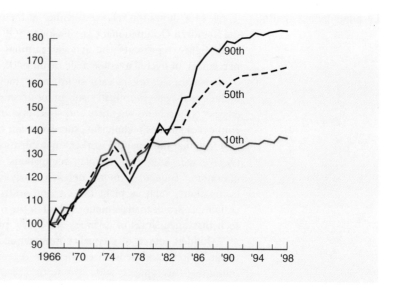

hourly (male) earnings between 1966 and 1992 of people positioned at three different points on the income distribution scale. The 50th percentile line traces the increases in the real hourly earnings of workers receiving the median ('average') wage over the period. Similarly, the 90th percentile represents the growth of real hourly earnings of workers who are 90% of the way up the income distribution, while the 10th percentile shows the growth of real hourly earnings for those whose income is only 10% of the way up the income distribution. Of course the 90th percentile is likely to include some of the people in the non-manual 'managers and administrators' category in Table 14.4, while the 10th percentile will include some of those in the manual 'other occupations' category.

Between 1966 and 1978 the three categories moved roughly in line with each other. However major differences have emerged since then between those on low and high pay. For example, the real pay for average earners (50th percentile) increased by 40% between 1978 and 1996, whilst the real pay for those near the top of the income scale (90th percentile) increased by as much as 55% over the same time period. On the other hand, those with earnings near the bottom of the income scale (10th percentile) hardly benefited at all over this period. The *relative position* of workers near the bottom of the income scale was in fact the lowest since records began in 1886.

The study by Gottschalk and Smeeding (1997) on the '90/10 ratio' confirms this pattern for the UK and considers the same ratio in other countries. For example in terms of the '90/10' ratio they found that the US had the highest *increase* in earnings inequality (rise in the ratio) between 1979 and the early 1990s for males as compared to other industrial countries. Their results show that the UK's increase in earnings inequality over the period was just over 80% of that of the US, followed by Canada and Australia, (in the range 50% and 80% of the US figure) and France, Japan, the Netherlands, Sweden and Finland (in the range 10–50% of the US figure). Finally, Italy and Germany experienced no measurable increase in earnings inequality. From these figures we note that the growth of male earnings inequality in the UK has been second only to the US over the recent past.

Explanation of earnings differentials

In seeking to explain the earnings distribution there are two main theoretical approaches, similar to those we considered above for factor shares.

Market theory   The first, the 'market theory', starts from an assumption of equality in *net advantages* for all jobs, i.e. that money earnings *and* the money value placed on working conditions are equal for all jobs. It also assumes that labour has a high degree of occupational and geographical mobility, so that if there is any inequality in net advantages, labour will move to the more advantageous jobs until equality is restored. Thus, differences in *actual* earnings must be caused by compensating differences in other advantages. Job satisfaction is one compensating advantage: enjoyable or safe jobs will be paid less than irksome or risky ones; this may partly explain the relatively high wage of manual workers such as coal-face miners and chemical, gas and petroleum plant operators. Still more important are differences in training. Training and education are regarded as investments in 'human capital', in which the individual forfeits immediate earnings, and bears the cost of training, in the prospect of higher future earnings; this may in part explain the high earnings of professional groups. Market theory therefore proposes that relative occupational earnings reflect non-monetary advantages between occupations, and the varying length and cost of required training.

Proponents of this theory agree that it is not wholly adequate, and would recognize differences in natural ability as also affecting earnings. However others, whilst still broadly advocating market theory, have suggested a more fundamental objection, namely that labour is in fact highly immobile. The most recent study of income immobility among the rich and poor found that groups of people at the extreme ends of the income distribution tend to be subject to intergenerational immobility (Johnson and Reed 1996). This research attempted to assess whether the income level and unemployment experiences of fathers was related to the subsequent experiences of their sons. The results were interesting in that the sons of those fathers who were unemployed were also more likely to end up being unemployed. Indeed, the sons of fathers whose income was in the bottom 20% of income earners were three times more likely to remain in the same income group than those sons whose fathers' incomes were above average. Similarly, the sons of fathers whose income was in the top 20% of earners were three times as likely to end up in the same income group as their father than those sons whose fathers' incomes were in the bottom 20% of income earners. However, the survey also showed that the more able children of poor parents do have a better chance of moving into higher income bands than less able children, making it very important to make sure that good quality education is available to all. From what we have noted above, a combination of social, occupational and geographic immobility can have a significant effect on the earnings distribution especially at the upper and lower ends of the distribution, contrary to the simple predictions of market theory.

Segmented markets   The second theoretical approach places 'immobility' at the very centre of its analysis. This approach sees the labour market as 'segmented', i.e. one which is divided into a series of largely separate (non-competing) occupational groups, with earnings determined by bargaining power *within* each group. Some groups, especially professional bodies, have control over the supply of labour to their occupations, so that they can limit supply and maintain high earnings. Other occupational groups have differing degrees of unionization and industrial power. The relatively high earnings of the relatively small number of printworkers and coalminers in the UK up to the mid 1980s, may be explained in part by their history of effective and forceful collective bargaining, whilst the fragmented nature of agricultural and catering work may have contributed to their low pay. In this approach bargaining power is held to outweigh the effects of free market forces. A recent UK study on the relationship between wage inequality and union density during the 1980s largely substantiated these conclusions (Gosling 1995). It found that wage inequality increased as trade union influence weakened. The significant weakening of trade union power in the UK in the 1980s may therefore have played a part in the observed increase in the inequality of income. In particular, various groups of labour which do not have strong market power will suffer more than proportionately as a result of any decline in trade union bargaining positions.

These two theoretical approaches to the distribution of earnings need not be regarded as mutually exclusive. Market theory can itself be used to analyse bargaining power, with professional bodies and trade unions affecting the supply of labour, and the elasticity of labour demand determining the employment effects of their activities. More fundamentally, it may be suggested that labour, whilst fairly immobile in the short run, is highly mobile in the long run. Thus, whilst the exertion of bargaining power may affect differentials in the short run, in the long run labour will move in response to market forces, and thereby erode such differentials.

However, it is obvious from Fig. 14.2 that the wage differential between those on low and those on high wages has *not* been eroded; in fact it actually *widened* between 1978 and 1996. Although the reasons for such a trend are complex, they seem to lie in both inter-industry and intra-industry shifts which have occurred in the UK labour market (Gregg and Machin 1994). For example, the *inter-industry* employment shift from manufacturing to services has tended to increase the number of lower-paid jobs. However, there also seem to have been *intra-industry* employment shifts, namely a shift in demand *within* industries in favour of non-manual, better educated, workers. Even when the proportion of workers with degrees rose from 8% to 11% during the 1980s, their wages continued to rise as demand for such workers rose even faster than their supply. At the other end of the scale, although the percentage of workers with no qualifications fell from 46% to 32%, the unemployment rate among this group actually rose from 6.5% to 16.4% over the 1980s. In other words the demand for such workers fell even faster than the fall in their supply. The drive towards international cost competitiveness and the introduction of new technology has increased the demands for a more skilled and flexible workforce (OECD 1996), leaving workers with low skills, poor family backgrounds and inflexible work attitudes to occupy the low-paid jobs. These trends are also linked to age. For example, young people who are poorly qualified and have low earnings, are less likely to experience increasing real earnings with age than are their predecessors (Gosling *et al.* 1994).

Another interesting theory linked to the segmented market hypothesis has been suggested by Daniel Cohen (Cohen 1998). He suggests that there is no longer a single market even for a particular kind of skill or occupation, i.e. there is an *intra-skill* dimension to earnings differentials. For example, top law firms may require secretaries whose pay will reflect their value to the company while secretaries of similar capabilities working for less profitable law firms will earn considerably less. In other words, an individual's earnings prospects may depend on the nature and profitability of the company which employs them, so that even modest differences in skill may be magnified into significant earnings differentials. In this sense earnings differentials may substantially exceed any skill differentials, even within a given occupation.

The above attempts to explain the presence of wage differentials did not explicitly seek to clarify the reasons for earnings differentials by *sex*, so clearly shown in Table 14.5. Such differentials could be due, for example, to some element of *discrimination* which might exist in the labour market between men and women, even though they were identical workers. For instance, until December 1975, when it was made illegal, collective agreements between employers and employees often included clauses which prescribed that female wage rates should not exceed a certain proportion of the male wage. The examples of wage differentials noted above were made possible because of the preponderance of males in most unions. The state has also been active in allowing this wage differential to exist. For example, up to 1970 when the Equal Pay Act was passed, the police pay structure provided for a differential wage structure for men and women up to the rank of ordinary sergeant, while the pay structure for more senior sergeant ranks included only male rates. Obviously, female policewomen were felt to be only able to achieve the lower grades and even here were not seen as of equal value to males (Tzannatos 1990).

On the other hand the observed differentials could be regarded as being due to *genuine differences* which exist (or are perceived to exist) between male and female labour. For instance it is often observed that employers make certain assumptions about the 'average' female worker, i.e. as being one who will not be working for long before leaving to have a child. As a result, employers may be more reluctant to train female workers, who are then placed at a disadvantage as compared to their male counterparts. By acquiring fewer skills, the female worker inevitably receives less pay. Again, female workers are often constrained in competing with male workers by the need to seek employment in the catchment area of their husbands' employment. Such restrictions can again result in a lower wage as compared to that received by the more mobile male counterpart.

Whatever the causes of wage differentials between males and females, there is no doubt that they still exist, even after the initial improvements in the early 1970s following the Equal Pay Act of 1970 and the Sex Discrimination Act of 1975.

Distribution of wealth

Definition of data collection   Wealth is notoriously difficult to define. The most obvious forms of wealth are land, housing, stocks and shares and other financial assets. In addition, many households hold several thousands of pounds-worth of durable goods: a car, carpets and furnishings, electrical goods and so on. All these together are known as 'marketable wealth'. But many ordinary families, whilst owning little land and few shares, may have substantial pension rights. In the case of private schemes these usually derive from contributions into a fund, which in turn is used to buy assets; whilst in the state scheme it derives from contributions which entitle people to future income from government revenues. It is the ownership of marketable wealth plus occupational and state pension rights which is often presented in the data (e.g. Table 14.6).

There are also considerable problems in obtaining information about wealth. Britain has no wealth tax, and so no regular wealth valuations are made. Attempts have been made to do this via sample surveys, but people are often reluctant to reveal their economic circumstances in sufficient detail to draw reliable conclusions. The only time that wealth *is* publicly evaluated is when substantial amounts are transferred from one person to another, usually at death, when wealth is assessed for capital transfer tax. By analysing these figures in terms of age and sex, it is possible to take the dead as a sample of the living, and so estimate the overall wealth distribution. Of course, there is an obvious likelihood of sampling error, especially in estimating the wealth of the young. The procedure also ignores certain bequests, such as those to surviving spouses, which are not liable to tax. Nevertheless, it is the best method available.

Concentration of wealth

Table 14.6 shows the Inland Revenue's estimate of the overall wealth distribution, including occupational and state pension rights. As we might expect, wealth is much more unequally distributed than income. For example, the most wealthy 1% of the population own 11% of the wealth, whilst the top 10% own as much as 36% of wealth and the top 50% own 83% of wealth (i.e. the bottom half own only 17% of wealth). If we *exclude* occupational and state pension rights and the value of dwellings, then the picture for *marketable* wealth becomes even more extreme. In this case the most wealthy 1% own 28% of wealth, the top 10% own 65% of wealth and the top 50% own 94% of wealth (i.e. the bottom 50% own only 6% of wealth).

But perhaps more significant than the absolute figures is the astonishingly rapid reduction in inequality, especially in the early 1970s. The wealth of the richest 1% fell in five years from 21 to 13% of the total, whilst for the richest 10% it fell from 49 to 36% (Table 14.6). This reflects the high rate of inflation in those years, which rapidly eroded the value of financial assets, and also the steep decline in the prices of stocks and shares and commercial land. Over a much longer period we observe a steady reduction in wealth inequality. In 1924 the wealthiest 1% owned 60% of *marketable* wealth (i.e. excluding occupational and state pension rights); this had fallen to 42% in 1951, and is now 28%. A major reason for this has been death duties, and more recently capital transfer tax (inheritance tax). This is a progressive tax, and helps break up the largest wealth holdings as they pass from one generation to another.

Despite the continuing influences of these factors, changes in the distribution of wealth have been much more modest in the 1980s and 1990s, as can be observed from Table 14.6. Recently, however, it has been argued that 'new wealth' is being created in the UK as the rapid spread of home ownership and the rise in house prices (during the late 1980s) means that inheriting such properties may allow both middle and working class people to benefit in the future. The percentage of UK households owning their own homes rose from 56% in 1980 to 74% in 1998. Although this may improve the wealth situation of many middle and working class income earners, it will create even more problems for the children of the 25% or more parents who may never own their

Table 14.6 Ownership of marketable wealth plus occupational and state pension rights.

Percentage of wealth owned by:	1971	1976	1986	1994
Most wealthy 1% of population	21	13	10	11
Most wealthy 5% of population	37	26	24	25
Most wealthy 10% of population	49	36	35	36
Most wealthy 25% of population	71	57	58	58
Most wealthy 50% of population	87	80	82	83

Source: Inland Revenue Statistics (1998) and previous issues.

own homes. It may also further increase the regional disparity of wealth as a result of regional house price differentials.

Though it is an emotive issue, one may doubt that the wealth distribution is a primary source of income inequality. We have already seen that the main source of income inequality is not between capital and labour, but between different groups of labour.

Poverty

Definition   There has been much debate as to the definition of poverty. Some have tried to define it in *absolute* terms. For example, Rowntree (1901), who made a major study of poverty at the turn of the century, concluded that poverty was having insufficient income to obtain the minimum means necessary for survival, namely basic food, housing and clothing. Others have sought to define it in *relative* terms: Townsend (1973) in his survey of poverty, saw it as the inability to participate in the customary activities of society, which today might include taking an annual holiday away from home, owning a refrigerator, having sole use of an indoor WC, and so on.

In some ways, the grinding poverty experienced in pre-World War II Britain is no longer present. For example, studies by the Department of Social Security on 'Houses Below Average Income' have shown that amongst the poorest 10% of UK income earners, the percentage who have access to some basic consumer benefits were as follows: fridge/fridge freezer (99%), washing machine (88%), central heating (77%), telephone (76%), video (72%) and car or van (53%). Although these figures suffer from measurement problems, the improvement over the last fifteen years in these percentages has been significant. However, such data does not always capture the more complicated aspects of poverty and the *relative* positions of different groups in UK society.

On a more practical level the 'official' poverty level (defined as the minimum acceptable income level) used by many researchers in the UK is given by the level of Income Support. On the other hand, the Child Poverty Action Group (CPAG) has defined the 'margins of poverty' as those people whose incomes are below Income Support plus 40%. Income Support is set by governments, and may be affected not only by the needs of the poor, but also by general political policy. It also ignores other aspects of economic deprivation not directly related to money income, such as inadequate housing, schools, health care and such like. However, the Income Support level has the advantage of being definite, and figures are readily available. A further measure of the poverty line is based on the *Households Below Average Income* statistics collected by the Department of Social Security. Using these statistics, the CPAG has defined poverty as a situation where households earn below 50% of the average UK income.

The Council of Europe also has a measure of minimum income which they call the 'decency level'; this is set at 68% of the average earnings of men and women in the country in question. These various measures, together with the information on poverty which can be obtained from government statistics (such as in Table 14.1), give a good general picture of low income and poverty, but often fail to account for other forms of poverty, such as those frequently shown in statistics of homelessness or of health.

Incidence of poverty   When we look at some of these suggested measures of poverty we find some disturbing results. Data show that the number of people *receiving* Income Support has varied from 3.0m in 1978 to the very high levels of 4.8m in 1987 and 5.2m in 1997. If we add to these figures the people who *depend upon* these benefits, e.g. children, then the total number dependent on these benefits in 1997 was 12.5m people, or 21% of the total population. Indeed, if we take the 'margins of poverty' definition of the CPAG it seems that some 18.5m or 33% of the UK population were living in poverty by the late 1980s (Child Poverty Action Group 1996).

To help clarify the reasons behind the growth of poverty it may be helpful to look at Table 14.7 (Piachaud 1998) which contains data from the 'Households Below Average Income' survey published in 1997. The definition of poverty used here is those whose income is below half of the average income adjusted for family size, after taxes and benefits and before housing costs. The table shows a breakdown of poverty according to economic/family status.

Table 14.7 shows that the total number of *all* people in poverty more than doubled between 1979 and 1995 from 4.4 million to 10.3 million, i.e. from 8% to 18% of all individuals. The key groups which make up this total include the elderly, lone parents, the unemployed and couples with only one working member. Each of these groups has shown an increase in both the number and the proportion who are classified as in poverty. By 1995 some 62% of all the unemployed were classified as in poverty, followed by lone parent families (39%), the elderly (23%) and one wage-couples(12%). If we look at the *growth* of poverty over the period, we find that one-parent families and one-wage couples account for most of the recorded growth. As a result the number of children in poor households has almost trebled over the period, both in number and percentage. In fact by 1995 around one-quarter of all children were living in households defined as in poverty. The elderly have also made a significant contribution to this recorded growth of poverty. A further insight into levels of poverty in groups other than the ones shown in Table 14.7 reveal that some 25% of self-employed people also found themselves in poverty, indicating the close relationship between poverty and the state of the economy in general.

Other indicators of poverty might also be considered, such as the fact that in 1997, of the total number of people reporting themselves as homeless to local councils, as many as 30% were lone parents with dependent children. Similarly, 33% of families with a lone mother and 27% of families with a lone father had a gross weekly income of £100 or less. Yet again a survey in 1997 showed that 3

Table 14.7 The growth of poverty* by status 1979–95.

	Numbers of individuals (m)		Numbers in millions and percentages (%) in poverty	
	1979	1995	1979	1995
Elderly	7.9	10.0	1.5 (19)	2.3 (23)
Lone parent family	2.3	4.5	0.4 (16)	1.8 (39)
Unemployed	1.4	3.4	0.7 (49)	2.1 (62)
Couple[†]	11.3	7.3	0.3 (3)	0.9 (12)
All types	54.0	57.5	4.4 (8)	10.3 (18)
(children)	(13.8)	(13.3)	1.2 (9)	3.3 (25)

*Poverty defined as below 50% of average income in each year (before housing costs).
[†]Couple – one full-time worker and one not working.
Source: Adapted from Piachaud (1998).

million or 27% of all the children in the UK are in families on income support (Middleton *et al.* 1997).

Research has also suggested a close relationship between poverty and illness. For example, poor people are one and a half times as likely to have a long-standing illness and twice as likely to have a disability than those who are better off. The problem of poverty would also seem to have an effect on the incidence of crime – for example the incidence of assault and theft in the most deprived neighbourhoods of the Merseyside region are, respectively, more than five and ten times higher than the incidence for the least deprived neighbourhoods (Hirschfield *et al.* 1996).

The prospects for government policy being able to reverse this situation rapidly would appear rather slim. For example it has been calculated that the introduction of the minimum wage (at £4 rather than the £3.60 actually selected) would reduce the number in poverty by only 300,000 out of a total of 10.3 million. Changes in the Government benefit system, such as the introduction of the Working Families Tax Credit (WFTC) in 1999 together with a 20% increase in child benefit, have been designed to help stem the tide of poverty (see Ch. 19). These changes are in addition to reforms of the tax system in 1998 which sought to reduce the poverty trap, as in the case of a family with two children who will now pay tax only when they earn over 50% of average income (as compared to previously being taxed when their income rose above 25% of average income). All these government initiatives should help reduce the numbers in poverty, as should any successes of the 'Welfare to Work' initiatives in reducing unemployment. Nevertheless, the large number and varied characteristics of the 'poor' suggest that poverty is most effectively tackled by a wide range of initiatives over a prolonged period of time.

Table 14.8 presents a forecast of likely changes in the numbers in poverty by 2002 on various assumptions (Piachaud 1998). Despite the hazards of such forecasts it is interesting to note that improvements in the various Social Security benefits (here growing at least in line with inflation) would appear to make the most impact in reducing the projected numbers in poverty. It would seem that appropriate benefit policies, together with policies which help achieve sustained macroeconomic growth (so as to attain the −400,000 scenario for possible reductions in unemployment) are perhaps the two most important contributions the government can make to poverty reduction. Of course economic growth rates depend at least as much on global economic conditions as on UK government policy!

The projections shown in Table 14.8 indicate an *increase* in poverty of between 0.35 million and 1.95 million persons by 2002 on 'best case' and 'worst case' scenarios. Such projections can only strengthen the case for vigorous and sustained attempts by government to reduce the numbers entrapped by poverty, however defined.

Table 14.8 Forecast effects on numbers in poverty 2002.

Ageing of population	Negligible
Growth in lone-parent families	−50,000 to +100,000
Level of unemployment	−400,000 to +800,000
New Deal and Welfare to Work	−400,000 to −150,000
Minimum wage (£4 per hour)	−300,000
Social Security price indexation	+1,500,000
Overall change	+350,000 to +1,950,000

Source: Adapted from Piachaud (1998).

Conclusion

After some move towards greater equality of income distribution between 1961 and 1979, the process has been significantly reversed since the end of the 1970s. Income from employment provides over 63% of all income received, and must be a focus for any attempt to explain the inequality that does exist. Variations in income by occupation, by sex and by skill levels clearly contribute to such inequality. Together with the rise of inequality of income from employment, the growth of self-employment in recent years has also contributed to greater inequality in overall income. Wealth is more unequally distributed than income, and although there has been a progressive tendency towards a more equal distribution since the early 1970s, this process slowed down markedly in the 1980s and 1990s. Poverty is a serious and growing phenomenon in the UK, no matter how we define it. The large numbers and varied characteristics of those in poverty suggest that government policy must be wide-ranging and sustained if poverty levels are to be reduced substantially.

Key points

- The Gini coefficient (G) is the ratio of the area between Lorenz curve and diagonal to the total area beneath the diagonal.
- Where G = 0, we have perfect equality; where G = 1, we have perfect inequality.
- Where Lorenz curves intersect, we must be particularly careful in using the Gini coefficient.
- Since 1979, the Gini coefficient has tended to rise in the UK.
- Inequality as measured by the Gini coefficient is higher in the UK than for the *average* of EU countries, but is lower than for the US.
- Since employment accounts for around 63% of all factor income, the labour market must be a major source of any income inequalities observed.
- Significant differences in earnings can be observed by type of occupation and by gender, though the latter gap has narrowed in recent years.
- Household characteristics such as age, unemployment, single parenthood, etc., also play a key role in income inequality.
- The distribution of wealth is even more unequal than the distribution of income, though inequalities in wealth have narrowed over the past two decades.
- Poverty can be expressed in both absolute and relative terms. Using a variety of indicators, the incidence of poverty has clearly increased in the UK in recent years.

References and further reading

Atkinson, A. B. (1996) Income Distribution in Europe and the United States, *Oxford Review of Economic Policy*, Vol. 12, No. 1.
Child Poverty Action Group (1996) *Poverty*, No. 93, p. 18.
Cohen, D. (1998) *The Wealth of the World and the Poverty of Nations*, MIT Press.
Department of Employment (1998) *New Earnings Survey*, Part A.
Goodman, A. and Webb, S. (1994) For Richer, For Poorer: The Changing

Distribution of Income in the United Kingdom, 1961–91, *Institute for Fiscal Studies,* Commentary No. 42.

Gosling, A. (1995) Wages and Unions in the British Labour markets, Working Paper, University College, London.

Gosling, A., Machin, S. and **Meghir, C.** (1994) What has Happened to Wages? *Institute for Fiscal Studies,* Commentary No. 43.

Gottshalk, P. and **Smeeding, M.** (1997) Cross-National Comparisons of Earnings and Income Inequality, *Journal of Economic Literature*, Vol. 35, No. 2, June.

Gregg, and **Machin, S.** (1994) 'Is the UK Rise in Inequality Different?' in R. Barrell (ed.) *The UK Labour Market: Comparative Aspects and Institutional Developments,* CUP.

Hirschfield, A. *et al.* (1996) *Crime and Spacial Concentration of Disadvantage*, ESRC Programme.

Jenkins, S. P. (1994) Winners and Losers: A Portrait of the UK Income Distribution During the 1980s, *University of Swansea Economic Discussion Paper*, No. 94-07.

Jenkins, S. P. (1996) Recent Trends in the UK Income Distribution: What has Happened and Why? *Oxford Review of Economic Policy*, Vol. 12, No. 1.

Johnson P. and **Reed, H.** (1996) Intergenerational Mobility among the Rich and Poor: Results from the National Child Development Survey, *Oxford Review of Economic Policy*, Vol. 12, No. 1.

Machin, S. (1996) Wage Inequality in the UK, *Oxford Review of Economic Policy*, Vol. 12, No. 1.

Middleton, S., Ashworth, K. and **Braithwaite, I.** (1997) *Small Fortunes: Spending on Children, Childhood Poverty and Parental Sacrifice*, Joseph Rowntree Foundation.

OECD (1996) *Technology, Productivity, and Job Creation*, April.

Oppenheim, C. and **Harker, L.** (1996) *Poverty: The Facts*, 3rd edn, Child Poverty Action Group (CPAG).

Pen, J. (1971) *Income Distribution*, Pelican.

Piachaud, D. (1998) The Prospects for Poverty, *New Economy*, March.

Rowntree, S. (1901) *Poverty – A Study of Town Life*, Macmillan.

Ryan, P. (1996) Factor Shares and Inequality in the UK, *Oxford Review of Economic Policy*, Vol. 12, No. 1.

Tzannatos, Z. (1990) Sex Differences in the Labour Market, *Economic Review*, May.

Chapter 15

Trade unions, wages and collective bargaining

This chapter first identifies the main institutions involved in the process of collective bargaining in the UK. The structure and growth of trade unions are then traced, and the role of employers and government examined. A simple 'marginal productivity' model of wage determination is presented, before assessing the degree to which unions can use their 'bargaining power' to modify the predictions of this model. Other factors affecting the wage bargain, such as comparability, work conditions, cost of living, and productivity agreements are considered. The role of government in setting a minimum wage is assessed, as are the likely impacts of the minimum wage. The chapter concludes by examining the impact of collective bargaining on pay differentials, restrictive practices and strike activity.

Types of trade union

A trade union has been described as 'a continuous association of wage-earners for the purpose of maintaining or improving the conditions of their working lives' (Webb and Webb 1896: 1). Although useful, this definition does not reflect the whole range of trade union objectives. The Trades Union Congress (TUC) outlines ten general objectives of unions, with improved wages and terms of employment at the top of the list. Other aims, such as 'full employment', 'industrial democracy' and a 'voice in government' are included, but the emphasis is on the unions' 'capacity to win higher wages through collective bargaining as one of their most effective methods of attracting membership'.[1]

Despite having some objectives in common there is still a considerable amount of diversity between unions in the UK (Table 15.1). Most unions are relatively small. In 1996 some 47% of unions had less than 1,000 members each, but together they accounted for only around 0.5% of total union membership. There has been a progressive reduction in the number of unions, from the peak of 1,384 unions in 1920, to 245 in 1996. The reduction has been particularly marked for small unions. The number of unions with less than 1,000 members has more than halved since 1979. In 1996 the ten largest unions accounted for over 68% of total membership. The trend towards fewer and larger unions, largely as a result of mergers, is well established, but the 245 British unions provide a contrast with the 17 industrial unions in the former West Germany.

Table 15.1 Unions and union membership, 1979 and 1996.

Members	Number of unions		All membership (000s)		Percentage of			
					No. of unions		Membership of all unions	
	1979	1996	1979	1996	1979	1996	1979	1996
Under 100	73	31	4	1	16.0	12.7	0.0	0.0
100–499	124	62	30	21	27.3	25.3	0.2	0.3
500–999	47	21	33	14	10.4	8.6	0.3	0.2
1,000–2,499	58	43	92	72	12.8	17.6	0.7	0.9
2,500–4,999	43	20	152	74	9.5	8.2	1.1	0.9
5,000–9,999	24	14	155	98	5.3	5.7	1.2	1.2
10,000–14,999	7	7	83	92	1.6	2.5	0.6	1.2
15,000–24,999	19	6	358	104	4.2	2.4	2.7	1.3
25,000–49,999	17	19	623	665	3.7	7.8	4.7	8.4
50,000–99,999	15	5	919	314	3.3	2.0	6.9	4.0
100,000–249,999	16	8	2,350	1,210	3.5	3.3	17.7	15.2
250,000 and more	11	9	8,490	5,271	2.4	3.9	63.9	66.4
All members	454	245	13,289	7,935	100.0	100.0	100.0	100.0

Source: Adapted from *Labour Market Trends* (1998) July.

Four broad headings have been traditionally used to classify trades unions in the UK, namely craft, general, industrial and 'white-collar' unions.

Craft unions

These were the earliest type of union, and are mainly composed of workers regarded as 'qualified' in a particular craft. Most craft unions now include workers with the same skill across the industry or industries in which they are employed, such as the Associated Society of Locomotive Engineers and Firemen (ASLEF). Another contemporary example is the Graphical, Paper and Media Union.

General unions

These unions originated in the 1880s in the attempt to organize semi- and unskilled workers not covered by the craft unions. General unions do not restrict their membership to workers with specific skills, or to particular industries or occupations. Examples include the Transport and General Workers' Union (TGWU) with 884,669 members and the GMB with 718,139 members.

The distinction between craft and general unions is not always clear. Over the last few years, this problem has been complicated by the growth of merger activity in the trade union movement. For example, in May 1992 the Amalgamated Engineering Union (AEU) merged with the Electrical, Electronic, Telecommunications and Plumbing Union (EETPU) to form the Amalgamated Engineering and Electrical Union (AEEU). The new union included occupations within the engineering and electrical sectors, which can be classified as 'craft' type occupations, as well as a variety of semi- and unskilled machine operators who could legitimately be placed in the 'general union' category.

Industrial unions

These attempt to place under one union all the workers in an industry, whatever their status of occupation. The National Union of Mineworkers (NUM) comes closest to this in the UK, covering most of the occupations engaged in mining operations, though now much reduced in size. Other examples of industrial unions include the Iron and Steel Trades Confederation (ISTC) and the Communication Workers Union. Most industrial unions in the UK are 'a matter of degree rather than kind'. In other words, they usually cover a large number of those engaged in the industry, but by no means all.

'White-collar' unions These restrict their membership to professional, administrative and clerical employees. 'White-collar' unions have expanded faster than any other type of union in the post-war period. Large numbers of professions are now organized as unions, such as the National Union of Teachers (NUT) with 271,299 members. The supervisory and managerial grades in industry have become more highly unionized with Manufacturing, Science and Finance (MSF) having 425,103 members.

As in the case of general and craft trade unions, the distinction between white-collar and manual unions is also becoming clouded by merger. This was exemplified in July 1993 by the formation of UNISON as a result of an amalgamation of the white collar National and Local Government Officers' Association (NALGO) with the two primarily manual workers unions, the National Union of Public Employees (NUPE) and the Confederation of Health Service Employees (COHSE). In fact, the overwhelming majority of unions now have features taken from more than one category of union, suggesting the need for new and alternative classifications. For example, some unions may now be more usefully classified as either 'closed' or 'open'. They may be said to be 'closed', in that they restrict membership to a clearly definable trade or profession such as the British Airline Pilots' Association (BALPA), or to a particular industry as with the National Union of Mineworkers (NUM). In contrast, 'open' unions seek to recruit a diverse membership, such as the large general unions, thereby making them less susceptible to decline as particular industries ebb and flow.

Table 15.2 The top ten largest TUC unions, 1996.

Rank	Name	Membership
1.	UNISON°	1,374,583
2.	Transport and General Workers' Union (TGWU)	884,669
3.	Amalgamated Engineering and Electrical Union (AEEU)	725,097
4.	GMB*	718,139
5.	Manufacturing, Science and Finance (MSF)	425,103
6.	Union of Shop, Distributive and Allied Workers (USDAW)	290,170
7.	Communication Workers Union△ (CWU)	274,820
8.	National Union of Teachers (NUT)	271,299
9.	National Association of School Masters and Union of Women Teachers (NASUWT)	238,472
10.	Graphical, Paper and Media Union (GPMU)	209,900

Notes:
*GMB is the formal designation of the Boilermaker and Allied Trades Union (composed of seven sections which cover both blue and white collar workers).
°UNISON was formed in July 1993 and is composed of the three main public sector unions, NALGO, NUPE and COHSE.
△This union was formed in 1995 as a result of a merger between the National Communications Union and the Union of Communications Workers.
Source: Adapted from Annual Report of the Certification Officer (1997).

It is difficult to provide an accurate pattern of trade union membership by *industry*, as over 4 million members belong to unions recruiting over several industries. The fact that the UK does not have just a few industrial unions as in West Germany, or enterprise unions as in Japan, poses problems not only for classification but also for collective bargaining. The 'multi-union' structure of the UK means that many unions are involved in negotiations at both plant and enterprise levels. This can cause problems for both management and unions. Management may experience difficulties in co-ordinating negotiations with several different unions, often in the same plant. Unions may have to compromise individual aims and policies when part of a 'team' negotiating with employers. Multi-union plants or enterprises may also lead to inter-union rivalry and conflict. For instance, the Rail and Maritime Transport union (RMT) and ASLEF compete for membership among London Underground employees. There is also rivalry among the teaching unions in both schools and university sectors for membership. In part, this has led to the negotiation of single-union deals by many companies establishing new plants in the last decade. The AEU and EEPTU have been at the forefront of unions in concluding such agreements, leading to their eventual merger in May 1992. In the public sector, the desire on the part of trade unions to combat the increasing decentralization of pay bargaining also led to merger between NALGO, NUPE and COHSE (Confederation of Health Service Employees) to form UNISON in July 1993. These trends, if continued, will also lead to more simplified bargaining structures, since there will be fewer unions for management to deal with at the plant level.

The Trades Union Congress

The TUC was founded in 1868 with the aim of improving the economic and social conditions of working people, and of promoting the interests of its affiliated organizations. In 1996 there were 68 affiliated trade unions representing over 82% of trade unionists in the UK. The TUC is mainly concerned with general questions which affect trade unions both nationally and internationally, and has participated in discussions relating to the national economy through its membership of the National Economic Development Office (NEDO), although the government's abolition of NEDO in 1992 has removed a major residual channel of communication. The General Council of the TUC represents the organization in the period between one annual Congress and another and is responsible for putting Congress decisions into effect. The General Council has no authority to call strikes, or to stop strikes called by its members, but can offer advice on disputes. Under Rule 11 the General Council can intervene in unofficial strikes and make recommendations to the unions and employers concerned.

In 1994, the TUC's structure was modified after criticisms that the institution was spending too much time on administration and on the servicing of committees, thus often failing to clearly identify union priorities. For example, the eight main committees which used to report to the General Council were replaced by one 'executive committee' which meets monthly. Also, General Council meetings were decreased from twelve to seven per year. To provide greater focus to the work of the TUC, 'task groups' were introduced to deal with specific problems which needed to be resolved within a given time remit. The aims of these changes and others were to make the TUC more effective and outward looking during a difficult period for the labour movement.

Trade unions and change

Until 1980 the fall in employment, and therefore the number unionized, in the primary and secondary industries was more than compensated for by the rise in employment, and so the number unionized, in the service industries. Since 1980 this trend has been broken (see Table 15.3) and with it the sustained growth in trade union membership over the post-war period. In fact, membership fell substantially by 40.2% between 1979 and 1996, with union density declining from a peak of 54.5% in 1979 to 31.7% in 1996. A breakdown of membership by sex reveals that of the 8 million or so union members in 1996, 41.6% were women, giving a density of around 28% compared to a density of 32% for men.

Factors affecting union growth and decline   Explanations of the factors which affect union membership (and in particular the decline in the density figure since its peak in 1979) can be grouped under *three* broad headings.

1. Labour force composition   This set of explanations highlights the role of changes in the *compositions of the workforce* as a factor affecting the decline in union density. The argument being that the composition of employment has moved away from the industries, occupations and regions where union density was relatively high, and towards those industries, occupations and regions where union density tends to be relatively low.

For example, union membership differs *by sector*. In the public sector, national government (65%) and local government (72%) tend to have high union densities. These figures remain above the average for manufacturing (30%). As far as *occupations* are concerned, union density is high for employees such as teachers (82%) and for the skilled engineering trades (57%), but low for secretarial (21%) and various sales occupations (16%). In terms of *employment status* (i.e. whether a person is full-time or part-time, self-employed or a trainee), the statistics show that union density is much higher for full-time workers (35%) than for part-time workers (21%)

Table 15.3 Trade union membership and density in the UK, 1979–96 (000's and %).

Year	Civilian employees in employment	Unemployed	Potential trade union membership	Trade union membership	Density* (%)
1979	23,173	1,295	24,368	13,289	54.5
1981	21,892	2,520	24,412	12,106	49.6
1983	21,067	3,104	24,171	11,236	46.5
1985	21,423	3,271	24,694	10,821	43.8
1987	21,584	2,953	24,537	10,475	42.7
1989	23,661	1,799	25,460	10,238	40.2
1990	22,918	1,665	24,583	9,947	40.5
1992	21,853	2,779	24,632	9,048	36.7
1994	21,967	2,796	24,763	8,278	33.4
1996	22,623	2,388	25,011	7,935	31.7

*Union density defined as: $\dfrac{\text{Actual union membership}}{\text{Potential union membership}} \times 100$

Sources: Labour Market Trends (1998) July, and previous issues.

or for full-time self-employed (10%). It also seems that the *size of workplace* is an important factor. For example, the average union density in workplaces employing 25 or more employees is 36%, while that for workplaces employing less than 25 employees is only 16%. *Gender* is also a factor, with union density higher for males (32%) than for females (28%) and increasing with age and length of service for both males and females. Finally, union density is affected by *region*, being highest in Wales (43%) and lowest in the South East (outside London) (21%). Given these figures, it is obvious that the recent changes in the structure of the working population (see Chapter 1, Table 1.4) have had an adverse effect on union density.

The privatisation of much of the public sector; the loss of engineering and related jobs via de-industrialisation; the sharp increase in the number of self-employed and part-time workers; the growth in the number of small companies; the growth of female participation in the labour force, are just some of the changes which have tended to decrease union density. The deindustrialisation process has also decreased employment in some of the highly unionised sectors such as coalmining, shipbuilding and textiles which were traditionally based in the North, while the relatively low unionised service sector grew rapidly in the South. An empirical assessment of the importance of *compositional changes in the workforce* on unionisation (Green 1992) showed that this factor could account for about 30% of the fall in union density between 1983 and 1989. Although this is a very significant factor, other explanations for the decline in union density must also be sought.

2. Macroeconomic factors   *Macroeconomic factors* such as economic growth, unemployment, as well as movements in prices and wages, also have an effect on union membership and density.

Unemployment has obviously had a significant negative impact on union growth. Historically the major upswings in trade union membership have occurred in periods when unemployment has been relatively low or falling – for instance, 1901–20 and 1934–47. A study by Bain and Elsheikh (1982) found that in fifteen of the nineteen industries studied during the inter-war and post-war years, slow growth of unionization was correlated with periods of high unemployment, and vice versa. The Bain–Elsheikh model suggests that relatively high unemployment will reduce union bargaining power, and therefore discourage union membership.

This conclusion is also supported by a survey which investigated the effects of the 1990–93 recession on TU membership (Geroski *et al.* 1995). That recession was shown to cause a still more rapid decline in Trade Union membership than might otherwise have been predicted.

However, some have suggested that the *threat* of unemployment may even act as a *stimulus* to union growth. Hawkins (1981) sees this as one factor in raising union density amongst white-collar workers threatened by technological and organizational change during the 1970s. Technology is something of a two-edged sword for unions; on the one hand it may create unemployment, whilst on the other it often confers substantial industrial 'muscle' on the few key workers operating the new computer-based systems.

Price and Bain (1976) suggest that the *rate of change of prices* and *the rate of change of wages* may also influence union growth. Rising prices have a 'threat' effect so that workers unionize to defend real wages, particularly in the early years of an inflationary period. Wage rises have a 'credit' effect for unions, in that they are attributed to their bargaining power, and this promotes membership. Bain and Elsheikh (1982) found that the real wage variable, in one form or another, had a significant and positive impact on union growth in fifteen of the nineteen industries studied. Also the desire to protect established *pay relativities* may affect union growth. For example, in advanced stages of incomes policies, when pay differentials have been substantially eroded, there is evidence that union membership increases. The suggestion here is that a series of injustices leads workers to seek greater bargaining power by joining unions in the hope of restoring differentials.

The rapid decline of both union membership and density in the 1980s and early 1990s suggests that macroeconomic factors may be having a negative influence on union growth. Some of the macroeconomic factors also appear to have different effects on union density than those shown by some of the earlier studies quoted above. For example, Carruth and Disney (1987) tried to capture the effects of the main macroeconomic factors on union density by separating out the changes in union membership into two components; a 'trend' component influenced by changes in total employment, and a 'cycle' component which varies with macroeconomic variables such as wages, prices and unemployment. They note that when unemployment and real wage growth are high relative to the trend, membership growth is depressed. The 'threat' and 'credit effect' noted in earlier studies seem to have become much less effective. Interestingly, a more recent study of the 1988–90 period (Metcalf 1994) noticed that the reverse relationship did not seem to hold; i.e. falling unemployment and slower real wages did *not* seem to halt the fall in union density. This may suggest that union density may be experiencing a long term, secular decline rather than being only affected by short run cyclical changes in macroeconomic variables.

3. Industrial relations environment   This set of reasons relates to the influence on union membership and density of such factors as government and employer policies, and the trade unions' own responses to such policies.

Carruth and Disney (1987) found that, in a historical context, *Conservative governments* have tended to exercise a negative impact on membership rates. Freeman and Pelletier (1990) and Minford and Riley (1994) also accord a strong negative impact on membership rates of the post-1979 legislative programme of the UK Conservative governments. Although it is difficult to be precise there is little doubt that the post-1979 legislative reforms significantly weakened the position of trade unions. To these legislative reforms should be added the effects of government supply side policies, with their emphasis on privatisation and cost savings. For example, the total number of public sector employees decreased from just over 7m in 1979 to 5m in 1995 – a fall of 29%. Central government employment fell by 29%, local government employment fell by 9% and employment in the public corporations fell by 21%, over the same period. Given that the density of unionisation is higher in the public sector than the private sector, it is hardly surprising that the government's economic policies have been directly associated with a decline in union density.

Changes in the *attitudes of employers* have also affected union membership over the last fifteen years. For example, the incidence of companies refusing to recognise unions has increased. 'De-recognition' refers to the complete withdrawal of a trade union's rights to negotiate pay on behalf of its members, although they may be represented for consultation purposes or during grievance and disciplinary hearings.

De-recognition was a feature of several heavily publicised disputes in the 1980s, notably News International's de-recognition of the print unions, P&O's of the seafarers union and the government's decision that union membership was incompatible with national security at Government Communications Headquarters (GCHQ). Although these were far from being typical instances, they did serve to indicate a change in management power and the declining attractiveness of union membership in such circumstances.

Decreases in union recognition appear to have continued into the 1990s. Research covering some 500 predominantly large firms over the 1990–93 recession showed that the decrease in union recognition was particularly significant in relatively smaller single-plant firms with annual sales of less than £50m (Geroski *et al*. 1995). A major survey carried out by the DTI in 1998 (Workplace Employee Relations Survey) found that the percentage of total workplaces recognizing trade unions had fallen from 66% in 1984 to 45% by 1997. This trend set the scene for the Labour government's White Paper 'Fairness at Work' which proposed a statutory right to union recognition for bargaining purposes in companies with more than 25 employees. This statutory right to union recognition would come into effect where an employer and trade union fail to agree on union recognition and where a majority of employees vote in a ballot in support of such recognition.

The employers

Employers' associations

Many employers in the UK are members of employers' associations which seek to regulate relations between employers and trade unions. These associations are usually organized on an industry basis rather than a product basis, as with the Engineering Employers' Federation with over 4,800 members. Their role includes negotiating with unions at industry level, the operation of procedures for the resolution of disputes, and the provision of advice to members on employment law, manpower planning and other personnel matters. In some industries there are local or regional employers' associations, combined into national federations, as with the Building Employers' Confederation. Altogether there are about 150 national employers' associations which negotiate the national collective agreements for their industry with the trade unions concerned, and most of these belong to the Confederation of British Industry (CBI). Table 15.4 presents the ten largest employers' associations.

Membership of employers' associations has tended to fall over the past fifteen years as the trend towards company bargaining has gained ground. Large companies, such as the car manufacturers, BP, ICI, and Shell, prefer to bargain on a company basis with unions rather than be part of a multi-employer bargaining team.

The Confederation of British Industry

This is the largest central employers' organization in the UK, representing over 12,000 companies which employ around 10 million people. Membership includes all sizes and types of company, both private and nationalized, and covers the primary, secondary and tertiary sectors of industry, although manufacturing predominates. Policy is determined by a council of 330 members, and there are 360 permanent staff members, including representatives with the EU in Brussels. The CBI seeks to represent the broad interests of businessmen in discussions with the government,

Table 15.4 The top ten employers' associations (in rank order of subscription income) 1996.

Rank	Name	Membership
1.	National Farmers' Union	121,454
2.	Engineering Employers' Federation*	4,884
3.	National Federation of Retail Newsagents	25,285
4.	Chemical Industries Association Ltd	179
5.	British Printing Industries Federation	3,078
6.	Newspaper Society	235
7.	Retail Motor Industry Federation Ltd	12,270
8.	Freight Transport Association Ltd	11,639
9.	Federation of Master Builders	15,238
10.	National Pharmaceutical Association Ltd	5,970

*Figure includes the EEF and 13 other separate associations in the engineering industry.
Source: Adapted from Annual Report of the Certification Officer (1997) Appendix 5.

with national and international institutions, and with the public at large. It nominates the employers' representatives for such bodies as the Advisory, Conciliation and Arbitration Service (ACAS).

Individual employers

Over the last decade the influence of management has increased as the pressures of unemployment and international competition shifted power away from unions and towards management. Recent management initiatives to increase employee flexibility, to improve quality, and to introduce more performance related pay, have begun to create a 'cultural change' within individual workplaces. One such change has been the issue of trade union recognition within the company.

The most difficult aspect of collective bargaining in the UK is the fact that workers of a given company often belong to different unions, i.e. multi-union companies. As a result, management often have to negotiate with each union separately. The changing competitive environment mentioned above has begun to cause a shift in the locus of power away from employers' association bargaining with unions and towards individual company bargaining. This shift in power has often resulted in company management attempting to limit bargaining rights to a single trade union within the workplace i.e. '*single unionism*'. The advantage to management of such arrangements is that it simplifies the bargaining process and prevents conflict over demarcations between different skill groups represented by different trade unions within the same enterprise. However only around 200 single union agreements have as yet been concluded; for example BICC Cables, Ikeda, Hoover, Bosch, Venture Pressings, together with those for several Japanese companies such as Nissan, Matsushita and Toshiba. Despite the relatively small number, it may be a guide to the future trends in union-management bargaining.

Another approach to collective bargaining has been the rise of '*single table bargaining*' which means that, unlike 'single unionism', more than one union is allowed to exist within the company but they have to bargain jointly as a single unit with management rather than separately. These arrangements are supported by the TUC and by individual unions as preferable to single union deals. Examples are to be found in engineering, the privatised water companies and in car manufacturing, e.g. Rover. Both single union and single table bargaining have tended to reflect a shift in power within the workplace, namely towards management and away from unions.

In addition to the issues of union representation, management have been involved in trying to increase employee flexibility by '*multi-skilling*', i.e. by widening the skills of each worker (functional flexibility) and by varying the hours worked or employing more part-time or sub-contracted workers rather than full-time workers (numerical flexibility). This trend has threatened union bargaining power since part-time or sub-contracted workers have a lower union density, as noted earlier in this chapter. Multi-skilling also tends to restrict the ability of shop stewards to negotiate such subjects as manning levels, job demarcations and the pace of work. Similarly the growth of performance related pay (PRP), by linking reward to actual performance, has weakened the trade unions because part or all of the annual pay award is no longer subject to collective bargaining.

Finally it is worth noting that the growth of quality consciousness in UK industry has enhanced the importance of *teamwork*. The introduction of such devices as quality circles, where groups of around ten workers meet to discuss their work and suggest improvements, has increased employee involvement in the firm. The large-scale survey of workplace practices by the DTI in 1998 showed that many 'new' management practices had been introduced to create more employee commitment. Such practices included teamwork activity, team briefings and also performance appraisal meetings in which staff were invited to participate in setting targets and goals. The net effect of these increased attempts by management to involve employees has been to circumvent or marginalise unions while retaining union recognition, leaving the future of 'collective' (i.e. union) representation of the workforce rather unclear.

The government

The government's role in industrial relations is threefold: as an employer, as a legislator and as an economic and social policy-maker.

The government is a major direct *employer of labour*, with central government employing 1.1 million persons, or 4% of the workforce in 1997. It influences not only these pay settlements but also those of the local authorities and the remaining nationalized industries, in total an extra 4.1 million persons. The government can, through its position as a primary source of finance, and by using cash limits (see Chapter 8), affect wage bargaining and employment levels in the local authorities and the nationalized industries.

As a *legislator*, the previous Conservative administration was particularly active, and made extensive use of the law in an effort to reduce what it perceived as excessive union bargaining power, resulting in high UK wage cost and low labour productivity. An examination of the major legal changes introduced since 1979, mainly in the 1980, 1982, 1988, 1989 and 1990 Employment Acts, and in the 1984 Trade Union Act, reveals important changes in the context of collective bargaining. The previous Conservative government consolidated its 'step by step' reforms with the passing of the Trade Union and Labour Relations (Consolidation) Act 1992 (TULR(C)A) as amended by the Trade Union Reform and Employment Rights Act 1993. The former Act was a measure designed to rationalise all previous relevant statutory provisions into a *single act* rather than to change the substance of the law. The latter Act aimed to modify some sections of the 1992 Act by enhancing the rights of individual employees and union members while also imposing certain regulations relating to industrial action. The incoming Labour government has pledged to retain most of these legal reforms, and indeed to introduce important new statutes (e.g. setting a national minimum wage), as will be discussed later in this chapter.

The closed shop   This is a situation where employees only obtain or retain a job if they become a member of a specified trade union. Its advantages to unions *and* management are discussed below. This practice was progressively weakened by legislation in the 1980s and 1990s making unions liable to legal action from both employees and management if they tried to enforce the closed shop. The relevant legislation which deals with this aspect is contained in Part III of TULR(C)A. A sample study of 529 firms in the mid-1990s found that only 9% of firms still had formal closed-shop arrangements (Geroski *et al.* 1995). However, two important studies (Wright 1996, and Addison and Siebert 1998) have shown that while formal union arrangements such as the closed shop may have collapsed among white-collar workers, manual workers and other groups have still retained informal methods of maintaining a closed shop, as in the case of closed-shop arrangements *agreed* between managers and labour.

Strikes and other industrial action   Since the end of the last century it has been impossible for a trade union to organize a strike without committing a *tort*, that is the civil wrong of interfering with the contract of employment between employer and employed. The committing of a tort enables the employer to obtain an injunction against, or claim damages from, the union. However, since 1906 Parliament has protected unions from this liability by providing them with immunity from civil action and a major aim of the post-1979 legislation has been to narrow the scope of this immunity by rendering certain types of dispute 'unlawful'.

Industrial action is unlawful when the union is no longer covered by immunity from civil actions brought by employers or other affected parties in the courts. If successful, the employer will obtain a court injunction prohibiting the dispute, and the union will face fines or the sequestration of its assets for failure to comply. An employer can also subsequently claim damages arising from losses sustained during the action.

An important provision in the 1982 Employment Act restricted 'lawful trade disputes' to those between workers and their own employer, making 'political' strikes and inter-union disputes unlawful (s. 219). Also rendered unlawful by the 1980 Employment Act was secondary action, i.e. action against an employer not party to a dispute (s. 224). Picketing is now almost wholly restricted in law to the union members' 'place of work', often even excluding another plant of the same employer. Restrictions on illegal picketing are effected by making unions liable to pay damages in civil actions brought against them by employers. The 1984 Act also meant loss of legal immunity in certain circumstances. Official industrial action, i.e. that approved by the union leadership, must be sanctioned by a secret ballot of the membership. The ballot must be held no more than four weeks before the event, and a majority of union members must be in favour of the action. If the action takes place without majority consent, then the union loses any legal immunity for organizing industrial action that it may have enjoyed in the past. These provisions were strengthened by the 1988 Employment Act which gave the individual union member the right not to be called out on strike without a properly held secret ballot and, most controversially, in view of the stated opposition of both the CBI and the Institute of Personnel and Development, the right not to be disciplined by his or her union for refusing to strike or for crossing a picket line. The Act also established a Commissioner for the Rights of Trade Union Members to provide funds and advice to individuals wishing to take legal action to exercise these rights (s. 62).

The 1990 Employment Act took the control of union behaviour even further by requiring that the union leadership must take positive steps to repudiate 'unofficial action', i.e. actions undertaken by union members without union consent (that is of the executive committee or president or general secretary). For instance, the union must do its best to give written notice to all members participating in the action that it does *not* receive the union's support. Failure by the union to take such steps could mean loss of immunity for the union, even though the action is unofficial. In addition, the Act allowed employers to dismiss unofficial strikers selectively at the place of work (e.g. the strike leaders) and deny those dismissed the right to claim unfair dismissal. Any industrial action because of such dismissal would now be deprived of immunity (s. 223).

The Trade Union Reform and Employment Rights Act 1993 passed three main provisions relating to the organization of industrial action. First, ballots held in support of action should be fully postal and subject to independent scrutiny, effectively restricting the initiation of action at 'rank-and-file' level. Second, unions are to be required to give seven days written notice before industrial action can be taken. This affords a longer waiting period to help settle any dispute. The unions argue, however, that it also gives employers rather longer to prepare for any dispute. Third, it created a new 'Citizen's Right' to restrain unlawfully organized industrial action which deprives a citizen of goods and services. This means that members of the public have the right to take legal action against unions who are involved in 'unlawful actions', e.g. those who have not had a properly conducted secret ballot, etc. An independent Commissioner may, on application, grant financial assistance to an individual who is deemed to merit such help.

Legal regulation of wages and conditions of work   Many legal regulations which had originally been designed to place a 'floor' on both wages and conditions of work were dismantled after 1979 by successive Conservative governments in order to remove alleged disincentives to employment and to help increase labour flexibility. For example, the abolition of the Wages Councils in 1993 took away minimum-wage guarantees for low-paid workers in the industries for which these Wages Councils existed. In addition, the UK also 'opted out' of the 'Agreement on Social Policy' contained in the Social Protocol of the Maastricht Treaty – commonly known as the Social Chapter. This absolved the UK government from the need to implement certain EU Directives regulating employer/employee relations.

Although also committed to workforce flexibility, the incoming Labour government has tended to reverse some of this earlier legislation. First, it has established the Low Pay Commission to make recommendations for a *National Minimum Wage* (NMW), subsequently accepting the proposal that the adult rate should be £3.60 per hour from April 1999, with a lower 'development rate' of £3.20 per hour for 18–21-year-olds. Those who are likely to benefit most will be female part-time workers, unskilled manual workers, and those employed in labour-intensive service sector industries. Second, the government has made it a statutory right that employees should be represented in disciplinary proceedings, and has promised to initiate other policy changes, such as preventing the blacklisting of trade union members and improving the rights of workers on 'zero hours' contracts, i.e. where workers have no guaranteed paid hours.

Trade union democracy   The Trade Union Act 1984 and Employment Act 1988 embodied a number of provisions for internal union democracy in addition to those pertaining to strike action. Members of the main executive committee of a trade union must have been elected in a secret ballot of the union's members within the previous five years. The Employment Act of 1990 contained the right of members to a postal vote in elections for all members of union governing bodies and for key national leaders. In addition, the 1984 Act required trade unions with political funds to ballot their members at least every ten years. Only if this is done, and majority assent for the fund achieved, can the union continue to spend money on 'political' matters, such as a campaign against new legislation or in support of a political party. To date, of all ballots which have been held on this matter, a substantial majority have been in favour of retaining the fund.

The Trade Union Reform and Employment Rights Act 1993 modified some sections of the TULR(C)A by taking the issue of democracy further. Firstly, it strengthened the rights of *individuals* by giving them greater feedom to belong to the union of their choice. For example, an individual could belong to more than one union and unions could not dismiss a member for failing to support a strike. This had obvious implications for relationships between unions and their members. Secondly, it also gave *trade union members* the right not to have union subscriptions deducted from their pay except with their written consent. The latter 'check off' arrangements were seen as threatening union membership levels and were repealed in 1998 by the Labour government.

In its legislative capacity therefore, the government can alter the balance of power between employer and employee. However, it is difficult to assess how far any legislation can be effectively used by employers, as this depends upon a complex array of factors, such as management style, the firm's size and position within both product and labour markets, the availability of alternative tactics and the anticipated repercussions of recourse to law on a firm's industrial relations.

The European Union and UK Industrial Relations

The European Union is discussed more fully in Chapter 28, but the current proposals of the European Commission are of potentially great significance to the UK. The most important measures are contained in the *European Social Charter* and the accompanying 'Action Programme' for its implementation. The Charter contains provisions relating to both the individual and collective rights of workers, but it is important to recognize that it is a statement of *principles* or intent and that by itself it creates no legally enforceable rights. However, the Commission plans to give legal form to the Charter's contents over the next few years, which at present enjoy majority support in the Council of Ministers.

Only a brief outline of the Charter can be given here, but measures pertaining to individual employee rights include greater freedom of movement within the Community; the right to training; protection regarding health and safety and against discrimination; provisions to safeguard the employment conditions of the young, disabled and elderly, and employees at large; minimum rules on work duration, rest periods and holidays, shift work and systematic overtime. Broadly similar rights are to be extended to part-time, casual and temporary workers. The Charter excludes a commitment to minimum wage legislation. Measures relating to collective labour law are more limited, and the Charter does not propose any legally enforceable right to bargain for trade unions where this is not already part of a member state's law.

However, the Charter does include important prospective rights to information and consultation plus the 'participation' of employees before companies make decisions on redundancies and closures.

EU Social Chapter

In 1997 the Labour government reversed the UK's 'opt out' from the Social Protocol of the Maastricht Treaty, commonly known as the Social Chapter. The UK was now able to adopt various EU Directives already in force in other member countries. For example the *Working Time Directive* was implemented in the UK in October 1998 and contained provisions for a legal right to paid holidays, an upper limit to the working week of 48 hours (averaged over 17 weeks), together with various other entitlements such as rights to rest periods, etc. Two other EU Directives were implemented in the UK in 1999. The *Parent Leave Directive* gave employees with at least one year's service a basic right to a period of three months' unpaid leave after the birth or adoption of a child, whilst the *Part-time Workers' Directive* established the principle of equal treatment for part-time and full-time employees, giving pro rata benefits to part-time employees for pay, holidays, etc.

The structure of collective bargaining

Collective bargaining has been defined by Clegg as referring to 'the whole range of dealings between employers and managers on the one hand, and trade unions, shop stewards and members on the other, over the making, interpretation and administration of employment rules'. These rules are both *substantive*, determining pay, hours, overtime, manning levels, holidays, etc., and *procedural*, governing the way in which substantive issues are settled. One of the most significant changes which has taken place in UK industrial relations over the last fifteen years has been the decrease in the percentage of employees covered by collective bargaining agreements. For example, between 1984 and 1998, the percentage of total employees covered by collective bargaining arrangements had fallen from 71% to 36%. The effects of decreased union density, the legal changes introduced by government, the privatization movement, and the increased power of management, all contributed towards this downward trend. Despite this radical change, collective bargaining between unions and employers is still of major importance in most of the UK's key sectors, and occurs at a number of levels.

National or multi-employer bargaining

This level of negotiation predominates in the public sector in which centralized bargaining gives rise to relatively formal, fixed-term and comprehensive agreements, leaving little scope for localized or workplace bargaining. However there is now a clear trend towards more decentralized bargaining in the public sector. The 'local management of schools' initiative, together with the creation of semi-autonomous NHS Trusts, necessarily imply further moves towards local bargaining. Moreover, both the privatized water companies and electricity generators have withdrawn from industry-level agreements and decentralization is becoming the norm for the privatized elements of British Rail. Finally, the 'contracting out' to private tender of many services previously supplied by local authorities, clearly reduces the coverage of national bargaining in this sector.

In the private sector national bargaining occurs on an industry level, between employers' associations and trade unions, or federations of unions. This was once the main type of collective bargaining, but has declined in importance in many industries so that by the late 1990s it only covered about 15% of employees in the private sector (e.g. electrical contracting). In fact, industry-wide and multi-employer bargaining has already disappeared from a number of sectors, including the clearing banks, the cable industry, provincial newspapers and independent TV companies.

Single-employer bargaining

This occurs at two levels: (a) *corporate*, i.e. at the level of the company or whole organization; and (b) *establishment*, i.e. at the level of the workplace, such as the factory, plant or office.

A major conclusion of the Donovan Commission in 1968 was that 'informal' workplace bargaining was primarily responsible for wage drift (i.e. the negotiation of bonuses and other wage premiums supplementary to industry rates), restrictive practices and unofficial strikes. Its 'informality' resided in its dependence on tacit, unwritten agreements between managers and shop stewards based on 'custom and practice', causing a fragmented bargaining system independent of corporate management or official trade union control, and often subject to conflict and renegotiation. The Donovan Commission therefore recommended the extension of 'formal' bargaining to the workplace; 'formal' in the sense of written agreements, of specified duration, on clearly delineated issues, in order to promote 'effective and orderly' industrial relations.

After the Donovan Report in 1968 there was a marked rise in formal, corporate-level bargaining. Bargaining at the company level usually integrated and formalized earlier practices at the workplace, with important consequences. First, there was a large increase in the number of full-time shop stewards involved in the negotiation of factory agreements and procedures with senior management. Rather than merely being parties to open-ended arrangements, these stewards were now joint negotiators of formal agreements, and as a result were responsible for their observance by union members. Second, by raising the level of substantive bargaining and incorporating shop stewards within it, the movement towards corporate bargaining reduced the involvement of shopfloor workers and their freedom of action.

However, this shift to company agreements, largely initiated by US-owned multinationals to exert greater control over collective bargaining, has not been universal. In fact, establishment or plant-level bargaining remains important in many industries, such as clothing, and the footwear, brick and timber industries. More significantly, recent changes in managerial practice, which have devolved more responsibility to middle management for running individual establishments as separate budget or profit centres, have enhanced formal plant bargaining at the expense of company-wide negotiation. The growth of multi-product or multi-divisional firms such as Unilever, Philips, Coates Viyella and Lucas are examples of such trends towards division and establishment level bargaining, However, this development has been accompanied by a decline in the range of substantive issues which many managements are prepared to negotiate with unions. Moreover, and of perhaps greater future importance for workplace bargaining, there has been a marked increase in systems of individual assessment and reward, some linked to the profit performance of the company, which could further undermine collective representation. A number of studies on wage bargaining have shown that corporate- or company-level bargaining occurs in around 25% of all the firms studied, and that establishment- or plant-wide bargaining occurs in around 30% of firms (Geroski *et al.* 1995). Bargaining had become more decentralized over time, moving from the multi-employer to the corporate level, and on the other hand from the corporate level to the establishment or plant level. The main reasons cited for the growth of establishment- or plant-level bargaining included better control of profitability levels by taking into consideration local labour market conditions and more ability to reward individual employees according to performance.

In a small number of industries with fragmentary collective bargaining procedures, there were statutory wage-regulating bodies, known as Wages Councils. Although they have now been abolished, it is still important to understand their nature and relevance as they remain the subject of much debate.

Advisory, Conciliation and Arbitration Service (ACAS)   ACAS was established as an independent statutory body on January 1st 1976 and is formally independent of direct ministerial intervention. The agency stemmed from the Department of Employment's Conciliation and Arbitration Service which had often been criticized as not being independent since it was directly under the control of a government minister. Its role is to promote improved industrial relations and to extend collective bargaining procedures. It conciliates in around 1,500 industrial disputes, in both public and private sectors, each year. It also provides, on request, arbitration in around 200 disputes each year, either by appointing single arbitrators or boards of arbitrators.[2] Arbitration by ACAS occurs when both management and employees cannot agree on either the interpretation of an existing written contract (rights issues) or on demands which are arguably outside legal contracts (interest issues). Pay and conditions of employment have comprised 60% of the arbitrations undertaken, followed by dismissal and discipline (22%), issues of employee grading (16%) and redundancy and demarcation (2%) (Mumford 1996).

The service is controlled by a council consisting of an independent chairman and nine others with experience in industrial relations. Three of these are nominated after consultation with the TUC, three after consultation with the CBI, and three are independent.

Wage determination and collective bargaining

The neo-classical view of wage determination is embodied in 'marginal productivity' theory. With many small buyers of labour (firms) and many small suppliers (i.e. non-unionized individuals), the wage rate would be determined by the intersection of demand and supply curves for labour.

The demand curve for any factor, including labour, is seen as being derived from the demand for the product or service it produces. Additional labour will always be required if the revenue gained from selling the output produced by the last person, the marginal revenue product of labour (MRP_L),[3] is greater than the extra cost of employing that person, the marginal cost of labour (MC_L). In a competitive labour market (see Fig. 15.1), the supply of labour (S_L) to each firm would be perfectly elastic at the going wage rate (W_1), so that the wage rate is itself the marginal cost of labour.[4] The profit-maximizing firm would then hire people until MRP_L equalled

Fig. 15.1. Wage determination in a competitive market.

MC_L, i.e. L_1 persons in Fig. 15.1. If more than L_1 persons were hired, then the extra revenue from their hire would fail to match the extra cost incurred.

Under these conditions the MRP_L curve becomes the demand curve for labour (D_L), since at any given wage rate the profit-maximizing firm will employ labour until MRP_L equals that wage rate. For example, if the wage rate falls to W_2 in Fig. 15.1, then demand for labour rises to L_2.

Wages and unions   If the labour force is now unionized, then the supply of labour to the firm (or industry) may be regulated. However, even though unions bring an element of monopoly into labour supply, theory suggests that they can only influence price *or* quantity, but not both. For example, in Fig. 15.1 the union may seek wage rate W_3, but must accept in return lower employment at L_3. Alternatively, unions may seek a level of employment L_2, but must then accept a lower wage rate at W_2. Except (see below) where unions are able to force employers off their demand curve for labour (MRP_L), then unions can only raise wages at the 'cost' of reduced employment. However, a *given rise* in wages will reduce employment by less, under the following circumstances:

1. The less elastic is final demand for the product.
2. The less easy it is to substitute other factors for the workers in question.
3. The lower the proportion of labour costs to total costs of production.

All of these circumstances will make the demand curve for labour, MRP_L, less elastic.

Unions and bargaining power   Unions may seek to force the employer off his demand curve for labour so that he makes less than maximum profits. It may then be possible for wages to rise from W_1 to W_3 with no loss of employment, i.e. point A in Fig. 15.1. How effective unions will be in such strategies will depend upon the extent of their 'bargaining power'.

Chamberlain defines union bargaining power as:

$$\frac{\text{Management costs of disagreeing (to union terms)}}{\text{Management costs of agreeing (to union terms)}}$$

Although this ratio cannot be measured, as it relies on subjective assessments, it is a useful analytical tool. If unions are to exert effective influence on management the ratio must exceed unity. That is to say it must be more costly for management to disagree (e.g. loss of profits, or market share as a result of strike action) than to agree (e.g. higher labour costs and manning levels). The higher the ratio, the more inclined management may then be to agree to the union's terms.

The level of the wage demand will affect union bargaining power. The more modest the wage claim, the lower the management cost of agreement, and the higher Chamberlain's ratio, i.e. the greater is union bargaining power. This will increase the prospects for securing higher wages with stable employment.

Union density will also affect bargaining power. The greater the proportion of the industry unionized, the less easy it will be to substitute non-union labour. The management costs of disagreeing to union terms will tend to be higher, so that the ratio, i.e. union bargaining power, rises. Equally, the higher is union density in the industry as a whole, the easier it is for any particular company to pass on higher wage demands as price increases to consumers without losing market share. This is because competing firms in the industry will also be facing similar wage-cost conditions. High union density therefore reduces the management costs of agreeing to union terms, and again raises the ratio, i.e. union bargaining power. High union density will therefore also increase the prospects for securing higher wages with stable employment.

Even macroeconomic factors can be brought into this analysis. The higher the level of real income in the economy, the higher will be demand for 'normal' goods. Management will then be able to pass on cost increases as higher prices with relatively less effect on demand. This will reduce management costs of agreeing to union terms, raise the ratio, and with it union bargaining power.

Another main factor which affects the bargaining power of trade unions is the degree of competition in the *product market*. For example, Gregg and Machin (1991) found that those unionized firms facing increased competition in the market for their product, experienced slower wage growth than those unionized firms that did not. In other words, increasing competition in the product market tends to *reduce* the bargaining power of unions to raise wages. This seems to indicate that unions are becoming more aware of the potential 'costs' to them in terms of unemployment if they bargain for higher wages when their firm is experiencing intense competition.

However, one must recognize the existence of many other dimensions to union bargaining power, such as the degree of unanimity or conflict within unions over bargaining goals and methods. Unions will also vary in the militancy of their members and the bargaining abilities of their leaders. All this makes the assessment of bargaining power extremely difficult. It is also important to note that the 'resource' theory of the impact of trade unionism on the firm does not accept that the exercise of this power will necessarily raise production costs. Instead, the theory argues that unions can significantly increase productivity by providing an efficient means for the management and settlement of disputes. Thus, collective bargaining reduces the costs of individual expressions of grievances, which may raise the 'quit' rate of key employees and the incidence of absenteeism or poor-quality work. Further, the 'shock' effect of unions' negotiation of pay rises may force managements to increase efficiency in order to absorb higher costs.

Wages and employers' associations

Wages are determined by a variety of factors, of which union bargaining power is but one, admittedly important, element.

Employers' associations are themselves able to create an element of monopoly on the *demand* side of the labour market (i.e. 'monopsony'). These associations bring together the employers of labour in order to exert greater influence in collective bargaining. Standard theory suggests that monopsony in the labour market will, by itself, reduce both wages and employment in the labour market.

In Fig. 15.2, under competitive labour market conditions the equilibrium would occur where the supply of labour ($S_L = AC_L$) equalled the demand for labour (MRP_L) giving wage W_C and employment L_C. If monopsony occurs, so that employers bid the wage rate up against themselves, then it can be shown that the MC_L curve will lie above the $S_L = AC_L$ curve. For example, if by hiring the fourth worker, the wage ($= AC_L$) of all workers is bid up from £5 to £6, then the AC_L for the fourth worker is £6 *but* the MC_L for the fourth worker is higher at £9 (£24 − £15). The profit-maximizing employer will want to equate the extra revenue contributed by the last worker employed (MRP_L) to the extra cost of employing the last worker (MC_L). In Fig. 15.2 this occurs with L_1 workers employed. Note however that the employer only has to offer a wage of W_1 in order to get L_1 workers to supply themselves to the labour market. The wage W_1 is *below* the competitive wage W_C and the level of employment L_1 is *below* the competitive level of employment L_C. This is the standard case against monopsony in a labour market, namely lower wages and lower employment as compared to a competitive labour market.

When monopoly on the demand side (employers' associations) is combined with monopoly on the supply side (trade unions), the wage and employment outcome becomes indeterminate.[5]

The existence of employers' associations will clearly affect the strength of union bargaining power. The greater the density of their coverage within an industry the smaller might be the management costs of disagreement, e.g. in the case of a strike there is less likelihood of other domestic firms capturing their markets. By reducing the numerator of the ratio, union bargaining power is reduced.

Fig. 15.2. Wage determination with monopsony in the labour market.

Wages and government: the National Minimum Wage

As already noted, the Low Pay Commission has recommended a National Minimum Wage (NMW) of £3.60 per hour from April 1999, with a lower 'development ratio' of £3.20 for 18–21-year-olds. There has been much controversy over the level at which the NMW should be set. The Unions had pushed for a rate considerably above £4.00 per hour, though the Low Pay Commission eventually recommended a lower rate.

Figure 15.3 illustrates the problem of setting too high a minimum wage. If the NMW is set above the competitive wage (W_C) for any labour market, then there will be an excess supply of labour of $L' - L^*$, with more people supplying themselves to work in this labour market than there are jobs available. In Fig. 15.3 the actual level of employment falls from L_C to L^*.

However, there have been a number of studies suggesting that in the US, a higher minimum wage has actually increased wages *and* employment (Atkinson 1996). But it has been noted that many of the US studies have involved labour markets (e.g. fast food) which are dominated by a few large employers of labour, i.e. *monopsonistic* labour markets.

In fact our earlier analysis of monopsony might have led us to expect this. For example, if in Fig. 15.4 the initial monopsony equilibrium was wage W_1 and employment L_1, then setting a minimum wage of W^* would result in a rise in both wages (W_1 to W^*) and employment (L_1 to L^*). Since no labour is supplied below the minimum wage W^* this is the *effective labour supply curve* at W^* ($W^* = AC_L = MC_L$). The profit-maximizing situation is at point 'A' on the MRP_L curve, where the marginal cost of hiring the last person (MC_L) exactly equals the extra revenue resulting from employing that last person (MRP_L). So imposing a minimum wage on a labour market that is already imperfect (here monopsony) can increase both wages and levels of employment.

Wages and other factors

Wages can also be influenced by institutional practices which bear little relation to market conditions.

'Spillover' and comparability The 'spillover' hypothesis argues that wage settlements for one group of workers are transmitted ('spillover') to other groups through the principle of comparability, irrespective of product and labour market conditions. For example, the pay awards achieved by 'wage leaders' often give rise to a

Fig. 15.3. Minimum wage (W^*) set above the competitive market wage (W_C).

Fig. 15.4. Minimum
wage (W*) raising both
wages and employment
with monopsony in the
labour market.

Fig. 15.4. Minimum wage (W*) raising both wages and employment with monopsony in the labour market.

sequence of similar settlements in the same 'wage round' for other workers. Settlements at Ford and in the coal industry have been regarded as important targets for pay settlements in the private and public sectors respectively. The 'going rate' established by powerful trade unions becomes a 'virility symbol for those who follow' (Taylor 1989), a bench-mark against which the performance of union leaders will be measured.

Non-pecuniary advantages or disadvantages   Not all jobs have the same conditions of work. Some are hazardous, dirty, boring, require the working of unsocial hours, or receive various perquisites ('perks'). These will inevitably form part of the collective bargain, and ultimately affect the wage outcome. In some circumstances wage demands may be modified as the union places greater emphasis on non-wage factors.

Cost of living   The cost of living is an important factor in determining the wage claim, and has even been a formal part of wage settlements. In the early 1970s, as part of the Heath government's incomes policy, cost-of-living rises beyond a certain 'threshold' would trigger additional payments to employees. Daniel (1976) found that the increase in the cost of living since the previous pay rise was by far the most important consideration for the claims of union officers in all circumstances. When inflation is accelerating, unions become still more preoccupied with securing cost-of-living increases. This can trigger off a wage-price spiral when unions overestimate future rates of inflation.

Productivity agreements   Part of the wage bargain may include the abandonment of restrictive practices, and the raising of production in return for higher wages. During the 1960s a whole series of formalized productivity agreements were concluded. The first and most celebrated of these was negotiated between Esso and the unions at the oil refinery at Fawley. A whole range of restrictive practices, including demarcation rules, excessive overtime, and time-wasting, were 'bought out' by management for higher wages. A similar agreement was signed between the British Oxygen Company and the unions covering 4,000 workers in 50 plants. Most of these productivity agreements were negotiated at plant level. In a rather less formal way it soon became accepted practice for shop stewards to 'trade' small concessions on work practices for higher wage increases.

The effects of collective bargaining

The process of collective bargaining has had a number of important effects on the UK labour market.

Pay differentials

A number of studies have suggested a significant pay differential between unionized and non-unionized workers. During the 1980s studies by economists such as Nickell and Andrews placed this differential as high as 20% in favour of unionized workers, though studies in the 1990s by Metcalf (1994) suggested a lower figure of around 10%. The more recent research of Blanchflower (1996) also suggests a pay differential of around 10% between unionized and non-unionized workers. The evidence also suggests that such differentials have decreased over time and that they depend, in part, on the degree of union density across sectors; the greater the union density, the greater the pay differential (Addison and Siebert 1998).

However, the nature of the pay differential observed between union and non-union labour may be due to more than simply collective bargaining. First, union labour may be of higher quality than non-union labour, with some of the pay differential due to the higher marginal revenue product of union labour. Second, employers may raise the wages of non-union labour in an attempt to forestall unionization, thereby eroding the pay differential. Third, incomes policies imposed by governments may affect the union/non-union pay differential. Flat-rate norms which are often a part of incomes policy will compress the pay differential that union bargaining power might otherwise have secured.

In practice, the particular effect of trade unions on pay is very difficult to disentangle from those of other labour market conditions. It is interesting to note, however, that both union and non-union workers have on average been able to secure very large increases in real wages, even during periods of high unemployment. This may suggest a fall in the price elasticity of demand for labour as the capital/labour ratio has increased, thereby reducing labour costs as a proportion of total costs (see above), and may also indicate a low and negative unemployment elasticity of real wages.[6] In fact, unemployed workers have perhaps ceased to exert a *permanent* influence on wage determination.

Restrictive practices and labour utilization

It has been suggested that the process of collective bargaining reinforces the unions' perception that they have 'property rights'. These rights may include a variety of established practices which have been used to protect jobs or earnings. These practices have important consequences for labour utilization and may form part of the collective bargain. They include the closed shop, minimum manning levels, demarcation rules, seniority principles, strikes, etc. We briefly review a number of the most important 'restrictive practices'.

The closed shop   Closed shops confer a number of advantages on trade unions. First, they permit monopoly control over labour supply. This increases the union's ability to disrupt production through industrial action, and therefore raises its 'bargaining power'. In terms of Chamberlain's ratio above, it raises the 'management cost of disagreeing', and therefore union bargaining power. Second, closed shops prevent the 'free rider' problem, whereby non-union labour benefits from union bargaining power. Third, closed shops make it easier to enforce agreements reached between unions and management. Indeed, despite restricting the freedom of employers to choose whom they will employ, the closed shop has the benefit of bringing more order and certainty to industrial relations.

As we have seen, legislation since 1979 has made the closed shop legally unenforceable, reflecting the government's desire to reduce union bargaining power and to protect the right of an individual not to join a trade union. The incidence of closed shops has decreased rapidly since 1979 with contemporary estimates suggesting that only some 9% of firms continue to have some form of closed shop agreement with unions.

Established practices   In industries such as printing, the railways, and car production, unions often have, by tradition, some control over manning levels, job speeds, the introduction of new technologies and demarcation issues. In other words, which type or grade of workers should undertake particular types of work. As a result, management decisions over the allocation of labour within an enterprise are subject to union influence.

Interestingly, Daniel (1987) found that trade union opposition to investment in advanced, new technology was unusual, though highly publicized when it did occur. In fact, where there was an association between change and working practices, it was *positive*, i.e. unionized firms in the survey were *more likely* to introduce technical and other forms of change than companies where unions were not recognized.

The seniority principle   This is the principle whereby union members with the longest service in a firm are the first to be promoted and the last to be made redundant. This principle may conflict with the firm's desire to employ younger, more flexible and cheaper workers. However, companies may sometimes wish to retain senior workers having already made a substantial investment in them through specific training.

These restrictive practices may enter into the collective bargain. Unions may seek to trade them for higher wages – as in the productivity agreements noted above. Through 'buying out' restrictive practices in this way, management seeks a more efficient utilization of labour, and thereby higher productivity.

The strike weapon   One of the most powerful 'property rights' perceived by the unions is their ability to affect the collective bargain by withdrawing their labour, i.e. going on strike. This is viewed by some as the ultimate form of restrictive practice. The use of the strike weapon by unions in the UK has been the subject of much research and debate.

Table 15.5 Strikes: international comparisons, 1985–96 (working days lost per thousand employees).

Country	1987–91	1992–96	1987–96
Spain	630	400	514
Canada	344	172	257
Italy	276	172	225
United Kingdom	126	29	78
France	98	97	97
United States	68	42	55
Denmark	39	46	42
Germany*	5	17	12
Japan	4	2	3
EU average	246	93	167
OECD average	148	65	105

Notes:
*From 1993 data covers entire Federal Republic of Germany.
Source: Adapted from *Labour Market Trends* (1998) April.

Table 15.5 demonstrates that compared to its major economic competitors the UK was less strike-prone than the OECD and EU averages over the whole period shown. It is often in the context of strikes that governments and employers see union 'property rights' as detrimental to Britain's economic performance, while the unions themselves perceive the withdrawal of labour as a response to the failure of management. Disputes over pay are the most common cause of working days lost, accounting for 71% of the total in 1995–97, followed by staffing and redundancy issues (9%) and work allocation issues (7%), although attributing strikes to a single cause often masks the existence of other contributory factors. The threat of industrial action by a trade union may alone be sufficient to achieve its aims, but one must be careful not to overestimate its role or that of actual strike incidence in the process of bargaining. The CBI has reported that both are only rarely given as a reason for employers conceding wage increases.

Although the improvement in Britain's strike record is clear and indisputable, there has been a dramatic rise in notified individual grievances. For example, the Advisory, Conciliation and Arbitration Service (ACAS) has reported a substantial rise in cases received for conciliation, i.e. prior to a hearing by an industrial tribunal. Perhaps the lack of actual strike activity may not be a good indicator of the actual stresses and strains experienced within the labour market!

Conclusion

We have seen that the trade unions play an important role in the wage-bargaining process, despite the recent decline in union density. The employers' associations and the government are also important role-players in the process of collective bargaining. In recent years there has been a shift in the private sector from national or industry-wide bargaining to single-employer and, increasingly, establishment bargaining of a largely 'formal' nature. Wage negotiation is, however, a complex procedure, and the outcome depends upon the relative 'bargaining power' of both management and unions. Wages are also affected by a variety of 'non-market' factors, such as comparability, work conditions, cost of living, and the 'trading' of restrictive practices. Government legislation in the form of the National Minimum Wage will also influence the wage outcome. Collective bargaining can have an important effect on pay differentials and may even help enshrine a variety of established (restrictive) practices which have been used to protect jobs or earnings. However, the use of the strike weapon appears to be limited to large plants in specific industrial sectors, though the fact that these are often the basic UK or export-orientated industries may still leave the UK at a disadvantage *vis-à-vis* her international competitors.

Key points

- Most Trade Unions are relatively small; around 47% have less than 1,000 members. However, these unions have less than 1% of total union membership. In fact very large unions with over 250,000 members have around 66% of total union membership.
- Trade Unions in the UK can be one of four types: craft, general, industrial or white-collar. In Europe most unions are industrial.
- There has been a sharp fall in union membership: in 1979, 54.5% of all employees were unionized, but by 1996 this figure had fallen to only 31.7%.
- Unions can usually only secure higher wages at the 'cost' of less employment unless their bargaining power is strong. If this is the case, they may be able to force employers off their labour demand curves, securing higher wages with no loss of employment.
- Chamberlain defined union 'bargaining power' as the ratio between the management costs of disagreeing and of agreeing to union terms. The larger the ratio, the greater the union bargaining power.
- A *given rise* in wages will usually reduce employment by less: (a) the less elastic the demand for the final product, (b) the less easy it is to substitute labour by other factors of production, (c) the lower the proportion of labour costs in total production costs.
- The government has legislated to reduce union power in various ways: e.g. removing the closed shop, imposing conditions on strikes and other union activities, deregulating the setting of wages and other working conditions, and promoting Trade Union democracy. It has also legislated to introduce a National Minimum Wage.
- Other factors influencing the wage settlement include: spillover and comparability, non-pecuniary advantages/disadvantages, the cost of living and any productivity agreements made between employers and employees.
- Less strikes currently occur in the UK than is the average for the advanced industrialized countries; e.g. over the period 1987–96, only 78 working days were lost per thousand employees in the UK compared to 105 for all advanced industrialized countries.

Notes

1. Trades Union Congress evidence to the Royal Commission on Trade Unions and Employers' Associations (1968).
2. It may also refer to a Central Arbitration Committee. This is an independent national body which provides boards of arbitration for the settlement of trade disputes.

3. The marginal revenue product of labour (MRP_L) equals the marginal physical product of labour (MPP_L) times the price of output. Because of diminishing returns to labour, the MPP_L curve will eventually begin to slope downwards. This is the part of the curve reflected in Fig. 15.1, since, if MPP_L slopes downwards, so will MRP_L.
4. In Fig. 15.1 we assume the firm to be small, so that changes in its demand for labour are insignificant relative to total demand for that type of labour. As a result it can purchase all the labour it requires at the going wage rate. For this firm, the supply curve of labour can be regarded as perfectly elastic at the market wage rate. Therefore wage rate = average cost of labour = marginal cost of labour.
5. This is often called 'bilateral monopoly'.
6. Unemployment elasticity of real wages =

$$\frac{\% \text{ change in real wages}}{\% \text{ change in unemployment}}$$

Oswald estimates a coefficient of about -0.10, i.e. 'we can expect a doubling of unemployment to lower wages by (*ceteris paribus*) a little under 10%.'

References and further reading

Addison, J. and Siebert, W. (1998) Union security in Britain, *Journal of Labour Research*, **XIX**, 3, Summer.

Atkinson, B. (1996) National Minimum Wage, *Developments in Economics*, **13**.

Bain, G. S. and Elsheikh, F. (1980) Unionization in Britain: an inter-establishment analysis based on survey data, *British Journal of Industrial Relations*, **18**, 2, July.

Bain, G. S. and Elsheikh, F. (1982) Union growth and the business cycle: a disaggregated study, *British Journal of Industrial Relations*, **20**, 1, March.

Barrell, R. (ed.) (1994) *The UK Labour Market*. Cambridge University Press.

Blanchflower, D. (1996) The role and influence of trade unions within the OECD, Centre for Economic Performance. LSE Discussion Paper, No. 310.

Carruth, A. A. and Disney, R. (1987) Where have 2 million trade union members gone?, *Economica*, **55**.

Claydon, T. (1989) Union derecognition in Britain in the 1980s, *British Journal of Industrial Relations*, **27**, 2, July.

Daniel, W. W. (1976) Wage determination in industry, *Political and Economic Planning*, **563**.

Daniel, W. W. (1987) *Workplace Industrial Relations and Technical Change*. Frances Pinter and PSI.

Daniel, W. W. and Millward, N. (1983) Workplace Industrial Relations in Britain: Survey by the Department of Employment, Policy Studies Institute, *Employment Gazette* (1992) May.

Disney, R. (1994) The decline of unions in Britain, *The Economic Review*, November.

Evans, S. (1987) The use of injunctions in industrial disputes, May 1984–April 1987, *British Journal of Industrial Relations*, **25**, 3, November.

Freeman, R. R. and Pelletier, J. (1990) The impact of British Union legislation on trade union density, *British Journal of Industrial Relations*, September.

Geroski, P., Gregg P. and Desjonqueres, T. (1995) Did the retreat of UK trade unionism accelerate during the 1990–93 recession? *British Journal of Industrial Relations*, **33**, March.

Green, F. (1992) Recent trends in British trade union density. How much of a compositional effect? *British Journal of Industrial Relations,* September.

Gregg, P. and **Machin, S.** (1991) Changes in union status, increased competition and wage growth in the 1980s, *British Journal of Industrial Relations,* **29**, 4, December.

Metcalf, D. (1994) Transformation of British industrial relations? Institutions, conduct and outcomes 1980–1990, in Barrell, R. *op. cit.*

Millward, N. and **Stevens, M.** (1987) *British Workplace Industrial Relations, 1980–1984.* The DE/ESRC/PSI/ACAS Survey, Gower.

Minford, P. and **Riley, J.** (1994) The UK labour market micro rigidities and macro obstructions, in Barrell, R. *op. cit.*

Mumford, K. (1996) Arbitration and ACAS in Britain; a historical perspective, *British Journal of Industrial Relations,* **34**, June.

Nickell, S., Wadhwani, S. and **Wall, M.** (1989) Unions and productivity growth in Britain, 1974–86. CLE Discussion Paper, No. 353.

Price, R. and **Bain, G. S.** (1976) Union growth revisited, *British Journal of Industrial Relations,* **14**, 3, November.

Price, R. and **Bain, G. S.** (1983) Union growth in Britain: retrospect and prospects, *British Journal of Industrial Relations,* **21**, 1, March.

Taylor, R. (1989) *The Fifth Estate: Britain's unions in the modern world.* Pan Books.

Towers, B. (1989) Running the gauntlet: British trade unionism under Thatcher 1979–1988, *Industrial and Labour Relations Review,* **42**, 2, January.

Webb, S. and **Webb, B.** (1896) *The History of Trade Unionism.* Longman.

Wedderburn, L. (1990) *The Social Charter, European Company and Employment Rights.* Institute of European Rights.

Wright, M. (1996) The collapse of compulsory unionism? Collective organization in highly unionized British companies 1979–1991, *British Journal of Industrial Relations,* **34**, December.

Macroeconomics

Chapter 16

Consumption and saving

Consumption is the most important single element in aggregate demand, so that its accurate estimation is essential to the management of the economy. J. M. Keynes related consumption to current disposable income, and for many years this was widely accepted. However, in the 1950s evidence began to appear of a discrepancy between the consumption function estimated from long-run time-series data, and the much flatter consumption function estimated from short-run time-series and cross-section data. The Keynesian consumption function could not resolve this discrepancy, and it was this, together with the need for more accurate forecasts of consumption, that led to the development of the Permanent Income and Life-Cycle Hypotheses. In this chapter the Keynesian and alternative theories of consumption are considered in detail, their predictions are compared with actual fact, and their different implications for policy analysis are noted. We also look carefully at the mirror image of consumption, namely the savings ratio.

Consumption

The consumption function – the relationship between consumer expenditure and income – is probably the most widely researched relationship in macroeconomics. The impetus to this research was given by Keynes's initial conceptual breakthrough in *The General Theory of Employment, Interest and Money* (Keynes 1936). In the Keynesian view of the economic system, both output and employment are determined by the level of aggregate demand. Consumer spending is by far the largest element in aggregate demand. Typically it accounts for between half and two-thirds of total final expenditure, so it is essential that the factors influencing consumer spending be identified in order that it may be forecast accurately. This forecast for consumer spending can then be added to forecasts for the other elements of aggregate demand, namely investment, government spending, and net exports (exports minus imports), to derive an overall forecast for *total aggregate demand*. Policy-makers can then decide whether this projected level of demand is appropriate for the economy, and if not, what corrective fiscal or monetary action should be taken.

The central position of the consumption function in Keynesian economics has therefore led to many attempts to estimate an equation that would indeed predict consumer expenditure. Unfortunately, most of the early Keynesian types of equation failed to explain some of the more interesting features of aggregate consumer behaviour. Alternative theories were therefore developed in the 1950s and 1960s which, it was claimed, fitted the facts rather better than the simple Keynesian view of consumption.

The development of these new theories, and the relative economic stability of the 1950s and 1960s, led economists to believe (over-optimistically as it turned out) that consumer spending was probably one of the best-understood and best-forecast variables in economics. We see from Table 16.1, however, that there was a sharp fall in the proportion of personal disposable income consumed (the average propensity to consume (a.p.c.)) in the early and late 1970s, which was *not* predicted by the existing equations. This fall in the a.p.c. was reflected in the sharp rise in the savings ratio, and we return to this, along with the subsequent changes in the savings ratio in the 1980s and 1990s, later in the chapter.

The Keynesian consumption function

In the *General Theory*, Keynes argued that 'The fundamental psychological law ... is that men are disposed, as a rule and on the average, to increase their consumption as their income increases, but not by as much as the increase in their income' (Keynes 1936: 96). From this statement can be derived the Keynesian consumption function[1] which is usually expressed in the following way:

$$C = c_0 + bY$$

where C = consumer expenditure;
c_0 = a constant;
b = the marginal propensity to consume (m.p.c.), which is the amount consumed out of the last pound of income received; and
Y = National Income.

The Keynesian view is that when income rises, consumption rises, but by less than income, which implies that b, the m.p.c., is less than 1. Keynes also argued that 'it is also obvious that a higher absolute level of income will tend, as a rule, to widen the gap between income and consumption' (Keynes 1936: 97). This is usually taken to mean that he thought that the proportion of income consumed, C/Y (i.e. a.p.c.), will tend to fall as income increases. In fact the positive constant c_0 in the above equation ensures that this will happen, since

$$\text{a.p.c.} = \frac{C}{Y} = \frac{c_0}{Y} + b$$

and this will decrease as Y increases if, and only if, c_0 is positive. This also implies, of course, that the a.p.c. is greater than the m.p.c. by an amount c_0/Y.

Drawing the consumption function as a straight line, as in Fig. 16.1, means that we are assuming that the m.p.c., b, is a constant, as it is the slope of the consumption function. The a.p.c. is found, for any level of income, by measuring the slope of the radian from the origin to the appropriate point on the consumption function. For example, if income is Y_1, then consumption would be C_1, and the a.p.c. would be

Table 16.1 Personal disposable income, consumption and savings ratio (£m at 1990 prices), 1960–98. *Source:* Adapted from *Economic Trends* (1998).

Year	1 Real personal disposable income	2 Real consumers' expenditure	3 Average propensity to consume (a.p.c.)*	4 Change in real personal disposable income	5 Change in real consumer expenditure	6 Marginal propensity to consume (m.p.c.)†	7 Personal savings ratio (%)‡
1960	169,199	156,735	0.93	10,461	5,822	0.56	7.4
1961	176,256	160,199	0.91	7,057	3,464	0.49	9.1
1962	178,286	163,925	0.92	2,030	3,726	1.84	8.1
1963	185,426	170,874	0.92	7,140	6,949	0.97	7.8
1964	193,247	176,044	0.91	7,821	5,170	0.66	8.9
1965	196,998	178,493	0.91	3,751	2,449	0.65	9.4
1966	201,207	181,550	0.90	4,209	3,057	0.73	9.8
1967	204,171	185,985	0.91	2,964	4,435	1.50	8.9
1968	207,772	191,209	0.92	3,601	5,224	1.45	8.0
1969	209,684	192,366	0.92	1,912	1,157	0.61	8.3
1970	217,675	197,873	0.91	7,991	5,507	0.69	9.1
1971	220,344	204,139	0.93	2,669	6,266	2.35	7.4
1972	238,744	216,752	0.91	18,400	12,613	0.69	9.2
1973	254,329	228,615	0.90	15,585	11,863	0.76	10.1
1974	252,360	225,317	0.89	-1,969	-3,298	1.67	10.7
1975	253,814	224,580	0.88	1,454	-737	-0.51	11.5
1976	253,012	225,666	0.89	-802	1,086	-1.35	10.8
1977	247,695	224,892	0.91	-5,317	-774	0.15	9.2
1978	265,925	236,909	0.89	18,230	12,017	0.66	10.9
1979	281,084	247,212	0.88	15,159	10,303	0.68	12.1
1980	285,411	247,185	0.87	4,327	-27	-0.01	13.4
1981	283,176	247,402	0.87	-2,235	217	-0.10	12.6
1982	281,722	249,852	0.89	-1,454	2,450	-1.69	11.3
1983	289,204	261,200	0.90	7,482	11,348	1.52	9.7
1984	300,037	266,486	0.89	10,833	5,286	0.49	11.2
1985	309,734	276,742	0.89	9,697	10,256	1.06	10.7
1986	323,316	295,622	0.91	13,582	18,880	1.39	8.6
1987	335,271	311,234	0.93	11,955	15,612	1.31	7.2
1988	355,945	334,591	0.94	20,674	23,357	1.13	6.0
1989	370,809	345,406	0.93	14,864	10,815	0.73	6.9
1990	377,977	347,527	0.92	7,168	2,121	0.30	8.1
1991	377,980	340,037	0.90	3	-7,490	-2,496.67	10.0
1992	385,506	339,652	0.88	7,526	-385	-0.05	11.9
1993	393,256	348,164	0.89	7,750	8,512	1.10	11.5
1994	399,572	357,845	0.90	6,316	9,681	1.53	10.4
1995	412,376	364,046	0.88	12,804	6,201	0.48	11.7
1996	425,821	377,166	0.89	13,445	13,120	0.98	11.4
1997	443,356	394,545	0.89	17,535	17,379	0.99	11.0
1998	450,400	409,300	0.91	7,044	14,755	2.09	9.1

Notes: *column 3 = column 2 divided by column 1; †column 6 = column 5 divided by column 4; ‡column 7 = personal saving as a percentage of disposable income.

C_1/Y_1, which is the tangent of the angle α. It can be seen that as Y increases, the slope of the radian from the origin to the consumption function falls, which means that the proportion of income consumed (a.p.c.) falls. Indeed some early Keynesian economists were concerned that private sector investment would not grow as a proportion of income to fill the gap left by a declining average propensity to consume, in which case the economy would be subjected to 'secular stagnation'.

For Keynes, the main influence on consumption in the short run was current disposable income, i.e. income minus direct taxes. When this fluctuated, so would consumption, but because the m.p.c. was less than 1, consumption would change by an amount less than the change in disposable income. If we look at the actual data for the UK and plot consumption against disposable income, both measured in real terms (using 1990 prices), we can see from Fig. 16.2 that over the period 1960–98 there appears to be a close positive relationship between consumption and disposable income.[2]

In order to find numerical estimates for c_0 and b for our consumption function, we can fit a regression line, or line of 'best fit',[3] to the data in Table 16.1. Using linear regression we can derive the following equation:

$$C = 3.89 + 0.89 Y_D$$

where Y_D is real disposable income (£000m).

This consumption function (1960–98) not only appears to fit the data well, as can be seen from Fig. 16.2, but also seems to support the Keynesian view that the m.p.c. is less than 1 (in our case 0.89). The equation also has a positive (if rather small) intercept of 3.89 (£bn) implying that the a.p.c. does indeed fall as income rises. However the intercept term is, statistically, not significantly different from zero and so we cannot be certain that the consumption function fails to go through the origin. If it did, this would mean that the a.p.c. does *not* fall as income rises.

As a first attempt, therefore, the above equation, which explains changes in consumption in terms of changes in current disposable income, seems to fit the facts and the Keynesian theory rather well. To take an example from Table 16.1, in 1997 real disposable income was £443.4bn; fitting this into our equation gives predicted consumption of £398.5bn. Actual consumption was £394.5bn, an error of around 1%. The equation also gives a predicted a.p.c. of 0.897 for 1997 whereas the actual a.p.c. was 0.890, again only a very small error.

Fig. 16.1. The consumption function.

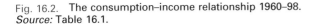

Fig. 16.2. The consumption–income relationship 1960–98.
Source: Table 16.1.

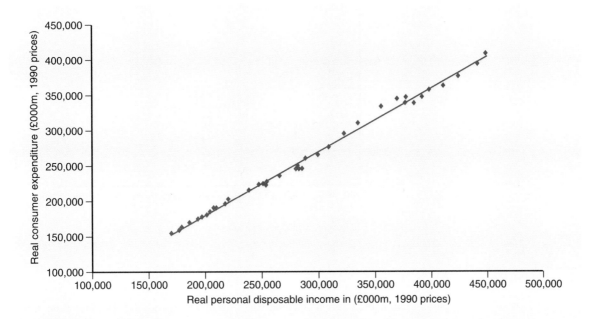

Closer examination of the data, however, indicates that using changes in current disposable income to explain changes in consumption may be less than satisfactory. It may help to look more carefully at the 'errors', i.e. the deviations of the *actual* observations for consumption from the *predicted* values on the regression line. At first sight, these 'errors' in our earlier Fig. 16.2 do not look very large. Nevertheless policy makers relying on the simple consumption function equation to forecast any future consumption would, in some years, still make substantial errors. A more striking picture of the errors can be seen in Fig. 16.3. Here the *differences* between actual and forecast consumption [C − (3.89 + O.89Y$_D$)] are plotted.

Very large *negative* errors occurred – from 1973–1976 and again from 1978–1982. In these periods actual consumption was very much *less* than forecast, given the levels of real disposable income. It appears that consumers were acting very cautiously because they were pessimistic about their future incomes. In both periods, uncertainty was caused in part by oil-price shocks and rising unemployment. Similarly, in the early 1990s actual consumption was also lower than forecast by our equation, again in part because of uncertain future incomes as unemployment levels increased, but also because of falling asset prices (houses) and the desire of consumers to pay off accumulated debt.

At the other extreme, large positive errors were made in the late 1980s. Here people actually consumed more than would be forecast by our equation, given the levels of real disposable income. This period was one of falling unemployment, inflated house prices and rising incomes, all of which made consumers more optimistic about the future.

It appears from the above that consumers are a good deal more sophisticated than the simple Keynesian consumption function would imply. Consumers not only take

Fig. 16.3. Error*
analysis of simple
consumption function.

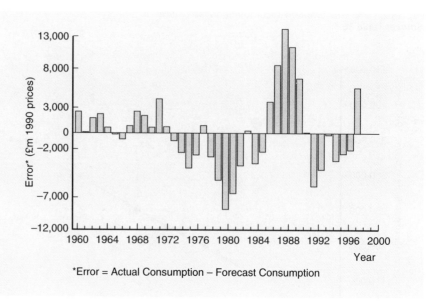

*Error = Actual Consumption – Forecast Consumption

into account their *current* income when deciding expenditure, but also their future *expected* income. Indeed one of the goals of the post-Keynesian theories of consumption considered in the next section is to attempt to include the influence of future income on consumer spending.

One other feature of consumer behaviour ought to be noted at this stage. In general, consumers attempt to keep a relatively smooth consumption pattern over the business cycle. In periods when disposable income is rising rapidly, consumption will rise but not in proportion. In other words, during the recovery period consumers behave cautiously, at least at first. Similarly, in periods when disposable income is falling, consumers will on the whole attempt to maintain their consumption as best they can despite their reduced circumstances. Put simply, in the *short run*, consumption fluctuates less than disposable income (i.e., the short run m.p.c. is smaller than the long run m.p.c.). Figure 16.4 illustrates this point for the UK.

The major exception to this pattern is the most recent cycle. Financial deregulation and asset price inflation encouraged consumer borrowing in the mid-to-late-1980s, which resulted in consumption increasing in those years by more than income. On the other hand the severe recession of the early 1990s, coupled with the collapse of house prices and the hangover of indebtedness from the previous period, has this time resulted in consumers cutting expenditure by more than income in an attempt to repay debt. It appears, therefore, that a Keynesian consumption function based only on *current disposable income* is insufficient to explain fully the short run changes in consumer expenditure.

Post-Keynesian theories of the consumption function

The newer theories of the consumption function differed from that of Keynes in that they were more deeply rooted in the microeconomics of consumer behaviour.

Fig. 16.4. UK annual percentage change in disposable income and consumption (1990 prices).
Source: Table 16.1.

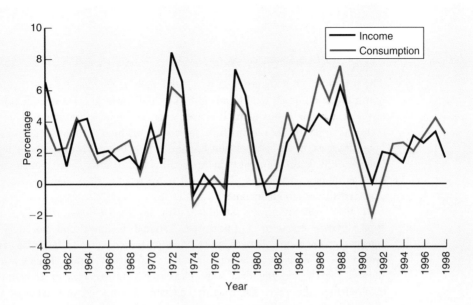

Two of the theories, Friedman's Permanent Income Hypothesis (PIH) and Modigliani's Life-Cycle Hypothesis (LCH), start from the position that consumers plan their consumption expenditure not on the basis of income received during the current period, but rather on the basis of their long-run, or lifetime, income expectations.

In both these theories, therefore, the link between current consumption and current income is broken. A consumer determines his or her consumption for a given period on the basis of a longer-run view of the resources available, taking into account not just current income but future expected income and any change in the value of their assets. Of course if consumers cannot borrow on the strength of future income, i.e. if they are liquidity constrained, then they will have to adjust current spending to current income, as in the Keynesian theory.

The Permanent Income Hypothesis (PIH) In Friedman's PIH an individual's consumption is based on that individual's permanent income (Y_p). Technically Y_p is defined as the return on the present value of an individual's wealth, and hence it is what can be consumed whilst leaving the individual's wealth intact. More generally Y_p could be thought of as some form of long-run average income, or 'normal income', which can be counted on in the future. An individual's actual or measured income (Y) in any time period will be made up of two parts – the 'permanent part' Y_p, and the 'transitory' part (Y_t). Transitory income might be positive, if the individual is having an unexpectedly good year, or negative, if the individual is having a bad year. It follows that measured income is

$$Y = Y_p + Y_t$$

In the simplest form of the PIH, consumption is a constant proportion of permanent income, i.e.

$$C = kY_p$$

where

$$k = F(i, w, x)$$

The proportion k is determined by factors such as the interest rate (i), the ratio of non-human to human wealth (w), and a catch-all variable (x) which includes age and tastes as a major component. If i rises, then individuals are assumed to feel more secure as to the future returns from their asset holdings, so that k increases. Equally, k will increase if the ratio of non-human to human wealth (w) rises in total wealth holding. This is also thought to increase individual security, since non-human wealth, such as money and shares, is assumed more reliable than human wealth, such as expected future labour income.

If the economy grows steadily, with no fluctuations, then Y_p would be approximately equal to Y (measured National Income), and not only would a constant proportion of permanent income be consumed, but also a constant proportion of measured National Income. A study by Simon Kuznets in the US showed that if *long-run* data were used (ten-year averages of consumption and income) then the a.p.c. was roughly constant. Taking ten-year averages effectively eliminates short-run fluctuations in income, and so Kuznets's results are consistent with the constant proportion k in the PIH.

This long-run consumption function derived from time-series data averaged over the business cycle, with its constant a.p.c., seemed, however, at odds with the short-run consumption function derived either from time-series data on an annual basis or from cross-sectional data. The short-run consumption function was flatter than the long-run function (see Fig. 16.5 below), having therefore a lower m.p.c. and an a.p.c. that was not constant, falling when incomes rose (booms) and rising when incomes fell (slumps). The answer to this puzzle, according to Friedman, is that in booms more people will think that they are doing better than normal than will think they are

Fig. 16.5. Long- and short-run consumption functions.

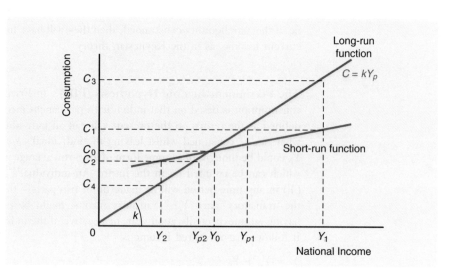

doing worse than normal. For the economy as a whole, therefore, there will be positive transitory income (Y_t), so that measured National Income (Y) will be above permanent income (Y_p). The unexpectedly high measured income will, however, have little impact on consumer views of their permanent income unless it lasts for several years. Since consumer spending plans are based on permanent income, any boom that is not long-lived will have little effect on consumer spending. The unexpected increases in income are therefore largely saved, with the result that in a boom the average propensity to consume falls. This is seen in Fig. 16.5.

As the economy expands along its long-run trend, then consumption is a fixed proportion, k, of income. In reality, however, the economy fluctuates around this long-run trend. Suppose we start in situation Y_0, with measured and permanent income equal, consumption (kY_0) equal to C_0, and a.p.c. equal to k. The economy then experiences a boom with measured income rising to Y_1. Permanent income will, however, be less affected by the sudden increase in income, and in our figure only rises to Y_{p1}. Consumption, being based on permanent income, now rises to $C_1(kY_{p1})$. Only if measured income remained at Y_1 *for several years* would permanent income be revised upwards to Y_1, and consumption to $C_3(kY_1)$. If this is *not* the case, then the proportion of income consumed will only be C_1/Y_1, i.e. the a.p.c. will have fallen below the initial level k during the boom.

In a slump, income will fall, say from Y_0 to Y_2, and although permanent income may be revised downwards a little to Y_{p2}, it will fall proportionately less than measured income. Consumption will therefore be $C_2(kY_{p2})$, falling much less than if Y_2 had been regarded as permanent (when consumption would fall further to C_4). The a.p.c. will then be C_2/Y_2, which is *above* the initial level k.

It can be seen from this analysis that Friedman is able to explain why the short-run consumption function is flatter, with a variable a.p.c., whilst the long-run consumption function is steeper, with a constant a.p.c. Booms will, unless long-lived, cause a.p.c. to fall. There will be little upward revision of consumption plans, when higher income is largely regarded as transitory. Slumps will, unless long-lived, in a similar manner cause a.p.c. to rise.

The Life-Cycle Hypothesis (LCH)   The LCH developed by Modigliani and his associates, is similar in many ways to the PIH. Consumption is again seen as being a constant proportion k of Y_p, with the same sort of variables affecting k as in Friedman's theory. Modigliani stresses, however, the age of the consumer, with the consumer trying to even out consumption over a lifetime in which income fluctuates widely. In youth and old age, when income is low, consumption is maintained by borrowing or drawing on past savings respectively, so that consumption is a high proportion of income; in middle life, when income is relatively high, a smaller proportion is consumed, with savings being built up to finance consumption after retirement.

One of the empirical facts that needed to be explained by any theory was why, from *cross-sectional* data, it was seen that low-income groups had a higher a.p.c. than high-income groups. The LCH argued that low-income groups contain a high proportion of very young and very old households, both of which have a high propensity to consume. On the other hand, the high-income groups contain a high proportion of middle-aged households, with a low propensity to consume.

The variations in a.p.c. observed using *time-series* data, when National Income rises or falls, can also be explained by the LCH. Any windfall or transitory income received in a boom is spread over the individual's remaining lifetime. For example, an unexpected increase in income of, say, £1,000 for someone with twenty more years to live, would mean that they would revise their Y_p upwards by about £50 per annum, so that consumption in the year in which the windfall is received would increase by a relatively small amount (some proportion of £50). The a.p.c. would therefore fall with higher income because consumption (the numerator) will have risen by only a small amount, based on Y_p, but measured income (the denominator) has risen by the full £1,000. An unexpected reduction in income in a recession would likewise be spread over an individual's lifetime, with borrowing and/or the running down of past savings leading to only a small cut in that individual's current consumption, thereby causing a.p.c. to rise. The LCH has therefore been able, like the PIH, to reconcile the flatter short-run consumption function with the steeper long-run consumption function (with constant a.p.c.).

Both theories imply that the m.p.c., which is the slope of the consumption function, is lower in the short run than it is in the long run. In the PIH any unexpected increase in income is not consumed, but largely saved, whereas in the LCH it is spread over the consumer's lifetime. It follows that the multiplier[4] predicted by these theories will be small in the short run, because m.p.c. is low in the short run. Changes in government spending and taxation aimed at stabilizing the economy will therefore be relatively ineffective, especially if these changes are seen as being only temporary. A by-product of Friedman's work on the consumption function appears, therefore, to be an attack on the effectiveness of Keynesian short-run demand-management policies.

The PIH and LCH appear to have broken the link between current consumption and current disposable income by arguing that consumption depends not only on current disposable income but also on all future disposable income. It could be argued, however, that there are two reasons why the influence of current income may be more important than these theories imply. First, it is unreasonable to believe that all consumers will be able to borrow and lend in different periods to even out their consumption pattern. An unemployed worker is unlikely to be able to borrow money to maintain his consumption, even though he is convinced he will be able to repay the loan out of future earnings. In this case, once past savings are exhausted, the constraint on consumption will be current disposable income. Second, estimates of future disposable income, on which permanent income is based, are highly uncertain. It is reasonable to expect, therefore, that the consumer uses his or her recent experience, and current income, as an important basis for estimating long-run or permanent income, and hence wealth. For both these reasons, therefore, one could still argue that current disposable income is still a major influence on current consumption, even under the PIH and LCH.

Rational expectations and consumption

The theories of consumption developed by Friedman, Modigliani and others all involve some concept of permanent or (long-term) 'normal' income on which households plan their consumption decisions. In order to arrive at this concept, households need to come to some view of their *expected* future income. The early post-Keynesian theories made convenient, if rather naive, assumptions about this process. Friedman, for example, used *adaptive expectations*, which means that consumers adapt or change their view of their expected income in the light of any 'errors' made in previous time periods.

In effect it can then be shown that 'permanent income' (which is supposed to capture future expected income) is simply a weighted average of past incomes.

Despite the empirical convenience of this method of modelling expectations (data on past incomes being readily available), economists have become increasingly dissatisfied with this approach to modelling the formation of expectations. This approach is too mechanistic, is backward looking and, apart from income, ignores all other relevant information that might affect future earnings. As an alternative many economists have adopted the hypothesis of *rational expectations*. Rational expectation theory argues that households form expectations not only on the basis of past experience but also on their predictions about the future. It is assumed that households possess some sort of 'model' of the economy which they then use to process relevant information and derive an expectation of future income. Of course most households do *not* possess any economic model of the economy. Nevertheless forecasts from actual models are freely available in the media and households can use these, together with any specific knowledge they might have of their particular industry and region, to make a rational forecast of anticipated future income. Although economists have had problems in applying this concept of rational expectations to empirical work, much of the current theoretical study of consumption is based upon it.

One application of rational expectations to the permanent income model has been developed by Robert Hall. Hall (1978) argued that under certain conditions a household's consumption should follow a '*random walk*'. If households have included all the available and relevant information in their forecast of future income then, assuming consumption smoothing, the only reason for a household to alter its consumption would be an unexpected change in income. Hence the best estimate of next year's consumption (C_{t+1}) will be this year's consumption (C_t), as this reflects all the available information on future incomes. That is to say, $C_{t+1} = C_t + e_{t+1}$ where e_{t+1} is a random amount that results from unexpected shocks. Hall found some evidence to support the view that next year's consumption is closely related to this year's consumption. However, he also found that other variables, including past income, influenced next year's consumption. One reason for this finding is, of course, the linkage between past income and current borrowing potential for householders as a means of financing future consumption.

The substantial variations in the savings ratio over the last economic cycle have, to a large extent, been explained by the impact of monetary policy. Monetary policy, operating through the house price channel, in an environment of financial liberalization, has been held responsible for the boom–bust cycle. Work by Catão and Ramaswamy (1996), however, suggests that although the monetary stance and wealth effects on consumption accounted for over half the contraction in economic activity, the role of 'true' shocks also played a significant role. True shocks are defined as those that cannot easily be explained by obvious economic factors. These could be caused by pessimism about the future or anxiety about the particular course of political or social developments. One policy conclusion that comes from their work is that although monetary policy is influential, it is difficult for monetary policy to fine tune the economy in the face of expectational shocks.

Windfall gains and consumption

In 1996 consumers received around £3.5bn in special payments, sometimes called windfall gains. In 1997 the figure was around £35bn. These windfall gains were mainly the result of the merger of building societies and their demutualization, which converted building society assets into tradable shares. There were also windfall gains via enforced (by the regulator) payouts to customers from the regional electricity companies and the sums received from maturing TESSA accounts.

Economic theory tells us that an increase in a consumer's wealth is unlikely to lead to a proportionate increase in consumption, with consumers maximizing utility by spreading the additional consumption over the rest of their lifetime. The increase in current consumption is likely, therefore, to be relatively small. The Bank of England Inflation Report in February 1997 adopted this viewpoint, arguing that previous windfall payouts by the Abbey National and TSB had resulted in only modest increases in current consumption. The Bank of England estimated that only around 5–10% of the £35bn of windfall gains expected in 1997 would be spent in the first year (i.e. up to £3.5bn). This view was further supported by a survey carried out by the Harris Research Centre, which found that only 36% of individuals who expected to receive a building society windfall in 1997 intended to spend all or most of it.

The *National Institute Economic Review* (1998) found that the effect of the windfalls on consumption had turned out to be larger than the Bank of England had anticipated a year earlier. It estimated that consumers' expenditure in 1997 had risen by a further £8bn because of the windfall gains received in that year. One explanation might be that more consumers had suffered from liquidity constraints in 1997 than the Bank of England had anticipated. If an individual is liquidity constrained then arguably they cannot achieve their optimum consumption pattern taking into account expected future income because they cannot, for various reasons, borrow on the strength of that expected future income. Any liquidity-constrained consumer who receives a windfall gain is then likely to spend more of it in the current period than they would have done had no such liquidity constraint been present.

The savings ratio

Consumer spending has clearly been one of the most widely researched areas in macroeconomics. Despite this there have been unexpectedly large movements in the proportion of income consumed, and hence saved, over the last twenty years. In the 1970s, personal savings rose as a proportion of personal disposable income, reaching a peak of 13.4% in 1980 (see the earlier Table 16.1). In the 1980s the savings ratio fell, reaching a low point of 6.0% in 1988, before rising again to 11.9% in 1992 as households sought to cushion themselves against uncertainty (and possible job loss) during a period of recession. These largely unanticipated swings in savings imply that the consumption function is less stable than Keynes had thought. The growth of consumer expenditure over the last sixteen years has therefore proved very difficult to forecast. In the boom years of 1985–88, consumption was consistently *underestimated*; whereas in the recession years of 1989–92, it was consistently *overestimated*. The impact of these forecasting errors on economic policy, and the subsequent welfare losses resulting from policy failures, are a cause for serious concern. As we shall see later in this section, this concern has led to a re-examination of the determinants of consumption and especially of the role played by financial liberalisation and the housing market.

Measurement of the savings ratio   The savings ratio for the personal sector is the *difference* between personal disposable income (PDI) and consumption, expressed as a percentage of PDI. Several practical and conceptual problems arise with respect to the savings ratio. Firstly, it is the difference between two large and fairly inaccurate aggregates, and hence it is inevitably inaccurate itself (up to 20% out either way, according to the government's own calculations). As a result the published figure is often revised; for example, the savings ratio for 1974 first appeared as 12.7%, was subsequently revised up to 14.4% and has since been revised down to 10.7%. Secondly, the personal sector includes not only households but also unincorporated businesses, non-profit-making bodies and life assurance and pension funds. The inclusion of businesses means that PDI, and therefore personal savings, will be influenced by *stock appreciation*. Thirdly, the savings ratio is sensitive to what is included in the respective definitions of consumption and capital expenditure. For example, in 1984 the Central Statistical Office reclassified expenditure on *home improvements*, moving this item out of consumption and into capital expenditure. This increased the savings ratio for 1983 by as much as 1.5% points. Finally it must be remembered that the personal sector includes unincorporated businesses. Stock appreciation during periods of high inflation increases the income of these companies and thus may raise the savings ratio.

Post-war behaviour of the savings ratio

From Fig. 16.6 and the earlier Table 16.1, it can be seen that over the post-war period there has been a long-run upward trend, at least until the late 1970s and early 1980s, in the proportion of personal disposable income saved. The period as a whole could be divided into five parts for further investigation.

Savings in the 1950s, 1960s and 1970s

The **first period**, from the end of the Second World War up to 1960, saw a rise in the savings ratio, from an exceptionally low level (0.1% in 1948) to what was considered at the time a more normal level (7.4% in 1960). The explanation for this appears to be that people in the early post-war years were catching up on

Fig. 16.6. Personal saving as a percentage of personal disposable income 1950–98.
Source: Economic Trends (various).

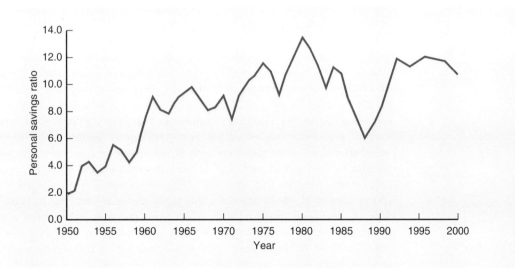

consumption that had been postponed during the war years, so that the savings ratio in the early post-war period was uncharacteristically low. The rise in the savings ratio after these early years can therefore be seen as a return to normality.

The **second period**, from 1960 to 1971, revealed no marked upward trend, with the ratio fluctuating around an average of 8%. The fluctuations in the ratio coincided with variations in the rate of growth of National Income; the savings ratio fell when the economy slowed down, and rose when the economy accelerated. This period could therefore adequately be explained by any of the post-Keynesian theories of consumption.[5]

In the **third period**, from the early 1970s to around 1980, the upward trend in the savings ratio was re-established, reaching a peak of 13.4% in 1980. As we noted, this has been puzzling, being associated with high rates of inflation, negative real interest rates, and periods when real disposable income actually fell (1974, 1975 and 1977).

A number of attempts have been made to explain why the savings ratio has risen under these conditions. For example, the Bank of England has argued that increases in contractual savings (regular contributions to pension funds and life assurance companies) have at times contributed to the high savings ratio, especially in the early 1970s. Rising unemployment and related uncertainties, in times of recession, may also have led to an increase in savings for precautionary reasons.

Savings and inflation   The greater part of the research, however, has been into the relationship between inflation and the savings ratio. Most of the studies have found a positive connection between these two variables, but there is some disagreement as to why the inflation rate should affect the savings ratio.

One theory (Deaton 1977) explains the relationship in terms of consumers failing to perceive the actual rate of inflation. The suggestion is that consumers *underestimate* the average price level and are therefore unduly shocked at the apparently 'excessive' rise in the price of particular commodities. Until such time as consumers recognize the true (and higher) level of average prices, purchases of these commodities will have been cut back in response to the assumed sharp increase in individual prices. Savings will therefore rise as a result of this 'inflation surprise' effect. This theory suggests that it is unanticipated inflation that matters, so that the effect on consumption, and therefore savings, will be particularly strong in the early stages of inflation when the rate of inflation is accelerating.

A study by Bulkley (1981) has supplemented the above theory, showing that even if inflation is fully anticipated the savings ratio will still increase as long as anticipated inflation is itself increasing. Even if inflation is fully anticipated, workers' real wages will still have fluctuated throughout the year, since money wages are usually set on only one occasion in the year. Real wages will therefore be at a maximum when the money wage is first set, falling to a minimum a year later as prices progressively rise. In order to smooth out his or her real consumption pattern over the year, an individual will save more each week early in the contract period, and correspondingly less later in the contract period. If inflation is constant, and if wage contracts are spread evenly over the year, then the additional savings of some will cancel out the reduced savings of others, and there will be no aggregate effect on the savings ratio. However, when anticipated inflation is increasing and with it the money wage, then the extra savings by those who have recently received higher wage awards will more than offset the reduction in the savings of those nearing the end of their nominal wage contracts, and the savings ratio will rise.

Other explanations (Cuthbertson 1982) stress the impact that inflation has on the real value of an individual's liquid assets, affecting the individual's desire to save. Liquid assets include notes and coins, bank and building society deposits, National Savings and other short-term assets. Because the real rate of interest (nominal rate minus the rate of inflation) on liquid assets over this period has often been zero or negative, the real purchasing power of a given stock of these assets has fallen. If consumers wish to maintain the real value of their liquid assets, for reasons of security or flexibility, they must choose either to cash in less liquid assets, or to save more from current income. The real rate of return on some non-liquid assets such as housing and consumer durables has been positive over this period as a whole, and so rather than cash these in, one would expect the holdings of these to increase in inflationary times. Other non-liquid assets, such as life assurance and long-term contractual saving, are expensive to cash in, as are government bonds when the interest rate is high. Thus the desire to rebuild a given stock of real liquid assets could really only come from a reduction in non-durable consumption, i.e. saving. People have tended, therefore, during the recent inflationary times to save a higher proportion of their disposable income in the attempt to maintain the real value of their liquid assets.

Savings in the 1980s and 1990s

The **fourth period** embraces 1980 to 1988. During this period the savings ratio fell from its peak of 13.4% in 1980 to a thirty-year low of 5.7% in 1988. There appear to be a number of reasons for this.

First, in inflationary times some savings are needed just to maintain the *real* value of assets, the values of which are fixed in money terms. As the inflation rate falls, as it did from 1980–83, the need for such saving declines. A second factor in the fall of the savings ratio seems to be the behaviour of pension funds. Conventionally, these funds are seen as the property of the personal sector and the income of these funds (including investment income and employers' contributions) is treated as part of personal income. However, movements in this element of personal income are unlikely to have much effect on consumption and for that reason are more likely to affect the savings ratio. As the earnings on the funds assets rose from the low levels of the 1970s, the savings ratio increased. But in the 1980s it became apparent that the value of these pension funds had risen above the sum needed to meet pension liabilities; as a result employers' contributions to pension funds stopped rising from 1981. Indeed in 1986 and 1987 they actually fell in *nominal* as well as real terms. This 'contributions holiday' lowered personal income and so the *personal savings ratio* fell in favour of higher company saving.

A third factor influencing the savings ratio in this period has been the increased financial liberalization of capital and money markets. Financial liberalization included the ending of quantitative controls on consumer credit in 1982 and the relaxation of the controls on mortgage lending. The average loan offered by building societies to first-time buyers rose from 76% of purchase price in 1980 to 86% by 1986. Deregulation at a time of rising house and other asset prices enabled consumers to gain easier access to credit markets at a time of growing consumer confidence. As a result, household borrowing rose rapidly in the 1980s with the ratio of debt to personal income rising from 57% in 1980 to 116% by 1990 (see Pain and Westaway 1994). Despite this increase in borrowing, the net wealth of the personal sector rose from 3.25 times income at the start of the decade to 5 times income by the end. This increase was mainly the result of the rise in home ownership and the buoyancy of share prices. Easier access to credit, and the confidence which came from rising incomes, falling unemployment and rising asset prices, all helped fuel the consumer boom and depress the savings ratio in the second half of the 1980s. Fig. 16.7 illustrates the rise in consumer credit and mortgage equity withdrawal (that part of new mortgage lending used for consumption rather than investment in housing) at this time.

The fourth factor influencing the savings ratio in this period has been a demographic one. Recent research carried out by the London Business School suggests that the fall in the proportion of the population in the 45–64 year age group during this period has influenced savings. It is the people in this age group that are the principal savers in our society; younger people are borrowing to set up home and older retired people are living on past savings. A decline in the 45–64 year age group is therefore likely to reduce the savings ratio.

Finally, it has been claimed that the official figures actually underestimate the true savings ratio. Personal income, it is argued, is *underestimated* in official statistics, whereas consumption is *measured* reasonably accurately. This would lower the level of *measured* or recorded saving.

It is extremely difficult to quantify the role of the various influences on consumption and savings behaviour over this period from 1980–88. However, recent econometric work by Muellbauer (1994) has attempted to identify the various factors that caused the unprecedented 10 percentage points rise in the consumption to income ratio (a.p.c.) between 1980 and 1988. In his view the contribution of *forecast income growth* was just over 2 percentage points (at the same time the rise in real interest rates reduced the ratio by 1 percentage point). *Reduced uncertainty* in the economy in the later part of the period was responsible for 3 percentage points upturn in the a.p.c.; of this some 2.5 points resulted from lower unemployment and 0.5 percentage points from reduced income volatility. By far the largest contribution however was a 5 percentage point rise in the ratio (i.e. half of the recorded total) caused by the rise in what Muellbauer calls *'spendability'*; more precisely the weighted net asset[6] to income ratio. Essentially not only was the net asset to income ratio increasing but, because of financial liberalization, asset backed credit was more easily available. A rise in net asset to income ratio clearly increased opportunities for spending via a wealth effect and a greater access to liquid funds (credit). One offsetting factor in this period was the growth of income inequality; the impact of this inequality was to *reduce* the consumption to income ratio by around 1 percentage point, because in general higher income households have higher saving ratios (lower a.p.c.).

Fig. 16.7. Percentage changes in mortgage equity withdrawal and consumer credit.

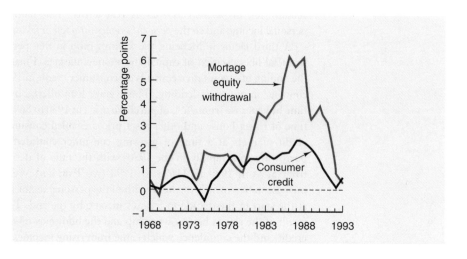

The **fifth period** for the savings ratio covers the years 1988 up to the present time. After 1988 the savings ratio began to rise, reaching a peak of 11.9% in 1992 (third quarter). The savings rate peaked (according to Muellbauer) *before* the net asset to income ratio peaked. Several factors can account for this, including a sharp fall in expected income growth, a steep rise in the rate of increase of unemployment, an increase in income volatility, a rise in the real interest rate and the downturn in current income growth. Certainly the doubling of short term interest rates over 1988–1990 led, both directly and indirectly, to a fall in the net asset to income ratio. The impact of this sharp rise in real interest rates contributed to a lower real value of shares, a fall in real and nominal house prices and a high level of debt and debt repayments. All this led to a fall in the a.p.c. and an associated rise in the savings ratio. It is interesting to note that the Bank of England estimated that three-quarters of a million home owners in 1992 had properties valued at less than their outstanding mortgage. The value of this 'negative equity' was worth £5.9bn and obviously had a depressing effect on consumer spending as households saved harder to reduce this debt burden. These factors taken together clearly help explain the depths of the UK consumer recession in the period 1990–92 and the relatively sluggish recovery of consumption since the fourth quarter of 1992 despite lower interest rates.

The savings ratio has fallen since economic recovery began in 1992, but it is worth noting that its fall has not been as pronounced as it was over the same period in the previous recovery in 1981. The debt burden, continued weakness in house prices and tax increases have all helped to undermine consumer confidence.

Some authors have taken a wider view of savings to include both the corporate and public sector as well as personal savings. On this basis, *gross domestic saving* as a percentage of GDP can be shown to have been remarkably stable in the UK over the last three decades at around 18% (Smith 1990). In contrast the gross savings ratios in Japan, Germany, France and the US have all shown long term declines. In a similar vein, Alec Chrystal (1992) has argued that the level of gross domestic savings in the UK is not out of line with international rates (see Fig. 16.8). The UK rate is about average for an industrial country; the extremes being the US at 13% and Japan at just over 30%.

Fig. 16.8. Gross domestic savings as a percentage of GDP (1996).
Source: Adapted from OECD, *Economic Outlook*, No. 63, June 1998+.

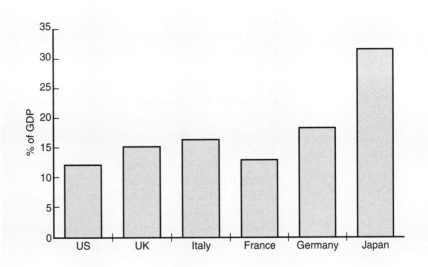

Conclusion

The importance of having a clear idea of what factors determine consumption cannot be overestimated. Consumption expenditure is the largest element in total expenditure and so any fluctuations in consumption will have important implications for the overall level of demand in the economy. The failure to appreciate the strength of consumer demand in 1987 and 1988 was an important contributory factor to the subsequent deterioration in the inflation and balance of payments position that has posed such problems for the UK economy. Similarly the fall in consumer spending in the current recession has been much sharper than in either of the previous two recessions of 1974–77 and 1979–82. Again this change in consumption expenditure was largely unforeseen by forecasters.

Post Keynesian theories stress that, when deciding on consumption, consumers have a longer term planning horizon than merely considering current income. The implication of post–Keynesian theories being that consumption is more stable than Keynesians thought. Evidence suggests, however, that in the face of uncertainty and liquidity constraints, current income may still be a key factor influencing consumption.

The experience of the 1970s and 1980s led to an intensified search for new variables to augment the existing consumption equations. Wealth, interest rates, inflation and the ease of access to credit, all seem to be factors influencing consumer spending plans. The relative importance of these variables is, however, difficult to unravel given the high degree of correlation between them.

| Key points |

- In the Keynesian view, current disposable income is the main determinant of consumer spending.
- The suggestion here is that the *average propensity to consume* (a.p.c.) will fall as disposable income increases.
- Further, the *marginal propensity to consume* (m.p.c.) will be less than 1.
- Using a line of 'best fit' to UK data over the period 1960–98, the consumption function has been estimated as $C = 3.89 + 0.89\,Y_D$, where Y_D is real disposable income (£000m).
- This suggests an m.p.c. of 0.89 and a low intercept term, suggesting a.p.c. will decline only slightly as disposable income increases.
- Evidence began to accumulate that the *short-run* consumption function was flatter than the *long-run* consumption function. In other words short-run m.p.c. is less than long-run m.p.c.
- Attempts to explain this discrepancy have resulted in independent variables *other than* current disposable income being proposed. The Permanent Income Hypothesis (Friedman) and Life-Cycle Income Hypothesis (Modigliani) have been suggested.
- Even models based on past experience and future expectations have been used (rational expectations).
- The policy consequences of errors in forecasting consumption (and therefore savings) have been serious: *underestimates* of consumption causing economic policy to be overexpansionary (inflationary); *overestimates* of consumption causing economic policy to be overcautious (deflationary).

Notes

1. This is a 'generalized' version of the Keynesian consumption function as it uses total income rather than disposable income as the independent variable.
2. However this is not always the case, as can be seen on the rare occasions when m.p.c. is negative. A negative m.p.c. means that when disposable income falls, consumption actually rises. In 1982 consumption even rose by *more* than National Income fell, giving a value of -1.69 for m.p.c.
3. 'Best' in the sense that it minimizes the sum of squared deviations from the line.
4. The simple National Income multiplier is defined as $1/1 - $ m.p.c. for a closed economy with no government sector, and indicates the extent to which National Income changes following a given change in injections or withdrawals. If m.p.c. is low, the multiplier is low.
5. Remember that a fall in the savings ratio during 'recession' is the same as a rise in a.p.c.; and a rise in the savings ratio during 'boom' is the same as a fall in a.p.c.
6. 'Net asset' is essentially the market value of assets such as houses, stocks and shares, etc., *minus* any debt still outstanding on their acquisition.

References and further reading

Bulkley, G. (1981) Personal savings and anticipated inflation, *Economic Journal*, **91**, March.
Catão, L. and **Ramaswamy, R.** (1996) Recession and recovery in the United Kingdom in the 1990s: identifying the shocks, *National Institute Economic Review*, **157**, July.
Chrystal, A. K. (1992) The fall and rise of saving, *National Westminster Bank Quarterly Review*, February.
Cuthbertson, K. (1982) The measurement and behaviour of the UK saving ratio in the 1970s, *National Institute Economic Review*, **99**, Feb.
Deaton, A. (1977) Involuntary saving through unanticipated inflation, *American Economic Review*, **67**, 5, December.
Hall, R. (1978) Stochastic implications of the life cycle permanent income hypothesis, *Journal of Political Economy*, **86**, December.
Kennally, G. (1985) Committed and discretionary saving of households, *National Institute Economic Review*, **112**, May.
Keynes, J. M. (1936) *The General Theory of Employment, Interest and Money*, Macmillan.
Kuznets, S. (1946) *The National Product Since 1869*, The National Bureau of Economic Research.
Leighton Thomas, R. (1984). *The Consumption Function*, in Demery, D. *et al.*, *Macroeconomics*, Surveys in Economics, Longman.
Muellbauer, J. (1994) The assessment: consumer expenditure, *Oxford Review of Economic Policy*, **10**, 2, summer.
National Institute Economic Review (1998) **165**, 3, July.
Pain, N. and **Westaway, P.** (1994) Housing, consumption and borrowing: an assessment of recent personal sector behaviour in the UK, *National Institute Economic Review*, **149**, August.
Smith, R. S. (1990) Saving policy and tax reform, IMF Staff Papers, **37**, 1, March.

Chapter 17

Investment

Although only around one-third as important as consumption in total aggregate demand, investment is arguably one of its most significant components. It is highly volatile, and through its impact on productivity affects both supply and demand sides of the economy. After briefly reviewing the definition and measurement of investment, this chapter considers the theory and evidence for a number of factors allegedly affecting fixed investment. The rate of interest, the Accelerator Theory, the Capital Stock Adjustment Model, profitability, 'crowding out', uncertainty, public policies and inadequate financial provision, are all considered. The chapter concludes by assessing the role of investment in economic growth.

Nature of investment

Resources in an economy can be used to produce goods and services for immediate use (consumption), or to add to the stock of fixed capital (investment). This chapter concentrates on the latter.

In one sense consumption and investment are quite distinct. The act of investment usually involves abstaining from current consumption in order to acquire assets, which raise the productive potential of the economy, and therefore the possibilities for future consumption. Yet in another sense they are similar, both being components of aggregate demand, i.e. types of spending which create income for others in the economic system. We noted in Chapter 16 that consumption was around 48% of total final expenditure (TFE) in 1997. Although smaller, fixed capital investment was 13% of TFE in 1997.

Stock and flow concepts
The total value of fixed capital at any time is a 'stock' concept. The rate of change of that 'stock' is a 'flow' concept. Investment in the National Accounts is entirely a 'flow' concept, as it is the addition to the stock of fixed capital in any given year. This helps explain why purchases of shares, paintings or antiques, although often termed 'investments' in everyday speech, are not regarded as such in the Accounts. Usually they merely represent a transfer of ownership from one person or institution to another, rather than an addition to the stock of assets. The difference between stock and flow valuations is often substantial.

Gross and net investment

'Gross' investment, though a flow concept, overestimates the change in size of the stock of capital or inventories in the year. In the course of the year some fixed capital will have worn out or become obsolete, and some inventories will have become unusable. A part of 'gross' investment will therefore be needed simply to replace these assets used up in the course of production. If we subtract this 'replacement' investment from 'gross' investment, then we are left with 'net investment'. Net investment is then the estimate of the addition, in any year, to the stock of fixed capital and inventories, having allowed for depreciation of that stock during the year.

Of course, quantifying depreciation presents a number of problems. Estimating the loss in value of a machine in a year is difficult in itself, and may be guided less by the physical state of the asset than by the possibility of tax concessions. Also different accounting conventions will yield different measures of depreciation. For instance, historical cost accounting yields much lower figures for depreciation than does inflation accounting.

The majority of investment expenditure is on fixed capital formation rather than inventories and it is to this that we now turn.

Gross Domestic Fixed Capital Formation

Gross Domestic Fixed Capital Formation (GDFCF) is defined in the National Accounts as 'expenditure on fixed assets (buildings, plant and machinery, vehicles, etc.), either for replacing or adding to the stock of existing fixed assets'. This apparently clear-cut definition turns out to be rather arbitrary in application. For instance, 'investment' in the National Accounts is restricted to the firm sector. If a household purchases a typewriter for personal use, it is classified in the National Accounts as 'consumption', yet the same purchase by a firm is classified as 'investment', even though in both cases the capital asset yields a stream of useful services throughout its life. This is because the National Accounts treat the household purchase as self-gratification, but the firm purchase as producing a flow of marketable goods and services.

The arbitrariness of this classification is well illustrated when an individual chooses, for tax purposes, to be regarded as self-employed. The purchase of a car by a teacher for travel to work as an employee is classed as 'consumption' expenditure. Should the teacher change his or her designation to self-employed and engage in privately contracted teaching, then the purchase of that same car could be classed as 'investment' expenditure.

Despite problems of classification, it is important to gauge changes in GDFCF through time, both in total, and by sector and type of asset. Table 17.1 presents data for selected time periods since 1979. Given the problems we noted in measuring depreciation, the 'gross' concept is perhaps the most useful for purposes of comparison, whether through time or across countries. GDFCF stood at around £128bn in 1997, which is some £45bn higher than the figure recorded in 1979. Over this period the level of investment spending was, however, quite volatile falling sharply in the recession of the early 1980s and, as the table indicates, more recently in the economic downturn of the early 1990s.

The components of GDFCF have changed substantially over the last fifteen years. There has, for example, been a significant shift in investment from the public to the private sector, with the latter now accounting for 91% of new capital spending

Table 17.1   Gross Domestic Fixed Capital Formation by sector and by type of asset (£m at 1990 prices).

| | | Sector | | | | Types of asset | | | | | |
| | | Private | | Public | | Dwellings | | | Other new buildings & works | Vehicles, ships & aircraft | Plant and machinery |
	Total	Total	Manu-facturing	Central govt..	Public corps	Total	Private	Public			
1979	82,840	62,795	13,558	9,147	10,992	22,149	16,871	4,974	23,549	11,062	22,390
1989	122,470	106,745	14,984	10,054	5,671	27,789	23,653	4,136	47,525	11,231	37,925
1992	108,973	87,225	11,828	13,787	4,961	20,280	17,524	2,811	47,249	7,787	32,602
1997	127,657	115,109	14,236	8,690	3,858	23,524	21,297	1,957	44,562	11,360	38,404

Source: Economic Trends (various editions).

compared with 76% in 1979. Indeed public sector investment is currently, in real terms, below the levels reached in the late 1970s. This is partly due to the privatization programme which has been implemented in recent years and has reduced the number of public corporations. However, it also reflects the desire of government to cut back on spending initiatives. Because of difficulties involved in cutting back on current expenditure plans, capital projects have been sacrificed in a bid to fulfil this objective.

Investment by type of asset has also changed since 1979. Investment in plant and machinery has grown most rapidly, increasing by around 72%. It now accounts for around 30% of total GDFCF. There has also been a healthy rise in the real level of investment in new building and work which in 1997 contributed around 35% of GDFCF. The level of investment in dwellings and in vehicles, ships and aircraft has been rather more modest; in fact both categories experienced roughly the same real investment in 1997 as in 1979 which corresponds to a decline in *share* of the (higher) total GDFCF in both cases. Within the housing investment component (dwellings) there has also been a significant transfer of resources from the public to the private sector. Investment in public sector housing fell from 22% of total dwelling investment in 1979 to only 8% in 1997.

Factors affecting fixed investment

Gross Domestic Fixed Capital Formation is so heterogeneous that any explanation must address itself to particular components. For instance, investment in dwellings is influenced by population trends, expected lifetime income, the availability and cost of mortgage finance, etc. Most attempts at theory and empirical work have, however, tended to concentrate on investment in plant and machinery, particularly in the manufacturing sector. Here we review the factors which allegedly affect this type of fixed investment.

The rate of interest

The earliest theories of investment placed considerable emphasis on the importance of the rate of interest, seen here as the compensation required for forgoing current consumption. Fisher used the rate of interest to derive the present value (PV) of an expected future stream of income. By calculating the PV of various alternative investment projects they could then be ranked against each other.

This approach was taken a stage further by Keynes who introduced the concept of the marginal efficiency of investment (MEI). The MEI was defined as that rate of discount which would equate the PV of a given stream of future income from a project, with the initial capital outlay (the supply price):

$$S = PV = R_1/(1+i) + R_2/(1+i)^2 + R_3/(1+i)^3 + R_n/(1+i)^n$$

where S = the supply price;
$\quad PV$ = the present value;
$\quad\ R$ = the expected yearly return; and
$\quad\ \ i$ = that rate of discount necessary to equate the present value of future income with the initial cost of the project.

The curve relating the marginal efficiency of investment (i) to the level of investment in Fig. 17.1 is negatively sloped, for two main reasons. First, the earliest investment projects undertaken are likely to be the most profitable, i.e. offering the highest expected yearly returns (R), and therefore having the highest marginal efficiencies of investment (i). As more projects are initiated, they are likely to be less and less profitable, with lower expected yearly returns, and therefore lower $MEIs$. Second, a rise in the level of investment undertaken is, at least in the short run, likely to raise the supply price (S), which in turn will reduce the MEI. This could follow if the capital goods producing industries faced capacity constraints in their attempt to raise output in the short run.

The decision on whether to proceed with an investment project will depend on the relationship between the rate of interest (r) and the marginal efficiency of investment (i). If r is less than i, then the annual cost of borrowing funds for an additional project will be less than the expected annual return on the initial capital outlay, so that the project will be profitable to undertake. In Fig. 17.1, with interest rate r_1, it will be profitable to invest in all projects up to I_1, with I_1 itself breaking even. The MEI schedule is therefore the investment demand schedule, telling us the level of investment that will be undertaken at any given rate of interest. Expectations play an important role in this theory of investment. If, as is often the case, expectations are volatile, then the expected yearly returns (R) on any project will change, causing substantial shifts in the MEI schedule. At *any given rate of interest* investment demand will therefore be changing, which will reduce the closeness of any statistical fit between

Fig. 17.1. **The investment demand schedule.**

the interest rate and investment. In fact, it may be via expectations that interest rates exert their major influence on investment. A fall in rates is often a signal to investors of better times ahead, raising expected returns, shifting the *MEI* curve to the right, and raising investment (and conversely). Although this may dilute the statistical fit between *r* and *I*, there may still be an underlying linkage between the two variables.

Evidence   One problem in testing the influence of interest rates on investment is the selection of an appropriate interest rate. The average yield on debentures is a rate frequently used, as this broadly indicates the cost of new borrowing for a company at any point in time.

Most UK studies have failed to show any close connection between interest rates and investment, suggesting that the latter is interest-inelastic. Savage (1978) in reviewing econometric evidence over a wide range of studies, concludes that the interest rate has been found to have little significance in influencing UK fixed investment. A more recent analysis of the relationship between the real rate of interest and gross fixed investment in plant and machinery in manufacturing was conducted by Turner (1989). He also found only a weak correlation between the two variables as did Whitaker (1998) in his study of investment in the UK in the recovery period 1992–96. However, a study by Osler (1994) covering not only the UK but also Germany, France, Japan and Canada, found that the high level of real interest rates between 1990 and 1993 had substantially depressed private investment and consequently reduced output in the five countries by between $2\frac{1}{2}$ and $4\frac{1}{2}$ per cent per year over the period.

In contrast to the rather weak relationships noted in the studies relating to the UK, the Bank of England's most up to date model suggests a much stronger impact of the interest rate on gross fixed investment (Easton 1990). It appears to show that a rise in interest rates of 1% would result in a fall in investment by 1.3% after four months, and 2.8% after twelve months. However most of the impact of the interest rate rise was on the residential investment (housing) component of gross investment, which fell by 3.2% and 4.1% over the same lagged periods.

Instead of focusing solely on the rate of interest some research has looked for alternative measures of the cost of capital to firms. Cummins, Hassett and Hubbard (1996), for example, have examined the role of the stockmarket in influencing investment trends. A rise in equity prices tends to make it cheaper to raise capital on the stockmarket while a fall can make it more expensive. They found that sudden share-price changes had a substantial impact on firms' investment plans in 12 of the 14 OECD countries examined, i.e. a rise in share prices leads to higher investment, and vice versa.

The rate of change of output – the Accelerator Theory

The Accelerator Theory relates net investment to the rate of change of output. If the capital stock K is fully utilized, and the capital/output ratio v is a constant, then net investment (I) can be expressed in the following way:

$$K_t = vY_t$$
$$K_t - K_{t-1} = v(Y_t - Y_{t-1})$$
$$I_t = v(Y_t - Y_{t-1})$$
$$I_t = v\Delta Y_t$$

where Y is output and t and t − 1 are time periods.

Net investment in year t is then a constant proportion of the change in output during that year. For example, if output rose by £2m for the economy ($\Delta Y_t = £2$m), and each extra £1 of output needed an average of £5 of capital equipment to produce it ($\nu = 5$), then $I_t = 5.2$m $= £10$m. A number of criticisms have been levelled at the Accelerator Theory. First, the assumption that there is no excess capacity is particularly suspect. If there is spare capacity then a rise in output ΔY_t can be met from the existing capital stock, with no need for new investment. It has been estimated by the CBI that in the period 1979–95, an average of just over 40% of firms were working at full capacity. Such a large amount of excess capacity must severely impair the effective functioning of the accelerator. Second, the assumption of a constant capital/output ratio, ν, is becoming less and less plausible. The advent of new generations of microelectronic technology is progressively reducing capital/output ratios. Third, it is also likely that prior to making an investment the firm would want to be sure that any upsurge in demand and in output is not a temporary phenomenon. *Expectations* of future demand, and therefore future changes in output, will then be important.

Evidence   Even when varying lag structures are introduced into more refined versions of the Accelerator Theory, the evidence in its support is far from convincing. McCormick *et al.* (1983) found that changes in real GDFCF by firms between 1962 and 1980 were not strongly related to the previous year's change in real consumer spending or demand. Black (1982) related changes in net fixed investment to changes in GDP over the previous three years. Again, the results were rather disappointing, with only 39% of the observed variation in net investment 'explained' by his equation. Black had already excluded investment in dwellings, in the social services, and in North Sea oil, on the grounds that investment in these sectors was unlikely to be affected by an accelerator principle.

The level of output and capital – the Capital Stock Adjustment Model

This was developed to overcome some of the problems of the simple Accelerator Theory. It states that investment is positively related to the expected level of output and negatively related to the existing capital stock. Any rise in investment will consequently depend not only on the expected level of output (demand) but also on the current size of the capital stock. Specifically,

$$I_t = b\,Y_{t-1} - cK_{t-1}$$

where I_t = gross investment in the current year;
  b and c = constant coefficients;
  Y_{t-1} = last year's level of output;
  K_{t-1} = the capital stock at the end of the preceding year.

If it is assumed that the expected volume of output is roughly equal to that experienced in the previous year, Y_{t-1}, then the higher is Y_{t-1} the greater will gross investment tend to be. However, the greater the inherited capital stock, K_{t-1}, the less need there will be for adding to the capital stock, or even replacing worn-out equipment.

Evidence   A variety of studies have introduced capacity utilization variables on the lines of the Capital Stock Adjustment Model, with encouraging results. Panić and

Vernon (1975) ran a series of tests in the mid-1970s relating GDFCF in six manufacturing industries to a number of variables. Their results confirmed the importance of capacity utilization in determining investment, in that investment tended to take place only when output increased sufficiently to stretch current capacity. Nobay (1970) came to a similar conclusion, and found a relationship between the change in output beyond 'capacity' and manufacturing fixed investment. Kennedy (1997) notes that the Capital Stock Adjustment Principle was useful in explaining manufacturing investment in the UK between 1955 and 1970, though less so since then. Similar support for a modified accelerator theory as a determinant of investment has come from the studies of Catinat (1987) and Ford and Poret (1990).

Profitability   There are at least three reasons why changes in profitability might be associated with changes in private sector investment:

1. Higher profits indicate a more favourable return on capital, which may encourage companies to reinvest any surplus rather than devote it to alternative uses.
2. Higher profits may improve business confidence and raise the expected future return on any project. An outward shift of the *MEI* schedule (see Fig. 17.1 above) might then raise investment at any given rate of interest.
3. Higher profits may raise investment by reducing its cost, as funds generated internally are cheaper than those obtained from the capital market, whether equity or debenture.

Evidence   Table 17.2 sets out the rates of return on capital in the business sector in the five major OECD economies over the past twenty-five years. From this it is evident that profitability in the UK has lagged some way behind the levels achieved by its key competitors.

In a major study of investment in the EU over the period 1961–90, the relation between net investment and the rate of profitability per unit of capital stock was found to be highly significant. Indeed variations in profitability were found to account for some three-quarters of the variations in capital stock during this period (European Economy 1991). In this study the profitability variable was lagged one period in order to take into account the unavoidable delays between changes in profit conditions and the effective realization of resulting investment decisions. More recent work by Schiantarelli (1996) concluded that the investment decisions of the firm are quite sensitive to the availability of internal funds, which in turn reflects profit levels. This is because internal funds tend to be cheaper than external funds as a source of cash.

Given the more open product markets implied by a global economy, it is not only profitability in the *domestic economy* which now influences investment decisions but that

Table 17.2 Rates of return on capital in the business sector (averages).

	USA	UK	Germany	France	Japan
1970–79	19.5	9.4	13.4	14.5	17.2
1980–89	20.8	8.9	11.9	13.0	13.7
1990–97	25.7	9.5	13.1	15.5	13.7

Source: Adapted from OECD (1998) *Economic Outlook*, June.

in the *global economy*. A recent study has found that an increase in costs in the UK *relative to those in other countries* leads to a more than proportionate reduction in the UK investment, and of course vice versa (Young 1994). In other words, *relative* changes in UK factor prices and tax policies, and thereby in profitability, have a significant effect on UK investment. For example, Young found that a 1% rise in UK *relative factor prices* would lead to a 1.62% decline in UK investment, with an 8-quarter time lag.

Uncertainty   During periods of uncertainty (for example, after a shock rise in oil prices) it has been argued that firms will reduce the value they place on expected future returns on investment projects. In terms of the earlier Fig. 17.1, the *MEI* will shift leftwards and less investment will take place at any given rate of interest. Faced with such uncertainty, therefore, businessmen and women become more inclined to delay any planned capital spending.

Evidence   The limited empirical work on the importance of uncertainty as a variable affecting investment decisions yields some support for this argument. For example, Ford and Poret (1990) compare *actual* investment expenditures with investment *intentions* as reported in various surveys. The expectation here being that *revisions* in investment intentions (i.e. the differences between planned and actual investment expenditures) would be greater in periods of low economic activity and greater uncertainty than in periods of high economic activity and greater certainty. Certainly Table 17.3 provides a measure of support for this view. Revisions in investment intentions were generally smaller in the more stable and buoyant economic environment of the mid to late 1980s than in earlier periods of greater uncertainty. More recent work by Heye (1995) has confirmed the importance of business expectations in influencing aggregate levels of capital investment and Price (1996) also concludes that 'aggregate uncertainty' has a negative effect on the level of manufacturing investment. The additional uncertainty implicit in certain types of public policy (e.g. 'stop–go' policies) has also been linked in empirical work to reduced levels of investment (see below).

Public policies   The post-war period until the late 1970s witnessed governments playing a positive role in stimulating demand through reflation of the economy. Booms were, however, generally interspersed with balance of payments crises. This prevented the application of reflationary policies over long time periods, since deflation of demand, to reduce spending on imports, was often used to correct balance of payments

Table 17.3   Revisions in Investment Intensions (average annual % difference between planned and actual investment expenditures).

	1974–78	1979–82	1983–88
USA	2.5	3.7	1.7
Japan	4.9	3.5	3.5
Germany	3.1	2.3	2.2
France	2.3	1.9	2.0
Italy	4.9	8.7	5.1
UK	4.8	4.1	2.9
Canada	3.2	8.3	4.6

Source: Adapted from Ford and Poret (1990).

deficits. The uncertainty of such stop–go policies arguably reduced business confidence and discouraged investment.

Other public policies may also influence investment in the private sector. For example, changes in the rate of taxation of company profits, or in the capital allowances which can be set against tax, are believed by many to significantly affect levels of investment.

Evidence   Nobay (1970) in his econometric study concluded that low profits were not so much the cause of low levels of investment, but rather the result of slow expansion of manufacturing output, accentuated by stop–go policies. Panić and Vernon (1975) also concluded that long-run instability in demand seriously undermined investment in the six manufacturing industries studied.

Studies on the impacts of the reform of corporation tax and the phasing out of accelerated depreciation allowances on UK investment have been undertaken by Sumner (1988) and Devereux (1989). The results suggest that such policies have relatively little impact on investment demand over the longer term. However a more recent study by Bond, Denny and Devereux (1993) re-opened the debate. It suggests that recent corporation tax changes and the loss of capital allowances have created a strong fiscal bias against investment, equivalent to companies facing permanently higher interest rates of between one and two per cent. This conclusion is not dissimilar to the results produced by Cummins, Hassett and Hubbard (1994). They found that investment behaviour responded in a significant fashion to any changes in the tax regime which affected the cost of capital.

Inadequate financial systems   It has been suggested that inefficiencies in the banking system and in the capital markets have prevented industry from obtaining the finance it requires for investment. Amongst the criticisms of UK financial institutions are the allegations that UK banks place too great an emphasis on lending to consumers, whereas overseas banks are primarily concerned with long-term industrial finance. Another criticism is that UK banks tend to concentrate on short-term lending, causing a shortage of long-term funds for investment. A further criticism is that financial institutions, which are major shareholders in many companies, place undue pressure on directors to distribute too high a proportion of total profit as dividend. The consequence then being that little profit is available, to be 'ploughed back' as investment.

Evidence   The most recent work carried out by Corbett and Jenkinson (1996) suggests that much of the criticism of the banking sector may be misplaced. Their study, which covers the period 1970 to 1994, suggests that banks provided a roughly similar share of funds for fixed investment in the UK as they did in Germany and the US. On average, bank finance in the UK accounted for 14.6% of investment spending. The corresponding figure for the US is 11.1% and that for Germany 10.8%. The economy where banks *have* played a more significant role is that of Japan. Over the period as a whole Japanese banks provided 27% of the funds required for Japanese fixed investment.

Even though this research suggests that the UK is not markedly out of line with its main competitors, there remains considerable unease that 'short-termism' by the city

Fig. 17.2. Dividend
payments as a
percentage of net
earnings of non-financial
corporations, 1982–93.
Source: House of
Commons Trade and
Industry Committee
Report (1994).

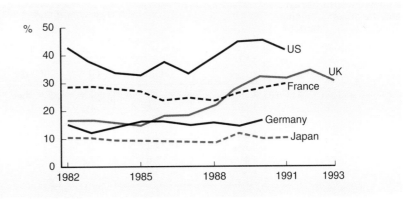

discourages investment in another way, by inducing companies to pay too high a
dividend in relation to profit. A related criticism is that dividend payments are too
inflexible, not varying as profits rise and fall, with the result that funds available for
investment are squeezed in times of recession. A House of Commons Trade and
Industry Committee Report (1994) substantiated some of these concerns, showing a
rising trend of dividend payments as a percentage of net earnings in UK companies,
reaching levels in the UK above most other advanced industrialized countries (Fig.
17.2), with the exception of the USA. The Report noted that: 'The Financial
Secretary to the Treasury accepts that relatively high dividend pay-out ratios are a
weakness in the UK economy' (p. 70). Whitaker (1998) concluded that relatively high
dividend payouts during the UK economic recovery of 1992–96 may have diverted
funds away from investment in fixed capital. Such concerns have resulted in changes
to the tax treatment of dividends, making it relatively more attractive for firms to use
profits for investment purposes rather than for dividend payments. Chapter 21
provides further background to this alleged cause of low levels of UK investment.

The importance of investment

Investment has a dual role to play within any economy. In the short run, investment
may be seen mainly as a component of aggregate demand which, if increased, will
have the effect of stimulating the economy and, through the multiplier, substantially
raising the level of National Income. Fixed investment made up some 13% of TFE in
1997.

In the long run, investment will also affect the supply side of the economy, raising
its productive potential and thereby pushing outwards the production frontier.
Economic growth is sometimes strictly defined in this way, being that increase in
GDP which results from raising productive potential. More usually it is loosely
defined as any increase in GDP, even when that is within the existing production
frontier.

There have been a number of studies into the importance of investment as a
generator of growth, though the results have not been conclusive. For example,
in 1961 Kuznets, using time-series data for a number of countries, found little
relationship between the *share* of investment in GDP, and the growth in output
over time. Similarly, a 1970 OECD survey based on cross-sectional data found

Table 17.4 Investment and the growth of output 1967–97.

| | Average annual growth (vol.) | | | | |
| | 1967–79 | | 1980–97 | | Share of GDFCF in GDP (av. 1970–97) |
	GDFCF	GDP	GDFCF	GDP	
Canada	4.5	4.5	3.6	2.4	16.8
France	2.6	4.1	1.1	1.9	22.4
Germany	3.7	3.4	2.4	2.5	22.1
Italy	3.5	4.5	1.1	1.9	20.8
Japan	8.4	6.7	3.3	3.1	29.6
UK	2.0	2.4	2.2	2.0	20.6
US	3.5	3.2	2.9	2.6	17.0

Source: Adapted from OECD (1998) *Economic Outlook*, June.

no clear well-defined relationship between investment shares and growth in output. Table 17.4 suggests that there may be some linkage between *growth* of investment (GDFCF) and growth in output. Countries which experienced the highest average annual growth rates for GDFCF in the time periods presented, tended to be the countries which also achieved the highest average annual growth rates for GDP, and vice versa. It could, of course, be argued that the growth in output is the *cause*, rather than the *effect*, of the growth in investment. To expand production may require additional capacity, giving rise to extra investment!

Whatever the validity of these arguments it is evident from Table 17.4 that the two countries (Japan and Canada) with the most impressive investment performances have also experienced the most rapid rates of economic growth. In contrast, the UK has suffered from a relatively low level of investment and achieved only a modest increase in GDP.

Not all economists accept that investment in the UK has been sluggish. Vittas and Brown (1982) reject the use of GDFCF as an appropriate measure of productive investment. The Department of Trade Industry (1996) adopted a similar argument, i.e. that GDFCF includes forms of non-productive investment which are irrelevant to economic growth, residential investment being a prime example. Table 17.5 shows the situation for the seven countries in Table 17.4 when residential investment is excluded from private sector GDFCF. In terms of annual average growth rates in *non-residential investment*, the UK fares reasonably well in the periods 1970–79 and 1980–89, but it has lagged behind somewhat during the 1990s.

Table 17.5 Annual growth in private sector non-residential investment.

	1970–79	1980–89	1990–97
Canada	8.1	6.9	5.3
France	2.7	3.1	−0.3
Germany	2.8	2.4	3.6
Italy	2.5	2.7	2.6
Japan	4.0	7.8	1.9
UK	3.1	6.6	0.7
US	5.2	2.6	4.8

Source: Adapted from OECD (1998) *Economic Outlook*, June.

Arguably an even better basis for comparison is provided by the figures produced by the OECD measuring *net business fixed investment* as a share of *business sector value added*, defined as GDP at factor cost less the government sector wage bill (Ford and Poret 1990). On this basis Japan once again comes top of the pile, reaching an average figure for this share or ratio of 14% over the past 20 years. Continental European economies have unexpectedly low ratios of between 9 and 10%, possibly reflecting the important role of government investment in these countries, but are still ahead of the UK (8%) and the US (7%).

Another criticism of the use of GDFCF as an appropriate measure of productive investment concerns its failure to take any account of variations in the rate at which past investment is 'scrapped'. A report by stockbrokers UBS (1992) draws attention to this factor, suggesting that *actual* rates of depreciation of capital in the UK have been well in excess of official assumptions as to rates of depreciation, aided by an overvalued exchange rate. In this case the true productive potential of the UK economy will be less than that implied by official gross or net investment data. The report points to the existence of a large deficit on non-oil current account in the middle of the last recession (see Ch. 26) as evidence of a more serious shortfall in the UK productive potential than could be gauged from official data on investment.

Efficiency and investment

The level of investment is not the only factor contributing to growth. A number of economists see investment as a necessary, but by no means *sufficient*, condition for economic growth. Growth also depends on the efficiency with which any investment is utilized. One method of measuring the efficiency of investment is through the gross incremental capital/output ratio, i.e. the extra capital required to produce an additional unit of output.

Table 17.6 presents incremental capital/output ratios for five major economies. It demonstrates what appears to have been a major weakness of the UK economy, namely that the UK has in the past required *a higher rate of gross investment* to produce a *given increase* in output, than have Germany, France, the USA or Japan. However, the data suggest a significant improvement in the efficiency with which investment in the UK has been utilized during the 1990s. Some have suggested that the more flexible labour market in the UK following earlier reforms (see Ch. 15) has allowed capital to be used more productively in recent times.

Table 17.6 suggests that increased capital intensity within the UK may result in *more than proportionate* increases in output during the 1990–97 period, with only a 0.4 unit of capital required to yield a one unit increase in output. It has been pointed out in Chapter 1 that *total* factor productivity must rise in UK plants and enterprises if growth is to be sustained. It follows that increasing the efficiency of labour, and improving the organizational structure of UK firms, may have been at least as

Table 17.6 Incremental capital/output ratios.

	1970–79	1980–89	1990–97
France	0.7	1.3	−0.2
Germany	0.9	1.5	1.6
Japan	0.8	2.1	0.9
UK	1.3	2.7	0.4
USA	1.6	0.9	2.1

Source: Adapted from ONS (1998) *United Kingdom National Accounts.*

important in generating economic growth as raising the absolute level of investment. However, as we have noted in Chapter 1, measure of total factor productivity for the UK can be subject to different interpretations.

Studies such as Young (1994) suggest that in a global market with 'footloose' multinationals continually re-appraising the location of investment decisions, it is *relative efficiency* which is becoming a crucial factor in investment decisions. Changes in total factor productivity (and thereby costs) in the UK relative to other countries may therefore have an increasingly significant influence on investment decisions in the UK.

Conclusion

Investment occurs in so wide a variety of assets and sectors that it must be disaggregated substantially if any close statistical fit is to be found. However, even when we concentrate on fixed investment in manufacturing, no single theory 'explains' much of the variation in investment. What evidence there is certainly suggests that UK investment is relatively interest-inelastic, reducing the effectiveness of the interest rate as a policy instrument. Nevertheless, in so far as changes in interest rates affect expectations, lower interest rates may still contribute to higher investment.

Although much less important than consumption in aggregate demand, investment has, through the multiplier, a significant effect on National Income, and is the most volatile element in aggregate demand. It also affects the productive potential of an economy. Even though the link between investment and growth is in some ways tenuous, it is interesting that higher growth rates of fixed investment in various countries have been accompanied by stronger growth performances. Some have also suggested that the observed increases in labour productivity suggest that UK investment is now being more efficiently utilized, as reflected by falls in the incremental capital/output ratio for the UK noted in Table 17.6. Increased globalization of production and investment decisions is placing a still greater premium on the UK matching, and surpassing, the efficiency with which investments are utilized in other countries.

| Key points |

- Investment is an important element of aggregate demand, contributing around 13% of total final expenditure (TFE).
- Investment also contributes to the 'supply side' of the economy, e.g. directly influencing real output per unit of factor input.
- Investment is a 'flow', as it involves a rate of change.
- Investment is volatile, having a significant impact on changes in National Income (via the multiplier).
- The public sector has taken a progressively smaller share of investment; only 9% of GDFCF in 1997.
- Expectations as to future profitability are a key factor in influencing the level of investment.
- Other relevant factors include the rate of interest, the rate of change of output (accelerator theory), levels of capital stock, size of public sector, financial support available, etc.
- In a global economy, changes in UK costs *relative to other countries* has been identified as influencing UK levels of investment.
- As well as the levels of investment, the *efficiency* with which any investment is utilized is also important.

| References and
further reading |

Bond, S., Denny, K. and **Devereux, M.** (1993) Capital Allowances and the Impact of Corporation Tax on Investment in the UK, *Fiscal Studies,* **14**.

Bond, S. and **Jenkinson, T.** (1996) The Assessment: Investment Performance and Policy, *The Oxford Review of Economic Policy*, 12.2.

Bond, S. and **Meghir, C.** (1994) Financial Constraints and Company Investment, *Fiscal Studies,* **15**.

Catinat, M. *et al.* (1987) The Determinants of Investment, *European Economy Annual Economic Report* **31**, March.

Corbett, J. and **Jenkinson, T.** (1996) *The Financing of Industry: An International Comparison*, mimeo, University of Oxford.

Cummins, J. G., Hassett, K. A. and **Hubbard, R. G.** (1994) A Reconsideration of Investment Behaviour using Tax Reforms as Natural Experiments, *Brookings Papers on Economic Activity* **2**, 1–74.

Cummins, J. G., Hassett, K. A. and **Hubbard, R. G.** (1996) A cross-country comparison of investment expenditures, *Tax Reform Journal of Public Economies and Investment*.

Department of Trade and Industry (1996) *UK Investment Performance: Fact and Fallacy*, June.

Easton, W. W. (1990) The Interest Rate Transmission Mechanism in the United Kingdom and Overseas, *Bank of England Quarterly Bulletin*, **30**, 2, May.

European Economy (1991) The Profitability of Fixed Capital and its Relation with Investment, *Annual Economic Report* 1991–92, **50**, Dec.

Ford, R. and **Poret, P.** (1990) Business Investment in the OECD Economies: Recent Performance and Some Implications for Policy, *OECD Working Paper* **88**.

Gordon, R. J. and **Veitch, J. M.** (1987) Fixed Investment in the American Business Cycle 1919–1983, in Gordon, R. J. *The American Business Cycle: Continuity and Change*.

Heye, C. (1995) Expectations and Investments, in Epstein, G. and Gintis, H. (eds) *Macroeconomic Policy after the Conservative Era*, Cambridge University Press.

House of Commons (1994) Trade and Industry Committee, *Competitiveness of UK Manufacturing Industry,* Second Report.

Kennedy, M. (1997) Economic Activity and Inflation, in Artis, M. J. (ed.) *The UK Economy*, 14th edn, Oxford.

Mullins, M. and **Wadhwani, S. B.** (1989) The Effects of the Stock Market on Investment, *European Economic Review,* **33**.

Nobay, A. R. (1970) Forecasting Manufacturing Investment – Some Preliminary Results, *National Institute Economic Review,* **52**, May.

Osler, C. L. (1994) High Foreign Real Interest Rates and Investment in the 1990s, *Federal Reserve Bank of New York Quarterly Review*, Spring 1994.

Panić, M. and **Vernon, K.** (1975) Major Factors Behind Investment Decisions in British Manufacturing Industry, *Oxford Bulletin of Economics and Statistics,* **37**, 3, Aug.

Price, S. (1996) Aggregate Uncertainty, Investment and Asymmetric Adjustment in the UK Manufacturing Sector, *Applied Economics,* **28**.

Schiantarelli, F. (1996) Financial Constraints and Investment: Methodological Issues and International Evidence, *The Oxford Review of Economic Policy*, 12.2.

Turner, P. (1989) Investment: Theory and Evidence, *Economic Review,* **6**, 3.

Vittas, D. and **Brown, R.** (1982) *Bank Lending and Industrial Investment*, Banking Information Service.

Whitaker, S. (1998) Investment in this Recovery: an Assessment, *Bank of England Quarterly Bulletin*, February, **38**, 1.

Young, G. (1994) International Competitiveness, International Taxation and Domestic Investment, *National Institute Economic Review*, May.

Chapter 18

Public expenditure

In this chapter we consider the growth of public expenditure and the difficulties surrounding its control. The next chapter will examine the burden of taxation.

Here we look at public expenditure, its form, size and apparently inexorable growth. Problems of definition and calculation are considered – for instance, current estimates for the ratio of public spending to National Income vary from as little as 25% to over 60%. Resolving such ambiguities is extremely important since entire economic and political platforms rest upon the outcome. Attempts to control public expenditure are nothing new; they began long before Gladstone. Although the last Conservative government was pledged to cut back public expenditure, the evidence suggests that successive Conservative governments failed. Real public spending between 1979 and 1997 showed an average growth rate of 1.4% per annum compared with an annual rate of 1% under the previous Labour administration. However, public expenditure has fallen as a *proportion* of GDP. In 1982/83 public expenditure was 47% of GDP; in 1998/99 it was only around 40% of GDP. This fall is largely because of the high growth rates of GDP in the mid- to late 1980s and 1990s. In fact public expenditure fell to as low as 39% of GDP in 1988/89, but in the recessionary years of the early 1990s the percentage started to rise once again, reaching 44% in 1993, before falling back to around 40% in the late 1990s.

Trends in UK public spending

Figure 18.1 shows the inexorable rise in the real value of general government expenditure under various administrations since the early 1960s. General government expenditure (GGE) covers spending by central and local government combined. The calculated figure for GGE usually excludes any proceeds from privatization during the year in question. The proceeds from a privatization will *reduce* the recorded value of GGE; in other words these privatization proceeds are counted as negative expenditure rather than tax revenue.

The present government's medium term objective for general government expenditure is that, over time, it should take a declining share of national income (see

Fig. 18.1. General government expenditure since 1963 in real terms.
Sources: Treasury (1998a); *Sunday Times* (1994).

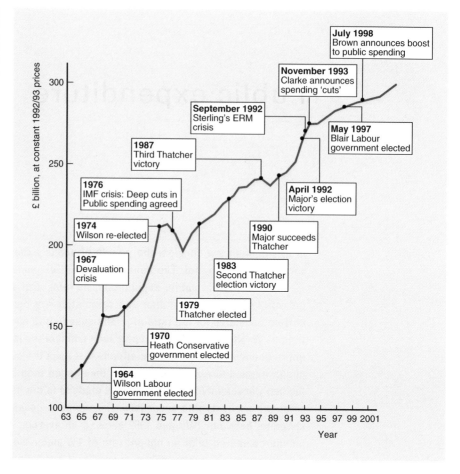

Fig. 18.2). Between 1996 and 1999 general government expenditure grew by under 1% per year on average, somewhat below the growth of the economy. The upward drift of general government expenditure as a percentage of National Income since 1988 has been sharply reversed.

As we can see from Fig. 18.2, the ratio of general government expenditure to GDP fell sharply during the growth years of the mid- to late 1980s. The Conservative government failed to sustain this objective during the early 1990s as the ratio rose, with social security and other demand-led expenditures placing upward pressure on public spending, and GDP falling relative to trend. Nevertheless the government reiterated its determination that, over time, public expenditure should continue to take a declining share of National Income and announced severe cuts in public expenditure in November 1993. The government believed that the result of such cuts would be lower borrowing which, combined with lower taxation, would mean that enterprise and efficiency would be encouraged and output and employment would grow.

What is clear from Fig. 18.2 is that there has been a sustained fall in general government expenditure as a percentage of GDP since 1993/94, and this has continued under the incoming Labour government.

Fig. 18.2. General government expenditure as % of GDP. *Source:* Adapted from Treasury (1998b).

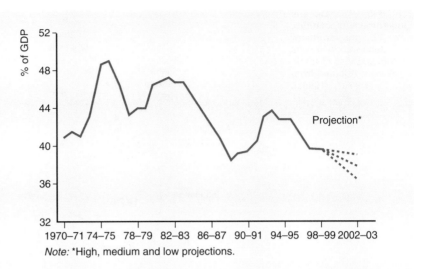

Note: *High, medium and low projections.

Components of UK public spending

We now consider a number of ways in which we can view the public spending figures recorded in the UK. Public expenditure can be identified in terms of the *programmes* on which money is spent, by *demand category* (goods and services or cash transfers) and by *source* (central or local government). Perhaps most interesting of all is the approach which seeks to identify public expenditure in terms of 'rescue', 'renewal' and 'welfare'.

General government expenditure by programme

In 1998–99, central and local government intended to spend approximately £332.5bn, divided between twenty programmes (roughly equivalent to the responsibilities of the main government departments).

Figure 18.3 reveals that Health, Personal Social Services and Social Security plans dominate expenditure by programme, with 47.9% of the total general government expenditure in 1998/99. The next most important item is Education with 12.2% of the total, followed by Defence with 6.9% of general government expenditure. Law and order accounts for 5.4%, Housing, Heritage and the Environment 4.8% and Transport 3%. Debt interest can be seen to take a sizeable portion of general government expenditure (8.1%) especially during times of high interest rates.

A large proportion of the expenditure in areas such as transport, law and order and education is carried out by the local authorities. However, central government expenditure is increasing its share of total spending on areas such as education (opted-out schools, FE colleges and sixth forms centrally funded) and housing (grants to housing associations). These programmes include capital spending (e.g. school buildings) and current spending on both goods (e.g. school books) and services (e.g. wages of policemen/nurses/teachers). The expenditure plans revealed in July 1998 showed that increased resources had been made available for health, housing and education.

Fig. 18.3. General
government expenditure
by programme or
department 1998/99
(percentages of total).
Source: Adapted from
Treasury (1998a).

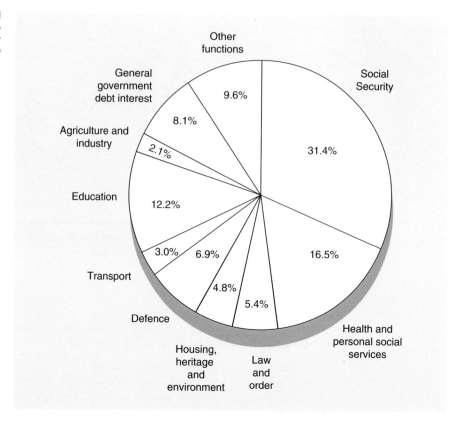

The above plans for public spending are an integral part of the government's medium-term financial strategy aimed at reducing inflation and maintaining the conditions for sustained growth, the creation of jobs and higher living standards.

**General government
expenditure by demand
or economic category**

A further way of presenting the above data is to divide public spending between goods and services (purchased by the state) and cash transfers (to individuals or industry). This particular classification is, as we note below, an important element in the debate on the size of the public sector and is reflected in Fig. 18.4. This figure reveals that around 50% of general government expenditure involves public sector pay plus the purchase of goods and services for consumption by the public. Almost 33% is absorbed by the 'disadvantaged' in the form of pensions, unemployment and supplementary benefits, etc. (transfers to personal sector). A further 2.4% goes into transfers to industry in the form of various subsidies (the corporate sector). Capital spending is seen to total only 2.1% of general government expenditure and covers spending on new construction, land, building and other physical assets, as well as grants to the private sector, the nationalized industries and other public corporations.

**Public expenditure by
source**

A further way of viewing public expenditure is to look at who spends the money (see Fig. 18.5). Central and local government dominate the total, with central government responsible for almost three-quarters.

Fig. 18.4. General government expenditure by demand or economic category in 1998/99. *Source:* Adapted from Treasury (1998a).

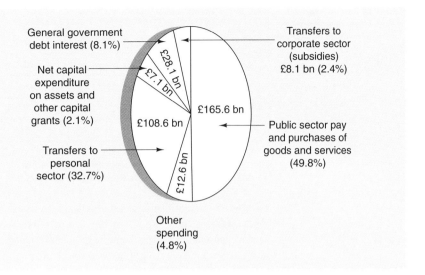

General government debt interest (8.1%)

Transfers to corporate sector (subsidies) £8.1 bn (2.4%)

£28.1 bn

£7.1 bn

£165.6 bn

Net capital expenditure on assets and other capital grants (2.1%)

£108.6 bn

Public sector pay and purchases of goods and services (49.8%)

Transfers to personal sector (32.7%)

£12.6 bn

Other spending (4.8%)

Fig. 18.5. Public expenditure by spending authority 1998/99; £bn and percentages of total. *Source:* Adapted from Treasury (1998a).

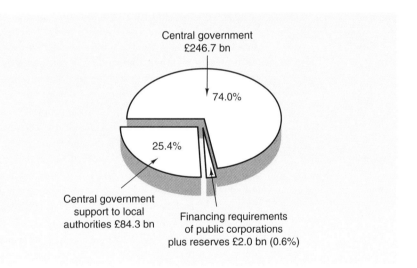

Central government £246.7 bn

74.0%

25.4%

Central government support to local authorities £84.3 bn

Financing requirements of public corporations plus reserves £2.0 bn (0.6%)

The size of public expenditure

So far we have looked at changing *shares* within total public spending, but has the *absolute* level of public spending grown as fast as critics suggest? Such people usually point to a single statistic for evidence; for instance, that the public sector employs about 25% of the labour force or, as with Milton Friedman, that if public expenditure grows to around 60% of National Income then it will threaten to destroy freedom and democracy. Actually, estimates for the ratio of public spending to National Income vary widely, depending on the definitions used for each item. Figures for 1998/99 put general government expenditure at around 39.9% of GDP at market prices (see Table 18.1 below). If, however, transfer payments are excluded from government expenditure, as they are from the measurement of National Income, then general

(a) Government spending as a proportion of GNP at factor cost (%)							
1790	1890	1910	1932	1951	1966	1970	1976
12.0	8.0	12.0	29.0	40.2	40.2	44.8	51.4
(b) Government spending as a proportion of GDP at market price (%)							
1978/79	1982/83	1986/87	1988/89	1990/91	1992/93	1995/96	1998/99
44.0	47.3	42.7	37.8	39.2	42.9	42.7	39.9

Note: From 1977 onwards, an approximately 6% upward revision should be made to any government spending/National Income ratio if comparison with pre-1977 figures is to be made. *Sources:* Treasury (1998b); Brown and Jackson (1982).

government expenditure falls dramatically to less than 30% of GDP at market prices. What, then, is the truth about the size of public expenditure?

An examination of data from the Office for National Statistics (ONS) suggests that as many as ten measures could be used for estimating the size of public expenditure. The measure selected will depend on the question at issue. If the intention is to assess the *financial resources* passing through the hands of government, then a ratio involving general government expenditure might be appropriate. However, the ONS's definition of National Income in the Blue Book excludes current grants and other transfers. Strictly, therefore, these same items should be excluded from government expenditure. They do not represent additional demand for resources, they are merely transfers of purchasing power from the taxpayer to other sectors of the community. Using this argument, a ratio of general government expenditure on goods and services of approximately 30% of National Income would appear to be the most appropriate measure.

No single measure of public expenditure has met with universal agreement, and even when one has been widely used for some time, it can be subject to change for a variety of reasons. In April 1977 general government expenditure was redefined to bring the UK into line with OECD accounting methods, and resulted in an apparent overnight reduction of some 6% in measured public expenditure. Again, what was previously tax relief may be reclassified as government expenditure, as with child tax allowances being replaced by child benefit in 1977. Public expenditure will also be affected by changes in the degree of 'privatization' (which is recorded as negative expenditure) or by changes in public sector pricing.

The National Income aggregate used for comparison will also influence our impression of the size of the public sector. Some ratios use domestic product, which measures resources produced *entirely within the domestic circular flow*. If, however, our interest was in the resources produced by UK nationals, *wherever they happen to be located*, then our ratio should use national product. Yet again, both domestic and national products could be valued 'gross' (including depreciation) or 'net' (excluding depreciation); at 'market prices', including the effects of taxes and subsidies, or at 'factor cost', excluding them.

For all these reasons, public spending ratios must be treated with caution when used in policy analysis.

Explanations of the growth in public expenditure

No matter what the definition, statistics show that the government sector of the economy has expanded over the last 150 years (see Fig. 18.6), both in money and

Fig. 18.6. General government expenditure as a percentage of GDP.

real terms, and as a percentage of National Income. In Table 18.1, Brown and Jackson (1982), quoting a variety of sources, show a dramatically rising trend of government spending as a proportion of GNP at factor cost up to 1976. The trend (using a different statistical series) continued upwards for data after 1976, reaching a peak of 47.3% in 1982/83. Since then there has been a sustained fall in government spending as a percentage of National Income, though for a few years during the recession of the early 1990s the percentage had risen before resuming its downward path.

The 1979 government was returned with a mandate to cut public expenditure. Initially the results were very disappointing as public expenditure continued to grow.

The explanation of the above trends and the difficulties involved in controlling public expenditure are based on two types of analysis: microeconomic and macroeconomic respectively.

Microeconomic analysis   Explanations based on microeconomic analysis suggest that additional public spending can be seen as the result of governments continually intervening to correct market failure. This would include the provision of 'public goods' such as collective defence, the police, and local amenities. An extra unit of such goods can be enjoyed by one person, without anyone else's enjoyment being affected. In other words the marginal social cost of provision is zero, and it is often argued in welfare economics that the 'efficiency' price should, therefore, be zero. Private markets are unable to cope with providing goods at zero price, so that public provision is the only alternative should this welfare argument be accepted. Microeconomic analysis would also cover extra public spending due to a change in the composition of the 'market', such as an ageing population incurring greater expenditure on health care.

Macroeconomic analysis   There are also explanations of the growth of public spending based on long-run macroeconomic theories and models. The starting point in this field is the work of Wagner (see Bird 1971), who used empirical evidence to support his argument that government expenditure would inevitably increase at a rate faster than the rise in national production. Wagner suggested that 'the pressures of social progress' would create tensions which could only be resolved by increased state activity in law and order, economic and social services, and participation in material production. Using the economists' terms, Wagner was in effect suggesting that public sector services and products are 'normal', with high income elasticities of demand. Early studies in the UK by Williamson during the 1960s tended to support Wagner, indicating overall income elasticities for public sector services of 1.7, and for public sector goods of 1.3, with similar results in other advanced industrialized countries. Further evidence in favour of Wagner's ideas came during the 1980s when studies by the OECD concluded that the proportion of GNP absorbed by public expenditure between 1954 and the early 1980s on 'merit goods' (education, health and housing) and 'income maintenance' (pensions, sickness, family and unemployment benefits) had doubled from 14% to 28%, as an average across all the advanced industrialized countries, with high income elasticities and low price elasticities playing a major part in this observed growth. Surveys of less developed economies were, however, more confusing, with econometric studies suggesting that little of the growth in public spending could be 'explained' by rising incomes (or low price elasticities).

Peacock and Wiseman's 'displacement theory', covering the period 1890–1953, suggested that public spending was not rising with the smooth, small changes predicted by Wagner, but that it was displaced (permanently) upwards by social upheavals associated, for instance, with depressions or wars leading to demands for new social expenditure (Fig. 18.6 above indicates the displacements of 1914–18 and 1939–45). Displacement theory has, however, been criticized for giving insufficient weight to political influences on the level of public expenditure. A further criticism of 'displacement' theory is the fact that for the UK there is little evidence that ratchet increases in public spending are long lasting. In fact, where the ratio of public expenditure to National Income has continued to rise in the 1970s and 1980s, it has been more easily explained by downward deviations of trend National Income in recession, with consequent increases in spending on unemployment benefits and social services, rather than through any upward revision of government expenditure plans.

The conclusion that must be drawn from reviewing such work is that there is no definite micro- or macro-explanation of the growth path for public expenditure. It then follows that there is no inevitable 'law' ensuring that public expenditure becomes a progressively rising proportion of National Income. However, in a recessionary period such as that of the early 1990s, increased spending on unemployment and social services may indeed cause a sharp increase in the share of public expenditure in National Income. Demographic changes may also conspire to raise the share of public expenditure. There was considerable debate in the mid-1980s of the mounting 'burden' on the working population likely to result from the growing number of pensioners in the second and third decades of the next century. It has been estimated that the UK dependency ratio – the non-working population divided by the working population – will have risen from the current 0.52 to 0.62 by 2030. By 2030, therefore, each worker will be required to contribute 18% more real income to sustain the current level of welfare provision. It is scenarios such as this which have led to renewed scrutiny of the practicability of a welfare state along present lines.

Table 18.2 Total outlays* of government as a percentage of GDP at market prices. Some international comparisons.

	1964	1974	1979	1989	1998
Australia	22.1	31.6	31.4	33.1	34.6
Austria	32.1	41.9	48.9	50.0	49.9
Belgium	30.3	39.4	49.3	55.7	51.6
Canada	28.9	36.8	39.0	44.6	41.6
Denmark	24.8	45.9	53.2	59.4	52.5
France	34.6	39.3	45.0	49.4	53.9
Italy	30.1	37.9	45.5	51.5	49.5
Japan	N/A	24.5	31.6	31.5	35.6
The Netherlands	33.7	47.9	55.8	55.9	47.5
Norway	29.9	44.6	50.4	54.6	45.3
Sweden	31.1	48.1	60.7	59.9	59.6
UK	32.4	44.9	42.7	41.2	39.2
US	27.5	32.2	31.7	36.1	31.6
Germany	32.4	44.6	47.6	45.5	47.4
Average EU countries	32.1	40.7	45.5	47.8	47.5
Average OECD countries	29.9	36.3	41.2	41.5	38.6

*Total government outlay = final consumption expenditure + interest on national debt + subsidies + social security transfers to households + gross capital formation.
Source: Adapted from OECD (1998) *Economic Outlook*, November.

International comparisons of public expenditure

Given that public expenditure has grown over time in the UK, how do we compare with other countries? Conclusions based on OECD surveys indicate that UK public expenditure patterns are similar to those in most other advanced industrialized countries, although inferences drawn from international surveys must be treated with caution. The OECD definitions are frequently different from national ones, public sector boundaries vary between countries, and fluctuating exchange rates compromise any attempt at a standard unit of value.

Table 18.2 indicates that the growing share of UK public expenditure in National Income has been paralleled in other countries. If anything, public expenditure has grown less quickly in the UK; in 1964 it was joint third highest, with Germany, of the fourteen countries shown in Table 18.2; by 1989 it was only eleventh highest of those same fourteen countries, and by 1998 it had retained its position of only being eleventh highest. Again, whereas the government outlay ratio averaged 47.5% across all the EU countries in 1998, the UK at 39.2% was considerably below that average. In comparative terms it would appear that there is little cause for alarm at the growth path of UK public expenditure.

Should public expenditure be restricted?

Freedom and choice

Arguments for controlling or reducing the size of public expenditure are wide-ranging but not always convincing.

One argument is that excessive government expenditure adversely affects individual freedom and choice. First, it is feared that it spoonfeeds individuals, taking away the incentive for personal provision, as with private insurance for sickness or old age. Second, that by impeding the market mechanism it may restrict consumer choice. For instance, the state may provide goods and services that are in little demand, whilst discouraging others (via taxation) that might otherwise have been bought. Third, it has been suggested that government provision may encourage an unhelpful separation between payment and cost in the minds of consumers. With government provision, the good or service may be free or subsidized, so that the amount paid by the consumer will understate the true cost (higher taxes, etc.) of providing him or her with that good or service, thereby encouraging excessive consumption of the item.

Crowding out the private sector

The previous Conservative government had long believed that (excessive) public expenditure was at the heart of Britain's economic difficulties. It regarded the private sector as the source of wealth creation, part of which it saw as being used to subsidize the public sector. Sir Keith Joseph clarified this view during the 1970s by alleging that 'a wealth-creating sector which accounts for one-third of the national product carries on its back a State subsidized sector which accounts for two-thirds. The rider is twice as heavy as the horse'.

Bacon and Eltis (1978) attempted to give substance to this view. They suggested that public expenditure growth had led to a transfer of productive resources from the private sector to a public sector producing largely non-marketed output, and that this had been a major factor in the UK's poor performance in the post-war period. Bacon and Eltis noted that public sector employment had increased by some 26%, from 5.8 million workers to 7.3 million, between 1960 and 1978, a time when total employment was largely unchanged. They then alleged that the private (marketed) sector was being squeezed by higher taxes to finance this growth in the public sector – the result being deindustrialization, low labour productivity, low economic growth and balance of payments problems (see also Chapter 17).

Control of money

Another argument used by those who favour restricting public expenditure is that it must be cut in order to limit the growth of money supply and to curb inflation. The argument is that a high Public Sector Borrowing Requirement (PSBR) following public expenditure growth, must be funded by the issue of Treasury bills and government stocks. Since there are inadequate 'real' savings to be found in the non-bank private sector, these bills and bonds inevitably find their way into the hands of the banks. As we will see in Chapter 20, they may then form the basis for a multiple expansion of bank deposits (money), with perhaps inflationary consequences.

A related argument is that public expenditure must be restricted, not only to limit the supply of money, but also its 'price' – the rate of interest. The suggestion here is that to sell the extra bills and bonds to fund a high PSBR, interest rates must rise to attract investors. This then puts pressure on private sector borrowing, with the rise in interest rates inhibiting private sector investment and investment-led growth. A major policy aim of the government has, therefore, been to reduce public sector borrowing.

Incentives to work, save and take risks

There are also worries that increased public spending not only pushes up government borrowing to fund a high PSBR, but also leads to higher taxes, thereby reducing the incentives to work, save and take risks. The evidence linking taxes to incentives is reviewed in Chapter 19. Suffice it to say here that the evidence to support the general proposition that higher taxes undermine the work ethic is largely inconclusive.

Balance of payments stability

A further line of attack has been that the growth of public expenditure may have destabilized the economy. During the 1970s and early 1980s this view was implied by the Cambridge Economic Policy Group (CEPG), who used an accounting identity (see Chapter 24) to demonstrate that a higher PSBR must lead to a deterioration in the balance of payments. The common sense of their argument is that higher public spending raises interest rates and attracts capital inflows, which in turn raise the demand for sterling and therefore the exchange rate. A higher pound then makes exports dearer and imports cheaper, so that the balance of payments deteriorates.

These various lines of reasoning have been challenged by, amongst others, the New Cambridge School which suggested that the relationships between the public sector and economic management may by no means be so simple. In fact, one adherent of the New Cambridge School, Lord Kaldor, went so far as to say that there was no empirical support for a high PSBR leading either to substantial growth in money supply or to high rates of interest. Similarly, the claim that resources liberated by the public sector would automatically find their way into the private sector was hardly supported by the rising unemployment trend of the early 1980s and early 1990s. Another criticism has pointed to the fact that public expenditure cuts, rather than helping to control unemployment (by cutting inflation in a monetarist model), have either caused or exaggerated current unemployment (see Chapter 23).

The debate on the role of public expenditure continues. Nevertheless, both the previous Conservative government and the present Labour government have accepted that, as a cornerstone of the medium-term financial strategy, they should squeeze inflation progressively out of the economy, through a close control of the rate of growth of public expenditure. Continuing fiscal rectitude is seen as important for a government committed to the Maastricht criteria for fiscal convergence (see Chapter 28). These include a 3% target for the overall ratio of PSBR to GDP, and a 60% target for the ratio of public debt to GDP.

Fiscal 'rules'

In addition to its commitment to the Maastricht criteria for fiscal convergence, in 1998 the Labour government committed itself to the following two important 'fiscal rules'.

- The 'golden rule'; over the economic cycle the government will only borrow to invest and will not borrow to fund current expenditure.
- The 'public debt rule'; the ratio of public debt to National Income will be held over the economic cycle at a 'stable and prudent' level.

In effect the 'golden rule' implies that current expenditure will be covered by current revenue (see Chapter 19) over the economic cycle. Put another way, any PSBR must be used only for investment purposes, with 'investment' defined as in the National Accounts.

The 'public debt rule' is rather less clear in that the phrase 'stable and prudent' is somewhat ambiguous. However, taken together with the 'golden rule' it essentially means that, as an average over the economic cycle, the ratio of PSBR to National Income cannot exceed the ratio of investment to National Income. Given that we have already seen that, historically, government investment has been no more than 2–3% of National Income (see Fig. 18.4 earlier), then clearly the PSBR as a percentage of National Income must be kept within strict bounds.

This inevitably brings into focus the procedure for the planning, monitoring and control of public expenditure.

Public expenditure planning, monitoring and control

Governments must seek to *plan* levels of public expenditure several years into the future, especially since any rise in public expenditure must either be financed by additional taxation or by increased borrowing. Governments must also develop and apply procedures to *monitor* and *control* public expenditure. All three elements are involved to some extent in the Public Expenditure Survey 'rounds', to which all the spending Departments must submit on a regular and ongoing basis.

Public Expenditure Survey (PES)

Planning public expenditure for the next three years begins with the Public Expenditure Survey (PES). As part of this process the spending Departments discuss their spending proposals with the Public Expenditure Division of the Treasury, with all proposals expressed in cash terms. This PES 'round' usually takes place between April and September of each year, with the results of the PES announced at the end of November when the Chancellor presents his Budget Statement to Parliament. To avoid any planning 'surprises' the major spending Departments, such as the Department of Social Security, actually undergo *two* PES rounds each year, the second lasting from October to April.

Control Total (CT)

We have already noted the importance attached to the 'golden rule', which has resulted in the government paying less attention to monitoring and controlling *cyclical* components of expenditure, such as unemployment benefit and various types of income support. This has led to the government establishing a new Control Total (CT) for public expenditure, which covers around 85% of the value of spending included in General Government Expenditure (GGE). An underlying objective of the CT is to help government focus on those items of expenditure which it can directly control and which are independent of cyclical fluctuations in the economy. As well as excluding unemployment benefit and income support, the CT also excludes central government gross debt interest (since borrowing and interest payments tend to rise during recession and fall during recovery).

Until 1992, the Ministers in charge of the spending Departments would seek to agree on spending limits for their Departments in *bilateral* negotiations with the Chief Secretary to the Treasury. The agreed sums for each Department would then be added together and announced in an 'Autumn Statement' on public spending plans.

Since 1993, however, the spending Ministers have had to meet face-to-face in Cabinet in October or November to fight for a share of the already established overall value for the Control Total. Any extra given to one spending Department must be funded at the expense of another spending Department by reallocating the provisionally agreed CT. Clearly this procedure is intended to restrict the possibility of 'upward drift' in total public spending, which many critics claimed to have been a constant feature of the previous system of simply aggregating the outcomes of bilateral negotiations between spending Departments and the Treasury.

Further, since 1993 we have had a unified Budget in March, in which both revenue raising and expenditure plans are discussed together. Prior to 1993, the spending totals were announced in the 'Autumn Statement' and the revenue-raising measures to finance them were announced some six months later in the March Budget. This separation of time between announcing planned expenditure and announcing methods for raising the tax revenue to fund that expenditure, was seen as encouraging public expenditure growth, since the public would be less likely to associate any need for higher taxes in the March Budget with announcements of higher public expenditure in the previous Autumn. To remedy this, since 1993 we have had a 'unified' Budget, with planned expenditure and planned tax revenue announced together, reinforcing the linkage between the two.

As already noted, the government still measures General Government Expenditure but now places greater emphasis upon the Control Total for planning purposes.

Forecasts   Since the expenditure plans for each Department must cover three years, *forecasts* are needed for the future expenditures required to implement the agreed policies over this time period. The expenditure forecasts for each Department are based on the work of both *internal* Departmental experts (e.g. statisticians and economists) and *external* experts (e.g. members of the independent Government Actuaries Department). Further, the basic assumptions on which these forecasts rest include estimates of future changes in variables such as retail prices, average earnings, unemployment rates, economic growth, etc. To ensure that the various departmental forecasts rest on *common* assumptions, the Treasury provides the spending Departments with projections of the data on expected values for all these variables over the next three years.

Agreement by the government on the future spending plans of a Department implies agreement on the policy proposals produced by that Department over the next three years. Such policy proposals are usually generated by the Policy Group which resides within each Department. Members of the Policy Group will seek to reflect the political priorities of both the government and the Departmental Ministers, as well as taking into account the representation of various pressure groups and any current research findings in the field. These policy proposals, once agreed, are then costed by a Specialist Group within the Department containing Statisticians and Economists, and these costings will in turn provide the basis for the Department expenditure forecasts.

An outline of the various processes involved in a Public Expenditure Survey has been provided by Weir (1998), with the Department of Social Security (DSS) used to illustrate a system common to most spending Departments (Fig. 18.7).

The DSS is the largest spending Department and accounts for around 30% of planned public expenditure. Expenditure on Social Security benefits, such as the Retirement Pension, Housing Benefit and Child Benefit, account for 95% of the total DSS bill. Social Security expenditure is almost entirely demand led, so estimating future expenditure requires projections as to how that demand is likely to change in the future. Factors influencing Social Security expenditure can usefully be grouped into four key headings.

- *Demographic*: the size and the structure of the population are key variables here, for example an ageing population will reduce spending on Child Benefit, but increase spending on Retirement Pensions.
- *Economic*: the projected levels of unemployment, earnings, prices and economic growth will affect the demand for various types of benefit and therefore the amount of benefit paid.
- *Social*: changes in family structures, for example the frequency of divorce and of lone parenthood, will affect benefit expenditures.
- *Policy*: the introduction of new benefits, changes to entitlement, changes to benefit rates, etc. will all affect benefit expenditure.

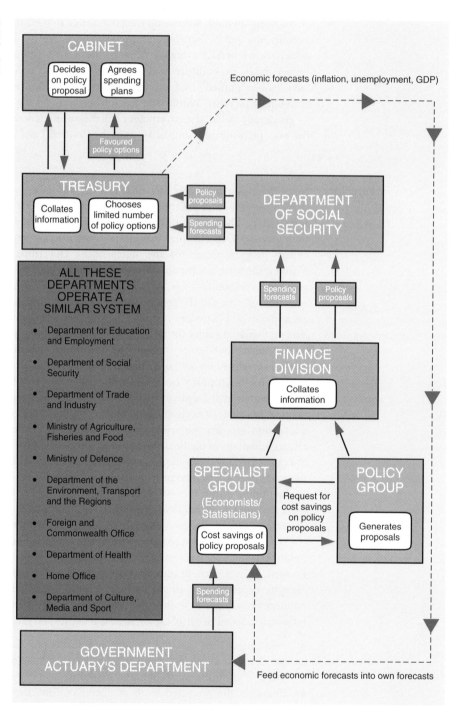

Fig. 18.7. The Public
Expenditure Survey (PES)
within the Department for
Social Security (DSS).
Source: Adapted from
Weir (1998).

The government is obliged to report the differences between *forecast* expenditure and *actual out-turn* for any given year; drawing attention to any discrepancies between what was planned to be spent and what was actually spent is seen as helping the process of monitoring and controlling public expenditure.

The planning, monitoring and control of public expenditure can therefore be seen to have undergone considerable change in recent years, with the underlying aim of curbing tendencies towards an upward drift in spending totals. The procedures involved in the PES, the introduction of a new Control Total, the unified budget, obligations to report any discrepancies between forecast expenditures and actual out-turn, are all parts of a more structured and accountable system for public expenditure.

A further element in such a system has been the so-called government drive for greater 'efficiency' in the public sector.

The drive for efficiency

Increasingly strident claims were made throughout the 1980s that, in the absence of competition, public services would always be produced inefficiently. One remedy might clearly be to increase such competition by privatizing the public services (see Chapter 8). Where this 'remedy' was not available then it was argued that efficiency could be improved by making sure that the delivery of public services conformed more closely to the needs of those who used them, rather than to the interests of those who provided them. This view led to a wave of reforms, including the introduction of contracting out and competitive tendering, the creation of Next Step Agencies, and the introduction of Value for Money Audits.

- *Contracting out and competitive tendering*: putting services previously provided through the public sector out to tender has led to cost savings of varying magnitudes. For example, there have been estimates of savings of 20% in the case of NHS catering and laundry, and savings of 14% in the case of highway services. In a number of other cases savings of 7% have been realized (Griffiths 1998).
- *Next Step Agencies*: these have been introduced within government departments with the intention of improving the management of such departments. The idea here has been to separate the management of policy (the responsibility of central government) from operational management (the responsibility of the Agencies). For example the Department of Social Security (DSS) has five agencies – the Benefits Agency, the Contributions Agency, the Child Support Agency, the War Pensions Agency and the IT Services Agency. Such Agencies have often been given the task of meeting a number of key performance indicators or targets, giving a yardstick against which their subsequent performance can be evaluated.
- *Value for money (VFM) audits*: these are part of the Financial Management Initiative (FMI) aimed at ensuring that public provision of goods and services is economic, efficient and effective. Under the FMI, central government departments have had to demonstrate to the Treasury that they have in place a VFM framework whereby audits are undertaken to check that managers are finding resource savings, while at the same time improving the quality of public services. Again, such procedures have often involved performance indicators.
- *Private Finance Initiative (PFI)*: the intention here has been to identify projects which can attract private sector finance to be used alongside public sector finance (see Myers 1998).

Conclusion

The definition of public expenditure is by no means clear-cut and must depend upon the question at issue. Since National Income also has many variants, any public expenditure/National Income ratio must be treated with caution. The estimate for 1998/99 puts general government expenditure at around 40% of GDP at market prices. If, however, we subtract grants and transfers from public expenditure, as we do from all the National Income measures, then the figure falls substantially to around 30%. Whatever the definition chosen, the proportion of government spending in National Income has risen steadily throughout the twentieth century. The reduction in the growth of National Income played an important part in raising the ratio in the early 1980s and early 1990s; both directly, by restricting the denominator, and indirectly, by causing unplanned increases in expenditure on social security. Whether a growing public sector 'crowds out', or otherwise adversely affects the private sector, is a matter of deep controversy. Certainly in comparative terms the UK is by no means exceptional, with the share of UK government spending in National Income well below the average for the EU countries. More 'rigour' has been imposed on procedures to plan, monitor and control public expenditure. This, together with renewed growth in National Income, has helped to progressively reduce the ratio of government spending to National Income to below 40% in 1998, with further falls projected over the next few years. The move, in late-1992, towards a new 'control total' for public spending, made it clear that the government would continue to seek a tight fiscal stance, especially on items of expenditure of a non-cyclical nature. The determination of the government to adhere to the Maastricht criteria of a ratio of PSBR to GDP below 3% and of public debt to GDP below 60%, suggest that public expenditure will remain closely controlled. This view is further strengthened by the announcement of fiscal 'rules' in 1998, especially the 'golden rule' whereby government borrowing will only be undertaken to support public investment and not current consumption.

Key points

- Although government spending is rising in real terms by around 1% per annum at present, this is less than the growth in real National Income.
- As a result the share of government spending in National Income is falling; from almost 45% in 1992–93 to just below 40% in 1998–99.
- Critics argue that too high a proportion of government spending goes on 'rescue' and 'welfare' and too little on 'renewal'. In this view more of the public purse should be used to support 'investment' type expenditures (on human or physical capital) directed towards raising future National Income.
- International comparisons do *not* suggest that UK public expenditure is exceptionally high as a percentage of GDP. In 1998 it was only 11th highest out of 14 countries investigated, and some eight percentage points below the EU average.
- Many of the reasons put forward for controlling public expenditure involve the desire to cut the PSBR. The government concern is that too high a PSBR will force higher taxes and interest rates, with adverse effects on incentives and investment in the private sector.
- Part of the 'convergence criteria' within the EU involves keeping the PSBR no higher than 3% of GDP, implying tight control of public expenditure.
- The government has also introduced two key 'fiscal rules', both of which imply a tight control of public expenditure.
- The procedures for planning, monitoring and controlling public expenditure have modified. These include changes to the departmental PES, a new 'Control Total', a unified Budget, relating spending forecasts to out-turns, and various initiatives to increase efficiency in the public sector.

References and further reading

Bacon, R. and **Eltis, W.** (1978) *Britain's Economic Problem: too few producers*, 2nd edn, Macmillan.

Bird, R. M. (1971) Wagner's Law of Expanding State Activity, *Public Finance*, **26**, 1.

Brown, C. V. and **Jackson, P. M.** (1982) *Public Sector Economics*, 2nd edn, Martin Robertson.

Flemming, J. and **Oppenheimer, P.** (1996) Are government spending and taxes too high (or too low)?, *National Institute Economic Review*, July.

Griffiths, M. A. (1998) Government expenditure and efficiency, *Money Management Review*, **51**.

Joseph, K. (1976) *Monetarism is not Enough*, Barry Rose.

Myers, D. (1998) The Private Finance Initiative – a progress report, *The Economic Review*, **15**, 4, April.

Papava, V. (1993) A new view of the economic ability of the government; egalitarian goods and GNP, *International Journal of Social Economics*, **20**, 8.

Rowthorn, R. (1992) Government spending and taxation in the Thatcher era, in Michie, J. (ed.) *The Economic Legacy, 1979–1992*, Academic Press.

Treasury (1998a) Public Expenditure: Statistical Supplement to the Financial Statement and Budget Report 1998–99.

Treasury (1998b) Financial Statement and Budget Report, 1998–99.

Weir, J. (1998) Government spending: a view from the inside, *Money Management Review*, **51**.

Chapter 19

Taxation

This chapter looks at the existing pattern of UK taxation and the changes that have taken place in recent years. We examine the degree of progressiveness of the UK tax system and the effects of the recent switches between direct and indirect taxation. The changing burden of taxation in the UK is charted, and international comparisons are presented. We then consider the effect of higher taxes on incentives to work, save and take risks, and on the rise of the 'black economy'. After a more general treatment of the direct vs indirect tax debate, we conclude with a brief look at recent reforms of local taxation and social security benefits.

The taxes that are collected: some taxation concepts

Taxes may be classified in a number of different ways.

- The method of collection.
- The tax base.
- The tax rate.

The method of collection

Taxes may be grouped by the administrative arrangement for their collection.

Direct or indirect

Income tax is paid *directly* to the Exchequer by the individual taxpayer (mainly through Pay As You Earn – PAYE), on the full amount of income from employment and investment in the fiscal year. The same is true of corporation tax, paid by firms on company profits. On the other hand, value added tax (VAT), though paid by consumers, reaches the Exchequer indirectly, largely through retailers acting as collecting agencies. Taxes may therefore be classified as either direct or indirect, according to the administrative arrangement for their collection. From Table 19.1 we see that direct taxes – in the form of income tax, capital taxes, corporation tax and petroleum revenue tax – were expected to produce 38.2% (126.1/330.1) of total government receipts in 1998/99. Income tax is by far the

Table 19.1 How public spending is paid for. Income of general government.

	General government receipts (£bn)		
	1997/98	1998/99 forecast	1998/99 %
Inland Revenue:			
Income tax	76.7	84.3	
Corporation tax	30.5	30.0	
Petroleum tax	1.1	0.5	
Windfall tax	2.6	2.6	38.2
Capital Gains tax	1.4	2.2	
Inheritance tax	1.7	1.9	
Stamp duty	3.4	4.6	
Total Inland Revenue	**117.4**	**126.1**	
Customs & Excise:			
VAT	51.0	53.3	
Fuel duties	19.1	21.5	
Tobacco	8.3	8.9	
Betting	1.5	1.6	
Alcohol	5.7	6.0	28.9
Customs duties	2.3	2.0	
Air Passenger duty	0.5	0.7	
Insurance premium tax	1.0	1.3	
Others	0.5	0.3	
Total Customs & Excise	**89.9**	**95.6**	
Vehicle excise duties	4.6	4.6	
Oil royalties	0.5	0.3	8.2
Business rates	14.7	15.0	
Others	7.6	7.2	
Total taxes	**234.7**	**248.8**	**75.3**
Social security receipts	50.5	53.7	16.3
Council tax	11.1	11.6	3.5
Interest and dividends	5.1	4.5	1.4
Trading surplus and rent	4.8	4.9	1.5
Other receipts	7.1	6.6	2.0
Total receipts	**313.3**	**330.1**	**100.0**

Note: Items may not add up to totals because of rounding.
Source: Treasury (1998) *Financial Statement and Budget Report* (modified).

most important direct tax, alone contributing almost 25.5% of government receipts. Strictly speaking we should add the various National Insurance contributions to the total for direct taxation. These are a compulsory levy on employers, employees and the self-employed, expressed as a fixed percentage of total earnings, and paid directly to the Exchequer (shown under the 'Social Security receipts' heading). They total some £53.7bn in 1998/99 and provide around 16.3% of government receipts. They are not, however, included in the Consolidated Fund revenue tables.

Indirect taxes – VAT, a range of excise duties on oil, tobacco, alcohol and motor cars, and import duties – were expected to produce 28.9% of total government receipts in 1998/99. Of these VAT (16.1% of total 'receipts') was the most important. The indirect taxes are collected by Customs and Excise.

This Consolidated Fund revenue (£248.8bn), together with Social Security

Table 19.2 Public sector borrowing requirement.

	£ billion					
	1993–94	1994–95	1995–96	1996–97	1997–98	1998–99
General government expenditure	278	288	303	309	317	332
General government receipts	231	250	269	286	313	330
General government borrowing requirement	47	38	34	23	4	2
Public corporations' market and overseas borrowing	−1	−2	−2	0	−1	0
PSBR	**46**	**36**	**32**	**23**	**3 (5)**	**2 (4)**
Money GDP	639	678	709	752	797	834
PSBR as percent of money GDP	**7.0**	**5.25**	**4.5**	**3.0**	**0.4 (0.6)**	**0.2 (0.5)**

Note: = excluding windfall tax
Figures rounded to nearest £1bn (estimates post 1997).
Source: Treasury (1998) *Financial Statement and Budget Report* (modified).

receipts (£53.7bn), business rates (some £15.0bn) and the Council Tax (£11.6bn) plus other miscellaneous receipts, including those from privatization, are necessary to pay for the government's expenditure plans of around £333bn in 1998/99.

Details of the main items of government income and expenditure are shown in Table 19.2.

The growing economy of the late 1980s helped contribute to increased tax revenue and the creation of *budget surpluses* from 1987/88 to 1990/91. However, these surpluses or PSDR (Public Sector Debt Repayment) shrank rapidly after 1989 as government revenue fell and government expenditure rose in the wake of the most protracted period of recession since the inter-war years. In March 1998 the government was projecting a maximum budget deficit or PSBR of £4bn for 1998/99 (excluding windfall tax), as can be seen in Table 19.2. If GDP growth remains relatively steady between 1997 and the end of the century, then the government forecasts that the PSBR will be in balance around the year 2000.

The tax base The tax base is essentially the 'object' to which the tax rate is applied. Excluding National Insurance contributions, taxes are usually grouped under three headings as regards tax bases: taxes on income (income, corporation and petroleum revenue taxes and fuel duties); taxes on expenditure (VAT and customs and excise duties); and taxes on capital (capital gains and inheritance tax).

Fig. 19.1. Government
revenue 1998/99 and the
tax base (as % of total tax
revenue of £248.8bn).

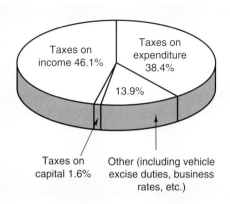

Fig. 19.1. Government revenue 1998/99 and the tax base (as % of total tax revenue of £248.8bn).

Figure 19.1 shows that for 1998/99, taxes on income were expected to yield 46.1% of the Total Tax Revenue of £248.8bn; taxes on expenditure 38.4% and taxes on capital, 1.6%. In addition to these taxes (not in Fig. 19.1) there were compulsory levies in the form of Social Security receipts (National Insurance contributions) from individuals and companies of £53.7bn and council tax of £11.6bn, raising the burden further on income.

Classifying taxes in terms of tax base, rather than method of collection, is often of more interest to economists, especially when calculating tax incidence (on whom the tax falls)! However, using the tax base does present problems of definition. For instance, Lord Wrenbury, in a legal judgment in 1925, defined income tax as being that which is 'within the Act, taxable under the Act'. National Insurance contributions, because they are based on calculations by actuaries, are not classified as a tax on income, yet they are levied as a percentage of income. Whatever the tax base, the taxes levied can be one of two types, either specific (lump sum) or *ad valorem*.

Specific and *ad valorem* taxes   A *specific tax* is expressed as an absolute sum of money per unit of the good. Excise duties are often of this kind, being so many pence per packet of cigarettes or per proof of spirit. An *ad valorem* tax is a percentage tax, levied not on volume but on value; e.g. in 1999 VAT is 17.5% of sales price, and corporation tax is 30% of assessable profits for larger companies and 20% for smaller companies.

Rate of taxation   Another useful classification is between progressive, proportional and regressive taxes. Tax is imposed as a rate or series of rates; e.g. income tax in 1999 is levied at just 20%, 23% and 40% of taxable income whilst VAT items that are not exempted are zero-rated or pay 17.5%. These tax rates can be regarded as progressive, proportional or regressive, though such terms must be defined strictly as they are often used loosely. For a tax to be regarded as progressive, its rate structure must be such that the tax takes a rising proportion of total income as income increases; a proportional tax takes a constant proportion, whilst a regressive tax takes a declining proportion.

The pattern of UK taxation

A broadly proportional tax system

Since a progressive tax means that the rich pay more, not only in an *absolute* sense, but *as a proportion of their total income*, we need to know more than that the *marginal* rate of tax rises with income.[1] If, for instance, tax allowances and exemptions are more easily acquired by higher-income groups (as with mortgage repayments, etc.) then, despite a rising marginal rate, the individual may pay a smaller proportion of a higher total income in tax. In fact, it is the *average* rate[2] that is the best guide to whether the tax or tax system is, or is not, progressive. If the average rate is rising with income, then the tax *is* taking a higher proportion of higher incomes, i.e. the tax *is* progressive.

As we know from any game, say cricket, only when an individual scores more on his last (marginal) innings than his average for all previous innings, will his overall average actually rise. In the same way, only when the *marginal rate of tax is higher than the average rate*, will the average rate rise as income rises, and the tax be progressive. If the marginal and average rates are equal, then the average rate will be unchanged as income rises, so that the tax is proportional. If the marginal rate is below the average rate, then the average rate falls as income rises, and the tax is regressive.

Figure 19.2 shows that, for the UK, direct taxes (the unshaded area in each bar) are progressive, taking a larger proportion of the total (gross) income of richer households. Indirect taxes are in contrast regressive, taking a declining proportion of such income. Overall, taking *both* direct and indirect taxes together, the UK tax system is broadly proportional to income.

Fig. 19.2. Direct and indirect taxes as a per cent of gross household income (1996/97). *Source:* Adapted from ONS (1998) *The Effects of Taxes and Benefits on Household Income, 1996/97*, No. 533, April.

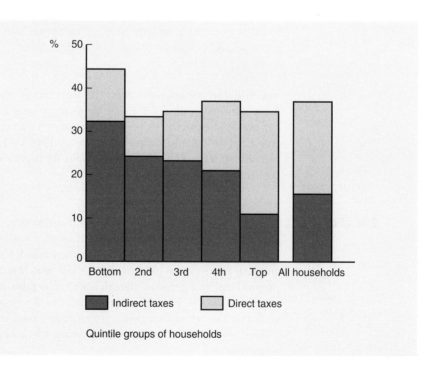

Table 19.3 The regressiveness of indirect taxes (1996–97).

Quintile groups of households	Indirect taxes as percentage of *disposable* income per household		
	VAT	Other indirect taxes	Total indirect taxes
Bottom fifth	13.9	22.4	36.4
Next fifth	9.5	16.4	25.9
Middle fifth	9.1	13.8	22.9
Next fifth	9.5	13.5	23.0
Top fifth	6.5	7.2	13.7

Source: Adapted from ONS (1998) *The Effects of Taxes and Benefits on Household Income, 1996/97*, No. 533, April.

Although indirect taxes as a whole are regressive, there is some variation between different types of indirect tax. As we observe from Table 19.3, VAT is a more mildly regressive tax, whereas other indirect taxes are strongly regressive.

A shift towards indirect taxation

We have seen that indirect taxes are more regressive than direct taxes. Here we chart the substantial changes that took place in the direct/indirect tax ratio during the 1970s and early 1980s.

As Fig. 19.3 indicates, throughout the 1950s and 1960s taxes on income (direct) and expenditure (indirect) maintained a steady relationship, with taxes on income yielding around 10% more revenue. During the early and mid-1970s, however, the balance changed in favour of direct taxes on income as revenue providers for central government, due in part to inflation raising money incomes (and therefore direct tax receipts) and in part to fiscal drag. Fiscal drag is the extra tax yield which results from the fact that changes in both tax allowances and tax bands may not occur until *after* inflation has had its impact on money incomes. By 1975 direct taxes on income had peaked, providing some 60% more revenue than taxes on expenditure. The ratio fell

Fig. 19.3. The ratio of central government taxes on income to taxes on expenditure. *Source:* Treasury (1998) *Financial Statement and Budget Report*, and previous issues.

substantially after that, and by 1986 direct taxes only provided some 10% more revenue than taxes on expenditure. After 1986 the ratio began to edge upwards again as incomes increased, with growing prosperity in the economy raising the yield from direct taxes. However, in 1988/89 the Chancellor once more reversed the trend by permitting a substantial over-indexation of tax allowances. This, together with the increase in VAT rates to 17.5% in the 1991 Budget, has caused the ratio to continue its downward path so that by 1994 it was below 1.

Income taxes are more 'visible' to individuals than expenditure taxes, which to some extent are hidden in product prices. This may well have contributed to the *feeling* that the UK was overtaxed, despite the fact that this is contradicted by the evidence (see Table 19.5 below). It may be helpful to look further into the factors helping to establish the pattern shown in Fig. 19.3.

With the slowing down of inflation in the mid-late 1970s, the ratio of direct to indirect taxes in total revenue began to fall. The new Conservative government in 1979 then made a deliberate switch away from direct income taxation towards indirect taxation, cutting the standard rate of income tax from 33 to 30%, and raising VAT from 8 to 15%. We might have expected this switch to reinforce the downward trend in the ratio of direct to indirect tax receipts. In fact, higher inflation in the early years of that government prevented the ratio falling. Since the early 1980s, the receipts from direct taxes on income have fluctuated around an average figure some 10% above those from indirect taxes on expenditure; we have returned to the broad pattern of the 1950s and 1960s. The restored importance of indirect taxes, whatever its source, must, in the context of our earlier analysis, have made the UK tax system less progressive than it would otherwise have been.

A rise in the UK tax burden

We have seen that the *structure* of UK taxation has changed in recent years. What about the *level* of taxation? The ratio of total tax take to National Income is a frequently used measure of tax 'burden'. We can see from Table 19.4 that between 1964 and 1970 the total receipts from all taxes (including National Insurance) rose sharply as a proportion of GDP. Between 1970 and 1974 the tax ratio fell from 37.5% to 33.75% but has risen since then. Even the substantial income tax *reductions* of the post 1988/89 budgets have left the total tax burden in 1998/99 at 37.7%, which is higher than when the Conservatives came into office in 1979. The fear that the tax burden will begin to rise rapidly in the second half of the 1990s to finance growing public expenditure on a population with more old people, led to proposals for radical changes in the Welfare State.

The UK tax burden: a comparative survey

Despite the projected rise in UK tax burden over the next few years, and contrary to popular public opinion, the UK is only a middle-ranked country in terms of tax burden. From Table 19.5 we see that in 1981 the UK was the eighth-ranked country out of twenty in terms of tax burden, below the Scandinavian countries and close to France. OECD data in 1996 gave the UK a lower ranking of twelfth. Despite the high level of tax revenue as a proportion of GDP over this ten year period, the UK tax burden in 1996 continued to lie well below that in the Scandinavian countries, where between 40% and 50% of GDP was taken in tax and social security contributions in that year, and below other major competitors such as France and Germany.

Table 19.4 UK tax burden.

Fiscal year	Tax as a percentage of GDP*
1964–65	30.00
1969–70	37.50
1973–74	33.75
1978–79	33.00
1979–80	33.80
1980–81	35.50
1981–82	38.50
1982–83	38.70
1983–84	37.90
1984–85	38.70
1985–86	37.80
1986–87	37.30
1987–88	37.10
1988–89	36.40
1989–90	36.00
1990–91	36.70
1991–92	35.80
1992–93	34.20
1993–94	33.50
1994–95	34.70
1995–96	35.60
1996–97	36.00
1997–98	37.20
1998–99	37.70

*Total taxes and National Insurance contributions as a percentage of money GDP.
Source: Adapted from Treasury (1998) Financial Statement and Budget Report.

Table 19.5 Comparative tax burdens and economic growth.

Tax* as a percentage of GNP	1981 Percentage	1981 Rank	1996 Percentage	1996 Rank	GDP growth† 1981–1997 Percentage	GDP growth† 1981–1997 Rank
Australia	33.5	14	30.7	16	2.5	=5
Austria	49.6	4	42.4	6	2.2	=7
Belgium	49.6	4	46.5	=3	1.9	9
Canada	40.0	12	37.2	11	2.0	8
Denmark	55.6	3	51.3	1	2.2	=7
Finland	39.6	13	46.5	=3	2.3	=6
France	47.6	7	44.5	4	1.8	=10
Germany	42.3	9	39.2	10	2.2	=7
Greece	31.6	16	41.4	8	1.7	11
Ireland	41.6	10	33.8	13	4.8	1
Italy	33.4	15	41.3	9	1.8	=10
Japan	28.3	19	28.5	18	3.0	=3
Luxembourg	40.0	11	44.0	=5	4.7	2
Netherlands	49.4	6	44.0	=5	2.3	=6
Norway	48.7	2	41.5	7	3.0	=3
Spain	27.2	20	34.0	14	2.5	=5
Sweden	56.9	1	49.7	2	1.5	12
Switzerland	30.8	18	33.9	15	1.2	13
United Kingdom	42.4	8	35.3	12	2.3	=6
United States	31.1	17	27.9	17	2.7	4

*Including social security contributions.
†Yearly averages.
Sources: OECD (1998) OECD in Figures, Paris; CSO (1995).

Tax burden and economic growth It can be concluded from the evidence of Table 19.5 that there is little relationship between low tax burdens and faster economic growth. Finland, with the third-highest tax burden in 1996, had an annual average growth rate of 2.3% in the period 1981–97, just above the OECD average of 2.1% per annum, and was also ranked as high as sixth in terms of growth rate. On the other hand, Switzerland, with one of the lowest tax burdens, had only the thirteenth-fastest growth rate of 1.2% in that period, well below the OECD average.

Tax schedules and tax rates We should, however, bear one or two cautionary points in mind before lapsing into complacency! A study by Messere, Owen and Teir (1982) suggests that published *tax schedules* are a greater disincentive to effort than the 'effective tax rates' (i.e. the tax actually paid after all personal and other allowances have been calculated). The argument here is that it is tax schedules as shown in Table 19.6, widely publicized in newspapers and annual tax returns, which form the basis for the ordinary citizen's notion of tax burden.

In analysing tax schedules, the Messere study found that a higher proportion of taxpayers (over 95%) paid the basic rate in the UK than elsewhere, and that both the initial and top rates of tax on earned income were higher in the UK than elsewhere. Nevertheless, the taxpayer on average income in the UK paid a marginal rate no higher than in other OECD countries. Since 1987/8 the Conservative and Labour governments have simplified the tax structure and reduced the tax rates (as shown in Table 19.6 and Fig. 19.4) in order to try to encourage incentives. By the late 1990s the Treasury could safely claim that the UK's top rate of income tax at 40% was below that of its major competitors, as can be seen from Fig. 19.5.

A further reason for taxpayers believing that the burden of taxation is higher than it actually is may arise from a failure to understand the method of collection of income tax. Income tax is *not* collected on the total amount of income. Each individual is granted allowances or exemptions that reduce the total amount of income liable to tax. In 1999/2000 each single person under 65 was, for example, given an allowance of £4,195; married couples were given an additional allowance of £1,900 over and above the single allowance and pensioners were given even higher allowances. These allowances, plus a few others, are deducted from the total income to produce the *taxable income*. Tax rates of 20%, 23% and 40% (on taxable incomes over £27,100) are then applied to this *taxable income*. Further tax relief is also given to mortgage

Table 19.6 UK income tax schedules 1987/88 and 1999/2000.

Rate of tax (%)	1987/88 Taxable income (£)	1999/2000 Taxable income (£)
20	–	0–4,300
23	–	4,301–27,100
27	0–17,900	–
40	17,901–20,400	Over 27,100
45	20,401–25,400	–
50	25,401–33,300	–
55	33,301–41,200	–
60	Over 41,200	–

Note: Investment income surcharge on unearned income was abolished in March 1984.

Fig. 19.4. Comparison of income tax between 1987/88 and 1999/2000.

□ 1987/88

▨ 1999/2000

27%   40%   45%   50%   55%   60%

20%   23%   40%

Taxable £4,301   £27,100
income

Fig. 19.5. Comparative maximum income tax rates 1997. *Source:* Adapted from OECD (1998) *OECD in Figures*, Paris.

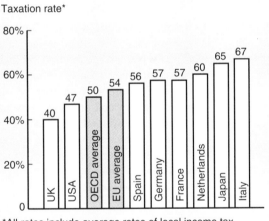

Taxation rate*

80%

60%

40%

20%

0

40   47   50   54   56   57   57   60   65   67

UK USA OECD average EU average Spain Germany France Netherlands Japan Italy

*All rates include average rates of local income tax where applicable.

payers. Such mortgage relief on interest payments to banks and building societies is worth some 15% of the gross monthly payments. Thus the average burden of taxation for the average taxpayer is considerably below the main 23 and 40% seen in the tax schedules.

Overall there appears little evidence that the UK has an excessive burden of tax in comparison to other countries. Although the proportion of GNP taken in tax has tended to rise in the UK since the early 1970s, the UK is, in comparative terms, a lower-ranked country in terms of tax-take, with tax (including community charge) amounting to 37.7% of GDP in 1998. However, particular groups of UK taxpayers at the lowest and highest taxable income scales did suffer unusually high marginal rates during the 1970s and 1980s. This, together with the growing 'visibility' of the income tax and social security payments system in the UK, may have created the impression of a comparatively high tax burden, but this impression was, in fact, misleading for the *average* taxpayer. Unfortunately the post 1988/89 reduction in tax rates and simplifications of the system have done little to improve the tax burden on low income earners, or to alter the overall burden of the tax system over the last fifteen years as seen in Table 19.4.

Does the level of taxation matter?

Clarke suggested in 1945, with the support of Keynes, that when taxation of all kinds was more than 25% of National Income, damaging pressures would follow. In fact, most industrial countries passed this figure over twenty-five years ago, with tax ratios of over 40% for some countries in the 1970s, yet they experienced low inflation and rapid growth of real incomes. However, perceptions of the benign nature of taxation have begun to change in more recent years, reverting back to those of Clarke and Keynes. Two of the major criticisms of a high tax burden relate to its (alleged) erosion of economic incentives and its encouragement of tax avoidance and evasion. We now consider these criticisms.

Impact of taxes on incentives to work, save and take risks

As the reader familiar with indifference curve analysis will know, a higher tax on income will have two effects, which pull in opposite directions. First, an 'income effect', with real income reduced via higher taxes, which means less consumption of all items, including leisure, i.e. more work is performed. Second, a 'substitution effect', with leisure now cheaper via higher taxes, since less real income is now sacrificed for each unit of leisure consumed. The substitution effect leads to cheaper leisure being substituted for work, i.e. less work. On grounds of theory alone we cannot tell which effect will be the stronger, i.e. whether higher taxes on income will raise or lower the time devoted to work rather than leisure (where, of course, the worker has some choice).

The only general conclusions that can be drawn from indifference analysis are the following:

1. Progressive taxes have higher substitution effects, and are therefore likely to cause a greater increase in leisure consumption (i.e. less work) than if the same sum of money were raised via a proportional tax.
2. Taxes on savings create a strong disincentive to future savings via their double-taxation effect. Since saving takes place out of real disposable (net) income, to tax the returns on savings is to impose a further tax on net income.
3. Taxes on investment may discourage high-risk projects. Investment projects involve combinations of risk and yield, those with more risk usually providing more yield. If yields on investment income are more heavily taxed, then this may discourage high-risk investments, such as North Sea oil-prospecting, and encourage low-risk investments (including cash-holding).

Theory can take us little further than this general analysis. Beyond it we must look at actual behaviour to assess the impact of higher taxes on incentives. Empirical studies have taken three forms: (a) controlled experiments, usually observing how selected persons respond to higher benefits (negative taxes); (b) questionnaires based on random samples, and (c) econometric studies using data on how people have responded in the past to tax changes.

Studies up to 1970   Brown and Dawson (1969) conducted an exhaustive review of tax studies in the UK and USA from 1947 to 1968. They concluded that higher taxation had a disincentive effect on work (income < substitution effect) for between 5 and 15% of the population. These were mainly people who had the greatest freedom to vary their hours of employment – those without families, the middle-aged, the wealthy, and rural workers. In contrast, higher taxation had an incentive effect on work (income > substitution effect) for a rather smaller percentage of the population, who were characteristically part of large families, young, less well-off, urban dwellers. From a national viewpoint the small *net* disincentive effect on the population of higher taxes was regarded by Brown and Dawson as of little significance; over 70% appeared neutral (income = substitution effect) in their work response to higher taxes.

As regards the UK, two of the most important studies reviewed by Brown and Dawson were those based on questionnaires by Break in 1956 and Fields and Stanbury in 1968. In 1956, Break found a small *net* disincentive effect, with an extra 3% of the population claiming higher taxes to be a disincentive to further work than claimed it to be an incentive. In 1968 Fields and Stanbury updated Break's UK study and found the *net* disincentive effect to have grown to 8% of the population. In both studies the *net* disincentive effect was greater for higher-income groups, as one might expect with these paying higher marginal taxes (stronger substitution effects). This small growth in overall *net* disincentive effect between 1956 and 1968, and its being more pronounced at higher-income levels, was really all the empirical support there was in the UK for those suggesting that higher taxes discouraged work effort.

Studies after 1970   Controlled experiments and questionnaire results after 1970 gave no clearer a picture than those before 1970. If anything, they again pointed to a slight disincentive of higher taxes. For instance, Brown and Levin found that an increase in marginal tax rates for 2,000 Scottish workers in 1974 reduced hours worked, at least for higher-income groups. Fiegehen and Reddaway conducted a study on incentives amongst senior managers at board level in 94 companies in 1978, just before the large tax cuts introduced by the (then) newly elected Conservative government a year or so later. Similarly to Break, and Fields and Stanbury (see above), they showed that 12% of managers reported an incentive effect of high taxation on hours of work, while an equal percentage reported a disincentive effect. The most common response from 41% was 'no reply or don't know'. Fiegehen and Reddaway concluded: 'it is clear that, in total, any disincentive effects that operated on senior managers had a minimal impact on the activities of British industry'. Such studies were hardly a basis for advocating that tax *cuts* would lead to an upsurge in work effort! An important study by the Institute of Fiscal Studies (Dilnot and Kell 1988) tried to assess the effects of the 1979/80 reduction in the top rate of UK income tax from 83% to 60% on tax receipts. The argument used to support these top-rate tax cuts was that the lower income tax rates should provide extra incentives to work harder and thus boost tax revenue. The study found that the subsequent increase in tax revenue during the period to 1985/86 could be explained mostly by factors such as employment growth, growth of earnings and growth of self-employment rather than by any 'incentive' effects. Dilnot and Kell felt that any 'incentive' effect which may have been present could only account, at most, for £1.2bn or 3% of the total increase in tax revenues over the period studied.

Flemming and Oppenheimer (1996) have also found little evidence to support the suggestion that reduced marginal tax rates at the upper end would unleash entrepreneurial talent and labour effort. They argue that if skilled or energetic workers supplied more effort (i.e. labour input/hours worked) as higher marginal tax rate fell, then one might expect that the *relative price* of their time/effort, i.e. wage per hour, would fall *vis à vis* other lower skilled groups via an increase in relative supply resulting in a decrease in relative price (i.e. wage per hour). However, as noted in Chapter 14, pre-tax hourly earnings between different skill and occupational levels have widened considerably over the last 15 years, indicating that the higher-income earners have *increased* their relative wages. This rather suggests that the higher income, higher skilled segment of the workforce may not have increased the number of hours worked, i.e. the supply of effort, but may merely have benefited from *demand* changes which have moved in their favour, as discussed in Chapter 14. Interestingly, the disincentive to work resulting from high real marginal rates of tax is arguably more of a problem for those on below-average incomes, as the discussion of the poverty 'trap' indicates below.

The Laffer curve   Professor Laffer derived a relationship between tax revenue and tax rates of the form shown in Fig. 19.6. The curve was the result of econometric techniques, through which a 'least squares line'[3] was fitted to past US observations of tax revenue and tax rate. The dotted line indicates the extension of the fitted relationship (continuous line), as there will tend to be zero tax revenue at both 0 and 100% tax rates. Tax revenue = tax rate × output (income), so that a 0% tax rate yields zero tax revenue, whatever the level of output. A 100% tax rate is assumed to discourage all output, except that for subsistence, again yielding zero tax revenue. Tax revenue must reach a maximum at some intermediate tax rate between these extremes.

The London Business School has estimated a Laffer curve for the UK using past data. Tax revenue was found to reach a peak at around a 60% 'composite tax rate', i.e. one which includes both direct and indirect taxes, as well as various social security payments, all expressed as a percentage of GDP. If the tax rate rises above 60% then

Fig. 19.6.   The 'Laffer' curve.

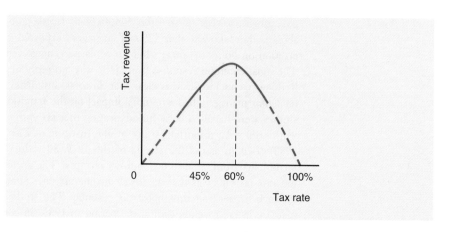

the disincentive effect on output is so strong (i.e. output falls so much) that tax revenue (tax rate × output) actually falls, despite the higher tax rate. The Laffer curve in fact begins to flatten out at around a 45% composite tax rate. In other words, as tax rate rises above 45%, the disincentive effect on output is strong enough to mean that little extra tax revenue results. Econometric studies of this type have given support to those in favour of limiting overall rates of tax. It is interesting to note that shortly after this study, the top rate of tax on earned income in the UK was indeed reduced from 83% to 60%.[4]

The reduction in the top income tax rate to 40% in 1988/89 was inspired by the Laffer curve and supply-side economics. The Chancellor of the Exchequer believed that the tax cuts would increase revenue. He based his tax cuts on American research by Lindsey that concluded that reductions in the top tax rates to the American government in 1981/82 were costless as the top 170,000 taxpayers ended up paying $26.6bn under new legislation instead of $26bn under the old. Lindsey argued that the tax cuts were not only incentive creating but they also increased the *cost of tax avoidance*.

This research has been criticized partly because it is American evidence and partly because the American rates were slashed by 23% over three years with the top personal rate being reduced from 70 to 50% whilst the UK moved from 60 to 40% in just one year. Finally, Lindsey and other tax experts have consistently argued that as tax rates are cut, economic efficiency is raised by reducing tax breaks and shelters at the same time. However fresh evidence on the impact of cuts in high rates of British taxation has been provided by Minford and Ashton (see Brown 1988). The latter study concluded that the cut in the higher British tax rates to 40% would increase hours worked by 8%.

In summary, those who advocate 'supply side economics', with tax reduction a key instrument for improving economic incentives, leading to an upsurge of productive activity, receive limited support from empirical studies. Only a small net disincentive effect has been found from studies using questionnaires, such as those by Break and Stanbury. This conclusion was reinforced by the later study of Dilnot and Kay. On the other hand, the Laffer curve constructed for the UK by the London Business School, and work by Minford in the UK and Lindsey in the US, do indicate that *reductions* in the composite rate of tax below 60% and down as far as around 45%, have strong incentive effects on output – the converse of *rises* in tax rate between 45 and 60% having strong disincentive effects. However, we noted in Table 19.4 that the UK composite tax rate is currently less than 40%, and reductions below this level receive little support from econometric studies.

Poverty and unemployment traps   One area where the facts do strongly suggest that the current level and type of taxation may have eroded incentives, concerns the 'poverty' and 'unemployment' traps. The families in these traps are enmeshed in a web of overlapping tax schedules and benefit thresholds, developed and administered by two separate departments (Department of Social Security and the Treasury) with differing objectives in mind.

The 'poverty trap' describes a situation where a person on low income may gain very little, or even lose, from an increase in gross earnings. This is because as *gross* earnings rise, the amount of benefits paid out decreases while income tax deductions increase. In extreme circumstances, *net* income may actually fall when a person's

	April 1998			
	(£ pw)	(£ pw)	(£ pw)	(£ pw)
Gross earnings	50.00	100.00	150.00	200.00
Plus: Child benefit	20.75	20.75	20.75	20.75
Family credit	92.40	81.12	55.49	31.75
Housing benefit	43.73	21.73	14.59	7.98
Council Tax Benefit	11.07	4.30	2.11	0.07
Less: Income tax	0.00	0.00	8.38	19.48
National Insurance	0.00	4.88	9.88	14.88
Net income	217.95	223.02	224.68	226.19

Notes:
Calculations are for a married man with two children aged 10 and 14, Local Authority rent of £50 a week and Council Tax of £13 a week.
Source: Adapted from DSS, Tax/Benefit Model Tables (April 1998).

gross earnings rise, i.e. an implicit marginal tax rate (or marginal net income deduction rate) of over 100%. After 1988, the government tried to resolve the gross disincentive effects of such high rates of deduction by relating benefits to net income after tax. However, the problems of the poverty trap dilemma still occur, if not to the same extent as before.

Table 19.7 shows the net income situation of a married man with two children in April 1998 when his gross income rises from £50 to £200 per week. We can see that net income rises very little over this range. For example, an increase in income from £100 to £150, i.e. £50 per week, gives only an extra £1.66 in income after deductions, i.e. £48.34 is lost. This results in an implicit marginal tax rate of about 97% (48.34/50). In 1992, using exactly the same family situation and gross income change, the rate was as high as 124%. The improvements in the family credit arrangements since 1992 has eased such extreme situations but the rates are still very high indeed and provide little encouragement for those in the area of the poverty trap to work harder. On a general level, the number of families where the head of the household faces a relatively high implicit marginal tax rate of 70% and over, doubled after 1988 to nearly 725,000 by 1997/98 (HMSO 1998).

A high implicit marginal tax rate can therefore act as a major disincentive to low income earners. This point is further exemplified by Fig. 19.7 which simulates the net income of a family with two young children and only one income earner, under different income circumstances (*Poverty* 1995).

The vertical axis presents *net* pay after all benefits (here income support) and tax payments have been taken into consideration. The horizontal axis presents the hours worked per week. The income support level for such a family under the Jobseekers Allowance would be around £125 per week and would correspond to the income that the family would receive if the only wage earner in the family was unemployed. The two other lines in Fig. 19.7 denote the change in net income which the family would receive if the person *was* in employment. The net income lines are plotted for wages of between £3.00 and £5.00 per hour and, as one would expect, net income tends to rise in line with increases in the number of hours worked. Notice however that when the wage per hour is only £3.00, net income

Fig. 19.7. Hours, wages and net family income: couple (one earner) with two children aged 4 and 6.
Source: Poverty (1998).

barely rises between 10 and 20 hours work per week, and for more than 30 hours work per week. For example, if the worker increases the number of hours worked from 30 to 80 hours a week, the net pay rises by only about 3p for every pound earned. In fact the 'plateaux' broadly represent the impact of the poverty trap. If wages increase to £5.00 per hour then there is much less evidence of any such plateaux. This analysis would seem to suggest that the reasons for the existence of a poverty plateau is a combination of the complexity of the benefit/tax structure (which creates very high implicit marginal tax rates at lower income levels), and the very low wages per hour paid to many workers. The extent of this problem can be gauged from the fact that there were still some 1.8m UK workers earning less than £3.40 per hour and some 3.75m earning less than £3.50 per hour prior to the introduction of the £3.60 hourly minimum wage in 1999.

As we have noted, the 'poverty trap' relates to people who are *in work* but find little incentive to improve their situation by extra work effort. On the other hand, some workers never even enter the labour market because of another problem, often called the 'unemployment trap'.

The 'unemployment trap' occurs when people find that their income when employed is no better than if they were unemployed. Table 19.8 shows that when the gross wage of the married man in our example is £150 per week, the net income after various allowances and deductions is £224.68. If he was unemployed, his net income would be £195.70, i.e. the *replacement rate* is 87%. The replacement rate measures the proportion of a person's net income that will be 'replaced' by the benefit system if that person loses his or her job. The introduction of family credit in 1988 has helped to decrease the number of people with replacement rates of over 100%. The

Table 19.8 Unemployed married couple (one earner previously working more than 30 hours per week) with two children aged 10 and 14 (rent £50, Council Tax £13.00 per week).

In work	(£ pw)	Out of work	(£ pw)
Gross earnings	150.00	Jobseeker's Allowance	132.70
Child benefit	20.75	Housing benefit	50.00
Family credit	55.49	Council Tax benefit	13.00
Housing benefit	14.59		
Council Tax benefit	2.11		
Income tax	8.38		
National Insurance	9.88		
Net income	224.68	Net income	195.70
Replacement ratio	$\frac{195.70}{224.68} = 87\%$		

Notes:
Calculations are for a married man with two children aged 10 and 14, Local Authority rent of £50 a week and Council Tax of £13 a week.
When employed he claims Family Credit and is entitled to the £10.30 thirty-hour premium. The figures when unemployed are illustrative for when the entitlement to Family Credit has run out. The Jobseeker's Allowance is income-based and includes allowances for children.
Source: Adapted from DSS, Tax/Benefit Model Tables (April 1998).

replacement rate for a person in exactly the same situation as our present example in 1992 was 104%, so things have got marginally better. However, the fact that the income of a person when out of work is still 87% of his income when in work provides little incentive to work. There were still 595,000 people in the UK with replacement rates of 70% and over in 1997/98 (HMSO 1998).

From these examples, we can see that both poverty and unemployment traps provide a disincentive to work because people caught in these problematic situations find it difficult, if not impossible, to improve their position through their own efforts.

Impact of taxes on avoidance and evasion

Tax avoidance is legal; tax evasion is illegal – involving concealment in one form or another, and therefore fraud.

The black economy   The Inland Revenue has estimated that tax evasion was equal to between 6 and 8% of GDP in the UK – often called the 'black economy'. However other estimates in 1996 suggested that the black economy may even be as high as 10–12% of GDP – i.e. £85bn per year. (Smith 1996). This would mean that the UK's black economy is the same size as Portugal's entire economy or is as much as the Treasury earns from income tax every year. One way in which the black economy can be estimated is through the difference between National Income when measured by the income method, and when measured by the expenditure method. Apart from errors and omissions these are defined in the National Accounts in such a way that they come to the same value. If, however, people receive income and do not declare it in tax returns, it will not appear on the income side, though expenditure will increase as the unrecorded income is spent on goods and services. In recent years the 'income' valuation – based on tax returns – has fallen short of the 'expenditure' valuation by progressively larger amounts.

Direct vs indirect taxes

In Fig. 19.3 above we observed a switch from direct to indirect taxation since the late 1970s. We noted that this switch entailed a move towards a more regressive system of taxation, i.e. one which takes a *smaller proportion* of higher incomes. This must follow since we move away from direct taxes which we saw to be progressive, towards indirect taxes, which at best are proportional (VAT), and more usually are regressive (the community charge – now the Council Tax, Uniform Business Rate, excise duties, import duties, etc.). It might be useful to consider in *more general terms* the advantages and disadvantages of direct and indirect systems of taxation. For convenience we shall compare the systems under four main headings, with indirect taxes considered first in each case.

Macroeconomic management

Indirect taxes can be varied more quickly and easily, taking more immediate effect, than can direct taxes. Since the Finance Act of 1961, the Chancellor of the Exchequer has had the power (via 'the regulator') to vary the rates of indirect taxation at any time between Budgets. Excise and import duties can be varied by up to 10%, and VAT by up to 25% (i.e. between 13.13% and 21.87% for a 17.5% rate of VAT). In contrast, direct taxes can only be changed at Budget time. In the case of income tax, any change involves time-consuming revisions to PAYE codings. For these reasons, indirect taxes are usually regarded as a more flexible instrument of macroeconomic policy.

Economic incentives

We have already seen how, in both theory and practice, direct taxes on income affect incentives to work. We found that neither in theory nor in practice need the *net* effect be one of disincentive. Nevertheless, it is often argued that if the *same sum* were derived from indirect taxation, then any net disincentive effect that did occur would be that much smaller. In particular, it is often said that indirect taxes are less visible (than direct), being to some extent hidden in the quoted price of the good. However, others suggest that consumers are well aware of the impact of indirect taxes on the price level. Let us look in more detail at the direct vs indirect argument, first in relation to incentives to work and second in relation to incentives to save and take risks.

Work effort In terms of effects on the supply of work effort, a case against the current system of direct taxes and in favour of a switch towards indirect taxes might be made in the *specific* cases of poverty and unemployment traps. However, no *general* case can be made for such a switch. In fact, both income and substitution effects of a rise in indirect taxes are in the same direction as those for a rise in direct taxes. By raising the prices of goods, higher indirect taxes also reduce real income, and at the same time reduce the cost of leisure in terms of goods forgone. In other words, the income and substitution effects we considered above apply to higher indirect taxes as well as to higher direct taxes. Whether the *magnitude* of the income and substitution effects will be the same for indirect as for direct taxes is quite another matter. It will partly depend upon which items are taxed. If indirect taxes are levied on goods with highly inelastic demand curves, then the indirect taxes will be largely passed on to consumers as higher prices. Both income and substitution effects will then be substantial in magnitude. Of course the converse also applies – if the indirect taxes are levied on goods with elastic demand curves, both income and substitution effects will be small. We can make no general claim for 'superiority' of either type of tax with regard to work incentives.

Saving and risk-taking   With regard to incentives for saving, indirect taxes have the advantage of avoiding the 'double-taxation effect' imposed by direct income taxes. Saving takes place out of net income, i.e. income that has already been taxed. To tax the return on savings, via a tax on investment income (e.g. dividends), is to impose a type of double taxation on that income, an obvious disincentive to saving. This is, however, a weak argument in support of indirect taxes as it is quite possible to devise a system of direct taxation that avoids double taxation (as currently with tax exemptions for returns on Post Office Savings and National Savings).

The argument that indirect taxes are to be preferred because they avoid the discrimination against risky investments of a direct tax system can also be rebutted. Risky investments do usually have higher yields, and do therefore pay more direct tax than less risky investments. However, such discrimination could be reduced, perhaps by raising the value of allowances (e.g. on exploration costs, etc.) that can be set against tax.

In terms of incentives, then, there is no general case to be made for or against one or other types of tax system. If we are to be more specific, we must compare one particular type of indirect tax system with one particular type of direct tax system.

Economic welfare   It is sometimes argued that indirect taxes are, in welfare terms, preferable to direct taxes, as they leave the taxpayer free to make a choice. The individual can, for instance, avoid the tax by choosing not to consume the taxed commodity. Although this 'voluntary' aspect of indirect taxes may apply to a particular individual and a particular tax, it cannot apply to all individuals and all taxes. In other words, indirect taxes cannot be 'voluntary' for the community as a whole. If a chancellor is to raise a given sum through a system of indirect taxes, individual choices not to consume taxed items must, if widespread, be countered either by raising rates of tax or by extending the range of goods and services taxed.

Another argument used to support indirect taxes on welfare grounds is that they can be used to combat 'externalities'. In Chapter 10 we noted that an externality occurs where private and social costs diverge. Where private costs of production are below social costs, an indirect tax could be imposed, or increased, so that price is raised to reflect the true social costs of production. Taxes on alcohol and tobacco could be justified on these grounds. By discriminating between different goods and services, indirect taxes can help reallocate resources in a way that raises economic welfare for society as a whole.

On the other hand, indirect taxes have also been criticized on welfare grounds for being regressive, the element of indirect tax embodied in commodity prices taking a higher proportion of the income from lower-paid groups. Nor is it easy to correct for this. It would be impossible administratively to place a higher tax on a given item for those with higher incomes although one could impose indirect taxes mainly on the goods and services consumed by higher-income groups, and perhaps at higher rates.

In terms of economic welfare, as in terms of economic incentives, the picture is again unclear. A case can be made with some conviction both for and against each type of tax.

Administrative costs Indirect taxes are often easy and cheap to administer. They are paid by manufacturers and traders, which are obviously fewer in number than the total of individuals paying income tax. This makes indirect taxes, such as excise and import duties, much cheaper to collect than direct taxes, though the difference is less marked for VAT, which requires the authorities to deal with a large number of mainly small traders.

Even if indirect taxes do impose smaller administrative costs than direct taxes for a given revenue yield, not too much should be made of this. It is, for instance, always possible to reform the system of PAYE and reduce administrative costs. The Inland Revenue is, in fact, considering a change from PAYE to an American system of income tax, with the obligation on taxpayers themselves to estimate and forward tax, subject to random checks. Also, the computerization of Inland Revenue operations may, in the long run, significantly reduce the administrative costs associated with the collection of direct taxes.

In summary, there is no clear case for one type of tax system compared to another. The macroeconomic management and administrative cost grounds may appear to favour indirect taxes, though the comparison is only with the *current* system of direct taxation. That system can, of course, be changed to accommodate criticisms along these lines. On perhaps the more important grounds of economic incentives and economic welfare the case is very mixed, with arguments for and against each type of tax finely balanced. To be more specific we must compare the particular and detailed systems proposed for each type of tax.

Tax and social security reform

The subject of tax reform is a topic in its own right and can only be touched upon here. Tax reform had been low on the political agenda before 1965, with the basic structure of taxes remaining unchanged for decades. Since then there have been more new taxes introduced than in any other equivalent peacetime period. Changes have included the introduction and repeal of selective employment tax; VAT replacing purchase tax; corporation tax replacing profits tax; the amalgamation of surtax and income tax; new taxes such as gambling and betting duties, and capital gains tax; and the replacement of estate duty first by capital transfer tax and subsequently by an inheritance tax.

Local taxation In the late 1980s the Conservative government increased the pace of its tax reform. It introduced the Community Charge in England and Wales during 1990 (in Scotland during 1989), together with the Uniform Business Rate (UBR) in the same year. The unpopularity of the Community Charge or 'poll tax' led to its replacement in April 1993 by the Council Tax.

The 'rates' system The Community Charge was introduced to replace what was seen as the 'unfairness' of the old local authority rates system. The rates were a property tax, paid by tenants and owner occupiers. The total amount paid per household in tax was based on two figures. First, on the rateable value of the property, which was a value based on an assessment of what the property could earn if it were let out on the open market. Second, on a 'poundage' expressed as 'so many pence in the pound'. This was calculated by the local authority in accordance with the revenue it needed to raise to pay for local services. For example, if the local authority valued a house at £30,000 and the local poundage was 2p in the pound, then the total rates for that house would be £30,000 × 0.02 or £600 per year. There were persistent complaints that the rates system was complicated and inequitable, for instance because it was difficult to properly assess the rentable value of any property. It was also based on the household unit, irrespective of how many people were actually living in the household. Also the rates had a regressive effect on some members of the public: e.g. on elderly people who sometimes occupied large, highly rated properties but who could no longer afford to pay the rates demanded since their incomes were insufficient. Finally, the total rates collected by this method were often inadequate to meet the increasing cost of local government spending on education, etc. As a result, this system was abolished for domestic premises and replaced by the Community Charge in 1990. For business premises the rating principle was retained in a modified form known as the Uniform Business Rate (UBR).

Hypothecation

A recent approach favoured by many as a means of raising the tax take whilst retaining public support, involves the idea of *hypothecation*. This is the allocation of current or additional taxes to *specific* spending outcomes. For example, the suggestion in the 1992 election manifesto by the Liberal Democrats that an extra 1% should be added to the basic rate of income tax and the entire extra revenue raised be used for education spending.

The Uniform Business Rate (UBR)

The UBR payable on any commercial property is based on two factors – the rateable value of that property, and a UBR 'multiplier'. The rateable value represents the annual rental value of the property on the open market and is fixed by an independent valuation officer, with rateable values reviewed periodically throughout the UK. To determine the actual amount of UBR to be paid per year, the rateable value is then multiplied by a rating 'multiplier' or poundage. The UBR multiplier in England in 1998 was 46.5p in the pound for rateable valuations of under £10,000 per year and 47.4p in the pound for rateable values above £10,000 per year. For example, business premises whose rateable value is above £10,000 would pay the actual rateable value multiplied by 0.474.

One of the inevitable problems with this new tax was that business properties in the more dynamic or prosperous areas would find their valuations rising overnight to a much higher level than before, while other businesses in less prosperous areas would experience a fall in their valuations. The UBR also represented a change in that the 'poundage rate' under this scheme was now set by central government and not by the local authority. Although the local authorities actually collect the UBR, the receipts are paid into a central fund outside local authority control. The fund is then redistributed to local authorities at a fixed rate per adult, with extra finance made available to those local authorities with special problems. This is clearly a further curbing of local authority financial control.

The Community Charge

Unlike the UBR, the *Community Charge* sought to depart from the old rating system method of calculating local taxes. The Community Charge was to be based not on the household, but on the individual. In other words, the Community Charge (or poll tax) was a personal tax assessed on each adult and expressed in the form of a lump-sum payment per year.

The Community Charge was unpopular because it meant an increase in tax for many families, especially those with a number of adults living in one household. It was also accused of being a regressive tax, in that the fixed charge per head tended to affect low income earners more than high income earners despite the existence of rebates for poor families. Also, the cost of administering the tax was high, at some 4% of its yield, whereas other taxes cost less than half that amount to collect. Many of these costs were associated with the need to register individuals and with the problems of chasing non-payers. The tax also created tensions between central government and some local authorities who felt that their 'needs' were greater than was implied by their Standard Spending Assessment (see below). As a result, some local authorities (often in hard pressed urban areas) put an extra levy on their Community Charge. This increase in the Community Charge in major urban areas resulted in a general dissatisfaction with this form of local taxation. The intense unpopularity of the Community Charge led to its replacement by the Council Tax on the first of April, 1993.

Council tax The *Council tax* is a hybrid tax, which is both part property or household tax and part personal tax. The Council tax is based on the capital value of each property, on the assumption that it contains two adult members. If the property contains only one adult, then he or she will pay only 75% of the bill of a two adult household. No additional tax is paid on a property where more than two adults reside. Also, personal discounts are given to certain classes of adults, e.g. those on very low incomes, handicapped people, those in full time education, and so on. It has been calculated that about 25% of all households are entitled to some form of Council tax rebate.

Properties are valued on a sample basis (e.g. one house may be taken as typical of that street or area) and assigned to specific property bands, as shown in Table 19.9. The average national property value is calculated and assigned to the appropriate band, i.e. band D in this case. From this base, the tax bills for properties in both higher and lower bands are calculated. For example, the average property value in England in 1998 was deemed to be £80,000, i.e. it is located in band D – between £68,000 and 88,000

Table 19.9 Council Tax: bands and property values 1998 (England).

Band	Property value (£)	Property value (% of national average)	Council Tax (% of average property)	Average bill* (£)
A	Under 40,000	up to 50	67	455
B	40,001–52,000	50–65	78	531
C	52,001–68,000	65–85	89	607
D	68,001–88,000	85–110	100	682
E	88,001–120,000	110–150	122	834
F	120,001–160,000	150–200	144	986
G	160,001–320,000	200–400	167	1,137
H	Over 320,000	400–500	200	1,365

*For a property in SE England.
Source: Adapted from Guide to 1998/9 Council Tax and Business Rate (1998).

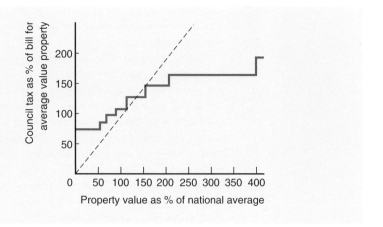

(column one). This means that this band ranges from between 85% and 110% of the average property value (second column). Therefore the tax paid by property owners in band D is regarded as the 'average', i.e. 100 (third column). Properties which are valued at under £40,000 will pay 67% of the average bill, and those valued at between £88,000 and £120,000 will pay 122% of the average bill, and so on.

The central government calculates a Standard Spending Assessment (SSA) for each authority based on its estimate of the amount of money the authority needs to provide a 'standard' level of service given the demographic and other characteristics of the local area. The government grant to each local authority is then equal to its SSA *minus* an estimate of how much the authority can raise from other sources, e.g. Community Charge and the UBR. If all authorities kept to their SSA, then the actual average household bill would be shown in column four of Table 19.9.

There are some points worth noticing about this scheme. First, the Council tax, as in the case of rates, is a regressive tax in that properties of below average value pay proportionately more tax, while properties of above average value pay proportionately less in tax. This can be seen from Fig. 19.8, in that the Council Tax line is flatter than the dotted 45% line, which would represent a proportionate tax. However, it may be said to be fairer than the Community Charge in that the tax does, at least, rise with the value of the house and it is reasonable to assume that those living in more expensive houses have higher incomes than those living in less expensive dwellings. Second, the administration of the scheme will be much easier because, unlike the Community Charge, collection is based on the household and not on the individual. Third, as with the Community Charge, the central government will still estimate the amount each local authority 'needs' to spend, i.e. the Standard Spending Assessment (SSA). If a local council exceeds this amount, then the local Council tax will be increased by a factor *greater than* the excess spending (i.e. the high spending councils are penalized).

It has been calculated that some 37% of families were better off, and 37% worse off, as a result of the change from Community Charge to the Council Tax.

**Other taxes and Social
Security benefits**

In addition to the significant changes which have taken place in local taxation, there have also been attempts by government to modify the tax structure in order to make it more equitable, while at the same time encouraging savings and increasing the base of UK share ownership. For example, the Approved Profit Sharing scheme (APS), the SAYE scheme and the Discretionary Share Option Scheme, all provide tax incentives for employees to buy shares in their companies. Also the Personal Equity Plans (PEPs) introduced initially in 1986 have encouraged small savers to invest in UK companies through unit and investment trusts. By making the income and capital gains from investing in such trusts free of tax, up to a maximum amount of £6,000 a year, it was hoped that savings would be encouraged, thereby helping to channel investment into UK industry. In April 1999, these were replaced by Individual Savings Accounts (ISAs). For example, during the 1999–2000 tax year, savers can invest up to £7,000 tax free in an ISA with the advantage that they can have instant access to the tax-free saving. ISAs will also be sold by a wider range of providers, e.g. by post offices and supermarkets, as well as by the financial institutions. It is difficult to measure the success of such share and savings schemes in stimulating UK industry since any increase in shareownership by employees does not necessarily improve company performance per se (Griffiths 1990).

On the personal taxation front, 1990 saw the introduction of a greater measure of equity, in that independent taxation for married couples was introduced. This gave married women independent status as taxpayers, i.e. they could control their own tax affairs. Since 1805 husbands had been legally responsible for the married couple's tax affairs and any married couple's allowance had been received by the husband. In the budget of 1992 it was announced that from 1993/94 onwards any extra married allowance can be claimed in its entirety by *either* husband or wife, or it can be shared equally between them, thus making the tax system fairer to married women.

As far as the social security system was concerned, the government introduced important measures in 1988 to modify the whole system. These covered unemployment benefits, pensions, income support, housing benefits, a family credit system and the social funds. The State Earnings Related Pensions Scheme (SERPS) which provided a pension based on National Insurance contributions was cut back. Designated occupational pension schemes could now 'contract out' of SERPS. This meant that state pensions would be reduced, but the private scheme must then guarantee to at least make up the difference. Contracted out workers pay a rate of National Insurance contribution reduced by 2%, as do their employers. At the same time the old supplementary benefit and heating allowances were abolished and a new system of income support was introduced.

The incoming Labour government of 1997 built on these reforms in order to tackle both the poverty and unemployment traps discussed earlier. A Jobseeker's Allowance (JSA) had already been introduced in 1996 to encourage more active job search during the first months of unemployment. Under the JSA the unemployed person and the Employment Service Adviser must draw up an agreement specifying what is expected of the unemployed person if they are to continue receiving the allowance. In April 1998 the government's 'New Deal' or 'Welfare to Work' initiative took such measures further by offering wage subsidies to employers to take on the unemployed and by offering new training and education opportunities. For example, young people between 18 and 24 who have been unemployed for more than six months can choose between various job options or study on a full-time approved course. If a New Deal place is refused, then benefits are reduced.

Further reforms of the tax and benefit system were introduced in the 1998 budget. For example, a single organization, the Contributions Agency, would now deal with both tax and national insurance matters for the self-employed and small businesses, the intention being to reduce 'red-tape' and simplify the move from welfare to work. In April 1999 the level at which employers and employees begin paying national insurance has been raised, with the result that employers no longer have to pay national insurance contributions for up to 1 million of their employees. This is designed to decrease the cost of employing such workers, although the cost to the exchequer in lost National Insurance receipts will be around £1.4bn per annum.

Perhaps one of the biggest changes on the welfare to work front was the introduction of the Working Family Tax Credit (WFTC) in October 1999 to replace Family Credit. Help is now to be given to the newly employed through the tax system rather than in the form of a 'hand out' from the benefit agencies, as under the old scheme. As a result the benefit will be included in the pay packet received by the worker, and such benefits will now fall more slowly as income rises. A child-care tax credit will also be incorporated in the WFTC to meet 70% of the eligible child-care costs for low-income working families. It is thought that the introduction of the WFTC will help some 1.2 million families as compared to the 0.8 million families covered under the old Family Credit scheme, at a cost of some £3.5bn per year. One of the aims of measures such as the WTFC is to tackle the 'unemployment trap', by making work pay more than being unemployed on benefit, and the 'poverty trap', by cutting the rate at which benefits are withdrawn as income rises.

Conclusion

The UK tax system is broadly proportional. Direct taxes are, as a group, *progressive* in the UK, taking a larger proportion of the income of richer households. Indirect taxes are, as a group, *regressive*, though this is not the case for all indirect taxes. VAT is broadly proportional with the exception of the top fifth of income earners. The movement towards indirect taxation has therefore made the UK tax system less progressive than it would otherwise have been. The overall tax burden measured as a *percentage of GDP* has fluctuated since the late 1960s and has risen during the 1990s to levels experienced in the early 1980s. However, the UK is *not* overtaxed compared to other countries. Neither does higher tax necessarily mean lower economic growth. Certainly the empirical case for higher taxes being a disincentive to effort and output is rather flimsy, whether from questionnaire or econometric study. There can be no general presumption in favour of either indirect or direct taxation, when we assess each system in terms of macro-management, economic incentives, economic welfare and administrative costs. The dilemma of how to construct an equitable and efficient form of local taxation remains, while the complicated relationships between tax changes and social security benefits still create difficulties for those families caught in the poverty or unemployment 'traps'. Various 'welfare to work' reforms are seeking to provide greater opportunities and incentives to those seeking employment.

Key points

- Taxes on *income* account for around 46% of all tax receipts, with taxes on *expenditure* around 38%.
- UK *direct* taxes are progressive while *indirect* taxes are regressive. Overall, the UK has a broadly proportional tax system.
- The UK tax burden as a percentage of GDP has remained fairly steady at around 36% of GDP over the past decade.
- The UK is a middle-ranked country in terms of tax revenue as a percentage of GDP, i.e. in terms of 'tax burden'.
- There is no clear relationship between high income tax rates and disincentives to work. Detailed surveys show only a potentially small disincentive effect.
- The 'poverty trap' has improved since 1992 with implicit marginal tax rates for some households falling from 124% in 1992 to around 97% by 1998. Low hourly wages tend to worsen the poverty trap situation, though the minimum wage may help in this respect.
- The 'unemployment trap' has eased slightly, with replacement rates for an unemployed married couple, two children, falling from 104% in 1992 to 87% by 1998.
- Labour market reforms, such as the Working Family Tax Credit (WFTC) and other 'Welfare to Work' initiatives should help further relieve the unemployment and poverty 'traps'.

Notes

1. Which it does in the UK, e.g. 20% on the first £4,300 of taxable income, 23% on taxable income up to £27,100 and 40% on higher income.
2. The average rate is total tax paid, divided by total income.
3. That is, that line which minimizes the sum of squared deviations from the line.
4. Though the Laffer curve strictly refers only to *overall* tax level, and not that for any particular tax.

References and further reading

Brown, C. (1998) Will the 1988 income tax cuts either increase work incentives or raise more revenue? *Fiscal Studies*, **9**, 4.

Brown, C. V. and **Dawson, D. A.** (1969) *Personal Taxation, Incentives and Tax Reforms.* Political and Economic Planning (PEP).

Crawford, M. and **Dawson, D.** (1982) Are rates the right tax for local government?, *Lloyds Bank Review*, 145, July.

CSO (1995) Taxes and Social Security contributions: an international comparison 1981–1993, *Economic Trends*, 505, Nov.

Dilnot, A. W. and **Kell, M.** (1988) Top-rate tax cuts and incentives: some empirical evidence, *Fiscal Studies*, **9**, 4, November.

Flemming, J. and **Oppenheimer, P.** (1996) Are Government spending and taxes too high? *National Institute Economic Review*, 157, July.

Griffiths, A. (1990) Shareownership and the economy, *British Economic Survey*, **20**, 1, Autumn.

HMSO (1998) The Government's expenditure plans 1998/99: *Social Security Departmental Report*, Fig. 14, p. 16 (poverty trap) and Fig. 13, p. 15 (unemployment trap).

House of Commons (1990) Low Income Statistics, Social Services Committee, Fourth Report, House of Commons.

Kay, J. and **King, M.** (1990) *The British Tax System*, OUP.

Messere, K., Owen, J. and **Teir, G.** (1982) Tax trends and impact of taxes on different income groups, *The OECD Observer*, 25 Jan.

OECD (1998) *OECD in Figures*, Paris.

ONS (1998) 1996/97, The effects of taxes and benefits on household income, **533**, April.

Poverty (1995) Fact and figures, *Journal of the Child Action Poverty Group*, 92, Winter, Fig. 1.

Poverty (1996) Fact and figures, *Journal of the Child Action Poverty Group*, 93, Spring, Table 1 (modified).

Poverty (1998) After the minimum wage: social security for working families with children, *Journal of the Child Action Poverty Group*, **99**, Spring, Fig. 1.

Smith, D. (1996) Moonlighters cheat taxman out of £85bn, *Sunday Times*, 31 March.

Treasury (1998) Financial Statement and Budget Report, 1998-99.

Chapter 20

Money and EMU

This chapter looks at the nature of money and the functions any money commodity must perform, before considering its importance from both monetarist and Keynesian perspectives. The money stock must be measured before it can be controlled: we therefore look at current definitions of the money stock, distinguishing between 'narrow' and 'broad' money. We review recent attempts to control the money stock, and analyse the problems which have arisen in the course of their implementation. A brief review of European Monetary Union (EMU) is presented (see also Chapter 28), with particular attention being paid to the advantages and disadvantages of a single currency.

The nature of money

We are all familiar with money. We use it almost every day of our lives, we recognise it when we see it, and most of us are all too aware that we don't have enough of it! Despite this, the effect of changes in the money supply on macroeconomic variables such as the rate of inflation, the rate of unemployment and the level of output are matters of deep controversy. One reason for this is that there is no completely watertight physical or legal definition of money. Instead, economists adopt a behavioural approach to the definition of money. This approach highlights the confidence element of money and emphasises the importance of its *acceptability*. At the most basic level, money can be thought of as anything generally acceptable to others as a means of payment. History is littered with examples of commodities that have functioned as money at different times and in different places. The word 'pecuniary' is derived from the Latin for cattle and 'salary' is derived from the Latin for salt, indicating that both these commodities have functioned as money in the past. Other commodities such as stones, shells, beads and metals have also functioned as money.

In the UK, notes, coins, cheques and credit cards are used as a means of payment to promote the exchange of goods and services and to settle debts, but cheques and credit cards are not strictly regarded as part of the money supply. Rather it is the underlying *bank deposit* of the cheque or credit card which is part of the money supply. Since cheques are simply an instruction to a bank to transfer ownership of a bank deposit. A cheque drawn against a non-existent bank deposit will be dishonoured by a bank and the debt will remain, as will be the case if an attempt is made to pay by using an invalid credit card. Therefore a general definition of money in the UK today is notes, coins and bank and building society deposits transferable by cheque.

In practice, for any asset to be considered as money it must perform certain functions and we turn now to a brief discussion of these.

Functions of money

Unit of account One of the most important functions of money is to serve as a numeraire, or unit of account. Distance is measured in metres, weight in kilograms and so on. In the same way, when we measure the relative value in exchange of a house, a car or a haircut, our measuring rod is money. Money is therefore a common denominator against which value in exchange can be expressed. We then know that a litre of petrol is less valuable than a litre of whisky because we are able to express relative values in money terms. In the UK the basic unit of account is the pound sterling and all values in the UK are expressed in pounds or fractions of a pound.

The existence of a unit of account facilitates rational decision taking by consumers and producers. To understand the importance of this, consider a *barter economy*, i.e. an economy in which there is no unit of account. As an initial simplification, assume that only *four* consumer goods are offered for sale in this economy. To make decisions about how much of each good to acquire, consumers would need to consider the value of each good in relation to the value of all other goods. Figure 20.1(a) shows that consumers would need to express the value of good A in terms of goods B, C and D. Similarly, the value of good B would need to be expressed in terms of goods A, C and D, and so on. Without money, each good or service offered for sale would require an exchange value (or ratio) expressed in terms of *each* of the other goods and service offered for sale; *six* exchange ratios in all would be required. Figure 20.1(b) shows that when a unit of account does exist, the number of exchange ratios is reduced (here to only three) because the value of each good can be expressed in terms of the money commodity.

Fig. 20.1. (a) In a non-money economy producing four goods, six exchange ratios are required. (b) In a money economy producing four goods where one of the goods is money, only three exchange ratios are required.

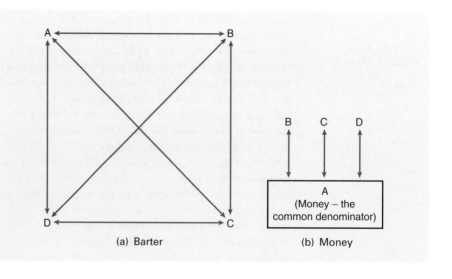

(a) Barter   (b) Money

This is important because the number of exchange ratios increases rapidly as the number of goods and services offered for sale increases. In fact, we can calculate the number of exchange ratios that would exist in a *barter economy* if we substitute into the formula:

$$R_b = \tfrac{1}{2}N(N-1)$$

where R_b = the number of exchange ratios in a barter economy;
    N = the number of goods and services traded in the barter economy.

For example, in an economy where 1,000 goods and services are traded (quite a modest number compared with the number of goods and services actually traded in a modern economy such as the UK) the number of exchange ratios that would exist is 49,500! Imagine trying to make rational decisions about what and how much to produce when it is first necessary to compare such a large number of exchange ratios!

Contrast this situation with the number of exchange ratios that exist in a *money economy* and you immediately see one of the main advantages of money. In this case the number of exchange ratios is simply:

$$R_m = N - 1$$

where R_m = the number of exchange ratios in a money economy;
    N = the number of goods and services traded in the money economy.

Again if 1,000 goods and services are traded, the number of exchange ratios is now only 999 for the money economy! Since each of these exchange ratios is expressed in the *same unit of account*, comparisons between relative goods and services as regards exchange value is very easy, taking the form of relative prices in a money economy. The fact that it is easy to compare relative prices makes it possible for consumers and producers to estimate the *opportunity cost* of any production or consumption decision. Economic theory tells us that in these circumstances resources are likely to be allocated much more efficiently than would otherwise be the case.

Medium of exchange   In this sense money is an interface between buyers and sellers which enables them to trade without the existence of a 'double coincidence of wants'. With a barter system those who trade must seek out others who have what they require and in turn require what they have! In functioning as a medium of exchange, money greatly improves the efficiency of the economic system and vastly increases the scope for specialisation, thereby allowing firms to reap economies of scale. So important is the role of money in the process of exchange that it would be impossible for all but the most primitive societies to function in the absence of money.

The restrictions on specialization and exchange that would characterise a barter economy are easy to illustrate. Consider a producer of wheat who requires cloth. First the wheat producer must find someone who requires wheat and who is simultaneously able to offer cloth in exchange. Having established such a double coincidence of wants, it is then necessary to agree a mutually acceptable rate of exchange for wheat in terms of cloth. In such cases, the time and effort devoted to exchange might well exceed that devoted to production and there would be a tendency towards self-sufficiency.

Compare this with a money economy where the process of trade simply involves the exchange of money in return for the receipt of goods or services. Money clearly makes specialization and trade viable but it also makes possible the vast economies of scale so characteristic of modern production. Remember, mass production is impossible without the existence of a mass market, and the existence of a common medium of exchange within an economy satisfies one of the conditions necessary for the existence of such a mass market. Without money it would be impossible for countries to support their current populations, far less for them to enjoy their current standard of living.

Store of value   The store of value function of money is closely bound up with its medium of exchange function. As a store of value, money permits a time-lag to exist between the sale of one thing and the purchase of something else. When goods and services are sold they are purchased with money which is then held by the sellers of goods and services until they themselves make purchases. In this sense money is an *asset* used for storing the value of sales until this value is required to make purchases. Most people receive payment for their labour at discrete intervals, usually a week or month, which do not coincide with the continuous flow of expenditures made over the same period. Money is therefore a convenient form in which to store purchasing power.

Money is not unique as a store of value and there are many forms in which wealth can be held, ranging from financial assets such as government bonds, to physical assets such as antiques. As a means of storing wealth these assets have advantages over money. For example, holders of government bonds receive interest income while holders of antiques usually experience a capital gain. Money, on the other hand, has the advantage of being immediately acceptable in exchange for goods and services. Economists use the term *liquidity* to describe assets which can easily and inexpensively be converted into money. Money is therefore the most liquid of all assets.

The liquidity which money possesses gives it a 'convenience value' over other assets, but whether it is an effective store of value depends on the behaviour of the price level. The nominal value of money is fixed by law but during periods of inflation, when prices rise, the real value of money falls. Clearly as inflation rises, money performs its store of value function less and less effectively. Indeed, inflation can be thought of as a tax on money holdings and the tax rate is equal to the rate of inflation. For example, between 1 January 1997 and 1 January 1998 the Retail Price Index in the UK increased from 154.4 to 159.5 This implied that the purchasing power of £1.00 on 1 January 1997 only had a purchasing power of £0.97 on 1 January 1998, as the following calculation shows.

$$£1.00 \times \frac{\text{RPI on } 1.1.97}{\text{RPI on } 1.1.98} = £1.00 \times \frac{154.4}{159.5} = £0.97$$

Between 1 January 97 and 1 January 98, the real value of money had fallen by some 3%.

The store of value function of money and the medium of exchange function are closely bound together. In periods of hyperinflation, money ceases to function both as an effective store of value and as an effective medium of exchange. Indeed those hyperinflations that have been documented are characterised by economic agents spending money balances as quickly as possible. A classic example of this occurred during the French Revolution of 1889 when assignants, the paper currency of the time, were issued in such quantity that their value declined so quickly that the

Fig. 20.2.   Liquidity
spectrum.

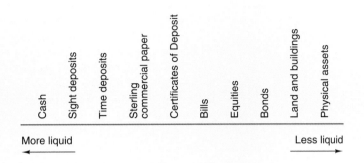

peasants regarded them as effectively worthless. The German experience with hyperinflation in the inter-war period provides another classic example of money becoming ineffective as both a store of value and a medium of exchange. In extreme cases such as this, the value of money falls so quickly that it becomes increasingly difficult to make production and investment decisions. The result is that economic activity declines and economic agents resort to barter and exchange goods and services directly.

Money provides a standard for deferred payments

Economists sometimes identify a fourth function of money: that it provides a standard for deferred payments. In this sense money provides a means of agreeing payments to be made at some future point in time, for example when contracts are signed. Arguably, this is simply a particular aspect of its unit of account function.

Near money

Commodities which fulfil only some of the functions of money cannot be classed as money. Credit cards and luncheon vouchers, for instance, can be used as a medium of exchange for transactions, but they are not money because they cannot always be used, nor do they fulfil the other functions of money. Paper assets such as government securities serve as a store of value, but they cannot be used as a medium of exchange. However, liquid assets, i.e. those which can be easily converted into money without loss of value, form a potential addition to the money stock, and are often referred to as 'near money'. Assets normally classed as 'liquid' include time deposits, treasury and commercial bills, and certificates of deposit (Fig. 20.2). Other assets become more liquid the nearer is their maturity date. Many of the assets shown in Fig. 20.2 are considered in more detail later in this chapter and in Ch. 21.

The importance of money

Economists are in no doubt that 'money matters', but there is considerable disagreement as to how changes in the money stock influence macroeconomic variables (the so called *transmission mechanism*) and as to the magnitude of its influence on these variables. Monetarists argue that although money supply growth may influence 'real' variables such as output and employment in the short run, in the long run it only affects nominal (or money) variables such as the rate of inflation, the rate of interest and the rate of exchange. The New Classical view is an extension of monetarist thinking and agrees that money supply growth affects only nominal variables, but contends that this is the case both in the long run and the short run. Keynesians, on the other hand, argue that as well as affecting nominal variables, money growth also affects real variables such as the level of output and employment in both the short run and the long run.

It is natural that we should focus on the differences between Keynesians and monetarists, but it would be a mistake to think that there are no similarities! Both groups agree that in the short run an increase in money supply growth will affect both real and nominal variables. They also agree that nominal variables will be affected in the long run, but they disagree over the nature of the transmission mechanism and over the influence of changes in money supply growth on the real economy in the long run. Keynes held the view that higher inflation was an acceptable price to pay for higher output and employment, whereas the monetarists argued that any changes in output and employment that occurred as a result of higher money supply growth would only be transitory, i.e. in the long run real variables would revert back to their equilibrium rates and higher money supply growth would only affect nominal variables.

The quantity theory of money

The connection between money on the one hand and output and prices on the other can be formally stated by means of the Fisher identity, known as the Quantity Theory of Money. It states that:

$$M \times V = P \times T$$

In other words, that the amount of money in the system times the velocity of circulation (the speed at which units of money circulate in a given time period) must be identical to the number of transactions in that time period multiplied by their average price.

The velocity of circulation (V) is a measure of the speed at which money circulates in the economy, and is determined by the following.

1. The *rate* at which money is passed from one person to another. This, in turn, is primarily determined by *payments practices* – by whether wages are paid weekly or monthly, for instance, or by how quickly credit accounts are settled.
2. The *length of time* for which money is held. Money is held for transactions purposes, but also as a wealth form. The greater the fraction of the money stock held as an asset (i.e. as a wealth form), the lower is the overall velocity of circulation (although that part of the money stock which is still circulating will have to circulate faster if a given volume of monetary transactions is to be maintained).

The Quantity Theory thus assumes that there is a long-term equilibrium relationship between private sector money holdings and nominal incomes. The 'theory' is of course an identity, in the sense that in the long term it must be true by definition. However, we can use it to illustrate the disagreement between monetarists and Keynesians in terms of the interrelationships between the four variables M, V, P and T. The two schools of thought differ in their views on such interrelationships, as well as on the question of the time perspective.

The monetarist view of money

Monetarism is interested in long-term relationships. Monetarist economists believe that money affects 'money things' such as prices, rather than 'real things' such as output and employment. They therefore believe that T, the volume of transactions (and therefore of output), is determined by factors outside the Quantity Theory itself – for instance, by supply-side factors operating on the labour and goods market such as productivity, production costs and profits. In other words they believe that T is exogenously determined.

Monetarists also hold that V is constant in the long run. If T is exogenously determined and V is constant, then there is a clear relationship between M and P. However, monetarists would argue that the relationship is not merely true in a definitional sense, but that there is a causal relationship whereby changes in M will actually cause changes in P. We must first examine how this can be the case. We then deal with some of the criticisms of this position.

The monetarist explanation for the connection between money and prices hinges on the effects of an increase in M in different markets. It would be simple to argue that an increase in the money stock, by giving people more purchasing power, causes goods, market prices to rise. In fact, the early Classical economist would have argued in this way, but in those days goods prices were market determined, whereas nowadays goods prices, as Keynes pointed out, are determined by costs of production which may not vary with changes in demand for a particular good. So modern monetarists do not attempt to account for the effect of changes in M on P by looking at the goods market alone. Instead, they concentrate on the *labour market* and the *asset market* in order to identify the ways in which the prices of goods are affected by changes in M.

Monetarists admit that changes in M may well be associated with temporary changes in output due to the way labour markets work and to the existence of inflationary expectations. If there is an *increase in the money stock* producers are likely to increase production to meet the increased demand for goods. Labour market conditions may mean that they have to pay higher wages to get the extra labour, but they know that they can pass these higher wage costs on in the form of higher prices. There will thus be both a rise in wages and a rise in output and employment.

Wages will rise from W to W_1 and employment from e^* to e^1 due to increased output (Fig. 20.3). However, workers will quickly realise that although their wages have risen in money terms, in real terms they are no better off since prices have also risen. Because it is assumed that the supply of labour depends not on the money wage but on the real wage, the supply of labour will now be reduced (supply curve, S_1) and output and employment will return to their original level at e^*, but money wages will have risen to W_2 leading to a rise in prices, i.e. inflation.

Monetarists also point to the effect of an increase in M on asset prices. Money is regarded by the monetarist as an *asset*, i.e. a form of wealth holding as well as a medium of exchange. It is, however, just one asset within a whole spectrum of assets, of varying degrees of liquidity, profitability and marketability.

The definition of the word 'asset' used here is so broad that it includes cash at one end of the spectrum and physical assets, including goods, at the other. All these assets will have different characteristics, not only in terms of liquidity, but also in terms of profitability and of marketability. Asset holders will hold a portfolio, or range of assets, which will depend on their preferences for these characteristics, as well as on the prices and relative rates of return of each asset.

An increase in M may mean that money holdings in the portfolio rise beyond an

Fig. 20.3. The labour
market response to an
increase in *M*.

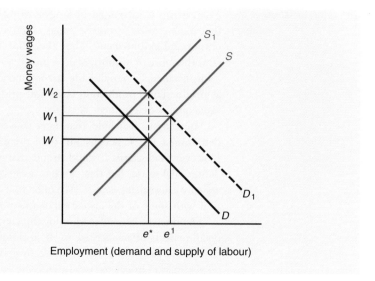

Fig. 20.3. The labour market response to an increase in *M*.

acceptable level. To avoid this, asset holders will readjust their portfolio, switching out of money towards the less liquid end of the spectrum. This will increase demand for relatively less liquid assets, raising their prices. This will be true not only for the prices of financial assets such as shares and bonds, but also for those physical goods held as assets. As a result, an increase in *M* will imply an increase in *P*.

It is important to note that monetarism changes the relationship between *M* and *P* (given *V* and *T*) from that of an identity, to a *causal* relationship. Although monetarism provides a theoretical rationale for doing this, a number of criticisms can be made of the view that a change in *M* will automatically lead to a change in prices.

The first, and perhaps the most damaging, relates to the assumption of a constant velocity of circulation. The velocity of circulation has always fluctuated in the short run, often in response to sudden fluctuations in the money stock. However, monetarists have always argued that in the longer term it could be assumed to be stable. Recent experience indicates that this is *not* the case. Velocity of the broader monetary aggregates such as M4 (see p. 440) fell dramatically in the 1980s and early 1990s, reversing a trend which had been rising since 1950, although as Fig. 20.4 shows, different monetary aggregates behave differently. Prior to 1980, the growth of deposits was restricted, and negative real interest rates made deposit holding unattractive. Velocity therefore rose. Since 1980, however, short-term interest rates have been historically high and real interest rates have been positive. People have therefore preferred to hold their wealth in interest-bearing deposits rather than in non–monetary forms. This decreased sharply the velocity of circulation of the broader monetary aggregates (e.g. M4) until 1992, when interest rates began to fall after leaving the ERM.

Velocity can therefore not be assumed to be constant, and any assessment of changes in the money stock on the economy has to take that fact into account. However, since 1992 there has been a considerable stability in the velocities of both M4 and M0 (Fig. 20.4).

Another problem with the monetarist explanation of the effects of changes in *M* relates to assumptions made about goods and labour market behaviour. Goods prices

Fig. 20.4. Velocity of the
monetary aggregates.
Source: Calculated from
Bank of England data
(1985 = 100).

are assumed to be demand rather than cost determined, changing as asset holdings change. Labour supply in the aggregate is assumed to be a function of the real wage, rather than dependent on the desire for employment. Whereas it can be argued that there may be circumstances where these assumptions might be relevant – for instance, where physical assets are goods which already exist such as houses or paintings, or where wages are so low as to be matched by social security payments – they cannot be said to be appropriate in all cases. The monetarist response to this is to point to the long-run emphasis of their argument. Of course in policy terms this perspective is unrealistic, since circumstances and policy problems are constantly changing, so that the long run is never in fact reached.

The Keynesian view of money

The perspective of Keynesian economics is essentially short run. Keynesians believe that changes in the money stock affect 'real' variables such as output and employment rather than money variables such as prices. Keynes envisaged people as holding money for speculative motives as well as for transactions purposes, and switching between financial assets and holdings of money in response to changes in financial markets. Each individual would switch money holdings into bonds when he or she considered the price low enough and the yield high enough to warrant the loss of liquidity. An increase in the money stock would have the effect of increasing the flow of money on to the bond market, hence driving up the price of bonds. The yield on the bonds would then fall, as their fixed interest return would remain unchanged, even though their market price had risen. In other words, the effective rate of interest would have fallen. Although the price of financial assets would have changed, no other prices in the economy would be affected.

The fall in the interest rate may then have the effect of encouraging investment (see Ch. 17), so that output, employment and incomes will rise in consequence as the multiplier effect works through the economy. We should ask ourselves why Keynes did not see this general expansion as causing a rise in prices. The answer is that, in the Keynesian view of the economy, different variables adjust at different rates. Market quantities, such as output or the number of jobs, adjust much more quickly than market prices. Prices may indeed rise as a result of an expansion in aggregate demand, but they will rise slowly, because it will take time for manufacturers to feel the effects of overall expansion on costs of production. Price rises will only accelerate when the economy nears full employment. The market is therefore in a permanent 'disequilibrium' state, because prices do not adjust fast enough to equate demand and supply.

The differences between the two positions can be summarised as follows. Monetarists believe that money affects money things (prices) through asset-switching behaviour which affects *all* relative prices, including goods prices. Real things (output and employment) are, at least in the long run, affected not by money, but by supply-side factors such as productivity, profits and costs. Their perspective is fundamentally a long-term one. Keynesians, on the other hand, believe that money affects real things because changes in M alter prices of financial assets and their yields. This affects interest rates in general, and thereby alters investment and consumption decisions. This change in aggregate demand leads to changes in output and employment. Prices are largely unaffected, since markets never fully adjust and remain in disequilibrium, with quantities responding more rapidly than prices to changes in demand.

This debate between monetarists and Keynesians is not just about the role of money, and the consequent nature of monetary policy, it is also about ideology. It is about whether the market can, and should, be allowed to allocate resources in a modern economy. However, the choice of economic policy tends to be based on pragmatic rather than ideological grounds, with the control of inflation having become an endemic part of every Western economy. The control of the money supply has therefore assumed major importance even for those of a broadly Keynesian persuasion who doubt the causal link between M and P, because even if a rise in P (inflation) is not actually *caused* by an increase in M, it must be *financed* by such an increase. In other words, the money stock must at the very least play a permissive role in the inflationary process, otherwise even inflationary factors such as wage increases would be choked off by a shortage of bank loans and rising interest rates. It is to the measurement and control of M, the money stock, that we now turn.

Issues in counting the money stock

Economists, governments and central bankers are interested in counting the money stock, not least because this is important if we are to test the propositions of monetary theory. Earlier we discussed the quantity theory of money in some detail but how would we be able to test this theory without a clearly defined measure of the money supply? Another reason we are interested in counting the money stock is that we wish to control its behaviour so as to achieve macroeconomic objectives, in particular controlling the rate of inflation. Without a measure of the money stock this would be impossible.

Narrow and broad money

Estimates of the money stock have been published in the UK since 1966 but there is no single measure of money that fully encapsulates monetary conditions. Indeed it is usual to distinguish between narrow measures of money and broad measures of money. *Narrow* measures of money include the more liquid assets and are therefore concerned with the medium of exchange function of money, whereas *broad* measures of money also include a variety of less liquid assets and therefore also focus on the store of value function.

Definitions of money include notes, coins and assets such as bank deposits. The narrowest measure of money in the UK is M0 (pronounced M zero), which is sometimes referred to as 'base money' or 'high-powered money'. This consists of notes, coins and operational deposits of the banking sector. This is a very narrow measure of money and consists only of the most liquid assets.

No one would seriously argue that M0 provides a comprehensive definition of money. For example, other deposits such as sight deposits at banks and building societies also function as money and would certainly be included in any comprehensive definition of money. Indeed there are other assets, such as time deposits, which function as a store of value and which, after the required notice of withdrawal has elapsed, can be converted into assets which perform the medium of exchange function of money. The problem is not simply to distinguish between assets which function as money and assets which do not, but rather to identify that group of assets which provides a reliable and stable link between money supply growth and prices.

This is no easy task and measures of the money stock have changed frequently since they were first introduced. This is not only because of changing asset behaviour by the public, but also because of financial deregulation and innovation. The public holds deposits with the banking sector not only for *transactions* purposes but also as an *asset* on which they receive interest. Anything which changes the asset behaviour of the public, i.e. the volume of bank deposits held by the public, will be reflected in changes in the different money aggregates. This would weaken the link between money growth and prices. It is precisely for these reasons that the long-run behaviour of the velocity of circulation of money has been less stable than it otherwise might have been.

In recent years financial innovation and deregulation have changed the nature of the assets which perform the functions of money and this in turn has changed the relationship between measures of the money stock and nominal income. Major changes occurred in the banking sector in the 1980s. For example, the Big Bang of 1986 removed the distinction between retail banks and wholesale banks, while the Building Societies Act of 1986 allowed building societies to offer transactions services (cheque books, cash cards and credit cards) and loans for purposes other than house purchase. This considerably blurred the distinction between banks and building societies and therefore rendered existing measures of the money supply, which excluded building society deposits, less reliable. In other words, measures of money supply growth failed to accurately predict changes in the rate of inflation, not necessarily because the demand for money was unstable, but possibly because existing measures of money no longer adequately measured the money stock! The increasing availability of new assets is sure to mean that measures of the money stock will continue to change for the foreseeable future.

In counting the money stock at least three issues are relevant.

Which deposits should be included?   Some measures of money include only sight deposits (chequing accounts where cash is available on demand) whereas others also include time deposits (requiring notice of withdrawal). In narrow measures of money[1] we are particularly interested in counting transactions balances and therefore the question arises as to whether we should count only retail deposits up to a certain limit; if so should wholesale deposits up to the same limit also be included (see Ch. 21 where we note that *retail deposits* are usually defined as individual deposits of £50,000 or less, and *wholesale deposits* as individual deposits in excess of £50,000)? There is a further problem about the ownership of deposits. In the UK only private sector deposits are counted as part of the money stock. Public sector deposits are therefore excluded, as are deposits of overseas residents. The same is not true in all countries.

Which liabilities should be included?   Traditionally only bank deposits have been counted as part of the money stock but, as the nature of the financial sector has changed, building society deposits are now included in some measures of the money stock. This simply reflects the fact that these institutions now provide banking services similar to those of the clearing banks. Some idea of the importance of this is illustrated by events in July 1989 when the Abbey National Building Society changed its status from a mutual society to that of a bank. To have included its very large deposits in measures of the money stock which did not already include building society deposits would have involved large breaks in the statistical series of those measures. Instead it was decided to discontinue publication of certain money aggregates and to introduce a new money aggregate (M4).

Which currencies should be included?   No money aggregate currently measured in the UK includes foreign currency deposits. However, these have been included in earlier measures of money and a dilemma certainly exists for the authorities. Capital controls have now largely been abandoned and the Single Market certainly allows the free flow of funds within the EU. One currency can readily be converted into other currencies and in particular euros can easily be converted into sterling. Foreign currency deposits might well become an even more significant component of the money supply in the future than they have been in the past.

Measures of money   Currently in the UK only two measures of money are published, M0 and M4.

M0   This is a *narrow* measure of money and consists of:

(a) notes and coin outside the Bank of England, plus
(b) bankers' operational (i.e. clearing) deposits with the Bank of England.

M0 is the cash base of the monetary system and is the only measure of the money stock which is unaffected by changes in the financial system. Indeed there are only two ways in which M0 can change:

1. the government issues more notes and coins, and/or
2. operational deposits change as a result of transactions between the private sector and the government. This might happen because of random factors, for example when a large company settles a tax demand, or it might happen because of government expenditure or as a result of open market operations. Any transactions between the private sector and the Bank of England will alter operational deposits at the Bank of England and will cause M0 to change.

M4   This is a *broad* measure of money first introduced in 1987, and now upgraded to the status of the sole broad measure of money in the UK. M4 consists of:

(a) notes and coins held by the M4 private sector (i.e. the private sector other than Monetary Financial Institutions (MFIs) such as the Bank of England and other banks and building societies), plus
(b) all M4 private sector retail and wholesale sterling deposits at MFIs in the UK (including certificates of deposit and other paper issued by MFIs of not more than five years' original maturity).

Table 20.1 **Components of M0 and M4 (£m) as at October 1998.**

M4	(£m)	M0	(£m)
Notes and coin in circulation with the M4 private sector	22,652	Notes and coin in circulation outside the Bank of England	27,186
Non-interest-bearing bank retail deposits	34,807	Bankers' operational deposits at the Bank of England	177
Other bank retail deposits	345,162		
Building societies retail shares and deposits	103,130		
Bank wholesale deposits (including CDs)	254,988		
Building societies wholesale deposits (including CDs)	8,099		
Total M4	768,838	Total M0	27,363

Source: ONS (1998) Financial Statistics, December (adapted).

This money aggregate was introduced in 1987 because of the evolving role of the building societies which ceased to offer loans solely as mortgage finance for the purchase of property. Indeed building societies began to compete aggressively with banks as providers of loans for purchases other than property. The nature of the medium of exchange function of various financial intermediaries therefore evolved and to accommodate this it became necessary to widen the definition of money to include deposits with building societies. Table 20.1 shows the importance of these different components of M0 and M4 at October 1998. In particular, we can see the importance of interest-bearing retail deposits at banks ('other bank retail deposits') and the larger denominated wholesale deposits at banks ('bank wholesale deposits'). The importance of retail deposits at the building societies ('building societies retail shares and deposits') is also shown, with this figure being about 27% of all bank retail deposits.

The Divisia Index   M4 items are simply summed to give a measure of the money supply. Each item in the aggregate has a weight of unity and so all assets are weighted equally. This approach takes no account of the 'moneyness' of the different assets. Thus notes and coin in circulation are treated in exactly the same way as interest-bearing time deposits and any substitution of one for the other has no effect on the measured magnitude of M4. However, notes and coin function as a 'pure' medium of exchange and are non-interest bearing, unlike interest-bearing deposits which function primarily as a store of value. The latter earn an explicit rate of return and, at different times, *switching* between assets is apparent. The implicit assumption of simple sum measures of the money supply, namely that all components are perfect substitutes, is therefore erroneous.

A different approach is to weight the different assets in the money stock according to their role in *transactions*, i.e. according to the extent to which they function as a medium of exchange. This is the reasoning behind the Divisia Index which is claimed to be more closely related to total expenditure in the economy than conventional money aggregates. There are, of course, problems as to which variables to include in such a Divisia Index and the weight to be accorded to each variable. In practice the basic approach has been to weight each component according to the *difference* between its interest yield and the yield on a safe benchmark asset. In a Divisia Index, notes and coin therefore have a weight of 1, while high interest bearing savings accounts have a weight closer to zero, because the interest paid on them approaches the benchmark market rate and switching into and out of such accounts makes them less useful as a measure of the medium of exchange function.

The money supply process

The creation of deposits

The existence of a legal definition of money enables us to focus on an important question: how is money created? The answer is not self-evident. Notes and coin are, of course, issued through the Bank of England and the Royal Mint, but they are not released without limit. If they were they would quickly lose value and would become unacceptable as a medium of exchange. However, before we focus on the importance of changes in base money (which includes notes and coin) in the money supply process, let us look at the creation of bank deposits. Even a cursory glance at the data for M4 in Table 20.1 shows that bank deposits are a significantly greater component of broad money such as M4 than of base (narrow) money such as M0.

In any discussion of the creation of bank deposits it is customary to begin by recognising that not all of the funds deposited with a bank will be withdrawn at any one time. Indeed, under normal circumstances inflows and outflows of funds will be such that on any one day banks will only require a fraction of the total funds deposited with them to meet withdrawals by customers. This implies that the remainder can be lent to borrowers. But this is not the end of the story because funds lent by one bank will flow back into the banking system, again a fraction will be retained and the remainder will be available for lending to other borrowers. It is easier to understand the process at work here if we consider a simple balance sheet approach to the banks' activities.

Consider the effect on the balance sheet of Bank A which receives a deposit of £100m. This deposit is a *liability* to the bank (as it is liable to repay it), but the cash value of the deposit is at the same time an *asset* which can be used for various purposes. The changes in the bank's balance sheet are shown below.

Bank A

Liabilities (£m)	Assets (£m)
+100	+100

Now suppose Bank A maintains a ratio of 10% cash to total deposits which it deems adequate to meet withdrawals by customers. If the opportunity to make a loan exists, Bank A will lend out £90m. Assume this happens and that, when spent, the £90m is deposited with Bank B. The changes in Bank A's and Bank B's balance sheets will therefore be as shown below.

Bank A				Bank B			
Liabilities (£m)		Assets (£m)		Liabilities (£m)		Assets (£m)	
Deposits	100	Cash	10	Deposits	+90	Cash	+90
		Advances	90				

If Bank B also maintains a ratio of 10% cash to total deposits, it will also be willing to lend out 90% of the additional funds deposited with it, i.e. £81 which will be an advance for Bank B but a deposit for some other bank(s). The effect on Bank B's balance sheet will be:

Bank B

Liabilities (£m)		Assets (£m)	
Deposits	90	Cash	9
		Advances	81

This process can continue until the entire initial deposit of £100m is held as cash by various banks in order to meet withdrawals by customers, at which point it will support deposits of ten times that amount, i.e. £1,000m.

The money supply multiplier

This process of multiple deposit creation is known as the *money supply multiplier* and in our example above the money supply multiplier has a value of 10, i.e. an initial deposit (£100m in our example) leads to an eventual increase in total deposits of ten times the initial deposit (£1,000m in our case). In fact, models of the money supply multiplier link the money supply to the monetary base in a relationship of the following form:

$$M = mB$$

where M = the money supply;
m = the money supply multiplier;
B = the monetary base.

In models such as this m tells us how many times the money supply will rise following an increase in the monetary base. But what determines the value of m? In fact, there are two factors: the decisions of depositors about their holdings of currency and deposits, and the level of reserves the banks hold to meet customer demands for currency. For simplicity let us assume that c is the desired ratio of currency (C) to total deposits (D) and that r is the desired ratio of reserves (R) to total deposits (D). Thus we have:

$$c = \frac{C}{D} \text{ and } r = \frac{R}{D}$$

Since $B = C + R$ and $M = C + D$, it follows that:

$$\frac{M}{B} = \frac{C+D}{C+R} \text{ which, dividing right-hand side by } D, \text{ can be written as: } \frac{\frac{C}{D}+1}{\frac{C}{D}+\frac{R}{D}}$$

Replacing C/D with c and R/D with r we have:

$$\frac{M}{B} = \frac{c+1}{c+r}$$

Since $m = \frac{M}{B}$ we can say that the money supply multiplier is determined by the public's desired ratio of cash to total deposits and the bank's desired ratio of reserves to total deposits.

Whether the money supply multiplier is an adequate explanation of the money supply process depends partly on the stability of the ratios c and r. For the UK, the evidence suggests that c, the ratio of the public's demand for cash to deposits, can be unstable and unpredictable. Of course, there are bound to be seasonal variations and it might be expected that over the Christmas period and during the summer months when more holidays are taken the c ratio will rise because of an increase in the public's demand for cash. However, empirical studies of the c ratio have concluded that the instability it exhibits arises for many reasons and changes do not always coincide with predictable changes in the seasons. One reason why the c ratio might be unstable is that changes in the rate of interest change the opportunity cost of holding cash. This is especially important because of the emergence of interest-bearing current account deposits. Whatever the reasons, for the UK it has been estimated that the c ratio varies between 0.16 and 0.21.

The empirical evidence on the stability of the r ratio is not so conclusive and some studies suggest that r is unstable while others suggest that it is relatively stable. Again, in the short run at least, changes in the rate of interest are likely to cause changes in the r ratio. For example, when interest rates are rising, banks have an incentive to reduce their holdings of reserves.

Certainly for the UK the general view is that the money supply multiplier is unstable in the short run and that in the long run, changes in the money supply depend more on changes in the monetary base.

The monetary base
In light of the above discussion an important issue presents itself: can the authorities control the *monetary base*? It can easily be shown that if public sector borrowing is not financed by sales of debt to the non-bank financial intermediaries or by sales of the foreign currency reserves, the banking sector will act as a source of residual finance and the monetary base will rise.

Let us begin with the following notation:

PSBR = public sector borrowing requirement
MAT = maturing government debt
MGD = marketable government debt
NMGD = non-marketable government debt
FE = sales of foreign exchange reserves
ΔB = change in the monetary base.

We can derive the following identity:

$$PSBR + MAT \equiv MGD + NMGD + FE + \Delta B$$

This simply tells us that total public sector borrowing requirement (plus redemption of maturing government debt) must be met by sales of debt and foreign currency or by an increase in the monetary base. Rearranging this identity tells us that changes in the monetary base represent the difference between public sector borrowing on the one hand, and sales of government debt and foreign exchange on the other. Thus:

$$\Delta B \equiv (PSBR + MAT) - (MGD + NMGD + FE)$$

The question naturally arises about the extent to which the authorities can control the determinants of the monetary base.

Controlling the PSBR The PSBR is largely the central government's budget deficit and therefore controlling the PSBR implies that fiscal policy is geared to limiting the size of the budget deficit. In principle the authorities might very well be able to set targets for the budget deficit, but the problem is that expenditure and tax revenue are subject to short-term fluctuations which cannot easily be predicted. Indeed, during the *medium-term financial strategy* (see below) declining targets were announced for the PSBR, but these targets proved difficult to meet and were abandoned after only a few years. It is therefore not feasible to control the monetary base by controlling the PSBR.

Controlling MAT The amount of government debt maturing at any given time depends on sales of debt in previous years. This is not under the immediate control of the authorities and indeed the size of the national debt is a particular problem for the authorities in the UK. Again, controlling the level of maturing government debt does not provide a feasible mechanism for controlling the monetary base.

Controlling MGD Sales of marketable government debt have become the main means of financing the PSBR and maturing government debt. If the authorities were unconcerned with the monetary implications of their borrowing, this could be financed by sales of securities (debt) to the Bank of England. In this case the government's account at the Bank of England would be credited with an amount equivalent to the value of debt purchased by the Bank. However, once the government spent its newly acquired deposits they would flow into the banking system and the monetary base would rise. This is the modern equivalent of 'printing money'.

In practice the authorities are much more concerned to sell debt to the non-bank private sector such as insurance companies, pension funds, joint stock companies other than banks, private individuals and so on. Such sales result in a *fall* in banks' operational deposits at the Bank of England and the monetary base will tend to fall back towards its previous level. However, the extent to which the government can persuade the non-bank private sector to purchase debt depends on its willingness to accept higher and higher rates of interest. Given that changes in interest rates have become the main instrument for controlling the rate of inflation, it is inconceivable that sales of government debt to the non-bank private sector can be varied so as to control changes in the monetary base.

Controlling NMGD Non-marketable government debt consists of such assets as national savings certificates, premium bonds and so on. Sales of the former depend again on rates of return but since these are unlikely to vary as freely as market rates on marketable government debt, it is not possible to rely on such sales as a means of controlling changes in the monetary base. The latter are sold on tap, that is, they are sold in response to public demand. The government makes no attempt to actively increase sales. Varying the sales of non-marketable government debt is not therefore an option open to the government in controlling the monetary base.

Changes in the foreign exchange reserves When the authorities intervene to stabilize the exchange rate they buy or sell sterling in exchange for foreign currency.

When imports exceed exports there will be downward pressure on sterling on the foreign exchanges. To preserve the exchange rate the authorities must sell foreign currency and purchase sterling on the foreign exchanges. The sterling deposits acquired by the Bank of England through intervention in the foreign exchange market imply an equivalent reduction in operational deposits of the banking sector and the monetary base therefore tends to fall. In the event of upward pressure on sterling, intervention would tend to increase the monetary base since the Bank would be compelled to sell sterling on the foreign exchanges. It might be argued that the authorities could *sterilize* the effect of sterling inflows by open market sales of securities. However, as argued earlier, increased sales of securities implies an increase in the rate of interest which would tend to further increase upward pressure on the sterling exchange rate.

Two conclusions emerge: the monetary base is not exogenously determined by the authorities, and the money supply multiplier is an incomplete model of the money supply process. The first of these conclusions simply tells us that the monetary base is not under the direct control of the authorities unless they are prepared to allow interest rates and the exchange rate to be entirely determined by market forces. Given that the authorities clearly regard the interest rate and the exchange rate as instruments of economic policy, it is inconceivable that they would allow them to be entirely determined by the market. The second conclusion follows from the first and tells us that the monetary base is functionally related to changes in the rate of interest. Given that the two ratios which determine the money supply multiplier are also dependant on the rate of interest, it follows that the three determinants of the money supply in the multiplier model are interdependent. Any attempt by the authorities to offset changes in the c and r ratios by changes in the monetary base to achieve a particular money supply target are, therefore, likely to lead to further changes in c and r ratios!

Monetary control

Over the years governments have used a variety of techniques as part of their monetary policy actions. In general, techniques of monetary policy have either attempted to control the rate of money growth or the rate of interest. They cannot, of course, fix both simultaneously. Before we survey the operation of monetary policy over the years, let us briefly review techniques that might be used.

The authorities might impose regulations on financial institutions requiring them to hold a proportion of their assets in cash or as *reserve assets*, i.e. liquid assets of a specified type. The authorities can then seek to control the growth of bank deposits by limiting the availability of reserve assets in a variety of ways.

(a) *Open market operations.* When reserve requirements were in operation the authorities made frequent use of *open market operations* to influence the liquidity positions of the banks. For example, if the authorities *sell* gilts in the open market there will be a transfer of deposits from the banks' operational balances at the Bank of England into the government's own account as cheques authorizing payment are cleared. This technique was particularly effective when the authorities had regulations of the type outlined above which compel the banks to hold a specified proportion of their total assets as cash. Since operational deposits at the Bank of England were counted as part of the banks' cash reserves, such an action was sometimes used to compel the banking sector to reduce its lending. The opposite happened when the Bank *bought* securities in the open market.

(b) *Funding*. Another way of constraining money growth open to the authorities when reserve requirements were operational was to fund the national debt. When this happens the Bank simply issues fewer short-term securities (such as treasury bills) and more long-term securities. Since treasury bills would be counted as part of the banks' stock of liquid assets but long-term securities would not, the implied shortage of liquid assets could again put pressure on banks to reduce their lending. Funding would be particularly effective when used in a complimentary way with contractionary open market operations.

(c) *Special deposits*. The Bank might also require the banking sector to make special deposits. Such deposits are 'frozen' at the Bank of England and the banking sector has no access to them (although they do earn interest at the average treasury bill rate) until they are released by the Bank. Payment of such deposits implies a reduction in the banks' operational deposits and again this puts pressure on them to reduce their lending. The bank has not made a call for special deposits since the 1970s and it is unlikely that it will do so again.

(d) *Credit ceilings*. The Bank has also operated credit ceilings, such as *supplementary special deposits* as a technique of monetary control. Supplementary special deposits were imposed on the banking sector when their liabilities (bank deposits) rose above a specified level. In such cases banks were required to make additional *non-interest-bearing deposits* with the Bank of England in proportion to the growth of their liabilities.

(e) *Interest rates*. The most comprehensive technique available to the Bank is changes in short-term interest rates. We shall see on pp. 451–2 and in Chapter 21 the way in which the bank operates to influence short-term rates, but the point to grasp here is that a change in interest rates affects all money market institutions equally and simultaneously.

Monetary control in the 1950s and 1960s

In the 1950s and 1960s the Keynesian view of money was the consensus view. There was a widespread belief that money growth exerted its influence on the economy through changes in the rate of interest which stimulated changes in the rate of investment. However, monetary policy was viewed as having a weak effect since the available empirical evidence strongly suggested that investment was interest inelastic. The prevailing view was that investment by firms in fixed assets and stocks, if it was influenced at all by monetary factors, was influenced more by the *availability of credit* rather than by its *nominal cost*. Consequently monetary policy consisted primarily of ceilings on lending, although open market operations and special deposits were also used during this period.

Competition and credit control (CCC) 1971

In 1971 the focus of monetary policy switched decisively. Interest rates were, ostensibly at least, to be market determined rather than imposed by the authorities. Furthermore, regulations were introduced compelling banks to observe a minimum 12.5% *reserve assets ratio* between eligible reserve assets and eligible liabilities.

Eligible liabilities were defined as total liabilities minus the deposits of the monetary sector institutions, i.e. eligible liabilities consisted of private sector non-bank deposits and building society deposits.

Eligible reserve assets were defined to include:

1. Balances at the Bank of England (other than special or supplementary special deposits) to be an average of 1.5% of eligible liabilities.
2. Secured money at call and short notice with the London Discount Market institutions.
3. British Government and Northern Ireland Treasury Bills.
4. British Government stocks with a residual maturity of less than one year, i.e. less than one year until they were repayable by the government.
5. Local authority bills eligible for rediscount at the Bank of England.
6. Commercial bills eligible for rediscount at the Bank (up to a maximum of 2% of eligible liabilities).

If holdings of eligible reserve assets fell below the 12.5% minimum, it followed that banks were obliged to reduce their lending so as to restore the required ratio.

Within the CCC framework, monetary policy could be implemented in two ways:

1. The Bank could call for special deposits. Since eligible reserve assets excluded special deposits, the effect was to reduce the liquidity position of the banks and so put pressure on them to reduce their lending.
2. Although the 1971 measures explicitly stated that interest rates were to be market determined, the Bank frequently used open market operations to leave the money market short of funds. In its role as 'lender of last resort' the Bank stood ready to relieve shortages in the money market – but it reserved the right to impose a penal rate of interest. In practice, shortages of funds were primarily felt by the discount houses because, as cheques cleared in payment for securities and operational deposits at the Bank of England fell, the banks called in their loans to the discount market which was then 'forced into the Bank'. By raising its Minimum Lending Rate (the rate at which it relieved shortages in the market) the Bank compelled the discount houses to raise their own discount rates, i.e. the rate at which they lend to the government or rediscount first-class bills. Consequently a ripple effect spread throughout the banking sector because banks, along with other customers, were now being charged higher rates by the discount houses. As a result the banks raised their own base rates and, since all other rates of interest charged by banks are linked to base rates, interest rates throughout the economy were forced upwards.

During the 1970s monetary policy therefore consisted of a mix of money supply control and interest rate changes. In other words, interest rates were adjusted to reinforce changes in the availability of reserve assets brought about by government action. Such action might involve a call for, or a repayment of, special deposits and/ or changes in the weekly treasury bill issue so that the government increased or reduced its short-term borrowing in relation to its long-term borrowing.

Breakdown of the eligible reserve assets system   The eligible reserve assets system failed to provide an effective mechanism of monetary control for several reasons.

1. The authorities were unwilling to allow interest rates to be entirely determined by the market and intervened to prevent them rising to the extent required to give effective control of money growth.
2. The 1971 measures applied only to designated institutions and were too narrowly focused to give effective monetary control. In particular, the restrictions applied to the clearing banks so that when monetary policy was tightened and the clearing banks were short of funds, the secondary sector (consisting of institutions such as foreign banks who were exempt from the eligible reserve requirements) were able to meet unsatisfied loan demand. In fact, the restrictions encouraged more competition, not just from overseas banks, but also by allowing certain financial intermediaries such as finance houses (hire purchase companies) to upgrade to full banking status.

Encouraging greater competition in the banking sector clearly conflicted with the efforts of the authorities to exercise monetary control.

3. The acceleration of inflation in the 1970s, to which the CCC policy was a contributory factor, led to rising central government budget deficits which resulted in a large and persistent public sector borrowing requirement (PSBR). Because of the disruption to long-term interest rates that 'funding' government borrowing would cause, this ensured a plentiful supply of treasury bills many of which were bought by the banking sector. The availability of liquidity made it difficult for the authorities to exercise effective monetary control.
4. As a consequence of (3) above the authorities introduced *supplementary special deposits* as an additional control measure. Again these only applied to the regulated sector, but in any case the controls were easily evaded, most notably via the 'bill leak'. Large firms raised their own finance by issuing bills of exchange which the banks 'accepted' or guaranteed. These bills then functioned as exchange media and provided firms with a credit facility they could not obtain from the banks.
5. Higher rates of inflation also led to rising interest rates and encouraged 'round tripping'. This involved customers borrowing from banks and re-lending at higher rates of interest in other parts of the money market. The result was that the money market was provided with additional liquidity which reduced the effectiveness of monetary control techniques.
6. The abolition of exchange controls in October 1979 greatly increased flows of deposits between countries (see Ch. 25) making effective monetary control even more difficult. In particular, UK residents were now able to open bank accounts overseas and to borrow abroad for current spending in the UK.

The medium-term financial strategy (MTFS) 1980

In March 1980 the government unveiled its new approach to monetary control, the *medium-term financial strategy* (MTFS). The MTFS was designed to provide a framework of control within which money growth could be targeted over a four-year period. The emphasis of control shifted in two ways:

1. From a short-term to a medium-term perspective.
2. From controlling the availability of reserve assets to controlling the growth of bank assets, the so-called 'counterparts' to the money stock.

Counterparts to the money stock   Apart from the narrowest measures of money, definitions of the money stock focus on bank deposits. There is a famous banking maxim that 'every loan creates a deposit' because every loan granted by a bank is redeposited with the banking sector after being spent by the borrower. One approach to monetary control might be to control the asset counterparts of the money stock. This was the approach adopted by the authorities to control broad money on the (now defunct) sterling M3 (£M3) measure of money.

Banks lend in different ways to different organisations and individuals. They lend to the government and acquire bills and bonds; they lend to the private sector via overdrafts and loans and they lend overseas. In general any such lending increases bank deposits and therefore money growth – the government spends its deposits which are returned to the banking sector, and lending to private organizations and individuals involves crediting their accounts with the appropriate amount.

Deposits can therefore be thought of as lending to the:

- government;
- private sector;
- overseas sector.

To exercise control, these categories of lending were quantified as follows:

1. Bank lending to the government is equal to total government borrowing minus the amount borrowed from the private sector, for example through treasury bill sales or National Savings.
2. Lending to the private sector is simply the sum of bank loans plus overdrafts.
3. Net lending to the overseas sector was calculated as:
   sterling lending to overseas customers *less*
   increase in sterling deposits held by foreigners[2] *plus*
   net purchases of foreign currency by the Bank of England[3] *less*
   purchases of government debt by overseas residents.
4. Any increase in the capital base of the banks was also deducted to obtain an overall figure for £M3.[4]

Each of these form the counterparts to the money stock and the authorities aimed to control each separately.

1. *Fiscal policy* was used to control the growth of the PSBR. Strictly this implies reducing expenditure and/or increasing tax revenue. However, the proceeds from privatization were treated not as might be expected, as a means of financing the PSBR, but as a means of reducing it!
2. *Debt sales to the non-bank private sector* were to be encouraged by adjusting interest rates to the level required to persuade the non-bank private sector to take up offers of treasury bills. We have already seen that when the non-bank private sector takes up government debt, the effect on the money supply is neutral because deposits taken from the private sector are returned to the private sector when the government spends them. However, the situation is different if the banking sector takes up part of the treasury bill issue. Here banks lend to the government by creating a deposit. When payment is made, operational deposits at the Bank of England initially fall but are then restored to their original level when the government spends its newly acquired deposits. Each additional deposit spent by the government therefore increases the money supply in the ratio one to one.

An additional technique known as *overfunding* was operational in the early 1980s with the aim of ensuring that as little of the PSBR as possible was taken up by the banking sector. Overfunding involved issuing more debt than was necessary to cover the borrowing requirement. As operational deposits fell the Bank pumped liquidity back into the system by buying eligible bills from the bill market which the financial institutions sold to replenish operational deposits.

3. *Private sector borrowing* was also to be controlled by changes in the rate of interest.
4. *Exchange rate policy* was to be used to influence the external and foreign currency counterparts of the money stock. Note that since in the short run the exchange rate is determined by the rate of interest, a dilemma existed here because interest rate policy and exchange rate policy are not independent.

Monetary control measures 1981

In August 1981 the Bank introduced additional measures designed to improve the effectiveness of monetary policy by addressing some of the problems that had arisen towards the end of the 1970s and to form the basis for implementing the new monetary strategy. These additional measures consisted of:

1. Henceforth, banking regulations were to apply to all institutions within the monetary sector (see Ch. 21).
2. The reserve assets ratio was abolished. Banks were simply required to keep balances they thought prudential and to inform the Bank of any changes in their liquidity policies.
3. Initially all banks and licensed deposit takers were required to hold 0.5% of their eligible liabilities at the Bank as non-operational deposits. This was reduced in January 1992 to 0.35% and, since these deposits do not earn interest, their function is to provide the Bank with operating income. In addition clearers are required to maintain appropriate operational deposits at the Bank.
4. A category of 'eligible banks' was created and required to lend an average of 5% of their eligible liabilities to the discount houses, money brokers and jobbers, and not less than a daily minimum of 2.5% to the discount houses. At the time this was to ensure that the money market had an adequate supply of funds but after the 'big bang', in October 1986, the arrangement was discontinued.
5. The Bank announced that it would no longer act as 'lender of last resort' but would, instead, support the market by dealing in bills by responding to offers made to it by the discount houses. If the interest rate implied in the offer was not acceptable, the offer would be rejected and the discount houses would be forced to make a revised offer. Despite this, the Bank did reserve the right to lend directly (at a penal rate if it thought necessary) on occasions when it judged that dealing would distort the workings of the market.
6. Interest rates were to be market determined within an undisclosed band and the Bank would intervene to iron out day-to-day fluctuations where interest rates threatened to move outside the band. Shortages and surpluses of cash in the system occur regularly because transactions between the government and the public vary from day to day, for example when a large plc pays its tax bill. The daily procedure is for the Bank, each morning, to make an estimate of the day's position. If necessary, it will then notify the discount houses that it is willing to consider offers to buy bills to relieve a shortage of cash or it will sell bills to mop up a surplus. In the case of a shortage of funds, should the day's dealing not result

in enough transactions at prices acceptable to the Bank, direct lending to the discount houses will almost certainly take place.

In simple terms, when the cash position in the money market is acceptable, the Bank is prepared to allow market forces to determine the rate of interest so long as it moves within an acceptable range. However, when there are shortages or surpluses of cash the Bank will act to relieve them in such a way as to keep interest rates at the desired level. In terms of Fig. 20.5, suppose the undisclosed band for the rate of interest is given by SR and that the supply of base money is given by SS, with the desired level of cash at $0\bar{M}$. The Bank will be prepared to allow the demand for cash to vary from D_1 to D_3 because interest rates remain within the required range. However, if demand increases to D_4 and the Bank does not act, the rate of interest will rise outside the required range. To avoid this the Bank will buy bills to relieve the shortage of funds and the effect will be to force bill prices upwards and yields downwards to the required level.

Assessment of monetary policy in the 1980s

In any assessment of the effectiveness of policy in the 1980s two questions need to be addressed:

1. Whether the authorities were successful in controlling money growth and if not, why not.
2. Whether money growth was correlated with inflation and if not, why not.

We have already seen that control of the money stock was to be achieved by setting target ranges for money growth and the targeted variable was initially £M3 and, after 1984, M0, the monetary base, was also targeted. Other narrow and broad measures of money were also briefly targeted during this period. However, none of the targeted aggregates performed well and in 1987 the government abandoned broad money targets and ceased publication of £M3.

M0 was (and is) still published as an indicator of monetary conditions despite the fact that it bears no obvious relationship to expenditure. Nevertheless the authorities argued that changes in the growth of M0 provided an early indication of growth in broad money.

In fact the authorities repeatedly failed to meet the targets for money growth during the 1980s and there were several possible reasons for this:

1. Private sector borrowing proved rather insensitive to relatively high real rates of interest in the early 1980s. In the personal sector consumer credit and mortgage finance both increased and in the company sector firms borrowed to build up their reserves.

2. The growth of lending was paralleled by a growth of deposits. What appears to have happened is that the personal sector chose to build up the liquid asset component of its portfolio, attracted by interest rates which were driven up by competition between banks and building societies for deposits. This is partly explicable by the fact that the increase in borrowing increased the funds available for the acquisition of financial assets, and partly due to the fact that rising equity values and house prices during the 1980s enabled the personal sector to realize gains in equity markets. Companies too benefited from the new competition between financial intermediaries which resulted in a narrowing of margins between borrowing and lending rates.

3. During the period under review financial deregulation and innovation distorted the money supply figures. For example, until 1987 building society deposits were not included in the money aggregates. Competition between banks and building societies for deposits resulted in changes in the relative size of both and therefore distorted the information in the money supply aggregates so that they became less reliable indicators of actual money growth. This particular problem was solved in 1987 when the money supply figures were reformulated to include building society deposits. However, alongside the problems of deregulation, product innovation such as the growth of securitisation whereby financial institutions transform otherwise illiquid assets into capital market securities, also distorted the reliability of the money supply figures.

Notwithstanding these problems, circumstances altered raising serious questions about the appropriateness of the overall monetary policy strategy embodied in the MTFS. In particular:

1. Overfunding ensured that the PSBR had little effect on money growth. For example, for part of the 1980s the UK had a public sector debt repayment (PSDR), that is public expenditure was less than revenue. Despite this, broad money grew rapidly even though the government was *repaying debt* rather than issuing new debt to finance the PSBR!

2. In the early 1980s interest rates proved ineffective in restraining private sector borrowing and this fuelled rising demand for property and a boom in house prices. However, by the late 1980s the private sector debt burden had grown rapidly so that changes in interest rates had a much larger impact on expenditure and inflation.

3. Towards the end of the 1980s, the exchange rate became the main instrument for controlling inflation. In particular an increasing balance of payments deficit prompted fears of a depreciating exchange rate which would raise the cost of imports and fuel inflationary expectations. Targeting the exchange rate was designed to reduce inflationary expectations and to send a signal to those involved in fixing wages and prices that inflationary increases would not be accommodated by the authorities and would result in rising unemployment. To prevent the

exchange rate depreciating, interest rates were increased and by the beginning of the 1990s UK interest rates were significantly higher than our major competitors, reaching 15% in October 1990.

In summary, during the MTFS monetary control failed to restrain money growth within the target ranges and the relationship between money and prices deteriorated to the extent that the target variables ceased to be reliable indicators of future inflation.

Changing attitudes towards monetary control

Targeting the exchange rate culminated in UK entry into the European Exchange Rate Mechanism (ERM) in October 1990. However, it soon became clear that the central rate of DM2.95 left sterling hopelessly overvalued on the foreign exchanges and in September 1992, with the UK deep in recession and interest rates still at 15%, the Chancellor of the Exchequer bowed to the inevitable and sterling withdrew from the ERM. The following day interest rates were reduced to 10% and, free of exchange rate constraints, the focus of policy changed. The rate of inflation is now targeted over the medium term and interest rates are adjusted as the mechanism for achieving this objective.

Inflation target   An inflation target was first announced by the then Chancellor, Norman Lamont, in a speech at the Conservative Party Conference on 8 October 1992. The target was initially set in the range 1–4% annually to be achieved in the life of the Parliament, i.e. by May 1997. This marked a decisive change in policy because the Chancellor also announced that no intermediate target was to be set to achieve the overall aim of policy. The authorities would continue to monitor money growth and the exchange rate. A speech delivered by the then Governor of the Bank of England, Robin Leigh Pemberton, on 11 November 1992, made the point abundantly clear:

> Experience leads us to believe that monetary policy cannot be conducted with reference to a single target variable. The overriding objective of monetary policy is price stability. Therefore policy must be conducted with reference to our expectations of future inflation ... Consequently policy makers should make use of every possible variable, with the importance attached to any given variable at any point in time dependant on its value as a guide to prospective inflation. (Leigh Pemberton, 1992, *Bank of England Quarterly Bulletin*, December)

Targeting the inflation goal directly was therefore seen as the only practical way of achieving that goal but the question of how to make policy credible was left unanswered. The question was answered towards the end of October 1992 when, in his Mansion House speech, the Chancellor announced that the Governor of the Bank of England would provide a regular report on progress towards the inflation target. This *Inflation Report* is compiled by the Bank in the expectation that this will give it more credibility than if it was compiled by the Treasury and it is released through the Bank of England's Quarterly Bulletin. Credibility is therefore to be achieved through a policy of openness and Kenneth Clarke (Lamont's successor as Chancellor) took this a step further in 1994 when he began to publish minutes of regular meetings between himself and the Governor to review the operation of monetary policy. Publication of these minutes was designed to give greater transparency in monetary policy actions.

In his Mansion House speech of 1995, Kenneth Clarke announced that henceforth a point target of 2.5% was to be set for inflation to be met on an ongoing basis. This might appear to compromise the aim of greater credibility. After all, the inflation target was initially set within a band, not to allow slippage and countercyclical monetary policy, but rather to reflect an admission that control and forecasting were imperfect. Nevertheless, it was felt that if inflation was at the upper end of the band, or indeed if the band was widened, this would be interpreted as a loosening of policy and credibility would be compromised. It was argued that a point target therefore gave greater flexibility by permitting short-run unavoidable deviations, while shifting the focus away from the values in the bands themselves.

Operational independence of the Bank of England   In furtherance of the aim of achieving credibility, on 6 May 1997, the Bank of England was given operational responsibility for setting short-term interest rates to achieve the inflation target, retained by the Labour government at 2.5%. However, the incoming Chancellor, Gordon Brown, made it clear that the government would retain a national interest in controlling inflation. This is effectively an escape clause allowing it to overrule the Bank's interest rates decisions in pursuit of the inflation target when it deems such action necessary. The government has not specified any formal process for implementing the escape clause nor defined a set of conditions under which the Bank would be overruled. Nevertheless the point target now has a one percentage point threshold either side and if inflation breaches this, the Monetary Policy Committee (which decides on interest rate changes, see below) is required to publish an open letter outlining the reasons for the deviation and to explain the policy changes to be adopted so as to bring inflation back to target.

In setting monetary policy the Bank was also instructed that, without prejudice to the inflation target, monetary policy was to support the government's economic policy including its objectives for growth and employment. Interest rate changes have therefore been elevated to become the main instrument of monetary policy and they are to be adjusted up or down whenever the expected rate of inflation rises above or falls below 2.5%.

It is the task of the Monetary Policy Committee, which meets monthly at the Bank of England, to decide on the timing and extent of any change in the rate of interest. The broad aim is to keep the growth of demand in line with supply-side capacity as reflected by consistently low inflation. Monetary policy is therefore loosened or tightened in order to moderate the fluctuations that occur over the business cycle. It is anticipated that this will facilitate steadier growth, higher levels of employment and rising living standards into the medium and longer term. To inform its decisions, the Monetary Policy Committee considers a vast array of evidence, and data on broad and narrow money growth are just a part of this evidence. Monitoring ranges exist for M0 and M4, but there is no return to monetary targeting which effectively disappeared from the policy framework as far back as 1986.

European Monetary Union (EMU)

Chapter 28 on the European Union considers the historical developments behind the move towards European Monetary Union. In this section we focus on the issue of a single currency, the euro, and the monetary framework within which that currency will operate.

Creating a new money:
the euro

For the eleven countries which replaced their national currencies with the euro on 1 January 1999, irrevocably fixed exchange rates had already been established between their domestic currencies and the euro on 3 May 1998. Figure 20.6 gives the value of the euro in all participating countries on that date and therefore the bilateral rates of exchange that operated before the euro became the common currency in those countries.

Some of the key elements in this transition to a single currency are outlined below.

European Central Bank (ECB) The primary responsibility of the ECB is to ensure the stability of prices within the euro area. It is directed by a Council composed of the members of the Executive Board and the governors of the eleven central banks. The Council sets the main lines of monetary policy, for implementation

Fig. 20.6. Bilateral exchange rates pre-announced on 3 May 1998.
Source: Adapted from European Commission (1998) *Newsletter*, No. 9.

	Germany 100 DEM	Belgium/ Luxembourg 100 BEF/LUF	Spain 100 ESP	France 100 FRF	Ireland 1 IEP	Italy 1000 ITL	Netherlands 100 NLG	Austria 100 ATS	Portugal 100 PTE	Finland 100 FIM
Germany	euro									
Belgium/ Luxembourg	2062.55	euro								
Spain	8507.22	412.462	euro							
France	335.386	16.2608	3.94237	euro						
Ireland	40.2676	1.95232	0.473335	12.0063	euro					
Italy	99000.2	4799.90	1163.72	29518.3	2458.56	euro				
Netherlands	112.674	5.46285	1.32445	33.5953	2.79812	1.13812	euro			
Austria	703.552	34.1108	8.27006	209.774	17.4719	7.10657	624.415	euro		
Portugal	10250.5	496.984	120.492	3056.34	254.560	103.541	9097.53	1456.97	euro	
Finland	304.001	14.7391	3.57345	90.6420	7.54951	3.07071	269.806	43.2094	2.96571	euro

by an Executive Board. Members of the Executive Board are appointed for eight-year non-renewable mandates (those of the first Executive Board run between four and eight years). The ECB's headquarters are in Frankfurt.

Convergence criteria   These are conditions that must be met by a member state for its currency to be included in the euro. The four principal criteria are: the public budget deficit should not exceed 3% of GDP unless it has already undergone a substantial reduction and any excess can be considered exceptional; public debt should not exceed 60% of GDP unless it is falling at a satisfactory rate towards this ratio; inflation should not be more than 1.5 percentage points above the three member states with the best performance on price stability; long-term interest rates should not be more than 2 percentage points above rates in the three member states with the best performance on price stability.

ECU   It was exchanged on 1 January 1999 at the rate of 1 Ecu = 1 euro. On 1 January 1999 it disappeared.

European Monetary Institute   The EMI made the preparations for setting up the ECB and the monetary policy tools. It also expressed its opinion on convergence within the Union. It disappeared when the ECB was launched.

European Exchange Mechanism   Also known as the ERM2, it governs the exchange rate relations between the euro and the currencies of the 'pre-in' countries.

Pact for stability and growth   An agreement between the member states to ensure respect for budgetary discipline and limits on public deficits. It provides for sanctions for countries participating in the euro in cases of failure to respect the budgetary criteria for inclusion in the euro.

Definitive conversion rates   The definitive conversion rates between the euro and each participating currency were fixed by the Council on 1 January 1999.

Treaty on European Union   The Treaty of Maastricht defined the three stages leading to the introduction of the euro.

The stages in the transition to a fully operative EMU system are outlined in Table 20.2.

The euro and the functions of money   It is interesting to consider the introduction of the euro in the terms of the functions of money. The euro is widely regarded as the world's newest currency and yet, if money is defined in terms of the functions outlined above, it is misleading to think of the euro as money in the way that we think of the pound sterling as money in the UK.

Table 20.2 Transitional stages to a fully operative EMU system.

Timing	Actions	Responsibility
May/June 1998	• Creation of the ECB and appointment of its executive board • Start production of euro banknotes and coins • Adoption of necessary secondary legislation	• Council (member states participating in EMU) • Member states and national central banks • Commission proposed, Council decides
1 January 1999	• Conversion rates are irrevocably fixed and legislation comes into force, notably on the legal status of the euro • Definition and execution of the single monetary policy in euro • Foreign exchange operations in euro • New public debt issues in euro, some outstanding debt redenominated in euro • Many large companies begin issuing invoices and making payments in euro • Banks begin converting payments in national currency units into euro for euro accounts	• Council based on a Commission proposal • ESCB • ESCB • Member states, European Investment Bank, Commission and other issuers
1 January 1999 to 31 December 2001	• Changeover to the euro by the banking and finance industry • Assist the whole economy in an orderly changeover (IT, accounting, dual display of prices, etc.) • Information campaigns for the citizen	• Commission and member states • Commission and member states
1 January 2002	• Start circulation of euro banknotes • Start circulation of euro coins • Complete changeover to the euro of public administrations	• ESCB • Member states • Member states
1 July 2002 at the latest	• Cancel the legal tender status of national banknotes and coins	• Member states ESCB

Notes:
ECB – European Central Bank.
ESCB – European System of Central Banks.
Source: Adapted from European Commission (1998) *Newsletter*, No. 9.

The euro as a unit of account The nominal value of a unit of account is fixed by law and, as we have seen earlier, is used to express nominal prices. On 1 January 1999, the euro became the unit of account in eleven European countries. The euro will certainly function as a unit of account but, for convenience, a system of dual pricing operates whereby prices are quoted in euros and in domestic currency.

The euro as a medium of exchange   Although prices in those states adopting the euro are quoted in euros and payment can be made in euros via the banking system, euro notes and coin are not scheduled to circulate until some time after 1 January 1999. It is almost certain that many people will prefer to be paid in domestic currency rather than euros and, initially at least, the euro is unlikely to function as a universal medium of exchange in those countries adopting it.

The euro as a store of value   Whether the euro will function as an effective store of value depends on the behaviour of inflation throughout the euro area. Controlling the rate of inflation within the euro area is a major function of the independent European Central Bank (ECB). It might be argued that the success achieved by so many independent central banks in recent years provides encouraging evidence that the euro might well be an effective store of value. However, whether the ECB will be successful in this area is not yet known, but there is no doubt the task is formidable.

Advantages of a single currency   The move to a single currency has many potential benefits which are briefly reviewed here.

Lower costs of exchange   When goods are imported the trader receiving the goods must obtain foreign currency to pay the exporter. Banks will happily supply foreign currency, but they will levy a service charge for the transaction. For the economy as a whole these charges are sizeable and, in general, they will be passed on to consumers through higher prices. For the EU as a whole the transactions costs associated with intra-community trade are estimated at 0.4% of EU GDP. These figures give an idea of the resource savings to those countries which adopted the euro and an encouraging argument about why these resource savings might be reflected in lower prices within the euro area.

Reduced exchange rate uncertainty   Inside the euro area, exchange rates are irrevocably fixed and there is no uncertainty over future rates of exchange. This is important because traders often negotiate contracts for delivery and payment stretching six months and longer into the future. Outside the euro area exchange rate risk exists for traders involved in international transactions. For example, if at the time a contract was agreed for DM3m between a UK importer and a German exporter, the exchange rate for the Deutschmark against sterling was DM2.95, and this fell to 2.76 by the time the contract became due for settlement, the importer would face an unanticipated increase in costs of more than £70,000.[5] It is, of course, possible for traders to hedge the foreign exchange risk in the forward market where rates of exchange can be agreed today for delivery of currency at some future point in time. However, such arrangements are costly and so raise the cost of a transaction. A different alternative might be for traders to find a domestic producer instead of trading internationally. The implication is that exchange rate risk might raise the cost of trading internationally or discourage international trade altogether. To the extent that this is the case, a single currency will reduce the cost of transacting business across frontiers (because of the costless elimination of exchange rate risk) and will increase international trade with all the associated benefits of comparative advantage. These advantages include the increased variety of products that become available, lower prices due to competition (because price differences between markets will no longer be masked by being quoted in different currencies) and greater economies of scale because of the larger market.

Eliminating competitive devaluations Between the two world wars, several European countries engaged in what became known as 'competitive devaluations' when a devaluation in one country was matched by a devaluation in other countries. While such competitive devaluations have been avoided in the latter half of the century, the possibility that they might recur still exists; in fact all devaluations adversely affect inflationary expectations in the devaluing country. Given the increasing scale of intra-European trade, any return to competitive devaluations (or any other form of protectionism) would have devastating effects on Europe's economies. The possibility of these disruptions disappears when a common currency exists.

Preventing speculative attacks Where different currencies exist, there also exists the possibility of a speculative attack on one or more currencies. The problem is exacerbated when a fixed exchange rate exists because speculators have a one-way bet. If the currency they have bet against is not devalued, all they have lost is their transactions costs on the deal whereas betting correctly can result in spectacular gains. Governments can defend currencies against such attacks, but this often involves raising interest rates which reduces business investment and hampers economic growth. The events leading up to sterling's withdrawal from the ERM provide a graphic example (see Chapter 28)! To the extent that exchange rate disruption is avoided, trade, investment and economic growth will be encouraged, there will be resource savings (e.g. no longer necessary for the authorities to hold reserves of foreign currency to defend the exchange rate) and lower interest rates (e.g. higher rates no longer needed to defend the exchange rate). The latter will again have a positive impact on investment and growth.

Disadvantages of a single currency

The advantages of adopting the euro seem encouraging, but these advantages do not come without costs. It is to a consideration of these that we now turn.

Loss of independent monetary policy Countries participating in the euro relinquish the right to implement an independent domestic monetary policy. Instead they accept the monetary policy implemented by the ECB. However, this 'one size fits all' monetary policy might not suit all countries equally, for example when there is a recession in one country but not in others. If that country is outside the euro area then the country's central bank could reduce interest rates and stimulate economic activity. However, the ECB is unlikely to respond in this way if the recession is only country specific because this will raise inflation throughout the Union.

The ECB has announced that monetary policy will target the rate of inflation. In other words, changes in monetary policy will be initiated whenever the forecast rate of inflation for the euro area as a whole rises above the ECB's target rate of 2%.

Monetary policy actions for the ECB, as with the Bank of England, will involve changes in the rate of interest. However, changes in the rate of interest might not affect all countries equally. It has been suggested that at present in some countries (Germany, the UK, the Netherlands, Austria, Belgium and Finland) changes in interest rates might take up to three years before exerting their full impact on the economy, while in others (Denmark, France, Italy, Portugal, Spain and Sweden) the effect of changes in interest rates is felt much sooner – perhaps within fifteen to eighteen months. Furthermore, the effect of changes in the rate of interest is, at present, almost twice as strong in the first group as in the second. The implication is that in the euro area, a tightening of monetary policy would take more time to affect some countries and would exert a stronger impact in some countries than in others. Again a 'one size fits all' monetary policy might be less effective than the policy an independent country could pursue.

In part, the different effects of monetary policy in the UK compared with some other European countries stems from the fact that there are important differences in the size and role of the property market in the transmission mechanism. Typically UK mortgage finance is based on a variable interest rate so that changes in official interest rates are quickly reflected in mortgage rates. The effect on the economy is further reinforced because the UK has a relatively high rate of owner occupation and housing-related debt (outstanding mortgage debt is equivalent to about 90% of GDP). The effects of monetary policy in the UK might therefore be relatively long-lasting because of the effect of interest rate changes on property prices and through this on the wealth portfolio of property owners. There is ample evidence from the UK that these wealth effects exert a powerful influence on consumer expenditure. However, because of differences in the extent of home ownership and the types of mortgage finance, these effects are not uniform across member states. It is certainly not at all clear that a 'one size fits all' monetary policy will be appropriate for all countries within the euro area at all times; in particular it is unclear whether such a policy will be appropriate for the UK should it decide to adopt the single currency!

Loss of an independent exchange rate policy   Similarly, when a common currency exists, countries lose the ability to devalue the exchange rate to offset a loss of competitiveness. The exchange rate, like the rate of interest, is a powerful weapon for bringing about changes in demand and economic adjustment. In the event of a balance of payments deficit inside a common currency area, the burden of adjustment is thrown on to the domestic economy. For example, cutting aggregate demand to reduce imports and curb any price inflation will be reflected in lower domestic output and employment. This will continue until rising unemployment depresses real wages far enough to restore competitiveness. Adjustment is less painfully achieved when the rate of exchange can be devalued to restore competitiveness.

Loss of an independent fiscal policy   It might be argued that fiscal policy could fill the vacuum left by loss of monetary policy sovereignty and exchange rate policy sovereignty. However, since the maximum allowable budget deficit for any country in the euro area is 3% of that country's GDP, scope for an active fiscal policy is clearly limited. It will be limited even further if current thinking on harmonising taxation within the euro zone is adopted!

Fig. 20.7. Output gaps
for the UK, France and
Gremany.
Source: UK membership
of the single currency: an
assessment of the five
economic tests,
HM Treasury, October
1997.

Note: The output gap is the difference between actual and trend output.
         When the real sectors of economies are convergent we would expect the
         output gap to follow a similar path and to be closely related.

Lack of convergence   Loss of policy sovereignty might not be so important if economies are reasonably convergent, in which case country-specific shocks are less likely to occur. However, the convergence criteria agreed at Maastricht in 1992 focused entirely on 'nominal' variables. The problem for the UK is that the business cycle (a 'real' variable) is not entirely convergent with business cycles in Europe – even though on the nominal criteria agreed at Maastricht the degree of convergence in the UK compares favourably with convergence in many other European countries. Figure 20.7 shows the *output gap* (the difference between actual and trend output) for the UK, Germany and France between 1979 and 1997. On this indicator of convergence the UK is clearly out of step with other major European countries. Therefore, a monetary policy which suits other European countries is unlikely at the present time to suit the UK. For example, if the output gap is widening because actual output is falling below trend in the UK, the appropriate response would be a loosening of monetary policy. However, if, at the same time, the output gap for the rest of Europe was negligible, there would be no policy response from the ECB. Until there is clear evidence that business cycles are convergent, joining the euro area and accepting a Europe-wide monetary policy may well impose heavy economic costs on the UK.

Conclusions

A number of conclusions might be drawn from the UK experience of money growth and monetary control over the last three decades.

1. Financial innovation and deregulation make it impossible to define a set of assets which alone function as money. This is the major reason the broad money aggregates have been subjected to continuous redefinition.

2. Controversy remains about how useful the definitions of money are. In the UK one measure of narrow money (M0) and one measure of broad money (M4) are monitored. However, different measures of money are published in different countries and the accepted view is that when interpreting monetary conditions, definitions of money do not always include all of the relevant variables. There is also a view that weighted measures of the money stock (Divisia) might be more useful than 'simple sum' measures.

3. Doubt remains as to whether the direction of causation is from money to prices or from prices to money. However, growing evidence does support the view that the velocity of circulation of money follows a relatively stable trend, though there are short-run fluctuations about this trend.

4. Controlling a particular money aggregate is difficult because of financial innovation, deregulation and disintermediation. Monetary control is especially difficult because of disintermediation (see also Ch. 21).

5. The focus of monetary policy has switched from controlling intermediate variables such as the money stock or the exchange rate which were formally thought to be linked to the rate of inflation, to direct targeting of the rate of inflation.

6. Monetary policy actions focus on changes in the rate of interest which affect all institutions simultaneously and equally.

7. There are a number of clear advantages from adopting a single currency, though these do not come without costs and the latter may prove excessive unless business cycles become convergent.

Key points

- Money functions as a unit of account, a medium of exchange and a store of value.
- Money avoids the inefficiency of a barter system, permitting greater specialization and associated scale economies.
- M0 is the official definition of money which most closely corresponds to the idea of a 'cash base'.
- Deposits at financial institutions are the most important component of broad money.
- Definitions of money are constantly evolving because of financial deregulation and innovation.
- Since the end of 1992 monetary targets have been replaced by 'monitoring ranges' for M0 and M4.
- The Bank of England was granted operational independence on 6 May 1997.
- A point target for inflation of 2.5% per annum has been set for the Bank of England to achieve on an ongoing basis.
- The eleven countries of the euro zone began operations on 1 January 1999 and the UK must carefully assess the costs and benefits of possible entry.

Notes

1. Narrow measures of money, with the exception of M0 (discussed later) are no longer published in the UK.

2. Sterling deposits held by foreigners were excluded from £M3 which only included domestically held deposits of sterling.

3. When the Bank purchases foreign currencies on the foreign exchanges it credits the accounts of foreign exchange dealers with sterling deposits.
4. If banks increase their own capital holdings instead of paying out profits, the money supply will fall by an amount equivalent to the increase in banks' capital.
5. The current sterling value of the contract is DM3m/2.95 = £1,016,949 and at the time of settlement the value of the contract is DM3m/2.76 = £1,086,956.5.

References

Bank of England Inflation Reports (various) Supplements to *Bank of England Quarterly Bulletins*.

Bank of England Quarterly Bulletin (1998a) The objectives and current state of monetary policy, **38**, 3, September.

Bank of England Quarterly Bulletin (1998b) UK monetary framework and preparations for EMU, the transmission mechanism of monetary policy, **38**, 1, February.

Chote, R. (1997) Treading the line between credibility and humility, *Financial Times*, 13 June.

Harrison, B. (1998) Monetary policy and the ECB, *Money Management Review*, **54**, Winter.

Minford, P. (1997) Why not a single currency? *The Economic Review*, April.

Rodgers, P. (1998) The new monetary policy and the Bank of England, *The Economic Review*, April.

Turner, P. (1997) Britain and the European Monetary System, *The Economic Review*, February.

Chapter 21

Financial institutions and markets

All modern, developed economies have a sophisticated financial system which incorporates both the financial institutions and financial markets. These institutions and markets exist to mediate between those who wish to save or lend and those who wish to borrow or invest. Mediation is necessary because lenders and borrowers have different needs in terms of maturity, liquidity and yield.

Lenders can be expected to prefer to lend for a short term before the loan matures, to get their money back quickly if their own need for liquidity changes, and to receive high returns on their loans. Borrowers can be expected to prefer to borrow over the long term and to offer low returns, though sharing the same desire for liquidity.

The whole process of matching the needs of lenders and borrowers is known as 'financial intermediation' and the institutions which play a part in this process are known as 'financial intermediaries'. Financial markets also play a key role in this system by allowing borrowers to issue IOUs such as bills or bonds which are acceptable to lenders and which can be traded on the secondary markets (i.e. markets dealing in securities which already exist).

Today, this whole financial system is undergoing rapid development and financial markets are becoming ever more complex, offering new types of financial instruments which reduce transactions costs, are more flexible and better targeted, whilst the traditional roles of the financial institutions are becoming increasingly blurred.

The role of the financial system

The basic rationale of a financial system is to bring together those who have accumulated an excess of money and who wish to save with those who have a requirement to borrow in order to finance investment. This process arguably helps to better utilise society's scarce resources, increase productive efficiency and ultimately raise the standard of living. Santomero and Babbel (1997) have usefully summarized this role of the financial system.

After considering the role of the financial system, the different types of financial asset are reviewed. The chapter then considers in some detail the different types of financial intermediary and the various financial markets on which they operate. The role of the Bank of England and other means of regulation are reviewed, as are issues involving the European Single Financial Market and increases in the competitive pressures facing the UK banking system.

Without a developed financial system, institutions, firms, and households would be forced to operate as self-contained economies. As a result, they could not save without deploying their resources somewhere, and they could not invest without saving from their own current output. A financial system allows trade between individuals to accomplish both these ends. It allows savers to defer consumption and obtain a return for waiting. Likewise, it permits investors to deploy resources in excess of those that they have available from their own wealth in order to gain the productivity that such investment yields. The economy also gains from the financial system, as both households and firms advance the economy, total output, and economic growth.

Figure 21.1 provides an overview of the structure of the financial system in the UK. Essentially we have three kinds of operator in the UK financial system.

Fig. 21.1. The financial system.

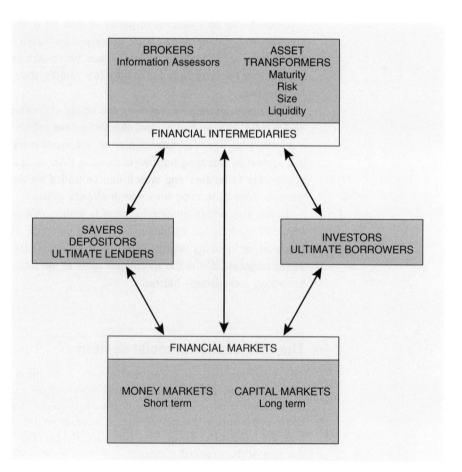

1. *Lenders and borrowers* – persons, companies, government.
2. *Financial institutions* – which act as intermediaries between lenders and borrowers, and manage their own asset portfolios. Financial intermediaries take one of two forms: brokers (bringing together lenders and borrowers by evaluating market information) and asset transformers (converting liabilities such as deposits into assets of varying maturity, risk, size, liquidity and yield).
3. *Financial markets* – where money is lent and borrowed, and paper assets are bought and sold. These include the short-term money markets and the long-term capital markets.

Financial assets

Before considering the operations of the financial institutions and financial markets in more detail, it may be useful to outline the various *financial assets* in which they deal.

Financial assets are issued by borrowers and traded on the financial markets by financial institutions who ultimately hold many of these assets in their portfolios. These assets are of two basic kinds: (a) bills and bonds, and (b) equities (shares).

Types of financial asset

Bills   Bills are short-term assets (e.g. three months) issued by the Treasury and companies when seeking to borrow money. The original purchaser (i.e. whoever has lent the money) will buy the bill at below its face (redemption) value and earn a return by holding it to maturity when its redemption value is paid in full. The yield to the purchaser then depends on the difference between the price paid for the bill and its redemption value when it matures. So, for example, a three-month bill of £100 face value bought for £98 and held to maturity, yields £2 on an investment of £98 over three months, a yield of just over 8% per annum. Alternatively the original purchaser can sell the bill in a secondary market for bills (e.g. the discount market) before the full term is up, in this case at a price somewhere between £98 and £100.

Bonds   Bonds are interest-bearing assets (or securities) issued by central and local governments, companies, banks and other institutions. The borrower undertakes to redeem the bond at 'par value' (£100) on a certain date, and to pay the bondholder an annual fixed sum (coupon rate) in interest each year. Bonds may be bought either as a new issue or second-hand on the secondary markets. The investor buying from the *secondary market* may have bought the bond at a price *below* par value, so that the annual fixed interest payment is still more attractive taking into account the lower price originally paid for the bond. For instance, if 5% government bonds (gilts) of par value £100 are bought on the secondary market at £50, the buyer receives £5 a year from the government. This will actually represent a yield higher than 5%, here 10% on an investment of £50. In addition there will be a further gain of £50 when the bond is redeemed by the government for £100 at the maturity date. As bonds normally bear a fixed rate of interest, there will usually be an *inverse* relationship between the market price of an existing bond and movements in current interest rates. In our example, a *doubling* of the current interest rate from 10% to 20% would mean that the 5% Treasury bond would *halve* in value to £25 (ignoring any later capital gain on maturity), since a £5 annual fixed interest payment only corresponds to a 20% return on an investment of £25.

This would certainly be the market price for an existing Treasury bond with no future redemption date (consols) and therefore no future capital gain. If the price of such bonds did *not* fall from £50 to £25 when interest rates doubled, then investors would simply move their funds to where they could earn a 20% return. Higher interest rates therefore reduce the market price or value of existing bonds, and lower interest rates increase the market price or value of existing bonds. This factor is key to the Keynesian 'speculative' demand for money.

Equities Equities (or shares) are non-redeemable assets issued by companies, and investors are actually buying part-ownership (a share) of a company. Investors in ordinary shares receive dividends if companies are able to pay them, but their major advantage as an asset lies in the possibility of capital appreciation if strong profits growth is anticipated. In the case of *preference shares* the company pays a fixed annual sum to the shareholder, and there is also the possibility of capital appreciation when the share is sold. *Ordinary shareholders* bear the largest risks since if the company goes out of business, the 'preferred' shareholders are entitled to a share of the money raised by selling assets first (although only after the Inland Revenue, Customs and Excise and secured bank borrowers are paid). However, in good times, the ordinary shareholder will earn the greatest returns as dividend payments may be much greater than the fixed return received by preference shareholders. As always in the financial markets, those who bear most risk have higher potential for returns.

Yields on financial assets If financial assets were *perfect substitutes* for one another, the yields on each would be identical. Any higher yield on one type of asset would cause financial institutions to adjust their 'portfolios' in favour of that asset. The higher demand would raise the market price of the asset and thereby reduce the yield. Any variation in yields therefore represents a lack of perfect substitutability between such assets. That there is such variation in yield between different types of asset is clear from any cursory glance at the financial press.

Assets are *imperfect substitutes* because they possess different characteristics with respect to liquidity, marketability and profitability. A *liquid* asset is one which can be transformed into cash quickly and without loss of value. The more distant the maturity date, the less liquid is the asset likely to be. *Marketability* varies between assets; some assets are easily realizable, but some – such as perhaps the shares of small companies – may not find ready buyers. *Profitability*, too, varies between the certain but perhaps unexciting rate of return paid by fixed-interest government securities, to the more uncertain possibility of large gains to be made on equities. Portfolio choice will depend on how individual investors evaluate the alternatives open to them, as well as on their expectations of future interest rate movements. Yields in general will tend to be higher for longer-term investments, because lenders require to be compensated for giving up their money for long periods of time, and uncertainty (risk) also increases with time. However, if investors expect interest rates to fall in the future they will wish to buy long-dated bonds today, thereby locking themselves into today's higher rates. This will have the effect of driving up the market price of long bonds, making their yield lower than normal, and perhaps even lower than short-term yields.

The role of financial intermediaries

Financial intermediaries come between these wishing to save (lend) and those wishing to invest (borrow). They provide a service that yields them a profit, via the *difference* which exists between the (lower) interest they pay to those who lend and the (higher) interest they receive from those who borrow. That they can earn such profits reflects the fact that they are offering a useful service to both lenders and borrowers, which can be disaggregated into at least four separate functions.

- Brokerage
- Maturity transformation
- Risk transformation
- Collection and parcelling

Brokerage   The brokerage function is rather different from the other three, which might all be regarded as including elements of 'asset transformation'. A broker is an intermediary who brings together lenders and borrowers who have complementary needs and does this by assessing and evaluating information. The *lender* may have neither the time nor the ability to undertake costly search activities in order to assess whether a potential borrower is trustworthy, is likely to use the funds for a project that is credible and profitable, and is able to pay the promised interest on the due date. By depositing funds with a financial intermediary the household avoids such information gathering, monitoring and evaluation costs, which are now undertaken by the specialised financial intermediary. The *borrower* needs to know that a promised loan will be received at the time and under the conditions specified in any agreement.

By bringing lenders and borrowers together in these ways, the various information and transactions costs are reduced, so that this brokerage function can command a 'fee'. The size of that fee will, of course, be greater the more difficult and expensive it is for the financial intermediary to develop procedures for evaluating and monitoring borrowers in order to minimise 'default risks'.

The next three functions involve elements of *asset transformation*, in which the liabilities (deposits) are transformed by the financial intermediaries into various types of asset with differing characteristics in terms of maturity, liquidity and risk.

Maturity transformation   Here the financial intermediaries bridge the gap between the desire of lenders to be able to get their money back quickly if needed, and the desire of borrowers to borrow for a long period. In fulfilling this function the financial intermediaries hold liabilities (e.g. deposits) that have a shorter term to maturity than their assets (e.g. loans), i.e. they borrow short and lend long. For example, a building society will typically hold around 70% of its liabilities in the form of deposits repayable 'on demand', i.e. which can be withdrawn at any time without penalty. In contrast, around 75% of its assets are only repayable after five years or more.

Financial intermediaries are able to perform this maturity transformation function in part because of the 'law of large numbers', which implies that while some depositors will be withdrawing funds others will be making new deposits. This means that, overall, withdrawals minus new deposits is likely to be small in relation to the value of total deposits (liabilities). As a result the 'funding risk', namely that depositors might wish to withdraw more funds than the banks have available in liquid form, is greatly reduced. This enables the financial intermediaries to hold a sizeable proportion of less liquid assets (e.g. long-term loans) in their portfolio.

Risk transformation   This involves the financial intermediaries in shifting the burden of risk from the lender to themselves. Their ability to do so depends largely on *economies of scale* in risk management. The large amounts of deposits (liabilities) the financial intermediaries collect allow them to diversify their assets across a wide variety of types and sectors. 'Pooling' risk and reward in this way means that no individual is exposed to a situation in which the default of one or more borrowers is likely to have a significant effect.

Collection and parcelling   Financial intermediaries also transform the nature of their assets through the *collection* of a large number of small amounts of funds from depositors and their *parcelling* into larger amounts required by borrowers. Often the financial intermediaries have relied on obtaining many small deposits from conveniently located branches of their operations. This process is known as 'size intermediation' and benefits borrowers because they obtain one large loan from one source, thus reducing transaction costs. Of course this loan is an asset to the financial intermediary and a liability to the borrower.

The common characteristics of all financial intermediaries are therefore as follows. First, they take money from those who seek to save, whether it be in exchange for a deposit or in exchange for an asset. Second, they lend the money provided by those savers to borrowers, who may issue a paper asset in return. Third, in exchange for such lending they acquire a portfolio of paper assets (claims on borrowers) which will pay an income to the intermediary, and which it may 'manage' by buying and selling the assets on financial markets in order to yield further profits for itself.

UK financial intermediaries

The UK financial system incorporates different types of financial intermediary, offering lenders and borrowers a variety of instruments which have different maturities, liquidities and risk profiles. A popular method of classification is to distinguish between the bank and non-bank financial intermediaries.

- *Bank sector*. All the UK financial institutions that have been issued with a *banking licence*, including the high street commercial banks, the corporate wholesale banks and the foreign banks, are regarded as being part of the bank sector. Currently there are 468 authorised banking institutions operating in the UK, a fall of almost 100 on the 1988 figure of 567.
- *Non-bank sector*. The other financial intermediaries, including the building societies, insurance companies, pension funds, unit trust and investment trust companies, are classified as part of the non-bank sector. A further disaggregation of the non-bank sector brings together those institutions which are *deposit-taking institutions*, such as the building societies, and those which are *investing institutions*, namely all the non-bank sector except the building societies.

However, even this simple classification of bank and non-bank sector is becoming more difficult to sustain with the growth of competition between these sectors (*inter-sector competition*) and between the institutions within these sectors (*intra-sector competition*), so that the distinction between banking and non-banking institutions has become increasingly blurred. Nevertheless it may be helpful to consider the UK financial intermediaries under the following three headings: banking financial intermediaries; non-bank financial intermediaries; Bank of England.

The UK banking financial intermediaries

The UK bank sector includes a range of financial intermediaries.

The retail banks   These include banks which either participate in the UK clearing system or have extensive branch networks. The retail banks are sometimes known as the MBBGs (Major British Banking Groups) and include Lloyds, NatWest, Midland, Barclays, Abbey National, The Standard Chartered, The Royal Bank of Scotland, The Bank of Scotland and, more recently, the Halifax, the Alliance and Leicester and the Woolwich.

Retail banks, through their extensive branch networks, have historically been primarily engaged in gathering deposits and creating loans, usually at high margins given that they could obtain deposits at low interest rates and could offer loans to individuals and firms at high interest rates. Activities in this sector were highly regulated until the early 1970s and were often described as being 'supply led', since most arrangements appeared to be in the interests of the providers rather than the customers.

Today, the retail banks are highly competitive and more responsive to the needs of their customers. The retail banks offer a wide array of services to personal customers, including savings accounts, unsecured and secured loans, mortgages, overdrafts, automated cash machines, home banking, foreign currency transactions and general financial advice. They also offer a range of services to corporate customers, including leasing and hire purchase, export and import facilities, payroll services, and international financial transfers.

Total assets in the banking sector have increased by over 150% in the past decade, from around £1,000 billion in 1988 to over £2,500 billion in 1998, a figure boosted by the recent trend of mutually owned building societies converting to banks (see p. 474).

The wholesale banks   These include around 500 banks which typically engage only in large-scale lending and borrowing transactions, namely transactions in excess of £50,000.

The wholesale banks include the following.

- *merchant banks*, of which there are about forty including the Accepting Houses;
- *other British banks*, a general category covering banks with UK majority ownership;
- *overseas banks*, which include American banks, Japanese banks and a variety of other overseas banks and consortium banks.

The wholesale banks actually include a large number of small providers. This, together with the fact that the majority of transactions are completed with knowledgeable corporate clients, usually results in margins being low. Nevertheless individual transactions are 'wholesale', that is of a high value (greater than £50,000) so that sizeable absolute levels of profit can still be made. Wholesale banking mainly takes place in foreign currencies, which reflects the substantial presence of Japanese and American banks in this sector. However, the sector also includes the British merchant banks, whose major business includes the acceptance of bills, underwriting, consultancy, fund management and trading in the financial markets.

Historically, retail banks could be distinguished from wholesale banks by the nature of their business, in that they dealt in a high volume of small deposits, operated an extensive branch network, were actively involved in the cheque clearing system and relied heavily on the personal sector for their deposits (liabilities). However, these distinctions are becoming increasingly blurred due to the participation of all banks and other financial intermediaries in corporate business and to the growth of the inter-bank market.

Much of this convergence between the retail and wholesale banking sectors has been due to retail banks entering the wholesale arena, largely because of diminishing margins in the retail sector. We consider the response of the retail banks to a variety of competitive pressures later in this chapter (p. 491). Wholesale banking, however, has remained relatively unchanged in that the vast majority of transactions remain with the corporate sector and are undertaken in foreign currencies.

UK non-bank financial intermediaries

The institutions in this sector fulfil a number of specialist functions, such as providing mortgage finance, insurance and pension cover. They typically specialise in matching the needs of borrowers for long-term finance with the needs of lenders for paper assets denominated in small units which are readily saleable. The UK non-bank financial intermediaries include the building societies, insurance companies, pension funds, unit trusts and investment trusts.

The building societies   These are mutually owned financial institutions which have traditionally offered loans in the form of mortgages to facilitate house purchase. Mutuality means that they are owned by their 'members', namely those who have purchased shares in the form of deposits, and those who have borrowed from them. Until the early 1980s, building societies were the only institutions offering mortgages and competition was restricted by various agreements and regulations between the various building societies.

Competition in this sector has, however, intensified since the early 1980s when deregulation of the retail banking sector allowed banks to offer mortgage finance and thereby to threaten the position of the building societies. This led to demands for deregulation to be extended to the building society sector in order to allow the building societies to respond by competing with banks in financial and other markets, where previously they had been restricted. The Building Societies Act of 1986, and subsequent Orders in Council of 1988, permitted building societies to offer a whole range of new banking, investment and property-related housing services, in addition to their traditional savings and home loan business.

Building societies can now lend amounts of up to £15,000 on an unsecured basis, lend money on second mortgages, buy life assurance companies, and run unit trust companies and stockbroking firms. They can also offer services such as tax advice, financial planning and executorship. Further, they need no longer rely on taking

Table 21.1 Bank and
building society shares of
gross lending for
mortgages and consumer
credit (£m).

	1994	1995	1996	1997	1998*
Gross mortgage lending					
Building societies	34,847	33,714	39,838	27,797	15,673*
Banks	20,248	21,238	28,727	44,601	45,636*
Gross lending for consumer credit					
Building societies	2,536	2,895	2,880	1,802	1,192*
Banks	57,347	66,002	76,884	87,774	75,991*

* 1998 January to September only.
Source: Adapted from *Bank of England Quarterly Bulletin* (1998).

deposits from savers to finance their lending since up to 50% of their deposits
(liabilities) can now be in the form of borrowings on the wholesale money markets. In
fact by September 1998, total wholesale liabilities in the building society sector were
over £26 billion.

Nevertheless building societies have remained predominantly mortgage finance
providers. Table 21.1 shows that the building society sector provided around
fourteen times more mortgage lending by value in 1998 than consumer credit
lending. In fact the table shows that the building societies have made little impact on
the consumer credit market, supplying less than 2% of gross lending for consumer
credit in 1998. Rather more significantly, the share of the building societies in gross
mortgage lending has declined substantially over the period, being only one-third in
value of gross mortgage lending by banks in 1998.

An important reason for bank domination of the consumer credit market is the
restriction that at least 75% of the building societies' commercial assets must be in the
form of loans secured by a mortgage on residential property, which only leaves 25%
of their assets available to finance other activities.

Table 21.2 shows that building societies are also losing their share of UK private
sector deposits. In 1985, some 45.1% of UK private sector deposits were held in
building society accounts, and 49.5% in UK banks. However, by 1997 the building
societies' share had dropped to 13.7%, whilst the share of the banks had risen to
84.4%. In fact such a trend had been long established, for example the building
societies witnessed a fall in their share of UK private sector deposits of nearly 5%
between 1985 and 1988. However, the trend accelerated as the larger building
societies themselves began to convert to bank plcs (see Table 21.3).

Table 21.2 UK private
sector deposits (£m) with
banks and building
societies 1985–97.

	1985	1992	1994	1995	1996	1997
UK banks private sector deposits	114,905	328,163	354,560	411,800	468,030	610,520
% of total	49.5	61.5	61.3	64.3	67.3	84.4
Building societies	104,816	190,451	210,420	211,206	212,820	99,302
% of total	45.1	35.7	36.4	33.0	30.6	13.7
Other UK private sector deposits	12,486	163,348	13,757	1,727	14,087	13,592
% of total	5.4	2.7	2.5	2.8	2.1	1.9
Total	232,207	534,982	578,737	640,733	694,947	723,414

Source: Adapted from British Bankers' Association Statistical Unit (1998).

Table 21.3 Building society conversions.*

Building society	Date of conversion	Total assets (£m)	Market capitalisation (£m)
Abbey National	July 1989	162,734	16,430
Alliance & Leicester	April 1997	26,777	5,069
Halifax	June 1997	134,011	19,467
Woolwich	July 1997	31,814	5,605
Northern Rock	October 1997	17,352	2,331
Birmingham Midshires (merged into Halifax)	January 1999	n/a	n/a
Bristol & West (merged into Bank of Ireland)	July 1997	n/a	n/a
Cheltenham & Gloucester (merged into Lloyds Bank)	August 1995	n/a	n/a
National & Provincial (merged into Abbey National)	August 1996	n/a	n/a

*Total assets mid-1998, market capitalization 2.11.98.
Sources: Building Society Association Yearly Handbook, Annual Reports and *Financial Times* (various).

Demutualization As we have already noted, the building societies have been losing market share to the banks in the deposit, consumer credit and mortgage markets. Indeed in 1997 the banking sector for the first time had a greater share of gross mortgage lending than the building societies, a trend which is set to continue. However, this comparison is not entirely fair, as it does not represent a like-for-like comparison over time. In fact a major reason for these losses of market share involve the demutualization and conversion of the larger building societies into banks, which means that their business is now counted as part of the banking sector. Table 21.3 shows those building societies which have converted into banks, the date of conversion, the total assets and the market capitalization involved. A number of reasons have been suggested for this trend towards demutualization.

- Banks are in a better position than building societies to compete in financial services and mortgage markets because they can issue shares. This will provide the funding to permit faster growth and enable speedier diversification into new areas.
- Building societies which convert to banks cannot be taken over for five years, giving them time to establish themselves and compete with the larger banks.
- Building societies which convert can now compete under the same regulatory environment as banks, which means that they no longer have restrictions on access to the wholesale markets and on the amount of unsecured lending. This provides them with improved access to corporate clients and to the consumer credit market.
- Diversification into new and risky areas of business should, it is argued, be undertaken by using newly issued capital raised by newly constituted institutions rather than by using historical capital derived from relatively safe savings and mortgage business.

Such arguments were present in the conversion documents of both the Alliance & Leicester and Halifax Building Societies. The Alliance & Leicester document (1996) stated that the society intends to expand its commercial lending activities, extend its use of wholesale money markets, and increase its provision of 'personal financial services, such as unsecured lending, telephone banking, life assurance and unit trust products'. This will allow it to reduce its 'dependency on the mature residential mortgage market ... and to build new sources of revenue from cross-selling'.

Expansion and consolidation was also a central theme in the Halifax Building Society's transfer documentation (1996). Their strategy statement read:

> Halifax plc are seeking significant earnings growth in the areas of long term savings and protection products and personal lines insurance ... Halifax must continue to focus on its key competitive advantages of providing innovative and competitive products together with a high level of customer service.

Those who doubt the benefits of conversion have, however, expressed their concern. First, the costs of paying large dividends to shareholders will increase the interest rate to borrowers and decrease the rate for deposit holders (lenders). Second, capital markets have a tendency to be short term in their evaluation of strategy and performance, which may hinder long-term growth. Third, there is little evidence that banks are more accountable to their owners than are building societies. Fourth, takeover threats by other banks may still exist. At least one building society waived its right not to be taken over after conversion and in any case the protection from takeover for five years is removed if another building society initiates the takeover, as when Birmingham Midshires was acquired by the Halifax in 1999. Fifth, there are increased costs resulting from conversion, including the cost of compliance with a new regulatory code and the cost of retraining staff.

However, the comparison of building societies with banks and the debate as to the respective advantages and disadvantages of conversion have arguably become redundant issues, having been superseded by events. Those building societies who wish to remain specialist mortgage providers are likely to stay in the building societies sector and by remaining as mutual institutions, may acquire a competitive edge in offering mortgages at lower interest rates. Much of the rationalization of this sector may already have occurred, there having been 481 building societies in 1970 but only 71 today.

On the other hand, most former building societies that have wished to expand their range of products and services having found regulations in the sector somewhat restrictive have already chosen to convert. Of the top ten building societies in December 1996, only four exist today, namely Nationwide, Bradford and Bingley, Britannia, and Yorkshire.

Insurance companies and pension funds About half of all personal savings are channelled into these institutions via regular and single-premium life assurance and pension payments. These savings from the personal sector are used to acquire a portfolio of assets. The institutions then manage these assets with the objective that they yield a sufficient return to pay the eventual insurance and pension claims as well as providing a working rate of return for the financial institutions themselves. The insurance companies and pension funds are major investors in the financial markets and exert considerable influence in these markets. They hold large amounts of long-term debt and help absorb ('make markets in') large volumes and values of new issues of various equities, bills and bonds. For example in 1998 they held around £660 billion of quoted UK company shares and around £220 billion of government bills and bonds, having total financial assets of almost £1,500 billion.

Although these insurance companies and pension funds compete strongly against each other in the personal savings market, their portfolio choices differ because the structures of their liabilities differ. For example the life assurance companies hold a larger proportion of assets as fixed interest securities, because many of their liabilities are expressed in nominal terms (e.g. money value of payments in the future on policies is known). Pension funds, however, hold a larger proportion of assets in the form of equities, which historically have yielded higher real rates of return, because many of their liabilities are expressed in real terms (e.g. pensions paid in the future are often index linked).

Unit and investment trusts Both unit and investment trusts offer lenders a chance to buy into a diversified portfolio of assets and thereby reduce risk while at the same time receiving attractive returns. These institutions can achieve this by pooling the funds received from a large number of small investors and then implementing various portfolio management techniques not available to such small investors.

There are over 1,400 *unit trusts,* provided by individual companies, banks and insurance companies. A lender looking to buy into a unit trust purchases the number of units they can afford at the current value and then pays a further 5% of the purchase price for the management of the fund. The price of each unit is given by the net value of the trusts assets divided by the number of units outstanding. The size of the unit trust fund varies with the amount of units currently in issue, which allows the fund to expand and contract depending on demand, thus unit trusts are termed 'open ended'.

There are over 300 *investment trusts* and they undertake a similar role, allowing individuals to benefit from a pooled investment fund. However, investment trusts are plcs and raise funds for investment by issuing equity and debt and by using retained profits. Unlike unit trusts they can also borrow money. If individuals or firms are to buy into an investment trust, they must purchase their shares, which are limited in supply, thus investment trusts are termed 'closed ended'.

Table 21.4 shows total investments by both unit and investment trusts. Two factors are worth noting. First, unit trusts hold over twice the value of assets held by the investment trusts. Second, both institutions invest heavily in foreign company shares, with around 40% of all investments of this type.

Table 21.4 **Total investments of unit and investment trusts 1996 (£m).**

Investment	Holdings
Unit trusts	
British Government Securities	2,716
UK company securities	72,765
Overseas company securities	50,271
Other	89
Total	125,841
Investment trusts	
British Government Securities	1,439
UK company securities	25,878
Overseas company securities	21,326
Other	1,408
Total	50,051

Source: ONS (1998) *Financial Statistics*, October.

An important issue is the extent to which insurance, pension fund, investment and unit trust companies are involved in *equity finance*. These institutions are responsible for holding around 50% of UK equity which means that share prices will be significantly affected by the portfolio preferences of these institutions. That preference will be influenced by overall 'environmental' factors, such as the inflation rate, the exchange rate and the state of business expectations, as well as by the particular needs of the institutions themselves. A concern is that such institutions may tend to be affected in the same way by the same set of factors, so that share prices may be more volatile than would otherwise be the case. This could have significant repercussions on the individual companies concerned because share prices may then fluctuate in ways which do *not* reflect their true valuation in terms of yield. It follows from this that the ability of companies to raise funds on the Stock Exchange may be affected by the activities of these institutions, and possibly in ways unconnected to their underlying profit potential.

The Bank of England   The Bank of England is at the head of the UK financial system, is owned by the government, having been nationalized in 1946, and has a monopoly on the note issue in England and Wales. Traditionally, the functions of the Bank of England can be divided into those which it performs as banker to the government and those which it performs as banker to the banks.

As *banker to the government* it must:

(a) implement monetary policy by manipulating interest rates, using direct controls or restricting bank credit as necessary;
(b) regulate the issue of legal tender;
(c) manage both the issue and redemption of government stock;
(d) keep the government's accounts;
(e) manage the Exchange Equalization Account and, when necessary, use official reserves to intervene in the foreign exchange market.

As *banker to the banks* it must:

(a) supervise the cheque clearing system;
(b) act as 'lender of last resort' to the banking system by supporting the discount market;
(c) exercise prudential supervision over the banking system as a whole.

The Bank also acts as banker to overseas central banks, as well as to international organizations and to a small number of other institutions, companies and private individuals.

In operational day-to-day terms the Bank of England has an important influence on three major markets: the sterling money market, the foreign exchange market, and the gilt-edged market.

1. The Bank is a major player in the *sterling money market* (see p. 481), buying and selling Treasury bills on a daily basis. The object is twofold; firstly the Bank buys or sells bills in order to ease cash shortages or to withdraw cash surpluses, which arise as a result of daily transactions between the government and the public. Such transactions by the Bank affect commercial bank clearing balances, alter the liquidity of these banks and hence their willingness to lend (e.g. to the discount

houses). Second, the Bank trades in bills with the government's interest rate policy specifically in mind. The buying and selling of bills by the Bank affects yields and therefore influences interest rates throughout the market (see p. 487). The Bank, in its daily dealings, attempts to reconcile these two separate objectives.

2. The Bank has a major role in the *foreign exchange market* as it is responsible for carrying out government policy with regard to the exchange rate. A strong pound has been seen by successive governments as essential if inflation is to be kept low. The combination in recent years of a floating pound and a weak balance of payments on current account has made it necessary to attract short-term funds on capital account by maintaining high interest rates. The Bank also uses the Exchange Equalization Account to intervene in the foreign exchange market by buying up surplus sterling should it need to support the external value of the pound.

3. The Bank is also influential in the *gilt-edged market* as it administers the issue of new bonds when the government wishes to borrow money. Various methods are used, depending on market circumstances. The 'tap' method is where bonds (gilts) are issued gradually in order not to flood the market and depress the price; the 'tender' method is where institutions are invited to tender for a given issue; and the 'auction' method is where bonds are sold to the highest bidders among the twenty or so gilt-edged market makers (GEMMAs). The Bank also manages the redemption of existing bonds in such a way as to smooth the demands on the government's financial resources. For instance it buys up bonds which are nearing their redemption date, so as not to have to make large repayments over a short period of time.

The Bank faces a continual problem in that its actions in each of these markets have repercussions for the functioning of the other markets. For instance, intervention to purchase sterling in the foreign exchange market in order to support the sterling exchange rate is often ineffective because of the size of speculative outflows of short-term capital from the sterling money and gilt-edged markets. As a result interest rates may need to be raised in order to deter these short-term capital outflows. This often proves difficult, however, because of the way in which daily transactions between the government and the public affect the balances of the clearing banks with the Bank of England. For example, if the banks are short of liquidity the Bank of England may be purchasing bills on the Open Market in order to help replenish their cash balances. However, purchasing existing bills by the Bank of England will raise their market price and lower their yield, i.e. lower interest rates. This may then conflict with the need to keep interest rates high to prevent short-term capital outflows from depressing the sterling exchange rate.

Bank of England supervision and regulation   Overall supervision of any banking system is essential to protect the interests of depositors, and although there was some degree of depositor protection in the 1960s it was not until the secondary banking crisis of the 1970s that formal supervisory structures were developed and embodied in the Banking Acts of 1979 and 1987.

The Board of Banking Supervision within the Bank concerns itself with three issues.

1. *Capital adequacy.* To what extent do banks have sufficient reserves of capital to cover the possibility of default by borrowers? This issue has become particularly important in recent years as the volume of Third World debt has grown to unmanageable

proportions (see Ch. 30). The 1989 Solvency Ratio Directive established an EU-wide rule that a bank's capital reserves must be at least 8% of its risk-adjusted assets and off-balance-sheet transactions. Off-balance-sheet transactions include such things as an advance commitment to lend (rather than an actual loan) which may or may not ultimately lead to a future balance sheet entry.

2. *Liquidity.* There is currently no formal requirement as to adequate liquidity holdings by banks. However, the Bank of England may require all banks under the Banking Act of 1987 to keep a ratio of 'primary liquid assets' to some definition of deposit liabilities. Such ratios may differ as between different types of banks, and deposits will be ranked according to their maturity. The shorter is the maturity structure of deposits, the higher will be the ratio of liquid assets required.

3. *Foreign currency exposure.* This issue relates particularly to banks which take deposits and lend in different currencies. Supervisors are concerned that banks should balance their assets and liabilities in each currency in such a way that their 'exposure' (to risk of loss on the foreign exchange market) should not exceed 10% of their capital base.

Recent regulatory changes In May 1997, the Chancellor of the Exchequer, Gordon Brown, proposed a number of institutional and operational changes to the Bank of England. First, the Bank of England was given operational independence in setting interest rates which would now be the responsibility of a newly created Monetary Policy Committee (MPC) working within the Bank. Second, the regulation of the banking sector was taken away from the Bank and given to a newly established 'super' regulator called the Financial Services Authority (FSA). Third, although the government retained responsibility for determining the exchange rate regime, the Bank could now intervene at its discretion in support of the objectives of the MPC, and fourth, the management of the national debt was transferred from the Bank to the Treasury. These changes were set out in The Bank of England Act which came into force on 1 June 1998. The most important of these changes involved the creation of the MPC and the FSA.

The Monetary Policy Committee (MPC) The Bank of England Act established that the responsibility for monetary policy and therefore for setting short-term interest rates was to reside with the MPC, a committee within the Bank of England. The MPC would be free from government intervention in all but extreme economic circumstances. The aim of short-term interest rate setting would be to restrict the growth of inflation to within a target range set by the government and announced in the annual Budget Statement. The present target has been set at 2.5% for annual retail price inflation, excluding mortgage interest payments (RPIX). Significantly, if inflation is more than 1% either side of this figure then the MPC is required to write an open letter of explanation to the Chancellor.

The MPC consists of the Governor of the Bank, two Deputy Governors, two members appointed by the Bank in consultation with the Chancellor and four 'experts' appointed by the Chancellor. The MPC meets monthly, publishes its decisions within days of concluding any meeting and publishes minutes of the meeting within six weeks.

There has been much discussion as to the merits of these recent changes. In essence, they are an attempt by the Chancellor of the Exchequer to take the 'politics' out of setting interest rate policy. Hall (1997) makes the following points.

> As a device for enhancing the credibility of monetary policy the current regime, if allowed to work with optimal efficiency, is vastly superior to its predecessors, which had confirmed the worst fears of outside observers by allowing the Chancellor to attempt to extract the maximum political advantage from the interest rate setting process ... Moreover, if one believes in a high and positive correlation between the degree of independence enjoyed by a Central Bank and that country's success in fighting inflation, then the recent changes can only but serve to reinforce one's optimism about the UK's future inflation prospects.

It has been argued that as a result of such independence, the financial markets will gain additional confidence in the UK's ability to control future inflation. Some have pointed to the fact that long-term interest rates for UK government borrowing have reached a thirty-year low since the Bank's independence was announced, as evidence of such confidence. Nevertheless, concerns over the new policy include fears that the Bank may set interest rates which are higher than necessary to control inflation, thereby stifling investment and raising the sterling exchange rate to levels which damage trading sectors of the economy, such as manufacturing. Others have argued that the MPC should have been given a target for economic growth as well as a target for inflation, to prevent an overemphasis on deflationary policies.

The Financial Services Authority (FSA)   The Chancellor has also reformed the regulatory structure of the financial system. Before this change, regulation and supervision of the *banking sector* was the responsibility of the Bank of England. However, regulation and supervision of the *non-bank sector* has historically been the responsibility of numerous different bodies, such as the Building Societies Commission and the Securities and Investment Board which itself headed three other self-regulating bodies. The Chancellor of the Exchequer highlighted problems with the then regulatory structure in a statement on 20 May 1997.

> It has long been apparent that the regulatory structure introduced by the Financial Services Act 1986 is not delivering the standard of supervision and investor protection that the industry and the public have a right to expect. The current two tier system splits responsibilities ... This division is inefficient, confusing for investors and lacks accountability and a clear allocation of responsibilities. It is clear that the distinctions between different types of financial institutions – banks, securities firms and insurance companies – are becoming increasingly blurred ... [therefore] there is a strong case in principle for bringing the regulation of banking, securities and insurance together under one roof.

The Bank of England Act of 1998 transferred the regulatory functions of the Bank to a new regulatory authority called the Financial Services Authority (FSA), which was now to be responsible for regulating all financial institutions, whether bank or non-bank.

The Bank of England is to retain responsibility for ensuring overall stability in the financial system, with the government establishing a structure whereby the Treasury, the Bank of England and the FSA work together to achieve such stability. In a Memorandum of Understanding published in October 1997 the Chancellor set out the various roles of the Treasury, the Bank, and the FSA, making it clear that these

Fig. 21.2. The regulatory
structure in the UK.

organisations should exchange information and consult regularly. A standing committee was established to provide the means for the three bodies to discuss any foreseeable problems.

The new regulatory structure was completed by the establishment of a new Financial Stability Committee whose functions were to oversee the stability of the system and detect any risk of system-wide failure. This Committee had the responsibility of liaison with the Standing Committee created by the Memorandum of Understanding. Figure 21.2 provides an overview of the new regulatory structure.

The UK financial markets

The financial markets within the UK perform a variety of functions which make them attractive to both borrowers and lenders. Such functions include providing a place or means by which to trade financial assets and a system by which to 'price' such assets. The major UK financial markets are located in London, which is one of three dominant financial centres, together with New York and Tokyo. One reason for London's domination is the large number of overseas banks transacting in foreign currencies on the UK financial markets.

As with the financial intermediaries there are a number of ways in which the financial markets might be classified. One of the most usual is to separate the UK financial markets into the sterling wholesale money markets and the capital markets.

The sterling wholesale money markets

Transactions undertaken in the UK 'money market' involve the borrowing and lending of short-term wholesale funds by financial institutions. 'Short term' means for periods varying from one day to one year, and 'wholesale funds' means amounts in excess of £50,000. Money market activity in London has developed rapidly over the last thirty years, partly due to the growth of the financial sector in general, but also because of the increasing demand for sophisticated financial services by clients both in the UK and abroad.

In the UK, the money markets were traditionally split into the *primary markets* issuing new securities and the *secondary (or parallel) markets* dealing in old securities. This distinction is no longer relevant today and it is best to think of the wholesale money market as one market issuing and trading in short-term financial debt. The sterling wholesale money market can, however, be broken down into a number of separate markets, such as the sterling inter-bank market, the certificate of deposit market, the commercial paper market, the Eurocurrency market and the discount market.

The sterling inter-bank market This market is now the largest and most significant of the wholesale money markets. The inter-bank market allows financial institutions to borrow and lend wholesale funds amongst themselves, dealing through money brokers, for periods ranging from overnight to five years. By using such borrowings, banks have been able to make (profitable) lending decisions which are to some extent independent of the amount of personal deposits that they have been able to attract, because they could now obtain any extra funding they might require on the inter-bank market. The amounts involved are large, ranging from £500,000 upwards, with transactions of £10–12 million not untypical. Banks today borrow on the inter-bank market to finance lending, to balance out fluctuations in their books, to speculate on future movements in interest rates, etc. The London Inter-Bank Offer Rate (LIBOR) in effect represents the marginal or opportunity cost of funds lent to the banks and is the major influence on their base rates.

The sterling certificate of deposit market Certificates of deposits (CDs) are paper assets issued by banks, building societies and finance houses to depositors who are willing to leave their money on deposit for a *specified* period of time. They are issued for periods ranging from three months to five years, but in the main tend to be towards the shorter end of this spectrum and are issued at a rate of interest which can either be fixed or floating. This system enables banks to engage in longer-term (and more profitable) lending because they can be certain of having deposits for specified periods of time. In addition, CDs are attractive to portfolio holders because the yield is competitive and the CD can be sold on the market at any time should the holder require liquidity. In 1998, banks held £131.8 billion in CDs and other short-term instruments as liabilities on their balance sheet.

The sterling commercial paper market. Since May 1986 companies have been permitted to issue short-term (7–364 days) unsecured promissory notes, which can then be traded at a discount. This provides a way of raising cheap short-term funds for companies who require finance for general business purposes. The 1989 Budget extended the right to issue these forms of sterling commercial paper to governments, overseas companies and certain overseas authorities, as well as to banks, building societies and insurance companies.

Large companies, or companies with high credit ratings, can borrow funds using this market at more competitive rates than they can obtain from the banks. The creation and growth of this market has led to *disintermediation*, whereby companies circumvent the various financial institutions and deal directly with the wholesale markets themselves. This could be a concern for banks in that they might be left with borrowers who are of 'lower quality' and therefore riskier should a larger proportion of the 'higher quality' companies deal directly with the wholesale markets.

As well as the three wholesale money markets already identified, it will be useful to briefly consider two other types of wholesale money market, namely the Eurocurrency market and the discount market.

Eurocurrency market   Eurocurrency is currency held on deposit with a bank outside the country from which that currency originates. For example loans made in dollars by banks in the UK are known as eurodollar loans. The eurocurrency market is a wholesale market and has its origins in the growing holdings of US dollars outside the US in the 1960s. Since that time eurocurrency markets have grown rapidly to include dealing in all the major currencies, and have become particularly important when oil price rises have created huge world surpluses and deficits, resulting in large shifts in demand for and supply of the major world currencies.

The major participants are banks, who use the euromarkets for a variety of reasons: for short-term inter-bank lending and borrowing, to match the currency composition of assets and liabilities, and for global liquidity transformation between branches. However, the market is also extensively used by companies and by governmental and international organisations. Lending which is longer term is usually done on a variable-rate basis, where the interest is calculated periodically in line with changing market rates.

There are two important factors which make eurocurrency business attractive. The first is that the market is unregulated, so that banks which are subject to reserve requirements or interest rate restrictions in the home country, for instance, can do business more freely abroad. The other factor is that the margin between the lending and borrowing rates is narrower on this market than on the home market, primarily because banks can operate at lower cost when all business is wholesale and when they are not subject to reserve requirements.

The discount market   The discount market has always played an important role within the financial system. In the last century its major function was the discounting of commercial bills of exchange which financed the increasing volume of international trade. Between the wars it provided a market for the growing volume of Treasury bills issued by the government to meet its short-term financing needs. As the volume of Treasury bills declined in the 1970s the discount houses facilitated the rapid growth in the commercial bill market.

The prime business of the eight members of the London Discount Market Association is to buy bills at a discount and hold them until redemption date, thereby taking a profit. Cash flow for this purpose is provided by overnight and short-term 'money at call' lent by the banking sector. Commercial bills must be 'accepted' (underwritten) by a discount house or a reputable bank in order to be eligible to be traded on the market. Commercial bills accepted by banks designated as 'eligible' banks by the Bank of England become first-class bills, which the Bank of England is willing to deal in on the market. The Bank of England as well as dealing with the discount houses, now also deals with the other firms or 'dealing counterparts' on this market.

The function of the discount houses may be summarised as follows:

(a) They underwrite the weekly tender issue of Treasury bills by bidding competitively for those not sold.

(b) They take surplus funds from the banking sector which can be recalled if banks are short of cash, thus effectively acting as a buffer between the banks and the Bank of England. The commercial banks' daily holdings of cash fluctuates as a result of transactions between the government and the public; deposits of the banking sector held by the discount houses are used to smooth out these fluctuations.

(c) They provide short-term finance for companies by discounting commerical bills.

(d) They maintain a secondary market in CDs and other short-term financial instruments.

Traditionally the Bank of England has supported the discount houses, and thus indirectly the banking sector as a whole, by lending to them at a rate of its own choosing, known since 1971 as *Minimum Lending Rate*. This enables the Bank to raise the Minimum Lending Rate when it wishes to make credit more expensive throughout the financial system. The current arrangement is that the Bank will support the discount market by dealing rather than lending. The Bank buys and sells securities daily in the market in a manner which is designed to achieve both its interest rate and liquidity objectives (see p. 487).

The UK capital markets   In contrast to the short-term transactions undertaken in the UK wholesale money markets, the capital market provides an arena in which private and public sector companies can trade medium and long-term financial claims. These financial claims can either be equity shares or interest-bearing debt instruments, or a mixture of the two.

Purchasers of *equity* have bought themselves a legal share in the ownership of the company, giving them the right to contribute to the determination of broad company strategy as well as a claim on the profits of the company. Any profits which are paid to shareholders are done so in the form of a *dividend*, which is usually paid annually. In addition, shareholders usually have voting rights in the election of directors and have a claim on any residual income should the company be liquidated.

Purchasers of *debt*, in contrast, have bought themselves a long-term financial instrument which provides them with a flow of cash interest payments at specific times in the future. The purchasers of debt are classed as creditors or lenders and do not have ownership rights on the company.

● *Primary capital markets.* New issues of equity and debt are originally placed on the primary capital markets and then subsequently traded in the secondary markets which include the London Stock Exchange (LSE). The majority of primary capital markets are *over-the-counter markets*, with no single location, reporting system or centralised market. In these markets information is widely dispersed and accessed via extensive computer networks.

● *Secondary capital markets.* These are organised markets which enable existing equity and debt to be traded. The ability to trade debt on a secondary market is an important part of any capital market because it allows holders of long-term financial debt to liquidate such debt for cash at any time, and for a known return.

This means that new issues are more likely to be purchased. Also the holders of marketable financial claims can more readily maximise their utility by rearranging their portfolios of assets over time.

At the heart of the capital market in the UK is the London Stock Exchange (LSE). The LSE has a physical location where equity and debt instruments can be traded. However, the amount of business transacted on the floor of the LSE is minimal with the majority of business taking place outside the physical location of the exchange using telephones and new technology. The market can be split into two: the *Main Market*, which is the largest and is where the majority of equity and debt prices are quoted; the *Alternative Investment Market* (AIM), which opened in July 1995, and allows smaller companies access to the secondary market (see Ch. 4).

A major factor concerning capital markets today is the growing competition between financial centres, especially those within Europe. Traditionally, London has been the busiest European capital market: for example, the amount of international banking business undertaken from London at the beginning of the 1990s was three times that of the next busiest European country. Reasons advanced for this dominance have included London's geographical position between New York and Tokyo, the large amount of foreign banks operating in London, the availability of trained staff, and London's convenience in reaching the rest of Europe.

However, with the evolution of the Single Market, the increasing globalization of businesses and the advancement of technology, the competition from other financial centres has become intense. This has meant that European companies requiring long-term finance are increasingly looking throughout the European financial centres and not just to London. We consider these competitive pressures in more detail later in the chapter.

Competition between financial centres in Europe

The move towards a single European currency, the deregulation of financial markets, and changes in technology, have increased the pressure on European financial centres. All the major European countries have been developing financial markets that will attract trade and boost their domestic economies. In recent years, London, New York and Tokyo have been the dominant centres, but within Europe, Frankfurt and Paris are evolving into a tangible threat to London.

Currently London remains dominant in both the size of its domestic markets and its share of international financial business. Evidence of this is shown by the market capitalization of the London Stock Exchange in 1998 which was around $2,000 billion, more than the combined capitalization of both Frankfurt and Paris. London also dominates international bank lending, having around 17% of the market share, and foreign exchange dealings, having around 30% of the market share. France has less than 10% of the market share in both these markets. In addition Britain has a head start on the other European centres because it is the largest net exporter of financial services in the world, reporting a trade surplus of over $8 billion in the late 1990s.

However, a number of factors are changing the ways in which the European financial centres conduct their business. These include the introduction of the euro, domestic financial market deregulation to entice business, and the growing use of electronic and telecommunication technologies. Such technical change is lessening the requirement of having to be located within a specific financial centre, lowering transaction costs and increasing efficiency.

The introduction of the euro will clearly be to the initial advantage of participating countries, benefiting Frankfurt and Paris. The German authorities have already passed a number of laws to deregulate the financial markets and have the advantage that the headquarters of the European Central bank is located in Frankfurt. Paris has also been reorganising its financial markets in preparation for the euro, evidenced by the fact that the proportion of French shares held by foreigners has increased to 35%. In addition, both Frankfurt and Paris have reorganised their stock exchanges, utilising new technologies to increase efficiency.

Despite this growing competition between European financial centres it is likely that, for the foreseeable future, London will remain dominant because of its lower costs and better infrastructure. London has a large, highly skilled workforce, lower personal taxation, a more flexible legal system and a regulatory system which distinguishes between retail and wholesale business, regulating wholesale business less stringently on the grounds that it represents business undertaken between well-informed professionals.

The Bank of England and the sterling wholesale money markets

Having introduced both the Bank of England and the sterling wholesale money markets it will be useful to consider the operations of the Bank of England in the money markets and the ways in which it seeks to influence the short-term interest rate.

We have already noted that setting interest rates is now the concern of the Monetary Policy Committee (MPC) which operates within the Bank of England. The aim of the Bank's operations on the money markets is to *guide* short-term interest rates to the level set by the MPC. The Bank does this by providing liquidity or cash to the banking system at the interest rate set by the MPC and by buying government securities at prices consistent with the interest rate set by the MPC. This exerts pressure on the short-term money market rate of interest to move to the 'official' rate set by the MPC.

To be able to do this, the Bank of England manages its accounts in ways which will ensure that the banking system as a whole is short of liquidity. The Bank of England can 'tighten' bank liquidity in the following ways.

- *Through taxation.* When people pay their taxes they do so from their bank accounts, the flow of these payments to the Bank of England (on behalf of the government) drains the banking sector of liquidity.
- *Through government borrowing.* Selling government securities (e.g. Treasury Bills) to individuals or institutions who pay for them from their bank accounts.
- *Through buying short-term claims on banks.* Such 'claims' are via the Bank of England lending to the banks for short periods. A number of these claims mature throughout the day and must be redeemed by the banks, draining them of liquidity.
- *Through regulations.* For example regulations which require the clearing banks to maintain positive end-of-day balances with the Bank of England.

The Bank of England is aware that banks will always look to the money markets in general, and the Bank of England in particular, should they need to restore their liquidity. At this point the Bank will offer such liquidity at a 'price', namely one which will reinforce the interest rate level set by the MPC.

Fig. 21.3. Open Market
Operations of the Bank of
England.

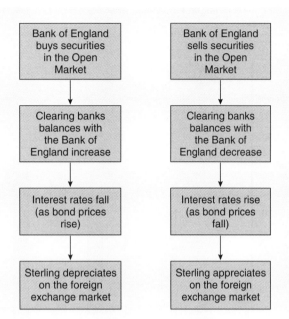

The Bank of England can, for example, raise short-term interest rates by first starving the banking sector of liquidity and then offering to restore that liquidity at its official rate of interest. This intervention often comes in the form of Open Market Operations (OMOs) on the money market. Figure 21.3 provides a simplified overview of such Open Market operations. Where the Bank of England wants to *raise* interest rates it *sells* securities, and vice versa.

The Bank of England conducts its Open Market operations by buying and selling high quality government securities such as Treasury bills and eligible bank bills, government foreign currency debt and gilt repos. By far the most significant of these securities are the gilt repos.

The introduction of the gilt repo market   In March 1997 the Bank introduced reforms to its daily operations in the money markets. The aim of these reforms were threefold. First, to increase the efficiency of liquidity provision in the banking sector; second, to increase competition by raising the number of eligible institutions with which the Bank would trade (these institutions are known as 'counterparties' and now include banks, building societies and securities houses); third, to introduce the gilt repo into its Open Market Operations, thereby providing the Bank with an additional instrument with which to influence short-term interest rates.

A *repo* is a transaction in which one party sells a financial asset to another party and agrees to repurchase an equivalent value of financial assets at some time in the future. The gilt repo market was introduced in January 1996 and quickly became a major tool with which the Bank of England could provide refinancing to the banking sector. Within three months of its introduction, over 50% of refinancing by the Bank was provided by the gilt repo and almost 50% of Open Market Operations by the Bank were undertaken using the gilt repo. The value of gilt repo's outstanding at banks and other financial institutions had expanded to over £104 billion by 1998.

Fig. 21.4. Gilt repos outstanding at banks and other institutions.
Source: Bank of England.

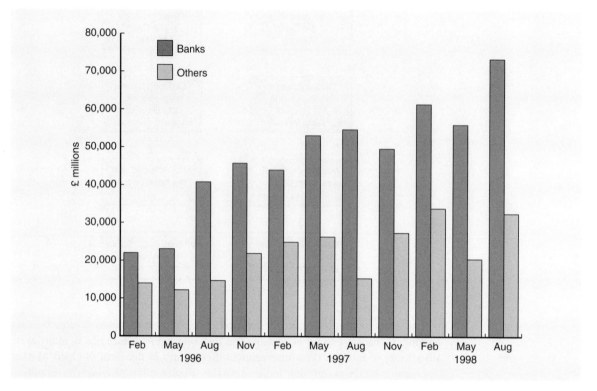

Table 21.5 The sizes of UK sterling money markets (£bn).

	Commercial paper	Treasury bills	CDs	Interbank	Gilt repo
1996 (November)	7	5	89	124	68
1997 (November)	8	3	100	135	72

Source: Adapted from Bank of England.

In addition the gilt repo market has made a considerable impact on the sterling money markets. As Table 21.5 shows, the gilt repo market is now the third largest market after the inter-bank and CD markets within the various sterling wholesale money markets.

The European Single Financial Market

The implementation of the Single Europe Act on 1 January 1993 provided for the EU-wide abolition of exchange controls and gave authorized financial institutions the right to undertake business anywhere in Europe. The aim was to create a European financial market where citizens and businesses in all member states would be free to invest their money, open accounts, and take out loans and insurance policies. Banks and other financial intermediaries are now free to offer their products and services without restriction, and securities from one EU country can be bought and sold on all EU stock exchanges.

European countries in recent years have been deregulating and modernising their financial services sector in order to be able to compete more efficiently in the new environment created by the single market. European financial institutions and financial markets have in the past been more heavily regulated and less developed than those within the UK financial sector. Therefore there has been more scope for innovation and change in Europe than there has been in the UK.

The European Single Financial Market was designed to allow companies and private individuals to be free to move funds around the EU without hindrance. The financial services market has been opened up on three main fronts:

- freedom of capital movement
- the right to sell financial services throughout the EU
- the right for financial organizations to establish themselves in any EU member state.

The essential characteristics of the new EU financial order are as follows:

- Financial institutions based in any member state can provide financial services in any other EU country. This also applies to financial institutions owned by an EU member state but which are located outside the EU.
- Financial institutions located in the EU can establish branches and subsidiaries in any other EU country.
- The principle of home country control is observed which means that foreign financial institutions must submit to their home, domestic regulatory authorities. This averts the complication of host country control.
- The new freedoms are counterbalanced by minimum general standards for the financial services industry which means that banking clients and investors throughout the EU will be afforded some measure of protection. Capital adequacy and institutional solvency regulations (see below) and minimum standards applied to EU brokerage and insurance markets, provide a basic level of EU-wide protection.
- The aim is for this single market to cover the whole financial services sector, so that both the freedoms to compete and the minimum regulatory standards will apply to all financial service activities in EU member states.

Financial Directives in the EU

Much of the legislation implementing the Single European Act is contained in a series of Directives. These bind members of the EU with respect to the objectives specified but allow individual countries to decide the precise form and means of implementing policies which meet those objectives.

The Second Banking Directive (SBD) This was adopted in December 1989 and implemented as a key part of the Single Europe Act in January 1993. The Second Banking Directive (SBD) applies to all credit institutions in the EU and was a significant step forward in the reform of financial services.

The most important feature of the SBD was the 'single banking licence'. This allowed any authorised 'credit institution' in the EU member country to establish branches or supply cross-border services as of right in all other member countries. The licence is limited to credit institutions authorised by their home authorities. This so-called 'single passport' covers a whole range of services, including deposit taking, lending, money transmission, leasing, participation in securities issues, issuing credit cards, travellers' cheques and other means of payment, securities trading and portfolio management and advice.

This measure has promoted widespread deregulation of financial services in previously highly regulated EU countries. Although the SBD does not legally require member states to remove any restrictions on their domestic banks etc., market forces resulting from increased competition from the EU banks now operating in their country has often resulted in their voluntarily doing so. Otherwise the constrained domestic banks will operate at a disadvantage *vis-à-vis* foreign banks.

The SBD also sought to protect investors by laying down minimum capital requirements of 5 million ECU (£3.3 million) for certain types of credit institutions to become authorized. This was taken further by the Capital Adequacy Directive (see below).

The most controversial and liberal aspect of the SBD is that it provides for reciprocal access to the single market for institutions from non-EU countries. Subsidiaries of third countries established in the EU will be considered to be EU undertakings and will benefit from the SBD's provisions. As a result, London remains a key EU entry point for US and Japanese banks. 'Reciprocal treatment' requires that EU banks in a third country are treated in the same way as the domestic institutions in that country or that effective market access is provided for EU banks which is comparable to that which the third country's banks receive in the EU.

Other important financial directives   Two other European financial services directives have played an important role in establishing a single market in financial services.

- *The Investment Services Directive* (ISD). This became effective on 1 January 1996 and gives non-bank investment firms opportunities for conducting business throughout the EU. These non-bank investment firms are involved in a range of services such as dealing, broking, underwriting and investment management. These firms in any EU country are now given the same freedoms to operate in other EU member countries as were given to other credit institutions under the Second Banking Directive.
- *The Capital Adequacy Directive* (CAD). This establishes minimum capital requirements for firms in the Financial Services sector and was implemented in 1993. The *capital* of any firm represents the value of the funds invested in the firm by the owners (shareholders). This capital base can be regarded as a kind of 'buffer stock', helping protect the firm against unexpected trading losses. The greater the capital base relative to total liabilities, the more secure the firm and the smaller the risk for any creditors of the firm. Such creditors (e.g. lenders via deposits) are protected by CAD, which sets minimum capital requirements of ECU 50,000 for firms not authorised to hold client money, ECU 125,000 for firms holding client's money but not dealing themselves (e.g. portfolio managers), and ECU 730,000 for all other firms.
- *The Deposit Guarantee Directive* (DGD). This was implemented in 1994 and provides a minimum level of protection for bank customers, as member countries must guarantee to refund at least 90% of the first 20,000 ECU (around £16,000) of any deposit with EU banks. Individual EU countries can *exceed* this minimum deposit guarantee should they wish.

Competitive pressures and the UK banking sector

The UK financial system is undergoing a phase of major structural change brought about by changing economic conditions and increasing pressures in traditional markets. This change has impacted on all areas of banking business, including customer profile, delivery strategies and the type of business undertaken. This in turn has changed the structure of the various balance sheets and the sources from which their income is derived.

Figure 21.5 indicates some of the competitive pressures facing the retail banking sector. Response to these pressures within the retail banking sector has, however, been rather slow. Historically the retail banks in the UK herald from a stable, regulated and largely uncompetitive environment, which remained largely untouched in the decades preceding the 1970s. The absence of competition meant that by the 1970s retail banks had evolved into monoliths, with extensive branch networks employing managers who operated within a highly regulated market, typified by the cartel arrangements for fixing interest rates between the large retail banks. In such a regulated, uncompetitive environment it is hardly surprising that bank managers have been characterised as adopting conservative, risk-averse strategies towards lending decisions. However, the progressive build up of competitive pressures on retail banks since the Competition and Credit Control Act of 1971 have brought about an entirely different landscape for the retail banks.

It will be useful at this stage to consider each of the factors identifed in Fig. 21.5 in rather more detail.

Increase in suppliers The increase in suppliers of services traditionally the preserve of the retail banks has come from three main sources: the financial markets, non-bank financial intermediaries and non-financial companies

The financial markets Traditionally, the retail banks have liaised between lenders and borrowers, using their deposits to benefit the economy by providing a variety of financial instruments with less risk and at a lower cost than would have been possible if the market had to rely on direct borrowing or lending. However, new

Fig. 21.5. Pressures on the UK banking sector.

financial instruments (e.g. repos) have been developed to enable borrowers and lenders to transact directly at lower cost. For example companies faced with a funding gap may now find that it is cheaper to transact directly with the financial markets. This trend towards *disintermediation*, i.e. direct transactions between ultimate borrowers and lenders, reduces the need for financial intermediaries.

Evidence to support this growing trend of disintermediation is provided by Table 21.6, which shows the proportion of external finance supplied by the banks and the capital markets to UK (non-financial) companies. Between 1979–82 UK companies obtained on average over 70% of their borrowing requirements from the banking sector. However, by the late 1990s this figure had fallen to under 40%, having even been negative during the early 1990s. In contrast, the capital markets have become an increasingly important source of external finance for the corporate sector, despite some volatility, far outweighing the contribution of the banking sector throughout the 1990s.

This increased use of the financial markets has been fuelled by the growing trend of *securitization*. Although technically the term securitization refers to the bundling up of mortgages into 'securities' which can be sold on the financial markets, it is more generally used to refer to the process of converting any existing (non-tradable) loan into a *security* (tradable). The seller of the asset (security) guarantees payment of interest in the new bundled security, which now becomes more liquid than the assets it replaces.

Although banks have lost business to the capital markets, securitization has enabled all financial institutions, including banks, to develop and market paper claims against what were previously non-marketable financial assets such as long-term loans, thereby reducing the risks and cost of holding them. Banks have also benefited by acting as advisor and broker to those companies wishing to finance future projects by issuing securities directly onto the markets.

Table 21. 6   Industrial and commercial companies' source of external domestic finance (£m and percentage).

	Borrowing from banks	Other loans and mortgages	Ordinary shares	Debentures and preference shares	Total UK capital issues	Total external finance	Per cent supplied by banks	Per cent supplied by capital markets	Per cent supplied by loans and mortgages
1979	3,981	1,402	879	−81	798	6,181	64.4	12.9	22.7
1980	6,340	831	896	14	910	8,081	78.5	11.3	10.3
1981	5,849	1,315	1,660	55	1,715	8,879	65.9	19.3	14.8
1982	6,562	1,496	1,033	−120	913	8,971	73.1	10.2	16.7
1983	1,619	1,196	1,872	364	2,236	5,051	32.1	44.3	23.7
1984	7,082	1,384	1,127	546	1,673	10,139	69.8	16.5	13.7
1985	7,454	2,508	3,407	1,586	4,993	14,955	49.8	33.4	16.8
1986	8,514	1,391	5,483	2,440	7,923	17,828	47.8	44.4	7.8
1987	12,096	3,928	13,410	3,304	16,714	32,738	36.9	51.1	12.0
1988	32,018	6,506	4,352	4,018	8,370	46,894	68.3	17.8	13.9
1989	33,746	10,031	1,882	5,606	7,488	51,265	65.8	14.6	19.6
1990	20,032	8,651	4,384	4,191	8,575	37,258	53.8	23.0	23.2
1991	−1,391	5,259	12,795	4,709	17,504	21,372	−6.5	81.9	24.6
1992	−1,941	−903	7,400	3,310	10,710	7,866	−24.7	136.2	−11.5
1993	−11,393	3,902	13,954	5,452	19,406	11,915	−95.6	162.9	32.7
1994	−4,807	2,878	11,435	7,796	19,231	17,302	−27.8	111.1	16.6
1995	13,945	2,857	12,574	12,345	24,919	41,721	33.4	59.7	6.8
1996	14,958	7,973	12,758	4,667	17,425	40,356	37.1	43.2	19.8

Source: Adapted from Datastream.

Non-bank financial intermediaries   These financial intermediaries include the building societies, insurance companies and unit and investment trust companies. They have utilized changes in market regulations and technology to offer new, cheaper and more flexible products and services to lenders. In many cases these institutions are not exposed to the high operating costs of the banking sector. For example the Halifax reported a cost/income ratio of 42.3% in 1996 covering its last year of trading as a mutual building society, whereas retail banks such as Lloyds and NatWest reported cost/income ratios of 57% and 68% respectively in the same year.

Non-financial companies   The threat of competition from non-financial companies to the retail banks has become real as the costs of entry into the banking sector have fallen. General retailers, such as Marks & Spencer and supermarkets such as Sainsbury's, Tesco, Asda, Safeway and Morrisons, all now offer many financial services and even car manufacturers such as Vauxhall are developing their own financial products. These retailers can benefit from cheaper entry costs to many banking activities due partly to advances in technology and also to their ability to utilise their extensive branch networks.

The term 'asymmetric competition' might be used to describe the competition pressures on the retail banking sector from these non-bank financial intermediaries and non-financial companies (Llewellyn 1997). It is asymmetric because changes in technology and regulation have made it easier for non-financial firms to diversify into banking business than for banks to diversify into non-financial business. This is mainly because of branding in that a strong reputation in general retailing gives a non-financial institution the possibility of using that reputation to sell financial products. However, the reverse is far less true, in that a bank with a strong reputation will find this of little help should it seek to diversify into general retailing. Further, whereas general retailers can put aside a small area within their current buildings to sell financial products, banks do not possess the spatial resources to sell tangible retail goods such as clothes or motor cars, etc. Generally speaking these non-financial companies have entered the financial services sector for three main reasons: first, they have an established distribution network to provide such financial services; second, they have a strong brand image, especially as regards reputation; third, in many cases (e.g. supermarkets) they can exploit information that they have gained from loyalty card and related schemes.

These new suppliers are clearly increasing the competitive pressures on the retail banking sector while at the same time restricting the ability of the banks themselves to diversify into new market segments. Further, the non-financial companies especially have the ability to cross-subsidise their financial services from other profitable activities and thereby out-compete the retail bank financial services.

Growing consumerism   At the same time there has been an increase in the awareness, expectations and demands of customers for newer, better and more targeted financial services. One possible reason for this growing 'consumerism' might include an increase in the number and quality of information flows available to consumers, for example via easier access to brokerage and other financial advice. Demographic changes might also have played a part, for example an ageing population has increased its demand for savings and pension-related financial products, especially in the context of a more

Table 21.7 The demand for PEPs and TESSAs in the UK (£m).

Year	PEPs	TESSAs
1990	2,600	n/a
1991	4,520	2,774
1992	6,970	3,532
1993	11,890	3,908
1994	20,090	4,193
1995	23,800	4,538
1996	34,120	4,682
1997	49,530	4,958
1998	77,850	–

Source: Adapted from ONS (1998) *Financial Statistics.*

restricted Welfare State in the future, including even less generous provision for the state pension. A longer life expectancy and reduced job security might be other important factors in this increased desire for newer, better and more targeted financial services.

Table 21.7 shows the rapid growth in demand for savings products such as PEPs and Tessas. *PEPs* are Personal Equity Plans and these were introduced in 1986 to encourage savings by being exempt from income tax on any dividends or interest received. PEPs can involve investments in a variety of market-based financial instruments, such as UK and European company shares and corporate bonds. The growth in PEPs has been extremely rapid, growing by more than thirty times in value between 1990 and 1998, with the value of PEPs in the UK reaching more than £77 billion in 1998. *Tessas* are Tax Exempt Special Savings Accounts and are also exempt from income tax on savings up to £9,000 over five years. Tessas have almost doubled in value since their introduction in 1991.

These identified trends suggest a shift in the balance of power from the suppliers of financial services to the consumers of financial services, and this shift is likely to continue as consumers demand more flexible, competitive and convenient financial products.

Single Market in financial services

The Ceccini report of 1988 had suggested that the Single Market Programme (SMP) for financial services would result in three main categories of benefit. First, financial institutions would benefit from economies of scale because they would be operating in a bigger market at higher volumes. Second, the increase in competitive pressure would reduce margins and financial institutions would be forced to reduce inefficiencies by reducing costs. Third, the increased competition would have non-price effects which would surface as higher product quality and more product innovation.

A major study has been published on the impacts of the SMP on credit institutions and banking since its initial implementation on 1 January 1993. The key findings of this study (Single Market Review, 1997) are presented below.

- Financial services firms have witnessed an increase in competition in the post-SMP period but the cost of loans to business has fallen only slightly in most markets.
- The cost of loans to the personal sector, including mortgages, has fallen by even less than those to business.

- The returns offered to depositors in both the personal and corporate sectors decreased slightly, but only 13% of financial institutions in the study believed this was due to the SMP.
- Smaller banks have been pressurized into mergers and overall the number of banks in Europe has declined post-SMP.
- There is little evidence that the SMP has increased productivity in European banking.
- Significant price differences for identical products, for example chequing accounts, still remain across Europe.
- The most common response by financial institutions to the SMP has been to diversify the range of products and services that they offer.
- Trade in off-balance-sheet business in financial institutions of the member states has increased but has not been mirrored by the retail financial sector.

Despite the comprehensive nature of the study, the trends identified have been difficult to disaggregate from changes which might in any case have occurred without SMP. What seems most likely is that the SMP has further intensified the competitive pressures that the European financial services industry was already experiencing.

Re-regulation   There are three broad categories of regulation, namely structural regulation, conduct (or prudential) regulation and investor protection. *Structural regulation* refers to rules about the actual separation of institutions. *Conduct regulation* refers to rules about the assets and liabilities of a bank, such as information disclosure, credit ceilings and capital adequacy requirements (CARs). *Investor protection* refers to rules which seek to prevent banks taking on excessive risk or undertaking fraudulent transactions.

Traditionally all three types of regulation were well represented in the UK banking sector given its importance within the economy and the need to restrict excessive risk-taking which might lead to system-wide bank failures. In more recent times the trend towards more competitive markets has led to a near disappearance of structural regulation but an increase in conduct and investor protection legislation in the UK and other EU financial markets (see p. 490). This has typically been applied to all credit institutions, further blurring the demarcation applied between banks, non-banks and non-financial companies. With investors in these non-bank and non-financial companies now being equally well covered as those in banks as regards conduct and investor protection regulations, such re-reglation has further increased the competitive pressures on the banking sector.

Ultimately, this trend towards re-regulation will have two effects on the incumbent retail banks. First, profitability in the banking sector will be reduced as competition increases with other credit institutions and margins are reduced. Second, the increase in conduct and investor protection regulation will add to overall costs and reduce profits still further. This suggests that the UK retail banking sector is facing both increased competition from other credit institutions and increased costs in order to comply with new regulatory structures.

Technology   New technologies have tended to replace labour-intensive and costly processes with more capital-intensive and efficient processes. This is especially so as regards methods of storing and analysing information and assessing risk, thereby substantially increasing the volume of financial transactions that can be processed and reducing the cost per unit transaction. A simple illustration of the impact of new technology can be found in the growth of automated clearing. Although only introduced in 1985, by 1988 it had exceeded the annual value of the more costly paper-based clearing mechanism, and is now more than ten times larger than paper-based alternatives, with an annual value of around £30,000 billion.

A significant impact of the new technologies has also been to reduce the costs of entry into the banking sector, thereby increasing competition. For example new competititors no longer need an extensively staffed branch-network given the availability of telephone and internet banking systems, which permit competitors to reach consumers in their homes.

It would seem that an increasing amount of future financial and non-financial business will be undertaken via the internet. Estimates for the UK suggest that there will be around 8.4 million households with computer facilities by the year 2000 (Llewellyn 1997). As yet retail banks would appear to have been slow to respond to such opportunitites. Most current providers tend to be technology based with little experience in banking, though this means that they are having to work jointly with a clearing bank in order to undertake such business. However, as these providers gain a greater market share of financial business over the internet, they themselves may become banks and remove the need for joint-ventures with the existing clearing banks.

A number of reasons have been suggested as to why the impact of the internet will be significant. These include:

- the marginal cost of transactions is extremely low
- there is no requirement to have a branch network
- easy access to service and product information which lowers search costs; customers can access information on all financial service providers quickly and cheaply and so price variation will fall, reducing margins in the sector
- costs of entry onto the internet are low, further eroding margins
- the consumer pays to connect to the service.

The increasing use of technology will therefore affect traditional banking business by increasing supplier access to customer information, reducing the costs of supplying various financial services and lowering entry barriers. Such impacts are forcing retail banks to reduce their cost structures in order to compete more effectively and maintain their profitability.

Responses of UK retail banks

Retail banks in the UK (and Europe) have made serious attempts to reduce their cost/income ratios in response to these various market pressures. The focus has been both to reduce cost and to increase income (revenue) in order to reduce this ratio.

Figure 21.6 suggests that retail banks have reduced fixed and variable costs by reducing the number of branches and staff. As can be seen there has been a substantial fall in the number of staff from around 280,000 in 1988 to around 200,000 today. These falls have been paralleled by a sustained increase in the number of Automatic Telling Machines (ATMs) from around 2,000 in 1979 to over 11,000 today.

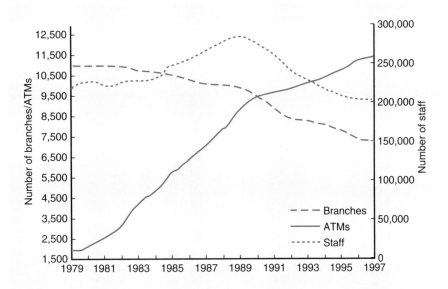

Fig. 21.6. Numbers of staff, branches and ATMs at the big four UK retail banks (Barclays, NatWest, Midland, Lloyds).
Source: Adapted from British Bankers' Association Statistical Unit (1998).

Figure 21.7 suggests that the cost/income ratios of retail banks have indeed fallen to around 60%. Many believe further falls must occur if retail banks are to become competitive. A target of around 50% is widely accepted, given that other credit insitutions such as building societies have cost/income ratios around 45%. It may be that more attention must be paid to generating extra *income* if further falls are to be achieved in this ratio.

Universal financial supermarkets   Although banks have reduced branch staff levels this policy has met some resistance on both the political and economic (customer) fronts. An alternative approach which seeks to tackle *both* sides of the cost/income ratio has involved the retail banks developing into 'universal financial

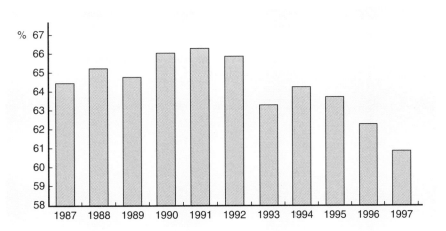

Fig. 21.7. Cost/income ratios of MBBGs 1987–97 (cost/income measured by operating expenses/ gross income). MBBGs are the Major British Banking Groups, which are the main retail banks.
Source: British Bankers' Association Statistical Unit (1998).

Fig. 21.8.   Net interest income and non-interest income as a proportion of average balance sheet total for UK MBBGs. *Source:* Compiled from various Annual Reports.

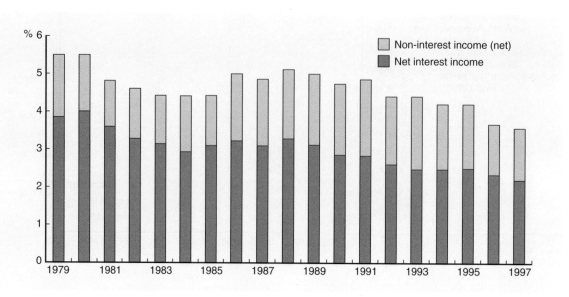

supermarkets'. This diversification into new markets has also helped to spread total costs over a wider product range. This allowed banks to spread their extensive assets into new areas using the same inputs and build on their solid reputation in the high street and access to customer financial data. Retail banks now offer a much broader array of products and services and increasingly receive income from other sources than interest payments, such as from foreign exchange and equity dealings and derivative-based income. This decline in importance of interest as a source of income is shown in Fig. 21.8. Whereas non-interest income was around 25% of all income in 1979, this figure had risen to over 40% of all income by the late 1990s.

The retail banks believe that by diversifying in these ways they are using their existing resources more effectively, including both tangible (branch networks and financial data) and intangible (reputation) resources, in order to benefit from economies of scale and scope. Economies of scale refer to cost reductions from increasing the size of their operations; economies of scope refer to cost reductions from changing the product mix of their operations. Further, the new financial supermarkets are meeting the demands of customers for more flexible and targeted financial products.

Key points

- Financial institutions exist to match the needs of borrowers and lenders, i.e. to *mediate* between them.
- Mediation may be necessary because borrowers and lenders have different requirements in terms of maturity, liquidity and yield.
- There are three main types of 'operator' in the UK financial system: lenders and borrowers, financial intermediaries and the various financial markets in which transactions take place.
- The Single Europe Act (1 January 1993) gave authorised financial institutions the right to do business anywhere in the EU.
- Financial intermediaries can take one of two main forms: brokerage intermediaries and asset-transforming intermediaries. *Brokerage intermediaries* assess information on lenders and borrowers but do not purchase or hold financial assets. *Asset-transforming intermediaries* acquire liabilities and transform them into assets with different characteristics in terms of maturity, liquidity and yield.
- UK financial intermediaries can also be categorized as *bank financial intermediaries* which includes the retail and wholesale banks and *non-bank financial intermediaries* which includes building societies, pension funds, investment and unit trusts.
- Financial intermediaton is becoming increasingly competitive and diversified. Not only are existing 'players' widening the range of activities in which they are involved but entirely new 'players' are entering the markets (e.g. supermarkets and banking services).
- The Bank of England has been granted independence in the setting of short-term interest rates and this is overseen by the Monetary Policy Committee (MPC) which is a committee within the Bank. The Bank manipulates short-term interest rates via open market operations in the money markets using predominantly gilt repos.
- Financial institutions are regulated by the Financial Services Authority (FSA). However, financial stability is maintained via frequent discussions between the FSA, the Bank of England and the Treasury department.
- Financial markets can be split into two main markets: the money markets which mainly deal in short-term financial assets, and the capital markets which mainly deal in long-term financial claims.

References and further reading

Apps, R., Goacher, D. and **Lipscombe, G.** (1996) *The Monetary and Financial System.* Banker Books, London.

Bank of England (1997) The Bank of England's operations in the sterling money markets, *Bank of England Quarterly Bulletin*, May

British Bankers' Association Statistical Unit (1998) Annual Abstract of Banking Statistics, *British Bankers' Association*, **15**.

Economist (1998) Capital of capital, *The Economist*, 9 May.

Greenbaum, S.I. and **Thakor, A.V.** (1995) *Contemporary Financial Intermediation*, Dryden Press. Orlando.

McKenzie, G. (1998) Financial regulation and the European Union, *The Economic Review*, April.

Pilbeam, K. (1998) *Finance and Financial Markets*, Macmillan.

Rodgers, P. (1997) Changes at the Bank of England, *Bank of England Quarterly Bulletin*, August.

Rodgers, P. (1998) The Bank of England Act, *Bank of England Quarterly Bulletin*, May.

Santomero, A.M. and **Babbel, D.F.** (1997) *Financial Markets, Instruments, and Institutions*. Irwin, Chicago.

Single Market Review (1997) Impact on services: credit institutions and banking, Subseries 2, Vol. 3, Kogan Page.

Webb, R.M. (1998) Operational efficiency of large UK retail banking groups, Middlesex University Business School, mimeo.

Chapter 22

Inflation

In this chapter we first examine a number of methods of measuring inflation. We then consider the 'costs' of inflation, both when it is fully anticipated, and when, as is usually the case, it is not. A basic theoretical framework for understanding inflation is presented and is used to explain recent UK experience. The issues of inflation targeting and central bank independence are also considered.

The definition and measurement of inflation

Inflation is a persistent tendency for the general level of prices to rise. In effect the rate of inflation measures the change in the purchasing power of money, i.e. how much more money you would have to have this year when faced with this year's prices to be as well-off as you were last year when faced with last year's prices. Until 1979 inflation in the UK was measured and reported almost exclusively by reference to the RPI; since then various additional measures have been introduced.

The Retail Price Index   The RPI, which was formerly compiled by the Department of Employment, is now the responsibility of the Office for National Statistics. It measures the change from month to month in the cost of a representative 'basket' of goods and services of the type bought by a typical household.

A number of stages are involved in the calculation of the RPI. The first stage is to select the items to be included in the index and to weight these items according to their relative importance in the average family budget. Obviously items on which a family spends a large proportion of its income are given heavier weights than those items on which the family spends relatively little. For example, in 1998 the weight given to tea in the index was 2, whereas that for electricity was 23 (out of a total 'all items weight' of 1,000). The weights used are changed annually to reflect the changes in the composition of family expenditure. The new weights are derived from the Family Expenditure Survey in which about 7,000 households, carefully chosen to represent all regions and types of household, take part each year. Each member of the household aged over sixteen years records his or her day-to-day expenditure on items over a two-week period, together with any longer-term payments, such as telephone bills, season tickets, etc. It is from these records that the weights for the RPI are based. The new weights, which begin in January each year, are largely based on the pattern of expenditure shown in the survey over the year to the previous June. For some items, however, such as selected consumer durables (e.g. furniture and carpets) where sales fluctuate widely from year to year, expenditure is averaged over a three-year period.

The weights for this 'general RPI' are obtained by excluding those pensioner households who derive 75% or more of their income from state benefits and any households who are in the top 4% of income earners (these categories together accounting for 16% of all households). These two groups are excluded because the pattern of their expenditure differs markedly from that of the great majority of households.

The weights used for groups of items are shown in Table 22.1. It can be seen that food has been replaced as the largest item by housing (rent, mortgage interest rates and council tax, water charges, repairs and dwelling insurance). This is part of a longer run trend associated with differing income elasticities of demand for the items in the 'basket'.

The second stage in deriving the RPI involves collecting the price data. For most items, prices are collected on a specific day each month, usually the Tuesday nearest the middle of the month. Prices are obtained from a sample of retail outlets in some 180 different areas. Care is taken to make sure a representative range of retail outlets, small retailers, supermarkets, department stores, etc. are surveyed. In all around 150,000 price quotations are collected each month. An average price is then calculated for each item in the index. For example on 16 June 1998, 496 price quotations were taken for tomatoes; the prices ranged from 39p to 66p per pound, with an average of 48p.

The final stage is to calculate the RPI from all these data. All index numbers must relate to some base period or reference date. In the case of the RPI the base period is January 1987 = 100. The index is calculated each month through a weighted price relative method.[1] Since the weights are revised each year to keep the index up to date, the index is calculated afresh each year with January counting as 100. Each yearly index is then linked back to the base year by means of a chain base method.[2] In June 1998 the RPI stood at 163.4, which means that average prices have risen by 63.4% between January 1987 and June 1998. As the index is an average, this figure conceals the fact that some prices have increased more rapidly (rent 123%, water 173% and beer 92%), whilst other prices have fallen (audio-visual equipment by around 43%).

Table 22.1 General index of retail prices: group weights.

	1987	1998
Food	167	130
Catering	46	48
Alcoholic drink	76	71
Tobacco	38	34
Housing	157	197
Fuel and light	61	36
Household goods	73	72
Household services	44	54
Clothing and footwear	74	55
Personal goods and services	40	40
Motoring expenditure	127	136
Fares and other travel costs	22	20
Leisure goods	47	46
Leisure services	30	61
	1,000	1,000

Sources: Adapted from Labour Market Trends (1998) Vol. 106, No. 9, September, and previous issues.

Fig. 22.1. Inflation is measured as the annual increase in the retail price index from 1946–74, and in the retail price index excluding mortgage interest payments from 1974–97.
Source: King (1997).

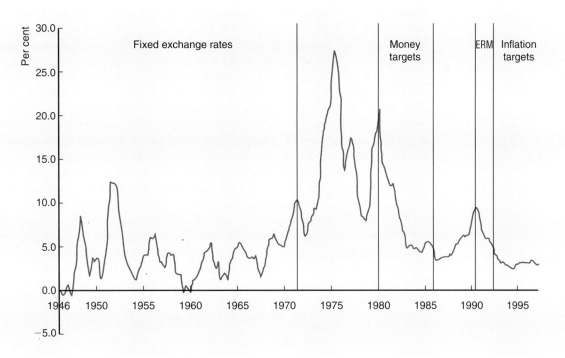

A separate index is calculated for one-pensioner and two-pensioner households. These have weights which differ from the general RPI because of the different pattern of expenditure of these households. For example, pensioners spend a higher proportion of their income on housing, fuel and food, and a smaller proportion on clothing, alcoholic drink, durable goods and transport. Despite this, 'pensioner' price indices have moved fairly closely in line with the general RPI for several years.

Once the RPI has been constructed, the rate of inflation can then be calculated, with the most usual measure being the twelve-monthly change in the RPI. For example, the RPI stood at 157.5 in June 1997. In June 1998 it stood at 163.4 and therefore the annual rate of inflation over that period is

$$\frac{163.4 - 157.5}{157.5} \times 100\% = 3.7\%$$

Inflation as measured by the RPI is shown in Fig. 22.1.

Housing costs   It has been argued that the way housing costs are treated in the RPI not only makes the RPI an unreliable indicator of the underlying inflationary trend in the economy, but also makes international comparisons of inflation invalid. The RPI includes *mortgage interest payments* as the main element in owner-occupiers' housing costs. Mortgage interest payments reflect changes in both house prices (a useful estimate of the increase in debt on 'standard' mortgages) and the interest rate charged to householders on this debt. It is, however, variations in the latter, namely interest rates, which tend to be the major short-term influence on mortgage costs. Frequent changes in interest rates can therefore generate erratic movements in the RPI. Indeed the anti-inflation strategy of the government in the late 1980s and early 1990s was based largely on high interest rates, which had the perverse effect of increasing the RPI. Inflation was then further fuelled by the fact that the RPI was the main indicator used by trade unions when formulating wage claims.

The problem is therefore how to treat housing costs in the RPI. Some European countries such as France and Italy *exclude* owner-occupation from their consumer price index. In many other countries which include owner-occupation in their consumer price index there is a large private rented sector, and so the measurement of housing costs for owner-occupiers can be *imputed* from the actual payments made by households living in similar rented accommodation. In Britain, it has always been thought that the private rented sector was too small to allow such imputation. As a result the RPI uses the interest on a standard mortgage as part of the calculation to capture owner-occupiers' housing costs.

There are a number of arguments against including mortgage interest payments in the RPI. For example, only one quarter of the housing stock is mortgaged and therefore mortgage interest is an unrepresentative measure. Also house purchase is an investment which produces a capital gain in the long run and arguably these capital gains should be *offset* against mortgage interest. On the other hand, most mortgage payers do regard these payments as part of their cost of living and would be disconcerted if they were removed from the index. The difference between the

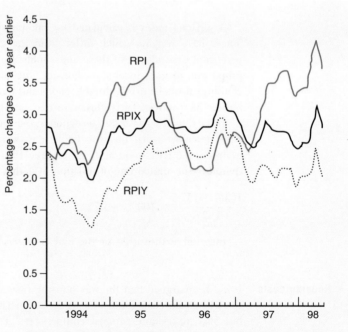

Fig. 22.2.   Retail price inflation.
Source: Bank of England Inflation Report, August 1998.

RPIX = Retail price index excluding mortgage interest payments.
RPIY = RPIX excluding VAT, local authority taxes and excise duty.

inflation rate measured by the RPI and the inflation rate measured by the RPI excluding mortgage interest payments (RPIX) can be seen in Fig. 22.2. The effect of the increases in the mortgage interest rate during 1997 can clearly be seen in the RPI beginning to diverge sharply from RPIX.

In 1993 the UK government introduced, for the first time, an explicit target for price inflation. The objective was to keep the underlying rate of inflation as measured by the RPI excluding mortgage interest payments (RPIX) within the range of 1–4%. Currently the Chancellor has charged the Bank of England's Monetary Policy Committee (MPC) with conducting monetary policy so as to achieve a target for the RPIX of 2.5%.

It is worth noting that both the measures of inflation discussed so far, the RPI (headline inflation) and RPI minus mortgage interest (the government's target), are influenced by changes in indirect taxes and the Council Tax. If indirect taxes increase, these indicators will show inflation increasing even though underlying inflationary pressures in the economy may not have changed. To assess the underlying inflation rate the Bank of England calculates another index, the RPIY, which excludes not only mortgage interest but also indirect taxes such as VAT and excise duty, as well as local authority taxes. The contribution since 1996 of higher rates of indirect taxes (e.g. petrol duty) to a higher inflation rate can be seen by the divergence of RPIY from both RPI and RPIX since that date (see Fig. 22.2).

Do the RPI and its related measures overestimate the cost of living?

The RPI (together with the various measures derived from it) is supposed to measure the movement in prices of goods and services that the average British family buys. In this respect the RPI has a pivotal role in the economy as a target for policy makers, for example in acting as a basis for indexing tax allowances and as a starting point for pay claims. The question might reasonably be asked as to how well the RPI reflects changes in the 'true' cost of living. In other words, if the RPI increases by 5% over the year do households really need a 5% rise in disposable income to maintain their living standards? Some studies suggest that there is potential for systematic discrepancies between the RPI and a 'true' cost of living index. For example Cunningham (1996) notes four sources of 'bias' which might cause the RPI to overestimate the true increase in the cost of living. The first is a *substitution bias* which arises from consumers choosing relatively cheaper goods and services over time. However, the RPI has a fixed basket of goods and services for each year, preventing a switch to cheaper sources being reflected during that year. The second is a *new outlet bias*. Price quotes are taken from a wide range of outlets but are unlikely to fully reflect short-term changes in retailing patterns which might cause consumers to move to cheaper discount stores. The third is an *upward bias* which arises from new consumer durable goods not usually being included in the RPI index until the initial phase of rapidly falling prices (often associated with new entry) is over. The fourth is a *quality improvement bias*, with quality gains in durable goods and services not being fully captured in the RPI. Cunningham estimates that the RPI may actually *overestimate* the cost of living by at least 0.35 to 0.8% points per annum as a result of these biases.

Other measures of inflation

Although the RPI (with or without the mortgage interest adjustment) is the usual measure of inflation, there are others (see Fig. 22.3). The *Index of Producer Prices*

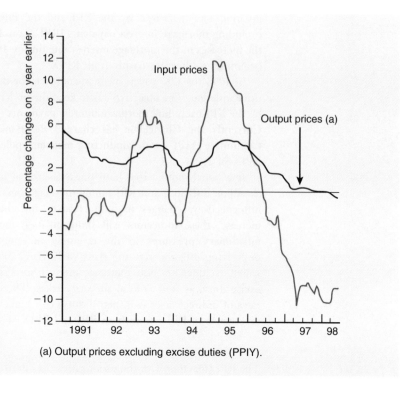

(a) Output prices excluding excise duties (PPIY).

(which has replaced the old Wholesale Price Index), for example, measures the rate of inflation before it is actually felt in the shops. This index has two parts, one giving the prices of raw materials and fuel as they enter the factory (input prices) and the other the rise in 'factory gate prices' as manufactured goods leave the factory (output prices). The main use of these two indices is to give an indication of the future trend of retail prices. The effect of the strong sterling exchange rate in 1996/97, together with the weakness in world commodity prices in the past few years, is clearly reflected in the *negative* input price inflation from mid-1996 to the present.

In contrast to the RPI, which measures movements in the prices of a 'basket' of goods bought by a representative UK household, the *GDP deflator* seeks to measure movements in the prices of the *entire basket* of goods and services produced in the UK and can in this sense be regarded as the most comprehensive price index in the economy. It is, however, less up-to-date than the other indicators and is liable to greater revision. It is obtained by dividing the GDP at current factor cost by the GDP at constant factor cost, and is sometimes called the 'implicit' deflator because it is derived in this indirect way. Between 1990 and 1998 the GDP deflator rose by 27.6% compared to 29.2% for the RPI.

EU comparisons of inflation

Harmonized indices of consumer prices (HICPs) have been calculated by EU members in order to enable more accurate comparisons as to progress towards meeting the Maastricht convergence criterion on price stability. HICPs are different from national calculations both in terms of method of calculation and coverage. For example, for the UK the RPI is calculated using the arithmetic mean, whereas the

Table 22.2 EU
harmonised indices of
consumer prices
(increase on year to
June 1998).

EU	UK	France	Germany	Greece	Italy	Netherlands	Spain	Sweden
1.6	1.7	1.1	1.0	4.9	2.1	2.2	2.0	1.4

Source: Adapted from *Labour Market Trends* (1998) Vol. 106, No. 9, September.

HICP uses the geometric mean; similarly the basket of goods and services included in the RPI does not include new car prices and air fares, both of which are included in the HICP, though around 87% of all items are common to both measures. In the UK, the HICP rose by only 1.7% in the year to June 1998, which compares with the headline RPI of 3.7% for the same period. Table 22.2 shows EU inflation measured by the HICPs.

Low inflation as a policy objective

Much of the recent debate on inflation centres around how best to defeat it. Less is heard, at least in public debate, about the actual economic costs of inflation. It is important to identify these costs and to try and quantify them, so that they can then be compared with the costs of the policies aimed at reducing inflation. These latter costs are usually seen in terms of higher unemployment, if restrictive monetary and fiscal policies are used to control inflation, or a misallocation of resources if prices and incomes policies are used. Traditionally the costs of inflation were seen in terms of its adverse effect on income distribution, as rising prices are particularly severe on those with fixed incomes, such as pensioners. However, Milton Friedman, in his Nobel lecture, shifted the focus of attention towards the adverse effects of inflation on output and employment.

In assessing the costs of inflation it is usual to distinguish two cases: that of perfectly anticipated inflation, where the rate of inflation is expected and has been taken into account in economic transactions, and that of imperfectly anticipated, or unexpected inflation. We will consider perfectly anticipated inflation first, as it provides a useful bench-mark against which to assess the more usual case of imperfectly anticipated inflation.

Perfectly anticipated inflation

Suppose we initially have an economy in which inflation is proceeding at a steady and perfectly foreseen rate, and in which all possible adjustments for the existence of inflation have been made. In this economy all contracts, interest rates, and the tax system would take the correctly foreseen rate of inflation into account. The exchange rate would also adjust to prevent inflation having any adverse effect on the balance of payments.

'Shoe-leather' costs   In such an economy the main cost of inflation would arise from the fact that interest is not normally paid on currency in circulation. The opportunity cost to the individual of holding currency would then be the interest the individual could have earned on other assets, such as deposits at the bank. Higher anticipated inflation will tend to raise interest rates and therefore the opportunity cost of holding currency, with the rational response to this being for the individual to economize on currency holdings by making more frequent trips to the bank. The costs of these extra trips to the bank are often called the 'shoe-leather' costs of inflation. Although these costs are small for low rates of inflation they have been estimated as rising to about 0.3% of GDP for perfectly anticipated inflation rates rising to around 10% per annum.

'Menu' costs   A second cost, when inflation is fully anticipated, is that of having to change prices frequently. This is sometimes called the 'menu' cost of inflation. Presumably the more rapid the inflation, the more frequently things like price tags, cash tills, vending machines and price lists have to be changed, and this takes time, effort and money.

A recent study (Bakhshi *et al.* 1997) has attempted to estimate the benefits and costs of reducing perfectly anticipated inflation in the UK by 2% (which, given the overstatement of true inflation by the RPIX, would amount to achieving price stability). The annual welfare benefits of such a reduction in inflation were estimated at around 0.21% of GDP. Of course the welfare benefits of lower inflation must be set against the lost output associated with the necessary deflation. Based on estimates of the UK 'sacrifice ratio' (the cost of cumulative lost output required for each percentage point reduction in inflation), Bakhshi calculated the annual welfare loss of such a reduction in inflation to be around 0.18% of GDP. In other words, based on his estimates, there would be a net welfare gain of 0.03% of GDP per annum as a result of policies which reduce perfectly anticipated inflation in the UK by 2%.

Further costs arise from inflation when it is either not foreseen correctly, or not adjusted to fully. It is to these additional costs from imperfectly anticipated inflation that we now turn.

Imperfectly anticipated inflation

Redistribution effects   Unanticipated inflation leads to a redistribution of income and wealth. Debtors will gain at the expense of creditors if contracts do not take inflation fully into account and those on fixed incomes will suffer. In general there is likely to be a transfer from the private to the public sector. For example, inflation causes fiscal drag, taking individuals into higher tax brackets, thereby raising tax revenue for the public sector. Inflation also reduces the real value of the national debt, with government securities maturing at specified future dates for sums that are fixed in *money* terms, so that inflation reduces the real cost to the government of redeeming them. Inflation can, in effect, be regarded as an implicit tax on the holding of cash.

Costs of decision-taking   Uncertainty about future price levels is likely to lead to a misallocation of resources. For example, such uncertainty may discourage long-term contracts. This in turn is likely to inhibit investment which by its very nature tends to be long term. Savers and lenders may react to the uncertainty about future price levels by demanding a premium to cover the perceived extra risk. This premium will push up real interest rates and again discourage investment. Capital will also be misallocated if savers and investors form different expectations of inflation and hence different views as to expected real interest rates. There is evidence to suggest that the rate of inflation and the level of uncertainty are positively correlated (see Briault 1995).

Inflation and relative price movements   In market economies, changes in relative prices act as signals which serve to guide the allocation of resource. It is argued that economic agents find it difficult to discern *relative* price movements from *general* price level movements in times of inflation, especially when the rate of inflation is uncertain. In this case incorrect decisions will be made and resources will be misallocated.

The effects of inflation on economic growth

The previous analysis suggests that inflation (and especially uncertainty surrounding the future inflation rate) will lead to a misallocation of resources and a lower rate of economic growth. Testing this hypothesis empirically is extremely complex.

One approach is to use *time-series* data for single countries. Grimes (1991) found a significant *negative* relationship for 13 countries, which implied that a sustained increase in inflation from 0% to 9% would lead to a full percentage point reduction in annual growth rates. Others have found weaker but still negative relationships. The problem with simple regression equations used in such analyses is that it is difficult to get unbiased results. Difficulties arise in interpreting the overall negative relationship between inflation and growth. For example, in most countries, at least in the short run, inflation and economic growth are likely to be positively related, as in periods of boom. It might also be the case that the negative relationship might just be picking up the effects of policy measures; for example, a period of high inflation might precipitate a deflationary policy response which would slow the growth rate. The interested reader should consult Briault (1995) for further discussion of these issues.

An alternative approach is to use *cross-country* data. One example of this is the work done by Robert Barro (1995). He looked at data for 100 countries from 1960 to 1990. His regression results indicated that an increase in average inflation of 10% points per year reduces the growth or real per capita GDP by 0.2–0.3% points per year, and lowers the ratio of investment to GDP by 0.4 to 0.6% points. Although these effects may not appear particularly large, a reduction in growth rate of the above order of magnitude (brought about by a 10% rise in the average inflation rate) would mean that after 30 years real GDP would be 4–7% lower than otherwise. This would represent an estimated £30–50 billion shortfall in GDP at current UK values of output.

Another study by Sarel (1996) suggests that the effect of inflation on growth is non-linear. He found a *structural break* in the relationship at an inflation rate of around 8%, with inflation below 8% per annum having no significant negative effects on growth, but inflation above 8% per annum having significant negative effects on growth. The suggestion here being that policy makers should always keep inflation below the level (8%) consistent with this structural break. Another implication of Sarel's study is that there is nothing particularly 'optimal' about the UK inflation target of 2.5% per annum.

Economic theory and inflation

The causes of inflation can be illustrated using the standard aggregate supply/demand framework found in most economic texts, such as Lipsey and Chrystal (1995) and Parkin *et al.* (1998). Figure 22.4 illustrates this framework. The first point

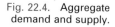

Fig. 22.4. Aggregate
demand and supply.

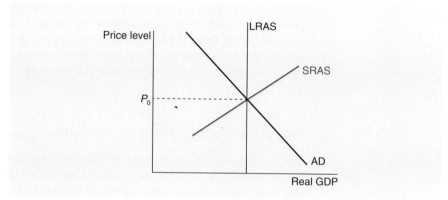

to make is that the distinction between the short-run and long-run aggregate supply curves is important.

The upward sloping *short-run aggregate supply* curve (SRAS) assumes that some input prices, particularly money wages, remain relatively fixed as the price level changes. It then follows that an increase in the price level, whilst input prices remain relatively fixed, increases the profitability of production and induces firms to expand output and employ more labour. An increase in the general price level will therefore lead, in the short run, to some increase in real GDP.

There are two explanations as to why wages may remain constant even though prices have changed. Firstly, many employees are hired under fixed-wage contracts. Once these contracts are agreed it is the firm that determines (within reason) the number of labour hours actually worked. If prices rise, the negotiated real wage will fall and firms will want to hire more labour time. Seondly, workers may not immediately be aware of price level changes, i.e. they may suffer from 'money illusion'. If workers' expectations lag behind actual price level changes, then workers will not be aware that their real wages have changed and will not adjust their wage demands appropriately. Both these reasons imply that as the price level rises, real wages will fall and the employment of extra labour hours will become more attractive to employers.

The long-run is defined as the period in which all input prices (e.g. money wages) are fully responsive to changes in the price level. Workers in the long run can gather full information on price level changes and can renegotiate wage contracts in line with higher or lower prices. It follows that in the long run, a change in the price level is likely to be associated with an equal increase in money wages, leaving the real wage unchanged and by implication leaving employment and output unchanged. The *long-run aggregate supply* curve (LRAS) is independent of the price level; in other words, it is vertical.

Because, in the long run, all wages and prices can be renegotiated in line with supply and demand, the labour market will be in equilibrium (the real wage equating labour demand and supply) at the full employment level, with unemployment at the natural rate (see Chapter 23). The level of output associated with this level of employment is variously called the *full employment* level of output or the *natural* level of output. This level of output is obviously not constant but is determined by supply-side factors, such as the labour force, the capital stock and the state of technology. Through time this full employment or natural level of output can be expected to increase as the economy grows, i.e. the vertical LRAS can be expected to shift to the right.

Demand pull inflation

One-off demand inflation Consider the case of a one-off increase in aggregate demand. The source of the increase could be an increase in the money stock, an increase in the budget deficit, or any autonomous change in consumption, investment or net exports. Whatever the cause, the aggregate demand curve AD_0 in Fig. 22.5 shifts to the right to AD_1 along the short-run aggregate supply curve $SRAS_0$. Excess demand now exists at the old price level P_0 and this pushes prices up to P_1. Such higher prices, with money wages lagging behind, increases the profitability of firms who then increase output beyond the full employment level Q_0, so that unemployment falls below the natural rate. However the new short-run equilibrium (B) with the output Q_1 is not sustainable; labour is relatively scarce and workers will negotiate money wage increases to compensate for the increase in prices. The short-run aggregate supply curve now shifts up and to the left (i.e. from $SRAS_0$ to $SRAS_1$) in response to the increased costs of production, returning the economy to a new long-run equilibrium (C).

The economy experiences a period of 'stagflation' as output falls back to its *natural* level Q_0 and the price level continues to rise to P_2. The reasons why a rise in price from P_1 to P_2 causes output to fall is usually explained in terms of rising prices reducing the real money supply, which in turn causes interest rates to rise and therefore interest-sensitive elements within aggregate demand to fall. Note that the inflation stops when the price level reaches P_2. A one-off increase in aggregate demand will not therefore generate a lasting inflation.

Continuous demand inflation Inflation proper, by which we mean a *sustained* upward movement in the price level, can only occur if the growth in aggregate demand is maintained. In this case output does *not* fall back to its natural rate but remains above it. It seems unlikely that autonomous shifts in private aggregate demand will be repeated period after period, which leaves either fiscal or monetary policy as the most likely causes of persistent demand inflation. However, expansionary fiscal policy, if funded by borrowing, is likely to lead to higher interest rates and therefore to the crowding-out of private spendings. This leaves monetary expansion as the most likely factor in turning a one-off inflation into a sustained inflation. The initial inflationary impulse could come from any demand side factor,

Fig. 22.5. A one-off increase in demand.

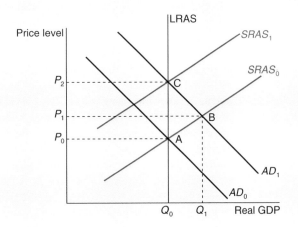

Fig. 22.6. Continuous
demand inflation.

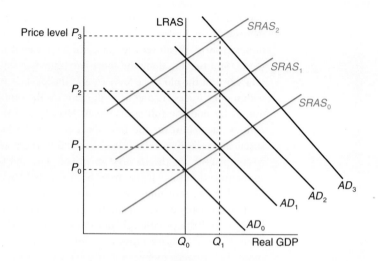

but an increase in the money supply is still necessary to prevent the price increases
from reducing the real money supply, pushing up interest rates and eventually
stopping the inflationary process. Figure 22.6 illustrates this case. As long as the
money supply is allowed to expand in line with increasing prices, the aggregate
demand curve continues to shift upward and the economy is kept above its natural
level of output Q_0. The cost of this money supply strategy, however, is continuing
inflation, with the price level rising in each time period.

Cost push inflation and supply shocks

Cost push or supply-side inflation results from an increase in costs of production
which firms pass on in the form of higher prices. The source of the cost increases
could be a rise in imported raw material costs, such as the two oil price shocks 1973–
75 and 1979–80. Alternatively, trade unions may use their market power to push
wages up irrespective of the pressure of demand in the labour market. In both these
cases one group, OPEC or unions, is using market power to try and secure a larger
share of output; firms, in response, attempt to protect their profits by increasing
prices. Figure 22.7 shows cost push/supply-side inflation.

Suppose the economy is initially in equilibrium (A) with output at the full
employment or natural rate Q_0 and the price level at P_0 with zero inflation. An
increase in oil prices then shifts $SRAS_0$, the short-run aggregate supply curve, to
$SRAS_1$. The economy now faces a period of stagflation with falling output, increased
unemployment and rising prices. The period of stagflation ends when the new short-
run equilibrium B is reached. If aggregate demand remains unchanged at AD_0 then
the excess supply in both goods and labour markets will eventually put downward
pressure on costs and wages, causing the SRAS curve to return to its original
position. This period of deflation returns the economy to its full employment
equilibrium (A). However this process is likely to be slow and painful, requiring a
major adjustment in relative prices and a fall in real wages.

Expansionary monetary policy which shifts the aggregate demand curve to AD_1
would speed up the process of returning the economy to full employment, but at the

Fig. 22.7. Cost push/
supply-side inflation.

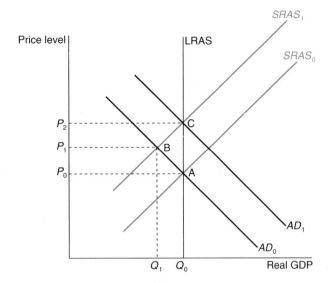

cost of additional inflation (Q_0/P_2 at point C). Indeed if the government got the
timing and strength of the demand expansion just right, the economy could move
from one long-run equilibrium to another, with very little loss of output. It is
highly unlikely, however, that the government has the appropriate information and
macroeconomic tools to stabilise output precisely at the full employment level Q_0.

Continued cost push inflation is unlikely, unless accompanied by accommodating
monetary policy. Union pressure for wage increases would be undermined by falling
output and increased unemployment, and even oil producers would eventually find that
the reduced activity of non-oil-producers would restrict their market power. Monetary
accommodation would, however, alter the story and might lead to repeated supply
shocks and continuing inflation. Unions, thwarted in their attempt to seek real wage
increases because of the higher prices associated with the monetary expansion and
without the deterrent of unemployment, might ask for wage increases in the next round,
causing the short-run aggregate supply curve to shift to the left a second time. The
choices for the government are, as before, either to allow unemployment to increase or to
accommodate the new price increases by increasing the money supply and stimulating
demand. The latter path could then lead to a continuous wage–price spiral.

There is no consensus as to the advisability of monetary accommodation of a
supply-side shock. The policy decision depends to some extent on judging the
relative costs to the state of extra unemployment against those of extra inflation. The
danger with accommodation is that once inflationary expectations become entrenched
in the wage–price setting process, they might only be eliminated after a prolonged
period of unemployment (see section on the Phillips curve).

In conclusion, the theoretical analysis of inflation indicates that the government
can always stop inflation, whether the cause is demand or supply-side factors. All the
government has to do is to halt the growth of the money supply. The bad news,
however, is that the cost of halting inflation is likely to entail a reduction in output
and a rise in unemployment.

Fig. 22.8. **The Phillips
curve.**

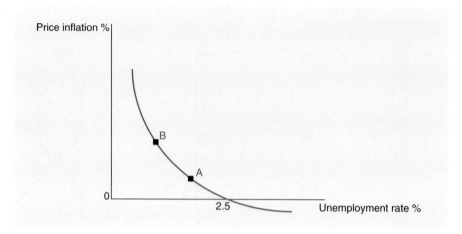

The relationship between inflation and unemployment (the Phillips curve)

Very few articles in economics have generated as much subsequent interest as A. W. Phillips' study of UK wage inflation and unemployment over the period 1861–1957. In the article (Phillips 1958) he appeared to find a stable and inverse relationship between unemployment and inflation (strictly, changes in wage rates). If unemployment was low, inflation would be high, and vice versa. The so-called Phillips curve suggested that with unemployment of around 5.5% there would be zero *wage inflation* and that with unemployment of around 2.5% the wage inflation generated would be covered by productivity growth, resulting in zero *price inflation*. This is depicted in Fig. 22.8. The relationship seemed to hold good over a long period of time and subsequent research found that it held good for many economies, and not just the UK.

The inverse relationship between inflation and unemployment was explained in terms of unemployment being an *indirect* measure of the level of excess demand in the economy. When unemployment is high and demand is low, the excess supply of labour holds wages and prices down; however when unemployment is low and demand is high, the excess demand for labour will push wages and prices up more quickly. The Phillips curve appeared to offer the policy-maker a menu of choices from which could be chosen the preferred combination of unemployment and inflation, whilst at the same time highlighting the trade-off between the two policy objectives. If the economy was, say, at point A and the government wished to reduce unemployment by expanding aggregate demand, then it could do so but only at the cost of higher inflation, as at point B. Using the previous AD/AS framework, the expansionary fiscal or monetary policy would cause the AD curve to shift to the right, so that it now intersected further along the SRAS curve, thereby causing the price level to rise. The rise in prices will then push real wages down (either because of fixed contracts or workers expectations lagging behind actual price increases), resulting in firms taking on more workers, unemployment falling and output rising. It is clear that some economists and policy-makers thought that point B could be maintained indefinitely if desired, but as we have seen and will confirm later, the existence of any such long-run trade-off (whereby a constant though higher rate of inflation can be achieved for a given fall in unemployment) is highly questionable.

Fig. 22.9. The relationship between the unemployment and inflation rates UK 1966–98.
Source: Adapted from *Labour Market Trends* (1998) Vol. 106, No. 9, September.

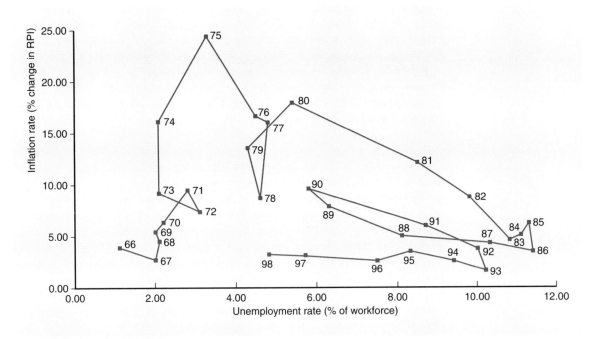

Breakdown of the Phillips curve   Evidence as to the breakdown of the Phillips curve came very soon after the 'discovery' of this relationship that had supposedly been stable for over 100 years. Figure 22.9 plots UK inflation against unemployment since 1966. Clearly the downward sloping Phillips curve is not always in evidence in the period 1966–98.

Supply-side factors.   One reason why the Phillips relationship might not be entirely stable is the existence of supply-side inflation. As we have seen, raw material prices or wage increases may push costs and prices up irrespective of the pressure of demand, at least in the short term. In this case, a given level of unemployment would be associated with higher levels of inflation than the original Phillips curve would predict. The two oil price shocks of 1973–75 and 1979–80 resulted in periods of increased inflation that were not associated with falling unemployment, as the demand-side theory would have led us to predict.

Time-period factors.   A more fundamental reason for the breakdown of the Phillips curve was proposed by Friedman (1968) and Phelps (1967). The new version of the Phillips curve makes the distinction between the short run and long run. It also assumes that markets are competitive enough in the long run to ensure that the real wage will be at the market clearing level. If this is the case, then labour supply will equal labour demand at the full employment level and unemployment will be at its natural rate. Note, however, that even when the market clears, not all workers who consider themselves to be part of the labour force will be either willing or able to accept a job at the going real wage. Some workers will be searching around for a better job offer; these are the *frictionally unemployed*, while other workers will not have the right skills or be in the right place; these are the *structurally unemployed*. The two groups together make up the *natural rate of unemployment* (NRU).

Figure 22.10 shows the market clearing or full employment real wage $(W/P)_F$ and the associated full employment level of employment (N_F); the natural rate of unemployment (NRU) is $N_1 - N_F$, the difference between the amount of labour demanded and the labour force.

Expectational factors. The final strand of the revised Phillips curve is to emphasize the role of *expectations* in the inflationary process. Friedman pointed out that what workers and firms are interested in is the *real* wages not the *money* wage. Wage bargaining takes place in money terms but when considering a money wage offer the expected inflation rate will be taken into account. The implication is that for any given level of unemployment (labour market tightness) there will be any number of possible money wage claims (for a given target real wage), depending on the expected level of inflation. As these money wage deals are passed on in price increases, it means that a given level of unemployment can be associated with any level of inflation which in turn means the existence of not just one Phillips curve but a whole family of Phillips curves, one for each expected inflation rate.

In Friedman's view, once expectations are taken into account the unemployment/inflation trade-off is only a short-term possibility. Assume that the economy is currently at the natural rate of unemployment U_n and that zero inflation has been experienced for some time and hence is expected to continue (point A in Fig. 22.11). The government attempts to increase output beyond the natural (full employment) rate by increasing the money supply. Aggregate demand shifts to the right and prices

Fig. 22.10.   The labour market.

Fig. 22.11. The
expectations-augmented
Phillips curve.

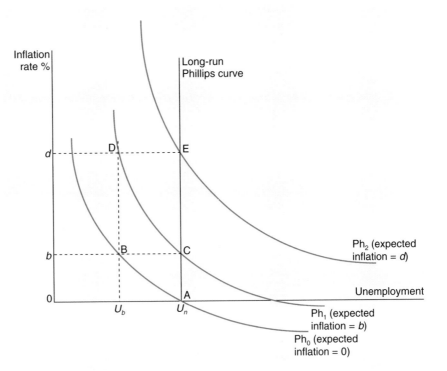

are forced up (as in Fig. 22.5 earlier). The increase in prices reduces real wages and so makes it profitable for firms to employ more labour. But why should previously unemployed labour take jobs they had previously rejected? As workers were expecting zero inflation, any money wage increase resulting from increased demand for labour will be interpreted as a *real* wage increase. As long as the money wage increase is less than the price increase, firms will be happy to employ the extra workers who have been 'fooled' into believing they have secured higher real wages by unexpectedly high inflation. Unemployment falls below the natural rate U_n to U_b, and inflation increases to b as the economy moves along the short-run Phillips curve (Ph_0) to B. (Note: this is equivalent to a movement up and to the right along the short-run aggregate supply curve in Fig. 22.5 earlier.)

If the inflation rate was to stay at b, workers would, sooner or later, adjust their inflationary expectations accordingly. Workers will then take the new and higher expected rate of inflation into account in their wage bargains. This is equivalent to the short-run aggregate supply curve shifting up and to the left, and the Phillips curve shifting up and to the right (Ph_1). The economy will now be at C, with unemployment and output falling back to their natural rates and with actual and expected inflation equal to b. In other words C is a long-run equilibrium possibility, with an inflation rate constant at b.

Suppose, however, that the government wishes to return unemployment to U_b. It must then increase the growth of the money supply more rapidly, so that actual inflation again exceeds expected inflation. If the government does do this the economy will move along the new short-run Phillips curve to point D. As before this short-run equilibrium cannot be maintained because expectations will again catch up with actual inflation, and the economy will then move to E as the short-run Phillips curve again shifts upwards (Ph$_2$). At E the economy is once more in long-run equilibrium, with expected and actual inflation equal and the inflation rate constant at d.

Several interesting conclusions can be drawn from this modern view of the Phillips curve.

- There is a short-run trade between unemployment and inflation but no long-run one.
- Any rate of inflation is consistent with long-run equilibrium, all that is required is that *expected* inflation should equal *actual* inflation.
- Attempts to push unemployment below the natural rate will result in accelerating inflation. In fact the natural rate of unemployment is sometimes known as the non-accelerating inflation rate of unemployment (NAIRU).
- Once inflationary expectations have become embedded in the system, a period of unemployment above the natural rate is required in order to lower the inflation rate. A movement down a given short-run Phillips curve to a level of unemployment above the natural rate will result in actual inflation being below expected inflation, leading to a downward revision of expectations, and hence decelerating inflation.

New Classical and New Keynesian views

Economists subscribing to either of these schools of thought would probably agree with the above distinction between the long-run and short-run Phillips curve. The disagreement would be over the length of the short run. In the Friedman view, expectations catch up with actual inflation over several time periods as economic agents *adapt* or adjust their expectations by some proportion of the error they made in the previous period.

New classical economists argue that using adaptive expectations is not rational in that it does not take into account all the relevant information available when forecasting next period's inflation. If all relevant information, including the government's monetary stance, is considered, there is no reason why expectations should lag behind actual inflation for any length of time. In addition, if prices and wages are extremely flexible in the short run, then there is no reason why the economy should move away from the long-run (natural) equilibrium level of employment or output. In this case the economy would move directly from A to C as a result of a monetary expansion that was anticipated. Only unanticipated policy impulses could drive a wedge between actual and anticipated inflation and hence influence short-run output and employment.

New Keynesians argue that an equilibrium position on the short-run Phillips curve can last for much longer because of the stickiness of wages and prices. Wage contracts often last for a year or more and cannot quickly be adjusted, even if expectations are rational and correct.

One important policy implication of the difference of views concerns how quickly the government can squeeze inflation out of the system. New classical economists would argue that if the government *announces* its commitment to lower inflation and if the government can establish the credibility of its declared policy, then economic agents will expect lower inflation, will quickly adjust their wage and price contracts, and lower inflation will very quickly follow without the need for unemployment to move above the natural rate. New Keynesians argue that because of downward stickiness of prices and wages, a long period of above-equilibrium unemployment is required before the adjustments are made.

Evidence from the UK seems to favour the New Keynesian view in that, despite public targets for the money supply, it took a prolonged and deep recession to reduce inflation in the early 1980s. Between 1980 and 1983 inflation fell from 18.0% to 4.6%, but unemployment rose from 6.4% to 12.5%.

UK inflationary experience

The worst inflationary episode experienced in the UK in recent history was in the mid 1970s. Inflation as measured by the RPI rose from 7.1% in 1972 to 24.2% in 1975. At the time many commentators laid the blame for the acceleration in the inflation rate at the door of OPEC, as oil prices had quadrupled in the aftermath of the Yom Kippur war and the subsequent oil embargo. However, as can be seen from Fig. 22.11, the UK economy had been growing very rapidly in the previous two years. The Autumn of 1971 had seen the beginning of a major expansion of the money supply as a result of the relaxation of controls on bank lending. In the following year the expansionary budget of the then Chancellor, Barber, injected further demand into the system at a time when the world economy was also booming as a result of US expenditure on the Vietnam War (US budget deficits led to an increase in the world money supply then linked to dollar availability).

In terms of our theoretical model this can be seen as a shift to the right in the aggregate demand curve which now intersects further along the short-run aggregate supply curve. The result was output was pushed beyond the full employment level and the inflation rate was given an upward boost. Our analysis tells us that even without the adverse supply shock of the oil price increase (crop failures meant that other commodity prices were also increasing at this time) prices would rise further and output would fall as the short-run aggregate supply curve shifted to the left under revised inflationary expectations. The adverse supply shocks further accelerated this shift, causing not only increased inflation but falling output in 1974/75, as can clearly be seen from Fig. 22.12. The resulting stagflation was further reinforced by the effects of tighter monetary controls introduced in late 1973.

A second inflationary episode occurred in the late 1970s when inflation rose from 8% in 1978 to over 18% in 1980. Again this period was marked by adverse supply shocks, including the doubling of oil prices and increases in wage costs, the latter being the result of a catching-up process after a period of wage controls. One difference from the previous bout of inflation was that the supply shocks were not preceded to any great extent by prior demand pressures. Unemployment in 1978 at 4.6% was more than twice the 1973 rate. The adverse supply shocks, together with the tighening of both monetary and fiscal policy in late 1979, led to a further period of stagflation (see Fig. 22.12). One further complication at the time was that the UK was now itself a major oil producer and this, together with the tight monetary policy, caused both a nominal and real appreciation of sterling. The appreciation of sterling helped moderate the inflationary pressures but contributed to the severity of the recession.

The third and final inflationary episode was, like the first, associated with excess demand in the economy. Financial liberalization, a relaxation of monetary policy, rising asset prices, tax cutting budgets in 1987 and 1988, growing consumer confidence and buoyant world demand, all conspired to push aggregate demand beyond the full employment level. In fact GDP was around 6% *above* its potential full employment level during this period (compare this with the current situation in 1996

Fig. 22.12.   UK price level and real output 1972–98.
Source: Economic Trends (various).

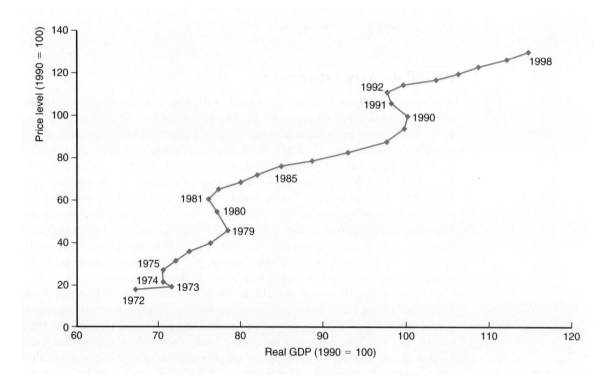

where output is estimated to be 2% *below* its potential). The excess demand pushed the RPI up to an annual rate of 10.9% by September 1990. Action to curtail the inflation rate was taken in late 1988 when monetary policy was tightened and interest rates increased. Entry into the ERM in 1990 also provided real exchange-rate discipline and meant that interest rates had to be kept higher, and for longer, than internal conditions probably required. The resulting recession pushed unemployment up above the natural rate and inflation subsided to below 2% by 1993.

The recession ended in 1992 and since then unemployment has fallen, whilst wage and price inflation has remained very low, leading some economists to question whether the nature of the UK labour market has changed. This issue will be discussed in Chapter 23.

Inflation targets   In recent years inflation policy, in several countries, has changed in its emphasis. Instead of using *intermediate policy targets* such as the money supply or the exchange rate to achieve price stability, the emphasis has moved towards the use of *explicit inflation targets*. Following the example of New Zealand and Canada, several European countries including the UK have adopted these inflation targets. In the UK, for example, the current inflation target is that the RPIX should average 2.5% or less over the medium term. The reason for the adoption of inflation targets seems to be disillusionment with monetary aggregates (Canada) or with exchange rates (Sweden) or with both (the UK).

The advantage of using explicit inflation tartgets, it is claimed, are that they act as an anchor for monetary policy and that they reduce the potential for inflationary bias in discretionary monetary policy (see King 1995).

Anchor for monetary policy   Because of the well-known time-lags inherent in monetary policy it is necessary to forecast inflation up to two years ahead. The Bank of England takes many variables into account when making its inflation projection, for example monetary aggregates, exchange rates, asset prices, price expectations, measures of activity and fiscal policy. The inflationary assessment in turn influences monetary policy. Essentially, if expected inflation is above the target then monetary policy will be tightened; and if expected inflation is below the target then monetary policy will be relaxed.

Reduced potential for inflational bias   Because targets are set and monitored this naturally leads to more openness and transparency in the policy making process. The UK has gone some way along this path, as can be seen by the publication of the Bank of England's quarterly *Inflation Reports* as well as the publication of the minutes of the monthly meetings of the Monetary Policy Committee (MPC). King (1995) argues that this has improved not only the quality of the public debate on monetary policy but also the information available to the public. Setting an inflation target raise the importance placed on inflation stabilization by the authorities, and so reduces the attractiveness of short-run output gains from any inflation 'surprise'. Not only will the reputation of the authorities be diminished but also, because of the increased transparency, economic agents will quickly spot any short-sightedness and revise upwards their inflationary expectations. The overall result is that there is less incentive to stimulate economies excessively in the first instance.

The introduction of an inflation target (goal) has introduced a distinction in policy making between goal independence and instrument independence. The government sets the goal and the Monetary Policy Committee of the Bank of England sets the

Table 22.3   Inflation and growth in countries with inflation targets.

	Decade preceding inflation target		Period following inflation target		Decade preceding inflation target		Period following inflation target	
	Average rate of inflation	Variance	Average rate of inflation	Variance	Average rate of GDP growth	Variance	Average rate of GDP growth	Variance
Australia	6.2	8.4	2.7	1.7	3.2	10.2	4.2	1.0
Canada	5.8	7.9	2.0	2.5	2.8	10.0	1.9	3.1
Finland	5.2	3.4	1.1	0.5	1.4	17.3	3.2	6.5
Sweden	6.6	6.7	2.3	2.3	1.6	4.7	1.9	5.1
New Zealand	11.6	25.7	2.5	2.7	1.8	7.0	2.4	7.8
UK	5.2	2.2	2.8	0.1	2.4	5.7	3.0	1.0
Average	6.8	9.0	2.2	1.6	2.2	9.2	2.8	4.1

Note: A lower variance implies less dispersion, i.e. a more *stable* value for that variable.
Source: Adapted from King (1997).

interest rate so as to achieve that goal. The Bank of England now has to operate with 'constrained discretion' in that it has to meet the 2.5% target, rather than with unfettered discretion.

It is probably too early to judge the success of this process of setting inflation targets and seeking to achieve them. However, the evidence from a number of countries (Table 22.3) does suggest that lower and more stable inflation rates can be achieved by setting inflation targets. Rather than inhibiting growth, such targets seem to have resulted in higher and more stable economic growth.

The National Minimum Wage and prices

The introduction of the National Minimum Wage in April 1999 is likely to have some impact on the inflation rate. It is estimated that 1.9m workers will be directly affected in terms of having a real wage increase, of which around 66% will be women. Of those directly affected, an increase of one-third in wages is expected on average, whereas others will be indirectly affected via attempts to restore wage differentials. The international evidence surveyed by the OECD suggests that minimum wages tend to compress earnings distributions, i.e. any pressure to restore wage differentials has little effect. Of course other factors may also influence the impact of the minimum wage on inflation, such as the degree of compliance by UK firms, the extent to which the minimum wage is increased in line with inflation, etc. The MPC of the Bank of England estimates that the likely effect will be to raise the overall wage bill by around 0.5%, with an equivalent rise in inflation of around 0.5% (see also Chapter 15).

Key points

- The RPI measures movement in the prices of a 'basket' of goods and services bought by a representative UK household.
- Items with higher income elasticities of demand (e.g. housing, leisure services, catering) are being given increasing weights in the calculation of the RPI.
- The RPI is linked back to January 1987 = 100 as base. With an RPI of 163.4 in June 1998, this indicates that average retail prices have risen by 63.4% since January 1987.
- RPIX is RPI *excluding* mortgage interest payments.
- RPIY is RPI *excluding* mortgage interest payments and indirect taxes.
- The GDP deflator seeks to measure changes in the prices of the *entire basket* of goods and services produced in the UK. It is found by dividing GDP at current factor cost by GDP at constant factor cost.
- The modern view of the Phillips curve is that there is a short-run trade off between unemployment and inflation, but no long-run trade off.
- Attempts to push unemployment below the *natural rate* will result in accelerating inflation.
- This natural rate of unemployment is sometimes known as the Non-Accelerating Inflation Rate of Unemployment (NAIRU).
- The government sets the inflation target and the Monetary Policy Committee (MPC) changes interest rates in trying to meet that target.
- There is evidence that setting an inflation target may itself help to reduce inflation without inhibiting growth.

Notes

1. If the price of an item in the index was 10p in January (P_0) and 12p in February (P_1) then the price relative would be 12/10 $(P_1)/(P_0)$ and this would then be multiplied by the weight (W) for that item. The index for period 1 (where period $0 = 100$) is given by $[\Sigma(P_1 \times W)/\Sigma(P_0 \times W)] \times 100$.

2. For example, if the index for January 1998 based on January 1995 was 120, and the index for July 1999 based on January 1998 was 110, then the July 1999 index, based on January 1995 = 100, would be calculated as follows: $120 \times 110/100 = 132$.

References and further reading

Bakhshi, H., Haldane, A. and Hatch, N. (1997) Some costs and benefits of price stability in the UK, *Bank of England Quarterly Bulletin*, 37, 3, August.

Barclays Bank Economic Review (1992) February.

Barro, R. (1995) Inflation and economic growth, *Bank of England Quarterly Bulletin*, 35, 2, May.

Briault, C. (1995) The costs of inflation, *Bank of England Quarterly Bulletin*, 35, 1, February.

Cunningham, A. (1996) Measurement bias in price indices: an application to the UK's RPI, *Bank of England Working Paper*, No. 47.

Friedman, M. (1968) The role of monetary policy, *American Economic Review*, 58, March.

Friedman, M. (1977) Inflation and unemployment, *Journal of Political Economy*, 85, 3.

Grimes, A. (1991) The effects of inflation on growth: some international evidence, *Weltwirtschaftliches Archive*, 127.

King, M. (1995) Do inflation targets work? *Bank of England Quarterly Bulletin*, 35, 4, November.

King, M. (1997) The inflation target five years on, *Bank of England Quarterly Bulletin*, 37, 4, November, speech by Mervyn King.

Lipsey, R. and Chrystal, K. (1995) *Positive Economics*, Oxford University Press.

Parkin, M., Powell, M. and Matthews, K. (1998) *Economics*, Addison Wesley Longman, London.

Phelps, E. S. (1967) Phillips curves, expectations of inflation and optimal unemployment over time, *Economica*, 34, August.

Phillips, A. W. (1958) The relation between unemployment and the rate of change of money wage rates in the United Kingdom, *Economica*, 25, November.

Sarel, M. (1996) Nonlinear effects of inflation on economic growth, *IMF Staff Papers*, 43, 1, March.

Soteri, S. and Westaway, P. (1993) Explaining price inflation in the UK: 1971–92, *National Institute Economic Review*, No. 144, May.

Wadhwani, M. L. (1984) Wage inflation in the United Kingdom, *Economica*, 52.

Chapter 23

Unemployment

In his conclusion to *The General Theory of Employment, Interest and Money,* Keynes wrote that 'it may be possible by a right analysis of the problem to cure the disease [of unemployment] whilst preserving efficiency and freedom' (Keynes 1936). The commitment to high and stable levels of unemployment of successive UK governments and the actual achievement of low rates of unemployment appeared to support Keynes' proposition, at least as far as unemployment was concerned. Indeed, in the 20 years after the Second World War the unemployment rate rarely exceeded 2%. This 'golden age', however, ended in the late 1960s and under the influence of two oil shocks during the 1970s and subsequent deflationary policy responses, unemployment in the UK rose to over 3 million by the mid-1980s, i.e. some 11% of the workforce. Although unemployment in the UK has fallen since then to its present level of around 5%, the 1990s average for the European Union has still exceeded 10% of the workforce. It appears that Keynes might have been over optimistic in his prediction. In this chapter we look at the methods of counting the unemployed and at who the unemployed are. We then consider the contribution of economic theory to the issue of unemployment before concluding with an attempt to identify those policies that might lead the economy in the direction of higher employment.

Unemployment in the UK

It could be argued that the adoption, after the Second World War, of Keynesian demand-management policies secured nearly two decades of historically low unemployment (see Fig. 23.1). In recent years, however, although government commitment to full employment (first stated in the 1944 White Paper on employment policy) has never been revoked, we no longer appear to have the tools with which to do the job. The traditional reliance on macroeconomic policies as a means of reducing unemployment has largely been replaced by a greater emphasis on microeconomic supply-side measures that take into account the changing nature of the labour market, society and the global economy. Labour market reforms of this type during the 1980s and 1990s and measures such as the 'New Deal' of the incoming Labour

Fig. 23.1. UK unemployment rate 1881–1998 (excluding school-leavers). *Sources: Labour Market Trends* (1998); London and Cambridge Economic Service (1967).

Rates (per cent)

Note: Vertical dotted lines indicate beginning of new series

government's have, however, resulted in a UK unemployment rate that compares favourably with our EU partners. Nevertheless, the UK unemployment rate is still twice as high as it was in the 1950s and 1960s and there is an uneasy feeling that this period of very low unemployment may prove to have been the exception rather than the rule!

Before attempting to assess the causes of high unemployment, and to consider what, if anything, can be done, it is important to examine the unemployment statistics themselves to see what light they shed on the issue.

Methods of measuring unemployment

There are two basic approaches to collecting the information from which to compile unemployment statistics.

(i) Survey method   One method is to conduct *surveys* specifically designed to provide information about the labour force. The UK government's quarterly Labour Force Survey (LFS) uses the International Labour Office (ILO) definition of unemployment: people without a job who were available to start work within the next two weeks and who had either looked for work within the four weeks prior to interview or who were waiting to start a job. For example, survey results for the 61,000 households interviewed in Spring 1998 showed that ILO unemployment in the UK was 1.81m, a fall of 277,000 over Spring 1997. This corresponded to an ILO unemployment rate of 6.3% in Spring 1998, defined as being the percentage of economically active people (the employed plus the ILO unemployed) who are unemployed on the ILO measure.

One advantage of the LFS in using the internationally standardized ILO definition of unemployment, is that inter-country comparisons can be easily made (see later). The major disadvantages of the LFS are the costs involved, the time taken to process and publish the data and the possibility of sampling and response errors.

As a result the UK government also uses *administrative records* to provide a second, alternative method, giving more up-to-date unemployment figures.

(ii) Claimant count method   The monthly *claimant count* (provided by the Benefits Agency) is the number of people who are claiming Jobseekers Allowance (JSA) or National Insurance credits on the day of the count. Recipients of the JSA must declare that although they are out of work, they are capable of, available for and actively seeking work during the week in which the claim is made. The results are usually published within five weeks, providing details on the level and duration of unemployment in relatively small geographical areas. Using this method the June 1998 claimant count was 1.34 million, a fall of 268,000 over the previous year. This corresponds to a claimant count unemployment rate of 4.8% in June 1998, defined as being the percentage of the workforce (number of employees + self-employed + HM forces + government-supported trainees) who are claimants on this measure.

Unfortunately, however, because the claimant count is based on the administrative system used to pay benefits, it is highly susceptible to changes in the rules governing people's eligibility for benefit. There have been around thirty changes since 1979, all but one of which have served to reduce the official unemployment claimant count. For example, it has been estimated that the change in benefit entitlement rules associated with the introduction of the JSA in 1996 removed between 100–200,000 claimants from the count compared with what might have been expected at the same point in the labour market cycle. Indeed, the Royal Statistical Society has suggested that the claimant count is 'very unsatisfactory as a measure of global unemployment'. Many regard the Labour Force Survey as providing a more complete measure of unemployment (under the ILO definition) than the claimant count method, especially as regards women who often do not qualify for benefit and therefore do not appear in the claimant count. Figure 23.2 compares the two measures.

Disaggregating unemployment statistics

Further insight can be gained by breaking down the total unemployment figures into a number of components as follows.

Regional unemployment   One feature of the unemployment pattern, at least until the latest recession, was the great disparity between regions. This regional problem is by no means a new one; away from the South and the Midlands unemployment has been well above the national average for over fifty years. In June 1998, when the UK average claimant count unemployment rate was 4.8%, Northern Ireland had 7.7% unemployment, Merseyside 9.4%, Wales 5.6%, the North of England 7.4% and Scotland 5.7%, whereas in the Eastern region it was 5.4% and in the South-East 2.8%.

Traditionally the explanation of such regional variation has been in terms of the depressed regions being over-reliant upon declining industries such as coal, textiles and shipbuilding. A study by Fothergill and Gudgin (1982) suggests that this *was* true until the mid-1960s, but that since then the main problem seems to be of regions, such as the North and Scotland, being dragged down by the fact that they have a disproportionate number of big cities in which unemployment is particularly high. In other parts of these regions unemployment trends are not so bad, but what is

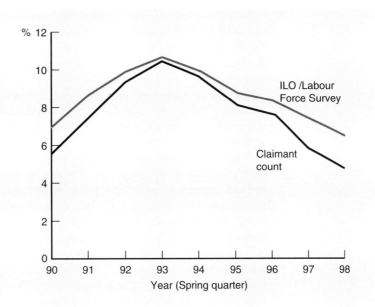

Fig. 23.2. ILO Labour
Force Survey and
claimant count measures
of the unemployment
rate (%).
*Source: Labour Market
Trends* (various).

happening throughout the UK is a massive shift of jobs from the cities to the smaller towns and rural areas on a scale that swamps most other trends in industrial location. Fothergill and Gudgin suggest that the main cause of this trend is the shortage of space in urban areas, with factories becoming less profitable than their rural counterparts because so many operate in unsuitable, old-fashioned buildings, with production organized less efficiently on more than one floor.

In the period following the recession of the early 1990s it appeared that the previously substantial variations in regional unemployment rates had largely disappeared. Indeed the Bank of England (1997) argued that the variation in regional unemployment rates was only half of what it had been 20 years earlier. Several reasons were offered for this, including the sharp downturn in the service sector and the collapse in house prices hitting the previously more prosperous regions of the South and South-East. It has also been argued that greater flexibility in the labour market has increased regional pay dispersion (e.g. the coefficient of variation in regional pay had risen to twice the level of the 1970s), with the result that employees in the less favourable regions may have priced themselves back into jobs. Such an observed narrowing of regional unemployment rates may, however, have only been temporary. The recovery in the housing market in the mid-1990s together with the rapid growth in sectors such as telecommunications, computers and financial services, all of which are better represented in the South and South-East, seem once more to have opened up a regional unemployment divide.

Finally it is worth noting that unemployment rates vary *within* regions more than they do *between* regions. For example, the Eastern region claimant count unemployment rate was 3.4% in 1998, yet within this region Cambridge had an unemployment rate of only 2.4% whereas Lowestoft had an unemployment rate as high as 8.9%.

Female unemployment   Whilst the overall employment rate in the UK has remained fairly constant at around 75% over the last 30 years, the *participation rate* of females has increased dramatically, from 57% in 1971 to 70% in 1998. The increasing flexibility of the UK labour market has helped the growth in female employment to take place. For example part-time working, mainly by women, has increased to about 25% of the workforce and in most cases (7 out of 8) the decision to work part-time is 'voluntary' in the sense that it is preferred to full-time working. Self-employment has also doubled in number over the same time period and many women are represented in this group.

The ILO unemployment rate for women was measured at only 5.4% in Spring 1998 compared to 6.9% for men. The UK is unusual within the EU in having its unemployment rate for females below that for males. Nevertheless there are still at least two areas of concern. First, the unemployment rate of single mothers has been rising; in 1998 almost 22% of workless households consisted of one adult (mainly female) with children under 16, much higher than the 13% recorded in 1984. Second, there is evidence to suggest that a disproportionate number of female jobs have gone to women whose husbands are already employed. This has led to a growing polarisation between work-rich households with both partners employed and work-poor households with neither partner employed.

Age-related unemployment   The unemployment rate in the UK amongst young people of working age is particularly high, though the duration of these periods of unemployment tends to be relatively short for most individuals. Where young people do spend long periods out of work, evidence suggests that the damage done can have a significantly negative impact on later labour market performance. Although the rate of 'youth unemployment' in the UK is less than the EU average, it is higher than in Germany, the Netherlands, Denmark and Austria. Table 23.1 indicates that the unemployment rate tends to decline with age; for example only 4.3% of those aged 35–49 years were unemployed in Spring 1998 compared to 18.2% for those aged 16–17 years.

However, these older workers who *do* become unemployed are particularly prone to long spells of unemployment. The long-term unemployed (a year or more) are disproportionately older, disproportionately male and disproportionately low skilled. Such *long-term unemployment* destroys skills and motivation and is often used by employers as an unfavourable filtering device, leading to the stark statistic that those workers who are still unemployed after two years stand only a 50% chance of leaving unemployment for a job within the following year. Table 23.2 indicates that 52.5% of the unemployed aged 50 and over had been unemployed for a year or more, compared to only 19.8% of the unemployed aged 18–24 years. The government's strategy towards both youth and long-term unemployment in the UK is discussed later in the chapter.

Table 23.1   ILO unemployment rates (%) by age.

UK	16–17	18–24	25–34	35–49	50–64 (m) 50–59 (f)
1992 Spring	17.9	15.8	10.4	7.3	8.4
1998 Spring	18.2	11.9	6.3	4.3	4.9

Source: Adapted from *Labour Market Trends* (1998) May.

Table 23.2 **Percentage of ILO unemployed out of work for a year or more, by age.**

UK	18–24	25–49	50 and over
1992 Spring	28.0	37.4	48.3
1998 Spring	19.8	36.4	52.5

Source: Adapted from *Labour Market Trends* (1998) May.

Qualifications and unemployment The demand for low-skilled and poorly educated workers has been declining throughout the OECD since the early 1980s, whereas the demand for skilled workers has outstripped the supply. The overall result is that the employment prospects and wages of poorly educated and unskilled workers have deteriorated relative to those for better educated and skilled workers. For example 33% of men aged 25–49 years with no qualifications are currently out of work, but this is true of only 5% of such men with a university degree. Similarly the wage gap between men aged 25–49 years with no qualifications and those with a university degree was 61% in 1979, but this gap had increased to 89% in 1998.

Ethnic unemployment One final area of inequality in unemployment statistics concerns its ethnic make-up (Fig. 23.3). As the unemployment rate for each group expresses the unemployed as a proportion of the 'total economically active' *for that group*, it reflects to some extent the differing age structure within ethnic groups; those groups with higher proportions of both older and younger people tending to have a higher unemployment rate. Even so, people of ethnic minority origins were more likely to be unemployed than whites of the same age-group, sex and educational qualifications. For example, in 1996 the unemployment rate for men aged 25–44 with qualifications higher than 'A' level was 4% for white males, but 14% for ethnic minority males.

Fig. 23.3. **ILO unempolyment rates by ethnic origin.** *Source:* Adapted from Labour Force Survey (1996), Spring.

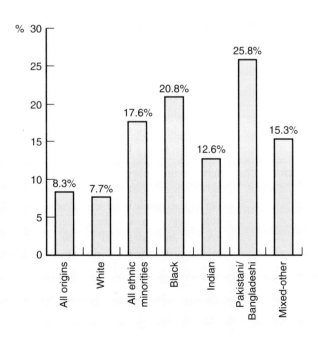

Table 23.3 Comparative
unemployment rates (%)
(standardised).
Source: Adapted from
OECD (1998) *Economic
Outlook,* June.

	1969–73	1974–79	1980–85	1986	1990	1992	1994	1996	1998
UK	3.4	5.0	10.5	11.2	7.1	10.1	9.6	8.2	6.3
USA	4.9	6.7	8.0	6.9	5.4	7.5	6.1	5.4	4.5
France	2.5	4.5	8.3	10.4	8.9	10.3	12.3	12.1	11.9
Germany*	0.8	3.2	5.9	6.5	4.9	4.6	9.6	10.3	9.7
Japan	1.2	1.9	2.4	2.8	2.1	2.2	2.9	3.3	4.0
Sweden	2.2	1.9	2.8	2.7	1.8	5.9	9.8	10.0	8.3
OECD	3.3	4.9	7.5	7.7	6.0	7.5	7.9	7.7	7.1
EEC/EU	2.9	4.8	9.3	10.3	7.9	9.6	11.6	11.4	10.1

*Germany – up to end 1990 W. Germany; from 1991 the whole of Germany.

International comparisons

Table 23.3 shows recent unemployment rates in selected countries. All of these countries, apart from Japan and Sweden, experienced high and rapidly rising average unemployment over the period to the mid-1980s. The consensus explanation, outlined in more detail in later sections, was that this was a result of the adverse oil price shocks of 1973–74 and 1979–80 together with the pursuit of tight monetary and fiscal policies aimed at eliminating inflation. The rise in unemployment in the late 1970s was, however, much sharper in the UK than in most other countries.

Although the unemployment rates have been standardized to allow for differences in national definitions care must be taken in making simple comparisons. Different countries' figures reflect different labour market practices. For example, the low Japanese rate is partly the result of the jobs for life agreement between firms and workers. This system leads to a certain amount of disguised unemployment.

Unemployment and economic theory

The traditional way of analysing the unemployment problem has been to try and identify the various types of unemployment by cause, this being seen as the first step towards formulating appropriate policy. Economists often distinguish between frictional, structural, classical and demand-deficiency (Keynesian) unemployment. Some would argue that a further type of unemployment should be distinguished, namely technological unemployment. We now consider each 'type' in more detail.

Frictional unemployment

Frictional unemployment results from the time it takes workers to move between jobs. It is a consequence of short-run changes in the labour market that constantly occur in a dynamic economy. Workers who leave their jobs to search for better ones require time because of the imperfections in the labour market. For example, workers are never fully aware of all the possible jobs, wages and other elements in the remuneration package, so that the first job a worker is offered is unlikely to be the one for which he or she is best suited. It is rational, therefore, for workers to spend time familiarizing themselves with the job market even though there will be costs involved in this search, namely lost earnings, postage, telephone calls, etc. These 'search' costs can, however, be seen from the workers' point of view as an investment, the gain being higher future income. In principle, the economy should also gain from this search behaviour, through higher productivity as workers find jobs that are more appropriate to their skills.

Any measures that reduce the search time will reduce the amount of frictional unemployment. Improving the transmission of job information, permitting workers to acquire knowledge of the labour market more quickly, is one such measure. A more controversial issue is how the level of unemployment benefit affects search time. It could be argued that by reducing the workers' cost of searching, increased unemployment benefit will lead to more search activity and a higher level of frictional unemployment. On the other hand, a reduction in unemployment benefit, though perhaps leading (via less search) to lower frictional unemployment, could also lead to a less efficient allocation of resources, with workers having to take the first job that comes along regardless of how appropriate it was to their skills.

Structural unemployment

Structural unemployment arises from longer-term changes in the structure of the economy, resulting in changes in the demand for, and supply of, labour in specific industries, regions and occupations. It could be caused by changes in the comparative cost position of an industry or a region, by technological progress or by changes in the pattern of final demand. Examples of structural unemployment are not difficult to find for the UK economy and might include shipbuilding, textile, steel and motor-vehicle workers, i.e. workers in manufacturing industries where the UK has largely lost its comparative advantage over other countries (e.g. newly industrialized countries). On the other hand, the emerging unemployment in the printing industry and in clerical occupations has more to do with technological progress, which enables information to be processed, stored and retrieved more quickly, so that fewer people are required per unit of output (see below). Yet again, structural unemployment may be due to a shift in demand away from an established product, as with the decline of the coal industry following the move to gas fired power stations.

The structurally unemployed are therefore people who are available for work, but whose skills and locations do not match those of unfilled vacancies. Structural unemployment is likely to reach high levels if the rate of decline for a country's traditional products is rapid and if the labour market adjusts slowly to such changes. Indeed, adjustments are likely to be slow since they are costly to make. From the workers' point of view it may require retraining in new skills and relocation, whilst from the firms' point of view it often means abandoning their familiar products and processes and investing in new and often untried ones. This process of adjustment is, of course, easier the more buoyant the economy.

At a broader level, one of the most important issues facing developed countries is whether they will be able to generate enough output to finance the necessary increase in service occupations required to absorb those released by the manufacturing sector. Whilst manufacturing accounted for 30.1% of employment in the EU in 1970, it only accounted for 26.6% in 1996, and most forecasts see this structural trend continuing (see Chapter 1). In Great Britain, for example, employment in manufacturing fell by 28% between 1979 and 1996. The way in which the developed world manages this structural transition over the medium term will be one of the key determinants of future levels of employment.

New technologies have substantially raised output per unit of *labour input* (labour productivity) and per unit of *factor input*, both labour and capital (total factor productivity). There has been much concern that the impact of these productivity gains has been to reduce jobs, i.e. to create technological unemployment. We now consider the principles which will in fact determine whether or not jobs will be lost (or gained) as a result of technological change.

Higher output per unit of factor input reduces costs of production, provided only that wage rates and other factor price increases do not absorb the whole of productivity gain. Computer-controlled machine tools are a case in point. Data from Renault show that the use of DNC machine tools resulted in machining costs one-third less than those of general-purpose machine tools at the same level of output. Lower costs will cause the profit-maximizing firm to lower price and raise output under most market forms, as in Fig. 23.4. A downward shift of the average cost curve, via the new technologies, lowers the marginal cost curve from MC_1 to MC_2. The profit-maximizing price/output combination ($MC = MR$) now changes from P_1/Q_1 to P_2/Q_2. Price has fallen, output has risen.

The dual effect on employment of higher output per unit of labour (and capital) input can usefully be illustrated from Fig. 23.4. The curve $Q = F(N)$ is the familiar production function of economic theory, showing how output (Q) varies with labour input (N), capital and other factors assumed constant. On the one hand the higher labour productivity from technical change shifts the production function outwards to the dashed line $Q' = F(N)$. The original output Q_1 can now be produced with less labour, i.e. with only N_2 labour input instead of N_1 as previously. On the other hand, the cost and price reduction has so raised demand that more output is required. We now move along the new production function Q' until we reach Q_2 output, which requires N_3 labour input. In our example the reduction in labour required per unit output has been more than compensated for by the expansion of output, via lower price. Employment has, in fact, risen from N_1 to N_3.

This analysis highlights a number of points on which the final employment outcome for a firm adopting the new techniques will depend:

1. The relationship between new technology and labour productivity, i.e. the extent to which the production function Q shifts outwards.
2. The relationship between labour productivity and cost, i.e. the extent to which the marginal cost curve shifts downwards.
3. The relationship between cost and price, i.e. the extent to which cost reductions are passed on to consumers as lower prices.
4. The relationship between lower price and higher demand, i.e. the price elasticity of the demand curve.

Suppose, for instance, that the new process *halved* labour input per unit output! If this increase in labour productivity (1 above), reduces cost (2 above), and price (3 above), and output *doubled* (4 above), then the same total labour input would be required. If output more than doubled, then more labour would be employed. The magnitude of the four relationships above will determine whether the firm offers the same, more, or less employment after technical change in the production process.

Although a more detailed treatment must be sought elsewhere, there is in fact a fifth relationship crucial to the final employment outcome. Namely, the extent to which any higher total factor productivity arising from a technological innovation can be separately attributed to capital or to labour. An innovation is said to be capital

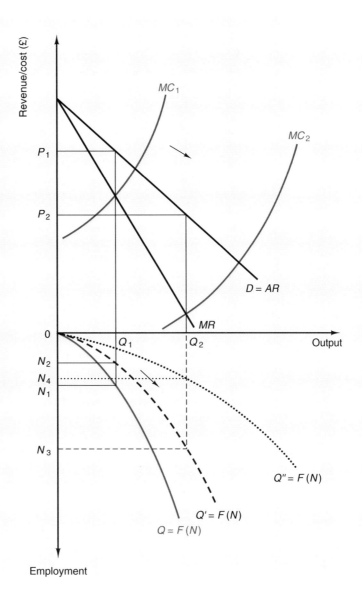

Fig. 23.4. Technical change and the level of employment.

saving when the marginal product of capital rises relative to that of labour, and labour saving when the converse applies. This whole issue is surrounded by problems of concept and measurement. We can, however, use Fig. 23.4 above to present the outline of the argument.

Suppose we take the dashed line $Q' = F(N)$ to represent a situation in which the new technology is capital saving (with only a small rise in labour productivity), so that the new and higher output Q_2 requires considerable extra labour to produce it (N_3 employment). If on the other hand the new technology were labour saving (with a substantial rise in labour productivity), then the new dotted line $Q'' = F(N)$ in Fig. 23.4 would be more appropriate. Output Q_2 would now only require employment N_4. The prospects for higher employment would therefore appear more favourable when innovations are capital saving, raising the marginal product of capital relative to that of labour.

Broadly speaking, the scenario most favourable to employment would be where a small increase in (labour) productivity significantly reduces both cost and price, leading to a substantial rise in demand.

Classical unemployment

Unemployment may be associated, in the classical view, with real wages that are 'too high'. In this case trade unions have used their power to force the *real wage* above the market clearing level or have prevented it from falling to the market clearing level after a change in the supply or demand conditions. A government minimum wage above the equilibrium wage could also generate such classical unemployment. In the 1970s there was a revival in this line of thought. The monetarist and new classical economists argued that whilst, for the most part, the economy would be at 'full employment', there might be times when firms and workers would *overestimate* the rate of inflation. If firms pay money wage increases based on such false price expectations, this will lead to (temporarily) higher real wages and reduced employment. Figure 23.5 illustrates classical unemployment using the familiar labour market diagram.

The *labour demand* curve has a negative slope to reflect the usual assumption that the demand for labour rises as the real wage falls. The *labour force* curve has a positive slope to reflect increased labour force participation as real wages rise. The *labour supply* curve represents those willing and able to take jobs at a given real wage. The market clearing real wage is $(W/P)_F$, giving employment equal to the full employment level N_F and unemployment equal to $N_1 - N_F$. This equilibrium level of unemployment is considered to be entirely *voluntary*. However if the real wage $(W/P)_2$ is above the market clearing level $(W/P)_F$ for whatever reason, then employment falls to N_2 and unemployment increases to $N_3 - N_2$ of which the portion $N_3 - N_4$ could be regarded as 'voluntary'. In the classical view the remaining 'involuntary' unemployment $N_4 - N_2$ could not persist for long. The unemployed would exert downward pressure on money wages, and the real wage would fall back to the market clearing level.

Fig. 23.5. 'Voluntary' or equilibrium unemployment and the real wage.

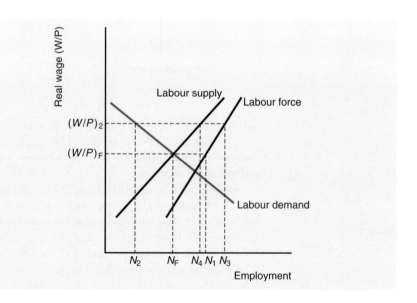

Fig. 23.6. Demand deficient unemployment.

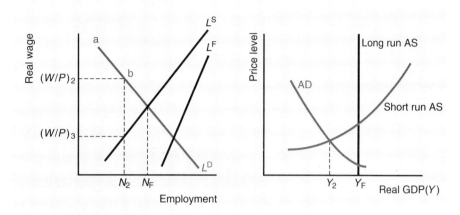

Keynes criticised the view that unemployment is caused by too high real wages. He considered that the cause of mass unemployment in the 1930s was not to be found in the market for labour, but was rather a result of too little demand in the *market for goods*. This lack of overall demand together with an assumed downward stickiness in wages and prices leaves the economy trapped for long periods with high levels of unemployment. The downward stickiness in wages (and therefore prices) thwarts the operation of the real balance effect, whereby lower prices raise *real incomes* and thereby increase consumer spending.[1] Since no automatic tendency exists to return the economy to full employment by generating sufficient aggregate demand in the goods market, Keynesians would advocate some form of expansionary government demand management policy. Demand deficient (Keynesian) unemployment is illustrated in Fig. 23.6.

Aggregate demand (AD) determines the level of output Y_2 (assume Y_F is full employment output – i.e. only 'voluntary' unemployment). Given this level of output and the production function in the economy, firms will only need to employ N_2 workers to meet the demand for their product. The *effective demand* for labour is traced out by the points $a–b–N_2$. Note that the real wage could be anywhere between $(W/P)_2$ and $(W/P)_3$. A cut in real wages would not restore employment to its full employment level (N_F) if aggregate demand for output remains unchanged at a level consistent with output Y_2.

A framework for thinking about unemployment

One useful way of thinking about unemployment, which is especially helpful from a policy perspective, is to distinguish between 'cyclical unemployment' which results from a deficiency of aggregate demand (e.g. during the downswing of the business cycle) and 'sustainable unemployment'. *Sustainable unemployment* is the level below which tightness in the labour market will lead to an increasing rate of wage and price inflation. The sustainable level of unemployment is variously referred to as the 'natural rate of unemployment' (NRU), the 'non-accelerating inflation rate of unemployment' (NAIRU) or, as in OECD publications, the 'structural' rate of unemployment.

Fig. 23.7.
Unemployment rates,
structural (sustainable)
and cyclical components
for OECD countries in
1997.
Source: OECD (1998)
Economic Outlook, June.

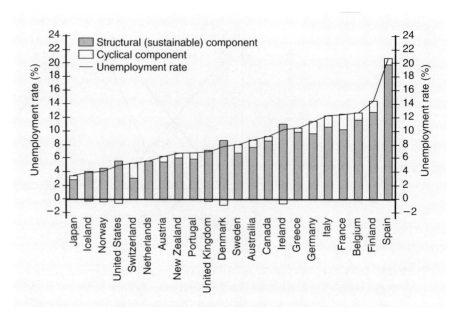

Fig. 23.7.
Unemployment rates, structural (sustainable) and cyclical components for OECD countries in 1997.
Source: OECD (1998) *Economic Outlook*, June.

At any moment in time therefore:

$$\text{Actual unemployment} = \text{Sustainable unemployment} + \text{Cyclical unemployment}$$

Figure 23.7 illustrates these two components for 22 OECD (advanced industrialised) countries in 1997. In some countries (United States, UK, Norway, Denmark and Ireland) the actual unemployment rate was *below* the sustainable (structural) rate. In these countries the relatively high level of aggregate demand might be expected to lead to future inflationary pressures unless corrective action is taken. In the majority of cases, however, the cyclical component was substantial so that the actual unemployment rate was well *above* the sustainable (structural) rate (e.g. Germany, France, Finland and Italy). In these countries aggregate demand might be expanded without serious inflationary consequences. Of course the uncertainties involved in decomposing unemployment into these two components must be borne in mind.

The natural rate of unemployment (NRU) and the NAIRU

Given the central role of these concepts in discussions of unemployment, it might be useful to consider the NRU and NAIRU in rather more detail.

Natural rate of unemployment (NRU) The NRU was introduced into economics by Milton Friedman (Friedman 1968). It can be thought of as being derived from a competitive labour market with flexible real wages, with the *natural rate* of unemployment being determined by the equilibrium of labour supply and demand. The usual labour market diagram of Fig. 23.8 can be used to illustrate this. Here labour demand, L^D, reflects the marginal revenue product of workers, i.e. the extra revenue contributed by employing the last worker. This is downward sloping in

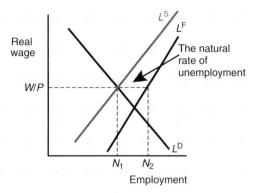

Fig. 23.8. Finding the natural rate of unemployment (NRU).

line with the assumption of a diminishing marginal physical product for workers (see Ch. 15). Labour supply, L^S, represents all those workers willing and able (i.e. they have the right skills and are in the right location) to accept jobs at a given real wage. The labour force, L^F, shows the total number of workers who consider themselves to be members of the labour force at any given real wage; of course not all of these are willing or able to accept job offers, perhaps because they are still searching for a better offer or because they have not yet acquired the appropriate skills or are not in an appropriate location. Note the convergence of L^S and L^F as the real wage rises. This reflects the reduction in the 'replacement ratio' (i.e. ratio of benefits when out of work to earnings when in work) when real wages rise, given the current level of unemployment benefits. Such a reduction in the 'replacement ratio' could be expected to result in a higher proportion of the labour force being willing and able to accept jobs as the real wage rate rises (see Ch. 14).

At the equilibrium real wage (W/P) in Fig. 23.8, N_1 workers are willing and able to accept job offers whereas N_2 workers consider themselves to be members of the labour force. That part of the labour force unwilling or unable to accept job offers at the equilibrium real wage ($N_2 - N_1$) is defined as being the natural rate of unemployment (NRU). In terms of our earlier classification of the unemployed the NRU can be regarded as including both the frictionally and structurally unemployed.

It can be seen that anything that *reduces the labour supply* (the numbers willing and able to accept a job at a given real wage) will, other things being equal, cause the NRU to increase. Possible factors might include an *increase in the level or availability of unemployment benefits*, thereby encouraging unemployed members of the labour force to engage in more prolonged search activity. An *increase in trade union power* might also reduce the numbers willing and able to accept a job at a given real wage, especially if the trade union is able to restrict the effective labour supply as part of a strategy for raising wages. A reduced labour supply might also result from *increased technological change* or increased *global competition*, both of which change the nature of the labour market skills required for employment. *Higher taxes on earned income* are also likely to reduce the labour supply at any given real wage.

Similarly anything that *reduces the labour demand* will, other things being equal, cause the NRU to increase. A fall in the marginal revenue product of labour, via a fall in marginal physical productivity or in the product price, might be expected to reduce labour demand. Many economists believe that the two sharp oil price increases in the 1970s had this effect, with the resulting fall in aggregate demand causing firms to cut back on capital spending, reducing the overall capital stock and hence the marginal physical productivity of labour.

Non-accelerating inflation rate of unemployment (NAIRU) Unlike the NRU which assumes a competitive labour market, the NAIRU is usually developed from a model that recognises imperfect competition in the labour market (Layard 1986). The 'sustainable' level of unemployment (i.e. the level consistent with the inflation rate being unchanged) is seen here as being the result of a bargaining equilibrium between firms and workers rather than a market clearing outcome. The two sides of the labour market are seen as engaged in a constant struggle over the available real output per head. If the claims of the two sides are inconsistent, in that they add up to more than the real output per head available, then each side will try to safeguard its own claim by using its market power. Workers will claim higher money wages and firms will raise their product prices. The result of such a power struggle will then be rising inflation.

Figure 23.9 illustrates the determination of the NAIRU. At any particular moment there is a limit to the real wage the economy can provide, given labour productivity and the mark-up that firms typically apply to costs. This limit is the *feasible real wage* $(W/P)^*$. At the same time, the *target real wage* reflects the aspirations of workers. It seems likely that this target will be influenced by the level of demand in the economy, as reflected by the unemployment rate. When demand is high and unemployment is low, workers will feel more able to negotiate wage increases than when demand is low and unemployment high. There will be some level of unemployment where workers' aspirations are *equal* to the real wage that firms are willing to offer; this is the NAIRU. In other words NAIRU is determined by the intersection of the target and feasible real wage curves in Fig. 23.9. If unemployment were pushed *below* the NAIRU by government expansionary policy, then workers would seek a real wage above the feasible level; in an attempt to secure this they would demand higher money wages. If they were successful in securing these, firms would maintain their mark-up over costs by raising prices. If unemployment were to *remain* below the NAIRU, then a wage-price spiral would ensue. At some stage the government would have to allow unemployment to rise toward the NAIRU to end the rising inflation rate.

Fig. 23.9. The determination of the NAIRU.

Table 23.4   Estimates of the UK NAIRU.

Time period	1966–73	1974–80	1981–87	1989–90	1996–
NAIRU range	1.6–5.6%	4.5–7.3%	5.2–9.9%	3.5–8.1%	6% approx.

Sources: Bank of England Quarterly Bulletin (1993), Vol. 33, No. 2, and Bank of England Inflation Report (1998), August.

To sum up then, the NAIRU is seen as being the level of unemployment necessary to keep inflation from rising. Anything which *shifts* the target or feasible real wage curves in Fig. 23.9 will affect the NAIRU.

Any factor that enables or encourages workers to *increase the target real wage* for a given level of unemployment will clearly increase the NAIRU, shifting the target real wage curve upwards and to the right. Such factors might include any or all of the following:

- an increase in benefits and their duration;
- an increase in trade union power or greater employment protection (both reducing the fear of unemployment);
- increased structural unemployment (the unemployed now compete less effectively with the employed because they have the wrong skills or are in the wrong place);
- an increase in the long-term unemployed as a proportion of total unemployment (the long-term unemployed compete less effectively with the employed for jobs);
- an increase in taxes on earnings which reduces the post-tax real wage and leads workers to seek a higher pre-tax real wage.

Similarly any factor that *reduces the feasible real wage* will increase the NAIRU. Such factors might include any or all of the following:

- reduced labour productivity;
- unfavourable movements in the Terms of Trade (i.e. fall in the ratio of export to import prices), reducing the share of output going to domestic employees and raising that going to foreign employees;
- higher dividends reducing the share of output going to employees and raising that going to shareholders;
- more 'leapfrogging' by which one group of workers use a pay increase by others to justify their own higher pay demands.

Although this idea of the NAIRU is a central concept in mainstream macroeconomics its actual level is not easy to pin down. Table 23.4 shows considerable variability in the estimates of the NAIRU that have been made for the UK over selected time periods.

Unemployment in the OECD

Two important puzzles face applied economists when considering the unemployment data in the advanced industrialised countries of the OECD (shown in Table 23.5). One puzzle involves explaining why unemployment has been much higher in almost all OECD countries during the 1980s and 1990s than it had been in the decades following the Second World War. The second puzzle involves explaining why there have been such large variations recorded in unemployment rates between the OECD countries.

Table 23.5
Unemployment rates in
selected OECD countries

	UK	France	Germany (W)	Italy	Netherlands	Spain	US	Japan
1960–68	2.6	1.7	0.7	3.8	1.2	2.4	4.7	1.4
1983–97	9.5	10.5	6.2	7.9	8.1	19.7	6.4	2.7

Source: OECD, *Economic Outlook*, various.

A recent study of cross-country differences in unemployment rates (Nickell 1998) has attempted to asses the impact on unemployment of a variety of factors. For example Nickell estimated that a 10% increase in the 'replacement ratio' and a one-year increase in the duration of entitlement to unemployment benefits would result in a 25% increase in unemployment, while a 10% increase in trade union density would result in a 60% increase in unemployment. On the other hand, a 5% reduction in the overall tax rate would reduce unemployment by 15% and a 2% cut in the real interest rate (a substantial cut) would reduce unemployment by around 10% . He found that policies involving an increase in labour market 'rigidity' (such as improved labour standards and greater employment protection) had little impact on overall unemployment. Nickell argues that such variables, despite problems of definition and measurement across countries, do shed some light on why unemployment varies a great deal between countries. For example, Spain with its high replacement ratios, long benefit duration, rather high tax rates on earnings and relatively 'rigid' labour market, suffers from high unemployment, as might be expected from Nickell's analysis, whereas the US, with its relatively low replacement ratios, short benefit duration, low tax rates on earnings, flexible labour market and low union coverage, has relatively low unemployment.

Nickell goes on to argue that although his variables usefully explain cross-country comparisons, they are less useful in explaining the time series pattern of OECD unemployment (see also Bean 1994). For example, when comparing the higher unemployment of the 1990s with the much lower unemployment of the 1960s, Nickell was surprised to find that today's replacement ratios are no more generous, trade union militancy no worse, real interest rates not much higher, and labour markets not much more rigid, than all of these factors had been in the 1960s and yet unemployment is so much higher.

Concentrating on the UK alone, rather than on cross-country comparisons, Nickell (1998) estimates that the fourfold rise in the numbers unemployed since the 1960s could comfortably be explained by a model including the replacement ratio, the Terms of Trade, skills mismatch, union pressure, industrial turbulence, the tax 'wedge' and the real interest rate. The variables making the most important (percentage) contributions in explaining the overall rise in unemployment have been skills mismatch 14%, union pressure 19%, tax 'wedge' 23%, but the real interest rate *only* 3.5%.

A rather different view is offered by Phelps and Zoega (1998) who suggest that two global forces, namely sharp rises in oil prices in the 1970s and in real world interest rates in the 1980s and early 1990s, have been the major factors responsible for the observed increases in world-wide unemployment since the 1960s.

Higher oil prices reduce labour productivity by reducing the proportion of the existing capital stock which can be regarded as 'economically efficient'; for example, oil-intensive capital equipment becomes effectively redundant. As well as diminishing the 'economically efficient' capital stock, and with it labour productivity, higher oil prices are seen by Phelps and Zoega as contributing to higher unemployment by diminishing net exports (exports minus imports) for many OECD countries. The

Table 23.6 Long-term real interest rates (average of US, Germany, UK and France).

	1956–73	1974–80	1981–93
Real interest rate	1.7	0.0	5.1

Source: Adapted from Rowthorne (1995).

non-oil exporting OECD countries have been particularly hard-hit by ever increasing import bills for oil and 'oil-based' products.

The Phelps and Zoega model sees hiring rates for workers as heavily dependent on both net productivity and the real interest rate. As well as the slowdown in productivity growth experienced in most countries following oil-price shocks, the steep rises in global real interest rates shown in Table 23.6 further reduce the hiring rate for labour, resulting in substantial increases in levels of unemployment. Higher real interest rates particularly discourage the hiring of workers who require a substantial investment in human capital, such as the large numbers of higher skilled and well-educated workers required by many high technology 'information age' industries.

Unemployment persistence and hysteresis

In the mid-1980s oil prices fell, trade union power diminished compared to the 1970s, the replacement ratio fell, and yet unemployment kept on rising, at least in Europe. One explanation might be that demand-deficient unemployment had risen because governments were trying to control inflation by running the economy with unemployment *above* the NAIRU. However, inflation did not fall in the mid-1980s, leading some economists to the view that a period of high unemployment resulting from contractionary demand management might lead to the NAIRU itself increasing. The idea that there might be a mechanism whereby a rise in unemployment increases the equilibrium (or natural) rate of unemployment is known as *hysteresis.* There are several possible mechanisms to explain hysteresis in European unemployment.

One explanation of hysteresis involves the *insider–outsider hypothesis* (Blanchard and Summers 1986, Lindbeck and Snower 1988). *Insiders* are the unionised employed who pay little attention to the interests of the unemployed *outsiders*. For a variety of reasons (such as turnover costs, firm-specific human capital and the possibility of refusing to cooperate with newly hired outsiders) insiders do not fear that they will be replaced by outsiders. Of course in practice, if the demand for labour falls, then some insiders may lose their jobs and become outsiders. Once labour demand recovers, however, the smaller pool of insiders who remain will exploit their relative scarcity by negotiating higher wages for themselves rather than accepting wage moderation and allowing the employment of more outsiders. The economy therefore settles at a higher wage, lower employment equilibrium.

A second explanation of hysteresis concentrates on the role of the *long-term unemployed;* in other words this approach concentrates on the role of the *outsiders* rather than on the wage-determining role of the insiders. The long-term unemployed are seen as effectively having withdrawn from the labour force (they search less effectively, they lose their skills and employers see them as a bad risk). The result is that they do not exert much downward pressure on wage setting, so that a higher level of unemployment is required to exert the same control on inflation when the long-term unemployed increase as a proportion of the total unemployed. Empirical evidence certainly suggests that when European unemployment persists the effect is to increase the proportion of the long-term unemployed in total unemployment, so that the equilibrium (or natural) rate of unemployment rises.

A third explanation of hysteresis involves the effect of recessions on the *capital stock*. As aggregate demand falls, firms go out of business and investment plans are shelved, reducing the capital-to-labour ratio and therefore the marginal productivity of labour (shifting the labour demand curve to the left). From the point of view of the NAIRU model there has been a reduction in the 'feasible real wage'. Whichever way we look at it, the equilibrium (or natural) rate of unemployment rises.

A fourth explanation of hysteresis involves the suggestion that a more highly regulated labour market discourages recruitment, and may lead to higher equilibrium unemployment after a downturn in demand (see Bean 1994).

What can be done to reduce unemployment?

The OECD *Jobs Study* (1994) made more than 60 policy recommendations for reducing unemployment. Following on from this, the OECD *Jobs Strategy* (1998) produced a blueprint aimed at creating jobs and reducing unemployment, whilst at the same time strengthening social cohesion. The key recommendations included the following.

- Set macroeconomic policy to encourage non-inflationary growth.
- Enhance the creation and diffusion of technology.
- Increase working time flexibility.
- Encourage entrepreneurship and eliminate restrictions on the creation and expansion of enterprises.
- Make wage and labour costs flexible and responsive to local conditions and skill levels, particularly for young workers.
- Reform employment security provisions that inhibit recruitment.
- Strengthen the emphasis on 'active' labour market policies.
- Improve the education and skills of the labour force.
- Reform 'unemployment and related' benefits and the tax system to improve the functioning of the job market, whilst not jeopardising societies' equity goals.
- Enhance product market competition to reduce monopolistic tendencies and weaken insider–outsider mechanisms, thereby leading to a more dynamic economy.

Country-specific recommendations were also drawn up and progress in implementing them is to be monitored by the OECD.

The situation as regards *structural* unemployment in the OECD countries over the period 1990–97 is summarised in Table 23.7. In only six out of 22 countries has structural unemployment decreased. In the view of the OECD these countries had undertaken many of the reforms outlined above as early as the 1980s; on the other hand, a number of countries that had undertaken significant labour market reforms in the 1990s were still waiting for structural unemployment to decrease. Nevertheless, the view of the OECD is that the *Jobs Strategy* is an effective response to the unemployment problems of its member states. The pace and scope of labour market reform in some countries is, however, constrained by the feeling that these reforms (like prolonged unemployment itself) might have negative effects on social cohesion and equity.

Table 23.7 Structural unemployment in OECD countries 1990–97 (as % of labour force).

	1990	1997
Increased		
Finland	7.0	12.8
Sweden	3.2	6.7
Germany	6.9	9.6
Iceland	1.5	4.0
Switzerland	1.3	3.0
Greece	8.2	9.8
Italy	9.7	10.6
France	9.3	10.2
Belgium	11.0	11.6
Austria	4.9	5.4
Remained stable		
Japan	2.5	2.8
Norway	4.2	4.5
Spain	19.8	19.9
Portugal	5.9	5.8
United States	5.8	5.6
Canada	9.0	8.5
Decreased		
Denmark	9.2	8.6
Australia	8.3	7.5
New Zealand	7.3	6.0
United Kingdom	8.5	7.2
Netherlands	7.0	5.5
Ireland	14.6	11.0
OECD structural unemployment rate (weighted average)	6.8	7.1
OECD actual unemployment rate (weighted average)	6.0	7.5

Source: OECD (1998) *Economic Outlook*, June.

The UK approach to reducing unemployment

The new Labour government of 1997 committed itself to a series of measures aimed at building upon and improving the labour market reforms of the 1980s, whilst at the same time putting greater emphasis on fairness and social inclusion (HM Treasury 1997). This strategy is in line with the OECD approach and includes the following elements.

- *Providing a framework for macroeconomic stability and economic growth.* Measures here include the operational independence of the Bank of England and two key 'rules' for fiscal policy (HM Treasury 1998). One of these, the 'golden rule', limits government borrowing to financing investment rather than current spending. The other, a 'sustainable investment rule', implies that net public sector debt will be reduced below 40% of GDP over the business cycle.
- *Promoting flexibility in the labour market whilst at the same time providing minimum employment standards.* Measures here include encouraging working practices that match the needs of both workers and employers, promoting real wage flexibility and encouraging competition. Signing up to the European Social Chapter and the introduction of a national minimum wage (see later) are attempts to provide some minimum standards in employment.

- *Providing investment in education and skills.* Measures here include improvements in school buildings financed by the 'windfall tax', raising standards of numeracy and literacy, allocating a larger proportion of the budget for vocational training and education and encouraging life-long learning opportunities to improve the situation of older unqualified workers.
- *Encouraging people to move from welfare to work.* Emphasis has been placed on getting young workers and the long-term unemployed back to work. The 'New Deal' was introduced in 1998 and provided wage subsidies to help secure work in the private sector for these groups. For those who do not secure work in the private sector there will be new opportunities for education and training, for work in the voluntary sector or on an Environmental Task Force. Sanctions will be taken against the young and long-term unemployed who do not participate. Similar schemes are also to be provided for lone parents, the disabled and ex-offenders.
- *Making work pay.* This involves the reform of the tax and benefit system together with the introduction of a national minimum wage in an attempt to minimise the unemployment and poverty traps (See Ch. 19). The UK Treasury has estimated that some 500,000 working people in the UK in 1997 had 'replacement ratios' of over 70%, whilst some 645,000 workers experienced marginal deduction rates (extra taxes and lost benefits) of over 70%. In addition to the national minimum wage, measures here include the reform of National Insurance contributions, the introduction of a working-family tax credit and a child-care tax credit, and a proposed 10% starting rate of income tax.

At the end of 1998, UK unemployment as measured by the LFS had fallen to 6.3%, which was below the minimum unemployment rate achieved by the UK in the previous cycle and amongst the lowest unemployment rates recorded in the OECD. Indeed evidence from earnings growth and vacancy/unemployment ratios suggest that this is probably below the sustainable natural rate of unemployment (Bank of England 1998).

Despite this success, a number of problems remain. For example the OECD estimates that in the UK a further 2.3 million people (6.5% of the working-age population) would like to work even though they are not classified as unemployed. It also notes that for the UK there has been virtually no growth either in the recorded labour force or in the employment rate over the 14 years to 1997.

Minimum wage and employment

A national minimum wage (NMW) has been introduced into the UK in April 1999. A rate of £3.60 per hour has been set for workers over 21 years and a lower rate of £3.00 per hour (rising to £3.20 in June 2000) has been announced for workers aged 18–21 years. An estimated 1.9 million workers will be affected by the minimum wage, of which two-thirds will be women. It is estimated that the rate of £3.60 per hour represents around 55% of median hourly earnings in the UK and around 45% of median hourly earnings for full-time males. This rate is lower than in France but higher than in the USA.

Most of the empirical work on the employment effects of an NMW has been undertaken in either the USA or France. Prior to the 1990s, most USA studies suggested that a NMW would have a small negative effect on employment. Typically the elasticity of employment with respect to the minimum wage was found to be between −0.2 and −0.1. The suggestion is that a 10% increase in the NMW would lead to a fall in employment of something between 2% and 1% as employers are discouraged from hiring the now more expensive but generally low-productivity workers. However, later studies in the USA by Card (1992) and Card and Kruger (1994), using cross-state data, were unable to find any significant negative employment effects of increases in the NMW. Indeed, the 1994 study of fast food restaurants showed that employment in New Jersey, where the minimum wage increased, grew relative to Eastern Pennsylvania, where the minimum wage did not increase. Both these studies have, however, been heavily criticised and their findings remain questionable (see Barro 1997).

French studies have tended to find a small negative effect of an NMW on youth employment, with typical employment elasticities of between −0.12 and −0.15. Other estimates have suggested that a 10% rise in the French minimum wage relative to the average wage would increase sustainable unemployment by around 0.9% points.

Most UK work has concentrated on the effect of rises in the minimum wage for specific industries covered by the former Wage Councils, so that it is difficult to generalise these results to a situation involving the imposition of a *national* minimum wage. The Bank of England's Monetary Policy Committee argues that the likely overall effect of the NMW on employment is uncertain, with a key factor being the degree of monopsony which prevails in a particular labour market. In their view, the greater the degree of market power (monopsony) which firms have in terms of recruitment, the smaller will be the negative effects on employment of the NMW (see Ch. 15). The Committee expects that the unemployment effects of introducing both the NMW and the Welfare to Work ('New Deal') initiatives will be small, tending in any case to work in opposite directions, with a broadly neutral overall effect on unemployment.

Key points

- Successive 'unemployment cycles' (peak to peak) have tended to result in higher unemployment rates.
- The ILO (survey) method of measuring the unemployed differs from the claimant (administrative record) method used in the UK. This difference suggests that unemployment is *under recorded* in the UK in terms of agreed international measures.
- Unemployment in the UK can be *disaggregated* into regional, occupational, gender, age, ethnically based and qualification-related unemployment.
- The major *types* of unemployment include frictional (temporary), structural (changing patterns of demand), technological (changing technology), classical ('excessive' real wages) and demand deficient (inadequate demand) categories.
- The *natural rate of unemployment* (NRU) is the voluntary unemployment (labour force–labour supply) existing at the real wage level which 'clears' the markets.
- The *non-accelerating inflation rate of unemployment* (NAIRU) is that level of unemployment which equates the *feasible* real wage with the *target* real wage. It is the unemployment rate at which inflation is constant.
- Estimates suggest that NAIRU has risen for the UK over the past two decades, though perhaps falling in recent years (e.g. via more flexible labour markets). Only where the actual unemployment rate is *above* NAIRU can unemployment be reduced (to NAIRU) without stimulating inflation.

Notes

1. The downward stickiness in wages (wage rigidity) and therefore prices also thwarts the interest rate and foreign trade effects which might stimulate recovery. In the 'interest rate effect', lower prices mean an increase in *real money supply*, lowering the 'price' of money (interest rates) and thereby raising the investment component of aggregate demand. In the 'foreign trade effect', lower prices mean more competitive exports and more competitive (home produced) substitutes for imports. A rise in exports and fall in imports again stimulating (net) aggregate demand.

References and further reading

Bank of England (1997) *Quarterly Bulletin*, **37**, 1, February.

Bank of England (1998) Inflation Report, February, August.

Barro, R. J. (1998) *Macroeconomics*. MIT Press, Cambridge, MA.

Bean, C. (1994) European unemployment: a survey, *Journal of Economic Literature*, **XXXII**, June.

Begg, D., Fischer, S. and **Dornbusch, R.** (1994) *Economics*, McGraw-Hill, London.

Blanchard, D. and **Summers, L.** (1986) *Hysteresis and the European Unemployment Problem*, NBER Macroeconomic Annual.

Card, D. (1992) Do minimum wages reduce unemployment? *Industrial and Labour Relations Review*, **46**, October.

Card, D. and **Kruger, A.** (1994) Minimum wages and employment: a case study of the fast food industry in New Jersey and Pennsylvania, *American Economic Review*, **84**, September.

Clark, A. and **Layard, R.** (1989) *UK Unemployment*, Heinemann Educational, Oxford.

Dawson, G. (1992) *Inflation and Unemployment: causes, consequences and cures*, Edward Elgar, Aldershot.

Fothergill, S. and **Gudgin, G.** (1982) *Unequal Growth: urban and regional change in the UK*, Heinemann, London.

Friedman, M. (1968) The role of monetary policy, *American Economic Review*, **58**, March.

HM Treasury (1997) United Kingdom Employment Action Plan.

HM Treasury (1998) Stability and Investment for the Long Term: Economic and Fiscal Strategy Report.

Keynes, J. M. (1936) *The General Theory of Employment, Interest and Money*, Macmillan, p. 381.

Labour Market Trends (1998) January, June.

Layard, R. (1986) *How to Beat Unemployment*, Oxford University Press, Oxford.

Layard, R., Nickell, S. and **Jackman, R.** (1994) *The Unemployment Crisis*, Oxford University Press, Oxford.

Lindbeck, A. and **Snower, D.** (1988) *The Insider–Outsider Theory of Employment and Unemployment*, MIT Press, Cambridge.

Nickell, S. (1998) Unemployment: questions and some answers, *Economic Journal*, **108**, 48, May.

OECD (1994) *Jobs Study: facts, analysis and strategies*, OECD, Paris.

OECD (1998) *Jobs Strategy: Progress Report*. OECD Working Paper, No. 196.

Phelps, E. and **Zoega, G.** (1998) Natural rate theory and OECD unemployment, *Economic Journal*, **108**, 48, May.

Rowthorne, R. (1995) Capital formation and unemployment, *Oxford Review of Economic Policy*, **11**, 1, Spring.

Chapter 24

Managing the economy

In this chapter the objectives of macroeconomic policy are discussed, along with the instruments for achieving them. After a short review of the interventionist theory of macroeconomic policy, we consider the conduct of policy in the UK. Adjusting the instruments of policy to 'best' meet a set of target values for various objectives seems to fit the actual conduct of policy in the UK until 1974. The emphasis then shifted away from such 'fine-tuning' and towards the adoption of medium- and long-term rules. This change of emphasis is well illustrated by considering the policies advocated by the Cambridge Economic Policy Group (CEPG) and by the monetarists. The fortunes of the Medium Term Financial Strategy are traced from its inception in 1979 to the late 1990s. An assessment is also made of the contribution of supply-side economics to macroeconomic policy. This chapter concludes with a study of economic policy in an international context.

The objectives of policy

The desire of most individuals is to live and work within an economic framework which gives them the prospect of steady employment, relatively stable prices and a rising standard of living. It is usually recognized that to achieve such a situation the economy must trade and 'pay its way' with other economies. Politicians realize that to attract votes and gain political power they must promise that these aspirations will be met, if only in the long run. Economic objectives at the macroeconomic level are therefore set in terms of full employment, price stability and rapid economic growth, together with long-term equilibrium in the balance of payments. All these objectives have attracted attention in the post-war period in the UK. Since they are unlikely to be achieved in their totality, they have usually been expressed in terms of target values. Whilst these target values have not always been explicitly stated, they seem to be influenced by achieved values within the recent past.

Full employment For instance, it is recognized that full employment can never mean zero registered unemployment if only because of dynamic change within society. Following the Beveridge Report of 1944, a 3% rate of unemployment (about half a million) was used in the 1950s and 1960s as the 'acceptable' upper limit. In the 1980s and the 1990s governments have been reluctant to commit themselves to any specific unemployment target.

Stable prices Stable prices have always been regarded as unrealistic, but the attainment of an annual inflation rate of around 2.5% seems to have been the approximate target in the first two post-war decades. More recently the reduction of the annual inflation rate to below 4% or to a rate equivalent to that of our industrial rivals, would appear to have been the target set during much of the 1980s and 1990s. With the advent of the new Labour government in 1997 and the establishment of an independent Monetary Policy Committee (MPC), a specific target of 2.5% for annual inflation has been given to the MPC to guide it in setting interest rate policy.

Economic growth Economic growth has received relatively little specific emphasis in the UK, although most governments have expressed some enthusiasm for it! We have, generally speaking, enjoyed rising living standards and have compared ourselves (favourably) with our parents and grandparents rather than with our contemporaries in Europe, the USA or Japan. A well-known statement concerning economic growth as an objective was made by the late R. A. Butler in 1954, when he suggested a doubling of living standards every twenty-five years as an explicit target. This was greeted as being over-ambitious, yet it entailed an annual growth rate of GDP of less than 3%. The Economic Plan of 1965 sought a growth rate of 3.8% per annum, but this was quickly seen to be unattainable and this attempt at long-term planning was soon abandoned. There has been criticism that the Monetary Policy Committee has not been given a growth target to set alongside the 2.5% inflation target when deciding the level of interest rates.

The balance of payments The balance of payments is often described as an objective of economic policy, the target being either equilibrium or a surplus over a period of time in order that accumulated international debts might be repaid. This can hardly be related to the aspirations of individuals and is thought by many to be more properly described as a constraint upon the achievement of other objectives. Nevertheless, target figures have been set in the past, e.g. the 1953 Economic Survey called for a surplus of £450m per annum as the target surplus on current account in the 1950s to finance the long-term capital outflow. It was not achieved, and since then the use of target figures has become less important. However a relatively 'healthy' external account is still an important consideration of policy.

This list of objectives could be extended to include others, such as the redistribution of income and wealth, but target values for employment, inflation and underlying economic growth have received most attention. The recent record of achievement is displayed in Table 24.1.

Table 24.1 shows that the efforts of successive governments simultaneously to achieve the four major objectives have failed. However, this by no means indicates that it is 'worthless' for governments to intervene in the economy, as the situation could have been still worse without such intervention.

Table 24.1 Achieved values for a number of policy objectives.

Year	Unemployment as a percentage of working population (excluding school-leavers)	Annual change in RPI (%)	Annual change in GDP (at factor cost) (%)	Balance of payments (current account) (£m)
1972	3.1	7.1	2.7	+203
1973	2.1	9.2	7.1	−998
1974	2.1	16.1	−1.7	−3,184
1975	3.3	24.9	−1.1	−1,524
1976	3.5	15.1	2.6	−772
1977	4.7	12.1	2.6	+53
1978	4.6	8.4	3.2	+1,123
1979	4.1	17.2	1.8	−453
1980	5.4	15.1	−2.4	+2,843
1981	8.5	12.0	−0.8	+6,748
1982	9.8	5.4	1.6	+4,649
1983	10.4	5.3	3.2	+3,529
1984	10.7	4.6	2.4	+1,482
1985	10.9	5.7	3.6	+2,238
1986	11.2	4.0	3.6	−864
1987	10.3	4.2	4.5	−4,813
1988	8.3	4.9	4.1	−16,475
1989	6.4	7.8	2.1	−22,398
1990	5.8	9.4	0.9	−18,746
1991	8.1	5.9	−2.3	−7,954
1992	9.8	3.7	−1.5	−10,133
1993	10.3	1.6	2.0	−10,756
1994	9.4	2.4	4.0	−1,655
1995	8.1	3.5	2.5	−3,672
1996	7.4	2.4	3.4	−600
1997	5.6	3.1	2.3	+8,006
1998*	4.9	3.6	2.5	−3,420

*Forecast.
Sources: ONS (1998) Economic Trends, October and previous issues.

The instruments of policy

Governments would have no macroeconomic problems if market forces in the economy automatically lead to 'full employment' equilibrium, with stable prices, and a rapid economic growth. The bulk of the evidence seems to indicate that market forces alone have failed to achieve these objectives, either in full or even at 'satisfactory' values. Such 'market failure' essentially constitutes the case for intervention by governments. If governments *are* to intervene in the economy, there still remains the problem of selecting the appropriate instruments for achieving the targets they set themselves.

In general terms the policy instruments available to the UK government are fiscal policy, monetary policy, prices and incomes policy, and policy instruments aimed at the balance of payments, such as the exchange rate or import controls. These policy instruments are sometimes called 'instrumental variables', i.e. variables over which the government has some control, and the values of which affect the behaviour of the economy itself in some reasonably systematic way.

Fiscal policy   Fiscal policy involves using both government spending and taxation to influence the composition and level of aggregate demand in the economy. Elementary circular flow analysis suggests that by raising the level of government expenditure and/or by reducing taxation, the level of aggregate demand can be raised (by a multiplied amount) with favourable consequences for economic activity and employment. Such an expansionary course of action might result in a larger budget deficit, or a reduced budget surplus, in this way affecting the Public Sector Borrowing Requirement (PSBR). This somewhat simplistic approach is the basis for fiscal interventionism as advocated by 'Keynesians', and carried out with some success in the UK for over twenty-five years after World War II. The Budget was viewed not as an accounting procedure, with expenditure and revenue to be balanced as a matter of good housekeeping, but as an instrument of policy to be manipulated as a means to an end. Deficits were financed by borrowing, short or long term, from home and abroad, with the increased National Debt seen as a means of spreading the costs of current policy over future generations.

Practical problems abound. Although tax rates can be set, the revenues they will yield are difficult to predict as income levels can vary. Also government expenditure and tax receipts are subject to time-lags, which can have destabilizing effects. For instance, the government may aim to raise spending to stimulate the economy during recession, but the effects may not be felt for several time periods, when the economy may be in a different situation. In other words, fiscal policy may move the economy away from desired values rather than towards them. There is even a problem in identifying the government's fiscal stance. A contractionary fiscal policy will, if successful, reduce incomes and tax yield, and might also have the effect of raising some government expenditures such as unemployment benefit. If we look, therefore, at the Budget *out-turn* for evidence of the government's fiscal stance, we may come to the wrong conclusion – the reduced tax yield and increased government expenditure may be the result of a contractionary fiscal policy, not evidence of an expansionary one! Problems such as these account in part for the relegation of fiscal policy in favour of monetary policy by Conservative governments during the 1980s.

Monetary policy   Monetary policy aims to influence monetary variables such as the rate of interest and the money supply, in order to achieve the targets set for the four major objectives. Although the rate of interest and the money supply are interrelated (see Ch. 20), for convenience we examine these separately.

The rate of interest – in practice there are many – is thought to be important because it is a cost of borrowing, influencing not only long-term investment decisions by firms but also their short-term borrowing to overcome cash-flow problems. Interest rates may influence consumer spending on durable goods by affecting the cost of hire-purchase finance. Interest rates also influence household decisions as to the composition of the assets they hold. For example, low interest rates offer little reward for those acquiring financial assets, thus encouraging consumer expenditure on goods and services. The balance of payments is also affected by interest rate policy, as capital inflow and outflow depend on UK interest rates relative to those in other countries.

The money supply, as we saw in Chapter 20, 'matters' to both monetarists and Keynesians. To monetarists, money supply mainly affects prices, at least in the long run, whereas to Keynesians, the major impact is on output and employm... measurement and control of money supply have therefore been widely regarded as an important policy instrument, and we return to this below.

Prices and incomes policy

Prices and incomes policy is used in an attempt to control inflation by directly influencing the rate at which prices, wages and salaries rise. Depending on political and economic belief, such a policy can be viewed as an irrelevance by the monetarists, or as a necessary means of influencing the institutional determinants of inflation by the Keynesians, particularly when expansionary fiscal measures are being used to overcome unemployment.

Since 1960 there have been few occasions on which this instrument of policy was not in use, either on a voluntary basis or in the form of statutory control. Prices have been directly controlled as well as wages, and wages themselves have been subject to various forms of restraint, such as 'freezes', or 'norms' for wage increases. The impact of the policy has, predictably, fallen most heavily on the public sector. Although during the operation of incomes policy the rate of wage inflation has usually been reduced below the previously prevailing figure, it has often been higher than the 'norm' set, and has always been followed, when controls have been relaxed, by a rapid and sharp increase in the rate of wage inflation. It is difficult to test the overall effects of the use of this instrument of policy, but it is generally regarded as having been less useful in the long term. Prices and incomes policy was last used formally in 1979, but an incomes policy has been used informally since then, with the introduction of cash limits for the public sector acting as a constraint on wage increases.

The exchange rate

The exchange rate is one of the instruments which can be used to influence the balance of payments. With the exception of the devaluations of 1949 (30%), and 1967 (14%), the sterling exchange rate was essentially fixed under the International Monetary Fund (IMF) system. In 1971 the convertibility of the dollar into gold at a fixed price was abandoned and the IMF fixed exchange rate system broke down. Since mid-1972 the UK exchange rate has fluctuated, in theory according to market forces (a 'clean' float), but in practice often 'managed' by the authorities (a 'dirty' float). Although the pound fell to record low levels against the dollar in early 1983, it would have fallen even lower had the Bank of England not intervened on the foreign exchange market to buy the pound with its foreign currency reserves.

A change in the exchange rate will affect the relative prices of domestic- and foreign-produced goods and services. For example, a lower exchange rate makes UK goods cheaper in the foreign markets, and foreign goods more expensive in the UK market (see Ch. 25). Given appropriate elasticities for exports and imports,[1] a lower exchange rate will improve the balance of payments.

One major difficulty in a lower exchange rate policy is that this will have an adverse effect on domestic costs, both directly and indirectly. The rise in price of imported foodstuffs and finished manufactures will have an immediate and direct effect on the price level, because these items are included in the Retail Price Index (RPI). The rise in price of imported raw materials and semi-finished manufactures will also have an indirect effect on the price level, by raising domestic costs of production. Higher prices could also stimulate higher wage demands to protect real incomes, further fuelling inflation. In these ways the competitive advantage of devaluation may well be eroded, and the objective of price stability (or reduced inflation) adversely affected. Between 1985 and 1988, the government sought to target the exchange rate at particular levels against various currencies. This was in order to prevent sterling depreciating too rapidly, thereby endangering the control of inflation. The entry of sterling into the ERM at a relatively high rate of 2.95 DM to the pound in October 1990 was also to help contain inflationary pressure in the UK. One of the concerns facing the government when the UK left the ERM in September 1992 was the fear that the 14% fall in sterling's value against the DM (and 20% against $US) by late 1992 would rekindle inflationary pressures. As it turned out such fears proved largely unfounded.

Import controls   Import controls are another policy instrument for affecting the balance of payments, but have been little used in the UK since the Second World War, other than to reduce import tariffs in line with other members of the General Agreement on Tariffs and Trade (GATT). Two examples may serve to illustrate their use. Between 1964 and 1966 there was an import surcharge scheme whereby most imported manufactured goods carried a levy of 15% in an attempt to reduce imports by over £550m per annum. It was a partial success, reducing them by perhaps half the intended sum. In 1968–70 there was an import deposit scheme whereby half the value of imported manufactured goods had to be deposited with the government for six months, with no interest paid. Little effect upon the balance of payments was discerned.

Renewed interest in import tariffs emerged in the early 1980s, stimulated by the Cambridge Economic Policy Group (CEPG) who, initially at least, saw a direct and close relationship between the size of the Budget deficit and the size of the balance of payments deficit. If expansionary domestic fiscal policy is to overcome unemployment and stimulate investment, they advocate imposing tariffs to prevent the extra domestic spending from being satisfied by overseas suppliers. Their aim was not to reduce imports below the initial pre-expansion figure, but to prevent them from rising above that level.

Problems in managing the economy

Before we consider the theory of economic policy, some general points can be made concerning the objectives of policy and the instruments available to the government.

Trade-off between objectives   With regard to objectives, the most obvious difficulty is that the objectives 'trade off' against each other. At the present time the policy instruments the government has used to achieve the objective of lower inflation have imposed a cost of higher unemployment. Curbing the money supply has reduced the value of spending,[2] and raised interest rates, resulting in the closure of many firms, with the loss of jobs. Curbing government spending as part of monetary policy has also reduced employment in the public sector. A higher exchange rate during 1981/82, from 1985 to 1988 and again from 1996 to 1998, made UK exports expensive, and imports cheaper, reducing domestic output and employment, especially in the more tradable manufacturing sector. Lower inflation has therefore been achieved, but at the cost of higher unemployment. High interest rates and low economic activity have discouraged investment, adversely affecting another important policy objective, that of economic growth. This raises the question of 'weighting' the objectives against each other, e.g. how much extra unemployment and lower growth will be tolerated in order to reduce the inflation rate by a further x percentage points?

Interdependence of instruments

Policy instruments are not independent of each other. For example, fiscal policy has implications for the money supply and for the rate of interest. In turn, the domestic rate of interest will, by its effect upon short-term capital flows, influence the sterling exchange rate, and will also affect the money supply.

Instruments as objectives

It has to be recognized that policy instruments sometimes become objectives in their own right. This was the case with the exchange rate instrument which was used only twice in the post-war period up to the early 1970s. This was because preserving the value of the pound had itself become an objective of policy, so that it could no longer be used as a flexible instrument of policy. Again in February 1987 the UK agreed to the Louvre Accord in Paris which stated that a period of exchange rate stability was desirable. This made it more difficult to use the exchange rate as a policy *instrument* and in some respects it then becomes an *objective* of policy instead! This became even more obvious between 1990 and 1992 when maintaining sterling's parity in the ERM was seen as a major objective of policy.

Political constraints

The set of policy objectives chosen, and the instruments used, may be constrained by the fact that it is politicians who are the ultimate decision-takers. Each course of action must therefore be evaluated in its political context. The use of some policy instruments may then be inhibited, as with the Conservative government's reluctance formally to use a prices and incomes policy given its views on the efficacy of a free market system. Similarly, the decision of the government to enter the ERM in October 1990 severely limited its ability to use the exchange rate as an instrument of policy, although its subsequent withdrawal in September 1992 eased this limitation. In 1997 the decision to establish an independent body, the Monetary Policy Committee, to set interest rates effectively removed this policy instrument from government control.

The theory of economic policy

Here we look at the basic theory of economic policy, concentrating on the 'fixed targets', the 'variable targets' and the 'satisficing' approaches to policy formation.

The fixed targets approach

Perhaps the best-known approach is that of Tinbergen (1952), the so-called fixed targets approach, which establishes the condition for the simultaneous achievement of fixed target values for a number of objectives. *Tinbergen's rule* states that if these target values are to be achieved simultaneously, then there must be at least the same number of instruments as there are objectives. The values of these instruments are determined by the desired-target values of the objectives, and they can then be assessed to see whether they are both feasible and acceptable to the decision-makers.

This rule can be illustrated in Fig. 24.1 where, for simplicity, the two-instrument/two-objective case is illustrated. Instruments I_1 (monetary policy), and I_2 (fiscal policy), are plotted on the axes of the graph. Movements along each axis and away from the origin will be used to indicate 'expansionary' policy. On the horizontal axis, for example, close to the origin we have 'tight' fiscal policy, with high taxation and low government expenditure. Movement along the horizontal axis and away from the origin indicates that fiscal policy becomes 'easier', with taxation falling and government expenditure rising. The Budget moves from surplus into deficit, with the deficit becoming greater as the movement to the right continues. On the vertical axis, points close to the origin indicate restrictive monetary policy, with high interest rates and static, or slowly growing, money supply. Movement along the vertical axis and away from the origin indicates an expansionary monetary policy, the money supply rising rapidly and interest rates falling.

The line O_1 shows the combinations of monetary and fiscal policy required to achieve the objective of *internal balance*, i.e. full employment (or something very close to it) with price stability (or a low and acceptable rate of inflation). O_1 will be negatively sloped, on the assumption that expansionary fiscal policy must be accompanied by contractionary monetary policy, if full employment is to be achieved without price inflation. If contractionary monetary policy did not accompany the expansionary fiscal policy then too high a level of aggregate demand would be generated, and with it price inflation.[3]

The line O_2 shows the combinations of monetary and fiscal policy required to achieve *external balance*, i.e. balance of payments equilibrium. It, too, is negatively sloped, reflecting the fact that expansionary fiscal policy raises domestic incomes, so increasing imports (and perhaps reducing exports). If balance of payments equilibrium is to be maintained, then these unfavourable effects on the current

Fig. 24.1.   Two-instrument/two-objective case.
Notes:
O_1 = Objective 1 (internal balance) at a particular target value.
O_2 = Objective 2 (external balance) at a particular target value.
I_1 = Instrumental variable 1, e.g. monetary policy.
I_2 = Instrumental variable 2, e.g. fiscal policy.

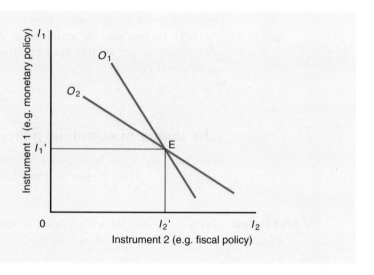

account must be offset by an improvement elsewhere in the accounts. This could be achieved by a contractionary monetary policy, which raises interest rates, attracting inflows of capital from overseas. Again, if fiscal policy is expansionary, a contractionary monetary policy will be necessary to preserve the external balance.[4]

Figure 24.1 shows that with two objectives (internal and external balance) and two instruments or instrumental variables (monetary and fiscal policy) then, by setting monetary and fiscal instruments at values I'_1 and I'_2 respectively, objectives O_1 and O_2 can be achieved simultaneously.[5] Tinbergen's rule is thereby illustrated.

Suppose now a third objective is added, perhaps a target rate of economic growth (Fig. 24.2). The line O_3 shows the combinations of monetary and fiscal policy required to achieve this target rate of economic growth. O_3 is positively sloped, on the assumption that an expansionary fiscal policy, involving extra government spending, will 'crowd out' private sector investment. Total investment can then only be kept at the level required to achieve growth rate O_3 by encouraging private sector investment through low interest rates, i.e. by expansionary monetary policy. Expansionary fiscal *and* monetary policy are in this case required to achieve the target rate of economic growth O_3.

We can now see that it would be a fortunate and unlikely coincidence if O_3 happened to pass through point E, i.e. if all three objectives could be achieved with just two policy instruments. If, as in the figure, it does not, then we can only achieve two of the three objectives with our two policy instruments. For instance, we could be at G (O_1 and O_3 achieved, but not O_2) or at F (O_2 and O_3 achieved, but not O_1) or at E (O_1 and O_2 achieved, but not O_3). To achieve the third objective now requires a third policy instrument, perhaps exchange rate policy![6] If we cannot find extra policy instruments, Tinbergen's rule will be violated, i.e. there will be fewer instruments (here two) than objectives (here three). Except in the fortuitous case that all three objectives intersect, at G, F or E, then an *explicit choice* will have to be made between the conflicting objectives. In our example we must choose between G, F or E.

Fig. 24.2. Two-instrument/three-objective case.

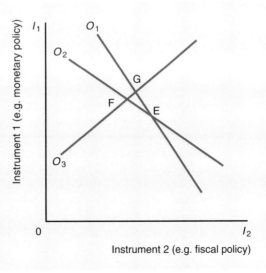

Instrument 1 (e.g. monetary policy)

Instrument 2 (e.g. fiscal policy)

Tinbergen's approach has the great merit of being fairly simple to understand. It has encouraged governments to be explicit about their macroeconomic objectives and has stimulated the search for new policy instruments, such as flexible exchange rates or prices and incomes policy. Its emphasis on 'fine-tuning' the economy by introducing additional policy instruments, and changing their values, reflects the spirit of 'Keynesian' interventionism.

The flexible targets approach

In Tinbergen's approach, when we were unable to achieve all three objectives simultaneously because we lacked sufficient policy instruments, the target then became the achievement of any two, i.e. at G, F or E in Fig. 24.2. A choice had to be made between these alternatives. In contrast Theil (1956) suggested that the target could be more flexible, and that any position could be chosen within the triangle GFE. In this case no single objective is achieved, instead a compromise between the three is reached, all three being 'missed', but by a narrow margin in each case. This might be preferred to achieving two objectives by missing the third by a considerable margin.

Theil's flexible targets approach therefore presupposes that since all the objectives cannot be met there must be some 'welfare loss' whatever choice of objectives is made. This approach also assumes that a social welfare function can be defined for society as a whole, the aim then being to minimize the welfare loss for any choice made. The welfare function will take into account the *deviation* between the actual value achieved for any objective and its target value, with any such deviation indicating a loss of welfare. The problem then becomes one of minimizing a welfare loss function bearing in mind that the objectives are presumably 'weighted' with respect to each other. For example, in the early 1980s a deviation between the actual and target inflation rate would appear to be weighted more heavily than a deviation between the actual and target unemployment rate. Weights W_1, W_2 and W_3 are introduced into the welfare loss function to be minimized below. The deviations between actual and target levels are conventionally squared in order to eliminate the problem of sign.

It follows that if the three objectives have *actual* values O_1, O_2 and O_3, and target values O_1^*, O_2^* and O_3^*, then the policy-makers would seek to minimize the social welfare loss function defined in terms of those three objectives, i.e.

$$\text{Minimize } U(O_1, O_2, O_3) = W_1(O_1 - O_1^*)^2 + W_2(O_2 - O_2^*)^2 + W_3(O_3 - O_3^*)^2$$

If there had been sufficient instruments to permit the simultaneous achievement of all three objectives, then $O_1 = O_1^*$; $O_2 = O_2^*$, and $O_3 = O_3^*$; in other words, the welfare loss function would equal zero. In terms of Fig. 24.2 all three objective functions (O_1, O_2 and O_3) have coincided at a single point. More sophisticated forms of such functions recognize that it is not only the extent to which the target objectives are fulfilled that matters, but also the values of the instrumental variables themselves. For example, high tax rates or higher interest rates may themselves reduce social welfare and might therefore be included in the loss function.

No one would suggest that political decision-makers study loss minimization functions of the form indicated above, but the approach is helpful in suggesting that attempts should be made to think seriously about the relative weights given to objectives, and that if fixed target values are unattainable then flexibility might have to be accepted.

The satisficing approach

Both the Tinbergen and the Theil approaches suggest that the economy is 'fine-tuned' by the policy-makers, i.e. instruments are continuously manipulated in order to achieve target welfare maximizing (or loss-minimizing) values. Mosley (1976) pointed out that in practice policy instruments are periodically manipulated, usually all at once, in response to a crisis. He has proposed a 'satisficing' theory of economic policy, which views the policy-maker as a 'satisficing' agent, i.e. one whose motive is not to achieve the best possible states at all times, but to achieve 'satisfactory' levels of performance. These 'satisfactory' levels are influenced, in the case of macroeconomic objectives, by recently achieved performance and are determined by compromise bargaining between such institutions as the Bank of England, the Treasury and the Cabinet. He suggests that a package of instruments will be used in order to respond to a 'crisis', which might be an unsatisfactory level of performance with respect even to one objective, with the strength of the response depending upon the amount by which the actual value differs from the 'satisfactory' level.

Testing the satisficing approach for the period 1946–71, Mosley found that *any* balance of payments deficit triggered a response – in other words only a zero or positive balance was regarded as 'satisfactory'. However, the unemployment figure considered 'satisfactory' varied over the years, following a rising trend. In 1953 it was below 1.6%, in 1965 below 2.5%, and by 1971 below 3.6%. Should a figure of below 5% be considered 'satisfactory' in the late 1990s?

The fixed and flexible targets approaches to macroeconomic policy predict that policy-makers will seek to find new and effective instruments of policy in order simultaneously to achieve a growing number of economic objectives. If that search is not successful, then compromises between the target values of the objectives will be sought; more pragmatically, the policy-makers will accept quite broad ranges of values for the objectives and will intervene only when one (or more) of the target values becomes 'unsatisfactory'. In this last, 'satisficing', case the economy is 'managed by exception'.

Until the mid-1970s this reflected the interventionist 'Keynesian' approach which prevailed in the UK after the Second World War. Target values and achieved values for the objectives rarely diverged significantly, and it was generally accepted that policy-makers, armed with the predictions of increasingly sophisticated forecasting models of the economy, and using an increasing range of instrumental variables, could and should manage the economy by 'fine-tuning' it on to a desired path. However, as the 1970s progressed, the fine tuning and satisficing approaches to policy making were being replaced by theories which began stressing the inherently stable nature of the economy. These advocated the need to set 'rules' which policy-makers should follow in the medium-term, instead of concentrating on short-term interventionism.

Post-war macroeconomic policy in practice

The first period – pre-1974

The major preoccupation as the Second World War ended was to put an end to the high levels of unemployment which had prevailed throughout the inter-war period when unemployment had averaged around 14%, even reaching 22% in 1932. The primacy of this objective was expressed in a famous sentence in the 1944

Government White Paper on Employment Policy: 'The Government accepts as one of their primary aims and responsibilities the maintenance of a high and stable level of employment after the War.' In the 1950s and 1960s unemployment figures of half a million led to reflationary measures, and the figure of 1 million unemployed (about 4% of the workforce) was first reached as late as 1972, when very strong measures were taken to expand demand and raise the employment level. Such expansionary measures usually took the form of fiscal activity (increased government spending and/or lower taxation), accompanied by relaxed hire-purchase controls and some stimulus to bank lending. This was the 'Keynesian' response to unemployment.

These measures had an effect upon the level of employment but also led to periodic balance of payments crises as the stimulus to aggregate demand raised not only incomes and employment but also imports. The resulting balance of payments crises could only be tackled, given our reluctance to use tariffs, by a deflation of aggregate demand resulting in greater unemployment. This 'stop–go' cycle had adverse effects upon the rate of long-term economic growth, which was a general objective of all post-war governments. The average inflation rate was generally low (4.8% in 1946–50, 4.6% in 1951–55, 2.1% in 1956–60, 3.5% in 1961–65, 4.6% in 1966–70 and 8.5% in 1971–73), and was dealt with partly by adjusting aggregate demand but also by the use of a prices and incomes policy, itself a reflection of the Keynesian view that trade unions and other institutional features of the labour market are major factors in determining inflation.

Up to the early 1970s we can broadly say that macroeconomic policy was based upon 'Keynesian' principles, emphasizing the management of aggregate demand, mainly through fiscal policy, backed up by some form of prices and incomes policy. This kind of interventionist policy has been described as an attempt to 'fine-tune' the economy, adjusting the various policy instruments in order to achieve a set of policy objectives, and reflects the three approaches dealt with above. After 1974 the emphasis began to move away from 'fine-tuning', with its continuous exercise of government 'discretion' in varying instruments to achieve target values, and towards a more ordered path of set 'rules'.

The second period – post-1974

The subsequent period saw dramatic changes. Inflation and unemployment increased appreciably (see Table 24.1 above), and the Keynesian approach was increasingly criticized as a basis for macroeconomic policy-making. New research programmes achieved prominence with their own theoretical bases, leading to new approaches to macroeconomic policy.

Money was increasingly recognized as an important factor, that is to say 'money mattered', and less emphasis was placed on the demand side of the economy and more on supply. Even to those for whom the demand side retained its Keynesian pre-eminence, there was an interest in the influence of net financial assets on consumer expenditure in addition to the influence of income. During the period two 'new' approaches seemed to reflect these trends – that of the CEPG and that of the monetarists. These two 'schools' of economic thought might at first sight seem to have little in common, for they advocated very different policy measures and disagreed about the way the economy worked. What makes them interesting from our point of view is that they agreed that the economy was inherently stable and that the

Keynesian fine-tuning interventionist approach was inappropriate. They advocated the use of 'rules' to be followed, a tax rule on the one hand and a money growth rule on the other. Short-run intervention was seen as likely to be at best irrelevant, and at worst counter-productive.

The Cambridge Economic Policy Group

The CEPG differed from traditional Keynesians in seeing fiscal policy as possibly *contributing to* the balance of payments problem rather than correcting it. They identified a strong link between the balance of payments on current account and the size of the public sector surplus/deficit.

In the conventional manner let

I = investment expenditure,
G = government expenditure,
X = exports,
S = savings,
T = taxation receipts,
M = imports. Then, for equilibrium:

$$I + G + X = S + T + M$$

rearranging

$$X - M = S - I + T - G$$

i.e. the surplus on the balance of payments current account is, by definition, equal to the private sector surplus $(S - I)$ plus the public sector surplus $(T - G)$.

The private sector surplus is the sum of household and company *net* savings and this, it is claimed, is so small that it can be ignored. Household saving in the UK is normally balanced by investment in housing (channelled by building society deposits), and company saving is the major source of company investment. That being so then:

$$S - I \simeq O$$

and

$$X - M \simeq T - G$$

i.e. the balance of payments current account surplus/deficit is approximately equal to the public sector surplus/deficit, and changes in the latter will lead to approximately equal changes in the former. The explanation is that the effect of expansionary fiscal policy will be to raise incomes and imports faster than exports.

The policy implication of the approach typified by the CEPG was that an expansion of domestic demand to alleviate unemployment must be accompanied by the use of import controls. If the expansion is not accompanied by import controls, then the balance of payments will rapidly move into a considerable deficit, with devaluation or depreciation of the exchange rate unable to correct the deficit. The favourable effects for employment of the expansionary fiscal policy will then be dissipated overseas as increased demand in the UK is met by increased purchases of foreign goods rather than domestically produced goods. Their reply to the argument that the imposition of import controls on the part of the UK would be met with retaliation from other countries, is that the aim would not be to *reduce* the level of imports into the UK but to keep the level from rising. If no other country is harmed there will be no need for retaliation! In fact, any rise in UK exports might subsequently create scope for imports to rise.

We have already seen that economists supporting the CEPG analysis believe that 'fine-tuning' the economy by pursuing an interventionist policy is actually counter-productive and destabilizing. They believe that the economy is relatively stable in the medium term and that the most appropriate policy is to apply a 'fiscal rule' within the context of a medium-term strategy. This rule takes the form of a composite tax rate – the par tax rate – set at such a level that desired targets for National Income (employment) and the balance of payments can be achieved in the medium term. This rule should be adhered to, and the par tax rate altered, *only* if the target values are themselves altered, or if there are major disturbances in the world economy, or in the trade-off between the employment and balance of payments objectives.

The monetarists   Monetarists similarly eschew the use of an armoury of policy instruments (instrumental variables) to achieve macroeconomic objectives. The monetarist economists believe that if the money stock is increased, real output is not affected in the long run, though prices are, i.e. control of the money supply is the key to the control of inflation.[7] They accept that in the short run changes in money supply will affect output as well as prices. However, there will be time-lags between the change in money supply and changes in output, making it inadvisable to use the manipulation of aggregate demand as a policy instrument for achieving target levels of output and employment. Output and employment will instead be determined at their 'natural' levels by microeconomic factors affecting aggregate supply. These are more easily influenced by measures designed to improve market efficiency or to increase the supply of factors of production.

Policy-makers are therefore encouraged to follow simple 'rules' which will influence the economy in the long run, and will not generally be subject to changes which might cause instability in the short run. The most obvious rule is to control the rate of monetary expansion, and to effect changes in it relatively gradually in order that disruption is not too great. To the monetarist the target rate for monetary expansion (given flexible exchange rates) becomes the proxy for the target rate of inflation, so that the 'target' is now set in terms of the value of the instrumental variable (money supply) rather than in terms of the objective (inflation). Short-run manipulation of the instrument to achieve the target objective was regarded as neither necessary nor even possible. Instead, the authorities are to control inflation through the long-run rate of monetary expansion. A rule for policy is therefore established.

Medium-term economic strategy

An important turning point in economic policy took place in 1979 with the election of the Conservative government under the leadership of Margaret Thatcher. The main thrust of macroeconomic policy moved towards the evolution of a non-inflationary economic environment within which a market economy could rapidly flourish. As in many aspects of Economics, a major shift in policy making often originates from a modification of economic thinking. In this case, the theoretical basis for the anti-inflationary policy was the breakdown of the Phillips curve relationship (which seemed to have underpinned Keynesian macroeconomic policy ideas in the 1960s) and the emergence of Friedman's 'expectations augmented' version of the Phillips curve. This latter version of the Phillips relationship combined the Friedmanite inflationary expectations theory with the concept of the 'natural rate of unemployment' (see Chapter 23). As far as policy making is concerned, the intention was to achieve the goal of lower inflation by influencing aggregate demand (through the money supply) and by improving aggregate supply responsiveness, thereby creating a fall in the 'natural rate of unemployment'. The Thatcher government therefore introduced an economic strategy directed towards the medium-term, which had two main components.

The first main component was **macroeconomic** in nature and was in line with monetary thinking. It involved a *Medium Term Financial Strategy* (MTFS) whose aim was to use constraints on the money supply (see below) to decrease the growth of money GDP over time, and thereby cut the rate of inflation. This obviously reflected the predominant use of monetary policy as the government's main economic policy instrument and the subordination of fiscal policy. As far as the latter was concerned, the government aimed to decrease the Public Sector Borrowing Requirement (PSBR), mainly by reducing public expenditure, since it felt that there was a close relationship between the size of the PSBR and the money supply. It was also argued that any increase in PSBR, and therefore in government borrowing, would mean that interest rates would have to rise in order to persuade the private sector to hold public debt. These high interest rates would, in turn, lead to a movement of funds from the private to the public sector, i.e. the private sector would be 'crowded out'. Therefore, the government saw the central aim of the MTFS as the control of inflation, which was to be achieved by reducing the growth of money supply and by keeping the PSBR under control. The second main component of the medium-term economic strategy was **microeconomic** in nature, making use of the so-called *supply-side policies* in order to improve the *output responsiveness* of the economy. In terms of the economic analysis used above, these supply-side policies sought to improve the workings of markets in order to decrease the 'natural rate of unemployment'. In the next section we will first follow the course of the MTFS before looking in more detail at the government's supply-side policies.

MTFS 1979–81   The MTFS was first published in March 1980. There have been annual policy statements since 1980 which set out *targets* for monetary growth and for the PSBR over a medium-term time horizon. As noted above, the prime aim of the MTFS was to eradicate inflation, in the belief that inflation actually caused unemployment by creating inflationary wage and price expectations. Creating a stable, non-inflationary framework was therefore seen as essential, and this became the cornerstone of policy.

In the early period, $£M_3$ was chosen by the government as the most reliable indicator of spending, and targets for the growth of $£M_3$ were set in each annual MTFS statement. Unfortunately, in order to control $£M_3$, interest rates had to be raised to record levels of 17% in 1979; even then this did not seem to bring $£M_3$ within the desired bands. Interest rates remained high throughout 1980 and this pushed up the exchange rate, making UK exports uncompetitive in international markets. The continued attempts to get £M$_3$ and the PSBR under control led the government to tighten its fiscal policy in 1981 and although interest rates fell during the early part of the year, they were back to 16% by later that year. The early monetarist experiment, plus the world recession, led to a fall in manufacturing output by 19.6% between June 1979 and June 1981 and a loss of 23% of manufacturing employment (see also Ch. 1).

Two interesting developments grew out of this early monetarist experiment. First, a difficulty arose in finding a valid measure of money which faithfully reflected movements in UK spending. Unfortunately, £M$_3$ was becoming unreliable as a measure of UK spending. For example, as the interest rate rose, depositors were induced to shift from non-interest to interest bearing accounts. Such a shift would not change the total money supply £M$_3$, but merely redistribute it from accounts where it was more likely to be spent (non-interest bearing) to accounts where it was less likely to be spent (interest bearing). As a result, although figures for £M$_3$ were not recorded as having fallen much in this period, the *actual spending* of the population decreased more significantly. Second, it was becoming clear that economic policy, whether short- or medium-term in aim, was still unable to reconcile conflicting objectives. For example, controlling money supply and the PSBR involved a policy of high interest rates; but these decreased industrial investment and also led to a fall in UK exports (as the exchange rate rose with interest rates). The early monetarist experiment was not immune to the traditional problems involved when trying to balance policy targets with policy instruments.

MTFS 1982–84   In 1982 the government overhauled the MTFS and began to abandon the policy of targeting a single monetary variable, i.e. £M$_3$. For example, it had became clear as early as 1981 that *narrower* definitions of money such as M$_0$ and M$_1$ were growing much more slowly than £M$_3$ and were reflecting more accurately what was happening to the real economy. As a result, other measures of money such as M$_0$, M$_1$, and PSL$_2$ began to be included as target aggregates, and £M$_3$ targets were adjusted to take into consideration some of the problems noted above. The doubling of unemployment between 1979 and 1982 also weakened the government's will to continue with its severe anti-inflationary policy. By Autumn 1982 interest rates had fallen to around 9% and remained reasonably steady until the middle of 1984, while at the same time the Lawson tax-cutting budgets from 1983 onwards provided some stimulus to aggregate demand. Much of the recovery of the 1982–85 period was due to a rise in consumer expenditure as earnings rose faster than inflation. This was further fuelled by a credit boom, brought about by easier access to credit and a fall in the savings ratio.

During this period the targets for the PSBR were gently eased, as money supply targets other than £M$_3$ were tried, with varying degrees of success. The government became more aware of the problems involved in using only monetary targets as the cornerstone of policy. Indeed 'squeezing' inflation out of the system by this method would not only be difficult, but might even be impossible. In a pragmatic sense, it seemed that by late 1984, both the government and the Bank of England had accepted that a 5% inflation rate might be a more realistic objective in the future. As money supply targets became less reliable, monetary policy began to shift towards targeting the exchange rate. This was to continue into the next period.

MTFS 1985–88 The government's MTFS took another turn at the beginning of 1985 when economic circumstances created an exchange rate crisis. The government had shown increasing unease at the apparent rise in the underlying trend of UK inflation in 1984, together with the continued problem of unemployment. At the same time the dollar was at its peak. The ensuing loss of confidence in the UK led to a fall in the value of the pound to $1.04; this caused the UK to experience inflationary pressure as the low exchange rate increased import costs. As a result of this volatility in the exchange rate, a more 'active' policy was adopted in order to stabilize the exchange rate at a 'desirable' level which would not increase inflation. It was felt that sterling would best be pegged to a stable currency such as the deutschmark, and for a while the unofficial government target for sterling was set at around 3.0DM to 3.2DM to the pound. It should be understood that the move towards stable and targeted exchange rates was not only a UK phenomenon. The major trading nations had agreed in the 'Plaza Accord' of October 1985 and in the 'Louvre Accord' of February 1987 to move towards co-ordinating their economic policies and to peg their currencies within agreed target zones.

What had clearly happened in 1985 was a shift in the role of monetary policy; instead of using the interest rate mechanism to control the *money supply*, it was now used to control the *exchange rate*. Inflation was now seen as being transmitted to the UK economy mainly through the exchange rate route. By November 1985, £M3 was downgraded from a 'target variable' to one which was now only to be 'monitored'; and, after 1987, M_0 was the only targeted monetary variable in government use during the period. The 1985–88 period saw a gradual fall in interest rates and a more relaxed approach to monetary policy in general; the interest rate weapon being used increasingly to achieve the desired exchange rather than any specific money supply targets. At the same time the UK experienced boom conditions, stimulated by easier credit conditions and higher post-tax incomes. Consumer expenditure on both durable and non-durable goods (such as housing) led the growth of aggregate demand. The unemployment rate fell, but many saw the rise in inflation by the end of 1988 as the inevitable 'cost' of such a policy.

This period shows that following simple monetary *rules* cannot always bring simple solutions to the economy. It also shows the conflicting nature of targets and instruments. Some members of the government (including the Prime Minister) believed that interest rates should have been higher during this period, in order to control the money supply and therefore aggregate spending and inflation. Others, such as the Chancellor, Nigel Lawson, felt that the best course was to keep interest rates rather lower in order to prevent the sterling exchange rate rising above a certain target level against currencies such as the deutschmark and dollar. In this way we could still control inflation, but without squeezing the domestic money supply and credit too much. In the end, a rise in M_0 above its target values and clear signs of a resurgence in inflation meant that in March 1988 interest rates rose once more.

MTFS 1988–1992 The period following the rapid expansion of the 1985–88 boom years was to prove 'costly'. As noted previously, consumer expenditure grew rapidly during these boom years as a result of lower interest rates, financial liberalisation measures, and a growth of the mortgage 'leak' (i.e. the financing of spending by re-mortgaging and using the cash to purchase goods). The boom came to an abrupt end around the middle of

1988, with interest rates rising sharply, curbing both consumer expenditure and house prices. The UK then entered the ERM in October 1990, tying the exchange rate to European currencies within a 'band' which gave some limited room for manoeuvre. It was hoped that maintaining sterling within a relatively high exchange rate band would help keep import costs low, thus easing inflationary pressures. The tightening of monetary policy after 1988 was also complemented by a tightening of the fiscal stance, resulting in a PSBR of $-£0.5$bn in 1990/91. However, the rise in unemployment due to the recession was soon to result in increased government expenditure, so that the PSBR of $-£0.5$bn in 1990/91 soon became a deficit of £16bn by 1991/92.

The Financial Statement and the Budget Report (the 'red book') for 1992/93 reaffirmed the government's commitment to bringing inflation down to a sustainable level. However, it had very little to say about monetary policy except that it was 'primarily directed at maintaining sterling's parity in the ERM', a clear sign that the government had effectively abandoned monetary policy as an independent policy instrument for influencing domestic conditions. As far as fiscal policy was concerned, its role was to 'balance the budget over a medium term'. By 1992 it was impossible to discern any policy guidelines as being clearly derived from the monetary side of the MTFS macroeconomic 'model', while fiscal policy continued to be seen as a passive instrument. These changes left the government with one main external target – namely keeping the exchange rate within the prescribed 'band' of the ERM, and one main instrument – the interest rate. However, events in late 1992 brought fiscal policy at least as regards public expenditure, into greater prominence. This new focus followed sterling being forced out of the ERM in September 1992. By late 1992, sterling had fallen by over 14% against the DM and over 20% against the $US. Fears of renewed inflationary tendencies, via higher import prices, and alarm at a rapidly expanding PSBR, forced the government into a sharp adjustment on the public expenditure side of fiscal policy.

MTFS 1993–1996

After the events of late 1992, it was unlikely that even a reconstituted ERM would provide the framework for macroeconomic policy as it had done in previous years. As a result it was essential that the UK's macroeconomic policy should be based on a sustainable *domestic* strategy.

By 1993 the scene was set for a reassessment of strategy. On the fiscal side, the minimal requirement of a sound policy was seen to be 'debt sustainability'. In other words the growth in the ratio of public debt to GDP should not accelerate too rapidly. The increase in this ratio from 0% to 7.0% between 1990/91 to 1993/94 involved major problems. For example, a high level of government borrowing left a heavy burden of debt to be financed in the future. This, in turn, led to instability in the financial markets as uncertainties about the future translated themselves into volatile interest rates. Further, a 'loose' fiscal policy placed more reliance on a 'tight' monetary policy to restrain inflation, again risking higher interest rates. The budget statements of 1994/95 included a programme to broaden the tax base together with measures to restrain public spending on defence, housing, social security and civil service running costs. The November 1995 and 1996 budgets remained somewhat restrictive in nature, with the long term aim of fiscal balance by the turn of the century.

Therefore one important medium term objective of the goverment in the late 1990s has been to achieve stable public finances, using fiscal policy as the main instrument for reducing the PSBR in the medium term. The problem about making medium term macroeconomic forecasts for the PSBR is that they have to be based on certain assumptions about the future behaviour of indices such as economic growth and various tax elasticities. If, for example, the economic growth forecasted four years ahead actually turns out to be lower than predicted, then *actual* tax receipts will fall faster than predicted, resulting in a higher PSBR than anticipated at the begining of the four-year period.

On the monetary side, the suspension of sterling from the ERM meant that a new strategy was needed for monetary policy (Hudson and Fisher 1994). In 1993, the government introduced for the first time an explicit target for the main objective of monetary policy, namely the inflation rate. The target was to keep inflation (i.e. the retail price index excluding mortgage interest payments) within a range of 1%–4% over the year. By 1995/96 the target for inflation was down to the lower end of the range, at around 2.5%. To do this, the Chancellor decided to *monitor* the variables which reflect the movement of inflation, i.e. the monetary variables M0 and M4. In previous years, M0 had been assigned a *specific target*, but in 1993 this was changed to a *monitored range* of between 0% and 4% for M0 and 3%–9% for M4. If the monetary variables moved outside these limits, there would then be some cause for concern. In addition to the monetary aggregates, indicators such as the exchange rate, asset prices and house prices were given more weight in judging the outlook for inflation.

Macroeconomic management during this period reflected two interesting aspects of the UK's fight against inflation. First, there was now a clear shift away from the 1988 to 1992 period, when the government seemed to have only one main objective to be targeted (the exchange rate) and one main instrument (the interest rate). Such a narrow focus for policy became increasingly inappropriate when an exchange rate policy designed to help the UK 'converge' with other European economies could be seen to be imposing major costs in terms of reducing both domestic output and employment. The Chancellor now began to consider a *wider range* of intermediate objectives and instruments, rather than concentrate on a narrow set of variables which had to be met precisely. In other words, a more flexible Theil-type approach was now envisaged. Although a more flexible approach has been adopted towards monetary policy, we should remember that the short term interest rate still remained the main instrument for controlling inflation. Second, a greater weight was now given to economic models in policy making. Models of the economy such as those produced by the Treasury, the National Institute of Economic and Social Research (NIESR), and the London Business School (LBS), regained their former importance as policy makers once again looked for the optimum relationship between various objectives and instruments (Bray, Kuleshov, Uysal and Walker 1993).

MTFS 1996–   Macroeconomic management took a new direction with the return of the Labour government in 1997. First, in May 1997 the Bank of England was given operational independence to set interest rates in order to meet the government's inflation objective. Second, the supervision of the banking sector was to be removed from the Bank of England and placed in the hands of the Financial Services Authority (FSA), and third, the Bank's responsibility for debt management was transferred to the Treasury. As far as monetary policy is concerned, theses changes suggest a greater focus on macroeconomic stability. The growth of money supply (i.e. M0 and M4) was still seen as playing an important role in the Bank of England's assessment of the inflation outlook, but setting targets for money supply was abandoned, being replaced by a specific target for inflation. Even the monitoring ranges for money supply were now regarded as being unhelpful, especially as the velocity of circulation had been seen to behave so erratically. The inflation target of 2.5% is to be 'policed' by an independent Monetary Policy Committee (MPC) of the Bank of England using one main instrument – the interest rate.

As far as the fiscal policy is concerned, the incoming Labour government sought to strengthen fiscal stability by the observance of two fiscal 'rules'. First, the 'golden rule', whereby over the economic cycle the government will only borrow to invest and not to fund current expenditure. Second, the 'public debt rule', whereby the ratio of public debt to national income will be held at a stable and prudent level over the economic cycle. In practice this means that the government will seek to achieve fiscal balance over an average cycle of 6–7 years.

On the fiscal side, these changes continued the trend of managing the economy using certain 'rules' in the medium term – now defined as the period covering the economic cycle. On the monetary side the main objective is to meet an inflation target of 2.5%, using the rate of interest as a key policy. Most of the problems involved in managing the economy noted at the outset of this chapter remain, for example 'trade-offs' between objectives such as inflation and unemployment (via growth) must still be considered, and the instruments available are still not independent, e.g. interest rates still affect exchange rates. The political constraints on policy making appear to have eased with the granting of independence to the Bank of England. However, it remains to be seen as to whether the political process can be divorced from the management of a nation's economy.

Supply-side strategy

As was explained previously, the Conservative government's medium-term economic strategy also revolved around improving the *output responsiveness* of the economy. Monetarists and 'New Classical' economists generally have sympathy with the view that output and employment are supply-determined, rather than with the Keynesian view that they are demand-determined.

Figure 24.3(a) represents the familiar Keynesian view, with prices and output (Real National Income) being determined largely by changes in aggregate demand.

Fig. 24.3. (a) The Keynesian approach; (b) the supply-side approach.

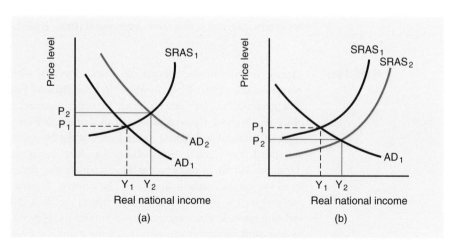

Our main interest here is to contrast this familiar diagram with Fig. 24.3(b), which uses the same axes to reflect the monetarist or supply-side view of economics.

In the Keynesian case, an increase in real output from Y_1 to Y_2 is most readily achieved by an increase in aggregate demand from AD_1 to AD_2. However, the supply side view is that an increase in real output from Y_1 to Y_2 is more effectively achieved by a downward (rightward) shift of the aggregate supply curve from $SRAS_1$ to $SRAS_2$. In the former case the average price level is likely to rise as real output rises, while the supply side approach predicts a fall in the average price level alongside a rise in real output.

In favouring the supply side approach, Conservative governments of the 1980s argued that there were certain features of the UK economy which tended to *prevent* the supply curve shifting downwards from $SRAS_1$ to $SRAS_2$. They felt that the main task of the government was to achieve such a downward shift in SRAS through 'supply side' policies aimed at increasing productive efficiency in the economy. However, before we look at the various policies advocated in support of this approach, it is useful to consider the factors which allegedly prevent the SRAS curve from shifting downwards.

First, there is the suggestion that unemployment and social security benefits encourage people to spend more time searching for the type of employment they consider appropriate. As a result they remain on the unemployment register longer, the unemployment figures are swollen, and aggregate output is restricted from the supply side. An ancillary argument is that the difference between some low-paid jobs and the rate of unemployment benefit is so marginal that such jobs are not taken up. This problem is aggravated by the UK tax system, which may result in some workers, previously unemployed, paying marginal tax rates in excess of 100% when moving into low-paid jobs – the 'unemployment trap' (see Ch. 19). Unemployment and social security benefits may in these ways cause the short run aggregate supply curve to remain at $SRAS_1$, in Fig. 24.3(b), thereby preventing output from rising to Y_2 and keeping the price level higher than it would otherwise be.

The second suggestion is that, quite apart from the 'unemployment trap', high taxation can affect the supply of labour (and so the level of output) through its disincentive effects. The reverse side of this is that a cut in taxes might so stimulate work effort that real output (and even total tax revenue) rises. In terms of Fig. 24.3(b) tax cuts would shift the supply curve to the right, i.e. from $SRAS_1$ to $SRAS_2$, so that output and employment would rise, and prices fall.

The third suggestion is that labour has priced itself out of the market, thereby reducing employment and output, because the trade unions have forced up the real wages of their members. It has been estimated by Minford and Peel (1981) that unions have 'marked up' members' wages by between 12 and 25%, so raising permanent unemployment figures by between 400,000 and 800,000, although more recent research has put the average mark-up at 10% or less. Another important study (Layard and Nickell 1985) showed that the unemployment rate in the UK had risen by 11.83 percentage points between 1956 and 1983 and that union 'push' on wages accounted for 2.27 of those percentage points. The policy implication is that trade union bargaining power should be curbed. In terms of *labour market* analysis the market wage is kept above the equilibrium wage so that unemployment is higher than market conditions warrant. In terms of the *goods market* in Fig. 24.3(b), the relatively high labour costs tend to keep the aggregate supply curve artificially high at $SRAS_1$. Output and employment are lower and prices are higher than they would otherwise be.

Finally, there is the suggestion that the very high unemployment and low output figures prevailing in the UK exaggerate the true situation because there is a considerable 'hidden' or 'black' economy, encouraged by a desire to evade taxation. Some of the 'black' economy would be conducted in monetary terms (e.g. payment in cash to a local handyman), some in non-monetary terms by means of barter. The 'black' economy has always been with us, and estimates as to its size vary from 2.5% of GDP (the gap between expenditure and declared income) to 7.5% (Inland Revenue estimates of tax evasion) and even to 15%.

As explained above, successive governments have implemented a wide range of measures consistent with the approach of supply-side economics (shown in Fig. 24.3 as a shift in the aggregate supply curve downwards to the right). We will briefly summarise some of the practical changes which have to be implemented in an attempt to increase the efficiency of markets.

Taxation

Successive governments have believed that the taxation structure has become distorted over the years and should be changed in order to create more incentives and to induce more output (supply) responsiveness. For example, the decrease in tax allowances on mortgages in the late 1980s from £30,000 per *person* to £30,000 per *dwelling* was partly designed to curb the amount of investment in housing and to stimulate investment in company shares, i.e. to channel investment into more productive forms which would help stimulate output. Similarly, tax relief on life insurance premiums had been abolished in 1984, in an attempt to encourage people to invest in company equities. Again the rate of Capital Gains Tax had long been *less than* the basic rate of income tax, giving, for example, a better return to a person who bought and sold oil paintings than to a person buying company shares. In 1988 the CGT and the basic rate of income tax were equalised to prevent this bias. As well as bringing down personal taxation in order to stimulate incentives, successive governments have also decreased corporation tax for large companies, from 52% in 1983/4 to 30% by 1999; for small firms the rate was reduced from 35% to 20% in the same period. Those cuts in corporation tax were an attempt to stimulate reinvestment in capital stock.

Labour supply, efficiency and training

Successive governments have also believed in the need to improve the workings of the UK labour market, in order to make it more 'efficient' (i.e . labour should be mobile, well trained and free from institutional – e.g. union – bias). As far as *mobility* is concerned, the government felt that the UK labour market needed to be 'flexible', with workers induced to take up jobs rapidly. It was thought that this process was being inhibited by narrow differentials between the income of those out of work, thereby preventing active job search. Continuous adjustments have therefore been made in national insurance benefits and income related benefits over the past years, with the aim of widening the gap in income levels between those in work and those out of work.

To improve the *institutional problems* surrounding the labour market, successive Conservative governments introduced a series of laws to regulate employment and the Trade Unions. The Employment Acts of 1980, '82, '88, '89 and '90, together with the Trade Union Act of 1984, all of which were consolidated into the Trade Union and Labour Relations (Consolidation) Act of 1992, have weakened the control of unions (see Ch. 15). In the area of training, one of the greatest problems for the UK has involved a dearth of vocational skills at the *intermediate* level as seen in Table 24.2. A recent study by O'Mahony (1998) confirms this situation, showing the UK to have only 36.2% of its workforce with intermediate skills qualifications compared to 63.2% for Germany. The study also found the UK to have 54.4% of its manufacturing workforce in the 'low skill' category, compared to only 29.5% for Germany.

As a result of these deficiencies, the UK government introduced a number of initiatives in the early 1990s. For example, by 1991 some 104 Training and Enterprise Councils (TECs) were in operation in Britain. These are independent business-led companies, funded by government, and charged with meeting the training, enterprise and vocational education requirements of local communities and employers. Similarly, the Technical and Vocational Educational Initiative (TVEI) was introduced in the early 1990s to influence the whole curriculum of schools and colleges to prepare pupils of 14–18 for the demands of working life. Other initiatives sought to encourage employers to invest more effectively in training and development. For example the 'Investors in People' initiative aims, through the TECs, to fund employers who attempt to meet a national 'Standard' of training set by a number of bodies including the CBI. The National Training Awards scheme was introduced to publicly reward good practice by identifying examples of exceptional training, holding national and regional award ceremonies to reinforce training campaigns. These changes, together with others relating to the basic school curriculum, have been aimed at increasing the quality of the UK's stock of 'human capital'.

The incoming Labour government of 1997 has continued with many such initiatives, including new training initiatives as part of its 'New Deal' and 'Welfare to Work' programmes (see Ch. 19).

Industrial policies   Very briefly, it should be realized that the whole process of privatization fits well into the supply-side ideology. Successive Conservative governments have felt that companies in the private sector are better at using resources than those in government hands. It is therefore no surprise that those governments sought to place the main utilities into private hands over the last decade (see Ch. 5). The more 'lenient' attitude towards Mergers and Acquisitions during the 1980s and 1990s was another by-product of this general view that the private sector can better utilise resources (see Ch. 8).

Policy effectiveness

As has already been noted, sound economic management from both the macroeconomic and microeconomic viewpoints is difficult to achieve at the best

Table 24.2 Percentage of the workforce with vocational qualifications.

	Britain	France	Germany
University degrees	11	7	11
Intermediate vocational qualifications	25	40	63
Of which: technician	7	7	7
craft	18	33	56
No vocational qualifications	64	53	26

Source: Adapted from Trade and Industry Committee (1994) Table 9.

of times, depending as it does on so many variables which are often hard to predict. The UK has been regarded by many commentators as having had some success in changing the microeconomic environment through supply-side policies, thereby increasing the flexibility of the labour market. However, praise for UK macroeconomic policy has not been so forthcoming (Oulton 1995). Oulton compared the UK's cyclical performance with that of a number of other main industrial countries since 1970 and found that boom periods were shorter and recessions longer in the UK than in the other industrial countries. Further, countries such as the UK which have spent longer periods in recession have also experienced lower average growth rates. The point here is that more effective macroeconomic policy in the UK could provide a more balanced cyclical growth path, thereby reducing the duration of those otherwise long recessions which so damage confidence and reduce investment.

Economic policy in an international context

While there has been a natural tendency in this chapter to concentrate on the macroeconomic environment of the UK, it would be instructive to place UK experience into an *international* context. Following the failure to control inflation in the late 1960s and 1970s, most industrial countries conducted macroeconomic policies in the 1980s which were designed to reduced inflation to low levels in order to achieve sustained economic growth. During the 1990s these countries often had to face the same problems resulting from the post 1988 slowdown in the world economy, namely government deficits increasing rapidly in all major countries (see Table 24.3).

It was therefore difficult for these countries to use an active Keynesian-type *fiscal policy* to help their recoveries because this would add further to budget deficits. As a result they concentrated on the longer term aim of *fiscal consolidation*, i.e. in decreasing the burden of government deficits. The reasons for the world-wide growth of fiscal deficits apparent in Table 24.3 (at least until the mid 1990s) can be traced to five main factors.

- First, some argue that there has been a growth across the major industrialized countries of more generous and widely avaliable public pensions, social security benefits and other government transfers.

Table 24.3 Industrial countries: general government fiscal balances including social insurance (% of GDP).

	1981–91	1994	1997	2000*	2003*
Major industrial countries	−2.9	−3.7	−1.4	−0.6	0.3
United States	−2.8	−2.3	−0.2	0.5	1.4
Japan	−0.4	−2.3	−3.4	−2.1	−1.1
Germany	−2.1	−2.4	−2.7	−2.2	−1.1
France	−2.2	−5.6	−3.0	−2.4	−1.1
Italy	−11.1	−9.2	−2.7	−1.9	−1.4
United Kingdom	−1.9	−6.9	−1.6	0.7	1.7
Canada	−4.2	−5.3	1.0	1.5	2.0

*Forecast.
Source: Adapted from IMF (1998) *World Economic Outlook*, May.

- Second, higher rates of unemployment have led to increased payments of unemployment benefit while, at the same time, government tax revenues have fallen because unemployed workers have not been earning income.
- Third, the overall productivity slow down experienced by the major industrialized countries since the early 1970s has meant that the tax base of the government has become became smaller than expected while at the same time governments have failed to adjust their spending patterns to the new reality.
- Fourth, higher real rates of interest have added to the budget deficits.
- Finally, greater exchange rate flexibility since 1973 together with more open capital markets have allowed governments to borrow more easily on an international basis, thereby allowing them to run up excessive deficits.

Persistent budgetary problems create serious difficulties. For example, the mounting government debts over the last 15 years have led to an increase in global real interest rates as various governments have competed for international savings to cover their deficits (Heibling and Wescott 1995). In turn, high real interest rates have led to lower global investment rates, and thus lower rates of economic growth. Large debt burdens have further meant that fiscal policy could not be used as an active policy instrument – thus overburdening the role of monetary policy. Large deficits have also influenced exchange rates, arguably contributing to a number of exchange rate misalignments.

Another likely contributor to future fiscal debt is the progressive ageing of the population. This will place increasing stress on government pensions and health budgets. The percentage of the population aged 65 and over to total population in the major industrialized countries is set to rise from 35% to 50% between 1995 and 2030. This 'invisible' (*future*) debt burden is also making countries take their existing budget deficits more seriously and to aim for fiscal consolidation in the short to medium term. Studies of countries which have introduced fiscal consolidation plans, i.e. have tried to decrease public debt as a proportion of GDP, have found that the countries which have been most successful placed more emphasis on cutting spending rather than increasing taxes (IMF 1996).

As far as *monetary policy* is concerned, most industrialised economies have managed to keep their inflation rates at relatively low levels as compared with the past. In the 1980s most central banks sought to rely on the control of monetary aggregates as a means of curbing spending and inflation. However it soon became obvious that the relationship between the various money aggregates, nominal income and interest rates was becoming increasingly imprecise. As a result, a growing number of economies moved away from targets for specific monetary aggregates during the 1990s and began focusing more directly on inflation. Although all of the major industrial countries pursued price stability as an objective of monetary policy, only a few central banks had statutory obligations to achieve price stability.

Indeed the main policy lesson of the past 20 years has been that the costs of allowing inflation to rise may be very high, with deep recessions often the only effective means of subduing inflationary pressures. This suggests that there is an *asymmetric* relationship between inflation and economic activity, i.e. excess demand has a much stronger effect in raising inflation than excess supply has in reducing inflation. This means that it is important to check inflation *before* inflationary pressures build up. Hence the reason why so many countries have adopted formal targets for inflation.

From this brief account it can be seen that formulation of macroeconomic policy in the UK has followed a similar route to that in other major economies during the 1990s, with similar global economic problems eliciting similar policy responses from individual countries.

As far as the *supply side* is concerned, the labour markets of most industrialised economies have experienced major changes over the last ten years. Unemployment has risen almost universally and countries have experimented with various methods for increasing labour flexibility. First, *wage flexibility* has been encouraged by linking pay to productivity and by simplifying complicated wage structures. Second, *functional flexibility* (reorganising methods of production to suit changing technical demands) has encouraged the growth of multi-skilling, reductions in job demarcation and more employee involvement. Finally, *numerical flexibility* has grown, i.e. the ability to adjust work levels or hours in line with changes in demand. This has involved the growth of self employment and the greater use of part timers and sub-contracting. To enable such labour market changes to occur with the least trauma, it has been essential for countries to introduce training schemes and more vocationally orientated courses.

The international movement towards the liberalisation of industry through privatisation (described in Chapter 8) was designed to introduce an efficient 'free market' discipline to previously government-owned industries. However, merely to shift more industry to the private sector may not, by itself, be a sufficient condition for a nation's economic success. This is because corporate strategy-making at the level of the firm merely reflects the ambitions of those who run the major corporations and these ambitions may not always coincide with the needs of the nation as a whole. It may be that the supply side policies of shifting more control to the private sector should be coupled with a more positive role for government.

Conclusion

We have seen how Keynesian interventionism placed a premium on finding a variety of policy instruments to achieve a number of target objectives. Until the 1970s the Keynes/Tinbergen/Theil approach was the theoretical basis for short-term macroeconomic policy. However, evidence began to accumulate that this activity could be counter-productive, even destabilizing. The search for alternative approaches was also encouraged by the oil crisis of 1974 which destroyed old-established trade-offs and relationships between objectives. In addition, the oil-price increases deflated the non-oil-producing economies of the West and stimulated inflation. 'Stagflation' and later 'slumpflation' became new problems which the traditional 'fine-tuning', interventionist theories could not easily handle. Emphasis switched to medium- and long-term strategies which now prevail over short-term fine-tuning. In the 1980s the setting of medium-term 'rules' for the conduct of policy became central to the ideas of groups of economists as diverse as the CEPG and the monetarists. However, attempts during the 1980s to adhere to various forms of the Medium Term Financial Strategy failed to provide a solution to the UK's macroeconomic problems. By the early 1990s, the control of inflation remained the main long-run objective of government policy. To achieve this objective, keeping the exchange rate within its prescribed ERM 'band' became the main 'target', and using interest rate policy became the main 'instrument' of policy.

With the enforced departure of the UK from the ERM in September 1992, both the exchange rate and interest rates fell sharply. The government re-focussed policy on economic growth as an objective, alongside the control of inflation. To achieve these objectives it would seek a tight fiscal policy as its key instrument, at least on the public expenditure side. The incoming Labour government in 1997 retained a tight fiscal stance, while placing still greater emphasis on achieving an inflation target of 2.5% per annum. To this end it created an independent Bank of England which, through its Monetary Policy Committee, was empowered to use its interest rate weapon to meet the inflation target laid down by Government. At the same time, fiscal 'rules' were introduced to achieve fiscal balance over the economic cycle whilst providing a framework for an eventual decline in the public debt/GDP ratio. Other targets and instruments appear less clear. For example, the exchange was left to find its own level with the interest rate being used primarily as an instrument for controlling inflation rather than influencing exchange rates.

Much attention has been given in recent times to the supply-side of the economy, i.e. to the efficient operation of a market economy in which the state plays a more limited economic role. Nevertheless, as noted elsewhere in this book (e.g. Chs 5–8), examples of 'market failure' still abound, and ironically more government intervention may be needed to remedy information defects and strategic alliances within the UK economy. Managing an economy is a difficult task both nationally and internationally and governments and their economic advisors will continue to grapple with the best ways of matching economic objects with policy instruments for some time to come.

Key points	

- Macroeconomic policy seeks to achieve various *target* values as regards objectives such as employment, prices, economic growth and the balance of payments.
- To achieve such 'target values', governments use various *policy instruments*, such as fiscal and monetary policy, prices and incomes policy, exchange rate policy and import controls.
- Governments often find that there are complex linkages between policy objectives and policy instruments.
- Tinbergen's *fixed target approach* emphasizes that there must be at least as many policy instruments as policy objectives if target values for a number of objectives are to be achieved simultaneously.
- Theil's *flexible target approach* suggests that no exact target value can be achieved for any single objective or group of objectives. Instead policy instruments are geared to minimizing the (squared) deviations between the actual and target value for one or more objectives in order to minimize overall welfare loss.
- The 'satisficing' approach of Mosley moves away from the fine tuning of Tinbergen and Theil, and suggests that 'satisfactory' rather than optimum levels of performance should be the aim of macro policy.
- Macroeconomic policy in the pre-1974 period largely followed Keynesian principles, i.e. managing demand mainly through fiscal policy, allied occasionally to prices and incomes policies.
- Macroeconomic policy in the 1974–79 period moved away from such Keynesian 'fine tuning' and towards the use of 'rules'. The CEPG and monetarists advocated such rule making.
- The Medium Term Financial Strategy (MTFS) began in 1980 and concentrated initially on controlling demand by using £M$_3$ and then the PSBR as the main *targets* for bringing inflation under control. The main *instrument* for achieving this was to be the interest rate.
- Between 1988 and 1992 the MTFS policy shifted its targets towards stabilizing the *exchange rate*, which was now seen as the main route through which inflation was transmitted to the economy. The *instrument* used to achieve this target was still to be the interest rate.
- Since the UK left the Exchange Rate Mechanism in 1992, a key target has been low inflation, seen as a prerequisite for economic growth. The main instrument for achieving this target has remained the interest rate, together with the observance of fiscal 'rules'.
- Macroeconomic policy also involved improving the responsiveness of the economy by concentrating on the *supply side* of the economy', for example by adjusting tax rates and improving labour efficiency and training.

Notes	

1. That is, provided the Marshall–Lerner condition is satisfied, with the sum of price elasticity of demand for UK exports and price elasticity of demand for imports into the UK greater than unity.
2. For instance, in Chapter 20 we noted that the money supply, M, times the velocity of circulation of money, V, would give the monetary value of spending.

3. If points on O_1 indicate internal balance, then points off it indicate imbalance. Check that above and to the right of the line there will be inflation, whereas below and to the left there will be unemployment.

4. Similarly, if points on O_2 indicate external balance, then points off it indicate imbalance. Check that a balance of payments surplus will occur below and to the left of the O_2 line, and a deficit above and to the right.

5. Provided that O_2 and O_1 cross! Economic objective O_2 is shown as having a shallower slope than O_1. Can you see why? Start at E, and move up the O_1, line; expansionary monetary policy reduces interest rates, so that the short-term capital inflow will diminish, and the balance of payments will deteriorate. To keep it in balance, a lower National Income would be necessary in order to reduce the import flow. This could be achieved by contractionary fiscal policy, i.e. above E, O_2 must lie to the left of O_1.

6. If the exchange rate is lowered then O_2 might shift to the right and so pass through point G (which had previously been a balance of payments deficit position). All three objectives are now achieved.

7. If $M.V \equiv P.T$, the equation of exchange where M = money supply, V = average velocity of circulation of money, P = average price level, and T = volume of transactions. Then, if both V and T are fixed (or change at a known rate), money supply M directly affects price level P. So $\Delta M = \Delta P$, and the inflation rate is determined by the growth of the money supply.

References and further reading

Bray, J., Kuleshov, A., Uysal, A. and **Walker, P.** (1993) Balance–Achieving Policies: A Comparative Policy–Optimization Study on Four UK Models, *Oxford Review of Economic Policy*, **9**, 3.

Cowling, K. and **Sugden, R.** (1993) Industrial Strategy: A Missing Link in British Economic Policy, *Oxford Review of Economic Policy*, **9**, 3.

Griffiths, A. (1990) Shareownership and the Economy, *British Economic Survey*, **19**, 3, Autumn.

Healey, N. (1990) Mrs Thatcher's Fight Against Inflation: Ten Years Without Cheer, *Economics*, **26**, Pt. 1, Spring.

Heibling, T. and **Wescott, R.** (1995) The Global Interest Rate, *Staff Studies for the World Economic Outlook*, IMF, Sept.

Hudson, S and **Fisher, P** (1994) Monetary Policy in the United Kingdom, *Economics and Business Education*, **II**, Pt. 2, 6, Summer.

IMF (1996) World Economic Situation and Short Term Propects, *World Economic Outlook*, May, Table 2.

Layard, R. L. and **Nickell, S.** (1985) The Causes of British Unemployment, *National Institute Economic Review*, **111**, Feb.

Minford, P. and **Peel, D.** (1981) Is the Government's Economic Strategy on Course? *Lloyds Bank Review*, **40**, April.

Mosley, P. (1976) Towards a Satisficing Theory of Economic Policy, *Economic Journal*, **86**, March.

O'Mahony, M. (1998) Britain's Relative Productivity Performance 1950–1996: estimates by sector, *National Institute of Economic and Social Research*, October.

Oulton, N. (1995) Supply Side Reform and UK Economic Growth: What Happened to the Miracle? *National Institute Economic Review*, **154**, Nov.

Savage, D. (1982) Fiscal Policy, 1974/5–1980/81: description and measurement, *National Institute Economic Review*, **99**, Feb.

Sentance, A. (1998) UK Macroeconomic Policy and Economic Performance, in *Britain's Economic Performance*, 2nd edn, Eds T. Buxton, P. Chapman and P. Temple, Routledge, London.

Theil, H. (1956) On the Theory of Economic Policy, *American Economic Review*, **46**, May.

Tinbergen, J. (1952) *On the Theory of Economic Policy*. North-Holland Publishing Co., Amsterdam.

Trade and Industry Committee (1994) Competitiveness of UK Manufacturing Industry. Second Report, House of Commons, April.

International economics

Chapter 25

Exchange rates

The exchange rate is the price of one currency in terms of another. The exchange rate for sterling is conventionally defined as the number of units of another currency, such as the dollar, that it takes to purchase one pound sterling on the foreign exchange market. In the market, however, it is usually quoted as the number of units of the domestic currency that it takes to purchase one unit of foreign currency. In general terms the sterling exchange rate is perhaps the most important 'price' in the UK economic system. It affects the standard of living, because it determines how many goods we can get for what we sell abroad. It influences the price of UK exports and hence their sales, thereby determining output and jobs in the export industries. It structures the extent to which imports can compete with home-produced goods, and thereby affects the viability of UK companies. Because the price of imports enters into the RPI any variation in the exchange rate will have an effect on the rate of inflation. This chapter will consider these various issues. Chapters 20 and 28 will provide additional insights into the role of exchange rate systems in general. These chapters will also consider the UK's specific experience both inside and outside the Exchange Rate Mechanism (ERM), together with the operation and likely impacts of European Monetary Union (EMU). The chapter concludes by reviewing the operation, over time, of various exchange rate regimes, such as the gold standard, the 'adjustable-peg' exchange rate system, and freely floating exchange rates.

The foreign exchange market

The foreign exchange market is the money market on which international currencies are traded. It has no physical existence: it consists of traders, such as the dealing rooms of major banks, who are in continual communication with one another on a worldwide basis. Currencies are bought and sold on behalf of clients, who may be companies, private individuals, or banks themselves. A distinction is made between the 'spot' rate for a currency, and the forward rate. The spot rate is the domestic currency price of a unit of foreign exchange when the transaction is to be completed within three days. The forward rate is the price of that unit when delivery is to take place at some future date – usually 30, 60 or 90 days hence. Both spot and forward rates are determined in today's market; the relationship between today's spot and today's forward rate will be determined largely by how the market *expects* the spot rate to move in the near future. The more efficient the market is at anticipating future spot rates, the closer will today's forward rate be to the future spot rate.

The spot market is used by those who wish to acquire foreign exchange straightaway. Forward markets are used by three groups of people. There are firstly those who wish to cover themselves (*hedge*) against the risk of exchange rate variation. For instance, suppose an importer orders goods to be paid for in three months' time in dollars. All his calculations will be upset if the price of dollars rises between now and payment date. He can cover himself by buying dollars today for delivery in three months' time; he thus locks himself into a rate which reduces the risk element in his transaction. Secondly there are *arbitrageurs* who attempt to make a profit on the difference between interest rates in one country and another, and who buy or sell currency forward to ensure that the profit which they hope to make by moving their capital is not negated by adverse exchange rate movements. And thirdly there are straightforward *speculators* who use the forward markets to buy or sell in anticipation of exchange rate changes. For instance, if I think that today's forward rates do not adequately reflect the probability of the dollar increasing in value I will buy dollars forward, hoping to sell them at a profit when they are delivered to me at some future date.

London is the world's largest centre for foreign exchange trading, with an average daily turnover of over US $600 billion (Cope 1998). The market is growing all the time; indeed the average daily turnover in 1998 was more than double the value recorded in 1992. Some 64% of transactions are 'spot' on any one day, 24% are forward for periods not exceeding one month, and 10% are forward for longer than one month. Increasingly, however, more sophisticated types of transactions are being done. For instance, there is a growth in the following types of transactions:

1. Foreign currency options, which give the right (but do not impose an obligation) to buy or sell currencies at some future date and price,
2. Foreign currency futures, which are standardized contracts to buy or sell on agreed terms on specific future dates,
3. Foreign currency swaps – spot purchases against outright forward currency sales.

Foreign exchange market business in London is done in an increasingly wide variety of currencies: £/$ business now accounts for only 11% of activity, and DM/$ for a further 22%. However trading transactions which do not involve the US dollar are becoming increasingly frequent.

Table 25.1 shows the average daily turnover in foreign exchange ($bn) in the UK in (April) 1998 compared to other major countries, and percentage growth rates since

Table 25.1 Daily foreign exchange turnover ($bn) in 1998 (April) across major centres. *Source:* Adapted from Cope (1998).

Country	Average daily turnover 1998 ($bn)	Percentage growth (over 1995)
UK	637	37
US	350	43
Japan	149	−8
Singapore	139	32
Germany	94	24
Switzerland	82	−5
Hong Kong	79	−13
France	72	24

1995. The predominance of London and the UK is clear, with a daily turnover almost twice that of the US and more than six times that of Germany.

Supply and demand for a currency

Prices of currencies are determined, as on any other market, by supply of and demand for the various currencies. Businessmen wishing to import goods will sell sterling in order to buy currency with which to pay the supplier in another country. Tourists coming to the UK will sell their own currency in order to buy sterling. Other types of transactions, too, will have exchange rate repercussions. For instance, if a German company wishes to buy a factory in the UK it will need to convert marks into sterling, as will foreign banks who wish to make sterling deposits in London, or residents abroad who wish to buy UK government bonds.

Another way of saying this is to say that in any given period of time the factors which determine the demand and supply for foreign exchange are those which are represented in the balance of payments account. The demand for foreign exchange arises as a result of imports of goods and services, outflows of UK capital in the form of overseas investment (short and long term), and financial transactions by banks on behalf of their clients. The supply of foreign exchange comes as a result of the export of goods and services, inflows of foreign capital and bank transactions.

It is clear from the balance of payments accounts that companies and individuals are not the only clients of foreign exchange market dealers. The Bank of England also buys and sells foreign currency, using the official reserves in the Exchange Equalization Account. In order to reflect on why this might be the case we have to remember that governments have an interest in the level of the exchange rate, and that they may on occasion wish to intervene in the workings of the foreign exchange market to affect the value of sterling. Indeed, it was estimated that on the day sterling was forced to withdraw from the Exchange Rate Mechanism (16 September 1992), the Bank of England spent an estimated £7bn, roughly a third of its foreign exchange reserves, in buying sterling. In particular it bought sterling with deutschmarks in an unsuccessful attempt to preserve the sterling exchange rate within its permitted ERM band.

Historically the policy stance on this has varied. As we note later in the chapter, it was only after the Second World War that foreign exchange markets began to function freely on a worldwide basis. Governments then had the option of allowing exchange rates to be market-determined, i.e. to 'float', or to establish some kind of fixed exchange rate system. The decision was taken at Bretton Woods in 1945 to adopt a fixed exchange rate regime; governments thus committed themselves to continual intervention in the market in order to offset imbalances in the demand and supply for their currencies. The Bretton Woods agreement collapsed in 1972, since when currencies have been allowed to float. However, the European Exchange Rate Mechanism (ERM) was established in 1979 to restrict the range within which member currencies could float against each other (see Chapter 28). For a variety of reasons, whether inside or outside the ERM, governments continue to 'manage' the floating exchange rate system by intervening in the foreign exchange market. In the UK the Bank of England deals in this market in order to smooth out short-term fluctuations in the value of sterling as well as to influence the exchange rate as part of its overall economic strategy. Whereas in the 1950s and 1960s the exchange rate was a policy objective, it is now a policy instrument, because the price of imports enters into the Retail Price Index and hence influences the rate of inflation. However, intervention in the market alone is insufficient to affect the sterling exchange rate, simply because the size of speculative trading on the world's foreign exchange markets dwarfs the size of any one country's official reserves. For instance, it has been estimated that daily dealings in the foreign exchange markets totalled around $1,000 billion, whereas the reserves of the six leading ERM nations in September 1992 only totalled some $250 billion. Governments must therefore attempt to increase the demand for their currencies by, for instance, attracting flows of short or longer-term investment from abroad by means of high interest rates.

We have argued that in everyday terms currency prices are determined by demand and supply on the foreign exchange markets. We must now examine in more detail the forces determining any given exchange rate in the short and long term. As we shall see, all the various theoretical explanations focus on the importance of one or other of the variables contained within the balance of payments accounts. The theories vary only in the time perspective considered. The function of theory is to explain and predict; we shall consider later to what extent recent experience in the UK validates the different theoretical arguments.

Exchange rate definitions

Before we do this, however, we must consider what we mean by 'the exchange rate'. In a foreign exchange market where exchange rates are allowed to 'float', every currency has a price against every other currency. In order to allow for measurability economists use three separate concepts:

1. *The nominal rate of exchange.* This is the rate of exchange for any one currency as quoted against any other currency. The nominal exchange rate is therefore a bilateral (two country) exchange rate.
2. *The effective exchange rate (EER).* This is a measure which takes into account the fact that sterling varies differently against each of the other currencies. It is calculated as a weighted average of the individual or bilateral rates, and is expressed as an index number relative to the base year. The weights are chosen to reflect the importance of other currencies in manufacturing trade with the UK. The EER is therefore a *multilateral* (many country) exchange rate.
3. *The real exchange rate (RER).* This concept is designed to measure the rate at which home goods exchange for goods from other countries, rather than the rate at which the currencies themselves are traded. It is thus essentially a measure of competitiveness. When we consider *multilateral* UK trade, it is defined as:

$$RER = EER \times P(\text{UK})/P(F)$$

In other words, the real exchange rate is equal to the effective exchange rate multiplied by the price ratio of home, $P(\text{UK})$, to foreign, $P(F)$, goods. If UK prices rise the real exchange rate will rise unless the effective exchange rate falls. We consider below the question of how one might measure this definition empirically.

Table 25.2 outlines the *nominal rate of exchange* for sterling against a variety of other currencies (columns ① to ⑤) and the overall *effective exchange rate* (EER) against a 'basket' of other currencies (column ⑥).

We can see that the £ sterling has fallen in terms of its *nominal exchange rate* against all the individual currencies over the period, except the Italian lira. A fall in these nominal exchange rates for sterling will make UK exports to these

Table 25.2 Sterling
exchange rates 1980–98.

	US dollar ①	French franc ②	Japanese yen ③	German mark ④	Italian lira ⑤	Sterling effective exchange rate (1990 = 100) ⑥	Consumer prices (1990 = 100)	
							UK	US
1980	2.33	9.83	526	4.23	1992	128.1	53.0	63.1
1981	2.03	10.94	445	4.56	2287	129.8	59.3	69.7
1982	1.75	11.48	435	4.24	2364	124.4	64.4	73.9
1983	1.52	11.55	360	3.87	2302	114.1	67.3	76.3
1984	1.34	11.63	317	3.79	2339	109.8	70.7	79.6
1985	1.30	11.55	307	3.78	2463	109.4	75.0	82.4
1986	1.47	10.16	247	3.18	2186	100.2	77.5	83.9
1987	1.64	9.84	237	2.94	2123	99.2	80.7	87.1
1988	1.78	10.60	228	3.12	2315	105.3	84.7	90.5
1989	1.64	10.45	226	3.08	2247	102.3	91.3	94.9
1990	1.79	9.69	257	2.88	2133	100.0	100.0	100.0
1991	1.77	9.95	238	2.93	2187	100.7	105.9	104.2
1992	1.76	9.33	224	2.76	2163	96.9	109.8	107.4
1993	1.50	8.50	167	2.48	2310	88.9	111.5	110.6
1994	1.53	8.48	156	2.48	2467	89.2	114.3	113.4
1995	1.58	7.87	148	2.26	2571	84.8	118.2	116.6
1996	1.56	7.98	170	2.35	2408	86.3	121.1	120.0
1997	1.64	9.56	198	2.84	2789	100.6	124.9	122.9
1998*	1.65	9.94	225	2.97	2925	105.3	126.4	124.4

*End 2nd quarter.
Sources: Economic Trends (various).

countries cheaper (in the foreign currency) and imports dearer (in sterling). For example, in 1980, an American resident would have had to give up $2.33 for each pound, whereas by 1998 he/she would only have needed to give up $1.65 for each pound. British goods would therefore have cost less in dollar terms in 1998 than in 1980.

Of course our trade with America is only part of our external transactions. The sterling *effective exchange rate* (EER) is a weighted average of 16 major national currencies, the weights depending on the relative importance of UK trade with each country. The dollar, deutschmark, franc and yen have the greatest weights at 21%, 20%, 12% and 9% respectively. The effective exchange rate is calculated as an index with 1990 = 100, and Table 25.2 suggests that the pound in 1998 was worth, *overall*, some four-fifths of its value in 1980.

The fall in both nominal and effective exchange rates for sterling means that it costs less to purchase each £1 worth of UK goods abroad in 1998 than it did in 1980. Does this then mean that UK goods have become more competitive on world markets? Of course the answer depends not only on changes in the exchange rate but on relative inflation rates between the UK and the countries with which we are comparing it. In other words, we must examine the *real exchange rate*.

Returning again to the *bilateral* exchange rate between sterling and the US dollar, we can now investigate the *real exchange rate* between the two currencies. As we can see from Table 25.2, although the nominal (bilateral) exchange rate between sterling and US dollar has fallen substantially over the period, consumer price inflation has been higher in the UK than in the US.

Using the information in Table 25.2 on nominal exchange rates and UK/US consumer prices, we can work out the real exchange rates between pound sterling and US dollar for 1980 and 1998.

$$\text{Real exchange rate} = \frac{\text{nominal } \pounds/\$}{\text{exchange rate}} \times \frac{\text{Price index of UK goods in } \pounds}{\text{Price index of US goods in } \$}$$

$$\text{Real exchange rate (1980)} = 2.33 \times \frac{53.0}{63.1} = 1.96$$

$$\text{Real exchange rate (1998)} = 1.65 \times \frac{126.4}{124.4} = 1.68$$

The fall in the real exchange rate ($\$/\pounds$) from 1.96 in 1980 to 1.68 in 1998 clearly indicates that fewer dollars need now be exchanged for each £1 worth of UK goods bought in the US. Although inflation has been higher in the UK than the US over the period, the fall in the nominal sterling exchange rate against the US dollar has *more than offset* the higher UK inflation. However sterling has only depreciated against the dollar by some 14.3% $\left(\frac{0.28}{1.96} \cdot 100 \right)$ over the period using *real* exchange rates, but by 29.2% $\left(\frac{0.68}{2.33} \cdot 100 \right)$ using *nominal* exchange rates. In other words, the loss of competitiveness via higher UK inflation has eroded *some* of the exchange rate gains between UK and US producers, though these still remain substantial.

This analysis of the fall in sterling exchange rates helping improve the UK's international competitiveness holds true over the period 1980–98. However, there has been a sharp upward revision since 1996 in nominal sterling exchange rates against individual countries and against the weighted average of 16 major industrial countries (i.e. the sterling effective exchange rate). This appreciation of sterling has led to a sharp *deterioration* in the UK's international competitiveness since 1996, making UK exports dearer overseas and imports into the UK cheaper (see Chapter 1). For example, the sterling effective exchange rate rose as an index from 86.3 to 105.3 (1990 = 100) between 1996 and 1998, a rise of over 22%. A lower price inflation in the UK than in its competitors would help modify any loss of competitiveness, resulting in a smaller rise in terms of *real* sterling exchange rates. However, Table 25.1 provides no evidence of a lower price inflation for the UK against the US during this period.

Exchange rate determination

We can distinguish four theoretical approaches to exchange rate determination. It must be emphasized that these are in no sense 'competing' theories. They are simply different ways of looking at what determines the exchange rate, depending on whether we are interested in the short run or the long run, in immediate or more fundamental determinants, and on what we consider to be the most empirically relevant factors at any given time.

Exchange rates and the balance of trade   The *traditional* approach sees the exchange rate simply as the price which brings into equilibrium the supply and demand for currency arising from trade in goods and services and from capital transactions, as explained above. This approach was

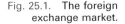

Fig. 25.1.   The foreign
exchange market.

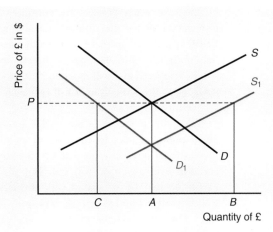

formulated in the 1950s when capital flows were small in relation to trade flows, and hence its major use is to illustrate the interrelationship between current account flows and exchange rate changes. Nevertheless, it can also accommodate capital account transactions. It is essentially a perspective which concentrates on short-run influences.

Figure 25.1 shows that the demand for pounds will increase as the price falls. This is because customers abroad will perceive that the price of UK exports has fallen in their own currency as sterling depreciates, increasing their demand for UK exports and therefore for pounds with which to buy them. The supply of pounds will rise as the price of sterling rises because the price of imports in sterling falls as the pound strengthens. With cheaper imports, UK consumers now buy more imported items and firms exchange more pounds in order to buy these imports.[1]

Demand and supply curves can shift for a number of reasons. A shift (increase) in supply from S to S_1 might be due to a change in tastes in favour of foreign goods. A shift (decrease) in demand from D to D_1 might occur because UK interest rates had fallen, leading to a decrease in the demand for pounds as investors switch their funds out of the UK money markets. In either of these cases there will be a fall in the exchange rate below its original level, P. In a floating exchange rate system the rate will be allowed to fall. Should the monetary authorities wish to keep the exchange rate at its original level they will be obliged to buy sterling. If the supply of sterling increases to S_1 they will buy up the excess quantity AB: if the demand for sterling has fallen to D_1 they will make up the shortfall by buying up quantity CA. In either case the price reverts to its original level.

This view of exchange rate determination predicts that the exchange rate will alter in response to macroeconomic policy, because the demand for imports (and hence the supply of pounds) will depend in part on the level of income. Fiscal policy will thus affect the exchange rate. It also regards short-term capital flows (and hence both demand and supply of pounds) as being sensitive to interest rate changes. Both fiscal and monetary policy will therefore have exchange rate repercussions. Expansionary policies, whether fiscal or monetary, which raise levels of income and employment, will cause the S curve to shift to S_1, as imports rise with income. Such policies will cause a balance of payments deficit and a fall in the exchange rate. The converse will

be the case when policies are contractionary. In addition, in so far as fiscal and monetary policies alter interest rates in a downward direction (if, for instance, the PSBR is reduced so that fewer bonds need to be issued, bond prices rise and yields fall, or interest rates are reduced directly by the monetary authorities) capital outflows will be triggered – S will move to S_1 as people move their money out of UK financial markets; at the same time D will fall to D_1 as investment in UK money markets is no longer forthcoming.

What this model does not enable us to do is to predict the overall effect of any given policy stance. In the case of an *expansionary monetary policy* spending will increase and interest rates will fall, the supply of pounds will increase in both cases and the exchange rate will fall. But in the case of an *expansionary fiscal policy*, expansion may be associated with an increase in government borrowing, which will lead to a fall in bond prices (as the supply of bonds increases) and a rise in the interest rate. The effect on the exchange rate will then be ambiguous, depending on the marginal propensity to import from a rise in income in relation to the interest elasticity of capital flows.

Marshall–Lerner elasticity condition

We have seen how the traditional explanation of exchange rate determination is based on balance of payments flows. However, there is also a 'feedback' effect in that these flows, in particular flows of imports and exports, are themselves partly determined by the level of the exchange rate. Suppose that an exogenous disturbance, such as a change in government policy, leads to a balance of payments deficit and a consequent fall in the exchange rate. Since the demand for exports and imports is dependent on their price, will the new exchange rate level result in a further deterioration in the balance of payments and a further fall in the exchange rate, or will the balance of payments improve and the exchange rate return to its former level?

The answer to this question depends on the elasticities of demand for imports and exports. The 'elasticities' approach to balance of payments adjustment predicts that if the sum of the elasticities of demand for imports and exports is greater than 1 (the *Marshall–Lerner condition*) then the balance between the change in export earnings and import expenditure will be such as to improve the balance of payments, and the exchange rate will rise in consequence. In practice this principle as it stands is not empirically useful for the following reasons:

1. Trade adjustments take time. The exchange rate may adjust instantaneously, but traders take time to adjust their orders. The initial effect of a depreciation may therefore be to make the deficit larger as export demand is slow to increase at new lower prices, and importers fail to cut back their purchases. There will thus be a 'J-curve' effect as the balance of payments worsens before it improves. At the time of the UK devaluation of 1967 it was estimated that it was only in the second year after the devaluation that the gain in export volume offset the loss in revenue due to lower export prices.
2. In a floating exchange rate regime exchange rates will alter again in the time it takes for these adjustments to be made. Stability is therefore unlikely to occur.
3. The analysis takes no account of supply conditions. In a full employment situation it may not be possible to cope with the increased demand both for exports and for import-competing goods, so that the beneficial effect of a depreciation may not be realized because of supply constraints.

4. The fall in the exchange rate will increase home prices, because import prices have risen, and may therefore cause an inflation which will wipe out the positive balance of payments effects of the devaluation. It was estimated that by 1972 the UK had lost the gain from the 1967 devaluation because of the effect of rising inflation.

5. It is assumed that only prices determine trade flows. In fact, there are several reasons why trade flows may be unresponsive to exchange rate changes. Quality and product differentiation are often more important in determining trade flows than prices (see Chapter 26).

6. The analysis takes no account of the effect of exchange rate changes on capital flows. If these latter are quantitatively unimportant this does not matter, but since they currently play a very large part in exchange rate determination the usefulness of the elasticities approach is weakened.

The 'traditional' analysis of exchange rate determination, which sees exchange rates as a function of the current balance of payments position, became less useful as historical circumstances have changed. Two major developments after the 1950s made it necessary to consider alternative theoretical approaches.

One of these was the growing importance of capital flows in the balance of payments accounts. These flows of international investment were partly caused by capital formation by multinational companies (see Chapter 7) but were also due to increasing preferences by asset holders for holding foreign assets as capital restrictions were eased. The last of these restrictions vanished in 1979 when the UK abolished exchange control. The other, later, development was the advent of worldwide inflation in the 1970s. The traditional view outlined earlier took no account of internal price changes when analysing exchange rate variations. In fact, in an inflationary situation internal and external price changes are interactive.

These two developments led to the *monetary* and *portfolio* approaches to exchange rate determination on the one hand, and to the revival of the *purchasing power parity* (PPP) theory on the other. Because the monetary and portfolio approach hinges on the validity of the PPP theory, we deal first with purchasing power parity.

Purchasing power parity

This theory originated in the nineteenth century, and was used in the 1920s to discuss the correct value of currencies in relation to gold. In general terms the proposition states that equilibrium exchange rates will be such as to enable people to buy the same amount of goods in any country for a given amount of money. For this to be the case exchange rates must be at the correct level in relation to prices in the different countries. In order to state the proposition more rigorously we must assume that goods are homogeneous (or that there is only one good), also that there are no barriers to trade or transactions costs, and that there is internal price flexibility. The 'law of one price' will then ensure that the price of a good will be equalized in domestic and foreign currency terms. For instance, the price of a car in the UK in sterling must be equal to the price of a car in US dollars times the exchange rate (the sterling price of dollars). If the exchange rate is too high or too low, it will adjust if exchange rates are flexible. If they are fixed, internal prices will adjust as there is an excess of demand in one country and a shortfall in the other.

There are two versions of the proposition:

(a) The 'absolute' version of PPP predicts that the exchange rate (E) will equalize the purchasing power of a given income in any two countries, so that

$$E = P(\text{UK})/P(\text{US})$$

(b) The 'relative' version of the principle states that changes in exchange rates reflect differences in relative inflation rates. If internal prices rise in one country relative to another, exchange rates will adjust (downwards) to compensate.

It is easy to see how the existence of high inflation rates in the 1970s increased the attractiveness of this theory as an explanation of exchange rate determination, because the theory concentrates on showing the relationship between exchange rates and relative price movements, unlike the more traditional view which, as we have seen, had nothing to say about prices. However, what can we say about the empirical usefulness of the principle? Let us consider the problems of applying the principle first, and then look at the extent to which it was in fact successful in explaining exchange rate changes.

A number of damaging criticisms of the theory can be made:

1. The major problem relates to the choice of price index used to give empirical content to the theory. Any overall price index includes non-traded as well as traded goods, and inflation rates may be differently reflected in these sectors, hence rendering the index unusable. Even the use of export price indices is problematic because the profitability element in export prices may vary over time. The appropriate measure would appear to be a measure of unit labour costs normalized as between countries (relative normalized unit labour costs – RNULC) which reflects differences in wage costs per unit of output and thus includes productivity measures.[2] The RNULC measures are the most accurate way of assessing the relative competitive strength of different countries in the traded goods sector (see also Chapter 1).

2. It is difficult to discuss an 'equilibrium' exchange rate without reference to some base year. The choice of representative year can pose problems in a world where inflation rates vary constantly.

3. Factors other than the prices of traded goods can affect the exchange rate. Barriers to trade such as tariffs can exist. Tastes can change, incomes can change, technology can change. The classic example of the latter is the effect on the exchange rate of North Sea oil.

4. Although in the long run the PPP theory may have some validity, exchange rates in the short run are more likely to be dominated by the effects of capital flows, particularly short-run flows. In other words, exchange rates may 'overshoot'.

Quite apart from these particular criticisms, it is doubtful whether the PPP theory provides us with an adequate explanation of changes in the sterling exchange rate. The theory would predict that if prices rise faster in the UK than in other countries the resultant trade deficit should cause a fall in the exchange rate. We can test this by examining the relationship between the effective exchange rate and RNULC. When costs rise the UK is becoming less competitive, so we might expect to see a consequent fall in the effective exchange rate if the 'relative' version of the PPP theory holds. In other words, there should be an inverse relationship between the two measures. This is clearly not the case. As Fig. 25.2 shows, relative prices (proxied by unit labour costs) and the effective exchange rate often tend to move together rather than inversely. There are various possible explanations for this:

Fig. 25.2.   Sterling exchange rate index (ER) and relative unit labour costs (RULC).
Source: ONS (1998) *Economic Trends*, October, and previous issues.

1. Price elasticities for imports and exports may not be such as to cause the exchange rate to improve with a rise in competitiveness. In fact, with a floating exchange rate a rise in competitiveness may cause the exchange rate to fall (the J-curve effect).
2. The effective exchange rate is affected by trade in invisibles and by capital flows as well as by the relative prices of manufactured goods entering into trade.
3. Price competitiveness is not the only factor affecting trade flows. Non-price competitiveness is also an important determinant. In other words, the crucial assumption of the 'law of one price' – that of homogeneous goods – does not hold in the real world.

We must also realize that RNULC are themselves affected by the effective exchange rate. This is because costs of production in the UK will rise faster than those in other countries if the effective exchange rate depreciates. Raw materials will become more expensive, production costs will rise, the rise in price may trigger wage demands, and RNULC will rise in consequence.

We may sum up by saying that the usefulness of the PPP theory as a theory of exchange rate determination is probably best thought of in a long-run context when changes in relative prices between countries represent the workings of inflationary forces rather than transient 'real' effects such as changes in tastes or technology. However, even in the long run it is still not possible to say whether relative price shifts determine exchange rate movements, or whether exchange rate changes influence price movements.

North Sea oil and the exchange rate

We have argued that little of the variation in the effective exchange rate can be explained by UK price competitiveness. Other factors have been more important: one of these has been the fundamental change in technological possibilities brought about by the advent of North Sea oil. North Sea oil came on stream in 1976, and the UK became self-sufficient in oil by 1980. This has been perhaps the main reason why the effective exchange rate has risen in spite of a loss of competitiveness.

There are three ways in which oil production has improved the balance of payments.

First, since 1976 the UK has been an exporter of oil and has reduced its own dependence on imported oil. As we can see from Table 25.3, the oil trading balance has been steadily improving since 1976, and moved into surplus in 1980. However, since 1985 oil production has begun to decline in volume, and this has been reflected in the reduced surplus since 1985. Nevertheless a modest recovery in world oil prices, new oil fields yielding extra output and the lower price of oil exports (after sterling depreciated on leaving the ERM) all contributed to an improvement in the oil trade balance in the 1990s.

Second, the inflows of capital needed to fund investment in the oil industry helped the UK balance of payments in the 1970s. However, this effect has to some extent been offset since then by outflows of interest, profits and dividends as companies remit their gains to the country of origin.

Third, the popularity of sterling rose as an asset currency during the late 1970s and 1980s, as international asset holders speculated on the strength of sterling deriving from the favourable oil trading balance. This explains particularly the sharp rise in sterling from 1980 to 1983, as oil trading figures became increasingly favourable. The more recent rise in sterling in 1990 and 1991 was again related to the possession of oil. Problems in the Gulf raised the profile of sterling as a 'petro-currency', attractive to investors at a time of potentially higher oil prices.

The net effect of the balance of payments impact of North Sea oil is likely to have been sufficiently favourable to keep the exchange rate higher than it would otherwise have been during the eighties and early nineties. This in itself had important consequences for competitiveness. A 'resource shock' can follow a higher exchange rate, as this will tend to raise the cost of other traded goods, and hence reduce competitiveness. In addition, there may be longer term structural adjustments as manufacturers find it impossible to maintain their position in world markets. The conventional wisdom has been to argue that this latter effect did *not* in fact happen in the UK, because the upward pressure on the real exchange rate was counterbalanced by a fall in the rate of inflation in the 1980s, as well as by a rise in domestic demand. These enabled UK firms and exporters to become more profitable and hence to compete more effectively abroad.

Of course, recession in the UK and other parts of the world economy in the early 1990s led to a renewed focus on the 'resource shock' aspect of an, allegedly, overvalued exchange rate. In more recent times, the sharp appreciation of sterling

Table 25.3 Balance on oil trading account (£m).

1976	1978	1980	1982	1983	1985	1987	1989	1991	1993	1995	1997
−3,947	−1,984	315	4,605	6,294	8,163	4,184	1,257	1,208	2,442	4,472	4,608

Source: Adapted from ONS (1998) *UK Balance of Payments.*

since 1996 has also brought the 'resource shock' debate to the fore, of particular concern being the negative impact of a high exchange rate on manufacturing output and employment. However, few have sought to link the rise in sterling since 1996 to North Sea oil.

The monetary approach to exchange rate determination

As we saw earlier, the growth in importance of capital account transactions led to attempts to explain the determination of the exchange rate by analysing financial flows between countries. The monetary approach to exchange rate determination, developed in the early 1970s, sees the exchange rate as the price of foreign money in terms of domestic money, determined in turn by the demand for and supply of money. If people are not willing to hold the existing stock of money there will be a shortfall in demand for it and its price will fall in relation to the currencies of other countries. What it in fact argues is that balance of payments, and hence exchange rate movements, are simply reflections of disequilibria in money markets.

Money is thought of as being an asset, the demand for which depends on income and interest rates. If the central bank in a country increases the money supply, income and interest rates remaining unchanged, people will be unwilling to hold more money and so the excess money holdings will be used to buy more goods from abroad. The result will be a balance of payments deficit and downward pressure on the exchange rate. If the authorities intervene to support the currency they will lose reserves, and so the increase in the money supply will be exactly offset by a reduction in the external component of the money stock (see Chapter 20). On the other hand, if exchange rates are flexible, the fall in the exchange rate will simply result in internal inflation (as the price of imports rises) which will exactly cancel out the original increase in the money supply.

Suppose now that there is no increase in the money supply, but that exogenous factors cause a change in the demand for money. Suppose incomes rise: the increase in demand for money balances will then lead to an appreciation of the exchange rate as less money is available for imports. Or suppose interest rates rise: the demand for money balances will be reduced, people will spend the money on imports, the exchange rate will fall and home inflation will result. (Note that the prediction here is at variance with the usual assumption that a rise in interest rates will cause an appreciation of the exchange rate because capital flows will be attracted into the country.)

The monetary approach to exchange rate determination, incorporating as it does a whole new perspective on the role of money in the balance of payments, provides a monetarist explanation of exchange rate determination. Its strength lies in the fact that it recognizes the importance of asset market changes in determining the exchange rate, as opposed to concentrating merely on the importance of current account flows in the short or long term, as the previous approaches did. That perspective allows for the possibility of introducing the question of the effect of expectations, which is essential if we are to explain exchange rate volatility. However, in evaluating the usefulness of this approach we must first of all remember that the validity of the argument rests on very limited assumptions:

1. The demand for money is a stable function of real income and interest rates.
2. Prices are determined by the world price level and the exchange rate, i.e. the PPP theory holds.
3. There is full employment domestically.

The validity of these assumptions may be criticized on several grounds:

1. The impact of a monetary disturbance on prices and hence the exchange rate may not be predictable in the short run because of the instability of the velocity of circulation (see Chapter 20).
2. Exchange rates do not conform to the naive PPP model.
3. Changes in the money stock may produce short-run changes in output (see Chapter 20) which may make it difficult to identify ultimate effects on prices and the exchange rate.

It may help to remember the restrictiveness of these assumptions when we examine some of the implications of this monetarist view. For instance, it is clear that the theory implies that there is no need to have a balance of payments policy because deficits are self-correcting, either because increases in the money stock are reversed by exchange market intervention or by the effects of resultant price rises. Also, under a system of fixed exchange rates it will not be possible to conduct an active monetary policy since all changes in the money stock will be offset by changes in the reserves. But perhaps the major problem with the monetary approach to exchange rate determination, and certainly the central problem when it comes to any empirical testing of its usefulness as an explanatory device, is that it considers there to be only one asset – money – which affects exchange rate determination. This is clearly not the case in practice. We must therefore look to a wider interpretation of asset-holding behaviour if we are to account for the actual behaviour of the exchange rate.

Portfolio balance approach to exchange rate determination

The portfolio balance approach to exchange rate determination sees exchange rates as determined mainly by movements on the capital account of the balance of payments. However, it recognizes that there are a wide variety of assets represented by these transactions. Wealth holders will hold their assets in domestic and foreign securities as well as money, and their asset preferences will be determined by their assessment of the relationship between risk and return on these assets. Given the difference between domestic and foreign rates of return, the exchange rate will be determined by investors' assessment of the degree of substitutability between domestic and foreign assets. If domestic interest rates rise, the extent to which this will cause an inflow of capital and a consequent appreciation of the exchange rate will depend on investor expectations. If expectations change, so that the perceived relationship between risk and return alters, the exchange rate will vary accordingly.

This approach, which was developed in the mid-1970s, represents the 'state of the art' in exchange rate theory. It does not discount the influence of the current account in trend movements of the exchange rate, but it does suggest a plausible explanation for the observed short-run variability in the exchange rate shown in Fig. 25.2 above. Exchange rates may vary sharply in response to asset-switching behaviour in the face of changing rates of return and expectations. Adherents of this view would argue that the major exchange rate changes of September 1992 were largely caused by asset-switching behaviour by portfolio holders. For example, once expectations moved sharply against the lira and pound sterling holding their central parities in the ERM, it became a 'low risk' one-way bet to move out of those currencies into 'harder' currencies such as D-mark and yen.

Fig. 25.3.   Sterling exchange rates and interest differentials.
Sources: Derived from ONS (1998) *Financial Statistics*, October, and *Bank of England Quarterly Bulletin* (1972–87).

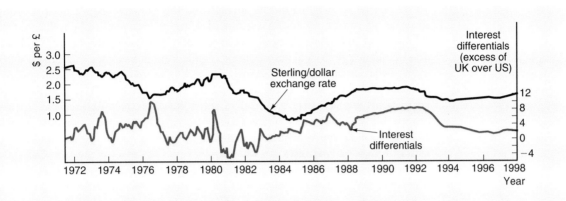

Short-term capital flows and the exchange rate   Here we consider the way in which the exchange rate is influenced by short-term capital flows. These consist mainly of borrowings from, and lending to, overseas residents by banks. Such short-term capital flows respond primarily to interest rate differentials. Asset switching between countries will take place so long as the interest rate differential is greater than any expected changes in the exchange rate. What happens is that if interest rates rise in, for instance, the US, people will buy dollars in order to invest in US money markets. This will drive the dollar rate up, but as people realize their gains by selling dollars the dollar rate will come down again. It is possible to try and hedge against potential loss by selling dollars bought today on today's forward market for delivery at some future date, but that will in turn drive today's forward rate down. In a perfect market the rise in dollar spot rate and the fall in forward rates (as investors try to make sure of their future gains today) will be just sufficient to cancel out the advantages of rising interest rates. But markets are never perfect, and some *arbitrage* is always possible.

We have no firm empirical evidence for such behaviour on the part of asset holders. There should be a positive correlation between interest rate differentials and exchange rates, as people switch funds into the UK when interest rates rise relative to US interest rates, thereby driving up the sterling exchange rate. Figure 25.3, which deals with the UK/US interest rate differential, shows as much evidence of negative as of positive correlation. There are various reasons for this. One is that the positive effect of interest rate differentials on the exchange rate may be outweighed by exchange rate *expectations*. For instance, in the period 1980–82, when interest rate differentials were very low because both the UK and the US had high interest rates, the UK exchange rate was high because people believed that a petro-currency such as sterling would remain strong.

Expectations about future exchange rates are formed by assessments about the potential demand for and supply of sterling. If asset holders see that the UK has a combined current and capital account deficit, they will *expect* the exchange rate to fall, and will move their money out of sterling, thereby exerting a further downward pressure on sterling. If the authorities do not wish this to happen, they must raise interest rates so that they are higher than those of other countries by a margin sufficient to attract funds into sterling.

Of course it is never possible to predict the effect on capital flows, and hence on the exchange rate, of any given interest rate differential. Capital flows will be more or less responsive, depending on the strength and the nature of expectations. Lacking adequate information in an imperfect market, speculators tend to be influenced by any item of information, however irrelevant. Money supply figures, political developments at home and abroad, unsuccessful Summit meetings – all these tend to trigger behavioural responses in terms of flows of 'hot' money in and out of sterling. Exogenous shocks, such as the consequences of oil price rises, or the threat of international conflict, may also lead to major flows of short-term capital. It may happen that, in spite of high interest rates, the exchange rate does depreciate. In this case there will be consequent structural changes both in competitiveness and in real rates of return on long-term investment.

Expectations would certainly seem to have outweighed interest rate differentials in September 1992, when a number of ERM currencies came under intense speculative attack. Despite sharp rises in Italian and UK interest rates, for example, the speculative pressure against the lira and pound was sustained. In the case of the UK, interest rates rose an unprecedented five percentage points (from 10% to 15%) within 24 hours. Even this, together with an estimated expenditure of £7bn by the Bank of England (roughly one third of total UK reserves) in purchasing sterling, and further support of over £2bn by the Bundesbank, could not withstand the continued speculative pressure. Eventually the UK was forced to withdraw from the system altogether (see Chapter 28) and the Italians had to reduce the central parity of the lira within the system.

Economic policy and the exchange rate

It has become increasingly clear that there is a direct relationship between changes in the exchange rate and the rate of inflation, because the price of imports enters into the Retail Price Index in different ways. We can illustrate this as follows. In Fig. 25.4 we consider in some detail the impact of a sterling depreciation on UK import prices. Sterling depreciation will raise the cost, expressed in sterling, of imported items. However, both the magnitude and the speed of price rise will vary with type of import. This can be illustrated for the 1980s by reference to a Bank of England short-term forecasting model. As we can see from Fig. 25.4, the full effect of the sterling depreciation on import prices will only be felt after more than two years. Imported fuel and industrial material prices will, with less elastic demands, respond most substantially and most rapidly to the depreciation. This is in part because the less elastic is demand, the easier it is to pass on cost increases to consumers. Imported finished goods' prices rise by a smaller amount, and less quickly, because some of these goods face extensive competition on home markets, i.e. face more elastic demand curves. Imported food prices will tend to be less affected, at least initially, because of the operation of the Common Agricultural Policy.

The final effect on consumer prices can be seen to be about one-quarter of the sterling depreciation, and then only after more than two years. For any depreciation, the final effect on consumer prices will depend on a number of factors:

1. The import content of production.
2. The extent to which cost increases can be passed on to consumers, i.e. price elasticity of demand.

Fig. 25.4. Impact on prices of a 10% depreciation. *Source:* Adapted from Bank of England.

Notes:
1 A 10% depreciation of sterling against the dollar is equivalent to an increase of 11.1% in units of sterling per dollar. As it is the latter rate which is relevant in this context, the 10% depreciation leads eventually to a rise slightly greater than 11% in some import prices.
2 The bank's short-term model assumes no wages response. The exchange rate is assumed to remain 10% below the level it would otherwise have been.

A = Consumer prices
B = Wholesale selling price
C = Imported foods
D = Imported finished goods
E = All imported goods
F = Imported industrial materials
G = Imported fuels

3. The import content of consumption.
4. The sensitivity of wage demands to cost-of-living increases.

Figure 25.4 is drawn on the assumption of no wage response, i.e. that (4) above is zero. Any such response would increase wholesale and consumer prices still further.

Whereas a fall in the sterling exchange rate will increase inflation, a rise in the exchange rate will reduce it. There is, of course, another side to the picture. A high sterling exchange rate, although helping the fight against inflation, may adversely affect output and employment. United Kingdom producers may now find it more difficult to sell their goods and services, first, because competition from cheaper imports drives them out of home markets and, second, because UK exports become expensive on foreign markets. Much of the deindustrialization of the early 1980s was attributed to the high pound, which has also been blamed for lost output and employment in UK manufacturing since 1996 (see Chapter 1).

The adherence of governments to a policy of high exchange rates has often been based on a belief that high exchange rates help fight inflation by making imports cheaper, and that on the export side reliance could be placed on the 'law of one price'. In other words, British manufacturers, seeing that they could not sell on world markets unless they observed world prices for their products, would restrain the rate of growth of labour costs, thereby raising exports and further contributing to the fight against inflation.

It will be useful to conclude this chapter by reviewing the various types of *exchange rate regime* which have operated over time, before considering the system under which the UK currently operates.

The gold standard system

As the nineteenth century progressed, and as world trade expanded, the use of gold as a means of international payment broadened to take in almost all the major trading countries. Although a few, such as the US, persisted for some time with silver, by about 1873 (with the passing of the Gold Standard Act in the US) a gold standard payments system could be said to be in effect. The 'price' of each major currency was fixed in terms of a *specific weight of gold*, which meant that the price of each currency was fixed in terms of every other currency, at a rate that could not be altered. The gold standard was therefore a system of *fixed exchange rates*. Any difficulties for the balance of payments had to be resolved by expanding or contracting the domestic economy. A rather stylized account of the adjustment mechanism will highlight the main features of the gold standard system.

Suppose a country moved into balance of payments surplus. Payment would be received in gold which, because domestic money supply was directly related to the gold stock, would raise money supply. This would expand the economy, raising domestic incomes, spending and prices. Higher incomes and prices would encourage imports and discourage exports, thereby helping to eliminate the initial payments surplus. In addition, the extra money supply would lead to a fall in its price (the rate of interest), encouraging capital outflows to other countries which had higher rates of interest – a minus sign in the accounts. A payments surplus would, in these ways, tend to be eliminated. For countries with payments deficits, gold outflow would reduce the gold stock and with it the domestic money supply. This would cause the domestic economy to contract, reducing incomes, spending and prices. Lower incomes and prices would discourage imports and encourage exports. The reduction in money supply would also raise the price of money (interest rate) – encouraging capital inflows – a plus sign in the accounts. Payment deficits would, therefore, also tend to be eliminated. This whole system came to be regarded as extremely sophisticated and self-regulating. Individual countries need only ensure (a) that gold could flow freely between countries, (b) that gold backed the domestic money supply, and (c) that the market was free to set interest rates. Of course, this meant that countries with payment surpluses would experience expanding domestic economies, and those with deficits contracting economies.

There seemed to be a general acceptance amongst the major trading nations that currency and payments stability took precedence over domestic production and employment. What was perhaps not realized was that the apparent 'success' of the system in the forty years between 1873 and 1913 was largely due to the additional liquidity provided by sterling balances. The growing value of UK imports had led to an increase in the holding of sterling by overseas residents, who then used sterling to settle international debts.

If the supply of gold and other precious commodities could not keep pace with the expansion of world trade, the obvious alternative was to make use of 'paper'. In practice, of course, exporters would only accept paper and a 'paper' system could only be used on a worldwide basis when it fulfilled a number of useful criteria:

1. it had to be freely exchangeable on a global basis;
2. it had to be available in sufficient quantities;
3. it needed to be of a fixed value which did not depreciate rapidly;
4. its value, ideally, needed to be guaranteed in terms of some other precious commodity such as gold.

The paper currency, in other words, had to be 'as good as gold'.

For a brief period in the late Victorian and early Edwardian eras sterling fulfilled the bulk of this role. Sterling continued to play a part in the funding of international debt in what was called the 'Sterling Area' well into the 1960s.

Although several attempts were made to revive the gold standard after the First World War, these largely failed. The dominance of the UK in world trade began to fade during this period, restricting the supply of sterling as a world currency. The Great Depression of the late 1920s and early 1930s also encouraged many countries to adopt protectionist measures. In such an atmosphere countries became less willing to abide by the 'rules' of the gold standard. Gold flows were restricted, and money supply and interest rates were adjusted independently of gold flow to help domestic employment rather than international payments. Wages and prices became much more rigid as labour and product markets became less 'perfect', which further impeded the adjustment mechanism. For instance, any deflation that did still occur in deficit countries, led *less often* to the reductions in factor and product price needed to restore price competitiveness. Countries began therefore to resort more and more to changes in the exchange rate to regain lost competitiveness.

This breakdown of the gold standard system during the inter-war period found no ready replacement. The result was a rather chaotic period of unstable exchange rates, inadequate world liquidity and protectionism. It was to seek a more ordered system of world trade and payments that the Allies met in Bretton Woods, in the US, even before the Second World War had ended. What emerged from that meeting was an entirely new system, under the auspices of the IMF.

The IMF system

Adjustable-peg exchange rate system

Imbalances in world trading patterns, and imperfections in world money markets have at least three implications:

1. That deficits and surpluses rarely self-correct, so that foreign exchange reserves are required to fund persistent payments deficits.
2. That although surpluses and deficits are supposed to balance as an accounting identity for the world as a whole, in practice surpluses are rarely recycled to debtor countries.
3. That even though in theory the world must be in overall balance, in practice there is a substantial imbalance. As far as these missing balances are concerned, the IMF reported in 1991 a global surplus of over $100bn. A number of factors may be involved; time-lags in reporting transactions, the non-recording of arrangements conducted through tax havens, and the problem of using an appropriate 'price' to evaluate trade deals when exchange rates fluctuate several times between initiation and completion.

In order to settle deficits, theory tells us that deficit countries should be able to run down their foreign exchange reserves, or to borrow from surplus countries. Both methods have, in reality, proved next to impossible. The countries most likely to suffer deficits are those with low per capita incomes and few foreign exchange reserves. They are also in consequence those with low credit ratings on the international banking circuit, making borrowing from surplus countries difficult. It was in order to solve just these sorts of liquidity problems for deficit countries that the IMF was established. As well as providing foreign currencies in times of need, its other major objective was to promote stability in exchange rates, following the uncertainties of the inter-war period.

Exchange rate stability

Under the IMF system, each country could, on joining, assign to itself an exchange rate. It did this by indicating the number of units of its currency it would trade for an ounce of gold, valued at $35. The dollar was therefore the common unit of all exchange rates. A country had a 'right' to change its initial exchange rate (par value) by up to 10%. For changes in par value which, when cumulated, came to more than 10%, the permission of the IMF was required. The IMF would only give such permission if the member could demonstrate that its payments were in 'fundamental disequilibrium'. Since this term was never clearly defined in the Articles of the IMF, any substantial payments imbalance would usually qualify. A rise in par became known as a revaluation; a fall in par, devaluation. As well as changing par value, a member could permit its exchange rate to move in any one year $\pm$ 1% of par, but no more. Because the IMF system sought stable, but not totally fixed, exchange rates, it became known as the 'adjustable peg' exchange rate system.

The IMF also introduced – in 1961 – the idea of 'currency swaps' by which a country in need of specific foreign exchange could avoid the obvious disadvantages of having to purchase it with its own currency by simply agreeing to 'swap' a certain amount through the Bank of International Settlements. The swap contract would state a rate of exchange which would also apply to the 'repayment' at the end of the contract.

Changes in exchange rate were a means by which deficits or surpluses could be adjusted. For instance, a devaluation would lower the foreign price of exports, and raise the domestic price of imports. The IMF system has, however, been criticized in its actual operation for permitting too little flexibility in exchange rates. Between 1947 and 1971 only six adjustments took place: devaluations of the French franc (1958 and 1969), sterling (1949 and 1967), and revaluations of the Deutschmark (1961 and 1969). It is true, of course, that adjustments of exchange rates are subject to an extremely fine balance: too many adjustments and the system loses stability and confidence; too few and the system generates internal tensions of unemployment and/or lower real incomes which may eventually destroy it.

By 1971, continuing US deficits (the expense of the Vietnam War was a major contributory factor), paid in part with US dollars, had led to an overabundance of dollars in the world system. Under the IMF rules all dollars could be converted into gold at $35 per ounce, and as confidence in the dollar declined, US gold stocks came under increasing strain. Although the US, even in 1971, still accounted for 30% of world gold reserves and 15% of total world reserves (gold, foreign currencies and SDRs), the enormous payments deficits of 1970 and 1971 ($11bn and $30bn respectively) imposed tremendous pressure on its gold and foreign currency reserves. President Nixon announced in August 1971 that the US dollar would no longer be convertible into gold.

The scrapping of dollar convertibility into gold at a *fixed price*, caused a crisis in the IMF exchange rate system, which had been founded on that very principle.[3] This was followed by two increases in the 'official price' of gold – in 1971 to $38 per ounce, and in 1973 to $42.22 per ounce – together with revaluations of other currencies against the dollar, and increases in the width of the permitted band within which currencies were allowed to drift from $\pm$ 1% to $\pm$ 2.25%. None of these had any lasting effect, however, as first sterling (in 1972), and then the dollar (in 1973) began to float freely against other currencies. By 1976 almost all IMF members had adopted some type of floating exchange rate system. The IMF meeting of that year in Jamaica officially recognized this new situation.

The floating exchange rate system

According to basic economic theory, a system of freely floating exchange rates should be self-regulating. If the cause of a UK deficit were, say, extra imports from America, then the pound should fall (depreciate) against the dollar. This would result from UK importers *selling* extra pounds sterling on the foreign exchange markets to buy US dollars to pay for those imports. In simple demand/supply analysis, the extra supply of pounds sterling will lower its 'price', i.e. the sterling exchange rate. As we have already seen, provided the Marshall–Lerner elasticity conditions are fulfilled (price elasticity of demand for UK exports and imports together greater than 1), then the lower-priced exports and higher-priced imports will contribute to an improvement in the balance of payments, perhaps after a short time-lag.

As it has developed since 1973, however, the system has not been one of 'freely floating' rates. Instead, governments have tended to intervene from time to time to support the values of their currencies (see Fig. 25.1). For instance, the UK has intervened in recent times to prevent the pound falling when cheap imports were part of its anti-inflationary strategy. The setting, for internal reasons, of particular 'targets' for the exchange rate has therefore resulted in a system of 'managed' exchange rates, picturesquely described as a 'dirty floating system'. The major advantages and disadvantages of fixed vs floating exchange rates are shown in Table 25.4.

Table 25.4 **Fixed vs floating exchange rates: the pros and the cons.**

Fixed	Floating
Advantages	
1. Exchange rate stability provides a realistic basis for expectations	1. Automatic eradication of imbalances
2. Stability encourages increased trade	2. Reduced need for reserves – in theory, no need at all
3. Reduced danger from international currency speculation	3. Relative freedom for internal economic policy
4. Imposes increased discipline on internal economic policy	4. Exchange rates change in relatively smooth steps
5. Domestic price stability not endangered through import prices	5. May reduce speculation (rates move freely up *or* down)
Disadvantages	
1. Requires large reserves	1. Increased uncertainty for traders
2. Internal economic policy largely dictated by external factors	2. Domestic price stability may be endangered by rising import prices
3. No automatic adjustment – danger of large changes in rates	3. May increase speculation through co-ordinated buying or selling

Sterling and the ERM

In the last fifty years we have moved, as we have noted, from a fixed to a floating exchange rate regime. With the advent of world inflation in the 70s it became impossible to maintain fixed exchange rate parities between countries because internal prices were accelerating at different rates. As world inflation subsided in the 1980s floating exchange rates became less necessary: in addition, the increased volatility of currencies led the major countries to seek some form of greater stability. The countries of the European Community had a particular problem in that it was clearly not possible to create a unified market without fixed parities. While it has not proved possible to implement any form of fixed exchange rate regime for countries as a whole, the European economies have, since 1979, operated an Exchange Rate Mechanism (see Chapter 28). This pegged currencies to the central unit, known as the 'ECU', within a permitted band of divergence. The value of the 'ECU' was based on a weighted average of the participating currencies. The ERM of the European Monetary System can now be seen to have been an intermediate step towards the European Monetary Union (EMU) which began its transition phase on 1 January 1999 with the launch of the Euro (see Chapters 20 and 28).

The UK did not join the ERM when it was established in 1979, as it was feared that sterling would not be able to maintain its position within the system. After that, when sterling rose as a result of the advent of North Sea oil, it seemed inappropriate to join an exchange rate system where the dominant currency, the mark, was a non-oil currency. After 1987, when the UK signed the Single Europe Act designed to create the single market by 1993, the question of joining the ERM again became a live issue. In fact, before the Chancellor, Nigel Lawson, resigned in 1989 it was clear that he was attempting to target the value of sterling at 3DM = £1. However, the UK government expressed a reluctance to join until various conditions were fulfilled. Behind what were clearly political arguments and bargaining positions lay a very real apprehension about the problems which the UK might face on entry. In particular there was the fear of losing the use of a policy instrument, namely the exchange rate, which might then make it more difficult to use depreciation/devaluation to remedy any trade imbalances with individual countries or the rest of the world. A full discussion of the UK's entry into, and exit from, the ERM can be found in Chapter 28, and more detail on the operation of the European Monetary Union (EMU) can be found in Chapters 20 and 28.

<table>
<tr><td>

Key points

</td><td>

- The exchange rate is usually quoted as the number of units of the domestic currency that is needed to purchase one unit of a foreign currency.
- London is the world's largest centre for foreign exchange trading, with an average daily turnover of $637 billion.
- Some 64% of transactions are 'spot' on any one day, 24% are forward for periods less than one month and a further 10% forward for periods greater than one month.
- The exchange rate is a key 'price', affecting the competitiveness of UK exporters and UK producers of import substitutes.
- A fall (depreciation) in sterling will, other things equal, make UK exports cheaper abroad and UK imports dearer at home.
- The Marshall–Lerner elasticity conditions must be fulfilled if a fall in the exchange rate is to improve the balance of payments. Namely the *sum* of the price elasticities of demand for exports and imports must be greater than one.
- Because short-term elasticities are lower than long-term elasticities, the initial 1 to 2 years after a depreciation may *not* lead to an improvement in the balance of payments (the so-called 'J curve' effect).
- The *effective exchange rate* (EER) for sterling is a weighted average of the 16 national currencies which are most important in terms of trade with the UK.
- The *real exchange rate* takes account of the nominal exchange rates between the various countries *and* of the relative inflation rates in those countries.

</td></tr>
</table>

Notes

1. This analysis assumes that the elasticity of demand for imports is greater than 1. In the case of exports foreign buyers will demand more pounds whatever the elasticity of demand, simply because they are buying more goods as the price in their own currency falls, and the sterling price of exports has not changed.
2. The RNULC are calculated by taking indices of labour costs in the UK and dividing by the weighted geometric average of competitors' unit labour costs. 'Normalization' involves adjusting the basic indices to allow for short-run variations in productivity – so eliminating cyclical variations.
3. During the exchange rate crisis of September 1992, three countries re-introduced exchange controls aimed at reducing the capacity of international banks to borrow in their money markets and then sell the currency for speculative gain. Portugal permitted only between half and one-third of escudos in Lisbon's money markets physically to be used for currency speculation. Spain demanded that the banks deposit funds interest free for a year to match the amount they plan to sell for foreign exchange. Ireland insisted that the government now take over the management of currency swaps, with the exception of those that are trade related.

References

Buxton, T. and **Lintner, V.** (1998) Cost competitiveness, the ERM and UK economic policy, in *Britain's Economic Performance*, 2nd edn, Routledge, London.
Cope, N. (1998) London's Forex trade is $637bn a day, *The Independent*, 30 September.

Kitson, M. and **Michie, J.** (1994) Fixed exchange rates and deflation: the ERM and the Gold Standard, *Economics and Business Education,* Spring.

ONS (1998) *Economic Trends,* October.

ONS (1998) *Financial Statistics,* October.

ONS (1998) *UK Balance of Payments.*

Thomas, D. (1995) The foreign exchange market in London, *Bank of England Quarterly Bulletin,* November.

Turner, P. (1997) Britain and the European Monetary System, *The Economic Review,* **14**, 3, February.

It would seem from Table 26.1 that had it not been for the oil shock of 1973/74, the UK current account would have remained in surplus, with the earnings on services and investment more than covering any deficit on the goods balance. With the advent of North Sea oil in the late 1970s, and with the UK becoming a net exporter of oil in 1980, the future of the current account would still seem secure! However, the underlying trends would warn us against any such complacency. For example, the fall in the price of oil and therefore oil revenue between 1986 and 1991 weakened the total goods balance significantly and further exposed the difficulties which the UK has experienced on its non-oil goods account. Although the balance on services has remained positive and grown substantially since the early 1990s, as has the investment income balance (capital inflows exceeding outflows), these have not been sufficient in total to offset the negative balances for non-oil goods and transfers (net payments to EU, foreign aid, etc.), so that the current balance has been negative in eleven of the past twelve years.

Goods trade   The UK's competitive weakness on her goods trade can be viewed from three main standpoints: first, the deterioration in the non-oil goods balance; second, the change in the area and commodity composition of goods trade; and third, the adverse trends observed for trade in manufactures.

The non-oil goods balance   From Table 26.1 we see that the non-oil goods balance has experienced alternate periods of deficit and surplus. Historically these periods have to some extent followed the business cycle. Deficits have tended to be more pronounced during periods of recovery and boom, and surpluses during periods of recession. The relatively high incomes experienced during periods of expanding economic activity have tended to attract imports (see below), with an adverse effect on the non-oil goods balance, as in 1973/74 and in the short-lived 'boom' of 1978/79. Conversely, lower incomes during periods of recession have tended to curb spending on imports, improving the non-oil goods balance. However, since 1980 this pattern has been disturbed, with the non-oil goods balance moving sharply into deficit in 1982–85 despite economic recession. The further deterioration of the non-oil goods balance during the 'boom' years of 1986–88 was not unexpected. Of greater concern is the fact that the significant fall in consumer spending after 1988, with the onset of recession, should only have led to such a modest 'improvement' in the non-oil goods balance after 1989. All these factors suggest that the UK is facing even greater problems in becoming competitive in goods other than oil.

The area and commodity composition of goods trade   Changes in the UK's pattern of goods trade, on both an area and commodity basis, also suggest further potential problems.

An area analysis of UK trade in goods, as seen in Table 26.2, shows a clear shift since 1960 towards Western Europe generally, and the EU in particular. Both the share of UK exports to, and imports from, Western Europe nearly doubled between 1960 and 1997, with most of the shift being due to increased UK trade with EU countries. On the other hand, the share of total trade in goods with North America has fallen, especially as regards imports, because although trade with the USA

		1960		1969		1979		1997	
		X	M	X	M	X	M	X	M
1	Western Europe	32	31	40	38	57	60	60	60
	(of which EU)	(21)	(20)	(29)	(26)	(43)	(45)	(56)	(54)
2	North America	16	21	17	20	12	13	14	15
	(of which USA)	(10)	(12)	(12)	(14)	(10)	(10)	(12)	(14)
3	Other OECD countries	13	12	12	10	6	6	6	8
	(of which Japan)	(1)	(1)	(2)	(1)	(2)	(3)	(2)	(5)
4	Oil-exporting countries	6	10	5	8	9	7	6	2
5	Rest of the World	31	23	23	20	13	11	14	15
	(of which Newly Industrial Asia	(4)	(3)	(3)	(3)	(3)	(4)	(5)	(8)
	E Europe and the former USSR)	(2)	(3)	(3)	(4)	(3)	(3)	(2)	(2)

*Exports are measured free on board (f.o.b.), but imports include cost, insurance and freight (c.i.f.). All figures are rounded.
Sources: ONS (1998) *Monthly Digest of Statistics*, July, and previous issues.

remained relatively steady, trade with Canada fell sharply. The share of UK trade with 'other OECD countries' such as Australia and New Zealand has also fallen, although trade with Japan, the remaining major country in this bloc, has increased (mainly on the import side). The oil-exporting countries (OPEC) account for a relatively steady share of UK exports of goods, but with the advent of North Sea oil their share of UK goods imports has declined. The remaining significant change is the rapid fall in the importance of the 'Rest of the World' in UK trade, with this category consisting mainly of Commonwealth countries and Latin American states. However, it is interesting to note the recent increase in importance of Newly Industrial Asia (Hong Kong, Singapore, Malaysia, South Korea, Taiwan, Thailand) in UK trade.

Table 26.3 shows the composition of UK trade in goods over the years 1960–97. On the *export* side, the share of manufactured goods has remained at around 84% over the period 1960 to 1997, while there has been an increase in the share of oil-based products from 4% to 6%. On the *import* side, there has been a significant decline in the share of food, beverages and tobacco in total goods imports, as has also occurred for basic materials, such as textile fibres, crude rubber and metal ores. In each case the volume of imports has increased, but much more slowly than total imports, so that their *share* has fallen. The opposite is true for manufactured goods,

	1960		1969		1979		1997	
	X	M	X	M	X	M	X	M
(0, 1)[†] Food, beverages, tobacco	5	33	6	23	7	14	7	9
(2, 4) Basic materials	4	23	4	15	3	9	2	3
(3) Mineral fuel and lubricants	4	10	2	11	11	12	6	3
(5–8) Manufactured goods	84	33	85	50	76	63	84	84
(5, 6) (i) Semi-manufactured goods	(36)	(22)	(35)	(28)	(31)	(27)	(26)	(25)
(7, 8) (ii) Finished manufactured goods	(48)	(11)	(50)	(22)	(45)	(36)	(58)	(59)
(9) Unclassified	3	1	3	1	3	2	1	1

*Exports (f.o.b.), imports (c.i.f.). All figures are rounded.
[†]Numbers in brackets relate to the Standard International Trade Classification.
Sources: ONS (1998) *Monthly Digest of Statistics*, July, and previous issues.

with the volume of imports growing so fast that the share of manufactured goods in total visible imports has more than doubled since 1960. In fact, the share of *finished* manufactured goods in total goods imports has increased more than fivefold.

Tables 26.2 and 26.3 show that the UK has shifted the geographical focus of her trade towards the industrialized countries of Europe, and in particular towards the EU. At the same time the UK is showing symptoms of being less able to compete with these countries in the important commodity sector of manufacturing. It may therefore be useful to look at this sector in more detail.

Trade in manufactures   The UK's problems as regards trade in manufactures manifest themselves in a variety of ways. Table 26.4 presents the share of selected countries in world *exports* of manufactures. Although not shown in detail on this table, the UK's share fell from about 17% in 1960 to an all time low of 7.5% in 1984, before rising to 8% by 1997. The significant fall in UK share of world exports of manufactures between 1960 and 1997 was not matched by any of her main competitors.

Table 26.5 shows *export intensity* figures for the manufacturing sectors of leading economies between 1971 and 1990. The four European countries have a significantly higher *average level* of export intensity (i.e. the ratio of exports to domestic production) than countries such as the US and Japan who have much larger domestic markets to entice their producers. The *average growth rate* of export intensity

Table 26.4 Share of world export of manufactures of major OECD countries (%).

	1960	1969	1979	1997
USA	22	19	16	16
Japan	7	11	14	14
France	10	8	10	8
Germany	19	19	21	16
Italy	5	7	8	8
UK	17	11	9	8
Others*	21	23	22	30

*All figures are rounded up, so that totals may not sum to 100.
Sources: OECD (1998) *Trade by Commodities*, Series C, and previous issues.

Table 26.5 Export intensity and import penetration in manufacturing.

	Export intensity (import penetration)		Average level
	Average growth rate		
	1971–80	1981–90	1985–90
US	6.9 (6.1)	1.3 (6.5)	8.4 (13.3)
Japan	2.8 (3.7)	−2.3 (0.8)	12.4 (5.4)
Germany	3.4 (4.2)	2.4 (2.6)	32.4 (24.6)
France	4.5 (4.0)	1.9 (3.4)	27.1 (27.7)
Italy	3.8 (3.0)	−1.1 (0.8)	23.2 (21.0)
UK	4.5 (5.1)	1.3 (3.3)	25.1 (29.3)

Notes:
Export intensity = Exports/domestic production.
(Import penetration) = Imports/apparent consumption*.
*Domestic production − exports + imports.
Source: Adapted from OECD (1994) *Assessing Structural Reforms: Lessons for the Future*, Paris.

Fig. 26.1. UK balance of
trade in manufactures.
Notes:
*Exports (f.o.b.), imports
(c.i.f.)
Sources: CSO (1968,
1973, 1987, 1988); ONS
(1998).

decelerated in all countries after 1980. The UK's recorded figure is similar to that of France and Italy, but still lags behind Germany whose average growth of export intensity has showed the steadiest increase of all the countries between 1971 and 1990.

Table 26.5 also provides information on import penetration in manufacturing – figures shown in brackets. The *average level* of import penetration (i.e. ratio of imports to domestic consumption) is higher in the UK than in the other economies. The *average growth rate* of import penetration has been increasing for all the major economies since 1970 as they progressively specialise in commodities for export while importing the rest. However, the growth rate of import penetration has been higher in the UK than in the other major economies, except for the US. At the same time import penetration statistics for certain UK *sectors* have been much higher than for the equivalent sectors of other countries. For example, the UK had particularly high import penetration ratios in electrical machinery (58%), motor vehicles (59%) and computers and office machinery (102%). The main problem for the UK is that its import penetration ratios are rising relatively more rapidly than its corresponding export intensity ratios. This points to progressively more serious problems for its balance of trade in manufactures.

The problems encountered by the manufacturing sector are also revealed in Fig. 26.1, which shows the balance of trade (value of exports/value of imports) for both finished and total manufactured goods. The ratios have fallen progressively since the early 1960s. In fact by 1982 the UK had, on an *Overseas Trade Statistics* basis, become a net importer of *finished* manufactures and of *total* manufactures. Data for the second half of the 1980s and the 1990s show some stabilisation of this trend, but the *overall* balance of trade in both finished and total manufactures still remained in deficit.

Reasons behind UK trade performance

This deterioration in UK performance on its non-oil account, and in particular in manufactures, may be due to a number of factors: an inappropriate trade structure, a lack of price competitiveness, or an inability to compete in terms of non-price factors such as marketing, design, delivery date and product development. We examine each of these possibilities in turn.

Trade structure   It is possible to argue that the UK's relatively poor trading performance, especially in exports, has been due to its inadequate response to the changing geographical and commodity composition of world trade. The fall in the UK's share of world trade could then be due to at least three main causes. First, a geographical composition of exports biased towards slow-growth areas. Second, an inappropriate commodity composition of exports, with the UK sluggish in shifting her exports to commodity sectors growing rapidly in world trade. Third, it may, of course, be that irrespective of area and commodity composition, the UK has basically failed to compete *within* each geographical area and *within* each commodity group. In many analytical surveys of competitiveness, this third factor is often called the 'residual effect' since it attempts to measure the importance of factors *other* than area or commodity – such as the effects of price and non-price competition within each area and commodity group.

A major study of UK export performance was conducted by the Bank of England (Dumble 1994). Using 'shift-share' analysis, it was possible to provide information on the relative magnitudes of the 'regional' (area) and 'commodity' composition effects for UK exports. These statistics are given in Table 26.6.

From Table 26.6 it can be seen that between 1970 and 1985 the UK lost export market share valued at $8,532m. A small part of this loss ($407m) could be attributed to the UK specialising in the export of manufactured goods the demand for which was growing more slowly than the demand for manufactured goods in general (*commodity composition effect*). A larger part of this loss ($1,017m) could be attributed to the UK concentrating its exports in regional markets which were growing more slowly than the average of all world markets (*regional composition effect*). However, the main factor causing the loss of UK export share over the period was the *residual effect*, which measures the loss of market share due to a host of factors *other than* the 'commodity' and 'regional' effects. Such residual factors included the forces of price and non-price competition which the UK faced across a range of commodities and regions over the period.

During the late 1980s the UK regained some of its export market share, to the value of $11,004m. This was due mainly to an improved performance in terms of the 'regional composition' effect. However it is interesting to note that the 'residual' still accounted for a third of the improvement. In short, the main determinant of the UK's export competitiveness over much of the post-war period has been her competitiveness in terms of price and non-price factors *within* particular commodity groups and *within* geographical regions. This study confirms earlier work by the OECD into the loss of UK share of world manufactured exports over the period 1970–87. The OECD study also attributed the loss of market share to the effects of

Table 26.6 **UK export performance in manufactures ($m).**

	Commodity composition effect	Regional (area) composition effect	Residual effect	Total effect
1970–85	−407	−1,017	−7,108	−8,532
1985–90	373	6,912	3,719	11,004

Note:
The total effect is the sum of the three effects. A positive figure represents an increase in market share.
Source: Adapted from Dumble (1994).

price and non-price factors as reflected by the size of the 'residual effect'. We now turn to an examination of UK competitiveness in terms of these price and non-price factors.

Price competitiveness

Price elasticity of demand is a traditional measure of demand responsiveness. In the trade context it can be expressed as a ratio of percentage change in quantity demanded of exports or imports, to the percentage change in price. As regards trade, however, it is not just the absolute price of UK exports or imports which is important, but UK prices *relative* to those of its main competitors. Such relative prices often reflect differences between countries in unit costs, inflation rates or exchange rates.

International competitiveness may be assessed in a number of different ways. One is to use the UK export price divided by a weighted average of competitors' export prices. Another is to look not at prices but at costs, since even where there is no change in price, a change in costs may still affect underlying competitiveness. For instance, if price is unchanged, a rise in costs will reduce profits, perhaps reducing future investment and eventually sales. Costs, and in particular unit labour costs, are therefore often used in assessing changes in international competitiveness. Let us now examine the evidence as to whether improvements in UK price or cost competitiveness will have an important influence on trade flow.

Writers do not fully agree on the responsiveness of UK export and import volumes to changes in price. For one thing it is often difficult to identify the effect of price on quantity demanded when other factors are changing. For another, measures of price elasticity are often calculated over varying time periods, which can lead to different results. The surveys that are available suggest that the *short-run* price elasticity of demand for total UK exports varies between 0.26 and 0.46, indicating a relatively inelastic response of export demand to price change. In the *longer run*, after a time-lag of around two years, the price elasticity of demand for total visible exports rises to between 1.5 and 2.6 (Thirlwall 1980). As regards total visible imports, most studies reveal a UK price elasticity less than 1, and sometimes near to zero. Manufactured imports are rather more price-responsive, with estimates ranging from 0.9 to 1.6 (Panić 1975; Morgan and Martin 1975).

Despite the difficulties of measurement, it seems that after a time-lag of around two years, UK exports are much more responsive to price than are UK imports. This suggests that an improvement in UK price competitiveness, *vis-à-vis* other countries, would significantly raise the volume of UK exports, but have much less effect in reducing the volume of UK imports.

Of course, it is not just volumes of trade flow that matter, but also *values*. The empirical measurements of UK price elasticities are encouraging in this respect in that they fulfil the Marshall–Lerner elasticity condition. This condition must be met if a fall in export prices and a rise in import prices (e.g. via devaluation) is to raise the *value* of exports relative to the *value* of imports, thereby improving the visible balance. The condition states that the sum of the respective price elasticities of demand for exports and imports must be greater than 1. Even taking the lower bands of the elasticity estimates for total visible exports and imports their sum is nearer 2 than 1, at least over the *longer-run* time period. In the *shorter run*, however, the sum may well be less than 1, so that observations in the UK of a J-curve effect, whereby an improvement in UK price competitiveness actually worsens the visible balance for eighteen months to two years, should therefore come as no real surprise.

Another way of assessing the importance of price factors in UK trade is to look at the *share* of UK exports and imports in world trade. If, for example, UK exports became relatively cheaper, one would expect other countries to substitute UK goods for their previous purchases, thus increasing UK share of world trade in these goods. We are, in effect, measuring the ease with which UK goods are substituted for foreign goods as the former become relatively cheaper. The basic question is this: will an improvement in UK price competitiveness increase our share of the world export market, and decrease import penetration as the home market switches to relatively cheaper UK goods?

A study by J. Fagerberg looked at the factors which determined the growth of the UK's share of world export markets between 1960 and 1983. It found that labour cost (a main determinant of price competitiveness) was much less important than non-price factors (such as the capacity to deliver goods and technological competitiveness) in accounting for the UK's relatively poor ability to compete in world markets (Fagerberg 1988). Interestingly, when the UK share of world export markets improved during the period 1985–90, the relative prices and costs of UK manufacturing *vis-à-vis* her main competitors actually *deteriorated* (Dumble 1994). This tends to suggest, once again, that factors *other than price* account for much of the UK's export competitiveness.

The picture is similar for imports. One early OECD survey found little link between UK price competitiveness and import penetration. A statistical survey by the present author has substantiated these results for the period 1963–97. The UK's ratio of imports to home demand was barely affected by observed changes in UK price competitiveness during this period, whatever the time-lags introduced. The analysis noted above should not be mistaken to mean that price factors are *not* important in the global trading environment. Indeed, price is an integral part of the 'marketing mix'. Lowering costs to enable prices to be set in a flexible manner is crucial to trading success. In 1995, the UK recorded average labour costs of $15 per hour, lower than all her main industrialised competitors. Countries such as Germany ($32) and Japan ($25) had average labour costs well above the UK level (*Economist* 1996). Despite this assertion, many major studies have shown that non-price factors have a crucial role to play in the complicated trading patterns of the 1990s.

Non-price competitiveness   Income   The level of world income is an important factor affecting demand for UK goods, and hence her trading position. As early as the 1980s, Thirlwall (1980) suggested that the income elasticity of demand for *total* UK exports (which measures the responsiveness of UK exports to changes in world income) had been relatively low over the previous thirty years, being in the main less than unity. The figure for *manufactured* exports was also generally below unity, although *individual sectors and products* often had elasticity figures which varied between 1.0 and 1.5. These values tend to be lower than those for our competitors. For Germany the income elasticity of demand for total exports is as high as 2.5, and for Japan 3.5.

However, it is well known that changes in the level of UK income have a significant effect on the UK demand for imports. In other words, the income elasticity of demand for *total* UK imports is high, ranging between 1.6 and 2. For *total manufactured* imports the value of income elasticity is even higher, between 2.6 and 3.0, and for *finished manufactured* imports higher still, around 4.6.

The UK income elasticity figure for *total imports* is not significantly different from other countries – USA 1.5, Germany 1.8 – but for *manufactured imports* it does seem higher in the UK than elsewhere. The study by Panić (1975) found the income elasticity of demand for manufactured products to be 3.1 in the UK, but only 2.2 in France and 2.1 in Germany. These elasticity values highlight three important points:

1. That income elasticity of demand for total UK imports is higher than for total UK exports.
2. That for manufactures, particularly finished manufactures, this gap between income elasticity of demand for UK imports and exports is even greater.
3. That other countries have similar or lower (as in manufactures) income elasticities of demand for imports, but experience higher income elasticities of demand for their exports.

The implications of these figures are clear. When income (and therefore demand) in the world economy rises, UK imports will tend to grow faster than UK exports, especially for manufactures. Other countries will not however suffer to the same extent as the UK. Whilst their imports may grow steadily, their exports will grow relatively faster than UK exports, so that their visible balance comes under less strain.

Unfortunately, the effect of higher income on imports is not easily reversed. The data suggest a sort of 'ratchet effect', so that although the ratio of manufactured imports to GDP rises on the upswing of the business cycle, it does not fall to the same extent on the downswing. There is then a real danger that higher import ratios for manufactures become a permanent feature of the economy.

One reason for exports rising relatively slowly when UK and world income increases, is the tendency for firms to concentrate on the more secure home market when domestic demand is high. This shift away from the export market and towards the home market has affected our export performance, with exports progressively becoming a 'residual' market for UK producers.

Another reason for the slow growth of exports when UK income increases, and with it domestic demand, might be the failure of firms to increase their total capacity in order to satisfy *both* home and foreign markets. For instance, an increase in total capacity may require UK companies to increase their investment in plant and equipment, and this is never easy.

Unfortunately, even if UK firms *do* manage to increase total capacity by channelling more resources into increased investment, the *composition* of this investment may be biased against export growth. For example, it has been argued that during the 1980s those UK sectors which invested most in plant and equipment were the ones which were least open to foreign competition (Muellbauer 1990). In his study, Muellbauer calculates 'tradeability' and 'investment growth' ratios for twenty-five sectors in the UK economy. The *tradeability ratio* is defined as the ratio of exports or imports to total sales (whichever is the largest). If this ratio is high, it indicates that the sector is relatively 'open' to trade, and thus to foreign competition. If the ratio is low, then the sector is less involved in trade and is not affected so much by foreign competition. The *tradeability ratio* of each sector was compared with the *growth of investment* in that sector between 1979 and 1987 (expressed as a ratio using 1979 as the base year). The general conclusion was that the investment ratio tends to be very *high* in sectors such as Distribution, Communications and Banking which have *low* tradeability ratios, i.e. which are not so open to foreign competition. In other areas (such as manufacturing) where the investment ratio is lower, the tradeability ratio is high, i.e. they are more open to foreign competition. The argument here is that investment has not grown sufficiently in those sectors most open to foreign competition. This obviously prevents many UK industries from competing effectively abroad. Similarly, too much investment may have gone into sectors such as banking, insurance, and distribution, which are not so open to foreign competition. This bias in the investment ratios may inhibit the UK's long run ability to produce goods for the world markets.

Quality, service and other effects Price and income are not the only factors influencing UK trade performance. In the home market, competition between oligopolistic firms often takes the form of non-price competition (see Chapter 6). Since much of world trade, especially in manufactures, involves competition between domestic and foreign multinationals (see Chapter 7), it is hardly surprising that it is often non-price competition that determines which nations will be successful in the export market. Indeed a major study by Hooley *et al.* (1988) of 1,380 UK companies found that only 7% of companies cited price as being a significant source of competitive advantage, with 26% citing company/brand reputation, 21% product performance, 18% product quality and 14% product design.

Two types of non-price competition seem particularly important for both domestic and overseas sales. First, competition in *product characteristics*, such as quality, design, ease of maintenance and the development of entirely new products. Second, competition in *sales characteristics*, such as delivery date, after-sales service, marketing strategies, and the use made of agents and subsidiaries at home and abroad.

To quantify the relative importance of non-price factors, such as quality and service, is a difficult task, made more so by a dearth of regular statistics in this area. However, some *ad hoc* attempts have been made at statistical analysis. One prominent method for evaluating the importance of non-price factors is to compare the average value per unit weight of exports from different countries. This figure is obtained by dividing the total value of goods exported by a certain sector, e.g. mechanical engineering, by the total weight of such exports. We should note that the 'value per ton' that results from this calculation is simply the average price per ton. The rationale behind value per ton comparisons is that if goods are identical in non-price characteristics such as quality, then international competition will tend to make value per ton (average price per ton) similar in whichever country those goods are produced. It then follows that any discrepancy in value per ton between countries in a given export product is an indication that non-price differences exist in that product.

Research based on the years 1962–75 found that the value per ton of UK exports from the non-electrical sector (essentially mechanical engineering) was the lowest of all the major industrialized countries. Apart from Italy, the rate of growth of value per ton was also lowest in the UK between those dates. Similar results were observed in a separate study of a wide range of manufactured exports traded between the UK and Germany (Connell 1980: Chapter 3). A number of inferences can be drawn from such evidence:

1. The lower value per ton of UK exports may reflect lower prices in the UK for *similar*-quality products. However, if UK exports were cheaper, and of the same

quality, then the UK's share of the world market in such products should increase! Since the UK's share did *not* increase it is unconvincing to explain lower value per ton of UK exports in terms of lower UK prices for similar-quality products.

2. It could still be argued that the lower-priced UK exports are similar in quality to those produced abroad, but that static or falling market share is due to inadequate sales back-up. United Kingdom exporters may have lowered prices (reducing value per ton) in the hope that relative cheapness would raise sales and help compensate for an inability to market the product adequately.

3. The relatively low value per ton of UK exports could be due to differences in product mix between different countries. The UK may be going progressively 'down market', exporting 'less technology-intensive' products. The price, and therefore value per ton, of UK exports would then tend to be lower than in those countries which export a higher proportion of the 'more technology-intensive' products (see Chapter 7).

Even if the precise cause of the low value per ton of UK exports is difficult to identify it seems reasonable to assume that it must be due to factors *other than* price competition amongst export goods of similar quality. Especially since in many cases the value per ton of other countries' exports was or three times higher than that of UK exports. Non-price factors – quality, design, marketing, after-sales service, etc. – must account for much of the substantial difference in value per ton.

Product quality   Product quality depends on many interrelated factors but it is clear that most high quality products are ones which tend to have a high research and development content, are technologically complex and are also skill intensive. The UK trade performance in high, medium and low technology manufactures[1] is shown in Table 26.7. This table gives the export market share for each category as a percentage of the total exports in that category of the 13 largest OECD countries. It also provides (in brackets) import penetration statistics for the same technological categories in each country.

Table 26.7 Export market shares and import penetration in manufactures in 1970 and 1990.

	High technology		Medium technology		Low technology	
	1970	1990	1970	1990	1970	1990
France	7.7	8.7	8.5	10.0	10.7	12.1
	(21.6)	(31.6)	(19.7)	(34.1)	(10.7)	(21.4)
Germany	17.7	16.2	23.1	24.7	15.0	17.9
	(14.9)	(37.0)	(17.2)	(29.5)	(11.1)	(20.9)
Italy	5.5	5.1	7.1	7.7	8.5	12.8
	(16.2)	(22.8)	(23.6)	(28.9)	(11.8)	(15.7)
UK	10.5	10.2	11.9	8.5	8.9	8.5
	(17.4)	(42.4)	(22.1)	(39.4)	(12.4)	(19.8)
Japan	13.2	21.1	8.5	16.9	13.2	7.1
	(5.2)	(5.4)	(4.5)	(5.9)	(3.0)	(6.6)
US	31.1	26.3	21.7	15.4	13.4	13.3
	(4.2)	(18.4)	(5.6)	(18.5)	(3.8)	(8.8)

Note:
Figures in brackets refer to import penetration.
Source: Adapted from OECD (1994) *Manufacturing Performance: a scoreboard of indicators,* Paris.

It is interesting to note the rapid improvement between 1970 and 1990 in Japan's *export share* in both high and medium technology categories and also its rapid shift out of the low technology category. In contrast, the UK has not increased its market share of the high technology category and has even lost out in the other two categories. The UK is the only country which has failed to gain market share in *any* of the three sectors. As far as *import penetration* is concerned, the UK had by 1990 reached a disturbingly high import penetration ratio in both the high and medium technology categories – above that of any other country shown in the table.

A range studies have been used to support the contention that the UK has gone 'down market' *vis-à-vis* the other advanced industrialized countries. Put another way, the UK has tended more and more to export cheaper, lower-quality products, embodying 'old' technology, and to import expensive, high-quality products, embodying 'new' technology. For instance, Katrak (1982) noted that during the 1970s UK exports contained a greater proportion of 'less skill-intensive' and 'less research and development-intensive' (and therefore less technologically advanced) products than did her imports. Katrak also noted that the UK tended to export mainly 'mature' products, i.e. those which have been on the market for a relatively long period, yet to import mainly 'less mature' products. This strategy is particularly dangerous when the growth of 'mature' products in world trade is slower than that of newer products. There is also the danger that domestic and overseas markets in 'mature' products will be increasingly vulnerable to competition, such as that from the newly industrializing countries.

These rather general studies on the 'down market' nature of UK production of both exports and import substitutes, may be backed up by specific industry case studies. For example, a tendency for the UK to produce, and often export, lower quality goods can be seen in a major survey of 29 manufacturing plants producing biscuits in four European countries, i.e. the Netherlands, France, UK and Germany (Mason *et al.* 1994). In this sector they found that the value-added per ton of biscuits was between 15% (Netherlands/France) and 75% (Germany) higher than in the UK, and that the reason for this differential had very little to do with the type of capital equipment used. Basically, the UK industry specialized in highly automated, mass-produced, low value-added biscuits – precisely the type of product which is prone to international competition from developing countries. Much of the reason for such a low value-added strategy was traced to the alleged lack of suitable labour skills at all company levels. Similarly, a study of the UK and German furniture industry (Steedman and Wagner 1987) showed that even though the industry was far from being in the 'high technology' class, it was still obvious that the UK furniture industry continued to use technically less advanced equipment and produced for the middle- to low-quality end of the market. German firms on the other hand used more advanced equipment and specialized in high-quality products, exporting some of these to the UK!

' However, it is interesting to note that in the more dynamic sectors of UK industry, there are signs of a *shift* towards the higher end of the quality market. This shift can be measured by taking the *revealed comparative advantage* figures for the main countries, as shown in Table 26.8.

'Revealed comparative advantage' is a *ratio* which is defined in the following way. A country's exports in a particular technological category are expressed as a percentage of its total manufacturing exports; this is then divided by OECD exports in the same technological category expressed as a percentage of the total OECD

Table 26.8 Revealed comparative advantage in manufacturing exports.

	High technology		Medium technology		Low technology	
	1970	1990	1970	1990	1970	1990
France	0.83	0.84	0.92	0.97	1.15	1.18
Germany	0.93	0.79	1.22	1.20	0.79	0.87
Italy	0.75	0.59	0.97	0.89	1.16	1.49
UK	1.01	1.16	1.14	0.96	0.85	0.95
EU 6	0.90	0.82	1.03	1.01	1.01	1.13
Japan	1.20	1.41	0.77	1.12	1.19	0.47
US	1.54	1.51	1.07	0.89	0.66	0.76

Source: Adapted from OECD (1994) *Manufacturing Performance: a scoreboard of indicators,* Paris.

manufactured exports. In other words, the ratio measures the distribution of each country's exports in a particular technological category as compared with that for the OECD as a whole. If the ratio is above 1, then it indicates that a country's exports are shifting in the same direction as the OECD countries as a whole, but at a faster rate.

Over the period 1970–90, the UK improved its performance in the *high technology* category revealing a higher ratio than that for Germany and the largest six EU countries. The UK's strength has been in chemicals, computers and aircraft. However, German strength is clearly seen in the *medium technology* category, whilst it is still difficult to compete with Japan and the US in the high technology categories. Although it seems that the UK is improving its *relative* trade performance in the high technology exports, it is important to note that it still has a long way to go before 'catching up' with Germany's higher *absolute share* of OECD high technology exports seen in Table 26.7 above.

Even the UK income elasticities of demand we noted earlier could be considered symptoms of 'product inferiority'. The low income elasticity of demand for UK exports, and high income elasticity of demand for UK imports, both suggest that at higher income, goods produced by the UK export industries and by the import substitute industries are replaced by more attractive, higher-quality goods from abroad. There is some evidence to show that European exports were moving in the direction of more highly skilled, capital-intensive products in the early 1980s and that the UK needed to become more involved in these high-technology products to increase its export share and to reduce import penetration. In 1987 an important study (Patel and Pavitt 1987) attempted to assess the relationship between the UK's technological competitiveness in world markets and her trading performance. Measuring the UK's trading performance in certain sectors of the economy was relatively straightforward, since figures for exports and imports are easily available. However, it was more difficult to devise a measure which reflected the UK's technological competitiveness in relation to other countries. They overcame this problem by studying the *number of patents* which were granted in the USA between 1963 and 1984 and calculated an index which measured the share of those patents which had *originated* in the UK. For example, it was obvious that if one sector of US industry used a large proportion of patents which had originally been invented in the UK, then this meant that the UK was technologically very competitive in this sector. Conversely, a sector with a low ratio of US patents originating from the UK indicated a relatively lower level of UK technical competence in this particular sector. By comparing these measures of UK technological competitiveness with UK trade performance, sector by sector, it was possible to see that the interrelationships between trade and technology were very close. For example in the electrical and electronics industry, the UK's technological competitiveness was medium to low and her trade competitiveness was also low. For the chemical industry, the UK's technological competitiveness was medium to high, and so was her trade competitiveness in this sector. In other words there seemed to be a strong relationship between technological competitiveness and trading performance. Since EU exports of high technology products have grown at a faster pace than manufacturing in general, it is important for the UK to improve its technological competitiveness in such products if it is to compete successfully with her main EU rivals. This point is further reinforced by the work of Lall (1998) which indicated that even the developing countries are increasing their share of world manufactured exports in both medium and high technology products. For example, between 1980 and 1996 the developing countries' overall share of world manufactured exports had risen from 10% to 23%, and interestingly their share of medium technology exports has risen from 3% to 11% and of high technology exports from 3% to 29% over the same period. The pressure on the UK to progressively improve its trade performance in medium to high technology products within manufacturing seems likely to continue.

The relatively low income elasticity of demand for UK manufactured exports does tend to indicate that UK producers are unable to react promptly to world demand with good quality products. However, it has been argued that the value of income elasticity of demand for UK manufactured exports has increased since the late 1970s. This would suggest that the UK manufacturing industry has become more responsive to changes in world demand since the recession of the early 1980s (Landesmann and Snell 1989). The crux of this theory is that the aggregate income elasticity of demand for UK manufactured exports has risen from 0.74 in 1979 to 1.0 by 1986, and that this may be due to the shake out of inefficient exporters during the 1979–81 slump which left a core of relatively more efficient exporters. By definition, 'poor' exporters have low income elasticities and 'good' exporters have high income elasticity figures. Improvements were found in many industries, with the income elasticity figure for electrical engineering rising from 0.78 in 1979 to 1.3 by 1986, the figure for textiles and clothing rising from 0.8 to 1.3, and for transport from 0.8 to 1.0 over the same period. These figures do tend to point to an export performance from UK industry which is more responsive to world demand since the early 1980s. Indeed, the UK has a number of companies which *export* a significant percentage of their UK turnover. For example, Lucas (vehicle/aircraft accessories), Caterpillar UK (earth moving equipment) and SIEBE (control devices and compressed air equipment) all export more than 80% of their turnover, while Rolls Royce and NEI plc (aero engineering), Allied Colloids (industrial chemicals), Amersham International (radioactive materials) and Polaroid (photographic and optical equipment) export over 70% of their turnover. Despite these encouraging signs, it should also be remembered that the UK manufacturing sector needs a greater *absolute number* of firms which are responsive to the market in order to increase total exports significantly. This is difficult to achieve when the manufacturing base of the economy is being eroded, as was seen in Chapter 1 of this book.

This conclusion is supported by a survey in 1994 which found that UK firms were much more likely to approve capital investment which was aimed at cutting production costs than investment to enhance new product development (Wardlow 1994). This suggests that the UK's investment growth in the early 1990s was more likely to *deepen* the industrial base rather than *widen* it across many companies. In other words, the UK's traditionally successful industries such as pharmaceuticals and aerospace have tended to strengthen their position, while the range of products offered by the UK as a whole has barely been extended.

However, even so-called successful industries should not be complacent, because research by the DTI into the office machinery and chemical industry has showed that while the UK has world-class companies in these areas, it still has a 'long tail' of relatively low productivity companies *within* each industry in comparison to Germany, France and Italy (HMSO 1996). Signs that this lower productivity and quality record might improve in the future have come from the growth of 'benchmarking' in the UK. Benchmarking occurs when companies set out to compare themselves systematically with the best in their industry, thus helping them to establish targets for improvement. In 1996 a number of benchmarking providers including the DTI, British Quality Foundation, the CBI PROBE initiative, and Cranfield University, agreed to work towards establishing a National Benchmarking Network. It is through such networks that the increased quality and productivity necessary for competitive exports might be secured.

Design   Improved design of new products, as well as product quality, is also essential for UK competitiveness. Research shows that firms in both traditional and new sectors which invest significantly in design are more successful than firms which pay less attention to this feature. Further, for those companies using professional designers, around 90% of the products which reached the production stage were found to be a commercial success, with an average payback period of under 15 months (HMSO 1996). Research by the London Business School in 1998 showed that an extra 1% of sales revenue devoted to product design and development was likely to increase company sales value and profits by around 3% to 4%.

Encouraging the design aspects of product competitiveness is also important, because there is often a close relationship between the design of a product and its cost of production. For example, it is not always realized that a significant proportion of the cost of a finished product is often dictated by the specific design which is chosen at the outset. Figure 26.2 indicates two aspects of the cost structure of a typical product development cycle, from the initial 'idea' stage through to the 'design' stage and then to the final 'ongoing production' stage. The lower line indicates the percentage of total development costs *actually spent* at each stage in the cycle; the upper line indicates the percentage of total development costs *committed* at each stage in the cycle. The importance of the 'concept' and 'detailed design' stages can be clearly seen from Figure 26.2. For example, while the absolute amount of money *actually spent* in the design stages is relatively low as compared to the production stages, it is obvious that it is in the 'concept' and 'detailed design' stages that the major share of the lifecycle development costs of the product are *committed*. From the graph, it appears that some 85% of a product's final costs have been committed by the end of the design stage.

According to executives of General Motors in the US, some 70% of the cost of producing the transmission mechanism of its trucks is determined at the design stage. Similarly, in a study of the Rolls Royce company, John Corbett found that 80% of the

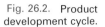

Fig. 26.2. Product
development cycle.

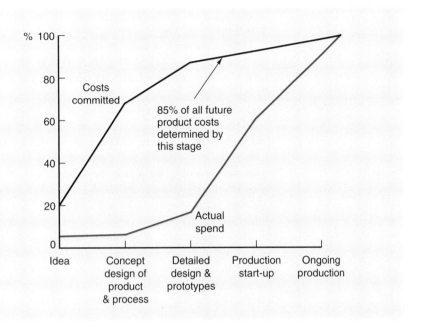

final costs of some 2,000 different components were determined by the design adopted. This means that good, efficient design is an essential requirement for keeping costs at a minimum when competing in international markets (Griffiths 1989).

An important survey by the Design Centre in 1993 found that 50% of all new UK products were late to market and that UK manufacturers were slow in adopting 'concurrent engineering techniques' which involve bringing the customer, designer, marketing manager, production engineer and supplier together from the start of the project. Such techniques tend to improve development times, quality, reliability and costs. The Design Council's conclusions have been reinforced by a more recent survey it conducted in 1998 into investment by 200 manufacturers in the three main design areas, namely product, engineering and graphic design. Such investment was shown to yield a high return, with some 48% of companies recovering their total design and tooling costs within a year of the project launch.

Product marketing and sales Apart from quality, marketing and selling operations can have a substantial impact on market share. Reports in the early 1980s indicated a declining UK share in total OECD exports in the majority of the thirty industrial sectors studied – with 'inadequate marketing' the single factor most often quoted as the explanation for this poor export performance. An earlier NEDO report on the UK textile industry had concluded that most of the UK's problems in competing with its EU counterparts arose from a poor performance in packaging, delivery date and after-sales service, rather than from price.

It does appear that other countries have devoted more sales effort to the export market than has the UK. There is considerable evidence to suggest that UK competitors have larger sales forces in the export sector, and that they also employ more highly skilled marketing specialists, and pay more attention to the activities of promotion, advertising, delivery date and after-sales service.

The importance of *early delivery* in determining export success has been stressed by many writers, such as Fagerberg (1988). He found that the loss of UK market share in manufacturing exports was very closely linked to the capacity of UK companies to deliver goods efficiently. This in turn was dependent on the diffusion of technology within companies, and on the growth of UK investment in plant and equipment. It can be seen, therefore, that an efficient delivery of goods depends on many interrelated factors. However, it should be understood that even if UK companies can produce good products, there is still the problem of cutting down the time between receiving a customer's order and actual delivery. It has been calculated that between 33% and 50% of the time taken between receiving an order and final delivery is taken up by sales and distribution activities, so that any effort to cut this time period will increase competitiveness and lower costs.

The importance of marketing efficiency for a successful product launch is standard knowledge. For example, a survey of 1,000 product launches in 320 firms based in Europe and North America, concluded that the failure of new product launches was closely correlated to a lack of market research and market testing, and ineffective market launches (Cooper 1994). Similarly, a survey of the Pacific Rim countries of Australia, New Zealand and Singapore, found that the companies which achieved the most impressive competitive advantage were those with a clear marketing orientation (Ghosh, Schoch, Taylor, Kwan and Kim 1994).

To achieve marketing effectiveness, UK firms must respond actively, rather than passively, to enquiries from foreign customers. It has been calculated that UK exports could be over 10% higher if passive exporters could match the average active performer. Similarly, there is the need to increase efforts on market research. An analysis of UK-based firms aiming to invest abroad in order to penetrate foreign markets found that less than 60% had undertaken any specific consumer research or done any work on assessing market demand, distribution channels or employment regulations in the countries in which they intended to operate (HMSO 1996). The irony is that while UK market research companies have a significant (23%) share of the EU market for such services, the status accorded by UK manufacturing firms to market research was the lowest (with the exception of Italy) recorded in a major seven country study (HMSO 1996)! The creation of the 'Marketing Council' in 1995 may help foster a greater understanding of the importance of this form of non-price competition.

The importance of trade in goods for the UK

It could be argued that there is no reason to worry about the problems facing the UK on her non-oil goods trade, because oil and services will rectify the financial imbalance. However, the situation is not as simple as this, involving long-term competitive problems within the UK economy which other parts of the accounts may not always be able to offset.

Problems of competitiveness for goods production in general, and manufacturing in particular, are important for a number of reasons.

1. The UK's dependence on trade in goods is as high, if not higher, than many other industrial countries of comparable size. The UK ratio of exports of goods to GDP

was 23% in 1997, compared to 22% in Germany, 21% in Italy, 19% in France, 9% in Japan and 8% in the USA. Since exports are an injection into the domestic circular flow of income, any lack of competitiveness in the international markets will have a particularly important effect on economies such as the UK's in which exports are an important component of aggregate demand.

2. The importance of manufactured goods is particularly vital to the balance of payments on current account. Around 43% of all export earnings on current account, and also about 45% of all expenditure on imports, derive from trade in manufactures. A less competitive performance in the manufacturing sector will, therefore, have a significant effect on the current account.

3. The rate of growth in the volume of exports of UK manufactured goods has, since 1969, been only half that of imports of manufactures. In fact by mid-1997, the volume of exports of UK manufactures was some 85% above its 1975 level, whilst the corresponding figure for the EU and Japan was 175%. This trend continued over the first half of the 1990s, with the volume of UK manufactured exports growing by only 7% while OECD manufactured exports grew by an average of 30% and the developing countries manufactured exports grew by an average of 77%. By 1997, the manufactured exports of Korea and Singapore combined were greater than that of the UK.

4. There is evidence that trade in manufactures between the developed industrialized countries is increasing at the expense of such trade with the newly industrialized countries, at a time when it is these developed countries which are the main threat to UK trade performance. For instance, in the particularly important sector of machinery and transport equipment (43% of total UK manufactured exports) the developed industrialized countries have been the source of 80% of total world exports in this category since 1965, with 60% destined for other developed industrialized countries. Complaints about competition from 'low-wage' countries although serious, may be rather less significant to the UK than competition from these highly industrialized nations. In any case, competition from the newly industrialized countries is itself often competition from other industrialized nations through the guise of multinational company activities in those developing nations. Therefore, the fact that more and more trade is conducted between the *developed* industrial nations, and that more of that trade is in manufactures, suggests that an open economy like the UK's will encounter serious problems if it becomes progressively less competitive in non-oil goods trade.

5. The import penetration ratio in manufactures has risen in the UK from 17 to nearly 46% between 1968 and 1996. Some have argued that this loss of UK competitiveness in the production of import substitutes matters little since the ratio of exports to total sales of manufactures (the export sales ratio) has also risen in the UK from 18% to 43% over the same period. However, it has been pointed out that the export sales ratio is often artificially high in times of recession. As demand falls, and with it total sales of manufactures, the ratio becomes artificially high since the denominator falls faster than the numerator. Although UK export performance has improved, it should be understood that a higher ratio during periods of slow growth or recession may be a misleading index of long-term UK export competitiveness. Also, it is worth noting that although the exports/sales ratio did rise up to 1985, it has not changed much since that date, while the import/home demand ratio continued to rise throughout the 1980s and 1990s.

Services, investments and the current account

Loss of competitiveness on the UK's non-oil goods balance *is* important for all these reasons. Although the UK oil surplus has alleviated many problems on current account (see Table 26.1), it would be short-sighted to see this as a cure for all our ills. The oil surplus has eased the immediate strains on the goods balance, but there is little evidence of improvement in UK price and non-price competitiveness. In fact oil has contributed to a high exchange rate for the pound (see Chapter 25), and in this sense has made UK producers less price-competitive in foreign and domestic markets.

Does the UK's deteriorating performance on non-oil goods trade in general, and manufacturing in particular, matter when we are still a major surplus country on services and investments? It is quite true that the UK has surpluses on services (in common with the US, France and Spain) and also surpluses on investment income (in common with Japan and Benelux countries), but there is no guarantee that such surpluses will *grow* fast enough to compensate for the deterioration in exports of manufactures. When we convert the UK surpluses on services and investment income into proportions of GDP (at factor cost) we find, over the last ten years, that the ratios of surpluses on services to GDP varied between 0.7% to 2.0% and the ratios of surpluses on investment to GDP varied from 0.03% to 1.6%, but with no discernible upward trend. Essentially, the invisible account is made up of three elements as seen in Table 26.1. First, net earnings on investments, i.e. from interest, profit and dividends (IPD). Second, earnings from services such as shipping, civil aviation, general government services and financial services (such as banking and insurance). Third, transfers between the UK government and other institutions in the form of overseas aid or payments to the EU.

On average, the only element which has been in continuous deficit over the last fifteen years has been the transfer element, while IPD has, in most cases, been in surplus. Earnings from services remain in surplus, with about 50% of the positive balance on services being provided by the financial services and 'other business services' sectors. It would be unwise for the UK to rely on the growth of such services to continue to compensate for the decline in manufactures and other visible items. This is particularly true when the future of London as an international banking and financial centre can depend on 'arbitrary' factors such as the decision to locate the European Central Bank in Frankfurt, and the implications of the single European Currency for European financial markets. Further successes in financial markets may therefore become increasingly difficult to achieve.

Other advanced countries are also concentrating on services as a means of increasing their incomes. For example, between 1970 and 1995 the UK's share of world trade in services fell from 12.5% to 5.8%. By the latter date, the UK's share of the market had fallen below that of the US (16.2%), France (8.5%) and Germany (8.2%). Indeed a major study by Humphries (1998) shows that by 1996 the UK had an overall deficit in its balance on services with the EU of almost £1.3bn, mainly due to its large surplus on financial services being insufficient to offset its even larger deficit on travel/tourism with the EU.

Table 26.9 suggests that most of the UK's surpluses derive from the financial services, engineering, and computing services sectors. On a country basis, the UK's surpluses in services appeared to be predominantly with the US, Germany and Japan. If these countries improve their own competitiveness in such services, as they have already done in manufacturing sectors, then it would be rash for the UK to rely on her trade in services to support progressive deterioration on the non-oil goods account.

Table 26.9 UK's balance on services with major competitors 1996 (£mn).

Country	Sea transport	Civil aviation	Travel and tourism	Financial services	Royalties	Engineering services	Managerial consultancy	Computer services	Communication services	Advertising and market research	R&D	Total
EU Total	-769	323	-3,773	1,550	295	476	123	344	-141	152	148	-1,272
Germany	-329	131	441	348	127	170	14	86	-13	62	108	1,145
France	-198	-14	-1,323	250	33	22	2	74	-35	4	1	-1,184
Italy	9	7	-276	248	40	35	13	12	-9	-9	15	85
Spain	13	-1	-2,217	96	42	24	8	14	-5	-5	1	-2,030
US	251	-50	-476	2,200	-658	279	80	118	20	22	161	1,947
Canada	6	-79	-37	160	36	5	3	5	4	0	–	103
Japan	46	62	323	449	-38	13	8	8	-4	19	120	1,006
Total	-971	379	-7,338	5,301	-123	1,024	251	661	-183	245	554	

Source: Adapted from Humphries (1998).

Table 26.10 Share of world exports of goods and services (%).

	1970–79	1980–89	1992	1994	1997*
US	12.1	12.1	12.9	13.3	13.7
Germany	10.2	9.4	10.4	9.2	8.7
France	7.0	6.7	7.3	6.5	5.2
Japan	6.3	7.8	8.0	8.4	7.1
UK	6.0	5.6	5.2	5.0	5.4
Italy	4.5	4.6	5.6	5.3	4.6
ANIEs	3.1	5.7	8.5	9.6	10.3

ANIEs = Taiwan, Hong Kong, Korea and Singapore.
Source: OECD (1998) *World Economic Outlook*, and other sources.

Interestingly, if we investigate the UK's share of world trade in goods *and* services, which is the format presented in the new UK trade accounts, then the results can be seen in Table 26.10.

From Table 26.10 it can be seen that the UK's share of world exports of goods *and* services has dropped since the 1970s, stabilizing at around 5% of world exports. The task in the future will be to keep the UK's share at this level in the face of pressures from both developed and developing countries.

A final point to observe is that the development of services is not necessarily divorced from manufacturing, in fact it is likely that some 25% of employment in the service industry depends directly on manufacturing. Service industries often need manufactured goods such as computer and data processing equipment, so that the contraction of manufacturing can have adverse repercussions on services. Indeed research in 1998 by the investment bank Paribas showed that for every 1% fall in manufacturing output there was a resulting fall of 0.4% in service sector output.

Given the strength of manufactured items, by value, in UK exports, it has been calculated that it would need more than a 2.5% rise in the exports of services to compensate for each 1% fall in manufactured exports. Members of the Cambridge-Harvard Research Group on UK Competitiveness calculated that for the period 1992–2003, even with economic growth at a modest average of 2.5% per year, the UK would continue to have a Balance of Payments deficit. For the accounts to balance, there would need to be a trebling in the exports of services, equivalent in value to the entire current international financial activity of New York and Tokyo put together!

Apart from these reservations, it should also be remembered that the UK export of services is only 39% of the value of manufactured exports, and only 31% of the value of total visible exports. A given percentage change in exports of manufactures or of total visibles will have a larger *absolute* impact on the current account than would the same percentage change in the export of services. The same is true of imports. To concentrate on developing the invisible sector may be an inappropriate response to any loss of competitiveness experienced in non-oil visible trade.

Conclusion

This chapter has attempted to analyse the trends in the UK balance of trade on goods, with special reference to trade in manufactures. Although UK goods trade has adapted along similar lines to that of her competitors as regards both geographical area and commodity composition, her ability to compete *within* these areas and commodities has come under greater strain. The chapter also stressed the role of non-price factors, such as income, quality, design and marketing, in accounting for both UK export performance and import penetration. Although price considerations are important, they are often given too prominent a place in explanations of trade flow. The fact that UK manufactures have moved down market in quality, design and marketing, should perhaps be given more recognition as an important factor in restricting the growth of UK exports and in encouraging import penetration. The high income elasticity of demand for UK imports of manufactures is but one reflection of the growing importance of such non-price factors.

Ironically, the UK's problem of matching other countries in terms of non-price factors has become a still more serious cause for concern over the last ten years with the progressive tendency for industrial countries to *specialize* in the production of traded goods. This has meant that countries have naturally increased their imports of specialized manufactured goods from each other, thereby increasing the import penetration ratio regardless of any change in other competitive factors. Although the UK has surpluses on oil, services and investment income, it would be a hazardous strategy to rely on these to 'subsidize' a progressive deterioration in trade in non-oil goods. The rapid fall in oil revenue between 1985 and 1991 has vividly demonstrated this point. There have been some signs that UK industry is becoming more supply responsive during the 1980s and that this has helped to increase the income elasticity of demand for UK exports, as shown by Landesmann and Snell. The health of the manufacturing sector is highly significant in this context because most manufactured goods are potentially tradeable across international boundaries, i.e. can be sold abroad, while only around 20% of services are internationally tradeable. This means that as resources move from manufacturing to services, the balance of trade may continue to deteriorate (Thirlwall 1992). The rise in the share of UK exports of manufactures between 1984 and 1993 which was noted previously in the text appeared encouraging. However, on closer scrutiny, the conclusions of Muellbauer and Murphy (1990) that UK exports had benefited from a fall in the growth of world trade relative to world production, and the findings of Landesmann and Snell (1993) that the US and Japan's share of world trade of manufactures weakened in the same period – may have been due to the same cause – namely trade friction between the US and Japan. As this problem has eased in the second half of the 1990s then we might have to look once more at whether the UK will lose the one per cent share of world manufactured exports which it recently regained. The question therefore remains as to whether UK companies in general have the flexibility to follow the ebb and flow of the international market. The evidence for this remains rather elusive and patchy.

Key points

- The UK current account was mostly in surplus until the late 1980s; problems on the non-oil goods account have subsequently resulted in the current account moving into deficit.
- The *area composition* of UK goods trade has moved strongly towards the EU and away from North America and other OECD countries since the 1960s.
- The *commodity composition* of UK goods trade shows a shift away from foodstuffs and raw materials, and towards manufactures, especially as regards imports.
- The UK's share of world exports of manufactured goods fell from 17% to 8% between 1960 and 1997, whereas various measures of import penetration of manufactured goods show a sharp increase.
- The UK's poor long-term performance in manufactured goods is due to a loss of competitiveness *within* particular commodity groups and *within* particular geographic areas.
- While *price* factors are important, *non-price* factors such as income, quality, design, service, etc. also crucially affect competitiveness.
- The UK shows symptoms of going 'downmarket', by exporting cheaper lower technology-based products and importing more expensive high technology-based products.
- Trade in goods is important for the UK, with 47% of the total value of exports being from goods.
- The UK usually achieves a balance of payments surplus from services and investment income etc., but only 20% of all services are internationally tradable. Manufactures and goods in general cannot therefore be neglected in trade terms.
- Some 25% of all income from services depends upon manufacturing industry itself, which also emphasizes the continued importance of manufacturing.

Notes

1. *High technology categories* include: pharmaceuticals, aircraft, computers, communications equipment, instruments, electrical machinery.
   Medium technology categories include: chemicals, motor vehicles, rubber and plastic products, non ferrous metals, non electrical machinery, other transport machinery and other manufactured goods.
   Low technology categories include: petroleum refineries, paper, stone, glass and clay, iron and steel, metal products, shipbuilding, food beverages and tobacco, textiles, apparel and leather, wood products and furniture.

References and further reading

Connell, D. (1980) The UK's performance in export markets – some evidence from international trade data, NEDO, discussion paper 6.
Cooper, R. G. (1994) New products: the factors that drive success, *International Marketing Review*, **11**, 1.
Dumble (1994) UK trade – long-term trends and recent developments, *Bank of England Quarterly Bulletin*, **34**, 3, August.
Fagerberg, J. (1988) International competitiveness, *Economic Journal*, **98**, June.

Ghosh, B. C., Schoch, H. P., Taylor, D. B., Kwan, W. W. and **Kim, S. T.** (1994) Top performing organizations of Australia, New Zealand and Singapore: a comparative study of their marketing effectiveness, *Marketing Intelligence and Planning*, **12**, 7.

Griffiths, A. (1989) Manufacturing competitiveness: new sources for old, *British Economy Survey* **18**, 2, Spring.

Hooley, G. J., Lynch, J. E., Brooksbank, R. W. and **Shepherd, J.** (1988) Strategic market environments, *Journal of Marketing Management*, **4**, 2.

HMSO (1996) *Competitiveness: Creating the Enterprise Centre of Europe*, HMSO.

Humphries, S. (1998) Geographical breakdown of export and imports of UK trade in services by component, *Economic Trends*, **530**, January.

Katrak, H. (1982) Labour skills, research and development and capital requirements in international trade and investment of the UK 1968–78, *National Institute Economic Review*, **101**.

Lall, S. (1998) Exports of manufactures by developing countries: emerging patterns of trade and location, *Oxford Review of Economic Policy*, **14**, 2.

Landesmann, M. and **Snell, A.** (1989) The consequences of Mrs Thatcher for UK manufacturing exports, *Economic Journal*, **99**, March.

Landesmann, M. and **Snell, A.** (1993) Structural shifts in the manufacturing export performance of OECD economies, *Journal of Applied Econonometrics*, **8**.

Mason, G., van Ark, B. and **Wagner, K.** (1994) Productivity, product quality and worker skills: food processing in four European countries, *National Institute of Economic Review*, February.

Morgan, A. D. and **Martin, A.** (1975) Tariff reductions and UK imports of manufactures 1955–71, *National Institute Economic Review*, May.

Muellbauer, J. (1990) A pattern biased against trade? *Financial Times*, 19 February, p. 17.

Muellbauer, J. and **Murphy, A.** (1990) Is the UK balance of payments sustainable?, *Economic Policy*, October.

Owen, C. and **Wren-Lewis, S.** (1992) *Variety, Quality and UK Manufacturing Exports*, July, Strathclyde University.

Panić, M. (1975) Why the UK propensity to import is high, *Lloyds Bank Review*, **115**, January.

Patel, P. and **Pavitt, K.** (1987) The elements of British technological competitiveness, *National Institute Economic Review*, November.

Steedman, H. and **Wagner, K.** (1987) A second look at productivity, machinery and skills in Britain and Germany, *National Institute Economic Review*, November.

The Sunday Times (1990) May, p. D7.

Thirlwall, A. P. (1978) The UK's economic problems: a balance of payments constraint? *National Westminster Bank Quarterly Keview*, February.

Thirlwall, A. P. (1992) The balance of payments and economic performance, *National Westminster Bank Quarterly Review*, May.

Wardlow, A. (1994) Investment appraisal criteria and the importance of low inflation, *Bank of England Quarterly Bulletin*, **34**, 3, August.

Chapter 27

Free trade, regional trading blocs and protectionism

Protectionist measures are aimed at reducing the level of imports, either because of the 'damage' they cause to particular domestic industries, or because of their adverse effects on the balance of payments. In this chapter we review critically the arguments in favour of free trade, and therefore against protectionism. We examine the international institutions which have been created to foster trade, particularly the General Agreement on Tariffs and Trade (GATT) and the World Trade Organization (WTO), and then note the measures available to countries wishing to pursue a protectionist strategy. The extent to which such measures have been used within both the European Union (EU) and the UK is considered, together with their alleged benefits and costs. We also consider the shift in trading patterns towards regional blocs and assess the implications of this development.

Free trade

Free trade was given impetus by 'The Theory of Comparative Advantage', outlined by Ricardo in the nineteenth century. Essentially, Ricardo sought to extend Adam Smith's principle of the division of labour to a global scale, with each country specializing in those goods which it could produce most efficiently. Even if one country was more efficient than another country in the production of all goods, Ricardo showed that it could still gain by specializing in those goods in which its *relative efficiency* was greatest. It was said to have a *comparative* advantage in such goods. This would raise total world output above the level it would otherwise be, with the benefits shared via trade between the two countries. The degree of benefit to any one country after specialization and trade would depend upon the terms of trade, i.e. the ratio of export to import prices.

The use of protectionist measures, such as tariffs, may distort the comparative cost ratios, by raising import prices and encouraging the domestic production of goods that could otherwise have been imported rather more cheaply. In addition to disrupting the efficient allocation of *domestic* resources, such protectionist measures are likely to reduce international specialization and to lead to a less efficient allocation of *world* resources.

Figure 27.1 shows that free trade could, in theory, bring welfare benefits to an economy previously protected. Suppose the industry is initially *completely protected*. The price P_D will then be determined by the interaction of domestic supply (S–S_H) and domestic demand (D–D_H). The government now decides to remove these barriers and to allow foreign competition. For simplicity, we assume a perfectly elastic 'world' supply curve P_W–C, giving a total supply curve (domestic and world) of SAC. Domestic price will then be forced down to the world level, P_W, with domestic demand being OQ_3 at this price. To meet this domestic demand, OQ_2 will be supplied from domestic sources, with Q_2Q_3 supplied from the rest of the world (i.e. imported). The consumer surplus, which is the difference between what consumers are *prepared* to pay and what they *have* to pay, has risen from DBP_D to DCP_W. The producer surplus, which is the difference between the price the producer receives and the minimum necessary to induce production, has fallen from P_DBS to P_WAS. The gain in consumer surplus outweighs the loss in producer surplus by the area ABC, which could then be regarded as the net gain in economic welfare as a result of free trade replacing protectionism.

Critics of free trade suggest that a number of drawbacks may outweigh the net gain shown above:

1. The theory is based on a 'full employment' model and fails to appreciate the problems raised by chronic unemployment. For instance, in Fig. 27.1 if domestic supply falls from OQ_1 to OQ_2 as a result of the removal of tariffs, then the reduced output may lead to unemployment. The welfare loss associated with this may more than offset the net welfare gain (area ABC) noted above.
2. It fails to analyse how the gains that arise from trade will be distributed. In practice, the stronger economies, through their economic power, have often been able to extract the greater benefits.

Fig. 27.1. Free trade versus no trade.

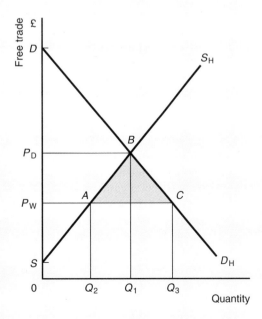

3. It assumes a purely competitive model of industry. If, in fact, industry includes both large and small firms, then area *ABC* may not represent net gain. For instance, a higher proportion of the remaining domestic output OQ_2 in Fig. 27.1 may now be in the hands of a monopoly. This growth in importance of monopoly could be construed as a welfare loss to be set against the area of net gain, *ABC*.

In practice a number of organizations have tried to encourage free trade in the post-war period.

General Agreement on Tariffs and Trade/World Trade Organization

The General Agreement on Tariffs and Trade (GATT) was signed in 1947 by 23 industrialized nations, including the UK, USA, Canada, France and the Benelux countries. Its successor, the World Trade Organization (WTO), now has 132 members with another 30 including China in the queue to join. WTO members in total account for more than 90% of the value of world trade. The objectives of the WTO are essentially the same as GATT's; that is to reduce tariffs and other barriers to trade and to eliminate discrimination in trade. In this way it aims to contribute to rising living standards and a fuller use of world resources.

Since GATT was formed, there have been eight 'rounds' of negotiations paving the way for considerable cuts in the level of tariffs being applied. In 1947, the average tariff in the industrialized world stood at some 40%, but by the late 1990s the figure had dropped to below 5%. The 'Kennedy round' of negotiations in the 1960s was particularly effective, with tariffs cut by about one-third, reducing the average duty on the manufactures to about 10% by 1972. The 'Tokyo round' in the later 1970s resulted in further reductions of approximately one-third. In the Tokyo round the negotiations favoured trade between the advanced industrialized nations, where the tariff cut was 38%; a rather smaller reduction, 25%, was agreed for trade between the advanced industrialized and newly industrializing nations.

There are a number of provisions which allow a country to deviate from the GATT strategy of reductions in tariff barriers. Article 6 permits retaliatory sanctions if 'dumping' (see below) can be proven. Article 18 provides a number of 'escape clauses' for the newly industrializing countries, allowing them to protect both infant industries and their balance of payments. Article 19 permits any country to abstain from a general tariff cut in situations where rising imports may seriously damage domestic production. Articles 21–25 are concerned with the protection of the national interest, permitting restrictions to be placed on imported products which might affect the nation's security.

In addition to tariff cuts, GATT has made efforts to eradicate discrimination in trade, by use of the 'most-favoured nation' clause. This requires that any trading advantage granted by one country to another must be accorded to *all* other member states. Exceptions to this are allowed in special cases, such as the creation of a free trade area or a customs union (i.e. protected free trade area).

A major criticism of GATT since its inception has been its inability to apply sanctions, forcing it to rely on voluntary compliance. Although the major trading nations have generally fallen into line with the recommendations made by GATT, there have been some instances where this has not been the case. The escalation of the conflict between the US and the EU over oilseed subsidies in 1992, was one example of this. While the EU complied with *some* of the conclusions reached by the GATT investigation of 1990, it only *fully* complied when the US threatened to impose retaliatory tariffs two years later.

The latest series of multilateral negotiations, known as the Uruguay round was settled in December 1993. This proved to be by far the most complex and ambitious round of negotiations. It consisted of twenty-eight separate accords designed to extend fair trade rules to agriculture, services, textiles, intellectual property rights and foreign investment. It was agreed to cut tariffs on industrial products by more than one third, to eliminate tariffs entirely in 11 sectors, and to substantially reduce the level of farm subsidies. Non-tariff barriers were to be converted into (more 'visible') tariff barriers (Greenaway 1994). GATT itself, the new accord on services and intellectual property, as well as the codes relating to government procurement and anti-dumping, now come under the umbrella of the WTO. Trade disputes between member states are settled in this arena by a streamlined disputes procedure with provision for appeals and binding arbitration. Since its creation in January 1995, more than 120 cases have been brought before the WTO. More than half of these have involved the US and EU while around one-quarter have involved developing countries. The WTO also seeks to provide a forum for further multilateral trade negotiations. In Autumn 1999 a decision will be taken as to whether to launch a new round which could focus on the trend towards regional trade agreements.

Trade and the world economy

The rapid growth of world trade over the last century reflects the fact that nations have become more interrelated as they have attempted to gain the benefits of freer trade. One way of measuring this increasing integration is to compare the *relative growth* of world trade and world output, as seen in Table 27.1.

Table 27.1 shows that the growth rate of world merchandise exports (Trade) has exceeded the growth of world output (GDP) in four of the five periods, clearly suggesting an acceleration of global integration through trade. The only exception to this pattern occurred in the period 1913 to 1950 when two world wars and a major world depression led to economic depression and the emergence of protectionist trade policies. The post World War Two period (1950–1973) saw an unprecedented growth of world trade which far outstripped the growth of world production. This period of freer trade reflected the desire to reduce the high protective tariffs introduced during the inter-war period as a means of increasing post-war prosperity for all countries. The founding of the GATT in 1947 was a positive step in this direction.

It may be useful to enquire at this stage whether the expanding role of world trade seen in Table 27.1 was accompanied by an increase in the share of that trade conducted on a *regional* basis. It would seem natural that nations would tend to trade more with their immediate neighbours in the first instance, thereby raising the share of world trade occurring between nations within a specific geographical region. This tendency towards *intra-regional* trade can be seen in Table 27.2.

Table 27.1 Growth in world GDP and merchandise trade 1870–1997 (average annual % change).

	1870–1900	1900–13	1913–50	1950–73	1973–97
GDP	2.9	2.5	2.0	5.1	2.8
Trade	3.8	4.3	0.6	8.2	4.2

Source: WTO, International Trade: trends and statistics (various) and Annual Reports (various).

Table 27.2 Share of
intra-regional trade in
total trade 1928–96 (% of
each region's total trade
in goods occurring
between nations located
in that region).

	1928	1938	1948	1968	1979	1996
Western Europe	50.7	48.8	41.8	63.0	66.2	68.3
Central/Eastern Europe/USSR	19.0	13.2	46.4	63.5	54.0	18.7
North America	25.0	22.4	27.1	36.8	29.9	36.0
Latin America	11.1	17.7	17.7	18.7	20.2	21.2
Asia	45.5	66.4	38.9	36.6	41.0	51.9
Africa	10.3	8.8	8.4	9.1	5.6	9.2
Middle East	5.0	3.6	20.3	8.7	6.4	7.4

Source: WTO, Annual Reports (various).

From Table 27.2 it can be seen that the share of intra-regional trade grew most rapidly in Western Europe between 1948 and 1996, while in Asia and North America the share of intra-regional trade also increased but at a slower pace. Intra-regional trade occurring in other regions remained largely unchanged or even declined (i.e. de-regionalization of trade), as seen in recent years in Central and Eastern Europe. It is also clear from Table 27.2 that intra-regional trading is not a new phenomenon and that geographically adjacent nations in many of the geographic areas of the world have been trading with each other for many years.

Regional trading arrangements

As we have noted above, the resumption of rapid growth in world trade after the Second World War was tied up with the desire for the resumption of *multilateral trade* under the auspices of the GATT. However, this movement towards free trade was accompanied by a parallel movement towards the formation of *regional trading blocs* centred on the EU, North and South America and East Asia. We noted in Table 27.2 that intra-regional trading is not a new phenomenon and has been active for at least a century or more. However, what is new involves the fact that the nations of a given region have begun to create more *formal* and comprehensive trading and economic links with each other.

There are four types of regional trading arrangements:

- *free trade areas*, where member countries reduce or abolish restrictions on trade between each other while maintaining their individual protectionist measures against non-members;
- *customs unions*, where, as well as liberalizing trade amongst members, a common external tariff is established to protect the group from imports from any non-members;
- *common markets*, where the customs union is extended to movements of factors of production as well as products;
- *economic union*, where national economic policies are also harmonized within the common market.

Three features have characterized post-war regional integration.

1. Post-war regional integration has been primarily centred in Western Europe. Out of 153 agreements notified to GATT between 1948 and 1996, more than half involved West European countries, with most of the post-1990 agreements with the EU involving the Central and Eastern European countries.

2. Only a small number of post-war regional agreements have been concluded by developing countries. This is mainly due to continuing competition between these countries involving trade in similar products (e.g. primary products) together with the difficulty of achieving the political stability in some developing countries which is so vital to trade.
3. The *type* of economic integration between the parties to agreements has varied quite significantly. Most of the notifications made to GATT have involved free trade areas, with the number of customs unions agreement being much smaller.

Table 27.3 provides examples of different types of regional trading arrangements across the globe. For example, the most advanced form of trading bloc is the EU, covering 15 nations with a combined population of over 370m and accounting for some 42% of world trade. This group originated as a customs union but moved towards the common market type of arrangement in the 1990s, with discussions progressing

Table 27.3 Regional trading schemes, intra regional exports and world exports.

	Founded	1960	1970	1975	1980	1985	1990
ANZCERTA	1983	5.7[1]	6.1	6.2	6.4	7.0	7.6
		(2.4)[2]	(2.1)	(1.7)	(1.4)	(1.6)	(1.5)
EU	1957	34.5	51.0	50.0	54.0	54.5	60.4
		(24.9)	(39.0)	(35.9)	(34.9)	(35.8)	(41.4)
EFTA[3]	1960	21.1	28.0	35.2	32.6	31.2	28.2
		(14.9)	(14.9)	(6.3)	(6.1)	(6.3)	(6.8)
Canada-US-FTA	1989	26.5	32.8	30.6	26.5	38.0	34.0
(NAFTA post 1993)		(21.9)	(20.5)	(16.8)	(15.1)	(16.7)	(15.8)
ASEAN[4]	1967	4.4	20.7	15.9	18.9	18.4	18.6
		(2.6)	(2.1)	(2.6)	(3.7)	(3.9)	(4.3)
ANDEAN PACT	1969	0.7	2.0	3.7	3.8	3.4	4.6
		(2.9)	(1.6)	(1.6)	(1.6)	(1.2)	(0.9)
CACM	1961	7.0	25.7	23.3	24.1	14.7	14.8
		(0.4)	(0.4)	(0.3)	(0.2)	(0.2)	(0.1)
LAFTA/LAIA[5]	1960/80	7.9	9.9	13.6	13.7	8.3	10.6
		(6.0)	(4.4)	(3.5)	(4.2)	(4.7)	(3.4)
ECOWAS	1975	–	3.0	4.2	3.5	5.3	6.0
		–	(1.0)	(1.4)	(1.7)	(1.1)	(0.6)
PTA	1987	–	8.4	9.4	8.9	7.0	8.5
		–	(1.1)	(0.5)	(0.4)	(0.3)	(0.2)

Note:
Definitions of regional integration schemes are: ANZCERTA – Australia-New Zealand Closer Economic Relations Trade Agreement; EU – European Union; EFTA – European Free Trade Area; ASEAN – Association of South East Asian Nations; CACM – Central American Common Market; LAFTA/LAIA – Latin American Free Trade Area/Latin American Integration Association; ECOWAS – Economic Community of West African States; PTA – Preferential Trade Area for Eastern and Southern Africa.
[1] Intraregional trade measured by share of intraregional exports in total exports.
[2] Share of regional integration scheme in total world exports.
[3] Originally formed in 1959 with seven countries; UK, Denmark, Sweden, Norway, Austria, Switzerland, Portugal. UK, Denmark and Portugal have subsequently joined the EU, as have Sweden and Norway. Effectively EFTA ceased to exist on 1 Jan. 1993 when it entered into arrangements with the EU.
[4] It is more a cultural and less an economic association; preferential trading among countries is minimal.
[5] LAFTA was founded in 1960, but renewed as LAIA in 1980.
Source: Adapted from De Melo and Panagariya (1992).

towards various forms of economic union. In August 1993 the North American Free Trade Agreement (NAFTA) was signed between the US, Canada and Mexico, having grown out of an earlier Canadian–US Free Trade Agreement (CUFTA). NAFTA, as the name implies, is a free trade arrangement covering a population of 372m and accounting for 31% of world output and 17% of world trade.

In South America, the economic and political instability of various trading blocs has prevented the success of arrangements such as LAFTA and LAIA, although the latter still provides a framework for discussions between countries seeking to increase bilateral trade between members. However, LAIA countries have developed more specific trading arrangements. For example, in January 1995 MERCOSUR (Mercado Comun del Sur) or a 'Southern Common Market' was formed, actually operating as a type of customs union with a common external tariff. It is hoped that this bloc, which covers a population of 200m people and £15m-worth of intra-bloc trade, will help integrate the economies of Brazil, Argentina, Paraguay and Uruguay. Other South American arrangements include the Andean Pact which agreed on a four-tier external tariff structure in 1994, and the CACM, which has extended its scope by negotiating a free trade area with Mexico.

In Africa, the Economic Community of West African States (ECOWAS) was formed in 1975 with the aim of creating a free trade area. In 1990 it launched its latest program to implement a free trade in all unprocessed products and progressively to liberalize industrial products, though significant economic and political differences have hampered this ultimate aim.

In Asia and the Pacific, the rather 'loose' Association of South East Asian Nations (ASEAN) with a population of 300m was formed in August 1967. In 1991 they agreed to form an ASEAN Free Trade Area (AFTA) by the year 2003. A Common External Preference Tariff (CEPT) came into force in 1994 as a formal tariff-cutting mechanism for achieving free trade in all goods except agricultural products, natural resources and services. Finally, in November 1994, the goal of an open trade and investment area was agreed in principle by members of the Asia-Pacific Economic Cooperation Forum (APEC) which includes the members of ASEAN, ANZCERTA and NAFTA as well as China, Japan, Korea, Hong Kong, Taiwan, and Papua New Guinea. It is hoped that this arrangement may be realised by 2010 for developed countries and by 2020 for developing countries. This group would account for 38% of the world's population (2.1bn), and 43% of the world trade in goods.

From the above examples it is possible to see that trading blocs have adopted various types of arrangements depending on their specific circumstances.

Table 27.3 shows the share of *intra-regional exports* of each specific bloc as a percentage of the total exports of that bloc. For example, in 1990 the exports of EU members *to each other* comprised some 60.4% of total EU exports. A significant shift towards intra-regional exports took place in Europe, North and Central America, and Asia between 1960 and 1970, but since that time there has been no major growth, except in the EU. Also shown (in brackets) in Table 27.3 are the shares of the exports of the various regional blocs as a percentage of total world exports. This ratio rose from 76% to 87% for *all* the blocs identified in Table 27.3 between 1960 and 1970, only to fall back again to 75% by 1990. In effect, the growth of intra regional trade and the importance of the trading blocs in total world trade has not changed dramatically since the mid 1970s, despite the increase in number of regional arrangements. This has been due to the fact that although the number of regional arrangements has increased (as smaller countries have sought to find havens inside larger trading blocs), there has been a still more rapid growth in total world trade.

The completion of the Uruguay round in December 1993 served as a step forward in the cause of *multilateral trade*. However, frustration with the slow progress of GATT during the 1990s, and continuing friction between the US, EU and Japan, have reinforced concerns that regional trading blocs may begin to look inwards and behave more like 'regional fortresses'. Thus, the trading blocs we have been discussing above have begun to be seen as initiators of a 'new regionalism', leading to potential problems for *inter-bloc* trade. Those who favour the regional approach argue that the setting up of trading blocs can enable individual countries to purchase products at lower prices because tariff walls between the member countries have been removed; this is the *trade creation effect*. They also argue that regional trading arrangements help to harmonize tax policies and product standards, while also helping to reduce political conflicts. Others argue that where the world is already organized into trading blocs, then negotiations in favour of free trade are more likely to be successful between, say, three large and influential trading blocs than between a large number of individual countries with little power to bargain successfully for tariff reductions.

On the other hand, the critics of regionalism warn that regional trading blocs have, historically, tended to be inward looking, as in the 1930s when discriminatory trade blocs were formed to impose tariffs on non-members. Some also argue that member countries may suffer from being inside a regional bloc because they then have to buy products from *within* the bloc, when cheaper sources are often available from outside; i.e. the *trade diversion effect*. Further, it is argued that regionalism threatens to erode support for multilateralism in that business groups *within* a regional bloc will find it easier to obtain protectionist (trade diversionary) deals via preferential pacts than they would in the world of non-discriminatory trade practices favoured by GATT. Finally, it is argued that regionalism will move the world away from free trade due to the increasing tendency for members of a regional group to resort to the use of *non-tariff barriers* (VERs, anti-dumping duties etc) when experiencing a surge of imports from other countries *inside* the group. Such devices, all part of the new protectionism, can then easily be used by individual countries against non-members from other regional groups.

Many studies have been made as to the trade and welfare effects of such regional blocs both on 'internal' participants and on countries outside the bloc.

- Analysis of the customs union formed between the original six members of the European Community (EC) show that trade creation exceeded trade diversion in the case of manufactures (Lloyd 1992, Srinivasan *et al.* 1993), but that the reverse was true in the case of trade in agricultural products – leaving the overall effect unclear.
- Studies of EFTA suggest that trade creation just outweighed trade diversion (Lloyd 1992).
- Studies for CUFTA suggest positive benefits for Canada but negligible benefits for the US, while trade with third countries declined (Primo Braga *et al.* 1994).
- For NAFTA, estimates indicate some net trade creation with small trade effects for third countries (Reinert *et al.* 1994).

The various studies noted above can only give a general idea of the net effects as they do not measure accurately the potential stimulus to third countries resulting from any higher rate of economic growth in the bloc being studied.

What then can be done to make sure that regionalism and multilateralism (general free trade) can co-exist? First, it has been suggested that article 24 of GATT which sets the rules for regional arrangements could be modified to allow only customs unions (i.e. regions which require a common external tariff) and to prohibit free trade areas which allow countries to retain a variety of national tariffs against other countries. If this were done, the more liberal members of the region would then be able to force down the overall regional tariff level, which could then be 'locked in' under GATT rules and prevented from being subsequently raised. Second, in order to fight the 'new protectionism', GATT articles 6 (anti-dumping) and 19 (VER) could be strengthened to minimise the use of non-tariff barriers against countries outside the regional arrangement (World Economic Outlook 1993).

Protectionism

There are a number of methods which individual countries or regional trading blocs can use to restrict the level of imports into the home market.

Methods of protection   Tariff   A tariff is, in effect, a tax levied on imported goods, usually with the intention of raising the price of imports and thereby discouraging their purchase. Additionally, it is a source of revenue for the government. Tariffs can be of two types: lump sum, or specific, with the tariff a fixed amount per unit; *ad valorem*, or percentage, with the tariff a variable amount per unit.

To examine the effect of a tariff, it helps simplify Fig. 27.2 if we again assume a perfectly elastic world supply of the good S_W at the going world price P_W, which implies that any amount of the good can be imported into the UK without there being a change in the world price. In the absence of a tariff the domestic price would be set by the world price, P_W in Fig. 27.2. At this price, domestic demand D_H will be OQ_2 though domestic supply S_H will only be OQ_1. The excess demand, $Q_2 - Q_1$, will be satisfied by importing the good.

If the government now decides to restrict the level of import penetration, it could impose a tariff of, say, $P_W - P'_W$. A tariff always shifts a supply curve vertically upwards by the amount of the tariff, so that in this case the world supply curve shifts vertically upwards from S_W to S'_W. This would raise the domestic price to P'_W which is above the world price P_W. This higher price will reduce the domestic demand for the good to OQ_4, whilst simultaneously encouraging domestic supply to expand to OQ_3. Imports will be reduced to $Q_4 - Q_3$. Domestic consumer surplus will decline as a result of the tariff by the area $1 + 2 + 3 + 4$, though domestic producer surplus will rise by area 1, and the government will gain tax revenue of $P'_W - P_W \times Q_4 - Q_3$ (i.e. area 3). These gains would be inadequate to compensate consumers for their loss in welfare, yielding a net welfare loss of area $2 + 4$ as a result of imposing a tariff.

The UK was extensively protected by tariffs until the 1850s. These were progressively dismantled in an era of free trade that lasted until the First World War. The first significant reintroduction of tariffs occurred in 1915 with the 'McKenna duties', a 33.3% *ad valorem* tax on luxuries such as motor cars, watches, clocks, etc. They were designed to discourage unnecessary imports in order to save foreign exchange, and thereby free shipping space for the war effort. In 1921, the Safeguarding of Industry Act extended protection to key industries. This was

Fig. 27.2.   **The effect of a tariff.**

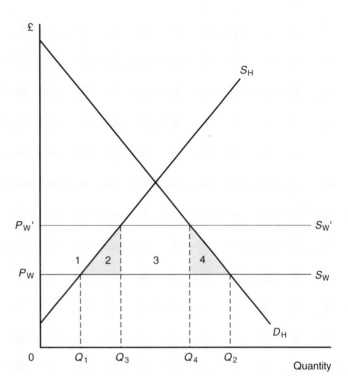

followed in 1932 by the Import Duties Act, which provided a comprehensive range of protection; a 20% *ad valorem* duty on manufactured goods in general, but 33.3% on articles such as bicycles and chemicals, and 15% on certain industrial raw materials and semi-manufactures.

Since the Second World War, the UK, along with others, has moved away from the protectionist doctrine of the inter-war period. We have already seen that considerable reductions in tariffs took place under the auspices of GATT. However, for the UK, entrance into the EU in 1973 has had a dual effect. Although tariffs on industrial products have been eliminated between member countries, permitting free trade, at the same time a Common External Tariff (CET) has been imposed on industrial trade with all non-member countries. For example, imports of trucks into the EU attract a tariff of 22% while the tariff on fruit juices ranges from 46 to 215%.

Non-tariff barriers   In recent years there has been a considerable increase in trade that is subject to non-tariff barriers, i.e. the rise of 'new protectionism'. This has been particularly noticeable with regard to trade in manufactures. In 1974 only 0.2% of UK trade in manufactures was recorded as subject to non-tariff regulation, whereas by the late 1980s, more than 10% of UK trade in manufactures was 'managed' in this way. As regards *total* UK trade, as much as 45% is still 'managed' by non-tariff regulation. As regards total *non-fuel imports* of the main industrial countries, some 22.6% are affected by selected non-tariff barriers.

Let us now consider the types of non-tariff barrier in use.

Quotas. A quota is a physical limit on the amount of an imported good that may be sold in a country in a given period. Its effects are examined in Fig. 27.3.

As in the case of a tariff, we assume for simplicity that the world supply curve is perfectly elastic at P_W. Once again, if there is free trade, the domestic price will be set by the world price, P_W. Domestic production would initially be OQ_1 though demand would be considerably higher at OQ_2. This excess would be satisfied by importing the amount $Q_2 - Q_1$ of the particular good.

If the government were now to decide that it wanted to limit the level of imports to, say, $Q_3 - Q_1$, it could impose a quota to this effect. The total supply curve to the UK market now becomes the domestic supply curve, S_H, plus the fixed quota permitted from abroad, Q. The new domestic price rises from P_W to P'_W which in turn reduces domestic demand from OQ_2 to OQ_5. Domestic supply will expand to OQ_4, with imports reduced to the quota level $Q_3 - Q_1$ ($= Q_5 - Q_4$).

As in the case of the tariff, the imposition of a quota will involve a loss in consumer surplus (i.e. area $1 + 2 + 3 + 4$). However, in contrast to the tariff, the only area of welfare gain will be the producer surplus of area 1, since the government receives no increase in tax revenue from the quota. This leaves area $2 + 3 + 4$ as the net loss of economic welfare. For *any given price rise*, the welfare loss is then greater for a quota than for a tariff.[1] Import quotas are still used on a whole range of products. They may be applied either unilaterally or as a result of negotiated agreements between the two parties. For instance, the EU has the authority to negotiate quota agreements on behalf of member states, including the UK, and does so on a whole range of products.

Fig. 27.3. **The effect of a quota.**

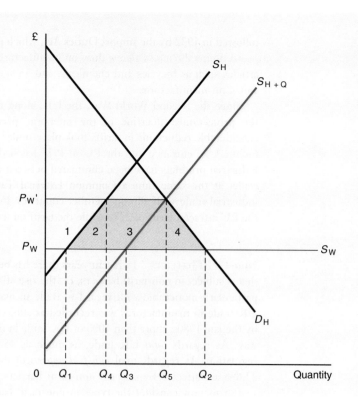

The import of textiles into the EU from the newly industrialized countries was until recently controlled by the Multi-Fibre Agreement (MFA), a negotiated settlement between developed and developing countries which first came into effect in 1974. A major aim has been to provide greater scope for newly industrialized countries to increase their share of world trade in textile products whilst at the same time maintaining some stability for textile production in the developed economies. The first agreement allowed for quotas to rise by approximately 6% per annum, though a subsequent agreement began to cut back on these concessions. The MFA was renewed for a third time in 1986 although there was considerable opposition from many of the textile producers who favoured a return to a more liberalised trading environment. As part of the Uruguay round, an accord was agreed which will gradually (by 2005) bring trade in clothing and textiles under normal GATT rules. The settlement provides for a phase-out period of ten years for all existing quota restrictions. However, the deal is heavily 'back-end' loaded.

An UNCTAD study in 1986 concluded that the complete liberalization of trade barriers would bring substantial benefits for developing countries. It was suggested that their total export of clothing would rise by around 135% while textile exports could grow by some 80%. A more recent analysis carried out by the World Bank put the potential gains at an even greater level. These figures seem to indicate quite clearly that the export quotas work against the interest of the *producers* rather than the *consumers*. But there is an argument that the developing countries actually benefit through the MFA arrangement. This is because, it is asserted, they receive what may be termed *quota rents*, i.e. higher prices than would be guaranteed through a free market.

Looking back to Fig. 27.3, this benefit would amount to area 3. However research into this by Balassa and Michalopoulos (1985) estimated that the value of lost output to the US exceeds the quota rent by nine times and to the EU by a factor of seven.

Apart from quotas imposed as a result of its membership of the EU, the UK, in common with other European Countries, until recently still applied a variety of nationally imposed quotas. These nationally imposed quotas were phased-out entirely on 1 January 1993, but in any case they had been declining for some time. In 1985 there had been close to 2,000 nationally applied quotas sanctioned by the EU. By 1990 this figure had fallen to below 200.

Voluntary Export Restraints (VERs).   These are arrangements by which an individual exporter or group of exporters agrees with an importing country to limit the quantity of a specific product to be targeted at a particular market over a given period of time. In effect, VERs are quotas and the consequent welfare implications of their application can be demonstrated in Fig. 27.3. An example of a VER involves the import of cars from Japan into the EU. At present there is an understanding that Japanese producers will limit their sales into the UK, France, Spain, Italy and Portugal to a maximum of 1.1m units (the figure excludes output from Japanese plants based in the EU). This particular arrangement is due to be phased out at the end of 1999.

Subsidies.   The first three forms of protection we have described have all been designed to restrict the volume of imports directly. An alternative policy is to provide a subsidy to domestic producers so as to improve their competitiveness in both the home and world markets. The effect of this is demonstrated in Fig. 27.4.

Fig. 27..4. The effect of a
general subsidy.

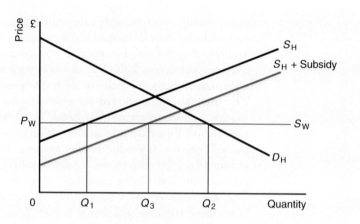

Once again we assume that the world supply curve is perfectly elastic at P_W. Under conditions of free trade, the domestic price is set by the world price at P_W. Domestic production is initially OQ_1 with imports satisfying the excess level of demand which amounts to Q_2-Q_1. The effect of a general subsidy to an industry would be to shift the supply curve of domestic producers to the right. The domestic price will remain unchanged but domestic production will rise to OQ_3 with imports reduced to Q_2Q_3. If, however, the subsidy is provided solely for *exporters*, the impact on the domestic market could be quite different. The incentive to export may encourage more domestic production to be switched from the home market to the overseas markets which in turn could result in an increased volume of imports to satisfy the unchanged level of domestic demand.

Subsidies have been quite widely employed over the last decade with agriculture a particularly significant beneficiary. The effective level of subsidy in the OECD agricultural sector rose from 30% to 50% of the value of domestic production during the 1980s. The 1990 European annual review of unfair US trade practices, for example, specifically focused on the use of agricultural export subsidies. Meanwhile, the US has itself had cause to complain about the protection afforded to farmers in the EU through the Common Agricultural Policy. In 1991, the EU provided almost $84bn in the form of subsidies to the agricultural sector; the US itself spent $35bn on such purposes. Interestingly, the Uruguay Round calls for domestic subsidies for agricultural producers to be lowered by 20% by the year 2000 from the levels prevailing in the second half of the 1980s. Significant subsidies still remain, however, in the manufacturing sector of the EU, in the form of general capital grants, export credit schemes and the state investment in its own sector. These amounted to subsidies of just over £1000 per worker in the late 1980s. Similarly, between 1991 and 1994, state aid to EU airlines totalled £10.4bn.

Exchange controls. A system of exchange controls was in force in the UK from the outbreak of the Second World War until 1979 when, in order to allow the free flow of capital, they were abolished. They enabled the government to limit the availability of foreign currencies and so curtail excessive imports; for instance, holding a foreign–currency bank account had required Bank of England permission. Exchange controls could also be employed to discourage speculation and investment abroad.

Safety and technological standards.   These are often imposed in the knowledge that certain imported goods will be unable to meet the requirements. The British government used such standards to prevent imports of French turkeys and ultra-heat-treated (UHT) milk. Ostensibly the ban on French turkeys was to prevent 'Newcastle disease', a form of fowl pest found in Europe, reaching the UK. The European Court ruled, however, that the ban was merely an excuse to prevent the free flow of imports. Problems with standards also occur between EU countries. For example, in the mid-1990s Germany effectively blocked imports of traffic cones from a UK manufacturer while it 'upgraded' its testing requirements no fewer than twelve times. The cones passed the test each time, but the German authorities refused to issue approval certificates or to publish their standards. Eventually pressure from the UK led to the standard for cones being published which allowed sales of cones to Germany to proceed. Similarly in 1996 Japan still continued to approve foreign truck imports on an 'individual' basis and not by 'type' of truck. Although it is argued that this is necessary to meet certain standards, it is nevertheless a clear form of non-tariff barrier.

Time-consuming formalities.   In 1990, the EU alleged that 'excessive invoicing requirements' required by US importing authorities had hampered exports from member countries to the US. In Asia these problems abound. For example Indonesian customs officials take at least a week to process imports, and this often involves considerable administrative and capital costs for many companies. A similar problem in China can lead to two or three weeks' delay.

Public sector contracts.   Governments often give preference to domestic firms in the issuing of public contracts, despite EU directives requiring member governments to advertise such contracts. A number of Australian states have continued to give price preferences of up to 20% to domestic bidders for public contracts in the latter half of the 1990s. Public contracts are actually placed outside the country of origin in only 1% of cases.

Labour standards.   This bears some resemblence to the point made above concerning safety and technological standards but is rather more controversial. Does the application of minimum labour standards represent a source of support for the poorest workers or is it simply a covert form of protection? Low cost producers, not surprisingly, believe the latter to be the case. The WTO is at present reluctant to go down this route but there is increasing pressure on governments in the industrialized world to take action on what is perceived as 'unfair' competition by countries with few, if any, effective minimum labour standards.

The case for protection   Protectionist measures may be applied on a selective or more widespread basis, with most of the measures currently in force falling into the first category.

Selective protection   A number of arguments have been used to justify the application of both tariff and non-tariff barriers on a selective basis:

1. To prevent dumping.
2. To protect infant industries.
3. To protect strategically important industries.
4. To maintain employment by preventing the rapid contraction of labour-intensive industries.

Dumping occurs where a good is sold in an overseas market at a price below the real cost of production. Under Article 6 of the GATT, the WTO allows retaliatory sanctions to be applied if it can be shown that the dumping materially affected the domestic industry. As well as using the WTO, countries within the EU can refer cases of alleged dumping for investigation by the European Commission. The Commission is then able to recommend the appropriate course of action, which may range from 'no action' where dumping is found not to have taken place, to either obtaining an 'undertaking' of no further dumping, or imposing a tariff.

There has been a significant increase in the number of anti-dumping cases initiated by the WTO in recent years, as Table 27.4 illustrates. Indeed, according to a World Bank study, average tariffs in the US manufactured goods sector would be 23% today as compared with a nominal level of less than 6% if anti-dumping duties were included.

As at the end of 1996 there were 900 cases of anti-dumping duties being applied. The US had imposed the most, over 300, with the EU around the 150 mark. Japanese exporters have suffered disproportionately. In 1997 the US applied a 454% anti-dumping duty on Japanese supercomputers sold in America after the US International Trade Commission had concluded that dumping had injured local producers. In an effort to circumvent the duties, there has been a growing trend towards establishing what are termed 'screw-driver' plants in Europe for the final assembly of the products. For example, when in 1984 a 28% duty was imposed on Japanese electronic typewriters, imports into the EU area amounted to 700,000. By 1988, a similar quantity were being *assembled* in various EU countries while only 35,000 were directly imported. Since the vast bulk of the production process was still taking place in the Far East, the EU reacted by bringing in limits on the extent of non-European content allowable in products if the dumping duty was to be waived. Research by Barrell and Pain (1996) confirms that the incidence of anti-dumping measures has influenced the level of Japanese foreign direct investment to the EU.

The use of protection in order to *establish new industries* is widely accepted, particularly in the case of developing countries. Article 18 of GATT explicitly allows such protection. An infant industry is likely to have a relatively high cost structure in the short run, and in the absence of protective measures may find it difficult to compete with the established overseas industries already benefiting from scale economies. The EU has used this argument to justify protection of its developing high-technology industries.

The protection of industries for *strategic reasons* is widely practised both in the UK and the EU, and is not necessarily contrary to GATT rules (Article 2). The

Table 27.4 **Anti-dumping: cases initiated.**

1983/84	1987/87	1989/90	1990/91	1991/92	1992/93	1993/94	1995/96
176	131	96	175	237	254	226	409

Sources: Financial Times (25 November 1993); Grimwade (1996); WTO, Annual Reports (various).

protection of the UK steel industry has in the past been justified on this basis, and the EU has used a similar argument to protect agricultural production throughout the Community under the guise of the CAP. In the Uruguay round of GATT, the developing countries used this argument in seeking to resist calls for the liberalisation of trade in the service sector. This has been one of the few sectors recording strong growth in recent years and is still a highly 'regulated' sector in most countries.

Criticisms of protectionism

Retaliation A major drawback to protectionist measures is the prospect of retaliation, which may arise in unexpected ways. For example, in July 1980 the UK imposed unilateral controls on the import of Indonesian clothes when that country exceeded its quota under the MFA. This involved imports worth around £10m. The Indonesian government immediately retaliated by cancelling an order with British Aerospace valued at £40m and began to reconsider other export contracts from the UK worth in excess of £350m. A more recent example of retaliatory measures involved the decision by the US, in Spring 1992, to publish a list of $1bn worth of European products on which it intended to impose tariffs of up to 100%. This American action was in direct retaliation against the EU for its continued subsidy of oil-seed growers.

The consequences of retaliation could be especially serious for the UK, given the importance of trade within its economy. In 1997 UK exports of goods and services totalled 34% of GDP, which is higher than most of its major competitors (e.g. France 28%, Japan 11%, USA 12%).

The widespread protection surrounding the Japanese economy has become increasingly widely criticized in recent years. In the late 1980s the US introduced the *Omnibus Trade Act*, under which Section 301 provides for the Administration to take retaliatory action against any countries deemed to be pursuing unfair trade practices. Recent analysis suggests that Section 301 made only a modest contribution to boosting US exports – around 1 per cent annually – but that it may have been instrumental in ensuring a successful outcome to the Uruguay round (Bayard and Elliot 1994). The US also initiated the *Structural Impediments Initiative* in 1989 in an effort to seek market opening reforms from Japan. By mid-1990 Japan had agreed to strengthen its anti-monopoly law to control the activity of Japan's large industrial groups, and to reform its Retail Store Law so as to allow more large stores which, it is hoped, would import more foreign goods. This, however failed to prevent a further widening in the trade imbalance between the two countries in the early 1990s. A new 'market access' package was put into effect by the Japanese government in 1994 in an effort to head off retaliatory action. This included further deregulation of trade, distribution and other business activities, stricter enforcement of anti-trust laws and another round of fiscal stimulation for the economy.

Misallocation of resources We saw in Figs 27.1–27.3 that protectionism can erode some of the welfare benefits of free trade. For instance, Fig. 27.2 showed that a tariff (and Fig. 27.3 a quota) raises domestic supply at the expense of imports. If the domestic producers cannot make such products as cheaply as overseas producers, then one could argue that encouraging high-cost domestic production is a misallocation of international resources.

A related criticism also suggests that protectionism leads to resource misallocation on an international scale, but this time concerns the multinational. We saw in Chapter 7 that multinationals are the fastest-growing type of business unit in Western economies, and that they are increasingly adopting strategies which locate particular stages of the production process in (to them) appropriate parts of the world. Protectionism may disrupt the flow of goods from one stage of the production process to another, and in this sense inhibit global specialization.

Work carried out by the OECD (Goldin and Van Der Mensbrugghe 1992) has attempted to quantify the costs of protection in terms of 'lost output'. The study considers two scenarios: (i) a 30% reduction in tariffs (roughly equivalent to that in the Uruguay round); and (ii) the complete elimination of tariffs. Under the first scenario, the report concludes that world output of goods and services would rise by an *additional* $195bn per annum within a decade, i.e. by around 0.75 per cent of current annual world output. Under the second scenario, world output is expected to rise by an *additional* $477bn per annum within a decade, i.e. by around 2 per cent of current annual world output. Although a few countries (mainly net food importers) were expected to be disadvantaged under both scenarios, the overall losses were calculated as being no more than $7bn. These anticipated losses are small in comparison to the anticipated gains from tariff reductions. Indeed the 'losses' could be fully compensated by a transfer of resources equivalent to only 3.5 per cent of the anticipated gains under scenario (i).

On the domestic level, various studies have found that profits were higher than normal in industries which were dominated by a few large firms, reflecting their use of market power (e.g. Turner 1980). However, excess profits were smaller in the industries which experienced most foreign competition. Protectionist measures, by removing such competition, may therefore allow large firms to exert their latent market power, causing prices and profits to be raised at the expense of consumers.

Conclusion

The completion of the latest GATT round after eight years of negotiation and the establishment of the WTO has eased concerns over the future of free trade. Indeed this completion of the Uruguay round of tariff reductions has been estimated as raising world GDP by 1% per annum compared to the non–completion scenario (Greenaway 1994). But there remains a number of reasons for caution. One is the increase in the number of bilateral barriers to trade which have been imposed outside the GATT framework. A second is the movement towards expanded Regional Trading Blocs (RTBs), such as the European Union, the North American Free Trade Agreement, and the Asian Free Trade Area. It remains to be seen whether RTBs ultimately promote or hinder multilateral trade! (Bhagwati 1992). For the time being, the volume of world trade is continuing to grow. But with globalization increasingly being seen as the cause of much upheaval and insecurity in industrial countries, the risk remains of a retreat towards protectionism. Unless there is a renewed recognition of the *world-wide costs* of such a development, the protectionist lobbies in various countries may still succeed in curbing the growth of international specialization and trade.

<table>
<tr><td>

Key points

</td><td>

- In a competitive, full employment framework, free trade can be shown to yield a net welfare gain *vis-à-vis* various protectionist alternatives.
- In the more realistic situation of 'market failures', the existence of monopoly power, unemployment, etc. may offset (in part or in whole) these welfare gains.
- The General Agreement on Tariffs and Trade (GATT) established in 1947, and its successor the World Trade Organization (WTO), seek to reduce tariffs and other barriers to trade, and to eliminate discrimination in trade.
- The GATT/WTO have had some success, cutting the average tariff in the industrialized world from 40% in 1947 to less than 5% in 1995.
- Since 1870, the growth of trade has *exceeded* the growth of world GDP in all but the period between the First and Second World Wars.
- *Intra-regional* trade (i.e. trade within a region) has grown substantially in recent decades. For example, 68% of all Western European trade occurs between countries in Western Europe.
- Various types of regional trading arrangement have promoted this trend. Free Trade Areas, Customs Unions (have an external tariff barrier), Common Markets (factors of production can also freely move) and Economic Unions (harmonization of member policies) have all been used to this end.
- Various types of protection have been used by countries including tariffs, quotas, voluntary export restraints, subsidies, exchange controls, and a range of restrictions involving technological standards, safety, etc.
- Arguments often advanced in *favour* of protectionist policies include the prevention of dumping, the protection of infant industries and of strategically important industries, the maintenance of high levels of domestic employment, etc.
- Arguments *against* protectionist policies include retaliation and a mis-allocation of resources on both a national and international scale, leading to welfare loss.

</td></tr>
</table>

Notes

1. It could, however, be argued that the welfare loss is overestimated by this analysis. Area 3, though no longer received by the government as tax revenue, may still be received by importers. Although only paying P_W to the foreign suppliers, the importers now receive P'_W when selling $Q_5 - Q_4$ on the domestic market.

References and further reading

Balassa, B. and **Michalopoulos** (1985) Liberalizing world trade, *World Bank Discussion Paper*.

Barrell, R. E. and **Pain, N.** (1996) Trade restraints and Japanese direct investment flows, *European Economic Review*.

Bayard, T. O. and **Elliot, K. A.** (1994) *Reciprocity and Retaliation in US Trade Policy*, Institute for International Economics, Washington DC.

Bhagwati, J. (1992) Regionalism and multilateralism: an overview, *Columbia University Discussion Paper* No. 603.

De Melo, J. and **Panagariya, A.** (1992) The new regionalism, *Finance and Development*, Dec.

Goldin, I. and **Van Der Mensbrugghe, D.** (1992) *Trade Liberalisation: What's at Stake?* OECD.

Greenaway, D. (1994) The Uraguay Round of Trade Negotiations, *Economic Review*, Nov.

Grimwade, N. (1996) Anti-dumping policy after the Uruguay Round, *National Institute Economics Review*, Feb.

Lloyd, P. J. (1992) Regionalisation and world trade, *OECD Economic Studies* No. 18.

Primo Braga, C. A., Safadi, R. and Yeats, A. (1994) NAFTA's Implications for East Asian Exports, *World Bank, Policy Working Paper* No. 1351.

Reinert, K. A., Roland-Holst, D. W. and Shiells, C. R. (1994) A general equilibrium analysis of North American regional integration, in *Modelling Trade Policy: Applied General Equilibrium Analysis of a North American Free Trade Area*, J. F. Francois and C. R. Shiells eds, CUP.

Srinivasan, T. N., Whalley, J. and Wooton, I. (1993) Measuring the effects of regionalism on trade and welfare, in *Regional Integration*, Kym Anderson and Richard Blackhurst eds, Harvester Wheatsheaf.

Turner, P. P. (1980) Import competition and the profitability of United Kingdom manufacturing industry, *The Journal of Industrial Economics*, **29**, Dec.

Vanston, N. (1993) What price regional integration? *The PECD Observer* No. 181.

Yannopoulos, G. N. (1990) Foreign direct investment and European direct investment: the evidence from the formative years of the European Community, *Journal of Common Market Studies* No. 23(3).

The area is seen as a precursor to full EU membership for the EFTA members (the UK, Denmark and Ireland had been EFTA members prior to joining the EEC in 1972). Switzerland has, of course, already applied to become a full member of the EU.

The Maastricht Treaty   The Treaty on European Union which was signed at Maastricht on 7 February 1992 represents one of the most fundamental changes to have occurred in the EU since its foundation. Although, legally speaking, merely an extension and amendment to the Treaty of Rome, Maastricht represents a major step for the member states. For the first time many of the political and social imperatives of the Community have been explicitly agreed and delineated. Maastricht takes the EU beyond a 'merely' economic institution (if it ever was such) and takes it towards the full political, economic and social union foreseen by many of its founders. Some of its major objectives are as follows:

1. to create economic and social progress through an 'area without internal frontiers' and through economic and monetary union (EMU);
2. to develop a common foreign, security and defence policy which 'might lead to common defence';
3. to introduce a 'citizenship of the Union'.

Table 28.1 presents some of the important characteristics of the fifteen member countries. It shows how diverse they are in terms of population, industrial structure, standard of living, unemployment level and inflation rate. In terms of population the UK is still the second-largest member, with a smaller proportion engaged in agriculture than in other EU countries but the second largest in services. In overall wealth however, the UK drops down the rankings. It has the third-largest GDP in absolute terms, but comes tenth in terms of GDP per capita, at around the EU average. In the thirty-eight years between 1960 and 1998 German GDP grew 23 times in money terms whilst Spanish GDP grew an impressive 38 times. The UK's GDP grew only 14 times – the lowest rate of overall growth of any of the EU member countries.

Quite apart from the political rationale behind the EU a number of economic arguments have been advanced in its support:

1. By abolishing industrial tariff and non-tariff barriers at national frontiers, the EU has created a single 'domestic' market of around 373 million people, with opportunities for substantial economies of scale in production. By surrounding this market with a tariff wall, the Common External Tariff (CET), member countries are the beneficiaries of these scale economies.
2. By regulating agricultural production through the CAP, the EU has become self-sufficient in many agricultural products.
3. By amending and co-ordinating labour and capital regulations in the member countries, the EU seeks to create a free market in both, leading to a more 'efficient' use of these factors. A further factor, 'enterprise', is to be 'freed' through increased standardization of national laws on patents and licences.
4. By controlling monopoly and merger activities, competition has been encouraged both within and across frontiers.
5. By creating a substantial 'domestic' market and by co-ordinating trade policies, the EU hopes to exert a greater collective influence on world economic affairs than could possibly be achieved by any single nation.

Table 28.1   The Fifteen: some comparative statistics.

| Member country | Population (million) | Economically active population | | | GDP ECU (bn) | GDP per capita ECU (000's) | Share of EU | | | Unemployment (%) 1998 | Inflation (%) 1998 |
		Agric. (%)	Industry (%)	Services (%)			GDP (%)	Population (%)	Index of GDP per capita		
Austria	8.1	7.2	33.2	59.6	181.0	22.4	2.6	2.1	113	4.2	2.1
Belgium	10.2	2.5	6.1	71.4	212.6	20.9	3.0	2.7	115	8.8	1.8
Denmark	5.3	4.0	27.0	69.0	144.0	27.3	2.0	1.4	113	5.4	2.5
Finland	5.1	7.1	27.6	65.3	103.3	20.1	1.4	1.4	98	12.6	2.0
France	58.6	4.6	25.9	69.5	1,230.9	21.0	17.2	15.6	104	12.3	1.5
Germany	82.2	3.3	37.5	59.2	1,862.6	22.7	26.1	21.9	109	9.8	2.2
Greece	10.6	20.4	23.2	56.4	105.6	10.0	1.5	2.8	69	9.3	4.5
Ireland	3.6	10.7	27.2	61.1	65.7	18.0	0.9	1.0	85	9.5	2.5
Italy	56.8	7.0	32.1	60.9	1,009.6	17.8	14.4	15.4	103	11.9	2.2
Luxembourg	0.4	2.8	30.7	66.5	13.7	32.6	0.1	0.1	175	3.8	1.7
Netherlands	15.6	3.9	22.4	73.7	317.2	20.3	4.3	4.1	106	4.8	2.4
Portugal	9.4	12.2	31.4	56.4	90.0	9.6	1.2	2.7	71	6.7	2.1
Spain	39.3	8.7	29.7	61.6	466.6	11.9	6.6	10.6	94	19.8	2.2
Sweden	8.9	2.9	26.1	71.0	201.5	22.7	2.8	2.4	94	9.9	2.0
UK	59.0	2.0	26.4	71.0	1,141.2	19.3	15.9	15.7	99	5.8	2.4
Total EU	373.1	3.9	28.2	67.9	7,145.8	19.2	100.0	100.0	100.0	10.3	2.2

Notes: 'Total EU' percentages for Agriculture, Industry and Sevices are *weighted averages.*
1 ECU = 70 pence approx.
Sources: European Economy (1998) No. 65; OECD (1998) *Economic Survey,* June; European Commission (1998).

These policies have been supported by a number of other arrangements, including a common form of taxation, a common currency, and policies directed towards transport, energy, education, social improvement and regional aid. Although our main concern in this chapter will be economic, we should not overlook the political objectives which lay behind the formation of the EU. As early as 1946, Winston Churchill had called for a 'United States of Europe' as a diplomatic and military counter to the Soviet Union. However, it was two Frenchmen – Robert Schuman and Jean Monnet – who were the founding fathers of the EC, with their vision of using economic involvement to tie Europe's warring countries together. Having attempted, on three occasions, to join the EU during the 1960s, the UK was finally accepted for membership in 1970, signed the Treaty of Accession in 1972, and became a full member with effect from 1 January 1973.

The UK's objectives in signing the Treaty of Accession in 1972 were a combination of the short- to medium-term economic, with the medium- to long-term political. There was an undeniable desire to share in the prosperity which the EU appeared to have stimulated for its six original members since 1958. The fact that the average growth rate of the Six had been 4.8% per annum between 1961 and 1971, compared to the UK's 2.7% per annum, seemed to show that entry into the EU might offer a solution to some of the UK's growth problems. In this chapter we examine the EU and the effect of UK membership of the EU under five broad headings:

1. Finance and the EU budget
2. Policy areas
    Competition
    Agriculture
    Structural
    Trade and balance of payments
    Monetary
    Commercial and industrial
3. Monetary Union
    EMU
    Convergence
    Single currency (euro)
4. Enlargement
5. Opting out?

For each of these headings we discuss both EU policy in general and how it has affected the UK in particular.

Finance and the EU budget

Between 1958 and 1970 the EU was financed by contributions from member states which, although politically determined, were still broadly based on the various countries' ability to pay. However, since 1970 the EU has financed its spending using a system of 'own resources', i.e. income it regards as its own *as of right*. The composition of 'own resources' is shown in Table 28.2 and consists of three main sources of revenue. First, Traditional Own Resources (TOR) which includes revenue raised from customs duties such as the Common External Tariff (CET) and agricultural duties. Second, revenue from each country up to a *maximum* of 1% of its

Table 28.2 Sources of
revenue for the EU
budget (ECU million
and %).

	1994	(%)	1996	(%)	1998	(%)
TOR	13,252.2	(20.6)	13,583.6	(19.1)	13,743.2	(16.7)
VAT	33,217.9	(51.8)	36,535.0	(51.4)	32,752.8	(39.7)
GNP	17,657.0	(27.5)	21,067.1	(29.6)	35,985.2	(43.6)
Total 'own resources'	**64,188.8**	**(100.0)**	**71,098.7**	**(100.0)**	**82,481.1**	**(100.0)**
Other revenue	1,813.3		10,176.4		1,628.0	
Total revenue	66,002.1		81,275.1		84,109.1	

Source: Adapted from European Commission (1998) *Funding in the European Union*, October.
Note: 1 ECU = 70 pence approx.

domestic VAT tax base. Third, a levy of up to a *maximum* of 1.27% of the value of GNP in each member country. This levy, which was introduced in 1988, is used as a 'buffer' to equate EU revenue with its expenditure. In other words, the actual percentage of GNP required can vary according to how much revenue is required to balance the EU budget (e.g. 0.40% of GNP in 1997 but 0.54% in 1998). Finally, the table also includes 'other revenue' which consists of revenue from a variety of sources such as interest on late payments, fines, taxes on salaries of employees of EU institutions, etc.

A notable feature of Table 28.2 is the decline in the relative importance of TOR and VAT as sources of revenue and the growth in importance of the GNP element. The impact of trade liberalization on tariff levels (e.g. reductions via GATT rounds) has meant that the total yield from TOR has failed to increase in line with the expansion of world trade, so that the share of TOR in total revenue has decreased. Similarly the share of VAT in total revenue has also decreased. This is partly because of decisions made by the Commission to decrease the percentage of GNP which acts as the *tax base* for calculating the VAT paid by member states. For example, the VAT base for member states has fallen from 55% of their GNP in 1995 to 50% of GNP by 1999. Once the absolute amount of the tax base has been calculated for each country, then a VAT tax rate is applied to this amount in order to arrive at the sum which each member has to pay. The maximum rate of VAT applied to this tax base has also fallen from 1.4% in the mid-1990s to 1% by 1999, which has further decreased the revenue derived by the EU from the VAT source. These curbs on the VAT source of revenue reflect the view that it is a regressive tax which tends to disadvantage poorer members of the EU because a greater proportion of their national income is devoted to consumption, resulting in a greater tax burden being placed on them than on richer members. As a result of the trends noted above, the importance of the GNP element in EU revenue has increased in order to fill the revenue gap. This is regarded as a more acceptable source because the contributions of the various member countries to the EU budget are more closely related to their affluence, i.e. to their ability to pay as indicated by GNP.

A breakdown of the expenditure side of the EU budget is shown in Table 28.3.

- During most of the 1990s, around 50% of the EU's total expenditure was spent on the *Guarantee* section of the European Agricultural Guarantee and Guidance Fund (EAGGF). This Fund is used to subsidize the farming community under the EU's Common Agricultural Policy (CAP) in various ways. The Guarantee section is responsible for a wide range of price support programmes (see p. 657).
- The second most important expenditure group involves 'Total Structural Funds' which account for some 32% of total expenditure. Within this group, the main

Table 28.3 Budgetary expenditure of the European Communities (ECU million).

Budget heading	1994	1996	1998
EAGGF Guarantee	37,465.0	41,328.0	40,937.0
Total Structural Funds	21,528.8	26,005.6	28,594.7
Structural Fund	17,555.7	21,099.2	23,084.4
Community Initiatives	1,860.2	2,204.6	2,558.8
Cohesion Fund	1,679.0	1,919.3	2,648.8
Others	433.9	782.5	302.7
Internal policies	3,733.8	4,780.3	4,678.5
External policies	3,348.3	4,718.2	4,528.5
Administration	3,617.6	4,128.6	4,353.4
Other	320.0	927.7	437.0
Total	70,013.5	81,888.4	83,529.2

Note: 1 ECU = 70 pence approx.
Source: Adapted from European Commission (1998) *Funding in the European Union*, October.

constituent is the 'Structural Fund' accounting for over three-quarters of the total. Although not shown in Table 28.3, the Structural Fund is made up of four sub-funds:

(a) the European Regional Development Fund (ERDF), which aims to reduce the inequality gap between the Community's regions;

(b) the European Social Fund (ESF), which is designed to improve the labour market in member countries by increasing employment opportunities, employment flexibility and equal opportunities for the work force;

(c) the EAGGF *Guidance* Fund, which helps to adapt the structure of agriculture by encouraging small (less efficient) farmers to leave the land;

(d) the Financial Instrument for Fisheries Guidance (FIFG), which helps the restructuring of the fisheries sector.

Over the second half of the 1990s, the average percentage shares of Structural Fund expenditure spent on these activities were ERDF (52%), ESF (30%), EAGGF (16%) and FIFG (2%).

The remaining parts of the Total Structural Fund expenditures are 'Community Initiatives' and the 'Cohesion Fund'. The main objective of the Community Initiatives is to stimulate transnational cooperation between member states in order to implement measures of common interest, e.g. projects to promote rural development. The Cohesion Fund is designed to help the least prosperous member states of the EU to take part in Economic and Monetary Union. For example it provides assistance to projects in Greece, Ireland, Portugal and Spain, such as those which contribute to improvements in the transport infrastructure and transport networks of these countries.

● 'Internal Policies' refers to the funds used to help improve EU competitiveness and includes spending on Research and Development (R&D) projects.

● 'External Policies' includes EU foreign aid to states such as the former Eastern bloc countries wishing to progress towards the market economy model.

In 1998 the European Commission reported on the revenue and expenditure aspects of the EU budget (European Commission, 1998). On the *revenue* side it was suggested that the performance of the budget should be assessed on five criteria, namely resources adequacy, equity in gross contributions, financial autonomy,

Table 28.4 GNP and EU budgetary balances, 1997.

	Share of EU GNP(%)	Share of EU budget(%)	Imbalance (ECUm)	Imbalance (%GNP)
Belgium	3.1	3.9	1,079	0.50
Denmark	1.9	2.0	69	0.05
Germany	26.0	28.2	−10,943	−0.60
Greece	1.5	1.6	4,371	4.13
Spain	6.6	7.1	5,936	1.28
France	17.2	17.5	−781	−0.06
Ireland	0.8	0.9	2,676	4.84
Italy	14.2	11.5	−61	−0.01
Luxembourg	0.2	0.2	725	4.89
Netherlands	4.5	6.4	−2,276	−0.71
Austria	2.6	2.8	−723	−0.40
Portugal	1.2	1.4	2,722	3.12
Finland	1.4	1.4	56	0.06
Sweden	2.7	3.1	−1,130	−0.59
UK	16.1	11.9	−1,799	−0.16
EU	**100.0**	**100.0**	78	**0.00**

Note: Figures are rounded; 1 ECU = 70 pence approx.
Source: Adapted from European Commission (1998) *Funding in the European Union*, October.

transparency and simplicity, and cost effectiveness. To fulfil these criteria the report proposed changes which would be simpler, fairer and more cost effective. In particular there was support for more *revenue* being derived from members' GNP contributions. On the *expenditure* side, the main proposal was to decrease spending on market support policies for agricultural products. Finally, the report suggested that those members with large budget imbalances (i.e. whose contributions are generally greater than their receipts) should be compensated by some form of correction mechanism. For example, Germany, the Netherlands, Austria and Sweden have found themselves with budgetary deficits which are arguably excessive in relation to their relative standards of living within the EU.

The nature of the imbalances problem can be seen from Table 28.4. This table shows the relative shares of member countries in total EU GNP and in relative contributions to the total revenue for the EU budget, together with figures for the imbalances, both in absolute amounts and as a percentage of the country's GNP (UK figures are net of its rebate). Some important points can be noted from this table. First, the UK had a 16.1% share of EU GNP but only contributed 11.9% (after rebate) to the total revenue for the EU budget. Even though the UK had a negative budgetary imbalance with the EU, in that it received less than it contributed, the burden of the imbalance relative to its GNP share was arguably quite reasonable. Second, although countries such as Germany, the Netherlands, Austria and Sweden were also experiencing negative imbalances with the EU, their situations are arguably less fair in that their negative budgetary imbalance is a much higher percentage of their respective GNPs than for other member states. Put another way, their relative contributions to the EU budget are greater than their relative prosperity within the EU. Germany's problems have been particularly difficult because, as a wealthy country with a relatively small agricultural sector, it attracts low shares of EU spending on both the Structural Funds and the CAP.

The four countries mentioned above want the budgetary correction to be replaced by a 'capping model' which would cut the UK rebate and reduce their own net contributions to the EU budget. Under the Fontainebleau agreement of 1984 any state which suffers a budgetary burden which is 'excessive' in relation to its relative prosperity may seek a correction 'at the appropriate time'.

The UK and the EU budget

It must be stressed that the terms 'net contributor' and 'net beneficiary' relate only to the EU budget and its relatively tiny amounts of expenditure, and *not* to the members' total experience within the Community. Merely to say that Germany and the UK have usually been large net contributors to the budget has no bearing upon whether they have or have not benefited overall from membership of the EU. It is also important to understand that being a 'net contributor' does not imply a transfer of German or UK funds to the EU. The budget is 'self-financing' to the extent that contributions to it are, by treaty, never the property of the member state. It is intended (although the results in practice are very different) to be a reallocation of resources from rich to poor in much the same way as national income tax. However, it is not so much being in the position of a net contributor to the budget that has worried successive UK governments, as the relative size of that contribution.

The calculation of the UK's net contribution involves the following procedure:

1. Customs tariffs paid directly to EU; *plus*
2. Agricultural levies paid directly to EU; *minus*
3. Administrative costs of collecting the above returned to UK government; *plus*
4. VAT contribution (according to the rate set by Council); *plus*
5. Direct UK government contribution (the GNP element)

equals gross contribution, *minus*

6. Amount due to UK for agricultural support (from Intervention Board); *minus*
7. Structural Fund payments

equals net contribution (or benefit for some members).

As a major importer of both manufactured goods and food (see Chapter 26), the UK collects large amounts under items (1) and (2). The VAT rate, as a tax on the value added is, of course, fairly closely related to economic activity and therefore the VAT contribution is reasonably proportional across member countries. Summing items (1)–(5) gives the UK's *gross* contribution to the EU budget. However, the UK must set against this the revenue it receives for agricultural support programmes, item (6), and for regional and social projects, item (7). Subtracting items (6) and (7) from gross contribution gives the UK's *net* contribution (or benefit).

Whereas the UK's gross contribution is relatively high compared with other members', her receipts from the EU budget, items (6) and (7), are relatively low. The UK receives little in terms of agricultural support because the operation of the CAP largely benefits less efficient producers, and not efficient ones like the UK. The modest increase in EU support for regional and social projects in the UK has been insufficient to correct this imbalance. As a result the UK has consistently found itself a net contributor.

The UK's net contributions to the EU budget are shown in Table 28.5. The fact that the UK was a large net contributor to the EU was addressed as early as 1984 when, under the Fontainebleau agreement of that year, the UK received a 'rebate' according to a set formula which the Commission calls 'a correction mechanism in favour of the UK'. The rebate was reviewed in 1988 and 1992 and on both occasions the European Commission decided that it should be continued.

Attempts to follow the history of British net payments to the EU budget are dogged by the changing nature of the agreements surrounding the budget and by the frequency of additional, 'emergency' payments made by member countries in order to keep the EU solvent whilst the larger budget issues were being settled.

Table 28.5 The EU
budget – UK payments
and receipts by financial
year.

£(m)	1988/89 Out-turn	1990/91 Out-turn	1992/93 Out-turn	1994/95 Out-turn	1997/98 Estimated
Gross payments	4,906	5,804	6,970	6,892	8,523
Gross receipts	−1,958	−2,035	−2,810	−3,603	−4,636
VAT abatement	−1,137	−1,317	−1,993	−1,648	−1,582
Net payments	1,811	2,452	2,168	1,641	2,305

Source: Adapted from Chancellor of the Exchequer's Departments (1998) Government's Expenditure Plans (and previous issues).

Policy areas

1. Competition policy

The theory behind European competition policy is exactly that which created the original EEC almost forty years ago. Competition brings consumer choice, lower prices and higher quality goods and services. The Commission has a set of directives in this area which are designed to underpin 'fair and free' competition. They cover cartels (price fixing, market sharing, etc.), government subsidies (direct or indirect subsidies for inefficient enterprises – state and private), the abuse of dominant market position (differential pricing in different markets, exclusive contracts, predatory pricing, etc.), selective distribution (preventing consumers in one market from buying in another in order to maintain high margins in the first market), and mergers and take-overs. The latter powers were given to the Commission in 1990.

Two of the most active areas of competition policy have involved mergers and acquisitions (see Chapter 5) and state aid. In the former, the power of the Commission was widened in 1998 to increase the range of mergers which can be referred to it. In the latter, the Commission has attempted to restrict the aid paid by member states to their own nationals through Articles 92 and 93 of the EC Treaty and Articles 4 and 95 of the ECSC Treaty. These Articles cover various aspects of the distorting effect that subsidies can have on competition between member states. However, it is likely that the progressive implementation of Single Market arrangements will result in domestic firms increasing their attempts to obtain state aid from their own governments as a means of helping them meet greater Europe-wide competition. Overall aid given by member states to their domestic industry has been running at around 2% of their respective GNPs during the 1990s.

Currently some 45bn ECU per year is spent on state aid to EU manufacturing. Germany tops the league of aid recipients as it tries to help its new *Länder* in the former East Germany to restructure their industry. The main problem with state aid is that the big, industrially powerful countries – Germany, France, UK and Italy – account for some 85% of the total state aid given by EU countries to their domestic industry. This arguably gives such economies considerable advantages over the four 'cohesion' countries – Greece, Portugal, Spain and Ireland.

To counter some of these trends, the EU Commission has begun to scrutinize state aid much more closely – especially where the aid seems to be more than is needed to ensure the ultimate viability of the recipient organizations. For example, in April 1998 the Commission decided that aid paid to the German porcelain firm, Triptis Porzellan GmbH, should be recovered because it believed it to be more than was needed to restore the firm's viability, thereby distorting competition in the market.

2. The Common Agricultural Policy

When the Treaty of Rome was signed in 1957 over 20% of the working population of the 'Six' were engaged in agriculture. In the enlarged EU of today that figure is only 3.9%, ranging from the UK with 2.0% to Greece with over almost 20.4% (see Table 28.1). Since one in five of the EU's workers were involved in agricultural production in 1957, it came as no surprise that the depressed agricultural sector became the focus of the first 'common' policy, the CAP, established in 1962. The objectives of this policy were to create a single market for agricultural produce and to protect the agricultural sector from imports, the justification being to ensure dependable supplies of food for the EU and stability of income for those engaged in agriculture.

Both the demand for, and the supply of, agricultural products are, for the most part, inelastic, so that a small shift in either schedule will induce a more than proportionate change in price. Fluctuations in agricultural prices will in turn create fluctuations in agricultural incomes and therefore investment and ultimately output. The CAP seeks to stabilize agricultural prices, and therefore incomes and output in the industry, to the alleged 'benefit' of both producers and consumers.

There are, of course, a number of ways of achieving such objectives. Prior to joining the EU, the UK placed great emphasis on supplies of cheap food from the Commonwealth. The UK therefore adopted a system of 'deficiency payments' which operated by letting actual prices be set at world levels, but at the same time guaranteeing to farmers minimum 'prices' for each product. If the world price fell below the guaranteed minimum, then the 'deficiency' would be made up by government subsidy. Under this system the consumer could benefit from the low world prices whilst at the same time farm incomes were maintained. Although the UK system involved some additional features, such as marketing agencies, direct production grants, research agencies etc., it was by no means as complex as that which has operated in the UK since 1972 under the CAP.

Method of operation   The formal title for the executive body of the CAP is the European Agricultural Guarantee and Guidance Fund (EAGGF), often known by its French translation 'Fonds Européen d'Orientation et de Garantie Agricole' (FEOGA). As its name implies, it has two essential roles: that of guaranteeing farm incomes, and of guiding farm production. We shall consider each aspect in turn.

Guarantee system   Different agricultural products are dealt with in slightly different ways, but the basis of the system is the establishment of a 'target price' for each product (Fig. 28.1). The target price is *not* set with reference to world prices, but is based upon the price which producers would need to cover costs, including a profit mark-up, in the highest-cost area of production in the EU. The EU then sets an 'Intervention' or 'guaranteed' price for the product in that area, about 7–10% below the target price. Should the price be in danger of falling below this level, the Commission intervenes to buy up production to keep the price at or above the 'guaranteed' level. The Commission then sets separate target and Intervention prices for that product in *each area* of the Community, related broadly to production costs in that area. As long as the market price in a given area (there are eleven such areas in the UK) is above the Intervention price, the producer will sell his produce at

Fig. 28.1. EU
agricultural pricing.

prevailing market prices. In effect the Intervention price sets a 'floor' below which market price will not be permitted to fall and is therefore the guaranteed minimum price to producers.

In Fig. 28.2, an increase in supply of agricultural products to S_1 would, if no action were taken, lower the market price from P_1 to P_2, below the 'Intervention' or 'guaranteed' price, P^*. At P^* demand is Q' but supply is Q^*. To keep the price at P^* the EAGGF will buy up the excess $Q^* - Q'$. In terms of Fig. 28.2 the demand curve is artificially increased to D_1 by the EAGGF purchase.

If this system of guaranteed minimum prices is to work, then EU farmers must be protected from low-priced imports from overseas. To this end levies or tariffs are imposed on imports of agricultural products. If in Fig. 28.2 the price of imported food were higher than the EU target price then, of course, there would be no need for an import tariff. If, however, the import price is below this, say at the 'world price' in Fig. 28.2, then an appropriate tariff must be calculated. This need not quite cover the difference between 'target' and 'world' price, since the importer still has to pay transport costs within the EU to get the food to market. The tariff

Fig. 28.2. EU and the
guarantee system.

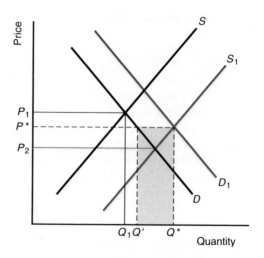

must therefore be large enough to raise the import price at the EU frontier to the target price minus transport costs, i.e. 'threshold price'. This calculation takes place in the highest-cost area of production in the EU, so that the import tariff set will more than protect EU producers in areas with lower target prices (i.e. lower-cost areas).

Should an EU producer wish to export an agricultural product then an export subsidy will be paid to bring his receipts up to the Intervention price (see Fig. 28.2), i.e. the minimum price he would receive in the home market. Problems involving this form of subsidy of oil-seed exports were a major threat to dealings between the EU and the USA, with the latter alleging a breach of GATT rules.

Reforms in the latter part of the 1980s had a significant effect on key sectors such as dairy products. In the cereals and oil-seeds market, intervention buying now occurs only outside the harvest periods. Maximum Guaranteed Quantities (MGQs) are also set for most products. If the MGQ is exceeded, then the intervention price is cut by 3% in the following year.

The system outlined above does not apply to all agricultural products in the EU. About a quarter of these products are covered by different direct subsidy systems, e.g. olive oil and tobacco, and some products, such as potatoes, agricultural alcohol, and honey are not covered by EU regulation at all.

Guidance system   The CAP was, as originally established, a simple price-support system. It soon became obvious that agriculture in the 'Six' required considerable structural change because too much output was being produced by small, high-cost, farming units. In 1968 the Commission published a report called *Agriculture 1980*, more usually known as the 'Mansholt Plan' after its originator, the Commissioner for Agriculture, Sicco Mansholt. The plan envisaged taking large amounts of marginal land out of production, reducing the agricultural labour force, and creating larger economic farming units. The plan eventually led to the establishment of a Common Structural Policy in 1972, which for political reasons was to be voluntary and administered by the individual member states. The import levies of the EAGGF were to provide funds to encourage small farmers to leave the land and to promote large-scale farming units.

Reform of the CAP   The relative failure of the guidance policy has meant the continued existence of many small, high-cost producers in many agricultural areas of the EU, with correspondingly high 'target' prices. High target prices have in turn encouraged excess supply in a number of products, requiring substantial purchases by the Guarantee section of the EAGGF, resulting in butter and beef mountains, wine lakes, etc. The net effect of the CAP has therefore been, via high prices, to transfer resources from the EU consumer to the EU producer. At the same time the CAP has led to a less efficient allocation of resources within the EU in that high prices made the use of marginal land and labour-intensive processes economically viable. Arguably, resource allocation has been impaired both within the EU *and* on a world scale, in that the system of agricultural levies distorts comparative advantages by encouraging high-cost production within the EU to the detriment of low-cost production outside the EU. Finally, through its import levies and export subsidies the CAP introduces an element of discrimination against Third World producers of agricultural products, for whom such exports are a major source of foreign earnings.

The growth of agricultural spending in the early 1980s placed increasing pressure on the EU's 'own resources'. By 1983 the 1% VAT ceiling had been breached and even the steady growth in imports (providing CET revenue) was not sufficient to meet the demands on the budget. The member governments were forced to agree to special additional payments to meet deficits which arose in 1983, 1984, 1985 and 1987. With no agreement on reform during the late 1980s, the CAP began to expand rapidly and the Council was forced to agree a series of 'supplementary' budgets.

The breakthrough occurred at the Brussels Heads of Government meeting in February 1988 during which a further, new source of finance was sanctioned (up to 1.2% of GNP) in return for legislative limits on the CAP. In 1988 the CAP was limited to a fixed sum of 27.5bn ECU and from then onwards could only expand, in future years, by three-quarters of the average rate of growth in EU GNP (see Table 28.6). Other significant limits were placed on the CAP in the form of a ceiling on cereal production (160 million tonnes), a cut in producer prices of about 3%, and a new 'co-responsibility' levy of 3% on larger farmers.[3]

The reform of CAP took a further step forward in June 1992 when the so-called 'McSharry proposals' for reform were adopted. The purpose of the reforms were, first, to control agricultural production which had been artificially stimulated by CAP: second, to make European agriculture more competitive by reduction of support prices: third, to discourage very intensive agricultural methods while still maintaining high employment on the land and supporting more marginal and vulnerable farmers.

To achieve these aims, support prices for cereals were to be reduced by some 30%. Also, arable land was taken out of production or 'set aside', with farmers receiving payment based on average yields for what is *not* produced. Livestock farmers were limited to a maximum head of cattle per hectare of available fodder. Other elements of the reform involved direct income-support for farmers in Less Favoured Areas (LFAs) and for those who use environmentally sound methods of farming. Finally, an early 'pre-pension' scheme was introduced to accelerate the retirement of farmers who operated unviable holdings.

In July 1997 the European Commission published Agenda 2000 which analysed the EU's past policies and considered certain long-term future trends. As far as agriculture was concerned, it recognized the need to extend the agricultural reforms of 1992. The recommendations of 1997 were designed to continue the post-1992 trend of reducing price support to farmers (through the intervention buying system) and providing more money payments direct to producers. For example, in the cereals sector the intervention price would be set much closer to world levels (see Fig. 28.1) and compulsory set-aside would be set at zero. The beef market would also see a

Table 28.6 **CAP spending as proportion of the EU budget.**

	% of EU budget
1984	65.4
1988	65.0
1990	59.4
1992	53.3
1994	55.7
1996	50.4
1998	49.0

Note: Figures exclude EAGGF guidance.
Source: European Commission (1998) *European Economy* No. 65 and *Eurostat* (various).

decrease in its intervention price, though farmers would be compensated by a rise in direct income payments per head of beef cattle (headage payments). It was recommended that the quotas on milk production would continue to 2006 and support prices would be gradually reduced, though farmers would be given a new yearly payment per head of dairy cattle. The Commission calculated that these proposals would save 3.7bn ECU in market intervention expenditure by 2006, but that it would still have to spend 7.7bn ECU in direct income support to farmers, i.e. in so-called 'compensatory aid'.

The pressure for agricultural reform has come from many sides – such as consumers who worry that CAP encourages higher prices, ministers afraid of the spiralling budget costs of agricultural subsidies, policy makers aware of the need to shift resources from an EU farming community of 7 million in order to help the 18.5 million Europeans who are unemployed, and supporters of the Single Currency who accept the need to cut member states' budget deficits in order to meet the Maastricht criteria. Agricultural reform has also been accepted as necessary by supporters of EU enlargement who recognize that if price supports are not decreased, then the enlargement of the EU to include Eastern Europe will cause severe budgetary difficulties. This is because farm prices in the potential new entrants are already 20–40% below the EU level and would require extensive (and costly) support to be raised to the EU levels. Such increases in agricultural prices to EU levels could, of course, also cause financial hardship for the consumers in those lower-income countries, as well as giving a cost-push stimulus to inflation.

3. Structural policy   This is the term given to a combination of what used to be called the Regional and Social Policies (together with several other minor policy areas). For clarity we have separated these two central policy areas in the discussion which follows.

Regional policy   Like the UK's own regional policy, the objective of that for the EU as a whole is to attempt to ease regional economic differences (Chapter 21). Almost a quarter of the current EU budget is devoted to 'regional policy' as part of what are called the 'Structural Funds' (Social plus Regional plus other policies).

Regional policy attempts to improve the structural base of the EU's poorer regions against a background of inequality in income per head, ranging from around 30% of the EU average in some poor regions to over 200% in some rich regions. The disparities in regional income per head will clearly grow still wider should the countries of eastern Europe join. Of even greater concern were the findings of a study by Dunford (1994). This showed that, although the regions of the EU were converging up to 1976, they actually diverged in terms of incomes per head after that date, casting doubt as to the effectiveness of EU regional policy. As a part answer to this problem a Cohesion Fund was introduced in 1993 to help certain countries achieve the convergence criteria necessary for economic and monetary union. Four countries have benefited from the Fund because they have GDP per head of less than 90% of the Community average. They are Spain (75%), Ireland (68%), Portugal (56%) and Greece (47%). Some 13 bn ECU has been spent on this Cohesion Fund over the 1993–99 time period.

The accepted wisdom during the 1970s and 1980s was that a European *core* existed which was highly developed and very wealthy. The core consisted of the northern and western parts of Germany, Benelux, most of northern France, and south-east England. Outside the core the picture was of a less-developed *periphery*. It is now understood that the EU's pattern of economic well-being is more patchy and far more complex than the 'core and periphery' model.

To address the patchy nature of EU regional development, the EU decided in 1997 to introduce new guidelines by the year 2000 in order to reduce the proportion of the EU population eligible to receive regional aid, as a step towards reducing the total value of such aid to industry. Initially it will more carefully scrutinize the eligibility of regions for the Objective 1 status which provides maximum grants, i.e. where GDP per head in the region is less than 75% of the EU average. In the UK, for example, 1999 data showed that Cornwall, West Wales, Merseyside and South Yorkshire could be classified as Objective 1 regions, having GDP per head of around 70% of the EU average. The intention is to progressively tighten eligibility rules so that only the most disadvantaged regions will qualify for regional aid.

Social policy   The development of European social policy has involved both the operation of the European Social Fund (ESF) and developments in the 'Social Chapter' of the Maastricht Treaty.

The European Social Fund is designed to develop human resources and improve the workings of the labour market throughout the EU. Expenditure is concentrated in those regions of the EU which are suffering from high unemployment and is designed to help with retraining initiatives, improving skills and providing educational opportunities in order to make the labour force more flexible. In March 1998 the European Commission formally adopted a series of draft regulations which will form the backbone of the ESF's plans for the 2000–2006 period. At the centre of these plans is the new European Employment Strategy (EES) which stipulates that each member state must submit an annual employment plan directed towards raising 'employability, entrepreneurship, labour force adaptability and equal opportunities'. A sum of 210bn ECU has been allocated to achieving these goals by 2006.

As far as the 'Social Chapter' of the Maastricht Treaty is concerned, the UK had been opposed to many of the regulations and directives associated with the Social Chapter, with successive Conservative governments arguing that attempting to impose regulations in such areas as works councils, maternity/paternity rights, equal pay, part-time workers issues, etc. merely increased labour costs and decreased UK competitiveness. For example German social/labour market policies have been criticized for making labour too expensive to employ! We have already noted in Chapter 1 that Germany's labour productivity in manufacturing was 20% above that of the UK in the late 1990s, yet its Relative Unit Labour Costs were 64% higher than in the UK. Part of the problem results from the fact that Germany's labour costs have been inflated by non-wage costs (e.g. social benefits) which are 32% of total wage costs in Germany as compared to only 18% in the UK. Nevertheless the Labour government in the UK has adopted many parts of the Social Chapter in order to provide basic minimum standards across Europe even if this does result in some increase in labour costs. In any case, even if the UK had remained outside the Social Chapter it would still have been subject to a great deal of EU social legislation introduced as part of other programmes for which there is no UK 'opt-out'. The UK has recently adopted the Working Time Directive (1998) and the Parent Leave Directive (1999) in an attempt to catch up with other EU members who had already adopted these directives (see Chapter 15).

4. Trade policy and balance of payments

The EU is the largest trading bloc in the world. It accounts for 20% of world GDP and around 40% of world trade. The EU runs a deficit on its visible trade with the rest of the world, largely due to its need for substantial imports of fuel and raw materials. As regards invisible trade the EU is roughly in balance with the rest of the world. By the early 1990s, almost 60% of both EU exports and imports involved other EU countries. The growth of this intra-European trade has been a significant factor in attracting inward investment into the EU (see Chapter 7).

The UK's trade with the EU   The UK's trade with the EU has shown important changes since the late 1960s. First, the area composition of UK visible exports and imports indicates a strong movement towards the Community. In 1969, for example, 29% of total UK visible exports were destined for the EU, whilst 26% of UK visible imports came from the EU. By 1997 the shares had increased significantly, to 56 and 54% respectively (see Table 26.2). Second, as can be seen from Table 28.7, the UK's trade with the rest of the EU has shown little improvement in either trade in goods or services. It is clear that the slight improvement in goods trade during the late 1970s and early 1980s was due, in no small degree, to Britain's exports of North Sea oil. The reduction in the value of these exports following that period has had a marked effect on the overall good balance, which has moved into substantial deficit. With trade in services with the EU itself moving into deficit by the late 1980s, the overall current account (visible and invisible) deficit with the EU peaked at over £23.5bn in 1988 (at constant 1994 prices), before falling back as the more severe recession in the UK during the early 1990s curbed visible imports from the EU.

The nature of the EU, as a bloc which allows free trade in manufactured goods, has worked to the disadvantage of the relatively less efficient British manufacturers. Similarly, the fact that the EU still remains a relatively closed market with respect to both agricultural goods and invisibles (particularly the two areas of relative British strength – insurance and banking) has restricted the UK from taking advantage of the areas in which she has had a small comparative advantage.

There has been an improvement in some sectors of UK trade with the EU since the mid-1980s (see Table 28.7), but this has been narrowly based upon North Sea oil, car exports and food-related products and has not been sufficient to reverse a long-standing disadvantage for the UK in its EU trade in manufactures. Any disadvantage for the UK in its trade in manufactures is particularly worrying since exports and imports of manufactures together constitute some 66% of total trade with the EU whilst food, drink, tobacco and oil, together account for only 25%. A major study

Table 28.7   UK current account transactions with the EU 1974–97.

£(mn)	1974	1978	1982	1984	1986	1988	1990	1993	1997
Balances									
Trade in goods	−2,617	−2,835	−1,513	−3,724	−10,109	−15,736	−11,743	−5,423	−4,087
Trade in services	−389	67	−1,177	−1,049	−1,229	−2,672	−2,283	−1,295	−1,301
Trade in goods and services	−3,006	−2,768	−2,690	−4,773	−11,338	−18,408	−14,031	−6,718	−5,388
Investment income	483	751	4,089	4,477	3,092	1,511	−2,013	−4,493	1,135
Transfers	−69	−903	−586	−733	−586	−1,278	−2,349	−1,996	−1,818
Current account transactions	−2,592	−2,920	+813	−1,029	−8,832	−18,175	−18,393	−13,207	−6,071

Source: Adapted from ONS (1997) *UK Balance of Payments; Economic Trends* (1998) December.

(European Commission, 1997) points out that the UK is still at a competitive disadvantage in high price/high quality goods compared to its European competitors.

5. Monetary policy

A single currency permitting trade at 'known prices', has been a long-standing goal of the EU. Such a currency would overcome the uncertainties created by currency fluctuations which discourage medium- and long-term contracts and therefore international trade. A common currency and common exchange reserves, together with a European Central Bank, are the major features of European monetary union (EMU). The 'Snake', and later the European Monetary System (EMS), were seen by many as steps towards European monetary union.

While now thoroughly integrated into the move towards economic and monetary union, we deal in this section with the background to EMU in the form of the EMS and its precursors and the European Currency Unit (ECU). The discussion of EMU and the Euro is presented in a separate section below.

The 'Snake' 1973–79 Consultations between the 'Six' and the three applicant countries between 1970 and 1972, led in 1973 to the establishment of a currency co-operation system called variously the 'Snake', or the 'Snake in the Tunnel'. It required each central bank to maintain its currency within a band of ±2.25% against the US dollar, limiting the fluctuations that could occur between member country currencies. This had the advantage of reducing uncertainty but it did restrict the use of the exchange rate as a policy instrument for adjusting trade deficits and surpluses between members.

The oil crisis of 1973 and ensuing world recession created balance of payments problems for many member countries. Fluctuations in the balance of payments in turn led to more volatile exchange rates, making it more difficult to maintain par values within the narrow bands of the 'Snake'. As a result the UK remained a member for only a few months, with France also leaving the system in January 1974. Although the 'Snake' itself continued, it did so in a truncated form, with three members outside (UK, Eire and France) and four non-members inside (Norway, Sweden, Austria and Switzerland). In effect the 'Snake' now contained only currencies with a historically close link to the Deutschmark and it was replaced in the late 1970s by the EMS.

European Monetary System (EMS) since 1979 The EMS was created in order to increase co-operation on monetary affairs within the Community, and like the 'Snake', was founded on the ultimate goal of European Monetary Union (EMU). The EMS was established in March 1979 with three main components, a European currency unit (ECU), an exchange rate mechanism, and the European Monetary Co-operation Fund (EMCF). In 1989 a fourth element was added – the Very Short Term Financing facility (VSTF). This is a means of funding deficits between member states to an unlimited amount, but for very short periods of time.

The ECU was, possibly, the most radical of the EMS innovations. Whilst superficially similar to the old unit of account in which EU dealings used to be denominated, the ECU was far more than a *numéraire*. It was valued according to a weighted basket of all the EU currencies. Being a weighted average it was more

Table 28.8 The European currency unit (ECU).

Weighting of national currencies in the ECU (%)	
Deutschmark	31.58
French franc	20.10
Sterling	13.35
Dutch guilder	9.87
Belgian franc	3.30
Italian lira	7.77
Spanish peseta	4.10
Danish krone	2.62
Irish punt	1.09
Portuguese escudo	0.69
Greek drachma	0.42
Luxembourg franc	0.13

Source: Adapted from European Commission (1998) *Directorate of Economic and Financial Affairs.*
NB Sterling remained part of the structure of the ECU in spite of the currency's withdrawal from the ERM in 1992.

stable than the exchange rate of any single currency (see Table 28.8). In addition to its role as a unit of account, it functioned as an international reserve currency. Each member of the EMS 'bought' ECUs with 20% of their gold and dollar reserves, which were then held by a new EU institution called the European Monetary Co-operation Fund (FECOM according to its French initials). The central banks used their holdings of ECUs to buy each other's currencies and to settle debts. Of course, as of 1 January 1999, the ECU was replaced on a one-to-one basis by the euro (see Chapter 20).

The second element of the EMS involved the exchange rate mechanism which was, essentially, a development of the 'Snake'. Like its predecessor, the scheme originally set a 2.25% divergence limit, but this time not against the more volatile individual currencies but against the ECU. The new scheme also differed from the old in that it encompassed a formally recognized method of 'warning' governments that they have to take action. Each currency had a 'divergence limit'[4] computed against each of the other currencies in the scheme which, because it did not include the 'home' currency whose divergence against itself was zero, was always slightly less than the official 2.25% limit. If a currency diverged by more than 75% of this limit it had reached its 'divergence threshold' and the government was expected to intervene, either to buy its own currency for ECUs (if the exchange rate has declined) or to sell it for ECUs (if the exchange rate has risen).

The European Monetary Cooperation Fund, the third element in the EMS, consisted of all the heads of the central banks of the member states and was intended to supervise the use of the 'official ECU'. This was the currency unit originally established, and acted as a means of settling deficits between the members; it was supported by an IMF-type system of deposits of gold and foreign currency. It held the members' 20% deposits of gold and dollars, was empowered to lend up to 25bn ECUs to countries in difficulties, and was intended ultimately to become a central bank for Europe acting to support the ECU against the dollar, yen, etc.

Until mid-1987 the development of the ECU as a private currency was hampered by the refusal of the West Germans to recognize it. The ECU had been developing as a major international bond currency and, indeed, as a private European currency but the objections of the West Germans meant that it could not be truly 'European'. In June 1987, however, the West German government removed their veto on the private holding of ECUs by their citizens and thereby opened the way for further liberalization of capital movements within the Community. Up to 1999 the ECU was used throughout the EU as a basis for travellers' cheques and the Belgian government even issued 50 ECU gold and 5 ECU silver coins in 1987 to celebrate the thirtieth anniversary of the founding of the EC. After 1999, the ECU was superseded by the euro.

The UK and the EMS   The UK has always been a member of the EMS but, until late 1990, did not join its exchange rate system (known as the 'parity grid'). The UK government felt in 1978 that sterling would be too volatile to cope with the confines of the parity grid system. The UK anticipated a continual need to defend a weak pound within the grid, thereby putting pressure on its gold and foreign exchange reserves. The UK also held that the restricted variation in exchange rate against other member currencies would impede the use of the exchange rate as a policy instrument. Finally, by setting limits for sterling, the exchange rate could less readily be used for economic management in the UK, e.g. a high pound helping to curb inflation.

Up to 1987 there had been 11 re-alignments in the EMS parity grid. The West Germans felt that these readjustments were too frequent, allowing several countries to avoid the macroeconomic discipline originally intended by adopting the system. Ironically, having remained out of the parity grid due to fears of sterling's weakness, the UK government experienced for a period the exact opposite. At least until the end of 1982 the problem would have been that of having to keep sterling down within the grid rather than of establishing a 'floor' for sterling.

As indicated in Chapter 26, UK trade has become less sensitive to price factors and therefore less easily influenced by exchange rate adjustment. Further, a third of UK trade is still invoiced in the dollar or in other EMS currencies, reducing the importance of EMS currency fluctuations to the UK. For these reasons it has been suggested that the restrictions imposed on the *sterling exchange rate* by the EMS parity grid were, from the point of view of trade, less important to the UK than to other EU member countries. It would therefore seem that the restrictions imposed upon *UK demand management*, via the parity grid, proved the greater deterrent to full UK participation within the EMS. However, the arguments in favour of the UK joining the EMS parity grid became stronger as the EU became more important in UK trade, and as dollar-invoiced oil took a smaller share in UK exports. The problem, once the UK joined in 1990, became the ability of the system to cope with three major currencies, in view of the difficulties it had experienced in coping with two, namely, the Deutschmark (DM) and French franc.

Black Wednesday   The initial phase of UK membership of the EMS lasted less than two years before the Conservative government of John Major withdrew sterling on Wednesday, 16 September 1992 – 'Black Wednesday'.

Underlying the events which led to the withdrawal of sterling and the lira from the EMS in September 1992 were two phenomena: the weakness of the US economy and the resulting low interest rates in that country, and the large amounts of capital required by Germany for economic reconstruction in the eastern part of that country and the resulting high interest rates needed in Germany to reduce inflationary pressure. Finance flowed towards the DM and out of US dollars and sterling. The UK government made it worse by refusing to realign sterling in the ERM in early September and there followed two weeks of momentous pressure on European currencies and the ERM itself.

Downward pressure on the Italian lira forced the Italian government first to increase domestic interest rates twice – first to 15% (4 Sept) and then to 20% (8 Sept). Continued speculative selling of the lira then forced the Italians to negotiate the first realignment in the EMS since 1987 – a 7% devaluation of the lira against the other EMS currencies (13 Sept). Finally, a small reduction in German interest rates (by 0.25% on 14 September) was not enough to prevent the lira being withdrawn from the EMS on Black Wednesday.

Sterling followed a similar path to the lira but without the intermediate rises in interest rates. On 3 September the Chancellor announced that the UK was borrowing £7.25bn in foreign currency to assist in the defence of the pound. At the same time the government made it clear that they had no intention of allowing sterling to be deflected from its rate and band in the EMS. Both German and French central banks, the Bundesbank and the Bank of France, assisted the Bank of England in trying to defend sterling's central rate in the EMS.

By Wednesday 16 September, however, the financial markets had driven sterling below its 'floor' in the EMS and the British government took drastic measures to attempt to maintain sterling's position. Unprecedented rises in British interest rates – by 2% and then by another 3% (from 10% to 15%) – were announced during Wednesday 16 September but neither was sufficient to prevent sales of sterling from reducing its rate against the DM well below the EMS 'floor' of DM2.78. Sterling was withdrawn from the EMS system – along with the lira – and allowed to 'float'. Viewed against an EMS central rate of DM2.95 and a 'floor' of DM2.78, sterling quickly fell and continued falling. By October of 1992 it had reached DM2.36 – a devaluation of some 20% on its previous central rate in the EMS.

These events seemed to indicate that a fixed system of exchange rates could not stand against the sheer scale of currency movements in the new global financial markets. A number of factors might, however, have exacerbated the situation for the EMS in September 1992 which need not have been allowed to hold sway. In the absence of these factors it might have been that the system could have weathered the period in a more effective manner.

It might have been the case that the attempt – unofficially – to 'fix' the EMS currencies together as early as the late eighties and early nineties was just too early. No realignment had taken place since 1987 in spite of significant underlying economic changes in the economies of the member states (reunification in Germany, lower inflation and better industrial performance in France, high inflation and poor economic performance in Italy, and persistent recession and falling industrial production in the UK). Rather than relieving pressures and differentials gradually by occasional realignments, the EMS had resisted changes in parity for five years. At the same time unusually large divergencies had built up between the United States and German economies. Interest rates of 3% in the USA and 9% in Germany carried sufficient differential to create massive currency flows between the two and between Germany and other less-successful economies. Large amounts of money were required by the German economy to finance reconstruction and high interest rates were deemed to be required both to encourage this investment and to keep inflation in check. Political and financial uncertainties over the future of the Maastricht Treaty and, therefore, over the future of Economic and Monetary Union following the Danish rejection of the Treaty simply added to the problem.

The crisis in the EMS in September 1992 did not imply that such currency arrangements were impractical or irrelevant; only that the member states of the EU needed to gain more experience of their management. The key seems to lie in achieving the correct balance in the degree of 'fixity' of the rates in the system and in ensuring that 'divergence indicators' require both strong and weak currencies to take action. Concerns about the degree of 'fixity' were met in late 1992 by extending the ERM fluctuation bands to ±15%. This band continued in operation for the non-eurozone currencies after the major EMU reforms of 1999.

6. Commercial and industrial policy

The Common External Tariff (CET) is imposed on all industrial imports from non-EU countries, though with a few exceptions. Since tariffs on industrial products traded between member countries have been dismantled, the application of the CET has created a protected free trade area or 'customs union' of some 375 million consumers.

The effect of creating a customs union is, however, double-edged. 'Trade creation' is the term used to refer to the extra trade between members of the customs union as a result of removing tariff barriers. Production of certain goods is then transferred from high-cost to low-cost producers within the customs union. It can therefore be argued that trade creation causes resources *within* the customs union to be used more efficiently. However, 'trade diversion' also occurs as a result of the CET imposed against non-members of the customs union. This may cause some production to be transferred from low-cost producers *outside* the union to high-cost producers inside. We shall see below that the two effects are extremely difficult to quantify. However, in general terms, the higher the original tariff between member countries, and the higher the original tariff against non-members, the more likely it will be that the efficiency gains from trade creation will outweigh the efficiency losses from trade diversion.

A major study of trade in manufactured goods in France, Germany, Italy and the UK over the period 1985 to 1995 showed a strong 'trade-creation' effect from the creation of the Single Market but found little evidence of a 'trade diversion' effect (European Commission, 1996). For example while the share of the domestic demand in these countries met from other member states (i.e. *intra-EU trade*) rose from 16.9% to 21.5% between 1985 and 1995, the share of domestic demand met from outside the EU also increased from 12.7% to 15.6%. In other words, there was a strong trade creation effect (rise in intra-EU trade) and no evidence of a trade diversion effect (fall in *extra-EU trade*).

UK industry and the EU   It is extremely difficult to evaluate the industrial effects of UK entry into the EU. Certainly the hope on entry was that the UK would secure 'dynamic gains' in this sector to offset the expected 'static costs' of the net budget contribution and higher food prices. The 'dynamic gains' were expected to include a boost to output and productivity from a large, protected market, with its potential for scale economies and greater export opportunities. However, for whatever reason, there seems little evidence in Table 28.9 of those gains in UK manufacturing output

Table 28.9 Comparisons
of manufacturing output
(1970 = 100).

	1970	1975	1980	1985	1992	1997
EU (excluding UK)	100	108	133	133	154	175
Germany	100	104	122	122	138	141
France	100	108	133	133	157	167
Italy	100	107	139	132	160	174
UK	100	102	110	113	128	144

Source: Adapted from OECD (1998) *National Indicators* (and previous issues).

anticipated after entry into the EU in 1973. In fact, the real output of UK manufacturing has grown more slowly than that of the other EU countries.

In fact Lord Kaldor suggested, prior to entry, that the alleged 'dynamic gains' might turn out to be 'dynamic costs', as the UK market in industrial products became more exposed to its European competitors with the dismantling of tariffs. It may be that the UK joined the wrong type of 'customs union'! If trade in agriculture and in service activities were freed between member countries, rather than trade in industrial products, then some of the alleged 'dynamic gains' might indeed have materialized. In Chapter 1 we noted that the trend towards service activities, though a feature of all advanced economies, has been most marked in the UK. It is arguable that it is in this sector that the UK's comparative advantages lie. The present industrial policy of the EU, which frees trade in industrial products whilst permitting (along with GATT) the protection of services, would seem to be to the particular disadvantage of the UK.

Monetary union

European Economic and Monetary Union (EMU)

As long ago as 1969 the Commission funded the 'Werner Report' which acknowledged what it called the 'political wish to establish economic and monetary union' and set a target of completion by 1980. Unfortunately the severe economic traumas of the 1970s intervened and it was 1979 before even the first stage – the setting up of the European Monetary System (EMS) – was accomplished.

In 1988 the Council decided to look into the matter again and set up a Committee under the then EC President, Jacques Delors. That Committee reported in June 1989 and the Council agreed to enter into Stage 1 on 1 July 1990.

The first stage of the Delors Plan – the establishment of a true Single European Market (SEM) – had, of course, already been put in train by the Single European Act of 1987. As the fundamental base of the EMU structure, the Commission felt that it was necessary to set out clearly what the economic benefits would be. They therefore commissioned a group of senior economists, financiers and business people to investigate the issues. The Committee under the chairmanship of Paulo Ceccini reported in 1988.

The Ceccini Report   Although published as a single report, the 'Ceccini Report' is simply the summary and conclusions of no less than 13 separate economic reports on aspects of the single market. It identifies two types of cost associated with what it calls, in shorthand, 'non-Europe'; i.e. a Europe of markets separated by physical, technical and fiscal barriers:

- first are those barriers which have an immediate benefit when they are removed;
- second are those which will have benefits spread over a period of time.

It should be noted that both types include elements of both static and dynamic benefits.

The parts which made up the 'Ceccini Report' examined the single market from the point of view of micro-economic benefits (the removal of non-tariff barriers, economies of scale, X-efficiencies, etc.) and of macro-economic benefits (the supply-side shock and its effects on GDP, inflation rates, employment, production, etc.).

Using a variety of methods, the Report came up with significant benefits which might accrue to EU members as a result of the single market. These included the following:

- total gains of around ECU 216bn at 1988 prices (between 4.3% and 6.4% of EU GDP)
- price deflation of an average 6.1%
- an improvement to the EU's external trade of about 1%
- an improvement to budget balances of about 2.2%
- around 1.8m new jobs (a reduction in unemployment of about 1.5%).

The Maastricht agreement set out a planned system for moving towards EMU, including the creation of a system of European central banks to precede the European Central Bank. The full schedule has been delineated in three 'Stages':

Stage 1   Theoretically this commenced on 1 January 1993 and involves the creation of an EU 'Monetary Committee' whose role includes general monitoring and review of monetary matters in EU states and throughout the EU as a whole, providing advice to the Council of Ministers and contributing to the preparation for the European System of Central Banks (ESCB) and the European Central Bank (ECB) (see below).

Stage 2   In theory this Stage was to commence on 1 January 1994 with the establishment of a new 'European Monetary Institute' to strengthen cooperation between EU central banks, coordinate monetary policy, monitor the functioning of the EMS and take over the role of the European Monetary Cooperation Fund (EMCF). The EMI will seek to obtain a 'high degree of sustainable convergence' against four criteria:

1. Price stability: This should be close to the performance of the three best performing members. In a protocol to the treaty 'close to' was defined as not more than 1.5% above the average inflation of the three best performers;
2. Government finance: This should adhere to a pre-ordained 'reference value' – defined as a government deficit of no more than 3% of GDP at market prices and a government debt of no more than 60% of GDP at market prices;
3. ERM fluctuations: Normal margins of fluctuation should not have been breached for *two years*;
4. Durability of convergence: This is to be measured by long-term interest rate levels. The rate for long-term government bonds should not have exceeded by more than 2% those of the three best performing countries.

The Maastricht Treaty required that the EMI should specify – by 31 December 1996 at the latest – the regulatory, organizational and logistical framework for the

ESCB (to be created in the third stage). It should also set a date for the beginning of the Third Stage. If this date is not set before the end of 1997 it will, according to the Treaty, automatically begin on 1 January 1999.

Stage 3   The establishment of the European System of Central Banks (ESCB) which would hold and manage the official reserves of all the member states. At this stage exchange rates would be fixed and the ECU would acquire full status as a currency throughout the Community. The ESCB will prepare for the establishment of the European Central Bank (ECB) which, when founded, will have the exclusive right to issue banknotes throughout the EU. It will accomplish this through the central bank of each of the member states. It would receive some 5bn ECU together with all members' reserves – excepting only member states' foreign currency, ECU holdings, IMF reserve positions and SDRs. Any reserves over 50bn ECU in value would also be left with the member country (in theory, of course, these would not be required and could be used in any way by the member state). The theoretical total reserves to be held by the ESCB would, therefore, be around 600bn ECU.

Maastricht established the shape and format of all of the institutions it envisaged. The Treaty provided for it to come into force on 1 January 1993 or on the date on which the last member country deposited an instrument of ratification with the Commission.

There were a number of protocols to the Maastricht Treaty involving most of the members. The UK had a lengthy protocol agreed which allowed it not to proceed to Stage 3 if it did not wish to and excluded it from most of the Stage 2 arrangements (in return the UK is not allowed to have a vote in Council on arrangements to do with the ESCB or the ECB).

The path to EMU seems now to have settled down into the following timetable:

1996-98	All member countries are to attempt to bring their economies into line to meet the Maastricht criteria (see Table 28.10).
1998	The countries which will form the first members of EMU will be selected.
1999	January 1 – the EMU process began with the launch of the Euro and the beginning of the transition phase (through to the end of 2001). During this phase national currencies will still exist but will be irrevocably fixed to each other and to the Euro.
2002	January 1 – the Euro will be introduced in coin and note form. A period of six months is to be allowed for national currencies to be withdrawn from circulation. On 1 July 2002 only the Euro will be legal tender in EMU member countries.

Convergence   In March 1998 the European Commission announced that eleven members had reached a sufficient degree of sustainable convergence as measured against the Maastricht Treaty criteria. The relevant criteria were (1) consumer price inflation must not exceed that of the three best-performing countries by more than $1\frac{1}{2}$ percentage points; (2) interest rates on long-term government securities must not be more than 2 percentage points higher than those in the same three member states; (3) the financial position must be sustainable. In particular, the general government deficit should be at or below the reference value of 3% of GDP. If not, it should have

Table 28.10   Performance of the member states in relation to convergence (1998).

	Inflation	Government budgetary position						Exchange rates	Long-term interest rates
	HICP (%)	Existence of an excessive deficit	Deficit (% of GDP)[1]	Debt (% of GDP)				ERM participation	
					Change from previous year				
	January 1998	1997	1997	1997	1996	1995		March 1998	January 1998
Reference value	2.7%		3%	60%					7.8%
Belgium	1.4	yes[2]	2.1	122.2	−4.7	−4.3	−2.2	yes	5.7
Denmark	1.9	no	−0.7	65.1	−5.5	−2.7	−4.9	yes	6.2
Germany	1.4	yes[2]	2.7	61.3	0.8	2.4	7.8	yes	5.6
Greece	5.2	yes	4.0	108.7	−2.9	1.5	0.7	yes	9.8
Spain	1.8	yes[2]	2.6	68.8	−1.3	4.6	2.9	yes	6.3
France	1.2	yes[2]	3.0	58.0	2.4	2.9	4.2	yes	5.5
Ireland	1.2	no	−0.9	66.3	−6.4	−9.6	−6.8	yes	6.2
Italy	1.8	yes[2]	2.7	121.6	−2.4	−0.2	−0.7	yes	6.7
Luxembourg	1.4	no	−1.7	6.7	0.1	0.7	0.2	yes	5.6
Netherlands	1.8	no	1.4	72.1	−5.0	−1.9	1.2	yes	5.5
Austria	1.1	yes[2]	2.5	66.1	−3.4	0.3	3.8	yes	5.6
Portugal	1.8	yes[2]	2.5	62.0	−3.0	−0.9	2.1	yes	6.2
Finland	1.3	no	0.9	55.8	−1.8	−0.4	−1.5	yes	5.9
Sweden	1.9	yes[2]	0.8	76.6	−0.1	−0.9	−1.4	no	6.5
UK	1.8	yes[2]	1.9	53.4	−1.3	0.8	3.5	no	7.0
EU	1.6		2.4	72.1	−0.9	2.0	3.0		6.1

[1] A negative sign for the government deficit indicates a surplus.
[2] The Commission recommended abrogation.
Source: European Commission (1998) Convergence Report (1998), *European Economy*, No. 65 (modified).

declined substantially and continuously and reached a level close to the reference value, or the excess over the reference value should be temporary and exceptional. The gross debt of general government should be at or below 60% of GDP or, if not, the debt ratio should be sufficiently diminishing and approaching the 60% reference value at a satisfactory pace. The exchange rate criterion is that the currency must have been held within the normal fluctuation margins of the ERM for two years without a realignment at the initiative of the member state in question. Table 28.10 indicates the degree of economic convergence that had been achieved in the EU by early 1998. Based on these figures it was agreed that eleven members of the EU had reached a sufficient degree of sustainable convergence against the criteria laid down in the Maastricht Treaty.

The countries which qualified and wished to join the single currency in January 1999 were Austria, Belgium, Finland, France, Germany, Ireland, Italy, Luxembourg, the Netherlands, Portugal and Spain. Sweden and Greece did not meet the convergence criteria at that time and the UK and Denmark had already decided not to take part in Stage Three of EMU in 1999.

Substantial progress had been made towards price stability and although some of the countries had not met the government debt criterion, they were 'abrogated' (i.e. allowed) to join the EMU because the debt ratios were deemed to have been brought down significantly from the high levels reached in the recession of 1993. The ERM seemed to have resulted in most countries meeting the exchange rate criterion with their currencies clustered close to their ERM target rate. Finally, long-term interest rates had generally fallen and differentials had narrowed, with the exception of Greece.

Single currency   **The euro**   The launch of the single currency, the 'euro', occurred on 1 January 1999, although it will not become a physical currency until 1 January 2002 (see also Chapter 20). However, from 1999 onwards the euro has become a legal currency in its own right and the vehicle for electronic and business-to-business transactions throughout the euro-zone. As early as January 1999 some 25% of Barclays Bank customers had already been asked to invoice or pay in euros.

The long-term effects of the euro, and with it EMU, will be to change the nature of the way business is carried out in Europe. For consumers, prices will be more 'transparent', making it easier to see whether different prices are being charged for the same product in various EU countries. For manufacturers and other traders, the introduction of EMU means the elimination of exchange rate risks, which should benefit smaller businesses which often lack the resources for foreign exchange management.

The EMU might also produce further corporate rationalization as firms merge in an attempt to grow larger in order to derive scale economies from operating within the single market. The foreign exchange market will be restricted in its dealings as fewer currencies are traded, with most dealings being in currencies outside the euro, together with euro-dollar or euro-yen. It is likely that a new market for government debt denominated in euros and a new pool of euro-denominated equity will be created.

For the potential benefits of the euro and EMU to be realized in the long run, three factors will be decisive.

- *Sustainable economic convergence*. For the smooth working of the euro, the economies of the participating countries must be in the same stage of the economic cycle and be relatively homogeneous.
- *Strong political commitments to EMU discipline*. The European Council of Economic and Financial Ministers (ECOFIN), consisting of the finance ministers of the EU, will be able to impose severe fines on member states whose budget deficits exceed the ratio of 3% of GDP. The fines could reach as much as 0.5% of GDP.
- *Credible European Central Bank* (ECB). The ECB's independence is enshrined in the Maastricht treaty, as is its commitment to price stability. Short-term interest rates are to be set with a view to achieving such price stability. However, political pressure for reflationary policies might arise if the EU experiences slow growth and high unemployment.

The question also remains as to how the national central banks will operate under EMU. Together with the ECB, the national central banks formed the European System of Central Banks (ESCB) in June 1998. This body, through its Governing Council and Executive Board, will define and implement monetary policy and foreign exchange and reserves policies. However, the operational responsibility to carry out agreed ESCB policy will be retained by the national central banks. As with the federal central banking systems of the US and Germany, the operations of the ESCB will therefore be highly decentralized. There is a risk that the national central banks may try to pressurize the independent ECB to adopt policies directed towards growth and employment in situations where the ECB might be more inclined to tighten control of inflation.

Enlargement

The economic objectives of the original EEC were centred on the creation of prosperity and growth through the creation of a 'customs union' involving both reduction in tariff barriers and the establishment of common external tariffs between the union countries and the rest of the world.

During the course of its history the EU has encouraged greater liberalization in trade (particularly in industrial goods) through a series of separate – usually bilateral – agreements with third countries. These 'association' agreements usually allowed their signatories preferential – 'Most Favoured Nation' – status with respect to EU tariff requirements while encouraging them to reduce their own tariff barriers. A number of countries with association agreements with the EU are currently seeking (or have indicated their intention to seek) full membership of the Community.

There is now a queue of twelve countries waiting to join the EU of which the majority is formed by the ex-Communist states of what used to be called the Eastern Bloc. Alongside the 'Mediterranean applicants' of Malta, Turkey and Cyprus, Poland, Hungary, the Czech Republic, Estonia, Latvia, Lithuania, Slovakia, Slovenia, Bulgaria and Romania have applied to join the EU and wish to do so at the earliest possible opportunity. The ten applicants from Eastern Europe have a combined GNP which is less than that of the Netherlands. The Commission believes that 2002 will be the earliest date on which the first of these applicants will be able to join. The first tranche is likely to consist of the Czech Republic, Hungary and Poland.

Under the Agenda 2000 programme initiated in 1997, it has been estimated that the budgetary position of the EU countries will deteriorate by around 0.15% of their GNP by 2006 as a result of enlargement. Consumers in these countries will have to adapt to the higher prices of the CAP, which might stimulate wage-push inflation. These economies will also face adjustment costs of improving their environmental standards in line with existing EU requirements. Such enlargement could also require redistribution of the EU budget to the detriment of poorer EU countries within the *existing* membership as well as the richer ones.

Opting out?

For the UK there are both advantages and disadvantages of making use of the 'opt-outs' which it negotiated at the Maastricht conference. The advantages lie mostly in the fact that it would leave the bulk of monetary policy firmly in the hands of the UK government, thereby making it possible to use the exchange rate as a policy instrument independently of other EU countries and without 'interference' from Brussels. In most respects this translates fairly clearly, into the ability to devalue in order to remain competitive (but, in so doing, probably to slip even further down the prosperity rankings).

The disadvantages stem from the opposite argument – that the UK needs external discipline over its exchange rate and monetary policy in order to ensure that difficult decisions are not fudged. Quite apart from the 'economic' arguments against opting out of EMU there is also the possibility that other member states might 'informally' discriminate against the UK and its products. There is a strong argument that remaining outside EMU would damage our financial services trade (the one area in which we claim – probably erroneously – to have a strong competitive advantage).

Non-EU companies might not regard the UK as such a good bet as far as inward investment is concerned if we did not have direct access to the single most important currency on the continent. If the effect of staying outside EMU was to create fear in financial markets (on the basis that UK policy outside EMU might result in higher inflation or continuing rounds of devaluation) then long-term interest rates may well be higher than on the continent. This would tend to deter inward investment and increase costs for UK businesses.

Conclusion

The purely economic effects of British membership of the European Union are extremely difficult to isolate and describe. It is increasingly irrelevant to speak of economic models of what Britain's experience might have been if we had not joined the EEC twenty-five years ago.

The economic debate has centred around two different 'models':

1. Britain as a permanent and irrevocable member of the EU; and,
2. Britain outside the EU – the 'non-Europe' model.

The viability of any economic argument which describes Britain outside the EC has become more and more suspect as the financial, economic and business environments have become intermeshed over the last two decades. There is little doubt that the UK has experienced a continuing budget deficit with respect to the EU, that its consumers may have suffered a slight welfare loss with respect to food and the policies of the CAP, and that there has been an observable displacement of UK manufactured goods in our own domestic market.

Alongside these factors one must recognize the interdependence of the member states in almost every commercial and economic area. The EU represents the UK's most important trading partner by far in both visible and invisible trade. Membership of the Community has also been responsible for significant amounts of inward investment from Japan and the US into the UK. Ironically this inward investment has been so large that the UK is becoming a major exporter of motor vehicles and electronic equipment, developing trade surpluses with the EU in these categories. In a similar fashion London's place as one of the pre-eminent financial centres in the world rests strongly on its position as the financial centre in which US, EU and Japanese banks and investment houses come together. Where portfolio investment is concerned the EU has become much more important to the UK (see Chapters 7 and 21).

The UK's experience in the European Monetary System has been fraught with problems but it is clear that a number of those problems were of the UK's own devising. International freedom in financial markets means that – even outside the EMS – the UK has had to ensure that sterling 'shadowed' the DM.

However, a further question has to ask why the benefits to the UK have been less than those which have accrued to other members. The UK has not gained massive benefits from Social and Regional funds and has a relatively efficient agricultural sector. There have been little or no net real benefits from the CAP and we have suffered from having a relatively inefficient manufacturing sector which has been only modestly successful in exporting to Europe. The UK has not, therefore, gained proportional benefits from the free-trade area. Outside the EU, however, we would still have had to survive, had to manage our own agriculture, and had to find markets for our exports in a world in which the ties of the Commonwealth and EFTA would almost certainly have counted for less and less as the years went by.

<table>
<tr><td>

Key points

</td><td>

- There are now 15 member states within the EU, with Austria, Sweden and Finland being the most recent additions.
- The EU is essentially a regional trading bloc with currently 373 million people within a protected free trade area, with a high per capita income of almost 20,000 ECU (euro) per annum.
- The EU is the largest trading bloc in the world. It accounts for 20% of world GDP and around 40% of world trade.
- Since 1992, the EU has established the European Economic Area which includes 19 countries altogether.
- Agriculture is the most regulated sector within the EU. Around 50% of the entire EU budget is spent on various price support and intervention policies involving agricultural products.
- The Regional and Social Funds are being targeted at poorer regions *within* each member state in order to relieve unemployment and poverty.
- The Social Chapter includes a number of 'directives' establishing minimum working conditions. The UK has an 'opt out', but the incoming Labour government sees many of the provisions of the Social Chapter as consistent with its policy objectives.
- The Maastricht Treaty in 1992 sought to widen the scope of the EU beyond a common market (see Chapter 27) to that of an economic and monetary union (EMU).
- Various 'convergence criteria' needed to be fulfilled before countries could join EMU, which began on 1 January 1999.
- These convergence criteria included consumer price inflation within $1\frac{1}{2}$%, and long-term interest rates within 2% of the average achieved by the 'best 3' EU countries. In addition the PSBR must be no higher than 3% of GDP and total public debt no more than 60% of GDP.
- EMU has a European Central Bank, a single currency (the euro) and a 'Stability Council' acting to monitor country compliance with the various criteria. Non-compliance can result in fines for the states in question.

</td></tr>
</table>

Notes

1. See, for instance, Lewis (1993).
2. The European Economic Area comprised the (then) 12 members of the EU plus Iceland, Norway, Sweden, Finland, Switzerland, Austria and Lichtenstein, though in 1995 Sweden, Austria and Finland joined the EU.
3. The 'co-responsibility' levy is a method by which farmers are penalized for over-production of agricultural products. Up to a certain level of production the farmer is entitled to sell his goods either on the open market, or to the EU's Intervention stocks. Above that, agreed, level of production the price allowed to the farmer will be reduced by a specific percentage called the 'co-responsibility' levy.
4. The divergence limit for any currency is calculated by the formula ± 2.25 $(1 - w)$ where w is the percentage weight of the currency in the ECU. For Germany this results in a limit of $2.25 (1 - 0.301) = 1.57\%$.

References and further reading

Ackrill, R. (1997) *Economic and Monetary Union, Developments in Economics*, Vol. 13, Causeway Press.

Barnes, Ian and **Barnes, Pamela** (1995) *The Enlarged European Union*, 2nd edn, Longman.

Barras, R. and **Madhavan, S.** (1996) *European Economic Integration and Sustainable Development*, McGraw-Hill.

Brittan, L. (1994) *Europe – The Europe We Need*, Hamish Hamilton.

De Grauwe, P. (1994) *The Economics of Monetary Integration*, OUP.

Dunford, M. (1994) Winners and losers: the new map of economic inequality in the European Union, *European Urban and Regional Studies*.

European Commission (1996) Economic evaluation of the internal market, *European Economy*, **4**.

European Commission (1997) Trade patterns inside the single market, *The Single Market Review*, Subseries IV, Vol. 2, Kogan Page, Earthscan.

European Commission (1998) Financing the European Union, 7 October.

Goodman, S. (1992) Agricultural policy, in Griffiths, A., *European Community Survey*, Longman.

Griffiths, A. (1992) *European Community Survey*, Longman.

Howe, K. (1992) The European Agricultural Industry, in D. Dyker (ed.) *The European Economy*, Longman.

Johnson, C. (1996) *In with the Euro, out with the Pound*, Penguin.

Kenen, P. (1995) *Economic and Monetary Union in Europe*, CUP.

Lewis, D. W. P. (1993) *The Road to Europe: History, Institutions and Prospects of European Integration 1945–1993*, Peter Lang.

McDonald, F. and **Dearden, S** (eds) (1998) *European Economic Integration*, 3rd edn, Addison Wesley Longman.

Wistrich, E. (1994) *The United States of Europe*, Routledge.

Wolf, M. (1996) Thinking the unthinkable, *Financial Times*, 18 June 1996.

Chapter 29

Transition economies

The process of economic transformation from central planning to a market economy in Eastern Europe has been neither smooth nor uniform. States in the vanguard of reform like Poland, the Czech Republic and Hungary quickly succeeded in creating thriving, dynamic private sectors, which are generating new jobs and contributing to economic recovery; together with Estonia and Slovenia, this group are on the verge of entry to the European Union. In contrast, in the twelve states of the former Soviet Union that now comprise the Commonwealth of Independent States (CIS) the slump in economic activity has been much more prolonged and earlier signs of recovery in 1997 are now overshadowed by fears that the so-called 'Asian crisis' will spread recession to the region. This chapter assesses the progress of the former centrally planned countries in their struggle to construct modern, competitive market economies. After a brief review of the size and economic structure of the twenty-eight 'transition economies', the chapter outlines the basic operation of centrally planned economies, highlighting the scale of the structural changes entailed by 'marketization'. It then documents the early phase of the transition process, in which all the transition economies have experienced a slump in output and hyperinflation following the breakdown of central planning and the liberalization of prices. The chapter then considers the main macroeconomic challenges involved in restoring stability to these economies together with the microeconomic (or 'supply-side') challenges of privatization, market liberalization and legal reform. It finally assesses the progress made over the ten years since the process began in 1989 and considers the outlook for the transition economies.

Central and Eastern Europe versus the Commonwealth of Independent States

The term 'communist bloc' was formerly used in the West to describe the countries that constituted the Soviet sphere of influence, implying a high degree of homogeneity between the twenty–eight independent states that have subsequently emerged. In reality these states vary considerably, in terms of living standards (as measured by, for example, per capita GDP), economic structure, population size, history, religion and culture.

Table 29.1   An overview of the transition economies.

	Population, millions (1997)	Per capita GDP, $PPP (1997)	Agriculture as % GDP (1997)	Industry as % GDP (1997)	Unemployment (%) (1997)
CEE countries					
Albania	3.2	708	55.9**	11.5**	13.9**
Bulgaria	8.3	1,239	11.4*	31.6*	13.7
Croatia	4.8	3,851	9.2*	20.3*	16.8
Czech Republic	10.3	5,052	5.1	34.9	5.2
Estonia	1.5	3,203	6.4*	18.9*	5.4
FYR Macedonia	2.1	1,494	17.8**	39.3**	30.0
Hungary	10.1	4,442	7.2**	23.5**	10.4
Latvia	2.5	2,181	9.1*	27.8*	6.7
Lithuania	3.7	2,473	11.4*	28.3*	5.9
Poland	38.7	3,467	6.0*	27.1*	10.5
Romania	22.6	1,521	20.7	34.5	7.0
Slovak Republic	5.4	3,540	5.7*	28.9*	11.5
Slovenia	2.0	8,995	3.8	27.1	14.4
CIS countries					
Armenia	3.7	428	38.3*	23.8*	9.3*
Azerbaijan	7.6	541	30.0*	23.0*	20.0*
Belarus	10.2	1,307	15.0	37.4	2.3
Georgia	5.4	969	32.6*	14.2*	n/a
Kazakhstan	15.7	1,343	9.2	20.2	4.2
Kyrgystan	4.6	356	46.6*	11.9*	3.2
Moldova	4.3	497	49.0**	25.0*	1.6
Russia	147.2	3,218	8.6*	39.3*	9.0
Tajikistan	6.0	177*	27.6	19.5	2.9
Turkmenistan	4.7	376	17.5*	50.0*	n/a
Ukraine	50.9	976	6.0	34.0	2.3
Uzbekistan	23.6	391*	27.5	16.3	0.5

* = 1996 figure; ** = 1995 figure.
Source: Adapted from EBRD (1998).

Table 29.1 gives some idea of the differences between the transition economies.[1] It shows the contrast in size, from Russia with a population of 147 million to Estonia with 1.5 million. It highlights the vast gulf in relative living standards, from Slovenia with a per capita income (calculated in terms of purchasing power parity) of $8,995 to Tajikistan with just $177. The importance of agriculture ranges from as little as 4–7% of GDP in Slovenia, the Czech and Slovak Republics, Hungary, Ukraine and Poland, to almost 50% in Moldova and 56% in Albania.

Table 29.1 also shows that, despite the differences between individual states, it is possible to draw a broad distinction between the Central and Eastern European (CEE) states, here defined to include the three Baltic states of the former Soviet Union and a further ten states in this geographical area, and the twelve states of the Commonwealth of Independent States (CIS). Taken as a group, the CEE states have a generally higher per capita GDP, a lesser reliance on agriculture and, reflecting the labour shedding which is an inevitable consequence of enterprise restructuring, much higher rates of unemployment.

The operation of the command economy

Despite the differences between the CEE and the CIS states, both groups started the transition process with an all pervasive central planning system, often termed a 'command economy'. The command economy dominated every aspect of life, telling factories where to buy their inputs, how much to pay their workers, how much to produce and where to sell their output; individuals were trained in specialist schools and universities and directed to work at specific factories, which provided their wages, houses, health care – even holidays in enterprise-owned hotels and sanatoria; the national bank was told how much to lend to which factories and how much cash to print to pay wages.

As a theoretical concept, central planning was very elegant. Using 'input–output' analysis (a planning framework which calculated the inputs required for each factory in order for it to deliver its planned outputs to the next stage in the production process), the planning ministry could calculate precisely how much labour, capital and raw materials each enterprise required to achieve its production targets. The various production targets for raw materials and intermediate and final products all fitted together to ensure a perfectly balanced expansion of the economy. Input and output prices were carefully set to ensure that all firms could pay their wage bills and repay loans from the national bank, while at the same time pricing consumer goods to encourage consumption of socially desirable goods (e.g. books, ballet, theatre, public transport, etc.) and discourage consumption of politically unfavoured goods (e.g. international telephone calls, cars, luxury goods).

The overall national plan was thus internally consistent. If each of the enterprises achieved its production targets, there could not be, by definition, shortages or bottlenecks in the economy. There would be full employment, with everyone working in an enterprise for which he/she had been specifically trained at school and university. The total wage bill for the economy, which was paid in cash, would be sufficient to buy all the consumer goods produced. There would be zero inflation and all the country's citizens would have access to housing, education and health care.

While the socialist nirvana of full employment and universal social security has been tarnished by the demonstrable failure of the command economy to deliver its promises in practice, it is important not to understate its emotional appeal. Market capitalism is plagued by social injustice. Large income inequalities, poverty, homelessness and mass unemployment are all characteristics of the advanced western economies. During the 'Great Depression' of the 1930s, for example, many western intellectuals readily embraced the principles of socialist planning as a way to end the misery of unemployment. Indeed, for some thirty years after the war, many western and developing countries used forms of national planning to support their growth policies, the latter group with the active encouragement of the World Bank. Japan and France, for example, both had well-developed national planning systems and, for a period during the 1960s, both Conservative and Labour governments tried to copy the French system in an effort to emulate that country's economic success.

Central planning ultimately failed, both in the west and, over a much longer period, in Eastern Europe. Much has been written about the deficiencies of central planning. Clearly, there are serious practical difficulties in implementing national plans. There are also fundamental, largely inherent contradictions. The Soviet model of central planning provided little incentive for either managers or workers to work harder or to innovate. The politicization of the whole economic system, with promotion at work based on service to the Communist Party rather than on-the-job performance, encouraged passivity and strongly discouraged risk-taking and individualism – the bedrocks of innovation and technological advance.

While central planning succeeded in turning Tsarist Russia from a feudal agricultural society into an industrial power, it became increasingly unwieldy after World War II. Internally, as economies developed, the complexity of the coordination problem grew explosively, as consumers demanded more choice and better quality. With innovation discouraged and the central planners being encouraged to set unrealistic targets for political reasons, productivity growth slowed and official statistics for production became ever more cosmetic. Absenteeism at work and false reporting of output became commonplace. Shortages of consumer goods emerged and, with people unable to buy goods with their wages, households' deposits with the national savings bank piled up. This state of affairs was summed up in the Soviet joke, 'the factories pretend to pay us and we pretend to work'. Meanwhile, in the west, scientific progress spawned a vast array of cost-saving technologies in the areas of transport, telecommunications, manufacturing and information handling, so that, relatively, the communist countries fell behind faster and faster.

Overlaid on the declining capacity of central planning to achieve its goals and promote technological advance was the geopolitical battle between the Soviet Union and the United States known as the 'cold war'. In the 'arms race' of the 1970s and early 1980s, the Soviet Union was increasingly unable to match the United Sates. With only 5% of GDP devoted to military expenditure, the United States was able to field a technologically advanced military force. Sluggish economic growth and an inadequate technological base meant that the Soviet Union was forced to divert an ever greater proportion of GDP to military spending. Estimates for the share of GDP absorbed by the military–industrial complex in the 1980s range from 20% to 40%. Attempts in the late 1980s to restructure the planning system ('perestroike') and liberalise the political system ('glasnost') paradoxically had the reverse of the effect intended, causing the whole economic and political system to unravel. Suddenly released from the threat of Soviet invasion, the CEE states opted for independence and market capitalism in 1989, quickly followed by the fifteen Soviet republics in 1991. By 1991, the integrated, centrally planned bloc that had comprised the Soviet Union and seven CEE countries had collapsed, splintering into twenty-eight independent countries[2] bent on constructing functioning market economies.

The road from Marx to the market

The decades of central planning meant that the transition economies began the reform process without functioning markets for labour, goods or capital. All three had been allocated by the central planner, in accordance with an internally coherent economic plan. Because all the means of production had been in state hands, there was, moreover, no legislative framework for the enforcement of property rights, the valuation and disposal of assets or the liquidation of unprofitable enterprises. Nor in a system of directed labour was there any official unemployment and, hence, no need for a social security system. As noted above, social welfare was provided by enterprises, with the central planners setting their aggregate employment equal to the size of the labour force, with services like education, health care and housing being provided by the enterprises to their employees. Banks in the central planning system were bookkeeping operations, allocating credit according to the demands of the plan rather than on the basis of objective risk assessments, and capital markets were non-existent. The challenge for the transition states at the end of the 1980s was to build a modern market economy on these foundations.

Table 29.2   Recession and recovery in transition economies (% annual change in GDP).

	1991	1992	1993	1994	1995	1996	1997	1998	1998 (1989 = 100)
CEE countries									
Albania	−28	−10	11	9	9	9	−8	12	89
Bulgaria	−12	−7	−2	2	3	−11	−7	3	64
Croatia	−20	−10	−4	1	2	4	6	6	77
Czech Republic	−14	−6	−1	3	5	4	1	2	100
Estonia	−11	−14	−9	−3	3	4	10	6	82
FYR Macedonia	−12	−21	−8	−4	−2	1	1	5	58
Hungary	−12	−3	−1	3	2	1	4	5	94
Latvia	−8	−35	−16	1	−2	3	6	6	59
Lithuania	−13	−38	−24	1	3	5	6	6	45
Poland	−7	3	4	5	7	6	7	6	118
Romania	−13	−9	1	4	7	4	−7	−2	81
Slovak Republic	−15	−7	−4	5	7	7	7	4	99
Slovenia	−8	−5	1	5	4	3	3	4	102
All CEE*	−11	4	1	4	5	4	4	4	99
CIS countries									
Armenia	−11	−52	−15	5	7	6	3	6	40
Azerbaijan	−1	−23	−23	−21	−8	1	5	7	43
Belarus	−1	−10	−11	−12	−10	3	10	2	72
Georgia	−14	−40	−39	−35	2	10	10	10	35
Kazakhstan	−13	−13	−12	−25	−9	1	2	3	60
Kyrgystan	−5	−19	−16	−27	1	6	10	6	62
Moldova	−18	−29	−1	−31	−3	−8	1	1	35
Russia	−13	−15	−9	−13	−4	−5	0	2	58
Tajikistan	−7	−29	−11	−22	−13	−4	2	4	42
Turkmenistan	−5	−5	−10	−20	−10	−8	−25	12	48
Ukraine	−9	−10	−14	−23	−12	−10	−3	1	38
Uzbekistan	−1	−11	−2	−4	−1	2	2	2	88
All CIS*	−12	−14	−9	−14	−5	−5	1	2	57

*Averages weighted by 1997 real GDP.
Source: Adapted from EBRD (1998).

The early 1990s ushered in a period of economic crisis in the transition economies of CEE and the CIS. The breakdown of central plan discipline and of trade between these economies, taken together with the highly concentrated, vertically integrated nature of production (particularly in the CIS), led to an early collapse in production across the region (see Table 29.2). Recovery began first in CEE, with all countries except Bulgaria showing positive growth in 1996. Nevertheless, only in Poland, Slovenia and the Czech Republic has recent growth been sufficient to regain the losses of the early years: in all other states, output in 1998 remains below the level in 1989. Recovery in the CIS countries started later and has been more hesitant. For the CIS countries as a group, output in 1998 remains at only 57% of its 1989 level.

Unemployment and underemployment in Russia   Given the calamitous fall in output that has taken place in Russia, the relatively modest increase in unemployment is, at first sight, surprising. However, as Table 29.3 shows, there are large numbers of employees working shortened hours or on compulsory leave. Between 20% and 25% of the labour force is either out of work, on unpaid leave or working reduced hours, with these numbers highest in the winter months.

Table 29.3   Underemployment at large and medium-sized enterprises in Russia.

	Numbers working shortened day[1] (million)	As % of the labour force[1]	As % of employed at large and medium-sized enterprises[1]	Numbers on compulsory administrative leave[2] (million)	As % of the labour force[2]	As % of employed at large and medium-sized enterprises[2]
1996 Q1	3.0	4.1	6.1	4.4	6.0	9.1
1996 Q2	3.3	4.5	6.8	6.1	8.4	12.7
1996 Q3	3.2	4.4	6.6	6.7	9.3	14.0
1996 Q4	3.4	4.7	7.2	7.5	10.4	15.9
1997 Q1	2.4	3.3	5.2	3.3	4.5	7.3
1997 Q2	2.6	3.5	5.6	4.9	6.8	10.9
1997 Q3	2.9	4.1	6.5	4.7	6.6	10.4

[1]End of quarter. [2]During the quarter.
Source: Adapted from Goskomstat (1998).

With national and regional governments heavily reliant on 'profit' and 'turnover' taxes on enterprises for state revenues, the early recession led to a sharp contraction of the tax base. In the absence of developed capital markets, which in market economies offer governments the opportunity of selling securities to finance themselves in a non-inflationary way, the resulting budget deficits were financed by printing cash through the central bank. Inflationary pressures were further compounded in many transition economies by the state's attempts to avoid wholesale job losses by granting heavy subsidies to loss-making enterprises. Whether these were provided by the state directly, thereby adding to its budget deficit, or in the form of 'soft' loans from the central bank, the result in both cases was to further fuel the rate of growth of the money supply. The slump in output was thus accompanied by hyperinflation in many transition states, as price liberalization brought repressed inflation out into the open. Table 29.4 shows the inflation rates suffered by countries in the region in recent years.

Clearly, the challenges facing the transition economies at the start of the process were profound in both macroeconomic and microeconomic dimensions. At the *macroeconomic* level, the main priority was to construct new instruments of fiscal and monetary policy and thereby stabilize economies suffering from collapsing output and spiralling prices. Under the former system, the central planners could set both production levels and final producer prices *directly* through the national plan. In the new emerging market economies, they needed to construct the tools to achieve these goals at the macroeconomic level through *indirect* means, by changing taxes and government spending and by altering interest rates and managing the exchange rate. At the *microeconomic* level, the priority was to transform an economy of large, state-owned enterprises (SOEs) into competitive, private companies capable of trading globally.

Macroeconomic reform

Governments in *market economies* use two main sets of policy instruments to indirectly influence economic activity: *fiscal policy* – the use of taxes and public spending; and *monetary policy* – the control of money supply and interest rates (and the exchange rate). Neither set of policy instruments exists in the same form in a command

Table 29.4 The inflationary price of transition (% annual change in retail prices, end-year).

	1991	1992	1993	1994	1995	1996	1997	1998
CEE countries								
Albania	104	237	31	16	6	17	42	14
Bulgaria	339	79	64	122	33	311	579	17
Croatia	249	937	1,150	−3	4	3	4	5
Czech Republic	52	13	18	10	8	9	10	12
Estonia	304	954	36	42	29	15	12	11
FYR Macedonia	115	1,935	230	55	9	0	5	5
Hungary	32	22	21	21	28	20	18	14
Latvia	262	958	35	26	23	13	9	7
Lithuania	345	1,161	189	45	36	13	9	7
Poland	60	44	38	30	22	19	13	10
Romania	223	199	296	62	28	57	152	47
Slovak Republic	58	9	25	12	7	5	6	7
Slovenia	247	93	23	18	9	9	9	8
CIS countries								
Armenia	25	1,341	10,996	1,885	32	6	22	13
Azerbaijan	126	1,395	1,294	1,788	86	7	1	5
Belarus	93	1,558	1,994	1,957	244	39	63	84
Georgia	131	1,176	7,488	7,144	65	14	8	8
Kazakhstan	150	2,567	2,169	1,160	60	29	11	9
Kyrgystan	170	1,771	1,366	87	32	35	15	12
Moldova	151	2,198	837	116	24	15	11	10
Russia	144	2,318	841	203	131	22	11	10
Tajikistan	204	1,364	7,344	5	1,500	41	165	19
Turkmenistan	155	644	9,750	1,330	1,000	446	22	50
Ukraine	161	2,000	10,155	401	182	40	10	19
Uzbekistan	169	910	885	1,281	117	64	28	35

Source: Adapted from EBRD (1998).

economy. In the central planning system, taxes were levied on SOEs, normally in the form of 'turnover taxes' (i.e. taxes on the enterprises' sales revenue or turnover), and on individuals in the form of income tax. These taxes ensured that the government could, as in a market economy, finance the army and other executive functions (e.g. law and order) that did not fund their activities by generating their own sales revenues. These taxes and associated government spending, like the configuration of input and output prices, were an integral part of the national plan and were set to ensure its internal consistency. Significantly, many social services that are provided by the state in market economies like public housing, public transport, pre-school education, vocational training and health care were often provided by SOEs to their employees and families and financed out of the enterprises' own operating surpluses.

As a consequence, the tax base at the start of the process in most transition economies was small relative to that in market economies (since so many social services were financed directly by SOEs) and tax and spending decisions were part of the broader process of national planning. In contrast, in a market economy, governments need to raise taxes to finance the whole range of public goods and social services, at the same time setting the balance between taxes and public spending (i.e. the budget deficit or surplus) in order to stabilise aggregate demand and output.

In a command economy there is a unified financial system, with different branches of the national bank acting as a bookkeeper for transactions between companies in different sectors and providing deposit, but not lending, facilities (through a national savings branch) to the general population. Credit was allocated by the national bank's sectoral branches according to the requirements of the national plan. Interest rates played no part in the allocation of, or demand for, credit. Lending facilities for retail customers were unknown. Domestic currencies were not freely convertible but could (with official approval) be exchanged for foreign currencies through the national bank at artificial exchange rates depending upon the purpose (a favourable rate for exporters, a higher, penal rate for importers). There were no financial markets of the sort recognisable in market economies.

However, the creation of financial markets which can 'price' risk and allocate savings to those projects and companies with the best, risk-adjusted, returns is essential to the transition process (see below). It therefore follows that macro-economic reform fundamentally alters the role of the national bank and of the private banks and financial institutions. Since these are now used to channel savings to private companies, the interest rate (and the exchange rate) become powerful tools for influencing saving, borrowing and spending in the economy as a whole.

Fiscal policy reform   Because the system of taxes and government spending had been constructed around the needs of central planning, the *fiscal policy* instruments at the disposal of governments in the early stages of the transition process were ill-suited to dealing with the emerging market economies. Fiscal policy was beset by two overriding problems. First, the tax base was small and not set up to deal with the tax affairs of small, private companies. As the central plan collapsed and SOEs' output and turnover slumped, the revenue from turnover taxes fell sharply. In the economic chaos that followed, many SOEs switched to bartering their outputs for inputs; other profitable SOEs took advantage of the confusion and simply stopped paying taxes. Attempts to bolster tax revenues by introducing new tax regimes for newly established private companies often foundered, because tax rates were set so high that the companies evaded taxes. The old tax systems in many countries proved unable to deal with the changing structure of economic activity and there was a slump in tax revenues as more and more economic activity shifted into the 'informal' or 'hidden' economy (see Table 29.5).

At the same time, the pressure on government spending increased. Many SOEs quickly found themselves in genuine financial distress, unable to pay their workforces or continue to fund the social services they had traditionally provided. Many of the associated 'social assets' (public housing, schools, hospitals, public transport systems) were taken into local government control. With widespread popular resistance to attempts to levy user charges which more closely approximated the true opportunity costs of providing these services, this 'nationalization' of social services, particularly in the former Soviet Union, added to government spending. Even more significantly, there was intense political pressure on governments to 'bail out' failing SOEs, by granting state subsidies to allow them to pay wages. The fear of social unrest, prompted by periodic strikes and demonstrations by powerful groups of workers (e.g. miners, shipyard workers) encouraged many transition governments to give large subsidies to their SOEs. The impact of declining tax revenues and increasing public expenditure on the government budget balances is shown in Table 29.6.

In the late 1990s, however, the fiscal situation in most countries is starting to stabilise, as new, market-oriented taxes begin to take effect. Budget deficits have gradually declined as compared to the early 1990s, particularly in the CEE, to levels

Table 29.5 Estimates of the unofficial economy as % of GDP.

	1989	1990	1991	1992	1993	1994	1995
CEE countries							
Bulgaria	22.8	25.1	23.9	25.0	29.9	29.1	36.2
Czech Republic	6.0	6.7	12.9	16.9	16.9	17.6	11.3
Estonia	12.0	19.9	26.2	25.4	24.1	25.1	11.8
Hungary	27.0	28.0	32.9	30.6	28.5	27.7	29.0
Latvia	12.0	12.8	19.0	34.3	31.0	34.2	35.3
Lithuania	12.0	11.3	21.8	39.2	31.7	28.7	21.6
Poland	15.7	19.6	23.5	19.7	18.5	15.2	12.6
Romania	22.3	13.7	15.7	18.0	16.4	17.4	19.1
Slovak Republic	6.0	7.7	15.1	17.6	16.2	14.6	5.8
CIS countries							
Azerbaijan	12.2	21.9	22.7	39.2	51.2	58.0	60.6
Belarus	12.0	15.4	16.6	13.2	11.0	18.9	19.3
Georgia	12.0	24.9	36.0	52.3	61.0	63.5	62.6
Kazakhstan	12.0	17.0	19.7	24.9	27.2	34.1	34.3
Moldova	12.0	18.1	27.1	37.3	34.0	39.7	35.7
Russia	12.0	14.7	23.5	32.8	36.7	40.3	41.6
Ukraine	12.0	16.3	25.6	33.6	38.0	45.7	48.9
Uzbekistan	12.0	11.4	7.8	11.7	10.1	9.5	6.5

Source: Adapted from Johnson *et al.* (1997).

Table 29.6 General government budget balances (% of GDP).

	1992	1993	1994	1995	1996	1997	1998
CEE countries							
Albania	−20.3	−14.4	−12.4	−10.4	−11.4	−17.0	−14.8
Bulgaria	−5.2	−10.9	−5.8	−6.4	−13.4	−2.7	−1.6
Croatia	−4.0	−0.8	1.7	−0.9	−0.5	−1.4	−2.1
Czech Republic	−3.1	0.5	−1.2	−1.8	−1.2	−2.1	−0.9
Estonia	−0.3	0.7	1.3	−1.2	−1.5	2.3	1.7
FYR Macedonia	−9.6	−13.6	−3.2	−1.3	−0.4	−0.6	−0.8
Hungary	−6.8	−5.5	−8.4	−6.7	−3.5	−4.6	−4.9
Latvia	−0.8	0.6	−4.1	−3.5	−1.4	1.3	−0.4
Lithuania	0.5	−4.3	−5.4	−4.5	−4.0	−2.4	−3.0
Poland	−6.6	−3.4	−2.8	−3.6	−3.1	−3.0	−3.0
Romania	−4.6	−0.4	−1.9	−2.6	−3.9	−4.5	−5.0
Slovak Republic	n/a	−7.0	−1.3	0.2	−1.9	−3.4	−2.1
Slovenia	0.2	0.3	0.2	0.0	0.3	−1.5	−1.0
CIS countries							
Armenia	−8.1	−56.1	−10.1	−12.0	−9.3	−6.7	−5.6
Azerbaijan	2.8	−12.7	−11.4	−4.2	−2.6	−2.8	−3.0
Belarus	0.0	−1.9	−2.5	−1.9	−1.6	−2.7	−3.3
Georgia	−25.3	−26.2	−7.4	−4.5	−4.4	−3.8	−3.0
Kazakhstan	−7.3	−1.3	−7.2	−2.0	−2.5	−3.4	−4.5
Kyrgystan	−17.4	−14.2	−11.6	−17.2	−9.6	−9.2	−9.0
Moldova	−26.2	−7.4	−8.7	−5.7	−6.7	−7.5	−7.5
Russia	−21.6	−7.4	−10.4	−5.7	−8.2	−7.5	−6.0
Tajikistan	−28.4	−23.6	−10.2	−11.2	−5.8	−3.5	−3.0
Turkmenistan	13.2	−0.5	−1.4	−1.6	−0.2	−0.5	−5.0
Ukraine	−25.4	−16.2	−7.8	−4.8	−3.2	−5.8	−4.0
Uzbekistan	−18.4	−10.4	−6.1	−4.1	−7.3	−2.3	3.0

Source: Adapted from EBRD (1998).

common in advanced market economies. Extending the tax base has not been easy, however, as companies used to trading in the informal economy have sought to resist the introduction of new company taxes and systems of value-added taxes (VAT).

Table 29.7   Enterprise arrears (Rbn).

	Total enterprise arrears 4 sectors	Total enterprise arrears 9 sectors	Of which: Arrears to suppliers 4 sectors	Of which: Tax arrears 4 sectors	Of which: Wage arrears 4 sectors	Government wage arrears Rbn
1994	90.4	–	56.8	19.3	4.7	–
1995	238.9	–	122.3	75.0	13.6	–
1996	514.4	–	245.9	203.4	34.7	9.3
1997	756.1	–	344.7	316.6	39.7	4.9
1998	936.3	1,082.0	417.2	391.1	56.4	10.0

Source: Adapted from *Russian Economic Trends* (1998).

Tax and wage arrears in Russia   Table 29.7 with its data on enterprise arrears provides a useful insight into some of the problems facing the fiscal authorities of Russia. The table shows the way in which Russian enterprises have financed their growing financial deficits, which has primarily taken the form of passing the deficits on to their suppliers (inter-enterprise arrears), workers (wage arrears) and, most significantly, the tax authorities (tax arrears). By the end of 1997, tax arrears had grown to 6.6% of GDP, a figure almost exactly equal to the federal budget deficit in 1997 (6.8% of GDP). Table 29.7 also illustrates the extent to which government wage arrears have increased over recent years.

Monetary policy reform   In a command economy, the national bank performs many of the functions of the central bank and the commercial banking system in a market economy, controlling the money supply, taking deposits from the general public and lending money to enterprises. The essential difference is that these activities are all part of a wider national economic plan: money emission, in the form of bank notes, is set to ensure that enterprises can pay their workers; and a separate credit plan allocates loans to enterprises to support their investment and finance stocks and work-in-progress. In the former communist countries, the *national bank* was normally structured into functional areas: the national bank which performed a coordinating role and liaised directly with the planning ministry; several sectoral banks (agriculture, industry, etc.) which managed the accounts of enterprises within their designated sector; an investment bank which made loans to enterprises for capital investment; and a national savings bank, which held the deposits of the general public.

In this system, there were, in effect, *two parallel monetary systems*, one cash based, one credit based. In the *cash economy*, the national bank, as part of the planning process, set the volume of cash to be printed within a given time period (Table 29.8). The production plan for each enterprise specified the amount of cash they could draw from their sectoral bank to pay wages; all wages and salaries were paid in cash. The general public then used their cash wages to buy goods and services and the state shops redeposited their cash takings in the national bank; household savings were deposited in the national savings bank. In the *credit economy*, the national plan set limits on the amount each enterprise could borrow from its sectoral or investment bank to finance investment and stocks. Inter-enterprise payments were all made by transfers between their accounts in the national banking system. Credits were not convertible into cash, so the two systems were separate, although integrated through the national plan.

Table 29.8   Broad money growth (% change per annum).

	1991	1992	1993	1994	1995	1996	1997
CEE countries							
Albania	104.4	152.7	75.0	40.6	51.8	43.8	41.3
Bulgaria	110.0	53.6	47.6	78.6	39.6	124.5	359.3
Croatia*	n/a	n/a	n/a	111.9	24.6	37.9	20.9
Czech Republic	26.8	20.7	19.8	19.9	19.8	9.2	10.1
Estonia	n/a	71.1	86.5	31.0	30.5	36.6	40.4
FYR Macedonia	n/a	n/a	n/a	n/a	0.3	0.5	8.0
Hungary	35.7	27.3	15.7	13.0	20.1	22.5	19.4
Latvia	153.0	169.9	84.1	47.7	−23.1	19.9	38.7
Lithuania**	143.0	245.3	100.4	62.9	28.5	−3.5	34.1
Poland	37.0	57.5	36.0	38.2	35.0	29.3	29.6
Romania	101.2	79.6	141.0	138.1	71.6	66.0	48.9
Slovak Republic**	n/a	n/a	16.8	20.1	19.2	16.5	8.9
Slovenia	n/a	131.6	64.2	50.7	30.2	19.4	22.6
CIS countries							
Armenia	n/a	n/a	n/a	684.0	68.7	35.1	20.6
Azerbaijan	n/a	n/a	685.9	486.1	122.2	25.8	14.3
Belarus	n/a	n/a	n/a	181.8	173.7	52.4	111.4
Georgia	n/a	464.0	4,319.0	2,229.0	146.4	41.9	29.0
Kazakhstan	211.0	391.0	692.0	576.0	103.8	14.7	12.9
Kyrgystan	84.0	428.0	180.0	125.0	76.7	22.4	19.9
Moldova	n/a	361.7	320.2	115.7	65.2	15.3	25.7
Russia	125.9	568.1	425.8	197.5	127.5	33.7	30.0
Tajikistan	68.0	579.0	1,429.0	159.0	413.0	144.0	112.3
Turkmenistan	n/a	n/a	n/a	984.0	448.0	429.0	82.0
Ukraine	n/a	n/a	758.0	573.0	117.0	35.0	28.0
Uzbekistan	n/a	468.0	784.0	680.3	158.0	100.0	34.6

* = M1; ** = M2.
Source: Adapted from EBRD (1998).

This feature of the command economy gave rise to curious monetary problems. It was possible, for example, for the two monetary systems to become misaligned. For example, if the national bank increased the *cash* issue to allow enterprises to pay higher wages, there could be increased demand for goods by households. At the same time, there may be restrictions on *credit* availability, so that enterprises could not expand production.

The immediate priority for the post-communist countries was to integrate the cash and credit systems and create a 'two-tier' financial system, in which the national bank could assume the responsibilities of a conventional central bank, setting interest rates and ensuring the viability of the system as a whole, and a lower tier of commercial banks could take deposits and make loans on market terms. In the former Soviet republics, there was an additional decision to be taken, namely whether to remain in monetary union with Russia after independence, or to secede and establish their own currency. In the event, the political difficulties of maintaining monetary ties with Russia during the turbulence of the transition process forced the issue and even those states which might have preferred to remain within the rouble zone introduced their own national currencies.

The restructuring of the national bank system was achieved fairly quickly, with most countries choosing to privatise the sectoral, investment and savings divisions of the national bank and allowing new joint-stock banks to be created. The core of the national bank which remained in state control was normally reconstituted as a central bank and, in most countries, given a high degree of legal autonomy from the government, along with a mandate to manage monetary conditions in the pursuit of price stability. Indeed, the constitution of the Bundesbank was widely used as a model for designing the new central banks of CEE and the CIS.

Establishing monetary stability has been made more difficult for the new central banks by two main factors:

1. Budget deficits.
2. The dollarisation of the economies.

Budget deficits and the money supply   In a cash-based economy where the government has the monopoly over currency issue, printing cash provides a straightforward alternative to raising taxes as a means of financing government spending. In the early years of the reform process, money emission was the primary way in which governments financed the growing gap between government spending and tax revenues. There are essentially three ways of financing government spending:

1. taxation;
2. printing currency or borrowing from the banking system – which increases the money supply;
3. borrowing from the general public or abroad – which increases government debt.

Transition governments have sought to rebuild their tax bases with varying degrees of success and, by western standards, budget deficits in the CEE and the CIS are generally modest. Nevertheless, monetary financing of the residual budget deficits remains a problem. The main reason is that, in western countries, budget deficits are normally financed by borrowing from the general public by selling bonds on the stock market. However, stock markets remain generally underdeveloped in many transition economies. The other alternative, borrowing from abroad, also has its drawbacks. While the IMF and the World Bank have been prepared to extend large loans to transition governments to assist them through the early stages, these loans are highly conditional upon the governments adhering to pre-agreed policies, restricting the government's subsequent room for policy manoeuvre. Unlike sales of bonds to the general public, which are normally in the local currency, transition governments borrow from the international agencies in foreign currency (usually US dollars) and this must be repaid, imposing a burden in terms of interest and capital payments (Table 29.9). Clearly the transition economies have borrowed heavily from abroad, so that their external debt is a large percentage of their annual GDP and export values. 'Servicing' this debt via interest payments etc. is also a substantial percentage of annual export values for many of these economies.

Dollarization   In a market economy, money performs the functions of a medium of exchange, a unit of account and a store of value. The ability of a currency to perform these functions is undermined by high rates of inflation. Typically, in many transition economies, US dollars first began to circulate as an alternative store of value: individuals would switch their wages from the local currency into dollars and only switch back when they had goods to purchase, preserving the value of their wages in the interim. At higher rates of inflation, the 'menu costs' of continually altering the prices of goods and services becomes intolerable and dollars have been

	External debt stock ($m)	External debt/GDP (%)	External debt/exports (%)	Debt service (% exports)
CEE countries				
Albania	815	35.4	447.8	6.7
Bulgaria	9,977	97.0	200.6	15.5
Croatia	6,300	34.3	145.1	10.1
Czech Republic	22,000	42.3	97.6	15.9
Estonia	563	12.1	28.8	n/a
FYR Macedonia	1,131	35.9	92.3	8.7
Hungary	24,300	54.0	123.7	23.3
Latvia	486	8.9	27.8	n/a
Lithuania	1,787	19.5	42.8	19.1
Poland	38,000	28.3	139.7	5.7
Romania	10,400	30.2	121.8	n/a
Slovak Republic	10,000	52.5	113.7	17.4
Slovenia	4,200	23.2	49.7	8.5
CIS countries				
Armenia	798	50.4	333.9	22.0
Azerbaijan	567	13.8	68.8	8.7
Belarus	970	7.3	13.6	2.0
Georgia	1,565	30.4	335.8	9.2
Kazakhstan	4,300	18.7	63.2	7.0
Kyrgystan	934	57.3	139.3	6.0
Moldova	969	46.5	133.6	22.7
Russia	131,900	27.8	148.5	10.2
Tajikistan	893	82.9	122.8	12.5
Turkmenistan	1,248	70.7	164.4	24.8
Ukraine	10,200	20.5	68.0	6.7
Uzbekistan	2,594	18.0	70.1	9.8

Source: Adapted from EBRD (1998).

used as the unit of account. Prices in a shop, for example, are shown in dollars and, at the checkout, the till operator converts the prices into local currency at the prevailing exchange rate for payment. Finally, when there is hyperinflation, dollarization often becomes complete, with goods and services being priced and paid for in dollars.

It is impossible to estimate accurately the volume of dollars (and other hard currencies, notably the deutschmark) in circulation in CEE and the CIS, but the sums are huge. The Federal Reserve Bank, for example, calculates that there are more dollars being used in the region than in the United States. This phenomenon presents major problems for monetary control, since a significant proportion of the 'money supply' in transition economies is unrecorded and outside the central bank's control. Transition economies which have succeeded in stabilising inflation have, however, been able to reverse the dollarization of their economies. The normal mechanism is that, as inflation comes under control and real interest rates for deposits in local currency become positive, it becomes more attractive to hold bank deposits in local currency than to hold dollar bills. Individuals begin to sell their dollars to the central bank and there is a virtuous circle, as stabilization leads to an increase in foreign exchange reserves.

The 'New Currency Boards': the case of Estonia   In June 1992, Estonia became the first of the former Soviet republics to leave the rouble zone and introduce its own national currency, the kroon. At the same time, Estonia set up a currency board, fixing the kroon to the deutschmark. The government's decision was heavily influenced by the return of 11 tonnes of gold reserves from abroad, which had been deposited by the Estonian government in 1940 shortly before the Soviet occupation in 1940. The early repayment of 4.8 tonnes of gold by the Bank of England in March 1992, which had a market value of DM80m, provided the capital for the initial currency issue.

Like the old colonial currency boards, the note issue was 100% backed by gold and hard currencies and the Bank of Estonia was legally obliged to exchange notes for deutschmarks, and vice versa, at the official rate. The advantage of the system is that, provided the government can obtain the necessary capital, it is simple to set up and operate. Latvia and Lithuania subsequently followed Estonia's example and set up currency boards of their own, also using gold reserves reclaimed from foreign central banks.

In analytical terms, a *currency board* is equivalent to using a foreign currency as the means of exchange and unit of account; that is, there is no difference in analytical terms between using dollars for domestic transactions and using local currency which is 100% backed by dollars. The obvious advantage is that a currency board provides a credible guarantee of monetary stability, thereby reducing inflationary expectations and restoring faith in the domestic currency. For transition economies which have experienced very rapid inflation rates and the resultant 'dollarization' of the economy as confidence in the domestic currency collapses, a currency board can provide a powerful mechanism for bringing about a sustainable disinflation.

There are two major risks to a currency board. One is related to the central bank's role in preserving the viability of the commercial banking system. In most countries, the central bank acts as 'lender of last resort', lending reserves to commercial banks with liquidity difficulties and thereby maintaining confidence in the banking system as a whole. Given the widespread problems of commercial banks in the transition economies, many of which have made non-performing loans to enterprises which are bankrupt, there is a danger that political and social pressure to rescue failing banks will force the central bank to issue local currency in excess of its holdings of foreign exchange reserves. The cost of avoiding a wholesale collapse of the commercial banking system may be the breakdown of the currency board.

The second risk, which applies to all forms of fixed exchange rate systems (since all involve the central bank losing control of the money supply) stems from the government's budget deficit. Introducing a currency board clearly closes off the option of financing the budget deficit through the creation of money. Indeed, it is precisely because a currency board forces the government to finance itself in non-monetary ways that this form of fixed exchange rate is so attractive to countries bedevilled by hyperinflation. However, if the government is politically incapable of reducing its budget deficit, it may be that resort to the 'inflation tax' (i.e. financing expenditure by printing money) is preferable to the social unrest that might follow from the non-payment of state workers, pensioners, etc. Unless achieving a more balanced budget is politically feasible, a currency board will fail.

The disadvantages of a currency board in economic terms are basically those of a fixed exchange system, namely the loss of monetary sovereignty. In the special case of transition economies, this can cause adjustment difficulties. Because high-inflation countries tend to be extensively dollarised, the introduction of a credible currency board will encourage residents to switch out of dollars into local currency. Under the currency board arrangements, the central bank's foreign exchange reserves and the stock of issued banknotes will grow. Because this portfolio reallocation out of dollars into local currency simply changes the form in which money is held, there need be no inflationary consequences from the subsequent rapid growth in the money supply. However, experience in the Baltic states and eastern Germany suggests that, as people switch from hoarded dollars into domestic currency, the *velocity of circulation* of money may rise. Because the exchange rate is fixed, any temporary increase in prices as a result of increased spending leads to a rise in the real exchange rate and may cause problems for exporters.

The balance of payments

Under the former centrally planned system, international trade of the transition economies was largely conducted within the framework of COMECON, the Council for Mutual Economic Assistance. Under this arrangement, trade between the economies of CEE and the former Soviet Union was organised through a central payments system (via 'trade roubles'). Exports to other COMECON members were recorded as credits, and imports as debits, in each country's 'account', with settlement for inter-country indebtedness made using trade roubles. This model of organising and financing international trade, together with a favourable configuration of export and import prices for trade with the former Soviet Union[3] and integrated national economic plans across COMECON, meant that the trade patterns of the smaller CEE countries were heavily skewed towards Russia and the other Soviet republics. Trade with capitalist countries outside the COMECON system was heavily restricted by a range of import and export taxes and, in the case of imported goods and services, by shortages of hard currencies; as a result, a high proportion of non-COMECON trade was conducted on a barter basis, with the government negotiating goods-for-goods exchanges with western manufacturers. PepsiCo's famous barter deal with the Russian government of Pepsi for vodka in the late 1980s was the most famous of the barter arrangements which characterised trade between the COMECON and capitalist world before 1989.

The breakdown of the centrally planned system, the weakening of the political ties between CEE and Russia and the liberalization of prices, exchange rates and trade regimes has led to a rapid reorientation of trade patterns towards the richer economies of the EU, notably Germany, and to a lesser extent towards the United States and South East Asia. Table 29.10 shows the predicted trade patterns for Russia and the former Soviet Union for the year 2000, illustrating the scale of this reorientation. The projections are based on the so-called 'gravity model' of international trade, which suggests that, in the absence of trade barriers, trade between countries will be a function of absolute GDP, per capita GDP and geographical distance (a proxy for transport costs).

This process of reorienting trade flows has been painful and most of the transition economies suffered a collapse in exports and trade deficits during the early and mid-1990s. The situation has since improved significantly, as Table 29.11 reveals, although some of the CIS countries still face major trading imbalances. As a major exporter of oil and other commodities, Russia stands out as one of only two transition

Table 29.10 Predicted shares of total trade in 2000 (%).

	EU	Japan	USA	CEE	Russia
Russia	45.6	17.4	12.2	7.4	7.3
Former Soviet Union	45.9	24.9	13.7	5.4	–

Source: Adapted from Gros and Steinherr (1995).

Table 29.11 Trade, the current account and foreign direct investment (FDI).

	Current account balance, 1997 (% GDP)	Trade balance, 1997 (% GDP)	FDI inflows 1997 (% GDP)	Cumulative FDI, 1989–97 ($m)	Per capita cumulative FDI, 1989–97 ($)
CEE countries					
Albania	−8.5	−18.0	1.4	369	115
Bulgaria	1.8	3.0	5.6	1,000	121
Croatia	−10.3	−26.1	2.7	1,276	267
Czech Republic	−6.1	−8.8	2.4	7,473	726
Estonia	−13.1	−25.6	2.8	809	557
FYR Macedonia	−8.1	−10.9	4.7	15,403	1,519
Hungary	−2.2	−3.8	7.6	1,287	515
Latvia	−6.4	−16.3	3.6	612	165
Lithuania	−10.3	−12.2	0.5	65	31
Poland	−3.2	−8.4	2.3	8,442	218
Romania	−5.5	4.1	2.9	2,389	106
Slovak Republic	−7.9	−7.9	0.8	912	169
Slovenia	0.4	−4.3	1.8	1,074	538
CIS countries					
Armenia	−27.0	−35.3	1.6	70	19
Azerbaijan	−23.4	−13.8	24.4	1,993	262
Belarus	−7.5	−11.2	0.7	267	26
Georgia	−6.2	−7.1	1.3	104	19
Kazakhstan	−4.8	−2.4	5.7	4,267	272
Kyrgystan	−11.5	−8.2	3.1	247	54
Moldova	−14.9	−13.2	3.4	249	58
Russia	0.8	3.5	0.8	9,743	66
Tajikistan	−1.3	−0.4	1.8	86	14
Turkmenistan	−26.1	−10.7	4.7	652	139
Ukraine	−3.1	−9.9	1.4	2,096	41
Uzbekistan	−5.2	−1.8	0.4	216	9

Source: Adapted from EBRD (1998).

economies with a current account surplus. Table 29.11 also shows the scale of foreign direct investment (FDI) relative to current account imbalances. Historically, developing economies attracted inward FDI which allowed them to finance current account deficits as their economies industrialised. While Azerbaijan and Kazakhstan, which have extensive oil reserves, have benefited from inward FDI from oil companies, per capita inward FDI over the period 1989–97 has been limited and concentrated in the richest CEE states (the link between inward FDI and microeconomic reform is discussed further below).

Microeconomic reform

A central planning system takes upon itself the responsibility for *resource allocation*. It therefore adopts its own procedures for the following activities which are performed in a market economy by:

1. dynamic, profit-seeking firms, which seek out profitable investment and production opportunities;
2. open competitive markets, in which domestic and foreign consumers and producers come together to set prices, sales and output;
3. the financial system, which channels resources from savers to investors which can earn the highest, risk-adjusted returns.

Building a fully-functioning market economy thus involves: transforming state enterprises into outward-looking, profit-oriented firms; opening up domestic markets to internal and external competition and establishing a banking system and capital market in which funds are allocated on the basis of objective risk assessments and prospective returns, rather than in accordance with the demands of a central plan.

Finally, transition requires the establishment of a functioning legal system to define and protect property rights, clarify ownership and, most importantly, to provide a legal framework which facilitates investment.

We now consider the issues involved in each in turn.

Creating a dynamic private sector

The creation of a dynamic private sector can be achieved in one of two ways: first, by encouraging entrepreneurs to start up new businesses; and second, by transferring the ownership of existing SOEs into private hands. Experience to date has highlighted the importance of maintaining a balance between the two. The crucial difference between business start-ups and the privatization of SOEs is that the former creates jobs, while the latter inevitably leads to job-shedding, at least in the short term. In Poland, for example, approximately half the jobs created between 1989 and 1995 have been in new, small-scale business ventures. When SOEs are privatized, on the other hand, the new management's first objective is often to eliminate over-staffing and thereby increase labour productivity. In the former centrally planned system, unemployment was officially non-existent; a result achieved, in part at least, by forcing SOEs to mop up all the available labour.

It is often asserted that promoting 'organic' private sector growth requires simple legal procedures for registering companies and a straightforward corporate tax structure. Strictly speaking, these conditions are essential for the growth of an 'official' private sector, rather than private sector activity *per se*. The former communist countries always had an unofficial private sector (sometimes called the 'hidden', 'informal' or 'black economy') which, despite being harshly repressed by the authorities, was active in selling smuggled goods and organizing currency trading. After 1989, state repression of the unofficial private sector was widely relaxed, while the accelerating disintegration of the command planning system created huge opportunities for entrepreneurs.

Mainstream economic theory suggests that, if markets are 'efficient' in the sense that markets are competitive and contestable and information is widely shared, then market operators cannot make abnormal profits in the long run; economic rent acts as a signal to attract new entrants, who compete down prices and eliminate the abnormal profit. In the aftermath of the democratic revolutions spreading around the CEE and CIS states, however, the fledging markets were characterized by massive inefficiency, with the debris of the central planning structures and the absence of clear property rights preventing normal market transactions. For the new entrepreneurs, the opportunities for hugely profitable arbitrage were everywhere. Extensive price controls meant that prices bore little relation to opportunity cost and, where official prices were far below world prices, moving goods across borders offered the prospect of spectacular returns. The much publicised Russian 'mafia' is a legacy of the early years of transition, when rational speculative activity in the presence of pervasive market inefficiency created opportunities for profit undreamed of in the west. This window of opportunity closed rapidly, as prices were deregulated and markets liberalized. Nevertheless, many governments are finding it difficult to draw their new class of small entrepreneur back into the official private sector.

Small-scale privatization

In the area of privatization, it is useful to distinguish between small-scale privatization and 'mass' privatization. The former refers to the transfer to private hands of small SOEs, mainly retail shops, restaurants and other service providers (e.g. hairdressers, bars, cinemas, etc.). In the west, such companies are typically owned by their managers. Replicating this arrangement through privatization involves either transferring ownership (either free of charge or for an agreed cash price) to the present managers and/or workers, or auctioning off the enterprise to the highest bidder. Most transition economies have experimented with small-scale privatization somewhere along the continuum from a straight give-away to the incumbents to a cash auction.

Small-scale privatization plays an important role in the transition process for two reasons. First, like business start-ups, small companies offer greater scope for job creation than large, overstaffed SOEs. In the communist days, for example, state restaurants were typically dour, unattractive places characterised by poor service. Freed from state control, such restaurants can expand into new markets (e.g. fast food, ethnic food, etc.), quickly increasing turnover and jobs. Second, small-scale enterprises are 'close' to people in a way that large SOEs are not. Their transformation, with the attendant changes in shop window displays, service to customers, range and quality of goods and services sold, provides an immediate and powerful psychological symbol of the benefits of transition.

Enterprise restructuring and large-scale privatization

At the other end of the scale, the region faces the problem of privatizing the huge SOEs that made up the Soviet military–industrial complex. Many of these enterprises employed tens of thousands of workers, often producing specialist intermediate and final products for the military. The breakdown of COMECON and the Warsaw Pact and the end of the Cold War (together with the budgetary problems of many CIS governments) have radically reduced the demand for the products of many large SOEs. At the same time, the liberalization of prices and the opening up of economies to international competition have resulted in many large SOEs making heavy financial losses. In the past, the central planners arranged input and output prices so that enterprises making 'socially necessary' goods could make a profit; liberalization and foreign competition has quickly driven input and output prices to world levels, making many previously profitable activities financially unviable.

Enabling the huge SOEs to respond flexibly to the changed configuration of input and output prices requires breaking the link between the state and enterprises, so that managements are free to maximize profits rather than meet political or social objectives imposed by their sponsoring ministries. The normal approach taken in most former centrally planned economies is to 'corporatise' the enterprises; i.e. transform them into joint stock companies. The stock (i.e. shares) created is initially held by the state, but the intention of corporatization is to enable the management to pursue commercial objectives free from political interference.

One difficulty widely encountered with corporatization involves the issue of 'corporate governance', a special case of the so-called 'principal–agent' problem. In market economies, companies are owned by private shareholders (the principals) who appoint managers (the agents) to run companies on their behalf. The principals clearly have different interests from their agents, the former wanting to see profits (or growth) maximized, while the latter are better served by targeting stable, secure markets (thereby promoting job security) and increasing the wages of senior management. A combination of annual general meetings – at which shareholders can assess the performance of the incumbent management and replace it as necessary – and an active stock market in which investors scrutinise the profitability of listed companies – driving down the market price of companies with underperforming managements and opening them up to hostile take-overs – ensures that the will of the principals is, by and large, imposed on the agents.

The process of corporatisation, of itself, means that corporate governance remains the preserve of the state and, quite probably, the ministry which previously managed the SOE. In such circumstances, it is difficult for corporatisation, *per se*, to break the link between state and SOEs. In countries where the state has effectively abdicated its role as principal (notably Bulgaria), presumably in the belief that freed from control the SOEs would act to maximize profit, the result has been predictably disappointing. The managers, rather than concentrating on increasing sales and profit, have instead taken advantage of their freedom of action to exploit the companies for their own benefit.

One solution to the principal–agent problem, widely employed in the developing world, is to transfer SOEs to indirect state ownership, through the creation of 'state holding companies'. Unlike a ministry, the state holding company is mandated solely to control the economic performance of the companies it owns, through *ex post* monitoring of its financial accounts. This solution permits a separation of the state's ownership and management functions, allowing a decentralised management to act more independently and thereby promoting restructuring and more commercial behaviour.

However, such 'half-way house' solutions have, in general, been rare in the transition economies, with most governments regarding corporatization as merely a first step on the road to full privatization. The transfer of the shares in SOEs from the state to the private sector, taken together with measures to create a vibrant stock market, is widely regarded as the only way of satisfactorily resolving the principal–agent problem and, in the process, revitalising large-scale industry in the CEE and CIS. The methods of privatization have varied widely and, amongst a wide array of different models, have included:

1. open-market auctions of SOEs for cash;
2. open-market auctions of SOEs for vouchers, which have previously been distributed amongst the target owners (who may be the incumbent workforce or the general public) either free or for cash at a discounted rate;
3. open-market auctions of SOEs for a mixture of cash and vouchers;
4. direct sales of SOEs to managers (so-called 'management buy-outs'), workers (in the form of cooperative enterprises) or, wholly or partially, to a foreign company; and
5. direct transfer of shares (free of charge) to the incumbent management and/or workers.

A key debate is whether restructuring of SOEs should precede or follow privatization. The British government, an early pioneer of privatization in the West, adopted a strategy of overhauling nationalized industries while they were still under public ownership. This meant that the heavy costs of redundancy were borne by the state; the enterprises themselves were not sold to the private sector until they were profit-making, thereby making them attractive to private investors. This model does not transfer easily to the transition economies of CEE and the CIS, where fiscal problems preclude the heavy investment of public funds in restructuring SOEs. In cases where companies are chronically inefficient, finding a foreign investor willing to invest in new plant and equipment is often the only way to revive the fortunes of a failing SOE. The German Treuhandanstalt, the privatization agency set up to sell off SOEs in the eastern *Länder* following the reunification of Germany in 1990, agreed sales on the basis of the new owner's commitment to invest and retrain workers, as well as the actual selling price.

As noted above, whether SOEs are sold to domestic buyers, who must improve their performance with only modest initial injections of capital, or acquired by foreign companies with funds to invest, large-scale job losses are inevitable – hence the importance of a vibrant private sector which can absorb the displaced workers through organic growth. The efficiency gains in countries in the vanguard of mass privatization have been impressive. For example, output per worker in the manufacturing sector in Poland and Hungary rose by 7–18% per annum between 1992 and 1995. While part of this increase reflects greater effort on the part of workers in the privatized SOEs and increased capital investment, the European Bank for Reconstruction and Development acknowledges that the shedding of staff was the dominant factor, especially in the early years of transition.

Given the huge scale of many SOEs, particularly in the CIS, the fear of wholesale job shedding following privatization provides a powerful political obstacle to progress in this area. The mass popular unrest and demonstrations that preceded the collapse of the former communist regimes provides a reminder of the anti-government riots which might result from massive, highly concentrated job losses in particular regions and industries. As noted above, SOEs traditionally provided their workers with a raft of social benefits (housing, education, health care), which explains why many workers continue to work in the CIS even when they are not paid for months at a time. The loss of their jobs threatens not just their incomes, but the continuation of these benefits-in-kind. It is clear that, while a vibrant private sector can act as a shock absorber, governments have to begin building a basic social welfare system (to provide basic income support and social services for the poor and unemployed) if the social costs of industrial restructuring and large-scale privatization are to be politically tolerable.

Income inequality and economic transition   Economic transition has meant a sharp increase in income inequality. Table 29.12 provides an overview of income distribution in Russia. It shows that for the poorest 20% of citizens, their share of total income has fallen from 11.9% to 6.2% over the period 1991–97, while the share of the richest 20% has risen from 30.7% to 46.7%. These changes are reflected in the Gini coefficient (the standard measure of equality, with the higher figure representing greater inequality), which has increased from 0.260 to 0.374 and the ratio of the income earned by the richest 10% to the income earned by the poorest 10%, which has trebled from 4.5 to 13.2.

Market liberalization

The operation of the 'invisible hand', namely the price mechanism, lies at the heart of a market economy, with high prices/profits encouraging an influx of producers to meet demand; and vice versa. Transition thus requires an end to the practice of

Table 29.12 Income distribution in Russia, 1991–97.

	1991	1992	1993	1994	1995	1996	1997
Income by quintile							
Poorest 20%	11.9	6.0	5.8	5.3	5.5	6.5	6.2
Next poorest 20%	15.8	11.6	11.1	10.2	10.2	10.9	10.6
Next poorest 20%	18.8	17.6	16.7	15.2	15.0	15.5	15.0
Next poorest 20%	22.8	26.5	24.8	23.0	22.4	22.4	21.3
Richest 20%	30.7	38.3	41.6	46.3	46.9	44.7	46.9
Total %	100.0	100.0	100.0	100.0	100.0	100.0	100.0
Gini coefficient	0.260	0.289	0.398	0.409	0.381	0.375	0.374
Richest 10% : poorest 10%	4.5	–	11.2	15.1	13.5	13.0	13.2

Source: Adapted from Russia–Europe Centre for Economic Policy.

setting prices and profit margins centrally, in accordance with the needs of the central plan and the planners' subjective judgements of the 'social value' of different goods and services. Price control was so fundamental to the central planning system that dismantling the apparatus by which prices and costs are fixed has proved lengthy.

The abolition of controls (both maxima and minima) on the prices of final goods was achieved in most countries relatively quickly, although at great social cost. Against a backdrop of rapid monetary growth and an already large 'monetary overhang' (i.e. money balances which people had accumulated in the years when they could not find the goods on which to spend their income), price liberalisation led to an explosion in retail prices, hitting vulnerable, fixed-income groups like pensioners disproportionately hard. The demonstrable social injustices occasioned by earlier price liberalization led governments in many countries to delay the ending of more subtle price controls (e.g. on 'essentials' like bread, milk, heat and light and public transport). Producers' input costs (notably energy) continue to be subsidized in some countries for fear of the inflationary consequences, while profit margins were often controlled long after final prices were liberalized for fear that consumers would be 'exploited' by the new 'capitalists'.

The opening up of foreign trade and the liberalization of the foreign exchange market are prerequisites for meaningful price liberalization. During the period of central planning, the states of CEE and the CIS traded relatively little with the outside world. The total exports of the former Soviet Union to countries outside the COMECON bloc were, in the 1980s, lower than Belgium's, for example. The isolation of domestic markets from outside competition, taken in conjunction with a regime of comprehensive import and export taxes and duties, was instrumental in ensuring that central planners could arrange internal costs and prices without reference to world prices. Artificial exchange rates, officially set and administered by national banks, achieved a similar result.

Allowing the invisible hand to operate freely implies that trade restrictions should be eased and, more importantly, that the tariff regimes should be simplified and purged of the distortions which hitherto served the purposes of the central planners. Similarly, true price liberalization needs 'current account convertibility', so that internal prices are not distorted by the government restricting access to foreign exchange. Under the former arrangements, exchange rates were administered (i.e. the rates were set by government decree), often with differential rates for importers and exporters, tourists and foreign investors. Current account convertibility does not mean that the government or the central bank cannot 'manage' the exchange rate by pegging its value to, say, the US dollar or the deutschmark; indeed, many of the more successful transition economies in CEE have exchange rate targets of one form or another. Rather, it means that the exchange rate should be one at which importers and exporters can freely buy and sell foreign currency, so that a process of arbitrage can bring internal and world prices into line. For example if the government pegs the exchange rate of currency X at, say, X1 = $1, then provided the government is prepared to accumulate or run down its foreign exchange reserves to maintain this parity, inflows and outflows of tradable goods and services will bring internal prices into line with the world price of (tradable) goods and services.

The final building block of market liberalization is, paradoxically at first sight, the creation of an effective competition or anti-monopoly policy. As noted above, central planners faced a rational incentive to try and maximise economies of scale, since, as the rulers of the economies they oversaw, they could prevent large state-owned monopoly producers exploiting their dominant market positions. At regional and local level, many similar dominant positions existed in the wholesale and retail sector. As former SOEs have been privatized, the risk that the new privately owned companies will abuse their inherited monopoly power is very real. Indeed, the fear that consumers will be exploited has deterred many governments from pressing ahead with privatization more aggressively and encouraged others to reimpose price and profit margin controls in an *ad hoc* way which threatens the viability of the newly privatized companies. The solution is a workable body of anti-monopoly legislation and, in cases where the scope for abuse is potentially extreme (e.g. in the case of a private monopoly electricity company), some form of state regulator along the lines of OFGAS and OFTEL in Britain.

Financial sector reform

In the central planning system, agencies of the national bank provided an accounting system to book the credits and debits of SOEs as intermediate and final products were transferred between one enterprise and another. These agencies of the national bank were typically organized on a sectoral basis, with an agricultural 'bank' for farms and food processors, an engineering bank for manufacturers of capital goods and so on. 'Soft' loans (i.e. loans at zero or artificially low interest rates) were available to loss-making enterprises, with decisions about credit being taken within the context of the central plan. Separate 'savings banks' provided a repository for individual citizens to save unspent income, but consumer loans were virtually unknown. Market economies, in contrast, are built upon competitive financial systems which allocate savings to their best uses – that is, to borrowers who can pay, after adjustment for credit risk, the highest rates of return.

The transition process thus implies creating a 'two tier' banking system, in which the state or national bank is split into a central bank (with responsibility for monetary policy and banking supervision) and a commercial banking system. This objective has generally been achieved by breaking up the national bank and privatizing the sectoral agencies as stand-alone commercial banks (albeit, initially, with a strong sectoral orientation). In Poland, for example, nine commercial banks were hived off from the national bank, of which four had been privatized by the end of 1996. In contrast to the industrial sector, moreover, new business start-ups in the banking sector have been very vigorous since 1989–91. In part, the rapid growth of a private sector banking system was based on market imperfections. Citizens socialized during the communist era often did not fully understand the principles of private banking, believing them to enjoy the same solid state backing as the former savings banks. The new breed of private bankers, initially loosely regulated by central banks unsure of their new role post-communism, only vaguely understood notions of capital adequacy and credit risk assessment, but quickly realised the scope for reinvesting depositors' funds at a profit in economies characterised by a lack of loanable funds and a huge demand for credit.

Recent years have seen a wave of private sector banking crashes and scandals. In Latvia, the activities of more than one-third of its commercial banks was suspended in 1995, after a number were found to be insolvent (i.e. to have deposit liabilities which exceeded its assets, due to loan defaults). In the same year, the Lithuanian central bank prohibited the planned merger of its two largest private banks after one was discovered to be insolvent. A number of medium-sized and local banks failed during a banking crisis in the Czech Republic in 1996. It has become clear that the challenge is not simply to promote the creation of a private sector banking system, but to properly regulate commercial banks (paying particular regard to the maintenance of minimum capital ratios – that is, the ratio of shareholders' capital to outstanding loans – and to supervise the accelerating numbers of mergers and acquisitions that will be necessary to transform the ranks of small, mainly local or regional banks that now characterise many former centrally planned economies into a much more select group of large, efficient commercial banks.

The second major area of financial sector reform concerns the development of functioning stock markets. As noted above, these are not only important as a means of mobilising savings and channelling them to their most efficient use, but also as an integral part of the process of corporate governance. For obvious reasons, the development of active capital markets has mirrored the pace of large-scale privatization (and to a lesser extent, the needs of government to sell securities to finance their budget deficits). The stock market capitalisation of the Czech Republic, for example, was 42% of GDP at the end of June 1996, reflecting the advanced nature of that country's comprehensive voucher-based privatization programme. In most CIS countries, in contrast, stock markets remains underdeveloped and illiquid.

Legal reforms

In the early stages of transition, investment was strongly inhibited by the absence of clear property rights and a generally murky picture with regard to the laws concerning the ownership of land and buildings (particularly the permissible extent of foreign investments), the valuation of assets and the outlook for taxes on profits and capital, as well as the future regime for the treatment of profits made by foreign investors. While all the transition economies have attempted to set in place new legal structures and regulations, legislation in one area (e.g. foreign ownership of land) often conflicts with laws passed in another (e.g. rules relating to the repatriation of profits by foreign-owned subsidiaries), resulting in a confused patchwork of inconsistent laws and regulations. Creating a transparent, internally consistent legal structure is thus essential for the promotion of investment, particularly foreign direct investment.

Foreign direct investment could potentially play an important part in the reconstruction of CEE and the CIS. Jeffrey Sachs, a US economist and advisor to governments in Eastern Europe, famously observed in the early 1990s that Singapore attracts more foreign investment each year than all the transition economies put together. While the picture has improved slightly, Table 29.11 above suggests that CEE and the CIS attract a relatively small amount of foreign investment. Moreover, creating a receptive investment climate not only holds out the promise of drawing more foreign capital into the transition economies, but also access to the latest western technology and management methods.

Progress in transition to date

Table 29.13 sets out the performances of the transition economies in each of these key areas. The indices are ranked from 1 (= little or no progress) to 4 (= complete or near complete reform). The key below sets out the meaning of the indices in more detail. Table 29.13 shows that the CEE countries are far more advanced in the transition process than their CIS rivals. Strikingly, of the twelve CIS countries, Russia is in the vanguard of reform, with the private sector now accounting for 60% of GDP following a successful and extensive privatization programme. Overall, Table 29.13 and its Key on the following page shows that most of the transition economies have completed (or nearly completed) the comprehensive liberalization of prices, foreign

Table 29.13   The transition picture in 1997.

		Firms			Markets			Finance		Law
	Private sector % GDP	Large-scale private	Small-scale private	Ent. restruct.	Price liberal.	Trade and forex	Comp. policy	Bank reform	Capital markets	Index of legal reform
CEE countries										
Albania	75	2	4	2	3	4	2	2	2	3
Bulgaria	50	3	3	2	3	4	2	3	2	3
Croatia	55	3	4	3	3	4	2	3	2	4
Czech Republic	75	4	4	3	3	4	3	3	3	4
Estonia	70	4	4	3	3	4	3	3	3	4
FYR Macedonia	50	3	4	2	3	4	1	3	1	2
Hungary	75	4	4	3	3	4	3	4	3	4
Latvia	60	3	4	3	3	4	3	3	2	3
Lithuania	70	3	4	3	3	4	2	3	3	4
Poland	65	3	4	3	3	4	3	3	3	4
Romania	60	3	3	2	3	4	2	3	2	3
Slovak Republic	75	4	4	3	3	4	3	3	2	3
Slovenia	50	3	4	3	3	4	2	3	3	3
CIS countries										
Armenia	55	3	3	2	3	4	2	2	1	3
Azerbaijan	40	2	3	2	3	2	1	2	1	1
Belarus	20	1	2	1	3	1	2	1	2	2
Georgia	55	3	4	2	3	4	2	2	1	2
Kazakhstan	55	3	3	2	3	4	2	2	2	2
Kyrgystan	60	3	4	2	3	4	2	3	2	2
Moldova	45	3	3	2	3	4	2	2	2	2
Russia	70	3	4	2	3	4	2	2	3	3
Tajikistan	20	2	2	1	3	2	1	1	1	n/a
Turkmenistan	25	2	2	2	2	1	1	1	1	n/a
Ukraine	50	2	3	2	3	3	2	2	2	2
Uzbekistan	45	3	3	2	3	2	2	2	2	2

Note: Key to numbers on following page.
Source: Adapted from EBRD (1997).

Key to Table 29.13.

	4	3	2	1
Large-scale privatization	More than 50% large enterprise privatized	More than 25% large enterprise privatized	Privatization scheme for large enterprises about to be introduced	Little or nothing done
Small-scale privatization	All small enterprises (e.g. shops, restaurants) privatized	Most small enterprises privatized	Significant proportion of small enterprises privatized	Little or nothing done
Enterprise restructuring	Corporatization of state enterprises completed	Corporatization in progress, but incomplete	Legislative reforms passed, but not fully implemented	Few reforms passed
Price liberalization	Complete price liberalization and anti-monopoly controls	Substantial price liberalization	Price controls remain for significant number of products	Most prices still controlled
Trade and foreign exchange system	No import/export quotas or controls, convertible exchange rate	Few quotas, near full convertibility of exchange	Few quotas, but exchange controls still in force	Widespread import/export quotas and/or exchange controls
Competition policy	Signification anti-monopoly enforcement	Some enforcement to control abuse of market power	Basic competition policy rules and institutions set up	No competition policy rules or institutions
Banking reform	Well-functioning banking system	Substantial progress towards competitive banking system	Interest rates main means of allocating credit	Little or no progress
Capital markets	Functioning, liquid capital market, with legal framework approaching international standards	Substantial issues of shares by private firms on capital market	Establishment of capital market and limited trading	Little or no progress
Legal reform index: rules on pledge, bankruptcy and company law	Comprehensive legal rules, independently and consistently enforced	Legal rules exist, but enforcement patchy	Legal rules are limited or contradictory, hard to enforce	Legal rules very limited in scope, unclear and not consistently enforced

trade and exchange rates; in almost all countries, small-scale enterprises have been largely privatized. The difference between the CEE and CIS countries is more stark in the field of large-scale privatization of SOEs and enterprise restructuring and financial sector reform, where the CIS countries lag markedly.

It is also worth noting that the pace of structural change is beginning to slow as compared with the early 1990s. This is because most of the 'easier' reforms have already been achieved. It is the 'hard core' of tasks that remain, notably the restructuring and privatization of large, loss-making SOEs and the creation of an efficient financial system. These are the reforms that promise to be the most socially or politically painful. The slowing of reform is also, in part, because the governments that were in power in the immediate aftermath of the collapse of communism enjoyed a popular mandate to undertake radical political change; but as the social pain of the transition process has mounted, the electorate's willingness to tolerate the further sacrifices necessary to maintain the rate of progress has waned. The blunting of voters' appetite for economic transformation, even in CEE where progress has been more swift and the beneficial results more tangible and evenly spread, is best illustrated by their growing propensity to elect left-wing administrations pledged to slow the pace of reform in the interest of promoting social harmony.

Conclusions

Taken together, the analysis above suggests a strong link between progress in reform and economic recovery. The CEE states have, as a group, moved furthest and fastest in transforming their economies into open, competitive market democracies and are now enjoying positive economic growth. In contrast, the CIS states have delayed reform and are still in economic decline. However, such a simplistic conclusion understates the importance of culture, history and geography. The CEE states started from a much better position, with a folk memory of capitalism and a popular antipathy towards their former Soviet colonisers and communism. With strong national identities and the massive markets of the European Union on their doorstep, transition has been economically, socially and psychologically easier than for their eastern neighbours in the CIS.

In the former Soviet Union, communist ideology pervades every aspect of the economy. The entire economic structure reflects the priorities of the plan, with mammoth, highly specialized state enterprises which have floundered outside the rigid framework of the central planning system. There is no generally shared belief that communism was fundamentally flawed and, given the large numbers of causalities of the reform process (pensioners, students, the military, employees of large state enterprises), the construction of a market system has taken place against a backdrop of growing popular hostility. Electoral resentment to the structural changes in the economy is further heightened by nostalgia for the days of the Soviet empire, which adds to a general feeling that things were better in the days of central planning.

Perhaps the most important conclusion from the transition experience to date is that transforming centrally planned economies into market democracies hurts; not only is the economy as a whole destined to undergo a painful negative output shock, with years of declining living standards, but income distribution is inevitably bound to become worse as the new entrepreneurs benefit at the expense of state employees and welfare dependants. The keys to success appear to be:

(i)   to rush through small-scale privatization and set in place the basic requirements for private business, so that small, dynamic start-up businesses in the private sector can begin to absorb the labour shed by state dinosaurs;

(ii) to establish a state welfare system which is independent of enterprises, to protect those who lose from transition in the short to medium term; and

(iii) to 'buy off' vested interest groups like large state enterprise managers and workers (e.g. by giving them shares when their enterprises are privatized), so that they support rather than block reform;

(iv) to liberalize trade and capital movements, in order to attract foreign investment to assist the transformation process.

Finally, the challenge which lies ahead in the twenty-first century for CEE and the CIS countries alike is to maintain high rates of domestic savings in order to finance the investment needed for restructuring and economic development. The European Bank for Reconstruction and Development estimates that the region will need to invest at least 20% of GDP in order to sustain annual growth rates in the region of 4%, the absolute minimum needed to regain the losses of the last decade and begin to catch up with the poorer west European states. While the consolidation and extension of market reforms remains the short to medium-term priority, the long-term objective must be to promote investment and savings and thereby accelerate development and raise living standards.

| Key points |

- CEE (Central and Eastern Europe) and CIS (Commonwealth of Independent States) economies can usefully be distinguished.
- The sixteen CEE economies consist of the three Baltic States and thirteen countries previously under the Soviet sphere of influence.
- Generally the CEE economies (as compared to the CIS economies) have experienced a higher per capita GDP, less dependence on agriculture, more industrialization and higher unemployment following enterprise restructuring.
- The former *command economies* depended upon highly structured national plans, using input–output techniques.
- The transition process requires the development of labour, goods and capital markets, largely absent from the command economy era.
- Disruption of the highly concentrated and vertically integrated production system of the command economies during the early transition years has caused major losses of output and employment, together with hyperinflationary tendencies as expanding money supply 'chased' an ever smaller output of goods and services.
- Macroeconomic policies restricting public sector deficits via reform of public expenditure and tax revenue, and microeconomic policies increasing productivity via supply-side reforms, are key elements in the transition process.
- Trade patterns of the transition economies have shifted towards the advanced industrialized countries and away from trade between themselves.
- Enterprise restructuring and privatization have played significant roles in the transition process, as have market liberalization and financial sector reform. However a basic prerequisite for 'success' is arguably an appropriate set of legal reforms concerning ownership and property rights.

| Notes |

1. The table includes Slovenia, Croatia and Macedonia, but excludes the other states of former Yugoslavia (Bosnia, Serbia and Montenegro) where war and economic sanctions have so far prevented economic transformation.
2. The Soviet Union's fifteen republics declared independence in 1991. In 1993, Czechoslovakia split into the Czech Republic and Slovakia, and after a series of conflicts, Slovenia, Croatia, Macedonia and Bosnia Herzegovina left Yugoslavia, leaving a federal rump of Serbia and Montenegro.
3. E.g. oil and natural gas from the former Soviet Union to CEE was exported at below world prices, while most studies now conclude that CEE countries were able to sell manufactured goods to the former Soviet Union at above world prices.

References and further reading

Aldcroft, D. and Morewood, S. (1995) *Economic Change in Eastern Europe since 1918*, Edward Elgar.

Aoki, M. and Kim, H. K. (1995) *Corporate Governance in Transitional Economies: insider control and the role of banks*, EDI Development Studies, The World Bank, Washington, DC.

Baldwin, R. (1994) *Towards an Integrated Europe*, Centre for Economic Policy Research, London.

Carlin, W. and Mayer, C. (1992) Restructuring enterprises in eastern Europe, *Economic Policy*, **15**, 311–52.

EBRD (1995) *Transition Report 1995: investment and enterprise development*, European Bank for Reconstruction and Development, London.

EBRD (1996) *Transition Report 1996: infrastructure and savings*, European Bank for Reconstruction and Development, London.

EBRD (1997) *Transition Report 1997: enterprise performance and growth*, European Bank for Reconstruction and Development, London.

EBRD (1998) *Transition Report Update*, London, European Bank for Reconstruction and Development.

Estrin, S. (Ed.) (1994) *Privatization in Central and Eastern Europe*, Addison Wesley Longman, London.

Gros, D. and Steinherr, A. (1995) *Winds of Change: economic transition in central and eastern Europe*, London, Addison Wesley Longman.

Healey, N. M. (1994) The transition economies of central and eastern Europe: a political, economic, social and technological analysis, *The Columbia Journal of World Business*, **XXIX**, 62–71.

Johnson, S. and Loveman, G. (1995) *Starting Over in Eastern Europe: entrepreneurship and economic renewal* Harvard Business School Press, Cambridge, MA.

Johnson, S., Kaufmann, D. and Shleifer, A. (1997) *Politics and Entrepreneurship in Transition Economies*, Working Paper Series No. 57, William Davidson Foundation, University of Michigan.

Kumar, A. (1993) *State Holding Companies and Public Enterprises in Transition*, Macmillan, London.

Lavigne, M. (1995) *The Economics of Transition: from socialist economy to market economy*, Macmillan, London.

UNECE (1995) *Economic Survey of Europe in 1994–1995*, UN Economic Commission for Europe, Geneva and New York.

Chapter 30

Economics of developing countries

The economic development of the less developed countries (LDCs) presents many important and challenging problems. These problems are many in number and diverse in nature. It is now acknowledged that political, social, historical and cultural factors work alongside the economic factors when LDCs go through a process of growth and structural change. This chapter will, however, focus on the economic issues, though reference will be made on occasions to these broader issues. The chapter begins by considering various ways of classifying countries, including those regarded as 'developing'. The nature and causes of poverty amongst the nations are very complex, and the remedies are neither easy nor quick. An analysis of the major features of LDCs will shed some light on the peculiar economic and social conditions of production, consumption and distribution of income and wealth which exist in LDCs. This will help us to understand some development theories and their policy implications. The 'debt crisis' facing many LDCs is considered and the policy responses of the IMF and other international institutions are reviewed.

Classification of economies

It may be useful to note at the outset that there are a number of ways of classifying countries in a world economy which consists of over 5 billion persons, living in 181 nation states and with an estimated average annual income of around $4,500 per person.

IMF classification One widely used method for classifying economies is that of the International Monetary Fund (IMF), which uses three broad groups.

- *Industrial countries*: this covers the 23 highly industrialized countries, including the so-called Group of Seven or G7 economies (Canada, France, Germany, Italy, Japan, UK and US), 14 other European economies and Australia and New Zealand.
- *Developing countries*: this is an extremely broad group of 130 countries covering the Western Hemisphere other than the US and Canada, Asia other than Japan,

the Middle East and Africa. It has been criticised as covering too wide a range of countries, from rural countries in extreme poverty to those close to being classified in the group of industrial countries. In an attempt to address this issue a sub-group of *newly industrializing countries* (NICs) has been separately identified within the 'developing countries', including countries such as Hong Kong, South Korea, Singapore and Taiwan.

- *Transitional economies*: these are the 28 countries that have emerged from the former Soviet Union (e.g. Ukraine, Belarus) together with the countries of Central and Eastern Europe which were closely allied with the former Soviet Union (e.g. Poland, Hungary). The transitional economies are considered in some detail in Chapter 29.

World Bank classification

The World Bank and a number of other bodies use annual Gross National Product (GNP) per head to identify three broad groups of countries, one of which is further subdivided, making four groups in all.

- *High income economies*: countries with an annual GNP per head of $9,656 or more (in 1997 values).
- *Middle income economies*: countries with an annual GNP per head from $786 to $9,655 (in 1997 values).

Because this group is so broad it has been subdivided into:

(i) *Upper-middle income economies*: annual GNP per head from $3,125 to $9,655.
(ii) *Lower-middle income economies*: annual GNP per head from $786 to $3,124.

- *Low income economies*: countries with an annual GNP per head of $785 or less (in 1997 values).

GNP data and classification   The use of GNP per head as a basis for classification has been much criticised in recent years. Nevertheless it does give some indication of the huge disparities in standard of living between countries, as can be seen from Fig. 30.1.

Before moving to alternative indicators of 'economic well-being' let us briefly review the usefulness of the GNP per head figures represented in Fig. 30.1. Students of macroeconomics will know that GNP can be measured in the local currency using output, income and expenditure methods. By dividing the figure for GNP (converted into US dollars at the official $/country exchange rate) by the country population, we obtain an average figure for output or income per head. Interesting as this figure undoubtedly is, it has a number of flaws as a measure of comparative living standards in the respective countries.

(a) *Inappropriate exchange rates*. Converting the value of GNP expressed in the local currency into a $ equivalent using the *official* exchange rate may misrepresent the actual purchasing power in the local economy. This is because the official exchange rate is influenced by a range of complex forces in the foreign exchange markets and may not accurately reflect the purchasing power of one country's currency in another country. A more accurate picture is given if we use *purchasing power parities* (PPPs) rather than official exchange rates when making

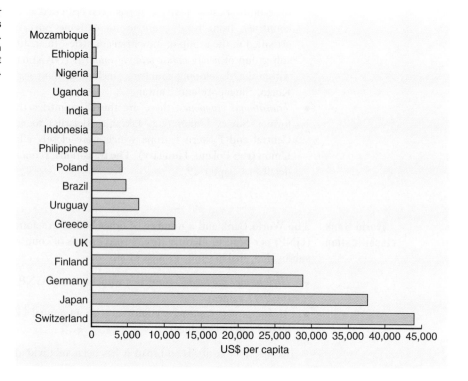

this conversion (see Table 30.1 on p. 709). Purchasing power parities measure how many units of one country's currency are needed to buy *exactly the same basket of goods* as can be bought with a given amount of another country's currency. On this basis the Mozambique figure rises from $90 to $959 per capita and the Switzerland figure falls from $44,320 to around $24,881 per capita using 1997 purchasing power parities.

(b) *Differing degrees of non-market economic activity.* GNP per capita only includes the money value of recorded (market) transactions involving goods and services. Non-market transactions are excluded. For example, the output of subsistence agriculture, whereby farmers grow food for their own consumption, are excluded from GNP figures. In many less developed economies where there is often a greater degree of non-market economic activity this fact may lead GNP figures to underestimate the true living standards.

(c) *Varying levels of inequality.* GNP per capita gives an indication of the 'average' standard of living in a country. However, this may reflect the experience of only a small number of people in that country because its *income distribution* may be highly unequal, being skewed in the direction of the wealthier sections of society. For example, instead of using the *arithmetic mean* for GNP per capita, the *median* might be a more useful measure of the 'average', i.e. that figure for which 50% of the population has a higher GNP per capita, and 50% has a lower GNP per capita.

(d) *Incidence of externalities.* Externalities occur where actions by an individual or group impose costs (or benefits) on others which are not fully 'priced'. Increased pollution is a by-product of many industrial processes, reducing the quality of life for those affected. However, this negative externality may not be reflected in the GNP calculations. Similarly, the GNP figure makes no allowance for the depletion and degradation of natural resources and for the social costs these may impose, e.g. deforestation as a factor in global warming, etc.

For these and other reasons (differing accounting conventions, economic and social practices, etc.) there has been a move towards the use of indicators other than the GNP per capita figure to reflect the 'true' standard of living in various countries, using various 'quality of life' indicators such as life expectancy, medical provision, educational opportunities, etc.

UN classification The United Nations has published a Human Development Report since 1990 in which two new methods of classification are presented, one involving a Human Development Index and the other a Human Poverty Index. We now consider each of these in turn.

Human Development Index (HDI) classification An interesting issue is whether the conventional GNP per capita figure can be merged with 'quality of life' indicators to give an overall index of economic well-being. A first step in this direction has in fact been made with the publication of the United Nations' Human Development Index (HDI). In Table 30.1 we present more comprehensive data for the 16 countries shown in our earlier Fig. 30.1 with the addition of the USA. We also show the rank of these countries (out of 174 countries) in terms of real GNP per head using purchasing power parities and in terms of the Human Development Index. Before commenting further on these rankings it will help if we explore the background to the HDI a little further.

Table 30.1 Selected country indicators and rankings (out of 174 countries, 1997).

	1 GNP per head ($)	2 Real GNP per head (PPP$)	3 Life expectancy at birth (years)	4 Adult literacy rate (%)	5 Enrolment ratio* (%)	6 Human Development Index (HDI)	7 Rank by real GNP per head (PPP$)	8 Rank by HDI
Mozambique	90	959	46	40	25	0.281	159	166
Ethiopia	110	455	49	36	20	0.252	173	169
Nigeria	260	1,270	52	57	38	0.391	137	160
Uganda	320	1,483	41	62	49	0.340	147	142
India	390	1,422	62	52	55	0.451	140	139
Indonesia	1,100	3,971	64	84	62	0.679	87	96
Philippines	1,220	2,762	67	95	80	0.677	109	98
Poland	3,590	5,442	71	99	79	0.851	69	52
Brazil	4,720	5,928	67	83	72	0.809	63	62
Uruguay	6,620	6,854	73	97	76	0.885	52	38
Greece	12,010	11,636	78	97	82	0.924	35	20
UK	20,710	19,302	77	99	86	0.932	21	14
Finland	24,080	18,547	76	99	97	0.942	23	6
Germany	28,260	20,370	76	99	81	0.925	16	19
USA	28,740	26,977	76	99	96	0.943	3	4
Japan	37,850	21,930	80	99	78	0.940	10	8
Switzerland	44,320	24,881	78	99	76	0.930	4	16

*Percentage of population at Levels 1, 2 and 3 (combined) of OECD Literacy Survey.
Sources: Adapted from Human Development Report (1998), UN; World Development Report (1998).

The Human Development Index (HDI) is based on three indicators.

- *Standard of living*, as measured by real GNP per capita (PPP$). Column 2 in Table 30.1.
- *Life expectancy at birth*, in years. Column 3 in Table 30.1.
- *Educational attainment*, as measured by a weighted average of adult literacy (two-thirds weight) and enrolment ratio (one-third weight). Columns 4 and 5 respectively in Table 30.1.

Each of these three indicators is then expressed in *index form*, with a scale set between a minimum value (index = 0) and a maximum value (index = 1) for each indicator.

- *Standard of living*: $100 real GNP per capita (PPP$) is the minimum value (index = 0) and $40,000 is the maximum value (index = 1).
- *Life expectancy at birth*: 25 years is the minimum value (index = 0) and 85 years is the maximum value (index = 1).
- *Educational attainment*: 0% for both adult literacy and enrolment ratios are the minimum values used for calculating the weighted average (index = 0) and 100% for both adult literacy and enrolment ratios are the maximum values used for calculating the weighted average (index = 1).

An index is then calculated for *each* of these three indicators, and the *average* of these three index numbers is then calculated, as shown for each country in column 6 of Table 30.1. This average of the three separate index numbers is the Human Development Index (HDI). The closer to 1 is the value of the HDI, the closer the country is to achieving the maximum values defined for each of the three indicators.

From columns 7 and 8 of Table 30.1 we can see that the rankings of the countries (in order from 1 to 174) do vary with the type of indicator used. In other words using a GNP per head indicator, even adjusted for purchasing power parities, gives a different ranking for countries than using the HDI index which brings quality of life aspects into the equation.

The HDI, by bringing together both economic and quality of life indicators, suggests a *greater* degree of underdevelopment for some countries than is indicated by economic data alone. For example Nigeria is 137th out of 174 countries when the GNP per head data is used for ranking (column 7) but *falls* a further 23 places to 160th when the HDI is used for ranking (column 8). For Nigeria it would seem that the relatively disappointing enrolment ratio into education has helped depress the 'education' index and with it the overall HDI. On the other hand, the HDI suggests a *smaller* degree of under-development for some countries than is indicated by economic data alone. For example Uruguay is 52nd out of 174 countries when the GNP per head data is used for ranking (column 7) but *rises* by 14 places to 38th when the HDI is used for ranking (column 8). For Uruguay it would seem that the relatively high adult literacy and enrolment ratios have helped increase the 'education' index which, together with encouraging life expectancy data, have raised the overall HDI.

Although only in its infancy, it may be that classifications of countries based on indices such as the HDI which bring together both economic and quality of life data, may give a more accurate picture of the level of development. Indeed Fig. 30.2 shows how countries with similar levels of real income per head can have markedly different scores in terms of the Human Development Index. For example both Paraguay and

Fig. 30.2.   Similar
income, different HDI.
Source: Adapted from
Human Development
Report (1998).

Fig. 30.2.   Similar income, different HDI. *Source:* Adapted from Human Development Report (1998).

Morocco have real GDP per head of around \$3,500, but the better quality of life indicators for Paraguay give it a much higher HDI than do similar quality of life indicators for Morocco.

Human Poverty Index (HPI)   A further step in this direction has been taken by the UN in 1997 with its introduction of the Human Poverty Index (HPI) This seeks to measure the extent of deprivation in terms of the percentages of people *not expected* to attain specified target levels for various economic and quality of life indicators. In this sense the HPI measures the proportion of people who are 'left outside' certain minimum standards for a country or community.

The Human Poverty Index (HPI) incorporates three indicators, P_1, P_2 and P_3, the last of which is a composite of three separate items.

● (P_1) Percentage of people not expected to survive to age 40.
● (P_2) Percentage of adults who are illiterate.
● (P_3) Percentage of people who fail to attain a 'decent living standard'.

This latter indicator (P_3) is subdivided into three (equally weighted) separate items.

(P_{31}) Percentage of people without access to safe water.
(P_{32}) Percentage of people without access to health services.
(P_{33}) Percentage of people with underweight children.

The P_3 indicator is then calculated as a simple average of these three separate items.

$$P_3 = \frac{P_{31} + P_{32} + P_{33}}{3}$$

The Human Poverty Index is then calculated by the following formula.

$$\text{HPI} = \left[\frac{1}{3}(P_1^3 + P_2^3 + P_3^3)\right]^{1/3}$$

Although rather complex, this formula gives an index number which is usually expressed as a percentage from 0 to 100%. The closer to 0% the HPI, the *smaller* the degree of deprivation in terms of the three indicators. The closer to 100% the HPI, the *greater* the degree of deprivation in terms of the three indicators.

We can illustrate the idea of the Human Poverty Index by considering the values of the three indicators for Egypt (Table 30.2).

To calculate P_3 we take the simple average of the three separate items.

$$P_3 = \frac{13 + 1 + 15}{3} = \frac{29}{3} = 9.67\%$$

Table 30.3 shows the HPI for the poorest 41 out of 77 countries for which data are available. HPI can be calculated as follows:

$$\text{HPI} = \left[\frac{1}{3}(13.0^3 + 48.6^3 + 9.67^3)\right]^{1/3}$$

$$= \left[\frac{1}{3}(2,197.0 + 114,791.3 + 904.2)\right]^{1/3}$$

$$= [39,297.5]^{1/3}$$

$$\text{HPI} = 34.0\%$$

Broadly speaking we can interpret this figure as suggesting that some 34.0% of people in Egypt suffer from 'poverty', in the sense of being deprived of a minimum standard of entitlement in one or more of the three poverty indicators.

Table 30.3 shows the extent of poverty as measured by the HPI in the poorest 41 out of 77 developing countries for which data were available. For Niger some 62% of people suffer from 'poverty' in terms of the HPI Index. In fact 32 countries have an HPI in excess of 33%, implying that for these countries at least one-third of their people suffer from human 'poverty' with five countries having an HPI in excess of 50%.

Notice that the ranking of countries by the earlier Human Development Index (HDI) and the Human Poverty Index (HPI) differs, at times considerably so. Arguably the HDI measures progress for the country as a whole, but the HPI measures the proportions of people in that country who are *excluded* from that progress. So, for example, in Table 30.3, out of the 77 countries ranked in terms of HPI and HDI, Oman is ranked 25 places *lower* on HPI than on HDI. This suggests that the *average* achievements in Oman in terms of Human Development Index are less evenly distributed amongst its population than is the case elsewhere (hence its lower ranking in HPI than in HDI). On the other hand Uganda is ranked 10 places *higher* on HPI than on HDI, suggesting that its *average* achievement in terms of the HDI are more evenly distributed amongst its population than is the case elsewhere.

Table 30.2 Deprivation indicators for Egypt (%).

	P_1	P_2	P_{31}	P_{32}	P_{33}
Egypt	13.0	48.6	13	1	15

Table 30.3   Human Poverty Index (HPI) for the 41 poorest countries.

	Human Poverty Index (%)	HPI rank	HPI rank minus HDI rank		Human Poverty Index (%)	HPI rank	HPI rank minus HDI rank
El Salvador	27.8	37	4	Uganda	42.1	57	−10
Oman	28.9	38	25	Sudan	42.5	58	−6
Guatemala	29.3	39	8	Guinea-Bissau	42.9	59	−10
Papua New				Haiti	44.5	60	−6
Guinea	29.8	40	−1				
Namibia	30.0	41	11	Bhutan	44.9	61	−2
Iraq	30.1	42	3	Mauritania	45.9	62	4
Cameroon	30.9	43	−1	Pakistan	46.0	63	14
Congo	31.5	44	4	Cote d'Ivoire	46.4	64	7
Ghana	31.8	45	0	Bangladesh	46.5	65	9
Egypt	34.0	46	14	Madagascar	47.7	66	5
India	35.9	47	−3	Malawi	47.7	67	−1
Zambia	36.9	48	−7	Mozambique	48.5	68	−2
Lao People's				Senegal	48.6	69	4
Dem. Rep.	39.4	49	2				
Togo	39.8	50	−4	Yemen	48.9	70	10
Tanzania	39.8	51	−8	Guinea	49.1	71	0
Cambodia	39.9	52	1	Burundi	49.5	72	−1
Morocco	40.2	53	16	Mali	52.8	73	−1
Nigeria	40.5	54	2	Ethiopia	55.5	74	2
Central African				Sierra Leone	58.2	75	−2
Rep.	40.7	55	−7				
Dem. Rep. of				Burkina Faso	58.2	76	1
the Congo	41.1	56	3	Niger	62.1	77	1

Note: HDI ranks have been recalculated for the 77 countries for which data are available.
Source: Adapted from Human Development Report (1998), UN.

Although not shown in Table 30.3, China has an HPI of 17.1% and an HPI ranking of 16 out of the 77 countries. The HDI calculated for China and Egypt turned out to be very similar, yet Egypt's HPI is much higher at 34%, a ranking of 46 out of 77 countries. This implies that although the average achievement in terms of the HDI are quite similar in China and Egypt, they are more inequitably distributed in Egypt than in China.

Major features of LDCs

Clearly the exact definition of which countries are regarded as the less developed countries (LDCs) may depend on the types of classification system adopted. Nevertheless, whatever the precise definition of an LDC, a number of *features* or characteristics are regarded as fairly typical of any country placed within this category.

1. *Low real income per capita*. This is a major indicator of underdevelopment. A comparison with the economically developed countries is striking. For instance, in 1998, an average Indian earned around 1.5% of the income of an average American. Most LDCs exhibit very low ratios of total income (however defined) to total population, resulting in a low value for real income per capita. This is often the result of low productivity, low savings, low investment, few resources and backward technology, often allied to high levels of population, the latter being determined by complex socio-economic factors.

2. *High population growth rate.* Most LDCs experience a high population growth rate, particularly in Africa. Many LDCs in Africa are experiencing a 'population explosion' even though the birth rate is stable, due mainly to a rapidly falling death rate. A major implication of such population explosion has been the growth of the proportion of people who live on the subsistence or 'poverty' line, defined as the minimum calorie intake necessary to stay alive. Even where the population growth rate is not very high (e.g. China) or falling (e.g. India), the *absolute size* of the population may be very high.

3. *Large-scale unemployment and underemployment.* This has been a common feature of many LDCs. Contributory factors often include a low level of economic activity, particularly in the industrial sector. Since labour in LDCs tends to be both more abundant than capital and poorly educated, labour productivity is often quite low. The pictogram shown in Fig. 30.3 indicates that today there are a huge number of people (each 'person' represents 10 million individuals) living on $1 a day or less (in constant 1985 international prices). As can be seen, the majority of these people are to be found in East and South Asia, Sub-Saharan Africa, Latin America and the Caribbean. Even with low wages, an even lower labour productivity can mean high 'relative unit labour costs' (see Chapter 1), which in turn can mean unemployment.

4. *Inequalities in the distribution of income.* The pattern of income distribution tends to be less equal in most LDCs in comparison with the developed countries.

Fig. 30.3.   Geographical location of the world's 'poor'.
Source: Adapted from World Bank (1998).

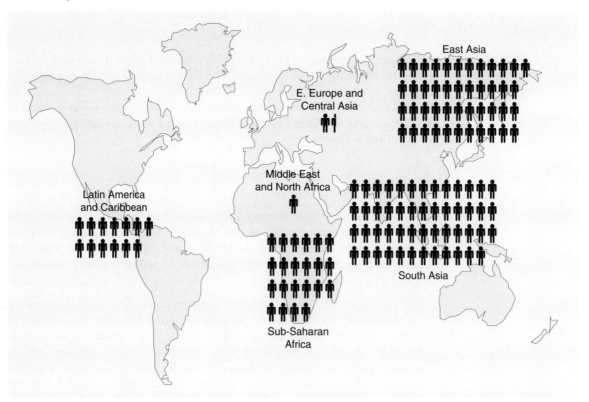

Note: Each figure represents 10 million persons living on $1 a day or less in 1998 (at 1985 international prices).

5. *Large but neglected agricultural sector.* In most LDCs, agriculture accounts for 40–85% of the real national income and about 60–90% of total employment. Nevertheless policy makers in many LDCs have opted for industrialization, often at the expense of agricultural development, in order to promote rapid economic growth. Such neglect of agriculture has often led to food shortages, poverty and famines, though the 1998 Nobel prize-winning economist A. Sen has also argued (1981) that to understand famine, it is necessary to understand the structure of ownership and food entitlement in the society. Nevertheless a well-developed agriculture would help to supply 'wage-goods', food, raw materials and foreign exchange for the development of both the industrial and the agricultural sectors.

6. *Volatile export earnings.* Foreign trade has tended to contribute relatively little to the national income of many LDCs. The pattern of foreign trade for most LDCs has often been determined by former colonial trade relationships, with today's LDCs remaining net exporters of primary goods and net importers of finished industrial goods.

   The export income of LDCs from primary goods (such as food and raw materials) sometimes fluctuates quite sharply, in part because of low income and price elasticities of demand for primary goods and in part because of the volatility of supply, as in extreme weather conditions. For example any substantial increase in supply allied to a relatively price inelastic demand curve will cause a fall in price and a fall in revenue for the exporter of primary goods. The tendency for such products to have a relatively low income elasticity of demand also means that rising prosperity in the developed countries results in only modest increases in demand for primary products. In addition the LDCs have historically often depended on a few key markets; such a narrow market base increases the risk factor as regards prospects of a sustained growth of export earnings.

7. *Market imperfections.* In many LDCs markets are imperfect; sometimes they do not even exist (e.g. forward markets). Indeed, the examples of market failures are all too frequent in the LDCs. For example there will often be a small *organized market* for money and other financial instruments and a larger *unorganized market* (see below) with few of the properties normally attributed to a market.

Theories of economic growth

Having noted these 'features' of the LDCs it may be useful at this stage to consider the causes, and possible remedies, to the situations in which these countries find themselves.

Neo-classical growth theory

Following the work of Solow and Dennison, neo-classical (NC) growth theory seeks to explain the contribution of different inputs to the overall growth of output of an economy. The underlying assumption is that variations in inputs such as labour (L) and capital (K), together with technological progress (A), can account for any observed changes in output (Y).

Thus, the change in output can be expressed in functional notation as:

$$Y = Af(L, K)$$

From the point of view of the developing countries, the neo-classical growth theory certainly points to increasing labour (L) and capital input (K) as a means of stimulating economic growth. This in turn suggests that encouraging savings (or at least access to savings) in order to finance investment in capital input (*K*) may be a useful policy direction. Unfortunately empirical investigations using the neo–classical model in the developed economies have pointed to a significant part of the growth process being correlated with changes in '*A*', the technological change or productivity growth 'residual'. This neo–classical model was able to 'account' for changes in output by attributing such changes to an increased use of labour and capital as factor input (*L*, *K*) and to technological change (*A*), the latter often referred to as 'productivity growth'. Unfortunately it *could not explain* how and why technological change (or productivity growth) has had its observed effect. In other words '*A*' was treated as a 'residual' in such neo–classical growth models rather than as a variable which could be manipulated for policy purposes. Since this 'residual' factor is assumed to be '*exogenous*' and yet has been found to be highly significant, economic growth seems to have fallen on developed countries like 'manna from heaven'!

Figure 30.4 provides an illustration of the significance of ('unexplained') productivity growth to changes in real GDP in Ghana and the Republic of Korea from 1956 to 1991. The two countries had rather similar (and low) real GDP per capita in 1956, but by 1991 Korea's real GDP per capita had grown by as much as seven times that of Ghana. Unfortunately only a small part of this large observed difference can be accounted for ('explained') by changes in physical capital (*K*) and human capital (*L*). The remaining (or residual) part is ascribed to the 'unexplained' factor of technological change (*A*) in terms of this growth accounting procedure.

This importance of the unexplained residual is further reinforced by the cross-country studies presented in Table 30.4. Capital was regarded as the only country-specific factor which could be accumulated and changes in capital per head were found to account for less than 30% of the recorded growth in GDP per capita in the two major studies, with the residual of Total Factor Productivity (TFP) growth accounting for 70% or more.

Fig. 30.4.   Trends in real GDP per capita in Ghana and the Republic of Korea.
Sources: Summers and Heston (1994); World Bank (1998).

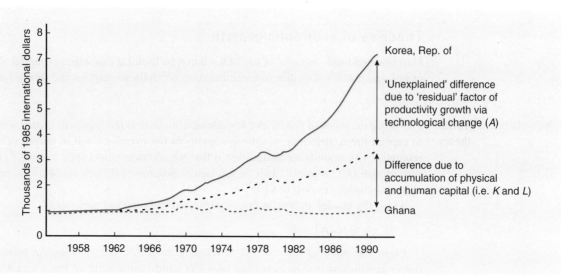

Table 30.4 Using growth accounting to decompose changes in GDP per capita.

Sources of variance in GDP per capita	Nehru and Dhareshwar, 1960–88	King and Levine, 1960–85
Growth in capital per capita	24	25
Unexplained by factor accumulation of which:	76	75
TFP growth	60	57
Covariance of TFP growth and capital accumulation	16	18

Source: Adapted from Easterly *et al.* (1998).

The absence of a sensible theory to explain the role of the 'residual' element of Total Factor Productivity simply led many to regard the measured value of '*A*' from empirical studies using the neo-classical growth accounting model as essentially a 'coefficient of ignorance'! In the late 1980s, however, a number of economists were prompted to analyse the nature and role of such a 'residual' element in growth theories by seeking to 'endogenise' it, as in the work of Romer (1990) and Barro *et al.* (1995).

Endogenous growth theory

The origin of the *endogenous growth theory* (EGT) can be traced back to the early 1960s when Arrow published his seminal work on 'Learning by Doing'. The EGT seeks to explain changes in Total Factor Productivity (TFP) by analysing the role of a number of variables which might explain the size and variation of the TFP residual over time. A number of variables are included in EGT, but at this stage we can illustrate this approach by considering one such variable, namely investment in training and education as a means of equipping labour to make better use of the technology available. By adding this human capital variable (*H*) to the neo-classical production function we derive the expression:

$$Y = Af(L, K, H)$$

Adding this extra variable *H* has helped reduce the 'unexplained' element of Total Factor Productivity growth in empirical work. Indeed Barro (1995) reported a study of 98 countries over the period 1960–86 which found that of the average recorded growth rate of output per worker of 2.24% per annum, around one-third (0.76 percentage points) could be 'explained' by changes in physical capital and a further one-fifth (0.45 percentage points) by changes in human capital accumulation. Even so just under a half (1.03 percentage points) still remained to be explained as part of the Total Factor Productivity 'residual'.

Convergence and divergence of growth rates Note that if we stick to the orthodox neo-classical (NC) growth theory and assume technical progress (*A*) as exogenous, then given the fact that knowledge is relatively inexpensive to input, the prediction is that all countries (rich and poor) should *eventually* attain the same value for *A* in their respective production function(s). Thus the orthodox NC growth theory indicates a 'convergence' or 'catching up' process in which in the long run LDCs acquire the more productive techniques and learn over time how to use them efficiently. Besides, LDCs with initially low capital/labour ratios should have a high marginal productivity of capital and thereby be better able to attract foreign capital to invest in equipment which may itself *embody* technical progress. In the long run, a system of *convergence* should therefore occur which results in broadly the same per capita GDP in the LDCs as in the developed countries. In other words LDCs with currently low per capita GDP should be able to grow *faster* to catch up with those with currently higher per capita GDPs. If this convergence theory *is* to be supported one would therefore expect that in empirical studies there should be a *negative correlation* between per capita GDP and the average growth rate. In practice, empirical evidence hardly supports this view, as in the report by Barro (1995) on a study of 98 countries over the period 1960–86.

The EGT tried to explain the lack of empirical support for convergence by introducing variables such as human capital, research and development, imperfect competition and knowledge accumulation into the production function. A key variable here is human capital (*H*) which is seen as involving education, training and other 'investments' in labour. Indeed human capital (*H*) as a factor of production is now seen as a *complementary* input to physical capital in the production function (rather than a substitute for capital) and this leads to some interesting theoretical results. For example, low (physical) capital to labour ratios commonly observed in LDCs are no longer necessarily associated with high marginal productivities of capital. In fact the combination of a low physical capital and human capital stock may imply a *low* marginal productivity for the composite 'capital' variable. Barro argues that by introducing human capital (*H*) into the production function in this way we can now better explain the 'manna from heaven' previously attributed to the exogenous variable '*A*' in neo-classical growth theory. In analytical terms, the more a country saves and invests in human capital (*H*) the faster its rate of growth of output.

Barro (1995), in reworking the empirical data for the 98 countries over the period 1960–86, argues that the main barrier to convergence seems to be inadequate investment in human capital among LDCs. To provide empirical verification of the new EGT, investment in human capital is measured by observing the disparities in levels of education between different countries. Lucas (1988) also argues that such disparities in the levels of education and labour skills can explain a good deal of the observed discrepancies in growth rates across nations.

If, over time, LDCs accumulate enough 'human capital', the prediction of EDG, as with earlier neo-classical growth theory, is that they should eventually 'converge'. Economic growth and convergence will then be faster for the LDC the more is saved and invested in both human and physical capital.

Public infrastructure   It is important to emphasise that in most LDCs '*public infrastructure*' (PI) can also be included in the aggregate production function alongside human capital and further help to explain Solow's 'residual' element. The term PI includes roads, schools, hospitals, communication systems and health care facilities generally provided by the government. Since PI is usually funded by public 'saving' (taxes) rather than by global markets, inadequate accumulation may readily occur in LDCs with low tax revenues.

Other endogenous variables   Research and development has been included as an additional endogenous variable in an attempt to explain the TFP residual, as have other variables which seek to proxy the accumulation and dissemination of information and knowledge.

Various types of 'market failure' in the LDCs may prevent many of these endogenous variables from being fully utilised in a 'catching up' process with the more developed economies. This will be especially true if these endogenous variables are associated with positive externalities and increasing returns when present, and negative externalities and decreasing returns when absent. The impact of such externalities and non-constant returns to scale could then 'explain' the observed failure of growth rates to converge over time. The policy implications of this are to place even greater emphasis on the role of governments in LDCs in supporting human and physical capital accumulation and 'favourable' public infrastructure programmes to stimulate output growth.

Dual economy models

The growth models examined in the previous section are highly aggregated since no attempt has been made to distinguish between different *sectors* of the economy, e.g. agriculture and industry. It has been argued that given the predominance of the agrarian sector in LDCs, the mechanics of economic development should be understood in the context of 'dual economy' models. It has been pointed out that unlike the developed countries, the LDCs do not suffer from a labour supply constraint. The problem in an LDC is thus to transfer 'surplus labour' (SL) from a largely unproductive agricultural sector to more productive industrial employment in order to promote economic growth. W. A. Lewis (1955) defines SL as that part of the labour force that can be removed without reducing the total output of the agrarian sector. This implies that the marginal productivity of labour in the agrarian sector is zero when such SL exists. Further, when the SL is redirected to the modern industrial sector there is the potential for creating what is in effect a highly elastic supply of labour to the industrial sector at a constant real wage. Of course when agricultural labour is in surplus, it may need some training and education for effective employment in industry. However, provided there is a modest surplus to employers over total wage costs resulting from industrial employment, then such funds should be available for profitable investment by the owners of capital to promote industrialization. This will in turn generate a greater demand for labour. Total industrial production will rise further with still greater employment of labour and this process will generate more reinvestible surplus funds and still greater capital accumulation. Eventually, however, industrial growth will lead to the exhaustion of all the surplus labour from the agricultural sector and the real wage will begin to rise in both the industrial and agricultural sectors, bringing this growth process via surplus labour to an end.

One of the many criticisms levelled at the Lewis model is that Lewis did not pay enough attention to the role of agriculture in economic development. Fei and Ranis in a study during the 1960s and more recently Jorgenson have tried to develop *dual economy* models, where they argue the case for a more balanced development of both the agricultural and industrial sectors without which overall economic growth would grind to a complete halt, as arguably happened in India and Pakistan during the 1960s. Such models emphasize the need to introduce technical progress in agriculture as part of the development process in order to generate sufficient additional food production to provide for an expanding industrial workforce without requiring expensive food imports, which would result in balance of payments problems.

However, supporters of such dual economy models have often underestimated the impact of high rates of population growth on the labour supply in LDCs, and failed to take sufficient account of the impact of inappropriate choices of techniques which have often occurred during industrialization (e.g. the choice of highly capital-intensive rather than labour-intensive techniques of production in 'labour-surplus' economies). It is therefore not entirely surprising that the dual economy models of development have themselves often failed to bring balanced and sustained growth for the LDCs. Another criticism is that the roles of an open economy and of the service sector in these dual economy models have hardly received any attention.

Money and economic growth

In many theories of economic growth, money does not play a significant role as it is not regarded as a real 'resource'. The sole purpose of money is seen as supporting exchange and determining the price level, i.e. money is regarded as a 'veil'. Of course, the progressive introduction of money into LDCs has the advantage of replacing barter and encouraging exchanges which are mutually beneficial to all parties. As a result the scope of exchange enlarges, division of labour increases and there is greater efficiency in the allocation of resources. Factors of production are now freed from producing for self-sufficiency alone as would have occurred in a bartering economy, so that the production possibilities of the economy increase.

Money markets in many LDCs are, however, far from perfect. This may present problems since a well-developed money market has a positive impact on economic growth by allocating savings into investment efficiently through financial institutions and the process of intermediation. The demand for loanable funds is brought into equilibrium with the supply of loanable funds in money markets via changes in the interest rate. A developed money market therefore leads to a more efficient allocation of resources, as well as providing for more liquidity and safety via trade in financial assets. In many LDCs savings and investments are rather low as people have less access to the wide variety of financial assets available in more developed economies. Savings too often take the form of holdings of land and gold rather than the financial assets which could help channel savings into productive investment.

The money markets of many LDCs are sometimes characterised by what is labelled as 'financial dualism'. This means that the money markets in LDCs can be divided into two broad categories: (a) organized; (b) unorganized. The *organized sector* generally consists of a central bank, commercial banks, co-operative credit banks and development banks. Division of labour and specialization does not always exist in such money markets, as with the absence of insurance companies. The *unorganised sector* mainly consists of moneylenders, indigenous banks, pawnbrokers, traders, merchants, landlords and friends.

While the organized sector is amenable to financial control, the unorganized sector is not. In many LDCs the unorganised sector still controls a significant section of the money market, chiefly because of its hold over the rural areas. Clearly the existence of such *financial dualism* has restricted the use of bank cheques and other means of payment. By reducing the volume of monetary transactions, it has also helped to perpetuate arguably wasteful non-monetary transactions of a barter or goods exchange variety. Further, it has deprived the society of an array of financial assets through which savings could have been more effectively mobilized and converted into investment for promoting economic growth. Evidently, a major policy objective in LDCs should be for the organized sector of the money markets to bring the unorganized sector more closely under its control.

'Inflation' and 'price stability' routes to development

It has been argued that money and physical capital are substitutes in the portfolio of economic agents. If the value of money balances falls, due to increases in money supply and a rise in inflation, then economic agents will hold more physical rather than money capital. Since output per head is directly related to capital per head, then inflation can actually raise capital and thus output per head. Many LDCs, chiefly those in Latin America, have followed this 'inflationary route' to economic growth, sometimes with unfortunate consequences. On the other hand, many East Asian countries, especially the 'Tiger' economies (i.e. Hong Kong, Singapore, Taiwan, Malaysia, South Korea) have followed the principle of price stability by holding the rate of inflation down. Despite recent difficulties in the Far East, the 'price stability route' to development would appear to be a surer method of stimulating development.

Financial repression

In the 1970s, Mckinnon and Shaw argued that many LDCs were following a monetary policy which leads to *financial repression* (FR). A system of FR occurs when the *real* rate of interest (i.e. nominal rate of interest minus the rate of inflation) is negative and below the equilibrium rate of interest. The policy of keeping the real rate of interest close to zero or even negative is based on the Keynesian idea that investment is very elastic with respect to changes in interest rates. Since investment is regarded as the prime mover of the economy, FR is advocated to stimulate investment and growth. Critics have pointed out, however, that in most LDCs investment is savings constrained. It is the *lack of availability* of savings rather than the cost of borrowing them that effectively determines the level of investment. Hence, LDCs should avoid FR and try to make the real rate of interest positive (rather than negative) in order to reward and encourage savers. A rise in real rates of interest would, it is argued, raise savings, raise investment and therefore raise economic growth. Further, a positive real rate of interest would arguably induce firms to choose only those investment projects which have a high output–capital ratio. Since only those projects with higher productivity are now chosen, the resulting gains in efficiency will lead to higher growth rates.

There is certainly some evidence to suggest that a system of FR has had an adverse effect on economic growth in many LDCs, particularly those in Latin America (Fry 1993). It should, however, be pointed out that a rise in real rates of interest can actually have a contractary effect on growth. For example such a rise could lead to cost-push inflation, as the interest rate is part of the cost to many producers. Further, given the financial dualism in LDCs, a rise in real rates of interest in the *organized* money market would very probably lead to a similar rise in the *unorganized* money markets. Small businesses in LDCs which frequently depend on the unorganised sector would then be driven out of business, reducing employment. Funds might also flow from the unorganized to the organised sector, leaving borrowers from the unorganized sector highly vulnerable to pressure for early debt repayment.

Clearly the final impact of the end of FR could vary from country to country. The weight of opinion seems to suggest that if the benefits claimed for the end of FR are to be realised, then it should be accompanied by prudent macroeconomic policies, e.g. price stability, a low public deficit to GDP ratio and a stable balance of trade.

Foreign aid and economic growth

In theory, foreign aid should raise both consumption and investment in a developing country, since in the absence of foreign aid an LDC will produce less of both consumption and investment goods given its limited resources. However, if the economy has a very high preference for consumption, then most of the foreign aid might be used for consumption purposes with little addition to its future productive capacity. To counter this the aid programmes often seek to designate aid for particular purposes; for example *food aid* is intended to increase consumption rather than investment, but *project aid* is usually intended to raise investment rather than consumption.

In the traditional economic models, an increase in access to savings from abroad should raise the growth rate of the borrowing country by increasing its rate of investment. If we aggregate aid from abroad with access to the savings from foreign capital markets, this gives us the variable 'financial resources' (FR). For some LDCs such as Bangladesh and Nepal in Asia and Mali and Senegal in Africa, foreign aid is a significant proportion of the GDP of these economies and hence the impact of additional aid on FR should help increase their growth rates. For countries such as China and India, however, foreign aid is only a small proportion of their GDP and hence the impact of additional aid on FR may have little effect on their growth rates.

Empirical studies in the 1970s seemed to suggest that the flow of 'financial resources' (FR) had a positive effect on real output growth rate in LDCs. The regression equations used in such studies were, however, rather simple and can be stated as follows:

$$Y = a + bFR + u$$

As long as the value of the co-efficient b is positive and significant, it was claimed that FR had an important positive role to play in stimulating economic growth.

However, some studies have found a negative relationship between the economic growth rates of LDCs and the flow of FR to the LDCs (e.g. Mosley *et al.* 1987). The explanation of such a negative effect of FR on growth rates in LDCs is not difficult to understand. A rise in the flow of FR may raise consumption at the expense of savings/investment, so that the overall growth rate suffers. Further, a rise in domestic consumption due to a rise in FR may increase imports and add to the balance of payment problems of many LDCs. They may then have to deflate aggregate demand to reduce imports, adversely affecting economic growth. In addition many governments of LDCs have used FR for increasing public expenditure on prestige projects which are relatively unproductive.

On the other hand, foreign aid has the potential to increase domestic economic growth rates by supplementing domestic savings to further increase investment and to allow imports of capital items previously restricted by scarce foreign exchange reserves. In this view foreign aid could have a positive and significant influence on growth rates for LDCs.

In recent years there seems little evidence of foreign aid having a 'crowding-out' effect on private sector investment, which had allegedly been observed in the 1960s.

Hence, the theory that the inflow of foreign aid generally strengthens the power of a regime which then restricts the flow of private capital, seems to have lost its force. This is not to deny that a corrupt government in a developing country seeking to maximise its own 'utility function' may use aid money to expand non-productive expenditures, e.g. on military capability, corrupt bureaucracy and very inefficient investments. In such cases, the impact of aid on economic growth will indeed tend to adversely affect growth. For aid to be effective may then depend on careful *targeting* of both the countries to support through aid and the specific projects to support within those countries. For instance it has been widely acknowledged that, despite the *absence* of a positive aid–growth correlation in India, aid inflows in the agricultural sector significantly helped to usher in the 'Green Revolution' in the late 1960s and early 1970s, thereby helping to overcome India's acute problems of food insecurity and famines. Such aid was generally well targeted, as in its allocation to specific areas in north-west India where irrigation facilities were available to reap the benefits of new seeds-fertilizer techniques. The inflow of foreign aid to such specific rural areas has helped India to import considerable amounts of new seeds and chemical fertilisers from abroad and to substantially increase the yields of major food crops.

The impact of foreign aid on the economic growth rates of LDCs is clearly likely to vary across different countries. More specifically, such impacts will depend on a number of factors.

(i)   the effective targeting of aid by both donor and recipient;
(ii) the effective use of aid by the recipient;
(iii) the current level of economic development and rate of output growth;
(iv) the rates of return on investment in both organized and unorganized financial markets;
(v)   the public infrastructure and the availability of physical human capital;
(vi) the level and types of economic regulation.

Without a careful analysis of such a complex set of dynamic socio-economic factors, it is difficult to draw a definitive conclusion about the real impact of foreign aid on LDCs.

Debt and development

An important economic issue in recent times has been the analysis of the impact of external debt on the economies of the less developed countries (LDCs). The main focus of attention has been the cost of servicing foreign debt and the potential benefits from default. It has been argued that if the cost of debt service is higher than the cost of default, then debt repayment by an LDC is not 'incentive-compatible'. However a highly indebted developing country may still have an incentive to repay because of the fear of losing access to the international capital market.

Reasons for LDC borrowing   The practice of borrowing from foreign countries as a method of promoting economic growth is not new. Historically, most of today's developed countries, including the USA, depended significantly on the imports of foreign capital for achieving a high standard of living. Besides the lessons of history, there are a number of sound reasons to explain the borrowing of LDCs from abroad.

(a) Most LDCs have low per capita income and savings. The required rate of economic growth to attain a better standard of living may need a higher level of investment (I) than can be financed by domestic savings (S). Thus, LDCs may wish to borrow foreign capital to eliminate the 'savings gap' i.e. ($I - S > 0$).

(b) Most LDCs suffer from serious shortages in their foreign exchange earnings as their imports (M) are generally much greater than their exports (X). Such an imbalance i.e. ($M - X$) > 0 is defined as a 'trade gap' which could be a serious constraint on achieving a higher rate of economic growth and per capita income. Many LDCs depend substantially on the import of capital and intermediate inputs to increase their production. Sometimes food imports may also play a crucial role in averting the threat of hunger and famine. Imports of foreign technology and skills may help ease the trade gap and accelerate economic growth.

(c) Many LDCs suffer from capital scarcity relative to labour supply which, according to orthodox theory, means that they should enjoy higher returns at the margin on capital flows from the developed countries. In capital-abundant countries, the marginal efficiency of capital (MEC) tends to be lower than in the LDCs. It follows that, as long as capital is fully mobile across nations, capital should flow, on efficiency grounds, from the rich to the poor countries to equalize the global MEC. Of course, such capital movements depend on the funds being invested in sectors where the rate of return is higher than the interest rate charged on the use of foreign capital.

It is now easy to see why the LDCs depended on foreign borrowing and debt accumulation throughout the 1950s and 1960s. Foreign debt helped to supplement low domestic savings to finance required investment in order to achieve high growth rates of real income and consumption. Besides, it was a vital ingredient in reducing the foreign exchange or trade gap. However, the suggestion that international debt – especially that of the lesser developed countries – has grown to such an extent that it has become a 'problem' gained ground during the 1970s and the 1980s. This trend continued through the 1990s with the total external debt of developing countries increasing from $1,374bn in 1990 to $1,748bn in 1998 – a growth of 27% in money terms.

The increase in oil prices during the mid-1970s created a surplus for the oil-exporting countries which they deposited with the banks of the US and Europe, who were only too happy to recycle the deposits as loans. Loans were advanced to LDCs for many purposes and competition between the banks ensured that the rates of interest were extremely low and that opportuniteies for profitable but risky investments in LDCs were aggressively pursued.

An indication of the extent of indebtedness can be gained from Table 30.5 which shows the position in 1984 and 1996 of the world's fifteen most heavily indebted countries. Of the fifteen countries, ten were located in South America, three in Africa, one in Asia (Philippines) and one in Europe (former Yugoslavia).

Over the given period, it can be seen that the total debt has grown. Its maturity structure, however, has lengthened, giving these countries greater opportunities for paying back debt. The major creditors have been the commercial banks, although they have been rather reluctant to play an expanding role in this regard, hence the increasing importance of official aid to those countries.

Table 30.6 gives a general overview of the external debt problem in a number of developing countries. A widely used indicator of international indebtedness is the *ratio* of total debt to the GDP. This provides a basic indicator of the relationship between total

Table 30.5 Fifteen most heavily indebted countries: total debt in 1984 and 1996.

Total debt ($bn)	1984	1996
By maturity	407.4	645.8
Short term	47.3	91.0
Long term	360.1	554.8
By creditor		
Official	73.0	241.2
Commercial banks	284.0	132.7
Other private	50.4	271.9

Source: Adapted from IMF (1998).

Table 30.6 The scale of external debt (1998).

	Total $bn	Debt (% of GNP)	Debt (% exports)	Debt service (% of exports)
Brazil	179	26	336	36
Mexico	157	44	238	35
China	128	17	84	9
India	90	22	254	27
Indonesia	129	64	211	32
Russian Federation	125	25	161	6
Turkey	80	47	217	33
Poland	41	31	195	4
Venezuela	35	51	209	21

Source: Adapted from World Bank (1998).

debt and the productive capacity of each economy. The table also shows the *absolute amount* of total debt outstanding, the *ratio* of this absolute debt to annual export earnings and the cost to each economy of paying interest on the debt plus capital repayments (*debt servicing*) as a percentage of the country's earnings from exports of goods and services.

The specific difficulties experienced by Mexico serve as a reminder of the complicated nature of external debt. For example, between 1982 and 1994, Mexico's total foreign debt doubled from $86bn to $165bn, with an accelerated rise in the first half of the 1990s. By early 1995 Mexico's problem was not only due to its high total debt, but also to the fact that some $58bn or 35% of the total debt fell due for repayment in 1995. Partly as a result of this the Mexico Peso suffered a spectacular depreciation in 1994 adding to that country's domestic (inflation) and trade (import costs) problems. Therefore Mexico had a short-term liquidity problem in addition to overall debt difficulties. In early 1995 the US came to Mexico's aid in the form of loan guarantees, with Mexico pledging its oil revenues in exchange for the guarantees.

Despite these problems, a combination of economic pressure and world assistance through the IMF and the World Bank has resulted in the needs of major debtor countries being reduced. The proportion of debt outstanding to exports has been falling; from a debt/export ratio of 1.80 for the developing countries in 1986, to less than 1.10 in 1998. The continuation of this trend will, of course, depend upon continued growth in the world economy.

Resolving the debt problem

The 1970s As the 1970s came to a close the main worry of the developed nations was that a large debtor would renege on debts and would, thereby, throw one or more of the world's largest economies into massive recession. The mechanism would have worked through the balance sheets of the major banks (some of which were extremely heavily committed) to their share prices and, thence, to the overall confidence of the public in the financial sector. Significantly efforts were made to avoid this and the IMF played a major role during the late 1970s and early 1980s in negotiating 'rescheduling' agreements in order to lessen the burden on the debtor nations. At the same time it attempted to encourage 'correct' economic policies which, it was hoped, would avoid the need for future loans. The IMF's medicine was administered to countries such as Argentina, Brazil, Peru and Uruguay but, even where it was accepted by the governments, it ran into considerable resistance from the public of those countries who objected to the economic stringency required.

The 1980s   By the early 1980s, and under the pressure of another world recession, many debtor countries were on the verge of reneging on their debts. In 1985 the 'Baker Plan' looked towards solving the problem by ensuring that the IMF amended its programmes. The 'Programme for Sustained Growth' was agreed in Seoul in October 1985 and aimed to reduce the burden of the IMF's austerity policies and the pressure on social stability brought on by both the austerity policies and those attempting to cut imports.

Within the confines of its restricted financial resources the IMF became a net recipient of money by 1987. Whereas in 1983 the Fund had been lending over $10bn per year to help offset the problems of debt repayment and economic adjustment, by 1987 it was actually a net recipient. In 1987, therefore, the Fund took a decision to reduce the amount of 'high-conditionality' lending it was doing and to increase lending under the *structural adjustment facility* (from SDR 3bn in 1987 to a peak of over SDR 9bn in 1990).

From 1982 the world economy grew more strongly (OECD growth averaged around 3% per annum) and imports grew particularly strongly (by around 7% per year). US and UK banks managed to reduce their exposure to the risk of Third World debt. For example, in 1982 US banks' exposure to problem debtors amounted to 6.8% of their total assets (UK banks 9.8%) but by 1987 the equivalent figures were 5.4% and 6.9% respectively. Even so, for the major debtor countries the proportion of debt to exports grew from around 165% in 1980 to over 330% in 1987. The result was that a series of the most heavily indebted countries reconsidered their options. Peru and Zambia placed limits on their debt-service repayments in 1987 and Brazil stopped paying interest due on their debts in February of that year. The annualised rate of inflation in Brazil in February 1987 was 377%.

World economic developments during the 1980s were mixed for the developing world. LIBOR (the London Inter-Bank Clearing Rate) fell by 5% between 1984 and 1988 and this had the effect of saving the debtor countries some $18bn per year in interest payments. On the same side of the balance sheet, oil importers such as Brazil benefited from the reduction in oil prices.

The 1990s   The late 1980s saw significant moves towards a more comprehensive and flexible approach to the ever increasing 'debt problem'. This was due, in no small measure, to the reluctance of debtor countries such as Mexico, Brazil and Nigeria to put their economies under unsustainable pressure by continuing to meet their interest and capital repayment obligations.

Given total world debt in the developing countries of over $1,700bn in 1996 (of which over $450bn was due from Latin America) the resources of the IMF (an absolute maximum of around \$135bn) were never going to be of significant help. Furthermore, the experience of the commercial banks during the late 1970s and early 1980s meant that they were not going to be interested in expanding their lending to those same countries.

In the event, the 1990s have seen a number of moves towards a 'package' of measures which, together, began to relieve some of the 'crisis' atmosphere. On the one hand the IMF continued to develop its facilities while, on the other, the commercial banks have begun to find ways around the roadblock of existing debt.

Role of the IMF and World Bank

As has been mentioned, both institutions have provided support for LDCs in various ways, but only under specified conditions.

IMF stabilization programmes   IMF stabilization programmes seek to address adverse balance of payments situations whilst retaining price stability and encouraging the resumption of economic growth. As Evers and Nixson (1997) have indicated, the main components of typical IMF stabilization policies include some or all of the following:

- fiscal contraction – a reduction in the public sector deficit through cuts in public expenditure and/or rises in taxation;
- monetary contraction – restrictions on credit to the public sector and increases in interest rates;
- devaluation of the exchange rate (this is often a pre-condition for the serious negotiation of a stabilization programme, rather than part of the programme as such);
- liberalization of the economy via reduction or elimination of controls, and privatization of public sector assets;
- incomes policy – wage restraint and removal of subsidies and reduction of transfer payments.

World Bank 'Structural Adjustment Lending'   Since 1980 the World Bank has been involved in various types of Structural Adjustment Lending (SAL) which accounts for over 20% of World Bank lending. These SAL programmes are non-project related, rather they involve lending to support specific programmes of policy which may involve elements of institutional change. These SAL programmes are generally directed towards improving the 'supply side' of the borrowing countries, intending to initiate and fund changes which will ultimately raise productive efficiency in various sectors of their economies.

Fig. 30.5 follows Evers and Nixson and provides a rather stereotyped but useful overview of the IMF 'stabilisation programmes' and the World Bank 'Structural Adjustment Lending' programmes.

Stabilization. As was noted above, most of the policies involved in the IMF stabilization programmes have been of a deflationary nature. This results in the

Fig. 30.5. Stabilization
and structural
adjustment.

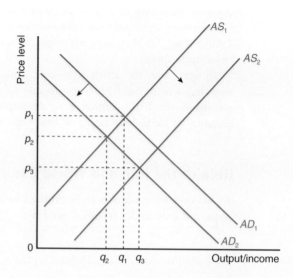

downward movement, to the left, of the aggregate demand curve (AD) from AD_1 to AD_2 thus reducing the price level (from p_1 to p_2) but also reducing output (from q_1 to q_2) The debtor country may be made more competitive in its exports and import-substitute sectors, benefiting its balance of payments and reducing its debt, but at the cost of lost output and employment.

Killick (1995) has provided a comprehensive review of the impact of IMF stabilization policies, providing evidence from Latin America and elsewhere that stabilization causes a fall in labour's share in the functional distribution of income. A wage freeze has often been involved, reducing the real value of all incomes from labour, especially those employed in the public sector where a wage freeze can be applied most effectively. Stabilization was often found to be associated with declines in public sector employment.

Cuts in public expenditure have been an important part of many stabilization programmes, such as health and education, with disproportional effects on the poor and particularly women. Stabilization has had differing effects on the urban and the rural poor, with the urban poor being hardest hit.

Structural adjustment. As was noted earlier, most of the World Bank SAL programmes have sought to improve the supply side of the economy. This results in the downward, to the right, movement of the aggregate supply curve (AS) from AS_1 to AS_2 thus reducing the price level (from p_2 to p_3 with AD_2) and increasing output (from q_2 to q_3). Clearly the 'medicine' via structural adjustment is rather more palatable in that output and employment rise, but only after possibly difficult changes to labour and capital market practices and institutions to improve supply-side conditions. (*Note:* for diagrammatic purposes we have assumed that the structural adjustment programme of the World Bank occurs *at the same time* as the IMF stabilization programme. Of course they may occur independently.)

Criticisms of IMF action

Criticisms of the IMF's activities in LDCs can be grouped as follows:

1. *That IMF programmes are inappropriate.* The criticism here is that its approach to policy has been preoccupied with the control of demand, and too little concerned with other weaknesses stemming from the productive system of LDCs, e.g. balance of payments problems. By deflating demand the IMF has imposed large adjustment costs on borrowing countries through losses of output and employment, further impoverishing the poor and even destabilizing incumbent governments.

2. *That IMF programmes are inflexible.* The criticism here is that the IMF has imposed its solutions on LDCs rather than negotiated a more flexible package. This has arguably infringed the sovereignty of states and alienated governments from the measures they are supposed to implement.

3. *That IMF support has been too small, expensive and short term.* The programmes have been criticised for having been too small in magnitude and too short term in duration for economies whose underlying problems are rooted in structural weaknesses and who often face secular declines in their terms of trade (fall in export prices relative to import prices).

4. *That the IMF is dominated by a few major industrial countries.* The criticism here is that the industrial countries have sometimes used their control of the IMF to promote their own interests, as for example in using the IMF to shift a disproportionate amount of the debt burden onto the debtor countries rather than forcing lenders (e.g. banks) to accept some of the debt burden. It has been alleged that successive American governments have used their influence to favour (or oppose) friendly (or hostile) LDCs.

Key points

- There are different ways of classifying countries, including those regarded as the less developed countries (LDCs).
- The conventional measure of real GNP per head has a number of weaknesses as a measure of the standard of living.
- New measures have been devised which also bring quality of life indicators into the equation. These include the Human Development Index (HDI) and the Human Poverty Index (HPI).
- Various theories of growth have been developed to identify policy measures which might raise output in the LDCs.
- Neo-classical models have been faced with a large unexplained 'residual'; as a result various 'endogenous' models of economic growth have been developed.
- The LDCs have a number of features which create additional problems for policies aimed at increasing growth.
- The world debt problem bears down heavily on the LDCs and the IMF and World Bank have sought to resolve some of these problems.
- There has been considerable criticism of the nature of the support mechanisms provided to LDCs, especially from the IMF.

References and further reading

Barro, R.A. (1995) *Economic Growth*, McGraw-Hill.

Collier, P. (1997) Africa, looking to the future, *Economic Review*, **15**, 2, November.

Easterly, W., Levine, R. and **Pritchett, L.** (1998) Stylized facts and the growth models who love them, *Development Research Group*, World Bank, Washington, DC.

Evers, B. and **Nixson, F.** (1997) *International Institutions and Global Poverty*, Developments in Economics, Vol. 13, Causeway Press.

Fry, M. (1993) *Money, Banking and Economic Development*, John's Hopkins University Press.

Ghatak, S. (1995) *An Introduction to Development Economics*, Routledge.

Ghatak, S., Levine, P. *et al.* (1996) Migration theories and evidence: a reassessment, *Journal of Economic Surveys*, July.

Ghatak, S. *et al.* (1997) Exports, export composition and economic growth: a co-integration analysis for Malaysia, *Applied Economics*, February.

Killick, T. (1995) *IMF Programmes in Developing Countries: Design and Impact*, Routledge, London.

Krugman, P. and **Obstfeld, M.** (1997) *International Economics*, Harper Collins.

Lewis, W. A. (1995) *Economic Development with Unlimited Supply of Labour*, Manchester School.

Lucas, R. (1988) On the mechanics of economic development, *Journal of Monetary Economics*, pp. 3–42.

Mankiw, G. *et al.* (1992) Empirics of economic growth, *Quarterly Journal of Economics*, **107**, pp. 407–37.

Mosley, P. *et al.* (1987) Aid, the public sector and the market in less developed countries, *Economic Journal*, **97**, pp. 616–41.

Romer, Paul (1990) Endogenous technical change, *Journal of Political Economy*, **98**, pp. S71–102.

Sen, A. (1981) *Poverty and Famine*, Oxford University Press.

Summers, R. and **Heston, A.** (1994) Differential productivity hypothesis and PPPs, *Review of International Economics*, **2**, October.

World Development Report (1998) World Bank, Oxford University Press.

A guide to sources

The following list, and associated discussion, is by no means intended to be exhaustive, but rather to highlight some of the more useful sources for statistical data and information on the UK economy. The sequence will be as follows:

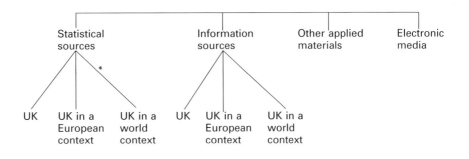

Statistical sources

The following contain important statistical series and, in some cases, articles commenting on those series or on related issues. The addresses given are those for enquiries about *orders* and *subscriptions*.

The UK economy Guide to Official Statistics HMSO, PO Box 276, London SW8 SDT.

This is, perhaps, the most useful starting point in any search for statistical sources relating to the UK. It has been published at irregular intervals since 1976 and the latest enlarged edition, compiled by the Office for National Statistics (ONS), was published in 1996. The first chapter of the Guide looks at the organization of the Government Statistical Office and gives the main contact points and publishers of statistics. The remaining 15 chapters contain one subject area per chapter, e.g. population, education, labour market, environment, the economy, etc. For each subject, the main datasets are described and the sources of statistics available are provided. Information on any specific topic can be obtained by using the extensive key word index at the back of the Guide.

The other UK statistical sources we consider are presented alphabetically.

Annual Abstract of Statistics (AAS)   HMSO, PO Box 276, London SW8 5DT.

Annual Abstract of Statistics gives annual figures, wherever possible, for the previous ten years, in some 400 tables. It presents the major statistics of the various government departments, grouped under eighteen section headings.

Bank of England Quarterly Bulletin (BEQB)   Publications Group, Bank of England, London EC2R 8AH.

The *Bulletin* is published quarterly, providing detailed statistics on assets and liabilities of the UK monetary sector institutions, though with less detail than in *Financial Statistics* (see below). Data are also provided for money stock components, government debt, official reserves, foreign exchange rates, comparative interest rates, and flow of funds analyses. Each issue contains a number of articles on recent economic and financial developments and on other topics in banking and finance. The Bank of England also publishes *Inflation Report* every quarter. This contains six sections covering topics such as the outlook for inflation over the next two years, monetary aggregates, financial market data, firm's pricing behaviour, etc.

Business Monitor (BM)   HMSO, PO Box 276, London SW8 5DT.

Business Monitor presents summary information on the annual census of production, with a two- to three-year time-lag. The annual summary tables (PA. 1002) present data for the latest, and previous four years, for mining and quarrying, the manufacturing industries, construction, gas, electricity and water. Detailed data are presented, by Minimum List Heading, on output, employment and costs, for both establishments and enterprises in each industry group. Separate annual (PA) reports are also available for each Minimum List Heading, together with quarterly (PQ), and monthly (PM), reports.

Economic Trends (ET)   HMSO, PO Box 276, London SW8 5DT.

Economic Trends is published monthly by the Office for National Statistics and contains tables and charts illustrating trends in the UK economy. Data are provided for the latest month, or quarter, as appropriate, and usually for at least the five previous years. As well as trends in the components of National Income, output and expenditure, trends in productivity, employment, trade, financial and corporate matters are outlined.

Financial Statistics (FS)   HMSO, PO Box 276, London SW8 5DT.

Financial Statistics is a monthly publication of the ONS. Data are provided on a wide range of financial topics, for the latest month or quarter, and for at least the previous five years. Financial accounts are presented for various sectors of the economy, central and local government, the public corporations, the monetary sector, other financial institutions, industrial and commercial companies, the personal sector and the overseas sector.

Key Data   HMSO, PO Box 276, London SW8 5DT.

Published annually, *Key Data* is a 'student version' of the key tables and charts from a variety of official publications involving economic and social data. Over 125 tables and charts cover topics such as Finance, Population, Transport, Employment, European Union, Law and Order, Leisure and Tourism, Education, Health and Personal Social Services, and Housing and the Environment.

Labour Market Trends   HMSO, PO Box 276, London SW8 5DT.

This is the successor to the Department of Education and Employment's *Employment Gazette* and is now published in an ONS series which includes *Economic Trends*, *Social Trends*, etc. It is published monthly and contains special feature articles which examine specific issues affecting labour markets – such as women's pay, trade unions, and flexible labour markets, etc. It does not include policy developments such as training, health and safety, as these are covered by the Department of Education and Employment's *Employment News*.

Monthly Digest of Statistics (MDS)   HMSO, PO Box 276, London SW8 5DT.

Again this is a monthly publication of the ONS. It gives up-to-date statistics on the output of various industries, covering a wider range of industries than *Business Monitor*. Statistics are also presented on the components of National Income and Expenditure, on demographic topics, on the labour market and on a variety of social issues.

National Income and Expenditure   HMSO, PO Box 276, London SW8 5DT.

Published annually by the ONS the so-called *Blue Book* is the single most comprehensive source of data on National Income, output and expenditure, and their components. As well as data for the current calendar year, those of the previous ten years are also provided. For some tables, data are even presented for twenty calendar years on a consistent basis and, in an annual supplement, as far back as 1946.

Regional Trends (RT)   HMSO, PO Box 276, London SW8 5DT.

Regional Trends is an annual publication of the ONS, and presents detailed data on the Standard Planning Regions of the UK. *Regional Trends* includes a wide range of economic, social and demographic indices, highlighting regional disparities in the UK.

Social Trends (ST)   HMSO, PO Box 276, London SW8 5DT.

Much of the material in *Social Trends* is of interest to the social scientist in general rather than the economist in particular. Nevertheless, it gives a detailed breakdown of patterns of household wealth, income, and expenditure, together with demographic, housing and social trends.

Transport Statistics: Great Britain HMSO, PO Box 276, London SW8 5DT.

Published annually by the Department of the Environment, Transport and the Regions, this is the main source of statistics on UK Transport. It is divided into nine parts covering Energy and the Environment, Vehicles and Roads, Road Traffic and Freight, Water and Air Transport and Public Transport. It also contains international transport statistics to place the UK in a world context.

UK Balance of Payments HMSO, PO Box 276, London SW8 5DT.

The so-called *Pink Book* is the most comprehensive single source available for balance of payments statistics. Published annually, it breaks down trade in goods and services, investment income, investment and other capital transactions, official financing, and external assets and liabilities, into their various components. Data for the previous ten years are presented for purposes of comparison.

UK Economic Accounts HMSO, PO Box 276, London SW8 5DT.

Published quarterly by the ONS it provides a useful update of some of the main components of National Income. It includes the financial accounts of industrial and commercial corporations together with those of central and local government This publication also provides details of the Balance of Payments on goods, services and investment accounts.

The UK economy in a European context

Economic Survey of Europe HMSO Books (Agency section), 51 Nine Elms Lane, London SW8 5DR.

Published by the UN annually. Data are presented by individual country, and by geographical groupings in Europe, including the Eastern bloc countries. Trends are identified for the various components of agriculture, industry, investment, consumer expenditure, National Income and foreign trade. The tables and charts are supplemented by written discussion.

European Economy HMSO Books (Agency section), 51 Nine Elms Lane, London SW8 5DR.

European Economy appears three times a year, in March, July and November, and is published by the Commission of the European Union. The November issue contains an annual report on the economic situation within the Union. A statistical annex presents the main economic indicators on an annual basis, and is attached to each issue.

Europe's 15,000 Largest Companies ELC International, 109 Uxbridge Road, Ealing, London W5 5TL.

This publication is regularly updated and contains information on the top companies of Europe. The volume contains data on the sales, profits, total assets, shareholder funds and employment of the largest companies in the Industrial, Trading and Services sectors.

Eurostat   HMSO Books (Agency section), 51 Nine Elms Lane, London SW8 5DR.

Annual publications on the major indices of economic activity are provided by the Statistical Offices of the members of the European Union under the *Eurostat* heading.

Panorama of EU Industry   HMSO Books (Agency section) 51 Nine Elms Lane, London SW8 5DR.

Published annually by DGIII of the European Commission it contains some 25 chapters covering all the main industrial and services sectors of the EU. Each chapter presents both a wealth of statistics and full commentaries. Each issue also contains special feature articles on topical subjects relating to industry and the Single Market.

The UK economy in a world context

International Monetary Fund publications   HMSO Books (Agency section), 51 Nine Elms Lane, London SW8 5DR.

World Economic Outlook. Published annually since 1980. This presents and analyses short- and medium-term projections for individual countries, together with a discussion of key policy issues. The industrial countries, the oil-exporting countries, and the non-oil developing countries, are considered as separate groups.

OECD publications   HMSO Books (Agency section), 51 Nine Elms Lane, London SW8 5DR.

OECD Economic Surveys. Individual country reports for the advanced industrialized economies, published annually.

OECD Economic Outlook. Presents economic trends and prospects in OECD countries. Published twice a year in July and December.

United Nations publications   HMSO Books (Agency section), 51 Nine Elms Lane, London SW8 5DR.

UN Statistical Yearbook. Published annually covering a wide variety of indices of economic activity for developed and developing nations.

World Economic Survey. Published every second year, examines fluctuations in the world economy, by individual countries and by groups of countries, for a variety of economic indicators. Problems and prospects are examined for the developed market economies, for centrally planned economies, and for the developing countries, together with the outlook for international trade.

Monthly Bulletin of Statistics. Published monthly, this volume contains a section on special statistics compiled for that specific issue and regular information on other statistical series, including population, wages, prices, production, manpower, etc.

Information sources

The following are helpful in locating new and past articles, in newspapers and periodicals. These often provide a fund of useful contemporary data on, and analysis of, applied issues. Also included are references to sources of documents and papers produced by various official and unofficial bodies.

The UK economy   Britain: an official handbook   HMSO, PO Box 276, London, SW8 5DT.

An annual publication by the ONS which provides a compact guide to the UK. It contains information and data on Government and Administration, External Affairs, Economic Affairs, the Environment and Social and Cultural Affairs. It is up-to-date and provides useful insights into the most recent changes in the UK economy and society.

British Humanities Index   Bowker-Saur, Windsor Court, East Grinstead House, East Grinstead, West Sussex RH19 1XA.

Published quarterly, this presents titles of articles, listed by subject and by author, for over 300 current periodicals.

Clover Newspaper Index   Clover Publications, 32 Ickwell Road, Northill, Biggleswade, Beds SG18 9AB.

Published monthly, this index covers all the main daily papers such as the *Times, Financial Times, Daily Telegraph, Guardian* and *Independent*, as well as the Sunday papers. It provides a single comprehensive source of all the articles written in these newspapers and is valuable for tracing most subjects of economic interest to the reader.

Monthly Index to the Financial Times   Primary Source Media Ltd, PO Box 45, Reading RG1 8HF.

Published monthly, this details all the articles, by subject, and by author, in the final edition of the *Financial Times* during that period.

Official publications   These are particularly difficult to track down.

HMSO Government Publications, PO Box 276, London SW8 5DT.

Published monthly (and even daily as a flysheet) this provides an index to new reports by parliamentary (e.g. House of Commons select committees) and non-parliamentary (e.g. Cabinet Office) bodies. Unfortunately a number of important reports from government departments and various official bodies are not included in the HMSO lists. A useful new publication seeks to document these.

Catalogue of British Official Publications. Chadwyck-Healey Ltd, The Quorum, Barnwell Road, Cambridge, CB5 8SW.

Published bi-monthly, this lists British official publications *not* published by HMSO. The majority of these publications are available on microfiche from the address above.

Also helpful is:

Government Statistics. A Brief Guide to Sources. ONS Press and Information Service, Great George Street, London SW1P 3AQ.

This is a free booklet from the Government Statistical Service listing the most important official statistical publications.

Research Index Broadmayne House Farm, Osmington Drove, Broadmayne, Dorset DT2 8EP.

A monthly index, by subject heading, and by company name, to articles and news items of financial interest in over 100 periodicals, and in the national Press, during the previous period.

Reviews of UK Statistical Sources Pergamon Press, Headington Hill Hall, Oxford OX3 0BW.

This is the successor to the previous series on *The Sources and Nature of the Statistics of the UK*, edited by M. Kendal. The reviews not only outline, but also evaluate statistical sources for a wide and expanding range of topics.

The Times Index Primary Source Media Ltd, PO Box 45, Reading RG1 8HF.

A monthly index, by subject heading and by author, to the pages of *The Times* newspapers (excluding the *Financial Times* – see above). Available on microfilm.

The UK economy in a European context

European Access Chadwyck Healey Ltd, The Quorum, Barnwell Road, Cambridge CB5 8SW.

Published six times a year. This is a useful source of information on articles covering various aspects of the EU. Each issue provides a brief commentary on recent events in the EU and a list of recent articles published under nineteen headings related to various EU activities, e.g. industry, business, money, environment, technology, education, etc.

European Business Intelligence Briefing Headland Business Information, Windsor Court, East Grinstead House, East Grinstead, West Sussex RH19 IXA.

Published eleven times a year. This is a newsletter which analyses the sources of European company, market and product information.

Publications of the European Community Alan Armstrong Ltd, 2 Arkwright Road, Reading, Berks RG2 0SQ.

This annual catalogue contains all the publications, including periodicals, issued during the year by the Institutions of the European Community. There is a breakdown by subject heading.

The Directory of the EU Information Sources Euroconfidentiel, Rue de Rixensart, Genval, Belgium.

This publication is regularly updated and presents useful details of various sources of information available on the EU.

The UK economy in a world context

HMSO International Organizations Publications PO Box 276, London SW8 5DT.

This annual catalogue contains all items placed on sale by HMSO in that year for the international agencies and overseas organizations for which HMSO acts as agent. These include: the European Commission; the IMF; the OECD; and the UN, amongst many others.

Information Sources in Official Publications Bowker-Saur, Windsor Court, East Grinstead House, East Grinstead, West Sussex RH19 IXA

This volume provides a guide to the Government/Official Publications available in a large number of countries across the world. It discusses the main guidebooks which can help readers access the myriad of official publications produced by various goverment and other official bodies.

Other applied materials

The following are a number of useful sources, readily available to the reader interested in applied economic issues.

Bank Reviews Often available free, on application.

Barclays Economic Review, published quarterly, Economics Dept, Barclays House, 1 Wimborne Road, Poole, Dorset BH15 2BB.

British Economy Survey York Publishing Services, 64 Hallfield Road, Layerthorpe, York YO3 7XQ.

A highly useful, twice-yearly, update on the current state of the British economy. Eight main sections: Industrial Structure; Public Sector; Monetary System; Public Finance; Industrial Relations and Employment; Balance of Payments; World Economy. Published in October and April.

Business Strategy Review   Oxford University Press, Pinkhill House, Southfield Road, Eynsham, Oxford OX8 1JJ.

This is produced three times a year by the London Business School's Centre for Business Strategy. It contains articles on practical issues which are relevant to decision making within modern business.

Business Studies   Anforme Business Publications Ltd, 2/3 Dukes Court, Princess Way, Prudhoe, Northumberland NE42 6DA.

Published four times a year. This journal provides useful reading for both business studies students and economists who wish to understand the interface between business and economics. Articles include topics such as marketing, human resource management, uses of marginal cost, and decision making under uncertainty.

Developments in Economics: An Annual Review   Ed. G. B. J. Atkinson, Causeway Press Ltd, PO Box 13, Ormskirk, Lancs L39 5HP.

A yearly publication in ring binder format. Each issue includes a number of clearly written articles which update student knowledge on various micro and macro economic issues.

Economics and Business Education   Economics and Business Education Association, 1a Keymer Road, Hassocks, West Sussex BN6 8AD.

This is the official journal of the Economics and Business Education Association and is published quarterly. As well as containing articles on various aspects of Economics, Business and related subjects, it also covers up-to-date teaching methods and reviews new literature.

Far Eastern Economic Review   GPO Box 160, Hong Kong.

A weekly publication available from main UK booksellers. It is a major source of up-to-date information about countries of the 'Pacific Rim' (such as SE Asia and Australasia) which have become an important part of the world economy. It contains sections which deal with regional issues in the Far East, and presents important articles on business and society in the different Far East countries.

Key British Enterprises   Dun & Bradstreet, Holmers Farm Way, High Wycome, Bucks HP12 4UL.

This yearly publication covers some 50,000 large and medium sized UK companies. It provides *financial* details (profit, turnover, etc.), *operational* details (line of business, markets, brand names, etc.), and *corporate* details (registration no., parent company, etc.).

Lloyds Bank Economic Bulletin   Economics and Strategy Planning, Lloyds Bank, PO Box 215, 71 Lombard St, London EC3P 3BS.

Bi-monthly, on request. Each issue covers a topic of current interest, presenting economic principles in a manner understandable to non-economists. Also included is a section on changes in the main economic indicators.

National Institute Economic Review   2 Dean Trench Street, Smith Square, London SW1P 3HE.

Published four times a year. Each issue of the Review contains comments on the economic situation in the UK and on the World economy as a whole. It also contains interesting articles on various aspects of the UK economy. This source is particularly strong in providing comparisons between the UK and her competitors in particular areas, e.g. labour costs, productivity, and education. There is a statistical appendix which offers updates on a wide range of economic variables relating to production, prices/wages, external trade, etc.

Oxford Review of Economic Policy   Oxford University Press, Great Clarendon Street, Oxford OX2 6DP.

A quarterly publication which includes articles on various topics of current relevance. Some issues concentrate wholly on *one* contemporary topic, such as Exchange rates, Education and Training, Finance, Health Economics, etc.

Regional Studies   Carfax Publishing Company, PO Box 25, Abingdon, Oxford-shire OX14 3UE.

Published six times a year. This is the standard source of articles for those students who are interested in various aspects of UK and world regional and urban issues.

The Economic Review   Philip Allan Publishers Ltd, Market Place, Deddington, Oxfordshire OX15 0SE.

Five issues are published each academic year in September, November, January, March and May. *The Economic Review* is aimed at introductory students in economics, and relates economic theory to contemporary economic problems. Each issue contains main feature articles, and a teaching section which reviews the various ways of tackling typical examination questions.

The Economist   25 St James Street, London SW1A 1HG.

This is the internationally known weekly, published by the Economist Newspapers Ltd. It includes articles on subjects such as World Politics and Current Affairs, together with Business, Finance and Science. It is an invaluable source of national and international business news and also has a useful update on basic economic statistics.

The Times 1000   Times Books, 16 Golden Square, London W1R 4BN.

This is a yearly update of the basic data on the world's top companies. It covers the top 1,000 UK companies and also the main companies of many other OECD countries. It also provides information on companies in the financial sector, such as Clearing banks, Acceptance houses and Discount houses, as well as an update on the year's main mergers and acquisitions.

United Kingdom in Figures   Central Statistical Office, Press and Information Service, Great George Street, London SW1P 3AQ.

This pocket-sized abstract provides current facts and figures on population, employment, the environment, the standard of living and the National Accounts. Free from the above address.

Who Owns Who · Dun and Bradstreet, Holmers Farm Way, High Wycombe, Bucks HP12 4UL.

This is a yearly publication which includes a mass of essential information about companies and their subsidiaries. It enables readers to find the main subsidiaries of UK companies, whether in the UK or abroad. It can also be used to trace the parent firm if the name of the subsidiary is known. This publication is therefore invaluable for unravelling the pattern of ownership and control in UK industry.

Electronic media

Many series of data and sources of information can now be accessed directly on-line or are available on disk or tape.

ONS Databank   ONS Sales Desk, Room 131/4, Office for National Statistics, Government Offices, Great George Street, London SW1P 3AQ.

The ONS Databank contains major series such as GDP, PSBR, RPI, Balance of Payments, National Accounts, index of production, etc. Time series data for these items are available on disk or paper.

NOMIS   Unit 3P, Mountjoy Research Centre, University of Durham, Durham DH1 3SW.

The National Online Manpower Information Service (NOMIS) is a database of labour statistics run on behalf of the ONS by the University of Durham. It contains a range of official statistics relating to the labour market.

ESRC Data Archive   University of Essex, Colchester, Essex CO4 3SQ.

This archive provides data across the full range of the social sciences and humanities and contains information about most areas of social and economic life including Family Expenditure Surveys, Labour Force Surveys, census data, etc. The Data Archive will endeavour to locate and obtain research data for those interested.

SINES   SINES Help Line, Room 285, Ordnance Survey, Romsey Road, Southampton, Hants SO16 4GU.

This source contains information about specific datasets through printouts, floppy disks or E-mail. It states the purpose, the sources, and frequency of updata, etc. of major economic, environmental and industrial, and other datasets.

CD-Rom   Many schools, colleges and public libraries now provide CD-Rom access to a range of UK and EU *databases* and *Information Sources*. The following items are indicative of what may well be available to you via this resource:

1. ABI/INFORM
   Gives 150 word abstracts and indexing to over 800 international academic business, economics and management journals.
2. ANBAR ABSTRACTS
   Abstracts and indexes articles covering business, management and IT topics from mainly UK and European journals.
3. BOOKBANK
   Gives bibliographic information on over 600,000 books from UK publishers and English language titles from overseas which are available in the UK.
4. BOOKFIND
   Includes over 2 million books, currently in print, from publishers in the UK, the US, Canada and other English speaking countries.
5. DISCLOSURE/WORLDSCOPE EUROPE
   Contains company accounts and financial information on over 10,000 companies in 27 countries. This information enables comparisons to be made between the major companies trading in Europe.
6. EC/EU INFODISK
   Contains the official bibliographic database of the European Union (SCAD) and detailed briefings on Britain's implementation of EU legislation prepared by the DTI (Spearhead).
7. FINANCIAL TIMES
   Full text of back issues of this newspaper.
8. THE GUARDIAN
   Full text of back issues of this newspaper.
9. JUSTIS
   This is the official legal database of the European Union. It contains the full text of most of the Treaties, regulations, directives, preparatory work, case law and parliamentary questions dealt with by the EU.
10. THE TIMES
    Full text of back issues of this newspaper.

Internet sources

The increasing use of the internet as a source of information for economics and business has grown rapidly over the last few years. The usefulness of the material on the internet largely depends on whether organizations keep their site up-to-date. The sources of information are growing daily so the list given below only provides a very brief idea of the type and range of websites available.

UK sites   British Library Catalogue   (http://opac97.bl.uk)
   This will provide details of books published in the UK enabling a search to be made to identify up-to-date books on many topic areas.

CCTA Government information   (http://www.open.gov.uk/)
This site will lead to most of the materials published by UK Government authorities, including the Departments of State and other Agencies.

Economist   (http://www.europe economist.com/)
This includes the current week's issue of the *Economist*, book reviews and surveys. It also provides links to other related sites.

Financial Times   (http://www.ft.com)
This covers current financial and business news. The user has to register (free) before using it but some of its services are not free.

HM Treasury   (http://www.hm-treasury.gov.uk)
Press releases, ministers' speeches, lists of research papers, together with details of economic forecasts and budget measures are available on this site.

HMSO   (http://www.the-stationery-office.co.uk)
This is a useful site to find out what is being published by HMSO.

European/international   EU Information (Europa)   (http://europa.eu.int)
This is the EU's central home page. It is the starting point for a search of the main sources of official information on the EU. It leads to an enormous range of sources, including the publications of the various Directors General (DGs) and Eurostat.

International Monetary Fund (IMF)   (http://www.imf.org)
This site provides a guide to the material available with the IMF on a wide range of economic issues.

United Nations   (http://www.un.org)
This site provides details of the publications and activities of the United Nations; for example it provides information about its yearly Trade and Development Report.

World Trade Organization (WTO)   (http://www.wto.org)
This site is dedicated to the publications of the WTO in the area of trade and trade policy.

FINANCIAL TIMES
Supplement

How to read the *Financial Times*

Philip Coggan, Markets Editor, *Financial Times*

The *Financial Times* was founded in 1888 and has been known for a century for its distinctive pink paper (an early marketing technique that stuck).

The paper is split into two, with the first section broadly covering politics, economics, social developments and industrial trends and the second section covering individual companies and stock, currency, bond and commodity market movements.

Pages covering UK and international companies

The UK results coverage includes an important feature in the form of comments on the figures. The aim is to guide investors through the morass; for example, to point out when profits have been boosted by one-off factors such as asset sales; when the trend in profits growth is slowing; when a healthy profits figure masks a weak cash position; when the performance is strong, but the shares already reflect all the good news.

Valuing shares

There are a number of techniques for valuing shares, based on the assets, profits, dividends or cash flow of a company. *Net asset value (NAV) per share* is calculated by adding up the value of the tangible assets of a company, deducting the debts, and dividing by the number of shares in issue. It can be a good way of assessing the value of some

companies; if the share price is 80p and the NAV per share is 100p, it would in theory be possible for a predator to buy up the company and sell off the assets at a profit. However, many modern companies are in the service sector and have few tangible assets, so NAV is of only limited use in valuing shares.

The *price–earnings ratio* (P/E) is a method of comparing a company's share price with its profits. The first step is to work out a company's profits, after tax and other deductions. These are known as the *earnings*, which are then divided by the number of shares in issue, to get the *earnings per share*. The last step is to divide the *share price* by the earnings per share to get the P/E ratio. Roughly speaking, this figure represents the number of years' earnings an investor is paying for a share; buying a company on a P/E ratio of 10 means one is paying 10 times current earnings. In theory, the lower the P/E the better. However, the markets are always looking ahead. Companies with a high P/E tend to be ones where investors are expecting earnings to grow quickly; companies with a low P/E are expected to show modest, if any, profits growth.

Another popular valuation measure is *dividend yield*, which shows the annual dividend as a percentage of the share price. Many investors own shares for their dividends, which over the long term make up a significant proportion of stock market returns. An advantage of divi-

dends is that they are real, in the sense that they have to be paid in cash; assets and profits can sometimes be accounting illusions. It would be a mistake, however, to assume that the company with the highest yield is the most attractive. Since the yield represents the dividend divided by the share price, as the price falls the yield rises. Sometimes shares offer a high yield because investors expect the company to cut the dividend, or not pay it at all; in other cases, they expect little in the way of growth. If a share has a low dividend yield, it may be that the company is currently paying only a small proportion of its profits out as dividends, so it can reinvest the money to help its business grow. Fast-growing companies tend to have low dividends; investors hope that eventually both profits and dividends will grow at an above average rate and they are prepared to accept a low yield for now.

The London share service pages give the P/E and the dividend yield (headed **yld gr s**) for most quoted companies.

Sometimes investors prefer to look at *cash flow*, rather than profits or dividends. In some cases, this may be because it is harder to manipulate cash flow than it is to fiddle the earnings or profits figure. In other cases, a company might look better value on cash flow than on an earnings basis; for example, if the company takes a heavy charge against its profits for depreciation of its assets.

Shares are divided by industrial sectors

so that ratios can be easily compared between, say, Sainsbury and Tesco, or Guinness and Allied Domecq. Other information shown includes the share price, the day's change, the 52-week high and low, and the market capitalization (the value placed by the stock market on the company, calculated by multiplying the share price by the number of shares in issue). Symbols direct the reader to footnotes which show where special circumstances apply.

The stock market

The back page of the UK edition contains coverage of the London stock market. The aim is to explain both why shares in individual companies rise and fall and why the overall market goes up or down. This is a difficult area; shares in, say, Acme Construction may rise on hopes of a bid from Megacorp. Even if the rumour turns out to be untrue, it is still the case that the story lifted the shares and it is our job to report it. One way of assessing the credibility of rumours is to look at the volume of shares traded. If it is greater than normal for that stock, it may indicate that the story has some substance; if volume is low, the chances are that few believe the rumours.

Individual shares may move for a whole host of reasons: stockbrokers' reports; bid rumours; executive departures; adverse press reports; results which beat, or fall short of, market expectations. This last factor is one of the most important. Outsiders are often puzzled when a company which reports a 30% rise in profits sees its shares fall.

Markets indulge in what one might call the White Queen syndrome, after the character in *Through the Looking Glass*. The White Queen screamed before she pricked her finger and when the injury actually occurred, made only a small sigh, as she had got all her screaming over with in advance. Similarly, stock markets are forever looking to the future and anticipating what will happen. Expectations are built into the market; thus if a company is expected to increase profits by 40% and only reports a rise of 30%, its shares will fall.

FTSE

Because there are so many quoted shares, investors use 'benchmarks', in the form of baskets of representative stocks, to track the market's overall movements. The most commonly used in the UK is the *FTSE 100*, which stands for the *Financial Times*/Stock Exchange 100 index and is designed to show the UK's 100 largest companies. Broader indices, such as the *FTSE All-Share* which includes around 800 stocks and the *FTSE SmallCap* which covers shares in smaller companies, are also used. Companies drop in and out of these indices as their shares rise and fall, or are subject to takeover.

The indices are also used to monitor the performance of fund managers who look after other people's money, whether it be pension funds, charities, or the portfolios of private investors. Experience has found that it is very difficult to beat these benchmarks. In part, this is because the index will inevitably represent the average performance of all shares, and thus all investors; by definition, therefore, half of all investors should not beat the index. On top of that factor is the burden of administrative and dealing costs, which investors have to pay, but the index does not reflect. More fundamentally, it seems as if very few people have the ability to pick successful shares. Academics have argued that this is because markets are efficient; share prices reflect all the available knowledge about a company. What will affect the price, therefore, is future news, which by definition cannot be known.

If picking the best shares is difficult, so is predicting the moves of the overall market. Over the long run, at least, it tends to go up. BZW's Equity–Gilt Study shows that £1,000 invested in equities at the end of 1945 would have grown, with net dividends reinvested, into £218,140 by the end of 1995. The same amount in a building society would have risen to just £10,400. But in the short term, it can fall very sharply. On Black Monday, 19 October 1987, the FTSE 100 index fell by 10.8%, and it then dropped another 12.2% on the following day.

The main factors which cause the market to rise and fall include the following:

Interest rates. Broadly speaking, rising interest rates are bad news for share prices and falling rates are good. Rising rates increase the cost of corporate borrowing and thereby reduce profits. Higher interest rates also increase the attraction of selling shares to hold funds on deposit. Factors which are likely to lead the government to raise interest rates – rising inflation, strong economic growth – are therefore often bad news for the markets.

Profits growth. Equities represent a share of the assets and profits of a company. The faster profits grow, therefore, the better for the markets. Tax changes which eat into profits hit the market.

Supply and demand. Flotations and rights issues increase the supply of shares in the market and drive prices down (other things being equal); dividends, share buy-backs and takeovers for cash increase the funds available for investment and push prices up.

International influences. Increasingly, stock markets are being dominated by global influences as investors move money round in search of the most attractive havens. There is a tendency for share prices to move up and down together; London, in particular, is heavily influenced by Wall Street and a sharp fall in the US market usually has a knock-on effect in the UK.

The global picture

For those who are interested in more than just the UK market, the *world stock markets page* covers the rest of the globe. The aim is to explain why each market rose and fell on the day and to give details of a few substantial movements of individual stocks. As with the UK, Wall Street often sets the tone, although Tokyo follows its own agenda. Having been amazingly strong in the 1980s, the Japanese stock market has been in a slump throughout the 1990s in the face of a sluggish economy and weakened financial system.

Investors are becoming increasingly interested in the so-called *emerging markets* of Latin America and Asia, which have faster rates of economic growth, and thus the potential for greater increase in corporate profits, than the developed world. Liberalization of these markets has also encouraged foreign investors to buy shares.

Bond markets

Daily coverage of the *bond markets* appears on the International Capital Markets page.

Government bond market

The market in government bonds is huge; at the end of 1995, there was some $22 trillion of outstanding debt or around $3,500 for every individual on the planet. Bond markets are curmudgeonly and rather misanthropic sorts; they tend to dislike news that pleases the rest of the population. A fall in unemployment, a pick-up in wages or a strengthening of economic growth will tend to cause the bond markets to fall. This is because the biggest enemy of bond markets is inflation. Even at 5% inflation, prices double every 14 years or so, so the real value of a 15-year bond will halve between issue and repayment. Bond investors tend to believe that strong economic growth (which in developed countries tends to be an annual rate of 2.5% or more) leads to inflation.

Apart from inflation, the other important factor in influencing bond markets tends to be supply. The supply of government bonds depends on the size of the country's budget deficit, so a larger-than-expected deficit tends to depress bond prices. In some countries, particularly the developing world, the debts become so large that countries have little hope of repaying the capital, or even the interest; such was the case during the debt crisis of the early 1980s, which centred on Latin America.

An important note for anyone reading the paper's bond market coverage is the relationship between the *yield* and the *price*. The yield is calculated by dividing the interest rate payable on the bond by the market price; as the price rises, therefore, the yield falls and vice versa.

Primary bond markets

The coverage of primary bond issues on the same page looks at how companies and governments are raising money, how much, at what rate, and in which currency. Trends change as borrowers seek to get the best terms available; it may, for example, be advantageous for a UK borrower to raise money in Australian dollars and convert back into sterling.

Foreign exchange markets

Coverage of the *foreign exchange markets* immediately follows the capital markets page. Here again, the market is huge

with daily turnover of around $500bn in London, and can be turbulent, as when the UK and other currencies were forced out of the Exchange Rate Mechanism in 1992. The main factors affecting a currency are economic; low inflation, a trade surplus, high real (after inflation) interest rates, tend to cause it to rise; high inflation, a trade deficit and low real rates tend to cause it to fall. But on a day-to-day or week-to-week basis, currencies can often move in a contrary direction to that implied by the economic fundamentals.

Commodites

Financial assets have tended to be good investments in the 1980s and 1990s but back in the 1970s, the smart money was in *commodities*. The era of high inflation saw price booms in most commodities, with the most obvious example being oil. Falling inflation, new sources of supply and improved production techniques combined to bring down commodity prices in the 1980s. Interest in the area has recently revived, however, and our commodities page covers the most important developments; the ups and downs of raw material prices can have important effects in individual sectors of the economy. A poor coffee harvest in Brazil, a cold winter in the US, political unrest in the Middle East; all can have knock-on effects which eventually become apparent to the consumer.

Notes on contributors

G. H. Black, FCA Senior Lecturer in Accounting, Anglia Polytechnic University (APU) and Principal Examiner in A-level Accounting for London Examinations. Author of a number of books, including *Accounting*, Addison Wesley Longman, 1994, and *Accounting Standards*, Letts Higher Education, 1998. Responsible for Chapter 2.

G. Burton, BSc, MSc Principal Lecturer in European Business, Anglia Business School, APU., with special reference to macroeconomics and quantitative methods. Author (with G. Carrol and S. Wall) of *Quantitative Methods for Business and Economics*, Longman 1998. He has taught economics at various levels and has lectured in Business Schools in France, Finland and the Netherlands. Responsible for chapters 16, 22 and 23.

P. Fenwick, BA, MA Senior Lecturer in Human Resource Management at the East London Business School, University of East London. Previous management experience in the British car industry. Responsible (with A. Griffiths) for Chapter 15.

E. Fuller, MSc, ACMA, FRSA Director of the Foresight Research Centre at Durham University Business School (DUBS). He has written and edited numerous publications, books, trainer manuals, expert systems and academic papers. Responsible for Chapters 3 (with Francis Greene) and 9.

S. Ghatak, MA, MSc, (Econ) PhD is a Professor and Director of Graduate studies in Economics at Kingston University. Before that he was a reader of Economics at Leicester University. He was a visiting Professor at the University of Florida, USA and Guelph University, Canada and acted as a consultant for many international agencies, including the UN and World Bank. He has written eight books and contributed numerous articles to leading international journals including, *Economic Journal, Journal of Public Economics, Empirical Economics, Applied Economics, Oxford Bulletin of Economics, Weltwirtschaftliches Archiv* and *Journal of Development Studies*. Responsible for Chapter 30.

A. Griffiths, BA, MSc Reader in Economics, Anglia Business School, APU, and previously Tutor in Economics at the University of Wales, Aberystwyth. Fellow of the Japan Foundation, Sophia University, Tokyo 1978, and visiting Professor of

Economics at Yokohama National University, Yokohama, 1987/88. Research Officer at the Research Institute for the National Economy, Tokyo 1987/88. Editor of *European Economy Survey*, Longman, 1992 and *British Economy Survey*, York Publishing. Co-author (with S. Wall) of *Intermediate Microeconomics: Theory and Applications*, Addison Wesley Longman, 1996. Responsible for Chapters 1, 5, 11, 19, 24 and 26, Chapter 15 (with P. Fenwick) and Chapters 4, 6, 10, 14 and 31 (with S. Wall).

B. Harrison, BA, MA Senior Lecturer in Economics, Department of Economics and Politics, Nottingham Trent University. Visiting Lecturer, NIMBAS Postgraduate School of Management, Utrecht. He has also held a visiting post at the National Institute for Management of the Economy in Baku, Azerbaijan. His main teaching and research interest are monetary economics and finance. Responsible for Chapter 20.

N. M. Healey, BA, MA, MBA Professor and Head of Department of Business Studies, Manchester Metropolitan University, where he is a member of the International Business research group. His research interests are European economic and monetary integration and economic transformation in the former communist countries of eastern Europe. He has worked extensively in eastern Europe, serving as economic advisor to the prime minister of Belarus and the Russian Ministry of Economy, and has held visiting posts at universities in the United States, Poland, Bulgaria and Lithuania. He is economics editor of *Teaching Economics and Business* (the journal of the Economics and Business Education Association). Recent publications include *The Economics of the New Europe* (Routledge, 1995) and *Central Banking in Transition Economies* (forthcoming). Responsible for Chapters 7 and 29.

S. Ison, BA, MA, MCIT Principal Lecturer in Economics, Anglia Business School, APU. Visiting Professor at California State University, Hayward. Author of a number of articles in the area of transport economics and specifically urban road pricing. Contributor to *British Economy Survey* and author of *Economics*, Financial Times Pitman Publishing, 3rd edition, 1999. Responsible for Chapter 12.

K. C. Pye, BA, MPhil Formerly Principal Lecturer in Economics and Politics at APU and Director of Economics, University of Cambridge Board Extra Mural Studies. Managing Director, Pye Tait Associates. Author (with J. Collier) of *The Organization and its Environment*, Hart Davis, 1985. Responsible for Chapter 28.

S. Rubinsohn, BA Portfolio Strategist with Capel-Cure Myers, and previously Lecturer in Economics at APU. Responsible for Chapters 17 and 27.

S. D. Wall, BA, MSc Formerly Principal Lecturer in Economics, APU, with special reference to microeconomics. He has returned to APU having acted as consultant to the OECD Directorate for Science, Technology and Industry and guest lecturer and examiner at the University of Cambridge. Author of a wide range of reports and articles on the economics of technical change, and (with A. Griffiths) of *Intermediate Microeconomics: Theory and Applications*, Addison Wesley Longman, 1996 and (with G. Carrol and G. Burton) of *Quantitative Methods*, Addison Wesley Longman, 1998. Editor (with G. Black) of Longman Modular Texts in Business and Economics. Responsible for Chapters 8, 13, 18 and 25 and (with A. Griffiths) for Chapters 4, 6, 10, 14 and 31.

R. Webb Lecturer in banking and programme leader for BA Money Banking and Finance in the economics department at Middlesex University Business School. He lectures on financial markets and institutions at both undergraduate and postgraduate level and is an active researcher. His main research interests are the structure, strategy and efficiency of domestic and international banks, asymmetric information in the provision of financial services, Japanese banking and data envelopment analysis. His PhD analysed the efficiency of large retail banking groups in the UK. Responsible for Chapter 21.

Index

The index covers Chapters 1 to 30. Index entries are to page numbers. Alphabetical arrangement is word-by-word, where a group of letters followed by a space is filed before the same group of letters followed by a letter, eg 'balance sheets' will appear before 'balanced growth'. Initial articles, conjunctions and prepositions are ignored in determining filing order.